CONTEMPORARY APPROACHES TO TRUSTS AND ESTATES

CONTEMPORARY APPROACHES TO TRUSTS AND ESTATES

SUSAN N. GARY
Orlando J. and Marian H. Hollis Professor
University of Oregon

JEROME BORISON
Associate Professor of Law
University of Denver Sturm College of Law

NAOMI R. CAHN
John Theodore Fey Research Professor of Law
George Washington University

PAULA A. MONOPOLI
Professor of Law and Marbury Research Professor
University of Maryland

Wolters Kluwer
Law & Business

Published by Wolters Kluwer Law & Business in New York.

Wolters Kluwer Law & Business serves customers worldwide with CCH, Aspen Publishers, and Kluwer Law International products. (www.wolterskluwerlb.com)

To contact Customer Service, e-mail customer.service@wolterskluwer.com, call 1-800-234-1660, fax 1-800-901-9075, or mail correspondence to:

 Wolters Kluwer Law & Business
 Attn: Order Department
 PO Box 990
 Frederick, MD 21705

Printed in the United States of America.

1 2 3 4 5 6 7 8 9 0

ISBN 978-0-7355-8927-8

Library of Congress Cataloging-in-Publication Data

Contemporary approaches to trusts and estates / Susan N. Gary . . . [et al.].
    p. cm. — (Aspen coursebook series)
  Includes index.
  ISBN 978-0-7355-8927-8
  1. Trusts and trustees — United States. 2. Wills — United States. 3. Estate planning — United States. 4. Casebooks. I. Gary, Susan N.
  KF730.C66 2011
  346.7305'6 — dc22

2011009854

About Wolters Kluwer Law & Business

Wolters Kluwer Law & Business is a leading global provider of intelligent information and digital solutions for legal and business professionals in key specialty areas, and respected educational resources for professors and law students. Wolters Kluwer Law & Business connects legal and business professionals as well as those in the education market with timely, specialized authoritative content and information-enabled solutions to support success through productivity, accuracy and mobility.

Serving customers worldwide, Wolters Kluwer Law & Business products include those under the Aspen Publishers, CCH, Kluwer Law International, Loislaw, Best Case, ftwilliam.com and MediRegs family of products.

CCH products have been a trusted resource since 1913, and are highly regarded resources for legal, securities, antitrust and trade regulation, government contracting, banking, pension, payroll, employment and labor, and healthcare reimbursement and compliance professionals.

Aspen Publishers products provide essential information to attorneys, business professionals and law students. Written by preeminent authorities, the product line offers analytical and practical information in a range of specialty practice areas from securities law and intellectual property to mergers and acquisitions and pension/benefits. Aspen's trusted legal education resources provide professors and students with high-quality, up-to-date and effective resources for successful instruction and study in all areas of the law.

Kluwer Law International products provide the global business community with reliable international legal information in English. Legal practitioners, corporate counsel and business executives around the world rely on Kluwer Law journals, looseleafs, books, and electronic products for comprehensive information in many areas of international legal practice.

Loislaw is a comprehensive online legal research product providing legal content to law firm practitioners of various specializations. Loislaw provides attorneys with the ability to quickly and efficiently find the necessary legal information they need, when and where they need it, by facilitating access to primary law as well as state-specific law, records, forms and treatises.

Best Case Solutions is the leading bankruptcy software product to the bankruptcy industry. It provides software and workflow tools to flawlessly streamline petition preparation and the electronic filing process, while timely incorporating ever-changing court requirements.

ftwilliam.com offers employee benefits professionals the highest quality plan documents (retirement, welfare and non-qualified) and government forms (5500/PBGC, 1099 and IRS) software at highly competitive prices.

MediRegs products provide integrated health care compliance content and software solutions for professionals in healthcare, higher education and life sciences, including professionals in accounting, law and consulting.

Wolters Kluwer Law & Business, a division of Wolters Kluwer, is headquartered in New York. Wolters Kluwer is a market-leading global information services company focused on professionals.

To Alec, Richard and George
— S.N.G.

To Meg, Spencer, and Georgia, who have had to endure
my countless hours at the laptop at the dining room table
and did so with unwavering support, smiles and,
in the end, benign resignation
— J.B.

To those who have given me the wealth of life:
my parents, Tony, Louisa and Abigail
— N.R.C.

To Marin, Richard, Victoria, Christopher and Patrick
— P.A.M.

SUMMARY OF CONTENTS

CONTENTS

4. NONPROBATE TRANSFERS — PASSING PROPERTY BY WILL SUBSTITUTES AND GIFTS 167

7. RIGHTS OF BENEFICIARIES AND CREDITORS IN TRUST PROPERTY; MODIFICATION AND TERMINATION OF TRUSTS 343

8. POWERS OF APPOINTMENT AND THE RULE AGAINST PERPETUITIES

401

9. WILL VALIDITY 443

11. REVOKING THE WILL AND WILL CONTESTS

13. PLANNING FOR INCAPACITY   719

14. ESTATE AND GIFT TAX PLANNING   787

15. ADMINISTRATION OF THE PROBATE ESTATE 829

16. CHARITABLE TRUSTS   907

PREFACE

The field of trusts and estates law is experiencing a transformation. The profound changes that have transformed the subject area over the past half-century have resulted in new laws and also in new ways of transmitting property. Demographic changes, such as the increasing number of multiple marriages, stepfamilies, nonmarital children and unmarried partners, have dramatically affected developments in trusts and estates. This book captures the rapid evolution of doctrine, introduces students to emerging policy debates and explores ethical and practical issues that arise in estate planning practice.

Based on recent developments in legal education, including the recommendations of the Carnegie Report, *Contemporary Approaches to Trusts and Estates Law* provides an approach that integrates legal analysis, judgment and perspective and practice skills. It focuses simultaneously on the theoretical foundations and practical applications of the material, teaching students by using traditional case analysis and, at the professor's option, innovative exercises.

While the casebook covers the customary elements of a trusts and estates course and focuses students on core trusts and estates issues of intent and statutory analysis, it does so with four innovations:

- It reverses the customary order of the course, covering lifetime planning issues before the wills component. The book proceeds chronologically, focusing on lifetime planning, including the use of trusts and other will substitutes, before turning to wills and the probate system.
- Early in the semester, it provides an overview of the status of all people involved in estate planning, addressing issues such as the meaning of "spouse" and "child" and the ethical obligations of lawyers who represent multiple clients.
- It includes exercises that are integrated into the more traditional casebook material and are designed to provide hands-on practical experience; these exercises involve skills ranging from counseling to drafting to litigation.
- It includes numerous problems to help students understand the complexities of the Uniform Probate Code and other statutes, as well as common law doctrines.

The book also presents important questions that arise in trusts and estates law, helping frame the law that provides the background to effective estate planning. Ultimately, our goal is for students to understand and appreciate the interrelated aspects of all forms of estate planning — the relationship of wills to trusts to gifts to tax to medical directives — and the necessity for everyone, regardless of their economic circumstances, to consider these issues.

Susan N. Gary
Jerome Borison
Naomi R. Cahn
Paula A. Monopoli

March 2011

ACKNOWLEDGMENTS

This casebook has involved an intensive collaboration among the four co-authors, and in writing the book we have each learned more than we could have imagined about teaching trusts and estates. As four professors who find trusts and estates endlessly fascinating, we hope this book gets you as excited as we are about the topic.

In the process of writing and editing this book, we benefitted immeasurably from the contributions of others, and we would like to thank the following people. Our deans and associate deans — Frederick Lawrence at George Washington University; Phoebe Haddon, Michael Van Alstine and Mark Graber at the University of Maryland School of Law; Martin Katz and Federico Cheever at the University of Denver Sturm College of Law; and Margie Paris and Michael Moffitt at the University of Oregon School of Law — have always encouraged and supported our work. Mary Kate Hunter, Reference Librarian at George Washington University, answered countless inquiries with expertise and good humor, and Lillian White ably assisted administratively. Susan McCarty, Senior Research Fellow, Kurt Meyer, Research Librarian, David Nolte, Research Fellow, and Megan McDonald, Program Manager at the University of Maryland provided excellent research and administrative support, and thanks to Lillian White for her excellent administrative support at George Washington University. Stephanie Midkiff, Research Librarian at the University of Oregon School of Law also provided valuable research support. Law students Alissa Marque, Lindsey Nelson, Jill Paul, Jose Recio, Peter Weiss and Alisa Yasin at George Washington University; Sadia Sorathia and Kobie Pruitt at the University of Maryland; Benjamin Hager at the University of Denver Sturm College of Law; and Brian Kirks and Sims Ely at the University of Oregon provided excellent research assistance. Several semesters of students at different schools have helped us develop these materials, providing useful critiques to guide us as we finalized the book.

Jerome Borison would like to specially thank Professor JoAnne Jackson, Case Western Reserve University School of Law, for her mentorship when he first began teaching Trusts and Estates oh so many years ago. It was she who was in the forefront of modern experiential learning, and her material and method have been important to the development of this book. For her generosity in allowing us to use whatever material of hers that we wished, the authors are most appreciative. We also thank Professor

Robert Tuttle, George Washington University Law School, for his help with professional responsibility issues, and we thank Randall W. Roth for assistance with the materials on charitable trusts.

Our work with the editorial staff at Aspen, particularly Richard Mixter and Barbara Roth, has been crucial to the publication of the book. Troy Froebe has helped us with the final stages of editing.

We thank our families for their gifts of supporting our work on this book.

In addition, we gratefully acknowledge the following sources for permission to reprint portions of their work:

"Brothers living in cave to inherit billions from lost grandmother" by Henry Samuel, 2nd December 2009 © Telegraph Media Group Limited 2009. Reprinted with permission. All rights reserved.

"The Estate and Gift Tax: The Law and Its Application." © Raymond Sutton, Baker & Hostetler LLP, Denver, CO. Reprinted with permission. All rights reserved.

"The Estate Tax: Myths and Realities." © Center on Budget and Policy Priorities, http://www.cbpp.org. Reprinted with permission. All rights reserved.

"Billionaire's Heirs First to Win 2010 Estate Tax Jackpot" © Scott Martin copyright, published April 10, 2010 on The Trust Advisor Blog (http://thetrustadvisor.com). Reprinted with permission of The Trust Advisor Blog. All rights reserved.

"Estate Planning with 529 Plans" © Money-Zine.com. Reprinted with permission of Money-Zine.com. All rights reserved. http://www.money-zine.com/Financial-Planning/College-Loan/Estate-Planning-with-529-Plans/.

"Steve McNair's Estate — And You Thought Settling Michael Jackson's Estate Would Be a Thriller" © 2010 Julie Garber (http://wills.about.com/). Reprinted with permission of About, Inc. which can be found online at www.about.com. All rights reserved.

American Law Institute, Restatement (Second) of Conflict of Laws (1971); Restatement (Second) of Property: Donative Transfers (1986); Restatement (Third) of Agency (2006); Restatement (Third) of the Law Governing Lawyers (2000); Restatement (Third) of Property: Wills & Other Donative Transfers (1999, 2003, T.D. No. 5, 2006); Restatement (Third) of Trusts (2003, 2007). Copyright © 1971, 1986, 1999, 2003, 2006 & 2007 by the American Law Institute. Reprinted by permission.

Authors' Note: Footnotes and textual citations of courts and commentators have been omitted without so specifying. Numbered footnotes are from the original materials and retain the original numbering.

Contemporary Approaches to Trusts and Estates

1 INTRODUCTION TO ESTATE PLANNING AND THE LAWYER'S ROLES

A. GENERAL INTRODUCTION

Trusts and estates is an ancient area of law that is integrally related to property ownership. Once society establishes laws on private property, it can create rules specifying how — and whether — property can be transferred upon the death of the owner. Great Britain enacted the Statute of Wills in 1540, a law which provided legal recognition that property could be transferred by will, a document executed with the requisite formalities. In the United States, each of the 50 states developed its own laws, largely built on the law of the country of origin of the initial settlers, generally England, France or Spain.

Early laws on the transmission of property at death were generally filled with formalistic requirements, such as the rule that there be three witnesses in order for a will to be valid. They were characterized by a single-minded focus on wills as the only means by which an individual could indicate how property should be distributed post-death.

Over the past 50 years, there have been dramatic changes in trusts and estates law throughout the country.

- The field has moved away from the formalism that traditionally characterized it towards an emphasis on effectuating the client's intent.
- The laws of the 50 states are becoming more similar as a result of the efforts of both the Uniform Law Commission (ULC) (formerly known as the National Conference of Commissioners on Uniform

State Laws (NCCUSL))[1] with its drafting of the Uniform Probate Code (UPC) and the Uniform Trust Code (UTC) as well as the American Law Institute (ALI) with its Restatements.

- Estate planning now typically involves the use of instruments in addition to wills. Trusts and beneficiary designation forms for life insurance and retirement plans are commonly used to convey property at death outside of the traditional probate process.
- Medical directives and various forms of powers of attorney that allow individuals to make advance arrangements for their incapacity have gained widespread legal and popular acceptance.
- The judicial process for probating wills or administering estates has been vastly simplified.

You will discover a mix of old and new doctrines throughout this material. One core principle that has resisted change, however, is the significance of freedom of donative intent, sometimes known as freedom of testation. The dominant norm in American trusts and estates law has always been to allow property owners to do what they want with their property, during life and at death. This norm has been and it continues to be subject to relatively few limitations. Property owners can make present or future gifts, transfer their property in trust to benefit someone else (or even themselves), place restrictions on property they own, share their interests with other owners and decide, upon death, who will own their property without the necessity of benefiting anyone in particular.

This respect for freedom of donative intent manifests itself most clearly in the general principle that a governing instrument, such as a will, dictates outcomes to the extent that it addresses a matter even if the choices made by the testator seem unfair. However, as you will see, even this bedrock principle is in a state of transition because of changing cultural norms concerning protection of dependent family members and various other public policy matters.

The respect for donative intent applies even when there is no explicit direction from the decedent, for example, when there is no written document or an estate planner failed to adequately consider various contingencies when drafting documents. In these situations, state laws provide a set of default rules designed to approximate what the decedent would have wanted. The ultimate default rules are intestacy rules, establishing who gets the entire probate estate where the individual died without a will at all. Even where there is a will, however, default rules may be necessary. For example, assume in her will, a testator left her house to her daughter. Before she died, she sold the house and bought a

---

1. The authors will be using both "ULC" and "NCCUSL" throughout the book to refer to the same organization. For further information about the ULC and to retrieve information about its uniform and model acts, see http://www.nccusl.org.

condominium. Does the daughter get nothing? Does she get the condominium? Or does she get the cash equal to the value of the house? In default of the testator's will addressing this question, a statute will apply to help resolve the situation.

This course provides you with an overview of American inheritance law. It explores the theoretical and constitutional underpinnings of the American system for distributing property at death, and also emphasizes the importance of lifetime planning for incapacity and property transfers. Through the course you will learn about a variety of subjects, ranging from: (1) the rules that govern one's ability to direct the allocation of property at death by drafting a will (testacy); (2) the laws that govern the allocation of property when one dies without a will (intestacy); (3) the method by which property passes at one's death through either intestacy or a will (the probate process); and (4) a series of other issues involved in lifetime estate planning, including gifting, using trusts and other will substitutes, planning for incapacity and minimizing taxes.

The themes of the book echo those throughout the field of trusts and estates. They include the need to consider freedom of disposition and respect for the testator's wishes balanced against rules dictated by the legislature and courts that restrict donative freedom in order to protect the living; the potential tension between seeking to fulfill the individual's intent and the formalities that, though designed to protect it, may actually thwart carrying out that intent; the use of other lifetime planning techniques; and the ethical issues that pervade estate planning.

The book is set up as follows, with a focus on planning over the course of a lifetime:

- Chapter 1 explores core trusts and estates issues of intent, testamentary freedom and the ethical obligations of lawyers;
- Chapter 2 provides an overview of the status of people involved in estate planning, addressing issues such as the meaning of "spouse" and "child" in a changing world;
- Chapter 3 examines intestacy laws that dictate the transmission of property when there is no will;
- Chapter 4 examines the process of planning with will substitutes (*e.g.*, trusts and beneficiary designation forms);
- Chapters 5 through 8 look at the law of trusts, exploring not only what is required in drafting, amending or terminating them, but also the responsibilities of the fiduciaries who are charged with administering them;
- Chapters 9 to 11 turn to wills, focusing on their drafting, interpretation, and revocation, as well as will contests;
- Chapter 12 examines protections for the family;
- Chapter 13 considers the fast-changing law associated with planning for incapacity;

- Chapter 14 introduces you to the tax laws involved in estate planning;
- Finally, Chapters 15 and 16 examine various specific issues: administering the estate and charitable trusts.

This book provides a distinctive approach to the study of trusts and estates. Like other textbooks, it includes cases, statutes, questions and problems that help in developing critical thinking about the field. It differs from many of those texts by offering you an opportunity to develop your understanding of the law through practical drafting and simulation exercises. In so doing, you will learn to make doctrinal and policy arguments in favor of or against the existing default rules.

The book is designed to help you look at the subject from a variety of roles — as drafters using best practices, as litigators dealing with a bad set of facts generated by another's poor drafting, as administrators or trustees (or their legal counsel) having to decide what to do when a beneficiary makes certain demands of them, as attorneys for disgruntled beneficiaries and a number of other perspectives. As you read the cases and address the assignments, we will ask you to assume one or more of these roles.

PROBLEMS

1.   Look through the syllabus for an overview of the course. Though you will notice that planning for the transmission of one's wealth is the principal focus, the course goes well beyond that: incapacity planning (for those not able to make decisions for themselves, such as injured persons or minors), elder law planning, tax planning and administering estates and trusts, asset protection planning, lifetime planning via gifts and trusts, etc. All these subjects are relevant to effective estate planning.

2.   In order to advise a client who, for example, owns a business on how best to pass the business along to her children, a lawyer might need to be familiar with business law and business tax law. With what other areas of law might you need familiarity as an estate planner? What should you do if you do not have the appropriate level of expertise?

3.   Look at the UPC definitions and the Glossary in Appendices A and B at the end of this chapter. These are some of the essential terms that we'll be discussing throughout the course. We will be reviewing some of the more critical ones in class.

4.   The guiding principle in estate planning and estate administration is effectuating the transferor's intent. UPC §1-102(b)(2) ("The underlying purposes and policies of this Code are . . . to discover and make effective the intent of a decedent in distribution of his property . . .). This requires that you fully understand the client's wishes when you are drafting the plan. Likewise, if litigation ensues, the parties and the court must be able to interpret the property-devising document. In this context, what evidence do

you think courts should allow into the record to determine the meaning of the instrument — what about direct, circumstantial and/or extrinsic evidence? Should courts have an expansive attitude and allow the introduction of any evidence that speaks to the testator's intent, or a narrow one focused on what is contained within the "four corners" of the document?

5.   Call your parents or grandparents! Seriously. (They'll love to hear from you.) Ask them whether they have a written will or created any trusts. Inquire whether they have done any planning in case they have health problems or become disabled and cannot make financial or medical decisions for themselves, such as having drafted a living will or durable powers of attorney.

6.   Has someone in your family or a friend experienced a messy situation dealing with the administration of a relative's estate?

B.   THE LEGAL SYSTEM GOVERNING TRUSTS AND ESTATES

Each year, almost 2.5 million people die in the United States, and a majority of them do not have a will. What happens to their property? What types of lifetime planning can people undertake to ensure their property is distributed as they wish? The readings in this section explore the structure of American probate law, and introduce some of the nonprobate mechanisms for distributing property.

As you learned earlier, each state borrowed from the law of its particular colonial tradition to develop its own approach to trusts and estates law; few federal laws apply in this area. To bring some uniformity and clarity to the law and to eliminate many of the formal rules that were intent-defeating, the ULC drafted the Uniform Probate Code (UPC) in 1969. After revisions to individual sections over the years, the ULC redrafted the entire UPC in 1990. The 1990 version has also been revised a few times, so it is difficult to describe one uniform act in terms of state adoptions. Some states have adopted the 1969 UPC, some the 1990 UPC as originally enacted and others have incorporated some of the revisions. In addition, some states have not adopted either act as a whole but have incorporated provisions from different versions.

Notwithstanding this lack of uniformity, the provisions of both UPCs, plus all the revisions over the years, have influenced statutes in states that are not on the list of "UPC states." Because of the impact of the UPC, this book uses selected provisions of the UPC to illustrate various aspects of American probate law. We primarily use provisions from the 1990 UPC, as most recently revised; where we use a different version, we indicate that fact. In addition, to show you some of the variations among the states, we use statutes and cases from states that have not adopted the UPC.

In the trusts area, the law developed primarily through cases and thus there were a variety of approaches as a result. In some states the Restatement was the primary source of legal rules because there was so little case law. So, in 2000, the ULC promulgated the Uniform Trust Code (UTC) to bring greater uniformity to the field and to provide a source of law in states with limited case law. The UTC codifies the common law in many respects, and to date, it has been adopted by slightly less than half of the states. Like the UPC, however, its influence extends beyond the states that have enacted it. The UTC provides precise, comprehensive and easily accessible guidance on trust law questions, and is a resource for trustees, lawyers and courts. Rather than attempting to discuss the law of 50 states, this book primarily uses UTC provisions to explain trust law. However, we occasionally include the law of other states where we think it is appropriate.

In addition to the UPC and the UTC, we frequently refer to the Restatements, which are particularly influential in this area of the law. While the Restatements in the wills and trusts areas often parallel the UPC and the UTC, they can differ in some respects. This is due to the fact that the authors of the Restatements are trying to restate the law not only as it exists in states that have adopted those uniform acts, but also as it exists in states that have not. Thus, when we refer to the Restatement, you should be aware that it may not accurately reflect either the law of your state or the UPC.

In the readings that follow, you will begin to explore the various mechanisms for transmitting property during one's lifetime and at death. You will — we hope — appreciate the dynamic nature of the field, as well as its jurisprudential and practical consequences.

1. *Wills*

Wills have been the traditional method for disposing of property. Singer Michael Jackson's will in Appendix D to this chapter is an interesting example of this kind of donative instrument.

Lawrence Friedman, Dead Hands: A Social History of Wills, Trusts, and Inheritance Law
(2009)

The whole edifice of the law of succession, legally and socially, rests on one brute fact: you can't take it with you. . . . In a rich country, the stock of wealth that turns over as people die is staggeringly large. In the United States alone, some $41 trillion will pass from the dead to the living in the first half of the 21st century. . . .

Only living people can "own" something. Once a person dies, owner-ship lapses, and the goods and assets pass into other hands. There are several ways in which society can deal with the property of a dead person. One way would be to cut off any rights the dead person might have had and leave the asset up for grabs. Or the state could confiscate the property and use it for whatever purposes it chooses. Or, to mention a third possibility, legal rules could dictate what becomes of the property — who gets what, and in what proportions. Fourth, we could let the dead person decide and honor whatever requests or arrangements he or she might have made.

In fact, our system has elements of all four, though the last two probably dominate. . . .

Law and custom allow people many ways to pass on their property. One of the simplest ways, of course, is to give most or all of it away while still alive. A rich father can make out checks to his children; or he can give them money in more complicated ways, for example, by setting up a trust. [In later chapters, we take a closer look at trusts — EDS.]

Most people, however, hold on to their money, or some of it. They pass on their property at death, and many of them do so through a document called a will. As we will see, the importance of the will has declined some-what in recent times. But the will is still a very common, fundamental, and genuinely popular document. . . .

The ordinary will, the most common kind, and the kind that is recog-nized as valid in every state, is a highly formal document. For one thing, it has to be in writing. . . .

[The will also needs a certain number of witnesses, who are] supposed to guarantee, through their testimony, that the will was executed properly and that all the legal details were buttoned up. Every will has to have the testator's signature. And the testator has to *intend* the document to be his will. . . .

Nobody *has* to have a will; the state will be happy to distribute your property without one, using its intestacy laws. Still, it is a good idea for any-body with money to make out a will, unless one is absolutely sure the intes-tacy laws are good enough and that the right person will be appointed your personal representative [*i.e.*, the person who administers the estate]. How many people actually do have wills? A telephone survey of 750 families in five states (Alabama, California, Massachusetts, Ohio, and Texas) in 1977 found that 45% of the people interviewed had a will. Age was an important factor. Eighty-four percent of those over 65 had a will; 92% of those under 24 did not. Richer and more educated people tended to have a will. . . .

The will once had a virtual monopoly over gifts at death. This is no longer the case. The rise of will substitutes has, in turn, affected the law of wills itself. This is probably a key reason why the law of wills has become less formal and formalistic. After all, now one can draw up a document that looks like a will, sounds like a will, and acts like a will, but isn't a will. . . .

The trust — or to be more precise a certain kind of trust — is one of the most important of the will substitutes. A trust is a legal arrangement in which certain assets — land, money, stocks and bonds — are put in the hands of a trustee, who manages the assets and has control over them, but who exercises his power on behalf of one or more beneficiaries.

---

2.   *The Emergence of Will Substitutes*

Only property that is owned by the decedent at death is included in the probate estate and disposed of by will or, in the absence of a will, through intestacy. In the past, wills or intestacy were virtually the only means available for determining to whom the decedent's property was distributed upon death.

Things have changed. You will see many references to *will substitutes* (the topic of Chapter 4), which can dispose of either property or contractual rights, and which have the effect of removing property from the probate estate. Will substitutes are established while the donor is still living, and they effectively: "(1) [shift] the right to possession or enjoyment of the property or to a contractual payment outside of probate to the donee at the donor's death; [while] . . . substantial lifetime rights of dominion, control, possession, or enjoyment are retained by the donor." RESTATEMENT (THIRD) OF PROPERTY: WILLS & OTHER DONATIVE TRANSFERS §7.1.

While wills must be executed with great attention to certain formalities, will substitutes are not subject to the same requirements, an issue Professor Friedman discussed in the excerpt above and to which we will return throughout the semester, including in the excerpt below. Will substitutes are also called "probate avoidance devices," and they take a variety of forms, including gifts, living trusts, certain bank and securities accounts and life insurance policies. In 1984, Professor John Langbein wrote the following landmark article.

John Langbein, The Nonprobate Revolution and the Future of the Law of Succession
97 Harv. L. Rev. 1108 (1984)

Over the course of the twentieth century, persistent tides of change have been lapping at the once-quiet shores of the law of succession. Probate, our court-operated system for transferring wealth at death, is declining in importance. Institutions that administer noncourt modes of transfer are displacing the probate system. Life insurance companies, pension plan operators, commercial banks, savings banks, investment companies, brokerage houses, stock transfer agents, and a variety of other financial intermediaries are functioning as free-market competitors of the probate system and enabling property to pass on death without probate and without will. The law of wills and the rules of descent no longer govern succession to most of the property of most decedents. Increasingly, probate bears to the actual practice of succession about the relation that bankruptcy bears to enterprise: it is an indispensable institution, but hardly one that everybody need use. . . .

Four main will substitutes constitute the core of the nonprobate system: life insurance, pension accounts, joint accounts, and revocable trusts. When properly created, each is functionally indistinguishable from a will — each reserves to the owner complete lifetime dominion, including the power to name and to change beneficiaries until death. These devices I shall call "pure" will substitutes, in contradistinction to "imperfect" will substitutes (primarily joint tenancies), which more closely resemble completed lifetime transfers. The four pure will substitutes may also be described as mass will substitutes: they are marketed by financial intermediaries using standard form instruments with fill-in-the-blank beneficiary designations.

The typical American of middle- or upper-middle-class means employs many will substitutes. The precise mix of will and will substitutes varies with individual circumstances — age, family, employment, wealth, and legal sophistication. It would not be unusual for someone in mid-life to have a dozen or more will substitutes in force, whether or not he had a will. . . .

The will substitutes differ from the ordinary "last will and testament" in three main ways. First, most will substitutes — but not all — are asset-specific: each deals with a single type of property, be it life insurance proceeds, a bank balance, mutual fund shares, or whatever. Second, property that passes through a will substitute avoids probate. A financial intermediary ordinarily takes the place of the probate court in effecting the transfer. Third, the formal requirements of the Wills Act — attestation and so forth — do not govern will substitutes and are not complied with. Of these differences, only probate avoidance is a significant advantage that transferors might consciously seek. . . .

Modern practice supplies only one theory that can reconcile wills and will substitutes in a workable and honest manner: the rule of transferor's intent. The real state of the law is that the transferor may choose to pass his property on death in either the probate or the nonprobate system or in both. The transferor who takes no steps to form or disclose his intent will be remitted to probate, the state system. The transferor who elects to use any of the devices of the nonprobate system will be protected in his decision, provided that the mode of nonprobate transfer is sufficiently formal to meet the burden of proof on the question of intent to transfer.

Transferring property of any type, whether it is treasured photo albums or the family farm, is serious business. While wills require a set of formalities that recognize the serious nature of these transfers, will substitutes are far more informal. Throughout the course, we will return to consider the benefits and drawbacks of requirements concerning formality. As you will see, the decline in formal rules, the increasing use of will substitutes rather than traditional wills and social changes in family structure have all had an impact on trusts and estates law.

Once again, consider Michael Jackson's will in Appendix D. Are you surprised by any of its provisions? Given the extent of his estate, does the length of the will surprise you? In what way does the will suggest that he used one or more will substitutes in developing his estate plan?

3.   The Probate Process

Probate is the process by which property from the estate is distributed to the appropriate recipients. A decedent's probate estate is "subject to administration under applicable laws relating to decedents' estates. The probate estate consists of (i) property owned by the decedent at death where the beneficiary is not already determined by a will substitute and (ii) property acquired by the decedent's estate at or after the decedent's death." RESTATE-MENT (THIRD) OF PROPERTY: WILLS & OTHER DONATIVE TRANSFERS §1.1(a) (2003). Probate has historical resonance with both law and equity. Professor Monopoli's book, excerpted below, explains the functions of probate and describes the development of the process for administering the probate estate. In the last 20 or so years, probate has become a less costly and time-consuming practice.

Paula Monopoli, American Probate:
Protecting the Public, Improving the Process
(2003)

The American states each developed their own methods of probating estates. In some states, the early probate courts were courts of equity that grew into what are now called chancery, surrogate, or orphan's courts. In other states, judges in courts of general jurisdiction were given authority over probate matters. The result was a patchwork of approaches that even today varies among states, and sometimes among counties in a single state. In an effort to promote a uniform set of probate court standards, the National College of Probate Court Judges in 1993 embarked on a systematic study of the nation's probate courts. They noted that, "Although individual cases involving wills, decedents' estates, trusts, guardianships, and conservatorships — traditionally, matters within the jurisdiction of courts exercising probate jurisdiction — have garnered considerable public and professional attention, relatively little is known about the administration, operation, and performance of courts with probate jurisdiction." In response to the dearth of relevant research, the National College gathered its own data, documenting the organization of the American probate courts. They found that, as of 1990, there were forty-four states (including the District of Columbia) with judicial structures that included a court of "limited or special jurisdiction" over probate matters. These courts only handle a limited class of cases for example, the probate of estates and the guardianships of incompetents. Within a given state, there can be as many as a thousand such courts.

Twenty-one states and the District of Columbia have a formal probate court or division. Some of these states use the term "probate" to designate the court that handles these cases, while states like New Jersey and New York use the term "surrogate." Connecticut has statewide probate courts, organized into 133 separate probate court districts. Its probate court system is managed by a probate court administrator who oversees a staff that includes a chief counsel, a staff attorney; coordinators for administrative, social, and financial services; and technical and administrative support.

A majority of states "have no formal probate court structure." For example, Arizona is one of thirty states where courts of general jurisdiction may have a probate department set up by local rule. Whether there is a separate court or not, there is wide variation in the jurisdiction of courts that handle matters loosely labeled "probate." The essential cases in a probate court's jurisdiction are wills, testamentary trusts, and decedents' estates. In the [] states and the District of Columbia that have a formal probate court organization, the courts hear wills, trusts, and estate cases. Seventeen of these and the District of Columbia hear guardianship cases in these courts. In eleven of them and the District of Columbia, the courts also hear conservatorship cases.

In addition to these basic duties, probate courts may hear cases as varied as involuntary civil commitment, adoptions, divorce, name changes, fish and game law violations, proceedings involving cemetery lots, and trusts related to community mausoleums. But when average Americans think of probate, it is the wills, trusts and estate cases that come to mind, and the oversight of decedents' estates in particular.

The probate process is intended to perform several useful functions. An executor is supposed to (1) collect or "marshal" all the decedent's assets and detail them on a list or "inventory"; (2) manage those assets during the several months or years it might take to administer the estate; (3) pay all those to whom the decedent owed debts, including hospital, doctor, and funeral bills and state and federal tax authorities; and (4) distribute what remains in the estate to the persons named in the will.

These important functions are performed by a "personal representative," either an "executor" or "administrator." Most probate courts oblige the decedent by making the person the decedent nominates the executor, but the court is not bound to do this. If someone objects, or if the court has misgivings about the nominee's ability to perform as a fiduciary, the court can name someone else. However, they rarely do.

If [someone dies] without a will, she would have died "intestate." In the event of intestacy, the probate court names an "administrator" rather than an "executor," usually a spouse, child or relative of the decedent. If there are no such relatives, then a lawyer or other court appointee will serve in this role. All fiduciaries must answer to the probate court, and judicial oversight is one of the major benefits the probate process offers. The requirement to account to the court is supposed to keep the personal representative honest in handling the decedent's cash, stocks and bonds, real estate, jewelry, and other valuable personal and real property.

Many Americans create "inter vivos," "revocable," or "living" trusts in order to avoid the probate process altogether. Even when people have established trusts, however, any assets not funneled to the trust before the death of the person creating it must go through probate before making their way into the trust.

In the American system, the government makes the first claim on its part of the estate, while the family must be content to wait for what is left. When the Internal Revenue Service has taken its share, it issues a "closing letter," indicating that all tax liabilities have been satisfied.

The term fiduciary, "is derived from the Roman law, and means a person . . . having [a] duty, created by his undertaking, to act primarily for another's benefit in matters connected with such undertakings." The fiduciary must act with "scrupulous good faith and candor."

The ethical rules in the legal profession have frowned on lawyers asking clients to name them as executor. . . .

Although the probate process is declining in importance as individuals engage in more lifetime planning that involves will substitutes and as jurisdictions provide for simplified probate procedures, it remains important to understand probate as the default procedure. Legal rules that now apply to will substitutes often developed as probate rules, and many of the cases you will read in this book were originally heard in probate courts.

C.   TESTAMENTARY FREEDOM AND LIMITATIONS ON "CONTROL FROM THE GRAVE"

Now that you've been introduced to the changing practice of estate planning, it is time to think about the purposes of estate planning. As set out above, the most fundamental principle concerns respect for effectuating the client's intent. Throughout the course, you will hear references to the "decedent's intent," or the "testator's intent," and most of the default rules in the trusts and estates field are attempts to establish what the decedent would have wanted. The following article explores how the law respects testamentary freedom as a cornerstone of American trusts and estates law.

Lee-ford Tritt, Sperms and Estates: An Unadulterated Functionally Based Approach to Parent-Child Property Succession
62 SMU L. Rev. 367 (2009)

The principle of testamentary freedom, the governing principle underlying American estates law, provides that individuals have the freedom (or right) to control the disposition of their property at death. From this follows the generally accepted principle that "succession law should reflect the desires of the 'typical person,' both with regard to protecting expressions of desire and anticipating situations where those expressions are inadequately presented."

The importance of testamentary freedom should not be underestimated. American society has long recognized the value inherent in protecting an individual's ability to acquire and transfer private property. Testamentary freedom is derived from general and well-established property law rights. Just as individuals have the right to accumulate, consume, and transfer personal property during life, individuals generally are, and should be, free to control the disposition of personal property at death. . . .

Rationales for testamentary freedom vary, and many theories have been proffered in support for the principle of this theory—some widely accepted, others more controversial. In general, testamentary freedom responds to basic human pleasures and desires and is supported by a variety of economic, philosophical, and societal values. The simplest rationale for testamentary freedom is that in a society based on the theory of private property, the freedom of testation might be the least objectionable arrangement for dealing with property succession at the testator's death. Others argue that robust testamentary freedom is natural; creates happiness; promotes wealth accumulation and responsibility; encourages industry, creativity, and productivity; reinforces family ties; and allows the testator to adapt to the needs and circumstances of his particular family. Each rationale has its proponents and skeptics, but the very breadth of jurisprudential and pragmatic justifications for testamentary freedom is, in itself, a testament to why this concept is at the core of Anglo-American succession law.

While testamentary freedom is a bedrock principle, the law does not allow an individual unfettered discretion; it sets limits on what someone attempts to do. For example, you are probably already familiar with the

Rule Against Perpetuities, which establishes parameters for the length of time that property can be encumbered. The law steps in at other points as well. For example, the elective share rules preclude an individual from denying a surviving spouse a portion of the decedent spouse's estate. Similarly, the law will not allow a person to avoid his creditors by leaving all of his property to others.

Outside of the statutorily created limitations or where the testator's plan promotes illegal conduct, courts are hesitant to limit testamentary freedom. *Feinberg*, the next case, shows a court struggling with where to draw the lines between following the testator's intent and fairness. The case concerns grandparents who sought to control the marital choices of their grandchildren through various means of estate planning. The laws of both wills and trusts (like that of contracts) will not enforce provisions that are contrary to public policy. The question, of course, is when is a provision contrary to public policy? Consider whether the court's approach reflects your own perspective. We return to these issues throughout the semester.

Feinberg v. Feinberg
919 N.E.2d 888 (Ill. 2009)

OPINION

. . . Max Feinberg died in 1986. He was survived by his wife, Erla, their adult children, Michael and Leila, and five grandchildren.

Prior to his death, Max executed a will and created a trust. Max's will provided that upon his death, all of his assets were to "pour over" into the trust. . . .

Upon Erla's death, any assets remaining in [the trust] were then to be distributed to Max's descendants in accordance with a provision we shall call the "beneficiary restriction clause." This clause directed that 50% of the assets be held in trust for the benefit of the then-living descendants of Michael and Leila during their lifetimes. . . . However, any such descendant who married outside the Jewish faith or whose non-Jewish spouse did not convert to Judaism within one year of marriage would be "deemed deceased for all purposes of this instrument as of the date of such marriage" and that descendant's share of the trust would revert to Michael or Leila. . . .

All five grandchildren married between 1990 and 2001. By the time of Erla's death in 2003, all five grandchildren had been married for more than one year. Only Leila's son, Jon, met the conditions of the beneficiary restriction clause and was entitled to receive [a distribution from the trust].

This litigation followed, pitting Michael's daughter, Michele, against Michael, coexecutor of the estates of both Max and Erla.

The trial court invalidated the beneficiary restriction clause on public ~T. ct~ policy grounds. A divided appellate court affirmed, holding that "under Illinois law and under the Restatement (Third) of Trusts, the provision in the ~Appellate~ case before us is invalid because it seriously interferes with and limits the right of individuals to marry a person of their own choosing." 383 Ill. App. 3d at 997. In reaching this conclusion, the appellate court relied on decisions of this court dating back as far as 1898 and, as noted, on the Restatement (Third) of Trusts. . . .

We note that this case involves more than a grandfather's desire that his descendants continue to follow his religious tradition after he is gone. This case reveals a broader tension between the competing values of freedom of testation on one hand and resistance to "dead hand" control on the other. This tension is clearly demonstrated by the three opinions of the appellate court. The authoring justice rejected the argument that the distribution scheme is enforceable because it operated at the time of Erla's death and could not affect future behavior, stating that its "clear intent was to influence the marriage decisions of Max's grandchildren based on a religions [sic] criterion." 383 Ill. App. 3d at 997. The concurring justice opined that while such restrictions might once have been considered reasonable, they are no longer reasonable. 383 Ill. App. 3d at 1000 (Quinn, P.J., specially concurring). The dissenting justice noted that under the facts of this case, grandchildren who had complied with the restrictions would "immediately receive their legacy" upon Erla's death (383 Ill. App. 3d at 1000 (Greiman, J., dissenting)), and that the weight of authority is that a testator has a right to make the distribution of his bounty conditional on the beneficiary's adherence to a particular religious faith (383 Ill. App. 3d at 1002).

We, therefore, begin our analysis with the public policy surrounding testamentary freedom and then consider public policy pertaining to testamentary or trust provisions concerning marriage.

When we determine that our answer to a question of law must be based on public policy, it is not our role to make such policy. Rather, we must discern the public policy of the state of Illinois as expressed in the constitution, statutes, and long-standing case law. We will find a contract provision against public policy only "if it is injurious to the interests of the public, contravenes some established interest of society, violates some public statute, is against good morals, tends to interfere with the public welfare or safety, or is at war with the interests of society or is in conflict with the morals of the time." Thus,

> "In deciding whether an agreement violates public policy, courts determine whether the agreement is so capable of producing harm that its enforcement would be contrary to the public interest. The courts apply a strict test in determining when an agreement violates public policy. The power to

invalidate part or all of an agreement on the basis of public policy is used sparingly because private parties should not be needlessly hampered in their freedom to contract between themselves. Whether an agreement is contrary to public policy depends on the particular facts and circumstances of the case." *Kleinwort Benson North America, Inc. v. Quantum Financial Services, Inc.*, 181 Ill. 2d 214, 226, 692 N.E.2d 269 (1998).

Because, as will be discussed below, the public policy of this state values freedom of testation as well as freedom of contract, these same principles guide our analysis in the present case.

Public Policy Regarding Freedom of Testation

Neither the Constitution of the United States nor the Constitution of the State of Illinois speak to the question of testamentary freedom. However, our statutes clearly reveal a public policy in support of testamentary freedom. . . .

Under the Probate Act, Max and Erla had no obligation to make any provision at all for their grandchildren. Indeed, if Max had died intestate, Erla, Michael, and Leila would have shared his estate, and if Erla had died intestate, only Michael and Leila would have taken. Surely, the grandchildren have no greater claim on their grandparents' testate estates than they would have had on intestate estates.

Similarly, under the Trusts and Trustees Act, "[a] person establishing a trust may specify in the instrument the rights, powers, duties, limitations and immunities applicable to the trustee, beneficiary and others and those provisions where not otherwise contrary to law shall control, notwithstanding this Act." Thus, the legislature intended that the settlor of a trust have the freedom to direct his bounty as he sees fit, even to the point of giving effect to a provision regarding the rights of beneficiaries that might depart from the standard provisions of the Act, unless "otherwise contrary to law." . . .

The record, via the testimony of Michael and Leila, reveals that Max's intent in restricting the distribution of his estate was to benefit those descendants who opted to honor and further his commitment to Judaism by marrying within the faith. Max had expressed his concern about the potential extinction of the Jewish people, not only by holocaust, but by gradual dilution as a result of intermarriage with non-Jews. While he was willing to share his bounty with a grandchild whose spouse converted to Judaism, this was apparently as far as he was willing to go.

There is no question that a grandparent in Max's situation is entirely free during his lifetime to attempt to influence his grandchildren to marry within his family's religious tradition, even by offering financial incentives to do so. The question is, given our public policy of testamentary freedom, did Max's beneficiary restriction clause []² violate any other public policy of the state of Illinois, thus rendering it void? . . .

Michele argues that the beneficiary restriction clause discourages lawful marriage and interferes with the fundamental right to marry, which is protected by the constitution. She also invokes the constitution in support of her assertion that issues of race, religion, and marriage have special status because of their constitutional dimensions, particularly in light of the constitutional values of personal autonomy and privacy.

Because a testator or the settlor of a trust is not a state actor, there are no constitutional dimensions to his choice of beneficiaries. Equal protection does not require that all children be treated equally; due process does not require notice of conditions precedent to potential beneficiaries; and the free exercise clause does not require a grandparent to treat grandchildren who reject his religious beliefs and customs in the same manner as he treats those who conform to his traditions.

Thus, Michele's reliance on *Shelley v. Kraemer*, 334 U.S. 1 (1948), is entirely misplaced. In *Shelley*, the Supreme Court held that the use of the state's judicial process to obtain enforcement of a racially restrictive covenant was state action, violating the equal protection clause of the fourteenth amendment. *Shelley*, 334 U.S. at 19. This court, however, has been reluctant to base a finding of state action "on the mere fact that a state court is the forum for the dispute." *In re Adoption of K.L.P.*, 198 Ill. 2d 448, 465, 763 N.E.2d 741 (2002). . . .

Third, Michele argues that the beneficiary restriction clause is capable of exerting an ongoing "disruptive influence" upon marriage and is, therefore, void. She is mistaken. The provision cannot "disrupt" an existing marriage because once the beneficiary determination was made at the time of Erla's death, it created no incentive to divorce.

Finally, it has been suggested that Michael and Leila have litigated this matter rather than concede to Michele's demands because they wish to deprive the grandchildren of their inheritance. The grandchildren, however, are not the heirs at law of Max and Erla and had no expectancy of an inheritance, so long as their parents were living, even if Max and Erla had died intestate. In addition, Michael and Leila are the coexecutors of their parents' estates and, as such, are duty-bound to defend their parents' estate plans. *Hurd v. Reed*, 260 Ill. 154, 160, 102 N.E. 1048 (1913) ("It is the duty of an executor to defend the will"), citing *Pingree v. Jones*, 80 Ill. 177, 181 (1875) (executor is "bound, on every principle of honor, justice and right" to defend the will, he "owes this, at least, to the memory of the dead who placed this confidence in him"). Although those plans might be offensive to individual family members or to outside observers, Max and Erla were free to distribute their bounty as they saw fit and to favor grandchildren of whose life choices they approved over other grandchildren who made

---

2. [Brackets indicate that the authors have omitted a few words that refer to extraneous issues. — EDS.]

choices of which they disapproved, so long as they did not convey a vested interest that was subject to divestment by a condition subsequent that tended to unreasonably restrict marriage or encourage divorce.

NOTES AND QUESTIONS

1.   *Who are these people?* Max Feinberg was a wealthy Chicago dentist who died in 1986. His wife Erla, who was the primary beneficiary of the trust, died in 2003. The case pitted one of their grandchildren against her father. Ron Grossman, *"Jewish Clause" Divides a Family*, CHI. TRIB., Aug. 25, 2008, at C1. What happens to a family after cases like *Feinberg*?

2.   *Dead hand control and public policy.* The intermediate appellate court in *Feinberg*, like other courts, struck down the use of financial incentives in estate planning "because it seriously interferes with and limits the right of individuals to marry a person of their own choosing." Courts generally find that conditions requiring a potential beneficiary to divorce or become separated are invalid as a violation of public policy. Is *Feinberg* such a case? *See* Shelly Steiner, *Incentive Conditions: The Validity of Innovative Financial Parenting by Passing Along Wealth and Values*, 40 VAL. U. L. REV. 897, 916-19 (2006). These clauses, it is argued, allow the dead to exert too much control over the personal choices of the living. *See* Jeffrey G. Sherman, *Posthumous Meddling: An Instrumentalist Theory of Testamentary Restraints on Conjugal and Religious Choices*, 1999 U. ILL. L. REV. 1273. To what extent should a testator be allowed to determine to whom to leave his property? *See* Aaron H. Kaplan, *Note: The "Jewish Clause" and Public Policy: Preserving the Testamentary Right to Oppose Religious Intermarriage*, 8 GEO. J.L. & PUB. POL'Y 295 (2010). Can you think of reasons why a state might wish to eliminate or reduce dead hand control or uphold it?

3.   *The only way?* The court noted that the parties conceded "that Max and Erla could have accomplished the goal of benefitting only those grandchildren who married within their religious tradition by individually naming those grandchildren as beneficiaries of the will or the trust, without implicating public policy." This was, however, physically impossible, the court pointed out, because when "Max prepared his estate plan, his grandchildren were too young to marry." While a will only becomes effective when the testator dies, the estate plan may be developed many years in advance of that event. If you were the estate planning lawyer for the Feinbergs, what alternatives could you have recommended to reward grandchildren who married within the faith and penalize those who did not? If the court had decided that the clause in issue was contrary to public policy, would not that have led to "game-playing" by people who wished to discriminate among beneficiaries but felt they could not do so forthrightly in the document?

D.   THE PROFESSIONAL STANDARDS ASSOCIATED WITH ESTATE PLANNING

1.   *Introduction*

Professional responsibility issues involving estate planning are raised in a variety of contexts, beginning with the initial client consultation and continuing after the death of the clients. Even if you have not yet taken a professional responsibility course, you know that lawyers are subject to a series of ethical restraints on their actions that are self-imposed by the legal profession, the violation of which may lead to sanctions such as suspension or disbarment through disciplinary proceedings. Attorneys may also become involved in will contests and malpractice cases as a result of their legal advice.

The Model Rules of Professional Conduct (MRPC) and the earlier Model Code of Professional Responsibility set the rules for how lawyers are to conduct themselves in the profession. Each state bar has adopted its variation of these rules. When lawyers are alleged to have violated their professional responsibilities, most jurisdictions enforce sanctions through disciplinary proceedings conducted by their state bar association, Supreme Court or a combination of the two. Sanctions against a lawyer who has breached the jurisdiction's professional rules can range from private or public reprimand to temporary or permanent disbarment. Legal disciplinary proceedings are designed to protect the public and ensure the integrity of the profession.

However, estate planning attorneys also have to be concerned that a disappointed beneficiary or heir may (i) challenge a will or other planning document, or (ii) bring a malpractice claim. In either situation, the attorney could be forced into the uncomfortable role of having to testify that what he did was consistent with the wishes of the client.

A will contest is an attack on the will. It is common for children or other relatives who have not received what they believe to be their "fair share" to contest a will, claiming, among other things, that the attorney failed to effectuate the decedent's intention. Where money and hurt feelings are involved, these actions can get very bitter.

Whether successful in the will contest or not, a disappointed potential beneficiary may also bring a malpractice claim against the attorney. Unlike disciplinary proceedings or will contests, these civil actions are designed to compensate individual victims by awarding damages. According to the American Bar Association, almost 9% of all malpractice claims filed against attorneys involve estates, trusts and probate, with many of the complaints alleging that the attorney had inadequate knowledge of the law or failed to consider or represent the interests of non-client family members. Henry Ordower, *Toward a Multiple Party Representation Model: Moderating Power Disparity*, 64 Ohio St. L.J. 1263, 1274 n.58 (2003).

In the material that follows, we first present the Model Rules along with relevant commentary focused on the estates and trusts field. Then we consider the application of the rules to various situations you might confront — joint representation, serving as drafting attorney or fiduciary and counseling. In addition, we explore the lawyer's obligations to clients and non-clients. We present the duties of care an attorney is expected to meet, the violation of which may be grounds for disciplinary proceedings or the basis for a malpractice action. As you review the materials on professional responsibility, reflect on how to conduct an estate planning practice that fulfills your obligations to your clients and that also serves: (1) to protect against a complaint filed with the licensing agency that might jeopardize your right to practice law; or (2) to show that you acted professionally and with due care to meet the client's intentions in case you are called as a witness in a will contest or as a defendant in a malpractice action.

2. The Model Rules of Professional Conduct and ACTEC Commentaries

The Model Rules, and the state rules adapted from them, are general statements that apply to all areas of the law; they are not focused on any specific field of law. In an effort to provide guidance in the estate planning context, the American College of Trusts and Estate Counsel (ACTEC), a nonprofit organization whose members are involved in the trusts and estates area, has developed commentaries on the Model Rules. The discussion below provides an example of how the ACTEC Commentaries give more specific guidance and adapt the general Model Rules to the particular problems encountered by estate planning lawyers.

a. Counseling

ACTEC COMMENTARIES ON THE MODEL RULES OF PROFESSIONAL CONDUCT (4th ed. 2006)[3]

MRPC 1.2. Scope of Representation and Allocation of Authority Between Client and Lawyer

(a) Subject to paragraphs (c) and (d), a lawyer shall abide by a client's decisions concerning the objectives of the representation and [] shall consult with the client as to the means by which they are to be pursued. . . .

---

3. *Available at* http://www.actec.org/public/CommentariesPublic.asp. All Commentaries throughout the book have been excerpted from the ACTEC COMMENTARIES ON THE MODEL RULES OF PROFESSIONAL CONDUCT (4th ed. 2006). All corresponding Rules are the Delaware Lawyers' Rules of Professional Conduct, *available at* http://courts.delaware.gov/rules/DLRPCFebruary2010.pdf, which closely resemble the Model Rules of Professional Conduct.

(b) A lawyer's representation of a client, including representation by appointment, does not constitute an endorsement of the client's political, economic, social or moral views or activities.

(c) A lawyer may limit the scope of the representation if the limitation is reasonable under the circumstances and the client gives informed consent.

(d) A lawyer shall not counsel a client to engage, or assist a client, in conduct that the lawyer knows is criminal or fraudulent, but a lawyer may discuss the legal consequences of any proposed course of conduct with a client and may counsel or assist a client to make a good faith effort to determine the validity, scope, meaning or application of the law.

* * *

ACTEC COMMENTARY ON MRPC 1.2

Facilitating Informed Judgment by Clients. In the course of the estate planning process the lawyer should assist the client in making informed judgments regarding the method by which the client's objectives will be fulfilled. The lawyer may properly exercise reasonable judgment in deciding upon the alternatives to describe to the client. For example, the lawyer may counsel a client that the client's charitable objectives could be achieved either by including an outright bequest in the client's will or by establishing a charitable remainder trust. The lawyer need not describe alternatives, such as the charitable lead trust, if the use of such a device does not appear suitable for the client. As indicated below, the lawyer should describe the tax and nontax advantages and disadvantages of the plans and assist the client in making a decision among them. The client might choose to ask the lawyer or another professional to prepare any tax returns that are required.

. . .

Defining and Refining the Scope of Representation.   As the lawyer obtains information from a client, the lawyer and the client are typically working together toward defining further the scope and objectives of the representation, which are often revised as the representation progresses. One of the lawyer's goals should be to educate the client sufficiently about the process and the options available to allow the client to make informed decisions regarding the representation. In furtherance of that goal many lawyers review with an estate planning client the appropriate alternative methods by which the client's general estate planning objectives could be implemented. In the course of doing so the lawyer should express to the client the relative cost advantages of the alternatives, including the present and future tax, legal and other costs, such as trustee's fees.

MRPC 2.1. Advisor

In representing a client, a lawyer shall exercise independent professional judgment and render candid advice. In rendering advice, a lawyer may refer not only to law but to other considerations such as moral, economic, social and political factors, that may be relevant to the client's situation.

* * *

ACTEC COMMENTARY ON MRPC 2.1

As advisor the lawyer may appropriately counsel the client with respect to all aspects of the representation, including nonlegal considerations. In doing so the lawyer should recognize his or her own limitations and the risks inherent in attempting to assist a client with respect to matters beyond the lawyer's expertise. Although it may be appropriate for the lawyer to suggest that a client consider either diversifying the client's investments or investing in a particular class of assets (e.g., municipal bonds), the lawyer ordinarily should not recommend specific investments to the client. In contrast, the lawyer may properly suggest that the client consider whether or not a particular course of action might generate adverse legal or nonlegal consequences. For example, the lawyer may properly ask a client to consider the legal and nonlegal consequences that might result if the client were to make unequal gifts to children or other equally related relatives. The lawyer may also appropriately recommend that the client consult with an expert in a particular field, whether it be mental health, investments, insurance, employee benefits, or any other matter that is not within the lawyer's expertise.

---

b. Confidentiality

MRPC 1.6. Confidentiality of Information

(a) A lawyer shall not reveal information relating to representation of a client unless the client gives informed consent, the disclosure is impliedly authorized in order to carry out the representation or the disclosure is permitted by paragraph (b).

(b) A lawyer may reveal information relating to the representation of a client to the extent the lawyer reasonably believes necessary:

(1) to prevent reasonably certain death or substantial bodily harm;

(2) to prevent the client from committing a crime or fraud that is reasonably certain to result in substantial injury to the financial interests or property of another and in furtherance of which the client has used or is using the lawyer's services.

(3) to prevent, mitigate or rectify substantial injury to the financial interests or property of another that is reasonably certain to result or has resulted from the client's commission of a crime or fraud in furtherance of which the client has used the lawyer's services.

(4) to secure legal advice about the lawyer's compliance with these Rules;

(5) to establish a claim or defense on behalf of the lawyer in a controversy between the lawyer and the client, to establish a defense to a criminal charge or civil claim against the lawyer based upon conduct in which the client was involved, or to respond to allegations in any proceeding concerning the lawyer's representation of the client; or

(6) to comply with other law or a court order.

* * *

ACTEC COMMENTARY ON MRPC 1.6 (Excerpts)

Obligation After Death of Client.   In general, the lawyer's duty of confidentiality continues after the death of a client. Accordingly, a lawyer ordinarily should not disclose confidential information following a client's death. However, if consent is given by the client's personal representative, or if the decedent had expressly or impliedly authorized disclosure, the lawyer who represented the deceased client may provide an interested party, including a potential litigant, with information regarding a deceased client's dispositive instruments and intent, including prior instruments and communications relevant thereto. A lawyer may be impliedly authorized to make appropriate disclosure of client confidential information that would promote the client's estate plan, forestall litigation, preserve assets, and further family understanding of the decedent's intention. Disclosures should ordinarily be limited to information that the lawyer would be required to reveal as a witness.

. . .

Joint and Separate Clients.   . . . [T]he same lawyer may represent a husband and wife, or parent and child, whose dispositive plans are not entirely the same. When the lawyer is first consulted by the multiple potential clients the lawyer should review with them the terms upon which the lawyer will undertake the representation, including the extent to which information will be shared among them. In the absence of any agreement to the contrary (usually in writing), a lawyer is presumed to represent multiple clients with regard to related legal matters jointly with resulting full sharing of information between the clients. . . .

Multiple Separate Clients. . . . [W]ith full disclosure and the informed consents of the clients, some experienced estate planners regularly undertake to represent husbands and wives as separate clients. Similarly, some estate planners also represent a parent and child or other multiple clients as separate clients. A lawyer who is asked to provide separate representation to multiple clients should do so with great care because of the stress it necessarily places on the lawyer's duties of impartiality and loyalty and the extent to which it may limit the lawyer's ability to advise each of the clients adequately. For example, without disclosing a confidence of one spouse the lawyer may be unable adequately to represent the other spouse. . . . The lawyer's disclosures to, and the agreement of, clients who wish to be separately represented should, but need not, be reflected in a contemporaneous writing. Unless required by local law, such a writing need not be signed by the clients.

Confidences Imparted by One Joint Client.   A lawyer who receives information from one joint client (the "communicating client") that the client does not wish to be shared with the other joint client (the "other client") is confronted with a situation that may threaten the lawyer's ability to continue to represent one or both of the clients. As soon as practicable after such a communication the lawyer should consider the relevance and significance of the information and decide upon the appropriate manner in which to proceed. The potential courses of action include, *inter alia*, (1) taking no action with respect to communications regarding irrelevant (or trivial) matters; (2) encouraging the communicating client to provide the information to the other client or to allow the lawyer to do so; and, (3) withdrawing from the representation if the communication reflects serious adversity between the parties. For example, a lawyer who represents a husband and wife in estate planning matters might conclude that information imparted by one of the spouses regarding a past act of marital infidelity need not be communicated to the other spouse. On the other hand, the lawyer might conclude that he or she is required to take some action with respect to a confidential communication that concerns a matter that threatens the interests of the other client or could impair the lawyer's ability to represent the other client effectively (e.g., "After she signs the trust agreement I intend to leave her . . ." or "All of the insurance policies on my life that name her as beneficiary have lapsed"). Without the informed consent of the other client, the lawyer should not take any action on behalf of the communicating client, such as drafting a codicil or a new will, that might damage the other client's economic interests or otherwise violate the lawyer's duty of loyalty to the other client.

. . .

c. Conflict of Interest

MRPC 1.7. Conflict of Interest: Current Clients

(a) Except as provided in paragraph (b), a lawyer shall not represent a client if the representation involves a concurrent conflict of interest. A concurrent conflict of interest exists if:

(1) the representation of one client will be directly adverse to another client; or

(2) there is a significant risk that the representation of one or more clients will be materially limited by the lawyer's responsibilities to another client, a former client or a third person or by a personal interest of the lawyer.

(b) Notwithstanding the existence of a concurrent conflict of interest under paragraph (a), a lawyer may represent a client if:

(1) the lawyer reasonably believes that the lawyer will be able to provide competent and diligent representation to each affected client;

1. Reasonably believes

(2) the representation is not prohibited by law;

2. Not against law

(3) the representation does not involve the assertion of a claim by one client against another client represented by the lawyer in the same litigation or other proceeding before a tribunal; and

3. Not 1 client vs another

(4) each affected client gives informed consent, confirmed in writing.

4. Informed consent

* * *

ACTEC COMMENTARY ON MRPC 1.7

. . .

Joint or Separate Representation. . . .

Example 1.7-1: Lawyer (*L*) was asked to represent Husband (*H*) and Wife (*W*) in connection with estate planning matters. *L* had previously not represented either *H* or *W*. At the outset *L* should discuss with *H* and *W* the terms upon which *L* would represent them, including the extent to which confidentiality would be maintained with respect to communications made by each. Many lawyers believe that it is only appropriate to represent a husband and wife as joint clients, between whom the lawyer could not maintain the confidentiality of any information relevant to the representation. The representation of a husband and wife as joint clients does not ordinarily require the informed consent of either or both of them. . . .

. . .

Conflicts of Interest May Preclude Multiple Representation.   Some conflicts of interest are so serious that the informed consent of the parties is insufficient to allow the lawyer to undertake or continue the representation (a "non-waivable" conflict). Thus, a lawyer may not represent clients whose interests actually conflict to such a degree that the lawyer cannot adequately represent their individual interests. A lawyer may never represent opposing parties in the same litigation. A lawyer is almost always precluded from representing both parties to a pre-nuptial agreement or other matter with respect to which their interests directly conflict to a substantial degree. Thus, a lawyer who represents the personal representative of a decedent's estate (or the trustee of a trust) should not also represent a creditor in connection with a claim against the estate (or trust). . . .

. . .

Prospective Waivers.   A client who is adequately informed may waive some conflicts that might otherwise prevent the lawyer from representing another person in connection with the same or a related matter. These conflicts are said to be "waivable." Thus, a surviving spouse who serves as the personal representative of her husband's estate may give her informed consent confirmed in writing to permit the lawyer who represents her as personal representative also to represent a child who is a beneficiary of the estate. The lawyer also would need an informed consent from the child that is confirmed in writing before undertaking such a dual representation.

---

3. Common Situations Raising Ethical Issues for Estate Planners

a.   Joint Representation

One of the most common situations that creates ethical concerns for an estate planning attorney is representing both a husband and a wife, who may have potentially different, and thus conflicting, interests. These issues are addressed above in MRPCs 1.6 and 1.7 and the related ACTEC Commentaries. The following article provides different perspectives on how to approach joint representation.

Naomi Cahn & Robert Tuttle,
Dependency and Delegation:
The Ethics of Marital Representation
22 Seattle U. L. Rev. 97, 100-03 (1998)

Under the Model Rules, few representations raise unwaivable conflicts; typically only those involving simultaneous representation of adverse parties in litigation are presumed unwaivable. . . .

The ethical analysis of multiple representation, then, usually turns on questions of informed consent. Did the clients receive sufficient information about the conflict? Was the clients' consent freely given? Has the lawyer continued to provide the clients with information relating to the conflict, especially where the information materially changes the extent or nature of the conflict?

Marital representation tracks the general ethical analysis of multiparty representation. Courts and bar associations have been somewhat reluctant to permit joint representation of spouses in divorce, though many jurisdictions do allow one lawyer to represent both spouses in an uncontested divorce (assuming, of course, fully informed consent). In other contexts, such as a married couple's purchase of a home, joint representation seems perfectly normal. Indeed, one would hardly think of suggesting a different form of representation where the spouses' interests are so closely aligned. Between these two polar contexts of complete dissolution or perfect harmony, a lawyer approached for representation by a married couple has four options: a separate lawyer for each spouse, the same lawyer representing each spouse individually, joint representation, and entity representation.

One possibility, of course, is that the lawyer can refuse simultaneous representation of spouses and request that one spouse, or both, seek another lawyer. This possibility fits perfectly into the "one lawyer for each client" ideal and may be appropriate where the spouses' interests are in conflict (e.g., the spouses have a serious disagreement about estate planning involving one spouse's children from a prior marriage, or a man and woman who intend to marry want to execute a prenuptial agreement).

Apart from such conflicts, the "separate attorneys" model leaves much to be desired. Separate lawyers means additional expense for the clients even though the additional protection is often unnecessary. In addition, separate representation may actually be counterproductive. Dueling lawyers may convert an otherwise harmonious process into an adversarial conflict.

A second possibility is separate representation by the same lawyer such that the same lawyer establishes two attorney-client relationships — one with each spouse. The Special Study Committee of the American Bar Association's Real Property Section accepts this model as one alternative for marital representation, provided that the relationship is established by express agreement of both spouses. In contrast to separate representation by separate lawyers, the Committee believes that separate representation by the same lawyer provides greater coordination of the spouses' mutual interests — especially important in estate planning — while still permitting each spouse the advantages of "independent" advice and confidentiality. However, separate representation by the same lawyer presents serious conflicts of interest that informed consent often cannot reliably cure. Since it would be extremely difficult even for the lawyer to describe the nature of possible conflicts that might arise between the spouses, the spouses will rarely be able to give sufficiently informed consent to this representation.

Third, the lawyer could represent the spouses as joint clients. . . . [J]oint representation [might mean] that the clients share control of the representation, and the lawyer shares all confidences with both clients. Both of these features distinguish the joint clients approach from separate representation by the same lawyer. While separately represented clients interact with the lawyer in isolation from each other, jointly represented clients work in concert with the lawyer, promoting the common development of their interests. The clients' isolation from one another, and the lawyer's potential possession of confidences from one spouse that are adverse to the other's interests, may lead the separate representation model into unavoidable conflicts. The joint representation model, however, obviates these concerns through its policy of full disclosure between the lawyer and client-spouses. Because clients need to understand the risks involved in full disclosure — that the lawyer must share all confidences with both clients, regardless of the disclosing client's preferences — the lawyer needs to obtain the spouses' informed consent before undertaking this form of representation.

[Joint representation might also be] the default model — the form spousal representation takes in the absence of express consent by the parties. As the parties have not consented, however, the mutual disclosure envisioned by the joint representation model becomes problematic. Full sharing of confidences depends on prior notice to the joint clients. Absent such notice, the lawyer should assume that "most confidences would not be imparted if the client were mindful of the lawyer's competing duty to the other spouse." Thus, the lawyer often should not disclose adverse consequences to the other spouse, but instead withdraw from the joint representation if failure to disclose would materially limit the lawyer's ability to represent both spouses. . . . If joint representation can raise troublesome conflicts with respect to client confidences, then why not require the lawyer to clarify the nature of the relationship, including the duty of full and mutual disclosure, at the outset of the representation?

The fourth model, the family as an entity, differs from the other approaches. Instead of representing the clients as individuals with shared interests and objectives, the entity model returns us to a "single client." This approach draws on the corporate client image of Model Rule 1.13, with the client as "the family unit." The lawyer represents the parties in and through their unity as husband and wife. [T]he entity model has the advantage of reflecting many spouses' self-understanding, i.e., that "families are prior to individuals." The marital relationship constitutes the spouses' identity in a way that other roles, such as being one among several partners or shareholders, do not. Because the lawyer represents and pursues the good of the family taken as a whole, the desires of individual members may sometimes stand in tension with the group's vision. Rather than taking such conflict as a reason for withdrawing and abandoning the representation, the lawyer for the marital entity has an obligation to seek a deeper reconciliation within the family.

. . . [H]owever, the entity approach seems counterintuitive given both the paradigmatic form of entity representation — the corporation — and our contemporary understanding of marriage. First, a lawyer representing a corporate client can usually distinguish between the corporation as a legal person and the corporation's constituents. A marriage or family may have its identity, but, for reasons we will develop in the next section, this identity is much more bound up with the individual identities of the spouses. Second, and closely related to the first observation, a strong account of marital unity may have been more plausible in an era of "entireties," of status relations rather than contract, when the family spoke and acted as one invariably through the husband's voice alone. That said, nothing prohibits the parties from adopting the entity model as an alternative option for spousal representation, so long as it is established by express agreement of the lawyer and clients.

The first two models, separate representation by separate lawyers or by the same lawyer, provide some potential benefits, but they also pose significant difficulties in operation — expense and disruption in the former and unavoidable conflicts in the latter. In contrast, the third and fourth models, joint and entity, seem to offer more constructive options for marital representation, especially when one spouse seeks to delegate decision-making authority to the other. Both these models recognize the importance of marriage as a shared project, although to differing degrees. Joint and entity representation respond to the realities of most marriages, such as cooperative and collaborative estate planning. Finally, assuming that mutual consent is required before entering the representation, each model also recognizes that the spouses are not totally subsumed within the marital relationship.

NOTES AND QUESTIONS

Who are you going to call? The issue of dual representation could occur when you are asked to represent (i) both a husband and a wife, (ii) the parent or spouse of a client whom you have represented in non-estate planning matters, or (iii) the personal representative of an estate who is also one of several beneficiaries. What benefits might arise from joint representation? What are the conflicts that might arise that you should disclose if you do agree to joint representation? Must all confidences be shared between joint clients? Are these benefits worth the potential costs? Do the Rules and Commentary strike the right balance? *See* John R. Price, *In Honor of Professor John Gaubatz: The Fundamentals of Ethically Representing Multiple Clients in Estate Planning*, 62 U. MIAMI L. REV. 735 (2008).

EXERCISE

You have just met with Hernando and Winona, a married couple, who are seeking joint representation. May you do so ethically? What documents or letters would you draft to address your professional responsibility concerns? As to each document or letter, what would be the key points you would wish to cover?

After the initial meeting, Hernando calls and says, "I didn't want to say this in front of my wife, but I've got an illegitimate child. The child is an adult, and we've had no contact for years. I don't want to leave anything to the child, but I thought you should know." What do you do? Does your answer change if the "blurted confidence" is that Hernando says he wants to leave property to the nonmarital child, using a trust that will be kept secret from Winona?

b.   Dual Roles

When a lawyer drafts planning documents, the client may feel so comfortable with the attorney doing the work that he asks him to serve as the estate administrator, as a trustee or in another fiduciary capacity. Is there an ethical bar to the attorney accepting the appointment? The ACTEC Commentaries indicate that so long as this occurs at the client's suggestion, and the lawyer does not attempt to influence the choice, it is generally permissible. ABA Comm. on Ethics and Prof'l Responsibility, Formal Op. 02-426 p.7 (2002) provides that "the lawyer may disclose his own availability to serve as a fiduciary" and that it is acceptable for the lawyer to be named:

> as a fiduciary under a will or trust that the lawyer is preparing for the client, so long as the lawyer discusses with the client information reasonably necessary to enable the client to make an informed decision in selecting the fiduciary. If there is a significant risk that the lawyer's interest in being named a fiduciary will materially limit his independent professional judgment in advising the client in her choice of a fiduciary, the lawyer also must obtain the client's informed consent, confirmed in writing.

QUESTION

This opinion appears to allow lawyers not only to accept an appointment, but also to "seek" it, subject, under certain circumstances, to the client's informed consent. Consider the point at which informed consent becomes necessary. Should the Rules instead specify that "in every case in which a drafting attorney is named as a fiduciary . . . such a transaction is a per se conflict of interest"? *See* Paula A. Monopoli, *Drafting Attorneys as Fiduciaries: Fashioning an Optimal Ethical Rule for Conflicts of Interest*, 66 U. Pitt. L. Rev. 411, 414 (2005).

PROBLEM

As a drafting attorney, you may be asked by clients to be their executor or trustee. How would you respond to such a request? Why? What if your client has no other close relatives or friends who can serve in this function?

If lawyer has interest there would be problems — undue

c. Counseling

A lawyer is responsible for exercising reasonable care in client matters, and for acting competently and diligently. Lawyers are responsible for communicating with their clients, and ensuring that clients understand matters adequately so that they can make informed decisions. *See* MRPC 1.4(b). While a lawyer need not share the client's perspective on any matter relevant to the representation, the lawyer is required to provide competent advice. A lawyer may not counsel or assist a client in commissioning crimes or frauds, although if a client requests advice on a particular course of action, the lawyer can advise the client on the legality of that plan. "A lawyer who proceeds reasonably to advise a client with the intent of providing the client with legal advice on how to comply with the law does not act wrongfully, even if the client employs that advice for wrongful purposes or even if a tribunal later determines that the lawyer's advice was incorrect." Restatement (Third) of the Law Governing Lawyers §94, cmt. c (2000).

EXERCISE

You are an attorney who is considering how to handle the requests of your client, Maxine Kreiter, for new provisions in her will. She wishes to make substantial gifts to her children and grandchildren. She tells you she loves them all but is terribly troubled by the facts that her son, Nathan, is married to an African-American woman, and her granddaughter, Susan, is intimately involved with another woman. She recognizes this is very bigoted but says she is old-school and just cannot accept these kinds of lifestyle choices.

Nathan - not / Susan - ok

She plans to give $50,000 to each of her children and grandchildren, other than Nathan and Susan. She also wants to include a clause in her will that revokes a bequest if any beneficiary (i) is married to or intimately involved with someone other than a Caucasian of the opposite sex at her death and does not terminate it within the next three years, or (ii) who, within the three years following her death, marries or becomes intimately involved with someone other than a Caucasian of the opposite sex.

According to Feinberg: legal.

Would you feel comfortable drafting gift documents or a will like she has in mind? Would they be legal? Can you figure out a way to write them so they are less likely to be challenged? What other matters would you want to discuss with her before she denies her descendants an inheritance based on their intimate partnerships?

4.   *Malpractice*

When the lawyer's actions create "a legal cause of injury" that damages "a person to whom the lawyer owes a duty of care," and the lawyer has no valid defense, a lawyer may be held liable for malpractice. RESTATEMENT (THIRD) OF THE LAW GOVERNING LAWYERS §52, cmt. a (2000). Lawyers generally owe a duty of professional care to act diligently and competently only to their clients. Because third parties are not in privity with the attorney, lawyers do not have the same duty of care to them. Consequently, disappointed potential beneficiaries historically have been barred from suing the estate planning attorney for any possible malpractice committed toward the client, even if the attorney's negligence was clear.

Because most estate planning cases do not arise until after the client is dead, the privity bar has protected lawyers from many malpractice suits. Over the past 50 years, however, most states have relaxed, or abolished, the privity bar. To give you a better understanding of the types of malpractice claims that estate lawyers face, the article below provides useful information on liability. It is followed by a case addressing the privity bar. A second case, *Sisson v. Jankowski,* presents an issue that is fundamental to any estate planning practice: If a lawyer may be liable to beneficiaries for negligently drafting a will, may a lawyer be liable to beneficiaries for failing to execute a will at all?

a.   Avoiding Malpractice?

The following article outlines some of the potential malpractice pitfalls for the trusts and estates attorney. Many of the cases throughout the book involve some type of lawyer malfeasance, even if there is no malpractice lawsuit. Appendix C provides a humorous alternative perspective on malpractice.

Stephanie B. Casteel, Letittia A. McDonald, Jennifer D. Odom & Nicole J. Wade, The Modern Estate Planning Lawyer: Avoiding the Maelstrom of Malpractice Claims
Prob. & Prop., Nov./Dec. 2008, at 46-50

The primary reason for not precluding liability of third parties may be that unless a third party has the right to sue a lawyer for breach of duty or malpractice, no one will have a right to bring an action for the damage. Even if an attorney is negligent in his planning, if the defect is not discovered until after the testator's death, which often is the case, the client is no longer alive to sue. Although the testator's estate may sue, frequently the estate itself may have suffered no harm, and the recovery may be limited to the relatively minor cost of the estate planning. Allowing a third party to sue provides accountability and thus an incentive for lawyers to use greater care in estate planning.

[F]or a third party to prevail he or she would have to show that the attorney breached a duty owed to the decedent.

The standard of care for an estate planning attorney is that the attorney should exercise the skill and knowledge ordinarily possessed by attorneys under similar circumstances. . . . [T]he duties of the estate planning attorney are defined in many states only by opinions rendered in malpractice actions, which provide incomplete and insufficient guidance regarding the ethical duties of lawyers.

So where does that leave the estate planning attorney? The requirement of privity has eroded, the standard of liability is ill-defined, and the specific duties are not well elucidated.

Estate planning attorneys have been sued for a number of alleged maladies. Specific causes of action have included:

- error in execution,
- failure to accomplish testator goals or effectuate testator intent,
- error of law,
- failure to update an estate plan based on new laws or facts,
- failure to investigate heirs and assets,
- failure to advice [sic] the testator on the effect of a testator's intent on taxes or other beneficiaries,
- breach of contract to make a will,
- negligent estate planning (which caused additional estate tax),
- errors in drafting,
- allowing execution when the testator lacked testamentary capacity,
- delay implementation of an estate plan,
- missed deadlines, and
- limiting representation to discrete issues.

Most of these causes of action are based on the tort of negligence and typically include breach of fiduciary duty, professional malpractice, infliction of emotional distress, fraud, breach of good faith and fair dealing, and/or negligent misrepresentation. . . .

_____

b.   Privity

States have developed different approaches to the issue of when a third party can sue an attorney for malpractice. The following case addresses whether an estate can sue a drafting attorney in the context of tax liability. As you read this case, the following background information is useful.

- You can purchase life insurance on your own life or on someone else's life. Life insurance is one of the most important forms of non-probate assets in today's estate planning world; and
- If the deceased owns a life insurance policy on his or her own life, the proceeds are subject to estate tax. If the deceased originally purchased the policy but transferred ownership to another at least three years before death, the proceeds are not taxable.

Schneider v. Finmann
933 N.E.2d 718 (N.Y. 2010)

JONES, J.:

At issue in this appeal is whether an attorney may be held liable for damages resulting from negligent representation in estate tax planning that causes enhanced estate tax liability. We hold that a personal representative of an estate may maintain a legal malpractice claim for such pecuniary losses to the estate.

The complaint alleges the following facts. Defendants represented decedent Saul Schneider from at least April 2000 to his death in October 2006. In April 2000, decedent purchased a $1 million life insurance policy. Over several years, he transferred ownership of that property from himself to an entity of which he was principal owner, then to another entity of which he was principal owner and then, in 2005, back to himself. At his death in October 2006, the proceeds of the insurance policy were included as part of his gross taxable estate. Decedent's estate commenced this malpractice action in 2007, alleging that defendants negligently advised decedent to transfer, or failed to advise decedent not to transfer, the policy which resulted in an increased estate tax liability.

Supreme Court granted defendants' motion to dismiss the complaint for failure to state a cause of action. The Appellate Division affirmed (60 A.D.3d 892), holding that, in the absence of privity, an estate may not maintain an action for legal malpractice. We now reverse and reinstate plaintiff's claim.

Strict privity, as applied in the context of estate planning malpractice actions, is a minority rule in the United States.[4] In New York, a third party, without privity, cannot maintain a claim against an attorney in professional negligence, "absent fraud, collusion, malicious acts or other special circumstances" (*Spivey v. Pulley*, 138 A.D.2d 563, 564 [2d Dept. 1988]). Some Appellate Division decisions, on which the Appellate Division here relied,

---

4. [FN 1] Now only a handful of jurisdictions apply strict privity to malpractice actions commenced by beneficiaries against estate planning attorneys. Numerous jurisdictions have either relaxed the principle of privity or have granted standing to beneficiaries or estates. Texas treats the malpractice claims brought by beneficiaries and personal representatives of decedent's estates differently.

have applied strict privity to estate planning malpractice lawsuits commenced by the estate's personal representative and beneficiaries alike. This rule effectively protects attorneys from legal malpractice suits by indeterminate classes of plaintiffs whose interests may be at odds with the interests of the client-decedent. However, it also leaves the estate with no recourse against an attorney who planned the estate negligently.

We now hold that privity, or a relationship sufficiently approaching privity, exists between the personal representative of an estate and the estate planning attorney. We agree with the Texas Supreme Court that the estate essentially "'stands in the shoes' of a decedent" and, therefore, "has the capacity to maintain the malpractice claim on the estate's behalf" (*Belt v. Oppenheimer, Blend, Harrison & Tate, Inc.*, 192 S.W.3d 780, 787 [Tex. 2006]). The personal representative of an estate should not be prevented from raising a negligent estate planning claim against the attorney who caused harm to the estate. The attorney estate planner surely knows that minimizing the tax burden of the estate is one of the central tasks entrusted to the professional. Moreover, such a result comports with EPTL §11-3.2(b),[5] which generally permits the personal representative of a decedent to maintain an action for "injury to person or property" after that person's death.

Despite the holding in this case, strict privity remains a bar against beneficiaries' and other third-party individuals' estate planning malpractice claims absent fraud or other circumstances. Relaxing privity to permit third-parties to commence professional negligence actions against estate planning attorneys would produce undesirable results — uncertainty and limitless liability. These concerns, however, are not present in the case of an estate planning malpractice action commenced by the estate's personal representative.

Accordingly, the order of the Appellate Division should be reversed, with costs, and defendants' motion to dismiss the complaint denied.

NOTES AND QUESTIONS

1. *Too strict?* New York and Texas are in the minority of jurisdictions that retain strict requirements of privity for malpractice actions. What policies support the New York and Texas approaches?

2. *Duties to the estate.* In *Schneider*, the court ruled that the personal representative may assert a claim of professional malpractice for negligent advice about the tax implications of life insurance. Would the personal representative also be permitted to assert a malpractice claim if the attorney

---

5. [FN 2] "No cause of action for injury to person or property is lost because of the death of the person in whose favor the cause of action existed. For any injury an action may be brought or continued by the personal representative of the decedent" (EPTL §11-3.2 [b]).

allegedly failed to comply with the statutory requirements for will execution, leading to the will being declared invalid? To understand the difference between the tax error and the negligent execution of the will, consider the damages suffered by the *estate*.

c. Malpractice for Not Executing a Will?

As the article indicated, there are numerous possible claims for malpractice liability in the trusts and estates context. Estate planning involves both the client's familial relationships and potential money, each of which separately may elicit strong emotions. *Sisson* continues our examination of the parameters of the lawyer's duties to a client.

Sisson v. Jankowski
809 A.2d 1265 (N.H. 2002)

BROCK, C.J.

The United States District Court for the District of New Hampshire (McAuliffe, J.) has certified the following question of law:

> Whether, under New Hampshire law and the facts as pled in plaintiff's verified complaint, an attorney's negligent failure to arrange for his or her client's timely execution of a will and/or an attorney's failure to provide reasonable professional advice with respect to the client's testamentary options (e.g., the ability to cure a draft will's lack of a contingent beneficiary clause by simply inserting a hand-written provision), which failure proximately caused the client to die intestate, gives rise to a viable common law claim against that attorney by an intended beneficiary of the unexecuted will.

For the reasons stated below, we answer the certified question in the negative. . . .

In December 1998, the decedent, Dr. Warren Sisson, retained the defendants, Attorney Jankowski and her law firm, Wiggin & Nourie, P.A., to prepare his will and other estate planning documents. According to the plaintiff, Thomas K. Sisson, the decedent informed Attorney Jankowski that he was suffering from cancer, did not want to die intestate, and, therefore, wished to prepare a will that would pass his entire estate to the plaintiff, his brother. The decedent told Attorney Jankowski that he was particularly interested in ensuring that none of his estate pass to his other brother, from whom he was estranged. The record, however, does not reflect any request by the decedent that the will be executed by a date certain.

Attorney Jankowski prepared a will and other estate planning documents and, in mid-January 1999, mailed them to the decedent for his review and execution. The decedent was injured in mid-January, however, and, therefore, did not receive the documents until January 22, 1999, when a neighbor delivered them to him at a nursing home. Three days later, the plaintiff contacted Attorney Jankowski to tell her that the decedent wanted to finalize his estate planning documents quickly because of his deteriorating condition.

On February 1, 1999, Attorney Jankowski and two other law firm employees visited the decedent in the nursing home to witness his execution of the estate planning documents. The decedent executed all of the documents except his will. After Attorney Jankowski asked him whether the will should include provisions for a contingent beneficiary, the decedent expressed his desire to insert such a clause, thereby providing that his estate would pass to a charity in the event the plaintiff predeceased him.

According to the plaintiff, the decedent's testamentary intent was clear as of the end of the February 1, 1999 meeting: the unexecuted will accurately expressed his intent to pass his entire estate to the plaintiff. Nevertheless, rather than modifying the will immediately to include a hand-written contingent beneficiary clause, modifying it at her office and returning later that day for the decedent's signature, or advising the decedent to execute the will as drafted to avoid the risk of dying intestate and later drafting a codicil, Attorney Jankowski left without obtaining the decedent's signature to the will.

Three days later, Attorney Jankowski returned with the revised will. The decedent did not execute it, however, because Attorney Jankowski did not believe he was competent to do so. She left without securing his signature and told him to contact her when he was ready to sign the will.

The plaintiff twice spoke with a Wiggin & Nourie attorney "to discuss Attorney Jankowski's inaction regarding the will." The attorney told him that he had spoken to other firm members about the situation. Nevertheless, after February 4, 1999, Attorney Jankowski made no attempt to determine whether the decedent regained sufficient testamentary capacity to execute his will.

The decedent died intestate on February 16, 1999. His estate did not pass entirely to the plaintiff as he had intended, but instead was divided among the plaintiff, the decedent's estranged brother, and the children of a third (deceased) brother. The plaintiff brought legal malpractice claims against the defendants, alleging that they owed him a duty of care because he was the intended beneficiary of their relationship with the decedent.

For the purposes of this certified question, there is no dispute as to the decedent's testamentary intent: he wanted to avoid dying intestate and to have his entire estate pass to the plaintiff. Nor does the plaintiff claim that the defendants frustrated the decedent's intent by negligently preparing his will. Rather, the plaintiff asserts that the defendants were negligent because they failed to have the decedent execute his will promptly and to advise him on February 1 of the risk of dying intestate if he did not execute the draft presented at that meeting.

The narrow question before us is whether the defendants owed the plaintiff a duty of care to ensure that the decedent executed his will promptly. Whether a duty exists is a question of law. A duty generally arises out of a relationship between the parties. While a contract may supply the relationship, ordinarily the scope of the duty is limited to those in privity of contract with one another. We have, in limited circumstances, recognized exceptions to the privity requirement where necessary to protect against reasonably foreseeable harm. "Not every risk of harm that might be foreseen gives rise to a duty," however. "[A] duty arises if the likelihood and magnitude of the risk perceived is such that the conduct is unreasonably dangerous."

"When determining whether a duty is owed, we examine the societal interest involved, the severity of the risk, the likelihood of the occurrence, the relationship between the parties, and the burden upon the defendant." *Id*. Ultimately, whether to impose a duty of care "rests on a judicial determination that the social importance of protecting the plaintiff's interest outweighs the importance of immunizing the defendant from extended liability."

In *Simpson v. Calivas*, 650 A.2d 318 (1994), we recognized an exception to the privity requirement with respect to a will beneficiary and held that an attorney who drafts a testator's will owes a duty to the beneficiaries to draft the will non-negligently. In *Simpson*, a testator's son sued the attorney who drafted his father's will, alleging that the will failed to incorporate his father's actual intent. The will left all real estate to the plaintiff, except for a life estate in "our homestead," which was left to the plaintiff's stepmother. The probate litigation concerned whether "our homestead" referred to all of the decedent's real property, including a house, over one hundred acres of land and buildings used in the family business, or only to the house, and perhaps limited surrounding acreage. The plaintiff argued that the decedent intended to leave him the buildings used in the family business and the bulk of the surrounding land in fee simple. The plaintiff lost the will construction action, and then brought a malpractice action against the drafting attorney, arguing that the decedent's will did not accurately reflect his intent.

We held that the son could maintain a contract action against the attorney, as a third-party beneficiary of the contract between the attorney and his father, and a tort action, under a negligence theory. With respect to the negligence claim, we concluded that, "although there is no privity between a drafting attorney and an intended beneficiary, the obvious foreseeability of injury to the beneficiary demands an exception to the privity rule."

Simpson is consistent with the prevailing rule that a will beneficiary may bring a negligence action against an attorney who failed to draft the will in conformity with the testator's wishes.

Simpson is not dispositive of the certified question, however. The duty in *Simpson* was to draft the will non-negligently, while the alleged duty here is to ensure that the will is executed promptly. Courts in several jurisdictions have declined to impose a duty of care where the alleged negligence concerns the failure to have the will executed promptly. The majority of courts confronting this issue have concluded that imposing liability to prospective beneficiaries under these circumstances would interfere with an attorney's obligation of undivided loyalty to his or her client, the testator or testatrix. . . .

The Massachusetts Supreme Judicial Court has similarly reasoned that:

> In preparing a will[,] attorneys can have only one client to whom they owe a duty of undivided loyalty. A client who engages an attorney to prepare a will may seem set on a particular plan for the distribution of her estate. . . . It is not uncommon, however, for a client to have a change of heart after reviewing a draft will. . . . If a duty arose as to every prospective beneficiary mentioned by the client, the attorney-client relationship would become unduly burdened. Attorneys could find themselves in a quandary whenever the client had a change of mind, and the results would hasten to absurdity. The nature of the attorney-client relationship that arises from the drafting of a will necessitates against a duty arising in favor of prospective beneficiaries.

We have recently reaffirmed the importance of an attorney's undivided loyalty to a client. . . .

Both parties cite compelling policy considerations to support their arguments. The plaintiff asserts that there is a strong public interest in ensuring that testators dispose of their property by will and that recognizing a duty of an attorney "to arrange for the timely execution of a will" will promote this public interest. He further argues that "the risk that an intended beneficiary will be deprived of a substantial legacy due to delay in execution of testamentary documents" requires the court to recognize the duty he espouses. The defendants counter that recognizing a duty to third parties for the failure to arrange for the timely execution of a will potentially would undermine the attorney's ethical duty of undivided loyalty to the client.

After weighing the policy considerations the parties identify, we conclude that the potential for conflict between the interests of a prospective beneficiary and a testator militates against recognizing a duty of care. "It is the potential for conflict that is determinative, not the existence of an actual conflict." Whereas a testator and the beneficiary of a will have a mutual interest in ensuring that an attorney drafts the will non-negligently, a prospective beneficiary may be interested in the will's prompt execution, while the testator or testatrix may be interested in having sufficient time to consider and understand his or her estate planning options. As the Massachusetts Supreme Judicial Court recognized:

> Confronting a last will and testament can produce complex psychological demands on a client that may require considerable periods of reflection. An attorney frequently prepares multiple drafts of a will before the client is reconciled to the result. The most simple distributive provisions may be the most difficult for the client to accept.

Creating a duty, even under the unfortunate circumstances of this case, could compromise the attorney's duty of undivided loyalty to the client and impose an untenable burden upon the attorney-client relationship. To avoid potential liability, attorneys might be forced to pressure their clients to execute their wills summarily, without sufficiently reflecting upon their estate planning options.

On balance, we conclude that the risk of interfering with the attorney's duty of undivided loyalty to the client exceeds the risk of harm to the prospective beneficiary. For these reasons, we join the majority of courts that have considered this issue and hold that an attorney does not owe a duty of care to a prospective will beneficiary to have the will executed promptly. Accordingly, we answer the certified question in the negative.

Remanded.

Nadeau, Dalianis and Duggan, JJ., concurred.

NOTES AND QUESTIONS

1. *The plaintiff.* Consider the identity of the plaintiff in this action. Could the estate have sued the attorney? Note that the estate was not the attorney's client at the time of the will consultation. What does the *Schneider* court tell you about the answer to this question?

2. *What duties?* The court distinguishes between a duty to draft a will non-negligently and a duty to make sure that a will is executed promptly. Why? Is the same group of beneficiaries harmed under each circumstance? Why does only the second situation lead, under the court's analysis, to a potential conflict in the attorney's loyalty? Would the result have been different if the decedent, whose only sibling was the plaintiff in this case, had executed the will and it had included a provision stating, "I leave all real property, stocks, and bonds to my sister"?

3. *Preventive planning.* What might you have done as a lawyer if faced with the situation Ms. Jankowski was when she went to the nursing home on February 1 or three days later?

EXERCISE

You have just opened your estate planning legal practice and met with your first client, Catherine. Catherine is in her early 70s, is separated from her husband and has two children. She would like to leave most of her considerable fortune to her younger daughter, a legal aid lawyer, and leave only a small amount to her older son, a partner in a large law firm. You've discussed this uneven allocation with her, but she is adamant. What steps might you take to ensure that you can defend against a malpractice action that might be brought by her son and estranged husband when they learn they did not get what they expected?

APPENDIX A

UPC Section 1-201. General Definitions

Subject to additional definitions contained in the subsequent articles that are applicable to specific articles, parts, or sections, and unless the context otherwise requires, in this Code:

(1) "Agent" includes an attorney-in-fact under a durable or nondurable power of attorney, an individual authorized to make decisions concerning another's health care, and an individual authorized to make decisions for another under a natural death act.

(2) "Application" means a written request to the Registrar for an order of informal probate or appointment under Part 3 of Article III.

(3) "Beneficiary," as it relates to a trust beneficiary, includes a person who has any present or future interest, vested or contingent, and also includes the owner of an interest by assignment or other transfer; as it relates to a charitable trust, includes any person entitled to enforce the trust; as it relates to a "beneficiary of a beneficiary designation," refers to a beneficiary of an insurance or annuity policy, of an account with POD designation, of a security registered in beneficiary form (TOD), or of a pension, profit-sharing, retirement, or similar benefit plan, or other nonprobate transfer at death; and, as it relates to a "beneficiary designated in a governing instrument," includes a grantee of a deed, a devisee, a trust beneficiary, a beneficiary of a beneficiary designation, a donee, appointee, or taker in default of a power of appointment, or a person in whose favor a power of attorney or a power held in any individual, fiduciary, or representative capacity is exercised.

(4) "Beneficiary designation" refers to a governing instrument naming a beneficiary of an insurance or annuity policy, of an account with POD designation, of a security registered in beneficiary form (TOD), or of a pension, profit-sharing, retirement, or similar benefit plan, or other nonprobate transfer at death.

(5) "Child" includes an individual entitled to take as a child under this Code by intestate succession from the parent whose relationship is involved and excludes a person who is only a stepchild, a foster child, a grandchild, or any more remote descendant.

(6) "Claims," in respect to estates of decedents and protected persons, includes liabilities of the decedent or protected person, whether arising in contract, in tort, or otherwise, and liabilities

of the estate which arise at or after the death of the decedent or after the appointment of a conservator, including funeral expenses and expenses of administration. The term does not include estate or inheritance taxes, or demands or disputes regarding title of a decedent or protected person to specific assets alleged to be included in the estate.

(7) "Conservator" as defined in Section 5-102.

(8) "Court" means the [. . . Court] or branch in this State having jurisdiction in matters relating to the affairs of decedents.

(9) "Descendant" of an individual means all of his [or her] descendants of all generations, with the relationship of parent and child at each generation being determined by the definition of child and parent contained in this Code.

(10) "Devise," when used as a noun, means a testamentary disposition of real or personal property and, when used as a verb, means to dispose of real or personal property by will.

(11) "Devisee" means a person designated in a will to receive a devise. For the purposes of Article III, in the case of a devise to an existing trust or trustee, or to a trustee or trust described by will, the trust or trustee is the devisee and the beneficiaries are not devisees.

(12) "Distributee" means any person who has received property of a decedent from his [or her] personal representative other than as a creditor or purchaser. A testamentary trustee is a distributee only to the extent of distributed assets or increment thereto remaining in his [or her] hands. A beneficiary of a testamentary trust to whom the trustee has distributed property received from a personal representative is a distributee of the personal representative. For the purposes of this provision, "testamentary trustee" includes a trustee to whom assets are transferred by will, to the extent of the devised assets.

(13) "Estate" includes the property of the decedent, trust, or other person whose affairs are subject to this Code as originally constituted and as it exists from time to time during administration.

(14) "Exempt property" means that property of a decedent's estate which is described in Section 2-403.

(15) "Fiduciary" includes a personal representative, guardian, conservator, and trustee.

(16) "Foreign personal representative" means a personal representative appointed by another jurisdiction.

(17) "Formal proceedings" means proceedings conducted before a judge with notice to interested persons.

(18) "Governing instrument" means a deed, will, trust, insurance or annuity policy, account with POD designation, security registered in beneficiary form (TOD), pension, profit-sharing, retirement, or similar benefit plan, instrument creating or

exercising a power of appointment or a power of attorney, or a dispositive, appointive, or nominative instrument of any similar type.

(19) "Guardian" is as defined in Section 5-102.

(20) "Heirs," except as controlled by Section 2-711, means persons, including the surviving spouse and the state, who are entitled under the statutes of intestate succession to the property of a decedent.

(21) "Incapacitated person" means an individual described in Section 5-102.

(22) "Informal proceedings" means those conducted without notice to interested persons by an officer of the Court acting as a registrar for probate of a will or appointment of a personal representative.

(23) "Interested person" includes heirs, devisees, children, spouses, creditors, beneficiaries, and any others having a property right in or claim against a trust estate or the estate of a decedent, ward, or protected person. It also includes persons having priority for appointment as personal representative, and other fiduciaries representing interested persons. The meaning as it relates to particular persons may vary from time to time and must be determined according to the particular purposes of, and matter involved in, any proceeding.

(24) "Issue" of an individual means descendant.

(25) "Joint tenants with the right of survivorship" and "community property with the right of survivorship" includes co-owners of property held under circumstances that entitle one or more to the whole of the property on the death of the other or others, but excludes forms of co-ownership registration in which the underlying ownership of each party is in proportion to that party's contribution.

(26) "Lease" includes an oil, gas, or other mineral lease.

(27) "Letters" includes letters testamentary, letters of guardianship, letters of administration, and letters of conservatorship.

(28) "Minor" has the meaning described in Section 5-102.

(29) "Mortgage" means any conveyance, agreement, or arrangement in which property is encumbered or used as security.

(30) "Nonresident decedent" means a decedent who was domiciled in another jurisdiction at the time of his [or her] death.

(31) "Organization" means a corporation, business trust, estate, trust, partnership, joint venture, association, government or governmental subdivision or agency, or any other legal or commercial entity.

(32) "Parent" includes any person entitled to take, or who would be entitled to take if the child died without a will, as a parent under this Code by intestate succession from the child whose

relationship is in question and excludes any person who is only a stepparent, foster parent, or grandparent.

(33) "Payor" means a trustee, insurer, business entity, employer, government, governmental agency or subdivision, or any other person authorized or obligated by law or a governing instrument to make payments.

(34) "Person" means an individual or an organization.

(35) "Personal representative" includes executor administrator, successor personal representative, special administrator, and persons who perform substantially the same function under the law governing their status. "General personal representative" excludes special administrator.

(36) "Petition" means a written request to the Court for an order after notice.

(37) "Proceeding" includes action at law and suit in equity.

(38) "Property" includes both real and personal property or any interest therein and means anything that may be the subject of ownership.

(39) "Protected person" is as defined in Section 5-102.

(40) "Protective proceeding" means a proceeding under Part 4 of Article V.

(41) "Record" means information that is inscribed on a tangible medium or that is stored in an electronic or other medium and is retrievable in perceivable form.

(42) "Registrar" refers to the official of the Court designated to perform the functions of Registrar as provided in Section 1-307.

(43) "Security" includes any note, stock, treasury stock, bond, debenture, evidence of indebtedness, certificate of interest or participation in an oil, gas, or mining title or lease or in payments out of production under such a title or lease, collateral trust certificate, transferable share, voting trust certificate or, in general, any interest or instrument commonly known as a security, or any certificate of interest or participation, any temporary or interim certificate, receipt, or certificate of deposit for, or any warrant or right to subscribe to or purchase, any of the foregoing.

(44) "Settlement," in reference to a decedent's estate, includes the full process of administration, distribution, and closing.

(45) "Sign" means, with present intent to authenticate or adopt a record other than a will:
(A) to execute or adopt a tangible symbol; or
(B) to attach to or logically associate with the record an electronic symbol, sound, or process.

(46) "Special administrator" means a personal representative as described by Sections 3-614 through 3-618.

(47) "State" means a state of the United States, the District of Columbia, the Commonwealth of Puerto Rico, or any territory or insular possession subject to the jurisdiction of the United States.

(48) "Successor personal representative" means a personal representative, other than a special administrator, who is appointed to succeed a previously appointed personal representative.

(49) "Successors" means persons, other than creditors, who are entitled to property of a decedent under his [or her] will or this Code.

(50) "Supervised administration" refers to the proceedings described in Article III, Part 5.

(51) "Survive" means that an individual has neither predeceased an event, including the death of another individual, nor is deemed to have predeceased an event under Section 2-104 or 2-702. The term includes its derivatives, such as "survives," "survived," "survivor," "surviving."

(52) "Testacy proceeding" means a proceeding to establish a will or determine intestacy.

(53) "Testator" includes an individual of either sex.

(54) "Trust" includes an express trust, private or charitable, with additions thereto, wherever and however created. The term also includes a trust created or determined by judgment or decree under which the trust is to be administered in the manner of an express trust. The term excludes other constructive trusts and excludes resulting trusts, conservatorships, personal representatives, trust accounts as defined in Article VI, custodial arrangements pursuant to [each state should list its legislation, including that relating to [gifts][transfers] to minors, dealing with special custodial situations], business trusts providing for certificates to be issued to beneficiaries, common trust funds, voting trusts, security arrangements, liquidation trusts, and trusts for the primary purpose of paying debts, dividends, interest, salaries, wages, profits, pensions, or employee benefits of any kind, and any arrangement under which a person is nominee or escrowee for another.

(55) "Trustee" includes an original, additional, or successor trustee, whether or not appointed or confirmed by court.

(56) "Ward" means an individual described in Section 5-102.

(57) "Will" includes codicil and any testamentary instrument that merely appoints an executor, revokes or revises another will, nominates a guardian, or expressly excludes or limits the right of an individual or class to succeed to property of the decedent passing by intestate succession.

[FOR ADOPTION IN COMMUNITY PROPERTY STATES]

[(58)   "Separate property" (if necessary, to be defined locally in accordance with existing concept in adopting state.)

(59)   "Community property" (if necessary, to be defined locally in accordance with exciting concept in adopting state.)]

APPENDIX B

Glossary — American Probate Glossary

Administration: Collecting, managing, and distributing the estate of a deceased person or "decedent." This is done by a court-appointed representative known as the "administrator" or the "executor."

Administrator: The person or institution named by the probate court to collect, manage, and distribute the estate when a decedent either dies without a will ("intestate") or does not name someone in his or her will to take on this task.

Attestation: The dual act of watching the testator of a will sign the will and then writing one's signature as a witness.

Beneficiary: The person who is to benefit from the income and principal of a trust or the person named to receive a bequest under a will.

Codicil: A document that modifies or amends a will and that is executed with the same formalities, including proper witnesses, as a will.

Conservator: The person or institution appointed by a probate court to manage the affairs of a person who is incapacitated. If the conservator is merely appointed to manage the financial affairs of the incapacitated person, this is known as a "conservator of the estate." If the conservator is to be accountable for the physical well-being and care of the incapacitated adult, this is known as a "conservator of the person." In many states, this function is also known as a "guardian of the estate" or a "guardian of the person."

Escheat: The general principle under most state inheritance laws that provides for an intestate decedent's estate to pass to the state where there are no heirs to inherit the property.

Execution: The act of putting one's signature on a will. Also the actual implementation of the provisions of a will.

Executor: The person or institution named or "nominated" by the testator of a will and appointed by the probate court to implement its provisions.

Fiduciary: In the probate area, someone who is appointed by the court to act in the best interests of another. For example, executors, administrators, trustees, and guardians are all fiduciaries who owe a legal duty to those for whom they manage property, and their breach of such duty is actionable.

Grantor: The person who creates a trust. Synonymous with the terms "donor," "settlor," or "trustor" in relation to a trust.

Guardian: The person or institution named or "nominated" by the testator of a will to assume responsibility for the testator's minor children. Also, the person or institution appointed by the probate court to act on behalf of an incapacitated adult. (See also "conservator.")

Guardian ad Litem: The person appointed by the probate court for the limited purpose of representing a minor child or unborn beneficiary's legal interests in the context of a legal proceeding. Unlike a "guardian," a guardian ad litem (typically an attorney) has no power to make decisions about the minor child's physical custody or financial assets.

Heirs: Those relatives who are legally entitled under state law to inherit the estate of a person who dies without a will or "intestate."

Inter vivos trust: A trust created during the grantor's lifetime (as opposed to a "testamentary trust" created at the time of death, under the terms of a will). Also known as a "living trust."

Intestacy: Having died without a will.

Intestacy statutes: State laws defining who is legally entitled to inherit a decedent's estate if that decedent dies without a will.

Issue: The lineal descendants of a person, including children, grandchildren, and great-grandchildren.

Joint Tenancy: The form of title to property that provides for co-ownership and which results in title to the property passing automatically to the surviving joint tenants when one co-owner dies, by "right of survivorship." The property passes outside of the probate process. To be distinguished from a "tenancy in common," which results in a co-owner's interest in the property being transferred by will or by intestacy statutes.

Letter of administration or letters testamentary: Official appointment papers signed by the probate court so that an administrator or executor may demonstrate they have the legal authority to manage, sell, or distribute the decedent's property.

Marshaling assets: The act of identifying and inventorying the decedent's assets in an estate. A legal duty of the administrator or executor.

Personal representative: The umbrella term used by some states and the Uniform Probate Code to designate either an administrator or an executor.

Power of appointment: A provision in a will or similar document that grants an individual (known as the "donee") the power to direct trust assets at termination of the trust to himself, his estate, or another individual or group named in the will or similar document.

Power of attorney: A document that grants authority to act on one's behalf to another (known as the "attorney-in-fact") creating an agency relationship between the two. The grantor of the power is the principal and the grantee is the agent. A "durable" power of attorney is one that survives the incapacity of the principal. Such agents may perform a variety of functions on behalf of the principal including buying, selling, and managing property.

Probate: The process of validating a will, if one exists, and administering a deceased person's estate.

Probate asset or probate estate: Property that passes under a will or by intestacy, in contrast to property that passes automatically, outside the probate process, like jointly held property and contractual assets such as life insurance.

Probate court: The court in each state that oversees the collection, management, and distribution of decedents' estates. Also known as "surrogate court" or "orphan's court" in some states.

Remainderman: An individual who is named in a trust to receive the principal or corpus when the trust comes to an end or "terminates." This is contrasted with an "income beneficiary" who is named to receive benefits from the trust during its ongoing existence.

Residuary estate: The assets that remain in an estate after the specific bequests have been made and any taxes and expenses of administration have been paid. The balance of the estate is also known as the residue or residual estate and is distributed under a "residuary clause" in a will.

Tenancy in common: A method of co-ownership between two or more persons under which the interest of a deceased co-owner passes in accordance with her will, or, if there is no will, in accordance with the laws of intestate succession.

Testamentary: This phrase denotes those matters having to do with a will. Wills become effective only upon the death of the testator who executes them, thus the phrase can also mean effective upon death.

Testamentary capacity: The requirement that a person making a will (1) understand that she is making a permanent disposition of her estate,

(2) understand the extent of her assets, and (3) is aware of which people constitute the "natural objects of her bounty," in other words, her relatives. All three must be present for the testator to create a valid will.

Testamentary trust: A trust created by the terms of a will. Such a trust comes into existence when the testator dies, as contrasted with an inter vivos trust, which comes into existence during the grantor's life.

Testacy: Having died with a will.

Testator: The individual who makes or "executes" a will is the testator. If one dies with a will one is said to have died "testate."

Trustee: The person or institution designated by the grantor of a trust or appointed by the court to assume the fiduciary duty of holding and administering a trust for the beneficiaries.

Uniform Probate and Trust Codes: Model probate and trust statutes promulgated by the National Conference of Commissioners on Uniform State Laws and adopted in whole or in part by many states.

APPENDIX C

20 Ways to Enhance Your Chances of Getting Sued for Malpractice

Professor Randall W. Roth, University of Hawaii School of Law[6]

I. Skip talks and articles on ethics — it all boils down to "the golden rule," doesn't it?

II. When pointy headed academics talk about potential problems, just tell yourself "if it was really a problem, someone would have told me about it before now."

III. Don't bother detailing the scope of your engagement in an engagement (or nonengagement) letter. After all, you know who your clients are and what you've agreed to do (or not do).

IV. Don't let it bug you if someone's file has been on your desk for quite some time (especially if the ball is in their court). If they aren't in a hurry why should you be?

V. Don't bother talking to a client about a theoretical option if you already know what he or she would eventually decide. After all, you're the expert.

VI. To heck with specialists. How hard can it be?

VII. Refer your clients to people who will scratch your back in return. And keep it simple — provide just one name.

VIII. Don't be a stickler for details and never double-check info provided by your client.

IX. Leave important details to the client's other advisors and just assume they are doing a good job.

X. Forget about unnecessary paperwork — don't document oral communications and always toss your research notes.

XI. Pay no attention to state lines.

XII. Never tell clients that they are now former clients.

---

6. Professor Roth prepared this list to stimulate a discussion of malpractice-avoidance procedures; his goal was not to identify what would be malpractice in all circumstances.

XIII. Summarize the effect of a complicated strategy in a simple letter to the client, and don't mention that it could be misleading.

XIV. Rely on a third party's description of what the client wants.

XV. Never explain the obvious.

XVI. Encourage your clients to make generous gifts to worthwhile charities; and, be generous with your time in serving on the boards of those same charities.

XVII. Make sure you are using every new idea being talked about at tax seminars, and don't mention that they are untested.

XVIII. Don't confuse (or worse yet, alienate) your married-couple clients by talking about possible conflicts of interest and stuff like that.

XIX. If your client wants you to serve as a trustee or personal representative, say yes quickly, but be sure to slip exculpatory language into the document(s).

XX. Make sure your clients realize that you are smarter and more important than them.

APPENDIX D

Last Will and Testament of Michael Joseph Jackson

I, MICHAEL JOSEPH JACKSON, a resident of the State of California, declare this to be my last Will, and do hereby revoke all former wills and codicils made by me.

I

I declare that I am not married. My marriage to DEBROAH JEAN ROWE JACKSON has been dissolved. I have three children now living, PRINCE MICHAEL JACKSON, JR., PARIS MICHAEL KATHERINE JACKSON and PRINCE MICHAEL JOSEPH JACKSON, II. I have no other children, living or deceased.

II

It is my intention by this Will to dispose of all property which I am entitled to dispose of by will. I specifically refrain from exercising all powers of appointment that I may possess at the time of my death.

III

I give my entire estate to the Trustee or Trustees then acting under that certain Amended and Restated Declaration of Trust executed on March 22, 2002 by me as Trustee and Trustor which is called the MICHAEL JACKSON FAMILY TRUST, giving effect to my amendments thereto made prior to my death. All such assets shall be held, managed and distributed as a part of said Trust according to its terms and not as a separate testamentary trust.

If for any reason this gift is not operative or is invalid, or if the aforesaid Trust fails or has been revoked, I give my residuary estate to the Trustee or Trustees named to act in the MICHAEL JACKSON FAMILY TRUST, as Amended and Restated on March 22, 2002, and I direct said Trustee or Trustees to divide, administer, hold and distribute the trust estate pursuant to the provisions of said Trust, as hereinabove referred to as such provisions now exist to the same extent and in the same manner as though that certain Amended and Restated Declaration of Trust, were herein set forth in full, but without giving effect to any subsequent amendments after the date of this Will. The Trustee, Trustees, or any successor Trustee named in such Trust Agreement shall serve without bond.

IV

I direct that all federal estate taxes and state inheritance or succession taxes payable upon or resulting from or by reason of my death (herein "Death Taxes") attributable to property which is part of the trust estate of the MICHAEL JACKSON FAMILY TRUST, including property which passes to said trust from my probate estate shall be paid by the Trustee of said trust in accordance with its terms. Death Taxes attributable to property passing outside this Will, other than property constituting the trust estate of the trust mentioned in the preceding sentence, shall be charged against the taker of said property.

V

I appoint JOHN BRANCA, JOHN MCCLAIN and BARRY SIEGEL as co-Executors of this Will. In the event of any of their deaths, resignations, inability, failure or refusal to serve or continue to serve as co-Executor, the other shall serve and no replacement need be named. The co-Executors serving at any time after my death may name one or more replacements to serve in the event that none of the three named individuals is willing or able to serve at any time.

The term "my executors" as used in this Will shall include any duly acting personal representative or representatives of my estate. No individual acting as such need post a bond.

I hereby give my Executors, full power and authority at any time or times to sell, lease, mortgage, pledge, exchange or otherwise dispose of the property, whether real or personal comprising my estate, upon such terms as my Executor shall deem best, to continue any business enterprises, to purchase assets from my estate, to continue in force and pay insurance premiums on any insurance policy, including life insurance, owned by my estate, and for any of the foregoing purposes to make, execute and deliver any and all deeds, contracts, mortgages, bills of sale or other instruments necessary or desirable therefore. In addition, I give my Executors full power to invest and reinvest the estate funds and assets in any kind of property, real, personal or mixed, and every kind of investment, specifically including, but not by way of limitation, corporate obligations of every kind and stocks, preferred or common, and interests in investments trusts and share in investment companies, and any common trust fund administered by any corporate executor hereunder, which men of prudent discretion and intelligence acquire of their own account.

VI

Except as otherwise provided in this Will or in the Trust referred to in Article III hereof, I have intentionally omitted to provide for my heirs. I have intentionally omitted to provide for my former wife, DEBORAH JEAN ROWE JACKSON.

VII

If at the time of my death I own or have an interest in property located outside of the State of California requiring ancillary administration, I appoint my domiciliary Executors as ancillary Executors for such property. I give to said domiciliary Executors the following additional powers, rights and privileges to be exercised in their sole and absolute discretion with reference to such property: to cause such ancillary administration to be commenced, carried on and completed; to determine what assets, if any, are to be sold by the ancillary Executors; to pay directly or to advance funds from the California estate to the ancillary Executors for the payment of all claims, taxes, costs and administration expenses, including compensation of the ancillary Executors and attorneys' fees incurred by reason of the ownership of such property and by such ancillary administration; and upon completion of such ancillary administration, I authorize and direct the ancillary Executors to distribute, transfer and deliver the residue of such property to the domiciliary Executors herein, to be distributed by them under the terms of this Will, it being my intention that my entire estate shall be administered as a unit and that my domiciliary Executors shall supervise and control, so far as permissible by local law, any ancillary administration proceedings deemed necessary in the settlement of my estate.

VIII

If any of my children are minors at the time of my death, I nominate my mother, KATHERINE JACKSON as guardian of the persons and estates of such minor children. If KATHERINE JACKSON fails to survive me, or is unable or unwilling to act as guardian, I nominate DIANA ROSS as guardian of the persons and estates of such minor children.

I subscribe my name to this Will this 7 day of July, 2002

Signed 'Michael Joseph Jackson'

On the date written below, MICHAEL JOSEPH JACKSON, declared to us, the undersigned, that the foregoing instrument consisting of five (5) pages, including the page signed by us as witnesses, was his Will and requested us to act as witnesses to it. He thereupon signed this Will in our presence, all of us being present at the same time. We now, at his request, in his presence and in the presence of each other, subscribe our names as witnesses.

Each of us is now more than eighteen (18) years of age and a competent witness and resides at the address set forth after his name.

Each of us is acquainted with MICHAEL JOSEPH JACKSON. At this time, he is over the age of eighteen (18) years and, to the best of our knowledge, he is of sound mind and is not acting under duress, menace, fraud, misrepresentation or undue influence.

We declare under penalty of perjury that the foregoing is true and correct.

Executed on July 7th, 2002 at 5:00 P.M., Los Angeles

2 INHERITANCE AND RELATIONSHIP

A. INTRODUCTION

Nothing provides a better illustration of how a society thinks about family than its inheritance statutes, which reflect its social, religious and cultural norms. In the United States, each state has a default rule or set of "intestacy statutes" that governs who is entitled to inherit from a decedent who dies without a will. These statutes typically favor family members over non-relatives. In addition to intestacy statutes, each state has laws — "statutes of wills" — that allow citizens to opt-out of these default rules and draft a will. The will allows them to specify someone other than family members, for example, friends, employees and favorite charities, as the recipients of their property upon their death. Finally, states have rules — "canons" or "rules of construction" — that help courts interpret those wills and other instruments like trusts that pass property at death.

The question of who constitutes a "family member" is essentially a question of *status*. American inheritance law is a status-based system. Certain people are entitled to inherit from the decedent because they are connected by blood or by marriage. For example, children inherit from their parents because of the relational status conferred on them by law as a result of biology or adoption. Wives inherit from husbands because of the relational status conferred by the marriage ceremony.

The status-based terms discussed in this chapter include "child," "issue," "descendant," "spouse" and "parent." These terms apply throughout trusts and estates law. For example, when a decedent dies without a will, the interpretive issues that arise involve applying the intestacy statutes. When an individual drafted a will or trust, the questions involve interpreting the meaning of the instrument.

In this chapter, we explore the meaning of these terms in American inheritance law in each of these contexts. We discuss the interpretive and policy questions raised by these terms historically and in the brave new world of assisted reproduction and of the increasing number of children born out of wedlock. We also consider blended families, same-sex marriage and domestic partnership.

The discussion in this chapter provides a foundation for many of the issues that arise in future chapters. The goal of the chapter is to familiarize you with the specific meaning of terms like "child" or "spouse" in inheritance law. These meanings may differ from how non-lawyers understand such terms. As you read statutes and instruments in subsequent chapters, you will have a greater understanding of how to interpret words like "child" and "spouse" as they appear in those statutes or instruments.

B.   WHO IS A CHILD?

1.   In General

As noted above, relational status is the dominant factor in whether someone may inherit from a decedent in American inheritance law. With a few notable exceptions, behavior is not a significant factor in whether someone may inherit. For example, whether a son will inherit from his mother does not turn on whether he called her every Sunday or took care of her when she became ill. Rather, it turns on his status as a biological or adopted child of his mother. Thus we have a dominantly status-based system of inheritance rather than a behavior-based system. There are only a few behavior-based exceptions like homicide and, in some states, abandonment of children or abuse of the elderly, which we explore below.

The following article explores how our status-based system has evolved in response to rapidly evolving shifts in cultural norms in the way we view family and thus how we think about who is entitled to inherit property.

Susan N. Gary, We Are Family: The Definition of Parent and Child for Succession Purposes
34 ACTEC J. 171 (2008)

Who is a child of a person for purposes of inheritance? The answer has far-reaching implications. The definition of parent and child matters for intestacy distributions and it matters for distributions under wills and trusts executed not only by the parent or child, but also by others who may direct distributions to children or descendants of someone named in the document. A trust document executed in 1950 might direct the trustee to make distributions to a beneficiary during the beneficiary's life, and then to distribute the remaining property to the beneficiary's "descendants" when the beneficiary dies. Does the term descendants used in a 1950 document include children or other descendants who are adopted into the family or adopted out, who are born outside of marriage and are genetically related to a man who may not act as a father, who are conceived the old-fashioned way or through some form of assisted reproduction, or who are conceived after the death of one of the genetic parents? The ways we construct our families continue to evolve, and the law of succession struggles to keep up. Recent changes have been dramatic, and changes, both in our legal constructs of family and in the technology that affects those constructs will likely continue and perhaps even accelerate. . . .

I.   Purposes of Intestacy Statutes

Drafters of intestacy statutes have considered decedent's intent an important, perhaps the most important, factor in creating patterns of intestate distribution. Intestacy statutes assume that most decedents will want property to go to "family." Scholars have noted that intestacy statutes provide support, both financial and emotional, to surviving members of the decedent's family. Further, the intestacy statutes serve an expressive function, indicating society's view as to who "counts" as a family member.

All of these purposes that underlie the intestacy statutes depend on a definition of family. In recent years, scholars have pointed out the problems of intestacy statutes that do not reflect the wide range of American families in existence today. Most intestacy statutes do not include unmarried partners and the families headed by those partners, stepchildren and foster children raised by parents who may not be their legal parents, and children who are adopted out but maintain contacts with their birth families. . . .

With respect to children, a number of recent changes have focused more discussion on the definition of parent and child. Increased use of DNA testing to establish the genetic relationship between a man and a child has raised questions about the determination of paternity. Children conceived through artificial reproductive technology may have connections, genetic and otherwise, to multiple adults. Children may be conceived after the death of a genetic parent, using gametes stored by the parent before his or her death. Blended families include stepchildren and foster children, and children may be adopted under a variety of circumstances. In some cases the adoption severs the child's functional ties to a genetic parent, but an adoption by a family member such as a stepparent, the same-sex partner of a genetic parent, or a grandparent, may leave ties to the genetic parent or the genetic parent's family intact.

These many changes in the ways people create parent-child relationships have led to several developments in the law. The Uniform Parentage

Act, approved by the Uniform Law Commission in 2000 and amended in 2002, sets forth rules for establishing the legal parent-child relationship. With respect to posthumously conceived children, cases in several states and a handful of statutes have begun to create rules to determine whether the genetic, deceased parent is a parent for intestacy purposes. And most recently, the Uniform Law Commission approved amendments to the Uniform Probate Code that change the definition of parent and child for intestacy purposes. The UPC Amendments, combined with recent case law and statutory efforts, should re-energize the debate about the best way to construct intestacy statutes.

The fundamental building-block of our status-based system is the parent-child relationship. Most inheritance statutes build this framework with the definition of "child" at the core. For example, UPC §§1-201(5) and (9) provide the basic definition of "child" and "descendant" for purposes of interpreting intestacy statutes and instruments like wills or trusts (with a few exceptions that we explore below). The premise of these two subsections is that a child is fundamentally a genetically connected or legally adopted child of either the decedent or a person named in an instrument. Note that "child" has a very specific meaning here. It only includes a person one step below the decedent, while "descendant" is multi-generational and includes children, grandchildren, great-grandchildren, etc.

UPC §1-201. General Definitions.

> Subject to additional definitions contained in the subsequent Articles that are applicable to specific Articles, parts, or sections, and unless the context otherwise requires, in this Code: . . .
>
> (5) "Child" includes an individual entitled to take as a child under this Code by intestate succession from the parent whose relationship is involved and excludes a person who is only a stepchild, a foster child, a grandchild, or any more remote descendant. . . .
>
> (9) "Descendant" of an individual means all of his [or her] descendants of all generations, with the relationship of parent and child at each generation being determined by the definition of child and parent contained in this Code.

Example: If Arun dies and he has one daughter, Azizah, and she has a daughter, Bettina, only Azizah is the "child" of Arun if he leaves a bequest to "my child" in his will or trust. Bettina is not a child of Arun for these purposes, but she is a descendant. Thus, "child" is a sub-set of "descendants," which includes Arun's child, grandchild, great-grandchild, etc. So, if Arun had left a bequest to "my descendants," Bettina would be included.

As you can see from subsection (5) and as Professor Gary notes in her article excerpted above, stepchildren and foster children are not generally considered "children" for purposes of most state intestacy statutes. And note that you will sometimes see the term "issue" used in statutes or instruments. Under UPC §1-201(24), the term "issue" means lineal descendants, *i.e.*, children, grandchildren, great-grandchildren, etc.

In order to inherit from a parent, a child must establish a parent-child relationship. That relationship qualifies the child to inherit under intestacy or as a member of a class for purposes of wills or trusts. A child who is either genetically related to the parent, who is legally adopted by the parent or whose parent has indicated his consent to be a parent to a child conceived with reproductive technology, even if there is no genetic connection, can now establish such a parent-child relationship. This was not always the case. Historically, many children who were genetically connected to their fathers were not entitled to inherit because they were born out of wedlock. Nor did legally adopted children always inherit from their adoptive parents or their parents' relatives. In other words, they were children (either genetic or adopted) but they were not eligible to inherit. In addition, mere intent to parent a child was not sufficient to establish a relationship for purposes of inheritance. However, there has been significant change in this area of the law over time. The most recent amendments to the UPC in 2008 illustrate these changes, and we explore them in detail below.

UPC §§2-103 and 2-705 illustrate why it is so important to be deemed a "child" for purposes of inheritance. These sections state that "descendants" are entitled to inherit either in intestacy or through inclusion in a class gift (a bequest to a group rather than to named individuals) in a will or trust.

UPC §2-103. Share of Heirs Other than Surviving Spouse.

> Any part of the intestate estate not passing to a decedent's surviving spouse under Section 2-102, or the entire intestate estate if there is no surviving spouse, passes in the following order to the individuals who survive the decedent:
>
> (1) to the decedent's *descendants* by representation; . . . [Emphasis added.]

UPC §2-705. Class Gifts Construed to Accord with Intestate Succession; Exceptions.

> **(b) [Terms of Relationship.]** A class gift [in a governing instrument] that uses a term of relationship to identify the class members [such as *"my children"* or *"my descendants"*] includes [those *children or descendants* determined] in accordance with the rules for intestate succession regarding *parent-child* relationships. [Emphasis added.]

NOTES AND QUESTIONS

1. *Status or behavior.* Do you think that courts should use the genetic connection between a parent and child as the basis for eligibility to inherit? Are there arguments for a functional approach that deviates from genetics and uses behavior — acting as a parent — as the primary factor?

2. *A cost/benefit analysis.* What are the costs and benefits of such a functional approach? *See* Lee-ford Tritt, *Sperms and Estates: An Unadulterated Functionally Based Approach to Parent-Child Property Succession,* 62 S.M.U. L. REV. 367, 368-401 (2009) (arguing for a completely functionally based approach to determining the parent-child relationship because modern familial relationships have rendered the status-based approach outdated).

2.   Intestacy — Interpreting Statutes

This section explores the rules that determine whether a person qualifies as a child for purposes of applying intestacy statutes. The rules for interpreting status-based relationships in instruments like wills and trusts are similar to those for interpreting intestacy statutes, but there are some differences that we explore in the next section.

This section discusses the varying rights of children depending on whether they are marital, adopted or conceived through assisted reproductive technology. As you read this section, remember that inheritance law incorporates various presumptions based on other state laws that define intrafamilial relationships. For example, the Uniform Parentage Act (UPA), which Professor Gary discusses in the article above, is incorporated into the UPC by reference. In defining "genetic father," UPC §2-115(5) refers to establishing the relationship pursuant to "applicable state law." The Legislative note to that section makes it clear that, "[s]tates that have enacted the Uniform Parentage Act (2000, as amended) should replace 'applicable state law' with 'Section 201(b)(1), (2), or (3) of the Uniform Parentage Act (2000), as amended.'"

a. Marital Children and the Marital Presumption

Perhaps the easiest way for a child to establish her eligibility to inherit is through the marital presumption. For example, the UPA presumes paternity when a man and woman are married (even if the marriage is or could be declared invalid) and the woman gives birth to a child during the marriage or within 300 days after the marriage is terminated. Children who fall within this presumption are referred to as "marital children." Under UPA §631(1), the presumed father can overcome the presumption of paternity only by introducing the results of genetic testing in an adjudication that either excludes him as the father of the child or identifies another man as the father of the child.

UPA §204. Presumption of Paternity

> (a) A man is presumed to be the father of a child if:
>
> (1) he and the mother of the child are married to each other and the child is born during the marriage;
>
> (2) he and the mother of the child were married to each other and the child is born within 300 days after the marriage is terminated by death, annulment, declaration of invalidity, or divorce[, or after a decree of separation];
>
> (3) before the birth of the child, he and the mother of the child married each other in apparent compliance with law, even if the attempted marriage is or could be declared invalid, and the child is born during the invalid marriage or within 300 days after its termination by death, annulment, declaration of invalidity, or divorce[, or after a decree of separation]; . . .
>
> (b) A presumption of paternity established under this section may be rebutted only by adjudication under [Article] 6.

Historically, the marital presumption was conclusive and virtually irrebuttable. Anyone other than the mother's husband who claimed to be a child's father was not even allowed to present evidence of paternity in court. While some courts now allow a man in this position to present evidence to rebut the presumption, the marital presumption is still very strong. For example, in *Michael H. v. Gerald D.*, 491 U.S. 110 (1989), the U.S. Supreme Court, interpreting California law, held that a man whose blood tests showed a 98.07% probability of being the father, was *not* denied due process rights when he was not allowed to demonstrate his paternity in an evidentiary hearing. The Court held that the presumption of paternity implements a substantive rule of law, thus making it generally *irrelevant* for paternity purposes whether a child conceived during and born into an existing marriage was begotten by someone other than the husband. The marital presumption continues to be a core principle in establishing the parent-child relationship, although states have developed somewhat differing approaches to its strength. In *Evans v. Wilson*, 856 A.2d 679 (Md. 2004), the Maryland Court of Appeals held that when a child is born during a marriage, the husband is presumed to be the father and the putative father has no absolute right to a DNA test. On the other hand, the court indicated that it would be willing to allow testing if that was deemed to be in the child's best interest. Thus, while the marital presumption is rebuttable, it remains very difficult for someone other than the husband of the mother to rebut the presumption and courts will consider the best interests of the child in allowing someone to do so.

NOTES AND QUESTIONS

1.   *Good reasons?* As a historical matter, the marital presumption was based, in part, on an effort to protect husbands from proceedings that would embarrass them. Is there any better reason to continue the presumption today? *Compare* Jana Singer, *Marriage, Biology and Paternity, The Case for Revitalizing the Marital Presumption*, 65 Md. L. Rev. 246 (2006) (critiquing the recent changes to the marital presumption and arguing that while the original reasoning for the presumption may no longer be relevant in today's society, the policy goals of the presumption continue to be valid) *with* Rebecca Moulton, Note, *Who's Your Daddy?: The Inherent Unfairness of the Marital Presumption for Children of Unmarried Parents*, 47 Fam. Ct. Rev. 698 (2009) (criticizing the marital presumption vis-à-vis nonmarital children).

2.   *Establishing paternity.* There are numerous critiques of the marital presumption in establishing paternity. *See* Veronica Sue Gunderson, *Personal Responsibility in Parentage: An Argument Against the Marital Presumption*, 11 U.C. Davis J. Juv. L. & Pol'y 335, 361 (2007) (discussing proposals to reform the marital presumption); Cynthia R. Mabry, *Who is the Baby's Daddy (and Why Is It Important for the Child to Know)?*, 34 U. Balt. L. Rev. 211, 215-18 (2004) (discussing different approaches to the application of the marital presumption as a determination of paternity); Paula Roberts, *Truth and Consequences: Part II. Questioning the Paternity of Marital Children*, 37 Fam. L.Q. 55 (2003) (analyzing various state approaches to the issue of paternity disestablishment for marital children).

PROBLEM

David and his second wife, Wanda, had a marriage ceremony seven years ago and have lived happily ever since in the same house. David died recently. At his death, the following facts exist:

- David and his first wife, Francie, had a child, Alice, during their marriage. David and Francie were divorced 10 years ago. Alice is 12 years old at David's death.
- David and Wanda had a child, Bob, during their marriage. Bob is six.

Who qualifies as David's "child" under the UPC for purposes of intestacy? Why?

Both children are David's children for intestacy d class gifts both born to intact marriages

b.   Nonmarital Children

Children who do not fall within the marital presumption outlined above are called "nonmarital children." Historically, nonmarital children could not inherit from either parent. By the mid-twentieth century, the law had evolved to allow nonmarital children to inherit from their mothers but not their fathers, paternity being more difficult to prove than maternity. The evidentiary challenge was much greater in establishing that a man was the father, especially before the advent of readily available genetic testing. In the 1970s, a pair of U.S. Supreme Court cases, discussed in the article below, established the constitutional requirement that states must provide some statutory mechanism by which nonmarital children could try to establish paternity and inherit from their fathers.

Paula A. Monopoli, Nonmarital Children and Post-Death Parentage: A Different Path for Inheritance Law?
48 Santa Clara L. Rev. 857 (2008)

I.   INTRODUCTION

The number of children born out of wedlock in this country has increased dramatically since the first half of the twentieth century. In 1940, there were 89,500 out-of-wedlock births, while by 2005, that number had increased to more than 1.5 million [and in 2008, almost 40% of all children were nonmarital]. . . .

The significant demographic shift in the number of nonmarital births makes the issues surrounding nonmarital children critical ones for society and inheritance law. Most of these children do not stand to inherit vast fortunes. They are often born into middle-income and low-income families. Their parents and grandparents are the least likely segment of the population to seek estate planning services and to opt out of the default system of intestacy to draft an inclusive will. This is the very reason why the rules of intestacy — the default or off-the-rack rules of inheritance law — should be streamlined to make it as easy for nonmarital children to inherit as possible. The impact of what might appear to be a small inheritance often proves very significant in the lives of nonmarital children, both as minors and adults . . .

II. SCIENTIFIC ADVANCES AND THE COURT'S ANALYSIS IN THE NONMARITAL INHERITANCE CASES

The United States Supreme Court and the federal courts have applied the Fourteenth Amendment's equal protection analysis to cases involving discrimination on the basis of illegitimacy in a number of areas, including inheritance law. In *Levy v. Louisiana*,[1] the Court found a violation of equal protection in a statute permitting only legitimate children to bring wrongful death suits. [] In *Parham v. Hughes*,[2] the Court used rational basis review to uphold a statute that barred the fathers of nonmarital children from bringing wrongful death suits. The next important illegitimacy discrimination case was *Clark v. Jeter*,[3] in which the Court first expressly applied intermediate scrutiny to such cases. "[T]he Supreme Court has recognized for several decades that classifications treating illegitimate children more harshly than legitimate children violate [the] [E]qual [P]rotection" Clause of the Fourteenth Amendment. . . .

In *Trimble*, the Supreme Court held unconstitutional an Illinois statute that prevented a nonmarital child from inheriting from the child's father unless the child's mother and father had later married. The state's purported rationales for this statute included promoting two parent families and enhancing the orderly disposition of estates. Justice Powell stated that the Court was using a "not . . . toothless" intermediate standard of scrutiny and that the state statute at issue had no more than an "attenuated relationship to the asserted goal." . . . One year later in *Lalli*, Justice Powell again wrote for the Court in a five-to-four decision that upheld a New York statute allowing a nonmarital child to inherit if paternity was established by adjudication. The New York statute was arguably broader than the Illinois statute struck down in *Trimble* because later marriage plus acknowledgment was not the sole mechanism by which the nonmarital child could establish his right to inherit. The state again argued that its interest in the orderly disposition of estates and the prevention of fraudulent claims was enough to justify the disparate treatment of nonmarital children. This time the Court agreed with the state and, using the new intermediate scrutiny test established in *Trimble*, held the statute constitutional. . . .

c.   The Legacy of Trimble and Lalli

Trimble and *Lalli* involved intestacy statutes — the default rules used to reallocate property at death when individuals choose not to opt out of this

---

1. [FN 21] 391 U.S. 68 (1968).
2. [FN 27] 441 U.S. 347 (1979).
3. [FN 29] 486 U.S. 456 (1988).

system by drafting a dispositive instrument. Since American inheritance law allows for freedom of testation, and it has little in the way of forced heirship (unlike civil law countries), individuals may use a custom-tailored instrument like a will or trust to alter the default inheritance scheme embodied in the intestacy statutes.

Trimble and *Lalli* provided the contours of the statutory proof barriers the Court would find constitutional, given the substantial state interest in the orderly disposition of estates and the prevention of fraudulent claims. *Trimble* established that a statute allowing a nonmarital child to inherit only if there has been a subsequent marriage plus acknowledgement was too narrowly drawn and not constitutionally sound. *Lalli* provided that a statute allowing for additional or alternative means of proving that a man was the nonmarital child's father — an adjudication of paternity pre-death — was sufficient to meet constitutional muster.

After *Trimble* and *Lalli*, most states responded by adding language to their intestacy statutes that provided nonmarital children with several ways by which they could establish paternity. Maine's statute, which is based on the original 1969 UPC, is an example of a law that includes these paths to establish paternity.

Maine Rev. Stat. tit. 18-A §2-109. Meaning of Child and Related Terms.

If, for purposes of intestate succession, a relationship of parent and child must be established to determine succession by, through, or from a person:

(2). . . . a person born out of wedlock is a child of the mother; that person is also a child of the father if:

(i). The natural parents participated in a marriage ceremony before or after the birth of the child, even though the attempted marriage is void; or

(ii). The father adopts the child into his family; or

(iii). The father acknowledges in writing before a notary public that he is the father of the child, or the paternity is established by an adjudication before the death of the father or is established thereafter by clear and convincing proof, but the paternity established under this subparagraph is ineffective to qualify the father or his kindred to inherit from or through the child unless the father has openly treated the child as his and has not refused to support the child.

Most states have similar statutes that lay out the ways in which a nonmarital child may establish paternity in order to inherit. For example, many states require that a nonmarital child prove that the alleged father "openly and notoriously recognized the child to be his child." *See, e.g.,* Md. Code Ann., Est. & Trusts §1-208(b)(3). More recently, some states have added statutory provisions that allow "a blood genetic marker test" which, together with other evidence, establishes paternity by "clear and convincing evidence." *See, e.g.,* N.Y. Est. Powers & Trusts. Law §4-1.2 (a)(2)(D).

However, the UPC itself does not specify the manner by which a nonmarital child may establish eligibility to inherit. For example, it does not mention acknowledgement or adjudication. The UPC simply states that there is no difference in status between a marital and a nonmarital child for purposes of inheritance from his genetic parents.

UPC §2-117. No Distinction Based on Marital Status.

> . . . , a parent-child relationship exists between a child and the child's genetic parents, regardless of the parents' marital status.

Instead, as noted above, the UPC suggests that states incorporate the UPA by reference in terms of the presumptions and procedures by which a nonmarital child can establish maternity and paternity in order to be eligible to inherit. The UPA provides that a nonmarital child may establish the paternity of the man from whom they are trying to inherit by either (1) statutory presumption; (2) by voluntary acknowledgement; or (3) through court proceedings, *i.e.,* an adjudication. Under UPA §631(1), if a man is presumed to be the child's father, has acknowledged himself to be the father or has been adjudicated the father, then paternity "may be disproved only by admissible results of genetic testing excluding that man as the father of the child or identifying another man as the father of the child."

Statutory Presumption of Paternity. With regard to establishing paternity, a nonmarital child must do more than a marital child to establish that a particular man is his legal father. UPA §204 provides the following helpful presumptions for nonmarital children who may be trying to establish paternity:

UPA §204. Presumption of Paternity.

> (a) A man is presumed to be the father of a child if: . . .
> (4) after the birth of the child, he and the mother of the child married each other in apparent compliance with law, whether or not the marriage is or could be declared invalid, and he voluntarily asserted his paternity of the child, and:

(A) the assertion is in a record filed with [state agency maintaining birth records];

(B) he agreed to be and is named as the child's father on the child's birth certificate; or

(C) he promised in a record to support the child as his own; or

(5) for the first two years of the child's life, he resided in the same household with the child and openly held out the child as his own.

(b) A presumption of paternity established under this section may be rebutted only by an adjudication under [Article] 6.

Voluntary Acknowledgement of Paternity.   In the absence of a presumption, a child can establish the man's paternity if the purported father executed an effective acknowledgment of his paternity (UPA §201(b)(2)).

Adjudication of Paternity.   Under UPA §601, in the absence of a presumption or voluntary acknowledgement of paternity, a child, his mother or other parties may bring an involuntary paternity action, and a court may issue an order establishing paternity after an adjudicatory proceeding. If the action is brought during the man's life, the court may use genetic testing to establish paternity under UPA §502. Even if the putative father has died, many courts will either order relatives of the father to provide genetic material for testing under UPA §508 or they may order exhumation of the body under UPA §509.

NOTES AND QUESTIONS

1. *Intent as a policy matter.* What do you think most parents would want in terms of a nonmarital child being able to inherit from them? Would they want a child who is clearly their genetic child to inherit even if they never met the child?

2. *Nonparents and intent.* What would most grandparents want if their son were dead and a nonmarital child fathered by their son, but who never knew him, showed up to claim a share of the grandparent's estate? In enacting our inheritance laws, should we simply implement what the majority of people would want? Whose interests should control?

3. *Where should the default rule lie?* A decedent can ensure that a nonmarital child inherits by writing a will. As a policy matter, if a decedent does not bother to make a will, what should the default rule be? Should we include or exclude nonmarital children? Can we exclude them?

4. *Should gender matter?* Consider why state statutes have evolved to make it easier for a nonmarital child to inherit from her mother than her father. Does this gender-based distinction make sense to you from an evidentiary perspective? What about from a constitutional perspective? This

issue arises when the nonmarital parent tries to inherit from the child as well. *See Estate of Hicks*, 675 N.E.2d 89 (Ill. 1996) below.

5.   *Proving paternity.* For further exploration of the complexities of proving paternity for nonmarital children, see Niccol D. Kording, *Little White Lies that Destroy Children's Lives — Recreating Paternity Fraud Laws to Protect Children's Interests*, 6 J.L. & FAM. STUD. 237 (2004); (analyzing the legal and emotional difficulties a father and child face when a mother incorrectly claims paternity); Laura Oren, *Thwarted Fathers or Pop-Up Pops?: How to Determine When Putative Fathers Can Block the Adoption of Their Newborn Children*, 40 FAM. L.Q. 153 (2006) (exploring the rights of unmarried fathers in adoption); Browne Lewis, *Children of Men: Balancing the Inheritance Rights of Marital and Non-Marital Children*, 39 U. TOL. L. REV. 1 (2007) (discussing the challenges that nonmarital children face in inheritance law); Stephen A. Sherman, Note. *You Ain't My Baby Daddy: The Problem of Paternity Fraud and Paternity Laws*, 5 AVE MARIA L. REV. 273 (2007) (exploring whether to allow victims of paternity fraud to seek reimbursement for childrearing from the biological father).

PROBLEMS

In the following scenarios, can Carol inherit from Daniel under the UPA? If so, what presumptions apply? Could she do so under the standards used by other states, *i.e.*, "open and notorious recognition" or "other evidence establishing paternity"? To the extent Carol will need to introduce evidence to prove Daniel was her father, what facts would you seek to discover during your investigation and via discovery that might help prove paternity?

1.   Daniel and Mary had a brief affair in college and then moved to opposite ends of the country. They never married. As a result of the affair, Mary became pregnant and gave birth to Carol. Mary raised Carol alone, never brought a paternity proceeding against Daniel and never sought child support from him. Until the day he died, Daniel did not know of Carol's existence.

2.   What if Mary and Daniel were living together when Carol was born? A year after Carol's birth, they went their separate ways. Daniel continued to visit Carol, told his family that she was his child, sent her birthday gifts and went to her school plays.

3.   What if Mary brought a paternity suit when Carol was five years old and the court adjudicated Daniel as Carol's father? Nevertheless, Daniel never visited Carol or paid child support.

c.   Adopted Children

Like both marital and nonmarital children, who are able to establish paternity, legally adopted children fall within the definition of "child" in the intestacy statutes of all states. Adopted children may inherit from and through their *adoptive* parents, and their parents may inherit from or through them.[4] Adoption generally severs the ties between the adopted child and the *genetic* parents and thus prevents inheritance from or through them, except in some states when a stepparent adopts the child. This was not always the case and historically, adopted children often did not inherit from or through their adoptive parents.

Naomi Cahn, Perfect Substitutes or the Real Thing?
52 Duke L.J. 1077 (2003)

Under the common-law approach to inheritance, only a legitimate, blood-related child served as his father's heir. Indeed, this principle was so strongly embedded in the law that illegitimate children were deemed to have "no" blood, and thus incapable of inheriting. [In the nineteenth century] [t]he early adoption statutes often provided that the adopted child was, with certain exceptions, the heir of his [sic] parents, but the adoptive parents could not inherit from the child. In addition, there was a series of differences between the other inheritance rights of adoptees and biological relatives. Moreover, regardless of what the statutes provided with respect to adoption, disappointed heirs mounted a series of challenges to adoption decrees, seeking to disinherit the adoptees. In applying the adoption statutes in the context of the common-law doctrine of blood-based inheritance, courts were chary of granting non-blood-related children significant intestacy interests, and thus scrutinized carefully the claims of adoptive children, lest they usurp "legitimate" children. . . .

1. Statutes. Though some early statutes provided that adopted children would have the same inheritance rights as "natural children," other statutes distinguished between the rights of adopted and biological children. First, some statutes explicitly specified differences between the rights of adopted and biological children to inherit from their parents. Second, historically, under the "stranger-to-the-adoption" rule, an adopted child generally could not inherit from relatives who were not a party to the adoption. Third, adoptive children could continue to inherit from their biological relatives in some states, and their biological relatives could inherit from them even after the adoption. Finally, even outside the general laws of

---

4. "Inheriting through" someone means that you do not inherit directly from them but have to establish a connection with them in order to inherit from someone else. For example, assume Grandma Alice had one child, Betty, and Betty has a child, Chloe. If Betty dies before her mother, Alice, and then Alice dies, in order for Chloe to inherit from Grandma Alice through Betty, Chloe must establish that she is Betty's child.

intestacy and wills, the adoption statutes allowed the adoption agreement to determine the adoptee's rights. . . .

[U]nder the stranger-to-the-adoption rule, the adopted child could inherit from her adoptive parents, but not from their relatives. Because they were "strangers" to the adoption process, these relatives were presumed not to have intended for their property to be inherited outside of the bloodline. The early treatises and articles on adoption do not question this precept. It is treated as a well-established exception to the general rule that adoption creates a substitute family relationship. As one court asked in 1881, in explaining why an adopted child could not inherit from a collateral relative, "[b]ut another person, who has never been a party to any adoption proceeding, who has never desired or requested to have such artificial relation established as to himself, why should his property be subjected to such an unnatural course of descent?" The court labeled the adoptee "an alien in blood." . . .

A third difference was that adoptees could often inherit from and through their biological parents, signifying recognition of the importance of passing property through the bloodline. Although the biological parents had no other parental rights and were explicitly deprived of the parental rights of maintenance and support from their children, the child could nonetheless inherit their property. The Maine statute explicitly provided that the decree of adoption would not affect the adoptee's inheritance rights. As late as 1925, Evelyn Foster Peck noted that adoptees could continue to inherit from their biological parents in many states, including New Jersey, New York, Ohio, and West Virginia. . . .

Even today, the intestacy rights of an adopted child are extremely complicated. As the South Dakota Supreme Court stated in 1978, inheritance follows blood. Today, in a few situations, an adopted child may have fewer rights to inherit from various relatives in the adoptive family than would a biological child. On the other hand, an adoptive child may have the same rights as a biological child of the adoptive family, and may also be able to inherit from her biological family.

Until 1996, in Vermont, an adoptee could not inherit from relatives of her adopted parents who had died intestate. In that year, the Vermont Supreme Court held that an adopted child could inherit from her uncle, her father's brother. In Mississippi, the right of adoptees to inherit from collateral relatives is still unclear. In some states, depending on the phrasing of the will, an adopted child may not be able to inherit through a "class gift," or a gift that is phrased as, for example, "to my descendants" or "to my grandchildren."

In Colorado, an adoptee may inherit from her biological parents if there are no other heirs. In Pennsylvania, when the biological relatives — other than the parents — have maintained a relationship with the adoptee, then she may inherit from those relatives. In other states, an adoption decree can protect the child's rights to inherit from her biological family. Under the model statute that governs inheritance, a child adopted by the spouse of one of her biological parents can still inherit from her other biological parent, even though all legal ties have otherwise been severed between that parent and the child. Though some of these statutes protect a child's relationship with her biological kin, the assumption behind these provisions seems, nonetheless, to be based on the assumption that the decedent would prefer that her estate be left to a blood relative rather than to distant relatives.

As you can see, over time states began to recognize that adoptive children should be treated as "children" for purposes of inheriting both from and through their adoptive parents. Consistent with this approach, they embraced the idea that the child would no longer be able to inherit from or through the genetic parents. UPC §§2-118 and 2-119 continue this basic approach of treating the child as a member of the adopting family and not of the genetic family. Adoption breaks the ties to the child's genetic family, and the adopting family becomes the child's legal family.

UPC §2-118. Adoptee and Adoptee's Adoptive Parent or Parents.

> **(a) [Parent-Child Relationship Between Adoptee and Adoptive Parent or Parents.]** A parent-child relationship exists between an adoptee and the adoptee's adoptive parent or parents.

UPC §2-119. Adoptee and Adoptee's Genetic Parents.

> **(a) [Parent-Child Relationship Between Adoptee and Genetic Parents.]** Except as otherwise provided in subsections (b) through (e), a parent-child relationship does not exist between an adoptee and the adoptee's genetic parents.

So if a child is given up for adoption, she is cut off from her genetic parents for purposes of inheritance law. She cannot inherit from them nor they from her.[5] This is the general rule. Exceptions to this general rule, like the "stepparent adoption" exception, are discussed below.

---

5. In discussing the technicalities of adoption, we often forget the human side of the legal process. For a powerful article discussing the process and the acute sadness that many birth mothers feel in giving up their children for adoption, see Maureen A. Sweeney, *Between Sorrow and Happy Endings: A New Paradigm of Adoption*, 2 YALE J.L. & FEMINISM 329 (1990).

PROBLEMS

Twelve years ago, Carmelo and Aiesha gave birth to Sebastian. Unable to afford to raise Sebastian, they gave him up for adoption when he was only six weeks old. Mario and Inez adopted Sebastian.

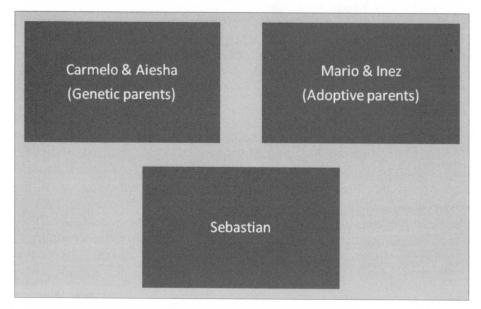

1.   If Mario died this year, may Sebastian inherit from his estate?
2.   If Carmelo died this year, may Sebastian inherit from his estate?
3.   If Mario's mother died this year, may Sebastian inherit from her estate?
4.   If Aiesha's father died this year, may Sebastian inherit from his estate?
5.   If Sebastian died this year due to the negligence of a driver and there were a large damage award, who could inherit from Sebastian's estate among the following individuals if the wrongful death statute in that state gives the award to Sebastian's intestate heirs: Carmelo, Aiesha's mother, Inez, Mario, Mario's mother?

i.   *Children Adopted by a Stepparent*

While the general rule in the United States is that adopted children are cut-off from their biological family for purposes of inheritance, some states and the UPC have established special rules for children adopted by the spouse of one of the genetic parents. These rules preserve the ability of the child to inherit from the biological family. Under this exception, the child may inherit both from the adopting stepparent and his family and from the genetic parents and their families. For example, the UPC provides:

UPC §2-119. Adoptee and Adoptee's Genetic Parents.

> **(b) [Stepchild Adopted by Stepparent.]** A parent-child relationship exists between an individual who is adopted by the spouse of either genetic parent and:
>   (1) the genetic parent whose spouse adopted the individual; and
>   (2) the other genetic parent, but only for the purpose of the right of the adoptee or a descendant of the adoptee to inherit from or through the other genetic parent.

Consider the following scenario.

Example: Assume Tom and Mary were married and had a child, Rocco. Mary died in a car accident. Tom later married Valerie, who adopted Rocco. Rocco is considered a child of Tom ("the genetic parent whose spouse adopted the individual") and Valerie (the adopting parent per UPC §2-118). He is also considered a child of Mary's for the purpose of inheriting from or through her. As such, Rocco could inherit from Tom and Valerie and, through them, from their families. Because he is also the child of Mary, Rocco could inherit from Mary's family.

In the example above, Tom, Valerie and their family members could inherit from Rocco if he were to die first. In a sense, inheritance travels both ways with respect to the continuing genetic parent-child relationship and the adopting parent-child relationship. However, Mary's family could not inherit from Rocco. Under the stepparent adoption exception, the right to inherit belongs to the child, not the other genetic parent or her relatives. It is a one-way street.

While inheritance law generally does not allow for such "double-dipping," the policy rationale for the UPC's allowing an adoptee in this situation to inherit from both genetic parents as well as the new stepparent is to facilitate the stepparent's bonding with the adoptee. As a societal matter, we want to connect the stepparent to the child by creating an emotional and legal bond between them. Adopting the child creates a legal support obligation on the part of the new adoptive/former stepparent as well. Thus, inheritance law's usual aversion to allowing double-dipping is outweighed by these benefits.

Most stepparent adoptions occur after the death of one of the genetic parents. If the two genetic parents are divorced and one remarries, the new spouse of the remarrying genetic parent cannot adopt the child because the other genetic parent retains parental rights. The only scenario in which there is a divorce and a new spouse of a genetic parent can adopt is when the other genetic parent's rights are terminated, typically based on abuse and neglect.

PROBLEMS

Twelve years ago, Ivan and Sasha gave birth to Zoltan. Sasha died and Ivan married Dori, who then adopted Zoltan.

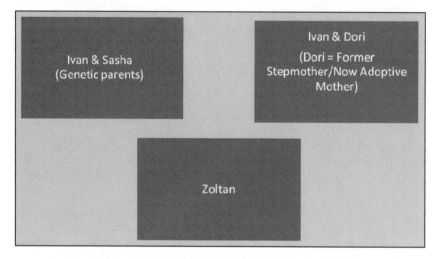

1. If Ivan died this year, may Zoltan inherit from his estate?
2. If Dori died this year, may Zoltan inherit from her estate?
3. If Sasha's mother died this year, may Zoltan inherit from her estate?
4. If Ivan's father died this year, may Zoltan inherit from his estate?
5. If Zoltan died this year due to the negligence of a driver and there were a large damage award, who could inherit from his estate among the following individuals if the wrongful death statute in that state directs that such an award is paid to the decedent's estate: Ivan, Dori, Ivan's father, Dori's mother, Sasha's brother?
6. From whom may Zoltan inherit if Ivan and Dori are not married and Dori adopts Zoltan?

ii.   Adult Adoption

While we generally think of adoption as involving minor children, a number of states allow the adoption of adults. One goal of adult adoption is to ensure inheritance by the "child" from the adoptive parent, even if the adoptive parent's will is challenged. Historically, some same-sex couples used adult adoption to thwart a potential attack by disapproving family members of a bequest in the decedent's will to a partner. These contests were often grounded in the doctrine of "undue influence," a doctrine that we explore in subsequent chapters.

A second goal of adult adoption is to alter who will inherit certain property. This goal is explored later in this chapter in the section that covers class gifts by someone other than the adopting parent.

UPC §2-115(1) defines an adoptee as "an individual who is adopted." The Comments are quite explicit in saying that this includes an individual who is adopted as an adult. Thus, under the UPC, adult adoptees are "children" for purposes of interpreting the intestacy statutes. Consider the following example:

> **Example:** Elizabeth, age 40, and Mary, age 30, are a same-sex couple who live in a state that does not allow same-sex marriage. Elizabeth inherited a beach house from her parents. She wants to make sure that Mary will inherit it. While Elizabeth has made a will to that effect, she is concerned that her family may challenge the will and succeed. If that were to happen, she would die intestate, and Mary would not be entitled to anything. If Elizabeth adopts Mary, Mary will inherit the beach house as Elizabeth's child under the intestacy statute even if the will is successfully challenged.

In many states, the fact that Mary is 30 years old when Elizabeth adopts her does not matter: Mary is now Elizabeth's legal child for purposes of intestacy and for purposes of inheriting from a parent under a will or trust. However, as we will learn later in the chapter, adult adoptees often may not inherit from nonparents who leave a class gift in a will or a trust to the "children" of the adoptee's parent or to their own "descendants." For an interesting analysis of the history of adult adoption and guidance for courts in this area, see Peter T. Wendel, *The Succession Rights of Adopted Adults: Trying to Fit a Square Peg into a Round Hole*, 43 Creighton L. Rev. 815, 854 (2010) (arguing for recognition of an exception from the classic adoption rule for adult adoptions and that doing so "would promote the typical decedent's intent . . . while simultaneously reducing litigation with respect to an adopted adult's succession rights under the testamentary instruments of others.")

iii.   Equitable Adoption

In some cases, a friend or relative takes in an orphaned child but fails to complete all the steps required for a legal adoption. The "parent" may hold the child out as a legal child. In many cases, the child may not know she is not legally adopted until the "parent" dies. Courts are often sympathetic to such children. In limited circumstances, courts use their broad power to promote justice to find that there has been an "equitable adoption" as opposed to a "legal adoption." This allows the children to inherit from their guardian even though the guardian had not become a parent through the formal adoption procedures.

Some courts require the child claiming from the guardian's estate to establish that an adoption proceeding had actually begun but had not been completed. They ground relief in an express or implied contract. Indeed, equitable adoption is also known as "adoption by estoppel." Other courts are more flexible, allowing a child to bring a claim for equitable adoption if the guardian and the child treated each other as legal parent and child. While a number of states have recognized equitable adoption, the UPC §2-122 takes no position on the doctrine.

Equitable adoption is hard to establish and thus will be successfully claimed in only rare cases. The evidentiary threshold is steep. For example, in *Wheeling Dollar Savings & Trust v. Singer*, 250 S.E.2d 369, 373-74 (W. Va. 1978), the Supreme Court of West Virginia held that the doctrine of equitable adoption would be recognized by West Virginia but that it must be established by "clear, cogent, and convincing proof." Justice Neely described what would be required to support the application of equitable adoption in a particular case:

> While formal adoption is the only safe route, in many instances a child will be raised by persons not his parents from an age of tender years, treated as a natural child, and represented to others as a natural or adopted child. In many instances, the child will believe himself to be the natural or formally "adopted" child of the "adoptive" parents only to be treated as an outcast upon their death. We cannot ascertain any reasonable distinction between a child treated in all regards as an adopted child but who has been led to rely to his detriment upon the existence of formal legal paperwork imagined but never accomplished, and a formally adopted child. Our family centered society presumes that bonds of love and loyalty will prevail in the distribution of family wealth along family lines, and only by affirmative action, i.e., writing a will, may this presumption be overcome. An equitably adopted child in practical terms is as much a family member as a formally adopted child and should not be the subject of discrimination. He will be as loyal to his adoptive parents, take as faithful care of them in their old age, and provide them with as much financial and emotional support in their vicissitudes, as any natural or formally adopted child.
>
> However, the equitably adopted child and the formally adopted child are not without differences. The formally adopted child need only produce his adoption papers to guarantee his treatment as an adopted child. The equitably adopted child in any private property dispute such as the case under consideration involving the laws of Inheritance or Private trusts must prove by clear, cogent and convincing evidence that he has stood from an age of tender years in a position exactly equivalent to a formally adopted child. Circumstances which tend to show the existence of an equitable adoption include: the benefits of love and affection accruing to the adopting party, the performances of services by the child, the surrender of ties by the natural parent, the society, companionship and filial obedience of the child, an invalid or ineffectual adoption proceeding, reliance by the adopted person upon the existence of his adoptive status, the representation to all the world that the child is a natural or adopted child and the rearing of the child from an age of tender years by the adopting parents. Of course, evidence can be presented which tends to negate an equitable adoption such as failure of the child to perform the duties of an adopted child, or misconduct of the child or

abandonment of the adoptive parents however, mere mischievous behavior usually associated with being a child is not sufficient to disprove an equitable adoption. Most of the cited cases predicate the finding of an equitable adoption on the proof of an expressed or implied contract of adoption. While the existence of an express contract of adoption is very convincing evidence, an implied contract of adoption is an unnecessary fiction created by courts as a protection from fraudulent claims. We find that if a claimant can, by clear, cogent and convincing evidence, prove sufficient facts to convince the trier of fact that his status is identical to that of a formally adopted child, except only for the absence of a formal order of adoption, a finding of an equitable adoption is proper without proof of an adoption contract.

In the case before us, appellant Singer alleges that she was taken from an orphanage when she was eight or nine by the Whartons; that she was given the surname of the Whartons; that she was raised as their child and that, until this action, she believed herself to be the adopted child of the Whartons. Furthermore it appears that Lyda Wharton devised and bequeathed her residuary estate to "my daughter, Ada Belle Singer." If the appellant Singer can prove these allegations at the hearing below, she has a strong case for equitable adoption, and one of the most important elements in her proof is that she was held out to all the world as a natural or adopted child. Clear, cogent and convincing proof of treatment as a "child" consistent with formal adoption is the highest possible standard of civil proof defined as "that measure or degree of proof which will produce in the mind of the trier of facts a firm belief or conviction as to the allegations sought to be established. It is intermediate, being more than a mere preponderance, but not to the extent of such certainty as is required beyond a reasonable doubt as in criminal cases."

NOTES AND QUESTIONS

1. *Virtual children?* Whose interests does equitable adoption recognize? Is this appropriate?

2. *Contract theory lives.* For an interesting case where the court refused to apply equitable adoption, see *O'Neal v. Wilkes,* 439 S.E.2d 490 (Ga. 1994). In that case, Hattie O'Neal was trying to establish her eligibility to inherit from decedent Rosewell Cook, who was not her biological father but who had raised her and paid for her education. O'Neal argued that under the theory of equitable or "virtual" adoption, her paternal aunt had placed her for adoption with Cook pursuant to a contract. The Georgia Supreme Court held that the aunt had no authority to enter into an adoption contract with decedent. Thus, the contract was invalid, and O'Neal was not entitled to share in decedent's estate. The dissent argued that the contract should be held valid and even if not, the practice of grounding equitable adoption in a contractual basis had correctly come under fire and should be abandoned as a requirement in Georgia. The dissent cites Jan Ellen Rein, *Relationship by Blood, Adoption and Association: Who Should Get What and Why*, 37 VAND. L. REV. 711, 766-806 (1984), which provides an excellent description of the policy and doctrinal aspects of equitable adoption.

3. *Standard of proof.* In 2003, the Georgia Supreme Court reiterated its holding in *O'Neal v. Wilkes*, stating that the appropriate standard for equitable adoption is clear and compelling evidence, including a showing that the contract was "made between persons competent to contract for the disposition of the child." *See Hulsey v. Carter*, 588 S.E.2d 717, 718 (Ga. 2003).

PROBLEMS

Frank and Lily had a daughter, Aurora. When Aurora was two months old, Lily died and Frank married Simone. Frank and Simone subsequently divorced when Aurora was two years old. Frank left Aurora with Simone and never saw her again. When Aurora was three, Simone married Dante. Aurora, who is now 17, has continued to live with Simone and Dante. Simone has just died. Simone and Dante began adoption proceedings several years ago and let Aurora know about this. Aurora was unaware of the fact that Simone and Dante never finalized the adoption. Simone and Dante always referred to Aurora as "Frank's daughter" in conversation with friends and family.

    1. What arguments can Aurora make to show that she should be eligible to inherit from Simone in intestacy?

    2. If you were her attorney, what facts would you introduce on her behalf? What is her likelihood of success?

d. Assisted Reproductive Technology (ART) Children

i. *In General*

The UPC defines assisted reproduction in UPC §2-115 as a means of causing pregnancy other than sexual intercourse. Assisted reproductive technology (ART) poses new and interesting issues for inheritance law. Parents may have used someone else's egg or sperm, or may have hired a surrogate mother to carry a child. ART children may be born to married heterosexual or same-sex couples, or to single parents, or to unmarried heterosexual or same-sex couples. There are additional issues raised by "posthumous" children, those conceived and born after one parent, typically the father, is dead. Many states have not yet grappled with all of these possibilities in terms of defining the parent-child relationship pursuant to inheritance law. Some of the uniform laws give guidance in this regard. For example, UPA §703 provides a consent-based rule to determine whether someone is the parent of an ART child. That section states, "A man who provides sperm for, or consents to, assisted reproduction by a woman . . . with the intent to be the parent of her child, is a parent of the resulting child."

The UPC provides the following framework for determining if there is a parent-child relationship between an ART child claiming from a decedent's estate and the decedent:

UPC §2-120. Child Conceived by Assisted Reproduction Other than Child Born to Gestational Carrier.

> **(a) [Definitions.]** In this section:
> (1) "Birth mother" means a woman . . . who gives birth to a child of assisted reproduction. The term is not limited to a woman who is the child's genetic mother.
> (2) "Child of assisted reproduction" means a child conceived by means of assisted reproduction. . . .
> (3) "Third-party donor" means an individual who produces eggs or sperm used for assisted reproduction, whether or not for consideration. The term does not include:
> (A) a husband who provides sperm, or a wife who provides eggs, that are used for assisted reproduction by the wife;
> (B) the birth mother of a child of assisted reproduction; or
> (C) an individual who has been determined under subsection (e) or (f) to have a parent-child relationship with a child of assisted reproduction.
> **(b) [Third-Party Donor.]** A parent-child relationship does not exist between a child of assisted reproduction and a third-party donor
> **(c) [Parent-Child Relationship with Birth Mother.]** A parent-child relationship exists between a child of assisted reproduction and the child's birth mother.

ii.   *Artificial Insemination (AI)*

As noted above, ART children can be conceived either within marriage or outside of it. The most basic form of assisted reproduction is artificial insemination (AI), whereby sperm from a donor is used to inseminate the birth mother. Under subsection (c) above, a child conceived by AI is the child of the birth mother.

In married couples, the donor may be the husband of the mother or may be a third-party donor. If the husband is the donor, then a parent-child relationship exists between the child and the husband of the birth mother under UPC §2-120(d). Note that if there is a third-party sperm donor other than the husband, there is still a presumption that the husband of the birth mother is the father of the child for purposes of inheritance unless there is clear and convincing evidence to the contrary under UPC §2-120(h)(1).

In cases of nonmarital children, a parent-child relationship exists between a person other than the birth mother who consented to the ART with the intent to be the other parent of the child under UPC §2-120(f)

UPC §2-120. Child Conceived by Assisted Reproduction Other than Child Born to Gestational Carrier.

(d) [Parent-Child Relationship with Husband Whose Sperm Were Used During His Lifetime by His Wife for Assisted Reproduction.] Except as otherwise provided . . . , a parent-child relationship exists between a child of assisted reproduction and the husband of the child's birth mother if the husband provided the sperm that the birth mother used during his lifetime for assisted reproduction. . . .

(f) [Parent-Child Relationship with Another.] Except as otherwise provided . . . , a parent-child relationship exists between a child of assisted reproduction and an individual other than the birth mother who consented to assisted reproduction by the birth mother with intent to be treated as the other parent of the child. Consent to assisted reproduction by the birth mother with intent to be treated as the other parent of the child is established if the individual:

(1) before or after the child's birth, signed a record that, considering all the facts and circumstances, evidences the individual's consent; or

(2) in the absence of a signed record under paragraph (1):

(A) functioned as a parent of the child no later than two years after the child's birth;

(B) intended to function as a parent of the child no later than two years after the child's birth but was prevented from carrying out that intent by death, incapacity, or other circumstances; or

(C) intended to be treated as a parent of a posthumously conceived child, if that intent is established by clear and convincing evidence. . . .

(h) [Presumption: Birth Mother Is Married or Surviving Spouse.] For the purpose of subsection (f)(2), the following rules apply:

(1) If the birth mother is married and no divorce proceeding is pending, in the absence of clear and convincing evidence to the contrary, her spouse satisfies subsection (f)(2)(A) or (B).

(2) If the birth mother is a surviving spouse and at her deceased spouse's death no divorce proceeding was pending, in the absence of clearly and convincing evidence to the contrary, her deceased spouse satisfies subsection (f)(2)(B) or (C).

Example: Lydia and Max have been married for five years. They have been unable to conceive a child. They visit a fertility clinic, where Lydia is artificially inseminated with sperm stored at the fertility clinic and donated by an anonymous sperm donor. Max signed a form that indicated he consented to the artificial insemination of his wife. Nine months later, Lydia gives birth to a little girl, Samantha. Under UPC §2-120(f), Max and Lydia are Samantha's legal parents for purposes of inheritance. UPC §2-120(b) makes it clear that the anonymous donor is not the father of the child.

iii.   In-Vitro Fertilization (IVF)

In-vitro fertilization (IVF) is a second type of assisted reproduction. With IVF, a woman's eggs are fertilized by a man's sperm outside of her body. The resulting embryo is implanted in the woman and she gives birth to a child. All kinds of combinations of eggs and sperm are possible.

Egg of wife	Egg of third-party donor	Sperm of husband	Sperm of third-party donor

If the wife's eggs and the husband's sperm are used, the child is clearly a marital child of both for the same reasons as discussed in the preceding section. Even if a third-party donor's sperm is used to fertilize the wife's eggs, the child would be a marital child of the wife and husband. If both the eggs and the sperm are donated by third-parties, you can see that the child might potentially have two mothers and two fathers!

Example: Steve and Ramona have been married for five years. They have been unable to conceive a child. They visit a fertility clinic, where Ramona is impregnated with an embryo that is the product of an anonymous third-party egg donor and an anonymous third-party sperm donor. The egg and sperm have been fertilized in the lab. Steve signed a form that indicated he consented to the transfer of the resulting embryo into his wife, Ramona. Nine months later, Ramona gives birth to a little girl, Lucy. Under the UPC, Ramona and Steve are the parents of Lucy.

Note that Steve can withdraw his consent to be a parent under ART if he does so before placement of the embryo. This situation can arise if, for example, embryos are frozen for future use. Steve's consent would also be withdrawn automatically by divorce if the couple divorces before placement of the embryo. In this regard, the UPC provides as follows:

UPC §2-120. Child Conceived by Assisted Reproduction Other than Child Born to Gestational Carrier.

(i) [Divorce Before Placement of Eggs, Sperm, or Embryos.] If a married couple is divorced before placement of eggs, sperm, or embryos, a child resulting from the assisted reproduction is not a child of the birth mother's former spouse, unless the former spouse consented in a record that if assisted reproduction were to occur after divorce, the child would be treated as the former spouse's child.

(j) [Withdrawal of Consent Before Placement of Eggs, Sperm, or Embryos.] If, in a record, an individual withdraws consent to assisted reproduction before placement of eggs, sperm, or embryos, a child resulting from the assisted reproduction is not a child of that individual, unless the individual subsequently satisfies subsection (f).

NOTES

1. *Same-sex couples and the parent-child relationship.* UPC §2-120(e) provides that "a birth certificate identifying an individual other than the birth mother as the other parent of a child of assisted reproduction presumptively establishes a parent-child relationship between the child and that individual." The UPC Comments note that this section, "could apply to a same-sex couple if state law permits a woman who is not the birth mother to be listed on the child's birth certificate as the child's other parent." *See e,g.,* D.C. CODE §7-205(e)(3) (2001) (requiring a domestic partner's name be added as a parent on a birth certificate, or if the mother is not in a domestic partnership, allowing the addition of the other parent's name if there is a written and signed agreement).

2. *Unintended consequences.* In the situation above, the woman who is not the birth mother could adopt the child under UPC §2-118, she could consent to assisted reproduction under UPC §2-120(f) or she could function as a parent of the child under UPC §2-120(f)(2) as a way of establishing a parent-child relationship. *But see* Nancy D. Polikoff, *A Mother Should Not Have to Adopt Her Own Child: Parentage Laws for Children of Lesbian Couples in the Twenty-First Century,* 5 STAN. J. C.R. & C.L. 201 (2009) (proposing legal changes that would allow both mothers in a same-sex relationship to be legal parents "from the moment of conception"). The other problem with this approach is that if the woman who is not the birth mother adopts the child, the birth mother is no longer a parent for inheritance purposes. This is a glitch under the UPC identified in Laura M. Padilla, *Flesh of My Flesh But Not My Heir: Unintended Disinheritance,* 36 BRANDEIS J. FAM. L. 219 (1997-1998).

3.   *Interesting case.* Singer Melissa Etheridge and her partner, film-maker Julie Cypher, wanted to have a child. They asked fellow singer-songwriter, David Crosby, to be the sperm donor. After being artificially inseminated with Crosby's sperm, Cypher gave birth to a daughter, Bailey, and two years later, a son, Beckett. Under UPC §2-120(e), a presumption of a parent-child relationship would arise if Etheridge's name is on the birth certificate or if she consented to parentage by a means specified in 2-120(f). In reality, Etheridge adopted both children. *See* http://www.cbsnews.com/stories/2000/01/17/60II/main150369.shtml, which discusses an interview with Etheridge during which she discusses the children's relationship with their genetic father, David Crosby. *See also* Jane S. Schacter, *Constructing Families in a Democracy: Courts, Legislatures and Second Parent Adoption*, 75 CHI.-KENT L. REV. 933, 948 n.44 (2000), in which the author discusses the rising public visibility of same-sex/second-parent adoption as illustrated by the Etheridge case.

iv.   Surrogacy

The situation becomes more complex where a woman provides donor eggs that are fertilized by her husband's sperm or by an anonymous donor and the resulting embryo is not carried by the wife but by a surrogate or "gestational carrier." In this case, the child has a birth mother who is different from her genetic mother. The UPC has a complicated framework for determining who is a child under these circumstances, but essentially the gestational carrier is generally not deemed to be the mother for purposes of inheritance. Rather, the woman who intends to be the mother of the child (the woman who entered into the "gestational agreement" with the surrogate mother) is the mother for purposes of inheritance.

UPC §2-121. Child Born to Gestational Carrier.

(a) [Definitions.] In this section:
(1) "Gestational agreement" means an enforceable or unen-forceable agreement for assisted reproduction in which a woman agrees to carry a child to birth for an intended parent, intended parents, or an individual described in subsection (e).
(2) "Gestational carrier" means a woman who is not an intended parent who gives birth to a child under a gestational agreement. The term is not limited to a woman who is the child's genetic mother.
(3) "Gestational child" means a child born to a gestational carrier under a gestational agreement.
(4) "Intended parent" means an individual who entered into a gestational agreement providing that the individual will be the

parent of a child born to a gestational carrier by means of assisted reproduction. The term is not limited to an individual who has a genetic relationship with the child.

(b) [Court Order Adjudicating Parentage: Effect.] A parent-child relationship is conclusively established by a court order designating the parent or parents of a gestational child.

(c) [Gestational Carrier.] A parent-child relationship between a gestational child and the child's gestational carrier does not exist unless the gestational carrier is:

(1) designated as a parent of the child in a court order described in subsection (b); or

(2) the child's genetic mother and a parent-child relationship does not exist under this section with an individual other than the gestational carrier.

(d) [Parent-Child Relationship with Intended Parent or Parents.] In the absence of a court order under subsection (b), a parent-child relationship exists between a gestational child and an intended parent who:

(1) functioned as a parent of the child no later than two years after the child's birth; or

(2) died while the gestational carrier was pregnant if:

(A) there were two intended parents and the other intended parent functioned as a parent of the child no later than two years after the child's birth;

(B) there were two intended parents, the other intended parent also died while the gestational carrier was pregnant, and a relative of either deceased intended parent or the spouse or surviving spouse of a relative of either deceased intended parent functioned as a parent of the child no later than two years after the child's birth; or

(C) there was no other intended parent and a relative of or the spouse or surviving spouse of a relative of the deceased intended parent functioned as a parent of the child no later than two years after the child's birth.

Example: Adam and Lisa discover that Lisa's health will not allow her to carry a pregnancy to term. They enter into a gestational agreement that provides for Joan to be impregnated with an embryo that has been fertilized at the fertility clinic. The embryo is the product of Lisa's egg and Adam's sperm. Joan becomes pregnant after the embryo transfer and nine months later she gives birth to a baby girl, Celia. Joan is the gestational carrier in this situation. She is not Celia's legal mother. Lisa is both Celia's genetic and legal mother though she is not Celia's birth mother. Lisa is the intended parent under UPC §2-121(a)(4).

If the gestational carrier changes her mind and wants to keep the child, there are very difficult questions for courts to resolve in terms of who is the legal mother for purposes of raising the child. These problems are beyond the scope of this book.

PROBLEMS

Donato and Walinda were married seven years ago. During their marriage, Walinda gave birth to a son, Bart. Bart was conceived via artificial insemination using donor sperm from Donato's best friend, Steve. Bart is six when both Donato and Walinda die this year.

1.   Does Bart qualify as a child of Donato?
2.   Would Bart be able to inherit from Steve if Steve died intestate?
3.   Would Bart be eligible to inherit from Donato if Donato had not been married to Walinda when Bart was conceived but had been in a committed relationship with her for seven years?

v.   Posthumous Conception

Most children who are the product of assisted reproduction are born during their parents' lifetimes. A few are born afterwards. This subcategory of assisted reproduction raises even more complex problems for inheritance law. The law has traditionally presumed that if a child were not born within 10 months (or 300 days) of a father's death, the child could not be a child of that father for purposes of inheritance. Now, genetic children can be conceived and born many years after either parent's death.

In this rapidly developing area of law, few cases have yet been decided on the issue of whether a child conceived after a person's death is his child. The few cases that have addressed this question involve remarkably similar situations where married men who have been diagnosed with cancer were able to "bank" or deposit sperm that was frozen prior to death. Their wives used the sperm to conceive children after their husbands' deaths through various ART procedures. Each of the wives had twins, and each applied for social security survivor benefits on behalf of their children. The Social Security Administration denied their claims. The women appealed the denials.

In *In re Estate of Kolacy*, 753 A.2d 1257 (N.J. Super. Ct. Ch. Div. 2000), the mother requested a declaration that her daughters were intestate heirs of her deceased husband. The court agreed they were. In a Massachusetts case, *Woodward v. Commissioner of Soc. Sec.*, 760 N.E.2d 257 (Mass. 2002), the court concluded that a child conceived posthumously could be a child under the intestacy statute if the child and parent were genetically related and the deceased parent had affirmatively consented to the posthumous conception and to the support of the resulting child.

In *Gillett-Netting v. Barnhart*, 231 F. Supp. 2d 961 (D. Ariz. 2002), *rev'd*, 371 F.3d 593 (9th Cir. 2004), the district court concluded that to "survive" a decedent, a person must be alive at the decedent's death, with an exception for after-born children *in gestation* before decedent's death. Therefore, said the court, a child who was not conceived until after decedent's death could not be an heir. On appeal, the Ninth Circuit reversed the district court's decision and remanded the case, holding that qualification as an intestate heir is not a requirement for qualification as a dependent under the Social Security Act.

UPC §2-120(k), drafted after these cases were decided, provides that a posthumously born child can be the child of a deceased parent for inheritance purposes, but it places a time limit on the child's conception and birth. The Comments explain that, "[t]he 36-month period in subsection [(k)] is designed to allow a surviving spouse or partner a period of grieving, time to make up his or her mind about whether to go forward with assisted reproduction, and a reasonable allowance for unsuccessful attempts to achieve a pregnancy. . . . Note also that [UPC] Section 3-703 gives the decedent's personal representative authority to take account of the possibility of post-humous conception in the timing of the distribution of part or all of the estate."

UPC §2-120. Child Conceived by Assisted Reproduction Other than Child Born to Gestational Carrier.

(k) [When Posthumously Conceived Child Treated as in Gestation.] If, under this section, an individual is a parent of a child of assisted reproduction who is conceived after the individual's death, the child is treated as in gestation at the individual's death for purposes of Section 2-104(a)(2) if the child is:

   (1) in utero not later than 36 months after the individual's death; or

   (2) born not later than 45 months after the individual's death.

Several states have also enacted statutes in this area. The following article discusses various state statutes that have tried to clarify when a post-humous child may establish a parent-child relationship for purposes of inheritance. Note that some state statutes require "consent in a record" while others, including the UPC, do not. The UPA §707 provides, "that the deceased individual is not a parent . . . unless the deceased individual consented in a record that if assisted reproduction were to occur after death, the deceased individual would be a parent of the child."

Raymond C. O'Brien, The Momentum of Posthumous Conception: A Model Act

25 J. Contemp. Health L. & Pol'y 332, 359-64 (2009)

B.   STATE STATUTES

A few states have recently enacted legislation that specifically addresses the issues raised by posthumous conception. . . . Those states that have made judicial determinations are Arkansas (denying status), New Hampshire (denying status), New York (permitting status), Massachusetts (permitting status), and New Jersey (permitting status). But the fact that states have begun to enact legislation, plus initiatives associated with the Model Act, indicates a movement towards recognition.

California now provides that:

> . . . [F]or purposes of determining rights to property to be distributed upon the death of a decedent, a child of the decedent conceived after the death of the decedent, other than a child conceived as a result of human cloning, shall be deemed to have been born in the lifetime of the decedent if the child or his or her representative proves by clear and convincing evidence that specified conditions are satisfied.

A review of the discussion offered concerning the new California legislation reveals a number of questions still unanswered. For example, when a posthumously conceived child is born, should the child have the right to recover from previous distributees? That is, if the estate was distributed and then an additional child was born and that child would qualify as taking from the estate, how should that posthumously conceived child take from the existing heirs? Such considerations are not insurmountable obstacles, such issues having been considered and disposed of through probate statutes already in existence. The legislature in Louisiana was among the first to enact a statute permitting posthumous children to inherit from parents who anticipated this possibility and then specifically consented to this eventual occurrence, thus legitimating the child for purposes of inheritance. Under the current version of the state statute, the child must be born within three years of the death of the decedent, and once born, the child is entitled to "all rights, including the capacity to inherit from the decedent as the child would have had the child been in existence at the time of the death of the deceased parent."

Consent of the provider of the gamete to posthumous conception is an essential element of any new legislation being considered. Illustrative is the Virginia provision requiring that before a provider may be considered a parent of a posthumously conceived child, that same decedent, prior to death, must have consented in writing to the implantation of the procedure resulting in birth. . . .

Likewise, Texas provides that,

> [i]f a spouse dies before the placement of eggs, sperm, or embryos, the deceased spouse is not a parent of the resulting child unless the deceased spouse consented in a record kept by a licensed physician that if assisted reproduction were to occur after death the deceased spouse would be a parent of the child.

Similar provisions may be found in North Dakota, Louisiana, and Washington. Florida, on the other hand, provides that a posthumously conceived child is not entitled to inherit under state intestacy statutes unless the decedent provided for that child in his or her last will and testament.

NOTES AND QUESTIONS

1. *What constitutes consent?* Do you think that most men would want a child conceived using their sperm post-death to inherit from them? What if the mother of the child were the man's surviving spouse? Does that imply consent? Should we require consent and if so, should it be written consent or should oral consent or circumstantial consent be sufficient? What if the man's parents had the man's sperm extracted after death to produce a grandchild using a surrogate mother? The banking or extraction processes are more intrusive for eggs than they are for sperm. What would most women want in these scenarios? *See* Mary F. Radford, *Postmortem Sperm Retrieval and the Social Security Administration: How Modern Reproductive Technology Makes Strange Bedfellows*, 2 Est. Plan. & Community Prop. L.J. 33 (2009), in which the author discusses the ethical, moral and legal inheritance dilemmas of extracting sperm from a decedent's body for future procreation.

2. *Posthumous children.* There are a number of articles on the topic of inheritance law and posthumously conceived children. *See, e.g.,* Kathryn Venturatos Lorio, *Conceiving the Inconceivable: Legal Recognition of the Posthumously Conceived Child*, 34 ACTEC J. 154 (2008), which provides a detailed examination of the legal rules concerning posthumously conceived children.

3. *Fairness vs. efficiency.* The most difficult problem in drafting statutes governing posthumous children and inheritance is balancing how long the estate will be left open for those children to come to fruition. The goal of efficiency, timely payment of creditors and distribution to beneficiaries may conflict with the goal of providing that a genetic child of the decedent is treated as her child for purposes of inheritance. What do you think is a reasonable time to leave the estate open? Would it matter if the decedent had no other living children?

PROBLEMS

Dietrich and Gretchen were married in a valid marriage ceremony seven years ago. Dietrich died on January 11th of the current year. At Dietrich's death, Gretchen was pregnant with Carol, who was born on January 21st of the current year, days after Dietrich's death.

1.   Does Carol qualify as a "child" of Dietrich for purposes of intestacy?

2.   Does your answer to Problem 1 change if Carol were born on November 25th of the current year?

EXERCISE

Draft a paragraph in a will in which Abdul leaves a bequest of $100,000 to the children of his sister, Alia. He wants to be assured that should she have any children after his death, they are provided for also. Consider the concerns raised in the article by Professor Gary.

e.   Foster and Stepchildren

Foster children and stepchildren are generally not included in the term "child" for purposes of intestacy or construction of wills and trusts. A foster child is a child who is unrelated to either a husband or a wife but for whom they provide care, typically as the result of a formal placement by a state social services agency. A stepchild is a spouse's child from a prior marriage or relationship who was not legally adopted by the stepparent.

UPC §1-201. General Definitions.

> (5) "Child" includes an individual entitled to take as a child under this Code by intestate succession from the parent whose relationship is involved and *excludes* a person who is only a *stepchild, a foster child*, a grandchild, or any more remote descendant. [Emphasis added.]

In some states, stepchildren may be eventual takers in intestacy when other heirs are exhausted. But even in those cases, they do not take as "children." For example, before allowing an estate to be paid over or "escheat" to the state, UPC §2-103(b) gives a stepchild and the stepchild's descendants an intestate share if there are no other blood relatives of the decedent within the first three degrees of relationship.[6]

---

6. Chapter 3 discusses the meaning of "degrees of relationship."

Section 6454 of the California Probate Court allows both foster and stepchildren to establish a parent-child relationship with the decedent for purposes of inheritance. It provides that a parent-child relationship exists if the relationship began while the child was a minor and continued throughout the joint lifetimes of the child and the deceased foster parent or stepparent, as long as there is clear and convincing evidence that the decedent would have adopted the person if there had not been a legal barrier to such adoption. What would the legal barrier to adoption be? In most situations, the legal barrier that exists is the other parent's refusal to give up parental rights. If that is the case, the barrier ceases to exist when the stepchild or foster child becomes an adult. What if the stepparent would have adopted the child when the child was a minor but could not and then when the child became an adult, the adoption no longer seemed important? The stepparent and child continued a parent-child relationship until the stepparent's death, but no adoption occurred. The Supreme Court of California refused to apply the statute on these facts, deciding that the legal barrier to adoption had to continue until the stepparent's death. *See Estate of Joseph*, 949 P.2d 472 (Cal. 1998).

However, the California statute is not typical, and most states do not include foster and stepchildren in the definition of child.

3. Interpreting Class Gifts in Wills and Trusts

In Section 2 we explored the rules that apply to interpreting an intestacy statute when a decedent dies without a will. These rules help guide the court in determining who qualifies as a "child" for purposes of inheriting in those circumstances. However, when a decedent dies with a will or trust, the court is faced with interpreting an instrument rather than a statute. Most states and the UPC simply extend the rules regarding who is a child for purposes of intestacy to wills and trusts, but there are some differences. This section describes those differences that arise in the context of class gifts. Class gifts are bequests in a will or trust that refer to the beneficiaries by relationship. For example, if Ellen leaves a bequest to "my grandchildren" in her will, that is a class gift.

a. Class Gifts from Parents

When a parent uses terms like "child" or "issue" as part of a class gift in a will or other governing instrument, like a trust, UPC §2-705(b) provides that the term shall be interpreted using the same rules used to interpret those terms in the intestacy statutes. Therefore, if a decedent leaves property to "my children" in a will or trust, the court will use the same analysis we discussed above in determining whether someone is a "child" of that decedent for purposes of inclusion in the class gift to her "children."

UPC §2-705. Class Gifts Construed to Accord with Intestate Succession; Exceptions.

> **(b) [Terms of Relationship.]** A class gift that uses a term of relationship to identify the class members <u>includes a child of assisted reproduction</u>, <u>a gestational child</u>, and, except as otherwise provided in subsections (e) and (f), <u>an adoptee</u> and a child born to parents who are not married to each other, and their respective descendants if appropriate to the class, *in accordance with the rules for intestate succession regarding parent-child relationships.* [Emphasis added.]

Example 1:   Hubert, a member of the armed forces, executed a will shortly before being deployed to a war zone. His will devised "90 percent of my estate to my wife, Gloria, and 10 percent of my estate to my children." At his death, Hubert's only child was the one he had with Gloria, Dora, who was 10 years old. Applying the intestacy rules we learned above to define child, Dora will inherit under Hubert's will since the marital presumption applies.

Example 2:   Hubert, a member of the armed forces, executed a will shortly before being deployed to a war zone. His will devised "90 percent of my estate to my companion, Gloria, and 10 percent of my estate to my children." At his death, Hubert's only child was the one he had with Gloria, Dora, who was 10 years old. Dora will inherit under Hubert's will since, even though the marital presumption does not apply, Hubert lived with Dora during the first two years of her life and held her out as his own. Since Dora would be a child under the intestacy rules, Dora is also considered a child of Hubert for purposes of interpreting his will.

Whether a child is a member of a class gift from a parent turns on the very specific language used by the parent in his will or trust. If a parent uses a broad term of relationship like "children" or "descendants" without further adjectives, a nonmarital child will be included in the class gift. But remember that parents are free to decide to exclude children from their wills. So what happens if a parent uses an adjective like "lawful descendants" in creating a class gift in his will? The following case explores this issue. Do you agree with the majority or the dissent in this case?

Hood v. Todd
695 S.E.2d 31 (Ga. 2010)

The opinion of the court was delivered by Chief Justice Hunstein

Appellee Regina Gordon Todd seeks to establish her right to a child's share of the estate of testator John E. Buffington. The probate court denied a motion for summary judgment filed by the estate's executors, appellants Beth Buffington Hood and Ginger Buffington Folger, by which they sought an adjudication as a matter of law that Todd was not a beneficiary under the testator's will. This Court granted appellants' application for interlocutory appeal, and, concluding that the probate court erred in finding a genuine issue of material fact regarding Todd's beneficiary status, we now reverse. . . .

[T]he undisputed evidence reflects that Buffington died in August 2006, leaving a will providing, in relevant part, for distribution of his personal and household effects to "[his] children surviving [Buffington]" and distribution of the residue of his estate to the Buffington Family Trust, under which "each then living child of [Buffington]" and "each deceased child of [Buffington] who shall leave issue then living" is to receive an equal share of the estate's entire residue, in trust. The term "children" is specifically defined in the will, in pertinent part, as "only the lawful blood descendants in the first degree of the parent designated." An introductory portion of the will reads, "I have two living children, Beth Buffington Hood and Ginger Buffington Folger." In addition to being named co-executors of the will, Hood and Folger are also each appointed as trustee of the respective residuary trust established for her benefit. No other trustees of any other potential trusts (other than a successor trustee) are named.

Todd claims to be Buffington's biological daughter, asserting that she was fathered during an extra-marital affair between Buffington and Todd's mother and that Buffington acknowledged her as his daughter during his life. As such, Todd claims that she is entitled to a child's share of Buffington's estate. Following the initiation of probate proceedings, Todd filed a separate action in superior court seeking a declaration of her beneficiary status under Buffington's will and related equitable relief. The superior court transferred that action to the probate court, and appellants then moved for summary judgment on the issue of Todd's beneficiary status, asserting that Buffington's will unambiguously evinced his intent to exclude Todd as a beneficiary. Finding the existence of genuine issues of material fact as to Todd's status under the will, the probate court denied the motion.

Though there may be a genuine issue of fact as to Todd's status as Buffington's daughter, we conclude that resolution of this issue is unnecessary in determining Todd's status under Buffington's will, as the will clearly and unambiguously expresses Buffington's intent that only Hood and Folger, the daughters born of his marriage, share as children thereunder. "In the construction of all wills, the court shall seek diligently for the intention of the testator and shall give effect to such intention as far as it may be consistent with the rules of law." "The court must look first to the 'four corners' of the will to discover that intent." Where the language of a will is clear . . . and can be given legal effect as it stands, the court will not, by construction, give the will a different effect."

A testator may make any disposition of his property he chooses, so long as not contrary to law or public policy, even to the exclusion of his spouse and/or descendants. The testator need not expressly name an heir in his will in order to disinherit her, so long as the intent to disinherit is clearly expressed. Mary F. Radford, *Redfearn Wills and Administration in Georgia*, §7:6(15), at 316 (7th ed. 2008). "'It is no proper concern of the court whether the disposition of one's property by will is wise or unwise, is justified or unjustified, so long as such disposition is legal and the intention of the testator is certain and clearly expressed by the terms of the will.'"

Here, the plain terms of the will clearly reflect Buffington's intent to exclude Todd. Todd is not mentioned in any portion of the will, as contrasted with Hood and Folger, who are specifically designated as Buffington's "two living children," are named co-executors, and are named as trustees of respective trusts created for each of them from the Buffington Family Trust. In addition, it is clear from the language creating the Family Trust that no other trusts were contemplated to be created therefrom, further illustrating Buffington's intent that only Hood and Folger be treated as his "children" for purposes of his will; the explicit provisions for the trusts for Hood and Folger reflect by negative implication that no trust was intended to be created for Todd.

Moreover, by defining the term "children" as "*lawful* blood descendants," Buffington also demonstrated his intent that his child born out of wedlock not be included as a beneficiary under his will. See *In re Estate of Wright*, 147 Wash. App. 674, 196 P.3d 1075(III) (2008) (use of phrase "lawful descendants" reflected testator's intent to exclude child born out of wedlock); *Carey v. Jaynes*, 265 S.W.3d 801, 804 (Ky. Ct. App. 2008) (same with respect to phrase "lawful blood descendants"); *Harris Trust and Savings Bank v. Donovan*, 145 Ill. 2d 166, 163 Ill. Dec. 854, 582 N.E.2d 120, 124 (1991) (same with respect to trust defining "children" and "descendants" as "only lawful blood children and descendants"); *Presley v. Hanks*, 782 S.W.2d 482, 489-490 (Tenn. Ct. App. 1989) (same with respect to "lawful issue" and "lawful children"); *Traders Bank of Kansas City v. Goulding*, 711 S.W.2d 872, 875 (Mo. 1986) (same with respect to "lawful issue"). But see *Bell v. Forti*, 85 Md. App. 345, 584 A.2d 77, 81-82 (1991) (finding genuine issue of material fact as to whether out of wedlock daughter fell within class of testator's "lawful descendants"). Indeed, to construe the term "children," "defined in the will as 'lawful descendants[,]' . . . as though [it was] instead defined simply as 'descendants' would be to simply ignore the modifier, giving it no effect." As we are required in the construction of a will to give effect to all provisions therein, we are compelled to assign meaning to the term "lawful" and can only conclude that its use, particularly in combination with the other operative language of the will, reflects Buffington's intent to exclude Todd.

This is the case despite the evidence adduced by Todd that Buffington acknowledged that Todd was his daughter and even provided support for her during his lifetime, as it is undisputed that Buffington never took any steps to formally legitimate Todd and was even known to have referred to her as "little bastard." In other words, though Buffington may have believed Todd to be his daughter in fact, it is clear that he did not believe that Todd was his child in the eyes of the law. Thus, Buffington's use of the phrase "lawful blood descendants" reflects a clear and conscious desire on his part to exclude Todd as a beneficiary under his will.

Similarly, Todd's effort to characterize the testamentary bequests as class gifts (i.e., to Buffington's "children") rather than as individual gifts to Hood and Folger fails to alter her status under the will. Again, because the class of "children" in which Todd claims to fall is defined as Buffington's "lawful blood descendants," Todd is explicitly excluded from taking as part of such class.

"We are mindful of the evolution in [the] law . . . with respect to recognizing the rights of illegitimate descendants. However, this is not a case of intestacy, and [Buffington] was free to dispose of his property as he provided in his will." Finding no genuine issues of material fact as to Todd's beneficiary status under Buffington's will, we conclude that the probate court erred in denying summary judgment to appellants and therefore reverse.

Judgment reversed.

All the Justices concur, except THOMPSON and HINES, JJ., who dissent.

HINES, Justice, dissenting.

I respectfully dissent because the opinion of the majority is premised upon an ill-supported finding of testamentary intent based upon the faulty and perilous legal conclusion that the term "lawful," when used to describe blood descendants named in a will, necessarily precludes biological children born out of wedlock.

As the majority sets forth, in this case the would-be biological child of the testator, Regina Gordon Todd, is attempting to obtain a child's portion of the estate of the late John E. Buffington. Buffington's legitimate daughters, Beth Buffington Hood and Ginger Buffington Folger, petitioned the probate court to exclude Todd, as a matter of law, from any inheritance under their father's will. And, construing the facts in a light most favorable to the non-movant Todd, as it was obligated to do, the probate court quite rightly refused to grant Hood and Folger the summary judgment they sought. The evidence, viewed in the appropriate legal posture, demonstrated that Buffington was aware of Todd, believed her to be his biological daughter, and apparently had a good relationship with her; Buffington went so far as to name Todd as the beneficiary of two life insurance policies. Buffington even acknowledged Todd as his daughter in sworn testimony in an unrelated legal proceeding. Thus, there is substantial evidence to support Todd's familial claim and to find, at a minimum, the existence of a genuine issue of material fact regarding her being Buffington's daughter.

Although the majority acknowledges this, it inexplicably proceeds to find that the unresolved issue of paternity is of no moment to the possibility of Todd's inheriting as one of Buffington's children. It does this by a mixture of factfinding in the guise of discerning testamentary intent and then reaching the legally dubious conclusion that the "plain terms of the will," without question, reflect Buffington's aim to exclude Todd.

The majority notes that Todd is not specifically named in the will, nor was a trust expressly created for her under the will, and thereby concludes by "negative implication" that Todd was purposefully bypassed as a beneficiary. However, any implication to that adverse effect should control only if there is "such a strong probability that an intention to the contrary can not be supposed." That is not the situation in this case. In fact, the general bequests and devises under the will do not specifically name the legitimate daughters either. And, while a testator's decision to designate beneficiaries by name, as a general matter, indicates the intent that the beneficiaries take under the will as individuals, there may exist other language in the will which demonstrates a controlling intention that the beneficiaries take as a class. Indeed,

> [m]ere designation by name does not . . . in all cases show that the persons were dealt with as individuals, and not as a class(;) the intention of the grantor or testator must be gathered from the whole instrument; and if there are other words used which show that he had the persons named in mind as a class, this intention will be allowed to control. Where persons are designated by name, and language is also used which indicates that the maker of the instrument had them in mind not as individuals but as members of a class, it must be determined which idea was uppermost or controlling in his mind.

So, key in this case is the designation "children," which is defined as "*lawful* blood descendants." (Emphasis supplied.) The majority then leaps to the conclusion that by using the term "lawful," Buffington meant for only Hood and Folger to share in his estate, and to exclude Todd, clearly as his "unlawful" issue. However, our precedent does not require this Court to interpret the ambiguous language "lawful blood descendants" to mean exclusively in-wedlock children. That is why the majority relies upon cases from foreign jurisdictions to reach its pivotal ruling that the term "lawful" equates to "legitimate," for the purpose of disinheriting Todd. Such ruling not only works a possible injustice in this case, but has an effect significantly more far-reaching; by so holding, this Court not only crafts a term of legal art that will control the construction of untold wills and the distribution of estates, perhaps contrary to the intentions of the testators, but takes a giant step backwards in the development of the law in regard to the rights of biological children born without the benefit of marriage. Simply, it is unwise for this Court to hold, as a matter of law, that a child born outside of marriage is to be deemed "unlawful" for the purposes of inheritance under a will which contains the above definition of "children." Even the foreign authority cited by the majority questions the wisdom of doing so. For example, in *Carey v. Jaynes*, 265 S.W.3d 801 (Ky. App. 2008), the Kentucky court construed the phrase "lawful blood descendants" to exclude an illegitimate child because Kentucky law had traditionally held the word "lawful" in that context to mean "legitimate or born of a lawful marriage." However, in so doing, the Kentucky court acknowledged the obvious conflict between such holding and the "evolution in constitutional law and statutory changes with respect to recognizing the rights of illegitimate descendants." This Court should not be quick to follow the example of issuing a holding so at odds with the evolving law regarding the rights of children born out of wedlock. The current probate code permits a child born out of wedlock to inherit from his or her father if the child presents "other clear and convincing evidence that the child is the child of the father." (2)(A)(v). Even though it appears that this case does not present a question of intestacy, the laws governing the construction of wills cannot be made in a vacuum, but rather with the full recognition of the laws of intestacy which, of necessity, are examined and modified by the General Assembly in order to keep pace with societal needs and realities.

Simply, this Court should not usurp either the broad province of the General Assembly in expressing the public policy of this State or the narrow role of the factfinder in this case. Unfortunately, the opinion of the majority does both.

I am authorized to state that Justice THOMPSON joins in this dissent.

————————————————

QUESTION

In *Hood*, what do you think about the majority's rationale for excluding this child—effectuating decedent's intent, assuming the child is indeed the genetic child of the testator?

b. Exception—Class Gifts from Nonparents

How would the *Hood* case come out under UPC §2-705 if the class gift had been in the will of the grandmother rather than the father? Different rules may apply to the terms "child" or "issue" if the decedent is not the parent but rather is someone other than the parent. For example, if grandmother leaves a gift in her will to "my grandchildren," or if sister leaves a gift to "the children of my brother Carlos," there are special rules that apply with respect to determining the members of the class. Marital children are automatically included under the marital presumption. However, nonmarital children (including posthumously conceived children) and adoptees who were not adopted as minors must meet certain additional requirements in order to be included in the class under the UPC.

Nonmarital Children.   UPC §2-705(e) provides as follows with regard to the inclusion of these children in class gifts by nonparent transferors:

UPC §2-705. Class Gifts Construed to Accord with Intestate Succession; Exceptions.

> **(e) [Transferor Not Genetic Parent.]** In construing a dispositive provision of a transferor who is not the genetic parent [*e.g.,* a grandparent or sibling], a child of a genetic parent is not considered the child of the genetic parent unless the genetic parent, a relative of the genetic parent, or the spouse or surviving spouse of the genetic parent or of a relative of the genetic parent functioned as a parent of the child before the child reached [18] years of age.

UPC §2-705 adopts a so-called "agency" approach, *i.e.,* the child will not be included unless her parent, a relative or a surviving spouse of the parent functioned as a parent when the child was a minor. This is called an agency approach because the son or daughter of the testator is the testator's "agent" in ascertaining whether or not a nonmarital child should be included in a class gift from someone other than the parent. So the theory is framed in terms of the son or daughter behaving in a way (thus the functional language) that indicates that the son or daughter would want the nonmarital grandchild to inherit from them and thus would want the child to take from the grandparent.

The UPC defines "functioning like a parent" in §2-115(4). That section provides that functioning like a parent means "behaving toward a child in a manner consistent with being the child's parent and performing functions that are customarily performed by a parent, including fulfilling parental responsibilities toward the child, recognizing or holding out the child as the individual's child, materially participating in the child's upbringing, and residing with the child in the same household as a regular member of that household."

Example: Bob and Carol met in college and became romantically involved. Carol subsequently gave birth to a daughter, Shakira. Bob and Carol never married. While Carol was in college, Shakira lived with her parents. After Carol graduated and found a job, Shakira moved in with her in a small apartment. Bob did not maintain any continuing contact with Carol or Shakira after Shakira's birth. If Bob were to die unmarried and intestate, Shakira would be entitled to inherit from him as his "child." However, if Bob's father died and left property in his will to Bob's "children," Shakira would not be entitled to inherit since no one in Bob's family ever functioned as a parent of Shakira before she reached 18 years of age.

Note that when you are in practice you must now consider carefully the potential issues involved in class gifts and posthumously conceived children (who are by definition nonmarital children) when drafting for your clients. The following article offers practical advice on how to do so.

Susan N. Gary, Posthumously Conceived Heirs: Where the Law Stands and What to Do About It Now
Prob. & Prop., Mar./Apr. 2005, at 32

Given the potential difficulties for those charged with distributing property to "descendants," clarifying the intent of the testator or the settlor of a trust takes on new significance for estate planners. A typical will form might define children to include "any child born to or adopted by me, before or after my death." As in the intestacy statutes, the form's intent is presumably to include children in gestation before the parent's death. With the developments in assisted procreation, the possibility of posthumous conception or the existence of frozen embryos at death should be considered at the drafting stage. If the testator prefers not to include posthumously conceived children, then the definition can be modified by placing a time limit on the birth of the after-born child. For example, the provision could state: "any child born to or adopted by me, before or within one year after my death." Because of uncertainties about the length of gestation, limiting the provision to children born within 10 months after death is probably safe, but using a time period shorter than 10 months could exclude a child conceived before death.

A client who has stored or plans to store genetic material should address the question of posthumous conception specifically in his or her will. The lawyer can include a provision either including or excluding any children created using the material after the testator's death. The lawyer can also include either a time limit on the posthumous birth or a direction that the child must be born "within a reasonable time" after the parent's death so that the estate will not be held in limbo indefinitely.

If the client wishes to provide for the possibility of posthumously conceived children, creating a trust for their benefit will allow the estate to close more quickly than it might otherwise. The trust should provide for alternative beneficiaries who will have interests in the trust either with the posthumously conceived children or in the event no children are later born. The trust should also provide a time limit for qualification of posthumously conceived children as beneficiaries, either a "reasonable time" or a period of years. The time limit, whether "reasonable" or a fixed period of years, can be longer than the period being considered for intestacy statutes, but some outside limit will provide closure for the surviving family members or other beneficiaries and will provide for better trust administration. The issues involved in setting the time limit differ somewhat from the concern of creating a time limit for an intestacy statute or for distribution under a will, but in all situations the time limit selected must balance the interests of living beneficiaries with the interests of beneficiaries who may or may not later exist.

STRANGER TO THE CONCEPTION

A lawyer advising a potential parent has an easier task than the lawyer advising someone whose beneficiary may procreate posthumously. The possibility that a beneficiary will have a child posthumously always exists, but a client will not likely imagine the possibility. If the document uses the term "descendants" in making a gift, the issue may arise, and if the document is a trust that continues for an extended period of time, the situation may occur many years after the settlor's death. Planning for situations that are unlikely but possible requires a sensitive discussion with the client and then appropriate language in the document. Simply providing for descendants "born before or after the death of the parent who is a descendant of mine" raises the question of how long to wait before determining who the descendants are. Adding a time limit for the birth of a child after the death of a parent or indicating that a child must be born "within a reasonable time" after the parent's death will help. Of course, a client may prefer to include only children who are actually in gestation before the death of the parent.

———————

Adopted Children.   Under certain circumstances, the UPC and some state statutes preclude an adopted child from taking as a "child" under a class gift from someone other than the adoptive parent. The UPC provides that:

UPC §2-705. Class Gifts Construed to Accord with Intestate Succession; Exceptions.

> **(f) [Transferor Not Adoptive Parent.]** In construing a dispositive provision of a transferor who is not the adoptive parent, an adoptee is not considered the child of the adoptive parent unless:
>
> (1) the adoption took place before the adoptee reached [18] years of age;
>
> (2) the adoptive parent was the adoptee's stepparent or foster parent; or

> (3) the adoptive parent functioned as a parent of the adoptee before the adoptee reached [18] years of age.

Some states have similar language. For example, Oregon Rev. Stat. Ann. 112.195 states, "that an adopted person so included must have been adopted as a minor or after having been a member of the household of the adoptive parent while a minor."

Example: Gertrude created a testamentary trust in her will that gives income to her daughter, Alice, for her life. At Alice's death, the property in the trust is to go to Alice's surviving descendants and, if Alice has no descendants who survive her, to the Red Cross. Alice and her husband, Bob, have no biological children. Rather than see the trust funds go to charity, Alice and Bob adopt Bob's 47-year-old friend, Xerxes, thus making him their descendant and the recipient of the inheritance.

Remember that in the example above, if it were Alice who executed a will or a trust containing a devise to her children, Xerxes would be included in the class. Under UPC §2-705(b), the general rules of intestate succession apply here. Alice is the adoptive parent and Xerxes would be Alice's child for purposes of intestate succession under UPC §2-118. However, while Xerxes would be a child of Alice for purpose of intestate succession, he would not inherit under Gertrude's trust because he does not meet the requirements of UPC §2-705(f).

Some courts have held that such statutes render the testator's actual intent irrelevant. For example, in *In re Estate of Bovey*, 132 P.3d 510 (Mont. 2006), the residue of a decedent's testamentary trust was to be distributed to her "then living heirs-at-law." The decedent's son had adopted his former wife's daughter, and that daughter claimed to be eligible to inherit the trust residue when her father died. The court held that the daughter, as an adopted individual, was not considered the child of the adopting parent unless the individual was a regular member of the adopting parent's household while a minor. Since the daughter had been an irregular member of the son's household from about the time she was 13, she did not meet the "regular member" test and thus could not inherit the trust residue. Interestingly, the court states in its analysis that testator's actual intent regarding whether the adopted daughter of the beneficiary of testamentary trust was a regular member of beneficiary's household while a minor would not be relevant when determining whether the adopted daughter was entitled to residue of the trust since the legislature had supplied the intent. Under what circumstances do you think the court should consider the testator's actual intent?

NOTES AND QUESTIONS

1. *Replicating intent.* Do you agree that the approach adopted by UPC §2-705 is justified because it replicates what most decedents would want? Is there an argument that this approach is actually regressive in terms of the rights of nonmarital and adopted children to be treated similarly to marital children under the law?

2. *Adult adoptions.* In the adoption example above, what do you think Gertrude would have intended had she known that Alice would adopt an adult? Would she have preferred Alice's obvious wish to have Xerxes inherit be carried out or would she have preferred that the Red Cross receive the trust corpus? If you represented the charity, what legal theories might you consider when (and if) filing a legal action? *See e.g., In re Trust Under Agreement of Vander Poel*, 933 A.2d 628, 635 (N.J. Super. Ct. App. Div. 2007), in which the court denied membership in a class gift to the plaintiff under the "stranger to adoption presumption" since the plaintiff was adopted as an adult and because the decedent had treated plaintiff differently than her natural children "when it came to the disposition of her fortune"; specifically, by not creating a separate trust for the plaintiff, excluding adoptees from a later trust and will and not describing the plaintiff as one of her grandchildren in her will.

PROBLEM

Dutch died on January 1st of this year. Eddie is the executor of Dutch's estate. Dutch had a will that left half of his residuary estate to "my wife" and the other half of the residuary "to my children." Eddie comes to visit you six months after Dutch's death. Eddie has been approached by Dutch's wife and his children, who would like Eddie to distribute their share of Dutch's estate to them now. How would you advise Eddie in terms of whether to distribute the proceeds of half the residuary to those persons claiming to be Dutch's children? Would you ask about potential nonmarital or ART children? If there are any, how would you advise Eddie about the possibility that they could establish paternity and be included in the class gift?

C. WHO IS A PARENT?

1. *In General*

The rules for establishing the parent-child relationship discussed above in the context of the child also apply to the inheritance rights of their parents.

For example, a parent would generally inherit from a deceased child in intestacy. In other words, inheritance typically flows in both directions.

UPC §2-116. Effect of Parent-Child Relationship.

> . . . [I]f a parent-child relationship exists or is established under this [subpart], the parent is a parent of the child and the child is a child of the parent for the purpose of intestate succession.

However, there are a few notable exceptions, including parents who have failed to support, or who have abandoned, their children or whose rights have been terminated. States vary widely in this area, and the next section explores those different approaches.

2.   Inheritance from or Through a Child by a Parent

As noted above, the "flip-side" of whether a child may inherit from or through a parent is whether the *parent* may inherit from or through a child. The UPC denies all parents — marital or nonmarital — the right to inherit from or through a child if their parental rights were or could have been terminated. It makes clear that traditional grounds for termination of parental rights are also grounds for disinheritance.

UPC §2-114. Parent Barred from Inheriting in Certain Circumstances.

> (a) A parent is barred from inheriting from or through a child of the parent if:
> (1) the parent's parental rights were terminated and the parent-child relationship was not judicially reestablished; or
> (2) the child died before reaching [18] years of age and there is clear and convincing evidence that immediately before the child's death the parental rights of the parent could have been terminated under law of this state other than this [code] on the basis of nonsupport, abandonment, abuse, neglect, or other actions or inactions of the parent toward the child.

A small number of states have a rule similar to UPC §2-114 whereby a parent — married or otherwise — who has abandoned or failed to support a child may be "taken out of the line of succession" or barred from inheriting.[7] This is one of the few behavior-based exceptions to our status-based system of inheritance.

However, in most states, while the parent of a *nonmarital* child must support and acknowledge the child in order to inherit from her, there is no similar rule for *marital* parents. A married father (or mother) who fails to support his child may still inherit.

Finally, the language of some state statutes still distinguishes between the manner in which a nonmarital mother and a nonmarital father may be eligible to inherit from their child. Historically, while nonmarital mothers could inherit, nonmarital fathers often could not. Many state statutes still include certain requirements that apply to nonmarital fathers but not to nonmarital mothers, such as requiring that the man was adjudicated to be the father, or acknowledged the child or openly and notoriously held the child out as his own. *See, e.g.* MD. CODE ANN., EST. & TRUSTS §§3-108 and 1-208 (2009).

The following case explores the very interesting constitutional aspects of such a differential approach. Before reading the case, consider the arguments that might be made on behalf of a father who has been denied an inheritance based on a state statute that permits only mothers, and not fathers, to inherit by intestate succession from their illegitimate children. Alternatively, consider the arguments that might be made by the attorney for the personal representative.

Estate of Hicks
675 N.E. 2d 89 (Ill. 1996)

The opinion of the court was delivered by Chief Justice BILANDIC.

At issue in this appeal is the constitutionality of section 2-2(d) of the Probate Act (755 ILCS 5/2-2(d) (West 1994)), which provides that the estate of an illegitimate intestate who dies without a surviving spouse or descendants shall be distributed to his or her mother and the mother's children/descendants. The circuit court of St. Clair County entered a judgment finding section 2-2(d) unconstitutional because it permitted only mothers, and not fathers, to inherit by intestate succession from their illegitimate children, and thereby unlawfully discriminated on the basis of gender, in violation of the equal rights provision of the Illinois Constitution of 1970 (Ill. Const.1970, art. I, §18). . . .

[Handwritten margin note: Equal Protection favors mothers who can inherit intestate not fathers]

---

7. *See* Anne-Marie Rhodes, *Consequences of Heirs' Misconduct: Moving from Rules to Discretion*, 33 OHIO N.U. L. REV. 975, 983 n.36 (2007) (listing, among others, Connecticut, North Carolina, Pennsylvania and Virginia).

FACTS

[The decedent, Ronadra J. Hicks, was a minor, nonmarital child whose mother asked the court to determine who would inherit Ronadra's estate. The circuit court originally determined that only Ronadra's mother and half-sisters could inherit the estate, relying on section 2-2(d) of the Illinois Probate Act, which excluded nonmarital fathers. The Code provided, "If there is no surviving spouse or descendant but the mother or a descendant of the mother of the decedent: the entire estate to the mother and her descendants, allowing 1/2 to the mother and 1/2 to her descendants per stirpes." The court appointed a bank (the Bank) as the administrator of the estate. Ronadra's father, who had been adjudicated her father by an Illinois court, filed a motion arguing that the statute that allowed mothers, but not fathers, to inherit from nonmarital children was unconstitutional. The trial court found the provision unconstitutional because it created a sex-based classification, and applied the Illinois test of strict scrutiny. The parties cross-appealed.] . . .

I.   Constitutionality

. . . We agree with the trial court that the statute creates a sex-based classification. The statute distinguishes between the parents of an illegitimate child based solely upon the gender of the parent. Because only females can occupy the status of motherhood, only females are entitled to inherit from their illegitimate offspring under the statutory scheme. By the same token, because only males have the family position of fatherhood, only males are unconditionally excluded under the statute from inheriting from their illegitimate offspring. Thus, the statute creates a sex-based classification and will be upheld only if it withstands strict scrutiny. . . .

The Bank first argues that the disparate treatment afforded to the mothers and fathers of illegitimate children is justified by the overriding purpose of section 2-2(d) and all laws governing intestate succession, which is to give effect to the presumed intent of deceased intestates. As the Bank notes, our intestacy laws apply only when a deceased leaves no will, and such laws represent a legislative effort to express the presumed wishes of a deceased intestate. The Bank argues that section 2-2(d) accurately reflects the presumed intent of illegitimate children who die intestate. The Bank contends that section 2-2(d) accords mothers of illegitimate children different inheritance rights than fathers because the legislature recognized that illegitimate children typically have a much closer relationship with their mothers than with their fathers. The Bank notes that mothers not only bear the physical and emotional ramifications of pregnancy, but also customarily assume a disproportionate share of the responsibilities of raising an illegitimate child. According to the Bank, fathers of illegitimate children often fail to support their children, unless compelled by court order to do so. In addition, the Bank asserts, fathers frequently have no meaningful personal relationship with their illegitimate children. It is reasonable, the Bank contends, for the legislature to presume that illegitimate children bear no affection for parents who fail to support and acknowledge them. Accordingly, it claims that section 2-2(d) simply carries out the deceased intestate's presumed wishes that his or her estate be distributed only to his or her mother and her descendants.

The state certainly has a legitimate interest in enacting laws that attempt to give effect to the presumed intentions of a deceased intestate. The state may also have a legitimate interest in enacting laws which allow only those parents who have demonstrated an interest in their illegitimate children to inherit by intestate succession. The United States Supreme Court has recognized that "[i]f one parent has an established custodial relationship with the child and the other parent has either abandoned or never established a relationship, the Equal Protection Clause does not prevent a State from according the two parents different legal rights." Lehr v. Robertson, 463 U.S. 248, 267-68. We assume, for the sake of argument, that the state's interest in enacting legislation which accomplishes these goals is compelling.

The question here is whether the discriminatory means employed in section 2-2(d) — which discriminates against fathers of illegitimate children — is narrowly tailored to achieve the state's asserted goals. We conclude that it is not narrowly tailored because the legislature did not employ the least restrictive means for accomplishing its asserted purpose. Here, the state's interest could be effectively achieved in a gender-neutral manner, by allowing intestate succession by any parent who has acknowledged and supported his illegitimate child.

Instead, the challenged statute "'make[s] overbroad generalizations based on sex which are entirely unrelated to any differences between men and women [and] which demean the ability or social status of the affected class.'" Section 2-2(d) is based upon the presumption that a particular parent will be involved or uninvolved in his illegitimate child's life simply because that parent happens to be a man or a woman. Not all mothers assume sole responsibility for their illegitimate offspring, and not all fathers abandon such offspring. In fact, by employing a gender-based classification, section 2-2(d) may actually thwart the legislature's desire to effectuate an illegitimate child's presumed intent in some cases. By employing a gender-based criterion, section 2-2(d) allows a mother who abandons her illegitimate child at birth to inherit from that child, while denying surviving fathers the opportunity to inherit even where there is conclusive evidence that they were objects of their child's affection. As stated, the objectives of the statute could be completely and effectively served by allowing intestate succession by any parent who has acknowledged and supported his illegitimate child.

The Bank argues that administrative concerns support the statute. The Bank, in effect, contends that it is more efficient for the legislature to presume that mothers and not fathers are the natural objects of their illegitimate child's affection than to require a case-by-case determination. The United States Supreme Court has held, however, that gender-based discrimination cannot be justified on the grounds of administrative convenience. . . . [W]e find that the gender-based classification found in section 2-2(d) cannot be justified on the ground that it effectuates the intent of an illegitimate who dies intestate, because the legislature did not employ the least restrictive (i.e., gender-neutral) means of accomplishing that purpose. . . .

One potential justification for gender-based classifications is the difficulties associated with proof of paternity. In this regard, we note that the state has a legitimate interest in ensuring that a decedent's estate is distributed only to actual members of his family. The United States Supreme Court has recognized that the danger of fraudulent claims against a decedent's estate is more problematic where illegitimate children and their parents are involved than in cases involving legitimate children. See *Trimble*, 430 U.S. at 770; *Lalli v. Lalli*, 439 U.S. 259, 268-69. The Supreme Court has also recognized that the danger of fraudulent claims is more apparent in cases involving fathers and their illegitimate children than in cases involving mothers and illegitimate children, for the simple reason that proof of paternity is more problematic than proof of maternity.

The Court has noted that the identity of the mother of an illegitimate child is rarely in doubt, since the birth of a child is a recorded or registered event usually taking place in the presence of others. The identity of the father, on the other hand, is frequently a subject of dispute where an illegitimate child is concerned. . . .

The distinction drawn in section 2-2(d) between mothers and fathers of illegitimate children, however, cannot be justified on this ground. Section 2-2(d) cannot withstand strict scrutiny, because the statute is not narrowly tailored to effectuate the state's interests in avoiding either the difficulties associated with proof of paternity after the illegitimate child's death or the danger of fraudulent claims by purported fathers against the estates of illegitimate children. Section 2-2(d) bars all fathers from inheriting from the estates of their illegitimate children. The statutory bar applies even in cases, such as this, where the father's paternity has been established in a judicial proceeding during the child's lifetime. . . .

Section 2-2(d) is similarly flawed. The problems associated with proving paternity might justify a statute that imposes a more demanding standard on fathers claiming under their illegitimate children's estates than that required for mothers claiming under their illegitimate children's estates. The difficulties of proving paternity in some situations, however, do not justify the total statutory disinheritance of all fathers of illegitimate children who die intestate. Section 2-2(d) cannot withstand strict scrutiny, because that statute does not adopt the least restrictive means of accomplishing the legislative goal of eliminating the danger of fraudulent claims by putative fathers against their illegitimate children's estates. Accordingly, we affirm the circuit court's determination that section 2-2(d) illegally discriminates on the basis of gender and results in a denial of equal protection of the laws in violation of section 18 of the bill of rights of the Illinois Constitution of 1970.

NOTES AND QUESTIONS

1. *Constitutionally permissible distinctions.* Do you think the court in *Hicks* was right? What legitimate reasons might a state have for treating mothers and fathers differently when it comes to inheriting from the nonmarital child? What does the court suggest about drafting a statute with constitutionally permissible distinctions between nonmarital mothers and fathers?

2. *Levels of scrutiny.* Note that the *Hicks* court used strict scrutiny as the standard of review when the U.S. Supreme Court has held that statutory differences based on gender will only be subject to an intermediate "rational basis with teeth" level of review. The Illinois test for the constitutionality of sex-based classifications differs from the federal test.

3. *Evidentiary issues.* In most states, grounds for termination of parental rights include nonsupport, abandonment, abuse, neglect or other actions or inactions of the parent toward the child. Do you think that parents who have abandoned, neglected or abused their children should not be allowed to inherit from their children if the state has not actually terminated their parental rights prior to the child's death? What evidentiary problems does this provide for a probate court whose main purpose is to redistribute property at death, not to make termination of parental rights decisions? If a parent's rights to a child are terminated, should the child still be entitled to inherit from that parent?

4. *Behavior vs. status.* As noted above, American inheritance law is dominantly status-based. Statutes that bar abandoning parents from inheriting in intestacy are some of the very few examples of a behavior-based model in American law. For further exploration of this issue, see Anne-Marie E. Rhodes, *Consequences of Heirs' Misconduct: Moving from Rules to Discretion*, 33 Ohio N.U. L. Rev. 975, 983 (2007), and Anne-Marie E. Rhodes, *Abandoning Parents Under Intestacy: Where We Are, Where We Need To Go*, 27 Ind. L. Rev. 517 (1994), in which the author discusses rules that provide equal shares to the abandoning and non-abandoning parent and suggests reform. *See also* Ronald J. Scalise Jr., *Honor Thy Father and Mother?: How Intestacy Law Goes Too Far in Protecting Parents*, 37 Seton Hall L. Rev. 171 (2007), which provides a historical overview of such statutes and proposes reform; and Paula A. Monopoli, *"Deadbeat Dads": Should Support and Inheritance Be*

Linked?, 49 U. Miami L. Rev. 257 (1994), in which the author defines American inheritance law as status-based rather than behavior-based, and proposes the adoption of a behavior-based model in the context of parents who abandon or neglect their children.

EXERCISE Marital presumption wins.

[handwritten margin note:] Finian's argument · marital presumption · No termination of parental rights.

Finian and Maura have one child, Claudine. After they divorce, Finian abandons Claudine. Finian does not pay court-ordered child support. Maura supports Claudine completely. At the age of 16, Claudine is killed in a car accident. A substantial monetary settlement of tort claims arising from the accident, totaling $350,000, is paid to Claudine's estate. Finian returns to claim his one-half share of Claudine's estate. Make an argument on behalf of Finian as to why he should be allowed to inherit. Then make an argument for Maura as to why Finian should not be allowed to inherit from Claudine's estate. See *Father Returns To Claim Estate Of Child He Left*, N.Y. Times, Jan. 17, 1994, at A10.

[handwritten margin note:] Maura's argument · abandonment.

D.   WHO IS A SPOUSE?

In terms of inheritance rights, there are several possible classifications for someone who had an intimate relationship with the decedent. The most advantageous classification for that person — the one that carries a right to inherit — is that of "surviving spouse." A surviving spouse is someone who was legally married to the decedent and who is entitled to a share in intestacy. Most of the time, the identity of one's spouse is clear. However, sometimes it is not clear whether someone is a "surviving spouse" and some survivors may successfully argue they come within that definition even if not legally married to the decedent.

To determine if someone is a surviving spouse, the court will first inquire as to whether there was a valid marriage and, if so, whether there was a subsequent divorce or annulment that would render the spouse an ex-spouse. A survivor may not meet the requirements to be a surviving spouse but successfully argue that she was a putative spouse who believed in good faith she was married to the decedent. She might fall into the category of common law spouse in the few states that recognize such marriages if she meets the state requirements, including the decedent and survivor having held themselves out as married for a specified period of time. The survivor and the decedent may have had a valid civil union or domestic partnership recognized in their state. Or they may simply have been mere cohabitants.

We explore each of these classifications and their implications for inheritance rights below.

1. Legally Married Spouses

The husband or wife of a decedent who was legally married in a sanctioned ceremony to the decedent in the absence of a divorce as of the date of death meets the definition of a surviving spouse for purposes of inheritance in all states. As long as there has been a valid marriage, the surviving spouse is entitled to inherit from the decedent in intestacy and under the terms of a valid will or trust that provide for a spouse. The surviving spouse will also be entitled to statutory benefits like the elective share and family allowances (discussed in Chapter 12).

Same-Sex Marriage. A handful of states recognize same-sex marriage, and others recognize valid same-sex marriages entered into in other jurisdictions. Massachusetts was the first state to recognize same-sex marriage, thus automatically conferring inheritance rights on same-sex married couples by virtue of their being included in the term "spouse" in the Massachusetts intestacy statute. As of the date of this publication, Connecticut, Iowa, Vermont, New Hampshire and the District of Columbia also grant marriage licenses to same-sex couples. Other states, like Hawaii and Wisconsin, offer some spousal rights. Some states explicitly recognize same-sex marriages from other jurisdictions. The status of same-sex marriages in California is unclear. The California Supreme Court ruled on May 15, 2008, that same-sex couples have the right to marry in California. Proposition 8, which limits marriage to one man and one woman, was passed on November 4, 2008. The decision was appealed. Same-sex marriages performed before Proposition 8 was passed remained valid, but same-sex marriages were no longer performed in California after November 4, 2008. On August 4, 2010, a federal district court judge ruled that the ban was unconstitutional. The case is being appealed, and marriages will not resume until the appeal has been decided.

2. Common Law Spouses

In a small number of states, cohabitants who have not participated in a formal marriage ceremony may be deemed "spouses" if they meet the criteria for a "common-law marriage."[8] "Even without solemnization or a license,

---

8. *See* http://www.unmarried.org/common-law-marriage-fact-sheet.html. These states include "Alabama; Colorado; Georgia (if created before 1/1/97); Idaho (if created before 1/1/96); Iowa; Kansas; Montana; New Hampshire (for inheritance purposes only); Ohio (if created before 10/10/91); Oklahoma (possibly only if created before 11/1/98.

parties could contract a valid common law marriage simply by (1) living together and (2) holding themselves out as married with (3) the mutual intention to be married. Once formed, a common law marriage was fully valid for all legal purposes, and could be dissolved only through formal divorce." *See* Douglas E. Abrams et al., Contemporary Family Law 161-71 (2d ed. 2009).

If the couple later moves to another state, that state will consider them "spouses" as well for purposes of inheritance, even if the second state does not recognize common law marriages, due to the full faith and credit and comity doctrines.

NOTE

Note that there is an interesting question about whether common law marriage applies to same-sex couples. *See* Peter Nicolas, *Common Law Same-Sex Marriage*, 43 Conn. L. Rev. (forthcoming 2011), *draft available at* http://ssrn.com/abstract=1630029 ("When courts and legislatures in Iowa, the District of Columbia, and New Hampshire extended the right to marry to same-sex couples, they did more than just join the small but growing list of jurisdictions to do so. In addition, they introduced the possibility that — for the first time in the United States — a same-sex couple might be able to enter into a legally recognized common law marriage.").

3. *Putative Spouses*

Spouses who think that they were legally married in good faith but who turn out to be wrong — because of some defect in the marriage ceremony or because of bigamy, for example — may be deemed "spouses" and entitled to equitable relief as "putative spouses." The drafters of *Restatement (Third) of Property: Wills & Other Donative Transfers* §2.2 (1999) note that, "A putative spouse is a person who cohabited with the decedent in the good-faith but mistaken belief that he or she was married to the decedent. The strongest evidence of a claimant's good-faith belief that he or she was married to the decedent is proof that they participated in a marriage ceremony."

The putative spouse doctrine is a common law doctrine in many states, reflecting the equitable power of the court. Some states have adopted the Uniform Marriage and Divorce Act §209, which explicitly gives the court authority to award some of the decedent's estate to the putative spouse.

Oklahoma's laws and court decisions may be in conflict about whether common law marriages formed in that state after 11/1/98 will be recognized.); Pennsylvania (if created before 1/1/05); Rhode Island; South Carolina; Texas; Utah; Washington, D.C."

Unif. Marriage & Divorce Act §209 [Putative Spouse].

Any person who has cohabited with another to whom he is not legally married in the good faith belief that he was married to that person is a putative spouse until knowledge of the fact that he is not legally married terminates his status and prevents acquisition of further rights. A putative spouse acquires the rights conferred upon a legal spouse . . . whether or not the marriage is prohibited or declared invalid. If there is a legal spouse or other putative spouses, rights acquired by a putative spouse do not supersede the rights of the legal spouse or those acquired by other putative spouses, but the court shall apportion property . . . among the claimants as appropriate in the circumstances and in the interests of justice.

As the section notes, putative spouses acquire the rights of a legal spouse and may be able to share a decedent's estate with a legal spouse.

Example: Wendy and Harold were validly married. Harold then left town and married Selina without divorcing Wendy. Selina would be a putative spouse at Harold's death (assuming she had a good faith belief in the marriage and did not find out about his lack of a divorce from Wendy). Both Wendy and Selina could claim a portion of Harold's estate at his death, Wendy as a legal spouse and Selina as a putative spouse.

Courts are obligated to apportion property among the claimants as appropriate and just. Courts would generally apportion Harold's estate based on length of time Wendy and Selina cohabited with Harold as a guideline. If Wendy lived with Harold for 15 years and Selina lived with Harold for 5 years, the court might award three-quarters of Harold's estate to Wendy and one-quarter to Selina.

NOTE AND QUESTION

Equity vs. efficiency. It seems fair to allow putative spouses to take some share of the decedent's estate if they believed in good faith they were married to the decedent. What is the downside of allowing putative spouses a process by which they may establish their right to take a share of the decedent's estate? For a general discussion of the putative spouse doctrine and its history, *see* Christopher L. Blakesley, *The Putative Marriage Doctrine*, 60 Tul. L. Rev. 1 (1985).

EXERCISE

You are retained to represent Selina, the putative spouse in the example above. What facts would you seek to introduce to strengthen your client's case for a larger share of the apportioned estate?[9]

4.   Civil Unions and Domestic Partnerships

A handful of states recognize civil unions and domestic partnerships that confer inheritance rights in intestacy. Some civil union or domestic partnership statutes state explicitly that couples are granted the same rights as if they were married, including inheritance rights.[9]

A civil union is a legal status that provides same-sex couples virtually the same legal rights as married couples, including inheritance rights. Vermont was the first state to allow civil unions, in 2000. It now recognizes same-sex marriages, and civil unions are no longer available. Connecticut, New Jersey and New Hampshire also allowed civil unions. However, both Connecticut and New Hampshire have recently recognized same-sex marriages, and civil unions will no longer be available.

California, the District of Columbia, Hawaii, Maine, Nevada, New Jersey, Oregon and Washington all offer some form of domestic partner status. The District of Columbia, Maine, Washington and California allow both same-sex and opposite-sex couples to enter into domestic partnerships (in California and New Jersey only if one partner in an opposite-sex couple is at least 62.) The Hawaii, Oregon and Wisconsin statutes are limited to same-sex couples.

The UPC and the *Restatement* do not currently provide for inheritance rights to those who are not "spouses," even if they have entered into a civil union. The *Restatement* drafters call this a "developing question," but they have not taken a position on it.

NOTES

1.   *Recognition of other state statutes.* A number of states, including Georgia, have enacted statutes or adopted constitutional amendments, or "Defense of Marriage Acts," that prohibit the state from giving full faith and credit to other states' same-sex marriages. One consequence is that the spouses would not be entitled to inheritance rights. *See* Barbara J. Cox, *Using an "Incidents of Marriage Analysis" When Considering Interstate Recognition*

---

9. This is a rapidly changing area of law. While the information in this section was accurate as of the date of publication, see the following sites for up-to-date information: http://www.ncsl.org/programs/cyf/samesex.htm. *See also* http://www.ncsl.org/default.aspx ?tabid=4244.

of Same-Sex Couples' Marriages, Civil Unions, and Domestic Partnerships, 13 WID-ENER L.J. 699 (2004), in which the author discusses cases in Connecticut, Texas and Georgia where courts refused to give full faith and credit to a Vermont civil union and a pair of cases in New York that reached opposite results on the issue. *See also* William C. Duncan, *Survey of Interstate Recognition of Quasi-Marital Statuses*, 3 AVE MARIA L. REV. 617 (2005), which analyzes how states that do not recognize same-sex marriage have decided whether to give legal status to out-of-state same-sex marriages; and Andrew Koppelman, *Interstate Recognition of Same-Sex Marriages and Civil Unions: A Handbook for Judges*, 153 U. PA. L. REV. 2143 (2005), in which the author discusses "evasive," "migratory," "visitor" and "extraterritorial" marriages in the context of growing state recognition of same-sex unions.

2. *Model statute proposed.* For an interesting study and model statute granting inheritance rights to domestic partners, see T.P. Gallanis, *Inheritance Rights for Domestic Partners*, 79 TUL. L. REV. 55 (2004).

3. *Planning for same-sex couples.* For practical guidance on counseling same-sex couples in estate planning, see Joseph Kapp & Nicholas E. Burkholder, *A Guide to Serving the Estate and Financial Planning Needs of Gay Men, Lesbians and Same-Sex Couples*, J. FIN. PLAN., Mar. 2008, at 54. *See also* DENIS CLIFFORD, FREDERICK HERTZ & EMILY DOSKOW, A LEGAL GUIDE FOR LESBIAN & GAY COUPLES (15th ed. 2010).

PROBLEMS

Dominic (Dom) and Xandra have lived together for 35 years. They have three children and six grandchildren who regularly come to visit them. Dom died intestate with $750,000 in stocks and securities in his name. In the following problems, analyze whether Xandra qualifies as a spouse for purposes of intestacy.

1. What result if Dom and Xandra had a valid marriage ceremony 35 years ago?

2. What result if Dom and Xandra went through a marriage ceremony 35 years ago but after Dom's death, Xandra discovers he was never divorced from his first wife, Sara? Would Sara be entitled to anything from Dom's estate? If so, how much?

3. What result if Dom and Xandra lived in a state where common-law marriage is recognized and they meet the criteria for a common law marriage?

4. What result if Dom and Xandra live in a state where common law marriage is not recognized?

     a. If Dom and Xandra came to you for advice as their attorney under these circumstances, what would you advise them about how to ensure that Xandra would receive Dom's property at his death?

   b. What other issues, in addition to inheritance, would you advise them to plan for?

  5. What result if Dom and Xandra were legally married but had been separated for five years at the time of Dom's death?

  6. What result if Dom and Xandra were legally married for 32 of the last 35 years but were divorced three years before Dom's death?

EXERCISE

Carla retains you to assert her claims against Consuelo's estate. She tells you that they were never married in a formal ceremony but that they always held themselves out as being married. You need to gather facts to support what she asserts. What facts would help you do this? What questions would you ask Carla or her friends and family, and what documentary items would you hope to discover in your investigation and trial preparation?

5. Cohabitants

Absent an explicit (or in some states an implied) contract, couples who live together without marital status (legal, putative or common law) are unlikely to be granted inheritance rights in most states. A different result might occur if the couple entered into quasi-marital arrangements like civil unions or domestic partnerships in those states that provide for these (see above). Taking affirmative action like getting married or entering into more formal arrangements like a civil union is a surrogate for intent to confer benefits like inheritance rights. In terms of policy, mere cohabitation without more does not give us an indication of a decedent's intent to confer these benefits.

3 INTESTACY—WHAT HAPPENS TO A DECEDENT'S PROPERTY IF THERE IS NO WILL?

A. INTRODUCTION

Intestate succession is the quintessential default rule. If the decedent dies without a will or if the will that is offered for probate is invalidated in whole or in part, the intestacy rules apply to determine who the beneficiaries are and to what portion of the probate estate they are entitled. "Intestacy statutes create, in effect, a statutory will—a will in which the government, rather than the individual, determines the dispositive terms." Susan N. Gary, *Adapting Intestacy Laws to Changing Families*, 18 LAW & INEQ. J. 1 (2000).

"When the wishes of a decedent are not known due to a lack of express intent (for instance, lack of a will, invalidity of a will or a valid will that only disposes a portion of the decedent's probate property), intestacy statutes attempt to further an individual's testamentary freedom by disposing of property in accordance with the probable intent of the average intestate decedent." Lee-ford Tritt, *Sperms and Estates: An Unadulterated Functionally Based Approach to Parent-Child Property Succession*, 62 SMU L. REV. 367, 379-80 (2008). While accomplishing the decedent's presumed intent is the primary goal of intestacy laws, there are, however, other goals that have been identified by commentators, as the following excerpt discusses.

> Many societal goals derive from a concern with support, both economic and otherwise, of the decedent's family. Other societal goals include "continuation of the regime of private property as dominant in the social order," avoiding complicated property titles and excessive subdivision of property, encouraging the accumulation of wealth, providing for ease of administration and maintaining respect for the legal system.

Of all of these goals, concerns for the family are paramount. . . . Intestacy statutes can support families by facilitating the transfer of wealth among family members. The statutes also can reduce the possibility of disputes among surviving family members. Constructing a statute that will be considered fair by all those who knew the decedent may lessen family disharmony and minimize disputes among surviving family members and others who have an interest in the decedent's estate.

Susan N. Gary, *Adapting Intestacy Laws to Changing Families*, 18 Law & Ineq. J. 1, 9-10 (2000).

With respect to determining who gets what portion of the probate estate via intestacy, the principal issues involve determining who qualifies as a family member entitled to take an intestate share, and calculating each family member's share. The first matter was considered in Chapter 2. Thus, in this chapter, after we reflect upon the policy, history and reasons underlying intestacy, we turn our attention to calculating the portions of the probate estate to which the surviving spouse, descendants (also sometimes called "issue") and other heirs are entitled under intestacy laws.

1. Who Dies Without a Will?

Do you have a will? If you answered "no," you are not alone. A significant percentage of the population does not have a will. The failure to have a will is common not only in the United States but also around the world.[1] While studies indicate that the majority of people who die intestate are young or of limited wealth, the fact is that people of all stripes die without a will, including the rich and famous and those with business — and legal — training.

Susan N. Gary, Adapting Intestacy Laws to Changing Families
18 Law & Ineq. J. 1, 9-10 (2000)

Three studies in particular have identified characteristics of those more likely to die without a will. [Mary Louise Fellows et al., *Public Attitudes About Property Distribution at Death and Intestate Succession Laws in the United States*, 1978 Am. B. Found. Res. J. 319; Joel R. Glucksman, *Intestate Succession in New Jersey: Does it Conform to Popular Expectations?*, 12 Colum. J.L. & Soc. Probs. 253 (1975-76); Contemporary Studies Project, *A Comparison of Iowans' Dispositive Preferences with Selected Provisions Of the Iowa and Uniform Probate Codes*, 63 Iowa L. Rev. 1041, 1070 (1978)]. That information, combined with information concerning who is more likely to die without leaving a

---

1. *Most People Have Yet to Make a Will* (Oct. 24, 2009), *available at* http://www.mirror.co .uk/news/latest/2009/10/24/most-people-have-yet-to-make-a-will-115875-21769314/.

probate estate, can prove useful in thinking about intestacy reform. The demographic characteristics of those whom the intestacy statutes will serve most often can guide thinking about appropriate intestate distributions.

. . . Not surprisingly, age shows a strong correlation with testacy in all three studies. Younger decedents are more likely to die intestate than older decedents. As individuals age they are more likely to think about their own death and about how they want their property distributed after death. Younger persons procrastinate preparing a will; older persons are more likely to have documents executed.

Wealth is also a significant factor identifying those who die testate. As an individual's estate increases in size the person is more likely to be concerned with its disposition. Wealth is also tied to age, since many people accumulate wealth as they get older. The studies show a direct correlation between greater wealth and greater likelihood of testacy.

The factors of occupation and education also affect likelihood of testacy. Greater education correlates with greater testacy and white collar workers are more likely to die testate than blue collar workers. Since education will affect occupation and both are likely to affect accumulation of wealth, the results of the studies confirm the findings with respect to wealth as a factor.

One study also found correlations between gender and testacy, reporting data that showed that women are more likely than men to die testate even though men are more likely to have greater wealth. Another study found comparable testacy rates between the men and women surveyed.

Two of the studies obtained data on marital status and found that widows and widowers are the most likely of any group (single, married, and divorced) to have wills. Widows and widowers have had the experience of dealing with the transfer of a spouse's assets and are aware of the need for a will. Also, with their spouse no longer alive, the transfer of property by joint tenancy is less likely to be an effective mechanism for disposition of their property than when their spouse was alive. . . .

WHY DO PEOPLE CHOOSE NOT TO EXECUTE A WILL?

If the majority of those who decide not to execute a will do so because they know that the intestacy statute will distribute their property in accordance with their dispositive preferences, then a reconsideration of intestacy law may not be necessary or advisable. Studies have shown, however, that actual knowledge of the intestate distributive scheme is limited and failure to execute a will results more often from procrastination than from planning.

Two studies asked specifically about the respondent's reason for not having a will. In the American Bar Foundation study, conducted in five different states, 63.6% of respondents who did not have a will cited "laziness" as the primary reason for not having a will. Other reasons included not having thought about it, being young and childless and having little property.

No one indicated that they were relying on the intestacy statute of their state.

Similarly, a study conducted in Iowa reported that 56% of one group of respondents and 57% of a second sample cited "have not gotten around to making a will" as the primary reason for not having a will. In that survey, 25% of the first group and 13% of the second group stated as their reason for not having a will either that the state would distribute their assets or that their "family" would get their assets automatically. The authors of the study suggest that these numbers do not reflect satisfaction with the Iowa statute, but may, in fact, reflect a lack of knowledge about what happens to the property when someone dies or a reliance on prior arrangements other than wills that distribute assets to chosen survivors. The authors concluded that the overall responses did not indicate informed reliance on the intestacy statute. Thus, in the results reported by these two studies, there is no evidence that any significant number of people are relying on intestacy statutes to distribute their property or that changes in the intestacy statutes would adversely affect expectations.

Finally, stepfamily members may be reluctant to discuss estate planning or to execute wills because of family dynamics. If relationships between a stepparent and stepchildren are strained, neither the legal parent nor the stepparent may want to address issues of property distribution on death. Unfortunately, the temptation to assume that family members will "do the right thing" after one parent dies, can lead to conflict. Inaction can result in greater difficulties, particularly for stepfamilies.

NOTES

1.   *Who dies without a will?* The percentage of people who die intestate is about 80%, according to Jeffrey A. Schoenblum, *Will Contests — An Empirical Study,* 22 REAL. PROP. PROB. & TR. J. 607 (1987). A 2007 survey by Harris Interactive on behalf of *lawyers.com* of 1,018 adults (aged 18 and over) found that "over half (55 percent) of all adult Americans do not have a will . . . a percent that has remained virtually unchanged over the past three years." The survey also found the following:

- Among non-white adults, the lack of wills is even more pronounced. Only one in three African American adults (32 percent) and one in four Hispanic American adults (26 percent) have wills, compared to more than half (52 percent) of white American adults.
- One in ten (10 percent) American adults who do not have any elements of an estate plan say it's because they don't want to think about dying or becoming incapacitated.

- Similarly, nearly one in ten (9 percent) adults say they don't have an estate plan in place because they don't know who to talk to about creating such documents. This percentage nearly doubled from 2004 (5 percent).
- Nearly one in four (24 percent) of adults say their biggest reason for not having an estate plan is a lack of sufficient assets. This was also the top reason cited in the 2004 survey (21 percent).

Majority of American Adults Remain Without Wills, available at http://www.lawyers.com/~/link.aspx?_id=910A52BD-D3AC-4A97-8B6E-0044D7424 9E5&_z=z .

2. *Famous intestates.* Among the famous people who died either without a valid will or with no will at all are Presidents Abraham Lincoln, Andrew Johnson, Ulysses S. Grant and James A. Garfield, industrialist and recluse Howard Hughes, civil rights leaders Martin Luther King, Jr. and Rosa Parks, world heavyweight boxing champion Rocky Marciano, philosopher Karl Marx, artist Pablo Picasso and entertainers Tupac Shakur, Kurt Cobain, Buddy Holly, Lenny Bruce, Billie Holiday, Marvin Gaye, Sam Cooke, Cass Elliot, James Dean, Sonny Bono and Tiny Tim.

3. *Lawyers, too.* Approximately 38% of accountants and 25% of attorneys surveyed had no will. Warren, *Advisors Often Fail to Heed Own Advice*, Tr. & Est., Jan. 1995 at 6.

2. The History and Development of the Intestacy Regime

Intestate succession has ancient roots, its origins lie in the common-law canons of descent, which determined inheritance of land, and the English Statute of Distribution, 1670, which governed succession to personal property. *Restatement (Third) of Property: Wills & Other Donative Transfers* §2.1 provides a good history of intestacy.

Intestacy has not always served as default law. It originated as mandatory law. Property was forced to pass by intestacy because there was then no power to make a will. The power to dispose of *personal* property by will was recognized early. The ecclesiastical courts asserted jurisdiction over succession to personal property on death, and encouraged bequests for religious and charitable purposes, as well as for the decedent's family. During the Anglo-Saxon period, testamentary disposition of *land* was possible, but recognition ceased within about a century after the Norman Conquest. The devise of land by will "stood condemned," Maitland wrote, "because it is a death-bed gift, wrung from a man in his agony. In the interest of honesty, in the interest of the lay state, a boundary must be maintained against ecclesiastical greed and the other-worldliness of dying men." 2 Frederick Pollock & Frederic W. Maitland, History of English Law 328 (2d ed. 1898). By contrast, the church courts never gained jurisdiction over succession to land, and the Crown courts were not concerned with seeing that a landowner atoned for his wrongs by devoting a portion of his property to pious objects.

By the English Statute of Wills of 1540, 34 & 35 Hen. 8, c. 5, §14, men (but not women) were granted some power to dispose of their land by will, in effect beginning the process of transforming intestacy from a rule of mandatory law into a default rule. It was not until the 19th century that the power of testation was granted to women by the Married Women's Property Acts.

Current state laws differ from their predecessors and tend to reflect modern thinking. The National Conference of Commissioners on Uniform State Laws (NCCUSL) (now the Uniform Law Commission — ULC), for example, reviewed several empirical studies (including many of those cited in the Gary article above) before drafting the structure that is in the UPC. In addition, each state legislature that has adopted the UPC reviewed the suggested language and decided whether it was right for that state or needed modification. For those states that have not adopted the UPC, legislatures followed a similar process, often consulting state bar committees on inheritance law and probate administration.

The studies reviewed by NCCUSL indicated that when people were asked who they wanted to receive their property if they died without a will, the vast majority of respondents wanted their spouses to get the entire estate. In other situations, those questioned said they would want their spouses to share the entire estate with their children, grandchildren or parents rather than leaving anything to their siblings or more distant relatives.

While the intestacy schemes differ from state to state, there are a couple of common themes. For example, spouses, and in some states registered domestic partners, are always entitled to some portion of the estate before others receive their shares. Also, the only takers under intestacy rules are relatives by blood or adoption (using the definitions we discussed in Chapter 2); friends and charities do not take. And, if a decedent has no spouse or other relatives alive to inherit, the property will be given to the state under "escheat," as the state is an heir per UPC §1-201(2).

3.   *The Limitations of Intestate Succession — Not All Things to All People*

As stated, only relatives as defined in the probate laws inherit via intestate succession. Moreover, the intestacy statutes generally give the decedent's property to the family members closest to the decedent, like the decedent's surviving spouse and descendants, to the exclusion of more distant family members, such as siblings and their offspring.

For many people, the rules work fine. This is particularly true for families that consist of a husband, wife and children solely of their marriage, as most of the statutes give the decedent's property exclusively to them. The rules do not work as well where there are stepchildren, blended families, unmarried heterosexual and gay and lesbian cohabitants with or without children — a situation that is increasingly true in our modern world — or where the decedent would like to give some of her property to remote family members, friends or charities.

Once an estate is subject to the intestacy laws, deviations from the statutory plan are not allowed for any reason, no matter how compelling the evidence is that the decedent would have wanted a different result. Any desired deviation from the statute must be accomplished by executing a will. For example, if you were to die intestate survived exclusively by your spouse and siblings, the UPC would give everything to your spouse, regardless of whether you and your spouse loved or hated each other and regardless of the comparative needs of your spouse and your siblings.

Before we delve into the mechanics of determining who gets what under the various intestacy schemes, we need to consider their limitations. Look over the problems below but do not spend more than a minute or two on any individual question. Try doing them *before* you read the UPC to avoid being influenced by what the rules presently are.

PROBLEMS

Assume you are being surveyed by the ULC as part of a study to determine whether the UPC reflects current trends and thinking. Give your personal opinion who you would like to receive your property upon your death and in what percentage. There are no right and wrong answers; the answers are strictly personal to you. We are looking for immediate reactions; don't think too hard and deeply about each situation.

1. At the time of your death, you are married and your spouse is living. You and your spouse have gotten along famously over the years and the two of you love each other very much. You have no living parents or children but you do have a very dear sibling.

    a. Would your answer differ if you and your spouse had three children together?

    b. Would your answer differ if you and your spouse had three children together and you also had two children from your first marriage who live with your ex-spouse and from whom you have been estranged for 10 years?

2. You and your spouse separated many years ago after years of bitterness and fighting. Your spouse was abusive and cheated and you hated him/her. You never divorced for religious reasons. You have no living parents or children but your very best friend had his savings decimated by convicted Ponzi schemer Bernard Madoff and, as a result, has experienced serious bouts of depression.

3.   The principal asset in your estate is a home in which your ancestors had been living since 1810, which your parents recently gifted to you as a wedding present. At the time of your death, your spouse and parents are alive. You have no living children.

4.   At the time of your death, your committed partner of 25 years is alive. You never married. You have three children and two grandchildren with the partner.

EXERCISE

You are on a ULC drafting committee. (Hopefully, when you graduate, you will become active in professional organizations like this.) You are to draft a provision for inclusion in an updated version of the UPC that leaves an intestate decedent's estate to the person(s) you identified in Problem (4) above. In doing so, remember that since you are drafting the equivalent of proposed legislation, the language must not only cover this situation but it must also be broad enough to handle situations of a similar nature. Be sure to define any new terms you use.

4.   The Intestate Estate

The intestacy laws only apply to probate property and then only to the extent a will does not effectively dispose of the property. Any property passing via will substitutes or valid wills is not affected by intestacy rules. (Will substitutes are discussed in Chapter 4.) Therefore, depending on the mix of property interests of the decedent and the validity of the will and will substitutes, intestacy may affect a large percentage of the property passing at decedent's death or a relatively small amount.[2]

It is possible for the intestate statute to apply unexpectedly. This could happen in the following situations:

- If the will is invalidated for some reason, such as the testator was not of sound mind when the will was drafted; or
- If one or more will substitutes fails. Examples of this would be where the decedent named his estate as the beneficiary of an

---

2. Moreover, while UPC §2-101 says the intestacy rules apply only when there is no will or the will does not dispose of all of the decedent's property, there are a few other times when they are enlisted. Of greatest importance are UPC §§2-301 and 2-302. They are sometimes referred to as the pretermitted spouse and child sections. They are discussed in greater detail in Chapter 12. These sections apply when a decedent wrote a will prior to getting married (UPC §2-301) or having one or more children (UPC §2-302) and failed to revise the will afterwards to include a bequest to these important people. Depending on the facts, these provisions give the "new" spouse or child a share in the probate estate equal to what they would have received if the decedent died intestate.

insurance policy or if joint tenants died simultaneously. (This is discussed in Section G of Chapter 4.) In these situations, what would otherwise have been non-probate property becomes probate property. If there is no will because the testator believed it was not necessary since all his property was being disposed of by will substitutes, intestacy would control its disposition.

UPC §2-101. Intestate Estate.

> (a) Any part of a decedent's [probate] estate not effectively disposed of by will passes by intestate succession to the decedent's heirs as prescribed in this Code . . .

The discussion that follows first analyzes the portion of the probate estate to which the surviving spouse is entitled. This is followed by an analysis of the portion made available to descendants and, if none, other "collateral" heirs. The chapter ends with a discussion of the effect of inter vivos transfers on the amount to which an interstate heir is entitled at the decedent's death, examining whether the transfers were pure gifts, which do not affect the amount the heir will receive in intestacy, or they were advances (prepayments) that reduce the heir's share. Before we delve into these topics, read the two stories that follow for perspective on how the law approaches distributing property for people who die without a will.

5. Stories About Intestate Succession

Here are two articles about what can happen when someone dies intestate. The first is from the perspective of the survivors and details what happened after the slaying of football great quarterback Steve McNair, who you will notice fumbled in his estate planning as badly as he fumbled against the Denver Broncos. The second tells of the good luck of two men who basically hit the lottery as beneficiaries when their German grandmother died intestate.

Steve McNair's Estate — And You Thought Settling Michael Jackson's Estate Would Be a Thriller[3]

Dying without a will is not a smart thing to do, particularly for a former NFL superstar who reportedly made over $75 million during his 13-year career.

---

3. Julie Garber (July 22, 2009), *available at* http://wills.about.com/b/2009/07/22/steve-mcnairs-estate-and-you-thought-settling-mjs-estate-would-be-a-thriller.htm.

Yesterday I summarized the sad contents of the Emergency Petition for Letters of Administration filed by Steve McNair's widow, Jonula "Mechelle" McNair. The gist of the petition — Steve McNair died at the age of 36 without a will and was survived by Mechelle and two minor children born of their marriage, as well as two minor children born out of wedlock and whose paternity Mechelle questions in the petition. And what did McNair own at the time of his death? A house in Nashville and some livestock located in Mississippi, but Mechelle McNair will need 60 days to figure out the rest.[4]

And you thought that Michael Jackson's estate would be a mess to clean up? MJ's estate plan is a dream compared to the intestate estate of Steve McNair, which will inevitably cost thousands, or possibly millions, of dollars to sort out. Here's why:

1. Even though she is the surviving spouse, Mechelle McNair will have to post a bond in order to oversee the administration of her husband's estate. A valid will or Revocable Living Trust could have avoided this problem.
2. Steve McNair left behind two minor children for sure and possibly two more. The mothers of the two children who were born out of wedlock will need to hire lawyers to establish the paternity of their children. In his will or Revocable Living Trust, McNair could have chosen to include or not include one or more of his children as beneficiaries of his estate.
3. Since all of the children are minors, their mothers will need to hire lawyers to set up court-supervised guardianships to oversee the management of their inheritances. In his will or Revocable Living Trust, McNair could have included trusts for the children that would have avoided the need for court-supervised guardianships.
4. Tennessee has a separate state estate tax in addition to the federal estate tax. According to the Emergency Petition, the value of McNair's estate at the time of his death will exceed the Tennessee estate tax exemption of $1,000,000 (the house in Nashville is currently on the market for $2,999,990), but it is unknown if the estate will exceed the federal estate tax exemption of $3,500,000. So at the very least, a tax lawyer or accountant will need to prepare and file a Tennessee Inheritance Tax Return, Form INH-301, and any estate taxes due will need to be paid within nine months

---

4. [When Mechelle filed an inventory with the court, it listed estate assets at around $20 million, most of which were securities — EDS.]

of the date of death. McNair could have eliminated 100% of Tennessee estate taxes and federal estate taxes by using an ABC Trust scheme in his estate plan.

The bottom line — spending a few thousand dollars on a basic estate plan prior to his death could have saved Steve McNair's family thousands or perhaps millions of dollars in legal fees, other costs and estate taxes after his death.

Penniless Cavemen Inherit $7.2bn[5]

Two penniless brothers who live in a cave outside Budapest are to inherit most of a reported $A7.2 billion after an astonishing twist in their family fortunes.

Zsolt and Geza Peladi have no fixed address and eke out an existence by selling junk they find in the street.

But their scavenging days are about to be over. The brothers have been told they are entitled to their long-lost grandmother's fortune, along with a sister who lives in America.

Charity workers in Hungary broke the news to them after being contacted by lawyers handling the estate of their maternal grandmother who died in Baden-Wurttemberg, Germany.

"We knew our mother came from a wealthy family but she was a difficult person and severed ties with them, and then later abandoned us and we lost touch with her and our father until she eventually died," Geza Peladi, 43, told ATV television.

Under German law, direct descendants are automatically entitled to a share of any estate.

---

5. Henry Samuel (Dec. 3, 2009), *available at* http://www.theage.com.au/world/penniless-cavemen-inherit-72bn-20091202-k673.html.

"If this all works out, it will certainly make up for the life we have had until now — all we really had was each other — no women would look at us living in a cave," he said.

"But with money, maybe we can find a partner and finally have a normal life. I understand it was only while they were carrying out genealogical research that lawyers found we existed."

Gyula Balazs Csaszar, a volunteer working for Budapest's Maltese Charity Service, said: "We were contacted by a lawyer asking us to find the brothers. He claimed he could help their lives with a large sum of money."

The grandmother's name has been kept confidential to prevent fraudsters trying to cash in. A spokesman for the lawyers handling the case said: "We know who we need to speak to and that is the two brothers who we are pretty sure are the grandchildren. There is no need for anyone else to be informed."

The brothers are seeking copies of their mother's death certificate and proof of their identity and family connections as the rightful heirs before claiming the fortune. . . .

B.   SHARE FOR SURVIVING SPOUSE

1.   *Introduction and Share in Non-UPC States*

Intestacy laws accord special status to spouses and issue. Surviving spouses and issue generally take to the exclusion of more remote heirs, including parents and siblings.

Usually, spouses get some bite of the "probate estate apple" before anyone else, even the decedent's children and grandchildren. This is derived from ancient concepts of dower and curtesy, which allowed spouses certain rights of use or inheritance with respect to the real or personal property of the decedent. Dower and curtesy have been abolished in all states. *See, e.g.* UPC §2-112. Whatever is not given to the spouse "off the top" goes into the "intestate pot" for sharing with descendants, if any. If there are no descendants, the intestate pot is shared by ancestors and then more distant heirs.

The amount provided for a surviving spouse differs from state to state. We will focus our primary attention on the UPC. However, before we do so, it is worth noting what surviving spouses receive in non-UPC states. The statutes of New York and California are representative of some of the many variations.

New York:

> (a) If a decedent is survived by:
> (1) A spouse and issue, fifty thousand dollars and one-half of the residue to the spouse, and the balance thereof to the issue by representation.
> (2) A spouse and no issue, the whole to the spouse.
>
> N.Y. EST. POWERS & TRUSTS LAW §4-1.1 (2010).

California:

> (c) As to separate property, the intestate share of the surviving spouse or surviving domestic partner . . . , is as follows:
> (1) The entire intestate estate if the decedent did not leave any surviving issue, parent, brother, sister, or issue of a deceased brother or sister.
> (2) One-half of the intestate estate in the following cases:
> (A) Where the decedent leaves only one child or the issue of one deceased child.
> (B) Where the decedent leaves no issue but leaves a parent or parents or their issue or the issue of either of them.
> (3) One-third of the intestate estate in the following cases:
> (A) Where the decedent leaves more than one child.
> (B) Where the decedent leaves one child and the issue of one or more deceased children.
> (C) Where the decedent leaves issue of two or more deceased children.
>
> CAL. PROB. CODE §6401 (2010).

Restatement (Third) of Property: Wills & Other Donative Transfers §2.2 summarizes what surviving spouses receive in non-UPC states in the following excerpt:

> Under non-UPC law, the surviving spouse usually inherits the entire intestate estate if the decedent leaves no surviving descendants or parents. If the decedent does leave descendants, the intestate estate may be divided between the spouse and the descendants. If the decedent leaves no descendants but does leave a parent or parents, the intestate estate may be divided between the spouse and the parent or parents.
>
> Non-UPC law commonly entitles the decedent's surviving spouse to one-third of the intestate estate if the decedent is survived by children (or descendants of deceased children), with the remaining two-thirds passing to the decedent's descendants. Other variations exist. Some non-UPC statutes

award half each to the surviving spouse and the descendants. Elsewhere the spouse receives half if one descendant survives but a third if more than one descendant survives; the remaining half or two-thirds goes to the descendants. Most pre-UPC statutes drew no distinction between the decedent's descendants who are also descendants of the decedent's spouse and any descendants who are not.

If the decedent is not survived by children (or descendants of deceased children), but is survived by one or both parents, the spouse's share under non-UPC statutes is often one-half, with the other half going to the decedent's parent or parents. Other variations exist. In a few states, the spouse shares the intestate estate with the decedent's siblings if both parents have predeceased. Other states have unique systems for allocating the intestate estate between the spouse and parents. Some non-UPC law gives the entire intestate estate to the surviving spouse and nothing to the decedent's parents.

EXERCISE

Look at the intestacy statute for the state where you grew up or where you intend to practice. Copy it so that you can refer to it throughout this chapter. *In your own words*, describe what the statutory scheme is for a surviving spouse. The purpose of this exercise is to get you used to explaining complex concepts in lay terms to a client.

2.   *The UPC Share for Surviving Spouses*

In the original version of the UPC in 1969, the decedent's surviving spouse was entitled to the entire intestate estate if the decedent did not leave either surviving issue or surviving parents. If the decedent left surviving issue (all of whom were also issue of the surviving spouse), or if the decedent left a surviving parent, the spouse's share was the first $50,000 plus one-half of the remaining balance of the intestate estate. If the decedent was survived by a child (or descendants of a deceased child) who was not also a child of the surviving spouse, the spouse's share was one-half of the intestate estate.

In 1990, the UPC was significantly amended in response to transformations in the law of wills and will substitutes and changes in society as identified in the empirical studies mentioned in the Gary article above. The UPC was slightly modified again in 2008 to increase the base amount for the surviving spouse and to add an automatic cost of living adjustment (COLA). UPC §1-109. The following excerpt from the Prefatory Note to Article II and Comments to UPC §2-102 explains the reasons for the changes.

Themes of the 1990 Revisions. In the twenty or so years between the original promulgation of the Code and 1990, several developments occurred that prompted the systematic round of review. Four themes were sounded: (1) the decline of formalism in favor of intent-serving policies; (2) the recognition that will substitutes and other inter-vivos transfers have so proliferated that they now constitute a major, if not the major, form of wealth transmission; (3) the advent of the multiple-marriage society, resulting in a significant fraction of the population being married more than once and having stepchildren and children by previous marriages and (4) the acceptance of a partnership or marital-sharing theory of marriage.

The 1990 revisions responded to these themes. The multiple-marriage society and the partnership/marital-sharing theory were reflected in the revised elective-share provisions of Part 2. As the General Comment to Part 2 explained, the revised elective share granted the surviving spouse a right of election that implemented the partnership/marital-sharing theory of marriage.

The children-of-previous-marriages and stepchildren phenomena were reflected most prominently in the revised rules on the spouse's share in intestacy.

Empirical studies support the increase in the surviving spouse's intestate share, reflected in the revisions of this section. The studies have shown that testators in smaller estates (which intestate estates overwhelmingly tend to be) tend to devise their *entire* estates to their surviving spouses, even when the couple has children.

The current version of the UPC is more complicated than the 1969 section. There are now several variables that affect the amount to which a surviving spouse is entitled, most important among them being who else survived the death of the decedent. Thus, the surviving spouse is entitled to differing amounts depending on whether the decedent was survived by parents, descendants who are also issue of the surviving spouse, descendants who are not also issue of the surviving spouse and descendants of the surviving spouse who are not also issue of the decedent. As you read the subsection, pay close attention to these differences.

UPC §2-102. Share of Spouse.

The intestate share of a decedent's surviving spouse is:
(1) the entire intestate estate if:
(i) no descendant or parent of the decedent survives the decedent; or
(ii) all of the decedent's surviving descendants are also descendants of the surviving spouse and there is no other descendant of the surviving spouse who survives the decedent;

> (2) the first $300,000 [+ COLA],[6] plus three-fourths of any balance of the intestate estate, if no descendant of the decedent survives the decedent, but a parent of the decedent survives the decedent;
>
> (3) the first $225,000 [+COLA],[7] plus one-half of any balance of the intestate estate, if all of the decedent's surviving descendants are also descendants of the surviving spouse and the surviving spouse has one or more surviving descendants who are not descendants of the decedent;
>
> (4) the first $150,000 [+ COLA],[8] plus one-half of any balance of the intestate estate, if one or more of the decedent's surviving descendants are not descendants of the surviving spouse.

Situation #1—Decedent survived by spouse or spouse and joint descendants: UPC §2-102(1) gives the surviving spouse 100% of the decedent's estate where, besides the surviving spouse, either of the following is the situation:

- The decedent is not survived by any of her descendants or parents.

- The *only* descendants of either the decedent or the surviving spouse that are alive at decedent's death are descendants of their relationship (sometimes herein referred to as "joint children" or "joint descendants").

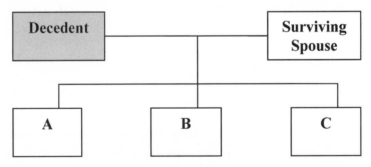

Situation #2—Decedent survived by spouse and parent(s): UPC §2-102(2) deals with the situation where, at death, the decedent is survived by her spouse and parents but not by any descendants. In this scenario, the spouse gets a large portion of the probate estate ($300,000) plus three-quarters of the amount in excess of $300,000, with the remaining one-quarter of the excess going to the parents.

---

6. Prior to the 2008 amendments, the base amount was $200,000 and there was no COLA.

7. Prior to the 2008 amendments, the base amount was $150,000 and there was no COLA.

8. Prior to the 2008 amendments, the base amount was $100,000 and there was no COLA.

Situations #3 and #4: The next two situations involve blended families and surviving stepchildren (or, more properly, step-descendants). The Reporter's Note to *Restatement (Third) of Property: Wills & Other Donative Transfers* §2.2 offers the following rationale for the treatment of blended families:

> When there are other than joint children in the family, the conduit theory [that the parent will support the child] becomes problematic. If the statute awards the entire estate to the surviving spouse of a decedent who leaves surviving children (or descendants of deceased children) who are not the surviving spouse's, the risks of permanent loss to those children appear greater because the surviving spouse is related to them only by marriage. Similarly, if the statute awards the entire estate to the surviving spouse who has children (or descendants of deceased children) who are not the decedent's, the risk exists that the surviving spouse will share at least some of the decedent's property with the decedent's stepchildren at the expense of the decedent's children. (The possibility exists that the same moral conflict will arise after the decedent's death, should the surviving spouse remarry and have children by his or her new spouse, but the law disregards this possibility because the share of the surviving spouse is determined on the basis of the facts existing at the decedent's death.) Thus, the dilemma in the stepparent situations becomes one of striking a reasonable balance between the objective of granting the surviving spouse an adequate share and the dual objectives of providing for the financial needs of a decedent's minor children and of reducing the risk of permanently disinheriting the decedent's adult children.
>
> The Revised UPC resolves that dilemma by invoking the lump-sum-plus-a-fraction device for these situations. The intent is not to restrict the spouse's share to the bare minimum necessary to provide him or her with the basic necessities of life, but to grant a share that is commensurate with the size of the estate and the circumstances of the family composition. In the typical intestate estate of small to modest size, this approach still allows the surviving spouse to take the entire estate. . . .
>
> The Revised UPC recognizes that the surviving spouse's conflicting loyalties are more intense when the decedent has children by a prior marriage than when only the surviving spouse has children by a prior marriage. In the former case, the surviving spouse is granted the first [$150,000] plus 50 percent of any remaining balance. In the latter case, the surviving spouse is granted the first [$225,000] plus 50 percent of any remaining balance.

Situation #3—Decedent survived by spouse, joint descendants and spouse's descendants: The UPC describes Situation #3 as where, in addition to being survived by her spouse, the decedent is survived by **both** joint descendants (*i.e.,* descendants who are related by blood or adoption to both the decedent and the surviving spouse) **and** step-descendants (*i.e.,* descendants of another relationship of the surviving spouse who were not adopted by the decedent). UPC §2-102(3) gives the surviving spouse $225,000 plus 50% of the amount in excess of $225,000. The other half of the excess goes into the intestate pot for distribution to the descendants of the decedent; **nothing** goes to the step-descendants. Interestingly, you will notice that the decedent's descendants are entitled to a share of the intestate estate even though they are joint descendants. This is in contrast to Situation #1 above.

> **Example:** Caroline died recently without a will. Her probate estate was worth $1,225,000. She is survived by her husband, Harry, two children with Harry (Lashaun and Letitia) and Harry's child Carrie (Caroline's stepdaughter) from his first marriage with Falore that ended in divorce 10 years ago. Harry is entitled to $225,000 plus 50% of $1,000,000 (the remaining value of the estate), for a total of $725,000. Lashaun and Letitia split the other 50% of $1,000,000 (or $250,000 each).

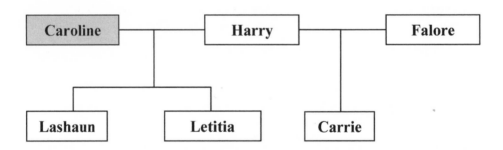

Situation #4—Decedent survived by spouse and descendants who are not joint descendants: In Situation #4, the decedent is survived by her surviving spouse and at least one descendant who is not a joint descendant. In this blended situation, the UPC §2-102(4) gives the smallest amount of all the scenarios to the surviving spouse — only $150,000 plus 50% of the balance — and places the greatest amount into the intestate pot for distribution to the decedent's descendants. *It is worth noting that this section applies in all cases where the decedent is survived by a descendant who is not a descendant of the surviving spouse, regardless of whether or not there are also joint descendants or descendants of only the surviving spouse.*

Example: Same facts as the previous example, except that Caroline is also survived by three children from her first marriage to Fritz. Harry is entitled to $150,000 plus 50% of $1,075,000 (for a total of $687,500) and her five children split $537,500 equally.

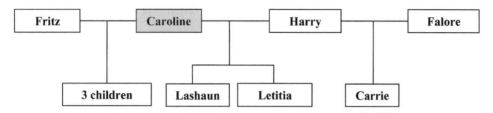

It is worth noting that Harry would get the same amount even if he and Caroline did not have Lashaun and Letitia together. That is because this paragraph applies in all situations where the decedent is survived by descendants who are not related to the surviving spouse by blood or adoption.

PROBLEMS

Having determined who the players are—the surviving spouse, descendants, step-descendants and parents—we must now calculate how much the statute gives to the surviving spouse. For purposes of the following questions, apply UPC §2-102.

1.   Donna dies without a valid will and with an ownership interest in the following nonprobate property: Donna had a joint tenancy with right of survivorship with her daughter in land worth $500,000, a $250,000 life insurance policy on her life with her son designated as the primary beneficiary and her estate as the secondary beneficiary, a $500,000 retirement account that designated her husband Steve as the beneficiary. She also had $75,000 in her separate checking account. To what is Donna's surviving husband, Steve, entitled under UPC §2-102? Can you answer this without knowing who the surviving family members of Donna and Steve are? How would your answer change if son had predeceased Donna?

2.   **For purposes of this problem, assume the following facts.** Dominic and Sally were married for seven years before Dominic's recent death. As of Dominic's death, the facts are:

- Dominic and his first wife (Fanny), from whom he divorced 10 years ago, had a daughter, Andrea, 26 years ago. Andrea died three years ago, survived by her child, Alice.
- Dominic and Sally gave birth to Bob five years ago.
- Sally was pregnant with Carlos, who was born 10 days after Dominic's death.

- Dominic's mother is alive at his death.
- Sally had a child, Richard, with her first husband, Henry.

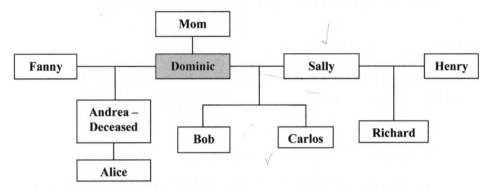

Dominic died without a valid will and with a total net probate estate of $1,000,000. Determine the dollar value of Sally's share under UPC §2-102. Be sure that you can identify the subsection that is applicable. (Disregard the benefits to which Sally might be entitled under homestead, family allowance and other support-based rights and the elective share.)

Assume Dominic is survived ONLY by:	Determine amount of distribution to Sally under the UPC (and give cite).	Who do you think receives the balance and in what amounts?
1. Sally	All	
2. Sally and Bob	150 K + half	
3. Sally and Bob and Carlos		
4. Sally, Alice and Fanny		
5. Sally, Richard and Fanny		
6. Sally, Alice, Bob, and Carlos		
7. Sally, Alice and Richard		
8. Sally, Bob and Richard		
9. Sally, Alice, Bob, Carlos, and Richard		
10. Sally and Dominic's mother		
11. Sally, Dominic's mother, Bob and Carlos		

C. SHARE TO LINEAL DESCENDANTS

1. In General

After the portion that is reserved for the benefit of the surviving spouse is trimmed off the top, or if there is no surviving spouse, then distribution of the remaining intestate estate is next made to the decedent's surviving lineal descendants or issue (the terms are synonymous). Only descendants by blood or adoption share under intestacy; stepchildren do not. If there are no surviving lineal descendants, then the estate is distributed to other heirs, referred to as "collateral heirs." If the decedent dies without a surviving spouse, the lineal descendants or other heirs share the entire probate estate.

It is worth recalling, as we saw in Problem 1 above, that if the probate estate is small, the share to which the surviving spouse is entitled may consume the entire estate to the exclusion of all other heirs. For example, under the UPC, if the intestate estate is $85,000, the surviving spouse will take the entire estate, regardless of whether there are children and grandchildren alive or not. Review UPC §2-102 (the least base amount available to a surviving spouse is $150,000 under subsection (4)).

While the share available to descendants and collateral heirs varies from state to state, one thing is certain: If there are any descendants of the decedent, they will take everything that is available and collateral heirs will receive nothing. The UPC is typical of this. For example, even if the decedent is survived by parents, many siblings, nieces, nephews, aunts, uncles and cousins, so long as the decedent is survived by a single grandchild, the grandchild will take to the exclusion of all the other heirs.

Here is how the UPC describes what is available to the lineal descendants:

UPC §2-103. Share of Heirs Other than Surviving Spouse.

> (a) Any part of the intestate estate not passing to a decedent's surviving spouse under Section 2-102, or the entire intestate estate if there is no surviving spouse, passes in the following order to the individuals who survive the decedent:
> (1) to the decedent's descendants by representation;

While all states give everything to the descendants instead of more remote relatives, the manner in which the descendants share the portion to which they are entitled differs among the states. Regardless of the differences, only living descendants are entitled to a share. If a descendant is not living at the time of the decedent's death, lower generation descendants and other heirs take by a system called "representation." In essence, these lower generations are entitled to share in the estate because they "represent" their parents or grandparents. We discuss the three principal representation models in Section E below.

EXERCISE

Look at the intestacy statute for the state where you grew up or where you intend to practice. Identify the state and which of the three representation models it is most like (see Section E below.). Then, *in your own words,* describe what the statutory scheme is for lineal descendants. The purpose of this exercise is to get you used to explaining complex concepts in lay terms to a client.

D. SHARE TO COLLATERAL HEIRS AND ESCHEAT TO THE STATE

If the decedent does not have a surviving spouse or descendants, the estate passes to ancestors and other collateral relatives of the decedent. As used here, a collateral heir is one who descends from both of the ancestors (parents or grandparents) of the decedent (in which case they are of the whole blood) or from only one of the ancestors of the decedent (in which case they are of the half blood). There is no uniform approach among the states on the shares to which collateral heirs are entitled.

This is a good time to look at the Table of Consanguinity (relationships by blood) in Appendix A to this chapter. You will notice the decedent is at the top of the column on the left. This column of relatives is alternately referred to as the "first degree of relationship" or the first "parentela." As discussed above, intestacy statutes dictate that the share of the probate estate not going to the surviving spouse goes to those in the first parentela, the decedent's lineal descendants (one's children, grandchildren and great grandchildren, etc.) employing whichever representation system is used by your state. To the extent there are any descendants alive, the entire share available to non-spouse heirs is distributed to them; nothing is left for collateral heirs.

However, if there are no descendants (having gone down the column in the first degree of relationship), most statutes move to the next (or second) degree of relationship on the right (up and over one column). This column is headed by the decedent's parents. Below them are their descendants, *i.e.,* the decedent's brothers and sisters, then nieces and nephews, and grand nieces and nephews, and so on. The parents and their descendants generally take under the same representation system in the state as is true for the decedent's descendants. As with the original degree of relationship, if there are heirs in this degree of relationship, nothing will be available for heirs in the next degree.

In the unusual event that the decedent is not survived by anyone in the first or second degrees of relationship, the same approach is followed in the third parentela, the column of people headed by the decedent's grandparents. Normally, the shares are divided into halves between the families of the maternal and paternal grandparents and then distributed to the appropriate heirs employing the same representation system in the state as is true for the decedent's descendants.

Finally, if there are no survivors in the first, second or third degrees of relationship, states take a variety of approaches. The system in about 10 states is to attempt to find more remote heirs. This is cumbersome. A more common alternative is that the intestate estate escheats to the state. It is justified on the grounds that it is better for it to go to the state than to "laughing heirs," those who are so distant from the decedent that, when told they inherited, laugh all the way to the bank and shed no tears. (Reflect back on the Pedali brothers).

Escheat to the state after no one is found through three parentela was the approach of the UPC prior to amendment in 2008. However, UPC §2-103 was amended to provide that before escheat occurs, the estate should go to the descendants of a deceased spouse to whom the decedent was married at the time of the spouse's death, in other words, the decedent's stepchildren and step-grandchildren. Consider the reasons that the UPC drafters made this change.

To see how the UPC approaches the share available for non-descendants, begin at subsection (a)(2); for escheat to the state, see UPC §2-105.

UPC §2-103. Share of Heirs Other than Surviving Spouse.

(a) Any part of the intestate estate not passing to a decedent's surviving spouse under Section 2-102, or the entire intestate estate if there is no surviving spouse, passes in the following order to the individuals who survive the decedent:

(1) to the decedent's descendants by representation;

(2) if there is no surviving descendant, to the decedent's parents equally if both survive, or to the surviving parent if only one survives;

(3) if there is no surviving descendant or parent, to the descendants of the decedent's parents or either of them by representation;

(4) if there is no surviving descendant, parent, or descendant of a parent, but the decedent is survived on both the paternal and maternal sides by one or more grandparents or descendants of grandparents:

(A) half to the decedent's paternal grandparents equally if both survive, to the surviving paternal grandparent if only one survives, or to the descendants of the decedent's paternal grandparents or either of them if both are deceased, the descendants taking by representation; and

(B) half to the decedent's maternal grandparents equally if both survive, to the surviving maternal grandparent if only one survives, or to the descendants of the decedent's maternal grandparents or either of them if both are deceased, the descendants taking by representation;

(5) if there is no surviving descendant, parent, or descendant of a parent, but the decedent is survived by one or more grandparents or descendants of grandparents on the paternal but not the maternal side, or on the maternal but not the paternal side, to the decedent's relatives on the side with one or more surviving members in the manner described in paragraph (4).

(b) If there is no taker under subsection (a), but the decedent has:

(1) one deceased spouse who has one or more descendants who survive the decedent, the estate or part thereof passes to that spouse's descendants by representation; or

(2) more than one deceased spouse who has one or more descendants who survive the decedent, an equal share of the estate or part thereof passes to each set of descendants by representation.

UPC §2-105. No Taker.

If there is no taker under the provisions of this Article, the intestate estate passes to the [state.]

E.   THE REPRESENTATION MODELS

Descendants and collateral heirs receive their shares under one of several representation models. "Representation" means that a descendant has died and left surviving descendants to "step-up" and represent them in the distributional scheme. The discussion that follows explains how each works.

There are many representational variations throughout the states. However, there are three basic models:

a.   Strict Per Stirpes,
b.   Modern Per Stirpes per 1990 UPC ("Per Capita with Representation"), and
c.   The Revised UPC Method ("Per Capita at Each Generation").

"Per stirpes" means per bloodlines or per roots or stocks. "Per capita" means per head or per person.

In certain situations, all of the models give the same result. In others, two may give the same result while the other one will not. At times, especially if there are several generations of descendants involved, all the methods produce different results.

The concept of representation is more significant today than in the past because people are living longer and because it is not unusual for families to be comprised of many generations. If members of the family die "out of order," in other words, some children or grandchildren die before the decedent or their parent, it becomes important to decide who is entitled to share in the decedent's probate estate.

1. Rules Common to All Representation Statutes

- If there is a surviving spouse, descendants and other heirs are entitled to a share of the intestate estate only from what is not reserved for the surviving spouse.
- If the decedent is survived by a descendant, the decedent's ancestors and more remote collateral heirs do not take.[9]
- If all of the decedent's children survive the decedent, the representation rules are not necessary. The children will share the portion of the estate to which they are entitled equally per capita. Thus, if the decedent is survived by all of her children (1st generation descendants), the entire portion of the decedent's intestate estate not going to the surviving spouse is divided equally among them. In the example illustrated below, A, B and C each get one-third of the intestate estate of the decedent available to the descendants regardless which representation model is the law of the decedent's state.

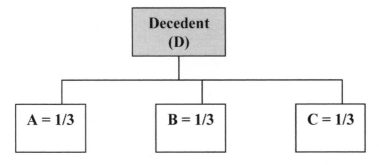

---

9. Colorado enacted an interesting rule effective July 1, 2009, that allows an individual to name another person as their "designated beneficiary" for a variety of purposes, including rights to inheritance, the ability to make medical decisions and hospital visitation rights. While not equal to marriage or a civil union, this offers gay and lesbian couples and other unmarried adults the ability to establish sweeping legal rights for each other. COLO. REV. STAT. §§101-12 (2010).

- If the decedent is survived by only some of her children (1st generation descendants) and if the child(ren) who predeceased the decedent did not leave any descendants of their own (as is true for child C below), the share of decedent's intestate estate available to descendants is divided equally among the surviving children.

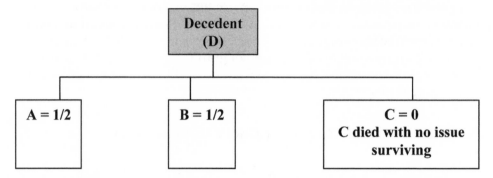

- An heir who predeceases the decedent cannot be represented by his spouse; or stepchildren. Only an heir's children and grandchildren can stand in his shoes as representatives. The representation rules require relationships by blood (consanguinity) or adoption, not marriage (affinity).

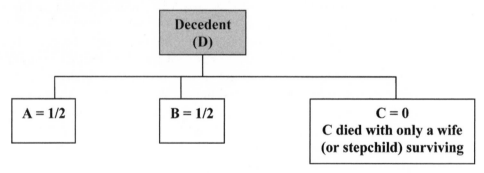

- Only the highest surviving generation member of a family may take. In the previous example, if B had a child (BB), B would take what is permitted in the statute (50%) and BB would not take anything.

2.   Strict Per Stirpes

This method of representation, sometimes called the **English, Classic or just "per stirpes"** method, distributes the decedent's property based on bloodlines or "roots" or "stocks" rather than based on generations. It relies exclusively on representation; there is no "per capita" aspect to it. Unless otherwise clarified, when people use the term per stirpes, this is the model that they normally mean. It is the method of representation originally used by almost all the states and still in place in just under a third of them.

All persons receiving an inheritance through a parent or grandparent who predeceased the decedent divide the portion that the deceased parent or grandparent would have taken. One might say that the shares are split on a vertical basis by bloodline as determined at the first generation. People who prefer this approach believe each child's descendants should get the same total amount as the descendants of the other children. They are less concerned with whether every person in a particular generation gets the same amount because the goal is to divide up the estate into equal shares at the first generation, regardless of the number of people in subsequent generations.

a.   Procedure for Determining the Per Stirpes Share

Step One: Determine the number of shares by dividing the estate into as many equal shares as there are:

(1)   living children of the decedent, if any, and
(2)   deceased children with descendants then living who will represent them.

> This "slicing of the pie" determines the number of bloodlines. Each bloodline will get an equal amount, no matter how many grandchildren or great grandchildren of the decedent there are in a given bloodline.

> **This system is unique in that the division occurs at the first generation even if everyone in that generation is dead!**

Step Two: Distribute one share to each *living* member of the highest generation.

Step Three: For the children who were not alive but whose bloodlines were entitled to a share because they were represented by their descendants, determine the portion allocated to that bloodline in the same manner as Step one above and distribute the probate property in the same manner as in Step two. Repeat this generation by generation, putting each descendant who is represented at the top of the chart.

Example 1: Decedent had three children — A, B and C. Decedent is survived only by her son C, who has a young son X. Decedent's son B died many years ago without any children. Daughter A died recently leaving three children of her own — U, V and W.

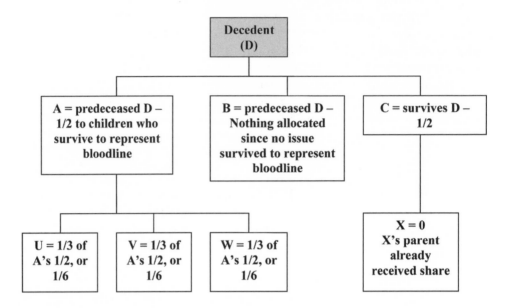

Procedure and Result: First, we determine the number of shares by dividing the estate into as many equal parts as there are living children of the decedent, if any, and deceased children who are represented by their living descendants. Since son B did not survive and did not leave any children to represent him, his potential share is lost. Thus, only two shares are created — one for the surviving child (C) and the other for the bloodline of A represented by A's descendants.

Second, we distribute to C the half to which he is entitled. (Note that his son X does not get anything since his parent is alive and has already taken the share reserved for their bloodline).

Third, we repeat steps one and two as to the 1/2 share to which A's bloodline is entitled. It helps to understand how we distribute the share reserved for A's bloodline by putting A at the top of the chart and then proceeding as reflected in Steps one and two. Doing this, U, V and W each get 1/3 of the 1/2 (*i.e.,* 1/6) of the intestate estate.

Example 2:   Decedent had three children — A, B and C. D is not survived by *any* of her children. Decedent's son B died many years ago without any children. Daughter A died recently leaving three children of her own — U, V and W. Decedent's son C died many years ago survived by child X.

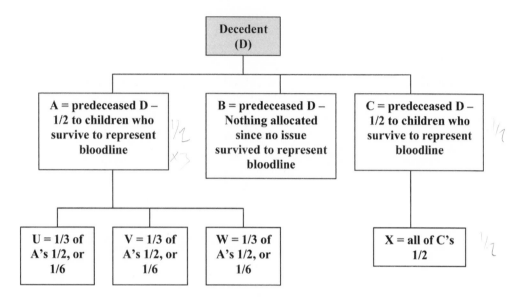

Result: With the exception that X now gets what C would have received, the result in this example is the same as the previous one. This follows because the determination of shares was made at the first generation regardless whether there was any child alive or not.

b.   Representative State Provisions

The states that use the per stirpes method of representation describe it in a variety of ways. Compare the language used by Florida and Maryland as examples.

Inheritance per stirpes (Florida)

> Descent shall be per stirpes, whether to descendants or to collateral heirs. FLA. STAT. ANN. §732.104 (2010).

Division per stirpes (Maryland)

> (a) When provision is made for representation in this article, the shares shall be determined in accordance with subsections (b) . . . of this section.
>
> (b) In the case of issue of the decedent, the property shall be divided into as many equal shares as there are children of the decedent who survive the decedent and children of the decedent who did not survive the decedent but of whom issue did survive the decedent. Each child of the decedent who did survive the decedent shall receive one share and the issue of each child of the decedent who did not survive the decedent but of whom issue did survive the decedent shall receive one share apportioned by applying to the children and other issue of each nonsurviving child of the decedent the pattern of representation provided for in this subsection for the children and other issue of the decedent and repeating that pattern with respect to succeeding generations until all shares are determined. MD. CODE ANN., EST. & TRUSTS §1-210 (2010).

c.   Drafting a Will Provision That Leaves Property to Descendants "Per Stirpes"

Our focus in this chapter is to determine the amount to which the survivors of a decedent are entitled if the decedent dies intestate. However, when you are drafting a will for someone, it is necessary to craft language that deals with multi-generational situations. Of course, before you can draft this provision, you need to explain the different representation models to the client and diagram or explain their operation. The following language could be used for a client who wishes to use the per stirpes method of representation.

> Where it is stated that property is to be distributed "per stripes," the property is divided into as many equal shares as there are (i) surviving children of the designated ancestor and (ii) deceased children who left surviving descendants. Each surviving child, if any, is allocated one share. The share of each deceased child with surviving descendants is divided in the same manner, with subdivision repeating at each succeeding generation until the property is fully allocated among surviving descendants.

To the extent possible, you should consider using the language of your state's statutes or case law to guide your drafting. This makes it easier for the personal representative and the courts to interpret because they are familiar with the terms used. Take a look at UPC §2-709 and you will notice that the language there and the language used in the provision above are basically identical.

3. Original UPC Version of "Per Capita with Representation"

This method, sometimes referred to as "modern per stirpes" or "modified per stirpes," is a hybrid between the "strict per stirpes" rule and the "per capita at each generation" rule in the current version of the UPC discussed next. Shares are determined on a per capita basis with representation available for lower generations.

There are two variations of this model — the traditional model and an original UPC variation. Except as noted in Step three of the below procedures, they are identical. We will focus on the version used in the UPC as it was adopted in 1969. One or the other of these methods is in force in almost half the states.

Like the strict per stirpes model, the per capita with representation rule allocates shares by bloodlines. Per capita with representation and the strict per stirpes rule discussed above will reach identical results if there is at least one descendant alive at each generation of a bloodline upon the decedent's death. If that is the case, the number of shares to be split among the descendants is determined by the number of children alive or represented at that generation.

Unlike the strict per stirpes rule, modern per stirpes does not make a determination of the number of shares at a particular generation until there is a generation with at least one descendant alive in the bloodline; *in other words, shares are not established for a generation if everyone in that generation is dead*. Whereas the strict rule will lock in the number of shares based on the represented bloodlines at the first generation even if there are no actual survivors at that generation, the modern rule jumps down to the first generation *where there are actual survivors*. Once that is determined, the lower generations who represent their parents are locked into the share determined for their parent, just as under the strict rule. If all takers are of the same generation, they take per capita, receiving equal amounts. If they are of different generations, they take per stirpes determining bloodlines based on the highest generation with survivors, the root generation.

a. Procedure for Determining the Per Capita with Representation Share

Step One: **Find the first generation where there are living descendants.** Determine the number of shares by dividing the estate into as many equal shares as there are:

(1) living children of the decedent, if any, and
(2) deceased children in the same generation who are represented by their living descendants.

Do not determine the number of shares at a generation where there are no living descendants and everyone is merely represented. There must be a living descendant at a generation to justify the share determination. In other words, perform step one at the highest generation where someone is alive.

Step Two: Distribute one share to each *living* member of the highest generation.

Step Three: For the children who were not alive but whose bloodlines were entitled to a share because they were represented by their descendants, determine the portion allocated to that bloodline in the same manner as Step one above (remembering that there must be a survivor) and distribute the probate property in the same manner as in Step two. Repeat this for each next generation.

Example 3:   Decedent had three children — A, B and C. Decedent is only survived by his son C, who has a young son X. Decedent's son B died many years ago without any children. Daughter A died recently leaving three children of her own — U, V and W. (Notice that these facts are the same as Example 1.)

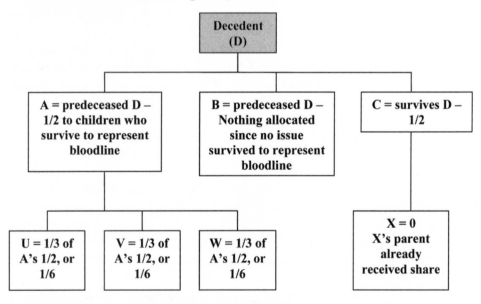

Procedure and Result: First, we determine the number of shares by dividing the estate into as many equal parts as there are living children of the decedent, if any, and deceased children who are represented by their living descendants. On these facts, we determine the number of shares at the "child" or first generation level because at least one child (C) is alive at the decedent's death. From here, the procedure and result are the same as in Example 1, reflecting the fact that this method is based in a per stirpes philosophy.

Example 4:   Decedent had three children — A, B and C. D is not survived by *any* of her children. Decedent's son B died many years ago without any children. Daughter A died recently leaving three children of her own — U, V and W. Decedent's son C died many years ago survived by child X. (Notice that these facts are the same as Example 2.)

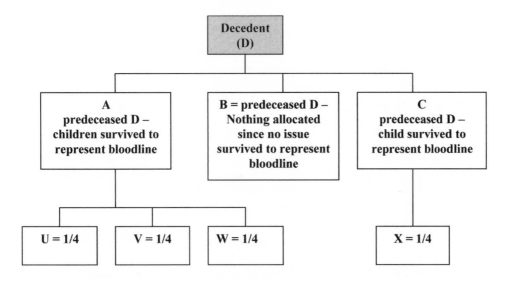

Procedure and Result: At the first generation where there is at least one descendant that survives the decedent, we divide the estate into as many equal shares as there are living descendants of the decedent and deceased descendants who are represented by their living descendants. Since there was no one alive at the first generation (*i.e.*, the child generation), we skip it and move directly to the second generation. At the second generation, there are four descendants of the decedent alive. There are no represented descendants. Therefore, four shares are created.

Second, we distribute one share to each living descendant at that generation. In this case, all four shares get distributed in Step two. U, V, W and X do not technically take by representation; instead, they take in their own right per capita.

Step three is not required on these facts.

b.   Representative State Provisions

The descriptions of the original UPC per capita with representation in the state statutes are reasonably uniform and track with the procedures described above. Set out below are the rules used by California and Arkansas.

Division into equal shares (California)

> If a statute calls for property to be distributed or taken in the manner provided in this section, the property shall be divided into as many equal shares as there are living members of the nearest generation of issue then living and deceased members of that generation who leave issue then living, each living member of the nearest generation of issue then living receiving one share and the share of each deceased member of that generation who leaves issue then living being divided in the same manner among his or her then living issue. CAL. PROB. CODE §240 (2010).

Per Stirpes Taking (Arkansas)

> (1) Heirs will take "per stirpes" if the intestate is predeceased by one (1) or more persons who would have been entitled to inherit from the intestate had such a person survived the intestate.
>
> (2) The intestate's estate shall be divided into as many equal shares as there are:
>
> (A) Surviving heirs in the nearest degree of kinship to the intestate; and
>
> (B) Persons, hereinafter called "predeceased persons," in the same degree of kinship as the heirs mentioned in subdivision (a)(2)(A) of this section, who predeceased the intestate leaving descendants who survived the intestate.
>
> (3) Each surviving heir in the nearest degree taking per capita shall receive one (1) share and the descendants of each predeceased person taking per stirpes shall collectively receive one (1) share. ARK. CODE ANN. §28-9-205(a) (2010).

EXERCISE

Draft a provision for inclusion into your client's will that results in her estate being distributed per capita with representation if some of her descendants predecease her and leave issue of their own. It should start out as follows:

> "I leave everything to my spouse. If my spouse should predecease me, I leave everything to my descendants . . ."

4.   *The Revised UPC Method — "Per Capita at Each Generation"*

This method, referred to as "per capita at each generation," is the one adopted by the NCCUSL when it revised the UPC in 1990. It establishes an approach that is more concerned with equality among members of a generation than with equality along bloodlines. It relies exclusively on a per capita methodology; no one takes by representation. It is the method of representation adopted by just over a quarter of the states.

The majority of states that have adopted the revised version of the UPC have accepted the definition intact or with only minor variations. The current version of the UPC describes this system as follows:

UPC §2-709. Representation; Per Capita at Each Generation . . .

(b) [Representation; Per Capita at Each Generation.] If an applicable statute or a governing instrument calls for property to be distributed "by representation" or "per capita at each generation," the property is divided into as many equal shares as there are (i) surviving descendants in the generation nearest to the designated ancestor which contains one or more surviving descendants (ii) and deceased descendants in the same generation who left surviving descendants, if any. Each surviving descendant in the nearest generation is allocated one share. The remaining shares, if any, are combined and then divided in the same manner among the surviving descendants of the deceased descendants as if the surviving descendants who were allocated a share and their surviving descendants had predeceased the distribution date.

While the amount one generation gets may differ from the amount other generations get, each living person at a particular generation gets exactly the same as other people within that generation who are entitled to take. Thus, for each generation that has survivors, the amount received by persons alive in that generation is the same.

Procedure:

Step One: **Find the first generation where there are living descendants.** Determine the number of shares by dividing the estate into as many equal shares as there are:

(1)   living children of the decedent, if any, and
(2)   deceased children in the same generation with descendants then living.

Step One is identical to the Original UPC modern per stirpes method. In other words, perform Step one at the highest generation where someone is alive.

Step Two: Distribute one share per capita to each living member of the first generation where there are living members.

Step Three: Combine the remaining shares, if any, into a pot for sharing by lower generations. It is at Step three that the Per Capita at Each Generation method breaks from the modern per stirpes method.

Step Four: Move down to the next generation and basically repeat Steps one to three until the entire estate is distributed.

Example 5:   Decedent had three children — A, B and C. Decedent is only survived by his son C, who has a young son X. Decedent's son B died many years ago without any children. Daughter A died recently leaving three children of her own — U, V and W. (Notice that these facts are the same as Examples 1 and 3.)

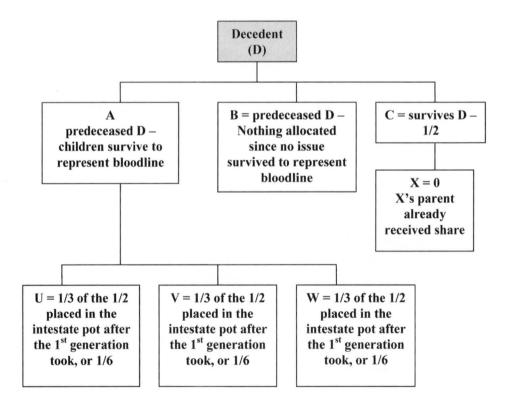

Procedure: First, at the highest generation where there is at least one descendant that survives the decedent, we determine the number of shares by dividing the estate into as many equal parts as there are living descendants of the decedent and deceased descendants who are represented by their living descendants. On these facts, we determine the number of shares at the "child" generation because at least one child (C) is alive at the decedent's death. Since son B did not survive and did not leave any children to represent him, his potential share is lost. Thus, only two shares are created — one for the surviving child (C) and the other for A's descendants.

Second, since C is alive, we distribute to C the half to which he is entitled per capita.

Third, we place the remaining 1/2 into a pot for sharing by the lower generation descendants.

Fourth, we repeat Steps one to three as to the amount in the pot. As a result, U, V and W each get 1/3 of the 1/2 (*i.e.,* 1/6) remaining in the intestate estate on a per capita basis. While the answer is the same as with per stirpes (Example 1) and the original UPC per capita with representation (Example 3), the reasons are different. Whereas with per stirpes and the original UPC, U, V and W acquired their share as representatives of A, with the revised UPC version they do so as members of the next generation per capita.

Example 6:   Decedent had three children — A, B and C. D is not survived by *any* of her children. Decedent's son B died many years ago without any children. Daughter A died recently leaving three children of her own — U, V and W. Decedent's son C died many years ago survived by child X. (Notice that these facts are the same as Examples 2 and 4.).

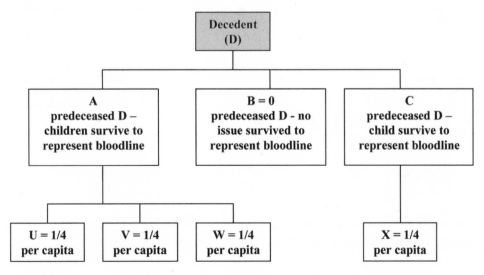

Result: The result here is the same as that in Example 4. The reason is that both are based on a per capita methodology for lower generations if there are no survivors at a higher generation.

Example 7: The facts are difficult to explain and might take 1,000 words. So, here's a picture instead.

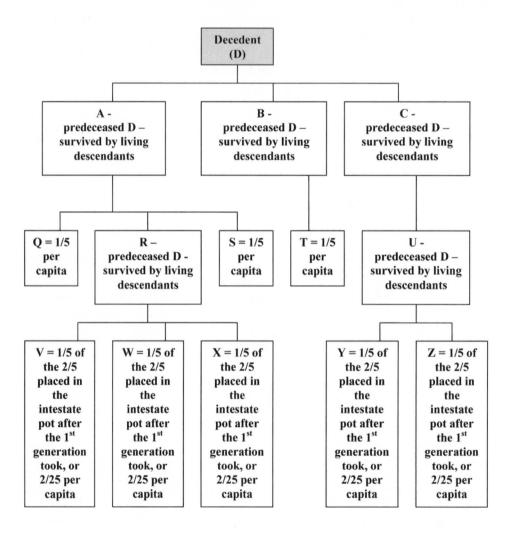

Procedure and Result: First, at the highest generation where there is at least one descendant that survives the decedent, we determine the number of shares by dividing the estate into as many equal shares as there are living descendants of the decedent and deceased descendants who are represented by their living descendants. Since there was no one alive at the first generation (*i.e.*, the child generation), we skip it and move directly to the second generation. At the second generation, there are three descendants of the decedent alive and two descendants who are represented. Therefore, five shares are created.

Second, we distribute one share to each living descendant at that generation per capita. In this case, three of the five shares get distributed (to Q, S and T).

Third, the two shares (out of the five) not distributed remain in the intestate pot to be shared by lower generations.

The fourth step repeats Steps one to three as to the remaining amount in the pot. As a result, V, W, X, Y and Z each get 1/5 of the 2/5 in the pot (*i.e.*, 2/25) of the intestate estate on a per capita basis.

QUESTION (AND ANSWER)

In Example 7, what shares would the surviving descendants get under the per stirpes and original UPC models?

Answer: Under strict per stirpes, Q and S would each get 1/3 of A's 1/3 by representation; V, W and X would each get 1/3 of R's 1/3 of A's 1/3 by representation; T would get 1/3 by representation; Y and Z each get 1/2 of C's 1/3 by representation.

Under the original UPC or modified per stirpes, Q, S and T each get 1/5 per capita; V, W and X each take 1/3 of R's 1/5 by representation; Y and Z each take 1/2 of U's 1/5 by representation.

PROBLEMS

In all the problems below, assume descendants designated as "X" predeceased the decedent.

1.   Determine the distribution of decedent's probate estate under the three models of representation. You may leave the answers in fractions if you find that easier.

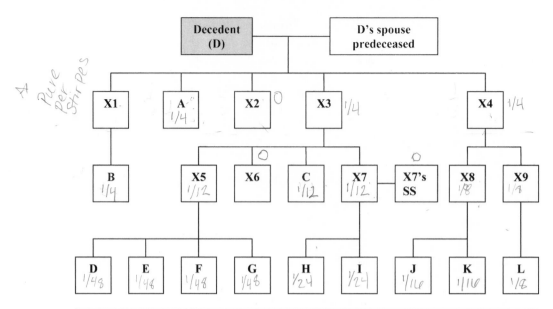

	Pure Per Stirpes	Modern Per Stirpes **Original UPC**	Per Capita at Each Generation **Revised UPC**
A			
B			
C			
D			
E			
F			
G			
H			
I			
J			
K			
L			
X7's SS			

2.   Determine the distribution of decedent's probate estate under the three models of representation. You may leave the answers in fractions if you find that easier. The difference between this problem and the previous one is that A is now dead also. (Are you starting to feel sorry for this family?)

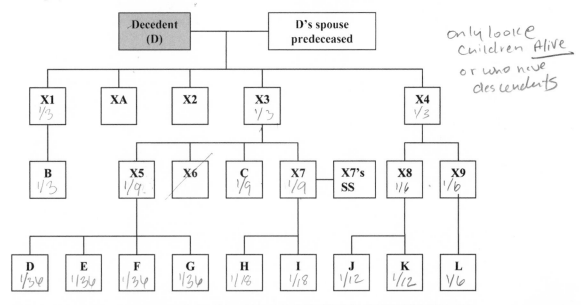

only looke
Children Alive
or who have
descendents

	Pure Per Stirpes	Modern Per Stirpes **Original UPC**	Per Capita at Each Generation **Revised UPC**
XA			
B			
C			
D			
E			
F			
G			
H			
I			
J			
K			
L			
X7's SS			

3.   Determine the distribution of decedent's probate estate under the three models of representation. You may leave the answers in fractions if you find that easier. This problem is different than the one above due to B's death also. (Come on, admit it, you have to feel sorry for this family now.)

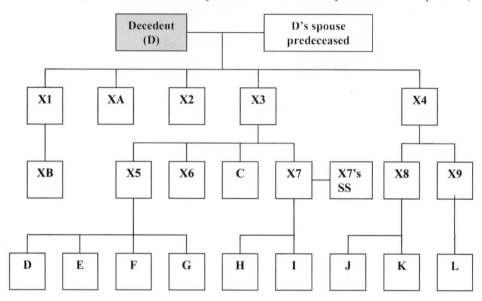

	Pure Per Stirpes	Modern Per Stirpes **Original UPC**	Per Capita at Each Generation **Revised UPC**
XA			
XB			
C			
D			
E			
F			
G			
H			
I			
J			
K			
L			
X7's SS			

4. Reflect back on Problem 1 above and consider these changed facts: Decedent dies without a surviving spouse or any surviving lineal descendants but with the collateral relatives diagrammed below. How would the amount that each heir is entitled to be the same or different than what your answer was in Problem 1?

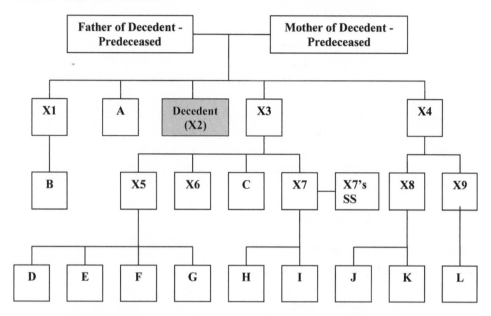

F. REDUCING THE INTESTATE SHARE FOR ADVANCEMENTS

1. Is an Inter Vivos Transfer a Gift, Advancement or a Loan?

An investigation of the facts by the personal representative after the decedent's death may uncover one or more inter vivos transfers of cash or other property that the decedent made to a surviving spouse or other intestate heir. The issue for the personal representative is to determine whether the transfer was intended by the decedent as a gift, a loan or an advance against the inheritance. Each characterization has different legal implications for the heir — and the estate.

A **gift** is an absolute and unconditional transfer which need not be repaid and does not diminish the donee's share of her inheritance from the estate. This characterization of the transfer is the one most favorable to the recipient.

By contrast, a **loan** from the decedent, if not repaid during the decedent's life, is an asset of the decedent's estate. Like any other asset, the personal representative should gather it and distribute it to the appropriate heir. This is the characterization least favorable to the recipient because the recipient must disgorge herself of the money.

Between a gift and a loan is an **advancement**, which is treated as a prepayment of some or all of the recipient's inheritance.[10] It reduces the amount the heir would have otherwise received. The transfer may have been made in fee simple to the recipient or in the form of a nonprobate transfer, such as through a gift of a joint tenancy interest or through being named the beneficiary of a life insurance policy.

Putting aside characterization as a loan for now, whether a transfer is presumed to be a gift or an advancement is different between the common law and the UPC. Under the common law, which is based on the English Statute of Distribution of 1670, all such transfers are treated as advancements unless the evidence establishes otherwise. The UPC takes the opposite position: All lifetime transfers to heirs are presumed to be gifts. In order to overcome the presumption of a gift, the UPC requires very specific kinds of evidence to establish that the inter vivos transfer was an advancement. You will need to consult your state's statute to determine which presumption applies.

UPC §2-109. Advancements.

> (a). If an individual dies intestate as to all or a portion of his [or her] estate, property the decedent gave during the decedent's lifetime to an individual who, at the decedent's death, is an heir is treated as an advancement against the heir's intestate share *only if (i) the decedent declared in a contemporaneous writing or the heir acknowledged in writing that the gift is an advancement or (ii) the decedent's contemporaneous writing or the heir's written acknowledgment otherwise indicates that the gift is to be taken into account in computing the division and distribution of the decedent's intestate estate.* [Emphasis added.]

As can be seen, the evidence necessary to establish a transfer as an advance must be in writing; oral (parol) evidence, no matter how persuasive, is not permitted. If the writing is from the *decedent*, it must have been drafted contemporaneously with the transfer and must specifically identify the transfer as an advancement or indicate in some clear manner that it was meant to reduce the amount to which the heir would have otherwise been entitled. Subsequent attempts at transforming an unqualified gift into an advancement are not allowed. If the writing is from the *recipient*, it need not be contemporaneous but it must make a similar acknowledgement. A writing from the recipient may be a simple note found among the decedent's papers saying, for example, "Thanks mom for giving me $10,000. I understand it will reduce my inheritance."

---

10. The analogous doctrine for prepayment of a recipient's share of a *testate* estate is "ademption by satisfaction." *See* UPC §2-609, discussed in Chapter 10.

Evidence to prove that a transfer was intended as a loan is not as restricted. Unless the Statute of Frauds applies and requires a written instrument, other evidence of a loan may be introduced, such as proof of repayments, perfection of a security interest with the state, an amortization schedule, etc.

Litigation may be necessary to determine the character of a transfer. The burden of proof is on those who benefit if the transfer is classified as a loan or an advancement, *i.e.,* the beneficiaries other than the recipient.

EXERCISE

A client tells you that he wants to make a $40,000 gift to his daughter to help her with a down payment on a home, but wants to be sure that the gift is counted against her inheritance. Draft a document for your client that satisfies the UPC's requirement of a contemporaneous writing evidencing an advancement.

2.   *How Do These Transfers Affect the Shares to the Heirs?*

Since a gift is an unqualified transfer and does not include an expectation of repayment in any way, the amount due the recipient heir under UPC §§2-102 and 2-103 is not disturbed by a finding that the transfer was a gift. The fact that the donee died prior to the decedent is irrelevant.

An advancement, being a prepayment of some or all of the recipient's share of the intestate estate, is treated differently. The value of the advancement will be brought into a "hotchpot" calculation (see below for details) to determine if the recipient's share has already been fully satisfied by the advance or if she is still entitled to more.

If the advancement exceeds the value of the recipient's calculated share of the estate, the recipient will not receive more from the estate but also has no obligation to return the excess. However, if the person to whom the advance was made predeceases the decedent, the descendants of the advancee are entitled to their share as if the advancement was never made. In other words, the descendants of the advancee do *not* "step into the shoes" of the advancee.

Under UPC §2-110, if the transfer was a loan, repayment is required. If the heir who is entitled to collect on the loan is other than the debtor, the debtor must pay the beneficiary according to the terms of the loan. If the debtor is the beneficiary of her own loan, the unpaid principal and interest on the loan can be set off against the borrower's intestate share. If the debt exceeds that share, then the debtor must return the excess to the estate. However, if the debtor fails to survive the creditor, the debt is not taken into account in determining the share given to the debtor's descendants. Presumably, the creditor had an opportunity to seek to collect on the debt from the deceased debtor's estate.

3.   Advancements and the "Hotchpot"

If the inter vivos transfer is determined to be an advancement, a calculation must be made to determine whether the heir who received the advance has already received the amount to which she is entitled or whether she is entitled to more. This is accomplished through a method known as the "hotchpot."

CALCULATION TEMPLATE FOR ADVANCEMENTS

Step 1. Start with probate estate.

Step 2. List advancements made to all beneficiaries.

Step 3. Add Steps 1 and 2. The result is the total preliminary hotchpot estate.

Step 4. Determine the intestate shares to which each beneficiary is entitled.

Step 5. Schedule the advancements made to each beneficiary.

Step 6. Subtract Step 5 from Step 4 on a beneficiary-by-beneficiary basis.

Decision Point. If no beneficiary received an advance that was larger than the amount to which he is entitled, this is the end of the calculation; each person gets the amount determined in Step 6. On the other hand, if any beneficiary received more in advances than his intestate share, it is necessary to do further calculations.

Step 7 (if necessary). Any beneficiary who received advances greater than his intestate share is not required to repay the excess. Repeat Steps 1-6 disregarding these beneficiaries, *i.e.*, without grossing up the amount for advances to that beneficiary or calculating an inheritance for that person.

Step 8 (if necessary). Repeat Step 7 until there are no excess advancements.

Example: This example comes from the comments to UPC §2-109, though the approach to the answer is based on the template. G died intestate, survived by his wife (W) and his three children (A, B and C) by a prior marriage. G's probate estate is valued at $190,000. During his lifetime, G had advanced A $50,000 and B $10,000. G memorialized both gifts in a writing declaring his intent that they be advancements.

Step 1. Start with probate estate = $190,000.

Step 2. List advancements made to all beneficiaries = $60,000 ($50,000 to A + $10,000 to B).

Step 3. Add Steps 1 and 2. The result is the total preliminary hotchpot estate = $250,000.

Step 4. Determine the intestate shares to which each beneficiary is entitled. W's intestate share of a $250,000 estate under UPC §2-102(4) is $200,000 ($150,000 + 1/2 of $100,000); the remaining $50,000 is divided equally among A, B and C, or $16,667 each.

Step 5. Schedule the advancements made to each beneficiary. A = $50,000 and B = $10,000.

Step 6. Subtract Step 5 from Step 4 on a beneficiary-by-beneficiary basis.

Decision Point.   A received an excess advance of $33,333 ($16,667 less $50,000). While A does not have to repay the excess advance, A also may not receive anything additional from the estate.

Since at least one heir received an excess advance, repeat Steps 1-6, disregarding child A.

Step 1. Start with probate estate = $190,000.

Step 2. List advancements made to all beneficiaries, disregarding A. B got an advance of $10,000.

Step 3. Add Steps 1 and 2. The result is the total preliminary hotch-pot estate = $200,000.

Step 4. Determine the intestate shares to which each beneficiary is entitled. W's intestate share of a $200,000 estate under UPC §2-102(4) is $175,000 ($150,000 + 1/2 of $50,000); the remaining $25,000 is divided equally between B and C, or $12,500 each.

Step 5. Schedule the advancements made to each beneficiary. B received a $10,000 advancement.

Step 6. Subtract Step 5 from Step 4 on a beneficiary-by-beneficiary basis. W's intestate share is $175,000; B's intestate share of $12,500 is reduced by $10,000 to $2,500; C's intestate share is $12,500. As there are no excess advancements, we stop here.

Under UPC §2-109(c), if the recipient of the advancement fails to survive the decedent, the advancement is **not** taken into account in determining the share to which the recipient's descendants are entitled unless the decedent's contemporaneous writing so requires. In the example above, if A predeceased G, the advancement of $50,000 would be disregarded in all respects when determining the amount due A's descendants by representation.

PROBLEMS

1.   The personal representative of Tyrell's estate discovers a letter from Joseph, Tyrell's son. Joseph's letter thanks Tyrell for paying $10,000 for his wedding and acknowledges that it is meant to be an advance against whatever he might have received at Tyrell's death.

      a.   Assume you are the personal representative and must decide who gets what. How does this note affect your decision?

      b.   Answer Problem 1.a, except that the note says thank you and nothing more.

      c.   You also learn that Tyrell gave Joseph $150,000 recently to start a business and told Joseph that it was in lieu of his inheritance in front of their friend, the family priest. As the personal representative, how would this affect what you are willing to distribute to Joseph?

2.   Donald died intestate recently with a probate estate worth $500,000. Donald and Sandy had two children, Brian and Clarissa. Donald also had a child (Angel), age 31, from a previous marriage. Donald is survived by Sandy, Angel, Brian and Clarissa.

      a.   Donald paid $100,000 toward Angel's college education 10 years ago and gave Brian $400,000 to start a dot.com business five years ago. As to the $400,000 only, Donald kept a letter in his file that was dated five years ago in which he stated to Brian that this would count against his inheritance when Donald died. Brian's business has since gone bankrupt. What share of Donald's probate estate goes to the survivors?

      b.   Brian died intestate a year before Donald died, leaving a spouse Bobbie and two children, Barry and Brian, Jr. How might that affect your answer to 2.a?

4.   Advancements and Disclaimers

In Chapter 10, you will learn that a beneficiary can disclaim the right to receive all or a portion of an inheritance. You will also learn that the effect of a disclaimer is to treat the disclaimant as having predeceased the decedent.

In our discussion of the representation rules that rely on a per capita approach, *i.e.*, the original and revised UPC methods, we learned that if all persons in a generation predecease the decedent, we make our determination of the amounts to which the next generation is entitled on a per capita basis, meaning that all descendants in that generation share equally. It would seem then that, based on the statement above, if there was a disclaimer, we would treat the disclaimant as dead for these and all purposes. However, this is not true for intestacy and advancement purposes. In this situation, we do not treat the disclaimant as dead when determining if there is a person alive at the same generation. If the law were not this way, depending on the facts, a manipulative heir in a higher generation could use a disclaimer to disproportionately increase the share to her children. The UPC does not allow this.

The problem can be highlighted by the following: Assume the illustration below represents the family tree. The decedent was a widow. Assume further that the probate estate is $50,000 and that A received a $50,000 advancement several years ago that was documented in a contemporaneous writing.

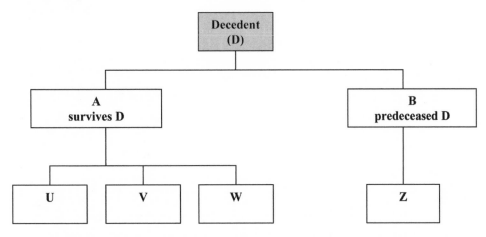

On these facts, under all of the representation schemes, both the original or revised UPC methodologies, both A and Z would be entitled to 1/2 of the $100,000 enlarged probate estate ($50,000 + the $50,000 advancement made to A). However, because of the advancement, A would not be entitled to anything further and Z would take the entire $50,000 probate estate.

Had A not survived D in fact, then U, V, W and Z would each receive 1/4 of the $50,000 probate estate. In other words, A's family (U, V and W) would receive an extra $37,500 of D's estate if A were dead at D's death as a result of the interplay of the representation system and the rule that disregards an advancement if the advancee predeceases the decedent.

A wise beneficiary might look at this result and think to disclaim her interest and be treated as predeceasing the decedent to give an advantage to her kin. However, the recipient of an advancement cannot use a disclaimer to increase the share passing to her lineal descendants either by taking advantage of the predeceasing advancee rule or the per capita model of representation.

In the illustration, A cannot use a disclaimer under UPC §2-1105 to give her children a larger share than that to which A was entitled. Under UPC §2-1106(b)(3)(A), the effect of a disclaimer by A is that the disclaimant's "interest" devolves to A's descendants as if the disclaimant had predeceased the decedent. The "interest" that A renounced was a right to a 1/2 share of G's estate reduced by the advancement. A's children merely step into A's shoes and will receive nothing.

APPENDIX A

Table of Consanguinity

Instructions:
Place the subject/decedent for whom you need
to establish relationships in the blank box. The
labeled boxes will then list the relationship by
title to the subject and the degree of distance
from the subject.

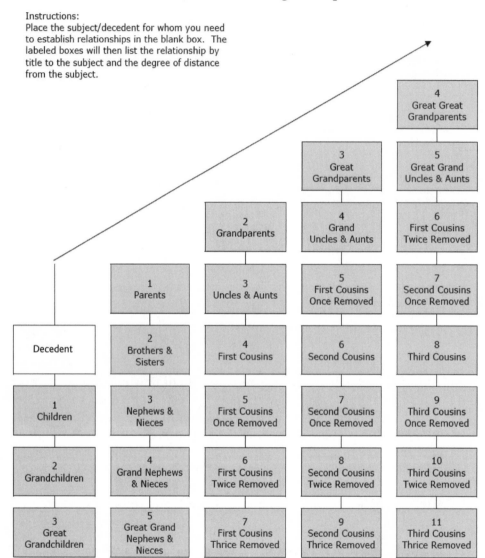

Source: http://www.dccourts.gov/dccourts/docs/probate/adm/FormsForDeaths
FromJan1_1981ToJune30_1995/TableOfConsanguinity.pdf.

4 NONPROBATE TRANSFERS—PASSING PROPERTY BY WILL SUBSTITUTES AND GIFTS

A. INTRODUCTION

This chapter picks up where the introduction to will substitutes in Chapter 1 left off. In that chapter, you were introduced to the concept of will substitutes and the fact that they reflect the revolution in the way property is transmitted at death. That chapter noted that some transfers at death are distributed *through the probate process* according to the terms of a will or, if there is no will, according to the intestacy statute of the state of the decedent's domicile at death. Other property, however, is distributed *outside of the probate process,* primarily through "will substitutes."

As you might expect, a significant portion of this book is devoted to the process of conveying property by trusts and wills. The principal focus of this chapter, however, is on will substitutes. While there is a brief discussion in this chapter of trusts (a major will substitute), we primarily address will substitutes that a client has created before coming to the attorney's office and for which the attorney's skills and advice are not sought. These include documents connected with life insurance, bank accounts, brokerage accounts holding stocks and securities, retirement plans and joint tenancies.

Even though an attorney is not usually involved with establishing these kinds of will substitutes, learning about them is important because they must be considered when an attorney develops a comprehensive estate plan for a client. The plan must coordinate both probate and nonprobate methods of disposition. For many people, the majority of their wealth is in their homes, insurance policies, stocks and securities, retirement accounts and bank accounts.[1] These kinds of property typically are passed to others via will substitutes rather than wills. Without developing an integrated plan, some beneficiaries may receive too much and others too little or none at all. In addition, if too much property is transferred outside probate directly to named beneficiaries, the estate may not have sufficient liquidity to pay taxes and debts of the decedent.

In the article below, Professor McCouch succinctly presents the history of wills (probate) and will substitutes (nonprobate) in the transmission of property at death and the role and significance each has in today's world.

Grayson M.P. McCouch, Probate Law Reform and Nonprobate Transfers
62 U. Miami L. Rev. 757 (2008)

The proliferation of probate avoidance techniques can be traced directly to several features of the probate process. Broadly speaking, probate refers to the body of substantive and procedural rules that govern the devolution of decedents' estates by will or intestacy. In this country, probate has traditionally been organized around judicial proceedings. Control over testamentary transfers is lodged firmly with the local probate court: A will has no binding effect until it is allowed by the court; estate administration cannot begin until the court appoints a personal representative; and the personal representative often remains subject to court supervision until the court orders a final distribution and discharge. Moreover, if estate assets are located outside the state of the decedent's last domicile, it may be necessary to open separate probate proceedings in several states [called "ancillary probate"]. Court-supervised administration also brings with it the need for lawyers to represent personal representatives and assist them in navigating a maze of arcane procedural requirements. The basic structure of the probate system has changed remarkably little since the nineteenth century, and some of its standard procedural safeguards — e.g., court-appointed referees, fiduciary bonds, notice by newspaper publication, and frequent court hearings on uncontested matters — seem hopelessly anachronistic in a world of electronic communication, paperless transactions, and automated recordkeeping. A growing number of states now provide for independent administration with minimal court supervision, as well as informal procedures for administering small estates and collecting specific types of assets,

---

1. "The law of wills and the rules of descent no longer govern succession to most of the property of most decedents. Increasingly, probate bears to the actual practice of succession about the relation that bankruptcy bears to enterprise: it is an indispensable institution, but hardly one that everybody need use." John H. Langbein, *The Nonprobate Revolution and the Future of the Law of Succession*, 97 HARV. L. REV. 1108 (1984).

but comprehensive reform proposals still encounter stiff resistance from lawyers, probate judges, surety bond companies, legal notice publishers, and other groups with vested interests in perpetuating the existing system. As a result, the probate process is widely perceived as costly, slow, and cumbersome, and many transferors actively seek to avoid it.

Will substitutes, as the name implies, are designed to achieve the practical effect of a will — designating beneficiaries to receive property at the owner's death — outside the probate system. The main doctrinal obstacle to nonprobate transfers is the conventional view that all property owned by a decedent at death automatically becomes part of the probate estate subject to administration and can be disposed of only by will or intestacy. Accordingly, will substitutes ordinarily take the form of a gift, trust, contract, or other nontestamentary arrangement that technically operates as a lifetime transfer while leaving the transferor with substantially undiminished ownership rights (i.e., access to the property as well as power to revoke or amend the beneficiary designation) until death. For example, life insurance has long been recognized as a nontestamentary vehicle that permits the insured policy owner to transfer property (i.e., proceeds) at death outside the probate system. Similarly, joint accounts with right of survivorship [or a "payable on death" designation] and tentative trusts serve a similar function for bank accounts [and stocks and securities]. The era of large-scale probate avoidance truly began, however, in the mid-twentieth century when courts decisively upheld the validity of revocable trusts, which, in many respects, are practically indistinguishable from wills. The decisions upholding revocable trusts, for all their doctrinal gyrations, are best understood as signaling judicial approval of a will substitute that offers a reliable, efficient, and socially useful alternative to probate.[2]

According to the standard account of the "nonprobate revolution," the rise of will substitutes is basically a story about deregulating the process of deathtime wealth transfers and allowing private-sector competitors to challenge the probate system's state-sponsored monopoly. Will substitutes flourish because they perform the essential functions of probate in a commercially viable, cost-effective manner. Today, decedents' wealth consists predominantly of financial assets (e.g., stocks, bonds, bank deposits, brokerage accounts, mutual funds, and life insurance), and financial intermediaries that routinely handle title registrations and transfers of such assets for living owners stand ready and willing to carry out nonprobate transfers

---

2. A revocable (living) trust is a trust created and funded by someone (the settlor) in which the settlor transfers property to a trustee but retains the right to revoke the trust at any time during life and regain the property. Normally, the settlor appoints himself as the trustee and income beneficiary for life. The terms of the trust also provide that on the death of the settlor/trustee a successor assumes the role of trustee and the property of the trust usually gets distributed to that person's spouse, descendants or a charity. Since the settlor has almost complete control over and rights in the property during life and since the property passes to another at death, this kind of arrangement is nearly identical to a testamentary transfer by will. The difference is that property passing by trust does not go through probate.

to designated beneficiaries of deceased owners. In the vast majority of cases, where no dispute arises concerning the validity or terms of a transfer, there is simply no need for probate court proceedings with their attendant costs and delays. Apparently, even creditors rarely find it necessary to use the probate safeguards designed for their benefit, preferring instead to protect their interests through informal methods or nonprobate alternatives such as credit life insurance and security interests.

Nevertheless, despite their practical advantages, will substitutes have not completely displaced wills or probate administration; indeed, they cannot do so. The probate system continues to serve the indispensable function of collecting and distributing property owned at death (i.e., property not otherwise disposed of by lifetime gift or by will substitute). Not all transferors avail themselves of will substitutes, and those who do should be aware that most will substitutes apply only to specific assets. Even revocable trusts, which can hold a virtually unlimited variety of assets, avoid probate only to the extent that they are funded with identifiable, existing property during life. Thus, while in theory a transferor in the last moments of life might be able to sweep every last item of property into a revocable trust, as a practical matter, there will almost always be some assets that remain outside the trust at death and become part of the probate estate subject to administration. By the same token, transferors continue to execute wills in order to direct the disposition of property — including failed nonprobate transfers [such as when a joint tenancy with right of survivorship is severed before the death of either tenant — *see* Part G below] — that otherwise would fall into intestacy. . . . Thus, wills and will substitutes should be viewed not as irreconcilable opposites, but rather as complementary components of an increasingly varied and complex system of deathtime transfers. . . .

A will substitute is sometimes referred to as a "nonprobate will." The phrase neatly captures the functional similarities between a will and a will substitute, but it should not be allowed to obscure the formal distinction between the two. Conventional doctrine insists that a will is the only instrument that can dispose of property at death — a logical conclusion from the premise that all property owned at death becomes part of the probate estate and passes either by will or by intestacy. By implication, to transfer property outside probate, a will substitute must be formally classified as a lifetime arrangement, even if it is functionally indistinguishable from a will. Arguably, it might be more candid to recognize that wills and will substitutes are alternative methods of transferring property at death, that the probate system is a default setting, and that transferors can freely choose to avoid probate by using will substitutes. But this approach puts increased stress on the formal manifestation of the transferor's intent. Most formal wills are readily recognizable as wills because they comply, literally or substantially, with statutory formalities that encourage standardized expressions of testamentary intent. As a practical matter, most will substitutes are also easy to classify, despite the absence of mandatory statutory formalities, because they usually exhibit some "alternative formality" — as, for example, in the case of a revocable trust instrument or a boilerplate beneficiary designation for financial assets. . . .

The advent of widespread, large-scale probate avoidance has added a new dimension to the project of probate law reform. When the Uniform Probate Code made its debut in 1969, its primary goal was to modernize traditional probate procedures and make them more uniform, flexible, and efficient. The Code's reforms were in part a response to the rise of will substitutes, which offered a ready means of transferring property at death outside the probate system. In the intervening years, however, will substitutes have continued to proliferate, while traditional probate procedures have resisted comprehensive reform. The probate system has not become obsolete — it provides valuable safeguards in many cases and remains indispensable in dealing with residual assets and resolving disputes — but it now plays a relatively modest role in regulating deathtime wealth transfers. Today, wills operate side by side with an ever-expanding array of will substitutes, and it no longer makes sense for reformers to focus exclusively, or even primarily, on the probate system. Accordingly, they have taken the first steps toward articulating a unified law of probate and nonprobate transfers. Much still remains to be done. Ultimately, the success of the reformers' project will require a sustained and vigorous effort to maintain conceptual coherence and achieve practical implementation.

This chapter first discusses the reasons will substitutes have become such a significant part of the legal landscape and examines their benefits and drawbacks. Then we look at some of the similarities and differences between the law of wills and will substitutes, which is based on the recognition that both accomplish the same thing (*i.e.*, the transfer of property on death) but with different legal justifications. After that, we analyze which property gets probated and which passes by will substitute instruments outside probate, ending with a consideration of gifts. Next, we discuss developing a comprehensive estate plan incorporating will substitutes and consider who the beneficiary of a will substitute is and the considerations that go into selecting the right one. Finally, we look at failed will substitutes and what happens when the will and a nonprobate instrument conflict, with each designating different beneficiaries.

QUESTIONS

1. *To have or not to have?* Do you have a will? Why or why not?
2. *Why did you do it?* Do you own an insurance policy on your life? Are you a participant in a retirement plan, such as an Individual Retirement Account (IRA) or a 401(k)? Do you own any real estate, stocks or bank

accounts jointly with another? If you do own any of these, did you complete a form designating someone to receive the property on your death? Did you enter into the arrangement to avoid probate? If not to avoid probate, what was your reason? What considerations went into your decision in naming the beneficiary? Reflect on these questions as you read the next section to determine which might apply to you or to a family member or friend.

B. WHY THE ADVENT OF WILL SUBSTITUTES?

1. Reasons Other Than Probate Avoidance

Most will substitutes developed (i) as the result of custom and commitment between spouses and other family members or (ii) as a by-product of contracts between companies and their customers — not to avoid probate.

Married people and others in a committed union frequently believe that their houses, stocks and bank accounts should be held jointly (with right of survivorship) in order to reflect the fact that they are a family unit. In addition, family members often hold property jointly because it is a convenient form of ownership for handling finances. This is especially true for multiple-party or convenience bank accounts because such accounts allow more than one family member to access the money to pay normal household bills. For example, this kind of account can be useful when a child needs to write checks from a disabled or elderly parent's account to pay the parent's expenses.

While joint ownership developed primarily for family reasons, beneficiary designation forms — another type of will substitute — resulted chiefly from business arrangements. Banks, investment firms, insurance companies and retirement plan administrators created these forms to let the company know who should receive the money on the death of their customer. An easy-to-understand example of this is life insurance: When an individual buys insurance, the owner is required to complete a form designating to whom the carrier should pay the proceeds on her death (and agreeing to notify the company if she wishes to change the beneficiary).

Will substitutes are attractive to many individuals for their convenience and because they may be executed and changed with few formalities. For example, if the insured wants to change the beneficiary on their insurance policy or securities account, they simply need to go online, download a new form and either complete it online or print it out and mail it back. Even for people who do not use the Internet, it is usually only a matter of calling the company and making the changes over the phone or getting someone to mail the form to them to complete and send back. (As we will see, by contrast, changing the beneficiary of a will generally requires returning to the attorney's office and undergoing various formalities to ensure the validity of the revised document.)

2.   Probate Avoidance

The probate process is the judicial procedure whereby the personal representative (the "P.R.") of the decedent (i) gathers the property of the decedent from all sources and inventories it, (ii) notifies creditors of the death of the decedent, determines which claims are legitimate and pays them, (iii) identifies the beneficiaries of the decedent's estate and the property to which they are entitled, and (iv) distributes the estate property to the beneficiaries with clear title, unencumbered by obligations. We discuss probate administration in depth in Chapter 15.

In the past, the probate process was almost always time-consuming, expensive and complicated by a potpourri of arcane rules. (Consider the Monopoli excerpt in Chapter 1.) The problem received much publicity in the 1960s in the bestselling book, *How to Avoid Probate!* by Norman Dacey. As a result of the book's influence, people began looking for ways to avoid probate, and the nonprobate revolution was born.

The publication of the Dacey book and the public reaction to it brought about significant change to the probate process. Most importantly, NCCUSL drafted the UPC in 1969 (and has revised it several times since). The UPC eliminates many of the offensive aspects of the process Dacey identified. Despite this, some individuals still actively seek to avoid probate.

a.   Should One Avoid Probate?

While the changes to the law have reduced the need to avoid probate, there are still several valid reasons to do so. However, many of the earlier reasons are no longer true (they are now myths). Additionally, there are other matters to consider in making the choice.

i.   *Reasons to Avoid Wills and Probate That Are Still True*

The will might be invalidated due to an infraction of one of the formalistic rules that apply to the drafting, amending and revoking of wills.   As we discuss elsewhere in the book, the execution of a will requires compliance with specific rules; failure to meet these requirements can result in an invalid will. The rules in most states today are less formalistic than in the past, but there are still many states that have rules that can defeat the intent of the person executing the will.

The formalities required to amend a will may be greater than those required for a will substitute.   A property owner may be able to change a beneficiary form more easily — and cheaply — than a will.

If one owns real property in another state, ancillary probate proceedings will be required there, adding time and cost to the process.   Owning out-of-state realty in a revocable trust or a joint tenancy with right of survivorship avoids this problem, since the realty passes outside probate.

For high profile individuals, a will is a public document, so the media might report on matters the individual would prefer to keep private.   Trusts, contracts and beneficiary designation forms are not available to the public; wills are. Think of the public nature of the Michael Jackson will from the first chapter and the private nature of the Michael Jackson Family Trust referenced therein.

Some statutory protections and restrictions apply to wills only.   As we discuss later in the course, rules protecting spouses and the liability of certain property to the claims of creditors may be avoided by using certain will substitutes.

ii.   *Some of the Stated Reasons to Use Will Substitutes Are Illusory*

Trusts are less expensive than wills.   The fact is that the cost of setting up and administering a plan that seeks to avoid probate may be greater than the cost of drafting a will. The attorney's fees for preparing a revocable trust agreement and the other documents needed to do a "complete" plan (including a will to capture property that might fall through the cracks of even the most well-crafted estate plan) are frequently greater than the fee for preparing a traditional will. In addition, if a revocable trust is created and lasts for many years, there will be fees for re-registering and transferring title of assets to the trust and annual fees for accountants and the trustee.

Probating a will is expensive.   Actually, the cost and time associated with probating most estates is not significant. It used to be that fees charged by personal representatives were based on a percentage of the value of the estate. That is still true in a few states. In most states now, fees are based on an hourly rate. In addition, the time and cost of probating a will is often not significant, especially for (1) smaller and simple estates where there are expedited or simplified procedures (filings that are handled exclusively by the clerk of the court without the involvement or oversight of a judge), and (2) estates where no one is contesting the will.

Estate taxes can be avoided if probate is avoided.   The reality is that most assets owned at death are includible in the decedent's gross estate and subject to estate tax regardless whether they are probated or not. Much of the delay and red tape customarily associated with probate is the result of the tax laws and tax filing requirements, which cannot be eliminated through revocable trusts or other probate avoidance instruments.

iii.   In Fact, There Are Advantages to Going Through Probate

The claims of creditors are addressed and resolved during probate.   Property that passes through a probated estate is distributed to heirs and devisees free of the claims of unsecured creditors if the statutory directives are followed. Creditors normally have a limited period to prove their claims after which the claims are no longer valid. Passing clear title to property can prevent many future headaches and legal expenses.

There is an "inheritance defense" associated with acquiring "superfund" property.   The inheritance defense allows one to avoid the costs of cleanup on "superfund" toxic sites. The defense is not available for property acquired outside probate. 42 U.S.C. §9601(35)(A)(iii) ("CERCLA").

The proceedings are controlled by a judge.   Even though a judge is not normally involved in the probate process these days, a judge is readily available if needed. This may expedite disputes between beneficiaries or between the beneficiaries and the personal representative.

In most cases, the personal representative is required to prepare an accounting and report of her activities.   This is a valuable safeguard against a less-than-honest personal representative.

iv.   Other Matters to Consider

It may be better to have the entire estate plan in one document.   As stated above, developing an integrated estate plan between nonprobate and probate property is critical. Rather than having beneficiaries receiving property from a variety of sources and at a variety of values, it may be wise to name the probate estate[3] as the beneficiary of all the client's will substitutes. In this way, the will can coordinate all the asset dispositions, including those to the surviving spouse, the children and grandchildren and charities, into one comprehensive plan. Where minor children are involved, this is a particularly valuable approach because it creates an easy vehicle for the property to be placed in trust for them (via a residuary testamentary trust for their benefit) rather than having them get the property outright on the decedent's death.

---

3. Alternatively, one could name the trustee of the testamentary trust created in the will or the trustee of an inter vivos revocable trust as the beneficiary of all the nonprobate property. As compared to a will, if a revocable trust is the repository of the client's assets it has the added advantage of not converting nonprobate assets into probate property.

The documents used to avoid probate may be confusing to an unsophisticated person.   Some of the planning devices that may be employed, especially trusts, can be complicated, and compliance with their terms over an extended period may be onerous. Some clients grow weary of them.

Some planning devices are forever.   Since some trusts are irrevocable and cannot be amended, clients frequently get frustrated by their inability to make changes as their family's circumstances change. By contrast, a will, being an ambulatory document, is always subject to change until the testator dies.

Even if one carefully plans to avoid probate, it is difficult to avoid it completely.   If the decedent owns any property at his death that was not titled in the name of a trust or dealt with by another will substitute, probate is required, no matter how informal or summary the proceedings may be.[4] This is especially likely for items like clothing, jewelry, simple art, computers and home entertainment centers that do not have registration documentation and therefore are more difficult to title in the name of a trust. It is also possible that some property that is meant to pass by a will substitute may be forced into the probate estate because of certain events. This is further discussed in Section G below.

C.   THE DIFFERENT LAWS OF WILLS AND WILL SUBSTITUTES

There are stark differences between the legal requirements related to drafting, amending, revoking, interpreting and contesting wills and those applicable to will substitutes. For example, the law of wills has historically required near-perfect compliance with certain arcane requirements associated with the testator's signature, witnessing, publication and other technicalities. These requirements were designed to serve an **evidentiary** function by showing how the testator wanted to distribute the property, a **ritual (or cautionary)** function to ensure that the testator was serious about the document serving as a will, a **protective** function to prevent against undue influences on the testator and a **channeling** function to ensure that the document looked like other wills and went through the

---

4. This problem is normally handled by drafting a simple will with a provision that transfers all probate property to the decedent's revocable trust. Such a will is referred to as a "pour-over will."

established probate process.[5] By contrast, will substitutes have fewer requirements and are controlled either by contract law (since many are commercial agreements between the company and the customer, for example, policies of life insurance and accounts with financial intermediaries) or by trust law.

The fact that probate law controls wills while contract and trust law govern most will substitutes also creates differences with respect to other matters, like the level of competency one must possess in order to execute the documents and, more importantly, the process employed for distributing the property that is subject to their provisions.

Given the similarities in function between wills and will substitutes (both transfer property at death) and the fact that the law of wills has an ancient pedigree, it is understandable that courts initially found will substitutes invalid because they failed to comply with the statutory formalities required of wills. Only during the latter part of the twentieth century have courts become more accepting of will substitutes. In part, this has been driven by the recognition that the evidentiary, ritual, protective and channeling functions that the formalities serve for wills are less critical when a third party is involved and where the form is part of a business contract. Today, will substitutes are widely accepted as nontestamentary, either by statute or case law, and therefore do not need to comply with the formalities that apply to wills. UPC §6-101 states this change in the law.

UPC §6-101. Nonprobate Transfers on Death.

A provision for a nonprobate transfer on death in an insurance policy, contract of employment, bond, mortgage, promissory note, certificated or uncertificated security, account agreement, custodial agreement, deposit agreement, compensation plan, pension plan, individual retirement plan, employee benefit plan, trust, conveyance, deed of gift, marital property agreement, or other written instrument of a similar nature is nontestamentary. This subsection includes a written provision that:

(1) money or other benefits due to, controlled by, or owned by a decedent before death must be paid after the decedent's death to a person whom the decedent designates either in the instrument or in a separate writing, including a will, executed either before or at the same time as the instrument, or later;

(2) money due or to become due under the instrument ceases to be payable in the event of death of the promisee or the promisor before payment or demand; or

---

5. John H. Langbein, *Substantial Compliance with the Wills Act*, 88 HARV. L. REV. 489, 492 (1975) ("The formalities are designed to perform functions which will assure that [the testator's] estate really is distributed according to his intention.").

> (3) any property controlled by or owned by the decedent before death which is the subject of the instrument passes to a person the decedent designates either in the instrument or in a separate writing, including a will, executed either before or at the same time as the instrument, or later.

The less formal law surrounding business contracts, joint ownership and trusts has profoundly affected the law of testamentary transfers and vice versa. While the law of wills and will substitutes is more alike today than in the past, they are still not the same. This has led many involved with the drafting of the UPC and state property inheritance laws to attempt to make the two even more uniform. Professor McCouch speaks to this in the following excerpt from the same article presented above. Some of what is presented in the article is beyond your present knowledge of the subject. However, when you have finished the course, it might be worthwhile to return to this article and compare how issues are handled differently between probate and nonprobate transfers.

Grayson M.P. McCouch, Probate Law Reform and Nonprobate Transfers (cont.)
62 U. Miami L. Rev. 757 (2008)

From the outset, the drafters of the Uniform Probate Code have acknowledged the utility and legitimacy of nonprobate transfers. To be sure, the Code, as originally promulgated in 1969, focused primarily on the law of wills and probate administration and promoted salutary reforms in both areas, including streamlined wills formalities and a flexible, informal system of administration. At the same time, the Code addressed nonprobate transfers in a separate article, which included detailed rules for bank accounts held in joint-and-survivor, pay-on-death, or trust form, as well as an open-ended provision declaring any pay-on-death direction or beneficiary designation in a written contract, deed of gift, conveyance, or trust agreement to be "nontestamentary" and hence not subject to wills formalities or probate administration. Initially, the drafters seem to have been content to affirm the validity of nonprobate transfers without attempting to prescribe comprehensive rules governing construction or creditors' rights. More recently, as nonprobate transfers continue to proliferate, the drafters of the Code, along with other law reformers, have sought to "bring the law of probate and nonprobate transfers into greater unison." Accordingly, in 1990, as part of a comprehensive overhaul of the Code's articles concerning wills and intestacy, the drafters rewrote several key rules of construction originally aimed at wills — notably those relating to survival, lapse, and divorce — and expanded them to apply more broadly to will substitutes.

The 1990 revisions reflect a growing awareness of the functional similarities between will substitutes and specific bequests, as well as a recognition that rules of construction, developed in the law of wills to discover a transferor's presumed intent, also lend themselves to filling gaps in the relatively fragmented and underdeveloped law of will substitutes. In keeping with the goal of unification, reformers have also sought to ameliorate some of the most rigidly formalistic aspects of traditional wills doctrine. For example, the 1990 Code revisions introduced a "harmless error" provision that allows an instrument to be admitted to probate as a will, notwithstanding defects of execution, upon a clear and convincing showing that the instrument was so intended. . . .

The unification project extends not only to intent-furthering constructional rules and protective or remedial doctrines, but also, in principle, to substantive restrictions that protect the interests of third parties such as a decedent's surviving spouse or creditors. One of the Code's most notable innovations is the concept of the "augmented estate" as the basis for the surviving spouse's elective share. The Code allows the surviving spouse to look beyond the decedent's net probate estate to other property, including the decedent's nonprobate transfers, in determining the size of the elective share and the sources available for its payment. In this way, the Code discourages transferors from attempting to defeat the surviving spouse's elective share by means of nonprobate transfers.[6]

In a similar vein, the Code seeks to prevent the use of nonprobate transfers to defeat creditors' claims. A provision added in 1998 makes the beneficiaries of nonprobate transfers personally liable to the decedent's probate estate for allowed creditors' claims to the extent the estate is insolvent. . . .[7]

As the McCouch article highlights, the drive to unify the laws of wills and will substitutes has continued for some time now. Do you agree with this movement to unify the two laws? As we proceed into the study of wills, the similarities and differences with will substitutes will be highlighted. Some of the similarities and differences are discussed in this chapter while others are presented in later chapters.

---

6. [A detailed discussion of the augmented estate and the elective share, including how nonprobate transfers are captured in the calculation, is reserved for Chapter 12 — Eds.]

7. [The obligation of the probate estate and the takers of nonprobate property to satisfy the claims of the creditors of the decedent and the estate of the decedent are more fully explored in Chapter 15 — Eds.]

D. DETERMINING WHICH PROPERTY IS PROBATED AND WHICH IS NOT

When we look at how property is transferred to others at a person's death, the world is divided into probate property and nonprobate property. To identify into which category property falls, it is first necessary to determine whether the decedent has an ownership interest in property in fact or in substance and then whether there is a will substitute instrument that governs its disposition upon the individual's death.

Property ownership interests can be divided into two categories: actual ownership and ownership in substance.

Actual ownership, for these purposes, means a beneficial ownership interest in property at the time of death, whether owned alone or jointly, present or future, vested or contingent, *so long as it does not terminate on the person's death*. It does not include a non-beneficial interest, such as that held by a trustee. While a trustee has title to the property in a trust, it is held in a fiduciary capacity; the trustee *qua* trustee does not own a beneficial interest in the property that she may pass along to others either through probate or outside of it.

> **Example 1:**   At his death, Chris owned the following property in fee simple: his principal residence in San Francisco, a condominium at Lake Tahoe at which he vacationed in the summer and winter, several cars, a checking account and 10,000 shares of Microsoft stock. Chris also owned a one-half interest in real estate with his sister, titled as tenants in common, and a 25% partnership interest in ABC Partnership. All of these items, including the one-half tenancy interest and the 25% partnership interest, represent actual ownership interests in property by Chris.

> **Example 2:**   Raja created a trust and funded it by transferring stocks to the trustee. The trust provisions gave his daughter the right to all the income for life and, on her death, the property would be distributed to Gilad, if living. If Gilad was not alive at daughter's death, the property would be paid to Riyad. Daughter, Gilad and Riyad all have property ownership; the trustee does not. Despite their having ownership interests, daughter and Gilad (if daughter is still alive) do not have anything to pass at their deaths since their interests terminate at that time.

"**Ownership in substance** refers to property that the decedent did not own but over which the decedent had sufficient control"[8] to become the owner, such as property subject to a power to revoke or a general power

---

8. Restatement (Third) of Property; Wills & Other Donative Transfers §1.1(b).

of appointment.[9] "[I]t is an arrangement respecting property or contract rights that is established during the donor's life under which . . . substantial lifetime rights of dominion, control, possession, or enjoyment are retained by the donor."[10]

Whether an ownership interest in property (actual or in substance) is probate or nonprobate property depends on the existence of a will substitute. If there is a valid will substitute, the will substitute controls the passing of property leaving nothing to be added to the probate estate. Probate property also includes property acquired by the probate estate after the decedent's death. This would include, for example, proceeds of a wrongful death action. Significantly, the probate estate also includes what would typically be nonprobate property where the individual exercises a power in favor of his estate, such as naming the estate through a general power of appointment, or designates his estate as the beneficiary of a contract, as might occur with an insurance policy. For other examples of situations that might lead property subject to a will substitute to be included in the probate estate, see the discussion of "Failed Will Substitutes" in Section G below.

While trusts and, to a lesser degree, joint tenancies in real property tend to be drafted by attorneys, most other will substitutes are prepared by financial institutions or insurance companies. As part of the package that accompanies the product they sell, companies provide the owner with the right to designate who should receive the property at death. This is accomplished on a beneficiary designation form. These forms perform the same function as bequests in a will by directing distribution of the property upon the death of the decedent. On presentation of a death certificate, the insurance company, retirement plan administrator, bank or other third party must pay the contracted amount to the primary or secondary beneficiary.

With the exception of trusts, which are only briefly discussed here because they are fully explored in Chapters 5-8, we are now going to examine the law associated with each of the will substitutes in greater detail.

But first we turn to the UPC, which uses the term "governing instrument" as an all-inclusive one to refer to wills, deeds and will substitutes. It is an important definition.

UPC §1-201. General Definitions

(18) *"Governing instrument"* means a deed, will, trust, insurance or annuity policy, account with POD designation, security registered in

---

9. Powers of appointment will be discussed separately in Chapter 8. For our purposes here though it is enough to know that the holder of a general power of appointment has the ability to direct that the subject property be paid to herself.

10. RESTATEMENT (THIRD) OF PROPERTY; WILLS & OTHER DONATIVE TRANSFERS §7.1(a).

> beneficiary form (TOD), pension, profit-sharing, retirement, or similar
> benefit plan, instrument creating or exercising a power of appoint-
> ment or a power of attorney, or a dispositive, appointive, or nomina-
> tive instrument of any similar type.

1.   Trusts

A trust is a legal relationship that separates legal ownership (the property is
titled in the name of "trustee") from beneficial ownership (the present and
future interests are held by the "beneficiaries"). The transferor (the "settlor") transfers title to the property (known as the "res," "principal" or "corpus" when in the trust) to the trustee to hold for the benefit of the present
and future beneficiaries.

Trusts are created for a variety of reasons, including the desire to avoid
probate, to minimize taxes, to have a professional trustee (like a bank)
manage the property for a donee who is young or unsophisticated with
investment strategies and money management, to allow someone in the
future to decide who needs property based on a set of criteria the settlor
establishes in the trust or to protect the property from the claims of the
creditors of the donee. Some trusts are better than others in accomplishing
these goals.

Trusts are categorized based on what rights or powers the settlor
retained and when they were created. As to the former, trusts are either
irrevocable (cannot be revoked or modified) or revocable (can be revoked
and amended). Trusts are either inter vivos (created during life) or testamentary (created in a will and funded with property of the estate).

From the perspective of ownership under state property law, the settlor no longer owns property that has been transferred into trust; the
trustee does. Thus, regardless of whether the trust is revocable or irrevocable, the property owned by an *inter vivos* trust is not probate property of
the settlor; by contrast, the property that funds a *testamentary* trust does go
through probate.[11]

a.   Revocable Trusts

In a revocable trust, the individual reserves the right to revoke all or a
part of the trust or amend its terms. With most revocable trusts, the individual wears many hats: The person is not only the settlor but is also the

---

11. Since this chapter focuses on nonprobate transfers, we postpone the expanded discussion of testamentary trusts until Chapters 5-8. A testamentary trust is established in the
decedent's will. Rather than having a separate document called a trust agreement with all
the terms of the trust stated in it, a testamentary trust is created in the will and all the terms
are embedded in the will. Since a testamentary trust only accepts property that has gone
through the will and been probated, by the time the testamentary trust takes effect, it is too
late to avoid probate.

trustee, the beneficiary of the income and a permissible distributee of the principal. Typically, all these interests are retained by the settlor until death (or disability), at which point the trust becomes irrevocable, a successor trustee takes over and the other beneficiaries' rights to income and principal come to the forefront.

Because the settlor wears so many hats, in some ways the transferor is not viewed as having parted with the property at all. It is as if the settlor still owns the property. Thus, for tax purposes and the right of future creditors of the settlor to garnish the principal, property in a revocable trust is treated as though it still belongs to the settlor.[12] Regardless of how revocable trusts are viewed for other purposes, they are valid will substitutes and result in the trust property bypassing probate. The trust, not the will or intestacy, determines what happens to the principal on the settlor's death.

A revocable trust is the closest will substitute to an actual will. It is the paradigmatic will substitute for several reasons: The trust's corpus typically includes most of the settlor's nonprobate property[13] not already covered by other will substitutes, the property is available to the individual with almost no restrictions during life and the property gets transmitted to others at the decedent's death pursuant to its terms. It should be apparent that this is very much like what happens with probate property owned by the individual during life that gets passed at death by will.

> **Example:** Alyssa created a revocable trust while she was alive, naming herself as trustee and retaining the right to the income for her life. The trust instrument provides that when Alyssa dies, the corpus of the trust is to be paid to Bertram, Alyssa's husband, if he survives her, and if Bertram does not survive Alyssa, then to Doctors Without Borders. If Alyssa dies without revoking the trust, the trust corpus will be distributed pursuant to the trust instrument and will not pass through probate. The corpus will go to Bertram, if he survives her, or if not to Doctors Without Borders.

---

12. If you are having trouble understanding what a revocable trust is at this early stage of your learning, it may be helpful to analogize a revocable trust to a bank account. Each contains property of the individual, one in a vehicle called a bank account (and held by the bank) and the other in a trust (held by a trustee). With a bank account, access is gained by withdrawing the funds or closing the account; with a revocable trust, the funds are similarly available to the settlor by exercising rights of withdrawal or revocation. As you can see, whether we are talking about a bank account or a revocable trust, the property is fully within the individual's control by the stroke of a pen, so to speak. The individual can do what she wants with the property during her life and, on her death, pass it to others. In the case of a bank account, absent joint ownership or a POD or TOD designation, the property passes by the terms of a will or by intestacy; while in the case of a revocable trust, the property passes by the terms of the trust. Of course, a bank account and a revocable trust have many differences: A bank does not own the money in the account, whereas the trustee holds legal title to property in the trust, and a bank, unlike a trustee, does not owe fiduciary duties to the beneficiaries of the bank account.

13. This is in contrast to most other will substitutes, which are more limited and consist only of a single asset, like an insurance policy.

b.   Irrevocable Trusts

When it comes to irrevocable trusts, the settlor does not retain the power to revoke or amend the trust. With some irrevocable trusts, the settlor may have parted with all rights and interests in the trust; with others, the settlor may have retained some interest in or right to the transferred property. The interests retained may be minor, such as the right to replace the trustee, or extensive, like the right to the income from the trust for life. As was the case with revocable trusts, the principal of an irrevocable trust is not included in the settlor's probate estate at death, even if the settlor retained significant rights and powers. The terms of the trust determine what happens to the principal, if anything, on the settlor's death.

> **Example:**   After her husband's death four years ago, Charlotte irrevocably transferred ownership of certain stocks and securities into a trust. According to its terms, Charlotte's son is entitled to income from the property for his life and, on his death, the trust terminates and the property will be distributed to son's children in fee simple. The gift is a complete transfer of her ownership rights: Charlotte has no continuing interest in the property of the trust. Charlotte's death has no effect on the trust, and the trust is neither her probate nor her nonprobate property.

> **Example:**   After her husband's death four years ago, Charlotte irrevocably transferred ownership of her principal residence into a trust, reserving the right to remain in the house for the rest of her life. According to its terms, the trust terminates on her death and the house will be distributed to her daughter in fee simple. The gift is only a partial one, represented by the remainder interest she gave to her daughter. When Charlotte dies, the trust property (the house) will pass to her daughter outside probate.

2.   *Joint Tenancies with Rights of Survivorship*

Joint tenancies have sometimes been referred to as the "poor person's will (substitute)" because most of them are created without legal advice. A joint tenancy is probably the most commonly used device to avoid probate because it is easy to understand and inexpensive to create.

Joint tenancies are a type of common ownership distinguished by the coexistence of what are referred to as the four unities: the unity of interest, the unity of title, the unity of time and the unity of possession. "In essence, the common law joint tenancy required that the several tenants have one and the same interests accruing by one and the same conveyance, commencing at the same time and held by one and the same undivided possession." *Minonk State Bank v. Grassman*, 432 N.E.2d 386 (Ill. App. Ct. 1982).

The most important aspect of a joint tenancy is that, assuming no previous severance (such as by one joint owner selling her interest to a third party), on the death of one of the joint tenants title passes exclusively to the surviving joint tenant or tenants.

> At common law, one could not create a joint tenancy in himself and another by a direct conveyance. It was necessary for joint tenants to acquire their interests at the same time (unity of time) and by the same conveyancing instrument (unity of title). . . . So, in order to create a valid joint tenancy where one of the proposed joint tenants already owned an interest in the property, it was first necessary to convey the property to a disinterested third person, a "straw man," who then conveyed the title to the ultimate grantees as joint tenants.

Riddle v. Harmon, 162 Cal. Rptr. 530, 532 (Ct. App. 1980).

However, most states have modified the common law with respect to the four unities by relaxing the requirements and providing that an estate with all the characteristics of a common law joint tenancy can be created through a conveyance from the grantor directly to herself and others as grantees, without the intervention of a third party.

Most husbands and wives and people registered as domestic partners or parties in a civil union own bank accounts, brokerage accounts and their homes and other real estate in joint tenancy with rights of survivorship. We will defer discussion of joint tenancies with bank accounts and brokerage accounts until Sections D.5 and D.6 below.

When real property is involved, the joint tenancy must be in writing to be in compliance with the Statute of Frauds. In some states, real property owned by spouses and, in some jurisdictions, by legally registered domestic partners, might be held as a tenancy by the entirety. Although similar to joint tenancy, tenancy by the entirety treats the estate as a unit, which means that neither spouse can sell assets without the other's consent. Tenancy by the entirety provides creditor protection.

3.   Life Insurance

Insurance can be a useful tool in estate planning. The governing instrument (*i.e.*, the will substitute) that transmits the proceeds on the death of the insured is the insurance company's beneficiary designation form completed by the owner of the policy. So long as the beneficiary is not the decedent's estate, the proceeds of a life insurance policy[14] are not probated. The greatest advantage of life insurance over other will substitutes is that, if

---

14. Other kinds of policies that may have a death benefit feature and a form to complete designating a beneficiary upon the insured's death include accidental death and dismemberment insurance and business travel accident insurance.

ownership is properly structured, life insurance proceeds not only bypass probate but also escape estate taxes.

Without getting into all the details of insurance law, anyone who has an insurable interest in a person may take out a policy on that person's life. Normally, the insured buys the policy on her own life. However, a family member or a trust whose beneficiaries are family members may also buy a policy on someone's life. The owner of the policy decides who the beneficiaries are. In addition, the owner may borrow against the value of the policy if the policy has an investment component to it, as is true with a whole life or universal life contract. These rights are sometimes referred to as "the incidents of ownership," especially in the tax context. The proceeds of a life insurance policy escape estate taxes if (i) the decedent was not the owner of the policy, (ii) the decendent did not have any incidents of ownership at any time during the three years prior to her death and (iii) the decedent's estate is not the beneficiary of the policy. Tax planning associated with life insurance is discussed in greater detail in Chapter 14.

> **Example:**   When she died, Emily owned a life insurance policy on her life. She had completed a beneficiary designation form for the policy, directing that on her death the insurance company should pay the proceeds of the policy to her husband, Roger, if he survived her, and if not to her estate. If Roger survives Emily's death, then the proceeds will pass to him directly and will not be part of her probate estate. If Roger does not survive her, then the insurance company will pay the proceeds to her estate and they will become part of the probate estate.

4.   Annuities and Retirement Accounts

Significant wealth resides in annuities and retirement plans, such as 401(k), 403(b), Keogh, pension, profit-sharing and self-employed plans (SEP) and individual retirement accounts (IRA). Like insurance contracts, the individual designates the beneficiary on a form provided by the investment company or retirement plan administrator. Much of the law associated with retirement plans in the workplace is preempted by federal law, the Employee Retirement Income Security Act (ERISA) of 1974. If the covered employee is married, then ERISA restricts the employee's choice of beneficiary — basically limiting the choice to the person's spouse unless the spouse signs a fully informed waiver of that right. So long as the beneficiary is not the individual's estate,[15] the annuity or retirement proceeds will escape probate.

---

15. Besides avoiding probate, it is wise to avoid naming one's estate as the beneficiary of an annuity or retirement plan because there are some adverse tax consequences for doing so and there are greater creditor protections if such items pass outside probate.

5.   *Contracts of Deposit with Financial Institutions*

Checking and savings accounts and certificates of deposit between a depositor and a financial institution can be set up in several different ways. Some ways will give rise to will substitute characterization and others will not. The ownership structure is designated in a form supplied by the institution. There are few formal requirements involved in the execution of the form. UPC §6-204 provides a form for use by banks, though it is rare to find a bank that uses it and has not created its own instead.

UPC §6-203. Types of Account; Existing Accounts.

> (a) An account may be for a single party or multiple parties. A multiple-party account may be with or without a right of survivorship between the parties. Subject to Section 6-212(c), either a single-party account or a multiple-party account may have a POD designation, an agency designation, or both.

Where only one person may access the funds in the account, it is a single-party account; if more than one person may have access, it can be established as a multiple-party account. A multiple-party account can be a tenancy in common or a joint tenancy with right of survivorship. A single-party account or a joint tenancy can be coupled with a payable-on-death designation.

Personnel at banks often do not make clear to their depositors the many variations that are possible. Can you recall when you opened an account at a bank whether someone explained all the possibilities to you?

a.   Single-Party Accounts

If a deposit account is owned by an individual and does not include a payable-on-death beneficiary designation (discussed below), the balance in the account passes as probate property. UPC §6-212(c).

b.   Multiple-Party Accounts

A multiple-party account is defined in UPC §6-201(5) as "an account payable on request to one or more of two or more parties, whether or not a right of survivorship is mentioned." According to the comments to the section, it includes any contract of deposit "having more than one owner with a present interest in the account . . . regardless of whether the terms of the account refer to it as 'joint tenancy' or as 'tenancy in common,' regardless of whether the parties named are coupled by 'or' or 'and,' and regardless of whether any reference is made to survivorship rights, whether expressly or by abbreviation such as JTWROS or JT TEN. Survivorship rights in a multiple-party account are determined by the terms of the account and by statute, and survivorship is not a necessary incident of a multiple-party account."

A bank may permit four different types of multiple-party accounts: a tenancy in common; a true joint tenancy account; an account with a pay-on-death designation; and an account which provides lifetime rights for the party added to the account but does not provide after-death rights (sometimes called a convenience account). In practice, almost all multiple-party accounts are joint tenancies.

A tenancy in common for a bank account is rare. If one exists, the share of the account owned by each party is "property of the decedent" and, assuming no payable-on-death provision, is probate property.

Joint tenancies are far more common in the case of bank accounts. A true joint tenancy account is one that provides each person named on the account the right to make withdrawals while both (or all) are alive and then provides that at the death of one joint tenant, the other joint tenant(s) becomes the owner(s) of the entire account. Spouses, parents and children and domestic partners often maintain joint tenancy accounts for savings and to pay household expenses. If an account is established as a joint account, *for example*, "John and Mary, as joint tenants" or "John and Mary, jointly," it is presumed to be a joint tenancy with right of survivorship, not a tenancy in common.

Sometimes the owner of a deposit account will add another person to the account merely to enable that person to withdraw money to pay the owner's bills or otherwise to use the money for the owner's care. An elderly parent might add a child or a caretaker to an account for this reason. The intention of the account owner is to allow the other person to have access to the account while the original owner is alive, but not to transfer the account balance to the other person at death. Unfortunately, the standard form used by banks usually creates a "joint account" and does not offer the account owner the choice of a "convenience" account. This has resulted in many disagreements about what the account owner intended when she added the other person to the account. In some states, evidence of the account owner's intent when she created the account can be used to show that the person named on the account should not receive the account at the original owner's death. In other states, the form is determinative and no other evidence is permitted. See the discussion of "convenience accounts" below.

> **Example:**   Katie and Stan created a joint bank account with right of survivorship. When they created the account, they both signed a signature card indicating their intent that the account be this type of account. If Katie dies first, the account will not be included in Katie's probate estate, and Stan will become the sole owner of the account. If

Stan dies later, with the account titled in his name alone, the account will be included in Stan's estate.

c. Payable on Death (POD) Beneficiary Designation

With this type of an account, the owner designates who should receive payment from the account upon her death. POD designations are generally only employed with single-party accounts; most multiple-party accounts are held in joint tenancy so that the funds already pass outside probate to the survivor. The POD designation converts what would otherwise have been a probate asset of the owner to a nonprobate one.

In all respects, the account holder is the owner and is the only person that has access to the funds in the account while she is alive. The beneficiary stated on the POD designation form is not a party to the account and cannot withdraw funds during the life of the owner. The only significance of the POD designation is that the account does not go through probate. The account holder can revoke the POD designation at any time.

> **Example:** Barbara had a savings account at Big Bank. She signed a POD designation form that said "pay on death to Yvette." Barbara also owned securities that were held in a brokerage account, and she had executed a Transfer on Death (TOD) form listing Yvette as the TOD beneficiary. When Barbara dies, neither account will be included in Barbara's probate estate. Yvette will become the owner of both accounts.

d. Convenience Accounts

A relatively new item in the banking world is a "convenience account." A "depositor" (primary account holder) can create such an account for the purpose of permitting a "convenience depositor" access to the funds in the account, both to make deposits and to withdraw funds. Obviously, this can be of great advantage to a family if the depositor is disabled and needs to have someone else have access to the account. The convenience depositor has neither an ownership interest in the account nor rights to the balance in the account upon the death of the depositor, which distinguishes it from a joint account or a POD account. As such, the designation of the account as a "convenience account" does not transform a probate asset into a nonprobate one. *See, e.g.*, Florida Banks and Banking Code §655.80.

The following case presents the difficulty sometimes encountered in distinguishing between a joint tenancy with right of survivorship account and a convenience account since access to the account by the parties during life is similar. Of course, the results at death are very different. Note also the comment in the opinion that "the party contesting the title of the survivor is required to establish one of the following: fraud, undue influence, lack of capacity to make a gift, or that the account was opened for the convenience of the deceased depositor. . . ." These are concepts that are explored in detail in Chapter 11 with respect to wills but apply equally to will substitutes.

Estate of Helen Butta
746 N.Y.S.2d 586 (Sur. Ct. 2002)

LEE L. HOLZMAN, J.

This proceeding, relating to the ownership of account 005701218918 opened at Chase Manhattan Bank (now J.P. Morgan Chase) on January 23, 1996 in the names of the decedent, Helen Butta, and the petitioner, Nicholas Pagani, was tried before the court without a jury. The "Statement of Issues" submitted pursuant to Uniform Rule 207.30 presents the following two questions: 1) Are the proceeds of the account an estate asset payable to the respondent, executor, because the account was a convenience account? 2) Are the proceeds of the account payable to the petitioner as the surviving joint tenant of a joint account with right of survivorship?

The decedent died at the age of 91 on August 18, 1999. Her will, executed on June 23, 1999, has been admitted to probate. The residuary estate is bequeathed to a revocable trust that was executed on the same day as the will. The petitioner, who is the decedent's great nephew, is not a beneficiary of the estate. In an accounting proceeding in this estate, the executor valued the estate assets at almost $4,000,000.00.

There is no dispute with regard to the history of the account. The $240,000.00 deposited to open the account was supplied by the decedent. On the date of the decedent's death the balance in the account was $151,485.75. All of the withdrawals from the account, whether by check or by "ATM," were made by the petitioner solely for his own benefit. All of the statements and canceled checks for the account were mailed to the decedent at her residence. The decedent also reported all of the interest earned on the account on her income tax returns.

One of the problems in ascertaining whether the presumption of section 675(b) of the Banking Law is applicable is that the bank has been unable to locate and produce the original signature card. Victoria J. Linton, who was a customer service representative at the bank when the account was opened, testified that she had probably opened between 500 and 1,000 accounts for customers during the years that she was employed as a service representative. Although she did not remember any specific conversation with the petitioner and the decedent on the date that the account was opened, she did recall that they came into the bank to open the account and that she told them among other things that the account would be payable to the survivor of them upon the death of the other. She believed that one of the reasons that she remembered the occasion was that she thought that the petitioner was a customer of the bank. In any event, she stated that she knows that she advised the petitioner and the decedent that this was a survivorship account because in January of 1996 Chase would not open an account in two names unless it was a survivorship account. She testified that since Chase did not have accounts without survivorship rights, the title to a joint account with right of survivorship might be any of the following: "A or B," "A and B," or "A and B JTWROS." The bank was able to produce an "electronic signature card summary" which is an electronic redacted version of the signature card. This summary contained: the account number, the names of both the decedent and the petitioner under the "Account Title," the letter "J" under the "Account Type" and the electronic signatures of both the decedent and the petitioner.

. . . The petitioner testified that after the death of the decedent's husband in 1989 he would go to the decedent's residence about once a week. He did various chores for her, including writing checks, making minor repairs and collecting rents from her apartment house tenants. He maintained that the decedent was the person who was primarily responsible for operating the property that she owned.

The last witness was the decedent's accountant who prepared both her personal and business tax returns. He confirmed that all of the interest earned on the account was reported on the decedent's returns. Although he did not testify that the petitioner was ever present when he discussed the decedent's affairs with her, he stated that the decedent depended upon the petitioner with regard to the operation of her real estate interests.

Section 675(b) of the Banking Law provides that when a deposit is made in the name of the depositor and another person to be paid to either or the survivor of them that "the making of such deposit . . . shall, in the absence of fraud or undue influence, be prima facie evidence in any action . . . of the intention of both depositors . . . to vest title to such deposit . . . and additions and accruals thereon, in such survivor." Any party who challenges the title of the survivor bears "the burden of proof in refuting such prima facie evidence."

The petitioner contends that the proof adduced brings into play the statutory presumption and that he should prevail because the respondent failed to rebut this presumption. The respondent contends that the statutory presumption is not applicable because the petitioner failed to produce the signature card containing the required survivorship language and that there is no credible evidence to establish survivorship rights in the petitioner. Additionally, he asserts that the proof adduced established that there was a confidential relationship between the decedent and the petitioner which creates an inference of undue influence that was not rebutted and leads to the conclusion that the account was created solely for the convenience of the decedent.

Numerous Appellate Division cases have stated that the presumption of title vesting in the survivor under section 675 of the Banking Law does not apply where the signature card for the account failed to contain the words "payable to either or the survivor" or similar survivorship language.

These cases as well as the leading case of *Matter of Fenelon*, 262 N.Y. 308, 186 N.E. 794, clearly hold that survivorship language on the signature card suffices to establish a prima facie case under the statute. However, it does not necessarily follow either from these cases or the language of section 675 of the Banking Law that the statutory presumption is restricted to cases where the signature card contains survivorship language. . . .

This court . . . holds that while survivorship language on the signature card itself is the best evidence to give rise to the statutory presumption, and, perhaps, in most cases the only practical way, it is not the exclusive way. The statutory presumption arises upon any proof that clearly establishes the deposit was made and credited in the name of both parties to be paid to either or the survivor of them.

In any event, the issue of whether survivorship language on the signature card is the exclusive means by which the statutory presumption arises is only a question of the quantum of proof that the survivor is required to adduce to prevail because it is well established that the surviving tenant will prevail, without the benefit of the statutory presumption, by establishing a common law joint account with right of survivorship. Once the survivor has presented a prima facie case for a survivorship account, whether it be established under the statutory presumption or by meeting the burden of proof required under common law principles, the party contesting the title of the survivor is required to establish one of the following: fraud, undue influence, lack of capacity to make a gift, or that the account was opened for the convenience of the deceased depositor. Furthermore, in those cases where an account is determined to be a true joint account each joint tenant is vested with a present one-half interest in the money deposited even though only one of them was the sole donor.

Here, the petitioner cannot be blamed for the failure of the signature card to be in evidence because it was the bank that inadvertently lost or destroyed the card. Under these circumstances it cannot be presumed that the signature card signed by the decedent and the petitioner did or did not contain survivorship language. However, the uncontroverted proof adduced established: that the redacted electronic signature card reflects that the type of account was "J," a joint account; that the only type of account that the bank would open at the time that this account was opened in the names of two depositors was a joint account with survivorship rights; and that the bank employee who opened the account told the decedent and the petitioner that the account upon the death of one of them was payable to the survivor. Although this employee appears to have been mistaken as to the reason why she remembered the decedent and the petitioner, there was no reason to doubt her credibility. Her testimony is similar to the testimony of an attorney who supervises the execution of numerous wills and can be positive that a particular will was executed with the required statutory formalities without necessarily being accurate as to all of the other details regarding the execution ceremony. Under the unique fact pattern presented the court holds, in the alternative, that the deposit was made in the names of the decedent and the petitioner payable to either or the survivor, entitling the petitioner to the presumption under section 675(b) of the Banking Law that the proceeds on deposit in the account vested in him as the surviving joint tenant of the account, or that the petitioner adduced sufficient proof to meet his burden of proof under common law principles that the account was intended to be a joint account with survivorship rights.

The bank statements and canceled checks for the account that are in evidence do not support the respondent's contention that the account was opened for the convenience of the decedent. Instead, they indicate that the decedent knew that the petitioner was using the account for his own benefit and that she did not object. The statements and canceled checks were mailed to the decedent's home from the time the account was opened in January, 1996 until her death in August, 1999 and there is no reason to believe that she did not read them. They reflect that the petitioner had issued more than 100 checks and made more than 100 withdrawals on an "ATM" card solely for his benefit, with the result that the initial deposit of $240,000.00 had dwindled to $151,485.75 on the date that the decedent had died. Although the proof adduced indicated that the petitioner assisted the decedent with chores, including her real estate interests, there was no proof that she relied solely upon the petitioner or that she was in any way incompetent. To the contrary, it appears that the decedent lived by herself, consulted with her accountant without anyone else being present and that, more than three years after the account was opened, she executed both a lifetime trust and a will under which the petitioner did not receive any portion of her substantial estate. The fact that the decedent decided to reward the petitioner, in gratitude for the services that he performed for her, with a joint account with survivorship rights in an amount equal to approximately 6% of the death value of her assets does not in any way reflect that he was in such a confidential relationship with her that it should be inferred that he exerted undue influence with regard to the account. To reach this conclusion, it would also have to be concluded either that the petitioner did not want to exert undue influence with regard to the balance of the decedent's assets or that he was unable to.

For the reasons stated above, the court holds that the account is a joint account with right of survivorship. Accordingly, a decree may be settled directing the respondent to deliver to the petitioner any tax waiver for the account that is in his possession, directing the bank to recognize the petitioner as the sole owner of the account and denying the claim of the estate to any portion of the account.

NOTES AND QUESTIONS

1.   *The correct presumption.* Do you think the court was correct in applying the presumption despite the absence of the signature card? Do you feel the evidence introduced by petitioner, Nicholas Pagani, was sufficient to raise the presumption? Do you think the result is sound as a policy matter?

2.   *Understanding what you are doing.* Do you believe Helen Butta knew the type of account she was opening and understood what would happen with the balance upon her death?

3.   *Presuming and rebutting.* The presumption in favor of joint tenancy with right of survivorship stated in §675 of the Banking Law in *Butta* is common. *See, e.g.,* FLORIDA BANKS AND BANKING CODE §655.79: "The presumption created in this section may be overcome only by proof of fraud or undue influence or clear and convincing proof of a contrary intent. . . ."

6.   Security Accounts

A security account, like one at Charles Schwab or e*trade, includes "(i) a reinvestment account associated with a security, a securities account with a broker, a cash balance in a brokerage account, cash, interest, earnings, or dividends earned or declared on a security in an account, a reinvestment account, or a brokerage account, whether or not credited to the account before the owner's death, or (ii) a cash balance or other property held for or due to the owner of a security as a replacement for or product of an account security, whether or not credited to the account before the owner's death." UPC §6-301(5). The rules for security accounts are sufficiently similar to those for deposit accounts with financial institutions that there is no need to repeat the discussion other than some nomenclature. UPC §6-301 *et seq.* Transfer on death (TOD) beneficiary designations are to security accounts what POD beneficiary designations are to contracts of deposit with financial institutions. While TOD is the term usually used regarding security accounts, UPC §6-305 also permits the term POD to be used because of the "familiarity, rooted in experience with certificates of deposit and other deposit accounts in banks, with the abbreviation POD as signaling a valid nonprobate death benefit or transfer on death." Comment, UPC §6-305.

7.   Transfer on Death Deeds for Real Estate

The ability to transfer assets using a TOD designation also can be useful for transferring real estate and avoiding probate in states that have authorized transfer on death deeds or TOD deeds, known in some states as beneficiary deeds. Thirteen states have authorized these deeds,[16] and the ULC, when it was known as the NCCUSL, has approved the Uniform Real Property Transfer on Death Act, so more jurisdictions will likely make TOD deeds available. An owner of real property can use a TOD deed to name the beneficiary who will succeed to ownership at the owner's death. The execution of a TOD deed creates no current interest in the beneficiary and is not a completed gift for property or tax purposes. The owner must record the deed in order for the deed to be given effect. The owner can revoke the designation at any time by recording a new TOD deed, recording a revocation of the deed or disposing of the property. If the owner records the deed and does not revoke it, the beneficiary can obtain title to the property at the owner's death without going through probate.

Sometimes property owners use a deed that creates a joint tenancy with right of survivorship to avoid probate. A TOD deed is a better option if the owner simply wants to transfer the property at death. Unlike a joint tenancy deed, the TOD deed creates no immediate interest in the beneficiary and can be revoked at any time before death. The property will not be subject to the creditors of the beneficiary while the property owner is alive because the beneficiary does not own an interest in the property.

Property subject to a TOD deed remains subject to the creditors of the property owner and the beneficiary takes the property subject to any claims, mortgages or liens.

See Susan N. Gary, *Transfer-on-Death Deeds: The Nonprobate Revolution Continues*, 41 REAL PROP. PROB. & TR. J. 529, 532 (2006).

EXERCISE

Go to the Internet. Search for copies of the documents identified in the chart in Appendix A. Download them for your files. Complete the chart.

E. GIFTING — NOT EXACTLY A WILL SUBSTITUTE

Gifting is a part of the arsenal of all estate planning attorneys. Inter vivos gifting can be either in fee simple or in trust. One can give away all rights in the property or only some, thus retaining others. Making gifts is not a will substitute in the strict sense of the term because the donor does not use or hold the property throughout life, nor is the property transferred to another as a result of the owner's death. Nonetheless, because successful gifting

---

16. Missouri (1989), Kansas (1997), Ohio (2000), New Mexico (2001), Arizona (2002), Nevada (2003), Colorado (2004), Arkansas (2005), Wisconsin (2006), Montana (2007), Oklahoma (2008), Minnesota (2008) and Indiana (2009).

causes the subject property to bypass the probate estate and because unsuccessful gifting means the property is still owned by the decedent and likely included in the probate estate, it is discussed in this chapter.

> **Example:**   Six years ago, Jasmine gave her daughter, Carrie, 200 shares of stock in the family's closely held corporation, retaining the remaining 300 shares. In her will, Jasmine transfers half her shares in the business to Carrie and half to Roberto, her son. If the gift six years ago was successful, only 300 shares are included in Jasmine's estate, half each going to Carrie and Roberto. If the gift was not effective for some reason, 500 shares are included in Jasmine's estate, divided equally between Carrie and Roberto.

While the effect of gifting is that the property avoids probate, gifting is not normally done for that reason.   Parents often make gifts to their children or grandchildren, providing money for things like schooling, buying a home, investing in a business or taking care of bills when things are not going well. Assuming the parents have the resources to help and are on good terms with the intended donees, they usually want to lend a hand. The gifts help the kids and make the parents feel good. In the above example, Jasmine may have given Carrie the stock because she was getting involved in the family business and she deserved to have an ownership interest.

Taxes frequently play a role in deciding whether to make gifts. As more fully developed in Chapter 14, if the circumstances are right and if the donor is selective about the assets transferred, the donor may be able to avoid, or at least minimize, gift and estate taxes. In addition, gifting may shift the responsibility for paying tax on income from revenue-generating property from a high income tax bracket donor (usually the parent) to a lower income tax bracket donee (usually the child), resulting in a tax savings for the family as a whole.

People also make gifts to protect their assets from the claims of creditors. If a person gives away her property prior to incurring debt, later creditors of the donor typically do not have the right to attach the property in the hands of the transferee. It is not uncommon for a person in a high-risk profession, like a surgeon or real estate developer, to want to protect assets in case of subsequent malpractice or other negligence-based actions.

1.   *What Distinguishes a Gift from Other Property Transfers?*

In what way is a gift, either outright or in trust, different from other transfers of property? There are a variety of transactions that transfer property from one person to another — a sale, compensation for services, a loan, a bailment or a gift. The principal distinction between the other transactions and a gift is the element of consideration — a gift is a gratuitous transfer while the others all have a quid pro quo element to them. In the non-gifting situations, the subject property is disposed of or pledged and something is received in exchange. The property itself or the replacement item, possibly cash or a receivable of some kind, is included in the decedent's probate estate if it has not been disposed of subsequent to the transaction. By contrast, if there is a completed gift, the decedent has nothing remaining to include in the probate estate.

2.   Methods of Gifting

As you likely remember from your first-year property course, if a person owns property in fee simple, the person possesses all the attributes associated with ownership. This means the individual can use it, invest it, pledge it for a loan, sell it and give it away. The vast majority of property owned in this country is held in fee simple. Unless an individual is married or in a domestic partnership and owns some assets jointly with a spouse or partner, the person probably owns everything (bank, investment and retirement accounts, life insurance, house, car, entertainment center, etc.) in fee simple.

Fee simple.   The most common way for someone who owns property in fee simple to give it away is to do so in fee simple. In this manner, the donee acquires all the ownership rights and the donor no longer has any.

Example: At the end of last year, Theo gave $20,000 in stock to his child, Margaret, in fee simple. He did not retain any rights in or powers over the property. It is a completed gift, and Margaret can do with the stock as she pleases. On Theo's death, the property does not pass through Theo's probate estate because he does not have any interest in it.

Gifts into trusts.   Rather than making gifts directly to the donee in fee simple, donors sometimes make inter vivos transfers using a trust. With some gifts in trust, the settlor retains no interest in the trust; in others, the settlor does. The reasons for one form over the other will be explored in later chapters. However, if the settlor wishes to make a completed gift so that there will not be any estate tax owed at death or if the goal is to deny subsequent creditors access to the property, the settlor must retain nothing. If the principal purpose is probate avoidance, then the settlor can retain significant interests in the trust. See the examples in Section D.1 above.

3.   *Was the Gift Successfully Made?*

The following problems and case ask the question whether Rita Genecin, the mother, made a completed gift of a painting to her son, Paul, or whether the painting was still owned by her when she died. The answer to that question determines whether or not the painting was included in her probate estate and passed pursuant to her will.

PROBLEMS

As you read the *Genecin* case, consider the following questions:

1.   What interests in the Lautrec painting, if any, did Rita transfer away in December 1999?
   a.   How do we determine if a gift was made and completed?
   b.   If the court had held Rita did not give title to the painting to Paul in December 1999 but rather intended for the gift to take place on her death, what impact would that have on Rita's probate estate, and who would have been entitled to the painting?
   c.   If the court had found that Rita gave Paul a remainder interest in the painting and that she retained the right to display the painting in her home for the rest of her life, how would that have affected the probate estate and the person entitled to the painting on her death?

Estate of Genecin
363 F. Supp. 2d 306 (D. Conn. 2005)

KRAVITZ, District Judge.

This lawsuit is the result of an unfortunate and bitter dispute between two brothers, Victor Genecin and Paul Genecin, over the rightful ownership of two assets — a lithograph and an individual retirement account — that once belonged to their mother, Rita Genecin, who is now deceased. Rita Genecin loved her sons very much and undoubtedly was very proud of them. Both are accomplished; one is a doctor and the other a lawyer. But the Court has no doubt that were she alive today, Rita Genecin would be deeply disappointed in her sons. For they have fought each other viciously over these assets when an amicable resolution was always evident, and in the process, they have leveled distressing allegations against each other — charging each other with fraud, falsifying documents and suborning perjury. Worse yet, in their headstrong battle over these assets, it appears that they may have expended more on legal fees than either could possibly hope to recover. . . .

I.

. . . Rita Genecin died suddenly and unexpectedly on or about August 5, 2000 in her home in Baltimore, Maryland, two years following the death of her husband Abraham. Rita Genecin is survived by her two sons — Victor, who resides in New York; and Paul, who resides in Connecticut. Victor Genecin is the sole personal representative of the Estate of Rita Genecin ("the Estate"). In her Will, Rita Genecin divided her residuary Estate as follows: 55% to Victor and 45% to Paul.

Throughout her life, Rita Genecin loved art. She was an artist herself, and, along with her husband, was an avid collector of art. Over the years, Abraham and Rita Genecin made gifts to their sons of many of the works of art that the Genecins had collected. The most valuable of the art works Rita Genecin owned in the year preceding her death was an 1897 color lithograph by French artist Henri de Toulouse-Lautrec entitled *Partie de campagne (Le chariot anglais)* (the "Lautrec"), which has been appraised as having a value of $150,000. At the time of her death, the Lautrec was hanging in the home in which Rita Genecin lived in Maryland. Immediately following her death, Paul brought all of the art from the Maryland home to Connecticut for safekeeping while the Estate was beginning its journey through the probate process.

Thereafter, Paul informed his brother Victor, the Estate's personal representative, and others, including Rita Genecin's personal lawyer and financial advisors, that his mother had given him the Lautrec as a Christmas gift during a visit that he and his family made to Rita's Maryland home in late December 1999, approximately six months before her death. Victor Genecin, as personal representative of the Estate, denied that his mother had made a legally valid gift of the Lautrec to Paul, and Victor brought this action on behalf of the Estate in Connecticut federal court to regain possession of the Lautrec for the Estate. Sadly, in pursuing that claim on the Estate's behalf, Victor has also been compelled to deny the effectiveness of a gift of two lithographs by French artist Edouard Vuillard entitled *Maternite* and *Avenue* that his mother appears to have intended to give him in January 2000 in the same manner that she gave Paul the Lautrec. . . .

III.

The parties agree that the validity of the Lautrec gift is governed by Maryland law. The parties also agree on who has the burden of proving a valid inter vivos gift, the standard of proof and the elements of a gift under Maryland law. Under Maryland law, the donee — Paul Genecin — has the burden of establishing every element of a valid gift, he must do so by clear and convincing evidence, and he must establish three elements: "an intention on the part of the donor to transfer the property, a delivery by the donor and an acceptance by the donee." While an admittedly close question, particularly because of the governing standard of proof, the Court concludes on the basis of the facts as the Court finds them that Paul has sustained his burden of proof on each element. Therefore, the Court finds that Rita Genecin made a valid gift of the Lautrec to Paul Genecin in December 1999.

A.   Donative Intent

In order to prove donative intent, it must be shown from the evidence that the donor clearly and unmistakably intended to permanently relinquish all interest in, and control over the gift. The Court concludes that Paul Genecin established by clear and convincing evidence that his mother intended to give him the Lautrec in December 1999.

In reaching this conclusion, the Court emphasizes at the outset that it did not rely on Paul's testimony regarding his mother's gift. . . . The Court . . . rules that with one exception noted below, Paul Genecin's testimony is barred by Maryland's Dead Man's Statute, which serves to "impose[ ] silence on interested parties as to transactions with or statements by the decedent."

[The court then goes on to discuss the Maryland Dead Man Statute.]

Having resolved these threshold evidentiary issues, the Court now turns to the evidence of donative intent. The admissible evidence presented at trial was overwhelming that Rita Genecin intended to give the Lautrec to Paul as a Christmas gift in December 1999. First, and most importantly, there is a deed of gift, which was undisputedly executed by Rita Genecin on or about December 1999, which states that "I, Rita Genecin, hereby give, grant, convey and transfer all my right, title and interest in and to the item listed below to you, Paul Genecin in fee simple, absolutely, without any reservations whatsoever." It is difficult for the Court to conceive of a clearer statement of Rita Genecin's intent than that contained in the deed of gift which she signed. Although there was considerable testimony about defects in the notarization of this document, the Court finds that evidence largely irrelevant given that Rita Genecin's signature on the deed of gift was verified at trial by her sons, Paul, and Victor, the personal representative of the Estate.

The Court finds it significant that the testimony and evidence showed that over the years Rita Genecin had made numerous gifts of art to Paul using deeds of gift nearly identical to the one at issue in this case. The Estate does not challenge the validity of any of those identical deeds of gift. In particular, the Estate does not challenge the validity of Rita Genecin's deed of gift in which she gave to Paul a wood cut print by Japanese artist Shiko Munakata entitled *Hawk Woman*. The Munakata deed of gift was executed by Rita Genecin on the same date as the identically worded Lautrec deed of gift.

Rita Genecin's intent to give the Lautrec to Paul Genecin was further evidenced by the testimony of three witnesses: Gregory Genecin; Ms. Sherlock, and Victor Genecin himself. The Court found Gregory Genecin to be a credible witness. He testified that after visiting an art museum with his grandmother during a family trip to Washington in March of 2000, his grandmother told him that "she gave [the Lautrec] to my dad at Christmas." Ms. Sherlock — who was the only truly disinterested witness to testify — also testified with great sensitivity and credibility. Ms. Sherlock testified that during a visit with her dear friend Rita Genecin in the spring of 2000, Ms. Sherlock observed that the Lautrec had been moved from its usual place in the Genecin home. When Ms. Sherlock noted the move to Rita, Rita explained that she had "given [the Lautrec] to Paul for Christmas." Significantly, Victor Genecin also conceded at trial that it was his view that his mother had intended to gift the Lautrec to Paul and/or his family. . . .

[T]he Estate's rebuttal case essentially asked the Court to draw a number of negative inferences from certain evidence in an apparent attempt to defeat Paul's claim on the basis of the clear and convincing standard of proof. The Estate's efforts are unpersuasive.

First, the Estate presented evidence regarding certain fractional deeds of gift that Rita executed in early January after executing the December 1999 deed of gift giving the Lautrec to Paul "in fee simple absolute." These fractional gifts, the Estate argues, show that Rita intended to give the Lautrec not to Paul alone, but to Paul and his family members, and that she intended to convey ownership of the Lautrec over time, not in December 1999, an intent that was defeated by her untimely death. Although the Court agrees that the Estate has provided one plausible interpretation for the subsequent fractional deeds, the Court does not find the Estate's theory the most compelling explanation. The explanation that the Court found far more persuasive is that Rita Genecin intended to give Paul full ownership of the Lautrec when she executed the deed of gift in December 1999 and that the subsequent fractional deeds — which were the brainchild of her financial advisor — were executed in order to create documentary evidence that would allow Rita Genecin to avoid paying gift tax on her gift of the Lautrec.

. . . Mr. Wagner [Ms. Genecin's financial advisor] testified that "[Rita] wanted to give within the gift tax limitations" and he said to her "you would have to divide up the painting . . . . We took the $150,000 [appraisal value] and divided by $10,000 per donee per year." (Victor testified affirmatively that the fractional deeds were "an attempt to address" gift tax).

. . . [W]hen Mr. Wagner did learn of the prior deed of gift transferring the entire Lautrec to Paul, he expressed his view that the subsequent fractional deeds were a "non-event," because, as he explained "You can't give away something twice." The Court agrees. . . . Finally, Rita Genecin never delivered the fractional gifts to the donees. Surely she would have done so had she truly intended to make the fractional gifts to the members of Paul's family. That she did not do so further supports this Court's finding that Rita Genecin executed the fractional deed of gift as a gift tax avoidance device and that they were not intended to supplant or negate Rita Genecin's December 1999 gift of the entire Lautrec to Paul Genecin. . . .

For the reasons previously stated, therefore, Court finds that Paul Genecin has established by clear and convincing evidence that Rita Genecin intended to give him the Lautrec in its entirety in December 1999.

B.   Acceptance

The Court also finds that Paul Genecin has met his burden of establishing acceptance in this case. To begin with, "[a]cceptance by the donee . . . is presumed, barring evidence to the contrary." The Estate presented no evidence to the contrary at trial. And while Maryland's Dead Man's Statute may bar testimony from Paul Genecin regarding what his mother said to him, there is nothing to prevent the Court from crediting the testimony of his assistant, Ms. Mulrine, that she saw the deed of gift in Paul's possession in New Haven in early January 2000. Nor does the Dead Man's Statute bar Paul's testimony that he did for a time, have the deed of gift in his possession and that he gave it to Ms. Mulrine to notarize in January 2000. The deed of gift itself was plainly admissible and was in fact admitted into evidence. Under these circumstances, Paul's testimony that he had the deed in his possession does not undermine or frustrate the purpose of the Dead Man's Statute. In any event even ignoring Paul's testimony in this regard, it is undisputed that the original deed of gift was produced by Paul in this litigation. The Court is not prepared to accept the Estate's speculation that Paul obtained possession of the deed of gift only after going through his mother's papers in August 2000 following her death. Therefore, the Court finds that Paul Genecin has satisfied the acceptance requirement.

C.   Delivery

In a very real sense, the adequacy of delivery has always been the critical issue in this case. Victor Genecin made this point crystal clear at trial when he was asked to explain why the Estate was not pursuing any claim with respect to the Munakata woodcut entitled *Hawk Woman* for which Rita Genecin executed a deed of gift to Paul at the same time as the Lautrec deed of gift. The reason, Victor confirmed, is that "the *Hawk Woman* was actually delivered to [Paul]; whereas the Lautrec was not."

The facts supporting delivery in this case are undisputed. As the Court mentioned earlier, although Rita Genecin did not physically deliver the Lautrec lithograph to Paul, she did execute and deliver to him (as she had often in the past) a very formal looking deed of gift. It is also undisputed that on the advice of her financial advisor, Mr. Wagner, and shortly after giving Paul a deed of gift for the Lautrec, Rita Genecin transferred ownership of her house into the names of herself and her two sons, apparently in the belief that this additional step would aid in perfecting her gifts of art to her sons. Thus, Mr. Wagner testified in the context of the fractional deeds of gift, "[W]e talked about moving the title to the house and effectively did it into the name of Paul, Rita and Victor Genecin as owners." Similarly, Mr. Hertzberg testified that "I recall Mr. Wagner advising Mrs. Genecin . . . that ownership of the house . . . should be changed to joint ownership with her two sons" in order to perfect her gift of the Lautrec. Thus, although the Lautrec lithograph itself never left the home where it had hung before the Christmas 1999 gift to Paul, after January 2000, the Lautrec hung in a home which Paul jointly owned.

On these facts, there is no question that if the *Restatement (Third) of Property: Wills and Other Donative Transfers* §6.2 (2003) governed, the delivery requirement for a completed gift would be satisfied. For the *Restatement* explicitly recognizes inter vivos transfers of property through delivery of a written instrument such as the deed of gift executed by Rita Genecin in this case. Section 6.2 of the *Restatement* provides: "The transfer of personal property, necessary to perfect a gift, may be made (1) by delivering the property to the donee *or* (2) by inter vivos donative document." (Emphasis added). Recognizing this latter method of effectuating delivery hardly represents a radical departure from existing law by the *Restatement* drafters. To the contrary, that method of satisfying the delivery requirement has long been embraced by courts of many jurisdictions. . . .

Indeed, Illustration 19 from the *Restatement* presents facts that are virtually identical to this case:

> G mails a letter to her son S. The letter signed by G states: "This is to let you know that you now own the painting that hangs in my living room. You can pick it up at your convenience." This letter is an inter vivos donative document, effective when mailed.

Restatement (Third) of Property: Wills and Other Donative Transfers §6.2, cmt. u, illus. 19 (2003). In fact, the present case is even stronger than the Illustration in view of Rita Genecin's gift to Paul of an ownership interest in the home in which the lithograph would hang until her untimely death.

Of course, the question in this case is whether a valid delivery has been effected under Maryland law. While the Estate argues that Maryland does not recognize transfer of moveable personal property through delivery of a donative writing, a more accurate assessment of the state of Maryland law is that Maryland courts have not yet had occasion to decide this issue presented by this case. Indeed, neither the parties nor the Court have been able to identify a Maryland case directly on point. Therefore, the Court must make an "*Erie* guess" as to whether Maryland courts would adopt the approach espoused by the *Restatement*. Although the Court candidly admits that the answer to that question is not entirely clear, the Court is nonetheless satisfied that Maryland courts would look to the *Restatement* for guidance in resolving this case and that they would adopt the *Restatement's* approach of recognizing that the delivery requirement can be met by inter vivos delivery of a donative document. . . .

. . . [A]s the *Restatement* drafters recognize, the evidentiary function of the delivery requirement can be equally well served by an effective donative instrument. The New York Supreme Court, Appellate Division persuasively made this point in *Gruen v. Gruen*, 104 A.D.2d 171 (N.Y.A.D. 1984), a case with facts strikingly similar to this one. The court in *Gruen* held that a father had successfully given a painting by artist Gustav Klimt to his son by sending him a gift letter, stating that "it is the delivery of the [written] instrument itself which fulfills the 'delivery' requirement of a gift *inter vivos*, and duplicative manual delivery is therefore unnecessary." As the court explained, "in the case of an oral gift, the fact of delivery serves to assist, in an evidentiary manner, to confirm the intent of the donor, and to prevent the assertion of fraudulent claims. . . . No such policy considerations are applicable to a gift made in writing."

Here, the Court finds that there has been no fraud and that Rita Genecin made her intent to give the Lautrec to Paul clear and unmistakable in numerous ways, including taking the rather extraordinary action of transferring ownership of her home to her two sons (to whom she had gifted art that remained hanging in the home). Like the drafters of the *Restatement*, the Court does not believe that it will encourage fraud to recognize that when a donor signs an instrument that clearly gives absolute ownership of a painting to a donee, delivers that instrument to the donee and (in this case at least) conveys to the donee a joint interest in the home in which the painting hangs, the donor has done more than enough to confirm an intent to make a gift.

Another reason to insist on physical delivery is to impress upon the donor that the gift now belongs to the donee and to ensure that the donor intended the gift to be irrevocable. . . . However, a donative writing is certainly capable of serving a similar function. As the court recognized in *Gruen*, "the delivery of a written conveyance . . . requires a high degree of deliberation on the part of the donor, substantially higher than a manual delivery, and affords the clearest and most convincing evidence of the fact that the gift has taken place." Similarly, the *Restatement* explains that, once a donee has a deed of gift in his possession, the gift is completed and irrevocable, and he may demand physical possession of the gifted property at any time. Here, the language of the deed of gift could not have been clearer. . . .

For the foregoing reasons, the Court concludes that Maryland courts would adopt the *Restatement's* position on delivery and would recognize that Rita Genecin's delivery of a deed of gift to Paul Genecin (combined with the virtually immediate conveyance of joint ownership to her home) would satisfy the delivery requirements for a valid inter vivos gift. Accordingly, the Court finds that Paul has established by clear and convincing evidence that his mother made him a valid gift of the Lautrec.

NOTES AND QUESTIONS

1. *Demonstrating a gift.* If you had been consulted by Rita Genecin to assist her with transferring ownership of the painting to Paul, what additional steps might you have taken to establish that she intended to make a completed gift and did not retain rights in it?

    a. How would you demonstrate intent, delivery and acceptance of a gift of other personal property like jewelry, furs and shares of stock or a recreational vehicle?

    b. How would you demonstrate intent, delivery and acceptance of a gift of real property?

2. *Who would have thunk it?* As attorneys who advise clients on planning transactions, you will have to balance the desire to do absolutely everything that is possible to protect the client's intent with the client's concerns about high legal fees. Maximum protection for the integrity of a transaction includes generating and retaining records of each step that was considered and how each decision was ultimately made as to what would be done. The more likely it is that someone might challenge a transaction, the greater attention you must pay to record generation and retention. Based on what you can glean from the facts, was this a situation that Rita Genecin (or her attorney) might have suspected would lead to litigation so that extra precautions should have been taken to document the facts at the time of the gift?

3. *Good old reliable.* Note the court's reliance on the *Restatements*. In wills and trusts law, more frequently than in other areas of the law, the *Restatements* often have significant weight and prove influential. For this reason, the authors of this book cite to them frequently.

4. *A thousand words or a picture?* Here is a picture of the painting over which the brothers were fighting. You might find it interesting to do an Internet search of the brothers as they are both remarkably accomplished individuals. This case underscores the fact that litigation in trusts and estates is not always only about money and that many emotional intangibles are also involved.

PROBLEMS

Tomasita is the decedent in the problems below. She is survived by her husband (Humberto), daughter (Delia), son (Spencer), grandchild (Georgia) and sister (Sally). As to each of the following, answer:

- Is the asset probate property or nonprobate property of the decedent? Be specific—identify whether the property passes through the will, the trust, a beneficiary designation form, a deed, a POD or TOD designation, etc.
- Identify to whom the property will pass on the decedent's death.
- What governing instrument or law controls disposition?

1. At her death, Tomasita had an ownership interest in a $1.0 million house and other real and personal property. Tomasita died with a valid will leaving all her property to Humberto.
    a. Tomasita owned the house and all the other property in fee simple.
    b. Tomasita owned the house and other property as a tenant in common with Sally.
    c. Tomasita owned the house and other property as community property with Humberto.
    d. Tomasita owned the house and other property in joint tenancy with right of survivorship with Spencer. Many years ago, Tomasita bought the property with her own funds and titled it in joint tenancy with Spencer.

2. At her death, Tomasita had an ownership interest in a checking account and an investment account. Tomasita died without a will.
    a. Tomasita owned the accounts in her name alone.
    b. Tomasita owned the accounts in her name and Spencer's names jointly.
    c. Tomasita owned the accounts in her name alone but there is a "payable-on-death" (POD) or a "transfer-on-death" (TOD) designation in favor of Spencer.
    d. Tomasita owned the account in her name alone but Spencer was added as a "convenience depositor."
    e. Tomasita owned the accounts in her name alone but there is a "payable-on-death" (POD) or a "transfer-on-death" (TOD) designation in favor of Spencer. The POD designation form provided that her estate was the secondary beneficiary in case Spencer did not survive Tomasita. For this problem only, assume Spencer predeceased Tomasita by two years.

3. Ten years before her death, Tomasita gifted stock to Spencer in fee simple that was worth $100,000 at the time. Tomasita died this year and the stock was worth $175,000.

4.   Tomasita created an irrevocable trust 10 years before she died to which she transferred $400,000 of stocks. She named Sally as the trustee and her cousin, Corinne, as the successor trustee on Sally's death. Delia is entitled to income from the trust for her life and on her death the corpus is distributed to Spencer, if living. If Spencer does not survive Delia, the corpus is to be distributed to Georgia or her estate. Tomasita died this year and the trust corpus is now worth $1.0 million.

5.   Tomasita created an irrevocable trust 10 years before she died to which she transferred $400,000 of stocks. She named herself as trustee with Sally as successor trustee upon her death or disability. Tomasita also named herself the income beneficiary while she was alive. On her death, the trust is to terminate and the principal is to be distributed to Delia as the remainder beneficiary. Tomasita died this year and the trust principal is worth $1.0 million at her death.

6.   Tomasita owned a life insurance policy on her own life. The primary beneficiary is Delia; the second beneficiary is Tomasita's estate.

    a.   Answer the questions asked re: Tomasita, assuming Delia is alive at Tomasita's death.

    b.   How would the answers change if Delia had predeceased Tomasita and Tomasita had not changed the beneficiary designation? Everyone knows (and is willing to testify) that Tomasita would have wanted her best friend of 20 years to get the proceeds of the insurance. However, she did not write a will because her insurance agent told her it was not necessary since all of her property was in will substitutes.

NOTE

Life insurance and estate taxes.   In Question 6 above, Tomasita was the owner of the policy. This is unwise from a tax perspective because the proceeds will be included in Tomasita's gross estate for estate tax purposes. The better approach is for someone else, usually the intended beneficiary, like a child or spouse or a trust established for the intended beneficiary's benefit, to apply for and purchase the policy on her life from the start. That person (or trust) is the owner and must pay the premiums. If the owner (spouse or child or trust for spouse or child) cannot afford to pay the premiums, the insured (parent) can make annual gifts to cover the cost (and if those gifts are below the annual exclusion amount, which in 2011 is $13,000, there will be no gift tax due). If Tomasita is already the owner of a policy on her life and she wishes to avoid inclusion of the proceeds in the taxable estate, she can gift or sell the policy to her spouse or child (or a trust for the spouse or child). If she does not die within three years of the gift, this will successfully avoid inclusion in the taxable estate. IRC §2035(a). This is discussed in greater detail in Chapter 14. Recall *Schneider v. Finmann*, discussed in Chapter 1.

F.　DEVELOPING A COMPREHENSIVE ESTATE PLAN INCORPORATING WILL SUBSTITUTES

When clients visit your office to develop an estate plan, all property in which they have an interest of any kind must be considered, whether probate or nonprobate property. A plan must be fashioned that coordinates these interests. After identifying the client's goals, the next step is to analyze an existing will and all existing will substitutes to determine if the beneficiaries designated fit within the client's present plans for the estate. Often, changes to who are named as the primary, secondary or contingent beneficiaries will be necessary because the client or a family member has gotten married or divorced, family members have been born or died, the client or a family member has had a significant increase or decrease in wealth or had some other major life-altering event occur. Additionally, the client may wish to have certain beneficiaries receive property only under certain situations.

When a lawyer drafts a will or trust, the lawyer can state which beneficiaries take or do not take given various circumstances and upon the happening of certain contingencies, but it is more difficult to build in this flexibility with other will substitutes. This is because beneficiary designation forms usually only have lines for naming the primary and secondary beneficiaries and do not often provide opportunities to state what is to happen upon the occurrence of a variety of events. This raises the question of who to name as the beneficiary of various will substitutes.

1.　Selecting the Beneficiary

Great care is required in naming the beneficiary of a will substitute. The following excerpt discusses the practical side of this decision.

Thomas E. Lund, Coordinating Beneficiary Designations with the Estate Plan
36 Est. Plan. 27 (2009)

Individual beneficiaries.　If the client wishes to have the asset pass directly to a specific person, the simplest method may be to name that person as the beneficiary. But even the simplest method requires thoughtful consideration. . . . If the client wishes to have the asset pass to a class of beneficiaries, how will the members of the class be described? . . . [W]hat will happen if that individual predeceases the client? . . . Is there a default beneficiary, or will the asset pass to the client's estate? . . .

Custodians.   A client with minor children and a simple estate plan may wish to designate a custodian under the state's Uniform Gifts to Minors Act or Uniform Transfers to Minors Act as the beneficiary for the minor children. The designation may need to be revised whenever the children move to another state so that the appropriate state law is referenced. . . .

Client's estate.   The easiest, if not the best method, of ensuring that the client's estate plan is fully coordinated is to designate the client's estate (or executor or personal representative) as the beneficiary of each asset requiring a beneficiary designation. All the assets will then be paid to the client's executor to be distributed in accordance with the client's will. This approach, however, may have significant adverse consequences [among them being subjecting the nonprobate property to the claims of creditors when they would otherwise be exempt and converting nonprobate property into probate property.]

Revocable trust.   The trustee of the client's revocable trust is the preferred beneficiary in almost every situation. With the trustee as beneficiary, the trust agreement can coordinate all the asset dispositions, including those to charities, the surviving spouse, or others that would have adverse income tax consequences if done incorrectly.

- The most important advantage is that, if substantially all of the client's assets pass through the revocable trust, implementation of the client's plan will be simplified.
- Because assets passing directly to the trustee of the revocable trust do not pass through the estate, their protection from claims of the client's creditors may be preserved. . . . [T]he trust instrument should explicitly prohibit the use of exempt assets for payment of the deceased settlor's obligations.
- Having the beneficiary designation assets paid to the trust makes it much easier to allocate and charge estate taxes appropriately among the beneficiaries because the trustee controls all the assets.

---

2.   What if the Beneficiary Predeceases the Decedent?

Upon the death of the decedent, the person who is to receive will substitute property is normally apparent. If a beneficiary designation form is used, it is the person so designated. The beneficiary of a joint tenancy is the survivor. The beneficiary of a trust is whoever is specified in the trust instrument, normally the remainder person. What is less clear is who is entitled to the property if the beneficiary predeceases the decedent.

With *probate* property, in order to inherit the heir or devisee must survive the decedent. If she does not, her right to inherit lapses or terminates. UPC §2-603, Comment, states:

> . . . a will transfers property at the testator's death, not when the will was executed. The common law rule of lapse is predicated on this principle and on the notion that property cannot be transferred to a deceased individual. Under the rule of lapse, all devises are automatically and by law conditioned on survivorship of the testator. A devise to a devisee who predeceases the testator fails (lapses); the devised property does not pass to the devisee's estate, to be distributed according to the devisee's will or pass by intestate succession from the devisee.

An exception to this rule is found in the "antilapse" provisions of UPC §2-603 and similar state statutes, which modify the devolution of lapsed devises in a will by providing a statutory substitute gift in the case of devises to specified relatives who leave descendants. "The statutory substitute gift is to the devisee's descendants . . . ; they take the property to which the devisee would have been entitled had the devisee survived. . . ." We discuss lapse and antilapse statutes in greater detail in Chapter 10.

In most states, the lapse rule and antilapse statutes apply strictly to wills; they do not apply to will substitutes. If the designated or POD or TOD beneficiary of a life insurance policy, retirement plan, bank or securities account dies before the decedent or is deemed to have died first, does the right lapse or terminate, does an alternate beneficiary take or does the statute establish a default rule of construction to further the decedent's probable intent?

Will substitutes, such as life insurance or retirement beneficiary designation forms, typically request the name of a secondary beneficiary. In such cases, since the contract states specifically what happens on the death of the primary beneficiary, the secondary beneficiary is entitled to the property and statutory or common law default rules are not required.

However, if neither the primary nor secondary beneficiary survives the decedent and if the form does not state that survival is a condition to taking, then the law is unsettled with regard to what happens to the property. In some states, the estate of the primary beneficiary takes the property; in states that have adopted UPC §2-706 (the antilapse rules for beneficiary designation forms), the descendants of the beneficiary, if any, receive the property if the beneficiary was one of several family members of the property owner; in other states, the estate of the secondary beneficiary is entitled to it; and in the remaining states, it reverts to the estate of the decedent for distribution by her will or by intestacy. You will need to check your state's law should this situation arise.

EXERCISE

This exercise is designed to be presented in class via role-playing with one student as the attorney and two students as the clients.

Malcolm and Iesha recently came to your office for estate planning. They have not done any estate planning before, and many of the beneficiary designation forms and ways property is titled were created years before they got married.

They tell you what they have in mind; it is a pretty traditional plan. They want to leave all their property to each other. If they were both to die at or about the same time, they would like to leave the property equally to their two sons, Jermain and Jamaal. If the boys have not reached 25 years of age at their death, Malcolm and Iesha would like the property to be held in trust for the children. Malcolm's parents will be both the trustees of the trust for the children and their guardians. Malcolm and Iesha are *very* interested in keeping things simple so as not to burden the survivor between them or Malcolm's parents.

They indicate that they are fine with their property either going through probate or not, so long as it is simple and accomplishes what they want to happen with their property and children.

At your suggestion, they have compiled the list of the property they own and who the present designated beneficiaries are (see table below). They state that they do not have any creditors other than credit cards with minor balances and a mortgage on the house of $100,000.

Depending on whether your professor assigns this as a memorandum that your senior partner can use for a meeting with Malcolm and Iesha later this week or has a roleplay with students acting as the attorneys, please (i) explain the differences between probate property and nonprobate property, (ii) discuss the advantages and disadvantages of each, (iii) whether they need to modify the beneficiary designations (and, if so, in what manner and any problems you see in doing so) and (iv) what would be a good estate plan for them considering their stated wishes.

Property Type	How Owned	Beneficiary	Amount
Stock in family business	Owned by Iesha in fee simple	No beneficiary named	$225,000
Checking account	Owned jointly by Malcolm and Iesha	N/A	$25,000
Life insurance	Owned by Malcolm on his life	Malcolm's brother, Keyshawn	$300,000
Life insurance	Owned by Iesha on her life	Iesha's mother, Dina	$250,000

| Retirement plan | Owned by Malcolm | Iesha | $100,000 |
| House | Owned jointly by Malcolm and Malcolm's brother, Keyshawn | N/A | $250,000 |

G.   FAILED WILL SUBSTITUTES

While property subject to will substitutes normally bypasses the probate estate, there are situations that might cause a will substitute to fail and result in the property being included in the decedent's probate estate. The most likely culprits include: (i) the naming of one's estate as the beneficiary in a designation form, (ii) the severance of a joint tenancy by the inter vivos actions of one of the tenants, (iii) the murder of the owner or joint tenant by the beneficiary or other joint tenant, (iv) a divorce between the beneficiary and the owner or one joint tenant by the other tenant or (v) the simultaneous death of the owner and designated beneficiary or of joint tenants. The first two of these are discussed here; the other three are discussed in the chapters that more fully analyze those concepts.

Naming one's estate as beneficiary.   Probate property embraces property acquired by the estate at or after the decedent's death. Since most people are not thinking of avoiding probate when they sign the beneficiary designation forms presented to them by a bank, insurance company, investment company or retirement plan administrator, it is not uncommon for them to designate their estates as either the primary or secondary beneficiary. If this happens and the estate receives the proceeds or account, what would have been a nonprobate transfer is converted into a probate transfer. In some situations, naming the estate as beneficiary may be the best way to coordinate dispositions of the entire estate, but the benefit of probate avoidance is lost.

The severance of a joint tenancy.   Joint tenancies with rights of survivorship create interesting problems in the context of whether the property will be probated or not. While the joint tenants are alive, they can terminate the joint tenancy by an act which is inconsistent with its continued existence, or which operates to destroy one or more of its essential unities. Typically, severance occurs when one of the tenants sells or gives away an interest or one or both of the parties seek its partition. If a severance occurs, the joint tenancy is transformed into a tenancy in common with no survivorship rights, which interest is a probate asset.

H. CAN A WILL OR OTHER DOCUMENT OR PROVISION OF LAW OVERRIDE A WILL SUBSTITUTE'S DESIGNATION OF A BENEFICIARY?

1. Will vs. Will Substitute

A common question faced by personal representatives of a decedent's estate is who should receive the property when a will names one beneficiary and a will substitute names someone else with respect to the same property. Does the will or the will substitute control? This is a particularly important issue when it comes to a beneficiary designation form filed with a bank, securities firm, insurance company or retirement plan administrator because there may be very specific ways required in the contract for modifying them. The case that follows is typical of the situations that arise when the decedent wishes to change the beneficiary via the will but has not necessarily complied with the procedures set out in the will substitute. The court states the majority view with regard to contracts that use a beneficiary designation form.

Lincoln Life and Annuity Co. of NY v. Caswell
31 A.D.3d 1 (1st Dept. 2006)

FRIEDMAN, J.

In *McCarthy v. Aetna Life Ins. Co.*, 92 N.Y.2d 436, 681 N.Y.S.2d 790, 704 N.E.2d 557 [1998], the Court of Appeals held that, where a life insurance policy sets forth a procedure for changing beneficiaries and does not authorize making such a change by will, a general testamentary statement in the insured's will does not override a prior designation of the policy beneficiary that was made in the manner provided by the policy. This appeal requires us to decide which instrument controls — the will or the prior beneficiary designation made in accordance with the terms of the policy — where, unlike *McCarthy*, the will *specifically* identifies the policy in question and purports to require a disposition of its proceeds inconsistent with the beneficiary designation under the policy. We hold that, under these circumstances, the purported testamentary disposition of the policy proceeds does not constitute "substantial compliance" with the policy and, therefore, cannot be given effect over the policy's beneficiary designation. As in *McCarthy*, this result is not affected by the insurance company's waiver of "strict compliance" with the policy terms by its commencement of an interpleader action to adjudicate among the conflicting claims to the policy proceeds.

There is no dispute as to the material facts. In April 1985, Aetna Life Insurance and Annuity Company (Aetna) issued Policy No. U1179854, a life insurance policy in the face amount of $200,000 (the '854 policy), to Martha L. Hubbard (hereinafter, the insured). The '854 policy provides that, to change the beneficiary, "[a] signed request must be sent to Aetna. When Aetna gives its written acceptance, the change will take effect as of the date the request was signed."

On two occasions, the insured changed the beneficiary designation in the manner provided by the '854 policy. Her last such change was made by a signed request dated October 9, 1987. That request, made on a printed form Aetna provided for the purpose, designated the insured's son, Robert W. Hubbard, Jr., as primary beneficiary, and defendant Bennie Caswell, Jr. (sued herein as Benjamin Caswell), as contingent beneficiary. Aetna's acceptance of that request is dated October 27, 1987. Since Robert W. Hubbard, Jr. predeceased the insured, giving effect to the October 1987 beneficiary designation would make Caswell the sole beneficiary of the '854 policy.

More than 15 years after she filed the October 1987 beneficiary designation with Aetna, the insured executed a last will and testament, dated June 16, 2003. This will specifically refers to the '854 policy by number, and purports to "devise and bequeath" portions of the proceeds of that policy to various individuals and charities. It appears that the will purports to leave Caswell only $25,000 of the proceeds of the '854 policy. There is no indication that the insured ever took any steps to have the legatees of the '854 policy under the will designated as beneficiaries of the policy in the manner provided by the policy itself.

The insured died on May 17, 2004, and her will of June 2003 has been filed in probate proceedings in Surrogate's Court. In June 2004, Caswell and the nominated executors of the insured's estate, by their respective attorneys, sent letters to the insurance company asserting conflicting claims to the proceeds of the '854 policy. Thereafter, plaintiff Lincoln Life and Annuity Company of New York, as Aetna's administrator, in accordance with CPLR 1006, commenced this interpleader action in the Supreme Court, Bronx County, seeking to be discharged of its obligations under the policy while allowing the competing claims to the proceeds to be resolved among the interested parties. . . .

By order entered on or about March 7, 2005, the motion court denied Caswell's summary judgment motion, based on the court's view that the dispositive consideration was the insured's intent, as to which, the court opined, there exists a triable issue of fact. . . . On Caswell's appeal, we now modify to grant Caswell's summary judgment motion to the extent of declaring him the sole beneficiary of the '854 policy, and otherwise affirm.

As the Court of Appeals stated in *McCarthy v. Aetna Life Ins. Co.*, the general rule is that "the method prescribed by the insurance contract must be followed in order to effect a change of beneficiary." As a corollary of this rule, it has long been recognized that, unless an insurance policy permits the beneficiary to be designated or changed by will, even a specific testamentary bequest of the policy proceeds generally will not override a prior beneficiary designation made in accordance with the terms of the policy.

Over the years, there has been some relaxation of the requirement of strict compliance with the procedures specified by an insurance policy for designating or changing beneficiaries. At first, it was held that "exact compliance with the provisions of the policy [would be excused] where the attempt at such compliance has been substantial and its full success prevented by some cause not within the control of the person attempting to make the change." As the law has evolved, the courts, recognizing that a primary purpose of specifying a procedure for changing beneficiaries is to protect the insurer from double liability, have come to hold that exact compliance with the contractual procedure will be deemed waived where the insurer, faced with conflicting colorable claims to the same policy proceeds, pays the proceeds into court in an interpleader action so that the opposing claimants may litigate the matter between themselves.

Although an interpleading insurer is deemed, by paying the policy proceeds into court, to waive exact compliance with the policy's procedures for changing beneficiaries, the question is still not purely one of the insured's intent. Rather, "[t]here must be an act or acts designed for the purpose of making the change, though they may fall short of accomplishing it. Mere intent is not enough." Thus, the controlling consideration as to whether a change of beneficiary has been effectuated in such cases is whether there has been *"substantial compliance* with the terms of the policy." Obviously, as the law has developed, it still seeks to encourage compliance with the requirements of the policy for changing beneficiaries.

Against the foregoing legal background, the dispositive question that emerges in this case is whether the insured's specific testamentary disposition of the '854 policy in her will can be deemed to constitute "substantial compliance" with that policy's requirements for effecting a change of beneficiary. Our answer to this question is "no." Although the will may constitute some evidence of the insured's subjective intentions, the making of the will plainly was not an attempt to comply with the simple change-of-beneficiary procedure set forth in the '854 policy. So far as the record shows, in the 15 years the insured lived after effecting the October 1987 change of beneficiary, she did nothing at all that could be characterized as an attempt to comply with the change-of-beneficiary procedure required by the policy, which, again, was simply to send the insurer a signed request — a procedure the insured herself had followed twice before she executed her will. Nor is there any evidence that the insured was "physically or mentally incapable of attempting to substantially comply with the requirements of the policy."

We recognize that at least two reported pre-*McCarthy* Surrogate's Court decisions have given effect to a specific testamentary bequest of an individual retirement account as a change of the beneficiary, although the bequest did not comply with the contractual requirements for effectuating such a change. In both, the court deemed the custodian of the account to have waived the contractual requirements for effecting a change of beneficiary, thereby rendering the question (in those courts' views) purely one of the decedent's intent. In the life insurance context, we do not believe that this position continues to be tenable in light of the Court of Appeals' *McCarthy* decision. *McCarthy*, after all, specifically rejected the view "that the requirement of substantial compliance with the requirements of the insurance policy is waived where . . . the insurance company becomes a stakeholder in an interpleader action." In this regard, we note that the policy consideration the *McCarthy* court invoked in support of its holding that a general testamentary statement in a will does not constitute substantial compliance — avoiding uncertainty on the part of the insurers that could lead to the delay of payment on life insurance policies — applies as much to specific testamentary bequests as to general testamentary statements.

---

2.   Intervening Divorce

Caswell presents a "pure" will versus will substitute situation. When there has been an intervening divorce, different problems arise in determining the rights of an ex-spouse to payment of the proceeds of a will substitute. The answer to who is entitled to the property will depend on whether or not the parties entered into a property settlement disavowing rights to the other's property or the state has a statute like UPC §2-804 that revokes all revocable governing instruments.[17] (This rule is discussed in detail in Chapter 11.) In addition, who might initially receive payment from the payor will depend on whether the payor was notified of the divorce.

   If the divorcing spouses have entered into a property settlement that purports to release each spouse's rights in all property of the other spouse, a court may conclude that the language in the property settlement revoked the designation of the spouse as a beneficiary. Unfortunately, a determination based on the property settlement will depend on the language used in the settlement agreement. If, however, the state has a revocation-on-divorce statute like UPC §2-804, then a former-spouse who is still the beneficiary of a contract is not legally entitled to the proceeds. Assuming the payor has been notified of the divorce, the payor should make payment to either the secondary beneficiary named on the form or, if no one is named, to the estate of the decedent. Since the property settlement or state law revokes the former spouse's rights, a change of beneficiary *in the will* is irrelevant to determining the correct beneficiary of the nonprobate instrument.

---

17. Comparable issues are involved when the beneficiary of a will substitute kills the decedent. UPC §2-803.

If the payor has **not** been notified, it would have no reason not to make payment to the former spouse, in which case it may be necessary for the rightful beneficiaries to institute legal proceedings to get the money back. What legal theories would you advance as the attorney, and what would be the prayer for relief? *See, e.g., Vasconi v. Guardian Life Insurance Co. of America*, 590 A.2d 1161 (N.J. 1991).

If the settlement agreement did not revoke the designation and the state does not have a revocation-on-divorce statute, the named beneficiary is entitled to receive the proceeds assuming a change of beneficiary form was not filed with the payor in the manner described in the contract. In such situations, it is critical following a divorce that the individual modify not only his will but also title to jointly held property and send revised forms to all companies with whom there is a beneficiary designation form on file.

NOTES AND QUESTIONS

1. *A word to the wise.* If, as part of the discussions leading to a comprehensive estate plan, you learn that your client wishes to change the beneficiary of a nonprobate contract, the *Caswell* case makes it clear that you should advise the client to file a change form with the company. Do you think it would be malpractice if you did not do so?

2. *Retirement plan designations are controlled by ERISA.* While UPC §2-804 and similar laws revoke beneficiary designations after a divorce, the Supreme Court has ruled that state law cannot change the rules that apply to retirement plans governed by ERISA (the "Employee Retirement Income Security Act of 1984"). *Egelhoff v. Egelhoff*, 532 U.S. 141 (2001). David Egelhoff had named his wife, Donna Rae, as the beneficiary of two employee benefit plans. When the couple divorced, they divided their assets and David kept the two plans. David died three months after the couple divorced, without changing the beneficiary designations. Donna Rae claimed the proceeds as the designated beneficiary, and David's children argued that Washington's revocation-on-divorce statute revoked the designation of the former wife. If the statute applied, the children would receive the proceeds as statutory heirs with respect to one plan and default beneficiaries with respect to the other. The Supreme Court ruled that ERISA preempted state law and that a state statute could not change an ERISA plan's agreement to pay a named beneficiary. The Court expressed concern about the burden on plan administrators if they could not rely on plan documents, particularly in situations involving multiple jurisdictions.

3. *Are banks special?* Banks, being the subject of extensive state regulation, have a special rule prohibiting wills from naming a beneficiary other than the person designated on the form on file with the bank. UPC §6-213(b) states, "A right of survivorship arising from the express terms of the account, Section 6212, or a POD designation, may not be altered by

will." No such statutory provisions exist for other will substitutes. Why do you think the UPC does not extend the same rule to other will substitutes?

4.   *Batman, The Green Hornet and Super Wills.* The State of Washington has statutorily created an exception to the rule presented in *Caswell*, creating what some refer to as a "super will." WASH. REV. CODE §11.11.020 (" . . . upon the death of an owner the owner's interest in any nonprobate asset specifically referred to in the owner's will belongs to the testamentary beneficiary named to receive the nonprobate asset, notwithstanding the rights of any beneficiary designated before the date of the will [except that if] the owner designates a beneficiary for a nonprobate asset after the date of the will, the specific provisions in the will that attempt to control the disposition of that asset do not govern the disposition of that nonprobate asset . . . "). Would the *Caswell* case have reached a different result if this statute existed in New York?

PROBLEM

Charles has a revocable trust with Fifth Bank as the Trustee. He retained an income interest for himself for life and named his daughter as the remainder person on his death. Charles had a falling out with daughter when she married someone he disliked, and he now wants to name his son as the beneficiary. Charles lives in a state that has adopted the Uniform Trust Code.

> The [Uniform Trust] Code [§602] eliminates [a] trap that has arisen for lay persons, in relations between the revocable trust and any subsequent will. When a testator attempts to revoke some or all of the trust by a later will, courts have often refused to enforce the attempted revocation. The reasoning has been that since the revocable trust is a lifetime transfer, the assets subject to the trust pass *inter vivos*, hence do not enter the estate, and thus cannot be subject to the decedent's will. The Code reverses this intent-defeating rule and permits a trust to be amended or revoked by a later will or codicil that expressly refers to the trust or specifically devises property that would have otherwise passed according to the terms of the trust.

John Langbein, *The Uniform Trust Code: Codification of the Law of Trusts in the United States*, 15 TRUST L. INT'L 66, no. 2, 2001 at 71.

What options does Charles have in terms of changing the beneficiary of his revocable trust? Do you agree with the change made in the Uniform Trust Code?

APPENDIX A

Chart for Exercise on Page 195

Type of property	URL address	Does form provide for a primary beneficiary to be designated? What does form or instructions say happens to the property on the death of the primary beneficiary?	What does form or instructions say happens to the property on the death of all the designated beneficiaries?	Does form or instructions indicate in what manner the individual makes later changes? If so, how?	What formalities, such as witnesses and notarization, are required to make form effective?
Beneficiary designation form for a life insurance policy					
Beneficiary designation form for a 401(k) retirement account					
Beneficiary designation form for an annuity					

	URL address?	What happens on death of owner? Does form allow for a POD or TOD designation?	Does form allow for joint ownership? If so, what happens on death of one of the owners?	Does form indicate in what manner the individual makes later changes? If so, how?	What formalities, such as witnesses and notarization, are required to make form effective?
Checking account registration with a bank, credit union or investment company reflecting alternative methods of ownership either as separate or joint and offering a payable on death (POD) option.					
A beneficiary deed form (hint - Mont. Rev. Stat. §72-6-121 or Ariz. Rev. Stat. §33-405 may be available via an Internet search).					

5 | *CREATION OF TRUSTS*

A. INTRODUCTION

1. *What Is a Trust?*

A trust is a *fiduciary relationship* and involves a settlor (who creates the trust), a trustee (who manages the trust) and a beneficiary (who benefits from the trust). These terms are further explained in Section A.2. The trust developed in England as a way to separate legal control from beneficial control. It has become a remarkably useful tool for estate planners. In this chapter we learn how title is held in a trust and why the trust has become so helpful.

 Settlor control plays a strong role in trust law. In general, a settlor can dictate the terms of a trust because the property being used to create the trust belongs to the settlor. We will consider the limits the law places on the settlor's control, and we will consider whether the law should give beneficiaries some ability to change the terms of the trust, especially after the passage of time.

 Trust law provides great deference to the settlor's intent, but it also establishes both *mandatory and default rules.* Mandatory rules apply to all trusts and cannot be changed by the settlor. The mandatory rules are, however, quite limited and serve to protect the interests of the beneficiaries who might otherwise have no way to protect their interests — and might not even know about the trust. Much of trust law, however, is default law; the settlor can establish the terms of the trust in a declaration of trust or a trust agreement.

Trusts are incredibly *flexible* estate planning tools, but once a trust becomes irrevocable, the trust can be exceedingly inflexible. Proper planning can build flexibility into a trust and permit the trustee to adapt to changing conditions over time. If a settlor tries instead to build in a great deal of control, the trustee will be bound by the terms, and if modification becomes necessary later, a court proceeding likely will be required.

Trust law developed in the common law over centuries of use. Some states have codified some aspects of trust law, and in 2000, the Uniform Law Commission finished the Uniform Trust Code (UTC) to provide consistent statutory rules for states to adopt. For the most part the UTC codifies the pre-existing common law, but in a few respects it changes the common law. As of 2010, 22 states have adopted the UTC. You can get the up-to-date list at www.nccusl.org.[1] As with all statutes, cases will continue to explain and interpret the statutes, and the statutes can be better understood by examining the case law preceding the UTC. We will use both the UTC and case law to examine trust rules. States often make changes to uniform laws before adopting new statutes, so even a state that has adopted the UTC may have a version that differs from the sections we will discuss. In general, however, the basic principles of trust law are the same in all states, whether the state has enacted a statute or merely follows the common law.

Estate planning lawyers use trusts for a variety of purposes — protecting assets from a spendthrift family member, managing assets for a minor child, holding assets in a way that will provide estate tax benefits or setting aside assets for a special needs child in a way that will not cause the loss of government benefits. Lawyers create most of the trusts we will discuss, but sometimes a person will create a trust relationship, governed by trust law, without realizing that the transfer is a transfer in trust. For example, Charlise might give money to her former husband, Elliot, to be used for the education of their daughter, Danielle. Elliot will have legal title to the money, but if Charlise intended the property to be held by Elliot for the benefit of Danielle, Elliot must use the money as Charlise directed and not as he wishes. Danielle will have the beneficial interest in the trust.

In this chapter we will learn about the elements of a trust: a valid purpose, a competent settlor, a trustee, the intent to create a trust, property and one or more beneficiaries. We will consider the lack of formalities required to create a trust, and we will look at some rules that apply to oral trusts. After we cover the requirements for a trust, we will look at the special uses of revocable trusts, a powerful will substitute. However, before we look at the elements of a trust, we need to learn the basic terminology for trust law.

---

1. As of October 2010, the following jurisdictions have adopted the UTC: Alabama, Arizona, Arkansas, District of Columbia, Florida, Kansas, Maine, Missouri, Michigan, Nebraska, New Hampshire, New Mexico, North Carolina, North Dakota, Ohio, Oregon, Pennsylvania, South Carolina, Tennessee, Utah, Vermont, Virginia and Wyoming.

2. *Terminology for Trusts*

Trust law, like all areas of the law, has terminology that must be understood and used correctly (although a court can find a trust even if the parties never used the word trust). The players in a trust are the settlor, the trustee and the beneficiary. As we will discuss shortly, an individual can play more than one role. The following diagram reflects the roles of the parties to a trust and their rights and duties. It might help you to think of a trust like a prism, splitting the settlor's fee simple ownership between the trustee, who holds legal title to the property, and the beneficiaries, who have the right to distributions.

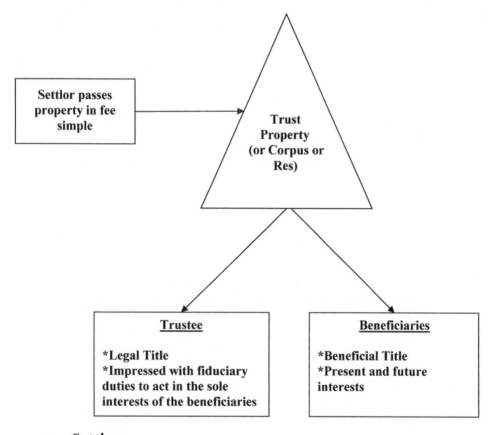

a. Settlor

The settlor is the person[2] (or persons) who creates a trust by transferring legal title to property to the trustee to hold for the benefit of the beneficiaries.

Two other terms are sometimes used to refer to a settlor. Trustor is an older term and is still used in some documents. Because the UTC uses the

---

2. We will discuss primarily trusts created by human persons, but a legal person, for example, a corporation, can also create a trust. *See* UTC §103(10) for its definition of person.

term settlor, that term is beginning to replace trustor, but lawyers comfortable with the term trustor continue to use it, even in UTC states. In states without the UTC, trustor may be the term of choice. In this text we will use the term settlor. Either is correct.

Grantor is also used to refer to the settlor, primarily in connection with some tax-planning trusts or in discussions of tax-related rules. For example, the "grantor trust rules" are the rules that describe the income and transfer tax consequences when the settlor retains some powers over or rights in the trust. This text uses the term grantor only in the tax context, when referring to the grantor trust rules or a "grantor trust" that has particular tax consequences.

b. Trustee

The trustee is the person who holds legal title to the property. A trustee can be an individual or a corporation authorized to act as a trustee (often a bank is used as a corporate trustee). A trust may have more than one trustee. The trustee manages the property, not for the trustee's own benefit but for the benefit of the beneficiary. The law imposes strict fiduciary duties on the trustee to protect the beneficiary. These fiduciary duties include the duty not to self-deal and duties connected with the management and investment of the trust property. We examine these duties in Chapter 6.

c. Beneficiary

The beneficiary is the person with beneficial or equitable title to the trust property. A trust may have many beneficiaries holding beneficial interests in the trust at the same time or at different times. Some of those interests may be present interests, and others may be future interests.

A trust may have several beneficiaries who have a current right to distributions from the trust. For example, Sheila could create a trust for her three children, with distributions to be made in the trustee's discretion to any or all of the children until the youngest child reaches a specified age, at which time the trust would terminate and all remaining property would be distributed to the children in fee simple.

A trust often has beneficiaries with rights that come at different times. For example, Diego might create a trust with a life estate for his surviving spouse and then a remainder interest for his descendants.

d. Qualified Beneficiary

The UTC uses this term for a subset of beneficiaries who have certain rights under the UTC. The comment to UTC §103 explains the decision to create a definition of "qualified beneficiary" and why the distinction between all beneficiaries and qualified beneficiaries is a useful one.

Comment to UTC §103

Due to the difficulty of identifying beneficiaries whose interests are remote and contingent, and because such beneficiaries are not likely to have much interest in the day-to-day affairs of the trust, the Uniform Trust Code uses the concept of "qualified beneficiary" (paragraph (13)) to limit the class of beneficiaries to whom certain notices must be given or consents received. The definition of qualified beneficiaries is used in Section 705 to define the class to whom notice must be given of a trustee resignation. The term is used in Section 813 to define the class to be kept informed of the trust's administration. Section 417 requires that notice be given to the qualified beneficiaries before a trust may be combined or divided. Actions which may be accomplished by the consent of the qualified beneficiaries include the appointment of a successor trustee as provided in Section 704. Prior to transferring a trust's principal place of administration, Section 108(d) requires that the trustee give at least 60 days notice to the qualified beneficiaries.

Here is the UTC section itself, followed by an example of how to apply the term.

UTC §103. Definitions.

(13) "Qualified beneficiary" means a beneficiary who, on the date the beneficiary's qualification is determined

(A) is a distributee or permissible distributee of trust income or principal;

(B) would be a distributee or permissible distributee of trust income or principal if the interests of the distributees described in subparagraph (A) terminated on that date without causing the trust to terminate;

(C) would be a distributee or permissible distributee of trust income or principal if the trust terminated on that date.

Example: Margaret creates a trust that provides income to her son, Shane, for Shane's life. On Shane's death, income is paid to Margaret's daughter, Olivia, for Olivia's life. When neither Shane nor Olivia are alive, the remainder is distributed to Margaret's descendants who are living on the date the trust terminates, but if no descendant is living on that date, the trust terminates and the property is distributed to the descendants of the settlor's sister, Selena, living on that date. The trustee, Margaret's brother, needs to determine the qualified beneficiaries as of today to provide notice of resignation.

If Shane and Olivia are both alive and both have two children, who are the qualified beneficiaries? Shane is a qualified beneficiary under UTC §103(13)(A) because he is a distributee of the trust income. Olivia is a qualified beneficiary under UTC §103(13)(B) because she would be a distributee if Shane died. If the trust terminated, that would mean that both Shane and Olivia had died. In that case, the children of Shane and Olivia, as Margaret's descendants, would be the distributees. Therefore, Shane and Olivia's children are qualified beneficiaries under UTC §103(13)(C). Selena's descendants are not qualified beneficiaries, although they are contingent beneficiaries. If neither Shane nor Olivia had descendants (and assuming that Margaret had no descendants other than Shane and Olivia), then Selena's descendants would be qualified beneficiaries under UTC §103(13)(C).

e. Corpus (Property or Res)

The *corpus* or *res* of a trust is the property held and managed by the trustee. The term *principal* is sometimes used to refer to all of the property in a trust, but the word may be used to mean the property in the trust that is not income. Trust accounting principles direct whether receipts and disbursements are classified as principal or as income, and we will discuss trust accounting in Chapter 7. Trust property may also be referred to as the trust estate.

f. Private Express Trusts

A private express trust is a trust created intentionally by the owner of property for private beneficiaries. Most of the trusts we discuss in this course are private express trusts.

g. Charitable Trusts

A charitable trust is a trust that has a charitable purpose or a charity as its beneficiary. Most trust law rules apply to charitable trusts, but some of the requirements and rules are different, and we will consider those differences in Chapter 16.

h. Inter Vivos and Testamentary Trusts

Trusts can be created during the settlor's lifetime (inter vivos) or, upon the settlor's death, through her will (testamentary trusts).

i. *Inter Vivos Trusts*

Inter vivos trusts are trusts created by a settlor while the settlor is alive. Here is an example of an inter vivos trust.

Example: Greta, the *settlor*, creates a trust to be used for college or graduate education of her grandchild, Linda, the *beneficiary*. Shortly after Linda's birth, Greta executes a trust instrument setting out the terms of the trust, and then transfers property to Caroline, Linda's aunt, as *trustee*, (with a bank as successor trustee) to invest until Linda begins attending college. Greta continues to make additional gifts to the trust each year. The terms of the trust provide that the trustee, in the trustee's discretion, can make distributions for Linda's health, education, maintenance or support, but emphasize that the primary purpose of the trust is to provide for Linda's college and graduate education. The trust continues until Linda reaches age 30, because Greta is concerned that Linda may not be ready to manage the money at an earlier age. When Linda reaches age 30, the trust terminates and the remaining assets are distributed to Linda. If Linda dies before age 30, the trust terminates on her death and the assets are distributed to her descendants, or if none, to Greta's descendants. (Linda's descendants and Greta's descendants are contingent beneficiaries.) This trust provides a way for Greta to set aside money to be used for Linda's education. By using a trust, Greta ensures that someone she trusts (Caroline in this case) will manage the property until Linda is 30 and old enough to manage any remaining money on her own.

ii. *Testamentary Trusts*

A settlor can provide for one or more trusts in her will, and any trust created under a will is referred to as a testamentary trust. When the settlor dies, the will directs the personal representative of the probate estate to distribute some amount of the estate's assets, often the residuary estate, to the trustee named in the will. The will, rather than a separate trust document, has embedded in it the terms of the trust — the beneficiaries, the standards of distributions and when the trust terminates.

Example: Maya's will makes a gift to the college from which she graduated. The will gives her jewelry to her daughter and then gives the rest of her tangibles (furniture, dishes, paintings, cars, etc.) to her children, to be divided among them as they agree. After the payment of debts and taxes, Maya's will divides all her remaining assets (known as the residue) into shares, one for each child who survives her and one for each child who does not survive her but who had children (or even grandchildren) who survive her. Each share is given to Thomas, as trustee, to be held as a separate trust. Each trust continues for the child's lifetime, during which the trustee may make distributions for the child's health, education and support. Each trust terminates when the child for whom it was created dies, at which time the trust assets go to the child's descendants or, if there are none, to Maya's descendants (the child's siblings or nieces and nephews), or if none, to Maya's alma mater. The terms of the trust are in the will, so this is a testamentary trust.

Like an inter vivos trust, a testamentary trust can provide for one or more beneficiaries, can be set up for a short time or can last as long as the Rule Against Perpetuities in that state permits and can provide whatever directions about distributions seem best for the purposes of the trust. We discuss the Rule Against Perpetuities in Chapter 8.

A testamentary trust will be subject to the supervision of the probate court. Avoidance of that supervision is one reason a settlor may prefer to establish an inter vivos trust.

i.   Revocable and Irrevocable Trusts

A trust can be revocable (the settlor retains the power to modify the terms of the trust or revoke the trust) or irrevocable (the settlor cannot amend, modify or revoke the trust). The default under the UTC is that all trusts are revocable unless the terms of the trust "expressly provide that the trust is irrevocable." UTC §602(a). This UTC provision does not apply to trust documents executed before the UTC becomes effective in a state, because the common law rule was to the contrary, *i.e.*, that a trust is presumed to be irrevocable unless the settlor reserves, in the terms of the trust, the right to revoke the trust.

i.   *Revocable Trusts*

If the settlor retains the power to modify or revoke the trust, the trust is revocable.

Example: Anthony creates a trust for his son, Aiden. The trust provides that the trustee can make distributions for Aiden's education. Anthony retains the power to modify or revoke the trust, so if Aiden engages in bad behavior, Anthony can revoke the trust and get the trust assets back. This sort of trust is unusual because, for tax reasons,

Anthony will probably want to make the trust irrevocable. But if Anthony has a small estate (and no transfer tax concerns) and wants to retain control of the money he sets aside for Aiden's education, Anthony could choose to set up the trust with a power to revoke.

ii. Revocable (Living) Trusts

When a lawyer assists a client in creating a revocable trust, the trust will typically be a revocable trust of a certain type — sometimes called a "revocable living trust." A trust can be revocable and not be a revocable living trust, like the trust described in the prior example, but for tax planning reasons, most inter vivos trusts are either revocable living trusts or are irrevocable.

A revocable living trust is created to hold the settlor's assets during the settlor's life, distribute to the settlor whatever income or corpus he needs and then distribute the remaining assets to others at the settlor's death. A revocable living trust provides a way to manage assets for the settlor, if the settlor becomes incapable of doing so, and also serves as a will substitute so that probate of the trust property is not necessary on the settlor's death. A settlor can create a revocable living trust by transferring the property to another individual or corporation as trustee (using a trust agreement or deed of trust) or by declaring that she holds the property as trustee and no longer holds the property in her individual capacity (using a declaration of trust). Revocable living trusts are discussed in detail later in this chapter. Because estate planning lawyers use the term "revocable trust" to mean revocable living trust, we will do the same in the rest of the text.

Example: Vania is 75. She is in good health but worries about slipping mentally as she ages. She agrees with her estate planner that she should set up a revocable trust. The estate planner drafts a declaration of trust, providing for management of the property by the trustee and distribution of the assets on Vania's death. Vania transfers title to her property to herself as trustee of the revocable trust. The trust provides a mechanism for Vania's daughter to step in as a successor trustee if Vania is unable to manage the trust later. On Vania's death, the successor trustee will make the distributions indicated by the terms of the trust. The trust also provides that the trustee will pay any debts remaining at Vania's death and any taxes due after her death. When the debts and expenses are paid and the assets are distributed, the trust will terminate.

iii. Irrevocable Trusts

All testamentary trusts are irrevocable. In addition, a settlor may create an inter vivos irrevocable trust. Revocable living trusts become irrevocable when the settlor dies. The trust created by Greta in the example in Section A.2.h.i above would most likely be an irrevocable trust. If Greta makes the trust irrevocable, the trust may provide income or estate tax benefits for Greta, depending on her situation. As in that example, irrevocable trusts, whether inter vivos or testamentary, are frequently created in lieu of giving the property outright to the donee. This is preferred in situations where the donee is either too young or too inexperienced to manage the property or because the settlor is interested in having someone else (the trustee) make decisions about the needs of the donee at a later time. Irrevocable trusts are also created for transfer tax reasons. For example, a settlor might create an Irrevocable Life Insurance Trust (sometimes called an ILIT) to hold a life insurance policy so that the proceeds are not included in the settlor's estate for estate tax purposes.

j. Constructive Trusts

A constructive trust is an equitable remedy, created by a court for the limited purpose of getting property to the right owner. The division of title — legal title to one person and equitable title to another — allows the court to transfer title as required by law to the legal owner but direct that the legal owner hold the property subject to a constructive trust, with the duty to transfer the property to the rightful owner. A constructive trust is a remedy and is not really a trust. For that reason, the UTC does not apply to constructive trusts. We discuss constructive trusts later in this chapter.

> **Example:** Guido and Belinda dissolved their marriage. They agreed to a property settlement, and Guido retained ownership of his pension. When Guido died just two months after the divorce, his children discovered that his pension still named Belinda as the beneficiary. Guido had the power to change the beneficiary, but he had not done so before he died. A court could decide to impose a constructive trust on the pension benefits. The court would direct the company to pay the benefits to Belinda as the legal owner (as the plan documents required) but provide that Belinda held the benefits as trustee with the duty to pay the benefits to Guido's children (who would take his estate under his will). The court is not legally bound to impose a constructive trust on the pension proceeds, but the court might chose to do so as an equitable remedy.

k. Resulting Trusts

The term resulting trust is used when an express trust fails because it no longer has a valid purpose. At that time the property returns to the settlor or to the settlor's estate, if the settlor is no longer alive. The UTC does not discuss resulting trusts.

Example: Charles creates a trust for his grandchild, Hayden, to pay for Hayden's college education. When Hayden graduates from college, the trust no long has a valid purpose. If the terms of the trust do not say what happens next, the trust property returns to Charles. Also, if Hayden dies in a car accident when he is eight and if the terms of the trust do not provide for other beneficiaries, the trust property returns to Charles, or to Charles' estate if he is no longer alive.

l. Merger

When a trustee and the trust's *only* beneficiary are the same person, the legal and equitable interests merge and the trust terminates. *See* RESTATEMENT (THIRD) OF TRUSTS §69 (2003). A comment to the *Restatement* adds that merger will occur even though the trust's "purposes have not been accomplished, and even though some or all of the equitable interest(s) of the trustee-beneficiary are subject to a spendthrift restraint." *See* RESTATEMENT (THIRD) OF TRUSTS §69, cmt. d (2003).

Example: Malika creates a trust for her son, Kofi. The trust provides for distributions for Kofi until he reaches age 40. When Kofi reaches age 40, the trust terminates and any remaining assets are distributed to him. If Kofi dies before age 40, the assets are distributed to his estate. Kofi and his uncle, Baraka, are co-trustees, with no provision in the terms of the trust for successor trustees and no requirement that a co-trustee be appointed. Baraka dies, leaving Kofi as the sole trustee. The trust terminates at that time under the doctrine of merger.

Example: Farid, Kofi's father, creates a trust for Kofi and names Kofi's sister, Samira, as trustee. Kofi gives his interest in the trust to Samira. If Kofi had a life estate and his descendants had the remainder interest, then merger will not apply because Samira will receive only Kofi's remaining income interest. But if the trust named Samira as the remainder beneficiary, then Samira will hold all beneficial interests and all legal interests and the doctrine of merger will apply to terminate the trust.

The issue of whether merger applies in the context of a revocable trust has been the source of concern for estate planners in the past because it is common for the settlor to be the trustee and the sole present beneficiary, although usually not the only beneficiary. The Comment to UTC §402(5) explains:

The doctrine of merger has been inappropriately applied by the courts in some jurisdictions to invalidate self-declarations of trust in which the settlor is the sole life beneficiary but other persons are designated as beneficiaries of the remainder. The doctrine of merger is properly applicable only if all beneficial interests, both life interests and remainders, are vested in the same person, whether in the settlor or someone else. An example of a trust to which the doctrine of merger would apply is a trust of which the settlor is sole trustee, sole beneficiary for life, and with the remainder payable to the settlor's probate estate.

The concern about merger and revocable trusts has been resolved in some states by case law. *See, e.g., Welch v. Crow*, 206 P.3d 599 (Okla. 2009). In other states, legislation provides that the doctrine of merger does not apply so long as there is one other beneficiary, even if the interest is a future interest and even if the interest is contingent. Here is the New York statute:

N.Y. Est. Powers & Trusts Law §7-1.1.

A trust is not merged or invalid because a person, including but not limited to the creator of the trust, is or may become the sole trustee and the sole holder of the present beneficial interest therein, provided that one or more other persons hold a beneficial interest therein, whether such interest be vested or contingent, present or future, and whether created by express provision of the instrument or as a result of reversion to the creator's estate.

Creditors of a beneficiary may seek to terminate a trust using the merger doctrine so that impediments to collection, such as spendthrift clauses and discretionary provisions (*see* Chapter 7) are eliminated. If a beneficiary is aware of the potential for merger, the beneficiary may be able to avoid the termination of the trust by refusing to accept the position of trustee. *See* Restatement (Third) of Trusts §69, cmt. d (2003). Most trusts have different present and future beneficiaries, so the issue of merger does not often arise.

Example: In the trust created by Malika for Kofi, if Kofi and Baraka are co-trustees, Kofi could resign as a trustee before Baraka's death or resignation. A court proceeding might be necessary to appoint a successor trustee when Baraka dies, but Kofi would have avoided the doctrine of merger. If the trust assets are protected from Kofi's creditors, keeping the property in trust may be in Kofi's interest.

QUESTIONS

1.   *The power to revoke.* Under the common law, a trust is presumed to be irrevocable and the presumption must be overcome by evidence (usually a statement in the trust agreement) that the settlor intended to make

the trust revocable. The UTC reverses the presumption. Under the UTC, a trust is presumed to be revocable. Why do you think the drafters of the UTC did this? Do you agree that this change is best for most people? What are the risks?

2. *What is equitable?* When should a court impose a constructive trust? Should a constructive trust be used in any case involving unjust enrichment or only if one party has acted fraudulently or in bad faith?

B. CREATION — ELEMENTS OF A TRUST

In determining whether a trust exists, courts focus on what the settlor intended when the settlor transferred property to someone else. When the settlor transferred the property, did the settlor intend to impose a mandatory duty on a trustee to act on behalf of a beneficiary or did the settlor intend something else? The inquiry into the elements of the trust assists us — and a court — in making that determination. The elements we will discuss are as follows:

- **The trust must be established for a valid purpose.**
- **The settlor must be competent when creating the trust.**
- **The trust must have a trustee.**
- **The settlor must have intended to create a trust.**
- **The trust must be funded, *i.e.*, must have some corpus (property or res).**
- **The settlor must identify an ascertainable beneficiary so there is someone who can enforce the trust. (As we will see, the UTC modifies this requirement.)**

A few states require some sort of writing for a trust, and if the trust holds real property, most, if not all, states require a writing.

A trust will not fail for lack of a trustee because a court will appoint a trustee for the trust. Each of the other requirements must be met before a trust will be created.

1. Valid, Legal Purpose

A trust must have a valid purpose — a reason the trustee holds and manages the property. Most trusts have a valid purpose when created, but if the purpose is accomplished and a valid purpose no longer exists for the trust, the trust terminates. At that point, the trustee will distribute the trust assets as directed by the terms of the trust, or if the terms do not state where the assets should go, the trust will become a resulting trust and will revert to the settlor or the settlor's estate.

A purpose cannot be illegal or against public policy, UTC §404, and a term of a trust that is illegal or against public policy will be held invalid and unenforceable. For example, if a settlor creates a trust to hide beneficial ownership of the settlor's assets from known creditors or from the government (before applying for government benefits such as Medicaid), the trust purpose is illegal and the trust will be unenforceable, at least as to those creditors or the government. Similarly, a trust that directs the trustee to purchase illegal drugs for distribution is invalid due to its illegal purpose.

A trust provision that is against "public policy" is also unenforceable, but public policy in this context can be difficult to determine. A decision that a trust term is invalid cuts against the deference usually paid to the settlor's ability to do what he wants with his property. The legal rules must balance the goal of permitting a settlor to address the needs and circumstances of the people the settlor chooses to benefit with the goal of limiting dead hand control on the personal freedoms of the beneficiaries. Courts rarely use public policy to invalidate a trust provision.

If a trust term encourages beneficiaries to engage in criminal or tortious behavior, perhaps by providing that the trustee will pay any fines incurred, that term may be held invalid as against public policy. The trust itself can continue without that provision. A trust term that restrains religious freedom by providing an incentive for a beneficiary to change religious faith may also be invalid. RESTATEMENT (SECOND) OF TRUSTS §62 (1959). Provisions that interfere with family relationships, for example, by encouraging divorce, discouraging marriage, encouraging neglect of parental duties or discouraging contact between siblings, likewise may be found to be against public policy. *See, e.g., Estate of Romero*, 847 P. 2d 319 (N.M. 1993) (holding invalid a provision that permitted the decedent's minor sons to live in his house as long as their mother — the decedent's ex-wife — did not live there with them). *See also* RESTATEMENT (THIRD) OF TRUSTS §29, cmt. (2003) ("A trust or a condition or other provision in the terms of a trust is ordinarily invalid if it tends to encourage disruption of a family relationship or to discourage formation or resumption of such a relationship.").

With respect to limiting a beneficiary's choice of spouse, a shift occurred between the *Restatement (Second)* and the *Restatement (Third) of Trusts*. The comments to Section 62 of *Restatement (Second)* explain that a provision stating that a beneficiary would lose an interest in the trust if the beneficiary married a person unacceptable to the settlor is invalid, but noted that restraints on a beneficiary's marrying before reaching the age of majority or marrying outside a particular faith would usually be upheld. The *Restatement (Third)* contains a new comment to Section 29 that suggests that a provision that limits the freedom to obtain a divorce or to marry should ordinarily be invalid. Despite the shift in the *Restatement of Trusts*, the Illinois Supreme Court reversed a decision of the Illinois Court of Appeals and upheld a restraint on marriage in *In re Estate of Feinberg*, 919 N.E.2d 88 (Ill. 2009), as discussed in Chapter 1.

PROBLEM

Sophia was concerned about the logging of old growth forests. In her will she created a testamentary trust to educate the public about the importance of old growth forests, to organize protests against logging in old growth forests and to pay the legal costs of anyone arrested for civil disobedience in connection with protests against logging in old growth forests. Is this trust valid?[3]

2.   *Competent Settlor*

The settlor of a trust must be competent to establish the trust. In some situations the competency required to create a trust and to execute a will are the same; in others, it is different.

The standard of capacity required to execute a will is discussed in detail in Chapter 11. In general terms, the testator must understand the natural objects of his bounty, the nature and extent of his property and how those interrelate — the plans the testator has for the disposition of his property. Because a testamentary trust is created in a will, the standard of capacity required to create a testamentary trust is the same as the standard to execute a will.

For an inter vivos trust, the level of capacity required is the standard required to transfer property free of trust — to enter into a contract. However, because the transfer is gratuitous, the settlor must also understand the effect that creating a trust has on her future financial security and ability to support any dependents. The law imposes this requirement because a decision to part with property during life affects the settlor's ability to care for herself and any dependents. Thus, the standard to create an inter vivos trust is higher than the standard to execute a will or create a testamentary trust. *See* Restatement (Third) of Trusts §11.

For revocable trusts, the question of what standard to use is complicated by the fact that a revocable trust serves both lifetime and testamentary functions. The UTC section that follows applies the wills standard to revocable trusts.

UTC §601. Capacity of Settlor of Revocable Trust.

> The capacity required to create, amend, revoke, or add property to a revocable trust, or to direct the actions of the trustee of a revocable trust, is the same as that required to make a will.

---

3. Note that although this trust does not have an identifiable beneficiary, one of the elements required for a private express trust, the trust will not fail if it is a charitable trust. You can assume that the educational purpose of the trust will qualify it as a charitable trust.

The comments to UTC §601 explain that the primary purpose of a revocable trust is to transfer property at death, and because a revocable trust operates as a will substitute, the standard should be the same as the will standard. This explanation ignores the fact that a revocable trust is often used to manage property during the settlor's lifetime and is likely to serve as more than a will substitute. If a settlor transfers all of her property to the control of the trustee, then the settlor will depend on the assets in the revocable trust for the remainder of her life. If someone takes advantage of a settlor who is beginning to lose capacity and encourages the settlor to transfer her assets to a revocable trust, the transfer may be upheld due to the low level of capacity required, even though the person no longer has the capacity to contract.

Although the lower standard for revocable trusts may create some risk, it is helpful to remember that a trust can be set aside on the same grounds used to invalidate a will: undue influence, fraud or duress. These issues are discussed in Chapter 11.

> **Example:** Bob knows that his elderly neighbor, Beulah, is beginning to lose capacity. She still understands what her property is and who her beneficiaries are, but she is confused about how her property will be managed during her lifetime. Bob encourages her to set up a revocable living trust, with Bob as trustee. After he tells her that the trust will save taxes, Beulah agrees. Bob talks to a friend of his who is a lawyer. The lawyer drafts a trust agreement creating the trust. The document provides that on Beulah's death, her property will go to Bob. She has several nephews who would inherit if she died intestate.
>
> On these facts, Beulah might have capacity to execute the revocable living trust under the UTC standard. The nephews could challenge the creation of the trust based on Bob's undue influence of Beulah and based on Bob's fraud in telling Beulah that the trust will save taxes (it will not). The longer the trust exists before Beulah's death, however, the more difficult a challenge will be. A challenge to a will focuses on the time of execution of the document. For a trust, the ongoing relationship between the trustee and the beneficiary means that a challenge has to consider the settlor's ongoing approval of the creation of the trust.

3. Trustee

A trustee holds title to the property interests held in trust. For example, the title of a bank account opened to hold trust assets would read like this: "Wayne Grimaldi, as trustee of the Theresa Grimaldi Trust dated January 22, 2010."

A trust must have a trustee to hold and manage the assets, but a trust will not fail for lack of a trustee. A court will appoint a trustee if necessary. Usually the trust instrument names a trustee and may appoint more than one trustee to serve at the same time or as successor trustees, to serve one at a time, in sequence. A trust created without a written document usually involves the transfer of property by the settlor to the trustee. Whether the person receiving the property holds the property as a trustee depends on the intent of the person transferring the property. *See* Section B.4. We will examine three issues in connection with the trustee: how the settlor chooses a trustee, how a trustee accepts the duties of a trustee and how a trustee resigns.

a.   Choosing a Trustee

Given the important role a trustee plays in administering the trust on behalf of the beneficiaries, a settlor must choose a trustee carefully. A settlor can serve as the trustee, or she may wish to ask a family member, a close personal friend or a professional like a bank to serve as the trustee. The settlor should discuss the trust with the intended trustee in advance and make sure the person or institution is willing to serve and understands the duties involved. Some lawyers provide clients with informational brochures outlining the duties of a trustee, and that can be helpful to the new trustee. A trustee may accept compensation for serving, but typically family members and close personal friends refuse to be paid or serve for less than the fees charged by a professional or corporate trustee. If the trustee is also a beneficiary of the trust, the trustee may serve without compensation.

In deciding who should serve as trustee, the settlor must consider possible conflicts of interest and family dynamics. A trustee has to act impartially with respect to all beneficiaries, which becomes more challenging if the trustee is also a beneficiary of the trust. For example, if a settlor creates a testamentary trust providing a life estate for his second wife and the remainder in the trust to the children of a first marriage, naming either the wife or a child may cause difficulties. Also, a family member who is a trustee, whether or not she is a beneficiary, is placed in a difficult position if she is given discretion in making distributions among different family members. Other considerations may include a person's experience in managing money, general sense of responsibility and ability to work with people whose interests conflict.

For any of the reasons just described, some settlors decide to use a professional trustee. A corporate trustee may be appropriate for a large trust. Many banks have trust departments and will serve as trustee for a trust, but each bank has minimum asset requirements before it will agree to accept a position as trustee. Bank fiduciaries charge fees based on the size of the assets being managed.[4] The settlor (or the lawyer) should interview a possible bank trustee in advance to be certain that the bank is willing to act as trustee. Banks and trust companies are regulated by state law.

If the assets are small but a trust is warranted, the settlor may decide to use an individual who is a professional fiduciary. Professional trustees have emerged in recent years to provide services for clients whose assets are not sufficient to warrant the expense of a corporate trustee. In California, concerns emerged about the quality of the services provided by professional fiduciaries, and a statute regulating these fiduciaries went into effect on July 1, 2008. CAL. BUS. & PROF. CODE §6501 *et seq.* (West Supp. 2010) (Professional Fiduciaries Act). The statute makes licensing mandatory and requires initial and continuing training, record keeping and reporting.

b.   Acceptance

As we discuss in Chapter 6, the law imposes serious fiduciary duties on trustees, and for that reason a person may not want to be a trustee. A person or institution named as a trustee need not accept the designation as trustee. However, although no formal acceptance of the position is required, if the person named in the trust document takes control of the property, the person may have accepted responsibilities as trustee.

If a lawyer drafts a trust agreement, the lawyer typically provides for a signature by the settlor (to signify intent) and a signature by the trustee (to signify acceptance). UTC §701(a) provides for two ways the trustee may accept the duties, and UTC §701(b) and (c) provide guidance for rejecting an appointment as a trustee.

UTC §701. Accepting or Declining Trusteeship.

(a) Except as otherwise provided in subsection (c), a person designated as trustee accepts the trusteeship:

---

4. An example of fees charged by American Estate and Trust, a Nevada trust company, as of June 2009: $750.00 annual base fee plus charges noted below, and plus Transaction Fees (see below) $500.00 (minimum) for annual federal & state tax returns combined. Special schedules are additional. For trusts which fall under this fee schedule, this tax preparation service from AE-Trust or its appointees is mandatory. In most cases AE-Trust will not accept tax work performed by outside or unknown tax professionals.

For managing and investing financial assets, the following annual fees are applied in addition to the above base fees if AE-Trust performs this service, which is not mandatory. These fees are calculated and charged at the end of each calendar quarter or portion of a quarter:

- 1% of managed assets with a net value up to $500,000.00
- + 3/4% of managed assets with a net value from $500,000 to 1,000,000
- + 1/2% of managed assets with a net value from $1,000,000 to 2,000,000
- + 1/4% of managed assets with a net value above $2,000,000

http://www.trusteeamerica.com/pdf/Trustee%20Fee%20Schedule.pdf

(1) by substantially complying with a method of acceptance provided in the terms of the trust; or

(2) if the terms of the trust do not provide a method or the method provided in the terms is not expressly made exclusive, by accepting delivery of the trust property, exercising powers or performing duties as trustee, or otherwise indicating acceptance of the trusteeship.

(b) A person designated as trustee who has not yet accepted the trusteeship may reject the trusteeship. A designated trustee who does not accept the trusteeship within a reasonable time after knowing of the designation is deemed to have rejected the trusteeship.

(c) A person designated as trustee, without accepting the trusteeship, may:

(1) act to preserve the trust property if, within a reasonable time after acting, the person sends a rejection of the trusteeship to the settlor or, if the settlor is dead or lacks capacity, to a qualified beneficiary; and

(2) inspect or investigate trust property to determine potential liability under environmental or other law or for any other purpose.

A signature on the trust agreement is usually the method of acceptance provided in the terms of the trust, but only substantial compliance and not to-the-letter compliance is required. If the terms require that the signature be notarized, for example, the acceptance will still be valid if the trustee signs the document, even if the signature is not notarized. Remember that a trust is valid even if there is no trustee, so if the trustee fails to sign the trust agreement, the trust is still valid.

Note that a person can also be held to be the trustee by "indicating" acceptance. As one can imagine, in a situation in which acceptance is not clear, arguments may develop around whether a person has agreed to act and has acted as a trustee or not. To encourage protection of trust property, without imposing the responsibility to act as a trustee, a person designated as trustee can act to protect the property without that action being considered an acceptance. If the person takes actions with respect to the property, the person must send a refusal of the trusteeship to the settlor, or if the settlor is dead or incapacitated, to a beneficiary. UTC §701(c)(1).

Example: Gina has a vacation house in Idaho. She uses the house for two weeks each summer and rents it to visitors the rest of the year. Gina's friend Rachel lives in Idaho, and Gina decides to put the house into a trust, with Rachel as trustee. Without asking Rachel, Gina transfers the title to the house to "Rachel, as trustee of the Gina Family Trust." Gina informs Rachel that she has created this trust and then leaves to visit relatives in Slovenia for two months. Rachel does not want to be trustee, but she finds that yard care and some fire prevention maintenance is necessary. Rachel can take care of the yard and clear brush that might be a fire danger, but she should also immediately notify Gina that she does not want to be the trustee. If Gina changes the title for the house and then dies, Rachel should notify the successor beneficiary. If Rachel does not notify Gina and manages the rentals on the house for six months, she will be treated as having accepted the duties of trustee.

c.   Resignation of a Trustee

A trustee can resign from the position, but the trustee remains liable for any acts or omissions that occurred while he was acting as trustee. Usually, the trust instrument gives a trustee the right to resign, identifies the procedures involved and names a successor trustee. If the trust instrument is silent on trustee resignation, then the trustee must look to common law or statutes. Under the common law, a trustee had to get court approval to resign. UTC §705 follows standard drafting practice and permits the trustee to resign after 30-days' notice to the qualified beneficiaries, the settlor (if living) and any co-trustees. In the alternative, a trustee can get court approval for the resignation so that the court can approve the trustee's final account and release the trustee from liability with respect to the trust.

After a trustee resigns, the successor trustee named in the trust instrument will become the next trustee. The trust instrument may, instead of naming a successor, direct the beneficiaries to appoint a successor. If the trust instrument neither names a successor nor provides a way to name a successor, the court will appoint a successor. UTC §704(c) provides that qualified beneficiaries can name a successor, without the necessity of going to court, even if the trust instrument does not provide for that process. UTC §§704 and 705 provide the rules for resignation by a trustee and for filling a vacancy. As with much of the UTC, these rules fill in the gaps for trust instruments that have not been optimally drafted and do not provide for these situations.

UTC §704. Vacancy in Trusteeship; Appointment of Successor.

(a) A vacancy in a trusteeship occurs if:
    (1) a person designated as trustee rejects the trusteeship;
    (2) a person designated as trustee cannot be identified or does not exist;
    (3) a trustee resigns;
    (4) a trustee is disqualified or removed;
    (5) a trustee dies; or
    (6) a [guardian] or [conservator] is appointed for an individual serving as trustee.

(b) If one or more cotrustees remain in office, a vacancy in a trust-eeship need not be filled. A vacancy in a trusteeship must be filled if the trust has no remaining trustee.

(c) A vacancy in a trusteeship of a noncharitable trust that is required to be filled must be filled in the following order of priority:

(1) by a person designated in the terms of the trust to act as successor trustee;

(2) by a person appointed by unanimous agreement of the qualified beneficiaries; or

(3) by a person appointed by the court.

UTC §705. Resignation of Trustee.

(a) A trustee may resign:

(1) upon at least 30 days' notice to the qualified beneficiaries, the settlor, if living, and all cotrustees; or

(2) with the approval of the court.

(b) In approving a resignation, the court may issue orders and impose conditions reasonably necessary for the protection of the trust property.

(c) Any liability of a resigning trustee or of any sureties on the trustee's bond for acts or omissions of the trustee is not discharged or "affected by the trustee's resignation.

PROBLEMS

1.   Hana tells her friend, Kyung, that she is going to give him $20,000 to keep in trust for her mother, to be used to buy books and flowers for her mother, until her mother's death. Hana writes a check to Kyung, and he cashes it. He puts the money in a separate bank account in his name and makes no withdrawals from the account. A year later, Hana dies and the money remains in the bank account. Kyung does not want to be a trustee and is willing to give the money to Hana's mother or daughter. Hana's daughter is her only heir.

a.   Would you advise Hana's mother to sue Kyung for violating his duties as trustee and, if so, on what basis?

b.   If you represented Kyung, could he argue that he never agreed to be a trustee and was just keeping the money safe for Hana?

c.   Who has the right to the money?

2.   Nicole has an estate valued at $5.0 million. She has no spouse, no partner and no children. She wants to create a trust under her will to provide for her mother for the rest of her mother's life and then to be

distributed to her nieces and nephews. While her mother is alive, the trustee can distribute trust principal to her mother and to her nieces and nephews for their health, education, maintenance and support. Nicole is considering three possible trustees: her sister (Rachel), her brother (Edward) and the local bank. Rachel is a full-time homemaker who cares for her three young children. Rachel's husband is a high school teacher. Edward is an investment banker. His wife is a banking lawyer, and they have two children. Nicole lives in a small town, and the bank is the one she uses for her personal banking business. How would you advise Nicole on choosing a trustee (the possible advantages and disadvantages of each of the three options she is considering)?

3.   Jeffrey has acted as trustee of his cousin's testamentary trust for five years. His cousin died leaving a wife and two adult children from a previous marriage. Jeffrey is tired of the squabbling and wants to resign as trustee. The trust document (the cousin's will) did not provide for a successor trustee. What would you advise Jeffrey to do?

4.   *Intent to Create a Trust*

The creation of a trust requires a "manifestation of intention" to create the trust. *See* Restatement (Third) of Trusts §2 (2003). When a court decides whether the settlor intended to create a trust, the court may consider various forms of evidence. Written evidence of intent is not required; a court can consider any admissible extrinsic evidence to determine intent, such as documents or testimony of witnesses. A settlor's undisclosed intent is irrelevant; a court cannot consider bare assumptions about why a deceased settlor transferred property to someone.

In most estate planning situations, a trust document will have been executed and establishes the settlor's intent to create a trust. Two types of documents are used to create an inter vivos trust: If another person is going to be the trustee (or a co-trustee with the settlor who is the other co-trustee), the settlor transfers property pursuant to a trust agreement; if the settlor is going to be the original trustee, the settlor declares himself trustee using a declaration of trust.

A document labeled "Trust Agreement" or "Declaration of Trust" usually suffices to establish intent to create the trust, although the trust may fail for some other reason or questions may arise as to the property that constitutes the trust (see discussion of corpus, *infra*). (But see *Palozie v. Palozie, infra.*)

Sometimes, however, it is not clear whether the property owner intends to create a trust with the recipient of the property acting as trustee or intends something else. Possible alternatives include:

- The transfer may have been intended as a testamentary transfer.
- The transfer may be an outright gift with explanatory or precatory language. (*Palozie v. Palozie* and *Matter of Estate of Bolinger*).

- The transfer may be a promise to make a gift in the future (*Hebrew Univ. Assn. v. Nye*).
- The transfer may be the creation of a power of appointment over the property (powers of appointment are discussed in Chapter 8).

A determination of what the property owner intended will establish whether a trust exists, which in turn will affect the ultimate ownership of the property: The property may still belong to the property owner, the property may have been transferred to someone else who now owns the property outright or the property may have been transferred to a trustee to hold for a beneficiary.

a.   Testamentary Transfer or Inter Vivos Gift in Trust?

A court may be asked to decide whether the owner of property had transferred the property during life or intended for the transfer to occur at death. The question often arises in connection with a declaration of trust, because in that situation the owner is "transferring" the property to herself as trustee. In the next case, the court considers a number of factors in determining whether the property owner created a trust.

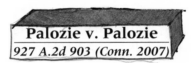

Palozie v. Palozie
927 A.2d 903 (Conn. 2007)

BORDON, J.

The plaintiff, Donald L. Palozie, appeals from the judgment of the trial court affirming the judgment of the Probate Court denying the plaintiff's application for title and right of possession to a twenty-three acre parcel of land situated on Crane Road in Ellington (Crane Road property). The plaintiff claims that the trial court improperly concluded that a declaration of trust executed by the plaintiff's deceased mother, Sophie H. Palozie (decedent), was invalid and unenforceable because the decedent had not manifested an unequivocal intent to create a trust and to impose upon herself the enforceable duties of a trustee. We affirm the judgment of the trial court. . . .

After conducting a trial on the merits of the plaintiff's application, the trial court found the following facts. "On February 23, 1988, [the decedent] asked her grandson David Palozie, who is also the plaintiff's son, to visit her. It was David's birthday and he did go to [the decedent's] home with his wife Susan. While there [the decedent] asked David and his wife, Susan [Palozie], to witness her signature on a document and they did so. The document . . . is entitled '[d]eclaration of [t]rust.'" At the time David did not know what the document purported to be, nor was there any evidence that Susan did either. The signature of the settlor appears to be that of [the decedent] and it has not been shown otherwise.

At the same time [the decedent] asked David and Susan [Palozie] to witness a second document purporting to be a quitclaim deed to the Crane Road property, again with the witnesses having no knowledge of what the document was. . . . The quitclaim deed purports to convey to herself as trustee under the terms of the [d]eclaration of [t]rust, the Crane Road property. The quitclaim deed was not acknowledged and neither it nor the [d]eclaration of [t]rust were recorded on the land records.

No one, other than [the decedent] was aware of the nature of these documents. Apparently, she kept them in either a small metal box or a suitcase in her home. [The decedent] died, in her home on March 13, 1991, intestate.

Family members, including the plaintiff and [the decedent's] daughter, Gaye Reyes, gathered at the house. They retrieved a small metal box and a suitcase. The contents of the metal box were briefly examined and then taken by the plaintiff to the house trailer in which he lived, which was located on the property. ([The decedent] lived separately in a house on the same property.)

Gaye [Reyes] was appointed administratrix of the estate and filed an inventory on March 24, 1992, which included the Crane Road property as an asset of the estate.

Gaye Reyes was removed as administratrix approximately ten years later because the administration of the estate was not proceeding timely. Two of [the decedent's] grandchildren, Richard Palozie and Joanne Palozie-Weems were appointed as successor coadministrators in June, 2002. In January, 2003, they filed an application to sell the real estate in question. The plaintiff objected to the proposed sale claiming, for the first time since [the decedent's] death in 1991, that he, and not [the decedent's] estate, held legal title to the property by virtue of the purported trust."

On the basis of the foregoing facts, the trial court concluded that the plaintiff had failed to prove, by clear and satisfactory evidence, that the decedent had "adequately manifest[ed] an intention to create a trust and to accept the enforceable duties of trustee." The trial court observed that the decedent had not informed "[t]he witnesses to the '[d]eclaration of [t]rust' . . . what the instrument was," and had "kept the document under her total control during her lifetime with no obligation . . . to the supposed beneficiaries." "The likelihood is that [the decedent] wished to retain total control of the property during her lifetime for her own benefit, and not as a trustee for the plaintiff . . . [and, therefore, the trust instrument] was a poorly designed effort to establish a testamentary document, rather than a trust with the requirements that would entail." In arriving at this determination, the trial court found it noteworthy that: (1) "there was evidence that [the decedent] and . . . [the plaintiff] were not always without conflict in their relationship," as reflected by a family violence protective order issued against the plaintiff on behalf of the decedent in 1990; and (2) the quitclaim deed "was never recorded, nor was it properly acknowledged as required by General Statutes §47-5. Accordingly, the trial court determined that the declaration of trust was void and unenforceable and, therefore, rendered judgment in favor of the defendants. This appeal followed.

The following additional facts are relevant to our resolution of the present appeal. The declaration of trust provides in relevant part: "Whereas I, Sophie H. Palozie, of the Town of Ellington, County of Tolland, State of Connecticut, am the owner of certain real property located at (and known as) 315 Crane Road in the Town of Ellington, State of Connecticut . . . NOW THEREFORE, KNOW ALL MEN BY THESE PRESENTS, that I do hereby acknowledge and declare that I hold and will hold said real property and all my right, title and interest in and to said property and all furniture, fixtures and personal property situated therein on the date of my death, IN TRUST being of sound mind to wit I make this my last private verbal act . . . [f]or the use and benefit of . . . Donald L. Palozie, Trustee [under declaration of trust] February 23, 1988 . . . [but] if such beneficiary be not surviving, for the use and benefit of . . . Gaye M. Reyes. . . ." The instrument further provides: "Upon my death, unless the beneficiaries shall predecease me or unless we all shall die as a result of a common accident or disaster, my [s]uccessor [t]rustee is hereby directed forthwith to transfer said property and all my right, title and interest in and to said property unto the beneficiary absolutely and thereby terminate this trust. . . ."

The plaintiff claims that the trial court improperly found that the decedent had not manifested an intent to create a trust, or to impose upon herself the enforceable duties of a trustee, based on her failure to communicate her intent and on her exclusive retention and control of the trust instrument and quitclaim deed during her lifetime. We disagree and, accordingly, we affirm the judgment of the trial court.

Before addressing the merits of the plaintiff's claim, we briefly review the basic principles that govern the validity and enforcement of trusts. The requisite elements of a valid and enforceable trust are: "(1) a trustee, who holds the trust property and is subject to duties to deal with it for the benefit of one or more others; (2) one or more beneficiaries, to whom and for whose benefit the trustee owes the duties with respect to the trust property; and (3) trust property, which is held by the trustee for the beneficiaries." 1 Restatement (Third), Trusts §2, comment (f), p. 21(2003). . . .

"One owning property can create an enforceable trust by a declaration that he holds the property as trustee for the benefit of another person." A trust may be created "without notice to or acceptance by any beneficiary or trustee"; 1 Restatement (Third), supra, §[2]at 14, p. 216; and in the absence of consideration. Id., §[2]at 15, p. 222. . . . Moreover, "the settlor may reserve extensive powers over the administration of a trust"; and may reserve the right to modify or revoke the trust at will. "No trust, however, is created unless the settlor presently and unequivocally manifests an intention to impose upon himself enforceable duties of a trust nature. . . . If what has been done falls short of showing the complete establishment of a fiduciary relationship, as where the intent to become a trustee is doubtful because what was said or done is as compatible with an intent to make a future gift as with an intent to hold the legal title to property for the exclusive benefit of another, the proof fails to show more than a promise without consideration."

To determine whether the decedent manifested an intent to create a trust and to impose upon herself the enforceable duties of a trustee, we begin with the language of the trust instrument. This is because "where the manifestation of the settlor's intention is integrated in a writing, that is, if a written instrument is adopted by the settlor as the complete expression of the settlor's intention, extrinsic evidence is not admissible to contradict or vary the terms of the instrument in the absence of fraud, duress, undue influence, mistake, or other ground for reformation or rescission." 1 Restatement (Third), supra, §[2] at 21, comment (a), p. 322. . . .

If, however, the trust instrument "is an incomplete expression of the settlor's intention or if the meaning of the writing is ambiguous or otherwise uncertain, evidence of the circumstances and other indications of the transferor's intent are admissible to complete the terms of the writing or to clarify or ascertain its meaning. 1 Restatement (Third), supra, §[2] at 21, comment (a), p. 322. Under such circumstances, the question of the decedent's intent to create a trust and to impose upon herself the duties of a trustee is a question of fact subject to review under the clearly erroneous standard.

In the present case, we conclude that the trust instrument is ambiguous with respect to whether the decedent intended to create a trust and to impose upon herself the enforceable duties of a trustee. Although the instrument plainly states that the decedent intended to hold the Crane Road property in trust, it also contains the following language, "being of sound mind to wit I make this my last private verbal act," which imports ambiguity into the trust instrument. . . . Of particular significance for purposes of our analysis, however, is not the decedent's characterization of the execution of the trust instrument as a verbal act, which appears to have little or no bearing on her intent to create a trust or to impose upon herself the duties of a trustee, but, rather, her characterization of it as her *last act.* In light of this language, it is unclear whether the decedent intended to create a presently enforceable trust, with all of the rights, duties and responsibilities that such a trust entails, or whether she intended to execute a testamentary document, which would become effective and enforceable only after her death. . . .

Although communication of intent to create a trust and delivery of the trust instrument are "not essential to the existence of a trust [they are] of great importance in determining the real intent of the alleged declarant." 90 C.J.S., Trusts §66, p. 192 (2002). This is because a settlor's failure to communicate his or her intent and to deliver the trust instrument "is some indication of the absence of a final and definitive intention to create a trust." . . .

In the present case, it is undisputed that the decedent informed neither the beneficiaries of the trust nor anyone else that she had intended to hold the Crane Road property in trust. Additionally, it is undisputed that she never delivered the trust instrument or the quitclaim deed to the beneficiaries or any other third party, and that she never recorded the trust instrument or the quitclaim deed on the town land records. These undisputed facts amply support the trial court's finding that the decedent had not arrived at a final and definitive intention to create a trust and to impose upon herself the enforceable duties of a trustee.

NOTES AND QUESTIONS

1. *Deed requirements.* Connecticut, unlike many states, requires acknowledgement of a deed. CONN. GEN. STAT. ANN. §47-5. In Connecticut, in order to transfer property into the name of a trustee, the deed making the transfer must be in writing, signed by the property owner (grantor), acknowledged by the grantor and signed by two witnesses.

2. *Legalese.* In *Palozie v. Palozie*, Sophie Palozie had signed a document titled "declaration of trust," yet the court finds that Ms. Palozie had not shown her intent to create a trust. The court makes much of language on the document, "I make this my last private verbal act," which may be language on a form or language she added to make the document sound more "legal." Does this language suggest that she intended something other than a trust? If so, what?

3. *Fact and factors.* The court suggests that Ms. Palozie might have intended to create a testamentary document rather than a presently enforceable trust. What are the arguments that this is an inter vivos trust? A testamentary document?

4. *Advice and duty.* If Ms. Palozie consulted you about giving the property to Donald, what might you have advised to anticipate the problems identified by the court? If after talking with Ms. Palozie you suspected elder abuse, what duties do you have as an attorney?

b. Gift in Trust or Outright Gift with Explanatory or Precatory Language?

When a document purporting to create a trust exists, the language will be important in determining whether the author of the document actually intended to create a trust. A property owner need not use the word "trust" or "trustee" in creating a trust, but the intent to create a trust must be clear. If the property owner makes a gift to someone and expresses the "hope" or "desire" that the recipient use the property in a particular way, perhaps for the benefit of someone else, the property owner may be merely explaining the reason for the gift or recommending how the gift should be used. Unless the owner intended to create a trust, precatory language may create a moral obligation, but it does not create a legal obligation with respect to the use of the property. Unfortunately, language does not always clearly convey the intent of the property owner.

Example: Mara writes: "I am giving Julius $10,000. It is my wish that he will use it for his children's college education." Mara has probably made an outright gift to Julius, with precatory language that expresses her wishes for the use of the gift. Julius is not required to hold the gift as a trustee (with all the fiduciary duties that involves) for his children's college education.

Example: Derek sends a check to his brother with a note that reads: "Jason, I'm delighted to hear about your son's successes in high school. I know that college is expensive, and I hope that you will use the enclosed check to help with his college tuition." The enclosed check is made out to Jason. Words like "hope," "wish" and "desire" are precatory words. In this example, while the directions from Derek are more explicit than those in the writing by Mara, and may provide Jason's son with a stronger argument that the transfer created a trust, the language is probably only precatory.

Example: Norman sends a check to his daughter. The check is made out to her, and his note enclosing the check says, "Jeanne, please use this for Amanda's college education." Amanda is Jeanne's daughter. This language may be precatory, but there appears to be a stronger argument that Norman intends to create a fiduciary duty in Jeanne to use the money for Amanda's education.

The following case takes a look at precatory language and raises the question of whether the property owner intended the person to take the property as trustee or in the person's individual capacity. As you read the case think about what you think the decedent intended. Do you think the majority or the dissent has the better reasoned opinion?

Matter of Estate of Bolinger
943 P.2d 981 (Mont. 1997)

NELSON, Justice
Harry Albert Bolinger, III, (Decedent), died March 23, 1995. . . . The November 15, 1984 will so offered for probate devised all Decedent's estate to Hal [Bolinger, decedent's father], or, in the event that Hal predeceased Decedent, to Hal's wife (Decedent's step-mother), Marian.

Specifically, the Fifth paragraph of the will, the language of which is at issue here, provides:

> I intentionally give all of my property and estate to my said father, H.A. Bolinger, in the event that he shall survive me, and in the event he shall not survive me, I intentionally give all of my property and estate to my step-mother, Marian Bolinger, in the event she shall survive me, and in that event, I intentionally give nothing to my three children, namely: Harry Albert Bolinger, IV, Wyetta Bolinger and Travis Bolinger, or to any children of any child who shall not survive me. I make this provision for the reason that I feel confident that any property which either my father or my step-mother, Marian Bolinger, receive from my estate will be used in the best interests of my said children as my said beneficiaries may determine in their exclusive discretion.

The will nominated Hal as personal representative with Marian as the alternate. Hal subsequently renounced his right to serve as personal representative and suggested the appointment of Marian, who petitioned to be appointed on November 6, 1995. Decedent's children objected, contending, among other things, that the will was void as a matter of law because of undue influence or constructive fraud on the part of Hal, and, in the alternative, that the will created a trust on behalf of the children. [The court found no undue influence or constructive fraud.] . . .

On the basis of the discovery responses and depositions provided as part of the summary judgment proceedings, the District Court found that both Hal and Marian believed that the language in the *Fifth* paragraph of Decedent's will created a trust (although in a second deposition Marian contended that she was mistaken in her initial impression in this regard). The court also found that Marian believed that at the time Decedent's will was drafted and executed, the children were minors and that Decedent used the language in the will to prevent his ex-wife from obtaining control over his estate. The court also agreed with Professor Folsom that, when read in its entirety, the *Fifth* paragraph of the will expressed Decedent's intention that all of his property must be used in the best interests of his children. The court found that the subject or res of the trust was all of Decedent's property and that the testator's purpose in creating the trust was to ensure that his assets would be used in his children's best interests. The court then concluded that Decedent having thus manifested his intention, and, on the basis of the criteria and authorities argued by the children, an express trust for the children's benefit was created under the *Fifth* paragraph of Decedent's will.

On appeal from the District Court's decision, Marian argues that proof of an express trust requires clear and convincing evidence that the trustor intended to create a trust and that devises, bequests and gifts that do not contain any restrictions on use or disposition of the property involved do not create an express trust. She contends that the use of "precatory" words by a testator, that is words which express only a wish or recommendation as to the disposition of property, are not sufficient to establish an intention

to create a trust. She cites, among other cases, our decision in *Stapleton v. DeVries*, 535 P.2d 1267 (Mont. 1975), in support of her position in this regard. Furthermore, she maintains that the trial court erred in considering the affidavit of Professor Folsom [a professor of English] because the question of whether given language in a will creates an express trust is one of law, and, as such, is not a proper subject of expert opinion.

In support of the District Court's decision, the children argue that where the testator manifests his intention to create a trust, no particular form of words or conduct is necessary, and that, providing that the trustor indicates with reasonable certainty the subject, purpose and beneficiary of the trust, an express trust is created. The children contend that, under the facts here and under these criteria, the language used by Decedent in the *Fifth* paragraph of his will created an express trust in their favor. They maintain that a trust must be construed in a manner so as to implement the trustor's intent and that, here, Decedent clearly expressed his intention that his property be used for the benefit of his children. The children cite a 1894 [sic] New York case, *People v. Powers*, 29 N.Y.S 950 (N.Y. Sup. Ct. 1984), *rev'd on other grounds*, 41 N.E.432 (1985), for the proposition that a testator's expression of "confidence" that a bequest will be used to benefit another is sufficient to create a trust. Finally, as to the matter of the Folsom affidavit, Decedent's children maintain that the professor did not express an expert opinion on the ultimate legal question, but, rather, his opinion went simply to "the *factual* issue of the grammatical construction of [the *Fifth* paragraph] — not on whether the language creates an express trust."

At the outset, we note that there are differences in the statutory law in effect at the time that Decedent executed his will in November 1984 and when he died in March 1995. . . .

. . . in the case at bar, we will address the first issue [creation of a trust] in the context of those legal principles which, we believe, have remained historically constant regardless of the changes in the statutory law over the time period in question. In this regard, we also note that under the present Trust Code, §72-33-103, MCA, provides that "[e]xcept to the extent that the common law rules governing trusts are modified by statute, the common law as to trusts is the law of this state."

Taking this approach, it is clear that a trust is created only if the testator demonstrates that he or she intends that a trust be created. This rule, followed in *Wild West Motors*, was set forth prior to 1989 at §72-20-107, MCA:

> a voluntary trust is created, as to the trust or and beneficiary, by any words or acts of the trust or indicating with reasonable certainty: (1) an intention on the part of the trust or to create a trust; and (2) the subject, purpose and beneficiary of the trust.

Since 1989, under the Trust Code the law is that "[a] trust is created only if the trust or properly [sic] manifests an intention to create a trust." Section 72-33-202, MCA.

Moreover, in our case law, we continue to cite to the general rule that in the construction of trusts it is the trustor's intent that controls and that to determine that intent we look to the language of the trust agreement. In that regard, our rules of construction with respect to testamentary instruments are well settled:

> The words of the instrument are to receive an interpretation which will give some effect to every expression, rather than an interpretation which will render any of the expressions inoperative. The will is to be construed according to the intentions of the testator, so far as is possible to ascertain them. Words used in the instrument are to be taken in their ordinary and grammatical sense unless a clear intention to use them in another sense can be ascertained. In cases of uncertainty arising upon the face of the will, the testator's intention is to be ascertained from the words of the instrument, taking into view the circumstances under which it was made, exclusive of his oral declarations. . . .
>
> "The object, therefore, of a judicial interpretation of a will is to ascertain the intention of the testator, according to the meaning of the words he has used, deduced from a consideration of the whole instrument and a comparison of its various parts in the light of the situation and circumstances which surrounded the testator when the instrument was framed."

Furthermore, "[n]o particular form of words or conduct is necessary for the manifestation of intention to create a trust," Restatement (Second) of Trusts §24 (1959), and "words of trusteeship are not necessarily conclusive," George T. Bogert, Trusts §11 at 24 (6th ed. 1987). Nonetheless, we have held that "express trusts depend for their creation upon a clear and direct expression of intent by the trustor," and that the burden of proof to establish the existence of a trust is upon the party who claims it and must be founded on evidence which is unmistakable, clear, satisfactory and convincing. . . .

From [the language in the will] it is clear that Decedent intended to accomplish several things under this paragraph of his will. First, he "intentionally" devised outright all of his property and estate to his father, and in default of that bequest, then to his step-mother, Marian. Second, it is also clear that Decedent "intentionally" devised nothing to his three children. Third, Decedent desired to make some explanation as to why he disposed of his estate in the foregoing manner. To this end, he added to the otherwise unequivocal language of the first sentence of the *Fifth* paragraph, a second sentence with the explanation that he made this provision because he felt "confident" that any property which either his father or his step-mother, Marian, received from his estate would ["will"] be used in the best interests of his said children as Hal or Marian may determine in their exclusive discretion. It is the language in this second sentence which is at issue and which the District Court determined created an express trust in favor of the children.

Precatory language @ issue
Not trust ethical obligation

The use of this latter sort of qualifying language in a will or instrument is referred to as "precatory" language. As stated in Bogert, *supra* §19 at 41:

> Usually, if a transferor of property intends the transferee to be a trustee, he directs him to act in that capacity, but sometimes he merely expresses a wish or recommendation that the property given be used in whole or in part for the benefit of another. Words of this latter type are called "precatory" and are generally construed not to create a trust but instead to create at most an ethical obligation.

In weighing the effect of precatory expressions the courts consider the entire document and the circumstances of the donor, his family, and other interested parties.

The author of this treatise notes that the primary question in construing precatory language is whether the testator meant merely to advise or influence the discretion of the devisee, or himself control or direct the disposition intended. Bogert, *supra* §19 at 42. Here, in Marian's favor, the author notes that "the settlor must have explicitly or impliedly expressed an intent to impose obligations on the trustee and not merely to give the donee of the property *an option to use if for the benefit of another.*" Bogert, *supra* §19 at 42 (emphasis added). Put another way, considering the language of the entire instrument and the situation of the alleged settlor, his family, and the supposed beneficiaries at the time the will was executed, "was it natural and probable that the donor intended the donee to be bound by an enforceable obligation *or was he to be free to use his judgment and discretion?*" Bogert, *supra* §19 at 42 (emphasis added). Moreover, "[w]here a donor first makes an absolute gift of property, without restriction or limitation, and later inserts precatory language in a separate sentence or paragraph, the courts are apt to find that there was no intent to have a trust." Bogert, *supra* §19 at 43.

We have addressed the use of such language in a prior decision relied on by Marian. In *Stapleton*, 535 P.2d at 1268, the decedent's will provided as follows:

> I give, devise and bequeath to my beloved wife, Amanda DeVries, all the balance, residue and remainder of my property of whatever nature, kind or character which I may own at the time of my death to have and to hold as her sole and separate property. I do this with the knowledge that she will be fair and equitable to all of my children, the issue of myself and my former wife as well as the issue of herself and myself.

When Amanda died leaving all her property to her children and nothing to the decedent's children by his first marriage, the latter sued claiming that a constructive trust was created by decedent's will in their favor. Reversing the trial court's summary judgment in the plaintiffs' favor, we ruled that the language was clear on its face—Amanda was given decedent's property outright and the remaining precatory language did not create a trust for the benefit of the children by decedent's first marriage. . . .

Similarly, in the case at bar, the language used by Decedent clearly and unambiguously makes an outright gift to his father, and in default of that gift, to his step-mother and specifically excludes his children. Then, in a separate sentence, Decedent explains the reason for this distribution, expressing his "confidence" that the devisees will use his estate for the children's "best interests" in the devisees' "exclusive discretion." This language does not impose any sort of clear directive or obligation (other than, perhaps, a moral or ethical one) on either Hal or Marian. The purported trustee is given no direction as to how the supposed settlor intends his estate to be used to further the "best interests" of the children and neither does Decedent provide any guidance as to what those best interests might include. Decedent imposes no restrictions on the purported trustee, but, rather, leaves in that person the "exclusive discretion" as to how the estate will be used for the children's best interests, expressing his "confidence" that will be accomplished. Decedent's statement of reasons for devising his estate to Hal and Marian, neither limits nor restricts the gift to them any more than did the language at issue in *Stapleton* and in *Miller* limit or restrict the bequests made in those cases. The bottom line is that, under the precatory language used by Decedent, his devisees had complete discretion as to how to use the property given them outright. . . .

We hold that the District Court erred in its legal conclusion that the *Fifth* paragraph of Decedent's will created an express trust for the benefit of Decedent's three children. Accordingly, we reverse and remand for further proceedings consistent with this opinion.

Reversed and remanded.

LEAPHART, J., dissenting.

I dissent . . . .

The language used in the Bolinger will is distinguishable from and more conclusive than that used in *Stapleton*. In *Stapleton*, the decedent's will devised the property to the beneficiary "to hold as her sole and separate property." Such a "sole and separate property" provision is absent in the Bolinger will. Secondly, in *Stapleton*, the testator made the devise knowing that the beneficiary would be fair and equitable to all his children (i.e. children from both marriages). The beneficiary was thus under no obligation to segregate the devised property or to treat it any differently than her sole property. In contrast, Bolinger provided that "any property" received from his estate was specifically tagged for use "in the best interests of [his] children." In other words, his father or step-mother were not to commingle the property with their own property, nor were they to treat it as their sole and separate property with some vague understanding that they would then be fair and equitable to all concerned. Rather, Bolinger was confident that this *specific property* **"will be used in the best interests of my children."**

[Emphasis in original.] The language in the Bolinger will is more than precatory, it is peremptory.

As the court recognizes, no particular form of words is necessary for the manifestation of an intent to create a trust, Restatement (Second) of Trusts §24, express trusts depend upon a clear and direct expression of intent by the trustor. Bolinger clearly intended that the property passing maintain its separate identity and that his father or step-mother, as trustees, use the property solely for the benefit of his children, who were, at the time of the will, minors.

I would affirm the decision of the District Court.

NOTES AND QUESTIONS

1. *Divine the intent.* How does the court determine Harry Bolinger's intent? What documents or other evidence does the court consider? What words does the court analyze? The dissent reaches a different conclusion based on the same language. Why? What evidence as to the existence or nonexistence of a trust do you find most persuasive?

2. *Words matter.* Proper drafting would have avoided the need for a court proceeding in *Bolinger*. What language might the drafting attorneys have used?

3. *For the family law lawyers.* A trust may be created in an estate planning document, but trusts arise in other circumstances, too. For example, a property settlement agreement entered into in a divorce might be adequate to create a trust. In *Penney v. White*, 594 S.W.2d 632 (Mo. App. W.D. 1980), a dispute between a former husband and wife included a disagreement about the following provision in their property settlement agreement:

> property shall be held by (the wife) and that upon the sale of the property by (the wife) or her remarriage, (the husband) requests that his equity conveyed (t)herein be held by (the wife) in trust for their children.

The court had to determine whether this provision created a trust, and the word "requests" created an ambiguity. The trial court found no trust, stating that this provisions was "at least ambiguous and at most a nullity," and awarded the husband his equity in the house (which had been sold). The appellate court reversed and held that a trust was created when the property was sold. The court explained:

> The predominant circumstance which removes the doubt and determines the intention to create a trust for the children is the very nature of the transaction which encompasses the precatory clause: a property settlement agreement in contemplation of a family dissolution . . . The extrinsic evidence shows that

the husband intended, despite the supplicative words, to command that the equity from the sale of the home be taken by the wife as trustee for the children.

c.   Transfer into Trust or a Promise to Make a Gift in the Future?

When a donor makes a gift, the gift is considered incomplete until delivery to the donee has occurred. Delivery can be constructive or symbolic, but delivery must be completed. Sometimes when delivery is not completed before the donor dies, the intended donee will argue that the donor had intended to hold the property in trust for him. A declaration of trust — "I now hold this property as trustee for the beneficiary" — does not require delivery of the property to the trustee (the settlor is the trustee) or to the beneficiary.

In *Hebrew University Ass'n v. Nye*, the Connecticut Supreme Court overturned the trial court's finding that a trust had been created. A donor had attempted to make an inter vivos gift and failed to complete the gift before her death, but the facts did not show that she had intended to create a trust. The case was remanded, and the donee won on different grounds. This text includes two opinions from the multi-year litigation. In the first opinion by the Supreme Court, the court made clear that it did not want to muddy trust law by finding the creation of a trust when the donor did not intend to create a trust. In the second case, the court got the property where the donor wanted it to go using different means. As you read these cases, remember the discussion in Chapter 4 of what makes a transfer a gift.

The Hebrew University Ass'n v. Nye (I)
169 A.2d 641 (Conn. 1961)

KING, Associate Justice

The plaintiff obtained a judgment declaring that it is the rightful owner of the library of Abraham S. Yahuda, a distinguished Hebrew scholar who died in 1951. The library included rare books and manuscripts, mostly relating to the Bible, which Professor Yahuda, with the assistance of his wife, Ethel S. Yahuda, had collected during his lifetime. Some of the library was inventoried in Professor Yahuda's estate and was purchased from the estate by his wife. There is no dispute that all of the library had become the property of Ethel before 1953 and was her property when she died on March 6, 1955, unless by her dealings with the plaintiff between January, 1953, and the time of her death she transferred ownership to the plaintiff. While the defendants in this action are the executors under the will of Ethel, the controversy as to ownership of the library is, in effect, a contest between two Hebrew charitable institutions, the plaintiff and a charitable trust or foundation to which, as hereinafter appears, Ethel bequeathed the bulk of her estate.

The pertinent facts recited in the finding may be summarized as follows: Before his death, Professor Yahuda forwarded certain of the books in his library to a warehouse in New Haven with instructions that they be packed for overseas shipment. The books remained in his name, no consignee was ever specified, and no shipment was made. Although it is not entirely clear, these books were apparently the ones which Ethel purchased from her husband's estate. Professor Yahuda and his wife had indicated to their friends their interest in creating a scholarship research center in Israel which would serve as a memorial to them. In January, 1953, Ethel went to Israel and had several talks with officers of the plaintiff, a university in Jerusalem. One of the departments of the plaintiff is an Institute of Oriental Studies, of outstanding reputation. The library would be very useful to the plaintiff, especially in connection with the work of this institute. On January 28, 1953, a large luncheon was given by the plaintiff in Ethel's honor and was attended by many notables, including officials of the plaintiff and the president of Israel. At this luncheon, Ethel described the library and announced its gift to the plaintiff. The next day, the plaintiff submitted to Ethel a proposed newspaper release which indicated that she had made a gift of the library to the plaintiff. Ethel signed the release as approved by her. From time to time thereafter she stated orally, and in letters to the plaintiff and friends, that she 'had given' the library to the plaintiff. She refused offers of purchase and explained to others that she could not sell the library because it did not belong to her but to the plaintiff. On one occasion, when it was suggested that she give a certain item in the library to a friend, she stated that she could not, since it did not belong to her but to the plaintiff.

Early in 1954, Ethel began the task of arranging and cataloguing the material in the library for crating and shipment to Israel. These activities continued until about the time of her death. She sent some items, which she had finished cataloguing, to a warehouse for crating for overseas shipment. No consignee was named, and they remained in her name until her death. In October, 1954, when she was at the office of the American Friends of the Hebrew University, a fund raising arm of the plaintiff in New York, she stated that she had crated most of the miscellaneous items, was continuously working on cataloguing the balance, and hoped to have the entire library in Israel before the end of the year. Until almost the time of her death, she corresponded with the plaintiff about making delivery to it of the library. . . .

. . . [The trial court found] that "a trust [in relation to the library] was created by a declaration of trust made by Ethel S. Yahuda, indicating her intention to create such a trust, made public by her." We construe this language, in the light of the finding, as a determination, that, at the luncheon in Jerusalem, Ethel orally constituted herself a trustee of the library for future delivery to the plaintiff. The difficulty with the trust theory adopted in the judgment is that the finding contains no facts even intimating that Ethel ever regarded herself as trustee of any trust whatsoever, or as having assumed any enforceable duties with respect to the property. The facts in the finding, in so far as they tend to support the judgment for the plaintiff at all, indicate that Ethel intended to make, and perhaps attempted to make, not a mere promise to give, but an executed, present, legal gift inter vivos of the library to the plaintiff without any delivery whatsoever.

Obviously, if an intended or attempted legal gift inter vivos of personal property fails as such because there was neither actual nor constructive delivery, and the intent to give can nevertheless be carried into effect in equity under the fiction that the donor is presumed to have intended to constitute himself a trustee to make the necessary delivery, then as a practical matter the requirement of delivery is abrogated in any and all cases of intended inter-vivos gifts. Of course this is not the law. A gift which is imperfect for lack of a delivery will not be turned into a declaration of trust for no better reason than that it is imperfect for lack of a delivery. Courts do not supply conveyances where there are none. . . .

It is true that one can orally constitute himself a trustee of personal property for the benefit of another and thereby create a trust enforceable in equity, even though without consideration and without delivery. 1 Scott, op. cit. §28; §32.2, p. 251. But he must in effect constitute himself a trustee. There must be an express trust, even though oral. It is not sufficient that he declare himself a donor. 1 Scott, op. cit. §31, p. 239; 4 id. §462.1. While he need not use the term 'trustee,' nor even manifest an understanding of its technical meaning or the technical meaning of the term 'trust,' he must manifest an intention to impose upon himself enforceable duties of a trust nature. *Cullen v. Chappell, supra*; Restatement (Second), 1 Trusts §§23, 25; 1 Scott, op. cit., pp. 180, 181. There are no subordinate facts in the finding to indicate that Ethel ever intended to, or did, impose upon herself any enforceable duties of a trust nature with respect to this library. The most that could be said is that the subordinate facts in the finding might perhaps have supported a conclusion that at the luncheon she had the requisite donative intent so that, had she subsequently made a delivery of the property while that intent persisted, there would have been a valid, legal gift inter vivos. The judgment, however, is not based on the theory of a legal gift inter vivos but on that of a declaration of trust. Since the subordinate facts give no support for a judgment on that basis, it cannot stand.

[The court concluded that no trust had been created, and then remanded the case for a new trial, after giving the plaintiff some suggestions as to how it might proceed on other theories.]

The Hebrew University Ass'n v. Nye (II)
223 A.2d 397 (Conn. 1966)

PARSKEY, Judge.

Most of the facts in this case are recited in *Hebrew University Ass'n v. Nye*, 169 A.2d 641 (1961). Additionally, it should be noted that at the time of the announcement of the gift of the "Yahuda Library" the decedent gave to the plaintiff a memorandum containing a list of most of the contents of the library and of all of the important books, documents and incunabula. At some time prior to the summer of 1954 and during the lifetime of Mrs. Yahuda, the Hebrew University began the project of erecting its library. In setting up this plan for the library building, the Hebrew University designated a room in the building as the Yahuda room and indicated upon its plan that such room was not open for subscription or contribution because it had already been assigned for the Yahuda collection. The assigned value of this room was $21,600. By thus removing such room from possible subscription or contribution, the Hebrew University deprived itself of a possible source of substantial revenue. . . .

[The court considered three theories: completed gift with constructive or symbolic delivery, constructive trust due to reliance by the Hebrew University and constructive trust for reasons of equity.]

For a constructive delivery, the donor must do that which, under the circumstances, will in reason be equivalent to an actual delivery. It must be as nearly perfect and complete as the nature of the property and the circumstances will permit. The gift may be perfected when the donor places in the hands of the donee the means of obtaining possession of the contemplated gift, accompanied with acts and declarations clearly showing an intention to give and to divert himself of all dominion over the property. It is not necessary that the method adopted be the only possible one. It is sufficient if manual delivery is impractical or inconvenient. Constructive delivery has been found to exist in a variety of factual situations: delivery of keys to safe deposit box; pointing out hiding places where money is hidden; informal memorandum.

Examining the present case in the light of the foregoing, the court finds that the delivery of the memorandum coupled with the decedent's acts and declarations, which clearly show an intention to give and to divest herself of any ownership of the library, was sufficient to complete the gift. . . .

If it be assumed that there was an insufficient constructive delivery to consummate the gift, the question arises whether the facts justify the imposition of a constructive trust. It is undisputed that the decedent intended to give the Yahuda Library to the Hebrew University. Her purpose in so doing was to establish a "centre for Biblical and Semitic research and a meeting place for scholars" as a memorial to her illustrious husband, Professor Abraham Shalom Yahuda. She had reason to expect that the plaintiff would act in reliance on the eventual delivery of the library. In fact it did so act. It removed from the fund-raising market a room which was set aside to house the Yahuda collection. "A promise which the promisor should reasonably expect to induce action or forebearance of a definite and substantial character on the part of the promisee and which does induce such action or forbearance is binding if injustice can be avoided only by enforcement of the promise." Restatement, 1 Contracts s90. . . .

There is authority for the proposition that where an owner of property makes an ineffective conveyance of it as an intended gift he will not ordinarily be compelled to complete the gift, but if he dies believing that he has made an effective gift and if the donee was a natural object of his bounty, such as a wife or child, the donee can obtain the aid of the court of equity to complete the gift as against the heirs or next of kin. 1 Scott, Trusts (2d Ed.) s31.5; Restatement, Restitution §164. The question here presented is whether the rule should be extended to cover gifts to charities. . . .

Although it is true that even in the case of a charity an imperfect gift will not be turned into a declaration of trust for no better reason than that it is imperfect; there is ample reason on the facts of this case for equity to impose a constructive trust. [The decedent's intent to make the gift was "abundantly clear" and should not be frustrated. The court finds a constructive trust appropriate on the facts.] . . .

The court recognizes, in arriving at this result, that it is abrogating in some respects the requirement of delivery in a case involving an intended gift inter vivos. Obviously, it would be neither desirable nor wise to abrogate the requirement of delivery in any and all cases of intended intervivos gifts, for to do so, even under the guise of enforcing equitable rights, might open the door to fraudulent claims. But neither does it mean that the present delivery requirement must remain inviolate. . . .

PROBLEMS

1.   Sofia owns several bonds. She writes "These bonds are for Marco when he turns 22" on the outside of an envelope and puts the bonds inside.
     a.   Sofia dies and the envelope with the bonds in it is found in her safe deposit box. Sofia's intestate heirs seek the bonds. Advise Marco. What if Marco is 19 when Sofia dies? What if he is 40?
     b.   Before Sofia's death, she tears up the envelope and sells the bonds. What rights does Marco have if he is 20? If he is 25?
2.   Dana writes a letter to Stan that says "Stan, I want you to have my grand piano when I die. I will keep it for you until you have a house big enough for it, but you should consider it yours." When Dana dies, the piano is still in Dana's house. Dana's will leaves her personal effects to Justin. Advise Stan.

3.   Alan devises Blackacre to Jennifer "hoping she will continue it in the family." Assume no other evidence of Alan's intention. Jennifer sells Blackacre and keeps the proceeds. Alan's heirs sue Jennifer for conversion and breach of her fiduciary duty not to self-deal. Advise Jennifer.

5.   *Corpus (Property or Res)*

A trust must have corpus to be a valid trust. The corpus can be as minimal as a $20 bill stapled to the trust document, especially if it is meant to be a standby trust awaiting funding from the settlor's estate upon her death, but usually the trust corpus is the property the settlor transfers to the trustee for management in the trust. Even if a settlor signs a trust agreement, until the settlor transfers property to the trust, the trust does not exist. The trust document, by itself, does not create the trust. The Uniform Testamentary Additions to Trusts Act, discussed below, now permits a trust funded at death to be considered created during the settlor's life, but that is a statutory exception to the rule that a trust cannot be created without corpus.

Any interest in property can be considered trust corpus. A settlor can transfer to the trustee the right to receive income from a contract, as long as the settlor has an enforceable right and the settlor makes an irrevocable transfer of the interest. A mere expectancy, however, is not a property right, and the transfer of an expectancy will not serve to create a valid trust. *See* Restatement (Third) of Trusts §41 (2003). An expectancy is the possibility or hope that the person will receive property but does not give the person an enforceable right. For example, an expected inheritance is an expectancy because the right may disappear if the property owner changes her mind and leaves the property to someone else. If the settlor cannot enforce a right with respect to the property, then neither can the trustee.

Property held in trust should be titled in the name of the trustee because the trustee, not the trust, has legal ownership of the property. The best practice for transferring property to a trust is to change the title to indicate that the property is now held by the trustee. A typical way to title property, to show ownership by the trustee in the trustee's fiduciary capacity, would be as follows: "Betty Tuan, as trustee of the Marjorie Tuan Trust, dated December 10, 2008."

The date of the trust is often used as an identifier for the trust. Marjorie Tuan may have more than one trust, and although the trusts may have different names, using the date will clarify which trust this is.

Can Ms. Tuan transfer her tangibles — furniture, jewelry and silver — into the trust? Unless a piece of jewelry or silver is quite valuable, the item is not likely to have a separate document establishing ownership. Tangibles can be "scheduled" to show that they have been transferred into the trust. The trust instrument will have a schedule attached identifying the assets Ms. Tuan is transferring to the trust. That will be sufficient to establish that her tangibles are now the property of the trustee.

Now imagine that Ms. Tuan lists on Schedule A, attached to the trust instrument, "Bank Account #4589, in the Second Bank of New York." Will listing the bank account on the schedule, without changing the title at the bank, cause the account to be subject to the terms of the trust? Bank accounts, stock accounts, houses and many other assets have formal title documents, unlike furniture and jewelry. The question is whether listing these assets on a schedule is enough to transfer legal title to the settlor in her capacity as trustee, when the registration has not been changed. If the settlor creates a trust with someone else as trustee, the title must be transferred to the name of the trustee, but if the settlor declares herself trustee, perhaps the declaration that she now holds the property as trustee is sufficient. The settlor is still the legal owner, although now in a different capacity.

Whether a declaration of trust, stating that the settlor now holds assets listed on a schedule as trustee, will be effective as to those assets depends on state law, but in most states no clear legal answer exists. New York, for example, requires "recordation of the deed" or "completion of registration of the asset in the name of the trust or trustee" for any assets that are "capable of registration." Thus, tangibles may be transferred through scheduling, but real property and bank accounts may not. N.Y. Est. Powers & Trust Law 7-1.18(b).

Cases in at least three states suggest that scheduling may be enough, but the results are not sufficiently conclusive that a good lawyer would rely on a schedule when helping a settlor establish a trust. In each of the three cases, a settlor declared himself trustee of assets listed on Schedule A attached to the trust document. Title to the assets was never transferred to the name of the trustee, but in each case the court held that the property was held in the trust. *See Samuel v. King*, 64 P.3d 1206 (Or. Ct. App. 2003); *Taliaferro v. Taliaferro*, 921 P.2d 803 (Kan. 1996); *Estate of Heggstad*, 16 Cal. App. 4th 943 (Cal. Ct. App. 1993). In both *Samuel v. King* and *Estate of Heggstad*, the scheduled property included real property.

In another case, *Estate of Meyer*, 747 N.E.2d 1159 (Ind. App. 2001), the court held that the settlor's trust agreement and a direction letter requesting a bank to transfer title to stock the settlor owned in the bank provided adequate evidence of the settlor's intent to fund the trust with the bank stock, even though title had not actually been transferred before the settlor's death.

The UTC permits the inclusion of property in a trust by declaration, but the comment explains that re-registration of the property is best.

UTC §401. Methods of Creating Trust.

> A trust may be created by:
>   . . . (2) declaration by the owner of property that the owner holds
>   identifiable property as trustee . . .

Comment to UTC §401(2)

> A trust created by self-declaration is best created by reregistering each
> of the assets that comprise the trust into the settlor's name as trustee.
> However, such reregistration is not necessary to create the trust . . . A
> declaration of trust can be funded merely by attaching a schedule list-
> ing the assets that are to be subject to the trust without executing sepa-
> rate instruments of transfer. But such practice can make it difficult to
> later confirm title with third party transferees and for this reason is not
> recommended.

PROBLEMS

For each question indicate whether a trust was created under UTC §401.

1. At a time when her father is alive but terminally ill, Rachel writes
and signs a document that says "I hereby transfer all my rights and interests
in the estate of my father to Terry as trustee for Liam for life, remainder to
Liam's issue." She gives the document to Terry.

2. The same facts as in (1) except that Rachel's father died shortly
before she signed the document and gave it to Terry.

3. Rachel writes and signs a document that says "I hold the property
listed on the attached Schedule A as trustee, in trust for my son Liam for life,
remainder to Liam's issue." On Schedule A she writes, "the furnishings of
my house, my bank account in Central Bank, my house." She does not have
the document witnessed, and she puts the document in her safe deposit
box. What should the court do with the property?

6.   *A Beneficiary*

The beneficiary plays a key role in a trust — and is a necessary element of a
trust — because the beneficiary has standing to enforce the trust. That
means that the beneficiary can require the trustee to carry out the terms of

the trust and if necessary, the beneficiary can go to court to do so. Without someone with the legal authority to force the trustee to comply with the terms of the trust, a trust would not work. A trust will fail if the settlor has not named a beneficiary, unless the trust qualifies as a charitable trust, the court is willing to find an honorary trust or, under the UTC, the trust is an animal trust or a trust for a purpose.

a. Person or Class

Under the common law, a beneficiary has to be either an identifiable person or a class of persons who can be identified. The beneficiary has to be specifically identifiable so that the court knows who has the authority to enforce the trust. A class like "children" or "descendants" works because the members of those classes can be identified, even if the membership will change over time and even if some members are not yet born. Other people can represent minor and unborn beneficiaries and can enforce the trust on their behalf. (In Chapter 6 we discuss UTC §§ 303 and 304, which provide rules for representation.) A class like "friends" does not work under the common law, because a court cannot determine for certain who the settlor's friends were and therefore who has rights in the trust. In the following case, the intended beneficiaries are friends of the decedent, so if the transfer is a transfer in trust, the transfer fails. As you read the case think about how else this transfer might be construed.

Testamentary trust.

Clark v. Campbell
133 A. 166 (N.H. 1926)

Snow, J.

The ninth clause of the will of deceased reads:

> My estate will comprise so many and such a variety of articles of personal property such as books, photographic albums, pictures, statuary, bronzes, bric-a-brac, hunting and fishing equipment, antiques, rugs, scrap books, canes and Masonic jewels, that probably I shall not distribute all, and perhaps no great part thereof during my life by gift among my friends. Each of my trustees is competent by reason of familiarity with the property, my wishes and friendships, to wisely distribute some portion at least of said property. I therefore give and bequeath to my trustees all my property embraced within the classification aforesaid in trust to make disposal by the way of a memento from myself, of such articles to such of my friends as they, my trustees, shall select. All of said property, not so disposed of by them, my trustees are directed to sell and the proceeds of such sale or sales to become and be disposed of as a part of the residue of my estate.

Stuff given to trustee
↓
If not distributed by trustee
→ Sold and incorporated in Residue of estate.

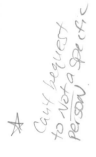

By the common law there cannot be a valid bequest to an indefinite person. There must be a beneficiary or a class of beneficiaries indicated in the will capable of coming into court and claiming the benefit of the bequest. This principle applies to private but not to public trusts and charities. . . . The basis assigned for this distinction is the difference in the enforceability of the two classes of trusts. In the former, there being no definite cestui que trust to assert his right, there is no one who can compel performance, with the consequent unjust enrichment of the trustee; while, in the case of the latter, performance is considered to be sufficiently secured by the authority of the Attorney General to invoke the power of the courts. . . .

Where a gift is impressed with a trust, ineffectively declared, and incapable of taking effect because of the indefiniteness of the cestui que trust, the donee will hold the property in trust for the next taker under the will, or for the next of kin by way of a resulting trust. The trustees therefore hold title to the property enumerated in the paragraph under consideration to be disposed of as a part of the residue, and the trustees are so advised. . . . Case discharged.

In Chapter 8 we examine powers of appointment, useful tools that allow a property owner to give someone the authority to make decisions about who will take property. Unlike a trustee, the holder of a power of appointment does not owe fiduciary duties to the people who may receive the property, if the power holder chooses to exercise the power. These "permissible appointees" need not be identified specifically because they have no authority to enforce the power. The power holder can exercise the power however he chooses, including choosing not to exercise the power at all. Can you see why using a power of appointment might have accomplished the testator's intentions in *Clark*?

QUESTION AND PROBLEM

1.   In *Clark v. Campbell*, the court concluded that the testator had attempted to create a trust but the trust failed for want of identifiable beneficiaries. Why do you think the following arguments failed? Look closely at the language from the ninth clause of the will.

- The testator was making an outright gift to the three trustees (named earlier in the document) in their individual capacities, with the precatory request that the property be distributed to his friends.
- The testator was creating a power of appointment, in the three trustees, giving them the power to appoint the property to his friends.

2.   How would you redraft the ninth clause to make the gift an absolute gift to the persons named as trustees so that they could give the property to the testator's friends?

b. Honorary Trusts

Courts sometimes find an "honorary trust" when the owner of property attempts to transfer the property to a devisee in trust for a noncharitable purpose and without an identifiable beneficiary. Unless state law provides for such a trust, the trust will fail as a private express trust for lack of a beneficiary. The devisee will hold the property for the benefit of the owner's beneficiaries or heirs, but with a non-mandatory power to make distributions to carry out the settlor's wishes. Thus, the person the owner intended to make the trustee is actually trustee for the benefit of the heirs, but can also carry out the owner's wishes if the person chooses to do so. Honorary trusts have been upheld for the care of graves and the care of animals and may also be used for the making of "benevolent" gifts. An honorary trust usually cannot last longer than 21 years, so that it will not violate the Rule Against Perpetuities. An honorary trust must be established by a court; a person planning for a particular purpose cannot be assured that an honorary trust will be created and if created that the honorary trustee will carry out the purpose. The UTC has responded to the desire to create trusts for a purpose (and not for a beneficiary) and trusts for animals by adopting UTC §§408 and 409, discussed next.

c.   Trust for a Purpose

As *Clark v. Campbell* demonstrates, under the common law, beneficiaries must be sufficiently specific so that the court will know who can enforce the trust. A charitable trust, in contrast with a private trust, need not have an identifiable beneficiary. The UTC now permits the creation of a "trust for a noncharitable purpose" without an ascertainable beneficiary. UTC §409 provides that the trust cannot last longer than the Rule Against Perpetuities, and each state that enacts the UTC will need to provide the appropriate provision with respect to that state's Rule Against Perpetuities. UTC §409(2) provides for enforcement of the trust by a person designated by the settlor or, if the trust does not designate someone, then a person appointed by the court.

UTC §409. Noncharitable Trust Without Ascertainable Beneficiary.

(1) A trust may be created for a noncharitable purpose without a definite or definitely ascertainable beneficiary or for a noncharitable

but otherwise valid purpose to be selected by the trustee. The trust may not be enforced for more than [21] years.

(2) A trust authorized by this section may be enforced by a person appointed in the terms of the trust or, if no person is so appointed, by a person appointed by the court.

(3) Property of a trust authorized by this section may be applied only to its intended use, except to the extent the court determines that the value of the trust property exceeds the amount required for the intended use. Except as otherwise provided in the terms of the trust, property not required for the intended use must be distributed to the settlor, if then living, otherwise to the settlor's successors in interest.

NOTES AND QUESTIONS

What's going on? Think of a situation in which someone would want to create a trust without an ascertainable beneficiary. What might the purpose be? Who would enforce the trust? Why would a settlor want to do this? Is the creation of a trust without an ascertainable beneficiary a good idea? For a policy discussion about trusts without ascertainable beneficiaries, see Adam Hirsch, *Trusts for Purposes: Policy, Ambiguity, and Anomaly in the Uniform Laws*, 26 Fla. St. U. L. Rev. 913 (1999).

d.   Trust for a Specific Animal

Under the common law, a trust that named an animal as a beneficiary created two problems. First, an animal does not have legal rights and therefore cannot enforce any rights in a trust. For that reason, an animal did not "count" as a beneficiary. Second, an animal does not "count" as a life in being for purposes of the Rule Against Perpetuities, so a trust for an animal violated the Rule and was void.

Despite these difficulties, people attempted to create trusts for pets and animals like horses. Sometimes a court would find an honorary trust, but other courts would hold the attempted trust invalid. A pet owner could give a bequest to a friend, with the hope that the friend would care for the animal, but many pet owners want more assurance that the pet will receive proper care. A trust can provide greater certainty, so many states now permit pet trusts or animal trusts. Most states have adopted either UPC §2-907(b), providing for pet trusts, or UTC §408, providing for animal trusts (trusts that can include animals that might not be considered pets, such as farm animals). Here is the UTC provision for animal trusts. How is the trust enforced? What is the purpose of subsection (c)?

UTC §408. Trust for Care of an Animal.

> (a) A trust may be created to provide for the care of an animal alive during the settlor's lifetime. The trust terminates upon the death of the animal or, if the trust was created to provide for the care of more than one animal alive during the settlor's lifetime, upon the death of the last surviving animal.
>
> (b) A trust authorized by this section may be enforced by a person appointed in the terms of the trust or, if no person is so appointed, by a person appointed by the court. A person having an interest in the welfare of the animal may request the court to appoint a person to enforce the trust or to remove a person appointed.
>
> (c) Property of a trust authorized by this section may be applied only to its intended use, except to the extent the court determines that the value of the trust property exceeds the amount required for the intended use. Except as otherwise provided in the terms of the trust, property not required for the intended use must be distributed to the settlor, if then living, otherwise to the settlor's successors in interest.

NOTES

1. *Trouble for Trouble.* When Leona Helmsley died in 2007, she left $12.0 million in her will in trust for her dog, Trouble. The probate court reduced the trust to $2.0 million, still enough to keep little Trouble in dog biscuits for quite awhile. How was the court able to reduce the amount Ms. Helmsley wanted to put into the trust? (Clue: New York had adopted a statute similar to UTC §408.) The $10.0 million that would have gone to the trust for Trouble was distributed instead with the residue of Helmsley's estate to the Leona M. and Harry B. Helmsley Trust. One of the purposes of that charitable trust was to benefit dogs. In Chapter 16 we look at what happened to that trust.

2. *How much is enough?* When Oregon enacted the UTC, the Humane Society asked that §408(c) be removed from the bill. Oregon enacted §408 without that subsection. What was the Humane Society's concern?

3. *More animals.* The subject of animal trusts makes interesting reading. *See* Gerry W. Beyer & Jonathan P. Wilkerson, *Max's Taxes: A Tax-Based Analysis of Pet Trusts*, 43 U. RICH. L. REV. 1219 (2009); Trusts and Estates Law Section, NY State Bar Association Annual Meeting, January 2010, at http://ssrn.com/abstract=1519123 (forms, links to pet trust statutes and a client handout).

Jennifer Graylock/Associated Press

Leona Helmsley and Trouble in New York
in January 2003

QUESTIONS

1.   Could the gift in Mr. Clark's will to his "friends" be carried out as an honorary trust? As a trust for a noncharitable purpose under UTC §409? Would any changes in the language of the gift be needed?

2.   If a pet owner does not want the expense of creating a pet trust or the state in which the owner lives has not yet adopted a pet trust statute, what are the other options?

EXERCISE

Geraldo asks you to help him draft his will. He wants to leave his estate to "his friends." When you ask him who he means, specifically, he explains that he would like his best friend, Steve, to decide who gets what. "Steve knows who my friends are," says Geraldo, "and he'll do the right thing." Write a letter to Geraldo, discussing his options. How can you help him accomplish what he wants to do? What are the costs, financial and otherwise, of each method?

7.   *Formalities — Written Trusts vs. Oral Trusts and Secret Trusts*

The elements of a trust do not include a requirement of a writing, a signature by the settlor or signatures by witnesses. Nonetheless, a lawyer helping a client typically drafts a trust instrument with places for the settlor to sign (to help indicate intent to create a trust) and for the trustee to sign (to indicate acceptance of the trusteeship). If the trust is a declaration of trust, only the settlor will sign (as settlor and as trustee), but a careful lawyer may have a declaration of trust notarized. Because only the settlor normally signs a declaration of trust, a notarization provides extra evidence if, for some reason, the settlor's signature and intent to create the trust are challenged.

a.   Oral Trusts of Personalty

Consistent with the common law, the UTC permits an oral trust. UTC §407 requires a high standard of proof — clear and convincing evidence — to establish an oral trust. This standard of proof is higher than the standard in effect in some states. Although the UTC authorizes oral trusts, a lawyer would not recommend using an oral trust given the difficulty of proving its existence. An oral trust can occur, however, in situations in which a property owner acted without the advice of a lawyer.

UTC §407. Evidence of Oral Trust.

> Except as required by a statute other than this [Code], a trust need not be evidenced by a trust instrument, but the creation of an oral trust and its terms may be established only by clear and convincing evidence.

At least one state, Indiana, requires some type of writing in support of a claim of an oral trust of personalty. Such a trust "is enforceable only if there is written evidence of its terms bearing the signature of the settlor or the settlor's authorized agent." IND. STAT. ANN. §30-4-2-1(a) (2010).

Florida requires that the testamentary portions (the provisions that will take effect at the death of the settlor) of a revocable trust be executed with will formalities — written, signed and witnessed. Because a revocable trust acts as a will substitute, the Florida legislature decided to apply the rules for executing a will. FLA. STAT. ANN. §736.0403(2)(b) (2010).

In Nevada, trusts may be written and stored in pure electronic format. NEV. REV. STAT. §163.0095 (2010).

b.   Oral Trusts of Real Property

Most U.S. states have adopted the English Statute of Frauds, either by statute or as part of the common law. Consequently, in these states, a trust of land must be stated in a writing that is signed by either the settlor or the trustee. RESTATEMENT (THIRD) OF TRUSTS §23 (2003). A few states appear to have no Statute of Frauds requirement for trusts of land. *See id.* §22, cmt. a. West Virginia requires a writing for a declaration of trust in land but not for a conveyance of land in trust (a trust agreement). W. VA. CODE §36-1-4.

What happens in a state that has adopted the Statute of Frauds if a property owner attempts to transfer land to a trust but does not do so in writing? The trust is not void, but it is unenforceable against the transferee (the trustee). The transferee now has legal title to the property, and if she is allowed to keep the property for herself and not subject to the trust, the transferee will be unjustly enriched. A number of rules have developed to address this problem, and we now turn to them.

i.   Voluntary Trust

Because an oral trust of real estate is not void, the trustee can carry out the terms of the trust voluntarily. If the trustee does so, the settlor cannot use the lack of writing as a way to terminate the trust. However, if the trustee refuses to carry out the trust, the trustee cannot be held in breach because the lack of writing provides a defense, and the trust is unenforceable against the trustee.

ii.   Partial Performance

If the trustee partially performs the trust and then stops, the trust can be enforced under the doctrine of partial performance. Partial performance can consist of the trustee taking action with respect to the trust property (investing it, paying income to a beneficiary) for some period of time and then deciding to stop carrying out the trust. Alternatively, the doctrine of partial performance applies if the beneficiary has acted in reliance on the trust (*eg.*, by making improvements to land held in the trust) and the trustee has permitted that reliance.

iii.   Constructive or Resulting Trust

Under some circumstances, a court will impose a constructive trust. The transferee holds the property on a constructive trust for the *intended beneficiaries* if (1) the transferee used fraud, undue influence or duress to cause the property owner to transfer the property, or (2) at the time of the transfer, the transferee was in a "confidential relation" to the property owner.

If neither of these conditions applies, a court may find that the transferee holds the property as a resulting trust (the trust fails and the property returns to the settlor) or as a constructive trust for the benefit of the *property owner*, unless the property owner is dead or incapacitated, in which case the transferee will hold the property for the *intended beneficiaries.*

If the property owner declared herself trustee of the property and there is no transferee, the property owner holds the property outright, free of trust. If the property owner declared herself trustee but then became incapacitated or died, the court may impose a constructive trust for the intended beneficiaries to avoid unjust enrichment.

For fraudulent behavior to result in the imposition of a constructive trust, the transferee must have intended not to act as trustee at the time of the transfer. The rule does not apply if the transferee intended to act as trustee but then, after accepting the property, changed her mind. In that situation, the transferee has assumed fiduciary responsibilities. Proving fraud or the lack of fraud (or undue influence or duress) may be difficult.

A determination of who is in a "confidential relation" to the property owner may also be difficult. As *Gregory v. Bowlsby*, excerpted below, shows, a parent-child relationship may not be the sort of confidential relationship that gives rise to a constructive trust; but on other facts, overreaching by a parent — or a child if the parent is of diminished capacity — could establish a confidential relationship. Courts have found some family relationships confidential and others not. See cases discussed in *Restatement (Third) of Trusts* §4, cmts. d-g.

The following case considers whether a land transfer warrants the imposition of a constructive trust.

Gregory v. Bowlsby
88 N.W. 822 (Iowa 1902)

DEEMER, J.

It appears from the amended and substituted petition, which, under the record, must be treated as presenting the facts, that plaintiffs are the children and heirs at law of defendant Benjamin Bowlsby and of Catherine S. Bowlsby, now deceased, and that the defendant M.J. Bowlsby is the second wife of her codefendant; that Catherine S. Bowlsby died intestate, seised of the real estate in dispute; that at the request of defendant Benjamin Bowlsby certain of the plaintiffs met the father at the home of Frank Davison, a son-in-law, and that the father then and there requested them to deed him their interest in the real estate left by his deceased wife, in order that he might use and farm the land to better advantage, and that he then and there verbally agreed that he would hold the land, would not sell or dispose of the same, and that the net proceeds and accumulations thereof should and would at his death descend to the children of Catherine Bowlsby, as provided by law; that, believing in said promises, and that such an arrangement was valid, they executed a deed of bargain and sale to their father of their interest in the real estate theretofore owned by their mother, which deed recited a consideration of $1, the receipt whereof was acknowledged by the grantors; that by reason of the relations existing between them and their father these plaintiffs accepted his statements and promises without taking legal advice, and relied on him to advise them as to their rights and protect them in the premises; that neither defendant nor his attorney, who was present with him, advised them that the arrangement could not be enforced. It further appears from the allegations of this petition that the conveyance was procured by mistake on the part of these plaintiffs, induced by the representations made to them by said defendant; that said defendant paid nothing for the conveyance, and that the sole consideration therefor was his agreement as aforesaid. It is further alleged that said defendant did not intend to carry out the arrangement or agreement on his part, but made the representations and agreement aforesaid for the sole purpose of cheating and defrauding plaintiffs out of their interest in the land of their deceased mother; that after his marriage to his codefendant he conveyed to her an undivided one-third interest in the property received from plaintiffs, but that this conveyance was without consideration, and was made with intent to cheat and defraud these plaintiffs; that his codefendant, when she took the conveyance, knew of the terms and conditions under which her husband received his deed from these plaintiffs. The prayer is that these deeds be canceled, that plaintiffs be adjudged to be the owners of an interest in the property, that their title be quieted, and that an accounting be had of the rents and profits of the real estate. The demurrer was the general equitable one, and as further grounds therefor it is claimed that the alleged oral agreement is within the statute of frauds.

[The court states that a trust with respect to land cannot be established without a writing based on the Statute of Frauds.]

As an express trust cannot be shown by parol, and as there was no resulting trust, we have one question left, and that is, was there such a fraud perpetrated by defendant Benjamin Bowlsby as entitles plaintiffs to the relief asked? . . . If there is any cause of action stated, it is for the declaration and establishment of a constructive trust, growing out of the alleged fraud of the defendants. While some facts are recited for the purpose of showing fiduciary relations between the parties, we apprehend they are insufficient for that purpose. A father bears no such confidential or fiduciary relations to his adult children as to bring transactions between them relating to the lands of either under suspicion. He may deal with them as with strangers, and no presumption of fraud or undue influence obtains. It is charged, however, that, with intent to cheat and defraud, defendant made the representations charged, fully intending at the time he made them not to carry them out, but to obtain the title to the land, and thus defraud the grantors. Does this make such a case of fraud as that a court will declare a constructive trust in the land in favor of the grantors? This instrument was in the exact form agreed upon by the parties, and there was no promise to execute defeasances or other instruments to witness the trust. The sole claim is that defendant made the promises and agreements with intent to cheat and defraud the plaintiffs. Mere denial that there was a parol agreement as claimed will not constitute a fraud. If it did, the statute would be useless. Nor will a refusal to perform the contract be sufficient to create a constructive trust. But the statute was not enacted as a means for perpetrating a fraud; and if fraud in the original transaction is clearly shown, the grantor will be held to be a trustee ex maleficio. If, then, there was a fraudulent intent in procuring the deed without intention to hold the land as agreed, and pursuant to that intent the grantor disposed of the property, or otherwise repudiated his agreement, equity will take from the wrongdoer the fruit of his deceit by declaring a constructive trust. Mere breach of or denial of the oral agreement does not, as we have said, constitute a fraud. . . .

We think the petition on its face recites facts showing a constructive trust, and that the demurrer should have been overruled. Reversed.

QUESTIONS

1.   *Confidence in whom?* Why did the court not find a confidential relationship between the father and his children?

2.   *Constructing a relationship.* Given that there was no confidential relationship, why did the court say a constructive trust might be imposed, if the facts recited were true?

c.   Oral Trusts to Be Given Effect at Death — Secret and Semi-Secret Trusts

Sometimes — one hopes not too often — someone will try to hide a gift or bequest by making a "secret trust." Usually, if a problem arises it will be a problem with an attempted testamentary trust — a trust created under a will. As we discuss in Chapter 10, strict rules apply to what documents can be given effect as a will. All testamentary devises made pursuant to a will must be in the will itself or included through one of the doctrines we will study (incorporation by reference, events of independent significance and integration). References to oral instructions do not fit within any of these doctrines, and oral instructions cannot be given effect because the instructions do not comply with the formalities required for a will.

Imagine two possible scenarios: (1) Jane's will says, "I give my house to Sebastian." Jane and Sebastian have discussed the gift, and Sebastian has orally agreed to give the house to Jane's cousin, Julia. This is a secret trust. (2) Jane's will says, "I give my house to Sebastian. I have given him instructions, and he has agreed to transfer the house as I have instructed him." This is a semi-secret trust. The question is whether a secret or semi-secret trust should be given effect — Sebastian must give the house to Julia — or whether the trust should fail and the assets go to the Jane's residuary takers or if none to Jane's heirs. In either case, Jane's intent is to give Sebastian the house as a trustee, not for his personal use.

An early case, *Oliffe v. Wells*, 130 Mass. 221 (1881), developed a distinction between a secret trust (a gift to someone under a will with no indication that the property is intended to be held in trust for someone else) and a semi-secret trust (a gift to someone under a will with an indication that the person is supposed to hold the property as a trustee but with no information about the terms of the trust). Under *Oliffe*, a secret trust will be enforced and the person named to take the property will acquire only legal title to the property and will hold it for the beneficiaries of the trust. A semi-secret trust will not be enforced. The trustee will hold the property as a resulting trust, and the property will be distributed through the estate of the person who attempted to create the trust — to the residuary takers under the will or to the decedent's heirs. The rationale for the distinction is that if the trust is a secret trust, the person named to take the property will acquire both legal and beneficial title unless the court enforces the trust, in which case the named person will acquire only legal title. A trustee of a semi-secret trust is identified as a trustee and thus has only legal title. The trust fails and the person named in the will is not unjustly enriched.

The *Restatement (Second) of Trusts* §55, cmt. h (1959) stated that a court should impose a constructive trust on behalf of the intended beneficiaries whether the trust was secret or semi-secret. The *Restatement (Third) of Trusts* §18 (2003) agrees. Despite the *Restatement* position, the distinction set forth in *Oliffe* remains the majority rule. The following case is a recent example.

Pickelner v. Adler
229 S.W.3d 516 (Tex. App. 2007)

T, J.

Shirley Alpha ("Shirley") executed a will in May 1997. Her long-time friend and attorney, Pickelner, drafted the will. The will made Pickelner the sole devisee:

> I give, devise and bequeath all the rest and remainder of my property of which I may die seized or possessed, or to which I may be in anywise entitled, whether real, personal or mixed, wherever situated and however acquired, to my long-time friend ROBERT S. PICKELNER, to be distributed in accordance with the specific instructions I have provided him.

The instructions to which the above-quoted provision refers were verbal, and Shirley did not reduce them to writing. The trial court received testimony of what Shirley's verbal instructions to Pickelner were. From that testimony, it is evident that Shirley's instructions to Pickelner did not cover all of the property that she bequeathed to him. Among her verbal instructions, Shirley required that Pickelner receive one of her homes and that Hurwitz, Shirley's close friend and portfolio manager, receive the other. Neither Pickelner nor Hurwitz was related to Shirley, and neither is her heir at law. . . .

The only reasonable interpretation of the devise in Shirley's will of all of her property to Pickelner "to be distributed in accordance with the specific instructions which I have provided him" is that Shirley intended for Pickelner to receive only legal title to her property, *i.e.*, to hold her property in some kind of trust, rather than outright. See *Heidenheimer*, 19 S.W 382, 385 (1892) (indicating that following language created semi-secret trust: "I give, devise and bequeath to my brother . . . in trust, to be disposed of by him as I have heretofore or may hereafter direct him to do"); . . . .

We further hold that the trust that Shirley attempted to create in her will was a semi-secret trust because it lacked essential terms, in particular because it completely failed to identify the beneficiaries. A semi-secret trust is, in essence, a failed express testamentary trust. Because an express testamentary trust was attempted, but failed, the trust terms could not be proved by parol evidence. . . . Because the semi-secret trust could not be proved by parol evidence, and because the will contained no residuary clause, Pickelner held all devised property under the remedy of a resulting trust for the benefit of Shirley's heirs at law. That is, her heirs at law take under her will.

Hurwitz urges this Court to adopt the rule from the Restatement (Third) of Trusts that, when the will contains a semi-secret trust, the intended beneficiaries of the semi-secret trust, rather than the heirs, receive the intended bequest under the remedy of a constructive trust. *See* Restatement (Third) of Trusts §18(1), cmt. c (2003). We decline to adopt this rule — which, incidentally, the same Restatement reveals is the minority rule in America, *see id.* cmt. c, *see also* GERRY BEYER, 10, 45.3 (3rd ed.) — because it runs contrary to the rule followed in Texas for 115 years.

QUESTIONS AND PROBLEMS

1. *Oral trusts.* What is the policy reason for allowing oral trusts? Do you think they should be permitted?

2. *Constructive solution.* On the facts in *Gregory v. Bowlsby*, how would a constructive trust work?

3. *Irrational?* What is the policy distinction between secret and semi-secret trusts? Is it rational?

4.   *Who was Pickelner?* Take a close look at the facts in *Pickelner*. What is the other problem Mr. Pickelner faces in getting control of the decedent's property?

5.   Charles wants to leave $10,000 to his friend, David, but he does not want knowledge of the gift to be public. In his will he gives the money to his brother, Brandon, as an outright gift. Privately, Charles explains to Brandon that although he is making the gift to him under the will, he expects him to give the money to David. He asks Brandon not to tell their sister, Zoe, because she dislikes David. Charles also tells David about the gift and assures him that Brandon will follow through as promised.

   a.   After Charles dies, Brandon tells David that he intends to keep the money. What can David do?

   b.   Assume that the will said, "I give $20,000 to Brandon, not for him personally but to distribute as he and I have discussed." The problem now is that although the intent to create a trust is clear, the identity of the beneficiary is not. What can David do?

8.   Exculpatory (Exoneration) Clauses

An exculpatory clause, sometimes also known as an exoneration clause, is a clause included in a trust document to excuse the trustee from liability for ordinary negligence although generally not from bad faith or willful neglect. A typical "boiler plate" clause is as follows:

> No individual Trustee shall be liable for any act or failure to act in the absence of such Trustee's own bad faith.

A court will usually give effect to an exoneration clause and limit a trustee's liability to a situation involving bad faith. A problem with an exoneration clause can arise if the person drafting the trust (and inserting the clause) is the person acting as trustee. In *Marsman v. Nasca*, 573 N.E.2d 1025 (Mass. App. 1991), the trust document included the following clause: "No trustee hereunder shall ever be liable except for his own willful neglect or default." James Farr, the lawyer who drafted the document that created the trust, was named as the trustee. The court determined that the trustee had breached his duties to the beneficiary of the trust, and then had to determine whether the trustee would be subject to personal liability. The court noted, "exculpatory clauses are not looked upon with favor and are strictly construed," but then determined that the trustee had not behaved with "willful neglect or default." No claim had been made that the exculpatory clause had been inserted as a result of the abuse of the fiduciary relationship between the lawyer and his client, so the court concluded that even though the lawyer/trustee had drafted the clause, the issue on review was limited to whether his behavior as trustee fell within the behavior covered by the clause.

In response to cases like *Marsman*, the UTC includes the following provision on exculpatory clauses.

UTC §1008. Exculpation of Trustee.

(a) A term of a trust relieving a trustee of liability for breach is unenforceable to the extent that it:

(1) relieves the trustee of liability for breach of trust committed in bad faith or with reckless indifference to the purposes of the trust or the interests of the beneficiaries; or

(2) was inserted as the result of an abuse by the trustee of a fiduciary or confidential relationship to the settlor.

(b) An exculpatory term drafted or caused to be drafted by the trustee is invalid as an abuse of a fiduciary or confidential relationship unless the trustee proves that the exculpatory term is fair under the circumstances and that its existence and contents were adequately communicated to the settlor.

Under the UTC, a trustee who drafted an exculpatory clause and caused it to be included in the terms of the trust must show that the trustee explained the clause to the client and that the clause is fair. Often the person drafting the clause is a lawyer who will act as trustee, but the UTC is worded to include a bank trustee who causes the clause to be included. The UTC provision puts the burden of proof on the trustee, rather than on the beneficiary. Because the settlor will be dead when the disagreement arises, the beneficiary is at a significant disadvantage in proving what the lawyer told the settlor unless the attorney documents the conversation contemporaneously.

In agreement with the UTC position is *Rutanen v. Ballard*, 678 N.E.2d 133 (Mass. 1997). In *Rutanen*, the court refused to enforce an exculpatory clause because the lawyer/trustee had not adequately advised the settlor about the clause. The comment to UTC §1008 explains that subsection (b) disapproves of cases such as *Marsman* and "responds to the danger that the insertion of such a clause by the fiduciary or its agent may have been undisclosed or inadequately understood by the settlor." The comment states that "the court may wish to examine: (1) the extent of the prior relationship between the settlor and trustee; (2) whether the settlor received independent advice; (3) the sophistication of the settlor with respect to business and fiduciary matters; (4) the trustee's reasons for inserting the clause; and (5) the scope of the particular provision inserted."

QUESTIONS

1.   *How bad?* If a trust included an exculpation clause like the one in *Marsman*, what type of trustee behavior would lead to personal liability for the trustee?

2.   *Would you serve?* What would you do if a client asked you to serve as the personal representative of his estate or the trustee of his trust?

9.   *Mandatory Rules*

A settlor can set the terms of a trust; state law acts as a set of default rules — a back-up if the settlor has not addressed a particular issue. On a few points, however, the settlor cannot change underlying legal rules. For example, a settlor cannot create a trust with a purpose that is unlawful. The UTC lists a number of mandatory rules in §105(b). These mandatory rules include the requirements for creating a trust, the trustee's duty to act in good faith and in the interests of the beneficiaries, the power of a court to take actions with respect to the trust that are necessary in the interests of justice, limitations on the settlor's ability to exculpate the trustee, the trustee's general obligation to keep beneficiaries informed about the trust and specific requirements about notice to beneficiaries. The rules on notice are discussed in more detail in Chapter 6.

C.   REVOCABLE TRUSTS

Revocable trusts are sometimes called "revocable living trusts," "RLTs" or "Rev Trusts." A revocable trust provides management of the trust property for the settlor during the settlor's life and then acts as a will substitute on the settlor's death. The settlor retains the power to revoke the trust at any time. Most of the trust rules discussed in this chapter apply equally to revocable trusts, but the particular purposes and functions of revocable trusts deserve separate description. Given their role as a will substitute, some rules from wills law apply to these trusts. In this section we consider the advantages and disadvantages of revocable trusts, including some common misconceptions about the benefits these trusts provide. In this regard, you may want to review the portion of Chapter 4 dealing with reasons to avoid probate. We also look at several UTC rules that apply to revocable trusts that differ from general trust law.

1.   Structure

A settlor creates a revocable trust during life, and the settlor retains control over the property, often serving as the trustee. The trust typically provides that a successor trustee can step in if the settlor becomes incapacitated. Thus, revocable trusts can be used to plan for the possibility of incapacity.

At death, the settlor's power to revoke the trust ends and the trust becomes irrevocable. Usually the settlor will have also drafted a pour-over will, which will transfer any probate assets (assets not already in the revocable trust) to the trustee of the revocable trust. Other nonprobate assets, such as life insurance, may name the trustee of the trust as the beneficiary for that asset so that those assets will be distributed to the trust outside of probate. The revocable trust will then serve as the dispositive document when the settlor dies, and the settlor's assets will pass under the terms of the trust to the desired beneficiaries.

A revocable trust has two parts: (1) the terms for the management and disposition of the trust during the lifetime of the settlor; and (2) the terms for the management and disposition of the trust after the settlor's death. During the settlor's lifetime, the trust will direct the trustee to distribute trust assets to or for the benefit of the settlor under a broad standard and will allow the settlor to withdraw assets from the trust. After death, the trust terms typically direct the payment of claims and taxes (and should be coordinated with the will if the settlor also has probate property) and then direct the distribution of the assets or the creation of further trusts to be held for beneficiaries.

2.   Funding the Trust

When a settlor creates a revocable trust, the settlor should fund the trust with something, even if most of the assets will be transferred later. As we have learned, corpus is an essential element of a trust; the trust will not be created until an asset is held in trust. If the settlor wants to avoid probate, then the settlor should transfer all his assets to the trustee before death. Any assets left in the decedent's name at death will go through probate, unless a beneficiary designation applies. The probate assets may be distributed to the trust through the probate process, but the benefits of probate avoidance will have been lost.

Sometimes a settlor creates a revocable trust as a "standby trust," to be funded primarily at death. The settlor funds the trust with a small amount of money or other assets, so that the trust is created, but then provides for the rest of the funding to occur at death. The settlor might name the trustee as the beneficiary of a life insurance policy or other will substitutes, or the settlor might rely on a will to distribute probate property to the trustee.

An estate planning lawyer will always pair a revocable trust with a "pour-over will." A pour-over will is a will that distributes the residue of the probate estate to the trustee of the revocable trust, to be held in the trust. It "pours" those assets into the revocable trust. Michael Jackson's will in the Appendix to Chapter 1 is a pour-over will. A pour-over will can pick up an asset that the settlor may have acquired and forgotten to transfer into the trust or an asset like a wrongful death settlement that arises by reason of the settlor's death and becomes part of the settlor's estate. The pour-over will can also be useful if the settlor simply forgets to transfer property into the trust. A typical pour-over provision is as follows:

> I give my residuary estate to the trustee, acting at the time of my death, of the Marjorie M. Black Revocable Trust, created by the declaration dated January 22, 2008, by me as settlor and trustee, as the trust shall exist at the date of my death, to be added to and administered in all respects as property of the trust. I expressly direct that the trust shall not be considered to be a testamentary trust. If and only if no such trust is in effect at my death, then I give my residuary estate to my trustee subsequently named in Article __, in trust. Such estate, together with any other sums payable directly to the trustee, shall be referred to in this will as the Residuary Testamentary Trust and shall be administered in accordance with the provisions of Article __.

Often when a lawyer finishes the estate planning documents, the lawyer will offer to transfer title to assets but will also explain that the settlor can save legal fees by transferring title himself. The settlor may prefer to transfer the property himself, but then he may procrastinate or forget, resulting in an unfunded trust. If a revocable trust remains unfunded at the settlor's death (no assets at all), then the trust does not exist. Prior to adoption of the Uniform Testamentary Additions to Trusts Act (UTATA), the fact that the trust did not exist raised questions about whether the provisions for distribution of the decedent's property could be given effect. Remember that under traditional rules a transfer at death — a testamentary transfer — cannot be given effect unless it meets the requirements of a will. UPC §6-101, discussed in Chapter 4, treats will substitutes as "nontestamentary" in order to avoid this rule. A transfer occurring through a revocable trust is not testamentary, either by statute or case law, although early cases raised this issue. *See, e.g., Farkas v. Williams*, 125 N.E.2d 600 (IL 1955) (holding a revocable living trust to be a valid inter vivos trust). If the trust exists, any property transferred to the trust through a pour-over will can be distributed through the trust because the trust is then an "event of independent significance" with respect to the will. We discuss events of independent significance in Chapter 10.

If the trust does not exist at the settlor's death, then the doctrine of incorporation by reference can be used to incorporate the written trust instrument into the will. See Chapter 10 for the rules on incorporation by reference. Only the document in existence at the time the will is executed can be incorporated by reference, so if the will was executed before the trust document was prepared or if the trust document was amended after the will was executed, anything written later cannot be given effect.

Faced with settlor mistakes that resulted in unfunded revocable trusts and ineffective dispositive documents, the Uniform Law Commission developed UTATA, now included in the UPC. A revocable trust will be considered an inter vivos trust as long as the will identifies the trust and the trust is funded either during the settlor's life or at the settlor's death.

UPC §2-511. Testamentary Additions to Trusts.

(a) A will may validly devise property to the trustee of a trust established or to be established (i) during the testator's lifetime by the testator, by the testator and some other person, or by some other person, including a funded or unfunded life insurance trust, although the settlor has reserved any or all rights of ownership of the insurance contracts, or (ii) at the testator's death by the testator's devise to the trustee, if the trust is identified in the testator's will and its terms are set forth in a written instrument, other than a will, executed before, concurrently with, or after the execution of the testator's will or in another individual's will if that other individual has predeceased the testator, regardless of the existence, size, or character of the corpus of the trust. The devise is not invalid because the trust is amendable or revocable, or because the trust was amended after the execution of the will or the testator's death.

(b) Unless the testator's will provides otherwise, property devised to a trust described in subsection (a) is not held under a testamentary trust of the testator, but it becomes a part of the trust to which it is devised, and must be administered and disposed of in accordance with the provisions of the governing instrument setting forth the terms of the trust, including any amendments thereto made before or after the testator's death.

(c) Unless the testator's will provides otherwise, a revocation or termination of the trust before the testator's death causes the devise to lapse.

Note that subsection (a) permits the written instrument setting forth the terms of the trust to be executed "before, concurrently with, or after the execution of the testator's will . . . ." This provision revises a prior version of UTATA that required the trust to be executed before or concurrently with the will. Some states may not have revised their statutes to reflect this change, so a safe practice is to have a client execute the revocable trust first and then the will.

3.   Purposes and Advantages

In Chapter 4, we discussed a number of will substitutes and the reasons property owners use will substitutes. In this section, we focus on the purposes and advantages of revocable trusts, one type of will substitute.

a.   Lifetime Purpose — Planning for Incapacity

A revocable trust provides a means to manage property if the settlor becomes incapacitated. If a person has done no advance planning and begins to lose mental capacity, a family member or other person may need to file a conservatorship over the property, so that someone else — the conservator — can manage the property for the incapacitated person. In some cases, the person may be forgetful but not legally incapacitated, and a legal conservatorship may not be appropriate. Even if a conservatorship is appropriate, the public process of declaring the person incapacitated can be a painful and upsetting experience for the person and for family members as well. An advantage of a revocable trust is that a trustee can manage the person's property and no conservatorship will be needed. The person can choose the successor trustee and can provide guidance in the terms of the trust as to how the determination of incapacity is to be made and how the property should be managed and used thereafter. We discuss planning for incapacity in Chapter 13.

b.   After-Death Purposes — Avoiding Probate

Revocable trusts have grown in popularity as a way to avoid probate. In the 1960s, probate in most states was a cumbersome, expensive process. Lawyers had to make numerous court appearances in connection with a probate estate, and court fees were significant. Some states still have expensive probate systems, but in many states probate reform has made probate much less difficult. See Chapter 15, discussing probate administration.

i.   Costs

Transferring property through probate may cost more than transferring property using a revocable trust, depending on the type of property and the state rules on probate. The costs of probate in states that use a statutory formula for determining probate fees can be high. For example, in California statutory fees are set on a sliding scale as a percentage of the gross value of the estate. For an estate of $250,000, the minimum statutory fees would be $16,000 for the executor and his or her attorney. The court could award more for "extraordinary service." The concerns over the cost of probate must be balanced with the greater cost at the front-end: Drafting a revocable trust typically costs more than preparing a will. In a state with high probate fees, however, the cost of preparing a revocable trust should be significantly less than the minimum probate fees.

ii. Privacy

Probate is a public process, and a will is a public document. If a person is famous or even well known locally, national or local publicity may follow the probate. If a person wants to keep the identity of the recipients of his gifts private, a trust can do that. A wealthy person may prefer privacy, and a person whose family arrangements differ from local societal norms may also prefer privacy. When Michael Jackson died, his will, which is a public document, gave his estate to the trustees acting under a Declaration of Trust dated March 22, 2002. The Declaration of Trust provided for the actual distribution of his assets. That document is not part of the public proceedings and will remain private unless released by the family or made public in connection with a legal battle over Jackson's estate.

iii. Challenges

An unhappy heir can challenge a revocable trust on the same grounds used to challenge a will: lack of capacity, undue influence, fraud or duress. It is, however, much more difficult to invalidate a trust than a will. To challenge a will, the plaintiff must show that the cause for the challenge existed at one point in time — the time the decedent executed the will. The person challenging a trust must show that the undue influence, for example, continued during the trust: The trust is an ongoing relationship, and the transactions involved in a trust continue from the time the settlor establishes the trust until the settlor dies.

iv. Avoiding Delays

Estate administration can be a lengthy process, and the probate process can take a year or longer. Administering a revocable trust takes time, but often distributions can be made more quickly than under a will.

v. Avoiding Ancillary Probate

Real property must be probated where it is located. If a person owns property in a state other than the state where the will is probated, the real property will be subject to probate in that other state through a process called ancillary probate. An ancillary probate can be expensive because local counsel may be necessary and some of the estate administration filings must be duplicated. Property held in a revocable trust will not be subject to probate, so any real property located in another state will not be subject to ancillary probate if held in a revocable trust.

vi.   Avoiding the Elective Share

In a few states the elective share (property available to the surviving spouse if she is disinherited — see Chapter 12) is determined based on the value of the probate estate. In those states, a spouse can shield his estate from the elective share by putting property into a revocable trust.

4.   Disadvantage — Statute of Limitations for Creditors

A popular misconception about revocable trusts is that they can be used to avoid creditors. In fact, using probate may provide greater creditor protection than using a revocable trust. The probate process includes a short statute of limitations for claims against the decedent's estate. The personal representative must notify known claimants and must publish notice of the decedent's death (see Chapter 15), but when the personal representative takes those steps, the statute of limitations for claims begins to run and can often be as short as four months. Claims filed against property in a revocable trust may have a longer statute of limitations, because the UTC does not provide for a limitation on the claims period. The statute of limitations for the underlying claim will continue to apply.

5.   Misconception — Taxes

Revocable trusts have no income or transfer tax benefits. Promotional material discussing revocable trusts is sometimes misleading in this respect. A revocable trust will be taxed for income tax purposes with the rest of the settlor's income. The trust does not need a separate tax identification number, and the income will be reported on the settlor's income tax return. The assets held in a revocable trust will be included in the settlor's gross estate for estate tax purposes. IRC §2038. See Chapter 14.

6.   Rules for Revocable Trusts That Differ from Those Applicable to Other Trusts

a.   Capacity

Under the UTC, the capacity to create a revocable trust is the same as that required to execute a will. UTC §601. Other inter vivos trusts are subject to the higher contract standard. In states that have not enacted the

UTC, the rule for inter vivos trusts may still apply to revocable trusts. See Section C.2.

b. Duty to Beneficiaries

While the settlor is alive, the trustee owes fiduciary duties *only* to the settlor/beneficiary. UTC §603(a). This provision changes the common law, and differs from the rule applicable to other trusts, because for other trusts the trustee owes fiduciary duties to all beneficiaries, not merely the current beneficiaries. Some states that have adopted this UTC provision have made the limit on the trustee's duties applicable only if the settlor has capacity. UTC §603(a) (bracketed provision). Under this version of the UTC, if the settlor is still alive but lacks capacity, then the trustee must provide notice to other beneficiaries and will owe all the applicable fiduciary duties to them as well. Fiduciary duties of trustees, including the different rules that apply to revocable trusts, are discussed in Chapter 6.

c. Rules That Apply to Wills

In some states, certain rules that apply to wills also apply to revocable trusts, but not to any other type of trust. The UPC takes this approach by applying a number of provisions relating to probate transfers to nonprobate transfers, including revocable trusts. These rules are discussed in Chapter 11 and include: effect of divorce, annulment and decree of separation, UPC §2-804; and effect of homicide of the settlor by a beneficiary, UPC §2-803.

D. JOINT REVOCABLE TRUSTS

The use of joint revocable trusts has grown in recent years, particularly in states with community property systems or in states to which couples with community property have moved. (We discuss community property in Chapter 12.) A joint revocable trust is one in which two settlors contribute property to a single trust. The two settlors may contribute the same amount of property or different amounts of property, and they may contribute property they hold as community property or as separate property. The settlors may both serve as trustees, or one may serve or neither may serve. The trust remains completely revocable as long as both settlors are alive, but when the first settlor dies, half the trust usually becomes irrevocable.

The settlors of a joint revocable trust are typically spouses or domestic partners. Clients often like joint trusts for emotional reasons, because property that was held jointly (or as community property) remains in a joint form rather than being divided between two revocable trusts, one for each spouse. The property is still "ours" rather than "yours" and "mine." Joint trusts can also be useful as a way to hold community property in a non-community property state. For example, if a married couple lives in California (a community property state), property earned during the marriage will be community property. If the couple moves to Oregon (a separate-property state), the couple may use a joint revocable trust to maintain the community property status of the property.

Lawyers find joint trusts difficult, but useful. The tax consequences, if the estate of either of the joint settlors will be taxable for estate tax purposes, must be carefully considered and planning for a taxable estate is complicated. At the other end of the economic spectrum, if one or the other settlor might need to qualify for government benefits at some time in the future, the fact that assets are held in a joint trust may complicate planning. If one spouse lacks the capacity to revoke the trust, planning with those assets may be impossible. Lawyers can plan for this possibility, which should be considered when counseling clients to consider a joint trust. The planning that may be needed, both tax planning and Medicaid planning, is beyond the scope of this textbook.

PROBLEM

Lisa executed a will that stated that the residue of her estate should "be added to and become part of the Lisa Family Trust, if I have created such trust during my lifetime, and be managed in accordance with the provisions of the trust as they exist at my death." Immediately after she executed the will, Lisa signed a declaration of trust establishing the Lisa Family Trust. She named the trust as the beneficiary of her life insurance policy. The trust provided that on Lisa's death the assets in the trust would be distributed to her three children. Lisa subsequently amended the dispositive provisions of the trust so that the remainder interest was no longer to be distributed to all three of her children but rather was given to only one of them. When Lisa dies, who will take the residue of Lisa's probate estate — her husband as her intestate heir (he is the father of the three children), the three children under the terms of the trust at the date the will was executed or the one child identified when the trust was amended?

EXERCISE

Flora is 70 years old. Her husband died several years ago. She is in good health, with the usual aches and pains that come with being 70. She has two children, Rita, who lives in town near her, and Alberto, who lives in another state. Alberto has had some problems with drug abuse, and she intends to put his share of her estate into a trust for his benefit. Flora was mayor of her small town and is something of a public figure. She has managed to keep Alberto's problems private because he lives so far away.

Flora has assets with a current value of $400,000. She has a bank account in joint tenancy with Rita; a stock account that names Rita and Alberto as the payable-on-death (POD) beneficiaries; her house, which is in her name; and a condo that Alberto lives in, but which she owns and has kept in her name.

Discuss with Flora whether you recommend a will or a revocable trust for her, and why. You will want to provide her with an understanding of the comparative benefits of each.

6 FIDUCIARY DUTIES

A. INTRODUCTION

As we have learned, a trust divides title between the trustee, who holds legal title, and the beneficiary, who holds equitable title. Because the trustee controls the trust property, strict duties developed in trust law to govern the behavior of the trustee and ensure that the trustee was accountable to the beneficiary. Without these strict duties, a trustee might be tempted to use the property for her own benefit or to manage the property in a way that would prefer the interests of one beneficiary over another or would harm the interests of all beneficiaries. In this chapter we focus on the fiduciary duties that apply to trustees of trusts. These duties also apply to personal representatives of decedents' estates, and in modified forms to directors of for-profit and nonprofit corporations. The rules governing fiduciary responsibilities developed in trust law. While any fiduciary managing property belonging to another will be subject to fiduciary duties in some form, the rules are least flexible as they apply to trustees.

Because trusts developed at a time when settlors used trusts primarily for the management of land, fiduciary duties limited the trustees' management powers over trust property. During the twentieth century, trusts increasingly held complex investments and trust law changed to accommodate the needs of trustees for greater management powers. The need for rapid changes in fiduciary duties resulted in new statutory law because the incremental development of law through cases could not keep pace with the need for modification of the rules. *See* John H. Langbein, *Why Did Trust Law Become Statute Law*, 58 ALA. L. REV. 1069, 1073 (2007).

The extent of a trustee's powers and fiduciary duties depends on the trust instrument, statutory law and the common law. Remember that most of trust law is default law. Although a settlor can modify, increase or limit the trustee's powers and duties by the terms of the trust, the settlor cannot create a trust with no fiduciary duties. In the following excerpt, Professor Langbein discusses mandatory rules in connection with fiduciary duties. He addresses the role of mandatory rules in trust law and the balancing of settlor's intent with a general principle that a trust be managed "for the benefit of the beneficiaries."

John H. Langbein, Mandatory Rules in the Law of Trusts
98 Nw. U. L. Rev. 1105, 1121-22 (2004)

2. Enforceable Duties. — Explaining the Code's [the UTC's] requirement that a trust must create enforceable duties, the official comment explains: "A settlor may not so negate the responsibilities of a trustee that the trustee would no longer be acting in a fiduciary capacity." If the trustee has no enforceable duties, the beneficiary would have no enforceable interest.

It is important to see how the rule mandating fiduciary obligation fits within the larger structure of trust fiduciary law. The starting point is that each of the fiduciary duties is a default rule, including the core duties of loyalty (the duty to administer the trust solely in the interests of the beneficiaries), impartiality (the duty of due regard to the interests of all the beneficiaries of a trust), and the duty of prudence in the conduct of trust administration (the care norm, requiring the exercise of reasonable care, skill, and caution). None of these fiduciary duties appears on the Code's list of mandatory rules, hence none is protected from settlor modification.

The recognition of the default character of trust fiduciary law is long-standing. Speaking of the duty of loyalty, the Second Restatement provides: "By the terms of the trust the trustee may be permitted to sell trust property to himself individually, or as trustee to purchase property from himself individually, or to lend to himself money held by him in trust, or otherwise to deal with the trust property on his own account."

Hence, even the duty of loyalty, the "most fundamental" rule of trust fiduciary law, yields to contrary terms of the settlor. Trust law allows the settlor to conclude that particular fiduciary rules would overprotect or otherwise complicate the particular trust and its purposes; hence, the beneficiaries would be better served by abridging them.

Oddly, however, although the various fiduciary rules are default rules, the settlor may not abrogate them in their entirety, because eliminating all fiduciary duties would make the trust illusory. To illustrate: If I am the owner of Blackacre, I am allowed to give Blackacre to T, or to make T the beneficiary of a trust of Blackacre. What the rule forbids me from doing is effecting that transfer by means of an illusory trust, a trust nominally for the benefit of B, rather than T. A purported trust to T as trustee for B, pursuant to trust terms providing that T shall owe B no fiduciary duties, would be illusory because B could not enforce a trust that is shorn of fiduciary duties. T could, therefore, deal with the trust property as though it had been transferred to T beneficially.

The requirement that a trust have enforceable duties speaks to means, not to ends; hence, it is intent-implementing as opposed to intent-defeating. Nothing in my example prevents me from making T the beneficiary of my trust rather than B. What the mandatory rule forces me to do is to spell out that my intent is to allow T to take beneficially. The concern is I may not understand that, by eliminating all fiduciary duties, I am effectively making T, rather than B, the donee. By forbidding me from eliminating all fiduciary duties, the rule protects me and my intended beneficiary (whether T or B) by requiring me to make my transfer in a forthright manner.

In this way, the requirement that a trust must have enforceable duties has the consequence of placing aggregate limits on the manner and the extent to which a settlor can oust the default law.

In this chapter we look at the roots of fiduciary law and the strict duties that grew from those roots, and we also look at the changes that have occurred to create more flexible powers for fiduciaries. We will discuss the key fiduciary duties: obedience, loyalty and care or prudence. In connection with the duty of loyalty we will review the duty of impartiality and explore the duty to allocate receipts and expenses to principal and income. In connection with the duty of care or prudence we will consider duties relating to investing trust assets, in particular the prudent investor rule.

B. DUTY OF OBEDIENCE (TO THE TERMS OF THE TRUST)

A trustee must carry out the terms of the trust, as directed by the settlor. As the following article explains, this duty is often merely mentioned in passing because it seems obvious. The duty of obedience underlies the other two primary fiduciary duties, the duty of loyalty and the duty of care or prudence.

Rob Atkinson, Obedience as the Foundation of Fiduciary Duty
34 J. Corp. L. 43, 48-49 (2008)

The duty of obedience is often overlooked or included in one of the other two fundamental fiduciary duties, precisely because it is so basic as to be almost invisible. To see why this is so, we need to examine the very foundation of fiduciary duty. The irreducible root of the fiduciary relationship is one person's acting for another. The duty of obedience derives directly from — indeed, is virtually synonymous with — that basic principle. The root of the fiduciary relationship is this directive from the principal to the fiduciary: Serve the one the principal designates, as the principal designates. The fiduciary must, at the most basic level, obey that directive; that directive is the duty of obedience.

Seen from this perspective, the duties of loyalty and care are derivative from, and grounded upon, the more fundamental duty of obedience. The duty of care requires, as the very term suggests, that fiduciaries must, upon pain of legal penalties, manage the assets committed to them at the direction of another with at least a legally mandated degree of effort and skill — in a word, care. Even more basically, the duty of loyalty requires fiduciaries to manage the assets in their care for the good of those whom the principal designates, not for their own private, personal gain or for the advantage of third parties.

If fiduciaries are to benefit the parties designated by their principals, the core of the duty of obedience, then they must not violate the duty of care by stealing or diverting the assets in their hands, and they must not violate the duty of care [loyalty] by affirmatively wasting or unreasonably jeopardizing those assets. These are the three analytic essentials; you cannot have a fiduciary relationship without them, any more than you can have a triangle without three sides. And at the base of the fiduciary triangle is the duty of obedience: to benefit those designated by another, one must be both loyal and careful.

Here is the way the UTC codifies the duty of obedience:

UTC §801. Duty to Administer Trust.

> Upon acceptance of a trusteeship, the trustee shall administer the trust in good faith, in accordance with its terms and purposes and the interests of the beneficiaries, and in accordance with this [Code].

C.   DUTY OF LOYALTY TO BENEFICIARIES

The duty of loyalty, simply put, is the trustee's duty to "administer the trust solely in the interests of the beneficiaries." UTC §802(a); RESTATEMENT

(THIRD) OF TRUSTS §78. This duty means that the trustee cannot (i) engage in self-dealing with the trust assets or (ii) enter into transactions in which the trustee has a conflict of interest. In addition, the trustee must deal fairly with the beneficiary and must keep the beneficiary informed about the trust. We will discuss this last aspect of the duty of loyalty, described as the duty to inform and report, in a separate section. The "interests of the beneficiaries" described here are the beneficiaries' interests *in the trust*, not the beneficiaries' other, more general, interests as individuals.

1. Self-Dealing

In order to protect the beneficiaries and to ensure the trustee's undivided loyalty, the duty of loyalty prohibits the trustee from entering into a transaction on behalf of the trust with himself in his individual capacity. Any self-dealing transaction is voidable. This means that any beneficiary can void the transaction, but if no one does, it will stand. As the Comment to UTC §802 explains, "The right of a beneficiary to void a transaction affected by a conflict of interest is optional. If the transaction proves profitable to the trust and unprofitable to the trustee, the beneficiary will likely allow the transaction to stand."

> **Example:** Caleb Jefferson is the settler of the Jefferson Family Trust. The trust holds a variety of investment assets and also holds a piece of real property that is currently undeveloped. Amos, a family friend of Caleb Jefferson, serves as trustee of the Jefferson Family Trust. Amos is a real estate developer and thinks the property could be more valuable if developed. If Amos (the real estate developer) buys the property from Amos (the trustee) the risk to the beneficiaries is that Amos (the real estate developer) may not pay a fair price for the property. The beneficiaries might have recourse against Amos (the trustee) if the beneficiaries could determine that the transaction was unfair to them, but the beneficiaries in most situations will have difficulty monitoring the trustee's behavior. An absolute prohibition (unless waived by the settlor as discussed below) against self-dealing will protect beneficiaries who may not be in a good position to uncover wrongs committed by a trustee. The fiduciary duty of loyalty creates that absolute prohibition.
>
> What if Amos, the trustee, gets three appraisals for the property from reputable appraisers and then Amos, the real estate developer, pays the trust the amount of the highest of the three appraisals? Under the "no further inquiry" rule, even if the trustee can prove that the transaction was fair, the trustee acted in good faith and the trustee did not profit from the transaction, the transaction will still be self-dealing and will still be voidable.

Now assume that Amos buys the property for a fair price and then one year later, hazardous wastes are found on the property. Amos would like to undo the transaction. Can he, as trustee, return the property to the trust? The answer is no because although the transaction is voidable, it is voidable only by the beneficiaries. *See* RESTATEMENT (THIRD) OF TRUSTS §78, cmt. b for a discussion of the no further inquiry principle.

The case that follows provides an example of self-dealing by the trustee.

Hosey v. Burgess
890 S.W.2d 262 (Ark. 1995)

HOLT, Chief Justice.

This case involves an appeal from a decision by the Phillips County Chancery Court, finding that appellant Leneva Judy Hosey and her late husband, N.R. Hosey, as trustees for the late Florence R. Watkins (whose executrix was appellee Marysue Robinson Burgess), were guilty of self-dealing to the detriment of Mrs. Watkins by subleasing a farm and not giving Mrs. Watkins as the trust beneficiary the benefit of the enhanced rental. . . .

Julian J. Watkins, who owned a farm in Phillips County, Arkansas, married Florence Robinson on March 25, 1975, after the death of his first wife, Lonette Watkins. Several years later, he retired and, on April 10, 1980, entered into a twenty-five-year lease of his property with his daughter by Lonette Watkins, appellant Leneva Judy Hosey, and her husband N.R. Hosey, who owned a substantial farming operation. The lease, which began on January 1, 1980, provided that the property must be used "for the purpose of planting, cultivating and harvesting agricultural crops and for purposes incidental thereto and for no other uses or purposes." Mr. and Mrs. Hosey, as lessees, agreed to make annual payments of $35 per acre for the approximately 400 acres of cultivated land. Among the conditions set forth in the lease was a requirement that the lessees "not assign or sublet said premises, or any part thereof, without the consent, in writing, of Lessor first obtained. . . . "

On March 25, 1982, Julian Watkins executed his last will and testament and a codicil. In it, he named Mr. and Mrs. Hosey his co-executors. He also created a testamentary trust consisting of his land holdings, including the 400 leased acres, to be administered by Mr. and Mrs. Hosey, as trustees, on behalf of his wife:

5.1. If my spouse, Florence R. Watkins, survives me, I give, devise, and bequeath all the balance and residue of the real property of which I die seized and possessed to my trustees herein named, in trust, to hold, manage, and invest the same, to collect the income thereon, and to pay to, or apply for the benefit of, my spouse the net income thereof in quarterly or other convenient installments, but at least annually, for and during the term of my spouse's life.

5.2. Upon the death of my spouse, my trustees shall assign, transfer, and pay over the then principal of this trust to my then living issue, per stirpes. . . .

In 1989, Mr. Hosey, whose health was declining, ceased active farming. He and Mrs. Hosey, as lessors, entered into a lease with Dixie Hill Farms, a partnership composed of Chris Kale and Clark Hall, as lessee. The lease, which embraced the farmlands owned by Mr. and Mrs. Hosey and involved a sublease of the 400 acres of Julian Watkins's farm, was to run for a three-year term from January 1, 1989, to December 31, 1991. The lease did not specify any rental on a per-acre basis for the two farms, which together contained approximately 1,316.5 acres; instead, the annual rental for all of the property was set at $88,000.

N.R. Hosey died on August 14, 1991, leaving his wife as the surviving trustee of the Watkins trust. In 1992, she entered into another three-year sublease of the trust land, extending through 1994, for the same rental amount.

On November 24, 1992, Mrs. Watkins died, leaving her daughter, appellee Marysue Robinson Burgess, as her sole beneficiary and executrix of her estate. Mrs. Burgess filed suit against Mrs. Hosey on March 5, 1993, seeking to recover the *pro rata* portion of the 1992 trust income and the difference between the rental under the twenty-five year lease and the amount received "at a rental greatly in excess of the rental paid to Florence R. Watkins" under the sublease for the years 1989, 1990, and 1991. . . .

Self-dealing by a trustee or any fiduciary is always suspect, and it is a universal rule of equity that a trustee shall not deal with trust property to his own advantage without the knowledge or consent of the *cestui que trust* [the beneficiary].

Mrs. Hosey cites the following exception to the general rule, stated in 76 Am. Jur. 2d Trusts §380 (1992), that a trustee, in administering a trust, is under the duty of acting exclusively and solely in the interest of the trust estate or the beneficiaries within the terms of the trust and is not to act in his or her own interest by taking part in any transaction concerning the trust where he or she has an interest adverse to that of the beneficiary:

> An exception exists to the well-recognized rule that a trustee may not place himself in a position where his interest may conflict with the interest of the trust property. When the conflict of interest is contemplated, created, and expressly sanctioned by the instrument, the conflict may be permitted. Thus, there is an exception when the trust clearly evidences the settlor's intent that there be identity between trustees and a corporation partially owned by the trust.

Id. See also Bogert, *The Law of Trusts and Trustees*, §543(U) (Repl. 1993): "In some cases where the settlor knew when his trust was drawn that the trustee whom he proposed to name was then in a position which, after acceptance of the trust, would expose him to a conflict between personal and representative interests, it has been held that there was an implied exemption from the duty of loyalty in so far as that transaction was concerned." . . .

Here, Mrs. Hosey was simultaneously trustee of the Watkins trust and remainder beneficiary under the testamentary trust established in the Watkins will. While the duality of identity is certainly not enough, in itself, to establish a violation of fiduciary duty, the circumstances of this case placed the trustee outside the bounds of fiduciary responsibility. The benefit to Mrs. Hosey was not merely coincidental but was, in fact, a breach of an explicitly defined duty to pay proceeds from the trust property to Mrs. Burgess.

Granted, the powers given Mrs. Hosey as trustee were exceedingly broad, as the sections quoted in the recitation of facts indicate. She was, for instance, empowered to "dispose of any . . . property, real or personal, . . . to any person . . . in such manner, and upon such terms and conditions as the executor or trustee shall deem advisable. . . . " Yet this general language was subject to the specific, overriding terms of §5.1 in Mr. Watkins's will, quoted earlier, in which the testator clearly set forth the extent of the duties of the trustees of the testamentary trust: "to hold, manage, and invest the same [real property], to collect the income thereon, and *to pay to, or apply for the benefit of, my spouse the net income thereof. . . . "* (Emphasis added.)

This court held, in *Hardy v. Hardy*, 263 S.W.2d 690, 694 (1954), that:

> A trustee is at all times disabled from obtaining any personal benefit, advantage, gain, or profit out of his administration of the trust. . . . Any benefit or profit obtained by the trustee inures to the trust estate, even though no injury was intended and none was in fact done to the trust estate[.]

In the present case, Mrs. Hosey and her late husband, however innocently, failed to adhere to the creating instrument's express directive that they apply the entire net income of the subject property to the benefit of Mrs. Watkins for her life. By the terms of the will, they were prohibited from deriving any personal monetary benefit from the 400 acres. . . .

We hold that the chancellor's findings that Mrs. Hosey and her husband engaged in self-dealing, albeit innocent and unintentional, were not clearly erroneous. . . .

Affirmed.

NOTES AND QUESTIONS

1. *Settlor's intent.* Mrs. Hosey argues that the terms of the trust authorized her self-dealing. What is the basis for her claim? Why does the court disagree?

2. *Should innocence matter?* In *Hosey v. Burgess*, the court makes a point of noting that the trustees acted "innocently." Why did the court conclude that the trustees breached their duty of loyalty? What do you think the damages were?

3. *Who wants to be a trustee?* In an Illinois case, *In re Will of Gleeson*, 124 N.E.2d 624 (Ill. App. Ct. 1955), a trustee entered into a lease to prevent loss to the trust. The court found a breach of the duty of loyalty because the trustee dealt with himself in his individual capacity. The person named as trustee had leased property from the settlor for two years. The settlor died 15 days before the start of the planting season in the third year. The trustee renewed the lease to himself because "satisfactory farm tenants are not always available, especially on short notice." *Id.* at 626. The trust suffered no loss and the court noted that the trustee had acted in good faith, but the court awarded the beneficiary the profits the trustee earned in his individual capacity as a farmer to the trust. What do you think the trustee in *Gleeson* should have done?

2. Conflict of Interest

A trustee must avoid not only transactions in which she participates in her individual as well as her fiduciary capacity, but also transactions in which her loyalty may be divided for more indirect reasons. A transaction might involve a conflict between the trustee's fiduciary duties and her personal interests. For example, if the trustee sits on the board of a company or holds a significant interest in the company, buying shares of that company as trustee or hiring that company to provide services to the trust would present conflicts of interest. If the company wanted to buy property owned by the trust, selling that property to the company would present conflicting interests for the trustee.

A conflict of interest can also develop if the trustee is involved in a transaction with a family member — a spouse, parent or child. For example, a trustee might want to hire a family member to perform services for the trust, to sell trust property to a family member or to engage in a transaction with a business in which a family member holds a significant interest. The trustee's concern for the well-being of the family member could affect the trustee's ability to consider the transaction with only the interests of the trust beneficiaries in mind.

A trustee must avoid any transaction that serves the interests of a third person, even one not related to the trustee, or serves an interest other than the interests of the beneficiaries. A decision to sell property to a city for a city park will breach the duty of loyalty if the trustee chose the seller based on the intended use of the property rather than on the interests of the beneficiaries. (Later in this chapter we discuss whether and when a trustee may consider factors other than the best investment return when dealing with trust property.)

The duty of loyalty prohibiting both self-dealing and conflict of interest transactions developed in the law based on the assumption that beneficiaries cannot be expected to have the information or ability to review all instances involving these conflicts. The strict duties were necessary because monitoring by the beneficiaries may be difficult or impossible. Beneficiaries may be unborn or incapacitated, or otherwise unable to monitor the trustees. As Professor Sitkoff has written, "After all, tax exigencies to one side, the settlor did not trust the beneficiaries enough to make an outright transfer, favoring instead a trust. . . . " Robert H. Sitkoff, *An Agency Costs Theory of Trust Law*, 89 Cornell L. Rev. 621, 680 (2004). The very reason for the trust may be that the beneficiaries are not capable of protecting their own interests, so the law developed to remove all possible temptations faced by the trustee.

The management of assets in trusts has changed since the early development of the fiduciary rules. Trustees provide more information to beneficiaries than in the past, and trustees increasingly need to engage in transactions that involve conflicts but benefit the trusts. In response to the changes, the law has developed exceptions to the duty of loyalty, undermining the absolute prohibition against self-dealing to a large extent. We will look first at specific exceptions and then consider a proposal by John Langbein that the absolute prohibition against divided-loyalty transactions be replaced with a rebuttable presumption that a self-dealing or conflict of interest transaction breaches the duty of loyalty.

3.   Exceptions to the Duty of Loyalty

Exceptions to the duty of loyalty exist. A trustee can engage in a divided-loyalty transaction — either self-dealing or conflict of interest — if (i) authorized to do so under the terms of the trust, (ii) with consent of a court, or (iii) with the consent of all the beneficiaries. Even if authorized in one of these ways, the trustee must act in good faith, in the interests of the beneficiaries and in fairness. In addition, specific types of transactions are no longer subject to the absolute prohibition. Transactions with family members and transactions by a corporate trustee with its proprietary funds are examples of transactions that are sufficiently common and useful to be subject to exemptions.

UTC §802(a) states the duty of loyalty, and subsection (b) lists some of the exceptions the UTC now codifies.

UTC §802. Duty of Loyalty.

> (a) A trustee shall administer the trust solely in the interests of the beneficiaries.
>
> (b) a sale, encumbrance, or other transaction involving the investment or management of trust property entered into by the trustee for the trustee's own personal account or which is otherwise affected by a conflict between the trustee's fiduciary and personal interests is voidable by a beneficiary affected by the transaction unless:
>
> > (1) the transaction was authorized by the terms of the trust;
> >
> > (2) the transaction was approved by the court;
> >
> > (3) the beneficiary did not commence a judicial proceeding within the [applicable] time;
> >
> > (4) the beneficiary consented to the trustee's conduct, ratified the transaction, or released the trustee in compliance with [the UTC]; or
> >
> > (5) the transaction involves a contract entered into or claim acquired by the trustee before the person became or contemplated becoming trustee.

Comment to UTC §802

> Subsection (b) states the general rule with respect to transactions involving trust property that are affected by a conflict of interest. A transaction affected by a conflict between the trustee's fiduciary and personal interests is voidable by a beneficiary who is affected by the transaction. Subsection (b) carries out the "no further inquiry" rule by making transactions involving trust property entered into by a trustee for the trustee's own personal account voidable without further proof. Such transactions are irrebuttably presumed to be affected by a conflict between personal and fiduciary interests. It is immaterial whether the trustee acts in good faith or pays a fair consideration. *See* RESTATEMENT (SECOND) OF TRUSTS SECTION 170, cmt. b (1959).

a. Terms of the Trust

The settlor can authorize the trustee to engage in self-dealing or conflict of interest transactions with the trust. The terms of the trust may permit the trustee to buy property from the trust or to borrow money from the trust. If a family business will be part of the corpus and a family member active in the business will be trustee, the settlor may want to authorize the trustee to buy shares of stock from the trust, to vote shares in favor of herself or one of her immediate family members and to engage in transactions between the trust and the family business. Whether the settlor should authorize divided-loyalty transactions will depend on who the settlor names as trustee and the types of assets held in the trust. Even if the trust authorizes these transactions, the trustee must act fairly, in good faith and with the interests of the beneficiaries paramount. A court will permit a transaction only if the authorization is sufficiently specific to cover the particular transaction. *See* UTC §802(b)(1). In the case that follows, the court considers whether the trust instrument authorized self-dealing by the trustee.

In re Estate of Stevenson
605 N.W.2d 818 (S.D. 2000)

SABERS, Justice.

Elmer Stevenson established the Elmer Stevenson Trust on August 8, 1990 and funded it with all his property. Elmer died on September 15, 1992. Pursuant to the terms of the trust, Elmer's surviving wife, Clara, is the primary beneficiary with a life estate interest in the estate. Clara's granddaughter, Tamara, is the second beneficiary as well as the sole trustee.

The trust assets consisted of 1,515 acres of farmland. Approximately 800 acres were leased to Larry Hebbert for 30 years. On November 12, 1998, Hebbert received a letter, prepared by Tamara's attorney and signed by both Clara and Tamara, informing him that his lease was being terminated. After the letter was sent, Clara, however, changed her mind and decided that she did not want to terminate Hebbert's lease. She told Tamara to reinstate the lease, but Tamara refused.

On December 16, 1998, Tamara executed two new leases. One lease was to Tamara's husband, Randy Luke, for 456 acres and the second lease was to Randy's cousin, John Cap (Cap), for 312 acres. Cap's father, Steve Cap, is Randy's uncle and employs Randy as a farm laborer.

Clara petitioned the trial court for an Order to Show Cause seeking to void the leases with Tamara's husband and Cap. The trial court found that the trust document contained "specific authorization in Article IX for the Trustee, Tamara K. Luke, to lease property either in her name or in her husband's name." It also found the "terms and conditions of the written lease agreements . . . to be fair and reasonable." Based on those findings, the court concluded that "[state statutes] do not lead to a contrary conclusion."

Clara made a motion for reconsideration. The motion for reconsideration specifically set forth Clara's objections:

> SDCL [s]ection 55-2-3 prohibits a trustee from taking part in any transaction concerning the trust in which he has an interest adverse to that of the beneficiary. SDCL [s]ection 55-4-13 also prohibits a trustee, unless expressly authorized by the trust instrument, from leasing any property from the trust or from or to a relative, employer or other business associate . . . .

This part of the trust document [Article IX] does not expressly authorize the [T]rustee to lease trust property to herself or a relative of hers. Although this paragraph does state the Trustee may operate directly[,][t]his provision simply allows the Trustee to operate the farm on behalf of the Trust and does not give permission for the Trustee to operate the farm for the Trustee's own profit.

This part of the trust document also authorizes the [T]rustee to lease trust property on a sharecrop basis. However, it does not expressly authorize the Trustee to lease to herself or her spouse such trust property.

The motion for reconsideration was denied. Clara appeals. We reverse and remand.

Because the facts are not in dispute, we determine the legal questions de novo. The issue is whether the findings support the conclusions of law. They do not because there is an error of law. . . .

Clearly, there is a general rule against self-dealing. However, our statutes set forth specific exceptions to this general rule. A trustee is allowed to participate "in any transaction concerning the trust in which [s]he . . . has an interest, present or contingent, adverse to that of h[er] beneficiary" *if* "the instrument creating the trust *expressly* grants permission to the trustee to buy, sell or lease property for the trust from or to the trust." SDCL 55-2-3(4) (emphasis added). SDCL 55-4-13 provides that: "a trustee may lease, purchase or sell property from or to the trust [s]he represents as trustee if *specifically* authorized to do so in a decedent's will or the instrument creating the trustee relationship . . . . " (emphasis added). Consequently, the question is whether the trust instrument "expressly" or "specifically" authorized Tamara to lease property to herself, her husband, or a relative.

Clara argues that the trust instrument does not authorize Tamara to lease land to herself or to her husband. She specifically points to SDCL 55-4-13 to support her argument that the lease to Tamara's husband constituted self-dealing and a breach of loyalty; therefore, she argues that the lease is presumptively invalid and void. She contends that the trust instrument merely allows the trustee to farm the property for the trust by performing the labor herself or by hiring employees or by renting the land to someone else to farm.

Tamara, on the other hand, argues that she had authority under SDCL 55-2-3(4) to lease the property because the trust instrument expressly allows her to do so.

In interpreting a trust instrument, we must first attempt to ascertain and give effect to the settlor's intention. Thus, we must interpret the instrument as written. . . . However, if the language is not clear, construction of an ambiguous trust instrument is a question of law to be decided by the court. "In addition, an ambiguity is not of itself created simply because the parties differ as to the interpretation of the [trust instrument]." *Johnson v. Johnson*, 291 N.W.2d 776, 778-79 (S.D. 1980). . . .

In this case, Article IX of the Stevenson trust provides, in part:

All of the powers granted to the Trustees in this Article, however, are subject to any express limitation or contrary directions contained elsewhere in this Trust. The powers set forth therein shall not be a limitation of but shall include the power to sell, lease, transfer, exchange or otherwise dispose of, or grant options with respect to, any and all property forming a part of the trust estate . . . and may make and deliver such deeds, leases or other instruments as it considers proper under the circumstances, and may deal with the trust estate in any and all other ways in which any natural person could deal with h[er] own property. . . .

> My Trustees may retain, acquire and continue any farm operation; engage in the production, harvesting and marketing of farm products either by operating directly or with management agencies, hired labor, tenants, or sharecroppers. . . .

Although these provisions provide the trustee the *powers* to deal with the trust property as if it were her own, the powers must always be used *for the trust* and its beneficiaries, not for the trustee. That is the nature of a fiduciary relationship. The trustee can farm the property herself, or hire it done, but all transactions must be done for the trust, not for herself. Therefore, the grant of these powers does not authorize Tamara to engage in self-dealing by leasing the property to herself, her husband, or a relative. Clearly, it does not "expressly" or "specifically" authorize self-dealing as claimed. Despite the fact that the parties' interpretations differ, no ambiguity exists here. In other words, Article IX does not provide "clear and unmistakable language" authorizing the trustee to engage in self-dealing. Therefore, the leases to Tamara's husband and Cap are void.

Tamara also argues that Clara had the capacity to contract and had full knowledge of the facts when she authorized Tamara to lease the property to Tamara's husband. Therefore, she asserts that SDCL 55-2-3(1) allowed her to engage in a transaction that may otherwise be considered self-dealing.

SDCL 55-2-3(1) provides, in part, that a trustee may participate in a transaction that is adverse to the beneficiary's interest when:

the beneficiary [has] the capacity to contract and, with a full knowledge of the motives of the trustee and of all other facts concerning the transaction which might affect h[er] own decision and without the use of any influence on the part of the trustee, permits the trustee to do so. . . .

However, SDCL 55-2-8 provides that when a trustee obtains an advantage from the beneficiary, it is presumed that the beneficiary entered into the transaction "without sufficient consideration and under undue influence."

All transactions between a trustee and h[er] beneficiary during the existence of the trust or while the influence acquired by the trustee remains, by which [s]he obtains any advantage from h[er] beneficiary, are presumed to be entered into by the latter without sufficient consideration and under undue influence.

Therefore, any claimed "consent" by Clara is presumed to be entered into without "sufficient consideration and under undue influence." Consequently, Tamara's argument fails.

We reverse the trial court's determination that Article IX "expressly" or "specifically" authorized Tamara to lease the trust property to herself, her husband, or a relative. We remand for proceedings consistent with this opinion.

---

b.   Court Authorization

A trustee can ask the appropriate court for authorization to purchase property from a trust or to engage in some other transaction that breaches the duty of loyalty. Court authorization will protect the trustee as well as the beneficiaries. A court will review the transaction for fairness and will authorize the transaction only if it is in the interest of the beneficiaries. The trustee can then proceed without concerns about later charges that she has breached the duty of loyalty. Trustees have always been able to seek court authorization, and the UTC has codified this exception to the rule that self-dealing transactions are voidable. UTC §802(b)(2).

After reviewing the transaction and the trustee's personal interest in the transaction, a court may decide that instead of authorizing the trustee to carry out the transaction, it will appoint a trustee ad litem to handle only that particular transaction. *See* UTC §802(i); *Getty v. Getty*, 252 Cal. Rptr. 342 (Cal. App. 1988) (appointing a "trustee ad litem" to conduct certain litigation).

UTC §802. Duty of Loyalty.

> (i) The court may appoint a special fiduciary to make a decision with respect to any proposed transaction that might violate this section if entered into by the trustee.

Although a trustee can seek court approval of a sale to himself, if the beneficiaries oppose the sale the court may be reluctant to authorize the sale. In the following case, the trustee was one of a number of beneficiaries — children and grandchildren of the settlor. He wanted to buy some farmland held in the trust. Other beneficiaries wanted to keep the family farmstead intact. The Nebraska Supreme Court upheld the lower court's decision not to authorize the sale.

In re Trust Created by Inman
693 N.W.2d 514, 521-22 (Neb. 2005)

STEPHAN, J.

Historically, the law has looked with disfavor upon a trustee selling trust assets to himself. While such transactions are not absolutely prohibited under current law, they are voidable by a beneficiary unless specifically authorized by the trust instrument, approved by a court, or consented to or ratified by the beneficiary. It logically follows that a court should not approve such a transaction over the objection of a beneficiary unless it can be clearly demonstrated that the transaction is consistent with the trustee's duty to administer the trust solely in the interests of the beneficiaries. *See* Restatement (Third) of Trusts §170, comment *f.* at 196 (1992) (noting that "court will permit a trustee to purchase trust property only if in its opinion such purchase is for the best interest of the beneficiary"). We agree with the county court that the evidence in this case does not meet this test. [The trustee] presented no specific plan for investment of the proceeds from the proposed sale, and thus, any potential benefit to the beneficiaries in the nature of increased income without a corresponding increase in risk to the principal is speculative. There is no evidence that additional income is needed in order to carry out any specific purpose of the trust, and the beneficiaries have articulated a legitimate interest in maintaining the geographic integrity of the farm that has been in their family for many years.

---

c.   Consent of the Beneficiaries

The beneficiaries can consent to permit a divided-loyalty transaction. For the trustee to be protected, all beneficiaries of the trust must consent. If only some of the beneficiaries consent, then those beneficiaries cannot sue the trustee for breach of the duty of loyalty, but any beneficiaries who did not consent may still do so. The UTC provides for consent of beneficiaries in UTC §802(b)(4).

Some beneficiaries may be minor children or even unborn children or may otherwise lack legal capacity. If all the beneficiaries must consent, how can unborn children consent? The common law has developed different types of representation rules, and the UTC now has extensive provisions on representation in UTC §304. We discuss representation later in this chapter, when we discuss the duty to inform and report, another time when the trustee may need to rely on representation.

Review the facts of *Hosey*. Do you think the trustees could have obtained the consent of the beneficiaries to enter into the sub-lease?

d. Trustee Compensation

Although a payment of compensation by the trustee to herself is self-dealing, trustee compensation is, nonetheless, routinely permitted. Often the terms of the trust explicitly authorize trustee compensation, but if not, the common law and now statutes also permit it. Compensation must be reasonable, and excessive compensation will be considered a breach of the duty of loyalty. *See, e.g., Nickel v. Bank of America*, 290 F.3d 1134 (9th Cir. 2002) (overcharging fees violated the trustee's duty of loyalty); UTC §802(h)(2) (providing that "payment of reasonable compensation to the trustee" will not be a violation of the duty of loyalty "if fair to the beneficiaries").

Here is an example of a clause authorizing trustee compensation:

> The trustee shall have the power to pay all expenses incurred in the administration of the trust, including reasonable compensation to any [corporate] trustee, and employ and pay reasonable compensation to agents and counsel (including investment counsel).

e. Intra-Family Transactions

As discussed above, a trustee may want to engage in a transaction with a spouse, parent, child or other family member. Although a transaction with a family member is a conflict of interest transaction to which the duty of loyalty applies, some cases have exempted the transaction from the general prohibition on conflicts of interest and have considered fairness to the beneficiaries in determining whether the transaction should stand. *See, e.g., Culbertson v. McCann*, 664 P.2d 388, 391 (Okla. 1983) (involving a sale to the fiduciary's sister). The UTC has now codified this exception, providing for a rebuttable presumption of invalidity rather than an absolute prohibition on the transaction. UTC §802(c)(1),(2). Here is the UTC's treatment of the presumption.

UTC §802. Duty of Loyalty.

(c) A sale, encumbrance, or other transaction involving the investment or management of trust property is presumed to be affected by a conflict between personal and fiduciary interests if it is entered into by the trustee with:

(1) the trustee's spouse;

(2) the trustee's descendants, siblings, parents, or their spouses;

(3) an agent or attorney of the trustee; or

(4) a corporation or other person or enterprise in which the trustee, or a person that owns a significant interest in the trustee, has an interest that might affect the trustee's best judgment.

Comment to UTC §802

The rule is less severe with respect to transactions involving trust property entered into with persons who have close business or personal ties with the trustee. Under subsection (c), a transaction between a trustee and certain relatives and business associates is presumptively voidable, not void. Also presumptively voidable are transactions with corporations or other enterprises in which the trustee, or a person who owns a significant interest in the trustee, has an interest that might affect the trustee's best judgment. The presumption is rebutted if the trustee establishes that the transaction was not affected by a conflict between personal and fiduciary interests. Among the factors tending to rebut the presumption are whether the consideration was fair and whether the other terms of the transaction are similar to those that would be transacted with an independent party.

If a trust holds interests in a family business and a family member is the trustee, the trustee may have a conflict when dealing with the business. The settlor may anticipate this problem and include a provision in the trust authorizing the trustee to deal with the business assets, vote shares of stock and even buy and sell stock of the business. Here is an example from a will:

Special Assets

The Trustees of each trust created hereunder and the Personal Representatives of my estate are expressly authorized to continue to hold any stocks, bonds or other securities issued by, or any other interests in [name of family business]. The Trustees and my Personal Representatives are also expressly authorized to make further investments therein from the trust estate of any trust or from my estate from time to time. These authorizations apply even though such stocks, bonds, securities or interests (hereinafter referred to as "special assets") may constitute all or substantially all of the trust estate of any trust created hereunder or my estate. I hereby request, but I do not direct or require, that the Trustees of each trust created hereunder and the Personal Representatives of my estate continue to hold any such special assets absent a significant change in circumstances. However, if a trust hereunder or my estate is unable to meet certain obligations, the Trustees of each trust created hereunder and my Personal Representatives, in their discretion, may sell such special assets to meet such obligations. Such obligations may include the payment of taxes due by reason of my death, or provision for the health, support, maintenance and education of my spouse or my then living descendants. The Trustees of each trust created hereunder and the Personal Representatives of my estate are further authorized, in addition to other powers herein granted to or conferred upon the Trustees and my Personal Representatives, to buy or sell any such special assets or any other assets. The Trustees and my Personal Representatives may make sales to and purchases from any one (1) or more of themselves, individually, or to or from any other person who is then acting as a Trustee of any other trust created hereunder or as a Personal Representative, or to or from any other person (including, without limitation, any individual, trust, estate, corporation or partnership). Such sales or purchases may be at a price equal to the fair market value of such special assets or other assets at the time of such transaction, but in no event for less than adequate consideration in money or money's worth. No Trustee or Personal Representative shall be liable to any beneficiary hereunder or to any other person for any act or failure to act pursuant to this Article in the absence of his or her or its own bad faith.

---

f.   Proprietary Mutual Funds

The UTC authorizes a corporate trustee to invest in proprietary mutual funds (funds the corporation manages). UTC §802(f). That section provides that the trustee will not be presumed to be engaged in a conflict transaction if the trustee complies with the prudent investor rule (discussed later in this chapter). The trustee can receive compensation for investment services in addition to compensation as trustee, but the trustee must provide information about the rate and method by which the amount of compensation was determined to the qualified beneficiaries and any other beneficiaries who have requested an annual report.

UTC §802. Duty of Loyalty.

> (f) An investment by a trustee in securities of an investment company or investment trust to which the trustee, or its affiliate, provides services in a capacity other than as trustee is not presumed to be affected by a conflict between personal and fiduciary interests if the investment otherwise complies with the prudent investor rule of

> [Article] 9. In addition to its compensation for acting as trustee, the trustee may be compensated by the investment company or investment trust for providing those services out of fees charged to the trust. If the trustee receives compensation from the investment company or investment trust for providing investment advisory or investment management services, the trustee must at least annually notify the persons entitled under Section 813 to receive a copy of the trustee's annual report of the rate and method by which that compensation was determined. . . .
>
> (h) This section does not preclude the following transactions, if fair to the beneficiaries: . . .
>
> (4) a deposit of trust money in a regulated financial-service institution operated by the trustee;

g. Advances by Trustee

A trustee can advance her own funds to the trust and be repaid, without interest, if the advance will protect the trust estate or is necessary for expenses of administration. A trustee may also lend money to the trust and be repaid with reasonable interest, if funds are not otherwise available on equal or better terms. *See* RESTATEMENT (THIRD) OF TRUSTS §78, cmt. c(6).

h. Voting Stock

If a trust owns corporate stock, the trustee will need to vote the stock. The UTC contains a reminder that the trustee must vote the stock in the best interests of the beneficiaries. Thus, if the trustee owns stock in the same company in the trustee's individual capacity, the trustee must be careful to vote the trust's stock in a manner that benefits the beneficiaries, regardless of how the trustee votes the individually owned stock. Also, the trustee cannot use the corporate form to avoid fiduciary duties such as the duty of impartiality. The Comment to this subsection of UTC §802 explains the potential problems the trustee could face.

UTC §802. Duty of Loyalty.

> (g) In voting shares of stock or in exercising powers of control over similar interests in other forms of enterprise, the trustee shall act in the best interests of the beneficiaries. If the trust is the sole owner of a corporation or other form of enterprise, the trustee shall elect or appoint directors or other managers who will manage the corporation or enterprise in the best interests of the beneficiaries.

Comment to UTC §802

> Subsection (g) addresses an overlap between trust and corporate law. It is based on Restatement of Trusts (Second) Section 193 cmt. A (1959), which provides that "[i]t is the duty of the trustee in voting shares of stock to use proper care to promote the interest of the beneficiary," and that the fiduciary responsibility of a trustee in voting a control block "is heavier than where he holds only a small fraction of the shares." ... When the trust owns the entirety of the shares of a corporation, the corporate assets are in effect trust assets that the trustee determines to hold in corporate form. The trustee may not use the corporate form to escape the fiduciary duties of trust law. Thus, for example, a trustee whose duty of impartiality would require the trustee to make current distributions for the support of current beneficiaries may not evade that duty by holding assets in corporate form and pleading the discretion of corporate directors to determine dividend policy. Rather, the trustee must vote for corporate directors who will follow a dividend policy consistent with the trustee's trust-law duty of impartiality.

QUESTION

Under the UTC, when does the absolute rule concerning the duty of loyalty apply (the trustee is in breach and the beneficiary can void the transaction) and when does a rebuttable presumption of an impermissible conflict apply (the trustee is not in breach if the transaction was fair and in the interests of the beneficiaries)? Give an example of each.

PROBLEMS

Savannah established a trust under her will, making her son, Tristan, the trustee. The trust provides for Savannah's second husband, Ralph, for his life and then on her husband's death, the trustee is directed to distribute the remaining assets to Savannah's descendants. Savannah and her first husband had two children, Tristan and William, and each of the sons has children. After Savannah's death, Tristan comes to you with the following questions:

    1.   Tristan would like to buy the family home from the trust. Ralph (who is Tristan's stepfather) has moved in with Ralph's daughter and is happy to have the house sold and the proceeds used for investments that will produce income. Can Tristan buy the house? How should he proceed if

William supports Tristan's buying the house? What if William is opposed and wants to buy the house for himself?

2. Savannah and her first husband owned a dry cleaning business. Tristan has managed the business for many years; his brother is not involved in the business. The trust owns 60% of the voting stock of the business, and Tristan and William each own 20%. Can Tristan vote the shares held in the trust? Can Tristan vote not to declare dividends (the business has paid dividends each year for the past eight years)? Can Tristan buy stock from the trust?

3. Tristan is spending a lot of time managing the portfolio of assets held in the trust. Can he pay himself a salary as trustee?

4. Now assume that Savannah comes to you before her death, with a will drafted by another lawyer, creating the trust described above. What provisions might Savannah want to include in her will in connection with the creation of the trust?

4. Best Interests of the Beneficiaries — Reprise

Before we leave our discussion of the duty of loyalty and its prohibition of divided-loyalty transactions, the following article excerpt will serve both as a review of the principles we have discussed and as an argument that the current rule should be changed. As you read the excerpt, consider which rule you think is best for trust law: the no-further-inquiry rule, which makes voidable any self-dealing or conflict of interest transaction, or Professor Langbein's proposal that trust law adopt a best interests rule and permit an inquiry into the merits of a conflicted transaction.

John H. Langbein, Questioning the Trust Law Duty of Loyalty: Sole Interest or Best Interest?
114 Yale L.J. 929 (2005)

The sole interest rule prohibits the trustee from "plac[ing] himself in a position where his personal interest . . . conflicts or possibly may conflict with" the interests of the beneficiary. The rule applies not only to cases in which a trustee misappropriates trust property, but also to cases in which no such thing has happened — that is, to cases in which the trust "incurred no loss" or in which "actual benefit accrued to the trust" from a transaction with a conflicted trustee. [citing GEORGE GLEASON BOGERT & GEORGE TAYLOR BOGERT, THE LAW OF TRUSTS AND TRUSTEES §543, at 217, 248 (rev. 2d ed. 1993).]

The conclusive presumption of invalidity under the sole interest rule has acquired a distinctive name: the "no further inquiry" rule. What that label emphasizes, as the official comment to the Uniform Trust Code of

2000 explains, is that "transactions involving trust property entered into by a trustee for the trustee's own personal account [are] voidable without further proof." Courts invalidate a conflicted transaction without regard to its merits — "not because there is fraud, but because there may be fraud." . . .

The underlying purpose of the duty of loyalty, which the sole interest rule is meant to serve, is to advance the best interest of the beneficiaries. This Article takes the view that a transaction prudently undertaken to advance the best interest of the beneficiaries best serves the purpose of the duty of loyalty, even if the trustee also does or might derive some benefit. A transaction in which there has been conflict or overlap of interest should be sustained if the trustee can prove that the transaction was prudently undertaken in the best interest of the beneficiaries. In such a case, inquiry into the merits is better than "no further inquiry." . . .

What is wrong with the trust tradition as embodied in the sole interest rule is the failure to take adequate account of the truth that prohibiting some conflicts is too costly, either because the compliance costs of prohibition outweigh the gain or because a conflicted transaction is benign. The very term "conflict" is an epithet that prejudices our understanding that some overlaps of interest are either harmless or positively value enhancing for all affected interests. To be sure, some conflicts of interest may harbor incentives so perverse, yet so hard to detect and deter, that categoric prohibition, as under the sole interest rule, is the cost-effective way to deal with the danger. The athlete betting on his or her team's performance is a good example, as is the lawyer representing both parties in a contested lawsuit. I demonstrate in this Article that trust administration is not a good example of a conflict worth prohibiting categorically, because there is so much evidence that various forms of trustee/beneficiary conflict promote the best interest of the beneficiary. Trust law has taken this lesson to heart in the numerous exclusions and exceptions to the sole interest rule that I discuss below. The view this Article advances is that the logic of the exclusions and exceptions should become the rule. . . .

B. THE CONCERN ABOUT CONCEALMENT

A main theme in the cases that developed the sole interest rule was the fear that without the prohibition on trustee self-interest, a conflicted trustee would be able to use his or her control over the administration of the trust to conceal wrongdoing, hence to prevent detection and consequent remedy. Lord Hardwicke, sitting in 1747, before the sole interest rule had hardened in English trust law, was worried about a self-dealing trustee being able to conceal misappropriation. In 1816 in *Davoue v. Fanning*, the foundational American case recognizing and enforcing the then-recently-settled English rule, Chancellor Kent echoed this concern: "There may be fraud, as Lord Hardwicke observed, and the [beneficiary] not able to prove it." In order "to guard against this uncertainty," Kent endorsed the rule allowing the beneficiary to rescind a conflicted transaction "without show-ing actual injury." In his Commentaries on American Law, Kent returned to the point that the sole interest rule "is founded on the danger of impo-sition and the presumption of the existence of fraud, inaccessible to the eye of the court."

Commentators continue to invoke this concern about trustee conceal-ment when justifying the severity of the sole interest rule. Says Bogert: "Equity will not inquire into the fairness of particular sales. It realizes that if it did, in many cases the unfairness would be so hidden as to be undiscov-erable." As a matter of logic, I find this line of reasoning dubious. The claim is that because some trustee misbehavior might be successfully concealed, the law should refuse to examine the merits of the trustee's conduct even in a case in which there has not been concealment.

There is a far deeper objection to the old preoccupation with the danger of trustee concealment: Changed circumstances have materially reduced the danger. However serious the hazard may have been in the days of Lord Hardwicke and Chancellor Kent, in modern trust administration the concern is no longer well founded.

[Professor Langbein explains that rules of evidence have changed — courts are now able to determine facts in a way they were not in the early 1800s when the no-further-inquiry rule was developed (think *Bleak House*). And modern recordkeeping requirements and norms mean that beneficiaries have access to information in ways that they did not in the 1800s. The UTC now requires disclosure in contrast with older law under which the beneficiary had the right to demand information, but the trust-ee's duty was only to respond to requests from beneficiaries.]

. . . Fixing the sole interest rule is not hard. Change the force of the presumption of invalidity that presently attaches to a conflicted transaction from conclusive to rebuttable. In place of "no further inquiry," allow inquiry. Allow a trustee who is sued for a breach of the duty of loyalty to prove that the conflicted transaction was prudently undertaken in the best interest of the beneficiary. That step would recast the trust law duty of loy-alty from the sole interest rule to the best interest rule. Precisely that step has now been taken in section 802(c) of the Uniform Trust Code, just dis-cussed, regarding affiliated providers and intrafamilial transactions. . . .

Recognizing a best interest defense would have the effect of clarifying the duty of loyalty, identifying the primacy of the best interest standard. Recall that the present Restatement (Second) rule provides: "The trustee is under a duty to the beneficiary to administer the trust solely in the interest of the beneficiary." Allowing the defense would effectively rework the rule as follows:

> (1) The trustee is under a duty to administer the trust in the best interest of the beneficiaries.
> (2) A trustee who does not administer the trust in the sole interest of the beneficiaries is presumed not to have administered it in their best interest.

The trustee may rebut the presumption by showing that a transaction not in the sole interest of the beneficiaries was prudently undertaken in the best interest of the beneficiaries. By comparison with the sole interest rule, a best interest rule would more accurately identify the policy that the sole interest rule has been meant to serve. The better focused a rule is on its true purpose, the greater the likelihood that those who work with the rule (in this instance, trustees and their legal advisers and the courts) will apply the rule in a fashion that carries out the purpose.

D. PROVIDING INFORMATION TO BENEFICIARIES—DUTY TO INFORM AND REPORT

1. Common Law Duty

In order for a beneficiary to enforce her interests in the trust, the beneficiary must have information about the trust, its assets, transactions engaged in by the trustee and income earned by the trust. The common law required the trustee to respond to requests for information from any beneficiary. The duty was a reactive one — the beneficiary had to ask and had to know to ask. In states that have not adopted the UTC reporting requirements described below, the duty to report remains a reactive one, defined in the common law. Nonetheless, most trustees, particularly those advised by lawyers, provide annual accountings to the beneficiaries of the trusts they manage. Providing reports and accountings is a "best practice" and protects the trustee because statutes of limitations begin to run once the beneficiaries have information about the trust.

2. The Uniform Trust Code

Historical changes in the types of assets held in trusts and the increasingly complex duties of trustees have led to the need for better reporting by trustees. UTC §813 incorporates the common law rule in paragraph (a) and then adds duties for trustees. Under the UTC, trustees now have affirmative duties to provide notice and reports, in addition to the duty to respond to requests for information. Certain of these duties are mandatory duties that cannot be removed by the settlor. UTC §§105(b)(8), (9) provide that the settlor cannot waive the duties provided in UTC §§813(a), (b)(2), (b)(3). States have not adopted §105 uniformly, however, and the uniform act now puts 105(b)(8) and (b)(9) in brackets.

UTC §813. Duty to Inform and Report.

(a) A trustee shall keep the qualified beneficiaries of the trust reasonably informed about the administration of the trust and of the material facts necessary for them to protect their interests. Unless unreasonable under the circumstances, a trustee shall promptly respond to a beneficiary's request for information related to the administration of the trust.

(b) A trustee:

(1) upon request of a beneficiary, shall promptly furnish to the beneficiary a copy of the trust instrument;

(2) within 60 days after accepting a trusteeship, shall notify the qualified beneficiaries of the acceptance and of the trustee's name, address, and telephone number;

(3) within 60 days after the date the trustee acquires knowledge of the creation of an irrevocable trust, or the date the trustee acquires knowledge that a formerly revocable trust has become irrevocable, whether by the death of the settlor or otherwise, shall notify the qualified beneficiaries of the trust's existence, of the identity of the settlor or settlors, of the right to request a copy of the trust instrument, and of the right to a trustee's report as provided in subsection (c); and

(4) shall notify the qualified beneficiaries in advance of any change in the method or rate of the trustee's compensation.

(c) A trustee shall send to the distributees or permissible distributees of trust income or principal, and to other qualified or nonqualified beneficiaries who request it, at least annually and at the termination of the trust, a report of the trust property, liabilities, receipts, and disbursements, including the source and amount of the trustee's compensation, a listing of the trust assets and, if feasible, their respective market values. . . .

(d) A beneficiary may waive the right to a trustee's report or other information otherwise required to be furnished under this section. A beneficiary, with respect to future reports and other information, may withdraw a waiver previously given.

Before enactment of the UTC, the trustee's duty to keep beneficiaries advised about the trust was a duty to respond to requests. Now the law imposes a duty to provide annual reports to certain beneficiaries. The problem is that sometimes a settlor may prefer that a beneficiary not know too much about a trust.

Example: Warren establishes a trust for his nephew, Brent. Brent is in college, doing well, and Warren wants the trust to be available for

Brent's future needs (Brent does not need additional funds for college). Warren's friend, Steena, is the trustee. Warren does not want Brent to know about the trust because he fears that knowing about the money will be a disincentive for Brent to study hard in school. Can Warren provide in the terms of the trust that the trustee cannot share information with Brent?

The answer is no, because if the beneficiary does not have information about the trust, the beneficiary cannot enforce the trust. The trustee has legal title only, and the beneficiary must be able to monitor the trustee in order to ensure that the trustee does not abscond with the money. Even if Warren has complete faith in Steena's trustworthiness, the law will not let Warren create a trust that is kept secret from the beneficiary.

The need to keep information from particular beneficiaries — a young person who might lose incentive to work hard, a beneficiary with a history of drug or alcohol abuse, a spendthrift — has troubled lawyers advising clients under the UTC. To provide an option in these circumstances, the District of Columbia modified the UTC to state that if the settlor provides, notice can be given to another person and not to the beneficiary. D.C. STAT. §19-1301.05(c) (2010). The other person must be designated by the settlor and is charged with protecting the interests of the beneficiary. Oregon has also adopted this designated-person idea. OR. REV. STAT. 130.020(3)(2009). The designated person solves the problem of giving notice to a beneficiary who is ill-suited to receive the information, but the statutes that have provided for this option have not addressed the status of the designated person. Does the person have fiduciary responsibilities to the beneficiary? Does the person have standing to sue the trustee for breach (the beneficiary would have standing to protect her interests, but the designated person has no beneficial interest in the trust)? For a discussion of these issues, see Kevin D. Millard, *The Trustee's Duty to Inform and Report Under the Uniform Trust Code*, 40 REAL PROP. PROB. & TRUST J. 373 (2005).

The trustee's duty to inform and report is an important one, and the trustee must determine who must receive information and who may receive information by requesting it. The rules are somewhat complicated, and we will not explore them further.

3.   Representation

In connection with the duty to inform and report and for other purposes, the UTC provides for representation for beneficiaries who lack legal capacity or are not yet born. The UTC provides for representation by fiduciaries, which is consistent with older law. In addition, the UTC permits the representation of minor and unborn children by a parent of the children.

UTC §303. Representation by Fiduciaries and Parents.

To the extent there is no conflict of interest between the representative and the person represented or among those being represented with respect to a particular question or dispute:

(1) a [conservator] may represent and bind the estate that the [conservator] controls;

(2) a [guardian] may represent and bind the ward if a [conservator] of the ward's estate has not been appointed;

(3) an agent having authority to act with respect to the particular question or dispute may represent and bind the principal;

(4) a trustee may represent and bind the beneficiaries of the trust;

(5) a personal representative of a decedent's estate may represent and bind persons interested in the estate; and

(6) a parent may represent and bind the parent's minor or unborn child if a [conservator] or [guardian] for the child has not been appointed.

The UTC also permits representation by a person who has an interest "substantially identical to" the interest of the person being represented. For example, if a trust provides a remainder interest for children of a person, an adult child can represent unborn or minor children — the child's siblings. The representation provisions apply only if the person representing another beneficiary does not have a conflict of interest that would affect the representation.

UTC §304. Representation by Person Having Substantially Identical Interest.

Unless otherwise represented, a minor, incapacitated, or unborn individual, or a person whose identity or location is unknown and not reasonably ascertainable, may be represented by and bound by another having a substantially identical interest with respect to the particular question or dispute, but only to the extent there is no conflict of interest between the representative and the person represented.

Example: A trust provides a life estate for Stephanie, the settlor's surviving spouse, and then on her death directs the trustee to distribute the trust to the settlor's descendants. The settlor had two children, Andrew and Bart. Andrew is 25 and Bart is 16. Andrew has a child, Clarice. Depending on the particular need for representation, Andrew may be able to represent Bart, because his interest is substantially identical to Bart's interest. Andrew may also be able to represent Clarice, as her parent. Representation for purposes of receiving annual reports should not create a conflict of interest in either situation. However, if the trustee wants to modify the trust in a way that benefits Andrew or to engage in a self-dealing transaction that could benefit Andrew but not Bart or Clarice, then Andrew will not be able to represent the other beneficiaries.

PROBLEMS

Suri creates a trust for her child, Cynthia. The trust provides income for Cynthia for life, with the remainder at her death to her then living descendants, by representation. Cynthia has two children, Darlene and Eloise. Darlene has two children, Frieda and Gabrielle. To answer the questions, you will need to review the definition of qualified beneficiary in Chapter 5.

1. Who must receive an annual report?
2. Who may request a copy of the trust document?
3. If a trustee resigns and a successor becomes trustee, to whom must the new trustee give notice?
4. If Cynthia becomes incapacitated, who can represent her?
5. If Gabrielle is a minor, who can represent her?

E. CARING FOR TRUST PROPERTY — DUTY OF PRUDENCE

As we noted at the beginning of this chapter, three duties serve as the foundation for fiduciary law: the duty of obedience to the purpose of the trust, the duty of loyalty and the duty of care or prudence. In this section we turn to the duty of care, now more often referred to as the duty of prudence. This duty, in general terms, is the duty to manage trust property and to administer the trust with "reasonable care, skill, and caution." *See* RESTATEMENT (THIRD) OF TRUSTS §77(2) (2003).

1. Duties to Protect the Property

The rules relating to the management of trust property address the trustee's duty to pay proper attention to the trust and to treat the property of the trust in a way that protects the property for the beneficiaries. For example, the duty to collect and protect trust property, UTC §809, the duty to enforce and defend claims of the trust, UTC §811, and the duty to redress a breach of trust committed by a former trustee, UTC §812, all serve to protect and increase the value of assets in the trust.

UTC §809. Control and Protection of Trust Property.

> A trustee shall take reasonable steps to take control of and protect the trust property.

UTC §811. Enforcement and Defense of Claims.

> A trustee shall take reasonable steps to enforce claims of the trust and to defend claims against the trust.

UTC §812. Collecting Trust Property.

> A trustee shall take reasonable steps to compel a former trustee or other person to deliver trust property to the trustee, and to redress a breach of trust known to the trustee to have been committed by a former trustee.

The settlor may want to provide in the terms of the trust that a successor trustee need not pursue a claim against the prior trustee if the costs of doing so outweigh the potential benefits. Section 812 directs the trustee only to take "reasonable steps" and a cost-benefit analysis belongs in a decision about what is reasonable, but guidance in the trust document could reassure the trustee that pursuing all claims against prior trustees is not necessary.

2. Duties to Keep Proper Records and to Keep the Property Separate

The trustee is also under duties to keep the property separate from the trustee's own property. Property that is commingled with the trustee's own property or property for which adequate records are not kept may be vulnerable to misuse by the trustee or to claims by the trustee's personal creditors. UTC §810 addresses these concerns. The duty to keep the property separate from the trustee's property, §810(b), is also referred to as the *duty not to commingle*, and the duty to label trust property as belonging to the trustee in her fiduciary capacity, §810(c), is often referred to as the *duty to earmark*. UTC §810(d) allows a trustee to invest assets in a common trust fund, as long as recordkeeping is sufficient to identify the property that belongs to the trust. UTC §810 requires that trust assets be identified as assets of the trust and that the trustee keep adequate records.

UTC §810. Recordkeeping and Identification of Trust Property.

> (a) A trustee shall keep adequate records of the administration of the trust.
> (b) A trustee shall keep trust property separate from the trustee's own property.
> (c) Except as otherwise provided in subsection (d), a trustee shall cause the trust property to be designated so that the interest of the trust, to the extent feasible, appears in records maintained by a party other than a trustee or beneficiary.
> (d) If the trustee maintains records clearly indicating the respective interests, a trustee may invest as a whole the property of two or more separate trusts.

Early cases held that if a trustee failed to earmark property belonging to the trust, the trustee would be liable for any loss incurred by the property, whether or not caused by the failure to earmark. In *Miller v. Pender*, 34 A.2d 663 (N.H. 1943), the court took the more modern view that the trustee should only be liable if the failure to earmark caused the loss, for example, because the trustee's creditors could reach the property.

3. Duty to Invest Prudently

A trustee must manage the trust's assets in a way that protects the value of the assets over time. For most trusts, the trustee will invest the assets with two goals: to produce income and to maintain the value of the trust. The legal understanding of what it means to invest prudently has evolved over the years. The duty has changed from strict rules with limited control by trustees to rules that facilitate investment decision making based on modern portfolio theory and other developments in investment strategies. The excerpt that follows explains the development of the prudent investor rule. In 1994, the Uniform Law Commission adopted the Uniform Prudent Investor Act (UPIA), which codifies the prudent investor rule. Professor Langbein, who served as reporter for UPIA, wrote the following article explaining the history of fiduciary investing and the changes UPIA makes. (The article also makes predictions for the future of trust investing, so you may want to read the entire article if you are interested in fiduciary investing.) After looking at Professor Langbein's description of the history of trust investing, we will examine the guidance UPIA provides for trustees.

John H. Langbein, The Uniform Prudent Investor Act and the Future of Trust Investing
81 Iowa L. Rev. 641, 641-46 (1996)

In recent years, American law has undergone a fundamental revision of the rules that govern how trustees invest. . . .

The Uniform Prudent Investor Act implements a tightly interconnected set of reforms. These adjustments to the legal regime were driven by profound changes that have occurred across the past generation in our understanding of the investment function. This new learning about the investment process is called the theory of efficient markets, or more broadly, Modern Portfolio Theory (MPT).

I. Older Standards of Prudent Investing

. . . English law got off to a bad start on trust investing. In 1719 Parliament authorized trustees to invest in shares of the South Sea Company. A number of them did, and when the South Sea "Bubble" burst the next year, share prices declined by 90 percent. The Chancellors took fright and developed a restricted list of presumptively proper trust investments, initially government bonds, later well-secured first mortgages. Lord St. Leonard's Act in 1859 added East India stock, and across the decades, some dribbles of legislation approved various other issues. Only in 1961 was the English statute amended to allow trustees to invest in equities more generally, and even then the investment was subject to a ceiling of half the trust fund. That legislation remains in force, although an official revision commission has begun to deliberate on reforming it.

Some American jurisdictions had a similar history in the nineteenth and early twentieth centuries, developing so-called legal lists of court-approved or legislatively-approved investments, which were initially restricted to government bonds and first mortgages, but grudgingly expanded in some states to include selected corporate issues.

The path of the future in American law led away from legal lists, however, and was forged in Massachusetts. In 1830, in the celebrated case of *Harvard College v. Amory*, the Supreme Judicial Court adopted what came to be known as the prudent man rule.

Trustees, said the Massachusetts court, should "observe how men of prudence . . . manage their own affairs, not in regard to speculation, but in regard to the permanent disposition of their funds, considering the probable income, as well as the probable safety of the capital to be invested." The Massachusetts rule represented a great advance by abandoning the attempt to specify approved types of investment. Prudence is another word for reasonableness, and the prudent man rule echoed the contemporaneously developed reasonable man rule in the law of negligence. The standard of prudent investing was the standard of industry practice — what other trustees similarly situated were doing. Investment practice under the prudent man rule led rapidly to judicial approval of the use of corporate securities, both equities and bonds, in trust accounts. By the 1940s many American states had adopted by statute a version of the Massachusetts rule that the American Bankers Association promoted on behalf of corporate fiduciaries. The Uniform Prudent Investor Act is designed to replace that act.

The prudent man rule as applied by the courts came to be encrusted with a strong emphasis on avoiding so-called "speculation," whatever that meant. (Recall the language from *Harvard College v. Amory*, cautioning the trustee to invest "not in regard to speculation" and to treat "the probable safety of the capital" as central.) As late as the 1959 Restatement we find the assertion that "the purchase of shares of stock on margin or purchase of bonds selling at a great discount because of uncertainty whether they will be paid on maturity" is speculative and imprudent. In some jurisdictions investing in junior mortgages, no matter how well secured, was per se imprudent. The view crystallized that an investment in a "new and untried enterprise" was inherently speculative and imprudent. Ludicrous judicial applications of the notion of speculation continued in some jurisdictions into recent times.

Trustees in the first half of the twentieth century, preoccupied with avoiding speculation and preserving capital, were inclined to emphasize long-term government and corporate bonds as the characteristic trust investment. Experience with inflation after World War II taught that bonds placed significant inflation risk on the bondholder. Investments in debt could therefore experience declines in real value as severe as in equities. We now know that, in inflation-adjusted terms, the long-term real rate of return on equities has greatly exceeded bonds. The Sinquefield/Ibbotson studies estimate the inflation-adjusted rate of return on stocks since the 1920s at about 9 percent per year, as compared to about 3 percent for bonds. Fiduciaries have adapted to this knowledge, and through the second half of the century, have tended to increase the proportion of equity in trust accounts, at least in those trust accounts that can bear the greater volatility of equities.

II. THE UNIFORM PRUDENT INVESTOR ACT

I turn now to the Uniform Prudent Investor Act, with a view to identifying and explaining its main reforms. As the title of the Act makes clear, the legislation retains the prudence standard. As did the 1992 Restatement, the Act takes the opportunity to unisex the prudent man, who has now become the prudent investor. The Act directs the trustee to invest "as a prudent investor would. . . . "

In giving content to the prudence label, the Act makes three great changes in the law. All three were presaged in the 1992 Restatement. First, the Act articulates a greatly augmented duty to diversify trust investments. Next, in place of the old preoccupation with avoiding speculation, the Act substitutes a requirement of sensitivity to the risk tolerance of the particular trust, directing the trustee to invest for "risk and return objectives reasonably suited to the trust." Finally, the Act reverses the much criticized nondelegation rule of former law and actually encourages trustees to delegate investment responsibilities to professionals.

---

a.   Interest, Dividends, Rents and Capital Gains

We do not need an advanced understanding of investment options (and estate planning lawyers should not act as financial planners unless qualified to do so), but some basic concepts are helpful in understanding the prudent investor rule, the allocation of principal and income in trust accounting and the duty of impartiality to beneficiaries.

Some investments produce "interest." These include bank accounts, treasury notes (backed by the U.S. government) and corporate bonds. Interest is considered "income" under trust accounting rules. Investment in stock in publicly traded companies will produce either dividends or capital gains or both. A company may pay a dividend as a way of distributing profits to shareholders. If the company is successful, the price of the stock will go up. The shareholder will not benefit from an increase in the value of the stock until the shareholder sells the stock, but at that time the shareholder will recognize "capital gain," which is the appreciation in the value of the stock from the time of purchase to the time of sale. Dividends are "income" under trust accounting rules, and capital gains are "principal." Some stocks distribute dividends but increase in value slowly; other stocks may appreciate in value rapidly but not distribute dividends. Both types of stocks may be "good" investments for a particular trust, as part of a portfolio of investments, but the types of return to the trust may be all "income" or all "principal" or some of each.

An investor may also invest in real estate. Rents from real property are "income," and capital gains are "principal." In addition, real property may have more significant costs than some investments, and costs are also allocated to the income or principal accounts. If a trust owns a building, for example, maintenance on the building may be a significant cost. The maintenance costs may reduce income while increasing the value of the building (and increasing the capital gain in the long run).

Each type of investment will, the trustee hopes, generate revenue. If the revenue is considered "income," then the income beneficiary gets a distribution. If the revenue is classified as "principal," then the remainder beneficiary will get more when the trust terminates. Changes in investment theory, in particular the development of modern portfolio theory, means that investing for "income" or "principal" no longer makes sense. Under modern portfolio theory a prudent investor should invest in a portfolio of assets that balances risk and return and that produces a reasonable rate of return for the trust. A prudent investor invests for overall return and doing so effectively may mean skewing the returns that are "income" or "principal." Thus, the success of the prudent investor rule depends on changes to the rules that determine income and principal for trusts. We examine the prudent investor rule first and then turn to the principal and income rules. Keep in mind that these interrelate.

Forty-four states have enacted UPIA, and even in states that have not enacted UPIA, its explanation of prudence will likely influence any determination of what it means to be a prudent investor. Trust law has long required that a trustee act with prudence in managing trust property. Now UPIA provides guidance on the standard. The Prefatory Note to UPIA explains the changes UPIA makes to legal rules on prudent investing.

Prefatory Note to the Uniform Prudent Investor Act

Objectives of the Act.

UPIA makes five fundamental alterations in the former criteria for prudent investing. All are to be found in the *Restatement of Trusts 3d*: Prudent Investor Rule.

(1) The standard of prudence is applied to any investment as part of the total portfolio, rather than to individual investments. In the trust setting the term "portfolio" embraces all the trust's assets. UPIA §2(b).

(2) The tradeoff in all investing between risk and return is identified as the fiduciary's central consideration. UPIA §2(b).

(3) All categoric restrictions on types of investments have been abrogated; the trustee can invest in anything that plays an appropriate role in achieving the risk/return objectives of the trust and that meets the other requirements of prudent investing. UPIA §2(e).

(4) The long familiar requirement that fiduciaries diversify their investments has been integrated into the definition of prudent investing. UPIA §3.

(5) The much criticized former rule of trust law forbidding the trustee to delegate investment and management functions has been reversed. Delegation is now permitted, subject to safeguards. UPIA §9.

The UTC has incorporated UPIA, so a state enacting the UTC would enact UPIA as part of the UTC. If a state had enacted UPIA before it enacted the UTC, the state would modify statutory section numbers to put UPIA into the state's trust code. We will use the UPIA section numbers.

b. Prudent Investor Rule

UPIA begins with a statement of the requirement that a trustee act as a prudent investor and a reminder that the prudent investor rule is a default rule.

Under UPIA, a trustee must use "reasonable care, skill, and caution" in making investment decisions. The standard of prudence established by UPIA is an objective standard, not a subjective one. A prudent trustee should make decisions that other similarly situated trustees would make. The comparative nature of the rule resembles the "reasonable person" rule in tort law. *See* UPIA, §1, cmt.

UPIA §1. Prudent Investor Rule.

> (a) Except as otherwise provided in subsection (b), a trustee who invests and manages trust assets owes a duty to the beneficiaries of the trust to comply with the prudent investor rule set forth in this [Act].
>
> (b) The prudent investor rule, a default rule, may be expanded, restricted, eliminated, or otherwise altered by the provisions of a trust. A trustee is not liable to a beneficiary to the extent that the trustee acted in reasonable reliance on the provisions of the trust.

c. Standard of Care; Portfolio Strategy; Risk and Return Objectives

UPIA §2 provides a list of factors the trustee should consider, including factors related to the trust as well as general economic factors. The trustee can, and should, make decisions with the entire portfolio in mind and should not make decisions on an asset-by-asset basis. The trustee must consider the purposes and beneficiaries of the trust, and the trustee's risk and return analyses will vary depending on the nature of the interests. An elderly person dependent on modest trust assets will have a lower risk tolerance than a young person with income and wealth apart from the trust. The trustee must balance the need for current income with the need to preserve and increase the principal of the trust, so that the interests of all beneficiaries become part of the decision-making process.

Here is UPIA's list of factors to consider.

UPIA §2. Standard of Care; Portfolio Strategy; Risk and Return Objectives.

> (a) A trustee shall invest and manage trust assets as a prudent investor would, by considering the purposes, terms, distribution

requirements, and other circumstances of the trust. In satisfying this standard, the trustee shall exercise reasonable care, skill, and caution.

(b) A trustee's investment and management decisions respecting individual assets must be evaluated not in isolation but in the context of the trust portfolio as a whole and as a part of an overall investment strategy having risk and return objectives reasonably suited to the trust.

(c) Among circumstances that a trustee shall consider in investing and managing trust assets are such of the following as are relevant to the trust or its beneficiaries:

(1) general economic conditions;

(2) the possible effect of inflation or deflation;

(3) the expected tax consequences of investment decisions or strategies;

(4) the role that each investment or course of action plays within the overall trust portfolio, which may include financial assets, interests in closely held enterprises, tangible and intangible personal property, and real property;

(5) the expected total return from income and the appreciation of capital;

(6) other resources of the beneficiaries;

(7) needs for liquidity, regularity of income, and preservation or appreciation of capital; and

(8) an asset's special relationship or special value, if any, to the purposes of the trust or to one or more of the beneficiaries.

(d) A trustee shall make a reasonable effort to verify facts relevant to the investment and management of trust assets.

(e) A trustee may invest in any kind of property or type of investment consistent with the standards of this [Act].

d. Special Skills

If a trustee is chosen based on a representation of "special skills or expertise," the trustee will be expected to use those special skills and will be held to a standard that includes those skills. Thus, the standard for a professional trustee is that of a prudent professional trustee, while the standard for a family member serving as trustee will be that of an ordinary prudent investor — an amateur rather than a professional.

UPIA §2. Standard of Care.

(f) A trustee who has special skills or expertise, or is named trustee in reliance upon the trustee's representation that the trustee has special skills or expertise, has a duty to use those special skills.

e.   Diversification

UPIA requires diversification unless the trustee determines that the trust is better served by not diversifying. Modern investment theory says that diversification reduces risk in a portfolio. *See* Jonathan R. Macey, *An Introduction to Modern Financial Theory* 20 (American College of Trust and Estate Counsel Foundation, 1991). Investments will not all increase or decrease at the same rate, so a diversified portfolio should protect against extreme swings in returns. In some circumstances, a trustee will decide not to diversify. If the sale of a block of stock will result in the realization of a large amount of income tax, the trustee may decide to continue to hold the stock. The trustee may also decide to retain stock in a family business, even if that stock represents the primary asset of the trust. Normally, the trust instrument will address issues raised by a family business and may authorize the trustee to continue to hold interests in the business to avoid potential breaches of the duty of prudent investment or the duty of loyalty (if the trustee holds an interest in the company in his individual capacity.)

UPIA §3. Diversification.

> A trustee shall diversify the investments of the trust unless the trustee reasonably determines that, because of special circumstances, the purposes of the trust are better served without diversifying.

Example: Jerry and Sandy ran their family store for many years. A fixture in the community, the store provided income for the family and also constituted the bulk of the family assets. Their children all work in the business and draw salaries from the business. When Jerry died, his will created a trust for Sandy and the children. Jerry and Sandy had each owned one-half of the business, and his shares were distributed to the trust created under his will. Although the trust holds primarily one asset — the shares of the family business — the trustee can continue to hold those shares rather than diversify the holdings without breaching the prudent investor rule. Jerry could have provided additional protection for his trustee by including in the terms of the trust a provision authorizing the trustee to retain the shares, even though retention of the shares might violate investment diversification principles.

In discussing the duty of loyalty, we briefly looked at *Inman*, a case in which the trustee, who was the grandson of the settlor, wanted to buy property from the trust. The court refused to permit the self-dealing transaction. One of the trustee's arguments was that selling the property was necessary to comply with the prudent investor rule and the duty to diversify. The trust held 189 acres of farmland and after selling 42 acres, the trustee planned to invest that money in other sorts of investments. We now return to the case to review the court's discussion of the duty to diversify.

In re Trust Created by Inman
693 N.W.2d 514, 517-22 (Neb. 2005)

. . . Dr. David Volkman testified on behalf of Brackett as an expert in economics and finance. Volkman reviewed the trust instrument, the assets held and income earned by the trust, the Nebraska Uniform Prudent Investor Act, information from the National Council of Real Estate Investment Fiduciaries, equity returns from a database, and the appraisals prepared by Wohlenhaus. Based upon this information, Volkman opined that because the assets of the trust were not diversified, the standards of the Nebraska Uniform Prudent Investor Act were not met. Volkman analyzed the diversification of the trust in relation to the return and risk of the investments and compared the rate of return on farmland as opposed to other types of investments. Asked to evaluate the risk associated with the trust assets as then held, Volkman stated:

> The greatest risk is that it's not diversified. It's invested all in one asset. And when you invest in one asset, you significantly increase the probability of not receiving the return that you would like to it. It would be similar if you went out and bought one stock and put all of your savings in one stock. There's a high probability you may not get the return that you want from that one stock.

Volkman further testified that farmland has a lower rate of return and higher risk for rate of return compared to the Dow Jones index, a higher rate of return and higher risk than treasury notes, and a significantly lower rate of return but also less risk than the NASDAQ Composite Index. He testified that the overall risk to the beneficiaries could be reduced by having a portion of the corpus invested in farmland and other portions in investments which would yield a higher rate of return.

Maryann Tremaine, Inman's other surviving daughter, testified as a spokesperson for the five beneficiaries who filed a written objection to the sale. She opposed the sale because of her belief that Inman intended the farmland to remain in trust for all of the beneficiaries and that it would increase in value over time. Another beneficiary who joined in the written objection testified that she opposed the sale for generally the same reasons. Two beneficiaries who did not file written objections also testified in opposition to the sale. Peters opposed the sale because she believed the property should remain "in the family" and was satisfied with the current income. One of Inman's granddaughters who is a beneficiary of the trust testified that she opposed the sale because "I truly believe my grandfather left the property for everybody to enjoy. It has sentimental value to the whole family, not just one person." . . .

ASSIGNMENTS OF ERRORS

Brackett assigns, combined and restated, that by denying him authority to sell the trust property to himself, the probate court (1) failed to allow him to diversify the assets of the trust in compliance with the Nebraska Uniform Prudent Investor Act and (2) erroneously allowed principles against self-dealing to trump statutory law and trust provisions that authorized the requested sale. . . .

Resolution of the issue prescribed by this appeal requires an examination of the relationship between two separate legal duties owed by a trustee to the beneficiaries of the trust. . . . [We will discuss] the trustee's duties of loyalty and compliance with the prudent investor rule.

The record reflects that Brackett has purely personal reasons for seeking to acquire the 42-acre parcel from the trust. Brackett, who described himself as one who invests, remodels, and sells real estate, testified that he moved the farmhouse which he had purchased at auction to the trust property because he had "nowhere else to put it." He further acknowledged that he sought more land than was necessary for a home site because "I wanted my kids to have a good sized piece of land. I've always worked the land when I was a kid there and played up there. And it has some sentimental value, and I wanted more of a farmstead for my kids to grow up on." Brackett argues, however, that the county court should nevertheless have approved the sale because investment of the proceeds in something other than agricultural real estate would provide diversification of trust assets in a manner consistent with the prudent investor rule, thereby benefiting all the beneficiaries.

The prudent investor rule applicable to trustees is now codified at §§30-3883 to 30-3889. Included in that rule is the principle that a "trustee shall diversify the investments of the trust unless the trustee reasonably determines that, because of special circumstances, the purposes of the trust are better served with-out diversifying." §30-3885. On the record before us, we conclude that there was no absolute duty to diversify the trust assets which would compel court approval of the proposed sale. The prudent investor rule is a "default rule" which "may be expanded, restricted, eliminated, or otherwise altered by the provisions of a trust." §30-3883(b). It is true, as Brackett argues, that the trust instrument in this case gave the trustee broad powers in dealing with trust assets, including the power "[t]o receive, hold, manage and care for the property held in trust," and "[t]o sell publicly or privately for cash or on time, property, real or personal, held in trust. . . . " However, the trust instrument also conferred upon the trustee the power

[t]o retain any property, whether consisting of stocks, bonds, other securities, participations in common trust funds, or of any other type of personal property or of real property, taken over by it as a portion of the trust, *without regard to the proportion such property or property of a similar character so held may bear to the entire amount of the trust,* whether or not such property is of the class in which trustees generally are authorized to invest by law or rule of court; *intending thereby to authorize the Trustee to act in such manner as will be for the best interest of the trust beneficiaries,* giving due consideration to the preservation of principal and the amount and regularity of the income to be derived therefrom.

(Emphasis supplied.) With respect to assets originally placed in trust, this provision modifies the general duty to diversify by authorizing the trustee to retain nondiversified assets if retention would be in the best interests of the beneficiaries.

Furthermore, the trustee's statutory duty to diversify trust assets is subject to the general "prudent investor" standard of care which requires a trustee to consider various circumstances relevant to the trust or its beneficiaries in investing and managing trust assets. §30-3884(c). These circumstances include "[a]n asset's special relationship or special value, if any, to the purposes of the trust or to one or more of the beneficiaries." §30-3884(c)(8). We agree with a commentator who has noted that a similar provision in the Nebraska Uniform Prudent Investor Act could be utilized as a basis for justifying "non-diversification" of a family farm or ranch held in trust in favor of retaining the asset "for future generations of the family." Ronald R. Volkmer, *The Latest Look in Nebraska Trust Law*, 31 Creighton L. Rev. 221, 246 (1997). Brackett's professed "sentimental" attachment to the farmland which has been in his family for many years is clearly shared by the other family members who are beneficiaries of the trust. Those who filed an objection or testified in opposition to the proposed sale expressed the view that excising a 42-acre parcel from the 189-acre farm would have a detrimental effect upon their special relationship with the asset without achieving any appreciable benefit. . . .

We conclude that the judgment of the county court conforms to the law, is supported by competent evidence, and is neither arbitrary, capricious, nor unreasonable. Finding no error appearing on the record, we affirm.

A trust may contain a provision that permits the trustee to retain assets, but the trustee must still exercise that power while following the duties of loyalty and prudence. A power to retain does not mean the trustee *should* retain, and a court reviewing a decision to retain an asset will look for a good reason not to diversify. In *Inman*, the court found that reason in the beneficiaries' desire that the family property be kept in the trust for the entire family.

Occasionally, a trust will require a trustee to retain a particular asset, and a court will usually give effect to that sort of clause, if the direction is clearly stated. *See* Jeffrey A. Cooper, *Speak Clearly and Listen Well: Negating the Duty to Diversity Trust Investments*, 33 Ohio N.U. L. Rev. 903 (2007). A trustee may be able to ask a court for permission to sell anyway, if the corpus of the trust is at risk. *See, e.g., Matter of Pultizer*, 249 N.Y.S. 87 (Sur. 1931), *aff'd mem.*, 260 N.Y.S. 975 (App. Div. 1932). In that case the settlor, Joseph Pulitzer, had directed the trustee to retain shares of the Press Publishing Company, the publisher of the *New York World*, the *Sunday World* and the *Evening World* newspapers. The court agreed that the trustee should be permitted to sell the assets of the company based "upon the power of a court of equity, in emergencies, to protect the beneficiaries of a trust from serious loss, or a total destruction of a substantial asset of the corpus. The law, in the case of necessity, reads into the will an implied power of sale. The law also assumes that a testator had sufficient foresight to realize that securities bequeathed to a trustee may become so unproductive or so diminished in value as to authorize their sale where extraordinary circumstances develop, or crisis occurs." *Id*. at 93.

f.   Costs

UPIA §7 imposes a duty on the trustee to incur only costs that are "appropriate and reasonable" for the trust. The comment to that section describes the provision as a direction to "minimize costs." Certainly a decision to incur unnecessary or excessive costs would not be prudent. The trustee must consider the assets in the trust and the skills of the trustee in determining whether hiring an investment advisor, for example, is appropriate.

UPIA §7. Investment Costs.

> In investing and managing trust assets, a trustee may only incur costs that are appropriate and reasonable in relation to the assets, the purposes of the trust, and the skills of the trustee.

Example: Catherine Gonzalez is trustee of the Gonzalez Family Trust, a trust created under the will of her husband and funded with significant assets (a large stock portfolio). Catherine is a high school teacher with no particular investment experience. As a prudent investor, Catherine may decide to hire an investment advisor to assist with management of the assets of the trust.

Now assume that Best Bank is the trustee of the Gonzalez Family Trust. Best Bank charges a fee for managing the investments, maintaining records for the trust and making distributions to the beneficiaries. If Best Bank decides to hire an investment advisor, it would be appropriate for Best Bank to reduce its fees related to investment decision making for the trust.

g. Not by Hindsight

A trustee must make decisions based on the information available at the time the decision is made. The trustee has a duty to investigate the truth of information relating to the investments and must be diligent in seeking information, but will not be judged by the success — or lack of success — of the investments. UPIA §8 confirms that decisions are judged by the facts and circumstances that existed at the time of the decision "and not by hindsight." In a time of market downturn, beneficiaries will be tempted to second-guess trustees. *See Ditmars v. Camden Trust Co.*, 76 A.2d 280, 291 (N.J. Ch. 1950), in which the beneficiaries of a trust argued that the trustee should have prevented losses incurred during the Great Depression of the 1930s. The court responded, "However loudly it may now be said that people should have foreseen, most men of that degree of prudence and caution that we call ordinary did not foresee. Wisdom after the event is not the test of responsibility." *Id.*

UPIA §8. Reviewing Compliance.

> Compliance with the prudent investor rule is determined in light of the facts and circumstances existing at the time of a trustee's decision or action and not by hindsight.

h. Delegation

Historically, a trustee could delegate ministerial but not discretionary functions. The settlor had reposed trust in the trustee and expected the trustee to carry out that trust, so the law limited the trustee's power to delegate. This nondelegation rule worked well when trusts held only real property, but as the types of assets managed by trustees changed, the nondelegation rule presented significant problems. Investment decisions are not ministerial, so a delegation of some level of decision making to investment advisors constituted a breach of the duty not to delegate.

Even before the promulgation of UPIA, states began enacting laws that permitted the delegation of investment decision making when it was prudent to do so. UPIA §9 sets out the rules a trustee must follow when delegating authority to act. The trustee must exercise reasonable care, skill and caution in selecting the agent, establishing the scope of the delegation and monitoring the agent. A trustee cannot "turn things over" to an investment advisor but must continue to monitor work done on behalf of the trust. The rules governing delegation balance the potential benefits to the trust of appropriate delegation with the risks of overbroad delegation. The comment explains: "If the trustee delegates effectively, the beneficiaries obtain the advantage of the agent's specialized investment skills or whatever other attributes induced the trustee to delegate. But if the trustee delegates to a knave or an incompetent, the delegation can work harm upon the beneficiaries." UPIA §9, cmt.

UPIA §9. Delegation of Investment and Management Functions.

(a) A trustee may delegate investment and management functions that a prudent trustee of comparable skills could properly delegate under the circumstances. The trustee shall exercise reasonable care, skill, and caution in:
> (1) selecting an agent;
> (2) establishing the scope and terms of the delegation, consistent with the purposes and terms of the trust; and
> (3) periodically reviewing the agent's actions in order to monitor the agent's performance and compliance with the terms of the delegation.

(b) In performing a delegated function, an agent owes a duty to the trust to exercise reasonable care to comply with the terms of the delegation.

(c) A trustee who complies with the requirements of subsection (a) is not liable to the beneficiaries or to the trust for the decisions or actions of the agent to whom the function was delegated.

(d) By accepting the delegation of a trust function from the trustee of a trust that is subject to the law of this State, an agent submits to the jurisdiction of the courts of this State.

F.   DUTY OF IMPARTIALITY

A trust typically provides for more than one beneficiary, and the beneficiaries' interests may occur at different times. For example, a trust might provide income to Zoe for Zoe's life, remainder to Vanessa. The duty of impartiality tells the trustee to manage the trust in a way that keeps the interests of the current beneficiary and the future beneficiary in mind. The duty of impartiality is not a duty to treat all beneficiaries in the same way. The settlor may have instructed the trustee to prefer one over another, either directly or by requiring the trustee to exercise discretion based on a standard of distribution. The duty of impartiality requires the trustee to act with regard to the interests of all beneficiaries. As the comment to UTC §803 provides:

> The duty to act impartially does not mean that the trustee must treat the beneficiaries equally. Rather, the trustee must treat the beneficiaries equitably in light of the purposes and terms of the trust. A settlor who prefers that the trustee, when making decisions, generally favor the interests of one beneficiary over those of others should provide appropriate guidance in the terms of the trust.

The duty of impartiality is related to the duty to invest prudently and to the rules governing the allocation of income and principal. The trustee must make investment decisions that do not prefer income beneficiaries over remainder beneficiaries or vice versa.

Example: A trustee invests the entire trust corpus in corporate bonds. The income beneficiary receives a steady stream of income payments, but over time the purchasing power of the principal — the bonds — decreases in value. When the remainder beneficiaries receive the remainder, they may be disappointed with the lack of growth in the asset value of the trust.

Example: A trust's sole asset is an apartment building. The trustee collects rents and distributes them to the income beneficiaries. The trustee does little to maintain the building, and over time the building decreases in value, due either to its worsening condition or to falling values in the neighborhood. The remainder beneficiaries will likely be upset.

Example: A trust's sole asset is a piece of vacant land. The land will generate no income, so the income beneficiaries will receive nothing. If the land appreciates in value, the remainder beneficiaries may receive a substantial benefit.

The old rules for determining whether receipts were income or principal made prudent investing difficult if a trustee wanted to comply with the duty of impartiality. As we have learned, a prudent investor invests the portfolio (the trust assets) for total return and not with a focus on which investments will produce the most "income." In order for a trustee to engage in portfolio investing, under the standards of UPIA, the rules that govern the determination of "income" and "principal" in a trust had to change. We turn to those rules next.

G. ALLOCATION OF PRINCIPAL AND INCOME

A typical trust might provide a life estate to one or more people and a remainder interest to others. For example, the terms of the trust may direct the trustee to pay the income to the settlor's husband, and then distribute the remainder to the settlor's descendants. A determination of what constitutes "income" will determine what amount to distribute to the husband and what amount to leave in the trust for eventual distribution to the descendants. Special trust accounting rules have developed specifically for tracking income and principal in trusts. These rules differ from tax accounting, and income for tax purposes may not be the same as income for trust accounting purposes. Trust accounting allocates receipts and expenses to either the income account or the principal account. The allocations will affect the shares of the income beneficiary and the remainder beneficiary.

The Uniform Principal and Income Act provides the current version of trust accounting rules and allows more flexibility than the traditional rules on trust accounting provided. Professor Langbein explains the relation between trust accounting (the Uniform Principal and Income Act) and UPIA in the following excerpt from his article about UPIA. Note that this article was written before the adoption of the Uniform Principal and Income Act in 2000.

John H. Langbein, The Uniform Prudent Investor Act and the Future of Trust Investing
81 Iowa L. Rev. 641, 667-68 (1996)

By distorting investment choices in order to maximize a particular form of return (whether dividends and interest or capital appreciation), conventional trust investment practices that are designed to satisfy principal-and-income concerns come into tension with Modern Portfolio Theory. Thus, for example, the trustee who is administering a trust that needs to achieve a high level of current income may feel obliged to invest heavily in bonds, even though it is known that equities outperform bonds across the long term on a total-return basis. The conventional principal- and-income rules drive that trustee to accept a lower total return in order to obtain a particular form of return — interest rather than capital appreciation. In many trust portfolios that could prudently tolerate greater risk by holding a higher proportion of equities, the trustees have refrained from investing appropriately in equities because such a portfolio commonly produces less current income.

The lesson, in the words of Joel Dobris, is that "investing should not be connected with principal and income allocation." Joel C. Dobris, *Real Return, Modern Portfolio Theory, and College, University, and Foundation Decisions on Annual Spending from Endowments: A Visit to the World of Spending*

Rules, 28 Real Prop., Prob. & Tr. J. 49 (1993). Instead, the trustee should first invest to maximize total return, and then, in a separate and subsequent step, "allocate the return as fairly as possible." In a prominent article published in 1986, Jeffrey Gordon observed that skewing the portfolio to achieve a particular income/principal allocation also impairs diversification. Jeffrey N. Gordon, *The Puzzling Persistence of the Constrained Prudent Man Rule*, 62 N.Y.U. L. Rev. 52, 100-01 (1987).

Our traditional notion that the current beneficiary automatically receives all the "income" has concealed from us the truth that the trustee's investment policy largely determines how much that income will be. Accordingly, an MPT-driven regime that would allow the trustee to invest for the maximum return suitable to the trust, regardless of form, and then to allocate to income that portion that the trustee determines to be appropriate for discharging the duty of impartiality, would involve no fundamental departure from the inner functional balance of the present law. Under either scheme, the trustee decides how much of the trust's investment return to devote to the income interest. But greater candor about the relationship between investing and allocating would allow the trustee to follow investment practices that would produce superior returns for both current and remainder beneficiaries.

The terms of a trust can provide guidance on allocating receipts and expenses, but if the terms do not include directions on principal and income, state law provides rules. Forty-two states plus the District of Columbia have enacted the Uniform Principal and Income Act (2000, as amended in 2008). This Act replaces two earlier uniform principal and income acts (1931 and 1962). The Uniform Principal and Income Act was created to establish rules for new situations and new financial instruments that had developed since 1962. The drafters also wanted to create a system of trust accounting that would enable trustees to invest for total return, following the Uniform Prudent Investor Act, rather than continuing to invest for traditionally defined "income."

The Uniform Principal and Income Act starts with traditional income allocation: interest, dividends and rents are allocated to income, while the settlor's contributions to the trust and proceeds from the sale of assets (capital gains) are allocated to principal. Investment choices have become more complicated, so the Act includes specific rules for certain assets, including zero-coupon bonds, timber, derivatives, options and asset-backed securities (we will not discuss how these investments work, although you should know they exist). Then, if the basic allocation rules do not result in a just division of income and principal, the Uniform Principal and Income Act gives the trustee the power to make adjustments in the allocations between income and principal. This power to adjust is a significant change.

The traditional allocation rules may make prudent investing on a portfolio basis difficult. Traditional rules allocate capital gains to principal. Thus, prior to the Uniform Principal and Income Act, if a trustee needed to make income payments to a beneficiary, the trustee had to balance investment for growth with investments that generated "income" for trust accounting purposes. If a prudent investment strategy based on modern portfolio theory resulted in gains overall but no "income," then the trustee might have violated her duty to act impartially as between the beneficiaries. The trust would have generated capital gains, but if those gains were allocated to principal for accounting purposes, then the remainder beneficiaries would get the benefit of all the gains.

The power to adjust solves this problem by permitting a trustee to make an adjustment between income and principal, if prudent investment decisions have led to accounting results that place an inequitable amount in either income or principal. The power to adjust allows trustees to engage in prudent portfolio investing while maintaining fair allocations for both income and remainder beneficiaries.

Uniform Principal and Income Act §103(b). Fiduciary Duties; General Principles.

> (b) In exercising the power to adjust under Section 104(a) or a discretionary power of administration regarding a matter within the scope of this [Act], whether granted by the terms of a trust, a will, or this [Act], a fiduciary shall administer a trust or estate impartially, based on what is fair and reasonable to all of the beneficiaries, except to the extent that the terms of the trust or the will clearly manifest an intention that the fiduciary shall or may favor one or more of the beneficiaries. A determination in accordance with this [Act] is presumed to be fair and reasonable to all of the beneficiaries.

Here is the Uniform Principal and Income Act's power to adjust, followed by three examples from the Comment to §104.

Uniform Principal and Income Act §104. Trustee's Power to Adjust.

> (a) A trustee may adjust between principal and income to the extent the trustee considers necessary if the trustee invests and manages trust assets as a prudent investor, the terms of the trust describe the amount that may or must be distributed to a beneficiary by referring to the trust's income, and the trustee determines, after applying

the rules in Section 103(a), that the trustee is unable to comply with Section 103(b). . . .

Comment to Uniform Principal and Income Act §104

Examples. The following examples illustrate the application of Section 104:

Example (1) — T is the successor trustee of a trust that provides income to A for life, remainder to B. T has received from the prior trustee a portfolio of financial assets invested 20% in stocks and 80% in bonds. Following the prudent investor rule, T determines that a strategy of investing the portfolio 50% in stocks and 50% in bonds has risk and return objectives that are reasonably suited to the trust, but T also determines that adopting this approach will cause the trust to receive a smaller amount of dividend and interest income. After considering the factors in Section 104(b), T may transfer cash from principal to income to the extent T considers it necessary to increase the amount distributed to the income beneficiary.

Example (2) — T is the trustee of a trust that requires the income to be paid to the settlor's son C for life, remainder to C's daughter D. In a period of very high inflation, T purchases bonds that pay double-digit interest and determines that a portion of the interest, which is allocated to income under Section 406 of this Act, is a return of capital. In consideration of the loss of value of principal due to inflation and other factors that T considers relevant, T may transfer part of the interest to principal.

Example (3) — T is the trustee of a trust that requires the income to be paid to the settlor's sister E for life, remainder to charity F. E is a retired schoolteacher who is single and has no children. E's income from her social security, pension, and savings exceeds the amount required to provide for her accustomed standard of living. The terms of the trust permit T to invade principal to provide for E's health and to support her in her accustomed manner of living, but do not otherwise indicate that T should favor E or F. Applying the prudent investor rule, T determines that the trust assets should be invested entirely in growth stocks that produce very little dividend income. Even though it is not necessary to invade principal to maintain E's accustomed standard of living, she is entitled to receive from the trust the degree of beneficial enjoyment normally accorded a person who is the sole income beneficiary of a trust, and T may transfer cash from principal to income to provide her with that degree of enjoyment.

H.   REMOVAL OF TRUSTEES

A court may remove a trustee for a variety of reasons. The most important reason for removal, both under the common law and the UTC, is a serious breach of trust. Not every breach will be grounds for removal, but if a trustee commits a serious breach of trust or commits a number of smaller breaches, the court may remove the trustee. Failure to care for trust property, self-dealing with trust property to the detriment of the beneficiaries or refusing to provide information to beneficiaries despite repeated requests (over a period of time) can be grounds for removal.

A court may also remove a trustee if co-trustees cannot or will not cooperate in managing the trust. Removal for lack of cooperation need not involve a breach of trust, but the failure to cooperate must significantly affect the management of the trust. For example, if a trust has two trustees (or any even number of trustees) and the two trustees cannot agree, no decisions can be made for the trust. The court may decide to remove one or both of the trustees.

The UTC also makes removal possible in the event of substantially changed circumstances affecting the trust, or the agreement of the beneficiaries that the trustee should be removed. The court needs to determine that removal is in the best interests of the beneficiaries and that removal is not inconsistent with a material purpose of the trust.

UTC §706. Removal of Trustee.

> (a) The settlor, a cotrustee, or a beneficiary may request the court to remove a trustee, or a trustee may be removed by the court on its own initiative.
>
> (b) The court may remove a trustee if:
>
> (1) the trustee has committed a serious breach of trust;
>
> (2) lack of cooperation among cotrustees substantially impairs the administration of the trust;
>
> (3) because of unfitness, unwillingness, or persistent failure of the trustee to administer the trust effectively, the court determines that removal of the trustee best serves the interests of the beneficiaries; or
>
> (4) there has been a substantial change of circumstances or removal is requested by all of the qualified beneficiaries, the court finds that removal of the trustee best serves the interests of all of the beneficiaries and is not inconsistent with a material purpose of the trust, and a suitable cotrustee or successor trustee is available.
>
> (c) Pending a final decision on a request to remove a trustee, or in lieu of or in addition to removing a trustee, the court may order such

appropriate relief under Section 1001(b) as may be necessary to protect the trust property or the interests of the beneficiaries.

I. POWERS TO DIRECT

Estate planners have begun to use trust protectors or advisors as a supplemental layer of direction or control for a settlor. A trust protector or advisor is someone other than the settlor who is named to handle a particular trustee function. While the person may be a trustee or a beneficiary, the person is usually someone not otherwise connected with the trust. The power held by the trust protector or advisor might be to modify or terminate the trust, to rearrange beneficial interests in keeping with the settlor's general intent, to change the trustee, to direct investment decision making or to manage a family business. The term "trust protector" developed in connection with off-shore asset protection trusts. In those trusts a trust protector might be given the power to remove the trustee or terminate the trust. Domestic trusts do not commonly include trust protectors or advisors, but the idea has gotten attention in recent years and the number of trusts with powers to direct has been increasing.

In a domestic trust, an advisor might have the power to handle investments or manage a family business. The advisor might not be an appropriate person to name as trustee, so the settlor would like to have both a trustee and an advisor. The settlor can do so by giving the advisor the power to direct the trustee with respect to a particular function. The trustee will need protection if the trustee is required to follow directions from the advisor. The terms of the trust can provide that the advisor — and not the trustee — will have fiduciary duties with respect to the particular function the advisor serves. The trustee will still have overall responsibility for the trust.

The UTC includes a section that permits the settlor to give powers to direct to a person (a corporation or individual) who is not a trustee. UTC §808. The trustee is required to follow the directions given to the trustee by the advisor. Section 808 adopts an approach that balances the need to relieve the trustee from liability for following directions from the advisor with the concern that the trustee protect the trust and the beneficiaries if things get too far out of line. The UTC does this by freeing the trustee from liability for following directions of the advisor but requiring that the trustee not follow a direction that is "manifestly contrary to the terms of the trust" or one that would constitute a serious breach of fiduciary duty. The UTC makes the advisor a fiduciary with respect to the particular power given to the advisor.

Example: Settlor names his brother as trustee of a trust for Settlor's children. Settlor thinks his brother will be an excellent trustee in most respects — attentive, concerned about the children and able to make good decisions about distributions. Settlor is less sure about his brother's ability to make good investment decisions for the trust. The amount involved is not large enough to justify a corporate trustee, and the brother is really the best person to serve as trustee in all other respects. Settlor has worked with an investment advisor who understands Settlor's risk tolerance and has done a good job for the Settlor for many years. Settlor can give the investment advisor a power to direct the trustee with respect to investment decision making. The trustee must follow the directions of the investment advisor, and in doing so will not have to worry about whether the investments are the ones a prudent investor would make. The advisor will owe a duty to the beneficiaries to act as a prudent investor.

UTC §808. Powers to Direct.

(a) While a trust is revocable, the trustee may follow a direction of the settlor that is contrary to the terms of the trust.

(b) If the terms of a trust confer upon a person other than the settlor of a revocable trust power to direct certain actions of the trustee, the trustee shall act in accordance with an exercise of the power unless the attempted exercise is manifestly contrary to the terms of the trust or the trustee knows the attempted exercise would constitute a serious breach of a fiduciary duty that the person holding the power owes to the beneficiaries of the trust.

(c) The terms of a trust may confer upon a trustee or other person a power to direct the modification or termination of the trust.

(d) A person, other than a beneficiary, who holds a power to direct is presumptively a fiduciary who, as such, is required to act in good faith with regard to the purposes of the trust and the interests of the beneficiaries. The holder of a power to direct is liable for any loss that results from breach of a fiduciary duty.

PROBLEMS

1.   Evan is the trustee of a trust created under the will of his wife, Miranda (Miranda died two years ago). Evan receives the income of the trust for his life, and on his death the remaining principal will be distributed to Miranda's descendants. Miranda had three children: Jesse (her son from a prior marriage) and two children with Evan.

a. Evan invests the trust property in two rental houses. He does the work himself on the rentals and then distributes income based on the rents received, less the costs of maintaining the houses. He pays himself a fee for managing the houses but takes no fee as trustee.

i. Is Evan acting as a prudent investor? (What additional information would you want to know?)

ii. Is Evan complying with his duty of impartiality?

iii. If Jesse requests a copy of the trust instrument, must Evan give him a copy?

b. Assume that Evan resigns as trustee. Pursuant to the terms of the trust, a family friend, Lewis, becomes trustee. Lewis sells the houses and invests the proceeds in government bonds.

i. How should the receipts from the house sales be reported for accounting purposes — income or principal?

ii. Is Lewis complying with his duty of impartiality?

iii. To whom should Lewis send annual reports?

c. Can Lewis hire an investment advisor to assist him?

2. When Maxine and Cyrus died in an automobile crash, their wills created a trust for their two children, who were eight and nine years old. The terms of the trust direct the trustee to use income and principal for the health, education, maintenance and support of the two children. When neither child is under the age of 25, the trust terminates and the trustee distributes the property to the then living descendants of Maxine and Cyrus. Maxine's brother, Ira, is the trustee and is also the legal guardian for the children. With respect to each of the following additional facts, indicate whether Ira has breached any of his fiduciary duties, and if so which one(s). If you find a breach, what remedy might the court impose?

a. Ira has had good success with investments, so he puts the trust's money ($500,000) in his investment account. With the additional funds and economies of scale, the account makes an even better return that it had before.

b. Two years after the accident, Ira's broker tells him about a start-up company that is a "sure thing." Ira takes $100,000 of the trust's money and invests in the new company. Unfortunately, the company goes under and the investment is basically worthless.

c. When the younger child turns 25, Ira gives each child $25,000 and says that he has spent the rest of the trust money taking care of them. He notes that he gave them each $10,000 a year for college and that the rest of the money had been spent on housing, food and clothing costs before they left for college.

3. Keisha set up a trust for her son, Luke. She named her sister, Cassandra, as trustee, and she named her friend and long-time investment advisor, Landon, as a trust advisor to make decisions about investments for the trust. The trust is to distribute income to Luke, and on Luke's death the

trust will be distributed to the Deschutes River Fund (a nonprofit charity that works to keep the Deschutes River clean). Cassandra asks for advice on the following questions:

a.   Landon has invested the trust assets in technology stocks, and the stocks have not done well. They have paid no dividends and have depreciated in value. Cassandra would like to allocate some money currently in the principal account to the income account so she can make a distribution to Luke. Can she do so?

b.   Is there any risk of liability for Cassandra because the stocks have performed so poorly?

7 RIGHTS OF BENEFICIARIES AND CREDITORS IN TRUST PROPERTY; MODIFICATION AND TERMINATION OF TRUSTS

A. INTRODUCTION

A trust beneficiary's rights and a trustee's duties depend on the terms of the trust established by the settlor. *See* RESTATEMENT (THIRD) OF TRUSTS §49. While a settlor may create an oral trust, most settlors choose to use a written trust instrument for the greater certainty it offers.

The trust instrument typically provides directions to a trustee concerning distributions of income and principal to the beneficiaries. These directions may be mandatory or discretionary, and they may establish standards that are considered ascertainable or nonascertainable. Regardless, in making these distributions, the trustee is bound by a reasonableness or good faith standard. A challenge for the lawyer drafting the trust instrument is to provide enough direction so that the trustee knows what the settlor wants, yet give the trustee enough flexibility to make good judgments about when, to whom and in what amounts to make distributions.

A beneficiary's interest in a trust may be a present interest or a future interest, may be contingent on the happening of an event, may be subject to revocation and may be subject to a power of appointment held by another person. As the *Restatement (Third) of Trusts* §49, cmt. says, "there is practically no limit to the variety of interests a settlor may create."

This chapter starts with an explanation of the different types of distribution provisions in trusts. These provisions not only provide guidance to trustees but also delineate the rights of beneficiaries. Because creditors of

343

the settlor or of beneficiaries may be able to reach assets in or distributions from a trust, we look next at the rights of creditors of the settlor and the beneficiaries and what estate planners may do to limit the reach of creditors.

Trusts may last for a long time, and due to changes over time in the economy as well as the situation of the beneficiaries, modification or early termination of trusts may become necessary. This chapter concludes with a section looking at the standards for modifying and terminating trusts.

B.   DISTRIBUTION PROVISIONS—RIGHTS OF BENEFICIARIES

1.   *Overview of Distribution Provisions*

The beneficiaries' rights in a trust depend on the provisions set forth in the trust instrument. The distribution provisions may be mandatory or discretionary and may be drafted in many different ways. We examine some of the standard forms for distribution provisions before we discuss the interpretation of these provisions.

a.   Mandatory Provisions

Mandatory distribution provisions direct the trustee to pay something to a beneficiary, without exercising discretion as to the amount or the timing. Mandatory provisions may affect present or future interests.

Example: "I give these assets to Mercedes, in trust, to pay the income to Sofia for life annually and on Sofia's death to pay the corpus to Luis." In such a situation, Mercedes must distribute to Sofia whatever income the trust generates as long as Sofia is alive and must distribute the corpus to Luis on Sofia's death. Mercedes cannot do more or less; she has no discretion with respect to distributions.

A beneficiary can require the trustee to comply with a mandatory provision and can go to court to enforce the provision, if necessary. The good faith or reasonableness of the trustee's actions is not a defense.

b.   Discretionary Provisions

Discretionary provisions direct the trustee to exercise some judgment in deciding what and how much to distribute, when to distribute or to whom to distribute. The trust instrument will usually provide guidance for the trustee. Discretionary standards can be narrow or broad, specific or general, ascertainable or nonascertainable.

The trust in the prior example provided for mandatory distributions of both income and principal. In contrast, some trusts are entirely discretionary: "I give these assets to T in trust to pay so much of the income and principal to my children as T, in his absolute discretion decides."

Most often, trusts contain a mix of mandatory and discretionary requirements, as in the next example. When considering discretionary provisions, only the wishes of the settlor limit the variations.

> **Example:**   "I give these assets to Mercedes, in trust, to pay all of the income to my children in equal shares and so much of the principal to my children as the trustee, in the trustee's discretion, determines is necessary for their health and education. When my last child reaches the age of 30 years, the trust shall terminate and the property be distributed to my descendants, per stirpes."
>
> In this example, before the last child reaches age 30, the trustee must pay all the income to the children in equal shares (a mandatory provision) and must decide whether to distribute any principal to any of the children and, if so, to which children (discretionary). The trustee must determine whether the children have health and education needs, and if they do, which expenses to pay (discretionary). When the last child reaches age 30, T must distribute any remaining income and principal to the settlor's descendants, per stirpes (mandatory). To the extent the trustee has discretionary authority, it is not absolute; the trustee's discretion is circumscribed because distributions from principal may only be made for the children's health and education and cannot be made for other reasons.

Discretionary standards will always provide some degree of flexibility, while guiding the trustee about the settlor's wishes for the trust. Here are several examples of standards of distribution frequently used in trust drafting:

> **Example:**   "I give these assets to the trustee, in trust, to pay to the beneficiary all of the income and so much or all of the principal, as the trustee determines to be [advisable] [necessary] [appropriate] . . .
>
> - . . . for the beneficiary's health, support, maintenance, and education."
> - . . . for the beneficiary's welfare and best interests."
> - . . . for the beneficiary's education."
> - . . . for the beneficiary's happiness."
> - . . . for the beneficiary's comfort."
> - . . . for the beneficiary's support in reasonable comfort."

The directions to the trustee also may include instructions about whether or not to consider other assets of the beneficiary in making decisions about distributions:

Example:

- . . . without regard to any other income or assets of the beneficiary" or
- . . . "after first taking into consideration any other income or assets of the beneficiary."

A discretionary provision requires the trustee to exercise judgment but does not require the trustee to act in any particular way. If the beneficiary thinks the trustee is not making distributions called for by the trust, the beneficiary can contact the trustee and urge the trustee to make the distributions the beneficiary wants. If the trustee refuses, the beneficiary may have to institute legal action to force a distribution.

The more discretion the terms of the trust give the trustee, the less ability the beneficiary has to force the trustee to make a particular distribution. The comments to UTC §814 explain: "A grant of discretion establishes a range within which the trustee may act. The greater the grant of discretion, the broader the range." Thus, if the standard for making distributions is one that gives the trustee broad discretion, a court will generally just require the trustee to exercise the discretion. While the court may make suggestions about the proper exercise of the discretion, a court will rarely order a trustee to make any particular distribution. When considering a beneficiary's claims, a court will consider whether the trustee acted in good faith or reasonably.

By contrast, the more precise and ascertainable the standard delineated in the trust, the greater the likelihood that the beneficiary can convince a court that the standard is not being followed and that the court should require action by the trustee.

c.   Spray or Sprinkle Provisions

The terms of a trust may direct a trustee to distribute income or principal among a number of named beneficiaries or to one or more of a class of beneficiaries. While the requirement to make distributions may be mandatory or discretionary, the fact that the trustee can "spray" or "sprinkle" the property pursuant to the terms of the trust among various beneficiaries makes the power as to whom to distribute discretionary. Some lawyers use the terms interchangeably, but some lawyers use the term "sprinkle" to mean the trust gives the trustee discretion to distribute income or principal to a beneficiary, while the term "spray" gives the trustee discretion to make distributions to a group of beneficiaries.

Example: "The trustee shall distribute all of the income of the trust, at least quarterly, to one or more of Damien, Edgar and Gregory, in such shares as the trustee determines to be in the best interests of these beneficiaries." While the group of permissible beneficiaries is narrow and the obligation to appoint all the income is mandatory, the standard is broad as to who should receive the income, and a court is unlikely to order the trustee to make particular distributions in the absence of bad faith.

Example: "The trustee shall distribute so much or all of the principal of the trust to one or more of my children, as the trustee determines to be necessary or desirable for the health, education, maintenance and support of each of my children." Here the class of beneficiaries is narrow and while the invasion of corpus is not mandatory, it is circumscribed by a standard considered ascertainable—health, education, maintenance and support—making it more likely that a court would require a distribution than in the previous example.

2. Interpreting Discretionary Standards of Distribution

Most trusts contain distribution provisions that require the trustee's discretion. The directions to the trustee in the trust instrument provide guidelines but do not answer all questions. Courts may be called upon to interpret the trust language and in doing so will consider factors such as the words used, the relationships between the settlor and the beneficiaries and all the terms of the trust. *See* GEORGE G. BOGERT, GEORGE T. BOGERT & AMY MORRIS HESS, THE LAW OF TRUSTS AND TRUSTEES §552.

A lawyer advising a trustee about making distributions or advising beneficiaries about their rights must have a sense of the range of discretion encompassed by the words used in the document. Unless a provision is mandatory, providing advice that predicts precisely how a court will interpret a provision is impossible. This section provides a sense of the scope of discretion created by words typically used in standards of distribution and a look at when and in what manner a court might intervene.

A trustee is governed by fiduciary duties, which we discussed in Chapter 6. A trustee must act with prudence and care and must act for the benefit of the beneficiaries and not for any self interest of the trustee. The trustee has a duty of impartiality and must treat the beneficiaries fairly, based on the instructions given by the settlor. Thus, in making decisions about distributions, the trustee must consider the directions provided in the trust instrument and must also get information about the beneficiaries' circumstances and needs. The fiduciary duties of trustees, including duties of prudence, loyalty and impartiality, will affect decisions the trustees make about distributions. As the court in *Copp v. Worcester County Nat. Bank*, 199 N.E.2d 200, 203 (Mass. 1964), explains:

The power which is given to the trustee is not unrestricted, for a court of equity may control a trustee in the exercise of a fiduciary discretion if it acts beyond the bounds of a reasonable judgment or unreasonably disregards usual fiduciary principles, or the purposes of the trust, or if it fails to observe standards of judgment apparent from the applicable instrument. This power, accordingly, is to be exercised after serious and responsible consideration, prudently, and in accordance with fiduciary standards.

a.   Judicial Review of Trustee's Exercise of Discretion—Reasonableness and Good Faith

When a court reviews a trustee's action or inaction, the court will intervene only to prevent misinterpretation or abuse of the discretion; it will not impose its own view of how a trustee should exercise discretion. The difficulty, as we will see, is that "abuse of discretion" tends to be one of those "I know it when I see it" concepts. It would be helpful, in advising trustees or beneficiaries, to be able to state what actions are within the trustee's scope of discretion and which are considered outside the scope and considered an abuse. Unfortunately, the best we can do is to review the standards of "reasonableness" and "good faith" courts have developed in reviewing the exercise of discretion. The determination of whether a trustee has acted reasonably and in good faith will be, necessarily, fact-specific.

If the trustee is given discretion in how and when to make distributions, the trustee must take action; the trustee cannot just refuse to do anything or dole out money without giving consideration to a variety of facts and circumstances. The trustee must act diligently in seeking information about the beneficiaries' needs and circumstances. After gathering the appropriate information, the trustee has the responsibility to determine how much to distribute, if anything, applying the standard of distribution based on the information gathered, the terms of the trust and the trustee's own view of what the settlor would have wanted. A court will not require a trustee to reach a particular decision. Rather, all a court will require is that the trustee make a carefully considered decision, one made in good faith and one that is reasonable given the terms of the trust.

Example: A trust instrument directs the trustee to make distributions for Amy's "health, support and maintenance." Amy asks the trustee to pay her rent, which is $600 a month. The trustee should consider the other directions in the trust, including who the other beneficiaries are and any guidance the settlor provided on the relative importance of the beneficiaries' interests. The trustee should get as much information as possible about Amy's resources and other needs. The trustee should also try to determine the settlor's intentions as expressed in the trust. If the trustee considers all this information and then makes a decision in good faith to distribute $200 a month to Amy, it is unlikely a court will require the trustee to distribute $600 a month.

The court will intervene only if the court thinks that $200 a month is unreasonable. If the trust holds a significant amount of assets, was created primarily to assist Amy with expenses during college, and if Amy shows that she needs help with the rent so that she can finish her education, a court might find the decision to distribute only $200 a month unreasonable. Even then, the court will not direct the trustee to distribute a specific amount (*e.g.*, $600) but instead will direct the trustee to exercise discretion reasonably (*i.e.*, to go back and re-think the decision.)

In the following case, the beneficiaries complained about insufficient distributions from a trust. The trial court directed the trustee to distribute a particular amount, but the appellate court reversed. The appellate court's deference to the trustee is typical, and the analysis shows the difficulty of determining with certainty what a settlor intended. The settlors chose a trustee to carry out their wishes, and a court is usually reluctant to substitute its own views for that of the trustee.

As you read this case and those that follow, think about the following questions:

1. What is the standard of distribution in the trust?
2. Who are the beneficiaries, and what does that tell us about proper exercise of the trustee's discretion?
3. What does the court say about the trustee's good faith and reasonableness?

Rowe v. Rowe
347 P.2d 968 (Or. 1959)

O'CONNELL, Justice.

This is a suit for a declaratory decree in which plaintiff prays for the construction of the provisions of two similar testamentary trusts under each of which he was named as one of the life beneficiaries. The defendant, Wilbur G. Rowe, was named as trustee. The other defendants are the remaindermen named in the trust. The defendants appeal from a decree construing the trust favorably to the plaintiff.

The trusts were created in the separate wills of Enoch J. Peterson and Nellie R. Peterson, husband and wife. Each of the wills contained the following provision (combined in the excerpt below for convenience):

Third: But, if my said wife [husband] should predecease me, then and in that event, I hereby give, bequeath and devise all of said rest, residue and remainder of my said estate unto her [my] cousin, Wilbur G. Rowe of Portland, Oregon; now the approximate age of forty-two (42) years, in trust nevertheless for the use and benefit of her [my] parents, George H. Rowe, now of the approximate age of seventy-four (74) years, and Katharine B. Rowe, now the approximate age of seventy-five (75) years, both of whom now reside at Glendale, Los Angeles County, California, providing, however, either and/or both of her [my] said parents should survive me, and for so long as either should survive. I hereby direct that my said Trustee hereunder shall have power to sell, mortgage, invest, re-invest, and otherwise convert and/or dispose of any or all of the assets of said trust estate, and to pay to and for the use and benefit of said two (2) trust beneficiaries and/or the survivor of them any or all rent, income and profits therefrom and any or all of the principal or corpus thereof entirely according to his own judgment and discretion. And I hereby further direct that said trust shall terminate upon the death of the last surviving of my said wife's [my] said two (2) parents, and that my said Trustee shall thereupon pay over and deliver whatever may then remain and be on hand, if anything, in the corpus of said trust estate, unto such legatees and devisees then living as are hereinafter named and mentioned in the Fourth clause hereof and in such amounts or proportion and in such manner as therein specified, and to which legatees and devisees I thus hereby give, bequeath and devise what may then remain, if anything, in said trust estate.

The testator and testatrix were killed in a common disaster; and their wills were admitted to probate in Multnomah County on January 12, 1951. Pursuant to the terms of the trusts, the estates were distributed to Wilbur G. Rowe, the named trustee, after the claims and expenses of the administration of the estate had been paid. From the time that he received the trust assets until this suit was brought approximately $7,500 accrued to the trust as income. Of this amount $600 was distributed to the plaintiff and his wife. The trustee paid $100 to the life beneficiaries on October 22, 1952; $100 to them on February 11, 1952; $200 to them on April 16, 1954; nothing was paid in 1955; $200 was paid to plaintiff on June 6, 1956; and nothing was paid thereafter. Katharine B. Rowe died on July 19, 1954.

The decree of the lower court ordered that the defendant trustee pay to plaintiff all of the net income which he had accumulated under the trust and to continue to pay the net income to plaintiff as it accrued in the future. The trial court construed the trust as vesting in the trustee the discretion only to divide the income between the two life beneficiaries and not to withhold from such beneficiaries any of the income. In its written opinion the court indicated that if the trust was construed to give the trustee the discretion to withhold the income from the beneficiaries there would be grave doubts as to the validity of the provision because no standard was provided to guide the trustee in exercising such discretion.

We cannot agree with the lower court's construction of the trust nor with the view that the trust provision is invalid for lack of a guiding standard. The provision in question was effective to create a discretionary trust. Such a trust may be created even though there is no *specific* standard to guide the trustee in exercising his authority. Stated differently, a settlor may create a valid trust which vests in the trustee the discretion to pay or apply only so much of the income or principal as the trustee sees fit. 2 Scott on Trusts (2d ed.) §§128.3 and 155; 3 Bogert, Trusts and Trustees, §560. The standard in such case is not a specific one, such as the beneficiaries' need, but is, rather, a general standard of reasonableness in exercising the discretion granted to him. The standard is stated in 2 Scott on Trusts, §128.3, p. 936 as follows:

> . . . If the settlor manifested an intention that the discretion of the trustee should be uncontrolled, the court will not interfere unless he acts dishonestly or from an improper motive.

The court will not interfere if the trustee acts within "the bounds of a reasonable judgment." 2 Scott on Trusts, §187, p. 1375. What these bounds are will vary with the terms and purposes of the trust and the circumstances of each case. . . .

If, then, we should construe the trust provision in the instant case as vesting in the trustee the power to pay to or withhold from the life beneficiaries the income or principal, the trust would, nevertheless, be valid.

We must decide, however, whether the language of the provision, read in light of the circumstances existing at the time of the creation of the trust, conferred upon the trustee a more restricted power.

When the specific purpose or purposes of the settlor can be ascertained the trustee's choice of action, if it is to constitute a reasonable judgment, must be within the limits set by the settlor's purpose. The difficulty in many if not in most of these cases is finding the purpose of the settlor with sufficient definiteness to be helpful in making out the limits beyond which the trustee should not be permitted to go in dealing with the trust property. The settlor's specific design in framing a discretionary trust is normally unexpressed or vaguely outlined. In looking outside of the terms of the trust itself the court is permitted to consider the circumstances attendant upon the creation of the trust in attempting to determine the scope of the trustee's power, but frequently these circumstances are not particularly illuminating.

The instant case presents an example of this difficulty of finding the settlor's purpose in the creation of a particular trust. We receive no aid to construction from the language directing the trustee "to pay to and for the use and benefit" of the life beneficiaries. This language is simply employed to complete the idea that the property transferred is to be held in trust, i.e., that the transferee holds the property "to the use of" and "for the benefit of" another rather than for his own use and benefit. . . .

As we have already stated, we do not regard the trust provision in question as conferring upon the trustee simply the authority to make an allocation of the income and principal between the two life beneficiaries. There is nothing in the terms of the trust or in the circumstances shown to have existed at the time of its creation which would support that conclusion. The life beneficiaries were husband and wife living together in harmony. There was no apparent reason for making an allocation between the beneficiaries and so we must assume that the discretion was not conferred upon the trustee for the purpose of making such an allocation.

We look then to the circumstances existing at the time of the execution of the trust for the settlors' purposes in creating it, from which purposes we may in turn define the trustee's powers.

The life beneficiaries were the parents and parents-in-law, respectively, of Nellie R. Peterson and Enoch J. Peterson, the settlors. The beneficiaries were the natural objects of Nellie's bounty; but not of Enoch Peterson's bounty. As the will recites, the life tenants were at an advanced age in life, one being 74 and the other 75 years of age. At the time of the death of the settlors the life beneficiaries owned property the total value of which was not made clear by the testimony, but it was at least $24,000. There was no other evidence of the circumstances existing at the time of the making of the wills from which we might derive the trust purpose.

The trustee indicated in his testimony that he understood that he had the duty to pay income to the life beneficiaries in case of "need." . . . [B]oth plaintiff and defendants have proceeded upon the assumption that trustee's power is limited to a determination of the needs of the life beneficiaries; it is assumed that the only question is whether the trustee properly interpreted the meaning of "needs" by limiting payments to such small amounts and to the few instances mentioned. The trustee understood that he was to pay over income to the beneficiaries only if they were in need in the sense that they lacked the essential things in life or were substantially inconvenienced by the lack of money. . . .

There is no question of the trustee's good faith in making his decision to limit the payments as he did. The only question presented is the reasonableness of his judgment. It is quite possible that we would have been more liberal in our treatment of the life beneficiaries had the power to decide been vested in us. But we have no right to substitute our judgment for that of the trustee. 3 Bogert, Trusts and Trustees, §560; 2 Scott on Trusts, §187. We are permitted to control the trustee only if we can say that no reasonable person vested with the power which was conferred upon the trustee in this case could have exercised that power in the manner in which it was exercised. We cannot say that the trustee's conduct in the instant case was unreasonable in this sense.

We hold, therefore, that the trustee is not required to pay over the accumulated income as ordered by the trial court, and that he may in the future continue to make or withhold payments to the plaintiff on the basis of the same criterion he has used previously in the administration of the trust.

It should be noted that the trust in question was created not only for the life beneficiaries but for the remaindermen as well. In vesting a broad discretion in the trustee it is possible that the settlors intended that the trustee should consider the needs of the remaindermen as well as the needs of the life beneficiaries. There is nothing in the record to show the needs of the remaindermen and as far as we know it is possible that there were such needs, that they were greater than those of the life beneficiaries, and that the trustee considered them in making his decision to limit the payments of income to the life beneficiaries. Irrespective of whether this was a consideration, we are without authority to interfere with the trustee's function under the circumstances of this case.

The decree of the lower court is reversed with directions to dismiss the complaint.

UTC §814 requires a trustee to act in "good faith." The comment to this section provides some additional explanation of the role of the court in supervising a trustee.

UTC §814. Discretionary Powers; Tax Savings.

> (a) Notwithstanding the breadth of discretion granted to a trustee in the terms of the trust, including the use of such terms as "absolute", "sole", or "uncontrolled", the trustee shall exercise a discretionary power in good faith and in accordance with the terms and purposes of the trust and the interests of the beneficiaries.

Comment to UTC §814

> Subsection (a) does not otherwise address the obligations of a trustee to make distributions, leaving that issue to the caselaw. Regarding the standards for exercising discretion and construing particular language of discretion, with numerous case citations, see Restatement (Third) of Trusts Section 50 (Tentative Draft No. 2, approved 1999); Restatement (Second) of Trusts Section 187 (1959). . . . Under these standards, whether the trustee has a duty in a given situation to make a distribution depends on the exact language used, whether the standard grants discretion and its breadth, whether this discretion is coupled with a standard, whether the beneficiary has other available resources, and, more broadly, the overriding purposes of the trust. . . .
>
> The obligation of a trustee to act in good faith is a fundamental concept of fiduciary law although there are different ways that it can be expressed. Sometimes different formulations appear in the same source. Scott, in his treatise on trusts, states that the court *will not* interfere with the trustee's exercise of discretion if the trustee "acts in good faith and does not act capriciously," but Scott then states that the court *will* interfere if the trustee "acts dishonestly or in [bad] faith, or where he acts from an improper motive." 3 Austin W. Scott & William F. Fratcher, The Law of Trusts Section 187.2 (4th ed. 1988).

Even when the settlor gives the trustee "absolute," "unlimited" or "sole and uncontrolled" discretion, a court will still require the trustee to act reasonably or in good faith. In the next case the court reminds the trustee of these duties.

Mesler v. Holly
318 So. 2d 530 (Fla. App. 1975)

McNulty, Chief Judge.

Plaintiffs-appellants seek a declaration of their rights under a certain Inter vivos trust created by Frederick L. Way, deceased. Their "amended complaint for declaratory judgment and for other relief connected therewith and for removal of Elaine J. Holly as trustee, for an accounting, and for other relief connected therewith" was dismissed for "failure to state a cause of action." We reverse.

The facts are these. On April 9, 1970 the settlor, Frederick L. Way, established two Inter vivos trusts: A Florida trust, for the joint benefit of himself for life and appellee, Elaine J. Holly, and of which he and Elaine J. Holly were named co-trustees, and a "Massachusetts Fund" trust under which plaintiffs-appellants, the settlor's great grandchildren, were the principal beneficiaries. The Florida trust instrument provided that upon the death of the settlor the aforesaid Elaine J. Holly would be the sole beneficiary with remainder over to the aforementioned Massachusetts trust. In his will, which he executed the following day, the settlor provided that the residue of his estate pour over into the Florida trust. Appellee O. Ray Gussler is a successor to the decedent as a co-trustee of the Florida trust.

Frederick L. Way died on October 20, 1972, and since that time Elaine J. Holly and the aforesaid O. Ray Gussler have acted as co-trustees under the Florida trust, although it is apparent that Gussler has been acting as such more nominally than actually. Indeed, it appears, at one point he ostensibly resigned but reconsidered and now remains at least a nominal co-trustee.

The dispute herein centers essentially on a provision of the Florida trust which plaintiffs-appellants allege has precipitated an abuse on the part of the co-trustees in the administration thereof, as a consequence of which the remainder is being wrongfully depleted. The critical provision, Paragraph EIGHTEENTH, is as follows:

A. The CO-TRUSTEES shall hold the trust estate for the use and benefit of ELAINE J. HOLLY under the following provisions:

2. The CO-TRUSTEES may in their absolute discretion distribute so much of the principal of the trust estate as the CO-TRUSTEES deem necessary to Maintain the standard of living to which ELAINE J. HOLLY has become accustomed.

4. It is the intent of the SETTLOR to grant a life estate to ELAINE J. HOLLY with right of invasion of principal in order to Maintain the standard of living to which ELAINE J. HOLLY has become accustomed.

Alleging that certain purposes for which the principal has already been invaded are unreasonable and excessive, appellants [the grandchildren] contend that this paragraph does not give unbridled discretion to the co-trustees to Determine or Establish a standard of living for Elaine J. Holly, but rather that the absolute discretion given relates solely to the manner, mode, and extent of distributing trust assets, including principal, in order to Maintain the standard of living to which she had "become accustomed." This, they contend, is an ascertainable fact which has been exceeded in this case. Appellees, of course, argue that the "absolute discretion" is all inclusive and the trial court agreed with them.

To begin with, even though a grant of "absolute discretion" to a fiduciary is very broad, it does not relieve a trustee from the exercise of good faith or from being judicious in his administration of the trust, which administration is always subject to review by the court in appropriate instance. Likewise, a trustee is always subject to accountability to remaindermen where discretion is improperly, arbitrarily or capriciously exercised.

Moreover, the courts recognize that where, as here, a trustee is also the sole lifetime beneficiary, such factor is a viable judicial consideration in determining whether the trustee is properly exercising discretionary powers. Concededly, determination of Elaine J. Holly's standard of living is, in the first instance, a function and responsibility of the trustees. While perhaps a court should not fix the criteria for exercise of the discretionary power of the trustees to invade the principal, it certainly may review the exercise of such power. We think, too, that when a trustee is peculiarly influential in making such determination for her own benefit, her discretion in the premises becomes particularly vulnerable to a challenge by remaindermen. And, we apprehend the legitimacy of the plaintiffs' concern where, as here, (1) there is no requirement for the trustees to post a bond for faithful performance of their duties, (2) either trustee may withdraw funds from any bank account in the name of the trust and (3), as the trial court determined, there is no specific requirement in the trust instrument to furnish any inventory, accounting or other information to the remaindermen beneficiaries until their eligibility for receiving distribution. Clearly, a trustee who is also a beneficiary and who is given a power, or discretion, to invade the trust principal has a fiduciary obligation to the remaindermen to keep her demands within reasonable limits. Even an unlimited power of invasion is subject to implied limitations to protect the remaindermen.

We hold, therefore, that allegations that a trustee is the sole lifetime beneficiary, that she has not furnished any accounts or reports of her administration to the remaindermen and that she is not confining her invasions of principal to reasonable limits, as may be set out in the complaint, give rise to an inference of abuse of discretion by the trustee and are sufficient to require the trustee to respond. Trustees are accountable to the courts and their performance may be controlled by the courts. If the evidence discloses any abuse of discretion on the part of a trustee or co-trustees in distributing principal to a lifetime beneficiary, particularly if such beneficiary is a trustee, then the trial court can order appropriate adjustments to correct any abuses in the past and take steps (e.g., to require bonding of trustees, periodic accountings to remainder-men and appropriate supervisory measures) to prevent abuses in the future.

In view whereof, the judgment appealed from should be, and it is hereby, reversed and the cause is remanded for further proceedings not inconsistent herewith.

NOTES AND QUESTIONS

1. *Trusty trustee.* The word trust should remind us that the settlor "trusts" the trustee to carry out the settlor's wishes as expressed in the trust instrument. The settlor has chosen the trustee for this task, and for that reason a court will rarely substitute its own judgment for that of the trustee. Only if the trustee abuses the trust will the court intervene. What do you think Mr. Way (the settlor of the trust at issue in *Mesler v. Holly*) intended the trustees of his trust to do?

2. *Options for the court.* As we have discussed, a court will not direct a trustee to distribute a particular amount. What can the court do to guide the trustee and help structure the trustee's exercise of discretion?

3. *Complicated impartiality.* A trustee must comply with the duty of impartiality, the duty to be fair to all beneficiaries. If the trustee is the current beneficiary, as was the case for Elaine Holly, she must make decisions that are fair to herself and to the remainder beneficiaries. Who will determine whether she has breached her duty of impartiality?

PROBLEMS

Marisa created a trust for her husband, Keenan. Keenan is the trustee and the trust provides, "the trustee shall, in the trustee's sole and absolute discretion, make such distributions as the trustee sees fit for my spouse's health, education, maintenance or support. On the death of my husband, the trustee shall distribute all remaining corpus to my niece, Elizabeth Jane Smith."

1. Keenan made distributions for lavish vacations, a fancy car and lots of designer clothes. Elizabeth Jane has come to you to ask whether she can curb his distributions. She asked Keenan to distribute less, but he pointed out that he is empowered to act in his "sole and absolute discretion" so he can distribute whatever he thinks best. Advise Elizabeth Jane.

2. If you had been Marisa's lawyer drafting the trust, what additional language might you have included in the trust to anticipate that Keenan might take the amount that he did? In doing so, assume: (1) that Marisa would have wished him to do so without challenge by Elizabeth; and (2) that she would not have wished him to take amounts for lavish items.

b. Specific Standards

A court will review a trustee's exercise of a standard of distribution to determine whether the trustee exercised the standard established by the settlor. The discussion below looks at several common standards and the difficulties courts face in determining what sorts of distributions are permitted or required under each standard. Remember that the trust instrument can provide additional guidance beyond simply listing the terms for the standard of distribution. If the settlor intends a particular meaning for any of the terms that follow, the settlor can spell out the meaning in the document. Clear information may mean that future disagreements between the trustee and the beneficiaries can be avoided.

i. Support and Maintenance

If the standard is limited to "support and maintenance," courts view this as an ascertainable standard. That is, a court can make a determination under state law about what the standard means in the context of a particular trust, even though the trustee still has discretion to interpret the standard. The court will start by looking at the beneficiary's basic needs, but "support and maintenance" goes beyond adequate food and housing. Courts normally will look to the amount of property the settlor placed in the trust and the relationship between the settlor and the beneficiary. Unless there is a reason to find otherwise, the terms will usually be interpreted to imply the beneficiary's accustomed standard of living. *See* RESTATEMENT (THIRD) OF TRUSTS §50, cmt. (d)(3). In *Cromwell v. Converse*, 143 A. 416 (Conn. 1928), the court explained that the terms "support and maintenance":

> . . . are not words of art, but have a relative meaning, which in these provisions of the will under our immediate consideration is revealed in the testator's intention and in the circumstances surrounding the testator and his son. It is quite obvious they are not here used in a restricted sense, nor are they to be measured by any fixed standards. The testator possessed large means; his children had been reared in luxurious living and were accustomed to its uses.

What was suitable for his son's situation and station in life is that which those possessed of great wealth and social position customarily adopt for their scale of living in these modern times. Unquestionably the testator had this in mind and understood its significant necessities in providing for his son's income. The funds which he placed in trust to provide an income for him were in size responsive to the considerations which we have suggested. They contemplated every expenditure necessary or incidental to the maintenance of his son and his family in the luxury accompanying one in his station in life.

On a related issue, *i.e.,* whether, absent specific direction in the trust, the beneficiary's other assets should be a factor in the trustee's decision to make distributions, the courts have reached inconsistent results. The *Restatement (Third) of Trusts* §50 adopts as a default view that a trustee should consider other resources, but the comment also indicates that no clear trend exists. RESTATEMENT (THIRD) OF TRUSTS §50, cmt. e.

Nations Bank of Virginia, N.A. v. Estate of Grandy, 450 S.E.2d 140 (Va. 1994), provides an example of a court's decision that the trustees could, but are not obligated to, consider outside assets. In this case, the trust provision being examined provided as follows:

> If it should become necessary or desirable, in the judgment and discretion of the said Trustees, to use a part of the corpus of any of the trusts herein-above in this item established for the benefit of any of the beneficiaries of the said trusts, then and in that event I hereby authorize and empower the said Trustees, in their uncontrolled judgment and discretion, to pay out of the corpus of the trusts any amount needed or required, in their opinion, for such purposes.

The trustee declined to make distributions to the beneficiary of one of the trusts because the beneficiary had significant assets of her own. The trial court required the trustees to pay from trust principal any expenses incurred by the beneficiary in excess of her cash on hand and income earnings. The appellate court reversed. After noting that any interpretation of a standard of distribution depends on the settlor's intent, the court explained:

> Generally, a trustee's discretion is broadly construed, but his actions must be an exercise of good faith and reasonable judgment to promote the trust's pur-pose. A trustee's exercise of discretion should not be overruled by a court unless the trustee has clearly abused the discretion granted him under the trust instrument or acted arbitrarily in such a way as to destroy the trust he is to maintain. Similarly, it is generally not within the power of a court to com-pel trustees to exercise their discretion.
>
> In this case, the trustees have not abused their discretion by refusing to invade the trust principal on behalf of Ms. Grandy. Ms. Grandy has substan-tial personal assets available for satisfaction of her debts and for payment of

her future medical costs as well as a competent guardian to oversee these assets. Cases in which courts have required trustees to invade principal generally have involved circumstances in which a beneficiary had no outside resources or the testator clearly anticipated the use of principal to support the beneficiary. Those factors are not present here. The language of the trust authorizes the trustees to make distributions of principal as deemed necessary in their "uncontrolled judgment and discretion." The trustees acted reasonably in exercising their discretion to preserve the corpus of the trust for both Ms. Grandy and the contingent beneficiaries.

For these reasons, we find that the trial court impermissibly substituted its judgment for that of the trustees by compelling them to invade the trust principal on behalf of Ms. Grandy. Accordingly, we will reverse the judgment of the trial court and remand the case for further proceedings consistent with this opinion.

In addition to whether and to what extent the beneficiary's outside resources may or must be considered in deciding whether to make distributions for someone's support, an issue that the trustee must address is the scope of the duty to affirmatively inquire into the needs of the beneficiary rather than wait for the beneficiary to request distributions. In *Marsman v. Nasca*, 573 N.E.2d 1025 (Mass. App. Ct. 1991), the trustee made only limited distributions to the beneficiary, even though the beneficiary direly needed money for his support. The court determined that, since the trustee was generally aware of the need and was therefore put on notice, the trustee had a duty to inquire into the beneficiary's needs. In this case, the court found that the trustee had not satisfied his responsibility to the trust and the beneficiary.

How extensive is the trustee's duty to inquire when attempting to fulfill the due diligence requirement? A trustee normally can rely on representations made by the beneficiary as to other available assets, but the trustee can also request the beneficiary to provide readily available information about other financial resources, especially if the trustee believes the beneficiary's representations are inaccurate. *See Hertel v. Nationsbank*, 37 S.W.3d 308 (Mo. Ct. App. 2001).

In sum, with respect to the exercise of a power to make distributions for support, the trustee must first consider the intent of the settlor to the extent it can be determined from the trust document and any information about the relationship between the settlor and the beneficiary. Support normally means the beneficiary's accustomed standard of living, so lavish vacations and fancy cars will not come within the standard, unless those sorts of expenses were usual ones for the beneficiary. After making reasonable inquiries about the financial situation of the beneficiaries, the trustee should consider the needs of future beneficiaries and the amount of property in the trust relative to the current beneficiary's needs as well as the needs of future beneficiaries. The trustee may be able to consider the beneficiary's other assets, depending on the terms of the trust or, if not specified, the law in the applicable state.

ii.   Education

A trust term that directs payments for "education" clearly covers tuition. It may also include room and board, books, fees and other costs. The term generally encompasses technical training as well as college or graduate education, depending on other evidence of the settlor's intent in the document. *See* Restatement (Third) of Trusts §50, cmt. (d)(3). Absent clear statements in the trust to the contrary, related costs for education, such as for private primary school, study abroad programs and music lessons or sports instruction, are less likely than those above to be viewed as within the term "education."

In deciding which costs the settlor intended the trustee to cover, the trustee must consider not only the standard for distribution but also other resources of the beneficiary (unless the trust says otherwise) and other purposes of the trust. The trustee cannot make a determination with respect to one distribution in isolation from the interests of other beneficiaries.

A settlor may choose to include a statement of his expectations in the trust instrument. If the settlor intends to limit distributions for education in some way or wishes the term to be interpreted broadly, that information should be clearly stated to avoid possible disagreements between the trustee and the beneficiary. Consider how such a trust term might be drafted, and the various issues that the settlor must decide. In thinking about possible definitions of "education," remember that the more specific the instructions to a trustee are, the less flexibility the trustee will have.

iii.   Emergency

"Emergency" is considered a restrictive standard, and a distribution can be made under the standard only if the sort of emergency the settlor envisioned has occurred. The terms of the trust normally do not provide guidance as to the type of emergency covered. The determination of what constitutes an emergency depends on the trustee's discretion and, if necessary, on a court's determination.

As is generally true with respect to a trustee's exercise of discretionary powers, courts tend to defer to the trustee's determination of whether an emergency has occurred and will define emergency narrowly when deciding whether the trustee acted unreasonably in not making a distribution. In *In re Tone's Estate*, 39 N.W.2d 401 (Iowa 1949), the beneficiary sought to force the trustee to make a distribution for legal expenses and attorney's fees incurred by the beneficiary and her husband to defend themselves against a civil assault claim, claiming this was an "unforeseen emergency." The terms of the trust provided: "If at any time or times, on account of serious illness or other unforeseen emergency, any beneficiary . . . shall, in the opinion of said Trustee, imperatively require the expenditure . . . or part of the accumulated . . . income or of the principal, said Trustee is hereby authorized to . . . expend for such purpose such an amount as in its discretion and judgment, it may think wise, prudent and necessary under the circumstances." The court defined emergency as "a sudden or unexpected happening which calls for immediate action," and did not require the trustee to make the payment.

The following case provides an example of a court's interpretation of the use of the word "emergency" as part of a standard to make distributions for the settlor's husband. The court considers each word in the standard as it determines the settlor's intent. While at first blush it appears the court's approach is excessively detailed, this case is a good reminder that when drafting trust standards, a lawyer should consider the significance of each word, as a court will rely on the exact definitions of words when interpreting their meaning.

Warner v. Trust Co. Bank
296 S.E.2d 553 (Ga. 1982)

JORDAN, Chief Justice.

The only issue we address is the intention of the testatrix, Elizabeth R. Bliss, as expressed in the following clause of her will: "(b) If my husband is without sufficient income from this and all other sources to provide comfortably for his wants according to the style of living which we have enjoyed, or to meet any emergency, such as prolonged illness, which may affect him, then I authorize my Trustees to invade the principal to such an extent and so often as may be necessary to provide ample funds for these purposes. I wish my Trustees to be generous in the interpretation of this provision, as my chief purpose in placing this property in trust is to see that my husband is well cared for."

The clause under construction appeared in the context of a will expressing an intention of Mrs. Bliss not to leave to her husband, Colonel William C. Bliss, either the bulk of her estate or a general power to control the disposition of the bulk of her estate; rather, that most of her property was to pass to her relatives, as by his will his property was to pass to his relatives, as they had no children.

The trial court found and concluded that the intention of Mrs. Bliss as expressed in the subject clause of her will paralleled her expressed intention to not give her husband a general power of appointment over her property, and that Mrs. Bliss intended (because of the language she used) any invasion of the corpus under the clause now under construction to be limited strictly by standards relating only to the health, support and maintenance of Colonel Bliss which are clearly ascertainable from the common meanings of the words she employed in the subject clause. We agree and affirm the judgment of the trial court.

Because each will is its own law, we now address the words of the clause under construction both individually and collectively.

"If," though brief, is eloquent. *Nothing* is to transpire under the clause unless Colonel Bliss is "without." What he is to be "without" is "sufficient income" from *all* sources ("from this and all other sources") with which "to provide comfortably for his wants." We give to those words their ordinary and accepted meanings, no other meanings having been ascribed to them by the testatrix.

The appellants insist that the word "wants" is vague and fits anywhere along a continuum of meanings which starts with the concept of "needs" and ends with the concept of "desires" or "whims." Certainly this would be correct had the testatrix not limited the word "wants" by the phrases "according to the style of living which we have enjoyed" and "as may be necessary to provide ample funds for these purposes." In common English parlance, a "want" which is "necessary" for a narrowly specified purpose is a "need", not a "desire" or a "whim." The English language will admit of no other reasonable construction. The other end of appellants' posited continuum of possible meanings is cut away and cast adrift by the limiting words and phrases employed by Mrs. Bliss to express her intentions.

The intentions of Mrs. Bliss readily are ascertainable from the common dictionary meanings of her chosen words. Not just any "want" is to authorize an invasion of the corpus. Only those "wants" (1) which are commensurate with "the style of living which we have enjoyed," and which also are (2) "necessary" for that purpose, are to be satisfied by invasion of the corpus, and such invasions of corpus are to occur only "if" Colonel Bliss is "without" any income sufficient for those purposes.

The fact that the trustees are enjoined to "provide comfortably" for these "wants" (which, born of necessity, must constitute "needs") by invading the corpus "to such an extent" and "often" to the end that "my husband is well cared for" does not remove the foregoing express limitations permitting invasion of the corpus only "if" Colonel Bliss is "without" funds from any source with which to provide for those wants necessary to his lifestyle, i.e., to provide his needs for his support and maintenance.

Appellants next insist that when Mrs. Bliss referred to "any emergency" she meant just that; no more, no less. However, this contention ignores, once again, a limiting phrase employed by the testatrix. The invasion may not be for "any emergency"; rather, it *only* may be for "any emergency, such as prolonged illness." The existence and proper application of the rule of *ejusdem generis* is too well known to permit cavil. The testatrix, speaking of the waning years of her husband's life after her death, provided for emergencies of later life "such as prolonged illness," i.e., health-related emergencies which might occur or recur until his death.

The trial court correctly ascertained from the words employed by the testatrix that invasions of corpus permitted to the trustees are strictly limited to those purposes specified in this opinion and to none other.

iv. Welfare, Best Interests, Happiness

Standards like "welfare," "best interests" and "happiness" create broad discretion in the trustee. A trustee can choose to honor any reasonable request from a beneficiary for a distribution, without concern about second-guessing by another beneficiary or the court. These standards are considered nonascertainable, both for state law purposes and for tax purposes.

A trustee must still be "reasonable" and must act in "good faith," but with one of these standards the court will give the trustee a lot of latitude in its exercise of discretion. A trustee can choose not to make distributions or a trustee can decide to make distributions for almost any purpose. Other beneficiaries will find challenging a distribution under a welfare, best interests or happiness standard difficult.

[handwritten: reversion ad litem for nephew]

Combs v. Carey's Trustee
287 S.W.2d 443 (Ky. 1956)

[handwritten: Trustee: Security trust company / Settlers Daughter. / Mrs. Walsh]

Waddill, Commissioner.

This action was brought to obtain a declaration of the powers and duties of the trustee under a deed of trust executed by Mrs. Sydney Sayre Carey.

Mrs. Carey executed the deed of trust in 1935, naming the appellee, Security Trust Company, trustee. She placed securities valued at $391,000 in the trust, including three notes previously executed by her daughter, Clara Bell Walsh, to H. W. Heidenrich, secured by certain property owned by Mrs. Walsh.

Under the terms of the trust the settlor received the income for life. Upon the settlor's death, the trustee was directed to pay the entire net income from the trust estate to the settlor's daughter, Mrs. Walsh, for life. The trustee was also empowered to invade the corpus for her benefit. Mrs. Walsh was given a testamentary power of appointment to dispose of the corpus, and in the event that she failed to exercise the power, the trust was to continue with the net income being paid to the settlor's great nephew, Sydney Sayre Combs. Upon his death the income was directed to be paid to his issue for 21 years, and at the end of this period the trustee was to distribute the corpus to the issue of Sydney Sayre Combs.

During the fourteen years following the settlor's death, which occurred in 1940, the net income from the trust, and a substantial portion of the corpus of the trust were paid to Mrs. Walsh by the trustee. In September, 1954, the corpus of the trust consisted of three notes of Mrs. Walsh, valued at $110,000 and $2,234.59 in uninvested cash. In view of the fact that Mrs. Walsh was no longer receiving any income from the trust, she requested the trustee pay over the three notes to her and release the lien on her property in order that the property could be utilized to meet her current expenses. The trustee has indicated its willingness to comply with Mrs. Walsh's request, but has sought a judicial declaration of its authority under the terms of the deed of trust.

[handwritten: Wants notes paid over to her and valore re lien on her property so she can use it]

The terms of the trust which define the trustee's authority to invade the corpus for the benefit of Mrs. Walsh are very broad. Paragraph (c) of the Deed of Trust provides:

> Upon the death of the Donor, the trustee shall disburse the entire net income from the trust estate to the Donor's daughter, Clara Bell Walsh, if she be then living, during the then remaining period of her natural life. In the event that the net income from the trust estate, together with such other income as Donor's daughter may have, shall not at all times be sufficient for the proper maintenance, support, comfort and welfare of Donor's daughter, Clara Bell Walsh, and especially should any emergency arise requiring surgical or medical treatment, nursing, travel or other unusual expense, the Donor directs the trustee, in addition to disbursing the income to Donor's daughter, to expend such part of the corpus of the trust estate as the trustee may deem necessary or proper for the comfort, welfare and happiness of Donor's said daughter at any and all times, even if it should require the entire corpus of the trust estate. But the trustee's discretion is to control and the exercise thereof in any reasonable and proper manner is not to be subject to question by anyone in any way. . . .

The trial court held that under this instrument the trustee was empowered to expend the corpus for the comfort, welfare and happiness of Mrs. Walsh, and therefore the trustee was authorized to deliver the three notes remaining in the trust to Mrs. Walsh and release the lien upon the property securing them. From this judgment the guardian ad litem for the infant children of Sydney Sayre Combs has prosecuted this appeal.

The evidence shows that Mrs. Walsh is a widow and has no children. She is now over seventy years old, and for many years has maintained an extremely high standard of living. She presently resides in the Plaza Hotel in New York City and maintains a chauffeur and several maids. She travels much and entertains extensively. It was shown that during the settlor's life she countenanced her daughter's lavish and imprudent manner of living, and the broad terms of the trust clearly indicate her intention that it continue.

The trustee's authority to invade the corpus is defined by the terms "comfort, welfare and happiness." These are very broad terms and indicate the extent of discretion given to the trustee. In *O'Bryan v. England*, 173 Ky. 12, 189 S.W. 1126, 1129, the trustee was authorized to invade the corpus whenever he deemed it necessary for the "support and maintenance" of the beneficiary. The trust further provided that the beneficiary's receipt should be a "full acquittance and discharge for any such payment." We said in that case that "It would be difficult to frame in any language a more absolute and unrestrained power and authority" in a trustee. The trustee's authority in the instant case is much broader. All that is necessary to authorize an invasion of the corpus is that Mrs. Walsh convince the trustee that such an invasion is necessary to her "happiness." While the language used in the trust instrument may not have created a prudent standard to guide the trustee in the administration of the trust, yet it is the standard chosen by the settlor, and the one followed by the trustee.

We therefore agree with the trial court that the powers of the trustee are plenary, and where such broad powers exist the court will not restrict the trustee in the exercise of his discretion unless it appears that he is guilty of bad faith or is acting in an arbitrary manner. 3 Bogert, Trusts and Trustees, Section 560, p. 478. Under the facts and circumstances of this case, the court cannot say that the delivery of the notes to Mrs. Walsh would constitute an abuse of discretion on the part of the trustee. . . .

QUESTIONS

1.   *Who does the trustee protect?* Why did the trustee in *Combs* bring the suit? Whose interests does the court protect? Why?

2.   *How bad is bad?* What types of actions might cause a court to find a trustee to be acting in bad faith?

PROBLEMS

1.   A trust provides: "The trustee shall distribute all the income to my son, Jeremy, and on Jeremy's death, distribute whatever remains in the trust to my daughter, Jacqueline." What discretion does the trustee have with respect to the amounts Jeremy and Jacqueline will receive?

2.   A trust provides: "The trustee shall make distributions from principal for the education of my grandchildren." What information would be helpful in advising the trustee?

   a.   Can the trustee pay tuition for a grandchild who is attending law school?

   b.   Can the trustee pay the expenses of a one-year trip around the world for a grandchild who wants to educate himself through travel?

   c.   For each of the requested distributions in (a) and (b), what due diligence would be required to establish reasonableness and good faith rather than an abuse of discretion for a decision to distribute or a decision not to distribute?

3.   A trust provides: "The trustee shall distribute so much or all of the trust principal as is necessary for the health, education, maintenance and support of my spouse. On my spouse's death, the trustee shall distribute the

corpus of the trust to my descendants, by right of representation." For each request below indicate whether the trustee *must* make the distribution and, if not, whether the trustee *can* make the distribution. If the trustee makes the distribution, would you advise the other beneficiaries to sue and, if so, on what legal basis?

    a.   The spouse requests a distribution to pay for elective cosmetic surgery.

    b.   The spouse requests a distribution to pay expenses for the vacation house at the coast that the settlor and spouse had used together before the settlor's death.

    c.   The spouse requests a distribution to pay for aerobics classes.

    d.   The spouse requests a monthly stipend of $1,000 to help cover expenses.

    4.   A trust provides: "The trustee shall distribute such amounts as the trustee determines, in the trustee's sole discretion, to be appropriate for Frieda's happiness and welfare." (Frieda is a niece of the settlor.) *Must* the trustee make distributions to cover the costs of a vacation for Frieda? *Could* the trustee make a distribution for that purpose? What if the trust has a relatively small corpus? What if the trust has a substantial corpus and Frieda has always lived a lavish lifestyle?

EXERCISE

Miranda wants to create a trust in her will, *i.e.*, a testamentary trust. She wants to provide for her husband, Zachary, for the rest of his life. At his death, she wants the assets remaining to go to her children from a prior marriage. All the children are adults. Miranda has a substantial estate, but not a huge one. She is concerned that income from her assets may not be enough to provide for Zachary, and she is willing to allow for some distributions of principal to supplement his income. "But," she says to her lawyer, "it's important that something be left for my kids. I certainly wouldn't want Zachary to spend my money on his next wife!"

Draft the terms of the trust that establish the trust and provide directions to the trustee for the distributions to Zachary. You do not need to draft other provisions for the trustee, and you do not need to draft the provisions directing distribution on termination. You should draft only the provisions that tell the trustee when and what to distribute to Zachary during his life. You can assume that Miranda's oldest child, Jenna, will be the trustee, and that Zachary will not be the trustee.

C. RIGHTS OF CREDITORS AND PLANNING TO PROTECT THE ASSETS IN A TRUST

1. General

A matter of great concern to the settlor and the beneficiaries is whether their creditors may require the trustee to turn over trust assets to pay off outstanding debts. Creditors normally have many sources from which to satisfy a claim, such as checking accounts, wages, stocks and securities, insurance, etc. A trust in which a debtor has an interest as a settlor or beneficiary is only one possible source and is likely not a favored one. While a trust may hold significant assets, creditors frequently do not attempt to attach an interest of a settlor or beneficiary because the protections we are about to discuss make doing so difficult. For example, the trust might include a "spendthrift" provision (discussed later in this chapter), designed to prevent the alienation of trust funds. The effort to shelter assets, especially through the use of trusts, is referred to as "asset protection planning."

In general, a creditor can only garnish what the debtor owns. A creditor essentially "steps into the shoes" of the debtor. This is the "doctrine of derivative title." If the debtor owns property in fee simple, a creditor can take possession of the property itself. If the debtor owns less than a fee simple interest, which is the case for beneficiaries of a trust, a creditor may only attach the interest of the beneficiary, which is a right to distributions of income or corpus. As we will see, because the rights of a beneficiary differ depending on whether the trust contains mandatory or discretionary distribution clauses, so do the rights of the beneficiary's creditors.

The focus of this part of the chapter is whether a creditor can get a court to order the trustee to turn over the trust property or pay distributions from the trust to the creditor instead of first making payment to the beneficiary (who may spend it before the creditor can garnish it). What we will learn is that with the exception of a settlor of a revocable trust, beneficiaries are not deemed to be the owners of the assets; they only own a right to distributions. Consequently, creditors may not normally garnish the assets of the trust; they may only intercept distributions to which the beneficiary is entitled. Regardless of the existence of the trust, however, creditors are free to pursue the debtor's other assets.

In the first part of this section, we consider the extent to which creditors of a *beneficiary* (other than a beneficiary who is also the settlor) can reach property held in trust or the distributions from it. After that, we consider what creditors of the *settlor* can reach with respect to a trust in which the settlor is also a beneficiary, sometimes referred to as a "self-settled trust." We do not separately discuss revocable trusts in which the settlor is not a beneficiary, because those trusts are uncommon and will be subject to the rules that apply when the settlor is a beneficiary. As we will learn:

- Where the **beneficiary is not the settlor**, the creditors of the beneficiary who have a judgment, whether obtained before or after the beneficiary's interest is created, can reach assets in the trust only to the extent the beneficiary has rights to demand assets or distributions. Thus, like the beneficiary, creditors of a beneficiary may be restricted in accessing the beneficiary's interest in distributions of income or property of the trust by (i) spendthrift provisions, (ii) the discretion of the trustee and (iii) the standards for distribution imposed by the terms of the trust. Like an onion, each of these restrictions adds a layer of protection for the beneficiary, warding off actions by the creditors to collect. These protections are more permeable with respect to "preferred creditors," like taxing authorities and children and ex-spouses who are owed child or spousal support. Once property is distributed to a beneficiary, it is fair game for the creditors.

- Where the **beneficiary is also the settlor**, creditors may be able to attach the property in the trust directly and not have to limit themselves to distributions. When a settlor creates either a revocable or irrevocable trust, *existing* creditors may attach the settlor's interest without restriction. With respect to a revocable trust, *later* creditors of the settlor can reach the assets in the trust unimpeded, either during the settlor's lifetime or after the settlor's death. Even with respect to irrevocable trusts containing a spendthrift clause, if the settlor has retained an interest in the trust, creditors may garnish the settlor's interest to satisfy their claims, unless the settlor established an asset protection trust in one of a few foreign or state jurisdictions that permit such trusts.

Existing creditors of the settlor are not affected by the rules we are going to discuss. The Uniform Fraudulent Conveyance (or Transfer) Act, adopted in one form or another by every state, establishes that if someone transfers assets to another for less than adequate consideration at a time when he is already indebted, the transfer is generally considered in fraud of creditors, regardless of intent to defraud. Consequently, not only does the transferor-debtor remain liable to the creditors but so does the transferee, even if innocent. These rules of general application apply with equal force to trusts. A court can order the trustee to turn over the value of the transferred property to the extent of the debt. Fraudulent conveyance statutes will apply whether or not the settlor is also a beneficiary.

Lastly, states differ with respect to the rights of creditors to access trust property to satisfy their claims. The UTC was promulgated generally to help make the law of trusts more uniform, and this is true regarding the rights of certain creditors and assignees to reach a trust. That being said, the UTC position on the rights of creditors and the common law of many states diverge in a number of respects, with the result that even some states that have adopted the UTC have modified a few of its creditor rights provisions.

2. *Creditors of a Beneficiary Who Is Not the Settlor*

a. **Mandatory Distributions**

As we learned earlier, mandatory distributions are those that must be made. No discretion on the part of the trustee is involved. For example, if the terms of the trust require the trustee to "pay income monthly to my wife and, on her death, to pay the remaining principal to my son, William," the distributions of income and principal are both mandatory.

With respect to distributions pursuant to a mandatory provision, and absent a spendthrift clause covering such distributions (see discussion of spendthrift provisions below), because the beneficiary has the right to demand payment of a distribution, a creditor *can* get a court order attaching present or future mandatory distributions to or for the benefit of the beneficiary. UTC §501. This is important to the creditor because the court order will require that the payments be made directly to it, thus avoiding the time-consuming, costly and often futile (if the income is already spent) procedure of garnishing the payments from the beneficiary after they have been distributed.

b. **Discretionary Distributions**

In contrast to mandatory distributions, the beneficiary's interest in distributions that are subject to the trustee's exercise of discretionary powers are difficult for a creditor to reach. Distributions of income or principal are treated as discretionary whether the discretion is expressed in the form of a standard of distribution, like health, education, maintenance or support, or the terms of the trust use language of discretion with language of direction, such as a provision that "my trustees shall, in their absolute discretion, distribute such amounts as are necessary for the beneficiary's support." (Despite the presence of the imperative "shall," the provision is discretionary, not mandatory.) Comments to UTC §506. Similarly, the power to sprinkle or spray distributions of income or principal among a number of named beneficiaries or to one or more of a class of beneficiaries is considered a discretionary power.

Just as a beneficiary has difficulty getting a court to intervene to force the trustee to make discretionary distributions, a creditor's lot is no better. In fact, under UTC §504(b), a creditor is in a worse position than a beneficiary, because under that subsection a beneficiary can seek judicial redress for an abuse of the trustee's discretion but a creditor cannot compel a distribution.

Because of the inconsistent and indefinite nature of discretionary distributions, courts usually will not grant an order requiring payments directly to the creditor. The creditor is left to go after distributions in the hands of the beneficiary once the trustee actually makes the distributions.

Unless the creditor is monitoring the situation closely, many distributions will go unnoticed and not be seized.

A special group of creditors are preferred in the eyes of the law and may be able to get a court order compelling a distribution. If an individual is in arrears in paying child or spousal support, UTC §504(c) says a court can order the trustee to make a distribution from the trust to the former spouse or children *even if the trustee's power is discretionary*, if it can be shown that the trustee "has not complied with a standard of distribution or has abused a discretion."

UTC §504(c) is controversial, because under pre-UTC law, even preferred creditors could not reach property subject to a discretionary standard. As a result, some states that have adopted the UTC have either left out UTC §504(c) entirely or modified it.

UTC §504. Discretionary Trusts; Effect of Standard.

(a) In this section, "child" includes any person for whom an order or judgment for child support has been entered in this or another State.

(b) Except as otherwise provided in subsection (c), whether or not a trust contains a spendthrift provision, a creditor of a beneficiary may not compel a distribution that is subject to the trustee's discretion, even if:

(1) the discretion is expressed in the form of a standard of distribution; or

(2) the trustee has abused the discretion.

(c) To the extent a trustee has not complied with a standard of distribution or has abused a discretion:

(1) a distribution may be ordered by the court to satisfy a judgment or court order against the beneficiary for support or maintenance of the beneficiary's child, spouse, or former spouse; and

(2) the court shall direct the trustee to pay to the child, spouse, or former spouse such amount as is equitable under the circumstances but not more than the amount the trustee would have been required to distribute to or for the benefit of the beneficiary had the trustee complied with the standard or not abused the discretion.

c.   Spendthrift Clauses

We now look at spendthrift clauses—how they work to protect the interest of a beneficiary from the claims of creditors, exceptions to the spendthrift clause rule and another controversial UTC section that gives certain creditors greater access to trust assets than the common law provides. A spendthrift clause adds another layer of protection from the claims of creditors beyond the protection that discretionary provisions already provide. The argument in favor of enforcing spendthrift clauses focuses on the right of the settlor to place conditions on the transfer of the settlor's assets into the trust, including protecting beneficiaries from their own frailties. The section also addresses arguments against enforcing spendthrift clauses.

A spendthrift clause is a clause in a trust that prevents *both* voluntary and involuntary alienation of trust interests by the beneficiary. An effective spendthrift clause precludes a beneficiary from assigning or selling her interest in a trust; it also prevents a creditor of the beneficiary from attaching the beneficiary's interest, with the result that the creditor must wait until after the payment is made and then attempt to collect from the beneficiary. The Comment to UTC §502(a) explains: "[A] settlor may not allow a beneficiary to assign while prohibiting a beneficiary's creditor from collecting, and vice versa." As the Comment to UTC §505 adds: "The effect of a spendthrift provision is generally to insulate totally a beneficiary's interest until a distribution is made and received by the beneficiary."

A well-drafted spendthrift clause should spell out the restrictions on both the beneficiaries and their creditors. The UTC provides that a trust term stating that "the interest of a beneficiary is held subject to a spendthrift trust, or words of similar import," restrains both voluntary and involuntary interests. UTC §502(b).

Lawyers typically include spendthrift clauses in trusts they draft. In fact, because spendthrift provisions are so beneficiary-friendly, they have become a boilerplate clause in most trust forms. They are so commonplace that lawyers are unlikely even to discuss with the client whether the difficult-to-fully-understand clause should be included.

Here is an example of a spendthrift clause. Note that the first sentence of the spendthrift clause prevents voluntary, and the second sentence prevents involuntary, alienation.

> No beneficiary shall have any right to anticipate, sell, assign, mortgage, pledge or otherwise dispose of or encumber all or any part of any trust estate established for his or her benefit under this agreement. No part of such trust estate, including income, shall be liable for the debts or obligations of any beneficiary or be subject to attachment, garnishment, execution, creditor's bill or other legal or equitable process.

As we know, the ability of creditors to reach and require distributions depends in part on whether the standard is mandatory or discretionary. Spendthrift provisions generally affect both. *See* UTC §503(c) below. To prevent a trustee and a beneficiary from collaborating to avoid a creditor by withholding a mandatory distribution of income or principal (including a distribution on termination of the trust to a remainder person), UTC §506 allows a creditor to reach a mandatory distribution if it has not been made "within a reasonable time after the designated distribution date." In essence, at this point, "payments mandated by the express terms of the trust are in effect being held by the trustee as agent for the beneficiary and should be treated as part of the beneficiary's personal assets." Comments to UTC §506.

Needless to say, creditors do not like spendthrift clauses. Third parties relying on payment from someone who is a beneficiary of a trust do so at their peril since most trust forms include a spendthrift clause and access to the trust is generally denied.

d.   Exceptions to Spendthrift Protection—"Super Creditors"

Most debtor-creditor relationships are created voluntarily after the creditor has had an opportunity to evaluate the risk of the debtor's nonpayment before extending credit. For these creditors, *caveat emptor* is the guiding philosophy. If they rely on assets held for the debtor in trust, they are stuck with a spendthrift limitation.

However, some creditors' claims do not arise voluntarily after a period of evaluation of the debtor's credit-worthiness. For this reason, the common law of numerous states has created exceptions to the spendthrift rule for these creditors. A child trying to enforce a court order for child support makes a sympathetic plaintiff, as does a former spouse trying to enforce an order for alimony. *See Hurley v. Hurley*, 309 N.W.2d 225 (Mich. Ct. App. 1981) (child support); *O'Connor v. O'Connor*, 141 N.E.2d 691 (Oh. Com. Pl. 1957) (alimony and child support). *See also Shelley v. Shelley*, discussed below.

The following case adopts exceptions to spendthrift protection. As you read the case, think about what interests Grant Shelley's children received, and why. The exception to the spendthrift clause provides only part of the answer.

Shelley v. Shelley
354 P.2d 282 (Or. 1960)

O'Connell, Justice.

. . . The trust involved in this suit was created by Hugh T. Shelley. The pertinent parts of the trust are as follows:

> (4) . . . it is my desire, and I direct, that, the United States National Bank of Portland (Oregon), as trustee, shall continue this estate in trust and pay all income derived therefrom to my son, Grant R. Shelley, as long as he lives, said income to be paid to him at intervals not less than three (3) months apart; Provided, Further, That when my son, Grant R. Shelley, arrives at the age of thirty (30) years, my trustee may then, or at any time thereafter, and from time to time, distribute to said son absolutely and as his own all or any part of the principal of said trust fund that it may then or from time to time

thereafter deem him capable of successfully investing without the restraints of this trust; Provided, However, That such disbursements of principal of said trust so made to my son after he attains the age of thirty (30) years shall be first approved in writing by either one of my brothers-in-law, that is: Dr. Frank L. Ralston, now of Walla Walla, Washington, or Russell C. Ralston, now of Palo Alto, California, if either of them is then living, but if neither of them is then living, then my trustee is authorized to make said disbursements of principal to my son in the exercise of its sole and absolute judgment and discretion; Provided, Further, That, said trust shall continue as to all or any part of the undistributed portion of the principal thereof to and until the death of my said son.

(5) I further direct and authorize my trustee, from time to time (but only upon the written approval of my said wife if she be then living, otherwise in the exercise of my trustee's sole discretion) to make disbursements for the use and benefit of my son, Grant R. Shelley, or his children, in case of any emergency arising whereby unusual and extraordinary expenses are necessary for the proper support and care of my said son, or said children.

(8) Each beneficiary hereunder is hereby restrained from alienating, anticipating, encumbering, or in any manner assigning his or her interest or estate, either in principal or income, and is without power so to do, nor shall such interest or estate be subject to his or her liabilities or obligations nor to judgment or other legal process, bankruptcy proceedings or claims of creditors or others.

The principal question on appeal is whether the income and corpus of the Shelley trust can be reached by Grant Shelley's former wives and his children.

Grant Shelley was first married to defendant, Patricia C. Shelley. Two children were born of this marriage. Patricia divorced Grant in 1951. The decree required Grant to pay support money for the children; the decree did not call for the payment of alimony. Thereafter, Grant married the plaintiff, Betty Shelley. Two children were born of this marriage. The plaintiff obtained a divorce from Grant in August, 1958. The decree in this latter suit required the payment of both alimony and a designated monthly amount for the support of the children of that marriage.

Some time after his marriage to the plaintiff, Grant disappeared and his whereabouts was not known at the time of this suit. The defendant bank, as trustee, invested the trust assets in securities which are now held by it, together with undisbursed income from the trust estate. The plaintiff obtained an injunction restraining the defendant trustee from disbursing any of the trust assets. Patricia Shelley brought a garnishment proceeding against the trustee, by which she sought to subject the trust to the claim for support money provided for in the 1951 decree of divorce. . . .

The trial court entered a decree subjecting the accrued income of the trust to the existing claims of the plaintiff and Patricia Shelley; subjecting future income of the trust to the periodic obligations subsequently accruing by the terms of the decrees in the divorce proceedings brought by plaintiff and Patricia Shelley; and further providing that in the event that the trust income was insufficient to satisfy such claims, the corpus of the trust was subject to invasion.

We shall first consider that part of the decree which subjects the income of the trust to the claims of plaintiff and of defendant, Patricia Shelley. The trust places no conditions upon the right of Grant Shelley to receive the trust income during his lifetime. Therefore, plaintiff and Patricia Shelley may reach such income unless the spendthrift provision of the trust precludes them from doing so.

The validity of spendthrift trusts has been established by our former cases. The question on this appeal is whether the spendthrift provision will be given effect to bar the claims of the beneficiary's children for support and the plaintiff's claim for alimony.

The question is whether a person should be entitled to enjoy the benefits of a trust and at the same time refuse to pay the obligations arising out of his marriage.

We have no hesitation in declaring that public policy requires that the interest of the beneficiary of a trust should be subject to the claims for support of his children. Certainly the defendant will accept the societal postulate that parents have the obligation to support their children. If we give effect to the spendthrift provision to bar the claims for support, we have the spectacle of a man enjoying the benefits of a trust immune from claims which are justly due, while the community pays for the support of his children. We do not believe that it is sound policy to use the welfare funds of this state in support of the beneficiary's children, while he stands behind the shield of immunity created by a spendthrift trust provision. To endorse such a policy and to permit the spectacle which we have described above would be to invite disrespect for the administration of justice. One who wishes to dispose of his property through the device of a trust must do so subject to these considerations of policy and he cannot force the courts to sanction his scheme of disposition if it is inimical to the interests of the state.

The justification for permitting a claim for alimony is, perhaps, not as clear. The adjustment of the economic interests of the parties to a divorce may depend upon a variety of factors, including the respective fault of the parties, the ability of the wife to support herself, the duration of the marriage, and other considerations. Whether alimony is to be granted and its amount are questions which are determined in light of these various interests. It is probably fair to say that the duties created by the marriage relation, at least as they are evaluated upon the termination of the marriage, are conceived of as more qualified than those arising out of the paternal relationship. On the theory that divorce terminates the husband's duty to support his former wife and that she stands in no better position than other creditors, some courts have held that the spendthrift provision insulates the beneficiary's interest in the trust from her claim. Recognizing the difference in marital and parental duties suggested above, it has been held that a spendthrift trust is subject to the claims for the support of children but free from the claims of the former wife. A majority of the cases, however, hold that a spendthrift provision will not bar a claim for alimony.

. . . The duty of the husband to support his former wife should override the restriction called for by the spendthrift provision. The same reason advanced above for requiring the support of the beneficiary's children will, in many cases, be applicable to the claim of a divorced wife; if the beneficiary's interest cannot be reached, the state may be called upon to support her. . . .

We hold that the beneficiary's interest in the income of the Shelley Trust is subject to the claims of the plaintiff for alimony and to the claims for the support of Grant Shelley's children as provided for under both decrees for divorce. These claims are not without limit. We adopt the view that such claimants may reach only that much of the income which the trial court deems reasonable under the circumstances, having in mind the respective needs of the husband and wife, the needs of the children, the amount of the trust income, the availability of the corpus for the various needs, and any other factors which are relevant in adjusting equitably the interests of the claimants and the beneficiary. . . .

The question of the claimants' rights to reach the corpus of the trust involves other consideration. For the reasons heretofore stated, the beneficiary's interest in the corpus is not made immune from these claims. But, by the terms of the trust, the disbursement of the corpus is within the discretion of the trustee (or, in some instances subject to the approval of others), and, therefore, Grant Shelley's right to receive any part of the corpus does not arise until the trustee has exercised his discretion and has decided to invade the corpus. Until that time, the plaintiff and Patricia Shelley cannot reach the corpus of the trust because the beneficiary has no realizable interest in it. It has been held that a discretionary trust for the "sole benefit" of the testator's son was enforceable by the son's destitute wife and children on the ground that the support of the son's family fell within the terms of the trust. But, assuming without deciding that such an interpretation is reasonable, it has not been extended to a case where there has been a divorce and the wife has ceased to be a member of the family and, therefore, has ceased to be a beneficiary of the trust. There is nothing in the trust before us which would indicate the testator's intent to make the plaintiff, either directly or indirectly, the beneficiary of the trust. Patricia Shelley could not be regarded as a beneficiary because the decree under which she claims called only for the payment of support money for the children and not alimony. In some jurisdictions a creditor of the beneficiary of a discretionary trust may attach the potential interest of the beneficiary. There is no such procedure in Oregon available to the creditor. And at least with respect to the corpus, ORS 29.175(2) makes the interest constituting the subject matter of the trust free from attachment. It follows that the decree of the lower court in making the corpus of the Shelley Trust subject to the plaintiff's claim for alimony was erroneous.

The claims for the support of Grant Shelley's children, provided for in the two divorce decrees, involve a different problem. The trust directed and authorized the trustee, in the exercise of its sole discretion upon the death of settlor's wife, to make disbursements for the use and benefit not only of Grant Shelley, but also for his children. The disbursements were to be made "in case of any emergency arising whereby unusual and extraordinary expenses are necessary for the proper support and care of my said son, or said children." Here the children are named as beneficiaries of the trust and need not claim derivatively through their father. However, they are entitled to a share of the corpus only if, in the trustee's discretion, it is determined that an emergency exists. The defendant bank contends that the expenses of supporting Grant Shelley's children claimed in this case were for the usual and ordinary costs of support and do not, therefore, constitute "unusual and extraordinary expenses" within the meaning of the trust provision. It is contended that there was no "emergency" calling for "unusual and extraordinary expenses" because there was no proof of an unexpected occurrence or of an unexpected situation requiring immediate action. We disagree with defendant's interpretation. We construe the clause to include the circumstances involved here, i.e., where the children are deserted by their father and are in need of support. We think that the testator intended to provide that in the event that the income from the trust was not sufficient to cover disbursements for the support and case of either the son or his children an "emergency" had arisen and the corpus could then be invaded. . . .

The decree of the lower court is affirmed and the cause remanded with directions to modify the decree in accordance with the views expressed in this opinion.

———————————

A tort judgment creditor also would seem like a sympathetic creditor because one does not choose one's tortfeasor, but the law has not looked upon tort creditors with the same favor as children and former spouses. Louisiana is currently the only state that provides an exception from spendthrift protection for certain tort judgment creditors. The statute permits a court to authorize seizure of a beneficiary's interest in a trust, in the discretion of the court and "as may be just under the circumstances" for "damages arising from a felony criminal offense committed by the beneficiary which results in a conviction or a plea of guilty." La. Rev. Stat. Ann §9:2005 (West 2010). In *Sligh v. First National Bank, Trustee*, 704 So. 2d 1020 (Miss. 1997), the Mississippi Supreme Court held that a tort creditor could reach assets held in trust for the tortfeasor despite the spendthrift clause. However, the Mississippi legislature quickly reversed this result by enacting a statute drafted by the estate planning bar. *See* Miss. Code Ann. 91-9-503. When presented with the opportunity to create an exception for a tortfeasor, the majority in a Maryland case, *Duvall v. McGee*, refused to do so. However, the strong dissent suggests that courts should reconsider this question. Here is the dissent.

Duvall v. McGee

826 A.2d 416 (Md. 2003)

BATTAGLIA, J. Dissenting.

I respectfully dissent.

Katherine Ryon was beaten to death during the course of a robbery that occurred in her home. After James Calvert McGee was convicted of felony-murder for his participation in the robbery and murder of Ms. Ryon, a money judgment was entered against him pursuant to a settlement agreement, in which McGee compromised civil claims brought against him by Robert Duvall, the Personal Representative of the Estate of Ms. Ryon. The majority today concludes that Ms. Ryon's estate cannot enforce its judgment against McGee's interest in an $877,000.00 spendthrift trust established for him by his deceased mother. The majority acknowledges that claimants seeking alimony, child support, and unpaid taxes may attach a beneficiary's interest in a spendthrift trust, but concludes that the victim of a violent tort may not, reasoning that such a victim is only "a mere judgment creditor." For the reasons expressed herein, I respectfully disagree. . . .

The majority concedes that tort creditors do not have the benefit of notice, which, as was discussed in *Smith, supra*, is a primary purpose for not allowing the invasion of spendthrift trusts. Despite this, the majority concludes that Ms. Ryon's estate cannot reach the corpus of the spendthrift trust because its claim is nothing other "than a debt" and that "its exemption from the bar of a spendthrift trust" is not "a matter of public policy." The majority, in my opinion, is wrong.

This Court has held that a beneficiary's interest in a spendthrift trust may be attached to satisfy claims for alimony arrearages and for child support. Also, a spendthrift trust was attached for the payment of federal income taxes in *Mercantile Trust Co. v. Hofferbert*, 58 F. Supp. 701, 705-06 (D. Md. 1944). "[N]one of these cases," the majority states, "was premised on there having been a lack of notice. . . . Rather, the courts recognized a fundamental difference between these obligations and those of ordinary contract creditors." The fundamental difference is essentially that these obligations were premised upon judicial intervention and determination of sound public policy.

Just as it is sound public policy to permit the attachment of a spendthrift trust for alimony, child support, and taxes, it is also as sound to permit invasion to make victims of tortious conduct whole. Indeed, a tortfeasor may be liable not only for compensatory damages, but also punitive damages, which we allow in order to "punish the wrongdoer and to deter such conduct by the wrongdoer and others in the future." Consequently, to equate victims of tortious conduct with contract creditors and distinguish them from recipients of alimony, child support, and tax claims, is without merit.

As the majority concedes, spendthrift trusts are considered valid in Maryland in large part because, by virtue of filing requirements, creditors are put on at least constructive notice of the limited interest of the beneficiary of such a trust. Such notice allows creditors to protect themselves, something that Ms. Ryon could not have done. Moreover, the "duty-debt" distinction set forth by the majority as the basis for its holding is unavailing. The obligation to restitute a wrong is commensurate with the obligations to pay alimony, child support, and taxes. I agree with the commentators that "it is against public policy to permit the beneficiary of a spendthrift trust to enjoy an income under the trust without discharging his tort liabilities to others." *See* Scott on Trusts, [4th ed., §157.5, p. 220.] Consequently, I respectfully dissent.

———————————

UTC §503 addresses the issue of which creditors are preferred and "may obtain from a court an order attaching present or future distributions to or for the benefit of the beneficiary . . . " despite a spendthrift provision. The section creates three exceptions to unenforceability: a child, spouse or former spouse with an order for child or spousal support, lawyers who provide services to the beneficiary with respect to the trust (guess who wrote this provision?), the state and the U.S. government (which might be a creditor for income taxes or for Medicaid reimbursement).

UTC §503. Exceptions to Spendthrift Provision.

> (b) A spendthrift provision is unenforceable against:
> (1) a beneficiary's child, spouse, or former spouse who has a judgment or court order against the beneficiary for support or maintenance;
> (2) a judgment creditor who has provided services for the protection of a beneficiary's interest in the trust; and
> (3) a claim of this State or the United States to the extent a statute of this State or federal law so provides.
> (c) A claimant against which a spendthrift provision cannot be enforced may obtain from a court an order attaching present or future distributions to or for the benefit of the beneficiary. The court may limit the award to such relief as is appropriate under the circumstances.

Contrary to the *Restatement (Third) of Trusts* §59(b) (2003), the UTC does not provide an exception from a spendthrift clause for goods and services provided as necessities to the beneficiary. Even these creditors cannot compel a distribution that is within the trustee's discretion.

Section 503 has had a mixed reception in the states that have adopted the UTC, and not all of those states have adopted this section.

For states that have not yet adopted the UTC, exceptions to spendthrift protection will depend on case law.

QUESTIONS

1. *Who got what?* In *Shelley*, what did the former spouses receive? Why? And what did the children receive and why?

2. *The English system.* The widespread use of spendthrift clauses in the United States means that inherited wealth can be protected from the next generation's creditors. In England, spendthrift clauses are not enforced, although British law has developed alternative trust provisions that can provide similar protection. *See* Edward C. Halbach, Jr., *Uniform Acts, Restatements, and Trends in American Trust Law at Century's End*, 88 Calif. L. Rev. 1877, 1893 (1983). From a policy standpoint, should spendthrift clauses be enforced?

3. *Worthy creditors.* You are a state legislator. The legislature is considering a statute that would permit some or all of the following creditors to reach property held in trust despite a spendthrift clause. As a legislator, you are being asked to balance the rights of creditors and trust beneficiaries. Which one or more of the following would you support? On what policy grounds?

- Under no circumstances can a creditor reach an interest of a beneficiary. No exceptions.
- A child support judgment creditor can reach an interest of a beneficiary.
- An ex-spouse enforcing an order for alimony can reach an interest of a beneficiary.
- A tort creditor can reach an interest of a beneficiary.
- The state government can reach an interest of a beneficiary to recover Medicaid payments.
- The federal government can reach an interest of a beneficiary to recover taxes due.
- Under all circumstances a creditor can reach an interest of a beneficiary. In essence, this would abolish spendthrift clauses.

How, if at all, would your answers change if you were a lawyer with the state Department of Justice? An estate planning lawyer representing clients? A family law lawyer representing clients? A personal injury lawyer?

PROBLEMS

1. Nitai created an irrevocable, inter vivos trust for his nephew, Dashiel. The trust directs the trustee to distribute all the income to Dashiel, at least annually, and also directs the trustee to distribute the amounts the

trustee determines to be necessary for Dashiel's health, education, maintenance and support. Answer each of the following questions twice, first assuming that the trust agreement does not include a spendthrift clause and then assuming that the trust agreement includes a spendthrift clause.

a.   Dashiel has fallen behind on a bank loan he took out personally to help pay for law school. Can the bank look to the trust to satisfy Dashiel's outstanding debt and, if so, in what manner and to what extent?

b.   Dashiel used his credit card primarily to buy food, clothing and other necessities. He also used it to travel to Hawaii for Christmas. He has fallen behind and cannot even make the monthly minimum payments. Can the bank look to the trust to satisfy Dashiel's outstanding debt and, if so, in what manner and to what extent?

c.   Dashiel was married and had a child. He dissolved the marriage three years ago and was ordered to pay child and spousal support. He has not paid either for two years. Can his child and former spouse look to the trust to satisfy Dashiel's outstanding debt and, if so, in what manner and to what extent?

d.   Dashiel asks the trustee to distribute some of the principal of the trust so that he can travel to his sister's wedding. Can the trustee do so? If the trustee makes a distribution, can the bank reach the money distributed?

2.   Now assume that the trust in Problem 1 included the following provision, "my trustee may distribute to any child of Dashiel the amount the trustee determines to be necessary for the child's support in reasonable comfort." Answer Problem 1.c with this additional information.

EXERCISE

Alexander is concerned about his grandchild, Jordan. Jordan is 29, has graduated from college but has never held a full-time job, asks his parents for financial help from time to time and has had a problem with substance abuse. Alexander wants to create a trust to provide a "safety net" for Jordon, but he does not want Jordan to be able to pressure the trustee to make distributions, and he does not want Jordan's creditors to be able to reach the assets in the trust. How should the trust for Jordan be structured? What sort of distribution standard do you recommend?

3.   Creditors of a Beneficiary Who Is also a Settlor

a.   Revocable Trusts

With most revocable living trusts, the settlor wears many hats—the settlor, the trustee, the life income beneficiary and the person with the power to invade principal without limitation. The settlor retains the ability to control the assets through the power of revocation and invasion. Thus, whether there is a spendthrift provision or not, the assets of a revocable trust (and not merely the settlor's interests in the trust) remain reachable by the settlor's creditors, both during lifetime and at death. UTC §505(a). If creditors could not reach assets in a revocable trust, these trusts would provide individuals with a too easy creditor-avoidance tool.

b.   Irrevocable Trusts

Since revocable trusts do not provide asset protection, people with significant wealth have, over the years, sought other ways to protect their assets from creditors. One method is to transfer property to an irrevocable trust for the settlor's benefit and attach a spendthrift clause to it. This approach has been rejected as a means of protecting oneself from present and future creditors, except, as discussed below, with foreign and domestic asset protection trusts, The traditional rule provides that if a settlor creates an irrevocable trust, with the settlor as one of the beneficiaries, the existing and future creditors of the settlor can attach the settlor's interest. This is true whether or not the settlor's interest is subject to a spendthrift clause. Specifically, UTC §505(a)(2) says: "With respect to an irrevocable trust, a creditor or assignee of the settlor may reach the maximum amount that can be distributed to or for the settlor's benefit."

Another method that can be employed is to transfer property to an irrevocable trust for someone else's benefit. A transfer to someone else, whether in trust or in fee simple, is an effective way for the settlor to avoid the claims of *future* creditors. The problem with this solution, of course, is that the settlor loses the ability to enjoy the property.

Thus, the search has continued for a way for settlors to protect themselves from creditors without giving up the use of their property. Following the lead of some island countries, a growing number of states have changed their common law by statute to permit self-settled trusts with spendthrift clauses to protect the settlor from claims by *future* creditors. (Remember— the settlor can never protect herself from the claims of *existing* creditors by gratuitously transferring assets to another, whether in trust or otherwise, because doing so is deemed to be a fraudulent transfer.) These asset protection trusts are discussed next.

c.   Asset Protection Trusts—Foreign and Domestic

In the 1980s, a number of "tax haven" countries created laws to encourage trusts to be established there by permitting non-residents to establish irrevocable trusts that benefit the settlor while denying the settlor's creditors the right to reach the assets in those trusts. In the Cook Islands, the Cayman Islands and various Caribbean and South Pacific islands, a settlor can establish a trust with a local trustee (based in the off-shore jurisdiction) and be certain that the local courts will not enforce a judgment obtained elsewhere.

While the foreign courts will not require the assets to be used to pay the settlor's future debts, what is uncertain is what U.S. courts will do when faced with a U.S. creditor, a U.S. settlor-beneficiary and an offshore trust. The *Affordable Media* case, better known as the *Anderson* case because the settlors were the Andersons, gave us a first look at the issue. *Federal Trade Commission v. Affordable Media, LLC,* 179 F.3d 1228 (9th Cir. 1999). In 1995, Denyse and Michael Anderson set up an irrevocable trust in the Cook Islands. Just a couple of years later, they illegally made over $6.0 million in a telemarketing Ponzi scheme and deposited the money in the Cook Islands trust. In 1998, the Federal Trade Commission charged them with violations of the Federal Trade Commission Act and the Telemarketing Sales Rule. The district court issued a temporary restraining order and an injunction, requiring the Andersons to repatriate any assets held for their benefit out-side the United States. The Andersons and a trust company licensed in the Cook Islands were co-trustees of their Cook Islands trust. The Andersons sent a letter to the corporate trustee, asking the trustee to repatriate the assets, but the corporate trustee notified the Andersons that it would not do so. (Surprise, surprise.) The district court held the Andersons in contempt for refusing to repatriate the assets, and they served six months in jail before the court purged the Andersons of their contempt. Eventually they settled with the FTC for $1.2 million, much less than the $20.0 million the FTC had sought.

Lawyers using offshore asset protection trusts usually suggest that the settlor name someone else as the trustee or trust protector. If the settlor is not the trustee, the settlor is yet another step removed from the assets. This structure helps mitigate the argument that the settlor has access to the trust assets. Offshore trusts continue to be used, but generally only for very wealthy clients, and, as the *Anderson* case shows, at some risk.

After watching trust business leave the United States, Jonathan Blatt-machr, a New York lawyer, and his brother, Douglas J. Blattmachr, who had trust and investment management experience, teamed up to convince the Alaska legislature to amend Alaska law to permit creditor protection for settlors in self-settled irrevocable spendthrift trusts if managed by an Alas-kan trustee. The concept is simple: permit a self-settled spendthrift trust to protect assets of the settlor-beneficiary from her creditors in the same way a spendthrift trust protects assets of a non-settlor beneficiary. Jonathan drafted the statute and Douglas set up a trust company, The Alaska Trust Company, to serve as the Alaskan trustee. The Alaska Trust Company's Web site provides information about the Blattmachrs' role in the Alaska legislation and the history of the company. *See* www.Alaskatrust.com. The Alaska statute provides that Alaskan law will apply to assets held in an Alas-kan trust by an Alaskan trustee; the settlor need not reside in Alaska. Alaska Stat. §13.36.035 (2008).

Following Alaska's lead, Delaware quickly enacted similar legislation, and Missouri, New Hampshire, Nevada, Oklahoma, Rhode Island, South Dakota, Tennessee, Utah and Wyoming did the same. Each statute provides that a specified number of years after the creation of the trust, a spendthrift clause will be effective against creditors of the settlor whose claims did not exist at the time the settlor created the trust.

There are certain common requirements among the state statutes that must be satisfied for protection:

- Shelter is not available for existing debts; only those liabilities that arise after the trust is established and funded are protected.
- The trust must be irrevocable.
- The settlor may not be a mandatory beneficiary, only a discretionary beneficiary.
- The settlor may not be a trustee.
- Some assets of the trust and the trustee must be located in the state where the trust is established and administered.

Conflict of laws rules remain untested with respect to asset protection trusts. For example, if a California resident sets up and transfers assets to an Alaskan trust, it is not clear whether California courts would agree to apply Alaska law if a California creditor sues the settlor in California. A number of scholars have raised concerns about domestic asset protection trusts. *See* Stewart S. Sterk, *Asset Protection Trusts: Trust Law's Race to the Bottom*, 85 CORNELL L. REV. 1035 (2000); Randall Gingiss, *Putting a Stop to Asset Protection Trusts*, 51 BAYLOR L. REV. 987 (1999).

Both the *Restatement (Third) of Trusts* §58(2) and the UTC §505(a)(2) provide that a settlor's creditors can reach a self-settled spendthrift trust, explicitly rejecting the protections allegedly offered by an offshore or Alaskan-style trust. The Comment to UTC §505(a)(2) explains:

> Subsection (a)(2) . . . follows traditional doctrine in providing that a settlor who is also a beneficiary may not use the trust as a shield against the settlor's creditors. The drafters of the Uniform Trust Code concluded that traditional doctrine reflects sound policy. Consequently, the drafters rejected the approach taken in States like Alaska and Delaware, both of which allow a settlor to retain a beneficial interest immune from creditor claims. Under the Code, whether the trust contains a spendthrift provision or not, a creditor of the settlor may reach the maximum amount that the trustee could have paid to the settlor-beneficiary. If the trustee has discretion to distribute the entire income and principal to the settlor, the effect of this subsection is to place the settlor's creditors in the same position as if the trust had not been created.

For an interesting look at self-settled spendthrift trusts, including a discussion of arguments in favor of and opposing the use and enforceability of spendthrift clauses, see Adam Hirsch, *Spendthrift Trusts and Public Policy: Economic and Cognitive Perspectives*, 73 WASH. U.L.Q. 1 (1995); Michael

Sjuggerud, *Defeating the Self-Settled Spendthrift Trust in Bankruptcy*, 28 FLA. ST. U. L. REV. 977 (2001) (analyzing self-settled spendthrift trusts from the perspective of creditors and offering suggestions about how creditors can reach assets in the trusts).

PROBLEM

The preceding discussion highlights how people might be able to reduce the risk that their interests in trust property will be attached by later creditors. Because of all the defenses available, creditors generally prefer to attach other assets before going after property in a trust. What other approaches could you ethically recommend to clients to reduce the risk of losing their income and property to the claims of future creditors, especially if they own a business or are engaged in a line of work that could lead to large liabilities? *See* Randall Roth, *Protecting Assets from Creditors Legally, Ethically and Morally (Part 1)*, ALI-ABA EST. PLAN. COURSE MATERIAL J. 43 (Oct. 2002).

D.   MODIFICATION AND TERMINATION OF TRUSTS

As we have discussed, the settlor's manifested intention in creating the trust governs the powers of the trustees and the rights of the beneficiaries. The terms provided in the trust document control a host of issues, ranging from the way the trustees make distributions to when the trust terminates. The terms also control the manner in which modification of the trust can be accomplished. The problem is that trusts can exist for a long time after they are created and things may change. The law is concerned with balancing the intent of the settlor with the beneficiaries' needs or desires to modify the terms of a trust or to terminate it.

American law has long permitted a settlor's wishes to control the circumstances under which a trust could be modified or terminated, regardless of whether the beneficiaries would like to do something else. Recent cases and the UTC, however, provide the beneficiaries with greater opportunities for amendment or early termination of a trust, even if doing so appears to be inconsistent with the wishes of the settlor. One reason for these changes is that with the repeal of the Rule Against Perpetuities in many states, more estate planners are using perpetual (or "dynasty") trusts in planning for clients. Also, the risk of human error increases as trusts become increasingly complex for tax reasons. In addition, many trusts are being established based on advice given by inexperienced lawyers and even by non-lawyers or by individuals getting the forms through the Internet. This leads to provisions that do not work well. Statutory changes that provide more flexibility in amending and terminating trusts may actually aid the settlor's objectives as well as serve the best interests of the beneficiaries over time. For more information about modification and termination, see Ron Chester, *Modification and Termination of Trusts in the 21st Century: The Uniform Trust Code Leads a Quiet Revolution*, 35 REAL PROP. PROB. & TR. J. 697 (Winter 2001).[1]

In this section, we look first at the rules that permit modification by the settlor under a retained power to modify or revoke. We then turn to irrevocable trusts and consider modification when the settlor is alive and then after the settlor's death. At the end of the chapter, we look specifically at the termination of trusts. As you read the materials on modification, however, keep in mind that the rules we discuss on modification typically also apply to termination of a trust.

1. Revocable Trusts

a. Power Retained by the Settlor to Modify or Revoke

As we discussed in Chapter 5, UTC §602(a) presumes a trust to be revocable unless the settlor states otherwise. In some states the common law presumption of irrevocability still applies, so a trust instrument should indicate whether the trust is revocable or irrevocable. A trust drafted by a lawyer normally will do so. If the trust is revocable, the settlor can modify or revoke terms of the trust according to the means specified in the trust instrument. UTC §602 provides guidance on revocation if the trust instrument does not indicate what the settlor must do to revoke the trust.

We will look at the rules for revocable trusts in connection with modification, but usually if a settlor has retained the power to modify a trust, she will also have retained the power to revoke (and terminate) the trust. Therefore, we will refer to the powers the settlor retains as the power to revoke the trust and discuss these trusts as revocable trusts.

Here are the UTC rules on revocation of a revocable trust.

UTC §602. Revocation or Amendment of Revocable Trust.

(a) Unless the terms of a trust expressly provide that the trust is irrevocable, the settlor may revoke or amend the trust. This subsection does not apply to a trust created under an instrument executed before [the effective date of this [Code]]. . . .

(c) The settlor may revoke or amend a revocable trust:

---

1. British law has long provided less deference to the intent of the settlor than does American law. British law views the trust as the property of the beneficiaries and significantly relaxes dead hand control (control by the settlor from the grave) over the trust. *See* English Variation of Trusts Act of 1958, 6 & 7 Eliz. 2, ch. 53 s1.

(1) by substantial compliance with a method provided in the terms of the trust; or

(2) if the terms of the trust do not provide a method or the method provided in the terms is not expressly made exclusive, by:

(A) a later will or codicil that expressly refers to the trust or specifically devises property that would otherwise have passed according to the terms of the trust; or

(B) any other method manifesting clear and convincing evidence of the settlor's intent.

A settlor normally revokes a trust by giving written notice to the trustee (often both positions are held by the same person) and taking back title to the property. A provision in a trust document might say:

Settlor reserves for settlor's lifetime the following powers, which settlor may exercise at any time or times:

(A) to revoke the trust by a writing;

(B) upon trustees' consent, to amend the trust, in whole or in part, by a writing, including the settlor's will; and

(C) to direct, by a memorandum which settlor may leave at settlor's death, distribution by trustees on settlor's death of any of settlor's tangible personal property, except such property used in any business in which settlor has an interest, together with any insurance policies covering such property and claims under such policies.

The settlor acting under this provision could write on a piece of paper, "I revoke the Maria Gonzalez Revocable Trust dated November 11, 2009." If the settlor is acting as trustee, delivery is automatic. If someone else is trustee, Maria must send the revocation to the trustee.

Exact compliance with the method prescribed in the trust instrument is not required. UTC §602(c)(1) permits "substantial compliance" for revocation, and UTC §602(c)(2) permits revocation by other means. The comments to the section explain that an act that demonstrates the settlor's intent may constitute revocation. That being said, the UTC sets a high standard of evidence—clear and convincing—for revocation to occur by means other that the method provided in the terms of the trust. Note also that if the terms of the trust do not provide a method or the method provided in the terms is not expressly made exclusive, UTC §602(c)(2)(A) permits revocation by a will or codicil that specifically refers to the trust or that devises property that would have passed under the terms of the trust. However, not all states that have enacted the UTC permit revocation by will. *See, e.g.,* OR. REV. STAT. §130.505 (2009).

b. Revocation by Someone Acting for the Settlor

A revocable trust does not necessarily become irrevocable if the settlor loses capacity. The settlor may regain capacity and be able to modify or revoke the trust herself, or someone may be able to modify or revoke the trust on the settlor's behalf. Whether someone else can modify or revoke the trust raises difficult questions, because a settlor often creates a revocable trust to plan for the possibility of incapacity. Under some circumstances an agent acting under a power of attorney or a conservator may be able to revoke the trust. We address the questions of when and how this can happen in Chapter 13. In that chapter we also examine UTC §602, which tries to limit disruption of the settlor's estate plan by providing safeguards for revocation or modification by others.

PROBLEM

William Grant created the William Grant Revocable Trust, which stated:

> "The settlor reserves the right to revoke or modify this trust at any time, by delivery of a written statement of revocation to the then acting trustee."

William's will, executed after the revocable trust, includes the following provision:

> "I hereby revoke the William Grant Revocable Trust."

Is this effective to revoke the trust as of the date the will is executed or the date William dies? Does it matter whether William or First Bank is the trustee? (Reflect back on the discussion in the will substitutes chapter, Chapter 4, about revoking a will substitute by means of a will and ask yourself whether revoking a revocable trust is different from trying to revoke a beneficiary designation with an insurance company.)

2. Irrevocable Trusts

a. Making Modification Unnecessary

Before we turn to the rules for modification or termination of irrevocable trusts, we should consider planning measures that can build flexibility into trusts so that modification will not become necessary, even as things change over time. The settlor may want to make it easier or more difficult for beneficiaries to make changes over time, and drafting can carry out these wishes. The settlor may want to consider including in the terms of the trust one or more of the following:

- Standards of discretion that give the trustee a broad range of discretion;
- A definition of spouse that would include only the person to whom the settlor or a beneficiary is currently married so that divorce will terminate any beneficial interest for the person;
- A provision giving the beneficiaries the power to replace the trustee with a different, independent trustee;
- A provision giving the trustee the power to make loans to beneficiaries;
- A provision giving the trustee the power to change nondispositive provisions of the trust;
- Powers of appointment exercisable by a spouse or other beneficiaries (see Chapter 8).

b.   Modification or Termination with Settlor's Consent

Irrevocable trusts are not meant to be modified or amended. As we have discussed, a settlor may build flexibility into a trust by granting broad discretion to the trustee or through the use of powers of appointment. If, however, the terms of the trust were narrowly drafted, or if circumstances change in unanticipated ways, modification may become necessary. The common law, *Restatement (Third) of Trusts* §65, and UTC §411(a) all provide that if the settlor and all the beneficiaries agree, they can modify (or terminate) an irrevocable trust. Because the settlor is included in the decision to modify, modification can occur even if the trust had a material purpose inconsistent with the modification. (See discussion below on the material purpose doctrine.)

UTC §411. Modification or Termination of Noncharitable Irrevocable Trust by Consent.

(a) [Alt. #1—A noncharitable irrevocable trust may be modified or terminated upon consent of the settlor and all beneficiaries, even if the modification or termination is inconsistent with a material purpose of the trust.]

[Alt. #2—If, upon petition, the court finds that the settlor and all beneficiaries consent to the modification or termination of a noncharitable irrevocable trust, the court shall approve the modification or termination even if the modification or termination is inconsistent with a material purpose of the trust. . . .

Although modification by the settlor and beneficiaries had long been part of the common law, when estate planners began to look at the UTC, they became concerned that the ability of the settlor to join with the beneficiaries to modify or terminate an irrevocable trust could have adverse tax consequences. They believed the IRS might view this power as a retained interest for life, which could cause inclusion of the value of the trust property in the settlor's estate for estate tax purposes under Internal Revenue Code §§2036 or 2038. *Cf.* Rev. Rul. 95-58, 1995-2 C.B. 191. Out of caution, some states chose to delete UTC §411(a) when they enacted the UTC, and the uniform version of the statute now puts this provision in brackets.

As we know, the terms of a trust supersede the default rules of the statute. So, if the trust says the settlor cannot participate in the modification or termination of the trust, that provision ends the inquiry. Due to the tax concern mentioned above, most attorneys draft a provision preventing the settlor from modifying or terminating the trust. A trust provision that speaks to the irrevocable nature of the trust might look like the following:

> This agreement shall be irrevocable and settlor shall have no right or power, whether alone or in conjunction with others, in whatever capacity, to alter, amend, revoke or terminate this agreement, or any of the terms of this agreement, in whole or in part, or to designate the persons who shall possess or enjoy the trust estate, or the income from the trust estate.

c. Modification or Termination Without Settlor's Consent (Usually After Settlor's Death)

If the settlor is dead and the settlor's consent is no longer available, or if the settlor is alive and refuses to consent to a modification, the beneficiaries of an irrevocable trust may nonetheless be able to terminate the trust or modify its terms. The law makes modification after the settlor's death difficult, however, especially when the desired modification may conflict with a material purpose that the settlor had in establishing the trust. If the settlor is still alive, modification will be even more difficult because the settlor can argue against the modification.

i. *Material Purpose Doctrine*

In 1899, *Claflin v. Claflin*, 20 N.E. 454 (Mass. 1899), established the rule that modification by beneficiaries will be permitted only if the modification is not contrary to a material purpose of the settlor. This rule, known as the *Claflin* doctrine or the material purpose doctrine, prevents modification of many common provisions in trusts. *Claflin* itself involved a provision that delayed termination of a trust until the beneficiary reached age 30. The beneficiary asked that the court terminate the trust when he reached age 21 and the court refused, noting that the settlor had the right to impose restrictions on property transferred in trust and to have those restrictions enforced. *See also In re Estate of Brown*, 528 A.2d 752 (Vt. 1987). In *Estate of Brown*, the beneficiaries wanted to terminate a trust and distribute the corpus to the lifetime beneficiaries. The lifetime beneficiaries were the parents of the remainder beneficiaries, and the remainder beneficiaries consented to the request to terminate the trust. The court refused, finding a material purpose in the management of the property for the lifetimes of the beneficiaries.

Some cases have found that the creation of a trust with life estate and remainder beneficiaries did not, without more information about the intent of the settlor, indicate that the trust could not be terminated early. For example, in *Bennett v. Tower Grove Bank & Trust Co.*, 434 S.W.2d 560 (Mo. 1968), the income beneficiary (the settlor's daughter) transferred her life estate to the remainder beneficiaries (her children). The settlor had imposed no restraint on his daughter's ability to sell or dispose of her interest, and nothing else indicated a concern that the trust be available for her throughout her life. In response to the request by the grandchildren to terminate the trust and allow the property to be distributed to them, the court said, "[Absent] other circumstances to show the intention of the testator, we are of the opinion that the mere creation of the trust for successive beneficiaries did not indicate a purpose other than the preservation of the corpus for the remaindermen and, therefore, the trust may be terminated by the action here taken."*Id.* at 564.

Although lawyers routinely include a spendthrift clause, the traditional common law view is that a spendthrift clause is presumed to be a material purpose, thus precluding modification by beneficiaries. *See* RESTATEMENT (SECOND) OF TRUSTS §337 (1959).

If the presumption is reversed, as both UTC §411(c) (see below) and *Restatement (Third) of Trusts* §65, cmt. e have done, then the mere existence of a spendthrift clause does not require evidence that the spendthrift provision was not intended as a material purpose. Under UTC §411(c), modification will be denied only if the court determines that the spendthrift clause constitutes a material purpose of the particular trust or that the modification would affect other material purposes of that trust. Whether the UTC and *Restatement* changes will become the majority approach is not yet clear. Revisions to the UTC in 2004 put §411(c) into brackets in recognition of the fact that the provision is not being uniformly adopted. It is worth noting that the trust in *Bennett*, discussed above, did not include a spendthrift clause. It appears from the court's reasoning that if the trust had included a spendthrift clause, the court might not have permitted the termination.

In re Trust of Stuchell
801 P.2d 852 (Or. App. 1990)

BUTTLER, Judge.

Petitioner appeals from the trial court's dismissal of her petition for approval of an agreement to modify a trust. The stated purpose of the proposed modification is to protect a retarded remainder beneficiary. We affirm.

Petitioner is one of two surviving life-income beneficiaries of a testamentary trust established by her grandfather, J.W. Stuchell, in his 1947 will. The trust will terminate on the death of the last income beneficiary, at which time the remainder is to be distributed equally to petitioner's children or their lineal descendants, *per stirpes*. One of petitioner's four children, John Harrell (Harrell), is a mentally retarded 25 year old who is unable to live independently without assistance. His condition is not expected to improve, and he will probably require care and supervision for the rest of his life. No guardian or conservator has been appointed for him. The Oregon Mental Health Division currently provides his basic care in the Eastern Oregon Training Center, a residential facility for mentally and physically disabled persons. He receives Medicaid and Social Security benefits, both of which have income and resource limitations for participants.

In December, 1989, petitioner requested the court to approve, on behalf of Harrell, an agreement, which had been approved by the other income beneficiary and remaindermen, to modify the trust. If the trust is not modified, Harrell's remainder will be distributed directly to him if he survives the two life-income beneficiaries. If and when that happens, his ability to qualify for public assistance will be severely limited. The proposed modification provides for the continuation of the trust, if Harrell survives the two life-income beneficiaries, and contains elaborate provisions that are designed to avoid his becoming disqualified, in whole or in part, for any public assistance programs. The stated purpose is to ensure that the trust funds be used only as a secondary source of funds to supplement, rather than to replace, his current income and benefits from public assistance. . . .

[Petitioner] contends that *Closset v. Burtchaell*, 112 Or. 585, 230 P. 554 (1924), is authority for allowing a court to approve her proposed modification. That case holds that a trust may be terminated, if (1) all of the beneficiaries agree, (2) none of the beneficiaries is under a legal disability and (3) the trust's purposes would not be frustrated by doing so. 112 Or. at 597, 230 P. 554. The court said:

> It is a well-established rule that where the purposes for which a trust has been created have been accomplished and all of the beneficiaries are *sui juris*, a court will, on the application of all of the beneficiaries or of one possessing the entire beneficial interest declare a termination of the trust[.]

Restatement (Second) Trusts §337 (1959) follows that rule. By its terms, that rule applies only to the termination of a trust under very limited circumstances. Petitioner, relying on *Restatement (Second) Trusts* §167(1) (1959), urges us to extend the rule to permit modification. That section provides:

> The court will direct or permit the trustee to deviate from a term of the trust if owing to circumstances not known to the settlor and not anticipated by him compliance would defeat or substantially impair the accomplishment of the purposes of the trust; and in such case, if necessary to carry out the purposes of the trust, the court may direct or permit the trustee to do acts which are not authorized or are forbidden by the terms of the trust.

Comment b to that section states:

> The court will not permit or direct the trustee to deviate from the terms of the trust merely because such deviation would be more advantageous to the beneficiaries than a compliance with such direction.

Even assuming that the *Restatement* rule were to be adopted as the law in Oregon, it is clear that the limitation imposed by the comment would preclude permitting the proposed amendment, the only purpose of which is to make the trust more advantageous to the beneficiaries. The most obvious advantage would be to the three remaindermen who have consented to the amendment.

There being no statutory or common law authority for a court to approve the proposed agreement modifying the trust, the trial court did not err in dismissing the petition.

Affirmed.

NOTES AND QUESTIONS

1. *Legislature to the rescue.* After the *Stuchell* case, the Oregon legislature adopted a statute permitting modification (or other nonjudicial settlement agreement with respect to the trust) without court approval if the settlor (if living), the beneficiaries concerned with the subject of the agreement and the trustee all consent. The rule has been incorporated into Oregon's version of the UTC. *See* OR. REV. STAT. §130.045 (2009).

2. *Planning.* If Mr. Stuchell had come to you for help in setting up the trust, what might you have suggested to build in flexibility? Remember that when Mr. Stuchell created the trust, the disabled beneficiary was not yet born.

ii. Modification by Consent of the Beneficiaries

If no material purpose of the trust would be frustrated by its termination or modification, the beneficiaries can agree to a modification, if *all* of the beneficiaries consent. UTC §411(b). Even if all beneficiaries do not agree, a court may authorize modification under certain conditions. UTC §411(e).

UTC §411. Modification or Termination of Noncharitable Irrevocable Trust by Consent.

(b) A noncharitable irrevocable trust may be *terminated* upon consent of all of the beneficiaries if the court concludes that continuance of the trust is not necessary to achieve any material purpose of the trust. A noncharitable irrevocable trust may be *modified* upon consent of all of the beneficiaries if the court concludes that modification is not inconsistent with a material purpose of the trust.

[(c) A spendthrift provision in the terms of the trust is not presumed to constitute a material purpose of the trust.] . . .

(e) If not all of the beneficiaries consent to a proposed modification or termination of the trust under subsection (a) or (b), the modification or termination may be approved by the court if the court is satisfied that:

(1) if all of the beneficiaries had consented, the trust could have been modified or terminated under this section; and

(2) the interests of a beneficiary who does not consent will be adequately protected.

iii. Representation

In order to obtain consent from all the beneficiaries, representation of some beneficiaries may be necessary. Some beneficiaries may be minors or under another legal disability, while others may not be born. Representation may be needed for a number of reasons, including consent for things like modification, receipt of required notices and in connection with the resolution of disputes involving the trust. Common law trust doctrine provides some rules on representation for these beneficiaries, but the law in many states has not adequately addressed representation.

As we discussed in Chapter 6, the UTC provides more complete rules for several types of representation. If a living, competent, adult beneficiary has exactly the same interest as beneficiaries who are not legally able to give consent, then the consent of the living, competent, adult beneficiary will bind unborn or unascertained beneficiaries. For example, a trust provision for "the children of Sarah" may include minor or unborn beneficiaries.

If Sarah has one child who is an adult and is legally competent, then that child's consent will bind any minor or unborn siblings. UTC §304 (reproduced in Chapter 6).

If a beneficiary is alive but not legally competent, a guardian, conservator, parent, agent or trustee can represent that beneficiary. UTC §303 (reproduced in Chapter 6). If the trust provides "for the children of Sarah," and Sarah has a minor child, then a parent or guardian can give consent for that child. If Sarah herself is alive, she can represent the child's interest as the child's parent, but only if her interest is not in conflict with the child's interest. For example, if the trust provides for distributions to Sarah for life and then the remainder to her children, their interests may be in conflict, at least with respect to some issues. Sarah might be able to represent the child in connection with the notice provisions but would not be able to represent the child in connection with a modification that would shift their interests. If no other representation is possible, a court can appoint a representative. UTC §305.

These representation rules apply to modification and termination, and, as we discussed in Chapter 6, they are used when the trust must distribute notices and reports to beneficiaries.

UTC §305. Appointment of Representative.

(a) If the court determines that an interest is not represented under this [article], or that the otherwise available representation might be inadequate, the court may appoint a [representative] to receive notice, give consent, and otherwise represent, bind, and act on behalf of a minor, incapacitated, or unborn individual, or a person whose identity or location is unknown. A [representative] may be appointed to represent several persons or interests.

(b) A [representative] may act on behalf of the individual represented with respect to any matter arising under this [Code], whether or not a judicial proceeding concerning the trust is pending.

(c) In making decisions, a [representative] may consider general benefit accruing to the living members of the individual's family.

QUESTIONS

1. *No consent.* Under UTC §411, a court can modify a trust even if all beneficiaries do not consent, if the interests of a beneficiary who does not consent will be adequately protected. How do you think the interests will be protected? Who will protect those interests?

2. *Consent of the unborn.* If a trustee needed to get the consent of unborn or unascertained beneficiaries through representation, how could the trustee protect against a conflict of interest?

iv. *Changed Circumstances—Equitable Deviation*

The doctrine of equitable deviation allows a court to modify a provision to give effect to the intent of the settlor rather than to change it. A court can modify a provision not only due to changed circumstances, but also due to unanticipated circumstances—something the settlor did not know about when the settlor created the trust. This approach applies to charitable trusts as well as to private trusts. In the past, courts were reluctant to permit modification based on changed circumstances, but the law in this area is changing.

Courts are more willing to use equitable deviation to modify administrative terms (those addressing operation of the trust) than dispositive terms (those addressing distributions). In fact, the *Restatement (Third) of Trusts* §66 (2003) imposes a duty on the trustee to request modification of an administrative provision that might cause substantial harm to the trust. In *Matter of Pulitzer*, 139 Misc. 575, 249 N.Y.S. 87 (1932), *aff'd mem.* 237 App. Div. 808, 260 N.Y.S. 975 (1932), the settlor, owner of two major newspaper publishing companies, directed the trustee to retain the stock of the companies. The court permitted the trustee to sell the stock when it became apparent that the trust would suffer extreme economic hardship if the stock could not be sold because the companies were losing large sums of money during the Great Depression of the 1930s. (We discussed this case briefly in Chapter 6 in connection with the fiduciary duty to diversify assets.) In *Donnelly v. National Bank of Washington*, 179 P.2d 333 (1947), the court allowed the modification of a termination provision imposed by the settlor. The settlor had directed that the trust created for his grandson's legal education be terminated when the grandchild reached a certain age. The grandson got drafted into the military and was unable to complete his legal education before the deadline. The court said that extending the trust furthered the settlor's intent to provide for the legal education of his grandson.

UTC §412 goes further and provides that dispositive as well as administrative provisions may be modified due to changed circumstances. In fact, the UTC says that even termination of the trust is possible if doing so will further the purpose of the trust.

UTC §412. Modification or Termination Because of Unanticipated Circumstances or Inability to Administer Trust Effectively.

(a) The court may *modify* the administrative or dispositive terms of a trust or *terminate* the trust if, because of circumstances not anticipated by the settlor, modification or termination will further the purposes of the trust. To the extent practicable, the modification must be made in accordance with the settlor's probable intention.

(b) The court may *modify* the administrative terms of a trust if continuation of the trust on its existing terms would be impracticable or wasteful or impair the trust's administration.

(c) Upon termination of a trust under this section, the trustee shall distribute the trust property in a manner consistent with the purposes of the trust. [Emphasis added by authors.]

v.   Modification to Fix a Mistake

The common law has always permitted reformation of inter vivos documents, including trusts, when there was a mistake of fact or law. UTC §415 applies this common law rule to all trusts. If a trust provision resulted from a mistake, then extrinsic evidence can be used to show the mistake. To avoid credibility issues when evidence beyond the document is used, the statute requires clear and convincing evidence to establish the mistake. The mistake may be either one of inducement, when the settlor was mistaken as to a fact or the law, or one of expression, when the language in the document fails to carry out the settlor's intent.

UTC §415. Reformation to Correct Mistakes.

The court may reform the terms of a trust, even if unambiguous, to conform the terms to the settlor's intention if it is proved by clear and convincing evidence that both the settlor's intent and the terms of the trust were affected by a mistake of fact or law, whether in expression or inducement.

vi.   Small Trust Termination

A trust document drafted by a lawyer will often contain a provision permitting termination if the value of the assets in the trust drops below a specified amount. The UTC provides this flexibility even if the terms of a trust do not. UTC §414 states that a trust may be terminated if the value of the trust falls below $50,000 and if the trustee determines that the value of the trust property is insufficient to justify the cost of administration. The trustee may decide not to terminate a trust with property below the indicated value if the trust has an important purpose that makes continuation of the trust important, even if doing so is expensive relative to the value of the assets.

UTC §414. Modification or Termination of Uneconomic Trust.

(a) After notice to the qualified beneficiaries, the trustee of a trust consisting of trust property having a total value less than [$50,000] may terminate the trust if the trustee concludes that the value of the trust property is insufficient to justify the cost of administration.

(b) The court may modify or terminate a trust or remove the trustee and appoint a different trustee if it determines that the value of the trust property is insufficient to justify the cost of administration.

(c) Upon termination of a trust under this section, the trustee shall distribute the trust property in a manner consistent with the purposes of the trust.

(d) This section does not apply to an easement for conservation or preservation.

vii. *Modification to Achieve Tax Objectives*

The UTC permits a court to modify a trust to achieve the settlor's tax objectives, as long as the modification is not contrary to the donor's probable intent, particularly with respect to dispositive provisions. UTC §416. For example, a trust that provides a life estate for the settlor's spouse with a power to appoint to herself or to their children as the need arises, might be modified to clarify that the right to invade is a general one not limited by ascertainable standards in order to obtain a marital tax deduction. A modification would still provide a payout to the spouse and remainder to the children but would be structured in a way that meets the requirements for a deduction.

UTC §416. Modification to Achieve Settlor's Tax Objectives.

To achieve the settlor's tax objectives, the court may modify the terms of a trust in a manner that is not contrary to the settlor's probable intention. The court may provide that the modification has retroactive effect.

viii. *Combining Trusts or Dividing a Trust*

A trustee may combine two trusts into one trust or divide one trust into two trusts if doing so would not adversely affect the purposes of the trust or any beneficiary. UTC §417. A trustee might decide to combine two trusts to save administrative costs. For example, Aunt Sue might have created a trust for Niece Nelly under her will and Aunt Liz, thinking this a good idea, might have done the same under her will. Combining these two trusts would make management more efficient and less expensive. A trustee might want to divide a trust for tax reasons or for management reasons, in order to keep shares for beneficiaries separate. A well-drafted trust might include provisions for combining trusts or dividing a trust, with instructions as to when and under what circumstances the trustee could make those decisions. UTC §417 now makes combining or dividing trusts possible when the terms of the trust did not anticipate the need for doing so.

UTC §417. Combination and Division of Trusts.

> After notice to the qualified beneficiaries, a trustee may combine two or more trusts into a single trust or divide a trust into two or more separate trusts, if the result does not impair rights of any beneficiary or adversely affect achievement of the purposes of the trust.

3.   Termination

a.   According to the Terms of the Trust

A trust will usually terminate pursuant to its terms. If a trust provides a life estate to Derek and then remainder to Eloise, the trust will terminate on Derek's death. At that time, the trustee will distribute the remaining assets to Eloise. A trust will also terminate if the corpus is gone. For example, assume a trust provides discretionary income and principal to Derek, and then remainder to Derek when he reaches age 30. If the trustee uses all of the trust assets to pay for Derek's education, the trust will terminate when no corpus remains.

UTC §410. Modification or Termination of Trust; Proceedings for Approval or Disapproval.

> (a) In addition to the methods of termination prescribed by Sections 411 through 414, a trust terminates to the extent the trust is revoked or expires pursuant to its terms, no purpose of the trust remains to be achieved, or the purposes of the trust have become unlawful, contrary to public policy, or impossible to achieve.

b. By Agreement

If the settlor and all the beneficiaries agree, they can terminate a trust. See the discussion above on modification if settlor and all the beneficiaries consent. *See* RESTATEMENT (THIRD) OF TRUSTS §65 (2003); UTC §411(a).

c. Without Settlor Consent or After the Settlor's Death

All the provisions discussed in connection with modification also apply to termination. For example, a court can terminate a trust if all beneficiaries agree and if the court determines "that continuance of the trust is not necessary to achieve any material purpose of the trust." UTC §411(b).

PROBLEMS

1. Cyrus created an irrevocable trust for his nephew, Gideon. The trust provides for distributions for Gideon's health, support, maintenance and education until he turns 30, when the entire trust is distributed to him. If Gideon dies before reaching age 30, the trust is distributed to his then living descendants, by representation, and if none, to Cyrus's then living descendants, by representation. Esther (Cyrus's sister and Gideon's mother) is trustee.

   a. Gideon is 26 and has finished college. The trust still has $60,000 in it. Cyrus, Esther and Gideon would all like to terminate the trust. How would you advise them to proceed? If Cyrus is dead, how would you advise Esther and Gideon?

   b. Assume the trust provides for distributions for Gideon's health, support, maintenance and education for his life. On Gideon's death the remaining corpus will be distributed to his then living descendants, by representation. Cyrus is no longer alive. The trust has $2.0 million in assets. How would you advise Gideon, who is 45 and would like to terminate the trust? Does it matter whether Gideon has children? How would you advise Esther?

2. When Gene died in 1969, his will created a trust for his daughter, Denise, and her descendants. Denise's brother is the trustee. The trust terms directed the trustee to pay Denise the income during her life and on her death to distribute the corpus to her descendants. When Gene died, Denise had two children, Angie and Benton. After Gene's death, Denise had a third child, Charlene, who was born with a serious mental disability. Denise kept Charlene at home when she was young, but in recent years Charlene has lived in a residential facility. She receives money for her care from the state through its Medicaid program. Denise is now in her late 70s and is worried about Charlene. The trust has $300,000 in assets. If the trust terminates and distributes $100,000 to Charlene, she will lose her govern-

ment benefits. The money can be spent on her care, but her care is so expensive that the money will not last long, and Denise worries that Charlene may then have trouble re-qualifying for benefits or that there may be a gap between the time the money is gone and she is able to re-qualify for government benefits.

  a. Advise Denise. Can the trust be modified? If so, how?
  b. Now assume that Gene consults you before his death. At the time he talks with you, Denise has two children, neither with disabilities. Denise plans to have more. Is there anything you can recommend in drafting the trust that would have made dealing with the later circumstances easier?

8 POWERS OF APPOINTMENT AND THE RULE AGAINST PERPETUITIES

In this chapter, we learn the terminology that applies to powers of appointment, and then we examine how a donor creates a power of appointment and how the donee exercises the power. We consider a number of problems that can arise in connection with the exercise of a power of appointment and what happens when a donor does not exercise a power or exercises it ineffectively. The chapter includes a look at the rights of creditors of the donee in property subject to a power of appointment. The chapter reviews briefly the tax rules that apply to nonfiduciary powers of appointment and to fiduciary powers held by trustees.

In this chapter we also examine the Rule Against Perpetuities. We do not analyze the Rule in depth; rather we address the key issues an estate planner must consider. Detailed discussion of the Rule is beyond the scope of this book.

A. WHAT IS A POWER OF APPOINTMENT?

1. Definition

Settlors can build flexibility into a trust in several ways. As we discussed in Chapter 7, the settlor can grant the trustee discretionary authority to make distributions to specified beneficiaries. The trustee's discretion can be substantial or limited. The fiduciary duties we discussed in Chapter 6 govern the trustee's exercise of the discretionary authority. The trustee's duties in exercising the powers depend on the grant of discretion, the beneficiaries and the general fiduciary duties that apply to trustees.

Another way to build flexibility into a trust is to give someone other than the trustee, often a beneficiary, a power of appointment. Through a power of appointment the settlor can give decision-making authority to another person, to be exercised at some later time. The settlor can create a trust that may last for many years, but allow a person holding a power of appointment to take into consideration changes in the family, the beneficiaries or economic conditions. A power of appointment means that someone the settlor names has the power to decide who will get the trust property at some future time. A power of appointment is a nonfiduciary power.

A person can also create a power of appointment over property that is not subject to a trust. While powers of appointment are most common in trusts, testators can create them in a will, and property owners can do so in property transferred by gift. We limit our discussion of powers of appointment to their use in trusts.

2.   *Distinguishing Between a Power of Appointment and Fiduciary Power*

A power of appointment, in contrast with a fiduciary power, is nonmandatory. The holder of a power to appoint property (the "donee") can choose to exercise the power or not and can choose to exercise it arbitrarily, as long as the property subject to the power is given to a permissible appointee. The holder of a fiduciary power, a trustee, must exercise discretion, even if the trustee decides not to make a distribution, and a trustee cannot act arbitrarily. In the past, some cases have described a trustee's discretionary power to distribute property as a power of appointment. Both the *Restatement (Third) of Trusts* §50, cmt. a and the *Restatement (Third) of Property: Wills & Other Donative Transfers* §17.1, cmt. g (T.D. No. 5, 2006) draw a distinction between fiduciary distributive powers and powers of appointment.

> **Example:**   Gloria transfers property to Mariko, as trustee. The trust instrument directs the trustee to distribute income and principal of the trust to Gloria's two children, Osamu and Natsuko, for their support and maintenance, so that they can maintain their accustomed standard of living. On the death of the survivor of the two children, the trust instrument directs the trustee to distribute the remaining principal to Gloria's descendants. In addition, the trust instrument gives Osamu a power of appointment to appoint so much or all of the trust property to anyone, including himself, during his lifetime or at death.
>
> Mariko holds a fiduciary power. She can distribute trust property only to Osamu and Natsuko while either of them is alive, and she must act in good faith to carry out Gloria's intentions. If the children have been accustomed to a modest standard of living, then she should not make distributions to fund lavish expenses. She has a fiduciary duty of

impartiality, which means that she should treat the two current beneficiaries and the remainder beneficiaries fairly. She cannot decide to make distributions only to Osamu because she likes him better. She may decide not to make distributions, but that decision must be made after considering the circumstances of the two beneficiaries and the decision must be reasonable. See Chapter 6 for a discussion of the fiduciary duties.

Osamu has a power of appointment. He can appoint the trust property entirely to himself, entirely to Natsuko or to anyone he chooses. He can choose not to appoint the property and need not even consider whether the settlor would prefer that he appoint the property. The settlor has given him the power of appointment because she expects him to exercise it appropriately, but his decisions about the exercise are entirely up to him.

Federal estate tax law does not draw a distinction between fiduciary distributive powers and powers of appointment. Instead, it treats the power to distribute or appoint property, whether held as a trustee or not and whether subject to fiduciary duties or not, as a power of appointment for purposes of Internal Revenue Code §2041. That section includes property subject to a general power of appointment (*see* definition below) as property included in the estate of the donee for purposes of the estate tax. See Section F.

3. Terminology

There is a special language that applies to powers of appointment and that specifies the parameters of the power:

- *Donor*: The person who creates a power of appointment.
- *Donee*: The person who holds the power and makes decisions using the power. The donee does not hold title to the property and does not have a beneficial interest in the property. The donee only holds a power to appoint the property.
- *Appointive Property*: The property subject to the power.
- *Permissible Appointees or Objects of the Power*: The persons in whose favor the power can be exercised.
- *Takers in Default*: The persons who will take the property if the donee fails to exercise the power and the donee's power terminates (often at the donee's death).
- *Testamentary Power of Appointment*: A power that can be exercised only by will.
- *Presently Exercisable Power of Appointment*: A power the donee can exercise during life, through an inter vivos instrument. A presently exercisable power is exercisable when it is granted.

Example: Eleanor is the settlor of a trust. In the trust she provides for her daughter, Juliet, for life. She also gives Juliet a power to appoint, by will, the property remaining in the trust at Juliet's death to any descendant of Juliet. If Juliet does not exercise the power of appointment, then on Juliet's death the property will be distributed to her descendants, by representation, or if no descendant is alive when Juliet dies, to the American Geographical Society.

In this example, Eleanor is the donor, Juliet is the donee, the trust property is the appointive property, Juliet's descendants are permissible appointees, Juliet's descendants are also the takers in default and the American Geographical Society is a contingent taker in default. The power is a testamentary power because Juliet can exercise the power only by will.

If Eleanor's trust had provided that Juliet could exercise the power at any time during her lifetime, in favor of any descendant of hers, by written instrument delivered to the trustee, then the power would be a presently exercisable power.

- *General Power of Appointment*: A power to appoint in favor of the donee, the donee's estate, the donee's creditors or the creditors of the donee's estate. A general power of appointment can be broad — to anyone — or can be limited to one or more of the four categories listed — for example, to the donee. The distinction between general and nongeneral powers comes from tax law, and different tax consequences follow depending on whether a power is general or nongeneral. See Section F below.

  Example: In the original example, Eleanor could have granted to Juliet the power to appoint the property not just to Juliet's descendants but also "to her estate." This would be a general power of appointment since Juliet could appoint to her estate, even though she could not appoint to herself.

- *Nongeneral Power of Appointment*: A power that cannot be exercised in favor of the donee, the donee's estate, the donee's creditors or creditors of the donee's estate. A nongeneral power can be broad — to anyone in the world other than the donee, the donee's estate, the donee's creditors or the creditors of the donee's estate — or it can be narrow — to the settlor's descendants or to Harry and Georgette. A nongeneral power may also be called a special power or a limited power.

  Example: In the original example, Eleanor gave Juliet a power to appoint, by will, the property remaining in the trust at Juliet's death to any descendant of Juliet; this is a nongeneral power because Juliet can appoint among her descendants, but she cannot appoint to herself, her creditors, her estate or the creditors of her estate.

- _Power of Withdrawal_: The right to withdraw property, or a specified amount of property, from a trust. A power of withdrawal is a general power of appointment, because the donee can withdraw property for her own benefit.

  Example: Eleanor could have provided Juliet with a power of withdrawal: "Juliet may withdraw from the trust an amount not exceeding $5,000 each year. If Juliet does not exercise the power of withdrawal in any year, the power shall lapse."

- _Exclusive Power of Appointment_: A nongeneral power of appointment that can be exercised in favor of one of a group of permissible appointees, to the exclusion of the other appointees. Most powers are exclusive powers.

  Example: In the original example, Juliet has an exclusive power of appointment because she can appoint the property "to any descendant." If she has two children and five grandchildren when she exercises the power, she can appoint all of the property in the trust to one grandchild if she wants to do so. She does not need to appoint some amount to each child and each grandchild.

- _Nonexclusive Power of Appointment_: A power that must be exercised in favor of all permissible appointees, so that each member of the group receives something. There is no requirement of equal distribution, and the amount each appointee must receive can be the subject of controversy among the group of permissible appointees. (Is $1 enough?) The default rule is that nongeneral powers are exclusive. Careful drafting should clarify the donor's intent.

  Example: Eleanor's trust could have provided: "to any descendant of Juliet, and when she exercises the power, she must appoint some amount of the trust property to each of her living descendants."

PROBLEMS

For each problem, identify (a) the donor, (b) the donee(s), (c) the appointive property, (d) the permissible appointees, (e) whether the power is general or nongeneral and (f) whether the power is presently exercisable or testamentary. All of the examples are exclusive powers.

1.   Nancy's will creates a trust for her daughter, Angela, for life, and on Angela's death it continues for Angela's descendants. Nancy gives Angela the power to appoint the property in the trust to one or more of her descendants. The power is exercisable exclusively by will.

2.   Kieran's will establishes a trust naming his sister, Phoebe, as the trustee. The trust directs the trustee to pay income to Kieran's brother, Seamus. The trust also provides that during Seamus's life, the trustee shall distribute up to $20,000 a year to any charity Seamus names in a writing that Seamus delivers to the trustee. On the death of Seamus, the trustee is directed to distribute all or some of the trust property to such person or persons as Seamus appoints by will. If Seamus fails to direct the distribution of all of the trust property, then the trustee is to distribute the property to Kieran's brother, Jervis, and if he is not then living, to his descendants.

B.   INTENT TO CREATE A POWER OF APPOINTMENT

As with the creation of a trust, the creation of a power of appointment requires that the donor of the power manifest the intention to create the power. *See* Restatement (Second) of Property: Donative Transfers §12.1 (1986). No special words are necessary, and the donor need not use the words "power of appointment." As a result, sometimes disagreements arise about whether the donor intended to create a power of appointment or instead gave the donee ownership of property, combined with precatory language that the donee use the property in a particular way. Much of what was discussed in Chapter 5 concerning intent to create a trust has equal relevance to intent to create a power of appointment.

> **Example:**   Edna's will provides: "I give my tangible property to Stephen, to divide among my children as Stephen thinks best." Is this an outright gift to Stephen, the creation of a power of appointment over the tangibles or a trust with Stephen as the trustee? Think about *Clark v. Campbell* in Chapter 5. How is the interest created in *Clark v. Campbell* the same as or different from the interest Edna created? Is the distinction important? If so, why?

In *Flynn v. Flynn*, 469 S.W.2d 886 (Ky. 1971), one party argued that the testator intended to transfer property in fee simple, and the other party argued that the testator had created a life estate with a testamentary power of appointment. Here is the language from Item Two of the testator's will:

I, hereby devise and bequeath all of my property both real and personal, tangible and intangible, wheresoever situate to my beloved wife, Eugenia Flynn, for and during her natural life, in fee simple absolute with the expressed desire that if she does not need to sell same, that she dispose of same to be effective at her death in an equitable manner to our son John, and my son Lewis.

The court then analyzed this language as follows:

Item Two describes an estate devised to appellee as a "fee simple absolute." The appellants would have us find that the other words used in Item Two restrict the estate to a life interest. Among the other words are ones giving the appellee the power to sell the property. This is not consistent with a life estate. Also, there is the statement of the testator's desire that appellee leave the remainder, if any, of his estate at her death to the testator's two sons. The word "desire" is a precatory term. It lacks the force necessary to limit a prior estate. *Kirk v. Lee, Ky.*, 402 S.W.2d 838 . The only words used in Item Two that could be regarded as limiting the fee simple estate are "for and during her natural life." Those words alone, in view of the other provisions of the will, cannot be taken as establishing an intent that appellee should have only a life estate.

The court concluded that the testator intended to leave his wife all his property in fee simple.

C.   EXERCISE OF A POWER OF APPOINTMENT

1.   *Effective Exercise*

When a donee chooses to exercise a power of appointment, she must ensure that the exercise is effective. The donee must follow any directions provided by the donor of the power. For example, if the power is a presently exercisable one, the donor will likely require the donee to exercise the power by giving a written document to the trustee. If the power is a testamentary one, the donee must exercise the power by will and the will must be valid.

In *Crook v. Contreras*, 116 Cal. Rptr. 2d 319 (Cal. App. 6 Dist. 2002), Florence and Lumir Kouba had executed a joint revocable trust. The trust provided that on the death of the first spouse the trust would become irrevocable and two trusts, Trust A and Trust B, would be created for the benefit of the survivor. The survivor would receive all the income from both trusts and had a right to withdraw from Trust A the amount designated "in a written notice served on the Trustee." In addition, the survivor had the power to appoint so much or all of the trust assets as the survivor "shall appoint and direct by specific reference to this power of appointment in his or her last Will admitted to probate by a court of competent jurisdiction." Some years after Lumir's death, Florence executed a document that purported to be an amendment to the trust. The document gave the family home to a friend, Louie Contreras, who had taken care of Florence. Florence signed the document and her lawyer notarized it. After Florence died, Mr. Contreras argued first that the document was an effective amendment to the trust. The trust was irrevocable, however, and could not be amended. He argued that the power of withdrawal gave her the power to revoke the trust, but the court disagreed. Then Mr. Contreras argued that the document was a codicil to Florence's will and that she intended to exercise the power of appointment. The document did not meet the requirements for a valid will (two witnesses must sign), and therefore Florence had not exercised her power of appointment. Even though her intent to give property subject to the power was clear, she had not complied with the requirement that the power be exercised by will. The property went to the takers in default.

2.   Specific Reference

To avoid inadvertent exercise of a power of appointment, many donors (or their estate planners) provide that a document exercising a power must include a specific reference to the power. What does "specific reference" mean when the power is exercised? In the case that follows, the donee knew where she wanted some of the property subject to the power to go, but her will did not include language that explained that she was exercising her power of appointment. The court was asked to determine whether the exercise was effective.

In re Estate of Carter
760 N.E.2d 1171 (Ind. App. 2002)

GARRARD, Senior Judge.

This appeal is from a determination by the Clinton Circuit Court that in her last will and testament Lucile Rogers Clark validly exercised a power of appointment given to her under the will of her deceased husband, James Cedric Carter. It is contended that the Clinton Circuit Court lacked jurisdiction to make the determination and that, in any event, the will of Lucile failed to exercise the power.

James Cedric Carter died testate in 1981, a resident of Montgomery County. His will was probated and his estate was administered there, and in due course the estate was closed. James' will established a testamentary trust to provide for his wife, Lucile, during her lifetime and which contained the following provision:

4. Upon the death of my wife after my death, the trustee shall distribute the trust property, as then constituted, to or in trust among the class of persons consisting of Robert R. Carter, Anne Fenton Carter, Junior Brownfield, Virgie Brownfield, and the then living descendants of any of such persons, upon such conditions and estates, with such powers, in such manner, and at such times as my wife appoints and directs by will specifically referring to and exercising this limited power of appointment. Nothing in this provision shall be construed as empowering my wife to appoint any of the trust property to herself, her estate, her creditors, or the creditors of her estate.

The trust then provided for a disposition of the trust property upon the death of James' wife "to the extent that she does not effectively exercise the foregoing limited power of appointment" (or upon James' death if his wife did not survive him).

Lucile died on August 9, 2000, a resident of Clinton County, and her will, executed May 6, 1998, was admitted to probate by the Clinton Circuit Court. Item III of her will leaves 16.19 acres of real estate, which is specifically described by metes and bounds, to Junior Brownfield and Virgie Brownfield, husband and wife. It is undisputed that the 16.9 acres is a portion of 80 acres left by James in trust and over which Lucile had a limited power of appointment, and it is undisputed that Junior Brownfield and Virgie Brownfield belong to the class of persons to whom Lucile could appoint by her will. It was also shown that on the same date Lucile executed her will, she executed a warranty deed in which she purported to convey the same 16.9 acres to Junior Brownfield and Virgie Brownfield, husband and wife. This deed was recorded in Tippecanoe County where the real estate was located.

Since Item III of Lucile's will did not expressly state that she was thereby intending to exercise the power of appointment granted her under James' will, the personal representative of her estate petitioned the court to construe her will and instruct it on how to proceed.

After a hearing the court found that Junior Brownfield and Virgie Brownfield were husband and wife. Within days of executing her will Lucile had adopted them as adults. They had lived on the 16.19 acres for more than thirty years, most of the time without direct payment of rent which was pursuant to the wishes of the Carters, and over the years they had made several improvements to the realty some of which they furnished and some of which the Carters furnished. The court then determined that in spite of Lucile's failure to specifically characterize the devise to the Brownfields as an "exercise of her limited power of appointment" her intention to do exactly that was clear and should be given effect. It then ordered the described tract conveyed to the Brownfields by Bank One Trust Company, N.A., the personal representative of Lucile's estate and the testamentary trustee of James' testamentary trust.

The appellant, Roger Carter, (hereinafter "Roger") [challenges the outcome].

In probate law it is axiomatic that the primary rule of construction is that the intention of the testator should govern (providing this can be done without contravening public policy or some inflexible rule of law.)

In the present case it is clear that James intended that Lucile have a limited power of appointment to dispose of certain assets by her will. The question thus arises as to whether she exercised that power.

I.C. §29-1-6-1(f) directs that a will will not operate as exercising a power of appointment "unless by its terms the will specifically indicates that the testator intended to exercise the power." Roger's brief characterizes the statutory requirement as "identical" to the one contained in James' will, and his argument attempts no distinction between the two. We, therefore, make no attempt to consider the two separately.

Roger contends that in order to have exercised the power Lucile's will must have explicitly stated that it was her intent to do so. He relies heavily upon the comment of the Probate Study Commission which stated,

> This subsection provides that the mere making of a will devising property over which the testator has a power of appointment will not constitute an exercise of such power of appointment unless the testator specifically indicates by the use of appropriate words his intention to exercise such power. It is believed that this rule of construction will avoid litigation.

We believe this comment adding the phrase "by the use of appropriate words" to the statutory requirement that the will specifically *indicate* that the testator intended to exercise the power, is simply an exposition of the statutory requirement rather than an attempt to further restrict the statute's meaning.

There can be little doubt that the general purpose of the statute is to resolve questions concerning the possible unintentional or accidental exercise of powers of appointment. The prime example is, no doubt, a general bequest of "all the rest, residue and remainder of my estate. . . ."[1] Yet Indiana legal history has long displayed an aversion to any notion that some shibboleth should be required for the exercise of powers of appointment. Thus, our supreme court in the early case of *Bullerdick v. Wright*, 148 Ind. 477, 47 N.E. 931, 932-22 (1897) stated that the authorities recognize three classes of cases as affording sufficient proof of intent to execute the power: (1) where the testator refers to, or recites, the power in his will; (2) where the property subject to be disposed of under the power is described; and, (3) where the will would be inoperative without acting on the property over which the power was given. Acknowledging that these "illustrations" do not afford the only proof, the court said they are considered as furnishing clear and unequivocal proof of intent to exercise the

---

1. [FN 1] A number of jurisdictions apparently still follow the view that a general residuary clause is rebuttably presumed to exercise a power. See, e.g., 2B Henry's Probate Law & Practice, §41, 2000 Cum. Supp., p. 68.

power. The court concluded, "The authorities uniformly affirm the doctrine that it is not essential to refer in express terms to the power, if an intention to execute it otherwise plainly appears; and any words or expressions indicating an intention to exercise the power will operate to that effect."

This view was followed in *Crawfordsville Trust Co. v. Elston Bank & Trust Co.*, 216 Ind. 596, 25 N.E.2d 626 636 (1940) where the court added, "The intent need not be shown in any particular way, but is to be determined by a construction of the whole instrument, with reference to the circumstances under which it was executed."

As already set forth, the court found that because Lucile's will specifically described property that was subject to the power and gave it to beneficiaries within the class permitted by the power and because of the other facts and circumstances surrounding her execution of the will it was clearly her intent to exercise her power of appointment. Roger's argument in opposition simply contends that in order to exercise the power, Lucile's will had to expressly state that she was thereby exercising her limited power of appointment. Since we have already held herein that express reference to the power is not the only manner of indicating that a testator intended to exercise it, this argument must fail. Moreover, we determine that the court's findings are sufficient to sustain its conclusion that the will did exercise the power of appointment granted under James' will.

Affirmed.

NOTES

1. *Substantially specific.* If a donor imposes formal requirements on how a donee should exercise a power, perhaps requiring a specific reference, the question courts — and legislatures — face is how precisely the donee must comply. The *Restatement (Third) of Property: Wills & Other Donative Transfers* §19.10 (T.D. No. 5, 2006) provides for substantial compliance with a donor's requirement. The *Restatement* says that an attempted exercise should be effective if evidence shows that the donee intended to exercise the power and that the way in which the donee exercised the power did not impair the donor's reason for imposing a requirement, including a requirement of specific exercise, on the manner of exercise. If the reason for the requirement is to prevent inadvertent exercise, then substantial compliance should be sufficient.

2. *Or strict compliance.* Some courts, however, apply the specific requirement rule strictly. In *Smith v. Brannan*, 954 P.2d 1259 (Or. App. 1998), Chester Dillinger's 1978 will created a marital trust for his wife, Doris, with a general power of appointment. The will required that the power be exercised "by specific reference to this provision of my will." Doris

exercised the power in her 1978 will, with an appropriately specific reference. In 1988, after Doris no longer had capacity to execute a new will (she had Alzheimer's disease), Chester revoked his 1978 will and executed a new will, changing the residuary beneficiaries. The language of the power of appointment in the marital trust created for Doris was identical to the language in the 1978 will. The court held that because Doris's 1978 exercise did not refer to Chester's 1988 will, the exercise was ineffective. *See also*, *Estate of Hamilton*, 593 N.Y.S.2d 372 (App. Div. 1993) (same result on similar facts).

EXERCISE

Assume that you are the lawyer advising Lucile and drafting her will. Draft the will provision exercising her power and giving the property to the Brownfields.

3. Exercise by General Residuary Clause

a. Specific Reference Not Required

Sometimes the donor simply requires a donee to exercise a power "by will." If the donor did not require a specific reference and the donee did not provide a clear expression of the intent to exercise the power, a will or other document may be ambiguous as to whether a power has been exercised. In this section we consider whether a residuary clause in a will exercises a testamentary power of appointment. Consider the following clause in a donee's will:

> **Example:** I give the residue of my estate to my descendants, by representation.

Does this clause indicate the testator's intent to exercise the power? The majority of states follow the rule that a general residuary clause like the one in the example, without more, does *not* exercise a power of appointment held by the testator. *See* RESTATEMENT (THIRD) OF PROPERTY: WILLS & OTHER DONATIVE TRANSFERS §19.4 (T.D. No. 5, 2006). The opinion in *In re Estate of Carter* explains that the Indiana statute that requires a specific reference was enacted to avoid inadvertent exercise by a clause like the one in the example. The clause is too general and makes no reference to the decedent's power of appointment in any way. Some of these states, however, permit the use of extrinsic evidence to establish that the donee intended to exercise the power. If the general residuary clause is not treated as the exercise of the power, the takers in default receive the property subject to the power.

In a few jurisdictions, unless a contrary intent can be established, a non-specific residuary clause is deemed to exercise a general power of appointment, but only if the residuary beneficiaries are permissible appointees under the power. In *Will of Block*, the New York Surrogate's Court applied this rule, emphasizing that New York cases and statutes "strongly favor finding a valid exercise, in furtherance of the presumed intention of most power holders." The result would have been different (no exercise of the power) in the majority of states. In *Block*, the court also had to determine how to treat an exercise that included an impermissible appointee.

Will of Block
598 N.Y.S.2d 668 (Sur. 1993)

Preminger, Surrogate.

Decedent, Dina W. Block, died in 1981, a domiciliary of New York. Her will established a trust of one half of her residuary estate for the benefit of her son Paul, Jr. and his twin sons, Allan and John. The trust terminated upon Paul Jr.'s death and he was given a limited power to appoint the trust principal by will "unto and among" these two sons in whatever proportion he chose. The twins' older half-brother Cyrus was not a permissible appointee. In default of the exercise of the power, the trust fund was to be divided into separate trusts for the life income benefit of Allan and John. U.S. Trust, Paul, Jr. and his brother William served as trustees under Dina Block's will.

Paul, Jr. died an Ohio domiciliary in 1987. His will, which was executed more than a year after his mother's death, did not refer to his power of appointment under her will. It left his entire residuary estate to a revocable inter-vivos trust he had created in 1974. Under the 1974 trust, after certain payments to his wife (not relevant here), there are separate subtrusts for all three of Paul's sons: 35% each to Allan and John, and 30% to Cyrus. . . .

The trustees seek direction whether Paul's disposition of his residuary estate without reference to the appointive assets, and in partial violation of the limitations Dina imposed, nevertheless effectively exercised his limited power of appointment. It is clear that this question must be answered by referring to the local law of New York rather than Ohio.

In New York, an effective exercise of a power of appointment need not refer to the power. EPTL 10-6.1(a) and (b). The legislature has abrogated the common law rule still in effect in Ohio which requires that a donee manifest a clear intent to exercise the power. . . . Under New York law a conventional residuary clause disposing of the testator's remaining assets exercises a power of appointment unless

"the intention that the will is not to operate as an execution of the power appears expressly or by necessary implication."

There is no question that Paul's will did not expressly negate an intention to exercise the power. The more difficult question is whether there is an adequate basis for finding "by necessary implication" that Paul did *not* intend to exercise the power.

The New York cases and statutes governing the exercise of powers of appointment strongly favor finding a valid exercise, in furtherance of the presumed intention of most power holders. . . .

Courts have also been restrictive in finding a "necessary implication" not to exercise a power. . . . Nothing in the text of Paul, Jr.'s will gives rise to the "necessary implication." The only possible indicia are: 1) the fact that this is the will of the domiciliary of a jurisdiction which would not deem it to have exercised the power, 2) the fact that the presumed exercise of the power was inconsistent with its limitations; and 3) the inference that the donee knew of the existence of the power because he was a trustee of the appointive assets. . . .

[The court determined that these factors were not sufficient to establish a "necessary implication" and held that the residuary clause exercised the power.]

. . . Having deemed the power exercised, it is now necessary to determine the extent of its exercise. It is undisputed that the power could not be exercised in favor of Cyrus. The question is what becomes of the 30% share invalidly allocated to him by Paul, Jr.'s will. Was the power of appointment exercised with respect to 70 percent only or the entire appointive property? Here the court's task is to further the valid portions of the testator's plan where to do so does not disturb his fundamental intention.

There is nothing in the pertinent instruments or in the applicable statutes which warrants the conclusion that the power of appointment was executed only partially. The provisions of Paul's will and trust dispose of property of much greater value than the appointive assets. The court determines that Paul, Jr.'s bequests of 35 percent each of the residuary estate to Allan and John demonstrate that his testamentary scheme was to benefit his twin sons equally. Consequently, the court concludes that the entire appointive property is to be disposed of for their primary benefit, in equal shares.

NOTES AND QUESTIONS

1. *Takers in default.* If the court had deemed the exercise ineffective, who would have received the trust property?

2. *Which rule?* Should the rule focus on the intent behind the attempted exercise or should the rule be the one followed by the New York

court—exercise presumed unless a strong reason exists not to allow exercise?

3.   *Intent to exercise.* Remembering that New York is not the majority rule, why do you think most states do not permit exercise by a general residuary clause?

4.   *Which law?* The court in *Block* applies the law of the donor's domicile to determine whether the exercise was effective. This is the majority view. A significant minority of states would apply the law of the donee's domicile, and the *Restatement* takes this view. RESTATEMENT (THIRD) OF PROPERTY: WILLS & OTHER DONATIVE TRANSFERS §19.1, cmt. e (T.D. No. 5, 2006). Which do you think is the better rule?

UPC §2-608 addresses the question of the circumstances under which a residuary clause should exercise a power of appointment. The policy behind the UPC provision is to limit exercise to situations in which permitting the residuary clause to exercise the power is likely to accord with the donor's intent.

UPC §2-608. Exercise of Power of Appointment.

> In the absence of a requirement that a power of appointment be exercised by a reference, or by an express or specific reference, to the power, a general residuary clause in a will, or a will making general disposition of all of the testator's property, expresses an intention to exercise a power of appointment held by the testator only if (i) the power is a general power and the creating instrument does not contain a gift if the power is not exercised or (ii) the testator's will manifests an intention to include the property subject to the power.

Example: Cheryl's will states: "On Jennifer's death, the trustee shall distribute the remaining trust property to such one or more persons, including the estate of Jennifer, as Jennifer shall appoint by will."

Jennifer's will says: "I give the residue of my estate, including any property over which I hold a power of appointment, to my daughter, Angelina."

The UPC would construe Jennifer's residuary clause as exercising the power if Cheryl's will did not provide for takers in default.

Now assume that the provision in Cheryl's will includes the following language: "and if Jennifer does not exercise the power of appointment granted under this Article 8, the trustee shall distribute the remaining trust property to my descendants, per stirpes." If Cheryl's will includes this additional language, Jennifer's residuary clause probably will not exercise the power, although extrinsic evidence could be used to show that Jennifer intended to exercise the power. See the comment to UPC §2-704 (discussing the use of extrinsic evidence to show the donee's intent to exercise a power).

b.   Specific Reference Required

If the creation of the power requires a specific reference to exercise the power, a general residuary clause will not exercise the power. But what is the effect of a residuary clause that refers to any powers held by the testator? Consider this clause:

Example: I give the residue of my estate, including any property over which I hold a power of appointment, to my descendants, by representation.

Is this language sufficient to exercise a power when the donor requested a specific reference? A statement that "I exercise any power of appointment I may have," may be boilerplate language or it may have been added with the intent that a power be exercised. The following case considers this problem.

Motes/Henes Trust Bank of Bentonville v. Motes
761 S.W.2d 938 (Ark. 1988)

HAYS, Justice.

The single issue presented by this appeal is whether a reference in the testator's will to a power of appointment was sufficient to exercise a power of appointment in a trust instrument.

Helen Fay Henes, deceased, executed a will in 1979 containing the following residuary clause:

I give, devise and bequeath all of the remainder and residue of my estate together with *property to which I may have a power of appointment at the time of my death,* to the trustee hereinafter named, to be held in trust for the uses. . . . [Emphasis added.]

In 1982, the Motes/Henes trust was established for Helen Fay Henes and her sister, Elizabeth Henes Motes, in which was placed approximately $6,000,000 from interests the sisters had redeemed from their ownership in certain businesses. The trust contained the following provision:

This trust shall terminate with respect to the separate trust share of each grantor [the two sisters] upon the death of said grantor. Upon such termination, the remaining assets of said separate trust shall be paid to such person or persons or trusts as grantor may, *by specific reference hereto, appoint in her Last Will and Testament.* [Emphasis added.]

Helen Fay Henes died in April 1983 and in February 1988 the trustee of the Motes/Henes trust petitioned for the consolidation of the probate and chancery proceedings and for construction of the power of appointment in the will. Consolidation was granted and following a hearing the trial court held that the language of the will was sufficient to exercise the power of appointment defined in the trust. The trustee and Elizabeth Henes Motes have appealed. Respondent-Appellees are the children of Elizabeth Henes Motes.

The question is: When a power of appointment requires a specific reference to it, as does the trust in this case, will a general reference in the will be sufficient to exercise the power requiring specific reference?

The general rule is defined in Restatement (Second) of Property, Donative Transfers (1986):

§17.1 Significance of Donee's Intent to Appoint.

In order for a donee to exercise a power effectively it must be established—

(1) That the donee intended to exercise it; and

(2) That the expression of the intention complies with the requirements of exercise imposed by the donor and by rules of law.

The problem here concerns the second requirement and the question we must decide is whether Ms. Henes' will provision, making reference to "property to which I may have a power of appointment at the time of my death," is sufficient to exercise the power of appointment in the trust, or does the law require that she must have made reference to the trust instrument itself.

Finding no cases of our own on this topic, we have turned to other sources for guidance. The Reporter's Note to section 17.1 of the Restatement is primarily devoted to the problem in our case. While the Restatement discusses cases it classifies as "supporting" the rule and those "contrary" to the rule, a closer examination of those cases reveals that the division would be more aptly placed between those cases that construe the "specific reference" requirement literally, and those that favor a flexible interpretation, focusing more on the intent of the donee. See also Annotation, 15 A.L.R. 4th 810 (1982), which distinguishes the cases between those that require specific reference and those that do not.

Our research does not produce a clear majority or trend on either side of the question. We prefer the approach focusing on the intent of the donor, however, as we regard it as the better reasoned view. It is also in keeping with our general approach to the interpretation of wills, which has as its paramount principle that the intention of the testator will govern, as well as the rule that wills should be liberally construed. And in *Moore v. Avery*, 225 S.W. 599 (1920), in construing a will, we held that the phrase, "all my property," was sufficient to refer to and exercise a power of appointment. While Moore does not involve a "specific reference" requirement, it nevertheless reflects the more liberal approach.

In *Roberts v. Northern Trust Co.*, 550 F. Supp. 729 (N.D. Ill. 1982), the court was faced with the same issue and reviewed Illinois law to determine the correct approach. The court found that in a significant power of appointment case, the Illinois court had drawn on three basic principles of will construction: 1) that the intent of the testator controls and courts should construe wills to give effect to that intention; 2) a devise or bequest should not be voided because of errors in describing the subject matter as long as enough remains to show the testator's intent; and 3) the court will use its equitable powers to correct technical defects in a will in order to effect the testator's intent. From those general rules the court fashioned the following test for the "specific reference" problem:

> Where the evidence of intent is powerful, the question of compliance should be examined in a light which favors fulfillment of both the donor's desire for assurance and the donee's intent. Where, however, evidence of the donee's intent is weak, a liberal construction of the condition of specific reference may well defeat the limitations of both donor and donee.

Following the approach in *Roberts, supra,* we find the evidence of intent in this case is very strong and therefore have no problem with a more liberal construction of the "specific reference" requirement. The evidence of Fay Henes's intent came from the testimony of John L. Johnson, who was the attorney for both sisters. He had drafted the wills for both, and had also drafted the trust agreement. He testified that at the time of drafting the will he had discussed with Ms. Henes how she wanted to dispose of her property and she told him she wanted her sister to be benefitted and the property to go to her nieces and nephews, her sister's children. The will was drafted to effectuate that intent, giving her sister a life estate through the trust, for her enjoyment during her lifetime, with the property ultimately going to the nieces and nephews.

When Johnson drafted the trust agreement he reviewed Ms. Henes' will and decided there was no need to make any changes in it. He noted that the provision in the will on the power of appointment would operate to exercise all powers of appointment that Ms. Henes would have, to pass the property under a trust arrangement that was set up under her will. Johnson stated that this was absolutely consistent with his view and understanding of Ms. Henes' intent.

Johnson further commented that in drafting the trust, which was irrevocable, he wanted to avoid placing Ms. Henes in the position of being unable to change the beneficiaries of her estate by naming them in the trust instrument. By not putting final testamentary disposition provisions in the trust, it retained for Ms. Henes the ability at any point to change her mind as to the disposition of her estate.

The trial court noted that another significant factor was the problem of estate taxes. If the power was not exercised by the will, double taxation would result, and the trial judge observed that people do not intend tax consequences of that nature. We agree.

Appellant urges that we must ascertain the intent of the testator at the time of the execution of the will, citing *Moore, supra*. That is true, but it does not mean that we eliminate after-acquired property from being disposed by way of a will executed previously. *See, e.g., Brock v. Turner*, 147 Ark. 421, 227 S.W. 597 (1921); *Fowler v. Hogue*, 276 Ark. 416, 635 S.W.2d 274 (1982). We held in *Brock, supra*, that when a will manifests the purpose to dispose of all the estate the testator might have at the time of death, it includes after-acquired property. In that case while there were other reinforcing considerations, the court looked primarily at the language of the will which included, "all . . . my property," and the phrase, "also all chattel, property of any kind, including money *on hand*," the court emphasising the phrase "on hand" as referring to the time of death. This is also the rule specifically as it relates to powers of appointment. Restatement (Second) of Property, Donative Transfers, §17.6 (1986).

In this case, Ms. Henes' will refers first to, "*all* of the remainder and residue of my estate," and then specifically refers to "property to which *I may have* a power of appointment *at the time of my death*." It seems clear that the testator's intent at the time of execution was to include any after-acquired property.

Affirmed.

NOTES AND QUESTIONS

1. *Malpractice anyone?* Contrast the result in *Henes* with the following case. Erma Surface's husband gave her a general power of appointment over the property in a marital trust created under his will. The grant of the power required a specific reference to the power in a "separate ITEM" in her will in which she did not attempt to dispose of other property. Erma's 1979 will effectively exercised the power, but some years later she went to a different law firm for estate planning services. The new lawyers drafted a will which attempted to exercise the power in the residuary clause of the will. The clause referred specifically to the power created under her husband's will, but the exercise was not in a "separate ITEM." After a court determined that the exercise was ineffective, the people who would have benefited from the exercise sued the lawyers who drafted the will for negligence. *See Calvert v. Scharf*, 619 S.E. 2d 197 (W. Va. 2005). Do you think the intended beneficiaries had standing? If they had standing, do you think this is malpractice?

2. *How hard is it?* The rule that the donor's requirements for exercise must be followed is an easy one to understand. Why then are there a number of cases in which the clause exercising the power is challenged? Is

it the lawyer's fault or the client's fault? As a lawyer, how would you attempt to provide for effective exercise of powers held by a client?

4.   Exercise in Further Trust

A general power may be exercised to appoint the property in fee simple as well as subject to further trust or to a new power of appointment. Since the donee of a general power could appoint to herself and then use the property to establish a trust or give the property to a donee subject to a further power, the law permits the original donee to accomplish this result without the intermediate step of appointing the property to herself.

If the power is a nongeneral power, however, the donee may be able to appoint in further trust only if the grant of the power so provides, depending on case law in the state. Some courts have held that the donee of a nongeneral power can appoint in trust so long as the trust is one for the benefit of the permissible appointees. *See Loring v. Karri-Davies*, 357 N.E.2d 11 (Mass. 1976).

Good drafting associated with the granting of the power should specify whether the donee has the authority to appoint in further trust or not. Here is an example of a power of appointment that includes the power to appoint in further trust:

> My husband shall have the power to cause all or any part of the Trust to be paid to such one or more persons, at such times, in such proportions and in such manner, in valid trust or otherwise, and with such powers of appointment, general or special, as he may appoint by his will, executed after my death, specifically referring to this power of appointment, and valid wherever probated.

Here is an example of an exercise of a power in further trust:

> I hereby exercise the power of appointment granted me under my wife's will and direct that all the property subject to that power be distributed to my friend, Eugene Tanaka ("trustee"), to be held by him as trustee for the benefit of my son, Simon Saldana. The trustee shall distribute to Simon so much or all of the income and principal of the trust as the trustee determines to be in Simon's best interests. On Simon's death the trustee shall distribute any remaining assets to my descendants, per stirpes.

In states that still follow the Rule Against Perpetuities, the Rule applies to an exercise of a power of appointment. The date of the gift of the power is the starting date for the Rule, and a gift in further trust may violate the Rule if the trust extends too far in the future. If the power is a general power, then the donee is treated as the owner and the Rule begins to run from the time of exercise rather than the time of creation, extending the period. In the example, the gift is a general power, so the rule will apply when the husband dies and appoints the property. If the power is a nongeneral power, then the power runs from the date of creation of the power, but facts at the date of the exercise control. In the example, because Simon was alive before his mother (the donor of the power) died, the trust for Simon would not violate the Rule even if the husband's power had been a nongeneral power.

5.   *Impermissible Exercise*

A power of appointment can only be exercised in favor of the permissible appointees. If a donee attempts to exercise the power in favor of someone who is not a permissible appointee, the attempted exercise is invalid. The property will go to the takers in default.

> **Example:**   Ella is the donee of a power to appoint among her descendants. Ella's will exercises the power, appointing the trust property subject to the power to "my children, Aiden, Noah, Caleb and Liam." Noah, Caleb and Liam are all descendants under the state definition of descendants, but Aiden is Ella's stepchild. Although Ella thinks of him as one of her children, he is not a permissible appointee (unless the document creating the power of appointment modified the state's definition of descendant). The attempted exercise in favor of Aiden is invalid. His one-quarter share will go to the takers in default (probably the other three children).

Look again at *Will of Block*. The court treated the donee's residuary clause as exercising the power of appointment, and the clause provided 30% to a child who was not a permissible appointee and 35% to each of two other children who were permissible appointees. The court had two options: (1) declare 30% of the exercise invalid or (2) treat the exercise as in favor of the permissible appointees (100% of the property would go in equal shares to the two permissible appointees). The court chose the latter approach, deeming that approach more in keeping with the donee's overall estate plan.

6.   *Predeceased Appointees*

What happens if a donee of a power exercises the power in her will and the appointee then dies before the donee dies? The exercise of the power takes effect when the donee dies, so the question is whether the appointee must survive the donee in order to take the property. The following case considers this question and reaches the same result as most other states that have decided the issue.

Sovran Bank v. Axelrad

23 Va. Cir. 237 (Va. Cir. Ct. 1991) (not reported in S.E.2d) Mar. 8, 1991

This case is before the court on a Bill For Aid and Direction filed by complainant Sovran Bank, N.A. ("Sovran") for guidance in resolving a number of issues arising from the will and codicil of T. Whitfield Harrison ("Whit") and from the will of Mary Bain Harrison ("Mary"). At the hearing on February 13, 1991, Mr. Hardy as counsel for defendants, Virginia Axelrad, Edwin Bain, Jeffrey Furman and Ann L.G. Gerard, moved this court to consider and decide only one of the issues presented in Sovran's bill at this time. The court granted Mr. Hardy's motion and the issue to be decided at this time is whether, under the terms of Whit's will, Mary effectively exercised her general power of appointment over the assets in Trust A. For the reasons set forth below, the court finds that Mary did not effectively appoint the assets in Trust A and therefore those assets "pour over" into Trust B in accordance with the provisions of Whit's will.

ROBERT L. HARRIS, Sr., Judge.

The parties proffered certain stipulations of fact which were accepted by this court's order of February 13, 1991. Copies of the wills referred to were made part of the stipulations. The relevant facts are as follows. Mary and Whit were married when Whit died on May 25, 1974. Both Mary and Whit were married only once and Mary was Whit's only heir. Whit's will, dated January 14, 1974, was probated before this court on June 14, 1974. Mary qualified as executrix and trustee under Whit's will.

In his will, Whit gave his residuary estate to his trustee to be divided into separate trusts, Trust A and Trust B. The trustee was to pay the net income from Trust A to Mary during her lifetime as well as so much of the principal as the trustee deemed necessary for Mary's support and mainte-nance. Whit also gave Mary an Unlimited Power of Withdrawal and a General Power of Appointment by Will with respect to Trust A. By the terms of Whit's will, the General Power of Appointment was exercisable only if Mary's will specifically referred to the power of appointment given to her under Whit's will.

Whit also provided that upon Mary's death, the assets in Trust A which were not "effectively appointed" by her should be added to Trust B and be disposed of in accordance with the provisions specified for Trust B. Whit made provisions for a number of specific bequests under Trust B and whatever remained in Trust B after those bequests were made was to pass in equal shares to defendants Children's Hospital, Sheltering Arms Hospital, Centenary Methodist Church, University of Richmond and Virginia Home for Boys in Richmond ("the charities").

On December 4, 1979, Mary was found to be incapacitated and a guardian was appointed for her. After Mary became incapacitated, First and Merchants National Bank qualified as successor trustee to Mary for both

Trust A and Trust B. Through mergers, Sovran succeeded First and Merchants National Bank.

Mary died on March 17, 1989. Her will, dated April 10, 1975, was probated on March 20, 1989. In her will, Mary "exercised" the general power of appointment over the assets in Trust A and named seven beneficiaries. She further provided that "(t)he balance of any funds remaining in the aforesaid Trust A established by [Whit], I give, devise and bequeath to my brother, E.L. Bain, and if he should predecease me, then to my sister-in-law, Mabel T. Bain." Mary went on to provide that if the balance of Trust A remaining at her death was insufficient to meet these bequests, she desired that the estate she owned prior to Whit's death be invaded to satisfy the bequests. E.L. Bain died on December 19, 1979 without descendants; Mabel T. Bain died on April 27, 1984 without descendants. Both predeceased Mary. . . .

The guiding principle in the construction of powers of appointment is that such "(p)owers are to be construed in accordance with the intention of the donor . . . to be gathered in general from the instrument itself." By the terms of his will, Whit's intent was to give Mary the power to appoint the assets in Trust A by her will and, to the extent she did not effectively do so, the remainder of Trust A would be added to Trust B. However, because Mary had a general power of appointment by will, a life interest in the income from Trust A and an unlimited power of withdrawal over the principal in Trust A, counsel have made alternative arguments regarding the exact nature of Mary's interest in the assets of Trust A. . . .

The key issue to be decided then is whether Mary's appointment was effectively exercised as provided in Whit's will. The effectiveness of Mary's appointment must be measured at the time of her death. A bequest under a power of appointment by will takes effect at the death of the donee, not at the death of the testator.

It is not disputed that Mary's attempted exercise of the power of appointment was procedurally valid under the terms of Code Section 64.1-50. Mary expressly referred to the power of appointment in her will as Whit required her to do. However, the fact that the appointment was lawfully exercised does not mean that it was effectively exercised.

Both E.L. Bain and Mabel T. Bain, the appointees, predeceased Mary. "An appointment to a person who is dead is ineffective except as provided by an antilapse statute." Restatement (Second) of Property (Donative Transfers) §18.5 (1984). Certain defendants have argued that because the appointment "lapsed" upon Mary's death, Virginia's antilapse statutes, sections 64.1-64.1 and 64.1-65.1, should apply to bring the assets of Trust A into Mary's estate to pass to her heirs. Both Virginia statutes are written in terms of the failure of devises and bequests, not ineffective exercise of powers of appointment, which contain no property interest. No Virginia Supreme Court cases have construed these statutes to encompass powers of appointment and it is this court's opinion that these statutes do not apply to the ineffective exercise of a power of appointment.

This court has also been urged to apply the doctrine of capture to find that Mary's attempted exercise of the general power of appointment brought the assets of Trust A into her estate to the extent of the failed appointment. Because the doctrine of capture is not recognized under Virginia law, this court declines to apply the doctrine in this case.

Because both E.L. Bain and Mabel T. Bain predeceased Mary, Mary's attempted exercise of her power of appointment was ineffective. Whit's clearly expressed intent was that if the Trust A assets were not effectively appointed by Mary, those assets would be added to Trust B. Because Whit's intent is controlling, the Trust A assets which were not effectively appointed by Mary must be added to Trust B to be distributed in a accordance with the provisions for Trust B set forth in Whit's will.

NOTES AND QUESTIONS

1. *Antilapse.* The court concludes that Virginia's antilapse statute does not apply to the attempted exercise of the power so the attempted exercise fails. Antilapse statutes provide substitute gifts in certain circumstances when a will beneficiary dies before the testator. We discuss lapse and antilapse statutes in Chapter 10. UPC §2-603 applies the UPC's antilapse rule to powers of appointment, and a number of states have adopted antilapse statutes that apply to the exercise of powers of appointment. The *Restatement (Third) of Property: Wills & Other Donative Transfers* §19.12 (T.D. No. 5, 2006) urges courts to apply a general antilapse statute to powers of appointment even if the state statute does not explicitly apply to powers. Under an antilapse statute, if the appointee is related to the donee as prescribed by the statute and the appointee predeceases the donee, the property will go to the donee's descendants. The question of applying antilapse statutes to powers of appointment is tricky because doing so may mean that the property will be distributed to persons who were not named by the donor as permissible appointees. For example, if the power is exercisable in favor of the donee's siblings and an appointee sibling predeceases the donee, an antilapse statute would give the property to the deceased sibling's descendants.

2. *Critical date.* If the court had found the exercise of the power effective, who would have received the property? Does that help explain why the critical date is the date of exercise and not the date the power was created? Should it make a difference that Mary had a general power of appointment and could have appointed the property to her estate?

D.   RELEASE, FAILURE TO EXERCISE AND AN EXPRESS STATEMENT OF NONEXERCISE

A donee of a power of appointment has several options of what to do with it. The most obvious is to exercise it consistent with the terms of the grant, as discussed in the prior section. However, if the donee does not wish to exercise the power, she can release it, not exercise it or expressly indicate her decision not to exercise it. The *Restatement of Property* refers to all of these situations as a lapse of the power (the donee did not exercise the power, so the power lapsed). *See* RESTATEMENT (THIRD) OF PROPERTY: WILLS & OTHER DONATIVE TRANSFERS §19.22 (T.D. No. 5, 2006). The law has developed rules that apply to all three forms of lapse in the same way. We consider definitions of the three types of lapse and the important question, which is what happens to the property when the power lapses.

- *Release*: If the donee releases a power of appointment, then the donee has given up control over the property and no longer has the ability to decide who will take it. The donee will notify the trustee of the release, and the takers in default, if there are any, will have certainty about the ultimate distribution of the property. The takers in default may not know about their interest in the trust, but if they do know about the trust, they will be assured that they have a remainder interest.

  Example: Jolene has a life estate in a trust, with a testamentary power of appointment to distribute the trust property among her siblings and their descendants. The trust provides that if she fails to exercise the power, the property will go to her niece, JiJi. If Jolene notifies the trustee in writing that she releases the power, then Jolene will have no further rights with respect to the power and JiJi will have a vested remainder in the property.

- *Nonexercise*: The donee may decide not to exercise the power if the donee thinks the takers in default should take the property. The donee may also forget to exercise the power, and it is even possible that the donee may not know about the power. If the donee does not release the power and does nothing that could constitute an exercise of the power, then the donee has failed to exercise the power.
- *Expressly refraining from exercise*: The donee may want to clarify in her will that she does not intend to exercise a power of appointment. Remember that sometimes a residuary clause may be considered to exercise a power, even if the residuary clause does not specifically refer to the power. For that reason, if a donee wants to be sure that the takers in default take the property, an express

statement is appropriate. The will might say, "I expressly do not exercise the power of appointment I have under the will of Grant Richardson."

1.   *Who Gets the Property?*

a.   Takers in Default

If the donee fails to exercise a power of appointment, releases it or expressly declines to exercise it, the question is who will take the property subject to the power. A well-drafted power of appointment will indicate who the takers in default are. If the original grant of power provides for takers in default, then if the donee does not exercise the power the takers in default will receive the property. *See* RESTATEMENT (THIRD) OF PROPERTY: WILLS & OTHER DONATIVE TRANSFERS §19.23 (T.D. No. 5, 2006). The takers in default are determined at the time set for distribution, so that if the takers are a class (children or descendants), the determination of membership in the class will be made at the time of distribution. Here are two examples.

> **Example:**   Jacob created a testamentary trust for his daughter, Miranda, with distributions during her life. The trust provides that on Miranda's death, the property will be distributed to such one or more charities as Miranda appoints, or, if Miranda does not exercise her power of appointment, to Miranda's two siblings equally. If Miranda releases her power of appointment, the contingent interests of the two siblings (as takers in default) become vested remainders in the trust. They know that they will receive the property when Miranda dies.

> **Example:**   Didier has a testamentary power to appoint to anyone other than himself, his creditors, his estate or the creditors of his estate (a broad, nongeneral power). The trust provides that the takers in default are his descendants. When Monique and Didier divorce, he agrees to release his power. When Didier releases the power, the living descendants take a vested interest in the property, although which descendants will take depends on who is alive at Didier's death. Didier will not be able to appoint the property to his next wife. His descendants living at the time of his death will take the property.

b.   No Takers in Default Stated

If the donor did not provide for takers in default, then who will take the property depends on whether the power was general or nongeneral.

If the power is nongeneral, the property will be distributed to the permissible appointees, if those permissible appointees are a defined and limited class. If the class is so broad that specific members cannot be determined, then the property will be distributed to the donor's estate as a reversionary interest. *See* Restatement (Third) of Property: Wills & Other Donative Transfers §19.23 (T.D. No. 5, 2006).

If the power is general and the donee fails to exercise the power, it will be distributed to the donee's estate, unless the terms of the grant of the power provide otherwise. The idea behind this rule is that because the donee could control the power, the default rule should be to distribute it through the donee's estate. If the donee releases the power though, or expressly refrains from exercising it, then the property is distributed to the donor or the donor's estate, as a reversionary interest. *See* Restatement (Third) of Property: Wills & Other Donative Transfers §19.22 (T.D. No. 5, 2006).

> **Example:** Daniel creates a trust for his daughter, Jeanne, with distributions during her life. The trust provides that on Jeanne's death the property will be distributed to such one or more charities as Jeanne appoints. The trust does not provide who will take the property if Jeanne does not exercise the power. Although this is a *nongeneral* power, the class of permissible appointees is not sufficiently specific for a gift to those appointees. The property will revert to Daniel or to Daniel's estate.

> **Example:** Daniel creates a different trust for Jeanne. This trust provides that on Jeanne's death the property will be distributed to such one or more of Jeanne's descendants as Jeanne appoints. This is a *nongeneral* power with a defined class. When Jeanne died, she had two living children and two grandchildren who are the children of one of her deceased children. On Jeanne's death the trust property will be distributed as it would be distributed to Jeanne's descendants under the state's intestacy statute, unless the document defines descendants in some other way. Thus, the trustee will distribute the property in three shares, one to each living child and one divided between the two grandchildren.

> **Example:** Daniel creates yet another trust for Jeanne and gives her a *general* power of appointment, to appoint to anyone including herself. In this case, assuming no takers in default, the trust property will be distributed to Jeanne's estate.

The rules that apply to distributions in default of exercise of a power of appointment are primarily common law rules, and the *Restatement* provides guidance on the rules, but a few states have enacted statements addressing the issue. Here is the California statute:

Cal. Prob. Code §672 (2010). Discretionary powers; general powers.

> (a) Except as provided in subdivision (b), if the donee of a discretionary power of appointment fails to appoint the property, releases the entire power, or makes an ineffective appointment, in whole or in part, the appointive property not effectively appointed passes to the person named by the donor as taker in default or, if there is none, reverts to the donor.
>
> (b) If the donee of a general power of appointment makes an ineffective appointment, an implied alternative appointment to the donee's estate may be found if the donee has manifested an intent that the appointive property be disposed of as property of the donee rather than as in default of appointment.

2.   *Contract to Exercise a Power*

The donee of a power of appointment that can be exercised currently can enter into a contract to exercise the power on behalf of a permissible appointee. If the power is a general power, the donee can exercise the power on behalf of himself, so entering into a contract to exercise the power will result in an enforceable power. If the power is a nongeneral power, the donee cannot exercise the power in a way that benefits himself because he is not a permissible donee, but the donee can contract to exercise the power in favor of one of the permissible appointees, as long as he does not benefit personally.

> **Example:**   Bernard is given a power to appoint among his children, during lifetime or at death. Bernard's daughter, Danielle, would like to buy a house. She would like Bernard to agree to appoint some of the trust property to her if she becomes unable to pay the mortgage. If Bernard agrees, his promise will be an enforceable contract, because he could currently appoint property to Danielle, who is a permissible appointee. *See* RESTATEMENT (THIRD) OF PROPERTY: WILLS & OTHER DONATIVE TRANSFERS §21.1 (T.D. No. 5, 2006). Note that Bernard cannot receive compensation for his agreement to appoint. Bernard is not a permissible appointee, so he cannot benefit indirectly from the exercise of the power. (This example comes from the *Restatement* section cited, and the section does not explain what the consideration for the contract would be.)

The donee of a *testamentary* power cannot enter into a contract to exercise the power in the future. A court will not enforce an agreement to exercise a testamentary power of appointment because the donee cannot exercise the power until the donee dies. If a donor creates a testamentary power of appointment, the donor intends the donee to be able to continue considering the best way to exercise the power. A contractual agreement to exercise it in a particular way operates like a current exercise because the donee cannot change her mind later.

If the person is not a taker in default and enters into a contract with the donee to exercise the power, then the person contracting with the donee will have a claim for restitution if the donee fails to exercise the power as required by the contract. The restitution claim will be based on the unjust enrichment of the donee. The contract will not be enforced against the property subject to the power, but the donee's own assets can be used to settle the claim.

In *Seidel v. Werner*, 364 N.Y.S.2d 963, *aff'd on opinion below*, 376 N.Y.S.2d 139 (1975), Steven Werner held a testamentary general power of appointment over property in a trust created by his father. He agreed, as part of a divorce settlement, to exercise the power of appointment in favor of two of his children, the two children of the marriage being dissolved. He died, with a will that exercised his power in favor of his next wife (she was wife number three). The court refused to uphold the contract to appoint and said that the children's only remedy was a claim for restitution against Werner. The trust property could not be used to satisfy that claim because the trust property did not belong to Werner, who only held a power of appointment over the property.

If the person hoping to get the property subject to a testamentary power is named as a taker in default, then having the donor release the power may be better than entering into a contact to exercise the power. In *Seidel* a release would have meant that Werner's four children (the takers in default) would have received the property.

E.   CREDITORS OF THE DONEES OF A GENERAL POWER OF APPOINTMENT

The donee of a general power of appointment may appoint some or all of the property to himself to the extent consistent with the grant. This may be viewed as the functional equivalent of ownership. Since the donee can make the trust property his own, the question arises whether the donee's creditors can look to the trust as a source to collect debts.

Under the common law, the donee of a general power of appointment has traditionally been treated as *not* owning the property until he exercises the power. *See* Restatement (Second) of Property: Donative Transfers §13.2 (1986). Thus, the donee's creditors cannot reach the appointive property before he appoints it to himself.

The UTC, the UPC and several states have changed this rule. UTC §505(b) provides that creditors of the donee can reach property subject to a power of withdrawal in much the same manner as they could have proceeded against the settlor of a revocable trust. The comments to §505 state, "If the power is unlimited, the property subject to the power will be fully subject to the claims of the power holder's creditors, the same as the power holder's other assets. If the power holder retains the power until death, the property subject to the power may be liable for claims and statutory allowances to the extent the power holder's probate estate is insufficient to satisfy those claims and allowances. For powers limited either in time or amount, [the creditors' rights are similarly limited]." A few non-UTC states have statutes that reach the same result. *See* N.Y. Est. Powers & Trusts Law §§10-7.2, 10-7.4 (2010); Cal. Prob. Code §682 (2010); Mich. Comp. Laws §556.123 (2010); Wis. Stat. Ann. §702.17 (2009). The UPC provision that grants creditors rights in nonprobate assets includes property subject to a general power of appointment. *See* UPC §6-102.

The *Restatement (Third) of Property: Wills & Other Donative Transfers* §22.3 (T.D. No. 5, 2006) also departs from the traditional rule. The *Restatement* provides that property subject to a general power will be subject to the donee's creditors, but only after the donee's other property has been used to satisfy the claims. Spendthrift clauses do not apply to powers of appointment.

F.   TAX ISSUES

In Chapter 14, we discuss the estate and gift tax. We need not discuss tax issues in depth here, but it is useful to note that giving someone a power of appointment or a fiduciary power to make distributions to herself may have estate or gift tax consequences.

Internal Revenue Code (IRC) §2041 imposes a gift or estate tax on any property subject to a general power of appointment. Section 2041 includes in its definition of a general power of appointment both the nonfiduciary powers we discussed in this chapter and the fiduciary powers over distribution of property we discussed in Chapter 6. For planning purposes, it is important to remember that giving a donee a general power of appointment causes the property subject to the power to be included in the donee's estate for gift and estate tax purposes, whereas giving someone a nongeneral power does not. If the donee has a significant amount of wealth, the donor will want to consider the donee's tax situation in making a decision about granting a power of appointment.

In this chapter we use the terms "general power" and "nongeneral power" as they are used in the tax code. A general power can include a fiduciary power, as explained below.

1. When the Donee Is Not the Trustee

Because a person holding a general power of appointment has the power to appoint the property for her own benefit, the IRC treats the property as the donee's property for estate and gift tax purposes. Even if the donee appoints the property to someone else and never benefits directly from the property, her control over the property is what matters for tax purposes.

A lifetime exercise, or a release, of the power is considered a taxable gift. If a person holds a general power at death, the property is included in the person's estate for tax purposes, whether she exercises the power or not.

2. When the Trustee Is a Beneficiary

An entirely discretionary power held by a trustee will be considered a power of appointment for tax purposes. Therefore, in choosing a standard of distribution for a trust, a lawyer should be aware of potential tax consequences, remembering that a general power of appointment is treated as the donee's property while a nongeneral power is not. Depending on the result preferred, the property owner may wish to give the trustee a general power or may wish to limit the power so that it is a nongeneral power.

> **Example:** "The trustee shall distribute so much of the income or principal of the trust to one or more of Damien, Edgar or Gregory, in such shares as the trustee determines to be in the best interests of these beneficiaries." If the trustee is Damien, he has a general power of appointment. Any exercise of discretion in favor of Edgar or Gregory will be considered a taxable gift by Damien.
>
> If the settlor wants to avoid the problem of creating a general power of appointment, the settlor can name someone other than Damien as the trustee. If the settlor names a friend, Franklyn, as trustee, then neither Damien nor Franklyn will have a general power of appointment. Franklyn cannot appoint the property to himself, so he holds a nongeneral power.

If the settlor wants to name as trustee someone who will be a beneficiary, the settlor can limit the standard of distribution to one that is considered ascertainable under the tax rules. In that case, what would otherwise appear to be a general power of appointment (the power to distribute to oneself) is converted to a nongeneral power for tax purposes.

Example: "The trustee shall distribute so much of the income or principal of the trust to one or more of Damien, Edgar or Gregory, in such shares as needed for their health and education." If the trustee is Damien, even though the power might appear to be a general one because he can distribute property to himself, he does not have a general power of appointment for tax purposes due to the standards imposed. Any exercise of discretion in favor of Edgar or Gregory will not be treated as a taxable gift and the property subject to the power will not be included in Damien's estate when he dies.

Whether a standard is ascertainable or nonascertainable depends on state law. However, for tax purposes, the Internal Revenue Code and Treasury regulations provide "bright-line" guidance. A standard that directs the trustee to make distributions for "health, education, maintenance, and support" (HEMS), or for any one of those purposes, is considered ascertainable. By contrast, a direction to distribute for a beneficiary's "welfare and best interests" is considered nonascertainable. Other standards are less certain. For example, "support in reasonable comfort" is ascertainable, but "comfort" by itself depends on how a state court interprets that standard.[2] Any standard deemed ascertainable under state law will be considered ascertainable for tax purposes, but a court proceeding may be necessary to determine whether the standard is ascertainable.

A decision to use a standard other than the "safe harbors" is dangerous, because the result is uncertain. A lawyer should use either one or more of the HEMS standards if the intent is to create a nongeneral power of appointment or the "welfare and best interests" standard, if the intent is to create a general power. Fortunately, UTC §814 affirmatively seeks to cure careless drafting by stating that, unless the terms of the trust expressly state otherwise, all general powers of appointment are to be exercised "only in accordance with an ascertainable standard, [unless the] power [is] held by the settlor's spouse who is the trustee of a trust for which a marital deduction . . . was previously allowed . . . . " This provision produces the "correct" tax result in the vast majority of situations.

---

2. The Treasury Regulations state that comfort is nonascertainable: "A power to use property for the comfort, welfare, or happiness of the holder of the power is not limited by the requisite standard." Treas. Reg. §20.2041-1(c)(2). Sometimes, however, "comfort" is used with other terms and may be interpreted to mean "support in reasonable comfort" or may in some other way be considered ascertainable. In *Estate of Vissering v. Comm'r*, 990 F.2d 578 (10th Cir. 1993) the court interpreted a power held by the decedent to invade corpus "to the extent required for [the decedent's] continued comfort" as an ascertainable standard. The safe thing is to avoid the word "comfort" when drafting a standard.

PROBLEMS

1. Amir's will created a trust with the following provision: "The trustee shall distribute all the income to Jasmine, at least monthly. The trustee shall also distribute so much or all of the principal of the trust to Jasmine, as the trustee determines necessary for her health, maintenance and support. On Jasmine's death, the trustee shall distribute the remaining trust corpus to such one or more of my descendants, in trust or otherwise, as Jasmine appoints by will, and if Jasmine fails to exercise this power of appointment, to my then living descendants, by representation." When Amir died, he was married to Jasmine. They had two children, Damien and Fatima. After Amir died, Jasmine married Ibrahim. They had a child, Nadia. To whom should the trustee distribute the trust property if, when Jasmine died, her will contained the following provision:

    a. "I appoint all property in the trust created under Article Five of my deceased husband's will and over which I hold a power of appointment to my husband, Ibrahim."

    b. "I appoint all property in the trust created under Article Five of my deceased husband's will and over which I hold a power of appointment in equal shares to my three children."

    c. "I give the residue of my estate to my descendants, by representation."

    d. "I give the residue of my estate, including any property subject to a power of appointment, to my daughter, Fatima."

2. Same facts as Problem 1. Five years before she died, Jasmine executed a document that said, "I hereby release the power of appointment I hold under the will of my former husband, Amir." To whom should the trust property be given?

3. Elvira created a trust for her daughter, Aubrey. The trust instrument directs the trustee to distribute the property to Aubrey, for her welfare and best interests. The trust instrument also directs the trustee to distribute property as Aubrey appoints either by an instrument executed during her lifetime or by will. If Aubrey fails to exercise the power of appointment, the trustee is to distribute the property to the nonprofit organization, Doctors Without Borders.

Aubrey enters into a contract with George, in connection with their divorce, in which she agrees to exercise her power of appointment in favor of their child, Bruno.

When Aubrey dies, her will contains the following provision: "I hereby exercise the power of appointment I was given under the will of my mother, Elvira, and appoint all remaining trust property to my partner-in-life, Hannah."

To whom should the trustee distribute the property?

4. In Problem 3, if Elvira's friend, Frederick, is the trustee, is the trustee's fiduciary power included in Frederick's estate as a general power of appointment? Same question if Aubrey is the trustee.

EXERCISE

Warren's trust contained the following provision: "My daughter, Violet, shall have the power during her lifetime or at death to appoint the trust property to any one or more of her descendants."

Violet has three children: Axel, Bernard and Claude. Axel has a child, Magda, and Bernard has a stepchild, Norine. Draft the following:

1.   A current exercise of the power giving the trust corpus to Magda and Norine.
2.   A testamentary exercise of the power giving the trust corpus to Axel, Bernard and Claude.

G.   CONTINGENT FUTURE INTERESTS AND THE RULE AGAINST PERPETUITIES

One of the oldest rules governing inheritance law is the common law Rule Against Perpetuities. The Rule was an attempt to force vesting of contingent future interests within a reasonable timeframe — couched in ancient parlance as a "life or lives in being plus twenty-one years." The Rule was an effort to constrain the dead hand of grantors long gone who wanted to keep tight control over the land they had left to their descendants. In policy terms, the Rule would cut off interests that prevented the free exchange of land and thus encourage a free flow of commerce. Without the Rule, contingent future interests in land could remain unvested forever. Those interests could lurk in the shadows until an event occurred that would trigger a shift from one interest holder to another, long into the future.

The focus of the discussion that follows is on the need for careful drafting to avoid the application of the Rule rather than a description of the many problems created by the Rule and the methods for solving those problems. This section explores the kind of future interests that are most likely to trigger the Rule and it describes the statutory reforms adopted in many states, including the Uniform Statutory Rule Against Perpetuities (USRAP). This section includes examples which will help you understand that careful drafting and a precise choice of the triggering event is the best way to prevent a Rule problem.

1.   In General

The common law Rule Against Perpetuities can be stated as follows:

A contingent future interest in property must either vest or fail to vest for certain within a life or lives in being plus twenty-one years.

If the interest vests during that time period, then the Rule has been satisfied; if the interest will not vest during that time and may continue to exist beyond the period of the Rule, then it is void. Note that only contingent future interests in a grantee trigger the Rule; a contingent future interest in a grantor does not trigger the Rule (an historical anomaly). Consider the following examples:

Example 1:   Carlos gives the family homestead, Evergreen, to Nina using the following language, "I hereby grant Evergreen to Nina." Carlos has given Nina a fee simple absolute in Evergreen.

Example 2:   Carlos gives Evergreen to Nina using the following language, "I hereby grant Evergreen to Nina for life." Carlos has created a present interest (a life estate) in Nina, and a future interest in himself (a reversion).

Example 3:   Carlos gives Evergreen to Nina using the following language, "I hereby grant Evergreen to Nina for life and then to Maria." Nina has a present interest (a life estate) and Maria has a vested future interest (a vested remainder). Maria is not at risk of losing her interest here because the common law Rule does not apply to vested future interests, only contingent ones.

Example 4:   Carlos gives Evergreen to Nina using the following language, "I hereby grant Evergreen to Nina for life and then to Maria, if Maria survives Nina." Nina has a present interest (a life estate) and Maria now has a contingent future interest (a contingent remainder). Maria is at risk of losing her interest here because the common law Rule *does* apply to contingent future interests. However, a court is able to tell at the moment this interest is created whether or not Maria's interest will either vest or fail to vest within a life or lives in being plus 21 years. Why? Because the event that will decide whether or not the interest in Evergreen shifts the interest from Nina to Maria — Maria's death — will happen within a life or lives in being — Maria's lifespan. The court will not even need the 21 years. Note that Carlos has a reversion. If Maria does not survive Nina, the interest goes back to Carlos or his estate. The common law Rule does not apply here even though Carlos technically holds a future interest that is contingent on Maria's failing to survive Nina. The Rule does not apply to contingent future interests in the grantor.

The Rule is applied as if the court has blinders on. The court does not look at what *might* happen in the future. It can only look to the language of the grant at the time it becomes operative (upon death if it is a will or testamentary trust and upon creation if it is a deed or inter vivos trust.)

Example 5: In 2000, Carlos gives Evergreen to Nina using the following language, "I hereby grant Evergreen to Nina but if someone swims the English Channel, then to Maria."

It does not matter if someone actually swims the English Channel a day after the grant is made. What matters is whether the court can tell, for sure, at the moment of creation whether or not the interest will either vest or fail to vest within a life or lives in being plus 21 years. The interest that matters in this case is Maria's interest. Nina is fine. She is not at risk of losing her interest because her interest is a present interest, not a future interest. Maria, however, has the vulnerable contingent future interest that triggers Rule application. If the grant violates the Rule, the remedy in most states under the common law would be that Maria's interest fails immediately. She does not even get a chance to wait and see whether someone swims the English Channel. And Nina would then be given a fee simple absolute.[3]

PROBLEM

Why does the grant in Example 5 above violate the common law Rule Against Perpetuities? How would you correct the language of the grant so it does not violate the common law Rule?

2.   Perpetuities Reform — Wait and See and USRAP

Over time, states began to modify the harsh results created by the Rule. They adopted statutory reforms that allowed courts to wait and see if the event that would trigger the shifting over from the present interest holder to the contingent future interest holder would actually happen. This so-called "wait and see" approach to reform was adopted by the Uniform Law Commission in 1986 with the promulgation of the Uniform Statutory Rule Against Perpetuities (USRAP), which combines "wait and see" with the common law Rule.

a.   USRAP

Under USRAP, if a grant is valid under the common law Rule, it is valid under USRAP immediately. The court does not even have to consider the alternative wait and see rule. That gives certainty to Maria — our contingent future interest holder. However, if her interest does violate the common law Rule, then Maria gets a second bite at the apple — the court

---

3. *See* Frederic S. Schwartz, A Student's Guide to the Rule Against Perpetuities (1988) for an excellent guide to the basic operation of the common law Rule.

can adopt a wait and see approach under USRAP. Maria does not lose her interest right away.

UPC §2-901. Statutory Rule Against Perpetuities.

> (a) [Validity of Nonvested Property Interest.] A nonvested property interest is invalid unless:
>
> (1) when the interest is created, it is certain to vest or terminate no later than 21 years after the death of an individual then alive; or
>
> (2) the interest either vests or terminates within 90 years after its creation.

Note that USRAP also applies to general powers of appointment subject to a condition precedent as well as nongeneral or testamentary powers of appointment.

UPC §2-901. Statutory Rule Against Perpetuities.

> . . . (b) [Validity of General Power of Appointment Subject to a Condition Precedent.] A general power of appointment not presently exercisable because of a condition precedent is invalid unless:
>
> (1) when the power is created, the condition is certain to be satisfied or become impossible to satisfy no later than 21 years after the death of an individual then alive; or
>
> (2) the condition precedent either is satisfied or becomes impossible to satisfy within 90 years after its creation.
>
> (c) [Validity of Nongeneral or Testamentary Power of Appointment.] A nongeneral power of appointment or a testamentary power of appointment is invalid unless:
>
> (1) when the power is created, the condition is certain to be irrevocably exercised or otherwise to terminate no later than 21 years after the death of an individual then alive; or
>
> (2) the power is irrevocably exercised or otherwise terminates within 90 years after its creation.

Example: Carlos gives Evergreen to Nina for life, then to Nina's firstborn child for life, then to such persons, including Nina's firstborn child or such child's estate or creditors, as Nina's firstborn child shall appoint after reaching the age of 25, and in default of appointment to Carlos' grandchildren. Carlos is survived by his daughter, Nina, who is childless at his death, and by his son, Geraldo, who has two children,

Xavier and Yolanda. The power of appointment is subject to a condition precedent. Since it is not valid under the common law Rule (section (1)(b)(1)) then the court must wait and see if it becomes valid under section (1)(b)(2). If Nina has a child, her child must live to be age 25 (or die before reaching age 25) within 90 years after Carlos' death or the power will be invalid under USRAP.[4]

USRAP provides that if an interest violates the common law Rule, the holder of the interest can petition the court to modify or reform the instrument so that it would be valid.

UPC §2-903. Reformation.

> Upon the petition of an interested person, a court shall reform a disposition in the manner that most closely approximates the transferor's manifested plan of distribution and is within the 90 years allowed by Section 1(a)(2), 1(b)(2), or 1(c)(2) if:
>
>   (1) a nonvested property interest or a power of appointment becomes invalid under Section 1 (statutory rule against perpetuities);
>
>   (2) a class gift is not but might become invalid under Section 1 (statutory rule against perpetuities) and the time has arrived when the share of any class member is to take effect in possession or enjoyment; or
>
>   (3) a nonvested property interest that is not validated by Section 1(a)(1) can vest but not within 90 years after its creation.

b. Perpetuities Savings Clause

As a matter of careful drafting, a lawyer will include a clause called a perpetuities savings clause in any instrument in which the Rule might be implicated. Savings clauses act as an override to cut off any contingent future interest that may be invalid under the common law Rule. The following is an example of the kind of "failsafe" provision that can be included in a will or trust instrument to ensure that no trusts created under the document will violate the rule.

Termination of Trusts. Notwithstanding any other provisions of the Declaration of Trust, each separate trust hereunder shall terminate twenty years after the death of the survivor of the settlor and such of the settlor's issue as were living at the date of this Declaration of Trust or, if amended, at the date of the

---

4. *See* Uniform Statutory Rule Against Perpetuities, Comment, Section E, Example 16, *available at* http://www.law.upenn.edu/bll/archives/ulc/fnact99/1990s/usrap90.htm.

latest amendment. Upon any termination provided for in this section, the property of the terminated trust shall be distributed, free of the Continuing Trusts provision of this article to or for the benefit of the beneficiaries who are then eligible to receive the income therefrom, in such amounts and shares as the trustees may determine.

NOTES AND QUESTIONS

1. *The new rules.* Under USRAP, how long does the court have to wait and see? Why do you think the drafters chose the number of years they chose? Why do you think the drafters retained the common law Rule at all? For an explanation of USRAP from the perspective of the principal drafter, see Lawrence W. Waggoner, *The Uniform Statutory Rule Against Perpetuities: The Rationale of the 90-Year Waiting Period*, 73 Cornell L. Rev. 157 (1988).

2. *Trust remainders.* The most common kind of contingent future interest in modern estate planning practice is a remainder in a trust. For example, Lily is the grantor of a trust that gives an income interest to her son, David, for his life with the remainder to David's daughter, Celeste, if she survives him. Lily has created a present interest in David and a future interest in Celeste that is contingent on her surviving David. Consider what will happen if more remote interests are created, such as an interest in Celeste's children or grandchildren — all descendants of Lily. These interests may not vest within a life or lives in being (typically using David and Celeste as measuring lives) plus 21 years. Will USRAP save such an interest in Celeste's children or grandchildren?

3. *Be careful with boilerplate.* The perpetuities savings clause reproduced above works for many client situations but not for all of them. Can you think of a family pattern for which a different clause would be necessary? How would you redraft the clause?

3. Complete Abolition?

An increasing number of state legislatures have abolished the common-law Rule altogether so that there is no check on when contingent future interests must vest. Others have adopted modifications to the Rule, suspending application of the Rule for a period of years ranging from 360 to 1,000 years. Often, the purpose of these statutory changes is to allow the creation of "dynasty trusts" — private express trusts that can provide for descendants in perpetuity. The goal is to attract trust business and capital to the states. Some inheritance law scholars have criticized this movement.

Lawrence W. Waggoner, Curtailing Dead-Hand Control: The American Law Institute Declares the Perpetual-Trust Movement Ill Advised
U. Mich. Pub. Law Working Paper No. 199 (2010)[5]

Recent years have seen a movement in the states to pass legislation repealing or modifying the Rule Against Perpetuities in order to allow transferors to create trusts that can last forever (*e.g.*, Alaska, Delaware, the District of Columbia, Idaho, Illinois, Maine, Maryland, Missouri, Nebraska, New Hampshire, New Jersey, North Carolina, Ohio, Pennsylvania, Rhode Island, South Dakota, Virginia, and Wisconsin) or for several centuries (*e.g.*, 1000 years in Colorado, Utah, and Wyoming; 500 years in Arizona; 365 years in Nevada; 360 years in Florida, Michigan, and Tennessee). In the *Restatement (Third) of Property: Wills and Other Donative Transfers*, adopted by the American Law Institute at its 2010 annual meeting, the Institute took a position that the perpetual-trust movement is ill advised. . . . The absence of a Rule Against Perpetuities or of a serious Rule Against Perpetuities has paid off for a few of the states that now allow perpetual or near perpetual trusts. In an empirical study, . . . the authors found that roughly $100 billion in trust assets had flowed into those states. . . . *See* Robert H. Sitkoff & Max Schanzenbach, 2 *Jurisdictional Competition for Trust Funds: An Empirical Analysis of Perpetuities and Taxes*, 115 YALE L.J. 356, 410 (2005); Max M. Schanzenbach & Robert H. Sitkoff, *Perpetuities or Taxes? Explaining the Rise of the Perpetual Trust*, 27 CARDOZO L. REV. 2465 (2006).

NOTES AND QUESTIONS

1.   *No more.* Do you think that complete abolition of the Rule is a good policy? Should people be allowed to control interests on behalf of their descendants forever? Put another way, should people be allowed to protect their descendants from creditors and estate taxes forever?

2.   *Stranger than fact.* An amusing way to "study" trusts and estates is to watch the 1981 movie *Body Heat* with William Hurt and Kathleen Turner. A plot twist turns on a supposed Rule violation, which the writers got wrong.

---

5. *Available at* http://ssrn.com/abstract=1614934.

4.   *Charitable Interests—Exception to the Rule*

One major exception to the application of the Rule Against Perpetuities is the transfer of a contingent future interest to a charitable organization. The policy rationale here is that society as a whole benefits from such interests being allowed to go on long into the future so that forcing them to vest early is not as great a concern. We explore charitable trusts in Chapter 16.

UPC §2-904. Exclusion from Statutory Rule Against Perpetuities.

> Section 1 (statutory rule against perpetuities) does not apply to:
>   (5) a nonvested property interest held by a charity, government, or governmental agency or subdivision, if the nonvested property interest is preceded by an interest held by another charity, government, or governmental agency or subdivision;

9 WILL VALIDITY

A. INTRODUCTION

The hallmark of American inheritance law is "freedom of testation." In other words, people can opt-out of the default system of intestacy by executing a will. A will is a donative instrument that is custom-tailored to reflect how an individual (the testator) wants property distributed at death. As you saw in Chapter 3, under the intestacy statutes the testator's close family members are the preferred recipients of the estate. However, the testator may prefer that property be distributed to those who do not fit within the statute's definition of family, to a favorite charity or to more distant relatives or friends. With a few limited exceptions discussed in Chapter 12, testators may devise property to whomever they wish.

In order for a probate court to enforce those choices after the testator's death, the will must meet certain requirements. These requirements concern the document itself as well as the testator's mental state or testamentary capacity. As noted in the excerpt below, American inheritance law has built upon both the 1677 English Statute of Frauds and the 1837 Statute of Wills in developing validity requirements.

Lawrence Friedman, Dead Hands: A Social History of Wills, Trusts, and Inheritance Law

(2009)

CHAPTER 3: THE LAST WILL AND TESTAMENT

In modern colloquial English, a will is a document that disposes of the man's property at death. No longer are there separate documents for real property and personal property; the two are combined and, while old-fashioned lawyers still pin on the label "Last Will and Testament," nowadays most of us simply call it a "will." The ordinary will, the most common kind, and the kind that is recognized as valid in every state, is a highly formal document. For one thing, it has to be in writing. In 1677, the (English) Statute of Frauds insisted that all dispositions of land at death had to be in writing, signed by the testator, and witnessed. Under the (English) Wills Act (1837), these requirements applied to all gifts at death, whether personal property or real estate. The texts of these two statutes had important influences on the way American statutes were drafted.

The law takes very seriously the requirement that a will must be in writing. If a man gathers a roomful of friends and relatives, and announces clearly and distinctly that he wants his money to go half to his daughter and half to a home for abandoned cats and then drops dead on the spot, he has died intestate, and his expressed wishes make no difference. Oral wills ("nuncupative wills") were at one time valid; but for two centuries or so, only under New York law, an oral will was invalid "unless made by a soldier while in actual military service, or by a mariner, while at sea." Most states no longer recognize such wills at all. They survive theoretically in a few states, but are virtually useless. In Indiana, only a person "in imminent peril of death" can make an oral will; it is valid, however, only if the person actually dies, and only if he declares this will before two witnesses who write down what he said within thirty days and submit it to probate within six months of the testator's death. Even then, this will can only dispose of property up to $1,000 in value, although people on active duty "in time of war" can bequeath up to a total of $10,000. My guess is that the total number of oral wills probated in Indiana, in any given year, is zero. I personally have never seen, in any probate file, the slightest trace of a nuncupative will.

How many witnesses are needed for ordinary wills? Holographic wills (handwritten wills) need none of at all. These wills, in a bare majority of American states, are as valid as any other kind of will. (More on these wills later.) Wills that do not qualify as holographs need at least two witnesses in every state [except Pennsylvania]. Some lawyers, out of caution, will throw in a third witness. This might spare the estate some trouble if one witness dies or moves to China or becomes demented. Witnesses were supposed to guarantee, through their testimony, that the will was executed properly and that all the legal details were buttoned up. Every will has to have the testator's signature. And the testator has to intend the document to be in his will. This is almost never a problem. After all, in the usual situation, the testator went to a lawyer for the specific purpose of asking the lawyer to draft him a will. The client tells the lawyer what he wants in his will, the lawyer draws up the document; the client signs it in front of witnesses, tells the witnesses (at the lawyer's prompting) that this is his will and asks them to witness it. As long as this little ceremony is carried out, nobody can question whether the document was a will and was meant to be a will, or that it was properly executed. [*citations omitted*].

———————————

This chapter explores these formal requirements in detail and the policy concerns that underpin them. The next section explores the complexities of these requirements for a valid will. It also describes a significant exception to the formalities for "holographic wills," and the relatively new doctrines of substantial compliance and harmless error, which are designed to mitigate some of the harshness of the formal requirements. Finally, we provide you with some exercises to develop your ability to interview clients, to draft a valid will and to perform a will execution ceremony.

B. LEGAL REQUIREMENTS FOR THE TESTATOR

1. Age and Testamentary Capacity

States typically require that the testator be age 18 and of sound mind to make a will.[1] For example, UPC §2-501 provides, "An individual 18 or more years of age who is of sound mind may make a will." While most states allow people under the age of 18 who are emancipated minors to make a will, the number of emancipated minors is quite small.[2] We explore the nature of being of sound mind or "testamentary capacity" more fully in Chapter 11. Suffice it to say at this point that the testator: (1) must understand she is making a will; (2) must know the extent and character of her

———————————

1. For some very interesting wills of the rich and famous, see http://www .megadox.com. *See also* Kevin Rawlinson, *Famous Wills: They Couldn't Take It with Them*, THE INDEP, (Aug. 11, 2010), *available at* http://www.independent.co.uk/news/people/news/ famous-wills-they-couldnt-take-it-with-them-2049101.html# ("A record of more than 6 million Victorian and early 20th-century wills has been made public for the first time, revealing the last wishes of some of the most important figures of the age, including Charles Dickens, Karl Marx and Charles Darwin.").

2. Emancipated minors are children under the age of 18 who have been legally recognized as having the rights of adults, either through court order or compliance with a statute.

property; and (3) must know the natural objects of her bounty, who are generally recognized as the testator's close relatives. *See In re Estate of Ellis*, 616 N.W.2d 59 (Neb. Ct. App. 2000).

2.   *Testamentary Intent*

In addition to testamentary capacity, all states require testamentary intent for the creation of a valid will. Testamentary intent means that the decedent intended the document to be a will and to become operative on her death. A strong but rebuttable presumption of testamentary intent exists if the will contains language to that effect, such as "This is my last will and testament." If such language is absent, a court may infer testamentary intent from other words in the document itself. In some states, courts allow extrinsic evidence to establish testamentary intent in the absence of an express provision. We explore testamentary intent more fully in Chapter 11.

C.   FORMALITIES REQUIRED IN THE WILL

In addition to the legal requirements of age, capacity and intent that are imposed on the testator, the will itself must meet certain formal criteria in order to be valid. The statutory formalities required by most states include that the will be in writing, it be signed by the testator and attested to by two or three witnesses. These requirements grew out of the English Statute of Frauds of 1677 and the Wills Act of 1837, both of which are mentioned in the excerpt from Professor Friedman's book at the beginning of this chapter. In addition, some states require "publication," *i.e.*, that the testator signify to the attesting witnesses that the document is the testator's will.

Will formalities serve four functions:

1.   *The Evidentiary Function.* They assure that permanent reliable evidence of testator's intent exists;
2.   *The Channeling Function.* They assure that the testator's intent is expressed in a way that is understood by those who need to interpret it. Formalism also assures that the document enters the legal system in a manner that courts (and personal representatives) can process routinely and without litigation;
3.   *The Ritual (Cautionary) Function.* They assure that the testator's intent to dispose of property is serious and that the testator understands this is a will. The formal requirements assure that the document is final and not a draft; and

4. *The Protective Function.* They assure that the testator is protected from her own lack of capacity. They assure that testator's intent is not the product of undue influence, fraud, delusion or coercion. The formal requirements also assure that the document and signatures are not the products of forgery or perjury.[3]

As we explore each of the formality requirements below—a writing, a signature, attestation and publication—ask yourself which of these functions the various requirements serve and how well they serve those functions.

Historically, inheritance law placed great weight on formalism. The law has shifted to the more relaxed approach we have today under the UPC. *See* John H. Langbein, *The Nonprobate Revolution and the Future of the Law of Succession*, 97 HARV. L. REV. 1108 (1984); John H. Langbein, *Substantial Compliance with the Wills Act*, 88 HARV. L. REV. 489 (1975). As we will see, UPC §2-502 requires only minimal formalities and UPC §2-503 even allows those to be waived if the error is harmless.

UPC §2-502. Formalities Required for a Valid Will.

(a) [Witnessed or Notarized Wills.] Except as otherwise provided in subsection (b) and in Sections 2-503, 2-506, and 2-513, a will must be:

(1) in writing;

(2) signed by the testator or in the testator's name by some other individual in the testator's conscious presence and by the testator's direction; and

(3) either:

(A) signed by at least two individuals, each of whom signed within a reasonable time after the individual witnessed either the signing of the will as described in paragraph (2) or the testator's acknowledgment of that signature or acknowledgment of the will; or

(B) acknowledged by the testator before a notary public or other individual authorized by law to take acknowledgments. . . .

(c) [Extrinsic Evidence.] Intent that a document constitute the testator's will can be established by extrinsic evidence, including, for holographic wills, portions of the document that are not in the testator's handwriting.

---

3. *See* Ashbel G. Gulliver & Catherine J. Tilson, *Classification of Gratuitous Transfers*, 51 YALE L.J. 1, 5-13 (1941); RESTATEMENT (THIRD) OF PROPERTY: WILLS & OTHER DONATIVE TRANSFERS §3.3, cmt. a.

1.   *The Writing Requirement*

States generally require that a will be in writing, although some states recognize nuncupative, *i.e.*, oral wills. As Professor Friedman notes in the excerpt above, if oral wills are allowed, they generally must be executed while in fear of imminent death, often on the battlefield, in order to be valid.[4] Courts prefer paper writings, but the writing requirement has been broadly construed to include a "medium that allows the markings to be detected." For example, the Licking County Probate Court in Ohio recently probated a will written on a piece of wood by a local woman.[5] The following example is based on the *Restatement (Third) of Property: Wills & Other Donative Transfers* §3.1, cmt. i.

> **Example.**   Arun writes his last will and testament with his finger on the dirty window of his car, just before he is to expire following a car accident. This would be considered a "writing" for purposes of meeting formality requirements. However, if Arun had drawn the same words in the air with his finger, in the presence of the ambulance driver who arrived on the scene, this would not meet the "writing" requirement.

Given this historical emphasis on the writing requirement, consider how new technology may have an effect on what constitutes a "writing." Nevada is in the forefront of allowing an electronic version of a will to meet the writing requirement. Other states have not yet followed Nevada's lead. What are the risks involved in allowing electronic documents to be deemed valid wills?

Nev. Rev. Stat. Ann. §133.085. Electronic Will.

> 1. An electronic will is a will of a testator that:
>   (a) Is written, created and stored in an electronic record;
>   (b) Contains the date and the electronic signature of the testator and which includes, without limitation, at least one authentication characteristic of the testator; and
>   (c) Is created and stored in such a manner that:
>   (1) Only one authoritative copy exists;

---

4. Note also that under 10 U.S.C. §1044d (2006), *Military testamentary instruments: requirement for recognition by States,* states are required to give effect to wills by service members which comply with this federal statute even though they do not meet the requirements of that state's statute of wills. This is a rare federal preemption of an area of law traditionally left to the states.

5. *See* L.B. Whyde, *Johnstown Woman's Will Recorded on Wood,* NewarkAdvocate.com, (Sept. 28, 2010), *available at* http://www.newarkadvocate.com/article/20100928/NEWS01/9280339/0/NEWS/Johnstown-woman-s-will-recorded-on-wood?odyssey=modllateststories.

(2) The authoritative copy is maintained and controlled by the testator or a custodian designated by the testator in the electronic will;

(3) Any attempted alteration of the authoritative copy is readily identifiable; and

(4) Each copy of the authoritative copy is readily identifiable as a copy that is not the authoritative copy. . . .

6. As used in this section:

(a) "Authentication characteristic" means a characteristic of a certain person that is unique to that person and that is capable of measurement and recognition in an electronic record as a biological aspect of or physical act performed by that person. Such a characteristic may consist of a fingerprint, a retinal scan, voice recognition, facial recognition, a digitized signature or other authentication using a unique characteristic of the person.

(b) "Authoritative copy" means the original, unique, identifiable and unalterable electronic record of an electronic will.

(c) "Digitized signature" means a graphical image of a handwritten signature that is created, generated or stored by electronic means.

Example: After John Smith died, his widow, Linda Smith, finds a document stored in his "My Documents" file on his laptop. The instrument says, "On this fifth day of September 2009, I hereby leave all of my property to my wife, Linda Smith." There is a date, *September 5, 2009,* and a digitized signature at the end of the document, *John Smith.* Under the Nevada statute, if this is the only copy of the will, it would be valid in electronic form since it is an authoritative copy in John Smith's control, on his laptop, with a date and a digitized signature.

NOTES AND QUESTIONS

1. *Formalism and electronic wills.* Does the Nevada statute serve all of the functions identified with formalities? In what ways, other than dispensing with the writing requirement, does it differ from the UPC? If you were to draft a Model Electronic Wills Act, what precautions against fraud would you include? What type of record would qualify as an "electronic will"?

2. *To witness or not to witness?* Notice there appears to be no witness requirement in the Nevada statute. What if John Smith's signature line were blank? Should it still be a valid electronic will?

3. *Change comes slowly.* Clearly there are policy concerns involved in allowing electronic wills. All of the evidentiary formalities that have grown up around will execution are aimed at ensuring that the will is the testator's own final wish as to the disposition of her property. For a discussion of these

policy concerns, see Joseph Karl Grant, *Shattering and Moving Beyond the Gutenberg Paradigm: The Dawn of the Electronic Will*, 42 U. Mich. J.L. Reform 105 (2008).

PROBLEM

Charlotte was 90 years old. She fell out of bed and broke her hip. Charlotte survived for a brief period of time but she died before anyone had a chance to check in on her. When Charlotte's neighbor, Lucy, found her, Lucy saw some scribbling in pencil on the floor next to Charlotte that read "I am dying and want my dear granddaughter, Monet, to inherit everything I own." If you represent Monet, what is the likelihood that you will be able to successfully argue that the scribbling on the floor qualifies as a "writing"?

2. The Signature Requirement

a. Where to Sign

All state statutes and the UPC require that the testator sign the will. The testator's act of writing her name, with the intent to adopt the document as her own, constitutes a valid signature. A signature provides evidence of finality, and serves to distinguish the final will from a preliminary draft, an incomplete document or simply notes about how the will might take shape in the future.

The testator's handwritten name in freestanding form at the end of the document unquestionably satisfies the signature requirement. This requirement is an outgrowth of the English Wills Act of 1837, which required the testator to sign "at the foot or end" of the will. A few states still require that the signature be at the end of the document, although the UPC does not.

> **Example:** Karina's attorney drafts a will for her. At the end of the document is a designated line for her signature. If Karina signs on the dotted line, this is a freestanding signature at the end of the document which will meet the signature requirements in all states.

LAST WILL AND TESTAMENT

I, Karina Klenke, being of sound mind, do make, publish and declare this to be my last will and testament . . .

. . . In testimony whereof, I have hereunto subscribed my name to this my last will and testament this 5th day of *June, 2010.*
Karina Klenke
Karina Klenke, Testator

However, in some cases, the testator fails to sign the will at the end, although his signed name may still appear in a provision of the will itself. For example, Jermaine executes a pre-printed will. He fills his name in his own handwriting in the first clause of the will which reads, "I, *Jermaine Johnson*, hereby make this last will and testament."[6] Jermaine does not sign again at the end of the will. The question for a court then is whether this type of handwriting of the testator's name is a sufficient "signature" for purposes of establishing that the formalities have been met.

In keeping with the relaxation of formalities embodied in the UPC, UPC §2-502(a)(2) does not require that the testator's signature be at the end of the will. The *Restatement (Third) of Property: Wills & Other Donative Transfers* §3.1 gives us guidance as to whether a signature that does not appear at the end of the document is valid. It notes that courts should not deem a name in an exordium alone to meet the signature requirement *unless* there is additional evidence that the person "adopted the document as his or her will." Thus, in those states that have adopted the UPC and in those non-UPC states that do not require a signature at the end, if such additional evidence exists, the written name will constitute a signature. *Comment k* to the *Restatement* above offers the following illustration of this rule and of the kind of evidence that will suffice to meet this standard.

> **Example:** Greta was 85 years old and ill in the hospital when she decided to make a will. She wrote out a will in her own hand on lined tablet paper. After the will was written out, she asked two friends to sign her will as witnesses, which they did at the bottom of the last page. Although Greta's will did not contain a freestanding signature other than her name in the exordium clause, that name suffices since she clearly evidenced her intent for the document to be her final will by asking the two witnesses to sign the will.

b. How to Sign

The best evidence that a testator intends the document she signs to be her will is a full name on the signature line, *i.e.*, what we normally think of as a "signature." However, there are cases where the testator is physically unable to put her full signature on the dotted line. In these cases, courts have recognized that testators may use other means to indicate that they have the intent to make this document their last will.

Both the UPC and the *Restatement (Third) of Property: Wills & Other Donative Transfers* note that the testator may sign her name or may make a cross or a mark, like an "X" or use a term of relationship like "Dad," "Mom" or "Auntie." These suffice, "if done with the intent of adopting the

---

6. This clause is called the "exordium clause" and it is the clause at the beginning of the will that establishes the testator's intent to make a will.

document as the testator's will." In addition, courts allow someone to guide the testator's hand in making the mark or the signature as long as there is evidence that this was done at the direction of a testator seeking to adopt the document as her will.

c. Who Can Sign

If the testator is physically unable to sign, even with the help of someone else guiding his hand, the UPC and state statutes allow someone else to sign at the testator's direction.[7] UPC §2-502(a)(2) allows for someone else to sign, but it provides certain safeguards against fraud by requiring that the other person sign ". . . in the testator's conscious presence and by the testator's direction. . . ." The UPC drafters expand on this test in the Comment to §2-502, which states that the person must be, ". . . within the range of the testator's senses such as hearing: the signing need not have occurred within the testator's line of sight." Courts have focused on whether the person signing is "so near at hand that [the testator] is conscious of where they are and of what they are doing, through any of his senses, and where he can readily see them if he is so disposed." *See* UPC §2-502 Comment (citing *Healy v. Bartless*, 59 A.617 (N.H. 1904)). The following illustration in the *Restatement (Third) of Property: Wills & Other Donative Transfers* §3.1, cmt. n reiterates that the person signing for the testator need not be in the testator's line of sight.

> **Example:** Gary directed a neighbor to sign his name to the will. Gary remained in bed while the neighbor went into an adjacent room, removed the will from a wall safe and wrote Gary's name in freestanding form at the end of the will. Gary maintained a conversation with the neighbor throughout these events. The neighbor's signing of Gary's name will suffice as a signature. The neighbor did not have to be in Gary's line of sight as long as he was in Gary's conscious presence and signed at his direction.

NOTES AND QUESTIONS

1. *Making your mark.* You can see the risk in allowing someone to guide the testator's hand in making her signature or mark and in allowing someone else to sign on behalf of the testator. It clearly opens the door to fraud. Why do you think the UPC, the *Restatement (Third) of Property: Wills & Other Donative Transfers* and state courts even allow for such a

---

7. *See, e.g.,* MD. CODE ANN., EST. & TRUSTS §4-102. Writing; signature; attestation. Except as provided in §§4-103 and 4-104, every will shall be (1) in writing, (2) signed by the testator, or by some other person for him, in his presence and by his express direction, and (3) attested and signed by two or more credible witnesses in the presence of the testator.

possibility? What factors should a court consider in evaluating whether the act was a volitional act of the testator, free of undue influence? In *In re Estate of Bernatowicz*, 649 N.Y.S.2d 625, 626 (App. Div. 1996), the court noted that "[t]he question whether a signature is assisted or controlled does not turn on the extent of the aid, but rather whether the act of signing was in any degree an act of the testator, acquiesced in and adopted by him."

2. *Providing for incapacity while safeguarding against fraud.* How would you draft a statute that provided more safeguards against fraud but still allowed for a flexible approach to validating wills executed by testators who did intend to make the will but were physically incapable of signing?

3. *Creating a record.* If you were representing an otherwise competent testator who was in the hospital and physically incapable of signing a will, what steps would you take to establish that someone else signed on the testator's behalf based upon the testator's wish? Should you sign on the testator's behalf? In *Muhlbauer v. Muhlbauer*, 686 S.W.2d 366 (Tex. App. 1985), the court refused to probate a will where a wife guided her blind husband's hand in making his signature on the will. The new will would have substituted the wife for the testator's children and would have made her the sole beneficiary. The court found that the wife had guided his hand without any direction by the husband, the husband had the physical ability to smoke a pipe and use his watch on his own and he had not attempted to sign or mark the will prior to the wife's assistance. The court noted that there was "no believable testimony that [the testator] ever specifically requested any person to assist him, and there is testimony that he was never asked to make his own mark." *Id.* at 377.

3. Publication

Historically, the testator was required to "publish" the will by signifying to the attesting witnesses that the document she was asking the witnesses to sign was her will. Strict publication consisted of the testator explicitly saying to the witnesses, "This is my last will." This requirement helped establish that the testator intended the document to be her will. Over time, many states relaxed the requirement. They began to allow the testator to manifest her intent by behavior that indicated that the document was her will. For example, the testator could ask the witnesses to come to her house and her lawyer could say to the witnesses, in front of the testator, that this was the testator's will. The testator's mere presence in the room to hear this statement by her lawyer would suffice as "publication." She need not say anything affirmative.

While there are a few states that still require publication, most do not. Nonetheless, estate planning attorneys routinely have the testator recite the particular "magic" words, "This is my last will," to the witnesses during the signing ceremony as a matter of good form. This recitation is helpful if the witnesses are later called to testify in a will contest as to the testator's capacity and intent to make a will.

Note that witnesses must know that it is a will they are signing. *See In re Estate of Griffith*, 30 So. 3d 1190 (Miss. 2010). In *Griffith*, the witnesses who signed the will identified their signatures on the will. However, they testified that they were not informed of what they were signing and that the testator did not identify the document as a will when they signed it. The majority ruled that as a matter of law the witnesses must have some knowledge that the document they are witnessing is a will.

NOTE AND QUESTION

Moving away from publication. The UPC does not require publication. The drafters note in the Comment to UPC §2-502 that, "There is no requirement that the testator 'publish' the document as his or her will, or that he or she request the witnesses to sign. . . ." Does this movement away from publication make sense to you? When we studied Will Substitutes in Chapter 4, were there any similar requirements when someone named a beneficiary of a life insurance policy for them to say out loud, "This is my beneficiary designation"? Why do you think the UPC drafters eliminated the publication requirement?

4.   The Witness Requirement

The will must be "witnessed," *i.e.*, signed by two or three people other than the testator, in order to be valid. The *Restatement (Third) of Property: Wills & Other Donative Transfers* §3.1, cmt. o notes that, "Nearly all states require two attesting witnesses. At one time, a substantial minority of states required three . . . but the number of states requiring three . . . has dwindled." Note that Pennsylvania requires only that the will be in writing and signed by the testator at the end. It does not require witnesses. However, if the testator is unable to sign and either simply makes a mark or has someone else sign for him, then there must be two witnesses. *See* 20 Pa. Cons. Stat. Ann. §2502 (West 2005).

A witnessed will is also called an "attested" will. In most states, notarization alone, without satisfying the witness requirement, is not sufficient to validate a will. The most recent version of the UPC allows acknowledgement by the testator before a notary public to substitute for witnessing by two other people.

UPC §2-502. Formalities Required for a Valid Will.

(a) [Witnessed or Notarized Wills.] Except as otherwise provided in subsection (b) and in Sections 2-503, 2-506, and 2-513, a will must be:
        . . . (3) either:

(A) signed by at least two individuals, each of whom signed within a reasonable time after the individual witnessed either the signing of the will as described in paragraph (2) or the testator's acknowledgment of that signature or acknowledgment of the will; or

(B) acknowledged by the testator before a notary public or other individual authorized by law to take acknowledgments.

The witnessing requirement is often viewed as a protective function for the testator to ensure that making the will is her wish and that it is not signed under duress. If there were a dispute about testamentary capacity or the proper execution of the will, the witnesses can be required to testify in court as to their view of the testator's capacity and the circumstances surrounding the execution of the will.

a.   Who May be a Witness

UPC §2-505. Who May Witness.

(a) An individual generally competent to be a witness may act as a witness to a will.

(b) The signing of a will by an interested witness does not invalidate the will or any provision of it.

b.   Where Must the Testator and Witnesses Be?

UPC §2-502(a)(3)(A) requires that two individuals "witness" the will. In other words, they must either observe the testator sign the will, or the testator must acknowledge to them that it is either his signature or his will. This raises two questions: Where must the testator be vis-à-vis the witnesses when he either signs or acknowledges the will, and where must the witnesses be when they sign the will?

i.   *Must the Testator Sign or Acknowledge in the Witnesses' Presence?*

The following case addresses the question of whether the testator must be in the presence of the witnesses when he signs the will. It also examines the purpose of the witness requirement.

Kirkeby v. Covenant House

970 P.2d 241 (Or. Ct. App. 1998)

The opinion of the court was delivered by Judge HASELTON.

This appeal and cross-appeal arise from an unusually convoluted probate dispute. The central issue on appeal is whether the trial court erred in determining that the testator's 1992 will was invalid because it was not acknowledged "in the presence" of witnesses. ORS 112.235(1)(c). . . . We conclude that the trial court correctly resolved those and other disputed matters. Accordingly, we affirm on both the appeal and the cross-appeal.

On *de novo* review, the material facts are as follows: The testator, Margaret Kirkeby (Margaret) and her husband, Orrin, were residents of the northeastern Oregon town of Wallowa. In May 1989, Margaret executed a will that provided that the proceeds of her estate be placed in trust, with "income earnings" to be distributed to Orrin during his life, then to other beneficiaries for a period not to exceed five years. The corpus was then to be distributed to a named charitable beneficiary, Mille Lacs Health System (Mille Lacs).

In June 1992, Margaret decided to revise some of the provisions of the 1989 will. She drafted a handwritten codicil dated June 10, 1992, which, among other things, included a specific bequest of the Kirkebys' home, including five acres of land, to two neighbors, Don Curtis and Gayle Lyman, in exchange for them providing physical care for both Margaret and Orrin until their deaths. However, the codicil was not properly executed, ORS 112.235.

In July 1992, Margaret again decided to change her will. After marking through the 1989 will and codicil and adding notes, she asked Gayle Lyman to type up a new will with the indicated changes. On July 15, 1992, Lyman took the document to her house, typed it on two pages and delivered it to Margaret, who signed it that same day. That 1992 will, although still providing that the assets be placed in trust with income distributions to Orrin for life, and then to other named beneficiaries, provided that the trust corpus be distributed to a different named charitable beneficiary, Covenant House. It also incorporated the specific bequest of the Kirkebys' house and land to Curtis and Lyman, which had been originally set out in the ineffective June 1992 codicil.

On July 15, after signing the will, Margaret telephoned Patricia Horton, a local notary whom she knew. Horton returned Margaret's phone call later that day, and Margaret, whose voice Horton recognized, told Horton that she had signed a document, that she wanted Horton to notarize it, and that Lyman would be bringing it to Horton's office. Still later on July 15, Lyman delivered the document to Horton who recognized Margaret's handwriting and notarized the second page. Horton did not know that the document was a will, and she did not see the first page, because it was not attached. Lyman then returned the document to Margaret. Although the dates are somewhat in dispute, it appears that

10 days later, on July 25, Margaret asked Lyman if she had had the will witnessed. Lyman replied that she had not and took the will to her house to type "witness" lines on the second page. Apparently while Lyman was gone, Margaret called Hazel Ortega, another neighbor. Margaret told Ortega that she had signed her will and that she wanted Ortega to witness it. Ortega arrived at Margaret's house, but Lyman had not yet returned with the will, so Ortega went home. When Lyman returned to Margaret's house, Margaret told her to take the will to Ortega's house. Lyman then took the second page of the document to Ortega, who signed as "witness." Another neighbor, James Pullen, also signed as a witness; unlike Ortega, he had not spoken to Margaret about the instrument or about signing as a witness. Once all the signatures were on the document, Lyman placed it in Margaret's satchel next to her bed.

Margaret died on September 2, 1992. In October 1992, Glenn Kirkeby (Glenn), Orrin's brother, filed a petition in probate alleging that the 1992 will was invalid as "not properly attested in that decedent did not sign her Will in the presence of the witnesses nor did she acknowledge to said witnesses that she had signed her Will," and that, consequently Margaret had therefore died intestate. Covenant House, Lyman, and Curtis, as named beneficiaries of the 1992 will (hereinafter, "objectors"), filed objections to Glenn's petition, alleging that the 1992 will was valid or, in the alternative, that Margaret's 1989 will and the June 10, 1992 codicil were valid.

In June 1993, the court issued a memorandum opinion and subsequent order, determining that (1) the July 1992 will and the June 1992 codicil to the 1989 will were both invalid as improperly executed; but (2) Margaret did not die intestate because, applying the doctrine of "dependent relative revocation," the 1989 will remained valid.[8]

On June 25, 1993, the court entered its order admitting the 1989 will to probate. . . .

All parties appeal. . . .

Objectors argue that the 1992 will was properly executed, ORS 112.235, because Horton, the notary, and Ortega, the neighbor, were both proper witnesses. In particular, objectors assert that Margaret properly acknowledged the 1992 will to both Ortega and Horton when she: (1) telephoned them, (2) told them that she had signed the will, and (3) told them that Lyman was bringing the instrument over for each to attest. Respondent Mille Lacs counters that the court properly declared the 1992 will invalid, even assuming that Horton's signature as a notary was sufficient to meet the witness requirements of ORS 112.235, because Margaret did not properly acknowledge her signature "in the presence" of either witness, as that term has been construed under Oregon law.

---

8. [We will be discussing the doctrine of dependent relative revocation in Chapter 11 — EDS.]

Assuming, without deciding, that Horton signed as a witness and not merely as a notary, we agree with respondents that the 1992 will was invalid and that the 1989 will was properly probated. As amplified below, the execution of Margaret's 1992 will did not comply with ORS 112.235, because Margaret's "acknowledgment" of her signature via the telephone in the circumstances presented here, was not "in the presence" of either of the witnesses, much less both.

ORS 112.235 provides, in part:

> A will shall be in writing and shall be executed with the following formalities:
>
> (1) The testator, *in the presence of each of the witnesses*, shall: [. . .]
>   (c) *Acknowledge the signature previously made* on the will by the testator . . .
> (3) At least *two witnesses* shall each: . . .
>   (b) *Hear the testator acknowledge the signature on the will; and*
>   (c) Attest the will by signing the witness' name to it. (Emphasis added.)

The "in the presence" requirement for acknowledgment by the testator was first codified in 1969, and has never been explicitly construed in a reported Oregon decision. However, before 1973, ORS 112.235 and its predecessor also included the requirement that attestation *by the witnesses* take place "in the presence of the testator and at his request." *See* ORS 112.235(3)(c) (1969). In several cases, most notably, *Demaris' Estate*, the Supreme Court construed the meaning of "in the presence" in that context and concluded that attestation was valid so long as the witnesses were in the testator's "conscious presence."

In *Demaris' Estate*, the testator made out his will with the assistance of his doctor. The doctor and the doctor's wife were present when the testator signed the will. However, 20 to 30 minutes later, and in a room 20 feet from where the testator lay, the doctor and his wife, as attesting witnesses, signed the will. Because of the layout of the office, the testator could not physically see the doctor witness the will, but he could have seen the doctor's wife, had he adjusted his position slightly. A contestant of the will argued that, in those circumstances, the statutory requirement that the witness sign "in the presence" of the testator had not been satisfied. The court, after noting "it is essential, not only that the signatures be genuine and that they be found upon an instrument which all three persons intended to sign, but also that the attesters signed in the testator's presence," concluded:

> We are, of course, satisfied that the attestation must occur in the presence of the testator and that no substitution for the statutory requirement is permissible. But we do not believe that sight is the only test of presence. We are convinced that any of the senses that a testator possesses, which enable him to know whether another is near at hand and what he is doing, may be employed by him in determining whether the attesters are in his presence as

they sign his will. . . . It is unnecessary, we believe, that the attestation and execution occur in the same room. And, as we just stated, it is unnecessary that the attesters be within the range of vision of the testator when they sign. If they are so near at hand that they are within the range of any of his senses, so that he knows what is going on, the requirement has been met.

Respondent Mille Lacs argues that the same "conscious presence" principle necessarily applies to the "in the presence" requirement with respect to testator's acknowledgment of a previously made signature. In particular, Mille Lacs suggests that the "in the presence" requirement is designed to avoid "bait and switch" tactics, and that that purpose is effectuated only if there is "concurrence in time and place" between (1) the testator's acknowledgment of the signature to each of the witnesses and (2) the presentation of the instrument to the witnesses. Thus, respondent reasons:

> [T]he presence requirement of ORS 112.235 . . . requires not only the presence of the testator and witness, but also implicitly requires the presence of the will. To put it another way, a signature can't be acknowledged to a witness if the signature isn't available to be perceived by the witness. The will must be present for the witness to know what signature on what document is being acknowledged.

We agree with respondent that to satisfy the "in the presence" requirement of ORS 112.235(1)(c), the will, bearing the signature that the testator acknowledges, must be before the witness at the time of the acknowledgment. Even if we were to assume that telephonic acknowledgment would otherwise satisfy the "in the presence" requirement — a question we do not resolve today — an "acknowledgment" made to a witness who cannot perceive what is being "acknowledged" is meaningless. If the "in the presence" requirement is to have any context, it must require *at least* the "concurrence" of the testator's acknowledgment and the witnesses' "perception."

Applying that principle here, neither Horton nor Ortega validly witnessed Margaret's "acknowledgment." In neither instance did the witness have the 1992 will before her at the time Margaret spoke with her. Thus, neither Ortega nor Horton was close enough at hand to have known that the instrument, which was later presented to them, was, in fact, the instrument upon which Margaret had previously "acknowledged" her signature, or whether Margaret had actually signed that instrument at the time she stated her "acknowledgment."

. . . The trial court did not err in admitting the 1989 will to probate. . . .

Affirmed on appeal and cross-appeal.

QUESTION

Thwarting testator's intent? The *Kirkeby* court notes that the will must be present for the testator to effectively acknowledge the will or his signature on it. Can you think of circumstances where that requirement might defeat a testator's best efforts to execute a valid will? What does UPC §2-502(a)(3)(A) require in terms of the testator signing or acknowledging the will in the presence of the witnesses?

ii.   Must the Witnesses Sign in the Testator's Presence?

In some states, the witnesses must sign in the presence of the testator. This has lead to a number of cases interpreting the word "presence." At first, presence was defined as being in the "line of sight" of the testator when signing. This is still the standard in some states. *See McCormick v. Jeffers*, 637 S.E.2d 666 (Ga. 2006), where the court held that the will was not properly executed because the witnesses did not sign the will in the testator's presence and she could not have seen them because they were in the dining room and she was in the bedroom. UPC §2-502(3) simply requires that there be, "at least two individuals, each of whom signed within a reasonable time after he [or she] witnessed either the signing of the will . . . or the testator's acknowledgement of that signature or acknowledgement of the will."

c.   When the Witnesses Must Sign

UPC §2-502(a)(3) requires that the witnesses sign "within a reasonable time" after witnessing either the signing of the will or the testator's acknowledgement. The following case analyzes the question of what constitutes a "reasonable time" in terms of the witness requirement. While the New Jersey statute interpreted by the court did not explicitly require the witnesses to sign within a reasonable time, the court read in such a requirement. As you read the case, consider why the court does so.

In re Estate of Peters
526 A.2d 1005 (N.J. 1987)

In December 1983, the testator was in the hospital for treatment following a stroke. While Peters was hospitalized, a will was prepared for his signature by Sophia M. Gall, Peters' sister-in-law. Ms. Gall had prepared an identical will for her sister, Marie Peters. The wills were drawn up at the request of Marie Peters, who apparently had discussed the need for these wills with her husband in mid-December, 1983. Although Conrad Peters was physically disabled as a result of the stroke, he suffered no mental disability; accordingly, his competency to make a will has not been questioned.

The dispositive provisions of the two wills complemented each other. Each provided for the distribution of the entire estate, after payment of debts and funeral expenses, to the surviving spouse. Both appointed the surviving spouse as executor. Additionally, both wills named Joseph Skrok, Marie Peters' son, as the alternate beneficiary and alternate executor.

On December 30, 1983, Sophia Gall came to the testator's hospital room with her husband and Marie Peters. Ms. Gall read the provisions of the will to Mr. Peters; he then assented to it, and signed it. Although Ms. Gall, her husband, and Mrs. Peters were present at the time, none of these individuals signed the will as witnesses. It was the apparent intention of Ms. Gall, who was an insurance agent and notary, to wait for the arrival of two employees from her office, who were to serve as witnesses.

When those two employees, Mary Elizabeth Gall and Kristen Spock, arrived at the hospital, Sophia Gall reviewed the will briefly with the testator, who, in the presence of the two women, again indicated his approval, and acknowledged his signature. Ms. Gall then signed the will as a notary, but neither of the two intended witnesses placed her signature on the will. Ms. Gall folded the will and handed it to Mrs. Peters. Conrad Peters died fifteen months later, on March 28, 1985. At the time of his death the will was still not signed by either of the witnesses. . . .

In an affidavit executed on June 28, 1985, Ms. Gall explained that her failure to obtain the signatures of the two witnesses was the result of her being "affected emotionally by [the testator's] appearance." . . .

The trial court found that the proffered instrument "was properly executed" because it was signed by the testator in the presence of two individuals, who were in his presence and that of each other. It further found that in such circumstances, the notary could be considered a subscribing witness and the probate action handled just as if one of two witnesses had died and the instrument were being proved by the testimony of the one surviving witness. According to the court, the failure of the intended witnesses to subscribe the instrument could be ignored as a mere "quirk," which should not be allowed to frustrate the obvious testamentary intent of the decedent. Where, as here, the alternative would be an escheat to the State, the trial court found that it had "equitable powers" to avoid what it perceived as a miscarriage of justice. Accordingly, the court ordered that the second witness, also present at the December 30, 1983, execution ceremony, be permitted to sign the document. Pursuant to this order, Skrok commenced an action in the Surrogate's Court, seeking to have the proffered will, now bearing the additional signature of a witness, admitted to probate in common form. Letters Testamentary were issued to Skrok.

As noted, the Appellate Division reversed the trial court and remanded the case for entry of judgment dismissing the action.

It cannot be overemphasized that the Legislature, in reforming the Wills statute, did not dispense with the requirement that the execution of a will be witnessed. Indeed, it is arguable that as the number of formalities has been reduced, those retained by the Legislature have assumed even greater importance, and demand at least the degree of scrupulous adherence required under the former statute.

It is generally acknowledged that witnesses serve two functions, which can be characterized as "observatory" and "signatory." A. Clapp, 5 N.J. Practice, supra, s 50 at 192.

The current statute, N.J.S.A. 3B:3-2, clearly requires the fulfillment of both functions; a testamentary writing proffered as a will, in the statute's terms, "shall be signed by at least two persons each of whom witnesses either the signing or the testator's acknowledgement of the signature or of the will."

The observatory function consists of the actual witnessing — the direct and purposeful observation — of the testator's signature to or acknowledgement of the will. It entails more than physical presence or a casual or general awareness of the will's execution by the testator; the witnessing of a will is a concomitant condition and an integral part of the execution of the will.

The signatory function consists of the signing of the will by the persons who were witnesses. The signatory function may not have the same substantive significance as the observatory function, but it is not simply a ministerial or precatory requirement. While perhaps complementary to the observatory function, it is nonetheless a necessary element of the witnessing requirement. The witnesses' signature has significance as an evidentiary requirement or probative element, serving both to demonstrate and to confirm the fulfillment of the observatory function by the witnesses. There is nothing, therefore, to suggest that in retaining the requirement that a will's execution be witnessed, the Legislature meant to imply that either witnessing function is dispensable. The statutory policy to reduce the required formalities to a minimum should not, in our view, be construed to sanction relaxation of the formalities the statute retained.

Resolution of the issue of when the witnesses must sign the will in relation to their observations of the execution of the will by the testator follows from the purpose of the requirement that the will be signed. Because, as noted, the signatory function serves an evidentiary purpose, the signatures of the witnesses would lose probative worth and tend to fail of this purpose if the witnesses were permitted to sign at a time remote from their required observations as witnesses. Consequently, because the witnessing requirement of the statute consists of the dual acts of observation and signature, it is sensible to infer that both acts should occur either contemporaneously with or in close succession to one another.

We are thus satisfied that it would be unreasonable to construe the statute as placing no time limit on the requirement of obtaining two witnesses' signatures. By implication, the statute requires that the signatures of witnesses be affixed to a will within a reasonable period of time from the execution of the will.

This reading of N.J.S.A. 3B:3-2 to require subscription within a reasonable time from observation is buttressed by a consideration of other statutory provisions. The Legislature clearly required that a witness actually observe directly and in his or her presence the testator's signing of the will or acknowledgement that the will bears the witness's signature. If, indeed, the will is to be "self-proving," that is, susceptible of being validated solely by the signed acknowledgement of the witnesses, the will must be signed by the witness in the presence of the testator either at the time the testator executed the will, N.J.S.A. 3B:3-4, or subsequent to the execution of the will, N.J.S.A. 3B:3-5. If a will cannot be "self-proving," then at the very least N.J.S.A. 3B:3-2 requires that the witness himself sign the will intending that the signature be that of a witness to the testator's signing or acknowledgement, and that the witness' signature be affixed to the will within a reasonable period of time following the testator's execution or acknowledgement of the will. In other words, since the witnessing of the will still constitutes a part of the formal ceremony entailed in the will's proper execution, it follows that the signing of the will by the witnesses must be within a reasonable period of time of the signing or acknowledgement of the will by the testator.

The requirement of subscription within a reasonable time follows also from the consistent policy of this state that execution formalities are substantive requirements, and, therefore, that execution defects are substantive. Because the purpose of execution formalities is to prevent fraud and undue influence, they have consistently been held by our courts to be substantive requirements. The fact that the Legislature has reduced the number of execution formalities required does not diminish the significance of the formalities it retained; if anything, in our view, their significance is heightened. What this Court stated in *In re Hale's Will, supra*, 21 N.J. at 297, 121 A.2d 511, is no less true under the reformed statute: the purpose of execution formalities is to "forestall [ ] fraud by the living upon the dead [and to] discourage imposition on the unwary. . . . "

As noted above, the UPC explicitly provides that the witnesses must sign within a reasonable time after having witnessed either the testator's signing the will or the testator's acknowledging his signature or the will. The witnesses can observe either one of these acts. The witnesses do not have to see the testator sign the will itself. For an extensive discussion of the UPC's attestation requirements, see Ronald R. Volkmer, *Formalities of Will Execution Addressed: Attestation Requirement: Role of Witnesses*, 29 EST. PLAN. 364 (2002).

NOTES AND QUESTIONS

1.   *Post-death signing.* The Comment to UPC §2-502 notes that there is no requirement that the witnesses sign *before* the testator's death; the witnesses can sign within a reasonable time afterwards also. What are the reasons for and against allowing such flexibility in the rule? *See In re Estate of Bernard William Jung,* 109 P.3d 97 (Ariz. Ct. App. 2005), where the court recognized that witnessing a will after the testator's death raised the possibility of fraud or mistake, but noted that "[t]hese concerns . . . do not support ignoring the effect of the legislative change to the statute," and it interpreted the phrase "reasonable time" to allow post-death signing. *Id.* at 102.

2.   *A bright-line rule?* Should states instead adopt a rule that requires the witnesses to sign before the testator's death? *See also* Matthew D. Owdom, Note, *Estate of Sauerssig and Post-Death Subscription: the Protection Function Reborn,* 39 McGeorge L. Rev. 359, 382-84 (2008), where the author discusses the costs and benefits of the reasonable time rule.

d.   Interested Witnesses

Historically, if one or both required witnesses were also beneficiaries of a will, then the entire will was void for failing to have the required number of witnesses. A beneficiary could not be a witness because that person was presumed to have an inherent conflict of interest and might provide false testimony about the matter in court. The law later evolved to invalidate only the bequest to the interested witness rather than void the entire will. Statutes that follow this approach are called "purging" statutes — automatically forcing the interested witness to forfeit her bequest. A more recent approach to such concerns is to create a rebuttable presumption that the gift to the interested witness was the product of undue influence, which gives the interested witness a chance to preserve her gift by rebutting the presumption. If she cannot, some statutes provide that such a witness only forfeits that part of her devise that is greater than the amount she would have taken in intestacy. *See* Restatement (Third) of Property: Wills & Other Donative Transfers §3.1, cmt. o.

Other states and the UPC do not have an "interested witness" rule at all. The general policy concern underlying this statutory approach is that many bequests, which are not in fact the product of undue influence, may fail unjustly if an interested witness rule is applied. The bad actors who procure wills that are in fact the product of undue influence are typically not so foolish as to be witnesses to those wills themselves. Most interested witness cases actually involve innocent family members who are pulled in to witness by a testator because there is no one else there. Consequently, the interested witness rule is not very effective in deterring intentional undue influence while it often invalidates perfectly legitimate bequests to innocent interested witnesses.

QUESTIONS

Selecting witnesses. What qualities would influence you as the drafting attorney in selecting the best witnesses? Would you be more or less inclined to pick a relative instead of a stranger, a young person instead of an old person or a home-care assistant instead of a neighbor?

PROBLEMS

Tia signed her will on January 1, 2010. Her son, Shaun, and her daughter, Dolores, acted as witnesses to Tia's will.

    1.   Shaun and Dolores do not sign the will for several weeks. Under the UPC, is this attestation valid?

    2.   Assume Tia leaves three-fourths of her estate to Dolores, her favorite daughter, and one-fourth of her estate to Shaun. How would the fact that Dolores and Shaun were both witnesses to the will affect the validity of the will if the state has adopted the UPC?

e. The Self-Proved Will

    When the proponent of a will seeks to begin the probate process, the proponent must "prove" the will before it can be admitted to probate. Proving a will requires the testimony of the witnesses, either in court or by affidavit. A number of states have a process by which one can present a will for probate without actually calling the witnesses to testify in court about whether the execution requirements were satisfied. Finding witnesses to testify is increasingly difficult in today's mobile society. A self-proved affidavit satisfies the requirements for execution without the testimony of the witnesses. See UPC §2-504 below, which includes an example of an affidavit that typically appears at the end of the will. *Remember that the notarization is not necessary to validate the will itself; the signatures of the testator and the witnesses are all that is required for a valid will.*

UPC §2-504. Self-Proved Will.

    (a) A will may be simultaneously executed, attested, and made self-proved, by acknowledgment thereof by the testator and affidavits of the witnesses, each made before an officer authorized to administer oaths under the laws of the state in which execution occurs and evidenced by the officer's certificate, under official seal, in substantially the following form:

I, _____, the testator, sign my name to this instrument this ___ day of _____, and being first duly sworn, do hereby declare to the under-signed authority that I sign and execute this instrument as my will and that I sign it willingly (or willingly direct another to sign for me), that I execute it as my free and voluntary act for the purposes therein expressed, and that I am eighteen years of age or older, of sound mind, and under no constraint or undue influence.

_____
Testator

We, _____, _____, the witnesses, sign our names to this instru-ment, being first duly sworn, and do hereby declare to the under-signed authority that the testator signs and executes this instrument as [his] [her] will and that [he] [she] signs it willingly (or willingly directs another to sign for [him] [her]), and that each of us, in the presence and hearing of the testator, hereby signs this will as witness to the testator's signing, and that to the best of our knowledge the testator is eighteen years of age or older, of sound mind, and under no constraint or undue influence.

_____
Witness

_____
Witness

The State of _____
County of _____
Subscribed, sworn to and acknowledged before me by _____, the testator, and subscribed and sworn to before me by _____, and _____, witness, this ___ day of _____. (Seal)
(Signed) _____

_____
(Official capacity of officer)

The procedural significance of the self-proved will is found in UPC §3-406 below. For these purposes, the notary is considered a quasi-judicial figure. Once having attested under oath before the notary that they were witnesses "to the testator's signing, and that to the best of [their] knowl-edge the testator is eighteen years of age or older, of sound mind, and under no constraint or undue influence," the witnesses do not have to do so again in court. While the witnesses to the will do not need to testify again about compliance with the formalities, they may still be called for other reasons, such as to speak to the facts surrounding the signing in case there are issues about the testator's competency or whether others appeared to be unduly influencing him.

UPC §3-406. Formal Testacy Proceedings; Contested Cases.

In a contested case in which the proper execution of a will is at issue, the following rules apply:

(1) If the will is self-proved pursuant to Section 2-504, the will satisfies the requirements for execution without the testimony of any attesting witness, upon filing the will and the acknowledgment and affidavits annexed or attached to it, unless there is evidence of fraud or forgery affecting the acknowledgment or affidavit.

(2) If the will is notarized pursuant to Section 2-502(a)(3)(B), but not self-proved, there is a rebuttable presumption that the will satisfies the requirements for execution upon filing the will.

(3) If the will is witnessed pursuant to Section 2-502(a)(3)(A), but not notarized or self-proved, the testimony of at least one of the attesting witnesses is required to establish proper execution if the witness is within this state, competent, and able to testify. Proper execution may be established by other evidence, including an affidavit of an attesting witness. An attestation clause that is signed by the attesting witnesses raises a rebuttable presumption that the events recited in the clause occurred.

PROBLEM

Claudia and Elizabeth witnessed Ralph's will. Ralph's will included an affidavit similar to the one included in UPC §2-504. The affidavit was executed and notarized. A relative of Ralph contests the will and alleges that Ralph was not of a sound mind at the time of the signing of the will and that the witnesses were not in the conscious presence of the testator when he signed the will. You are the attorney for the proponents of the will. What objection(s) would you make to Claudia and Elizabeth being called as a witness to testify about the execution formalities? What other areas of inquiry might Claudia and Elizabeth have to testify to regardless of the self-proved affidavit?

f. The Notarized Will

UPC §2-502(a)(3)(B) now provides that a will can be valid if the testator acknowledges the will before a notary, even if there are not two witnesses to the will. This provision for a notarized will is distinguishable from the provision above, the self-proved will, in that this rule substitutes the notary for the other witnesses and actually validates the will itself. Normally, notarization alone, without two witnesses, would not validate a will due to the requirement that there be two witnesses. This new provision, which provides for notarized wills, is a significant departure from traditional attestation. It allows a will to be validated without any witnesses, much like the holographic exception of UPC §2-502(b). Note that under UPC §3-406(2), in contested cases, a notarized will raises a rebuttable presumption of proper execution. A word of caution—this approach is very new and has not been widely adopted so the best practice is to make sure your client has two witnesses to a will. See Lawrence W. Waggoner, *The UPC Authorizes Notarized Wills*, 34 ACTEC J. 83 (2008).

g. Putting the Formalities into Practice

Once an attorney has interviewed the client and has successfully drafted her will, the next important step in the process is to have the client come to the attorney's office to execute the will (and any other documents included in the estate plan, like durable powers of attorney and revocable trusts.) As you will see in the *Snide* case below, this part of the job is one of the points at which the attorney is vulnerable to malpractice if not carefully conducted. The clients are nervous. They often joke and are distracted when visiting the lawyer's office for the actual signing ceremony. The following article gives sound guidance on this essential step on the road to executing a will that will withstand post-death scrutiny.

David Johns, Will Execution Ceremonies: Securing a Client's Last Wishes
Colo. Law., Jan. 1994, at 47

For centuries, people have had difficulty dealing with estate planning. Fear of death and a reminder of a person's own mortality usually lead to procrastination.

Moreover, superstitions have always surrounded the will execution ceremony. Wills were often made near the time of death and witnessed by clergy as one of the last acts of the testator. Thus, many people believed that once made, the will was an omen of pending death. This is one reason that will executions became "ceremonies": to impress upon all those involved the significance of the act and to evidence the testator's wishes for disposition of property after death.

Evidence of will execution ceremonies can be traced to the ancient Egyptians. For example, a ceremony conducted in 2548 B.C. involved an instrument written on papyrus and witnessed by two scribes. During Roman times, a free man could transfer up to three-fourths of his assets at death by executing an oral or written transfer of assets prior to death, which was enforceable by the Praetorium after death. This act was called a testamentum (testament) calatis comitiis. The testament had to be performed before at least seven witnesses who would, after death, then testify in front of the Praetor and prove (probate) the will.

Will execution ceremonies in the United States are based primarily on English statutes. The Statute of Wills of 1540, which gave power to devise certain lands held in fee simple, required devises to be in writing. There was no necessity that the writing be made by the testator, or that it be signed. The Statute of Frauds of 1676 provided more formal will execution requirements, including that the writing be signed by the testator and attested by three or four witnesses. The Wills Act of 1837 established the same requirements for disposing of real and personal property by will. Execution requirements included that the will be signed at the foot, or end, and further required that the testator sign the end of the will before at least two witnesses.

About one-half of the United States followed the formalities patterned under the Statute of Wills and Statute of Frauds, and approximately one-half adopted formalities under the Wills Act of 1837. The result is that wills validly executed in one state may not be formally valid in another, unless a curative statute has been adopted by the probating state, granting full probate dignities to a will executed under the formalities required in other jurisdictions. Execution formalities required by the Uniform Probate Code ("UPC") represent a compromise between different classifications of formalities. . . .

RECOMMENDED FORMALITIES

The possibility of adverse consequences warrants compliance by practitioners with formalities beyond those required by Colorado law. Laws of the jurisdiction which probates the will may, under certain circumstances, control the will's validity, rather than the laws where the execution takes place. For instance, a testator may be domiciled in Colorado when the will is executed, and in another state at death, or may own real property at the time the will is executed or at the time of death that is located in a state other than the domiciliary state (or even outside the United States). As a result, a will executed in Colorado may be held to the scrutiny of other states' statutory requirements.

The following guidelines and accompanying checklist go beyond those required in Colorado. If followed, they not only increase the acceptability of a will in other states, but also serve to safeguard against challenges based on fraud, undue influence and lack of mental capacity:

1. Location/Interruptions. The ceremony should take place in a room free from distractions. Once begun, the ceremony should not be interrupted.
2. Gathering/Seating of Participants. Participants should include only the attorney, testator, two disinterested witnesses and a Notary Public. To avoid the appearance of undue influence, no

family members should be present. Participants should be seated in such a manner that the witnesses and testator can see and hear one another.

3. General Introductions/Explanations. All parties should be introduced to one another. The practitioner should explain how the ceremony will proceed and the significance and general purpose of the ceremony. There should be no jokes or humorous statements during the ceremony.

4. Questions to Testator. The Notary Public should administer an oath to the testator. The testator's testamentary intent and mental capacity should be established by asking him or her questions demonstrating that the testator understands the transaction, comprehends generally the nature and extent of property to be disposed of, remembers who are the natural objects of his or her bounty and understands the nature and effect of the desired disposition. Answers should be clear and audible to each witness.

5. Execution by Testator. The will should be comprised of the same quality and color of paper, bound or stapled prior to the beginning of the ceremony. Witnesses should be standing or sitting, so all can see and hear the testator. The testator should sign or initial the margin of each page leading to the signature page, read aloud the testimonium clause, then fill in the date and sign his or her name at the end of the will.

6. Attestation by Witnesses. The Notary Public should administer an oath to the witnesses. The witnesses should initial each page of the will, sign their names and write their addresses next to their names in the attestation clause. The first witness should read aloud the attestation clause and write, under the clause, "The foregoing attestation clause has been read by us and is accurate," then place his or her initials immediately below this line, as should the other witness upon signing.

7. Notary Records. The Notary Public should complete the jurat and should be requested to record the events in the Notary's journal. Such a record can be used as evidence in a later trial, if necessary.

8. Announce End of Execution. The practitioner should announce to all present that the will has been executed.

9. Confirm Testamentary Intent. The practitioner should ask the testator if he or she has any second thoughts or regrets about signing the will.

10. Conclusion. The testator should be instructed as to the safekeeping of the will.

SPECIAL STEPS IF CONTEST IS ANTICIPATED

If the attorney feels there is a possibility of a will contest, additional precautions may be taken at the time of execution that will help defend against challenges of improper execution, fraud, undue influence or lack of mental capacity:

1. Prior to the ceremony, the practitioner should inquire about the testator's medications or history of mental disorders, if any. The testator should be tested for mental capacity, or a professional psychiatric evaluation should be obtained as evidence of the testator's level of competence.

2. Arrangements should be made for videotaping of the will execution ceremony, as evidence of the testator's mental state and appearance at the time of execution. A professional taping service should be used, to ensure proper lighting and equipment.

3. The number of witnesses should be increased, and the witnesses should be carefully chosen. Younger witnesses may prove better at recalling specific details of the ceremony. Conversely, older witnesses may prove more credible. People who have known and observed the testator for many years and are aware of his or her idiosyncrasies are much better testamentary witnesses than professionals (such as the client's accountant or clergy member). On the other hand, professionals such as physicians or nurses may be better trained to testify concerning a person's mental capacity.

4. During the execution ceremony, the attorney should ask additional questions of the testator, including details of his or her immediate family, business or profession and the extent of property owned. The document should be reviewed, paragraph by paragraph, with the testator and witnesses to confirm testamentary intent and understanding of the document. The testator should write the time and place of execution in the testimonium clause to establish being well-oriented as to time and place.

5. Subsequent to executing the will, the testator and witnesses should execute a self-proving affidavit. In addition, the testator should execute one or more codicils, not to change the substance of the will but to republish and reaffirm testamentary intent.

6. Prior wills that demonstrate a consistent desired plan of distribution should be saved. Conversely, prior wills should be destroyed if they provide for distributions inconsistent with those of the present estate plan.

QUESTIONS

Minimizing errors in the execution ceremony. Based on this chapter's discussion of will formalities, are all of the steps outlined in the article above legally required? Are there additional steps that could be taken? Are all these steps required in all situations?

D.   HOLOGRAPHIC WILLS

As we have just explored, state statutes have traditionally required two witnesses to validate a will. However, about half the states recognize a significant exception to this rule. If a will or a material portion of the will is written in the testator's handwriting, then the will may be validated without any witnesses as a holographic will. UPC §2-502(b) provides that such an unwitnessed or unattested will is still valid *"if the signature and the material portions of the document are in the testator's handwriting."* The UPC does not require that the will be dated. If the evidentiary benefits of having witnesses are so important, why do states allow holographs at all? Have the four functions of will formalities been satisfied because the will is in the testator's handwriting?

The *Restatement (Third) of Property: Wills & Other Donative Transfers* §3.2 notes that the statutory approaches to validating holographic wills can be divided into three "generations."

- A typical first-generation statute provides that: "A holographic will is one that is entirely written, dated, and signed by the hand of the testator. It is subject to no other form, and need not be witnessed."
- A typical second-generation statute provides that: "A will which does not comply with the requirements for an attested will is valid as a holographic will, whether or not witnessed, if the signature and the material provisions are in the handwriting of the testator." (The Arizona statute in the *Muder* case below is of the second generation.)
- A typical third-generation statute provides that: "A will which does not comply with the requirements for an attested will is valid as a holographic will, whether or not witnessed, if the signature and the material portions of the document are in the handwriting of the testator."

The following case involves the court's interpretation of a second-generation holographic statute.

In re Estate of Edward Frank Muder
765 P.2d 997 (Ariz. 1988)

The opinion of the court was delivered by Justice CAMERON:

II. ISSUE

We must determine whether the purported will is a valid holographic will pursuant to A.R.S. §14-2503.

III. FACTS

Edward Frank Muder died on 15 March 1984. In September 1986, Retha Muder, the surviving spouse, submitted a purported will dated 26 January 1984 to the probate court. The purported will was on a preprinted will form set forth as Exhibit A. [See below.]

The daughters of Edward Muder by a previous wife contested the will. They were unsuccessful in the trial court and appealed to the court of appeals. A divided court of appeals reversed. *In re Estate of Muder*, 156 Ariz. 326, 751 P.2d 986 (1988). We granted Retha Muder's petition for review.

IV. WAS THE DOCUMENT A VALID WILL UNDER A.R.S. §14-2502?

The right to make a will did not exist at common law. It is a statutory right. 1 W. Bowe & D. Parker, Page on the Law of Wills at 62-63 (1960). Because the legislature has the power to withhold or to grant the right to make a will, its exercise may be made subject to such regulations and requirements as the legislature pleases.

It is apparent that this was not a proper formal will pursuant to statute because only one witness signed. . . .

V. IS THE DOCUMENT A VALID HOLOGRAPHIC WILL?

To serve as a will, the document must indicate that the testator had testamentary intent. Testamentary intent requires that the writing, together with whatever extrinsic evidence may be admissible, establish that the testator intended such writing to dispose of his property upon his death.

Because this will fails under A.R.S. §14-2502, it is only valid if it can be considered a holographic will under the statute that provides:

A will which does not comply with §14-2502 is valid as a holographic will, whether or not witnessed, if the signature and the material *provisions* are in the handwriting of the testator. A.R.S. §14-2503.

[handwritten margin note: Used to require full will be in handwriting. Now only "material provisions"]

This section was enacted in 1973 ~~and replaced the previous~~ holographic will statute that stated:

A holographic will is one entirely written and signed by the hand of the testator himself. Attestation by subscribing witnesses is not necessary in the case of a holographic will. A.R.S. §14-123 (1956).

Under the previous statute, no printed matter was allowed on the document. Litigation resulted because often a testator would write his holographic will on paper containing printed letterheads. Such printed matter was obviously not in the testator's handwriting. To avoid the harsh result of denying such holographic wills admission to probate, courts created the "surplusage theory." This theory held that the statutory words "wholly" or "entirely" were satisfied when the material provisions of the will were "wholly" or "entirely" in the handwriting of the testator, and that other written or printed material could accordingly be disregarded as surplusage. Arizona adopted the surplusage theory to preserve the validity of such holographic wills.

~~With the increased use of printed will forms, states with statutes~~ similar to our previous statute requiring that a holographic will be entirely in the handwriting of the testator, applied the surplusage theory to the printed will forms by disregarding the printed matter and then looking to see if what was left made sense and could be considered a valid will. . . .

Indeed, our statute states:

B.[2]. The underlying purposes and policies of this title are [] to discover and make effective the intent of a decedent in distribution of his property. A.R.S. §14-1102(B)(2).

In the instant case, there is no question as to the testator's intent. We hold that a testator who uses a preprinted form, and in his own handwriting fills in the blanks by designating his beneficiaries and apportioning his estate among them and signs it, has created a valid holographic will. Such handwritten provisions may draw testamentary context from both the printed and the handwritten language on the form. We see no need to ignore the preprinted words when the testator clearly did not, and the statute does not require us to do so.

We find the words of an early California decision persuasive:

If testators are to be encouraged by a statute like ours to draw their own wills, the courts should not adopt upon purely technical reasoning a construction which would result in invalidating such wills . . .

VI. Relief

We vacate the opinion of the court of appeals and affirm the judgment of the trial court admitting the will to probate.

MOELLER, Justice, dissenting.

As the majority correctly notes, there is no common law right to make a will. To be entitled to probate, a document must meet the applicable statutory criteria. The majority opinion of the court of appeals and Judge Haire's persuasive special concurrence amply demonstrate that the document in this case does not comply with Arizona's holographic will statute, A.R.S. §14-2503. The statute is clear: in a holographic will the "signature and the material provisions" must be in the handwriting of the testator. The majority reads into the statute a provision that printed portions of a form may be "incorporated" into the handwritten provisions so as to meet the statutory requirements. I am unable to discern such expansiveness in the statute. Neither was the court of appeals in the recent case of *In re Estate of Johnson*, 129 Ariz. 307, 630 P.2d 1039 (App.1981), which was decided under the identical statute and in which we denied review. *Johnson*, if followed, compels the conclusion that the instrument in this case is not a valid holographic will; however, the majority opinion neither discusses, distinguishes, or disapproves of Johnson.

I am sympathetic to the majority's desire to give effect to a decedent's perceived testamentary intent. However, the legislature has chosen to require that testamentary intent be expressed in certain deliberate ways before a document is entitled to be probated as a will. Whether the holographic will statute should be amended to take into account the era of do-it-yourself legal forms is a subject within the legislative domain. I suspect the ad hoc amendment engrafted on the statute in this case will prove to be more mischievous than helpful. Because I believe there has been no compliance with the statute on holographic wills, I respectfully dissent.

Exhibit A

The Last Will and Testament

OF

Edward Frank Muder

I, *Edward F. Muder*, a resident of *Shumway*, in the County of *Navajo*, State of *Arizona*, which I do declare to be my domicile, being of sound and disposing mind and memory, do make, publish and declare this to be my last will and testament, hereby revoking all wills or codicils to wills previously made by me.

FIRST: I direct that all my just debts and obligations, including funeral expenses, and the expenses incident to my last illness be paid as soon after my death as practical.

SECOND: I give, devise and bequeath of this my gross estate, after all of my just debts, expenses, taxes and administration cost of the estate have first been paid, settled or compromised, to *A my wife Retha F Muder, Our home & property in Shumway, Navajo County; car = the w/o Frank Keiler, & all other earthly possessions belonging to me, Live stock cattle hay ect. Tacky, saddles the courts Checking Accounts, retirement benefits etc.*

THIRD: I nominate, constitute and appoint my *Wife Retha F Muder* as Executor (Executrix) of my estate.

FOURTH: I nominate, constitute and appoint my *wife; Retha F Muder* as guardian of the person and property of each minor child of mine who shall survive me.

IN WITNESS HEREOF, I *Edward F Muder* the testator (Testatrix), sign my name to this instrument this *26th* day of *January*

19 *84* and being first duly sworn, do hereby declare to the undersigned authority that I sign and execute this instrument as my last will and that I sign it willingly, that I execute it as my free and voluntary act for the purpose therein expressed, and that I am eighteen years of age or older, of sound mind, and under no constraint or undue influence.

Edward F Muder
TESTATOR (TESTATRIX)

_____ , the
witnesses, sign our names to this instrument, being first duly sworn, and do hereby declare to the undersigned
authority that the testator (testatrix) signs and executes this instrument as his (her) last will and that he (she)
signs it willingly, and that each of us, in the presence and hearing of the testator (testatrix), hereby signs
this will as witness to the testator's signing, and that to the best of our knowledge the testator (testatrix) is
eighteen years of age or older, of sound mind and under no constraint or undue influence.

Betsy Daniels Low _____ resides at _____

_____ resides at _____

_____ resides at _____

_____ resides at _____

ACKNOWLEDGEMENT *

STATE OF *Arizona*

COUNTY OF *Maricopa*

SUBSCRIBED, SWORN to and acknowledged before me by *Edward F.*
Mudar _____ the testator (testatrix) and subscribed and sworn to
before me by *Edward F Mudar* _____

the witnesses, this ___26___ day of ___February___ 19 84

Helene P. Matly
SIGNATURE OF OFFICER

Notary
OFFICIAL CAPACITY OF OFFICER

MY COMMISSION EXPIRES:

My Commission Expires Mar. 1, 1939

* NOTE: This is a Self-proved Will

© 1976, Alpha Enterprises — P.O. Box 26325 — Tucson, AZ 85726

As noted above, the *Muder* case involves a second-generation statute. The *Muder* court evaluates whether Mr. Muder's will is valid as a holographic will. The case introduces you to the "surplusage" theory of validating holographs. In other words, courts look at the will as a whole and strike out any provisions which are not in the testator's handwriting. If what's left evidences sufficient intent to make a will and identifies who is to get what, the court will validate the instrument. Do you think that what is left after the portion of Mr. Muder's will that is not in his own hand-writing is "struck out" clearly indicates his intent to make a will, who the beneficiaries are and to what they are entitled?

One of the most significant goals of recent probate reform efforts has been to simplify the process and enhance the ability of people to make their own wills. A problem with pre-printed will forms, which were designed to achieve this goal, is that they may have lured people into drafting their own wills only to have those wills later invalidated because of the technical rules of will validity. Who do you think has correctly analyzed the issues in the *Muder* case, the majority or the dissent?

The UPC has evolved to the "third generation" approach, moving from "material provisions" to "material portions" to "leave no doubt about the validity of the will in which immaterial parts of a dispositive provisions—such as 'I give, devise, and bequeath'—are not in the testator's handwriting. The material portion of a dispositive provision—which must be in the testator's handwriting under the Revised UPC—consists of the words identifying the property and the devisee." RESTATEMENT (THIRD) OF PROPERTY: WILLS & OTHER DONATIVE TRANSFERS §3.2. In other words, the words of gifting, such as "I give…," are not required to validate a holographic will in states that have adopted the material portions language.

UPC §2-502(b). Holographic Wills.

> A will that does not comply with subsection (a) is valid as a holographic will, whether or not witnessed, if the signature and material portions of the document are in the testator's handwriting.

With this distinction in mind, did the majority in *Muder* apply the law correctly?

A document written entirely by the decedent need not be witnessed to be a will, but not every handwritten document is intended to serve as a will. Another issue that arises in connection with holographs is whether the decedent intended the writing to constitute a will. Did the decedent have testamentary intent when he wrote the words? In the following case, the court analyzes whether a writing—a letter—meets the requirements of a holographic will. It is the first of two cases you will see in this chapter and the next that involve former CBS journalist, Charles Kuralt, and his complicated personal life.

In re Estate of Charles Kuralt

981 P.2d 77 (Mont. 1999)

OPINION

Justice W. WILLIAM LEAPHART delivered the Opinion of the Court.

On July 4, 1997, Charles Kuralt (Mr. Kuralt) died in a hospital in New York City. His widow, Suzanna "Petie" Baird Kuralt (Petie), thereafter filed a petition in the state courts of New York for probate of his estate. On September 15, 1997, Petie, as the Domiciliary Foreign Personal Representative of the Estate of Charles Kuralt (the Estate), secured Montana counsel and filed a Proof of Authority pursuant to *§72-4-309, MCA* (1995), in the Fifth Judicial District Court, Madison County, seeking to probate certain real and personal property owned by Mr. Kuralt in Madison County, Montana.

On September 30, 1997, Appellant Patricia Elizabeth Shannon (Shannon), an intimate companion of Mr. Kuralt for nearly thirty years, filed a Petition for Ancillary Probate of Will. This petition challenged the application of Mr. Kuralt's New York will to the real and personal property in Madison County. In part, the basis for Shannon's petition was a letter, dated June 18, 1997, which she had received from Mr. Kuralt shortly before his death indicating that he intended Shannon to "inherit" 90 acres along the Big Hole River. Shannon claimed that the letter constituted a valid holographic will that entitled her to Mr. Kuralt's real property in Madison County and, therefore, that the property should not be allowed to pass under the antecedent terms of Mr. Kuralt's New York will.

The Estate filed a Response and Objections to Petition for Ancillary Probate on November 10, 1997. On December 5, 1997, a hearing on Shannon's petition was set for March 3, 1998. Deposition and written discovery ensued. On the day of the scheduled March 3, 1998, hearing, the Estate filed a Motion for Summary Judgment and accompanying brief, arguing that Mr. Kuralt's June 18, 1997 letter expressed, at most, only a future intent to make a will, but not a present testamentary intent to devise the Montana property to Shannon.[9]

Notwithstanding the Estate's pending motion for summary judgment, the evidentiary hearing on Shannon's petition began on March 3, 1998, with the presentation of Shannon's case in chief. Thus, on March 3 and 4, 1998, the District Court heard "extrinsic evidence" bearing upon Mr. Kuralt's intent in writing the letter of June 18, 1997. This evidence

---

9. [FN 1] It is undisputed in this case that Mr. Kuralt's letter of June 18, 1997, meets the threshold formal requirements for a valid holographic will: Mr. Kuralt was of sound mind and sufficient age at the time that he wrote the letter, and the letter is entirely in Mr. Kuralt's handwriting and was signed by him. See *§§72-2-521* and *-522(2), MCA*. Thus, the only issue in dispute here is the question of whether Mr. Kuralt possessed the requisite testamentary intent in writing the letter.

showed, inter alia, that Mr. Kuralt had already transferred 20 acres of his land along the Big Hole River to Shannon in 1997, and that although that transaction had been structured as a "sale," it had been in substance a gift because Mr. Kuralt had secretly supplied the $80,000 in purchase money to Shannon before the ostensible transfer took place. Further, this extrinsic evidence suggested that, prior to Mr. Kuralt's fatal illness, Mr. Kuralt and Shannon had planned to transfer the remaining 90 acres of Mr. Kuralt's property along the Big Hole River in the same manner — as a sham "sale"-gift transaction — in the fall of 1998.

On April 30, 1998, the District Court heard argument on the Estate's motion for summary judgment and thereafter, on May 26, 1998, entered an Order and Memorandum granting partial summary judgment to the Estate. In this order, the court agreed with the Estate's position and held that the June 18, 1997 letter "clearly contemplates a separate testamentary instrument not yet in existence to accomplish the transfer of the Montana property." Shannon appeals from the order of the District Court granting partial summary judgment to the Estate. We reverse the District Court and remand for trial because there are genuine issues of material fact.

ISSUES PRESENTED

There are two issues on appeal:

(1)   Was the District Court correct in concluding that summary judgment was appropriate because the evidence raised no genuine issues of material fact?

(2)   Did the District Court err in concluding that the letter of June 18, 1997, was not a valid holographic will because it expressed no present testamentary intent?

FACTUAL BACKGROUND

Mr. Kuralt and Shannon first met in 1968 in Reno, Nevada, when Mr. Kuralt brought his CBS show "On the Road" to Reno to cover the creation and dedication of the "Pat Baker Park," a project which Shannon had spearheaded. During that weekend, Mr. Kuralt, a married man, invited Shannon to dinner. Thus began a protracted personal relationship between Mr. Kuralt and Shannon, lasting nearly thirty years until Mr. Kuralt's untimely death on July 4, 1997. Mr. Kuralt and Shannon took pains over the years to keep their relationship secret, and were so successful in doing so that even though his wife, Petie, knew that Mr. Kuralt owned property in Montana, she was unaware, prior to Mr. Kuralt's death, of his relationship with Shannon.

From 1968 to 1978, Shannon and Mr. Kuralt saw each other every two-to-three weeks for several days at a time. Indeed, Mr. Kuralt maintained close contact by telephone and mail, and spent a majority of his non-working time with Shannon during this ten-year period. Although Mr. Kuralt and Shannon spent less time together over the remaining twenty years of their relationship, they maintained meaningful personal and financial ties. The couple regularly vacationed together, frequently traveling around the United States, as well as Europe.

Mr. Kuralt also established close, personal relationships with Shannon's three children, acting as a surrogate father and providing them with emotional and material support which continued into their adult lives. For example, Mr. Kuralt paid the entire tuition for Shannon's eldest daughter to attend law school and for Shannon's son to attend graduate school. Over the years, in fact, Mr. Kuralt was the "primary source of support" for Shannon and her children, providing them with substantial sums of money on a regular basis — usually $5,000 to $8,000 per month.

In the 1980's, Mr. Kuralt and Shannon formed a limited partnership called "San Francisco Stocks," which packaged and sold frozen cooking stocks. Mr. Kuralt provided all the capital for the partnership, while Shannon and her two children ran the day-to-day operations of the business. San Francisco Stocks operated for approximately five years, closing in 1988. At that time, Shannon moved to London, England, where Mr. Kuralt paid for Shannon to study landscape gardening at the Inchbald School of Design. During this time period, Mr. Kuralt and Shannon traveled regularly around Ireland.

In 1985, Mr. Kuralt purchased a home in Ireland and then deeded the property to Shannon as a gift. That same year, Mr. Kuralt purchased a 20-acre parcel of property along the Big Hole River in Madison County, near Twin Bridges, Montana. On this parcel, Mr. Kuralt and Shannon constructed a North Carolina-style cabin. In 1987, Mr. Kuralt purchased two additional parcels along the Big Hole River which adjoined the 20-acre parcel, one parcel upstream and the other parcel downstream of the cabin. These two additional parcels constitute approximately 90 acres, and are the primary subject of this appeal. Also in 1987, Mr. Kuralt purchased the old Pageville Schoolhouse located on Montana Highway 41 between Twin Bridges and Dillon, and Mr. Kuralt and Shannon moved the old schoolhouse to one of the newly-purchased parcels with plans to renovate the structure and utilize it as a retirement home.

On May 3, 1989, Mr. Kuralt executed a holographic will, which stated as follows:

May 3, 1989

In the event of my death, I bequeath to Patricia Elizabeth Shannon all my interest in land, buildings, furnishings and personal belongings on Burma Road, Twin Bridges, Montana.

Charles Kuralt

34 Bank St.

New York, NY 10014

Mr. Kuralt mailed a copy of this holographic will to Shannon.

However, Mr. Kuralt thereafter executed a formal will, on May 4, 1994, in New York City. In this will, Mr. Kuralt proclaimed: "I, CHARLES KURALT, a resident of the City, County and State of New York, declare this to be my Last Will and Testament and revoke all my prior wills and codicils." With respect to real property owned by Mr. Kuralt, the will provided:

> *TWO*: I devise all my real property (including any condominium) which is used by me as a residence or for vacation purposes, together with the buildings and improvements thereon, if any, to my wife, PETIE, if she shall survive me. . . .
>
> *FIVE*: All the residue and remainder of my property and estate, real and personal, of whatever nature and wherever situate, including any property not effectively disposed of by the foregoing provisions of this Will, but excluding any property over which I have any power of appointment or disposal which power I hereby expressly do not exercise (hereinafter referred to as my "residuary estate"), I dispose of as follows: [the will then proceeds to gift the entire residuary estate outright to Petie, except for a credit shelter trust benefiting the Kuralts' two children].

The will makes no specific mention of the description or location of any of the real property, in Montana or elsewhere, that had been owned by Mr. Kuralt. The beneficiaries under Mr. Kuralt's Last Will and Testament are his wife, Petie, and the Kuralts' two children; neither Shannon nor her children are named as beneficiaries. In fact, Shannon was not even aware that Mr. Kuralt had executed his Last Will and Testament until institution of the probate proceedings at issue in this appeal. . . .

Tragically, Mr. Kuralt became suddenly ill and entered a New York hospital on June 18, 1997. On that same date, Mr. Kuralt wrote a letter to Shannon in which he expressed grave concern for his health and arguably sought to devise the remainder of the Montana property to Shannon:

> June 18, 1997
>
> Dear Pat —
>
> Something is terribly wrong with me and they can't figure out what. After cat-scans and a variety of cardiograms, they agree it's not lung cancer or heart trouble or blood clot. So they're putting me in the hospital today to concentrate on infectious diseases. I am getting worse, barely able to get out of bed, but still have high hopes for recovery . . . if only I can get a diagnosis! Curiouser and curiouser! I'll keep you informed.

I'll have the lawyer visit the hospital to be sure you *inherit* the rest of the place in MT. if it comes to that.

I send love to you & [your youngest daughter,] Shannon. Hope things are better there!

Love,

C.

Enclosed with this letter were two checks made payable to Shannon — one for $8,000 and the other for $9,000. After this letter was mailed, Mr. Kuralt did not have any formal testamentary document drawn up devising the 90-acres of Montana property to Shannon. [He died on July 4, 1997.] Thus, Shannon sought to probate the letter of June 18, 1997, as a valid holographic codicil to Mr. Kuralt's formal 1994 will, a claim which the District Court rejected in its summary judgment ruling. Shannon appeals.

DISCUSSION

(1.) Was the District Court correct in concluding that summary judgment was appropriate because the evidence raised no genuine issues of material fact?

Summary judgment is appropriate only where there are no genuine issues of material fact and the moving party is entitled to judgment as a matter of law. Rule 56(c), M.R. Civ. P. We review a grant of summary judgment de novo, and, in so reviewing, this Court employs the same Rule 56(c), M.R. Civ. P., criteria as a district court.

Shannon aptly labels the "strange procedural posture" of this case as "quixotic." From the outset of this dispute, Shannon and her attorneys pushed for an early resolution at trial because Shannon is presently experiencing "penurious circumstances." The Estate, in turn, sought to delay the institution of trial on the merits, repeatedly requesting additional time for preparation and discovery. At the start of the evidentiary hearing on March 3, 1998, the Estate again requested a continuance and, at that time, also filed its Motion for Summary Judgment. The District Court, while granting the Estate additional time in which to complete their anticipated discovery, denied the Estate's request for a continuance. In allowing Shannon to proceed with the presentation of her case in chief, the District Court stated:

Well, I'm going to expedite this case; and I'm going to do it by first denying the motion to continue. But I'm going to grant the Estate a right, after the evidence is introduced here today, which should be helpful to the Estate, to complete their contemplated discovery. I'm going to permit them to recall any witnesses which the Petitioner puts on today for cross-examination; and of course, . . . to call any witnesses of their own. We're in a search for the truth, and we're going to pursue it with dispatch if it takes all summer.

Then, during the "expedited" evidentiary hearing which ensued, counsel for the Estate objected to Shannon's presentation of "extrinsic evidence" bearing upon the question of whether Mr. Kuralt's letter contained the requisite animus testandi to render it a valid holographic will:

We're here for a June 18, 1997, document, and whether or not that document is a holographic codicil to Mr. Kuralt's May 4, 1994, will. The letter speaks for itself. We believe that it's clear and unambiguous; and in that matter, because of that, extrinsic evidence is not permitted to be considered. Now, this appears to be in the form of extrinsic evidence; and I make a standing objection to these proceedings, to any further evidence, because of that.

In response, counsel for Shannon cited Montana case law and a Montana statute in support of the argument that, irrespective of ambiguity, "extrinsic evidence is allowed on holographic wills." The District Court apparently agreed with Shannon since it overruled the Estate's "standing objection" to the presentation of extrinsic evidence on Mr. Kuralt's intent.

Thus, the District Court allowed the presentation of extrinsic evidence relevant to the question of Mr. Kuralt's intent in writing the letter of June 18, 1997. Regardless of whether the court admitted that evidence because it found the letter to be ambiguous or whether the court allowed the presentation of extrinsic evidence because it agreed with Shannon's argument that such evidence may be discretionarily admitted in any holographic will dispute, the result is the same: extrinsic evidence was admitted showing that Mr. Kuralt had previously gifted 20 acres along the Big Hole River to Shannon while disguising the transaction as a sale; that evidence also suggested that Mr. Kuralt intended to do the same with the remaining 90 acres of his Madison County property.

The District Court, having allowed the introduction of extrinsic evidence on testamentary intent, erred in granting summary judgment because that evidence raised a genuine issue of material fact which precludes the granting of judgment as a matter of law. Our role in applying the criteria of Rule 56(c), M.R. Civ. P., like that of the District Court, is to first determine whether the Estate, as the moving party, has met its burden of demonstrating that no genuine issues of material fact exist which would preclude judgment as a matter of law. Here, the Estate has failed to sustain that burden and, accordingly, the court erred in granting summary judgment.

We disagree with the Estate's position that Shannon's extrinsic evidence is "immaterial" to the question of testamentary intent, and is merely "an insubstantial attempt to manufacture a material issue of fact." Rather, we agree with Shannon that the District Court improperly resolved contested issues of material fact when it found, in support of its conclusion that the letter "clearly contemplates a separate testamentary instrument not yet in existence," that:

The extrinsic evidence — none of which is contested — confirms this conclusion. Petitioner herself testified during her deposition and at trial that decedent intended to "sell" — not "will" — the Montana property to her in the fall of 1998. While the extrinsic evidence substantiates a close and personal relationship between Petitioner and the decedent extending over 29 years, during which she and her children were apparently entirely housed, supported, educated and temporarily set up in business by the decedent, those facts are not sufficient to create a testamentary intent which the language of the letter clearly refutes.

When drawing all reasonable inferences in favor of Shannon, as the party opposing summary judgment, we conclude that the extrinsic evidence raises a genuine issue of material fact as to whether Mr. Kuralt intended to gift, rather than sell, the remaining 90 acres of his Madison County property to Shannon. The plain language of the letter of June 18, 1997, indicates, as Shannon points out, that Mr. Kuralt desired that Shannon "inherit" all of his property along the Big Hole River. While other language in the letter — "I'll have the lawyer visit the hospital . . . if it comes to that" — might suggest, as the Estate argues and as the District Court concluded, that Mr. Kuralt was contemplating a separate testamentary instrument not yet in existence, it is far from certain that that is the result Mr. Kuralt intended by the letter.

At the very least, when reading the language of Mr. Kuralt's letter in light of the extrinsic evidence showing the couple's future plans to consummate the transfer of the remaining 90 acres vis-a-vis a mock "sale," there arises a question of material fact as to whether Mr. Kuralt intended, given his state of serious illness, that the very letter of June 18, 1997, effect a posthumous disposition of his 90 acres in Madison County. Nor are the parties merely arguing different interpretations of the facts here; we have, in this case, a fundamental disagreement as to a genuine material fact which would be better reconciled by trial.

As this Court has firmly acknowledged, summary judgment "was not intended nor can it be used as a substitute for existing methods in the trial of issues of fact. . . . " The very purpose of summary judgment is to determine whether any genuine issues of material fact exist. See Rule 56(c), M.R. Civ. P. However, it is not the function of a trial court to adjudicate genuine factual issues by way of summary judgment. In this case, the District Court improperly resolved a disputed issue of material fact on a summary judgment motion when it should have instead deferred the determination of that issue to the trier of fact at trial.

We hold that, because there is a genuine issue of material fact, the District Court erred in granting judgment as a matter of law. Accordingly, we reverse the court's grant of summary judgment and remand, for trial, the factual question of whether, in light of the extrinsic evidence, Mr. Kuralt intended the letter of June 18, 1997, to effect a testamentary disposition of the 90 acres in Madison County to Shannon.

Our holding obviates the need for this Court to reach the second issue on appeal. . . .

[Chief Justice TURNAGE dissented from the opinion.]

NOTES AND QUESTIONS

Valid holograph? On remand the court decided that the letter was a holographic codicil. Why do you think they did so? What are the best arguments that it is not a holographic codicil?

PROBLEMS

1. Bob printed the following will form from a Web site on the Internet, and he filled in all the blanks with a pen in his own handwriting. How would a court evaluate the validity of the will under each of the three "generations" of holographic statutes outlined above? Consider the *Muder* case above. What would that court have done?

LAST WILL AND TESTAMENT

KNOW ALL MEN BY THESE PRESENTS that I, *Bob Harrison* , whose address is *212 Jasmine Street, Denver, CO 80220*, being of sound and disposing mind and memory, do make, publish, and declare the following to be my Last Will and Testament, hereby revoking all Wills made by me at any time heretofore.

FIRST:
I direct my Executor, hereinafter named, to pay all my funeral expenses, administration expenses of my estate, including inheritance and succession taxes, state or federal, which may be occasioned by the passage of or succession to any interest in my estate under the terms of this instrument, and all my just debts, excepting mortgage notes secured by mortgages upon real estate.

SECOND:
All the rest, residue, and remainder of my estate, both real and personal, of whatsoever kind or character, and wherever situated, I give, devise, and bequeath to spouse, *Carolyn Harrison*, to be hers absolutely and forever.

THIRD:

If my spouse does not survive me, all the rest, residue, and remainder of my estate, both real and personal, of whatsoever kind or character, and wherever situated, I give, devise, and bequeath to *Susan and Greta*, my *children* to be theirs absolutely and forever.

FOURTH:

I hereby appoint *John Peters*, as executor of this, my Last Will and Testament. If *John Peters* does not survive me, I hereby appoint *Charlotte Shaw* as executor of my estate. I direct that no executor serving hereunder shall be required to post bond.

IN WITNESS WHEREOF, I have hereunto set my hand and seal at this *20th* day of *March*, 2009.

Bob Harrison
Signature

212 Jasmine Street, Denver, CO 80220
Address

2. Assume there is an airplane filled with passengers on its way to Paris from New York City. The pilot has just finished telling the passengers that the plane is having mechanical trouble and may need to land in the ocean. After the shock wears off, many of the passengers aboard begin to realize that they have not written, or finished writing, a will.

Except for the bishop and the pastors in subpart c, assume all the passengers die as a result of the crash. How would you analyze each of these wills for compliance with the required formalities under the UPC?

    a. Passenger #1 pulls out her laptop and types out her last will and testament and saves it on the hard drive. The computer is found after her death with the hard drive still intact.

    b. Passenger #2 writes out her will on a smart phone. She was able to sign the "document" with her stylus and the two people in the seats next to her signed it also as witnesses. Consider also the Nev. Stat. 133.085 *supra*.

    c. Passenger #3 tells her fellow passenger, a bishop, within the hearing of two pastors, that she wants all her property to go to Sally, one of her two children. The bishop and pastors survive the crash and inform Passenger #3's attorney of her dying wish.

    d. Passenger #4 picks up the Skyphone, calls his attorney and leaves a lengthy message on the attorney's voice mail which includes all the terms of his will.

    e. Passenger #5 writes her will on the wall of the cabin with a permanent marker and then signs and dates it. The person in

488 Chapter 9. Will Validity

the seat next to her signs as a witness. The cabin wall and the markings on it are found intact.

f. Passenger #6 remembered a draft will sitting at her lawyer's office, waiting for her signature. On the plane, she pulls out a scrap of paper and writes: "I confirm that the draft will at the law offices of Appiah, Donovan & Howard is my final will although I have not yet signed it. If I die in this plane crash and this note is found, please probate that will." Then she signs her name. She dies in the crash and the scrap of paper is miraculously found at her death.

E. DISPENSING WITH FORMALITIES

This section illustrates how the law is evolving doctrinally so that wills might be validated without satisfying the witness requirements and other formalities. As you read about the judicial doctrine of substantial compliance and the statutory harmless error rule, consider the relationship between the formalities and these newer doctrines. First we will discuss the foundations of substantial compliance and then the evolution of harmless error.

1. Substantial Compliance

Holographic wills are, in some sense, the most common exception to the rule that wills must comply with certain formal requirements in order to be valid. Over the past 30 years, the law has moved to recognize another exception to the strict formalities requirements that govern wills. This movement began with the endorsement of the doctrine of "substantial compliance" by courts and prominent inheritance law scholars. Part of the push for courts to evaluate a will in terms of whether it "substantially complied" with the statute of wills was the rise of will substitutes and the nonprobate revolution.

As we studied in Chapter 4, will substitutes need not comply with the same formalities as wills despite the fact that they result in a reallocation of property at death just like wills. Courts began to try to bridge the gap between will substitutes and wills by recognizing that wills that clearly indicate the testator's intent but which might not strictly comply with all the formalities should be validated in order to effectuate the testator's intent. In other words, courts came to the view that they should not interpret wills statutes in a manner that is "intent-defeating." Adhering to the formalities in such cases made less sense as courts increasingly began to recognize the validity of transferring property at death through will substitutes. Substantial compliance also makes sense in terms of reconciling and closing the gap between attested wills and holographic wills. Professor John Langbein is the scholar most closely associated with encouraging the adoption of the intent-furthering doctrine of substantial compliance.

John H. Langbein, Substantial Compliance with the Wills Act
88 Harv. L. Rev. 489 (1975)

III. THE ELEMENTS OF THE SUBSTANTIAL COMPLIANCE DOCTRINE

The substantial compliance doctrine is a rule neither of maximum nor of minimum formalities, and it is surely not a rule of no formalities. It applies to any Wills Act, governing the consequences of defective compliance with whatever formalities the legislature has prescribed. Our major theme is that substantial compliance fits easily into the existing doctrinal structure and judicial practice of the law of wills.

Proper compliance with the Wills Act, so-called due execution, is the basis in modern law for certain presumptions which shift the burden of proof from the proponents of a will to any contestants. Unless the contestants advance disproof, the proponents need establish no more than due execution. Because there are usually no contestants, the effect of the presumptions is to limit the proofs in the probate proceeding to the question of due execution, and there are further presumptions which allow due execution to be easily inferred from seeming regularity of signature and attestation.

These presumptions are extremely wise and functional. They routinize probate. They transform hard questions into easy ones. Instead of having to ask, "Was this meant to be a will, is it adequately evidenced, and was it sufficiently final and deliberate?" the court need only inquire whether the checklist of Wills Act formalities seems to have been obeyed. In all but exceptional cases, a will is simply whatever complies with the formalities.

The substantial compliance doctrine would permit the proponents in cases of defective execution to prove what they are now entitled to presume from due execution—the existence of testamentary intent and the fulfillment of the Wills Act purposes. The substantial compliance doctrine necessarily impairs something of the channeling function of the Wills Act, because it permits the proponents to litigate issues which would otherwise be foreclosed. We shall see, however, that there is considerable reason to believe that the doctrine would also prevent species of probate litigation which now abound. This important question of the doctrine's impact on the level of probate litigation is best deferred until we have discussed the basics. Our immediate concern is with the feasibility of adjudicating the issues now presumed from due execution, and how they should be handled under the substantial compliance doctrine.

Consider the issues involved when an inadvertent defect occurs in executing documents. This can happen easily when lawyers are rushed or clients are nervous about taking such a serious and final act as signing their last will and testament.

> **Example:**   Azizah and her husband, Mohammed, visit their lawyer to sign two mirror-image wills (containing the same provisions, with each leaving the entire estate to the other). The lawyer seats them in the conference room, reads the clause about Mohammed being of sound mind and makes a joke to break the tension. Losing his concentration, the lawyer inadvertently puts Mohammed's will down in front of Azizah and puts Azizah's will down in front of Mohammed. They each proceed to sign the wrong will. Under most state statutes, the wills will not be valid since neither Azizah nor Mohammed intended to sign the will they actually signed.

The vast majority of states still require a two-step process of validation: (1) Are the formalities met; and (2) What was the testator's intent? If step (1) is not met in those states, then the court may not proceed to step (2). The *Snide* case illustrates the more modern approach, grounded in the substantial compliance doctrine and later codified in UPC §2-503, the harmless error rule, which is discussed below. This approach effectively collapses the two-step analysis and allows a court to dispense with the formality. Thus, the harmless error rule is sometimes called the "dispensing power." Consider whether the dissent in *Snide* is correct in terms of the risks of collapsing these two steps and relaxing the formalities.

In re Snide
418 N.E.2d 656 (N.Y. 1981)

The opinion of the court was delivered by Judge WACHTLER.

This case involves the admissibility of a will to probate. The facts are simply stated and are not in dispute. Harvey Snide, the decedent, and his wife, Rose Snide, intending to execute mutual wills at a common execution ceremony, each executed by mistake the will intended for the other. There are no other issues concerning the required formalities of execution nor is there any question of the decedent Harvey Snide's testamentary capacity, or his intention and belief that he was signing his last will and testament. Except for the obvious differences in the names of the donors and beneficiaries on the wills, they were in all other respects identical.

The proponent of the will, Rose Snide, offered the instrument Harvey actually signed for probate. The Surrogate decreed that it could be admitted, and further that it could be reformed to substitute the name "Harvey" wherever the name "Rose" appeared, and the name "Rose" wherever the name "Harvey" appeared. The Appellate Division reversed on the law, and held under a line of lower court cases dating back into the 1800's, that such an instrument may not be admitted to probate. We would reverse.

It is clear from the record, and the parties do not dispute the conclusion, that this is a case of a genuine mistake. It occurred through the presentment of the wills to Harvey and Rose in envelopes, with the envelope marked for each containing the will intended for the other. The attorney, the attesting witnesses, and Harvey and Rose, all proceeding with the execution ceremony without anyone taking care to read the front pages, or even the attestation clauses of the wills, either of which would have indicated the error.

Harvey Snide is survived by his widow and three children, two of whom have reached the age of majority. These elder children have executed waivers and have consented to the admission of the instrument to probate. The minor child, however, is represented by a guardian ad litem who refuses to make such a concession. The reason for the guardian's objection is apparent. Because the will of Harvey would pass the entire estate to Rose, the operation of the intestacy statute after a denial of probate is the only way in which the minor child will receive a present share of the estate.

The gist of the objectant's argument is that Harvey Snide lacked the required testamentary intent because he never intended to execute the document he actually signed. This argument is not novel, and in the few American cases on point it has been the basis for the denial of probate. However, cases from other common-law jurisdictions have taken a different view of the matter, and we think the view they espouse is more sound.

Of course it is essential to the validity of a will that the testator was possessed of testamentary intent, however, we decline the formalistic view that this intent attaches irrevocably to the document prepared, rather than the testamentary scheme it reflects. Certainly, had a carbon copy been substituted for the ribbon copy the testator intended to sign, it could not be seriously contended that the testator's intent should be frustrated. Here the situation is similar. Although Harvey mistakenly signed the will prepared for his wife, it is significant that the dispositive provisions in both wills, except for the names, were identical.

Moreover, the significance of the only variance between the two instruments is fully explained by consideration of the documents together, as well as in the undisputed surrounding circumstances. Under such facts it would indeed be ironic if not perverse to state that because what has occurred is so obvious, and what was intended so clear, we must act to nullify rather than sustain this testamentary scheme. The instrument in question was undoubtedly genuine, and it was executed in the manner required by the statute. Under these circumstances it was properly admitted to probate.

In reaching this conclusion we do not disregard settled principles, nor are we unmindful of the evils which the formalities of will execution are designed to avoid; namely, fraud and mistake. To be sure, full illumination of the nature of Harvey's testamentary scheme is dependent in part on proof outside of the will itself. However, this is a very unusual case, and the nature of the additional proof should not be ignored. Not only did the two instruments constitute reciprocal elements of a unified testamentary plan, they both were executed with statutory formality, including the same attesting witnesses, at a contemporaneous execution ceremony. There is absolutely no danger of fraud, and the refusal to read these wills together would serve merely to unnecessarily expand formalism, without any corresponding benefit. On these narrow facts we decline this unjust course.

Nor can we share the fears of the dissent that our holding will be the first step in the exercise of judicial imagination relating to the reformation of wills. Again, we are dealing here solely with identical mutual wills both simultaneously executed with statutory formality.

For the reasons we have stated, the order of the Appellate Division should be reversed, and the matter remitted to that court for a review of the facts.

Jones, Judge (dissenting).

I agree with the Appellate Division that the Surrogate's Court had no authority to reform the decedent's will and am of the conviction that the willingness of the majority in an appealing case to depart from what has been consistent precedent in the courts of the United States and England will prove troublesome in the future. This is indeed an instance of the old adage that hard cases make bad law.

Our analysis must start with the recognition that any statute of wills operates frequently to frustrate the identifiable dispositive intentions of the decedent. It is never sufficient under our law that the decedent's wishes be clearly established; our statute, like those of most other common-law jurisdictions, mandates with but a few specific exceptions that the wishes of the decedent be memorialized with prescribed formality. The statutes historically have been designed for the protection of testators, particularly against fraudulent changes in or additions to wills. "[W]hile often it may happen that a will truly expressing the intention of the testator is denied probate for failure of proper execution, it is better that this should happen under a proper construction of the statute than that the individual case should be permitted to weaken those provisions intended to protect testators generally from fraudulent alterations of their wills."

Next it must be recognized that what is admitted to probate is a paper writing, a single integrated instrument (codicils are considered integral components of the decedent's "will"). We are not concerned on admission to probate with the substantive content of the will; our attention must be focused on the paper writing itself. As to that, there can be no doubt whatsoever that Harvey Snide did not intend as his will the only document that he signed on August 13, 1970.

Until the ruling of the Surrogate of Hamilton County in this case, the application of these principles in the past had uniformly been held in our courts to preclude the admission to probate of a paper writing that the decedent unquestionably intended to execute when he and another were making mutual wills but where, through unmistakable inadvertence, each signed the will drawn for the other. Nor had our courts blinkingly invoked a doctrine of equitable reformation to reach the same end.

On the basis of commendably thorough world-wide research, counsel for appellant has uncovered a total of 17 available reported cases involving mutual wills mistakenly signed by the wrong testator. Six cases arise in New York, two in Pennsylvania, three in England, one in New Zealand and five in Canada. With the exception of the two recent Surrogate's decisions (*Snide* and *Iovino*) relief was denied in the cases from New York, Pennsylvania and England. The courts that have applied the traditional doctrines have not hesitated, however, to express regret at judicial inability to remedy the evident blunder. Relief was granted in the six cases from the British Commonwealth. In these cases it appears that the court has been moved by the transparency of the obvious error and the egregious frustration of undisputed intention which would ensue from failure to correct that error.

Under doctrines both of judicial responsibility not to allow the prospect of unfortunate consequence in an individual case to twist the application of unquestioned substantive legal principle and of *stare decisis*, I perceive no jurisprudential justification to reach out for the disposition adopted by the majority. Not only do I find a lack of rigorous judicial reasoning in this result; more important, I fear an inability to contain the logical consequences of this decision in the future. Thus, why should the result be any different where, although the two wills are markedly different in content, it is equally clear that there has been an erroneous contemporaneous cross-signing by the two would-be testators, or where the scrivener has prepared several drafts for a single client and it is established beyond all doubt that the wrong draft has been mistakenly signed? Nor need imagination stop there.

For the reasons stated, I would adhere to the precedents, and affirm the order of the Appellate Division.

———————————————

NOTES AND QUESTIONS

1.   *Significant departure from the rule?* The Judge who wrote the *Snide* opinion was Judge Sol Wachtler, at that time the Chief Judge of the Court of Appeals of New York (the highest appellate court in that state.) He often expressed his view that the court should try to achieve consensus and should speak with one voice. He also said that the legislature was often the better forum for unresolved issues. *See* Ruth Hochberger & Gary Spencer, *Sol Wachtler Tells Story of Drug Woe*, Nat'l L.J., Aug. 2, 1993. In the *Snide* case, the court was deeply divided and it chose to make a significant departure from accepted norms about dispensing with the formalities. For a general discussion about "crossed wills" and other "classic mistake cases" as well as proposed solutions, see Pamela R. Champine, *My Will Be Done: Accommodating the Erring and Atypical Testator*, 80 Neb. L. Rev. 387 (2001).

2.   *Proper forum for change?* Given the fact that *Snide* was contrary to the rules requiring strict adherence to will formalities that had existed in New York and the rest of the United States for several hundred years, do you think that Judge Wachtler was true to his convictions about the importance of consensus and the judicial deference to the legislature in this case? As a policy matter, should the court have created such novel and expansive policy changes or should they have deferred to the legislature to do so?

2.   Excusing Harmless Error

A court's use of substantial compliance is dependent upon its being willing to adopt a position contrary to the strict compliance approach supported by hundreds of years of precedent. To facilitate the broad use of intent-furthering doctrines, the drafters of the UPC adopted the harmless error rule in §2-503. The emphasis of this rule differs from that of substantial compliance. With substantial compliance, a court considers the level of compliance and determines whether compliance was "close enough" to make validating the will appropriate. The harmless error rule focuses instead on the intent of the decedent. If the decedent intended the document to be a will, then the document can be given effect as a will, but only if the proponent can establish intent by clear and convincing evidence.

UPC §2-503. Harmless Error.

Although a document or writing added upon a document was not executed in compliance with Section 2-502, the document or writing is treated as if it had been executed in compliance with that section if the proponent of the document or writing establishes by clear and convincing evidence that the decedent intended the document or writing to constitute (i) the decedent's will, (ii) a partial or complete revocation of the will, (iii) an addition to or an alteration of the will, or (iv) a partial or complete revival of his [or her] formerly revoked will or of a formerly revoked portion of the will.

This provision gives courts statutory authority to excuse a formality if a "defect in execution was harmless in relation to the purpose of the statutory formalities." RESTATEMENT (THIRD) OF PROPERTY: WILLS & OTHER DONATIVE TRANSFERS §3.3, cmt. b. Such defects would not likely include the writing requirement itself nor the signature requirement but might well include a failure to obtain a second witness or a situation where a husband and wife simply signed the wrong documents, each signing the other's will as happened in *Snide*. The proponent of the defective will must establish by clear and convincing evidence that the decedent intended the document to be his will. As the Reporter's Note to the *Restatement* section above notes, "The harmless-error rule effectively reduces the presumption of invalidity applicable to a defectively executed will from a conclusive one to one that is rebuttable by clear and convincing evidence."

The policy rationale underlying this doctrinal shift is to "retain the intent-serving benefits of Section 2-502 formality without inflicting intent-defeating outcomes in cases of harmless error." The statute instructs that the will *is to be treated* as if it had complied with the formalities if clear and convincing evidence is presented that the decedent intended the document to be his will. While UPC §2-503 has only been adopted, in whole or in part, in Colorado, Hawaii, Michigan, Montana, South Dakota and Utah, substantial compliance and the harmless error rule are clearly where courts and states are moving — albeit slowly.

The following case illustrates how a court might apply the harmless error rule to an instrument that appears not to be in compliance with traditional will formalities.

In re Estate of Wiltfong
148 P.3d 465 (Colo. App. 2006)

Domestic partner of decedent filed petition to have a letter from decedent admitted to probate as decedent's will, and the mother to decedent's nephews contested the petition. The District Court, Arapahoe County, John P. Leopold, J., ruled that the letter was not a will and that the nephews would take decedent's estate by intestate succession. Domestic partner appealed.

I.   BACKGROUND

The following facts are undisputed. Proponent and decedent were domestic partners for twenty years until decedent's death. They lived together and intermingled most of their finances.

On proponent's birthday in 2003, proponent and decedent celebrated with two friends. In the presence of the friends, decedent gave proponent a birthday card containing a typed letter decedent had signed. The letter expressed decedent's wish that if anything should ever happen to him, everything he owned should go to proponent. The letter also stated that proponent, their pets, and an aunt were his only family, and "everyone else is dead to me." Decedent told proponent and the friends the letter represented his wishes.

Decedent died from a heart attack the following year.

Proponent filed a petition to have the letter admitted to probate as decedent's will. Margaret Tovrea (contestant), the mother of decedent's three nephews who would be decedent's heirs if he died intestate, objected to the petition.

The trial court ruled the letter was not a will because it did not meet the requirements of §15-11-503(2), and therefore the nephews would take decedent's estate by intestate succession. This appeal followed.

Proponent contends the trial court erred in concluding decedent did not intend the letter to be his will. We conclude that further proceedings are necessary to resolve this question.

II.   GENERAL PRINCIPLES

We apply the following general principles regarding testacy proceedings, execution of wills, holographic wills, standard of review, and burden of proof.

A.   *Formal Testacy Proceedings*

Formal testacy proceedings to determine whether a decedent left a valid will are governed by statute. Section 15-12-401, et seq. In contested cases, proponents of a will have the burden of presenting prima facie evidence to show the will was duly executed. Once such evidence is presented, those contesting a will's validity have the burden of proving by a preponderance of the evidence lack of testamentary capacity, undue influence, fraud, or the like. Section 15-12-407.

B.   *Execution of Wills*

The underlying purposes of the Colorado Probate Code (Code) are to simplify and clarify the law concerning the affairs of decedents; to discover and make effective the intent of decedents in distributing their property; and to promote a speedy and efficient system for settling estates of decedents and distributing their property to their successors. The Code is to be liberally construed and applied to promote these purposes. Section 15-10-102.

As relevant here, §15-11-502(1) establishes three requirements for a will: (1) it must be in writing; (2) it must bear the testator's signature or be signed in the testator's name; and (3) it must also bear the signatures of at least two persons who witnessed either the testator's signature or the testator's acknowledgment of the signature. There is no need to publish the document as the testator's will or to have witnesses sign the document in the presence of the testator or the other witnesses.

Although these three formalities represent a reduction over time in the number of formalities surrounding the execution of wills, *compare* §15-3-502, C.R.S.1963, *with* §15-11-502(1), they "require strict adherence in order to prevent fraud because statutes governing execution are designed to safeguard and protect the decedent's estate." . . .

C. Holographic Wills

[The trial court found the letter was not a holographic will.]

D. Harmless Error

While scrupulous adherence to the formalities associated with executing wills serves the important purpose of preventing fraud, it can also "defeat intention . . . [or] work unjust enrichment." Restatement (Third) of Property: Wills & Other Donative Transfers §3.3 cmt. b (1999). To address this concern, among others, the Code was amended in 1994 to align Colorado's law with extensive changes suggested by the Uniform Probate Code.

One of these changes was effected by 15-11-503(1). This statute governs how potential donative documents are treated when they have not been executed pursuant to the three requirements established by §15-11-502(1). Sections 15-11-503(1) states:

> Although a document, or writing added upon a document, was not executed in compliance with section 15-11-502, the document or writing is treated as if it had been executed in compliance with that section if the proponent of the document or writing establishes by clear and convincing evidence that the decedent intended the document or writing to constitute:

The purpose of adding §15-11-503(1) was to provide a mechanism for the application of harmless error analysis when a probate court considers whether the formal requirements of executing a will have been met. Applying a harmless error standard in these circumstances supports the purposes of the Code and follows the general trend of the Uniform Probate Code extending the principle of harmless error to probate transfers.

Thus, the question is whether a defect is harmless in light of the statutory purposes, not in light of the satisfaction of each statutory formality, viewed in isolation. To achieve those purposes, the issue is whether the evidence of the conduct proves the decedent intended the document to be a will. Restatement, *supra*, §3.3 cmt. b.

Certain errors cannot be excused as harmless, like the failure of a proponent to produce a document. Other errors are difficult, although not impossible, to excuse as harmless, like the absence of a signature on a document. Restatement, *supra,* §3.3 cmt. b. In this regard, §15-11-503(2) reads: "Subsection (1) of this section shall apply only if the document is signed or acknowledged by the decedent as his or her will. . . . "

Adopted in 2001, Colo. Sess. Laws 2001, ch. 249 at 887, §15-11-503(2) was designed to limit the harmless error concept to minor flaws in the execution of wills. *In re Estate of Sky Dancer, supra;* Thus, §15-11-503(2) establishes the condition precedent that a document be "signed or acknowledged by the decedent as his or her will" before a court may move to the next step and decide whether there is clear and convincing evidence the decedent intended the document to be a will.

The kinds of errors viewed as harmless in Colorado are technical drafting mistakes that frustrate the testator's intent. [Emphasis added.]

E.   Burden of Proof Under §15-11-503

Under §15-11-503, a proponent of a document must show, by clear and convincing evidence, the decedent intended the document to be a will. This enhanced burden is "appropriate to the seriousness of the issue." Uniform Probate Code §2-503 cmt. Clear and convincing evidence is stronger than a mere preponderance; it is highly probable evidence free from serious or substantial doubt.

The greater the deviation from the requirements of due execution established by §15-11-502, the heavier the burden on the document's proponent to prove, by clear and convincing evidence, that the instrument establishes the decedent's intent.

III.   "SIGNED OR ACKNOWLEDGED BY THE DECEDENT AS HIS OR HER WILL"

Proponent contends the trial court erred in interpreting §15-11-503(2) to require a document to be both signed *and* acknowledged by a decedent as his or her will. We agree. . . .

The trial court found decedent signed the letter, but did not acknowledge the letter as his will. The court ruled the phrase "signed or acknowledged" must be read in the conjunctive and therefore, the letter could not be admitted to probate. We conclude the court's interpretation was erroneous. . . .

IV.   CONCLUSION

In this case, the court found decedent's letter did not satisfy the formal requirements of a will pursuant to §15-11-502(1) and that it was not a holographic will pursuant to §15-11-502(2). We agree.

Two of the formal requirements of §15-11-502 were met in this case because the letter was in writing and signed by decedent. However, the letter was not signed by at least two witnesses who had witnessed either decedent's signing of the letter or decedent's acknowledgment of the signature or of the document as a will. Thus, the letter was not a formal will.

The letter was also not a holographic will. Although it was signed by decedent, the material portions of the letter were typed, and, therefore, they were not in decedent's handwriting.

Thus, it was appropriate to determine whether the letter was a writing intended as a will under §15-11-503. However, the trial court erroneously interpreted §15-11-503(2) by holding decedent had to sign *and* acknowledge the letter as a will, even though decedent "stated his intent" in the letter.

In support of this ruling, the trial court added, "[T]he Legislature intends that a person has to say 'this is my will.'" However, §15-11-503 does not require a decedent to announce, "This is my will." The trial court's interpretation added a restriction not present in the statute. Because this legal error affected the trial court's decision, the order must be reversed and the case remanded for a new hearing.

On remand, the court should determine whether the defects in decedent's letter were technical drafting mistakes that should not be allowed to frustrate decedent's testamentary intent and, thus, harmless error under §15-11-503(1) and (2). *See In re Estate of Sky Dancer, supra.* Under a proper formulation of the harmless error analysis, once a court determines a decedent has signed or acknowledged a document as a will, as the trial court did here, the issue becomes whether the proponent can establish by clear and convincing evidence the decedent intended the document to be a will.

This proof may take the form of extrinsic evidence, such as decedent's statements to others about the letter. Section 15-11-502(3) ("Intent that the document constitutes the testator's will can be established by extrinsic evidence. . . . "); Tucker, *supra,* 32 Colo. Law. at 55 ("A critical adjunct to . . . §15-11-503 is . . . §15-11-502(3), which gives teeth to that statute.").

The language of the letter is also relevant evidence, including, for example, whether the letter disposes of all decedent's property and whether the letter identifies a beneficiary. . . .

Therefore, the trial court's order is reversed, and the case is remanded for further proceedings consistent with the views expressed in this opinion.

NOTE

Slow in coming. As noted above, there are only a small number of American states that have adopted the harmless error rule. Several foreign jurisdictions have adopted similar rules including several in Australia. *See* Stephanie Lester, *Admitting Defective Wills to Probate, Twenty Years Later: New Evidence for the Adoption of the Harmless Error Rule*, 42 REAL PROP. PROB. & TR. J. 577 (2007) (discussing historical development of the harmless error doctrine from Australia and analyzing cases and statutes in those American states that have adopted the doctrine); Samuel Flaks, *Excusing Harmless Error in Will Execution: The Israeli Experience*, EST. PLAN. & COMMUNITY PROP. J. (forthcoming 2011), *draft available at* http://ssrn.com/abstract=1675937.

F.   CHOICE OF LAW

An individual who validly executes a will in one jurisdiction and then moves to another which has different execution requirements does not need to execute a new will. States generally recognize the validity of wills executed in other states as long as the will was executed in conformity with the laws of the state or the country where it was initially executed. The UPC adopts this virtually universal approach.

UPC §2-506. Choice of Law as to Execution.

> A written will is valid if executed in compliance with Section 2-502 or 2-503 or if its execution complies with the law at the time of execution of the place where the will is executed, or of the law of the place where at the time of execution or at the time of death the testator is domiciled, has a place of abode, or is a national.

Testators may also seek to specify which state's laws control various provisions in their wills. A testator can choose to use the intestacy statute of another state to determine who is an heir but cannot specify that another state's probate laws will apply to the administration of the estate.

Example: Suri executes a will that provides, "I leave the rest, residue and remainder of my estate to those persons who are my heirs as determined under the Massachusetts intestacy statute. My will shall be administered according to the laws of Massachusetts as well." If Suri dies domiciled in New York, the court will use the Massachusetts statute to determine who qualifies as an "heir." However, the court will not follow the instruction by Suri in her will to probate her estate according to the probate administration rules of Massachusetts. In other words, the actual administration of the estate is not within the discretion of the testator.

G. ETHICAL ISSUES IN WILL DRAFTING

There are a number of interesting and important ethical concerns in drafting wills for clients. These include whether it is ethical for a lawyer (1) to name oneself as the executor or "personal representative," (2) to name oneself as a beneficiary in a client's will, (3) to include a clause limiting one's liability in a will and (4) to represent husbands or wives or testator and beneficiary. Another ethical issue is whether and when the attorney might have a duty to contact a client about changes in the law that affect her estate plan if the attorney keeps the will he drafted.

1. Conflicts of Interest

a. Drafting Attorneys as Fiduciaries

One of the most interesting ethical issues in will drafting is whether the lawyer who drafts the will should suggest that the client name the lawyer as the personal representative of the will, *i.e.*, the person who is in charge of marshaling the decedent's assets, paying creditors and distributing bequests under the will. Even if the lawyer does not suggest it, may the lawyer consent if the client asks her to be the personal representative? The traditional rule has been that the lawyer may not seek such an appointment as a fiduciary though she may accept if asked.

Why is this an ethical issue? Asking a client to name the lawyer as the personal representative of a will that the lawyer is drafting is arguably a conflict of interest because it will generate fees not only for acting as the attorney for the estate but also for acting as the personal representative. It also poses the risk that the lawyer-personal representative will retain herself as the attorney for the estate rather than exercising independent judgment when making this decision. Given these potential conflicts, drafting attorneys should avoid naming themselves as executors as a matter of good practice. The ACTEC Commentaries below give more specific guidance on this issue.

ACTEC COMMENTARY ON MRPC 1.7

Selection of Fiduciaries.   The lawyer advising a client regarding the selection and appointment of a fiduciary should make full disclosure to the client of any benefits that the lawyer may receive as a result of the appointment. In particular, the lawyer should inform the client of any policies or practices known to the lawyer that the fiduciaries under consideration may follow with respect to the employment of the scrivener of an estate planning document as counsel for the fiduciary. The lawyer may also point out that a fiduciary has the right to choose any counsel it wishes. If there is a significant risk that the lawyer's independent professional judgment in the selection of a fiduciary would be materially limited by the lawyer's self interest or any other factor, the lawyer must obtain the client's informed consent, confirmed in writing.

Appointment of Scrivener as Fiduciary.   An individual is generally free to select and appoint whomever he or she wishes to a fiduciary office (*e.g.*, trustee, executor, attorney-in-fact). None of the provisions of the MRPC deals explicitly with the propriety of a lawyer preparing for a client a will or other document that appoints the lawyer to a fiduciary office. As a general proposition lawyers should be permitted to assist adequately informed clients who wish to appoint their lawyers as fiduciaries. Accordingly, a lawyer should be free to prepare a document that appoints the lawyer to a fiduciary office so long as the client is properly informed, the appointment does not violate the conflict of interest rules of MRPC 1.7 (Conflict of Interest: General Rule), and the appointment is not the product of undue influence or improper solicitation by the lawyer.

The designation of the lawyer as fiduciary will implicate the conflict of interest provisions of MRPC 1.7 when there is a significant risk that the lawyer's interests in obtaining the appointment will materially limit the lawyer's independent professional judgment in advising the client concerning the choice of an executor or other fiduciary. See ACTEC Commentary to MRPC 1.8. (addressing transactions entered into by lawyers with clients).

For the purposes of this Commentary a client is properly informed if the client is provided with information regarding the role and duties of the fiduciary, the ability of a lay person to serve as fiduciary with legal and other professional assistance, and the comparative costs of appointing the lawyer or another person or institution as fiduciary. The client should also be informed of any significant lawyer-client relationship that exists between the lawyer or the lawyer's firm and a corporate fiduciary under consideration for appointment. . . .

Various state courts and state bar associations have issued opinions on this issue. For example, several state ethics opinions give guidance on lawyers naming themselves as fiduciaries. *See* Georgia Op. 91-1 (1991), which provides that a lawyer who neither promotes his or her appointment nor exercises undue influence on the client may draft an instrument appointing the lawyer as fiduciary if the lawyer makes full disclosure to the client, obtains the client's written consent and charges a reasonable fee. *See also* Montana Eth. Op. 951231 (1995). This opinion observes that neither MRPC 1.8(c) nor any applicable Comment admits of a broader prohibition than the prohibition against a lawyer preparing an instrument giving the lawyer or a person related to the lawyer any substantial gift, although it does observe that EC 5-6 (contained in the Model Code of Professional Responsibility) cautions attorneys to avoid "consciously influenc[ing] a client to name him as executor, trustee, or lawyer in an instrument." The opinion therefore concludes "it is appropriate for an attorney, upon the client's request, to draft a will in which the attorney is named personal representative or trustee." S*ee also* ABA Comm. on Ethics and Prof'l Responsibility, Formal Op. 02-426, at 7 (2002). This opinion appears to allow lawyers not just to accept an appointment, but also to "seek" it, subject, under certain circumstances, to the client's informed consent. It provides that such an appointment is not a gift to the attorney from the client and is not a prohibited transaction.

California restricts the ability of clients to name their attorneys as their fiduciaries. *See* CAL. PROB. CODE §§10804, 15642(b)(6). Anyone who has a fiduciary relationship with the transferor (including her lawyer) and who drafts an instrument is a "disqualified person." If the attorney is disqualified, he is restricted from acting as both the drafting attorney and the fiduciary unless (1) the attorney is related by blood or marriage to or are a cohabitant of the transferor, or (2) if an *independent* attorney certifies (on a statutorily prescribed form) that the transfer was not the product of fraud, menace, duress or undue influence. The legislation also places limits on double-dipping — receiving two different fees — by an attorney who is also acting as a fiduciary.

QUESTIONS

An absolute prohibition model? Rather than the vague language about conflicts, should the Model Rules actually specify that "in every case in which a drafting attorney is named as a fiduciary . . . such a transaction is a per se conflict of interest?" *See* Paula A. Monopoli, *Drafting Attorneys as Fiduciaries: Fashioning an Optimal Ethical Rule for Conflicts of Interest*, 66 U. PITT. L. REV. 411 (2005), which critiques the changes to ABA Model Rules and their impact on drafting attorneys as fiduciaries. What are the costs of such an absolute prohibition approach to rulemaking in this area?

b.   Exculpatory Clauses

If an attorney is drafting a will for a client and decides that it is appropriate to name himself as an personal representative in the will, he must be careful about including any clauses that limit the attorney's liability in acting as the personal representative. For example, this kind of clause might state that the lawyer is not liable for anything except "gross negligence" in his capacity as personal representative. Consider the following caution in the ACTEC Commentaries.

ACTEC COMMENTARY ON MRPC 1.8

Exculpatory Clauses.   Under some circumstances and at the client's request, a lawyer may properly include an exculpatory provision in a document drafted by the lawyer for the client that appoints the lawyer to a fiduciary office. (An exculpatory provision is one that exonerates a fiduciary from liability for certain acts and omissions affecting the fiduciary estate.) The lawyer ordinarily should not include an exculpatory clause without the informed consent of an unrelated client. An exculpatory clause is often desired by a client who wishes to appoint an individual nonprofessional or family member as fiduciary.

---

c.   Drafting Attorney as Beneficiary

An estate planning lawyer should absolutely avoid naming himself or his family members as the beneficiary of a will he is drafting for an unrelated client. Courts often view this as raising a presumption of undue influence and such gifts are likely to engender will contests from family members. In *Estate of Auen*, 35 Cal. Rptr. 2d 557 (Ct. App. 1994), *superseded by statute as noted in* Rice v. Clark, 47 P.3d 300 (Cal. 2002), the court noted that, "[t]he relation between attorney and client is a fiduciary relation of the very highest character. Transactions between attorneys and their clients are subject to the strictest scrutiny." 35 Cal. Rptr. 2d at 562-63 (citation omitted). Cal. Prob. Code §§21350 and 21351 do not allow testamentary gifts to drafters or their relatives unless the drafter is a relative or domestic partner of the testator. Consider the following ACTEC Commentary on this issue.

ACTEC COMMENTARY ON MRPC 1.8

Gifts to Lawyer.   MRPC 1.8 generally prohibits a lawyer from soliciting a substantial gift from a client, including a testamentary gift, or preparing for a client an instrument that gives the lawyer or a person related to the lawyer a substantial gift. A lawyer may properly prepare a will or other document that includes a substantial benefit for the lawyer or a person related to the lawyer if the lawyer or other recipient is related to the client. The term "related person" is defined in MRPC 1.8(c) and may include a person who is not related by blood or marriage but has a close familial relationship. However, the lawyer should exercise special care if the proposed gift to the lawyer or a related person is disproportionately large in relation to the gift the client proposes to make to others who are equally related. Neither the lawyer nor a person associated with the lawyer can assist an unrelated client in making a substantial gift to the lawyer or to a person related to the lawyer. *See* MRPC 1.8(k).

For the purposes of this Commentary, the substantiality of a gift is determined by reference both to the size of the client's estate and to the size of the estate of the designated recipient. The provisions of this rule extend to all methods by which gratuitous transfers might be made by a client including life insurance, joint tenancy with right of survivorship, and pay-on-death and trust accounts. As noted in ABA Formal Opinion 02-426, the client's appointment of the lawyer as a fiduciary is not a gift to the lawyer and is not a business transaction that would subject the appointment to MRPC 1.8. Nevertheless, such an appointment is subject to the general conflict of interest provisions of MRPC 1.7.

---

d.   Representing Multiple Clients

i.   *Husbands and Wives*

As you learned in Chapter 1, an estate planning attorney must always be cognizant of the possible conflicts inherent in representing husbands and wives since his representation of one may affect his ability to represent the other. *See* ACTEC Commentaries on MPRC 1.6 and 1.7; Naomi Cahn & Robert Tuttle, *Dependency and Delegation: The Ethics of Marital Representation*, 22 Seattle U. L. Rev. 97 (1998). Consider the following ACTEC Commentary on the representation of husbands and wives.

ACTEC COMMENTARY ON MRPC 1.7

Joint or Separate Representation.   As indicated in the ACTEC Commentary on MRPC 1.6 (Confidentiality of Information), a lawyer usually represents multiple clients jointly. However, some experienced estate planners regularly represent husbands and wives as separate clients. They also undertake to represent other related clients separately with respect to related matters. Such representations should only be undertaken with the informed consent of each client, confirmed in writing. *See* ACTEC Commentaries on MRPC 1.0 (e)) (defining "informed consent"); MRPC 1.0 (b) (defining "confirmed in writing"). The writing may be contained in an engagement letter that covers other subjects as well. [*See* Chapter 1 for the Example 1.7-1 included in this Commentary.]

---

ii. Beneficiary and Testator

Estate planning attorneys are often asked by someone other than the potential testator to draft a will for the testator. While this is not unethical, attorneys must be aware of potential conflicts. The ABA has issued an advisory opinion on this issue, *ABA Comm. on Ethics and Prof'l Responsibility*, Formal Op. 02-428 (2002), which provides that, "Under the Model Rules of Professional Conduct, a lawyer may, on the recommendation of a person who is a potential beneficiary, draft the testator's will, provided Rule 5.4(c) is satisfied and any informed consents required by other rules are obtained. If the person recommending the lawyer also agrees to pay or assure the lawyer's fee, the testator's informed consent to the arrangement must be obtained and the other requirements of Rule 1.8(f) satisfied. When the person recommending the lawyer is a current client of the lawyer, the lawyer should obtain clear guidance from the person and the testator as to the lawyer's use or revelation of protected information of each in representing the other. The lawyer also must assure compliance with any requirements of Rule 1.7 that are implicated under the circumstances."

What if the person asking the lawyer to draft the will is a very important current client of the lawyer's firm? Consider the following ACTEC Commentary on this issue when the person asking the lawyer to draft the will is an existing client.

ACTEC COMMENTARY ON MRPC 1.7

Existing Client Asks Lawyer to Prepare Will or Trust for Another Person.   A lawyer should exercise particular care if an existing client asks the lawyer to prepare for another person a will or trust that will benefit the existing client, particularly if the existing client will pay the cost of providing the estate planning services to the other person. If the representation of both the existing client and the new client would create a significant risk that the representation of one or both clients would be materially limited, the representation can only be undertaken as permitted by MRPC 1.7(b). In any case, the lawyer must comply with MRPC 1.8(f) and should consider cautioning both clients of the possibility that the existing client may be presumed to have exerted undue influence on the other client because the existing client was involved in the procurement of the document.

---

2. *Duty to Produce and Keep the Will*

Once a will has been executed, there are several alternatives for safeguarding the will. First, the client may want to take the will home. If she does, there is the possibility that it may be lost or that the client will make changes on the will that may later cause confusion about the client's final wishes. As an alternative, the lawyer might suggest retaining the original for safe-keeping in the lawyer's files. If the testator agrees, the lawyer, in most states, has a duty to keep the will in a safe place like a vault, regardless of whether the testator continues to use the lawyer's services. Often, a lawyer who is retiring will sell her practice to another lawyer. A lawyer who takes a will from another lawyer in this situation inherits the first lawyer's duty to keep the will safe. The UPC provides a third alternative, depositing the original will with the court.

UPC §2-515. Deposit of Will with Court in Testator's Lifetime.

> A will may be deposited by the testator or the testator's agent with any court for safekeeping, under rules of the court. The will must be sealed and kept confidential. During the testator's lifetime, a deposited will must be delivered only to the testator or to a person authorized in writing signed by the testator to receive the will. . . .

When a client or former client dies, the lawyer who has retained the will for safekeeping has a duty to produce it within a reasonable time. However, the sanctions for failure to do so are limited to contempt:

UPC §2-516. Duty of Custodian of Will; Liability.

> After the death of a testator and on request of an interested person, a person having custody of a will of the testator shall deliver it with reasonable promptness to a person able to secure its probate and if none is known, to an appropriate court. A person who willfully fails to deliver a will is liable to any person aggrieved for any damages that may be sustained by the failure. A person who willfully refuses or fails to deliver a will after being ordered by the court in a proceeding

> brought for the purpose of compelling delivery is subject to penalty for contempt of court.

A problem with retaining documents is that estate planning involves tax planning, and tax statutes change all the time. Questions arise as to how much of a duty a lawyer has to contact clients for whom she is retaining documents to let them know when a tax law that could affect their estate plans has changed. Consider the ACTEC Commentary below with regard to this issue.

ACTEC COMMENTARY ON MRPC 1.8

Retention of Original Documents. A lawyer who has drawn a will or other estate planning documents for a client may offer to retain the executed originals of the documents subject to the client's order. However, a lawyer who retains a client's documents for safekeeping should provide the client with a written receipt, which may be in the form of a letter, acknowledging that the documents are held subject to the client's order. The receipt may, but need not, also indicate that the fiduciary designated in the documents is not required to retain as counsel the lawyer with whom the documents were left for safekeeping. The documents should be held by the lawyer in a manner consistent with the requirements of MRPC 1.15 (Safekeeping Property) regarding the duties of a lawyer who receives and holds property on behalf of a client. In particular, the documents should be properly identified and appropriately safeguarded. Subject to otherwise applicable law, the lawyer should comply with the client's written directions regarding disposition of the documents.

The retention of the client's original estate planning documents does not itself make the client an "active" client or impose any obligation on the lawyer to take steps to keep informed regarding the client's management of property and family status. Similarly, sending a client periodic letters encouraging the client to review the sufficiency of the client's estate plan or calling the client's attention to subsequent legal developments do not increase the lawyer's obligations to the client. *See* ACTEC Commentary on MRPC 1.4 (Communication), for a discussion of the concept of dormant representation. . . .

ACTEC COMMENTARY ON MRPC 1.4

Example 1.4-1: Lawyer (L) prepared and completed an estate plan for Client C. At C's request L retained the original documents executed by C. L performed no other legal work for C in the following two years but has no reason to believe that C has engaged other estate planning counsel. L's representation of C is dormant. L may, but is not obligated to, communicate with C regarding changes in the law. If

L communicates with C about changes in the law, but is not asked by C to perform any legal services, L's representation remains dormant. C is properly characterized as a client and not a former client for purposes of MPRCs 1.7 and 1.9.

QUESTION

Retaining the original will. If the client agrees to the attorney's suggestion that the attorney retain his original will, his family must contact the attorney when he dies to obtain the will for probate. And in so doing, the attorney is making it more likely that they will hire her as the attorney for the estate (or conversely, making it more difficult for them not to hire her). Is this a conflict of interest, and if so, how would you address it?

3. Drafting Software, Mistakes and the Unauthorized Practice of Law

The burgeoning business of software that allows individuals to draft their own wills and other estate planning documents has led to problems for some people who use the programs. The issue for these testators is the potential mistakes non-lawyers may unwittingly make. Recent articles have cautioned against laypersons drafting their own wills using such software. *See* Deborah L. Jacobs, *The Case Against Do-It-Yourself Wills*, Forbes.com, Sept. 7, 2010,[10] which describes the case of a wealthy Texan who used a form copied from a book. This resulted in his forfeiting his $3.5 million federal estate tax exemption, and the author uses the case as an example of why she is "strenuously opposed to do-it-yourself-wills."

In addition to the issue of potential mistakes by non-lawyers who use such software, questions about the unauthorized practice of law have surfaced in connection with the providers of the software. Increasingly, state bars and plaintiffs in class action lawsuits are pursuing software producers and Internet sites under statutes that prohibit the unauthorized practice of law. *See Lawsuits Challenge Legal Zoom Document Business*, L.A. Daily News, June 20, 2010,[11] which notes two recent suits filed in California and Missouri against a company that provides legal documents

---

10. Deborah L. Jacobs, *The Case Against Do-It-Yourself Wills*, Forbes.com. Sept. 7, 2010, http://www.forbes.com/2010/09/07/do-it-yourself-will-mishaps-personal-finances-estate-lawyers-overcharge.html.

11. *Lawsuits Challenge Legal Zoom Document Business*, L.A. Daily News, June 20, 2010, http://www.losangelesdailynews.org/lawsuits-challenge-legalzoom-document-business/.

to the public. The suits allege that the company is engaged in the unauthorized practice of law since it provides legal documents without adequate lawyer supervision. Interestingly, the business was founded by two lawyers and uses famous O.J. Simpson lawyer Robert Shapiro in its television ads. It has been highly successful.

EXERCISES

The following exercises involve your meeting with two new clients, Alberto and Maria Juarez. As background, you should consider the following best practices. Prior to your initial meeting with new estate planning clients, you should send a questionnaire to them so they can list the assets they have, to whom they would like these assets to be distributed and who they would like to oversee their estate after they die. This makes the initial meeting with the clients go more smoothly and saves time for both the clients and the lawyer. At the initial meeting with the clients in your office, they may have a number of questions for you about how they should divide their estate and who their personal representative should be. Remember that ethical norms in the profession advise against suggesting yourself for the role of personal representative, but you are free to accept such an appointment if the clients ask you and you fully disclose to them fee information and who other candidates may be for the position.

Once you have fully interviewed your clients, discussed with them the applicable law of wills and will substitutes and have divined their intent, you will begin the drafting process of the will for their probate property. (For nonprobate property, you may need to discuss with the clients the need to update beneficiary designations to be consistent with the overall estate plan presently being devised.) Upon final completion of the draft, you should circulate it to the clients for their review. Ask them to take care in reviewing how beneficiaries are named and who is included to ensure that there are no mistakes or ambiguities. When they have sent the draft back to you and you have made any revisions, you will call them in for an execution ceremony. The following exercises will help you practice these three skills — interviewing, drafting and supervising the execution of the will.

1. Initial Client Interview

The following three exercises can be done in small groups of three students. The professor may call on one group to recreate the third exercise, the execution ceremony, in front of the class. Each group will simulate an initial meeting between an estate planning attorney and two clients, Alberto and Maria Juarez, draft a will for each of them and then conduct the execution ceremony. One student should play the role of the estate planning attorney and two others should play Alberto and Maria Juarez, the clients.

Alberto and Maria Juarez have called you to set up an initial appointment. You sent them an initial questionnaire which they completed with the following information:

Alberto and Maria own a family business. They have two children, ages 6 and 10. Their assets are as follows:

1. A house (valued at $600,000 with no mortgage);
2. 401(k) (Alberto) with a balance of $400,000;
3. 401(k) (Maria) with a balance of $350,000;
4. Term life insurance on each of their lives with a face amount of $1,000,000;
5. A stock portfolio valued at $650,000.

Other than the introductory phone conversation and the questionnaire information, you know little else about Alberto and Maria, their family, their finances and property, their intended beneficiaries and, most of all, their testamentary goals. You should elicit that information *in a general way*, recognizing that there will be more sessions together and that Alberto and Maria will be sent home with a to-do list. Open-ended questions, rather than leading ones that suggest an answer, tend to work better to learn what such clients know and wish.

Much of the purpose of this meeting is to get to know each other, put Alberto and Maria at ease, get basic information about their property and to start formulating a testamentary plan. In addition, you should focus on the basics of client counseling and explain matters of representation, such as the scope of the engagement, the fee, the attorney-client privilege, hiring of other experts, etc. Among other matters, the clients will need to be asked about what will substitutes they have and explained how these are handled, as compared to property that will be probated. A number of difficult questions may come up that you should consider. For example, if Alberto and Maria are not sure who to appoint as their personal representatives, discuss what you can or should suggest about who is an appropriate personal representative. What if they ask you if you would be their personal representative? How should you respond? How would you determine that Alberto and Maria have sufficiently aligned interests in how they wish to leave their property so that you can represent both of them ethically? Is there a way to assure that you will not be accused of a conflict of interest in this regard?

2. Drafting Exercise

After you have elicited the information you need from Alberto and Maria, draft a short will for each of them which includes an exordium clause, a provision that distributes their property and a residuary clause that leaves the remainder of their property to each other, if the other survives, and if not to the children by right of representation and if there are no children or lineal descendants, then to the Red Cross. Be sure to name a personal representative in each will.

3. Execution Ceremony Role-Play

Once you have drafted Alberto and Maria's will, you will need to have them execute the documents in a ceremony in your office. Consider each of the various will formalities required by probate codes and courts in the context of a controlled will ceremony environment (*i.e.,* at the law firm's office) with a "normal" client and a "normal" disposition plan.

Alberto and Maria are coming to your office in three days to sign the will.

a.   Consider what things you would do in advance of the meeting to prepare for the ceremony with Alberto and Maria, either alone or in conversation with the client;

b.   Role-play the ceremony itself (along with several students acting as Alberto and Maria, the two witnesses and the notary) (in this regard, you should use the will you drafted in Exercise 2 above and have the pages of the will where signatures are required ready for Alberto and Maria to sign); and

c.   Identify the things you would do with or say to Alberto and Maria and the witnesses at the conclusion of the ceremony (in this regard, a checklist might be helpful for the clients). Consider where the will should be kept after it is executed. If Alberto and Maria ask if they can keep the original with you, is this ethically acceptable? Is it wise?

10 INTERPRETING THE WILL

A. INTRODUCTION

The goal of each party involved in the probate process, from the drafting attorney to the personal representative of the estate to the courts, is to carry out the testamentary plan as the testator intended. The testator may draft a will that only becomes operative years later, after many changes have occurred in her life. If the drafting attorney drafts the governing instrument clearly and anticipates changes that could occur between drafting and the testator's death, then the testator's plan is less likely to be contested and more likely to be carried out. If the testator updates her will when she experiences major life events, or as her asset structure changes, then doing so helps clarify her ultimate intent. Thus, the drafting attorney plays an important role in making sure a client's plan is clear and easy to carry out.

No one can anticipate every eventuality, and some aspects of the testamentary plan may be ambiguous. This means that courts are often faced with the task of interpreting the instrument in a manner that is most consistent with the testator's intent. Courts look to rules (or "canons") of construction to help them discover or "divine" the testator's intent when it is not clear. These rules supply a presumptive intent to the court. Courts may also look to extrinsic evidence to rebut such presumptive intent and to clarify the testator's intent in a given case.

Many scholars have questioned whether individual intent can ever really be found since the testator is dead. Some have pointed out the inherent ambiguity of language, compounded by the fact that a lawyer was often interposed between the testator and the written word, creating somewhat of a legal fiction in the oft-stated rule that courts are to divine the "intent" of the testator. Professor Mary Louise Fellows describes the process of searching for the testator's sometimes elusive intent below.

Mary Louise Fellows, In Search of Donative Intent
73 Iowa L. Rev. 611 (1988)

The preeminent role that language plays in the search for the proper intent to impute in validly executed instruments is attributable to two factors. First, the system of legal rules designed to order and expedite the implementation of donative freedom, such as the Statute of Frauds and the Statute of Wills, defers to the written word. Second, the construction process operates on the assumption that communication through language, usually written, is the means by which most people would choose to be bound. In contrast to a situation in which a property owner is incapacitated and the absence of a transfer provides no basis for inferring continuing agreement with a previously executed estate plan or intestacy, a competent owner's deliberate and unrevoked language is an objective fact upon which to infer an intent to distribute the property exactly as the language directs. This jurisdiction for the states' deference to validly executed language, however, ignores the practical problems that verbal communication creates, and how it proves inadequate for imputing intent.

Words are imperfect means of communication because a word can stand for more than one object or event. Consider a will provision that provides: "I devise $10,000 to *A*, but if *A* and I both should die because of a common disaster, the $10,000 should pass to *B*." What does it mean to die in a "common disaster?" If *A* and the testator are in an automobile accident and the testator dies instantly, but *A* dies a short time later when a train strikes the ambulance taking her to the hospital, do the words "common disaster" apply to give the $10,000 to *B* rather than to *A*?

Second, the word's relation to the object is an indirect means of conveying the property owner's thought and, therefore, is susceptible to miscues. This indirect relationship leads to drafting mistakes when the thought does not adequately represent the object. An example is when a will contains a devise to "my Uncle John," who is a close friend of the testator, but unrelated. The indirect relationship also may lead to mistakes when the word does not correctly express the thought. An example is when a will misdescribes a parcel of land.

Third, words are an especially imperfect means of communication when they refer to abstractions because such thoughts are more detached from the persons and things to which they are to apply and lack sufficient specificity to give them effect. Further, abstractions involve generalities that inevitably encompass unintended situations. An example of an abstraction in a donative transfer is when a trustee is directed "to pay from time to time the net income and so much of the principal as it, in its absolute and uncontrolled discretion, may determine appropriate for the beneficiary's maintenance, comfort, and support." Such abstractions often raise more questions than they answer. For example, does the trustee have to exercise the discretion reasonably or only in good faith? Should the trustee consider the beneficiary's other resources in determining whether to pay income or principal? Should the state have a right to reimbursement from the trust for care it gives an institutionalized beneficiary? Careful drafting could address all of these issues, but the task is daunting.

The indirect relationship of the word to the object in the estate planning process is more problematic when the property owner hires an attorney. The language guiding the distribution of the property owner's wealth reflects two tiers of thought: the property owner's thought communicated by words to the attorney and the attorney's thought communicated by words to the state.

[The lawyer] searches for words to fit objects. He must probe his client's mind to ascertain his wishes for all the contingencies that are likely to occur, and then do his best to put into the document a phrase which describes the persons or things the client desires-every one of them and no more. Furthermore, the lawyer must be sure that when the document later gets before the court, the judge will reverse the lawyer's process and go back from the phrase to those very persons and things.

If the estate planning process is successful, the lawyer will avoid unique word usages and ambiguities and will consider many potential contingencies that can affect a disposition taking effect over a number of years. Legal boilerplate provisions in such professionally drafted instruments help to achieve estate plans, but also create a remoteness between property owners and the instruments purporting to reflect their donative intent. That remoteness is exacerbated further when a lawyer introduces issues the property owner never considered, considered only generally, or comprehends only vaguely. Adjustment of the form and nature of dispositions to reduce transfer tax liabilities is a primary contributor to this estrangement.

That clients are remote from their instruments does not mean that lawyers garbled their clients' donative intent. It does, however, increase the possibility that donative intent will be garbled because clients are less able to review the legal translations of their donative intent. Although a good lawyer will try to explain the various provisions to the client, the level of detail and the economic constraints of the planning process make it impossible for the property owner to understand, let alone make an informed choice about, all the issues that arise.

At best, a professionally drafted instrument may reflect the property owner's broad estate planning goals and decision to make a donative transfer. The specific provisions in the instrument, however, do not reflect the property owner's understanding of the plan because the property owner generally finds those specific provisions bewildering. As a result, the lawyer-drafted instrument can do no more than implement a plan that represents the client's probable intent.

The imperfect symbolism of language, the property owner's limited understanding of the instrument's details, the dynamics of the estate planning process, and the potential for lawyer error and incompetence leave the courts with a dilemma. On the one hand, deference to lawyer-drafted language is irrational because extrinsic evidence demonstrates the property owner's remoteness from the document and the likelihood that the document fails to manifest the property owner's intent. On the other hand, deference to lawyer drafted language is essential to providing certainty and predictability of interpretation. When extrinsic evidence clearly demonstrates a failure of expression in the executed language resulting from attorney error such as inadvertent omission, ambiguity, or misdescription, and when the extrinsic evidence clearly demonstrates how the property alternatively should be distributed, however, no dilemma exists and the courts ought to abandon the constraints of the executed language.

———————————

In this chapter, we first explore the rules or doctrines that help the court decide just what constitutes "the will." Then we review whether courts may use extrinsic evidence to determine intent when the terms of the will are ambiguous or the product of a mistake. After that, we look at the rules of construction that give courts a default meaning if the testator's intent is not clear. Finally, we end with several exercises to help you learn the nuances of these rules and to practice good, clear drafting in order to avoid ambiguities about your client's wishes in the first place.

QUESTIONS

The limitations of language. The excerpt above focuses on the ambiguity inherent in language. As you read this, consider whether permitting testators to speak, instead of write, their intended bequests would make any difference. If a testator were allowed to be videotaped talking about his final wishes, would it be sound policy for a court to accept that as the testator's valid will? Would such a process minimize the ambiguity inherent in the written word or would it create more ambiguity?

B.   WHAT CONSTITUTES THE WILL?

The first question that a probate court may face is which documents did the testator actually *intend* as her last will and testament. Typically, the pages that make up the will are clearly marked. This is especially true if an attorney drafted the will. The will usually consists of one document, with each page numbered and all paragraphs flowing one to the other, and with signatures of the testator, the witnesses and a notary. However, sometimes the will does not consist of one simple document. There may be several different pieces of paper that might arguably constitute the testator's will. (Remember the rules about safekeeping of a will in Chapter 9.) If an individual's will is not kept safely in a lawyer's vault or filed with the court, then questions about the testator's intent with respect to these papers are much more likely to arise.

In this section, we first look at this question in terms of the doctrine of "integration." Courts apply this doctrine to determine which papers actually constitute the will. We then look to whether certain documents or events outside the "four corners" of the will are treated as being part of the will itself. Courts apply the doctrines of incorporation by reference and acts of independent significance to resolve this question. Finally, we look at two statutory provisions that allow testators to draft instruments, after execution of the initial will, which may effectively dispose of property. As you read about these doctrines, consider whether they satisfy the underlying functions of will formalities and what tensions there may be between those functions and these doctrines.

1.   *Integration*

A probate court presented with a will must ensure that the document being probated consists of the pages that were present at the execution ceremony which the testator intended to be part of the will. Words, sentences, paragraphs or pages that are subsequently added or deleted should not be given effect. The process of recognizing various pages or documents as a single will is called "integration." If the pages of the will are fastened together, an inference arises that the testator intended them all to be part of one document. The testator need not sign every page.

There are many things a lawyer can do at the time the will is drafted and executed to lessen the likelihood that someone might contest the validity of the will being offered for probate on integration grounds. For example, the attorney can draft the will with the pages and lines numbered, use one font type and size and carry sentences from one page to the next so it is clear they were drafted at the same time. At the end of the execution, the document can be stapled together, with the testator and witnesses initialing and dating each page.

> **Example:**   Melinda arrives at her lawyer's office for the will execution ceremony. She initials each of the five pages and puts her full signature on the final page so that there is no question that the final document consists of all five pages. The attorney has two paralegals witness Melinda sign the will, and they place their signatures below the attestation clause. The attorney also has a notary take the oath from Melinda and the witnesses and complete the appropriate affidavit. On these facts, the court will read these pages as an integrated whole when probating the will and determining Melinda's testamentary intent.

If a testator executes a will in a sloppy manner, there may be litigation. The testator may have written the will himself on a variety of scattered papers, so it may be difficult for the proponent to establish which papers were present at the time of the execution. If the sheets are produced in the probate court in no particular order and are unnumbered, and if it appears that pages or provisions were later added or deleted, it is likely a court will conclude that the writing, or at least portions of it, do not constitute the testator's valid will.

2.   *Incorporation by Reference*

Certain documents in addition to the will itself may be relevant to understanding the testator's overall intent with regard to her estate plan. The "incorporation by reference" doctrine permits the court to include an additional document or writing as part of the testator's will if the testator intends it to be so included, the document or writing is in existence at the time the will is executed and it is sufficiently described so it can be readily identified. If the doctrine applies, the incorporated document — as it existed on the day the will was executed — is deemed to be part of the will, as if the document were literally typed into the will or attached to it as an exhibit. The UPC codifies the common law approach to incorporation by reference:

UPC §2-510. Incorporation by Reference.

> A writing in existence when a will is executed may be incorporated by reference if the language of the will manifests this intent and describes the writing sufficiently to permit its identification.

Later changes to the incorporated document generally are not incorporated by reference; like any other change to the estate plan, they require compliance with will execution formalities. Drafting attorneys typically avoid incorporating external writings by reference, preferring to type the contents into the will itself or attach it as an exhibit. However, incorporation by reference may be required if a document is not capable of easily being typed into the will itself or is attached as an appendix. This may be due to its length or complexity.

> **Example:** Sylvia executed a will providing that her $100,000 Bank of America checking account be distributed to the person identified in a letter to be found in her safe deposit box. Sylvia executed her will on August 1, 2010. After her death, her personal representative opened her safe deposit box, and it contained a letter dated July 31, 2010, which provided that Sylvia's $100,000 bank account should be distributed to Felix. The court must distribute the proceeds to Felix because the will specifically referenced the letter, and the letter was in existence as of the date the will was executed.

NOTES AND QUESTIONS

1. *Narrow construction.* In *Estate of Sweet*, 519 A.2d 1260 (Me. 1987), the court granted the beneficiary's probate challenge to the legitimacy of an external memorandum, which specified how funds should be distributed by decedent's personal representative. It found that the will's provision incorporating "any memorandum or memoranda of said indebtedness which shall have been prepared by me and is in existence at the time of my death" was too broad and that it did not describe the external writing with sufficient particularity to satisfy the requirement for incorporation by reference. Other courts have been similarly stringent in incorporating documents by reference. Why do you think courts construe the doctrine so narrowly? Would it better effectuate the testator's intent to apply the doctrine more expansively?

2. *The King of Pop.* Take a look at Michael Jackson's will, which you read in the first chapter. What document does his will incorporate by reference?

PROBLEM

Alice executed her will on January 2, 2010. Her will contains the provisions listed in (a)-(e). For each provision, decide whether the external writing referred to in the provision could be properly recognized by a court as part of the will.

a. I leave Bob all the African coins listed on the appraisal by Coin Collectors, Inc. dated July 23, 2009, that is located in my safe deposit box at Wells Fargo, 1666 Broadway St., Denver, CO.

b. I leave Ray all the European coins on the appraisal by Coins-R-Us that is located in my safe deposit box at Wells Fargo, 1666 Broadway St., Denver, CO.

c. I leave Dylan the South American coins listed in a notebook, labeled "Coins for Dylan," which I now keep in my safe deposit box at Wells Fargo, 1666 Broadway St., Denver, CO.

d. I leave Liam all Confederate coins listed in a notebook to be labeled "Coins for Liam."

e. In addition to all of the above powers, my personal representative and my trustee may exercise those powers set forth in the Colorado statutes relating to fiduciaries, as amended after the date of this instrument. I incorporate such Act, specifically Title 3B Chapters 4 and 20 or successor provisions, by reference and make it a part of this instrument.

3.   *Republication by Codicil*

Testators often execute subsequent instruments that partially revoke a prior will. These amendments or "codicils" to wills have the same force and effect as if they were executed as part of the original will. A codicil can be thought of as a "mini-will," which contains only limited provisions. It must be completed with the same formalities as a regular will. Pursuant to the doctrine of republication by codicil, a codicil incorporates all the provisions of the will it is updating. Republication by codicil is typically a common-law doctrine, although some states have codified it. *See, e.g.,* FLA. STAT. §732.5105. The doctrine provides that if a testator executes a will and later executes a codicil to that will, the will begins to "run again" from the date of execution of the second instrument, the codicil. In other words, the codicil not only includes its own provisions but it also includes the provisions of the original document. Both are deemed effective on the date the codicil is executed. Republication moves the date of the will forward and changes the applicable date for the application of other doctrines—incorporation by reference, revocation by marriage and omitted children.

> **Example:**   Mario executes a will in 2005 that leaves his property to his wife, Viviana. Their son, Marco, is born in 2006. In 2007, Mario executes a codicil to his will that adds a $10,000 bequest to his church. The codicil is attested by two witnesses. Mario dies in 2008. While Marco was an omitted child under the 2005 will, he can no longer claim such a status since 2007 codicil was executed after he was born.

4.   *Events of Independent Significance*

The doctrine of events of independent significance allows the probate court to look to events or acts outside the four corners of the will to determine which property goes to which beneficiaries. Were it not for the events of independent significance exception, class gifts and residuary clauses might otherwise fail to comply with the traditional rule that requires all the provisions governing which property is to be distributed to whom to be clearly stated in the four corners of the will itself. Events of independent significance are otherwise objective events that occur in the outside world without regard to the testator's specific intent as to who should receive what property at her death. Typical events include the birth, death and adoption of a child as well as the act of acquiring or disposing of property. The UPC codifies the common law rule in the following manner:

UPC §2-512. Events of Independent Significance.

A will may dispose of property by reference to acts and events that have significance apart from their effect upon the dispositions made by the will, whether they occur before or after the execution of the will or before or after the testator's death. The execution or revocation of another individual's will is such an event.

Example: Oona writes a will that says, "I leave my car and the savings account that I own at Wells Fargo Bank, #2222999, to my brother, Bono, if he survives me but if not to my sister, Lulu." Under the doctrine of events of independent significance, a court may declare this provision valid because Bono's survival (or not) is an event that has significance apart from its effect upon the dispositions made by Oona's will. In other words, the will as written and which complies with the required formalities anticipates this event.

As a matter of good drafting, it is best to refer to events that are clearly independent of the testator's dispositive plan, for example, stocks in a brokerage account or persons employed by the testator at his death. Other events are too closely linked to the testator's actions to qualify as events of independent significance. Such an event would include, for example, "the list of people and property I leave in a memo"[1] or "the property in the drawer next to my bed." Unless the event is clearly independent, using it in the will may invite a will contest.

---

1. Note that under UPC §2-513 described in more detail below, such a memorandum may be given the same effect as a will if it comports with certain requirements. However, this is not as a result of incorporation by reference but rather by the separate provisions of §2-513.

QUESTION

Events of independent significance as an exception. Given the general rule that all dispositive provisions and their terms must be included in the four corners of the will, why do you think this exception evolved under the common law and was then adopted by the drafters of the UPC?

PROBLEM

Are the devises listed below in (a)-(e) sufficient to be treated as part of a will? In other words, are these devises permissible in light of the fact that they require a court to look to documents or acts or events not ascertainable when the will was written?

a. A devise to "the party who may be farming my farm at my death."

b. A devise of "my stocks to the persons named in a document I will execute between now and my death. If I do not execute such a document, then to my children, per stirpes." Tony executed a document five years later that referenced his will and named his siblings as beneficiaries.

c. A devise of "the stocks and securities in my Schwab account #2345678 at my death to Lucinda and William Jefferies or the survivor of them."

d. A devise that provides, "I give Angela the diamond rings located in my safe."

e. A devise of "the residue of my estate to my children, or if any child does not survive me to that child's descendants, per stirpes."

5.   *Memorandum at Death*

In those states that have adopted the UPC, a testator may draft a memorandum after executing the will that leaves tangible personal property to certain people. The purpose of this exception to testamentary formalities is to enable a testator to make minor changes to his estate plan after executing the will without formally executing a new instrument. The testator must comply with certain requirements in order for such a memo to be enforceable, including signing the document and describing the items to be disposed of with some specificity. Note that a testator can use a memorandum only for tangible personal property and not for intangible property (stocks) or real property (a house).

UPC §2-513. Separate Writing Identifying Devise of Certain Types of Tangible Personal Property.

Whether or not the provisions relating to holographic wills apply, a will may refer to a written statement or list to dispose of items of tangible personal property not otherwise specifically disposed of by the will, other than money. To be admissible under this section as evidence of the intended disposition, the writing must be signed by the testator and must describe the items and the devisees with reasonable certainty. The writing may be referred to as one to be in existence at the time of the testator's death; it may be prepared before or after the execution of the will; it may be altered by the testator after its preparation; and it may be a writing that has no significance apart from its effect on the dispositions made by the will.

This section allows a testator to create a document after execution of the will that will be read together with the will and implemented by the court. It illustrates the trend toward fewer formalities in the process of validly passing property at death. That being said, the memorandum does need mini-formalities; while witnesses are not required, the memorandum must be in writing, the testator must sign it and each item of tangible personal property must be described "with reasonable certainty." The drafters of the UPC note that, "a document referring to 'all my tangible personal property other than money' or to 'all my tangible personal property located in my office' or using similar catch-all language would normally be sufficient," even though each particular item has not been specifically described.

Unless the testator specifies otherwise, the will itself takes precedence over an external memorandum if the two conflict. The following is an example of a typical clause in a will that clarifies that the separate writing will take priority over other dispositive provisions in the will itself:

> I might leave a written statement or list disposing of items of tangible personal property. If I do, then my written statement or list is to be given effect to the extent authorized by law and is to take precedence over any contrary devise or devises of the same item or items of property in this will.

PROBLEMS

1. Susan's will devised her antique desk to her granddaughter, Anika. It also contained a clause like the one reproduced above. After Susan's death, Susan's personal representative discovered the will in the

top drawer of Susan's antique desk. Susan's personal representative also discovered in the same drawer a typed piece of paper signed by Susan that says: "Antique desk to granddaughter, Betsy." Who will receive the desk, Anika or Betsy? Why?

   2.   Assume the facts are the same as in Problem (1) above except that the clause in Susan's will did not state that the list, "is to take precedence over any contrary devise or devises of the same item or items of property in this will." Who will receive the desk? Why?

6.   Pour-Over Wills

As we learned in Chapter 5, the increased use of revocable inter vivos trusts over the past 40 years has moved courts and legislatures to allow testators to include a provision in a will that transfers ("pours over") some of the estate (usually the residue) into the trust. If the revocable trust is created before the settlor's death, then the trust is an event of independent significance. Remember, however, that corpus is a necessary element of a trust and a trust will not be considered created if it is unfunded. Sometimes a settlor will have a revocable trust and pour-over will drafted by a lawyer, but will forget to transfer property into the trust. If the trust holds no property before the settlor's death, then the trust was not created and a transfer cannot be given effect as an event of independent significance. Also, the settlor's signature on the trust instrument provides evidence of the settlor's intent to create the trust. If the settlor does not sign the trust document, the element of intent may be missing. In either case, failure to take care of the details of the creation of the trust may cause the pour-over provision to fail.

   If the revocable trust is unfunded or the document is unsigned, the doctrine of incorporation by reference may be used to give effect of the terms of the trust, if the will adequately identifies the document and the intent to incorporate it. If incorporation by reference must be used, the trust will be considered a testamentary trust and the court will have jurisdiction over the terms of the trust, which will be considered part of the will. More importantly, any changes to the trust document after execution of the will cannot be given effect under incorporation by reference.

   Although the settlor's wishes at the time the will was executed may be given effect using incorporation by reference, the potential problems of having the trust be treated as a testamentary trust or having incorporation by reference not apply if the identification were insufficient led legislatures to enact statutes like UPC §2-511, the provisions of which were included in Chapter 5. UPC §2-511 incorporates the Uniform Testamentary Transfers to Trusts ACT (UTATA). It validates such pour-over provisions in a will. One of the most useful features of this section, and a significant reason why pour-over provisions are used, is that the trust (and thus, the estate plan) can be amended after the will is drafted as often as the testator/settlor wishes without having to re-execute the will.

EXERCISE

Review the Marjorie M. Black will in the Appendix to this chapter. Identify four aspects of the will that reflect its integration, and one paragraph each where there was reference to a document to be incorporated, an event of independent significance, a pour-over provision and a memorandum to be given effect at death.

C. INTERPRETING THE MEANING OF A WILL USING EXTRINSIC EVIDENCE

Given the uncertainty of language, courts are often faced with an ambiguity in a will. Under certain circumstances, courts may consider extrinsic evidence to divine the intent or to rebut the presumptive meaning supplied by a rule of construction. We will explore rules of construction below in Section D.

1. Resolving Ambiguities — The Historical View

The exercise of divining intent is to give expression to the testator's wishes and not to defeat them. In order for the court to do this, it must consider the language being interpreted in light of all of the surrounding circumstances. Courts generally try to use the plain meaning of language in their interpretive efforts to implement the testator's plan. The various provisions of the will should be read together to give effect to as many provisions of the will as possible. That approach alone may result in the court's being able to divine the testator's actual intent. However, a will may contain ambiguities that cannot be resolved using this approach.

Historically, courts distinguished between a so-called "patent" ambiguity, where extrinsic evidence was not allowed, and a "latent" ambiguity, where such evidence was allowed. This distinction has effectively disappeared over the years, with most courts allowing extrinsic evidence to be considered in either case. Note that extrinsic evidence should not be used to create an ambiguity in the first place. *See Matter of Estate of Frietze*, 966 P.2d 183 (N.M. Ct. App. 1998). (But note how circular that idea may be.) Courts generally find that a provision is ambiguous if it is susceptible to two reasonable interpretations.

A patent ambiguity is one that appears on the face of the will itself. For example, assume a will provides: "I leave all my property as follows: one-fourth to Alice, one-fourth to Bob and one-fourth to Carl." The testator says nothing else in the will. Did the testator make a mistake and forget to leave the final one-fourth to someone else, or did he mean to leave one-third to each of Alice, Bob and Carl? A court can tell that there is a problem here simply by looking at the will itself.

On the other hand, a latent ambiguity is a provision that is not apparent upon reading the will but rather becomes apparent when the provisions are applied. For example, "I leave $10,000 to John Smith." It turns out the testator knew two John Smiths very well and it is not clear which one he meant. The historic rationale for making the distinction was that in a latent ambiguity, the court had already looked outside the will to discover the facts that gave rise to the ambiguity itself. Thus, there was less reason to be concerned about the evidentiary concerns that generally limit courts to the four corners of the will.

Note how the appeals court in the following case adopted a more modern and flexible view than the more mechanical analysis of the lower court. It thus reached a different result in terms of whether extrinsic evidence should have been considered to resolve the ambiguity in Cora Black's will.

In re Estate of Black
27 Cal. Rptr. 418 (Ct. App. 1962)

The opinion of the court was delivered by Justice MOLINARI.

This is an appeal from that portion of an "Order and Decree" which directed the distribution of the rest and residue of the estate of the above-named decedent to the Regents of the University of California, a respondent herein, to be used at, on, and in the University of California at Los Angeles for educational purposes. A motion by the respondents to augment the record in certain particulars is presented in conjunction with said appeal.

THE FACTS

The decedent, Cora L. Black, died in Santa Clara County on December 3, 1957. [Her holographic will had a bequest as follows:

> To The University of Southern California known as The U.C.L.A. My entire Estate for Educations purposes.

The question raised was whether she meant the bequest to go to University of California at Los Angeles (UCLA), as the personal representative thought, or University of Southern California (Southern California). The trial court upheld the determination by the personal representative, finding no ambiguity and not considering extrinsic evidence.]

THE ISSUES

The issue [] raised on appeal [is] as follows: (1) Is the will ambiguous? . . .

The important consideration in each instance is whether or not extrinsic evidence is admissible. If it is not a proper case for the introduction of extrinsic evidence, and none has been considered, then it is also the rule that the interpretation placed upon a written instrument by the trial court, while not binding on appeal, will be accepted by the appellate court if such interpretation is reasonable, or if the interpretation of the trial court is one of two or more reasonable constructions of the instrument. On the other hand, where it is a proper case for the admissibility of extrinsic evidence and such evidence has been received, the appellate court will accept or adhere to the interpretation adopted by the trial court *where the parol evidence is such that conflicting inferences may be drawn therefrom.* When the terms or provisions of an instrument are clear and certain, extrinsic evidence to explain or interpret them is not admissible. But if the terms or provisions are ambiguous or uncertain extrinsic evidence may be admissible depending, apparently, on the kind of ambiguity involved. The parol evidence rule does not apply to every situation where an ambiguity may appear. Whether an instrument is, in any of its terms or provisions, ambiguous or uncertain is a matter of determination, in the first instance by the trial court.

It has been generally stated that where the ambiguity is patent parol evidence is inadmissible, but where the ambiguity is latent, such evidence is admissible. A patent ambiguity is one which appears on the face of the instrument. A latent ambiguity is an uncertainty which arises, not by the terms of the instrument itself, but is created by some collateral matter not appearing in the instrument. The distinction between patent and latent ambiguities with its incident of excluding or admitting extrinsic evidence, has not been strictly adhered to. Thus ambiguities appearing on the face of the instrument and apparently in the category of patent ambiguities have been explained or interpreted by extrinsic evidence. Accordingly, in *Estate of Torregano*, 352 P.2d 505, it is stated: 'Extrinsic evidence is also admissible to explain any ambiguity arising on the face of a will, or to resolve a latent ambiguity which does not so appear.'

Is the Will Ambiguous?

The trial court held that the provision in the decedent's will which states "To The University of Southern California known as The U.C.L.A." is not ambiguous. In reaching this conclusion the lower court did not resort to the aid of extrinsic evidence. This is clear from the narrative above set forth wherein the court stated in no uncertain language that it was considering *only* the provisions and terms of the will itself. Our inquiry must turn, then, to whether the said provision is ambiguous, and if it is, whether such ambiguity is such as to require the admissibility of extrinsic evidence.

A word or expression is said to be ambiguous when it is "[d]oubtful or uncertain"; when it is "[c]apable of being understood in either of two or more possible senses; . . ." (Webster's New International Dictionary (2nd ed., 1939).) Ambiguity is defined as "[d]oubtfulness; doubleness of meaning. . . . Duplicity, indistinctness, or uncertainty of meaning of an expression used in a written instrument. . . . Want of clearness or definiteness; difficult to comprehend or distinguish; of doubtful import."

The court below correctly concluded that there is no patent ambiguity. The provision in question is not, on its face, susceptible to one of two constructions. The language is clear, intelligible and suggests but a single meaning. A reader unacquainted with the fact that there are two universities in Southern California, one known as the University of Southern California and another commonly referred to by the initials U.C.L.A., would readily attribute to said provision the meaning that it refers to an institution named "University of Southern California," which is also known by the initials U.C.L.A.

The trial court was in error, however, in holding that there is no latent ambiguity. Such an ambiguity is created by a collateral matter not appearing in the will itself. The instant the attention of the lower court was directed to the fact that the University of Southern California is not known by the initials U.C.L.A., but that these designations are applicable to two different universities, there was created a necessity for interpretation as to which one the testatrix meant. Any reader of the will, upon being so apprised, would be cognizant that although the testatrix attempted to designate a sole beneficiary she did in fact name two separate institutions. It would be but to cavil to contend that this language does not engender a doubt and uncertainty as to which institution was meant to be the beneficiary. It is not the words used which cause the doubt and uncertainty but the ascertainment of the intended beneficiary from the words used.

In *Estate of Donnellan*, 127 P. 166, the court pointed out that there are two classes of wills which present latent ambiguities, for the removal of which resort to extrinsic evidence is permissible, to wit: "The one class is where there are two or more persons or things exactly measuring up to the description and conditions of the will. . . . The other class is where no person or thing exactly answers the declarations and descriptions of the will, but where two or more persons or things in part, though imperfectly, do so answer." In *Donnellan*, the following provision was presented for construction: "to my niece Mary, a resident of New York, said Mary being the daughter of my deceased sister Mary. . . ." The deceased sister, Mary, had two daughters, Annie Sheridan and Mary Smith. Annie was a resident of New York. Mary lived in Ireland and had never been in the United States. The court held that there was a latent ambiguity because no one person exactly fitted the description in the will.

In *Estate of Nunes*, 266 P.2d 574, the *Donnellan* case was cited and relied upon. In *Nunes* the provision presented for construction was as follows: "unto Joe E. Nunes, a nephew of mine. . . ." The estate was claimed by a Joseph E. Nunes who occasionally called himself or was called Joe. Joseph E. Nunes was the son of a half brother of the deceased and hence a nephew of the half blood of the deceased. The other claimant was a Joe E. Nunes, who occasionally called himself or was called Joseph. He was a second cousin of the deceased, but was usually referred to by the deceased as his "nephew." The court held that a latent ambiguity existed because no one person existed who precisely fitted the description of "Joe E. Nunes, a nephew of mine. . . ."

The basic statutory provision applicable to our inquiry is section 105 of the Probate Code. The limitations of this section do not apply once it is determined that extrinsic evidence is admissible because of a latent ambiguity as to identity. A latent ambiguity as to the identity of the legatee exists in the instant case once it is determined that there is no one university that completely fits the description "University of Southern California known as The U.C.L.A." Extrinsic evidence was therefore admissible to show who was intended. The lower court sought to make an interpretation from the context of the will without the aid of extrinsic evidence. Under section 105 of the Probate Code the court may look to other provisions of the will to determine the meaning of a doubtful provision. But here we have no other provision of the will which touches or can throw any light on the identity of the legatee. The lower court here eliminated one of two possible beneficiaries by an attempt to ascertain the intention of the testatrix from a mere reading of the will. It concluded as a matter of law that the words "University of Southern California" mean "the university *in* Southern California." (Emphasis added.) In arriving at this conclusion the trial court stated that when the testatrix used the word "of" she meant "in," and that she meant Southern California in the sense of a geographical area. The court stated further that the capitalization of the word "University" was of no significance because people sometimes capitalize the word and on other occasions they do not.

A court is not at liberty to read the language of a will with any other than its plain, ordinary meaning. Indeed, the words of a will are to be taken in their ordinary and grammatical sense, unless there be a clear intention to use them in another sense and unless that other sense can be ascertained from the will. The lower court has reached its conclusion by a strained construction of the pertinent language. In the face of the fact that it had judicial knowledge that there is a university whose full and proper name is "University of Southern California" it determined to disregard the capital "U" in the word "University" and then proceeded to substitute the word "in" for the word "of." We are not so much concerned with whether the word "of" may also mean "in," but with the propriety of changing a word which is an integral part of a proper name. In our opinion, the trial court was not warranted in making such an interpretation as a matter of law. The very fact that the court questioned the meaning of the words used by the testatrix in itself shows the existence of the ambiguity. Courts should not strain to find a clear meaning in an ambiguous document, and having done so exclude extrinsic evidence on the ground that as so construed no ambiguity exists. The crux of the matter is that we have a situation which falls in the second class mentioned in *Donellan*, i.e., no person exactly answers the description "University of Southern California known as The U.C.L.A.," but both the University of Southern California and U.C.L.A., in part, though imperfectly, so answer. This circumstance is sufficient in itself to raise the latent ambiguity. Whether or not the testatrix intended to leave her estate to the University of Southern California or to the university *in* Southern California known as U.C.L.A. was for the determination of the trier of fact upon a consideration of parol evidence. . . .

The exclusion of extrinsic evidence in the instant case constitutes reversible error.

The order and decree appealed from is reversed. The respondents' motion to augment the record is denied.

---

2.   *Resolving Ambiguities — The Modern View*

The more modern rule, as expressed in *Estate of Black,* focuses on the substance rather than the form of the ambiguity. For example, *Restatement (Third) of Property: Wills & Other Donative Transfers* §10.2 provides, "In seeking to determine the donor's intention, all relevant evidence, whether direct or circumstantial, may be considered, including the text of the donative document and relevant extrinsic evidence." The *Restatement* drafters provide the following guidance as to which kinds of extrinsic evidence a court may consider:

Restatement (Third) of Property: Wills and Other Donative Transfers §10.2 *Comments d, e, f and g.*

---

d. Surrounding Circumstances. Extrinsic evidence of the circumstances surrounding the execution of the donative document that might bear on the donor's intention, directly or circumstantially, may always be considered. Examples include evidence of the donor's occupation, property at the time of execution of the document, and relationships with family members and with other persons, including the designated or apparently designated donees. . . . Thus, when the fact tends to illuminate the meaning of the text employed, it is proper to show, for example, that a donor knew or believed a particular person to be incapacitated, dead, wealthy, in need of funds, friendly, unfriendly, or related by blood to the donor or to other affected persons.

e. Surrounding circumstances — skill of drafter. A significant element of the surrounding circumstances may be whether the drafter of the document was a layperson (usually the donor) or a person experienced in the use of legal or other specialized terminology (usually the donor's lawyer). . . .

f. Direct evidence of intention. Direct as well as circumstantial evidence relevant to the donor's intention may be considered. Direct evidence relevant to the donor's intention includes documents and testimony evidencing the donor's intention: the donor's own declarations of intention, written or oral; contents of the drafting agent's files; and written or oral statements made to the donor by the drafting agent or another concerning the contents or effect of the document, to the extent that the donor acquiesced, silently or expressly, in the other person's statements. . . .

g. Extrinsic Evidence — time to which evidence relates. Although the primary focus is on the donor's intention at the time of execution of the donative document, post-execution events can sometimes be relevant in determining the donor's intention. Post-execution statements of the donor, for example, can relate to the donor's intention at the time of execution. In addition, if the donative document was ambiguous when executed . . . post-execution indications of intention may properly be considered in resolving an ambiguity if they shed light on the donor's intention at the time of execution or on what the donor's intention would probably then have been had the ambiguity been recognized or the subsequent event been anticipated.

Note that the fact that the *Restatement (Third) of Property: Wills & Other Donative Transfers* includes broad authority for the court to consider extrinsic evidence to divine the testator's intent does not mean that courts do not impose constraints on considering such evidence if they determine that the will is not ambiguous. Thus, there is a threshold question as to whether there is any ambiguity with regard to intent in the first place. *See In re Estate of Flynn,* 606 N.W.2d 104 (N.D. 2000) (If the language of a will is clear and unambiguous, the testator's intent must be determined from the language of the will itself rather than through the use of extrinsic evidence.); *In re Estate of Pouser,* 975 P.2d 704 (Ariz. 1999) (if the language of the will is reasonably susceptible to two interpretations, court may consider extrinsic evidence to ascertain the testator's intent, but extrinsic evidence is not admissible to contradict the plain language of the will); *In re Estate of Frietze,* 966 P.2d 183 (N.M. Ct. App. 1998) (if a will is unambiguous, extrinsic evidence may not be accepted to determine the intent of the testator). *See also* Richard F. Storrow, *Judicial Discretion and the Disappearing Distinction Between Will Interpretation and Construction,* 56 Case W. Res. L. Rev. 65, 67 (2005) ("[The Third's] too flexible interpretive rules and limitless discretion tempt courts to ignore ambiguities in wills and unjustifiably streamline the interpretive process.").

QUESTION

Evidence of intent. Estate of Black was remanded for further findings of fact. Assume you represent U.C.L.A. What types of evidence would help you to prove your case that Cora L. Black intended to make a gift to U.C.L.A and not to U.S.C.?

EXERCISE

Review the Marjorie M. Black will in the Appendix. Can you identify three paragraphs where extrinsic evidence may be necessary to clarify her intent? What kinds of evidence would you seek? Are you certain that it would be admitted?

3. Extrinsic Evidence and Mistake — Reformation of Wills

In the sections above, we have discussed situations where the meaning of the language in the will is not clear — it is ambiguous. This section explores how courts have treated the use of extrinsic evidence to "fix" wills that are clear on their face but that are the product of a mistake on the part of the drafting attorney. Historically, courts were not allowed to use extrinsic evidence of testator intent to "reform" or rewrite the will to minimize the impact of mistake on the beneficiaries.

More recently, some courts, the *Restatement* drafters and the drafters of the UPC have supported the view that reformation for mistake should be allowed. *See* RESTATEMENT (THIRD) OF PROPERTY: WILLS & OTHER DONATIVE TRANSFERS §12.1 and UPC §2-805, which provides for reformation of a will (and other governing instruments) even if the will is unambiguous. The UPC provision applies a clear and convincing standard to the requisite finding that "the terms of the governing instrument were affected by a mistake of fact or law . . . ," and *Restatement (Third) of Property: Wills & Other Donative Transfers* §12.1 provides for consideration of "direct evidence of intention contradicting the plain meaning of the text" in determining whether the clear and convincing standard has been met. In addition, *Restatement (Third) of Property: Wills & Other Donative Transfers* §12.2 provides for modification of a donative document "in a manner that does not violate the donor's probable intention, to achieve the donor's tax objectives."

NOTES AND QUESTIONS

1. *A new era?* In *Erickson v. Erickson*, 716 A.2d 92 (Conn. 1998), the Connecticut Supreme Court held that extrinsic evidence should be allowed if the evidence could establish under the clear and convincing standard that

there was a "scrivener's error" that caused the testator to fail to clearly state that his new will, made several days prior to his marriage, should not be revoked. The court remanded the case for a new trial using this standard and allowing consideration of extrinsic evidence of such a mistake — thus allowing for the possibility of reformation in the face of mistake.

2. *No reformation for tax reasons.* In *Pellegrini v. Breitenbach*, 926 N.E.2d 544 (Mass. 2010), the testator left an income interest in his property to his sister and to a friend and then left the remainder to two charities. The lawyer was unaware of the value of the decedent's estate, which turned out to be subject to estate tax. If the transfer had been made to a charitable remainder trust, structured to provide payments to the sister and friend and then to distribute the remainder to the two charities, the estate would have saved $466,000 in estate taxes. The personal representative of the estate attempted to obtain that result by asking the court to reform the will to create a charitable remainder trust. Although courts have the authority to reform trusts, in this case no trust had been created. The request for reformation was a request to reform the will, and the court refused to do so, noting that "the relief sought by the plaintiff would contravene the Statute of Wills and that any change to the current statutory scheme is properly left up to the Legislature." The court found no mistake in the will because the lawyer had carried out the testator's intent as directed.

3. *Remedies.* As an estate planning attorney, if you were to make a "scrivener's error," what sanctions other than an embarrassing opinion from the court should you be concerned about and why? Why might some of these other remedies be insufficient to protect the beneficiaries who might suffer as a result of your mistake?

D. INTERPRETING THE MEANING OF A WILL USING THE RULES OF CONSTRUCTION

The testator's intent controls unless it is contrary to the law or public policy of the state. If the will does not clearly express the testator's intent, we must look elsewhere for guidance. Rules of construction and constructional preferences (both referred to herein as "rules of construction") are either statutes or judicial doctrines which assist the court in giving meaning where the testator's intent is not clear. Some rules of construction apply only to wills and others apply to a broader range of instruments, including the kind of will substitutes you studied in Chapter 4. We explore both kinds of rules below.

Since rules of construction apply only if the testator's intent is not clear, if the intent *is* clear, then the court must follow the testator's expressed intent. If not, then the court may deploy a rule of construction to give meaning to a provision in the will.

Example: Jeremy's will provides that, "I leave my house to my sister, Jillian." In this case there is no indication of whether Jeremy intends that his personal representative pay off the $300,000 mortgage that is attached to his house prior to giving the house to Jillian or not. There is a rule of construction that applies, UPC §2-607. It provides that if Jeremy does not make his intent clear on this issue then the house shall pass to Jillian with the mortgage obligation attached to it. Jeremy's will might have stated, "I leave my house to my sister Jillian and my personal representative shall pay off the mortgage prior to conveying the house to Jill." The court would then be obligated to follow Jeremy's specific intent as expressed in the will and the rule of construction would not apply.

If there is no rule of construction on point or if the rule supplies a rebuttable presumption as to what the testator meant, then the court may consider extrinsic evidence to determine the testator's intent under the circumstances described in the section above.

Rules of construction and constructional preferences are essentially default rules that are based on legislative and judicial choices about the normative preferences of most testators. For example, they reflect a preference for family members over non-family members and a preference for close family members over more distant ones. They also reflect a preference that the descendants of a predeceased beneficiary who is a family member take a bequest rather than let the bequest lapse to others and a preference for favorable tax results. The following excerpt from an article by Professor Adam Hirsch describes why such rules of construction are so important to courts in determining testator's intent. As you read his excerpt and study the rules in this chapter, consider whether American inheritance law should adopt an "expiration date" for wills, and whether such an automatic revocation after a specific number of years would solve the problem of "testamentary obsolescence" (stale wills) or exacerbate it.

Adam J. Hirsch, Text and Time: A Theory of Testamentary Obsolescence
86 Wash. U. L. Rev. 609 (2009)

Prior to the nineteenth century, Americans and Britons typically put off executing their wills until death was near. The resulting estate plans were timely but not always tidy, for testators often conceived them in haste. One of the early arguments against freedom of testation in Great Britain was that testators "visited with sickness, in their extreme agonies and pains," might dispose of their estates "indiscreetly and unadvisedly." Since the twentieth century, deathbed wills have grown comparatively rare, and as a consequence the risk of testamentary indiscretion has receded. But every silver lining has its cloud. Wills drafted in the prime of life implicate a different peril — the risk of being overtaken by events. If a hiatus separates the time when a will is executed from the time when it matures, intervening occurrences — changes in the testator's life — may render it less well adapted to his or her subsequent circumstances.

This is the problem of testamentary obsolescence or, to borrow a scholar's turn of phrase, the "stale will." Viewed structurally, it reflects a fundamental dilemma that recurs in our law. Whenever a court is called upon to apply the performative words of others, it must decide whether to read those words statically or dynamically, in spite of or in light of evolving facts. Time does its work, and contracts, statutes, and constitutions, inter alia, along with wills, are all subject to the march of anno domini. Ultimately, lawmakers confront the core problem of textual obsolescence and ought to examine that problem in all fields of law from a common perspective, even if it yields different outcomes within individual fields.

The replication of strategies to avoid textual obsolescence bears witness to the unity of the problem. Text makers themselves can update their words, of course, and codicils to wills stand beside statutory and constitutional amendments. . . . To the extent they can anticipate fortuities that would render a text anachronistic, text makers can also build into it preservatives against staleness. Contingency clauses often decorate wills and contracts. Within some statutes, fallback provisions (usually anticipating the possibility of unconstitutionality) and indexing provisions perform an analogous function. Alternatively, text makers may concede the futility of trying to anticipate every contingency and empower a delegate to revise their texts as circumstances evolve. In effect, that is what legislators do when they incorporate standards into statutes; a court can then reinterpret their application over time. In inheritance law, a power of appointment or discretionary trust serves this end. The donee of the power or the trustee will make distributive decisions as dictated by unfolding events.

The problem remains that text makers may decline or neglect to take any of these steps — a distinct possibility among the makers of testamentary texts. One estate planner offers a bleak assessment: "If truth were known, I believe we would be aghast at the number of outstanding wills of living persons in this country which are obsolete, as far as reflecting the present wishes of the testator." When, if ever, should courts step in to update a text on its maker's behalf? Specifically in the realm of wills, should courts ever infer textual revisions that testators themselves never formalized in an executed writing?

1. *Classification of Devises*

Devises in a will can be classified into four categories: specific devises, general devises, demonstrative devises and residuary devises. Demonstrative devises are not often used in wills. Classification matters because certain doctrines we will discuss shortly, like ademption, apply only to specific devises. Classification is also important in the doctrine of abatement, as we shall see below.

Restatement (Third) of Property: Wills and Other Donative Transfers §5.1. Classification of Devises.

Devises are classified as specific, general, demonstrative, or residuary:

(1) A *specific devise* is a testamentary disposition of a specifically identified asset.

(2) A *general devise* is a testamentary disposition, usually of a specified amount of money or quantity of property, that is payable from the general assets of the estate.

(3) A *demonstrative devise* is a testamentary disposition, usually of a specified amount of money or quantity of property, that is primarily payable from a designated source, but is secondarily payable from the general assets of the estate to the extent that the primary source is insufficient.

(4) A *residuary devise* is a testamentary disposition of property of the testator's net probate estate not disposed by a specific, general, or demonstrative devise.

Example: Taylor leaves a will that makes the following bequests: My house at 123 Main Street to Lulu (specific devise); $100,000 to the Red Cross (general devise); $25,000 from the proceeds of the sale of my IBM stock (demonstrative devise); and the rest, residue and remainder of my estate to Beth (residuary devise).

2. *Rules of Construction Applicable Only to Wills*

a. **What Is Included in a Bequest of "All My Property"?**

Testators often execute wills that include a residuary clause which provides that the testator leaves "all the rest of my property to X." The testator will most likely have assets at death that differ from those owned when the will was executed years earlier. How do courts construe this kind of provision? Does it include only the property owned at the date of will execution or does it cover property owned by the testator at death as well?

UPC §2-602 provides guidance to the court in answering these questions. Note the relationship between this provision and the events of independent significance doctrine discussed above:

UPC §2-602. Will May Pass All Property and After-Acquired Property.

> A will may provide for the passage of all property the testator owns at death and all property acquired by the estate after the testator's death.

Thus, courts are directed to interpret a residuary clause that bequeaths "all my property" to mean both property acquired prior to execution and property acquired after execution. Without such an interpretation, a partial intestacy would result as to the property accumulated in the testator's estate after will execution but before death. Construing a residuary clause to pass all property acquired prior to death, regardless of whether it was acquired before or after execution, is a far preferable result in terms of efficient disposition of property post-death and the law's preference for testacy over intestacy.

b. Lapse and Antilapse — What Happens to a Bequest When the Beneficiary Predeceases the Testator?

At common law, a bequest to an individual who died before the testator passed away would fail or "lapse." The bequest would go to an alternate beneficiary if one were named in the will. However, if the will did not name an alternate taker, a specific or general devise would "fall into" and be added to the residue. If the deceased beneficiary were a residuary beneficiary, the bequest would either be distributed through intestacy or be divided among the surviving residuary beneficiaries. UPC §2-604 outlines where such a bequest goes if it lapses:

UPC §2-604. Failure of Testamentary Provision.

> (a) Except as provided in Section 2–603, a devise, other than a residuary devise, that fails for any reason becomes a part of the residue.
> (b) Except as provided in Section 2–603, if the residue is devised to two or more persons, the share of a residuary devisee that fails for any reason passes to the other residuary devisee, or to other residuary devisees in proportion to the interest of each in the remaining part of the residue.

UPC §2-604(b) reflects the common law rule that if a bequest is made to members of a class and one of the class members predeceases the decedent, the gift to that class member lapses, and that gift is divided among the remaining members of the class.

Over time, states began to view lapse as a harsh and unintended result in certain circumstances. This change in thinking reflected a perception that if the bequest were to a family member, the testator would prefer that the descendants of the intended beneficiary take the bequest instead of letting the gift lapse and go to other beneficiaries. In essence, the bequest was construed to mean "to my relative, but if my relative predeceases me, to my relative's descendants." UPC §2-603 reflects this modern approach. If a beneficiary who is a close relative of the testator dies before the testator, a "substitute gift" to the beneficiary's descendant is created. Because most individuals leave their property to family members, antilapse is an exception that swallows the general rule.

There are four elements that must be met in order for the antilapse rule of UPC §2-603 to apply:

- The intended beneficiary must predecease the testator or be deemed to have predeceased the testator.
- The intended beneficiary must leave living descendants.
- The intended beneficiary must be a family member, defined as the testator's grandparents, a descendant of the grandparents or the testator's stepchild; the reach of the statute is very inclusive, covering almost all relatives who would receive property if the testator died intestate.
- The will must neither provide for an alternative gift (to a "taker in default") nor state specifically that the antilapse rules are not to apply, because such a statement of intent would supersede application of the default rules.

If all of these requirements are met, a substitute gift is created in favor of the surviving descendants of the intended beneficiary with the amount each descendant receives determined by the rules of representation we discussed in Chapter 3.

§2-603. Antilapse; Deceased Devisee; Class Gifts.

(b) [Substitute Gift.] If a devisee fails to survive the testator and is a grandparent, a descendant of a grandparent, or a stepchild of either the testator or the donor of a power of appointment exercised by the testator's will, the following apply:

(1) Except as provided in paragraph (4), if the devise is not in the form of a class gift and the deceased devisee leaves surviving descendants, a substitute gift is created in the devisee's surviving

descendants. They take by representation the property to which the devisee would have been entitled had the devisee survived the testator.

(2) Except as provided in paragraph (4), if the devise is in the form of a class gift, other than a devise to "issue," "descendants," "heirs of the body," "heirs," "next to kin," "relatives," or "family," or a class described by language of similar import, a substitute gift is created in the surviving descendants of any deceased devisee. The property to which the devisees would have been entitled had all of them survived the testator passes to the surviving devisees and the surviving descendants of the deceased devisees. Each surviving devisee takes the share to which he [or she] would have been entitled had the deceased devisees survived the testator. Each deceased devisee's surviving descendants who are substituted for the deceased devisee take by representation the share to which the deceased devisee would have been entitled had the deceased devisee survived the testator. For the purposes of this paragraph, "deceased devisee" means a class member who failed to survive the testator and left one or more surviving descendants.

(3) For the purposes of Section 2-601, words of survivorship, such as in a devise to an individual "if he survives me," or in a devise "to my surviving children," are not, in the absence of additional evidence, a sufficient indication of an intent contrary to the application of this section.

(4) If the will creates an alternative devise with respect to a devise for which a substitute gift is created by paragraph (1) or (2), the substitute gift is superseded by the alternative devise only if an expressly designated devisee of the alternative devise is entitled to take under the will. . . .

If the antilapse provisions of UPC §2-603 do not apply, the gift will lapse and under UPC §2-604, bequests that lapse become part of the residue.

Example: Gilbert's will devised "$10,000 to my sister, Susannah" and devised "the rest, residue, and remainder of my estate to Georgetown University." Susannah predeceased Gilbert, leaving a child, Naomi. Under the common law, the $10,000 bequest to Susannah would lapse and be added to the residue for Georgetown. However, under the antilapse rule of UPC §2-603(b)(1), Susannah's $10,000 devise goes to Naomi as a substitute gift, not to Georgetown. The default rule of UPC §2-603 overrides the default rule of UPC §2-604.

Class Gifts.   If a class gift is made to a group not covered by the anti-lapse statute and a member of the class predeceases the testator, the rest of the class will generally share in the gift.

> **Example:**   Leila executes a will which leaves a $15,000 devise to "my employees." When Leila executed the will in 2008, Ariela, Maura and Serena were employed by Leila in her small business. Leila died in 2010. Ariela had predeceased Leila in 2009 so that when Leila died, only Maura and Serena were her employees. Maura and Serena will each receive $7,500.

However, if the class gift is made to a group covered by the antilapse statute, there are two possible scenarios. The antilapse statute will not apply if the gift is to "issue" or a similar group that contains several generations. This is because the class gift itself is phrased in such a way as to auto-matically substitute a member of the younger generation if an ancestor predeceases.

> **Example:**   Leila executes a will which leaves a $15,000 devise to "my issue." At her death in 2010, Leila had a son, Benito, and a grand-daughter, Alexis, who was the child of Leila's deceased daughter, Antonia. Benito would receive $7,500 and Alexis would receive $7,500.

If, however, the class gift is not a "multi-generational" gift and the antilapse statute applies, then each surviving member of the class takes their share and the descendants of the deceased class member take her share.

> **Example:**   Leila executes a will which leaves a $15,000 devise to "my siblings." At her death in 2010, Leila had a brother, Alberto, and a sister, Martha, who predeceased Leila in 2009. Martha has a son, Nestor. Alberto would receive $7,500 and Nestor would receive $7,500.

If the deceased class member has no descendants, the remaining class members would benefit from her share so that in the example above, Alberto would receive $15,000 if Martha had died without descendants.

Sometimes a determination of whether a gift is a class gift or not will dictate the ultimate recipient of the property. A gift is more likely to be a class gift if the gift is one gift to be shared by the group ($15,000 or a piece of property) and if the members of the group all bear the same relationship to the testator (employees, siblings). If the testator makes individual gifts to named individuals, the result is less likely to be a class gift.

Example: Leila executes a will that leaves "$5,000 to each of my three employees, Ariela, Maura and Serena." Leila died in 2010. Ariela had predeceased Leila in 2009; Maura and Serena survived Leila. Maura and Serena will each receive $5,000 and the gift to Ariela will lapse and be distributed with the residue. The gifts are unlikely to be considered a class gift because each employee is named individually and the gifts are made individually.

i. Contrary Intent and Words of Survivorship

The antilapse rules are default rules. They are not mandatory and can be "drafted around" by the inclusion of a clear statement of the testator's intent that they not apply. Such an expression is known as "contrary intent";[2] silence requires courts to apply the rules of construction. A testator can trump the application of the antilapse rules by clearly expressing a preference in a will for who should receive the property in the event that the intended beneficiary dies first. The alternate beneficiary is generally referred to as a "taker-in-default."

Example: Donato's will provides, "I leave Carolyn $100,000, but if she predeceases me, it shall go to Ahmed." Ahmed is a taker-in-default; Donato has effectively overridden the antilapse provision by means of the alternate bequest to Ahmed.

Alternatively, the testator could simply express the intention that he does not want the antilapse rules to apply:

Example: Donato could say, "I leave Carolyn $100,000, but if she predeceases me, the devise shall lapse and pass under the residuary clause."

In the Comment to UPC §2-603, the drafters note that one of the most significant questions in lapse cases is whether "mere words of survivorship—such as in a devise 'to my daughter, Annabelle, if Annabelle survives me' or 'to my surviving children'—automatically defeat the antilapse statute." If they do, then Annabelle's gift would lapse and would not be saved for her descendants under the antilapse statute. If they do not, then Annabelle's gift will be preserved and will be given to her descendants.

---

2. *See* UPC §2-601 "In the absence of a finding of contrary intention, the rules of construction in this Part control the construction of a will."

Some courts have held that if the testator explicitly requires the beneficiary to survive, then that expresses an intent *not* to have the antilapse rules apply to save the bequest by giving the devise to the beneficiary's descendants. *See Estate of Stroble*, 636 P.2d 236 (Kan. Ct. App. 1981). However, there is a trend to deem the mere inclusion of survivorship words insufficient to override the application of the antilapse statute.[3] That policy approach is reflected in UPC §2-603(b)(3) above, and the Comment to that section states:

> In the absence of persuasive evidence of a contrary intent, however, the antilapse statute, being remedial in nature, and tending to preserve equality among different lines of succession, should be given the widest possible chance to operate and should be defeated only by a finding of intention that directly contradicts the substitute gift created by the statute. Mere words of survivorship — by themselves — do not directly contradict the statutory substitute gift to the descendants of a deceased devisee.

Thus, from a drafting point of view, it is essential that the testator clearly state his preference in this regard. If survivorship is intended to defeat antilapse, the testator should say something like, "to my surviving children and not to the descendants of a deceased child." Given these concerns, do you think the court was correct in finding a lack of contrary intent by the testator in the following case?

Estate of Tolman v. Jennings
104 Cal. Rptr. 3d 924 (Ct. App. 2010)

The opinion of the court was delivered by Judge LICHTMAN.

Deborah C. Tomlinson, granddaughter of decedent Nellie G. Tolman, appeals from the order denying her petition to determine persons entitled to distribution from Tolman's estate. Applying Probate Code section 21110, an anti-lapse provision, the trial court concluded that Tolman's grandson Michael Jennings (respondent) was among those entitled to inherit the residue of the estate, as issue of his mother Betty Jo Miller, the predeceased residual beneficiary. The court rejected appellant's contention that the will reflected Tolman's controlling intent that Jennings and other issue of Miller not take from the estate. We affirm the order.

---

3. Some courts have held that mere words of survivorship do not defeat the antilapse statute. *See In re Estate of Ulrikson*, 290 N.W.2d 757 (Minn. 1980) (residuary devise to testator's brother Melvin and sister Rodine, and "in the event that either one of them shall predecease me, then to the other surviving brother or sister."); *Henderson v. Parker*, 728 S.W.2d 768 (Tex. 1987) (devise of all of testator's property "unto our surviving children of this marriage.").

FACTS

The record reflects that Tolman was married to Lloyd E. Tolman, who predeceased her, and with whom she had two children, Lloyd C. Tolman and Betty Joe Miller. Appellant and Laurie Onan are the surviving children of Lloyd C. Tolman, and thus granddaughters of the decedent. Respondent is the surviving son of Miller, and grandson of the deceased. Additionally, Tolman was survived by three great-grandchildren, who are children of respondent's deceased sisters and grandchildren of Miller (hereafter Miller's grandchildren).

Tolman's 1981 will bequeathed all of her property to her husband. It provided, however, that if he predeceased her, her granddaughters, appellant and Onan, each would receive $10,000, and the remainder of the estate would go to Tolman's daughter, Miller. The bequests to appellant and Onan each provided that if the designee predeceased Tolman, "this gift shall lapse." No such proviso, or any alternative disposition, appeared in the residual bequest to Miller.

Paragraph seven of the will stated: "Except as otherwise specifically provided for herein, I have intentionally omitted to provide herein for any of my heirs who are living at the time of my demise, and to any person who shall successfully claim to be an heir of mine, other than those specifically named herein, I hereby bequeath the sum of ONE DOLLAR ($1.00)."

As stated, Miller died before Tolman, requiring resolution of the proper disposition of Miller's residual bequest. The named executor being deceased, appellant and respondent each filed petitions for probate of the will and for letters of administration with the will annexed. Appellant's petition estimated the value of the estate's property at slightly under $1 million.

Shortly after filing the petition for probate, appellant filed under section 11700 a petition to determine persons entitled to distribution. The petition alleged that neither Jennings nor Miller's grandchildren were entitled to inherit under the will, which did not provide for them. However, they were asserting entitlement under section 21110, subdivision (a). That subdivision provides that if a transferee by will fails to survive the transferor, "the issue of the deceased transferee take in the transferee's place." Subdivision (b) of section 21110 qualifies subdivision (a) by providing: "The issue of a deceased transferee do not take in the transferee's place if the instrument expresses a contrary intention or a substitute disposition. . . ."[4] Appellant alleged that the will's paragraph seven expressed

---

4. [FN 3] The full text of section 21110 is: "(a) Subject to subdivision (b), if a transferee is dead when the instrument is executed, or fails or is treated as failing to survive the transferor or until a future time required by the instrument, the issue of the deceased transferee take in the transferee's place in the manner provided in Section 240. A transferee under a class gift shall be a transferee for the purpose of this subdivision unless the transferee's death occurred before the execution of the instrument and that fact was known to the transferor when the instrument was executed. [¶] (b) The issue of a deceased transferee do not take in

Tolman's intention that an heir whom she had not named in the will should not inherit.

In its statement of decision, the trial court ruled in favor of respondent, and Miller's grandchildren. The court first observed that Tolman's gift of the residue to Miller, unlike her gifts to appellant and Onan, did not provide for lapse should Miller not survive Tolman. This omission did not "express an intention that the issue of Betty Jo Miller not succeed to her share."

It had been stipulated, the court noted, that Miller's descendants were "heirs." Appellant accordingly asserted that paragraph seven of the will barred them from taking pursuant to it, while the descendants argued that their right to take was not as heirs, but was solely based on their "being the lineal descendants of a deceased devisee, Betty Jo Miller." The court stated the issue as being whether paragraph seven was sufficient, under section 21110, subdivision (b), to preclude Miller's descendants from taking as lineal descendants.

The trial court concluded that paragraph seven did not have that effect. . . . The court ruled that paragraph seven "did not contain specific language that would be sufficient to bar a lineal descendant's right to inherit as the issue of a named deceased beneficiary," and therefore respondent and Miller's grandchildren should take under section 21110. The order denying appellant's petition followed.

DISCUSSION

Appellant contends that the trial court erred as a matter of law in its construction and application of paragraph seven, as not manifesting Tolman's intent to preclude respondent and Miller's grandchildren from taking in Miller's place, under section 21100. In support, appellant also argues that cases decided under former section 92, on which the court relied, were inapplicable, because the former statute provided for an "absolute" right to inherit, which was not rebuttable by the testator's expressed intent. Appellant is incorrect in both respects.

In paragraph seven of her will, Tolman expressed her intent not to provide for any of her unmentioned heirs, and limited to $1.00 the recovery of any person outside the will who successfully claimed to be her heir. The trial court ruled that this provision did not manifest an intention to preclude Miller's issue from succeeding to the residue of the estate under section 21110, subdivision (a). The court's ruling is strongly supported by the facts and reasoning of the two decisions on which it principally relied.

---

the transferee's place if the instrument expresses a contrary intention or a substitute disposition. A requirement that the initial transferee survive the transferor or survive for a specified period of time after the death of the transferor constitutes a contrary intention. A requirement that the initial transferee survive until a future time that is related to the probate of the transferor's will or administration of the estate of the transferor constitutes a contrary intention. [¶] (c) As used in this section, 'transferee' means a person who is kindred of the transferor or kindred of a surviving, deceased, or former spouse of the transferor."

In *Larrabee, supra,* 134 P.2d 265, the court affirmed a judgment for extrinsic fraud, obtained by the daughter of a predeceased legatee against an executor who had excluded her from the final decree. The executor contended that the plaintiff had been disinherited, under a clause in the will that disinherited all persons "'claiming to be or who may be lawfully determined to be my heirs at law, except as otherwise mentioned in this will.' The Supreme Court held that plaintiff had been entitled to her mother's bequest under former section 92."

The court explained, "Although a will may provide against the operation of this statute, the disinheritance clause . . . does not do so. It purports to exclude only those claiming as *heirs at law* of the *testator*, while [plaintiff] relies solely upon her status as the *lineal descendant of* [her mother] under section 92, *supra*. As said in *Estate of Tibbetts*, 119 P.2d 368 'the persons acquiring rights under said statute acquire such rights as 'statute-made' devisees or legatees. . . . Such rights are acquired regardless of whether such persons are or are not heirs of the testatrix.'"

Equally if not more instructive is *Pfadenhauer*. The will there contained a paragraph in which the testatrix declared her purposeful intent not to provide for any person not mentioned in the will, "'whether claiming to be an heir of mine or not,'" and bequeathed only $1.00 to anyone who contested or objected to the will's provisions. The provision concluded, "I specifically have in mind all of my relatives not herein specifically mentioned, and it is my will and wish that none of my said relatives other than those specifically herein mentioned receive anything from my estate." The will left shares of the residue to two of the testatrix's daughters, and also to the two children of one of those daughters (grandchildren). They sought a determination that they were entitled to the entire residue, because the other predeceased daughter's numerous descendants were excluded under the paragraph just quoted.

The court held that former section 92 defeated this claim. "[T]hat section must be read into this will and is operative unless a contrary intention appears in the will itself. Although this testatrix could have provided against the operation of this statute she did not expressly do so, and the language of her will does not indicate such intention." The court explained that the will's language sought to provide that no claim by an unmentioned relative would displace the specific gifts made to named relatives. There was no expressed intention flatly to exclude the descendants of those legatees, per se. *Larrabee* and *Pfadenhauer* support and confirm the trial court's holding with respect to the present applicability of section 21110, notwithstanding paragraph seven of the will. Both cases support the contention that exclusion of unmentioned heirs or relatives from the will's dispositions, or an intent to disinherit those who contest those dispositions, does not sufficiently express or manifest an intent to arrest the operation of the anti-lapse law following a legatee's death. These decisions provide a guide for measuring the intent of testators whose wills have been drafted with presumptive knowledge of the cases and their interpretations. From both perspectives, the trial court here reached a sound decision.

The significance of *Larrabee*, and *Pfadenhauer*, is not diminished by the fact that they applied former section 92, rather than its current successor, section 21110. Both cases turned on whether the expressed intention of the testator clearly displaced the application of former section 92. We do not agree with appellant's assertion that the predecessor statute operated without regard to the testator's intent. As stated in a decision that held section 92 not controlling because of the testator's expression of intent, "It is well settled that the California anti-lapse statute will not be applied where the testator has expressed, with sufficient clarity, a contrary intention." But that was not the case here.

DISPOSITION

The order under review is affirmed. Respondent shall recover costs.

NOTES AND QUESTIONS

1. *When is enough enough?* Do you think the court in *Tolman* was correct in finding that Paragraph Seven of the testator's will was not a sufficient expression of contrary intent? If not, what was the testator's intent in including the following clause?

> Except as otherwise specifically provided for herein, I have intentionally omitted to provide herein for any of my heirs who are living at the time of my demise, and to any person who shall successfully claim to be an heir of mine, other than those specifically named herein, I hereby bequeath the sum of ONE DOLLAR ($1.00).

2. *A comparative view.* Antilapse statutes in some other common law countries expressly provide that words of survivorship do not defeat the statute. *See, e.g.,* Queensland Succession Act 1981, §33(2) ("A general requirement or condition that [protected relatives] survive the testator or attain a specified age is not a contrary intention for the purposes of this section"). UPC §2-603(b)(3) adopts the position that mere words of survivorship do not — by themselves, in the absence of additional evidence — lead to automatic defeat of the antilapse statute. (. . . "words of survivorship, such as in a devise to an individual "if he survives me," or in a devise "to my surviving children," are not, in the absence of additional evidence, a sufficient indication of an intent contrary to the application of this section.") For an early discussion on the development and differences

of antilapse statutes in England, the United States and Canada, see *Anti-Lapse Statutes and the Conflict of Laws*, 47 YALE L.J. 1216 (1938).

3.   *Who is protected?* States may define the group of persons to which the antilapse statute applies in different ways. In Oregon, the antilapse statute applies to any beneficiary who is "related by blood or adoption to the testator. . . ." *See* OR. REV. STAT. §112.395.

PROBLEMS

In the following problems, Talia is the decedent and she has executed a will with the provisions discussed below.

1.   In her will executed in 2000, Talia left $100,000 to Art and $150,000 to Bertha, with the residue to Coty. Art died on January 2, 2010. Talia died on July 4, 2010, having been hit in the heart with a large stray firecracker. Bertha and Coty survived both deaths.
   a.   Identify who gets what by first applying the common law and then the UPC:
      i.   Assume Art left two children, Xerxes and Yolanda, and that Art is a friend of Talia's.
      ii.   Assume Art left two children, Xerxes and Yolanda, and that Art is Talia's spouse. Xerxes and Yolanda are Art's children from a prior marriage.
      iii.   Assume Art left two children, Xerxes and Yolanda, and that Art is Talia's nephew.
   b.   How would your answers differ if Art left no descendants?
2.   In her will, Talia left the residue of her estate to Coty. Coty died in 2005, and Talia died in 2010. Coty's two children survived Talia. Applying §2-603, how would the estate be distributed if Coty were Talia's son? What if Coty were Talia's friend?
3.   Talia left $90,000 total to Art, Bertha and Coty. Assume this is *NOT* a class gift. Art died in 2005. Talia died in 2010. At Talia's death, Bertha and Coty are alive. Applying §2-603, identify who would be entitled to the $90,000 assuming Art is a first cousin of Talia's and left two children? What if instead Art is Talia's friend?
4.   Talia left $90,000 total to "my children." Assume this *IS* a class gift and the class is closed. Talia had three children, Art, Bertha and Coty, when the will was executed. Art died in 2006. Talia died in 2010. At Talia's death, Bertha and Coty are alive as are Art's two children. Applying §2-603, identify who would be entitled to the $90,000? Who gets the $90,000 if Art left no descendants?
5.   Talia left $90,000 total to "my college roommates." Assume this *IS* a class gift. Talia had three roommates during college, Anne, Benita and Corinne. Anne died in 2006. Talia died in 2010. At Talia's death, Benita and Corinne are alive as are Anne's two children. Applying §2-603, identify

who would be entitled to the $90,000? Who gets the $90,000 if Anne left no descendants?

6.   Talia left $100,000 "to Ari, if he survives me; if he does not survive me, then the $100,000 should go to Bess." Ari died in 2008, and Talia died in 2010. Who gets what assuming Ari is Talia's first cousin and that he left three children? What if instead Ari is Talia's friend?

EXERCISES

1.   Adam comes to you for estate planning. After several meetings with you, he decides to leave $100,000 to his brother, Abel, and $150,000 to his brother, Cain, with the residue being added to a testamentary trust. The trust is to provide income to his surviving spouse, Eve, for her life and the remainder will then be distributed to Adam's children. Adam says that if Abel predeceases him, he would like the gift to go to Cain and vice versa. Adam also says that if Abel and Cain should both predecease him, he would like their bequests to go into the testamentary trust for his wife and descendants. Draft a provision that accomplishes this result.

2.   Review the Marjorie M. Black will in the Appendix to this chapter. Does it provide for any alternate bequests in the event that a beneficiary predeceases her or is a court left to apply the rules of construction?

c.   Ademption by Extinction

The testator may refer to property in his will that he owns at the date of execution but no longer owns many years later when he dies. If this happens, the question for the court is whether to ignore the bequest as if it does not exist, *i.e.*, to "adeem" the gift, or to substitute certain other property and give that property to the beneficiary. Note that ademption by extinction only applies to specific devises and not general or residuary devises.

If the testator's will is silent on what he would like to happen if he does not own the property at death, then the court must resort to the default rule of ademption by extinction.

> **Example:**   Jonah's will says, "I leave Billy my 1956 Mercedes." Jonah could include a provision that states, "If I no longer own the 1956 Mercedes at my death, I leave Billy the oldest antique car I own at that time." Alternatively, Jonah could include a provision that says, "I leave Billy my 1956 Mercedes. If I do not own the 1956 Mercedes at my death, I leave him nothing." In either case, the court will implement Jonah's specific intent rather than apply the default rules of ademption by extinction.

Example: Jonah's will says, "I leave Billy my 1956 Mercedes." The will was executed in 1980, and Jonah died in 2010. He did not own a 1956 Mercedes at his death. The court will first look at whether Jonah expressed his intent as to what should happen if he did not own the Mercedes at death. Since he did not, the court will apply the doctrine of ademption by extinction to evaluate whether Billy should receive any property in lieu of the Mercedes or nothing at all.

There are two theories of ademption by extinction that have evolved over time in the various states.

Identity.   The first is the "identity" theory. This approach is followed by the courts in a majority of states. It says that a specific devise is adeemed (rendered ineffective and fails) if the property is not owned by the testator at death. In applying the "identity" theory, courts do not inquire into the testator's intent; the only thing that matters is that the property is no longer owned at death and cannot be identified. The application of the "identity" theory of ademption has led to harsh results in a number of cases, where it was reasonably clear that the testator did not intend to revoke the devise even if the specific property identified in the will was no longer owned by the testator.

Intent.   In response to these harsh results, a recent trend is for courts to try to determine what the testator would have preferred to happen, the so-called "intent" theory. The intent theory recognizes that in certain limited situations, the property that was the subject of the gift has merely changed its form. In such cases, the "new form" should be substituted for the "old form." This approach is akin to the events of independent significance doctrine we explored earlier, in that the testator likely disposed of the old property and substituted the new property for reasons that are independent of a change in testamentary plan.

The UPC has adopted an intent theory of ademption by extinction. UPC §2-606 provides guidance to courts as to how they should handle various "change in form" scenarios. Subsections (a)(1)-(4) cover situations where the specifically devised property was disposed of and a balance is owed the testator at his death. These subsections give the beneficiary the right to collect the balance due in lieu of the property. (Any amounts already collected are not covered by the rule.) Subsection (a)(5) applies where it appears the property that was the subject of the gift was replaced with other property. Subsection (a)(6) applies when the testator manifested a plan of distribution at the time she executed the will and applying the rules of ademption by extinction would frustrate that plan. Ademption (failure of the gift) is still the outcome in the majority of cases because the nonademption rule is limited to only these few situations.

UPC §2-606. Nonademption of Specific Devises; Unpaid Proceeds of Sale, Condemnation, or Insurance; Sale by Conservator or Agent.

(a) A specific devisee has a right to specifically devised property in the testator's estate at the testator's death and to:

(1) any balance of the purchase price, together with any security agreement, owed by a purchaser at the testator's death by reason of sale of the property;

(2) any amount of a condemnation award for the taking of the property unpaid at death;

(3) any proceeds unpaid at death on fire or casualty insurance on or other recovery for injury to the property;

(4) any property owned by the testator at death and acquired as a result of foreclosure, or obtained in lieu of foreclosure, of the security interest for a specifically devised obligation;

(5) any real property or tangible personal property owned by the testator at death which the testator acquired as a replacement for specifically devised real property or tangible personal property [Author's note: The drafters note that "subsection (a)(5) does not import a tracing principle into the question of ademption, but rather should be seen as a sensible 'mere change in form' principle]; and

(6) if not covered by paragraphs (1) through (5), a pecuniary devise equal to the value as of its date of disposition of other specifically devised property disposed of during the testator's lifetime but only to the extent it is established that ademption would be inconsistent with the testator's manifested plan of distribution or that at the time the will was made, the date of disposition or otherwise, the testator did not intend ademption of the devise.

(b) If specifically devised property is sold or mortgaged by a conservator or by an agent acting within the authority of a durable power of attorney for an incapacitated principal or a condemnation award, insurance proceeds, or recovery for injury to the property is paid to a conservator or to an agent acting within the authority of a durable power of attorney for an incapacitated principal the specific devisee has the right to a general pecuniary devise equal to the net sale price, the amount of the unpaid loan, the condemnation award, the insurance proceeds, or the recovery. . . .

In the Comment to UPC §2-606, the drafters offer the following example to illustrate the intent theory as it is codified under UPC §2-606:

Example: Gretchen's will devised "my 1984 Ford" to her friend, Xavier. After Gretchen executed her will, she sold her 1984 Ford and bought a 1988 Buick; later, she sold the 1988 Buick and bought a 1993 Chrysler. She still owned the 1993 Chrysler when she died. Under UPC §2-606(a)(5), the court would give the 1993 Chrysler to Xavier.

Note that if, in the example above, Gretchen had used the proceeds from the sale of her Ford to buy IBM stock, which she owned at death, subsection (a)(5) does not give the court the authority to give Xavier the IBM stock in lieu of the Ford; the replacement property must be of the same character.

While §2-606(a)(6) appears to broadly include all specific devises not otherwise covered by the earlier sections, it is to be construed narrowly. The Comment to UPC §2-606 notes that, "subsection (a)(6) creates a mild presumption *against* ademption by extinction, imposing on the party claiming that an ademption has occurred the burden of establishing that the facts and circumstances indicate that ademption of the devise was intended by the testator or that ademption of the devise is consistent with the testator's manifested plan of distribution." The drafters offer the following example:

Example: Gloria's will devised, "that diamond ring I inherited from grandfather" to her son, Alonzo, and it devised, "that diamond brooch I inherited from grandmother" to her daughter Briana. After Gloria executed her will, a burglar stole the diamond ring (but not the diamond brooch which was in Gloria's safety deposit box). Under subsection (a)(6), the party claiming that Alonzo's devise was adeemed would be unlikely to be able to establish that Gloria intended Alonzo's devise to be adeemed or that ademption is consistent with Gloria's manifested plan of distribution. In fact, Gloria's equalizing devise to Briana affirmatively indicates that ademption is inconsistent with Gloria's manifested plan of distribution. The likely result is that, under subsection (a)(6), Alonzo would be entitled to the value of the diamond ring. Note that the person seeking nonademption in this example, Alonzo, is not getting the devised property or replacement property but rather a pecuniary devise (cash) equal to the value as of its date of disposition.

UPC §2-605 provides another exception to ademption by extinction. This exception applies to bequests of securities (whether specific or general) owned by the testator. A company may purchase the shares of stock of another company, and a shareholder in the acquired company may find his shares replaced by shares in the acquiring company. A company may also issue additional stock shares to shareholders as a result of "stock splits."

UPC §2-605. Increase in Securities; Accessions.

(a) If a testator executes a will that devises securities and the testator then owned securities that meet the description in the will, the devise includes additional securities owned by the testator at death to the extent the additional securities were acquired by the testator after the will was executed as a result of the testator's ownership of the described securities and are securities of any of the following types:

(1) securities of the same organization acquired by reason of action initiated by the organization or any successor, related, or acquiring organization, excluding any acquired by exercise of purchase options;

(2) securities of another organization acquired as a result of a merger, consolidation, reorganization, or other distribution by the organization or any successor, related, or acquiring organization; or

(3) securities of the same organization acquired as a result of a plan of reinvestment.

(b) Distributions in cash before death with respect to a described security are not part of the devise.

Example: Jonah's will provides that his friend Charlie is to receive all of Jonah's WorldCom stock. However, Jonah does not own any WorldCom stock at his death because Sprint bought out WorldCom. Jonah exchanged his WorldCom stock for that of Sprint. States that employ the "identity" theory strictly would deny Charlie any stock. Under UPC §2-605 Charlie would get the Sprint stock.

The pre-1990 version of UPC §2-605 was UPC §2-607. The following case illustrates how a court applied that section in the case of securities that were redeemed for cash. The Court of Appeals decision illustrates the "softer" intent approach in which the court reaches for a way to give the beneficiary something instead of applying the harsher "identity" theory, which results in the failure of the gift and the beneficiary's receiving nothing.

In re Estate of Magnus
444 N.W.2d 295 (Minn. Ct. App. 1989)

The opinion of the court was delivered by Justice FORSBERG.

Donald and Gerald Sweeney appeal from an order of the probate court finding a specific devise to a trust adeemed under Minn. Stat. §524.2-607 (1986). We affirm in part, reverse in part and remand.

FACTS

Dorothy B. Magnus died testate on August 17, 1988, at the age of 85. By order dated October 5, 1988, Magnus' last will and testament and the first codicil thereto (hereinafter, the "will"), were formally admitted to probate.

Article III of the will made the following provisions for Donald and Gerald Sweeney (appellants):

> I bequeath all of the shares of the capital stock of Heileman Brewing Company owned by me at the time of my death to my Trustees hereinafter named to hold, administer and distribute the same as follows, to-wit:
>
> 1. During the lifetime of my friends, Donald Sweeney and Gerald Sweeney, now residing in DelRay Beach, Florida, my Trustees shall pay all of the income of the said trust to said Donald Sweeney and Gerald Sweeney in equal shares and to the survivor thereof.
> 2. Upon the death of the survivor of said Donald Sweeney and Gerald Sweeney the said Heileman Brewing Company stock shall be distributed to Saint Mary's College, Winona, Minnesota, to be added to the scholarship endowment fund created by Paragraph B, Article V of this my Last Will and Testament.

In late 1987, Amber Acquisition Corp. and the Heileman Board of Directors completed a sale whereby Amber controlled 92.8% of Heileman shares by October 1987. In February 1988, the Heileman shareholders approved a reverse stock split in which Heileman made payments to all remaining shareholders of $40.75, in cash, for each share held. The new ownership made funds available in escrow accounts at various banks to enable former shareholders to present their certificates and receive the cash payments.

Prior to her death, Magnus tendered 17,549 shares and received for them $715,121.75 in cash. Following Magnus' death, the personal representative located certificates for 6,749 shares of Heileman in a safe deposit box. The personal representative surrendered the certificates and received proceeds of $275,021.75. . . .

ANALYSIS

The probate court ordered:

1. The bequest under article 3 of the decedent's will is fully adeemed and fails in its entirety under Minn. Stat. 524.2-607 because the decedent had no ownership interest in Heileman Brewing Co. at the time of her death.
2. All proceeds received by the estate for the Heileman stock certificates found in the decedent's safe deposit box are a part of the residue of the estate.

Therefore the only question under consideration by this court is whether the probate court properly applied Minn. Stat. §524.2-607 (1986). . . .

In relevant part, Minn. Stat. §524.2-607 (1986) states:

> (a) If the testator intended a specific devise of certain securities rather than the equivalent value thereof, the specific devisee is entitled only to:
>
> > (1) as much of the devised securities as is a part of the estate at the time of the testator's death;
> > (2) Any additional or other securities of the same entity owned by the testator by reason of action initiated by the entity excluding any acquired by exercise of purchase options;

[The court concluded the stock of Heileman was a security within the meaning of the statute.]

The next issue is whether these are securities "of the same entity." One could argue the "indebtedness" to testator is owed by the escrow agent rather than Heileman. However, the statute apparently foresees this situation by including a provision avoiding ademption when the amounts are owed "by reason of action initiated by the entity." We believe the stock redemption was the type of action contemplated by the framers of the UPC.

Additionally, the securities were acquired by testator as a result of ownership interest in Heileman. The framers of this law note this is an essential element in bringing the transaction within the purview of this statute.

The Joint Editorial Board considered amending Subsection (a)(2) so as to exclude additional securities of the same entity that were not acquired by testator as a result of his ownership of the devised securities. It concluded that, in context, the present language is clear enough to make the proposed amendment unnecessary. Unif. Probate Code §2-607, 8 U.L.A. 148, comment (1989).

We therefore conclude, as a matter of law, the probate court erred in holding the devise of the found stock certificates adeemed under Minn. Stat. §524.2-607 and remand with instructions to order the funds acquired thereof distributed to the trustee under the terms of article 3 of the testator's will.

NOTES AND QUESTIONS

1.   *The revised statute.* Note the new version of the statute uses a slightly different phrase. It requires that the securities be "of the same organization." The term organization is defined in UPC §1-201 as including, "a corporation, business trust, estate, trust, partnership, joint venture,

association, government, or governmental subdivision or agency, or any other legal or commercial entity."

2.   *Broad construction?* The probate court in the *Magnus* case found that the gift was adeemed, and the Minnesota Court of Appeals reversed that finding. Which court do you agree with? What is the court's rationale for its broad construction of the statutory requirement that the securities be "of the same entity" in order to avoid ademption by extinction?

3.   *Testator intent.* What do you think most testators intend with regard to property that is not in their estate at the time they die? Do they want a beneficiary to receive a substitute gift or not? Does it depend on the nature of the gift itself? Does it depend on who the beneficiary is? *See, e.g., Parker v. Bozian,* 859 So.2d 427 (Ala. 2003) (concluding that testatrix's split of a CD into two smaller CDs did not adeem the original CD because the original still existed, was numbered differently only for the convenience of the bank and the original funds of the CD were not increased or withdrawn).

PROBLEMS

1.   Tilly executed a will in 2005, naming Joshua as her personal representative. The will devises her house on Jasmine Street to Megan (worth $150,000 at the date of execution), her 10,000 shares in General Telephone & Electronics (GTE) stock to Nonnie (worth $100,000 at the date of execution), $75,000 to Oliver and the residue of her estate (worth about $300,000 at the date of execution) to Paul.

At Tilly's death, Tilly still owned the house on Jasmine Street, which was worth $500,000 on her date of death, and $1,250,000 in investments, stocks and bonds. Included in the stocks and bonds are the same 10,000 shares of GTE stock (worth $250,000 at date of death). Tilly only had $2,500 in her checking account at her death.

   a.   Assume the will was silent on subsequent changes to the assets. As the lawyer for the estate, counsel Joshua as personal representative as to who should get what assets.

   b.   Assume instead that there was no GTE stock in Tilly's estate at her death because she sold it many years ago. What would you give to Nonnie?

   c.   Assume again that there is no GTE stock in Tilly's estate at her death. However, you discover that GTE was merged into Verizon. Tilly owned 75,000 shares of Verizon on her death, 65,000 shares of which were the result of the merger and subsequent stock dividends and stock splits attributable to the shares in GTE. Ten thousand of the Verizon shares were shares that Tilly bought eight months before her death. How would these facts influence who gets what?

   d.   Assume instead that Tilly did not own the house on Jasmine Street at her death. She sold the house on Jasmine Street in 2009 for cash and moved into an assisted living facility where she paid rent, never having purchased a new home. How would these facts influence who gets what?

   e.   Assume again that Tilly did not own the house on Jasmine Street at her death. She sold the house in 2009, took the proceeds from the sale and used them to buy a house on Olive Street, where Tilly lived until her death. The Olive Street home is worth $500,000 on Tilly's death. How would these facts influence who gets what?

   How or would your answer change if Tilly's will included a provision that stated, "If any specific bequest or devise given to any beneficiary under this will shall fail because such property is not in my estate at the time of my death, I direct that my personal representative *shall not* substitute other property for it."

   f.   Assume again that Tilly did not own the house on Jasmine Street at her death. Four years before her death, the court appointed a conservator for Tilly because she had lost capacity. The conservator sold her house and used the proceeds to pay Tilly's expenses. How would these facts influence who gets what?

   g.   Assume again that Tilly did not own the house on Jasmine Street at her death. Four years before her death, Tilly appointed Paul as her agent under a power of attorney so that Paul could handle her financial matters. Three years before her death, Paul sold the house, moved Tilly into an assisted living facility and used the proceeds from the sale of the house to pay her expenses. How would these facts influence who gets what?

2. Tilly wanted to treat her two daughters equally. She gave Jane $100,000 worth of AT&T stock (when it was selling for $10 per share) and Jenny $100,000 worth of Procter & Gamble stock (when it was selling for $4 per share). Her will says, "I give 10,000 shares of AT&T stock to Jane and I give 25,000 shares of P&G stock to Jenny." On Tilly's death, she no longer owned the AT&T stock because she sold it a year ago for $185,000. She did, however, still own the P&G stock, which was worth $250,000 at the time of her death.

The personal representative must decide who gets what. If you are the lawyer for the estate, what advice would you give the personal representative after considering the provisions of UPC §2-606(a)(6).

EXERCISES

1.   Tilly comes to you to draft her will. She wants to devise her house on Jasmine Street to Megan, her 10,000 shares in General Telephone & Electronics (GTE) stock to Nonnie, $75,000 to Oliver and the rest and residue of her estate to Paul. Draft a provision that anticipates possible changes that could occur with regard to these assets — for example, sale, loss or gift — between the time Tilly executes the will and her death.

2.   Review the Marjorie M. Black will in the Appendix to this chapter. Does it provide for any alternative gifts in the event that she does not own property bequeathed at her death?

d.   Ademption by Satisfaction

A court probating a will may be faced with another interpretative question — whether a lifetime transfer from the testator to a beneficiary was meant to be in lieu of a bequest in the will or whether it was meant to be in addition to the bequest. Courts apply the doctrine of "ademption by satisfaction" in these cases.

> **Example:**   Nigel gives his daughter, Bettina, a check for $20,000 the month prior to his death, so that she can buy a new car. Nigel dies a month later, and his will provides that his daughter Bettina shall receive $40,000. Does Nigel intend that the first $20,000 check that he gave to Bettina be in addition to the $40,000 bequest under his will, or should it be deducted from the $40,000 so that Bettina only receives $20,000 under his will? In other words, is the bequest partially adeemed by satisfaction?

Note that it is often the residuary beneficiary who argues to the court that the bequest should be adeemed by satisfaction, given the likelihood that the residue would be increased if the general bequest were reduced or eliminated. Historically, some courts allowed parol evidence (oral testimony) of the testator's intent that the lifetime transfer be in satisfaction of the bequest under the will. The more modern rule is to require a writing of some sort either by the testator or by the beneficiary to evidence the testator's intent. The evidence of intent may be contained in the will itself, in a writing from the testator at the time he makes the lifetime transfer or in a writing from the recipient of the transfer when she receives it, acknowledging that it is in satisfaction of a bequest she is to receive under the testator's will.

UPC §2-609. Ademption by Satisfaction.

(a) Property a testator gave in his [or her] lifetime to a person is treated as a satisfaction of a devise in whole or in part, only if (i) the will provides for deduction of the gift, (ii) the testator declared in a contemporaneous writing that the gift is in satisfaction of the devise or that its value is to be deducted from the value of the devise, or (iii) the devisee acknowledged in writing that the gift is in satisfaction of the devise or that its value is to be deducted from the value of the devise.

(b) For purposes of partial satisfaction, property given during lifetime is valued as of the time the devisee came into possession or enjoyment of the property or at the testator's death, whichever occurs first.

(c) If the devisee fails to survive the testator, the gift is treated as a full or partial satisfaction of the devise, as appropriate, in applying Sections §2-603 and §2-604, unless the testator's contemporaneous writing provides otherwise.

The rule discussed here should sound familiar. It is closely related to the doctrine of advancement that we looked at in Chapter 3. The UPC drafters note that UPC §2-609 parallels "Section 2–109 on advancements and follows the same policy of requiring written evidence that lifetime gifts are to be taken into account in the distribution of an estate, whether testate or intestate." Of course, a testator can actually provide for ademption by satisfaction in the will itself, which of course someone who dies intestate cannot.

NOTES

1. *Drafting considerations.* If the testator wants to be clear about whether or not such lifetime transfers should be deducted from a beneficiary's eventual inheritance, a will might include one of the following provisions:

> All advancements I have made, or may subsequently make, to any of my children in excess of the annual Internal Revenue Code gift tax exclusion then in effect shall be in full or partial satisfaction of any legacies or other benefit given them by my will.

> or

> All advancements I have made, or may subsequently make, to any of my children shall be in addition to, and not in satisfaction of, any legacies or other benefit given them by my will.

A number of states have adopted the approach taken in the *Restatement (Third) of Property: Wills & Other Donative Transfers* §5.4 and UPC §2-609 that written documentation is required to prove ademption by satisfaction. *But see YIVO Inst. for Jewish Research v. Zaleski*, 874 A.2d 411 (Md. 2005) (declining to limit proof of a testator's intent when determining ademption by satisfaction to written evidence and stating that extrinsic evidence such as verbal statements could be proffered to prove or rebut ademption).

2.   *Is there someone else?* The UPC drafters note that this section can apply when there is a lifetime transfer to someone other than the devisee to satisfy the devise. For example, Thomas's will made a $20,000 devise to his child, Arnold. Thomas was a widower. Shortly before his death, Thomas, in consultation with his lawyer, decided to take advantage of the $10,000 annual gift tax exclusion and sent a check for $10,000 to Arnold and another check for $10,000 to Arnold's spouse, Belinda. The checks were accompanied by a letter from Thomas explaining that the gifts were made for tax purposes and were in lieu of the $20,000 devise to Arnold. The $20,000 devise here would be fully satisfied by the gifts to Arnold and Belinda.

3.   *Will substitutes.* Lifetime transfers in the form of will substitutes may satisfy devises also. Such transfers need not be outright gifts. For example, a testator may designate the devisee as the beneficiary of the testator's life insurance policy or the beneficiary of the remainder interest in a revocable inter vivos trust. If the terms of UPC §2-609 are met and the testator either provides for deduction of the face amount of the policy or the remainder interest in the trust, or declares in a contemporaneous writing that the transfer is in satisfaction of the devise or if the beneficiary acknowledges in writing that the transfer is in lieu of the bequest under the testator's will, then the lifetime transfers will be treated as an ademption by satisfaction by the court.

e.   Exoneration

At common law, if a devise of property did not specifically instruct the personal representative to pay off the mortgage prior to distributing it to the beneficiary, the silence on that point was construed to mean that the personal representative was to pay off the mortgage prior to distribution. The more modern rule, embraced by the UPC, reverses the common law and provides that, if the will is silent, the devised property is distributed with the mortgage attached. In other words, the beneficiary will take the property encumbered by the mortgage.

UPC §2-607. Nonexoneration.

A specific devise passes subject to any mortgage interest existing at the date of death, without right of exoneration, regardless of a general directive in the will to pay debts.

This rule applies even if there is a general provision that instructs the personal representative to pay all debts, such as the following: "I direct my personal representative to pay my funeral and burial expenses and the unpaid cost of the perpetual care and maintenance of the burial plot in which I should be buried, claims against my estate, and expenses of estate administration." For exoneration to occur, the testator must give the personal representative a specific instruction to pay the particular debt, for example, "I direct my personal representative to pay the mortgage on my personal residence before transferring title to the beneficiary named above who will be receiving it."

f. Abatement

Sometimes there is a question of what to do if there is not enough property in the estate to fully satisfy all creditors and all bequests. Perhaps the testator thought he would have a larger estate, or perhaps he incurred significant debts that must be repaid. If the testator made bequests to individuals that cannot be fully satisfied, the doctrine of "abatement" helps the probate court decide who gets what. The doctrine of abatement specifies which bequests will be reduced or eliminated altogether and in what order that will be done.

Abatement is meant to provide guidance where the testator did not specify his own order of priority in paying bequests, and it is intended to replicate the testator's intent not defeat it. To prevent the doctrine from applying, the testator can include a provision in the instrument that explicitly states the testator's preference, such as "I direct that the gifts made in this will abate in the following order [specify order]." If the testator does not specify a preference for the order, statutes like UPC §3-902 act as default rules to supply the court with an order of abatement:

UPC §3-902. [Distribution; Order in Which Assets Appropriated; Abatement].

(a) Except as provided in subsection (b) and except as provided in connection with the share of the surviving spouse who elects to take an elective share, shares of distributees abate, without any preference or priority as between real and personal property, in the following order: (1) property not disposed of by the will; (2) residuary devises; (3) general devises [normally monetary bequests]; (4) specific devises. . . . Abatement within each classification is in proportion to the amounts of property each of the beneficiaries would have received if full distribution of the property had been made in accordance with the terms of the will.

(b) If the will expresses an order of abatement, or if the testamentary plan or the express or implied purpose of the devise would be defeated by the order of abatement stated in subsection (a), the shares of the distributees abate as may be found necessary to give effect to the intention of the testator.

Example: Viviana dies with a will that provides that Tabitha is to receive her diamond ring valued at $10,000, Yale is to receive a general devise of $10,000 and Ben is to receive the residue. If there is only $10,000 and the diamond ring in Viviana's estate at her death, then Yale will receive the $10,000 bequest and Tabitha will receive the diamond ring. However, Ben will receive nothing since the residuary devise abates before the general and the specific devises.

PROBLEMS

Tabitha died testate. There is nothing in her will indicating how debts should be paid by the personal representative. The probate estate consists of the following assets: cash of $100,000, a house worth $500,000, stock in the family business worth $250,000, jewelry and furs worth $50,000 and other property worth $100,000. (Total = $1,000,000). The bequests in the will are as follows:

- House to Alexis.
- Jewelry and furs to Bertrand.
- Stock in the family-owned business to Carlotta.
- $150,000 cash to Derek.
- Rest and residue to Eloise.

1. Tabitha died with general debts of the estate and/or the testator (other than taxes) of $75,000 plus a mortgage on the house of $50,000. Explain from what sources the debts will be paid.

2. Assume the same facts except the debts are $200,000, plus a mortgage on the house of $50,000.

3. Assume the same facts except the debts are $600,000, plus a mortgage on the house of $50,000.

4. Do your answers to (1)-(3) change if the will said specific bequests were to be abated first?

g. Apportionment

Historically, if a testator failed to specify from what source taxes were to be paid, the default rule was that they would be paid from the residuary estate. However, many states have reversed that rule by statute and provide that in the absence of a clear direction to pay taxes out of the residue, each bequest shall share the tax burden pro-rata. This rule evolved as will substitutes became more popular since taking the taxes out of the residue may eliminate a residuary beneficiary altogether if there are large will substitutes that trigger tax to the decedent's estate.

As always, the default rules yield to direct statements of intent stated in the will. Most form books give the attorney the option of directing that estate taxes be deducted from the residue, or that each gift, either limited to those stated in the will or all gifts including nonprobate transfers, must contribute its pro-rata share. The attorney should always consider the preferences of the testator and the overall estate plan in drafting a provision that will best carry out the testator's wishes. The following clause allocates the burden among all takers:

> I direct that all estate, inheritance and succession taxes payable by reason of my death shall be apportioned as provided under the law of North Carolina in effect at the date of my death. In so doing, my personal representative shall charge such taxes against the property generating the tax, whether or not such property passes under my will. To the extent practicable, it shall deduct the amount of such taxes from the property distributable under my will and recover from the beneficiaries of property passing other than by my will their allocable share of such taxes, unless my personal representative in its discretion determines that the cost of recovery is greater than such recovery warrants.

The sometimes seemingly draconian effect of burdening the residuary estate with all the estate taxes rather than apportioning them may be seen in the following case, another decision involving the well-known and folksy CBS newsman, Charles Kuralt.

In re Estate of Kuralt
68 P.3d 662 (Mont. 2003)

The opinion of the court was delivered by Justice RICE.

Appellants, Susan Bowers and Lisa Bowers White (Bowers and White), the daughters of Charles Kuralt and personal representatives of the Estate of Charles Kuralt (the Estate), appeal from the decision of the Fifth Judicial District Court, Madison County, ordering that all estate taxes due as a result of the administration of the estate of Charles Kuralt be imposed on the residual estate. We affirm.

We address the following issue on appeal:

Did the District Court correctly apply New York law to the Kuralt codicil when it ordered that the taxes on the property conveyed therein shall be imposed on the residual estate?

PROCEDURAL BACKGROUND

This is the fourth appeal to come before this Court in the *Matter of the Estate of Charles Kuralt. . . .*

Charles Kuralt died testate in a hospital in New York City on July 4, 1997. While the bulk of his estate was in New York, he also owned property in Madison County, Montana, on the Big Hole River. Mr. Kuralt's widow, Suzanna "Petie" Baird Kuralt, thereafter filed a petition in a New York state court seeking to probate the estate. On September 15, 1997, Petie, as the Domiciliary Foreign Personal Representative of the Estate of Charles Kuralt, through Montana counsel, filed a Proof of Authority seeking to probate the real property owned by Kuralt in Madison County.

On September 30, 1997, Kuralt's long-time and intimate companion, Patricia Elizabeth Shannon, filed a Petition for Ancillary Probate of Will, challenging the application of Kuralt's New York will to the Madison County property based, in part, on a letter which she had received from Mr. Kuralt shortly before his death a letter that this Court, in *Kuralt II*, determined to be a valid holographic codicil conveying the Madison County property to Shannon. . . .

Left undetermined in the previous cases was the question of whether the Estate or Shannon was responsible for the estate taxes associated with the bequest to Shannon of the Big Hole River property in Madison County. . . .

On January 4, 2001, Shannon filed and served a "Demand upon Estate of Suzanna Baird Kuralt for Payment of Taxes" demanding that the co-personal representatives, Bowers and White, pay from the residuary of the Estate all federal, state and gift taxes due as a result of the bequest of the Big Hole River property to Shannon.

Bowers and White opposed Shannon's demand for payment out of the residuary of the Estate and argued that, under both New York and Montana law, estate taxes should be apportioned under the New York apportionment statutes, notwithstanding language to the contrary in Kuralt's 1994 will. They contended that the conveyance of the property to Shannon created adverse tax consequences against the Estate, contrary to the "dominant purpose or plan of distribution" of the 1994 will to take full advantage of the marital deduction and to protect Mrs. Kuralt from burdensome taxation.

Shannon responded that, under the applicable New York statutory and case law as well as Montana law, where the language of the will makes it clear that there is to be no apportionment of estate taxes according to state statute, the courts of both states will abide by the explicit language in the will.

The District Court agreed with Shannon and concluded that, under substantially similar laws of New York and Montana, the court must adhere and give effect to the testator's plan if such plan can be ascertained. The District Court further concluded that, under Article Twelve of Kuralt's 1994 will, wherein it states that all death taxes "shall be paid without apportionment," all taxes are to be paid by the residual estate and thus ordered that the taxes generated from the bequest of the Big Hole River property to Shannon be paid accordingly.

Bowers and White now appeal the District Court's decision.
Did the District Court correctly apply New York law to the Kuralt codicil when it ordered that the taxes on the property conveyed therein shall be imposed on the residual estate?

STANDARD OF REVIEW

The issue before this Court is a question of law. When reviewing a district court's conclusions of law, we determine whether the court's interpretation of the law is correct.

DISCUSSION

. . . The applicable New York statute provides:

> Unless otherwise provided in the will or non-testamentary instrument, and subject to paragraph (d-1) of this section: (1) The tax shall be apportioned among the persons benefited in the proportion that the value of the property or interest received by each person benefited bears to the total value of the property and interest received by all persons benefited. . . .

EPTL §§2-1.8(c). When interpreting the earliest version of this statute, the Court of Appeals of New York stated that the statute "requires apportionment of Federal and State estate taxes among the legatees and devisees 'in the proportion that the value of the property or interest received by each such person' . . . except where the testator 'otherwise directs in his will.'"

This holding was affirmed by the Supreme Court, Appellate Division of New York in *In the Matter of the Estate of Dewar* (1978), 404 N.Y.S.2d 750, 62 A.D.2d 352. In *Dewar*, the decedent's last will and testament, dated December 4, 1972, provided:

> I direct that all my just debts and funeral and administration expenses be paid. I further direct that all inheritance, estate, transfer, succession and death taxes imposed by any jurisdiction upon property passing under this, my Will, be paid out of the general estate as expenses of the administration thereof, without apportionment as to any legatee.

The will in *Dewar* clearly provided that all estate taxes imposed upon property passing under the will be paid out of the residual estate and "without apportionment" as to any legatee. The remainder of the will made bequests to individuals and charities and left the residuary to five charities.

However, in a later codicil dated June 22, 1973, the decedent increased the amount of some bequests to certain individuals previously named in her will, and further provided:

> In all other respects, I hereby ratify and confirm the provisions of my Last Will and Testament dated December 4, 1972.

With the increase of the bequests in the codicil, it was later determined that the estate and transfer taxes would consume all of the residuary, requiring abatement of pre-residuary bequests. The residuary legatees thereafter commenced proceedings in the New York Surrogate Court to determine whether the gifts bequeathed in the codicil should receive the same tax treatment as the gifts contained in the 1972 will.

The Surrogate determined that the gifts in the codicil should receive the same tax treatment as the gifts in the 1972 will and the Supreme Court, Appellate Division, affirmed, concluding that "[e]state taxes are apportioned among recipients of estate assets 'unless otherwise provided in the will or non-testamentary instrument' and such a contrary direction must be clear and unambiguous. Here there is no question but that the direction to avoid apportionment against the legatees named in the will is both clear and unambiguous and, indeed, it is undisputed that such was the intention of the testatrix."

In *Dewar*, the appellant argued that, because the codicil contained only general language in ratifying the terms of the will without expressing specific intent that the additional gifts be exonerated from statutory apportionment, pursuant to the apportionment statute, EPTL §2-1.8, the estate and transfer taxes generated by the codicil should be apportioned according to the specific property generating the tax. The Court of Appeals disagreed, and, citing to *Matter of Nicholas* (1973), 33 N.Y.2d 174, 350 N.Y.S.2d 900, 305 N.E.2d 911, stated: "Since a will and a codicil must be construed together, where the provisions of the will contain a tax exoneration clause broad enough to encompass all testamentary dispositions, the clause also applies to gifts contained in the codicil in the absence of a manifest intent to the contrary. . . . "

Bowers and White contend that the rule in *Dewar* is inapplicable to the current case because Kuralt's 1994 will did contain a "manifest intent to the contrary," that intent being Kuralt's intent to take full advantage of the marital deduction, thus ensuring that Mrs. Kuralt's share would be tax free. They argue that the Surrogate's conclusion, and the Court of Appeal's affirmation in *Dewar*, was not only consistent with the anti-apportionment clause in the will, but was also consistent with the undisputed intention of the testatrix in *Dewar* to opt out of the apportionment statute.

Bowers and White contend that, in the instant case, it is likewise undisputed that Kuralt's "dominant purpose or plan of distribution" was to insure that Mrs. Kuralt's share would be tax free, and that this dominant purpose is inconsistent with the tax burden now generated by the bequest in the codicil of the Big Hole River property to Shannon. They contend that this inconsistency generates an ambiguity such that there is no clear and unambiguous direction that the taxes generated from the Big Hole Property should not be apportioned to its recipient, and that such taxes should, therefore, be paid by Shannon, notwithstanding the language in Article Twelve of Kuralt's 1994 will. Article Twelve provides:

> A. All estate, inheritance . . . and other death taxes . . . which shall be imposed by reason of my death . . . shall be paid without apportionment in the following manner:
>
>> (a) first, out of that portion, if any, of the balance of my residuary estate disposed of under Paragraph B of Article FIVE of this Will with respect to which my wife shall have made a qualified disclaimer;
>> (b) second, out of the fractional share, if any, of my residuary estate disposed of under Paragraph A of Article FIVE of this Will; and
>> (c) third, out of (the balance of) my residuary estate disposed of under . . . Article FIVE of this Will . . .

While Bowers and White agree that Article Twelve presents a clear and unambiguous direction that taxes should not be apportioned among the recipients of the Estate, thus opting out of the default apportionment provision of EPTL §§2-1.8(c), they also contend that, pursuant to *Matter of Fabbri* (1957), 2 N.Y.2d 236, 240, 159 N.Y.S.2d 184, 140 N.E.2d 269, 271, where a reading of the entire will reveals a "dominant purpose or plan of distribution," the individual parts must be interpreted in light of that purpose, and be given effect accordingly, despite the fact that a literal reading might yield an inconsistent meaning. In other words, they argue that Kuralt's holographic codicil renders ambiguous the otherwise clear language of the will, and that, in light of this ambiguity, there exists a conflict between the dominant purpose of the will and the anti-apportionment language of Article Twelve.

Thus, they argue that the alleged ambiguity created by the holographic codicil requires this Court to look to the overall scheme of the will, and that, pursuant to *Matter of Pepper*, and given the strong policy in favor of statutory apportionment, any ambiguity in the testator's intent must be resolved in favor of the EPTL apportionment scheme, thus requiring Shannon to pay the estate taxes generated by the Big Hole River property. . . .

We disagree with Bowers and White that *Dewar* is distinguishable by virtue of the fact that the codicil in *Dewar* specifically "ratified and confirmed" the provisions of the decedent's previous will. Under New York law, a valid codicil, by definition, alters and supplements or adds and subtracts from an already existing will, whether or not the codicil contains specific language to that effect. A codicil that is silent on method of payment of estate taxes, therefore, does not add or subtract from clear and unambiguous language in the original will specifically directing how estate taxes should be paid, even if the bequest in the codicil generates a tax burden not previously existing under the original will. Similar to *Dewar*, in the instant case there is no question but that the direction to avoid apportionment against specific devisees in Kuralt's 1994 will is both clear and unambiguous, and that this, indeed, was Kuralt's intention.

While there is a strong public policy in favor of statutory apportionment under New York law, we hold that the District Court correctly concluded that Shannon satisfied the burden of proving that Kuralt's will directs, clearly and unambiguously, in Article Twelve, against statutory apportionment, and that all estate taxes are to be paid by the residual Estate, including those generated by the bequest of the Big Hole River property to Shannon.

The decision of the District Court is affirmed accordingly.

The UPC specifies that apportionment is the default rule where the testator has not declared specifically that estate taxes are to be paid in a different manner. In other words, in the absence of clearly stated contrary intent, estate taxes will be shared pro rata among the beneficiaries. In Part 9A, the UPC incorporates the Uniform Estate Tax Apportionment Act (2003) (UETAA). The General Comment to Part 9A reiterates the principle of apportioning the tax burden among all the beneficiaries:

> The new UETAA continues to advance the principle of the former UETAA that the decedent's expressed intentions govern apportionment of an estate tax. Statutory apportionment applies only to the extent there is no clear and effective decedent's tax burden direction to the contrary.

The interplay of responsibilities for the tax between the estate and the recipients of property is interesting. Transfer taxes are the primary responsibility of the estate to pay, though the ultimate responsibility lies with the beneficiaries. The UETAA allows the personal representative to withhold payments to probate beneficiaries until taxes are paid (UPC §3-9A-108(a)) and "may collect from any person the tax apportioned to and the tax required to be advanced by the person." UPC §3-9A-109(a). If not paid in full, the estate and gift tax liabilities create a lien on the gross estate or gift. The IRS can seek payment from anyone who receives property that was subject to the tax as a transferee, whether it is from probate or nonprobate transfers. Int. Rev. Code §§2205-2207B entitles the personal representative to collect the apportioned estate tax from recipients of certain nonprobate transfers.

NOTES AND QUESTIONS

1. *Burdening the residue.* Do you think the court really implemented Kuralt's intent when it put the entire tax burden on his residuary estate? For an interesting interview with Kuralt's intimate companion, Pat Shannon, see http://transcripts.cnn.com/TRANSCRIPTS/0102/14/lkl.00.html. *See generally* Mark R. Siegel, *Who Should Bear the Bite of Estate Taxes on Non-Probate Property?*, 43 CREIGHTON L. REV. 747 (2010) (in which the author identifies the question to be resolved in these cases as whether the testator who "provides for a beneficiary through a pre-residuary bequest or non-probate transfer necessarily intends for that person to be exonerated from state law apportionment of estate taxes so that such beneficiary receives the financial benefit of the property in full").

2. *Burdening the residue redux.* For another interesting case that illustrates the problems that poor planning can cause, see *Estate of Sheppard ex rel. McMorrow v. Schleis*, 782 N.W.2d 85 (Wis. 2010). When James F. Sheppard, who co-founded the sandwich chain "Cousins Subs," died intestate and left his goddaughter $3.7 million in two nonprobate accounts, his estate sought to get her to pay her portion of the estate taxes attributable to her inheritance. His estate was worth $12.0 million when he died. The Wisconsin Supreme Court affirmed a lower court ruling which held that the probate estate, and not the goddaughter, was responsible for the tax since Wisconsin does not have an apportionment rule as its default.

EXERCISE

Taunya has called you to meet with her about estate planning. After you have met with her and conducted the initial client interview, you determine that she has many assets that will be probated and many that will avoid probate through will substitutes. The bulk of her estate is going to the residuary beneficiaries. There will be expenses of dying, like the fees for the attorney, the personal representative and trustee, debts owed by Taunya incurred during life and taxes due.

   a.   Without more information, can you draft a provision for a will or trust that identifies how debts, taxes and other expenses of the decedent should be paid?

   b.   What additional information do you need from Taunya before doing so?

   c.   Taunya wants the expenses to be paid out of the residuary estate. Draft a provision in the will to that effect.

   d.   Taunya says she wants all recipients of her property to pay their fair share of all these items. Can you draft the provision now or do you think you still need more information? If so, what information would you like to have?

3. Rules of Construction Applicable to Both Wills and Will Substitutes

In the prior section, we explored rules of construction that apply only to wills. There are several rules that apply both to wills and wills substitutes under the UPC. These rules help determine the important issue of when one person survives another — a determination that is essential to deciding whether a gift under a will lapses and whether a beneficiary under a will substitute has met a requirement of survival.[5] These default rules determine when death occurs as well as what it means to "survive" a decedent, if a will or will substitute does not provide a different definition for "survive."

a. Determining Death

Determining who survives whom is an essential component of deciding who gets which assets in inheritance law. It is often easy to determine that someone has died. Hospitals do it every day, and they issue a death certificate which constitutes evidence that death has occurred and what time it occurred. However, when someone is kept alive through medical intervention or has disappeared, legislative or judicial presumptions apply. Without those presumptions, it would be very difficult to close certain probate estates. UPC §1-107(1)(2) and (5) provide guidance for the court as to when "death" occurs. This framework applies to both wills and will substitutes:

UPC §1–107. Evidence of Death or Status.

In addition to the rules of evidence in courts of general jurisdiction, the following rules relating to a determination of death and status apply:

1. Death occurs when an individual [is determined to be dead under the Uniform Determination of Death Act] [has sustained either (i) irreversible cessation of circulatory and respiratory functions or (ii) irreversible cessation of all functions of the entire brain, including the brain stem. A determination of death must be made in accordance with accepted medical standards].

2. A certified or authenticated copy of a death certificate purporting to be issued by an official or agency of the place where the death

---

5. Note that the rules imposed by state probate statutes cannot alter beneficiary rights under retirement plans governed by the Employee Retirement Income Security Act of 1974 (ERISA), the federal statute that governs such plans. The federal statute preempts state statutes in this regard.

purportedly occurred is prima facie evidence of the fact, place, date, and time of death and the identity of the decedent. . . .

5. An individual whose death is not established under the preceding paragraphs who is absent for a continuous period of 5 years, during which he [or she] has not been heard from, and whose absence is not satisfactorily explained after diligent search or inquiry, is presumed to be dead. His [or her] death is presumed to have occurred at the end of the period unless there is sufficient evidence for determining that death occurred earlier.

b.   Requirement of Survival

What happens when the decedent and his beneficiary die close together from a temporal perspective? Does it make sense to pass the decedent's property to the named beneficiary who has not lived long enough to enjoy it? The property would have to be probated a second time and then pass to the beneficiary's heirs or legatees when the testator may have preferred that the property pass to someone of her own choosing if the beneficiary could not enjoy it.

As we have discussed, a beneficiary under a will must survive the testator in order to take a bequest. For will substitutes, survival is not required unless the document says so, but most will substitutes require that a beneficiary survive. The document — either a will or the document creating a will substitute — can define what "survive" means. For example, a will might say, "I give my car to Geneva, if she is living on the 30th day after the day of my death." If Geneva dies a week after the testator, she has not met the requirement of survival provided in the will.

In many cases, a will or will substitute may simply say that the beneficiary must "survive" in order to take. A number of states and the UPC require that a beneficiary survive by a specific number of hours or days in order to "survive" to receive a bequest. In effect, all wills (and other governing instruments that require survival) are read to include a condition that the beneficiary survive the decedent by the specified time period. These statutes usually require clear and convincing evidence of survival in order to establish that the beneficiary met the required condition.

UPC §2-702 adopts a 120-hour rule, in the absence of any contrary provision in the testator's will. From a policy perspective, this type of survival rule prevents the bequest or devise from being probated in the testator's estate and then again immediately in the beneficiary's estate, incurring additional probate fees and perhaps taxes. The rule also ensures that the testator's property passes to her beneficiaries rather than those of the named beneficiary. And finally, the rule may avoid difficult evidentiary questions that arise in connection with simultaneous death (discussed further below).

As discussed below, if the beneficiary does not survive the decedent or is deemed not to have survived, the bequest will pass to alternate beneficiaries under the terms of the will or the antilapse statute. In the case of will substitutes, the alternate beneficiaries designated in the instrument itself will take the property.

UPC §2-702. Requirement of Survival by 120 Hours.

(a) [Requirement of Survival by 120 Hours Under Probate Code.] For the purposes of this Code, except as provided in subsection (d), an individual who is not established by clear and convincing evidence to have survived an event, including the death of another individual, by 120 hours is deemed to have predeceased the event.

(b) [Requirement of Survival by 120 Hours under Governing Instrument.] Except as provided in subsection (d), for purposes of a provision of a governing instrument that relates to an individual surviving an event, including the death of another individual, an individual who is not established by clear and convincing evidence to have survived the event by 120 hours is deemed to have predeceased the event.

(c) [Co-owners with Right of Survivorship; Requirement of Survival by 120 Hours.] [if there are more than two co-owners and it is not established by clear and convincing evidence that at least one of them survived the others by 120 hours, the property passes in the proportion that one bears to the whole number of co-owners.]

(d) [Exceptions.] Survival by 120 hours is not required if:

(1) the governing instrument contains language dealing explicitly with simultaneous deaths or deaths in a common disaster and that language is operable under the facts of the case;

(2) the governing instrument expressly indicates that an individual is not required to survive an event, including the death of another individual, by any specified period or expressly requires the individual to survive the event by a specified period; but survival of the event or the specified period must be established by clear and convincing evidence;

As subsection (d) indicates, a testator who wants to override the 120-hour rule must specify the alternate period required for survival. It is common to use a period of 30, 60 or 90 days. The following is an example of such a provision:

For purposes of this will, if any beneficiary in fact survives me but dies within 90 days following my death, he/she shall be deemed to have predeceased me.

UPC §2-702(b) also applies to will substitutes.[6] Thus, a named beneficiary of the decedent's life insurance policy that requires the beneficiary to survive must survive the decedent by 120 hours in order to receive the proceeds of the life insurance policy. Similarly, beneficiaries under a will substitute like an inter vivos trust must survive the grantor by 120 hours in order to take their interest under the trust, if the trust requires "survival."

i.   Simultaneous Death

While very rare, occasionally two people die in a common disaster, and it cannot be forensically determined who died first. This was true "simultaneous death" under the common law.

> **Example:**   Tai Shan and Ling Ling are married. They are on a plane to Hawaii for a vacation when the plane crashes in the Pacific Ocean. It is not possible for the rescue operation to recover any remains, and it is thus impossible to determine who died first. Tai Shan's will leaves all of his property to Ling Ling and Ling Ling's will leaves all of her property to Tai Shan. This is true simultaneous death.

In those jurisdictions that have adopted the 120-hour rule, true simultaneous death results in a failure of each person to survive the other and the bequest to that person lapses. In some cases, this has a negative tax result. If Tai Shan and Ling Ling are spouses, they may lose the opportunity to use both spouses' unified credits for estate tax purposes. In order to hedge against such an event, estate planning lawyers often include a provision in the will which provides that in the event of simultaneous death, the wealthier spouse shall be deemed to have died first. This has historically resulted in a more favorable tax outcome for the combined estates and maximizes the amount that will likely end up in the hands of the couple's children, if they have any. Under the tax legislation enacted in December 2010, which we explore in Chapter 14, this may be less important given the portability of unified credits as between spouses.

Note that the Uniform Simultaneous Death Act (1993) (USDA) and UPC §2-702 (to which the USDA conforms) adopt a broader view of simultaneous death than the common law. They extend the rule to those cases where it can be determined that one person survived the other but the survival time was "insubstantial."[7] In such a case, if the two decedents are

---

6. Note that the same rule applies in intestacy under UPC §2-104. If a decedent dies intestate and it cannot be proved by clear and convincing evidence that the heir did not survive the decedent by 120 hours, the heir is treated as having predeceased the decedent for purposes of intestate succession, homestead allowance and exempt property.

7. Those states that have adopted UPC §2-702 need not adopt the Uniform Simultaneous Death Act since §2-702 incorporates the same principles as the USDA. The drafters of

co-owners of property and it is not established by clear and convincing evidence that one survived the other by 120 hours, then one-half of the property passes as if one had survived by 120 hours and one-half as if the other had survived by 120 hours.

> **Example:**   Tai Shan and Ling Ling owned a beach house in Malibu as joint tenants with right of survivorship. In the example above in which the plane went down in the Pacific, one-half of the house in Malibu would pass to Tai Shan's alternate beneficiaries and the other half would pass to Ling Ling's alternate beneficiaries. Tai Shan and Ling Ling's wills provided that all of their assets should pass to the other but in the event that the other did not survive, then to their undergraduate colleges. Tai Shan graduated from Stanford while Ling Ling graduated from Berkeley. Thus, one-half of the Malibu house would pass to Stanford and the other half to Berkeley.

NOTES AND QUESTIONS

1.   *Strategic planning?* From our discussion above, it is clear that "death" or the moment thereof is a more malleable concept than most people think. Given that idea, do you think it would have been ethical to keep a testator alive long enough to have lived into the year 2010 when the federal estate tax "disappeared" for the year?

2.   *The 120-hour rule.* For a recent discussion of the pros and cons of the 120-hour rule, see Victoria J. Haneman & Jennifer M. Booth, *120 Hours Until the Consistent Treatment of Simultaneous Death Under the California Probate Code*, 34 Nova L. Rev. 449 (2010).

PROBLEM

Tom and Stella were married. While driving together, Tom and Stella were in a serious car crash. Tom died immediately. Stella remained in a coma after the crash. Under the following factual scenarios, would Stella inherit from Tom if his will provides, "I leave all of my estate to my wife, Stella"?

   a.   Stella survived the coma but she suffered a significant brain injury and had a conservator appointed on her behalf.
   b.   Stella died after two days in the coma.
   c.   Stella died after two months in the coma.
   d.   Stella died after two weeks in the coma but she had met the definition of "brain dead" the entire time. Her daughter from her first

---

the USDA note that it is "appropriate for enactment in those states that have not enacted §1-107 . . . and §2-702 of the Uniform Probate Code."

marriage, Ella, had refused to agree to the withdrawal of the life support systems prior to that time.

E.   DISCLAIMERS AND "DEEMED DEATH"

An intended beneficiary may wish to renounce, or "disclaim," all or a part of the bequest to which he is entitled. A "disclaimant" is *deemed* to have predeceased the decedent, and the interest to which the disclaimant would otherwise have been entitled (the "disclaimed interest") passes as if the decedent died before the testator (even though he did not actually die.)

The disclaimant may not specify who will take the property after he disclaims it. It must pass to the person or persons who would have taken if the disclaiming beneficiary had died before the testator. If the disclaimant tries to exercise any control over where the property goes, this will disqualify the disclaimer and interfere with the reason for disclaiming the property, which is often to avoid having the property included in the disclaimant's estate for tax purposes and to avoid triggering a gift tax on the transfer.

Note that the disclaimant is not considered dead for purposes of determining the interest to which she is entitled, but is considered dead for purposes of determining who gets the property. Therefore, the beneficiary of the disclaimed interest will be either (1) a taker in default if one is named in the will, (2) a descendant of the disclaimant per the substitute gift rules of UPC §2-603(b) if a taker in default is not named and the antilapse rules apply or (3) others consistent with UPC §2-604 if the gift lapses (a pre-residuary gift passes to the residuary beneficiaries, a residuary gift passes to the remaining residuary beneficiaries, if any, or via intestacy, if there are no other residuary beneficiaries).

> **Example:**   Tammy's will leaves all of her property to her sister, Susan, if she survives her, and if not, then to her brother, Bill. When Tammy dies, Susan has become the CEO of a very successful high tech company and does not need the inheritance that Tammy has left her. Bill, however, is a struggling artist. If Susan disclaims the property, then the property will pass as if Susan died immediately before Tammy. Since Tammy's will provides that the property shall go to Bill under these circumstances, Bill will receive the inheritance. If Tammy's will did not name Bill as the alternate taker and if Susan did not survive Tammy, the property would pass to Susan's descendants per the antilapse statute, and if she had none, to Tammy's heirs in intestacy.

Disclaimers are important post-death or "post-mortem" estate planning tools. They can minimize taxation and can be used to avoid the beneficiary's creditors. Thus, the UPC has a separate part, Part 11, dedicated to the rules that govern disclaimers. It incorporates the Uniform Disclaimer of Property Interests Act (1999). We have discussed disclaimers of property received under a will, but a beneficiary of property under a will substitute can also disclaim the interest. The following sections of Part 11 present the requirements for a valid disclaimer:

UPC §2-1105. Power to Disclaim; General Requirements; When Irrevocable.

(a) A person may disclaim, in whole or part, any interest in or power over property, including a power of appointment. A person may disclaim the interest or power even if its creator imposed a spendthrift provision or similar restriction on transfer or a restriction or limitation on the right to disclaim . . . .

(c) To be effective, a disclaimer must be in a writing or other record, declare the disclaimer, describe the interest or power disclaimed, be signed by the person making the disclaimer, and be delivered or filed in the manner provided in Section 2-1112. . . .

(d) A partial disclaimer may be expressed as a fraction, percentage, monetary amount, term of years, limitation of a power, or any other interest or estate in the property . . . .

(f) A disclaimer made under this Part is not a transfer, assignment, or release.

UPC §2-1106. Disclaimer of Interest in Property.

. . . (b) Except for a disclaimer governed by Section 7 or 8, the following rules apply to a disclaimer of an interest in property:

. . . (2) The disclaimed interest passes according to any provision in the instrument creating the interest providing for the disposition of the interest, should it be disclaimed, or of disclaimed interests in general.

(3) If the instrument does not contain a provision described in paragraph (2), the following rules apply:

. . . (B) If the disclaimant is an individual, except as otherwise provided in subparagraphs (C) and (D), the disclaimed interest passes as if the disclaimant had died immediately before the time of distribution.

UPC §2-1113. When Disclaimer Barred or Limited.

> . . . (b). A disclaimer of an interest in property is barred if any of the following events occur before the disclaimer becomes effective:
> (1) the disclaimant accepts the interest sought to be disclaimed;
> (2) the disclaimant voluntarily assigns, conveys, encumbers, pledges, or transfers the interest sought to be disclaimed or contracts to do so; . . .

Note that federal tax law also contains a provision regarding what is necessary for a valid disclaimer, the tax "qualified disclaimer" under IRC §2518. While it may seem counter-intuitive for someone to turn down an inheritance, there may be good reasons for doing so. Disclaimers may accomplish positive tax results or avoid negative ones. For example, disclaimers avoid the multiple estate or gift transfer tax consequences that result if property is conveyed one generation at a time. In addition, the judicious use of a disclaimer may help take advantage of the unified credit that allows significant amounts of wealth to be transferred without estate tax consequences. The tax uses of disclaimers and qualification under IRC §2518 are discussed further in Chapter 14.

Example: In his will, Charles leaves his property to his child, Roberta. The property is included in Charles's gross estate and, assuming Charles has a taxable estate, the estate will have to pay tax on the property. This cannot be avoided. If Roberta were to receive the inheritance and at some point give it to her children, the property received from Charles will be taxed a second time, this time to Roberta or her estate. To avoid the tax imposed on the transfer of property from Roberta to her children, Roberta could disclaim her inheritance. If she did so, the property would pass to her children, and it would be treated as if it came directly from Charles.

Disclaimers also have non-tax benefits. They may be used to rewrite the plan of disposition to more accurately reflect the plan of the testator. They can also be used for asset protection. For example, a beneficiary who has significant debt might disclaim the inheritance, with the property passing to a child of the beneficiary, rather than having the property go to the beneficiary's creditors. This may be effective to defeat creditors' rights and some courts have not treated this as a fraudulent conveyance because the disclaimant is treated as if he were dead and therefore his interest never arose. *In re Colacci's Estate*, 549 P.2d 1096 (Colo. App. 1976). A contrary result, though, occurs when federal tax obligations are involved. *Drye v. United States*, 528 U.S. 49 (1999) (cannot avoid tax lien by disclaimer). The effect of a disclaimer on government services is mixed. The majority view is exemplified by *Tannler v. Wis. Dep't of Health & Soc. Serv.*, 564 N.W.2d 735 (Wis. 1997) (the disclaimed assets are counted toward the eligibility requirements for Medicaid benefits); the minority view by *Estate of Kirk*, 591 N.W.2d 630 (Iowa 1999) (disclaimer was allowed to defeat government from collecting Medicaid claims).

The procedural requirements for an effective disclaimer are, in most regards, similar under state law and Internal Revenue Code §2518. They require that (i) the disclaimer be in writing and delivered to the personal representative or other person holding the property before the transfer if the property will transfer under a will substitute, (ii) the disclaimed interest pass without direction of the disclaimant and (iii) the disclaimant may not have received any benefits from property disclaimed nor received consideration in money or money's worth, directly or indirectly, from anyone in exchange for the disclaimer.

> **Example:** Lisetta's mother, Marni, had a stock portfolio valued at $2,000,000, which her will left to Lisetta's father. Marni's will also provided that her entire estate was to go to her husband, but if he predeceased her, it would go to Lisetta. When Marni died, Lisetta's father disclaimed the $2,000,000 stock portfolio in writing and timely delivered the disclaimer to the personal representative. Thus, when Lisetta's father disclaimed the stock, it went directly to Lisetta per the terms of the will — meeting test (ii) of IRC §2518. Through the disclaimer, Lisetta's father has avoided making a taxable gift to her by accepting the inheritance and then giving it to her. If Lisetta's father had ordered the brokerage house to liquidate some of the stock and had benefited from it, it would invalidate the disclaimer per (iii) above.

To have an effective federal tax law disclaimer, written notice must be filed within nine months of the decedent's death.

PROBLEM

David died on January 12, 2010. David and his second wife, Sara, had two children, Beryl and Carlene. David also had a child, Aniken, age 31, from his previous marriage. David is survived by Sara, Aniken, Beryl and Carlene. David's probate estate is worth $2,000,000. David's will bequeaths $100,000 to each of his children and the rest of his property to Sara.

    a.   Aniken died three days after David died, as the result of the same car accident.

        i.   What share of the estate goes to Aniken?

        ii.   If David had owned $200,000 worth of real estate with Aniken as joint tenants with rights of survivorship, how would the property be distributed?

b.   Sara wishes to disclaim all interests she has in the estate.
  i.   In what manner and by when must she do so?
  ii.   What is the effect of the disclaimer? In other words, what happens to the portion devised to Sara?
  iii.   Sara would like one-third of the interest she is disclaiming to go to her siblings. How can she accomplish that?

F. EXERCISES

Ademption, Exoneration, Accessions, Satisfaction, Lapse

Our client, Marie Simon, has asked us to draft her will. Marie is not married and has no children. Her parents are deceased. Her family consists of the following persons:

- Her sister, Natalie Simon, who is married but has no children;
- Her brother, Otis Simon, who is married and has one child, Ophelia Simon; and
- Rachel Wells, Sarah Wells and Trevor Wells, the children of her deceased sister, Patricia Simon Wells.

All of the nieces and the nephew are minors. You should assume that Natalie may have children in the future and Otis may have more children. At our first meeting with Marie, she told us the following:

- She has a coral necklace that belonged to her mother. She wants to leave the necklace to Natalie. She also has a gold pocket watch that belonged to her father. She wants to leave the gold pocket watch to Trevor, her only nephew. She wants to leave the rest of her jewelry to her sister or her nieces.
- She wants to leave a painting by local artist Emmet Sanchez to her friend, Frances Martinez.
- She wants to leave her other tangible personal property to Natalie and Otis, equally.
- Marie owns a rental house in Seaside, Oregon. The house was recently appraised for $250,000. Marie wants to give the house to Natalie.
- Marie owns 1,000 shares of HappyCo stock (worth about $250,000, but expected to keep going up). This was stock she inherited from an uncle. The company started as a family business but recently went public. Marie wants to leave the stock to Otis or to Ophelia if Otis dies before Marie.
- Marie wants to leave the rest of her property in equal shares to Natalie, Otis and to Patricia's children.

Instructions:

Draft dispositive provisions for Marie's will. The rest of Marie's will follows these instructions, and you do not need to retype those portions of the will. If you do not have all the facts you need, make reasonable assumptions as to what Marie would want. Do not take the above statements as precise instructions as to how to draft. The above statements reflect the client's wishes, but underlying assumptions are unstated. In general, Marie wants to give the property to her family. In general, she wants to give each sibling an equal share of the estate, although the two living siblings get more than the children of the deceased sibling (due to the specific bequests). You need to think about how to take her statements of what goes to whom and draft dispositions that creates reasonably equal shares for the three siblings (with Rachel, Sarah and Trevor taking Patricia's share).

Be sure to consider issues of lapse, ademption, exoneration, accessions and satisfaction. You can assume that Marie will have adequate assets to make all bequests and you need not consider abatement. Be sure to identify any specific bequests adequately.

In drafting, be consistent with your language. That is, if you say "to X, if he survives me," then use the same language for Y, rather than saying "to Y, if Y is living on the date of my death." Be careful when you use pronouns — watch the prior antecedent and do not use the plural pronoun "they" for a singular noun (use "he or she" if necessary, or use the noun if possible).

WILL OF MARIE SIMON

I, Marie Simon, of Eugene, Oregon, hereby revoke all prior wills and codicils and make this my Will as follows:

ARTICLE I

I give . . .

[The articles you draft will be inserted here.]

ARTICLE —

APPOINTMENT OF PERSONAL REPRESENTATIVE

A.   Personal Representative. I nominate my sister, Natalie Simon, as Personal Representative of this Will. If for any reason Natalie Simon fails or ceases to act as Personal Representative, I name my brother, Otis Simon, as Personal Representative of this Will.

B.   Waiver of Bond. To the extent allowed by law, I direct that either of the fiduciaries named above, or their successors, shall be entitled to serve without bond or other undertaking and without reporting or accounting to any court.

C.   Payment of Debts, Expenses and Taxes. I direct the Personal Representative to pay out of the residue of my estate passing hereunder, without apportionment, all expenses of my last illness, funeral, burial and administration of my estate, and all estate, inheritance, transfer and succession taxes (including any interest and penalties thereon) which become due by reason of my death, without reimbursement or contribution from any person.

D.   I give the Personal Representative the following powers and discretions, in each case to be exercisable without court order:

[The powers of the personal representative would be listed here. You do not need to list them.]

ARTICLE —

DISTRIBUTIONS TO MINORS

If any beneficiary hereunder has not attained age twenty-one (21) at the time any property becomes distributable to him or to her, such property shall vest in such beneficiary, but the Personal Representative may distribute any part or all of such property to a custodian for such beneficiary under any Uniform Transfers to Minors Act (and the Personal Representative shall not be liable for any act or failure to act of any such custodian), or to a parent or adult relative of the beneficiary, or to any person having custody of the beneficiary, as trustee, against such person's receipt and upon such person's written undertaking to hold the property in trust, to use the property for the benefit of the beneficiary, and at the time the beneficiary attains age twenty-one (21) to deliver the then remaining property to the beneficiary. The distribution to such a custodian or such receipt and written undertaking shall discharge the Personal Representative.

ARTICLE —

MISCELLANEOUS

A.   Table of Contents, Titles, Captions. The table of contents, titles and captions used in this instrument are for convenience of reference only and shall not be construed to have any legal effect.

B.   Interpretation. The laws of the state of Oregon shall govern with respect to the validity and interpretation of this instrument.

IN WITNESS WHEREOF, I execute this Will on the _____ day of _____, 20__.

_____
Marie Simon

The foregoing instrument, consisting of _____ (__) pages, this page included, was on this _____ day of _____, 20__, signed by Marie Simon who declared this to be her last will and testament; we saw the testator sign such instrument and at her request and in her presence and in the presence of each other have signed our names as attesting witnesses. At the time this will was signed, we believe the testator was of sound mind and memory and was acting voluntarily.

[signature lines for 2 witnesses — you do not need to provide]

[self proving affidavit — you do not need to provide]

APPENDIX A

LAST WILL AND TESTAMENT OF MARJORIE M. BLACK

I, Marjorie M. Black (formerly known as Marjorie M. Green) revoke any prior wills and codicils made by me and declare this to be my will. Specifically, I revoke the wills dated June 15, 1989 and December 2, 1995 and all codicils thereto. If for any reason this will is not valid and is not probated, I declare it is my intention to revive the June 15, 1989 will, a copy of which can be found in the same safe deposit box in which this will is located.

ARTICLE 1 — FAMILY INFORMATION

1.1   I am presently not married. Any references in this will to my ex-spouse refer to Dr. Howard Scott Black. I hereby direct that the terms of this will are not to be affected by my remarriage, should that occur. My children now living are Robert Black, born June 22, 1964, Sara Black Blue, born October 15, 1968, and Joel Black, born September 21, 1970. Any reference in my will to my children is to such children as well as any children subsequently born to or legally adopted by me. Any reference in my will to my issue is to my children and their issue.

ARTICLE 2 — SPECIFIC AND GENERAL GIFTS

2.1   SPECIFIC BEQUESTS.

(a)   I give the sum of $10,000 to my son, Robert Black, and his heirs. I have specifically excluded Robert and his heirs from all other provisions of this will and it is my intent that they take no other benefit from my estate. I do this not for any lack of affection for my son, but because I believe that he and his heirs already have been adequately provided for by me and by his father and his family.

(b)   I give the engraved gold pocket watch and chain which I inherited from our grandfather to my brother, Jerome Green, if he survives me, or if not, to my cousin, Walter Pickett Clayton, who now resides in Buffalo, New York. I ask the recipient to continue the family tradition that the watch and chain be devised in a direct line of descent from the original maker of the watch, our common great grandfather, John Pickett Clayton.

(c)   I give the sum of $25,000 to my sister, Hedy Redd, if she survives me, on the further condition that prior to receipt of this gift she shall establish to the satisfaction of my executor that she has refrained from smoking tobacco for a period of at least one full year. If this condition is not met within five years after the date of my death, this gift shall lapse and be distributed as a part of my residuary estate.

(d) I give my collection of scrapbooks, diaries, papers, medals, uniforms, weapons and other memorabilia relating to the Vietnam War to George P. Petarsky, who now resides in Atlanta, Georgia, in deep appreciation for his wisdom.

(e) I give my collection of twenty-one (21) autographed major league homerun baseballs to my stepson, Cory Lewis, if he survives me. I hope he will remember the many great afternoons we've shared in ballparks all across the country and that he will continue to build the collection together with his own children.

(f) I give $50,000 to whoever is awarded the Nobel Science Prize in the year prior to my death if such recipient is an American.

2.2 PERSONAL EFFECTS.

Except as otherwise provided in a memorandum left at the time of my death pursuant to Article 2.3, I give all my household goods, personal effects, and other articles of tangible personal property, except such property used in any business in which I may have any interest, together with any insurance policies covering such property and claims under such policies, to my children, to be divided between them as they may agree, or, in the absence of agreement within three months after the appointment of my personal representative, then as my personal representative may determine to achieve a fair and equitable division of said property. Notwithstanding the foregoing, should my personal representative determine that it would not be in the best interest of my children to receive possession of any item of such property, my personal representative may sell such item and add the proceeds to my residuary estate. All reasonable expenses of storage, packing, shipping, delivery, insurance or of sale shall be paid as an expense of administration

2.3 SEPARATE MEMORANDUM.

I reserve the right to give such property as specified in Article 2.1 in accordance with any memorandum directing their disposition signed by me or in my handwriting which I may leave at my death.

ARTICLE 3 — RESIDUARY ESTATE

3.1   DEFINITION.

All of the rest and remainder of the property which I shall own at my death, including property referred to above that has not been properly disposed of and any property over which I might have an unexercised general power of appointment, and after payment of expenses and taxes which are paid pursuant to this will, shall be referred to as my "residuary estate."

3.2   GIFT TO ISSUE.

If both my children survive me and both have reached the age of forty-five years, I give my residuary estate outright in equal shares to each of them. Alternatively, if none of the persons mentioned as possible trustees in Article 5.2 below are alive at my death and I have not named a successor trustee in a codicil, I give my residuary estate in equal shares to my children or, if one or both should predecease me, equally to their issue, per stirpes. If one child has reached the age of forty-five years and the other is not living at my death, I give the deceased child's interest in equal shares to his/her issue, if any, pursuant to the schedule in Article 4.2, but if that deceased child has no issue, I give my entire residuary estate to my surviving child.

3.3   GIFT IN TRUST.

If I am survived by issue and Article 3.2 does not apply, I give my residuary estate to the trustee, acting at the time of my death, of the Marjorie M. Black Revocable "Living" Trust, created by the agreement dated _____, between me as settlor and trustee, as the trust shall exist at the date of my death, to be added to and administered in all respects as property of the trust. I expressly direct that the trust shall not be considered to be a testamentary trust. If and only if no such trust is in effect at my death, then I give my residuary estate to my trustee subsequently named in Article 5.2, in trust. Such estate, together with any other sums payable directly to the trustee, shall be referred to in this will as the Residuary Testamentary Trust and shall be administered in accordance with the provisions of Article 4.

3.4   REMOTE CONTINGENT DISPOSITION.

If no issue of mine survive me, I give my entire estate, both the specific gifts in Article 2 and the residuary estate in this Article 3, in equal shares to the then-living children of my sister, Hedy Redd, and my brother, Jerome Green. If any of such children are not living at my death but they are survived by issue, the issue shall be entitled to their parent's share per stirpes in equal amounts.

3.5   ELECTIVE SHARE.

Should I remarry and should my husband exercise his statutory right after my death to take an elective-share of my augmented estate, then all gifts to him or for his benefit under this will shall be void and my estate shall be distributed as if my husband had not survived me.

ARTICLE 4 — RESIDUARY TESTAMENTARY TRUST

4.1   DIVISION IN EQUAL SHARES.

The Residuary Testamentary Trust, if it is created pursuant to Article 3.3, shall be divided into equal separate shares for the benefit of my children, if they are living at the time of my death, or if either or both is not then living, into equal separate shares for the benefit of the then-living issue of my children, per stirpes. If either child is not living at the time of my death and leaves no issue, that child's share is to be held in trust for the benefit of my remaining child or, if not then living, in equal shares for that remaining child's issue, per stirpes. Except as just mentioned, the share of one child or issue is not to be invaded in any way for the benefit of another child or issue.

4.2   INCOME AND PRINCIPAL DISTRIBUTIONS.

The income and principal of each child's or issue's share, as the case may be, shall be distributed as follows.

(A)   The Trustee shall distribute to or for the benefit of each child or issue as much of the net income and principal as shall be necessary or appropriate, in the sole discretion of the trustee, for such child's or issue's medical care, support, maintenance, education or opportunities in business, house purchasing and the like, without the necessity of equalization among them at any time. Without limiting the absolute discretion of the trustee, I suggest the trustee should be receptive to all reasonable requests of my child or issue but should also consider all funds and other resources available to him/her, including income from other trust funds, before making a distribution to a child or issue. Any net income not distributed shall be accumulated and added to principal.

(B)   When (i) each child reaches the ages listed below (and for the entire five year period thereafter) or (ii) when he/she would have reached that age if he/she had lived, or (iii) if upon my death the child has already then reached such age (or would have reached such age if he/she had lived), my child or their issue, as the case may be, shall have the right to withdraw the following percentages of the balance in their share. The trustee should convey my wish to the beneficiaries that they not squander their inheritance and, as such, should be discouraged from exercising their power to withdraw except when truly necessary.

AGE	FRACTION
40	1/2
45	all

(C)   In the event of the death of a child prior to complete distribution of such child's share, all property presently subject to the deceased child's power to withdraw shall be included within his/her estate, unless such child directs otherwise. However, subsequent powers to withdraw, if any, shall be exercisable by such child's issue living on the date of the distribution in equal shares per stirpes in the same manner as would have been the case if their parent were still living.

(D)   If the deceased child dies without issue, all property presently subject to the deceased child's power to withdraw shall be included within his/her estate, unless such child directs otherwise. However, subsequent powers to withdraw, if any, shall be exercisable by my remaining child, if living, his/her issue if not and by those persons entitled to the remote contingent interests specified in Article 3.4 if I have no living issue.

(E)   Except as otherwise provided herein, if any income or principal becomes payable to any beneficiary who is a minor, or who in the sole judgment of the fiduciary responsible for making such distribution is legally incapacitated, then such amount shall vest in such beneficiary, but shall be held in a separate trust for such beneficiary by my trustee during such minority or incapacity; and my trustee shall apply as much of the income and principal as the trustee determines necessary for the health, maintenance, education and support in reasonable comfort of such beneficiary. Such amounts may be applied directly, or may be paid to such beneficiary's guardian or conservator, to said beneficiary's custodian under the Uniform Gift to Minor's Act or Uniform Transfers to Minor's Act, or to any person or organization for the benefit of such minor or incapacitated person. Any amounts not so expended shall be retained by the trustee and paid to the beneficiary upon such beneficiary's reaching the age of majority or upon termination of the incapacity as the case may be, or earlier if trustee deems it advisable. In the event the beneficiary dies while still a minor or while still incapacitated, any principal and income shall be paid over to such beneficiary's estate, unless otherwise provided. For purposes of this instrument, the term "minor" shall mean a person under the age of twenty-one (21) years, any statute to the contrary notwithstanding.

(F) No interest in income or principal shall be assignable by, or available to anyone having a claim against, a beneficiary before actual payment to the beneficiary.

(G) The trustee shall have the power to make payments of any income or principal for a beneficiary (i) to such beneficiary; (ii) to the individual, other than the settlor, who is, in the judgment of the trustee, in proper charge of such beneficiary, regardless of whether there is a court order to that effect; (iii) in the case of a minor, to a custodian, other than the settlor, named by the trustee to be held under the Uniform Transfers to Minors Act; or (iv) by distributing or applying any part or all thereof for a beneficiary's benefit or on a beneficiary's behalf; and in every such event distribution may be made without any necessity to account to, qualify in or seek the approval of any court, and any such distributions made in good faith shall be deemed proper and shall be a complete release of the trustee therefore.

ARTICLE 5 — DESIGNATION AND SUCCESSION OF FIDUCIARIES

5.1   PERSONAL REPRESENTATIVE.

I nominate my ex-spouse, Dr. Howard Black as my personal representative. If Howard Black fails or ceases to act as my personal representative, I nominate my brother, Jerome Green as the personal representative of my estate. If Jerome Green fails or ceases to act as my personal representative, I nominate my brother-in-law, Joel Redd as my next successor personal representative. If Joel Redd fails or ceases to be my personal representative, I nominate my cousin, Margo Heilweil Gordon, as my next successor personal representative.

5.2   TRUSTEE OF THE RESIDUARY TESTAMENTARY TRUST.

I nominate my ex-spouse, Dr. Howard Black as the trustee of the Residuary Testamentary Trust. If Howard Black fails or ceases to act as my trustee, I nominate my brother, Jerome Green as the trustee of the Residuary Testamentary Trust. If Jerome Green fails or ceases to act as my trustee, I nominate my brother-in-law Joel Redd as the next successor trustee of the Residuary Testamentary Trust. If Joel Redd fails or ceases to act as my trustee, I nominate Margo Heilweil Gordon as the next successor trustee of the Residuary Testamentary Trust.

5.3   GUARDIAN.

I appoint my ex-spouse as guardian of each child or issue of mine for whom such appointment becomes necessary. If my ex-spouse fails or ceases to act as guardian or to do so would represent a conflict of interest, I appoint as guardian the individual or individuals designated in a separate writing signed by me in the presence of two witnesses. If no such separate writing exists, I appoint Margo Heilweil Gordon as guardian of each child of mine for whom such appointment becomes necessary.

5.4   CONSERVATOR.

I nominate the guardian of any minor child or issue of mine as conservator of the estate of such child if such appointment becomes necessary.

5.5   APPOINTMENT OF CO-TRUSTEE OR SUBSTITUTE FIDUCIARY.

If for any reason my fiduciary is unwilling or unable to act as to any property of any trust herein or with respect to any provision of my will, my fiduciary may designate in writing a person to act as co-trustee or co-personal representative as to such property or with respect to any provision, and may revoke any such designation at will. Each such co-fiduciary shall exercise all fiduciary powers granted in this instrument. Any co-fiduciary may resign at any time by written notice to the fiduciary who appointed him/her. When a co-trusteeship situation exists, each trustee may act without the concurrence and approval of the other.

5.6   RIGHTS OF SUCCESSOR FIDUCIARIES.

Any successor fiduciary at any time serving hereunder shall have all of the title, rights, powers, and privileges, and be subject to all of the obligations and duties, both discretionary and ministerial, as herein and hereby given and granted to the original fiduciary hereunder, and shall be subject to any restrictions herein imposed upon the original fiduciary.

5.7   RESIGNATION.

Any fiduciary may resign by giving written notice to settlor, if living, or to any adult beneficiary and to the parents of any minor beneficiary then eligible to receive current income, and to any other fiduciary then serving. Such written notice shall be delivered by hand or by certified mail and shall become effective upon the, acceptance of appointment by the successor fiduciary.

5.8 REMOVAL OF FIDUCIARY.

Any fiduciary may be removed, without cause, by settlor, or if settlor is deceased or incapacitated, by a majority of the beneficiaries then eligible to receive income, by giving written notice to such fiduciary and to any other fiduciary then serving, effective in accordance with the provisions of the notice. In the case of a minor or incapacitated beneficiary, the conservator of the estate or, if none, the guardian of the person of such beneficiary may act on behalf of such. A trustee shall be removed if the trustee's personal physician in consultation with Margo Heilweil Gordon, Hedy Redd or Jerome Green (or the court) determines they are disabled or incapable of exercising reasonable decision-making ability. If the trustee is deemed to be incapacitated or disabled, the trustee shall be removed as trustee and the next successor shall automatically, without order of the court, assume the role of trustee.

5.9 REPLACEMENT OF FIDUCIARIES.

If any fiduciary shall cease to serve for whatever reason, a majority of the beneficiaries then eligible to receive income, may designate a successor fiduciary. In the case of a minor or incapacitated beneficiary, the conservator of the estate or, if none, the guardian of the person of such beneficiary may act on behalf of such beneficiary. If any vacancy is not filled within 30 days after the vacancy arises, then any beneficiary or his or her legal guardian or conservator may petition a court of competent jurisdiction to designate a successor fiduciary to fill such vacancy. By making such designation, such court shall not thereby acquire any jurisdiction over the trust, except to the extent necessary for making such designation. Any successor fiduciary designated hereunder may be an individual or may be a bank or trust company authorized to serve in such capacity under applicable federal or state law. If a fiduciary other than a family member, by blood or marriage, or someone not approved by a majority of the beneficiaries is appointed by the court, the fiduciary so appointed shall serve merely to fulfill the liquidation of the estate and/or trust to those beneficiaries then presently entitled to the property.

ARTICLE 6 — POWERS OF FIDUCIARIES

6.1 GRANT.

My fiduciaries may perform every act reasonably necessary to administer my estate and trust. Specifically, my fiduciaries may exercise the following powers: hold, retain, invest, reinvest and manage without diversification as to kind, amount, or risk of non-productivity in realty or personalty and without limitation by statute or rule of law, partition, sell, exchange, grant, convey, deliver, assign, transfer, lease, option, mortgage, pledge, abandon, borrow, loan, contract, distribute in cash or kind or partly in each at fair market value on the date of distribution, without requiring pro rata distribution of specific assets and without requiring pro rata allocation of the tax bases of such assets, hold in nominee form, continue businesses, carry out agreements, deal with itself, other fiduciaries and business organizations in which my personal representative may have an interest; establish reserves, release powers, and abandon, settle or contest claims; employ attorneys, accountants, custodians of the trust assets, other agents or assistants as deemed advisable to act with or without discretionary powers and compensate them and pay their expenses from income or principal or both. Despite the broad grant hereby given to the fiduciaries to invest the corpus of my estate as he or she believes appropriate, I request that he/she consider adopting the investment philosophy I have engaged in during my lifetime, i.e. to invest in no load mutual funds with a proven long-term record of appreciation in the range of 10% to 15% per annum. If the fiduciary continues with my investments and philosophy, he/she is to be held harmless for their performance by the beneficiaries.

The trustee shall have the specific power at the expense of the trust estate, to place all or any part of the securities or other property at any time held by the trustee in the care or custody of any bank or trust company as "custodian," and to employ investment counsel. While such securities or other property are in the custody of any such bank or trust company the trustee shall be under the obligation to inspect or to verify the same at least semi-annually but shall not be responsible for any loss or misapplication by such bank or trust company.

6.2   BROAD GRANT OF FIDUCIARIES' POWERS.

In addition to all of the above powers, my fiduciaries may exercise those powers set forth in the New Jersey statutes controlling his/her actions, as amended after the date of this instrument. I incorporate such Act, specifically Title 3B Chapters 4 and 20 or successor provisions, by reference and make it a part of this instrument.

6.3   EXONERATION OF FIDUCIARY.

No fiduciary shall be obligated to examine the accounts, records, or acts or in any way or manner be responsible for any act or omission to act on the part of any previous fiduciary or of the personal representative of settlor's probate estate. No fiduciary shall be liable to settlor or to any beneficiary for the consequences of any action taken by such fiduciary which would, but for the prior removal of such fiduciary or revocation of the trust created hereunder, have been a proper exercise by such fiduciary of the authority granted to fiduciary under this agreement, until actual receipt by such fiduciary of notice of such removal or revocation. Any fiduciary may acquire from the beneficiaries, or from their guardians or conservators, instruments in writing releasing such fiduciary from liability which may have arisen from the acts or omissions to act of such trustee, and indemnifying such fiduciary from liability therefore, and such instruments, if acquired from all then living beneficiaries, or from their guardians or conservators, shall be conclusive and binding upon all parties, born or unborn, who may have, or may in the future acquire, an interest in the trust.

6.4 DISTRIBUTION ALTERNATIVES.

My fiduciaries may make any payments under my will or trust: directly to the beneficiary; in any form allowed by applicable state law for gifts or transfers to minors or persons under disability; to the beneficiary's guardian, conservator, or caregiver for the benefit of the beneficiary; or by direct payment of the beneficiary's expenses. A receipt by the recipient of any such distribution, if such distribution is made in a manner consistent with the proper exercise of one's fiduciary duties hereunder, shall fully discharge my fiduciary.

6.5 CONSOLIDATION OF TRUSTS.

Trustee may consolidate and merge for all purposes a trust created hereunder with any other trust created by settlor or any other person at any time, which other trust contains substantially the same terms as this trust for the same beneficiary or beneficiaries and is being administered by the same trustee, and thereafter may administer such consolidated and merged trusts as one unit; but if such consolidation and merger does not appear desirable or feasible, trustee may consolidate the property of such trusts for purposes of investment and administration while retaining separate records and accounts for the separate trusts.

6.6 EARLY TERMINATION.

If trustee shall determine, in trustee's discretion, that a separate trust established hereunder has become uneconomical to administer, trustee may terminate such trust and, in such event, shall distribute the principal and any accrued and undistributed income to the then income beneficiary of the trust, and if at that time there is more than one such income beneficiary, then such trust property shall be distributed among such beneficiaries, by representation.

ARTICLE 7 — ADMINISTRATIVE PROVISIONS

7.1 NO BOND.

I direct that no fiduciary shall be required to give any bond in any jurisdiction and if, notwithstanding this direction, any bond is required by any law, statute, or rule of court, no sureties be required.

7.2 COMPENSATION.

Fiduciaries under this instrument are to serve without the commissions otherwise allowed for their "normal" responsibilities, as provided in N.J.S.A. 3B:18-13 to 3B:18-15 and 3B:18-24 to 3B:18-25. To the extent there are actual, out-of-pocket expenses incurred or extraordinary time involved, he/she shall be entitled to be reimbursed for expenses properly incurred and to reasonable compensation commensurate with services actually performed as provided in N.J.S.A. 3B:18-16 and 3B:18-29. To the extent the fiduciary must retain the professional services of an attorney, accountant or other professional to assist with the administration of this instrument, he/she is directed to get a fixed dollar estimate of the cost of the services or, if that is not practical, to monitor closely the number of hours expended by said professional in performing the retained services.

7.3 ANCILLARY FIDUCIARY.

In the event ancillary administration shall be required or desired and my domiciliary fiduciary is unable or unwilling to act as an ancillary fiduciary, my domiciliary fiduciary shall have the power to designate, compensate, and remove the ancillary fiduciary, which may either be a natural person or a corporation, and delegate to such ancillary fiduciary such powers granted to my original fiduciary as my fiduciary may deem proper, including the right to serve without bond or surety on bond, and the net proceeds of the ancillary estate shall be paid over to the domiciliary fiduciary.

ARTICLE 8 — TAX AND DEBT PROVISIONS

8.1 DEATH TAXES AND PAYMENT OF EXPENSES.

The trustees of the trust referred to in Article 3 of this will are authorized to pay my funeral and burial expenses and the unpaid cost of the perpetual care and maintenance of the burial plot in which I should be buried, claims against my estate, and expenses of estate administration. Accordingly, I direct my personal representative to consult with the trustees to determine the preferable source for payment of such amounts and which, if any, should be requested. I direct that all taxes imposed by reason of my death, with respect to property passing under my will or otherwise, including but not limited to estate, inheritance, gift, generation-skipping transfer, and income taxes, together with interest and penalties thereon, shall be apportioned among my beneficiaries in a manner which fairly reflects the share of my estate which each beneficiary receives, under this will or otherwise, taking into consideration (a) the value of all property includible in my estate for purposes of the tax imposed which passes to such beneficiaries other than pursuant to the provisions of this will; and (b) in the case of each beneficiary, the share of all such taxes which is attributable to the share of such property which passes to such beneficiary. My personal representative shall charge each such tax against the property which gives rise to liability for such tax, whether or not such property passes pursuant to the provisions of this will, and to the extent practicable, shall recover from the beneficiaries of property passing other than pursuant to the provisions of this will their allocable share of such tax, unless my personal representative in his/her discretion determines that the cost of recovery is greater than such recovery warrants. In no event shall any of such taxes be allocated to or paid from property which is not included in my gross estate for federal estate tax purposes or which qualifies for the federal estate tax marital or charitable deductions. Notwithstanding the foregoing, if any property is included in my gross estate for federal estate tax purposes under Section 2044 of the IRC, as amended, as "qualified terminable interest property," because of the previous allowance of a federal estate tax or gift tax marital deduction, my personal representative shall recover from the persons receiving such property, or, if applicable, from the trust estate of which such property comprises all or a part, that maximum amount to which my estate is entitled pursuant to Section 2207A of the IRC; and shall pay that portion of the federal estate tax imposed by reason of my death which is attributable to the inclusion of such property in my gross estate out of my residuary estate as an expense of administration, without apportionment and without right of contribution from any person.

8.2 TAX AND ADMINISTRATIVE ELECTIONS.

My personal representative may exercise any available elections under any applicable income, inheritance, estate, succession, or gift tax law. This authority specifically includes the power to select any alternate valuation date for death tax purposes and the power to determine whether any or all of the administration expenses of my estate are to be used as estate tax deductions or as income tax deductions, and no compensating adjustments need be made between income and principal as a result of such determinations unless my personal representative shall determine otherwise, in the discretion of my personal representative, or unless required by law. My personal representative shall not be liable to any beneficiary of my estate for tax consequences occasioned by reason of the exercise or non-exercise of any such elections or by reason of the allocation and distribution of property in kind in full or partial satisfaction of any beneficiary's interest in my estate.

ARTICLE 9 — GENERAL PROVISIONS AND DEFINITIONS

9.1   ADOPTED CHILDREN.

A child adopted by any person and the issue by blood or adoption of such child shall be considered the issue of such adopting person and of such person's ancestors if the adoption is by legal proceeding while the child is under the age of 21 years.

9.2   DESCENDANTS.

"Descendants" means only the legitimate children of the person designated and the legitimate lineal descendants of my children, and includes any person legally adopted prior to reaching age 18 and such adopted person's legitimate lineal descendants.

9.3   DISTRIBUTIONS TO DESCENDANTS.

Whenever a distribution is to be made to the descendants of any person, the property to be distributed shall be divided into as many equal shares as there are (1) living members of the nearest generation of descendants then living and (2) deceased members of that generation who leave descendants then living. Each living member of the nearest generation of descendants then living shall be allocated one share, and the share of each deceased member of that generation who leaves descendants then living shall be divided among his or her then living descendants in the same manner.

9.4   DISINHERITANCE.

I have, except as otherwise provided in this will, intentionally and with full knowledge, omitted to provide for my heirs who may be living at the time of my death, including any person or persons who may, after the date of this will, become my heir or heirs by reason of marriage or otherwise.

9.5   ADVANCEMENTS.

All advancements I have made, or may subsequently make, to any of my children shall be in addition to, and not in satisfaction of, any legacies or other benefit given them by my will.

9.6 APPLICABLE LAW.

The validity and construction of my will shall be determined by the laws of New Jersey.

9.7 CONSTRUCTION.

Unless the context requires otherwise, words denoting the singular may be construed as denoting the plural, and words of the plural may be construed as denoting the singular, and words of one gender may be construed as denoting the other gender as is appropriate.

9.8 HEADINGS AND TITLES.

The headings and paragraph titles are for reference only.

9.9 IRC.

IRC shall refer to the Internal Revenue Code of the United States. Any reference to specific sections of the IRC shall refer to any sections of like or similar import which replace the specific sections as a result of changes to the IRC made after the date of this instrument.

9.10 OTHER DEFINITIONS.

Except as otherwise provided in this instrument, terms shall be as defined in the New Jersey Probate Code (Title 3B) as amended after the date of this instrument and after my death, regardless of the state in which I may die domiciled.

9.11 SURVIVORSHIP.

For purposes of this will, if any beneficiary in fact survives me but dies within 180 days following my death, he/she shall be deemed to have predeceased me for purposes of this will.

9.12 DISCLAIMER.

At any time before receiving the benefits of an interest in property under this will, a beneficiary (or his/her personal representative in case of his/her prior death) may disclaim all or any part of that beneficiary's interest if done so in accordance with New Jersey law. After any disclaimer or release, the interest disclaimed or released shall be administered and distributed as if that beneficiary did not survive me.

9.13   PROTECTION AGAINST PERPETUITIES RULE.

All trusts created hereunder shall in any event terminate no later than 21 years after the death of the last survivor of the group composed of settlor, settlor's spouse, and those of settlor's issue living at settlor's death. The property held in trust shall be discharged of any trust and shall immediately vest in and be distributed to the persons then entitled to the income there-from in the proportions in which they are beneficiaries of the income, and for this purpose only, any person then eligible to receive discretionary payments of income of a particular trust shall be treated as being entitled to receive the income, and if more than one person are so treated, the group of such persons shall be treated as being entitled to receive such income as a class, to be distributed among them, by representation.

IN WITNESS WHEREOF, I have hereunto set my hand and seal this_____ day of _____, 20_.

_____(seal)
Marjorie M. Black

The foregoing Will was SIGNED, SEALED, PUBLISHED AND DECLARED by the said Testatrix as and for her Last Will and Testament, in the presence of us, who afterward, at her request, and in her presence and the presence of each other, all being present at the same time, have hereunto subscribed our names as witnesses.

_____   _____
_____   _____
_____   _____

Names   Addresses

I, Marjorie M. Black, sign my name to this instrument consisting of pages including this page on _____, 20 ___, and being first duly sworn, do hereby declare to the undersigned that I sign and execute this instrument as my last will and that I sign it willingly, that I execute it as my free and voluntary act for the purposes therein expressed, and that I am eighteen years of age or older, of sound mind, and under no constraint or undue influence.

_____
Testator/Testatrix

We, _____, _____ and_____ the witnesses, sign our names to this instrument, being first duly sworn, and do hereby declare to the undersigned authority that Marjorie M. Black signs and executes this instrument as his/her last will and that he/she signs it willingly (or willingly directs another to sign for him/her) and that he/she executes it as his/her free and voluntary act for the purposes therein expressed, and that each of us, in the presence and hearing of Marjorie M.

Black, hereby sign this will as witness to his/her signing, and that to the best of our knowledge Marjorie M. Black is eighteen years of age or older, of sound mind, and under no constraint or undue influence; we further declare that entirely prior to the foregoing there was exhibited to us an original copies of the Trusts referred to in the foregoing instrument, and that as so exhibited, the same were fully and finally executed.

_____   _____
Witness   Address

_____   _____
Witness   Address

_____   _____
Witness   Address

STATE OF NEW JERSEY   )
)ss.
COUNTY OF_____   )

   Subscribed, sworn to, and acknowledged before me by , and subscribed and sworn to before me by _____, _____ and_____, witnesses, on_____, 20____.

   Witness my hand and official seal.

   My commission expires,

                              _____
                              Notary Public

11 REVOKING THE WILL AND WILL CONTESTS

A. INTRODUCTION

Once the testator has created a valid will, it will become effective upon her death unless she revokes it or unless it is successfully challenged. The requirements to *revoke* a will are far less onerous than the formalities required to *create* a valid will in the first place. In this chapter we explore how a will, or a part of it, can be effectively revoked by the testator, which circumstances can effectuate a revocation even in the absence of testator action, and various doctrines that give the court guidance as to whether the provisions of a validly revoked (or ineffectively revoked) will can somehow be probated. We also discuss how some of the rules regarding revocation apply to will substitutes. Finally, we explore the most common theories for challenging a will.

B. REVOCATION BY SUBSEQUENT INSTRUMENT OR BY PHYSICAL ACT

American jurisprudence, with its emphasis on freedom of testation, has always recognized that wills are by their very nature revocable up until the moment the testator dies. The testator does not need to reserve the power to revoke the will in the instrument in order for it to remain revocable. A testator may revoke her will in one of two general ways — by documentary means or through a physical act.

> **Example:**   Lara executes a valid will in 2005 that leaves all of her property to the Red Cross. In 2010, she changes her mind and decides that she wants all of her property to go to the United Way. Lara executes a new will in 2010 that says, "I hereby revoke all prior wills." This documentary act effectively revokes the 2005 will. Alternatively, Lara could simply execute a new will that leaves all of her property to the United Way. That act revokes the 2005 will by inconsistency. Finally, Lara can tear up the 2005 will. That physical act effectively revokes the 2005 will.

The UPC codifies these methods of revocation. UPC §2-507 provides:

UPC §2-507. Revocation by Writing or by Act.

> (a) A will or any part thereof is revoked:
>
>   (1) by executing a subsequent will that revokes the previous will or part expressly or by inconsistency; or
>
>   (2) by performing a revocatory act on the will, if the testator performed the act with the intent and for the purpose of revoking the will or part or if another individual performed the act in the testator's conscious presence and by the testator's direction. For purposes of this paragraph, "revocatory act on the will" includes burning, tearing, canceling, obliterating, or destroying the will or any part of it. A burning, tearing, or canceling is a "revocatory act on the will," whether or not the burn, tear, or cancellation touched any of the words on the will.
>
> (b) If a subsequent will does not expressly revoke a previous will, the execution of the subsequent will wholly revokes the previous will by inconsistency if the testator intended the subsequent will to replace rather than supplement the previous will.
>
> (c) The testator is presumed to have intended a subsequent will to replace rather than supplement a previous will if the subsequent will makes a complete disposition of the testator's estate. If this presumption arises and is not rebutted by clear and convincing evidence, the previous will is revoked; only the subsequent will is operative on the testator's death.
>
> (d) The testator is presumed to have intended a subsequent will to supplement rather than replace a previous will if the subsequent will does not make a complete disposition of the testator's estate. If this presumption arises and is not rebutted by clear and convincing

> evidence, the subsequent will revokes the previous will only to the extent the subsequent will is inconsistent with the previous will; each will is fully operative on the testator's death to the extent they are not inconsistent.

1. Revocation by Subsequent Instrument

Express revocation. A testator may revoke a will by including an express revocation clause in a subsequent will. In the example above, Lara executed a new will that stated, "I hereby revoked all prior wills." That is an express revocation.

Implied revocation. Testators may also revoke a will by executing a subsequent will that is inconsistent with the first, either in whole or in part. In doing so, the testator need not include an express revocation clause in her new instrument. Instead, she may simply execute a new will that changes the disposition of the original will completely. In the example above, if Lara were to execute a second will that leaves her entire estate to the United Way, the second will would be presumed to have revoked the first will under most state statutes and the UPC. This is because the second will is completely inconsistent with the first and it disposes of all the property Lara owns. This presumption can only be rebutted by clear and convincing evidence.

If the second will is only partially inconsistent with the first, a presumption arises that the second will revokes only those provisions in the first will with which it is inconsistent. In essence, the second will is deemed to be a mere amendment or "codicil" to the first will. As with the presumption above, this presumption can only be rebutted by clear and convincing evidence to the contrary.

> **Example:** Assume that Lara's first will leaves her house to the Red Cross and the remainder of her property to the March of Dimes. She later drafts a new instrument that simply says, "I leave my house to the United Way." Only the provision regarding her house is revoked in Lara's first will. The second instrument is treated as a codicil to the first. The United Way will receive her house, with the March of Dimes receiving the rest of her property.

Cash Devises. Cash devises pose a more difficult interpretative problem for the court because it may be difficult to discern whether the cash bequest in a later will revokes the cash bequest in the first will or is in addition to it. Under the common law, bequests under codicils were presumed to be cumulative rather than substitutional.

Example: Lara's first will provided that $50,000 should go to her neighbor, Dakota. Her second will provides that $25,000 should go to Dakota. Under the common law presumption that such additions are cumulative rather than substitutional, the second amount would be added to the first and Dakota would receive $75,000.

The UPC does not establish a presumption one way or the other. If the court finds that the cash devises are inconsistent with one another, *i.e.*, if the court finds that the cash devise in the second will was intended to replace rather than supplement the cash devise in the first will, the beneficiary will take only the amount included in the second instrument. However, if the court finds that the cash devises are not inconsistent with one another and that the second will was meant to supplement the first will, then the beneficiary will receive the amounts in both the first and second instruments. The court may consider extrinsic evidence in divining revocatory intent.

PROBLEMS

1. Assume the following exordium was included in a will executed on November 1, 2010.

> *I, Marjorie M. Black, revoke any prior wills and codicils made by me and declare this to be my will. Specifically, I revoke the wills dated June 15, 1999, and December 2, 2005, and all codicils thereto.*

Does the statement adequately revoke prior wills? Does it state what would happen if the current will were to be invalidated for one reason or another? How would you draft such a provision?

2. In her will executed in 2000, Tallulah left her Picasso to her friend, Xavier, her Monet to her friend, Yolanda, $50,000 to her niece, Zelda, and the rest of her property to her children by right of representation.

    a. In a properly attested 2006 codicil, Tallulah left her Picasso to her friend, Paul, her Monet to her friend, Mary, and the rest of her property to her son, Carl, without stating explicitly that she was revoking the earlier bequests. Under the UPC, who gets what?

    b. Assume there had been no 2006 codicil. In a properly attested 2009 codicil, Tallulah left $75,000 to her niece, Zelda, without stating explicitly that she was revoking the earlier bequests. Under the UPC, how much would Zelda get and what kind of evidence would you use to divine Tallulah's intent with regard to this question?

2.   Revocation by Physical Act

A will may also be revoked by physical acts performed by the testator or another individual, if performed in the testator's conscious presence and at the testator's direction. The physical acts may be done to the will or on it. Whether the will is effectively revoked depends upon whether the testator undertook the act with the intent to revoke it. Accidental acts should not be given revocatory effect since they are not done with the proper intent. Complete revocation may be accomplished by doing something to the document, such as burning it, tearing it up or throwing it away.

> **Example:**   Lara's will provided that her house should go to the Red Cross, $50,000 should go to her neighbor, Dakota, and the residue of her estate should go to the March of Dimes. Lara subsequently changes her mind and tears up her will. That act effectively revokes the will because Lara performed the physical act of tearing with the clear intent to get rid of the will in its entirety.

A testator may also decide to revoke only a part of the will. She may do this by "cancelling" a provision, *i.e.*, by lining through a provision of the will.

> **Example:**   Lara's will provided that her house should go to the Red Cross, $50,000 should go to her neighbor, Dakota, and the residue of her estate should go to the March of Dimes. Lara subsequently changes her mind about the bequest to Dakota. She takes a pen and lines out the bequest. Lara has effectively revoked the bequest. This is a partial revocation of the will.

Note that the effect of the revocation in the example above is that the bequest to Dakota falls into the residue, by operation of UPC §2-604 and thus the amount given to the March of Dimes.

Lara may also decide to revoke the bequest to Dakota in order to give it to someone else. In order to do this, she may line out or "cancel" Dakota's name and write in the name of the new beneficiary, for example, "Benno." The problem here is that this act consists of two parts: It is both an act of revocation *and* an act of bequest. While striking out the gift to Dakota suffices as an act of partial revocation, the second act of making the bequest to Benno must satisfy the normal formalities for executing a will. This means that in order for it to be valid, the changes must be signed by the testator and must either be witnessed or satisfy the requirements for a valid holographic will. If it is determined the new provision is not validly executed, it will be disregarded. That yields a result that the testator did not intend — the original bequest is effectively revoked but the new bequest is not effectively created. We address this conundrum below in the context of the doctrine of "Dependent Relative Revocation."

UPC §2-507(a)(2) provides that not only can the testator revoke the will but she can direct "another individual [to] perform[] the act in the testator's conscious presence and by the testator's direction." Thus, the UPC codifies the "conscious-presence" test: If the testator does not herself perform the revocatory act, but directs another to do so, it is sufficient if the other individual performs it in the testator's conscious presence. The act need not be performed in the testator's line of sight. We learned about a similar concept in terms of will execution in Chapter 9.

In order to have a valid revocation, whether by subsequent document (express or implied by inconsistency) or by physical act, it must be established that the testator: (i) had the capacity to revoke; (ii) had the intent to revoke; and (iii) did it in the proper way. *See* Frederic S. Schwartz, *Models of Will Revocation*, 39 REAL PROP. PROB. & TR. J. 135 (2004) (analyzing the statutory history and legal issues surrounding will revocation and its requirements). Courts are often asked to determine who actually revoked the will, when the revocation occurred, whether the act was intentional or accidental and whether it was done properly. For example, marks on a will may indicate intent to revoke all or part of the will by cancellation or the marks may be notes for a planned meeting with a lawyer. Extrinsic evidence is generally needed to resolve questions about intent. What kind of evidence might you seek to introduce to prove intent to revoke?

PROBLEMS

1. Your client, Trey, is leaving tomorrow for Europe. He calls and says the plan of distribution in the will you drafted for him many years ago is no longer what he wants. He would like to revoke several of the bequests he made to some people and make new bequests to others. He says he is too busy packing to come into your office.

    a. If Trey has the will in his possession, what would you recommend he do? Think "outside the box" — what would be practical suggestions? How might UPC §2-503 be helpful?

    b. Assume you kept the original of the will and that Trey only took a copy. What would you recommend he do? Can you make the changes for him without his coming in? How might UPC §2-503 be helpful?

2. Tommy had a six-page will, executed in 2001, that left "$100,000 to my child, Alice, $100,000 to my child, Bob, two-thirds of the residue to my wife, Margaret, and one-third of the residue to my mother, Ruth." Are the following acts deemed to be an effective revocation? How will the property be distributed if they are? What would be your arguments if you represented the persons affected?

    a. Tommy burned all six pieces of paper representing the will.

b.   Tommy wrote the word "Revoked" across the first page of the will. What if he did so across each of the six pages? What if he did so across his signature only?

c.   Tommy drew a line through the words "$100,000 bequest to Alice." How will the $100,000 be distributed?

d.   Tommy drew a line through the number "$100,000" in the bequest to Bob, wrote $200,000 above it and initialed and dated the change. Ask yourself (i) is the revocation of the $100,000 effective, (ii) is the bequest of $200,000 in compliance with attested or holographic will formalities and (iii) can the formalities be waived per §2-503?

e.   Tommy drew a line through the words "and one-third of the residue to my mother, Ruth."

3.   *Presumptions with Regard to Revocation*

a.   **Mutilated Will**

What if a will is found at the testator's house with cancellation marks or is found torn up but retained? Were the revocatory acts performed with the intent to revoke the will or were they the result of carelessness or an indication that the testator intended to engage in further estate planning?

    If the will is found with revocatory marks, the law creates a rebuttable presumption that the testator intended to revoke the will. The presumption can be rebutted by evidence that establishes that the testator did not mutilate the will with the intent to revoke it. For example, a single mark or tear could be the result of a mishap if the will was not stored in a protected place. Lots of annotations on the will could represent changes the testator had considered but did not make. It is also possible someone else made the marks. Depending on the evidence, the will may or may not be treated as revoked. *See* RESTATEMENT (THIRD) OF PROPERTY: WILLS & OTHER DONATIVE TRANSFERS §4.1, CMT. J. (1999).

b.   **Lost Will**

What if the family knows that the decedent had executed a will but the will is missing when the person dies? Is the will missing because it is lost or is it missing because the testator revoked it by throwing it away? Did someone with access to the will destroy the will to increase that person's share of the estate?

    If the will is missing, the common law creates a presumption that the testator destroyed the will with the intent to revoke. Extrinsic evidence can be used to overcome the presumption. The following case explores the presumption that the revocation was done with the proper revocatory intent and under what factual circumstances the presumption arises.

In re Estate of Beauregard
921 N.E.2d 954 (Mass. 2010)

Steven D. Knight appeals from a decree of the Probate and Family Court dismissing his petition for probate of the will of Marc R. Beauregard (decedent). The decedent died at the age of forty years, unmarried and childless, leaving his parents as his sole heirs and next of kin. After his death on July 19, 2003, a judge in the Probate and Family Court appointed Raymond L. Beauregard (Beauregard), the decedent's father, as administrator of his estate. Subsequently Knight, who had the same residential address as the decedent, filed a petition for probate of a "copy of a will." He contended that a document dated June 11, 2003, which bequeathed significant assets to Knight, was a copy of the decedent's last will and testament. Beauregard, the decedent's mother, and his four siblings filed objections to the petition. Following various pretrial proceedings, an evidentiary hearing was held during which the June 11, 2003, document was entered in evidence. All parties agreed that no original will could be located.

The trial judge found that the decedent had executed a will on June 11, 2003, and had himself retained the original. Despite the objectors' contention that the will was a forgery or not properly executed, the judge found that the will had been witnessed by two persons in accordance with G.L. c. 191, §1, and was otherwise proper. Five weeks after the execution of the will, the decedent was murdered.

Because Knight proffered only a copy of the decedent's will, the judge applied the evidentiary presumption that "where a will once known to exist cannot be found after the death of the testator, there is a presumption that it was destroyed by the maker with an intent to revoke it." The judge concluded that Knight had failed to rebut the presumption, and dismissed his petition. Knight appealed, and the Appeals Court affirmed in an unpublished memorandum and order pursuant to its rule 1:28. We granted Knight's application for further appellate review and now affirm.

Discussion.   When a will is traced to the testator's possession or to where he had ready access to it and the original cannot be located after his death, there are three plausible explanations for the will's absence: (1) the testator destroyed it with the intent to revoke it; (2) the will was accidentally destroyed or lost; or (3) the will was wrongfully destroyed or suppressed by someone who was dissatisfied with its terms. Restatement (Third) of Property (Wills and Other Donative Transfers) §4.1 comment j (1999). Of these, Massachusetts law presumes the first-that the testator destroyed the will with the intent to revoke it. ("It is settled law that where a will once known to exist cannot be found after the death of the testator, there is a presumption that it was destroyed by the maker with an intent to revoke it"). See also Restatement (Third) of Property (Wills and Other Donative Transfers), *supra*; 3 W. Page, Wills §29.139 (Bowe-Parker rev. 2004). Knight argues that the presumption should not apply in this case because the will opponents failed to raise it in their pleadings or at trial. The argument is without merit. For more than one century we have recognized the presumption as evidentiary, not an affirmative defense that must be pleaded or otherwise invoked by the opponents. See 3 W. Page, Wills, *supra* at §29.139, at 845 ("if a will which was in the custody of testator, or to which he had ready access cannot be found, the burden of proof is upon the proponent to show that it was not destroyed by testator with the intention of revoking it"). Knight knew he did not have the original will; he was on fair notice that the presumption would apply.

Whether the presumption is overcome in a given case "presents a question of fact," that we will not reverse unless it is clearly erroneous. The presumption may be rebutted by a preponderance of the evidence (in "absence of a statutory provision to the contrary, the preponderance of evidence standard is the standard generally applied in civil cases"). Because of "the other plausible explanations for a will's absence," the presumption should not "be such a strong one" that clear and convincing or another higher burden is required to rebut it.[1]

Accordingly, the proponent of a will that has been traced to the testator's possession (or to which the testator had ready access) but cannot be found after his death must demonstrate by a preponderance of the evidence that the testator did not destroy the will with the intent of revoking it. Whether the evidence is sufficient to meet this burden is determined by the facts and circumstances in each case. ("It is difficult to lay down any general rule as to the nature of the evidence which is required to rebut the presumption of destruction"). It is not necessary that the proponent establish that the will was in fact accidentally lost or destroyed, or that it was wrongfully suppressed by someone who was dissatisfied with its terms. The presumption is rebutted if a preponderance of the evidence demonstrates that the testator did not intend to revoke his will, regardless of whether the proponent can demonstrate what may ultimately have become of the will.

In this case, the judge concluded that he "could not draw any inference that the will was accidentally lost by the decedent." We do not read this to mean that the judge required Knight to prove what had become of the original or that the judge did not consider evidence tending to show that the deceased did not destroy the will with the intent to revoke it. It is apparent that the judge considered all the evidence and made findings sufficient

---

1. [FN 5] Some jurisdictions require a more stringent standard of proof to rebut the presumption. See, e.g., *Matter of the Estate of Crozier*, 232 N.W.2d 554, 556 (Iowa 1975) (whether presumption of revocation has been rebutted "is one of fact which must be proved by clear and convincing evidence"); *Bowery v. Webber*, 181 Va. 34, 36, 23 S.E.2d 766 (1943) (evidence required to overcome presumption of revocation of will must be "strong and conclusive"). We have not previously had occasion to state that a preponderance of the evidence is the standard of proof by which the presumption of revocation may be rebutted under Massachusetts law. We follow the Restatement (Third) of Property (Wills and Other Donative Transfers), *supra*, on this point, for the reasons explained.

to support his conclusion. The judge first reasoned that the decedent was young, healthy, and fully competent at the time of his death, so it would have been unlikely that he would have lost the original will accidentally. The judge further noted that there was a short period of time between the date on which the will was executed (June 11, 2003) and the decedent's death (July 19, 2003). Presumably, the judge reasoned that there was little time for the decedent to lose his will or to give it to someone who suppressed or destroyed it against the decedent's wishes. Both factors the judge cited — the competency of the decedent and the temporal proximity of the creation of the will and the decedent's death — support his finding that the decedent destroyed the original will intending to revoke it. We read the judge's decision to mean that the will proponent had not overcome the presumption by a preponderance of the evidence.

This is not to say that the facts in this case could not have been weighed differently. A copy of the will was discovered in the decedent's home. If he were competent, as the judge found, then he likely would have destroyed any copies, as well as the original, had he intended to revoke the will. Also, the temporal proximity between execution of the will and death provided little time for the decedent to change his mind. However, it is "not enough to show that a different conclusion might well have been reached." Our examination of the evidence does not lead to the inevitable conclusion that the judge's findings, based on his view of the evidence and his evaluation of the witnesses' credibility, are clearly erroneous.

Decree affirmed.

NOTES AND QUESTIONS

1. *Supplying the intent to revoke.* In *Beauregard*, how did the trial court weigh the evidence? The court stated that, "In this case, the judge concluded that he 'could not draw any inference that the will was accidentally lost by the decedent.'" Is that a reasonable inference given the facts?

2. *Revocation and formalities.* What is the best way to reduce the likelihood that someone may challenge the revocation of a will? Should there be more formalities attached to effective revocation? What are the arguments against doing so?

C. REVOCATION BY CHANGED CIRCUMSTANCES

An individual's will or will substitute may not anticipate all changes in circumstances, including divorce or remarriage. States have developed statutes that address some of these changed circumstances. If the person dies with a will or will substitute that gives property to a former spouse or fails to give property to a new spouse, the law may change the provisions to adapt the instrument to the new circumstances. These are default rules that can be changed by the testator, but the goal of the statutes is to fix problems created because the testator did not address them. In addition, the law revokes gifts to someone who killed the testator, both because the testator would probably not want to give property to his murderer but also because the murderer should not benefit from his wrongdoing.

1. Revocation by Marriage — Omitted Spouse

As we will learn in more detail in Chapter 12, early statutes in some states provided that "changes in circumstances" revoked a testator's will. Those statutes were used to revoke the will of a testator who already had a will and then got married. The policy rationale was the protection of the new spouse. The automatic revocation of a prior will would typically result in the testator's dying intestate, and the spouse would therefore inherit under the state intestacy statute. Many states have now moved away from such a rule because it is a cumbersome way to protect the spouse, and it often disrupts the testator's estate plan.

A few states still revoke the will in its entirety if the testator marries, but marriage will generally not revoke the will if evidence shows the testator did not intend that the marriage revoke the will or that the testator executed the will in contemplation of marriage. *See, e.g.*, OR. REV. STAT. §112.305 (2009).

Most states now provide that marriage only revokes the will to the extent necessary to give the spouse an intestate share. The UPC expands this rule to limit the spouse's share to amounts not devised to the testator's children born before the marriage who are not children of the spouse and to the descendants of those children.

2. Revocation on Divorce

In most cases where someone divorces his spouse, he no longer intends to leave property to his former spouse at death. During the divorce process spouses divide their marital assets. After the dissolution, each spouse can, and should, execute a new will, but if a former spouse dies with an old will, the will may devise property to his ex-spouse.

In most states, statutes revoke bequests to a former spouse and any nomination of the former spouse as a fiduciary. Some statutes stop there, while others also prevent family members of the former spouse from receiving property. The former spouse and her family members are deemed to disclaim the property or predecease the decedent and are precluded from taking or serving as a fiduciary. The policy rationale is that this is what most testators would want if they had drafted new wills after the divorce. Thus, this is in effect a revocation of a provision of a will that occurs without the testator taking any affirmative action at all.

Although typically someone who is divorced will not want a former spouse to inherit, testamentary intent with respect to the former spouse's relatives is more difficult. A testator may have provided that children of his former spouse (his stepchildren) will inherit. In some cases that wish will survive the dissolution of the marriage because the testator helped raise the stepchildren and had a close relationship with them. In other cases, the relationship with the stepchildren will end with the dissolution of the marriage. Because revocation-on-divorce statutes are default statutes, a testator should always execute a new will after divorce to clarify the testator's own wishes.

UPC §2-804. Revocation of Probate and Nonprobate Transfers by Divorce; No Revocation by Other Changes of Circumstances.

> **. . . (b) [Revocation upon Divorce.]** Except as provided by the express terms of a governing instrument, a court order, or a contract relating to the division of the marital estate made between the divorced individuals before or after the marriage, divorce, or annulment, the divorce or annulment of a marriage:
>
> (1) revokes any revocable (i) disposition or appointment of property made by a divorced individual to his [or her] former spouse in a governing instrument and any disposition or appointment created by law or in a governing instrument to a relative of the divorced individual's former spouse, (ii) provision in a governing instrument conferring a general or nongeneral power of appointment on the divorced individual's former spouse or on a relative of the divorced individual's former spouse, and (iii) nomination in a governing instrument, nominating a divorced individual's former spouse or a relative of the divorced individual's former spouse to serve in any fiduciary or representative capacity, including a personal representative, executor, trustee, conservator, agent, or guardian; and
>
> (2) severs the interests of the former spouses in property held by them at the time of the divorce or annulment as joint tenants with the right of survivorship [or as community property with the right of survivorship], transforming the interests of the former spouses into equal tenancies in common.
>
> **(c) [Effect of Severance.]** A severance under subsection (b)(2) does not affect any third-party interest in property acquired for value and in good faith reliance on an apparent title by survivorship in the

survivor of the former spouses unless a writing declaring the severance has been noted, registered, filed, or recorded in records appropriate to the kind and location of the property which are relied upon, in the ordinary course of transactions involving such property, as evidence of ownership.

   (d) [Effect of Revocation.] Provisions of a governing instrument are given effect as if the former spouse and relatives of the former spouse disclaimed all provisions revoked by this section or, in the case of a revoked nomination in a fiduciary or representative capacity, as if the former spouse and relatives of the former spouse died immediately before the divorce or annulment.

The revocation-on-divorce statute is based on the presumed intent of testators, but consider the facts in *Langston v. Langston*, 266 S.W.3d 716 (Ark. 2007). The testator executed a holographic will on April 7, 2000, while his divorce was pending. The will left his entire estate to his wife, whom he referred to solely by name without any reference to her marital status. After their divorce decree was entered on May 23, 2000, they maintained a close relationship until the 67-year-old testator died in 2005, without issue. The trial court held that the will was revoked by the divorce. The Arkansas statute provides that "[i]f, after making a will, the testator is divorced . . . all provisions in the will in favor of the testator's spouse so divorced are revoked."

The Arkansas Supreme Court agreed with the trial court. The couple's divorce, finalized by entry of the decree, occurred after the testator's execution of the will, and thus under the statute and case law, his bequest was revoked by operation of law. The Supreme Court rejected the ex-wife's claim that testamentary intent must prevail over the statute, noting that in *McGuire v. McGuire*, 631 S.W.2d 12, 14 (Ark. 1982), after holding that the statute rendered any bequest to a former spouse void, the court said that "[i]t is not necessary for us to try to reach the intent of the testator because the statute solves that problem for us." Thus, even though it may have been the testator's intent that his soon-to-be ex-wife would inherit his estate, the court held that such testamentary intent is irrelevant under the statute.

QUESTIONS

Presumed intent. Should the timing of the will's execution in *Langston* give rise to a different assumption in that particular case? Do you think the testator in *Langston* really wanted his former wife to inherit? Should the court be allowed to consider evidence of intent at all if the terms of a statute otherwise apply?

Will Substitutes.   A number of states have statutes that revoke a bequest to an ex-spouse in a will but have not extended that rule to will substitutes. As noted above, this approach can easily cause inconsistent results. Like UPC §2-803 and homicide described below, UPC §2-804 applies both to wills and will substitutes. It revokes bequests to former spouses and converts interest in jointly held property to a tenancy in common.

> **Example:**   Luther is married to Betty. They divorce. Betty has a $500,000 life insurance policy on her life. Luther is the named beneficiary. They also own a house as joint tenants with right of survivorship. Betty dies after the divorce, not having changed either the beneficiary designation on the life insurance policy nor the title to the house. Luther will not receive the life insurance proceeds. They will pass as if he disclaimed them and will go to the alternate beneficiary under the policy. Luther will only receive his own interest in the house. He will not receive Betty's half. The house will, in essence, be treated as if it were owned by the two as tenants in common.[2]

3. Revocation Due to Homicide

If a beneficiary named in a will killed the testator, most state statutes provide that the beneficiary should not receive the bequest. If the will named the killer as personal representative for the estate, the statutes remove the killer from that position. A question under the statutes is what kind of killing should result in the loss of benefits? The beneficiary might have stabbed her husband with the intent to kill him, or she might have killed him in self-defense as he tried to strangle her. The beneficiary may have accidentally caused a house fire that resulted in the death of her mother, or she might have started the fire hoping that her bedridden mother would die. The testator might have died under suspicious circumstances, but the evidence may not have been sufficient to convict anyone of murder.

UPC §2-803 revokes a bequest if the killing was "felonious and intentional." Other statutes may use different language, but they typically apply only to killings that could be prosecuted as felonies and that involve the element of intent. The revocation statute is a civil law so application of the statute does not require a conviction and the evidentiary standard is lower than that required for a criminal conviction. The UPC provides that if the killer is convicted of a felonious and intentional killing, then the conviction,

---

2. Remember, as we noted in Chapter 4, that rules imposed by state probate statutes cannot alter beneficiary rights under retirement plans governed by the Employee Retirement Income Security Act of 1974 (ERISA), the federal statute that governs such plans. The federal statute preempts state statutes in this regard, as discussed in Chapter 4.

after all right to appeal has been exhausted, will cause the application of the revocation provisions. Even if the killer is not convicted, or if the conviction is not final, an interested person (someone who will take if the killer does not) can petition the probate court for a determination of felonious and intentional killing under a preponderance of the evidence standard for purposes of inheritance. One high-profile example of the application of a "slayer statute" is the 1989 case of Lyle and Erik Menendez, who killed their parents in Los Angeles in order to accelerate their inheritance. Their subsequent conviction caused them to forfeit that inheritance. *See* Ann Burke, *Depletion of Menendez Estate Expected*, DAILY NEWS, Aug. 29, 1993.

UPC §2-803. Effect of Homicide on Intestate Succession, Wills, Trusts, Joint Assets, Life Insurance, and Beneficiary Designations.

> . . . **(c) [Revocation of Benefits Under Governing Instruments.]** The felonious and intentional killing of the decedent:
>
> (1) revokes any revocable (i) disposition or appointment of property made by the decedent to the killer in a governing instrument, (ii) provision in a governing instrument conferring a general or nongeneral power of appointment on the killer, and (iii) nomination of the killer in a governing instrument, nominating or appointing the killer to serve in any fiduciary or representative capacity, including a personal representative, executor, trustee, or agent; and
>
> (2) severs the interests of the decedent and killer in property held by them at the time of the killing as joint tenants with the right of survivorship [or as community property with the right of survivorship], transforming the interests of the decedent and killer into equal tenancies in common.
>
> . . . **(e) [Effect of Revocation.]** Provisions of a governing instrument are given effect as if the killer disclaimed all provisions revoked by this section or, in the case of a revoked nomination in a fiduciary or representative capacity, as if the killer predeceased the decedent.
>
> **(f) [Wrongful Acquisition of Property.]** A wrongful acquisition of property or interest by a killer not covered by this section must be treated in accordance with the principle that a killer cannot profit from his [or her] wrong.
>
> **(g) [Felonious and Intentional Killing; How Determined.]** After all right to appeal has been exhausted, a judgment of conviction establishing criminal accountability for the felonious and intentional killing of the decedent conclusively establishes the convicted individual as the decedent's killer for purposes of this section. In the absence of a conviction, the court, upon the petition of an interested

> person, must determine whether, under the preponderance of evidence standard, the individual would be found criminally accountable for the felonious and intentional killing of the decedent. If the court determines that, under that standard, the individual would be found criminally accountable for the felonious and intentional killing of the decedent, the determination conclusively establishes that individual as the decedent's killer for purposes of this section. . . .

If the statute applies, the provisions of the will take effect as if the killer disclaimed the gift or predeceased the decedent. Although the statute prevents the killer from taking, the application of the disclaimer rules means that the killer's descendants may take the property, either under the document or if the antilapse rules apply. The UPC would give the property to the killer's descendants if the will so provided, but some states bar the killer's descendants from inheriting. *See, e.g.,* CAL. PROB. CODE §250 (West).

There are a few states that do not have a statute that provides for forfeiture in the case of homicide. *See* Tara L. Pehush, Comment, *Maryland Is Dying for a Slayer Statute: The Ineffectiveness of the Common Law Slayer Rule in Maryland,* 35 U. BALT. L. REV. 271 (2005). However, even in those states, courts have applied a common law slayer rule. *See Cook v. Grierson,* 845 A.2d 1231 (Md. 2004) (summarizing the common law slayer rule in Maryland).

Will Substitutes.   A number of states have statutes which revoke a bequest to a killer in a will but have not extended that rule to will substitutes. However, the drafters of the UPC, with their focus on uniformity, have extended the rule to will substitutes. Thus, like UPC §2-804 on divorce, UPC §2-803 applies both to wills and will substitutes. More specifically, this section revokes "any revocable (i) disposition or appointment of property made by the decedent to the [killer] in a governing instrument . . . and severs the interests of the decedent and [killer] in property held by them . . . as joint tenants with the right of survivorship transforming the interests . . . into equal tenancies in common."

> **Example:**   Luther is married to Betty. He kills Betty in a drunken rage. Betty has a $500,000 life insurance policy on her life. Luther is the named beneficiary. They also own a house as joint tenants with right of survivorship. Luther will not receive the life insurance proceeds. They will pass as if he disclaimed them and will go to the alternate beneficiary under the policy. Luther will only receive his own interest in the house. He will not receive Betty's half. The house will, in essence, be treated as if it were owned as tenants in common.

PROBLEMS

Harry, a married man, drafted a will that left his residuary estate (worth $1,000,000) to a testamentary trust. He also left several specific bequests of cash and property, totaling $50,000. Harry named his wife, Wanda, as the executor of his estate and the trustee of the testamentary trust. The terms of the trust give Wanda income for her life and then give half the remainder to his children and half of the remainder to Wanda's children from a prior marriage, *i.e.*, his stepchildren.

1.   What result under each of the following scenarios?
   a.   One of Harry's children (Alice) paid a killer to "knock off" Harry. The killer was successful. What effect does this have on the distribution of the estate?
      i.   Alice has two children — what effect on them? Does it matter whether she is treated as a murderer under UPC §2-803?
   b.   Harry died in a car accident while a passenger in Alice's car. Alice survived the accident. Assume Alice was 22 years old and it can be established that she was driving carelessly. What effect does this have on the distribution of the estate?
   c.   Harry died in a car accident while a passenger in Alice's car. Alice survived the accident. Assume Alice was 22 years old and Alice is convicted of involuntary manslaughter based on a jury finding that she was incoherent due to drug use when the accident occurred. What effect does this have on the distribution of the estate?
   d.   Harry died in a car accident while a passenger in Alice's car. Alice survived the accident. Assume Alice was 22 years old. It can be determined that Alice had tampered with the brakes so they did not work around a vicious curve. Nevertheless, Alice was acquitted of all charges in her criminal trial because the police performed an unconstitutional search of Alice's home where the plans were discovered. What effect does this have on the distribution of the estate?
   e.   If Alice had received a distribution and later it was determined that she had murdered Harry, what legal doctrine(s) might you employ to seek its return to the rightful beneficiaries?
2.   Wanda and Harry divorced several years after the will was drafted, and Harry did not draft a new will. What effect does this have on the distribution of the estate?
   a.   In addition to the effect divorce has on Wanda's interest, who else would be affected?

3.   Now assume that Wanda is the named beneficiary on Harry's $1,000,000 life insurance policy and his $500,000 401(k) account. She and Harry are joint owners with rights of survivorship in the $2,000,000 family home.

     a.   If Wanda divorces Harry before he dies, who takes what?

     b.   If Wanda is found guilty of killing Harry, who takes what?

4.   Revocation Due to Abuse

A few states have adopted statutes that bar inheritance by someone who abused the decedent. These include California, Pennsylvania, Illinois, Oregon and Maryland.

Cal. Prob. Code §259 (West). Predeceasing a Decedent.

    (a) Any person shall be deemed to have predeceased a decedent to the extent provided in subdivision (c) where all of the following apply:

    (1) It has been proven by clear and convincing evidence that the person is liable for physical abuse, neglect, or fiduciary abuse of the decedent, who was an elder or dependent adult.

    (2) The person is found to have acted in bad faith.

    (3) The person has been found to have been reckless, oppressive, fraudulent, or malicious in the commission of any of these acts upon the decedent.

    (4) The decedent, at the time those acts occurred and thereafter until the time of his or her death, has been found to have been substantially unable to manage his or her financial resources or to resist fraud or undue influence . . . .

    (c) Any person found liable under subdivision (a) or convicted under subdivision (b) shall not (1) receive any property, damages, or costs that are awarded to the decedent's estate in an action described in subdivision (a) or (b), whether that person's entitlement is under a will, a trust, or the laws of intestacy; or (2) serve as a fiduciary . . . if the instrument nominating or appointing that person was executed during the period when the decedent was substantially unable to manage his or her financial resources or resist fraud or undue influence. This section shall not apply to a decedent who, at any time following the act or acts described in paragraph (1) of subdivision (a), or the act or acts described in subdivision (b), was substantially able to manage his or her financial resources and to resist fraud or undue influence . . .

PROBLEM

You are advising your state legislature's probate committee. Would you recommend adopting a statute that bars inheritance due to elder abuse? What are your arguments in support of such legislation, and what do you anticipate will be the arguments against it? Should the legislation cover abuse other than elder abuse? *See Estate of Lowrie,* 12 Cal. Rptr. 3d 828 (Ct. App. 2004) for an interesting case where a niece who was a beneficiary under the abuse victim's trust was allowed to bring an action under this California statute.

D. THE IMPACT OF REVOCATION

A will that is validly revoked cannot be probated. If the testator does not have an earlier will, the testator is treated as having died intestate. If the testator had executed an earlier will or wills, then the most recent valid, unrevoked will may be probated if one of the doctrines that we discuss in the next section applies.

If the will is only partially revoked, then questions arise as to the disposition of the property that is the subject of the revoked bequest. If the testator anticipated such a revocation, she might have provided for a taker-in-default.

> **Example:** Tara's will provides that, "I leave my car to Sally. However, if this bequest is subsequently revoked for any reason, then I leave my car to Connie." If Tara effectively revokes the bequest to Sally, then Connie will receive the car.

If testator fails to provide an alternate taker, the default rules of UPC §2-604 (or a state's equivalent provision or common law) apply to determine who will receive the revoked bequest. UPC §2-604 differentiates between the revocation of specific and residuary bequests. Specific bequests, like the car to Sally above, "fall into" the residuary estate and are distributed to the residuary beneficiaries.

> **Example:** Tara's will provides that, "I leave my car to Sally and the rest of my estate to Connie." If Tara effectively revokes the bequest to Sally, then Connie will receive the car since the specific bequest of the car is added to the residue when it is revoked and there is no alternate taker specified.

If there are no residuary beneficiaries, the revoked bequest is distributed according to the rules of intestacy.

As noted above, a validly revoked will cannot be probated. Or can it? It certainly raises questions about what the testator was thinking with regard to other wills or codicils she may have had prior to the revocation. In essence, it creates ambiguity as to the testator's intent. Professor Adam Hirsch outlines these questions in the excerpt below, and the following sections describe the doctrines that have evolved to help courts answer such questions.

Adam J. Hirsch, Inheritance and Inconsistency
57 Ohio St. L.J. 1057 (1996)

Given, at any rate, the undoubted legal authority of the testator to revoke her will by act, questions can arise about the substantive effect on the estate plan induced by that act. Of course, if a testator has a single testamentary instrument, the consequence intended by revoking that instrument is unequivocal: the testator seeks to become intestate. Where, however, a string of executed documents exists and the testator intentionally incinerates only one of them, the estate plan we are left with after the smoke clears is not self-evident.

The problem emerges in two essential contexts: a testator may execute two instruments sequentially and then revoke by act only the *first* one; or a testator may execute two instruments sequentially and then revoke by act only the *second* one. What effect does she intend her act to have on the legal operativeness of the other document? Curiously enough, depending on the circumstances, the act can be interpreted either to deprive the other document of legal force, *or the opposite* — to reinstate with legal force a document previously deprived of it. Alternatively, the act could be considered to have no legal effect whatsoever on any document other than the one directly acted upon. And that, ultimately, is the rub: for once we permit an act to substitute for executed words, both the testator's intent to render that act legally performative *and the substantive outcome she intended thereby* may be impossible to infer. Acts, alas, are ambiguous in more ways than one. . . .

Under the original version of the Code . . . an original will, whether revoked *completely* by a subsequent will or *partially* by a subsequent codicil, was presumed to remain revoked despite the later revocation of the subsequent instrument unless extrinsic evidence showed that the testator intended the contrary. The revised Code treats subsequent wills and codicils differently. When a will is entirely superseded by a subsequent will that the testator eventually revokes, the Code continues to presume an intent *not* to revive the original will unless extrinsic evidence shows otherwise. But when a will is partially superseded by a subsequent codicil that the testator eventually revokes, the rebuttable presumption flip-flops: now an intent to revive the original will *is* presumed, unless contradicted by extrinsic evidence.

1. *Revival*

If a will is revoked in whole or in part, what effect does that have on the validity of prior wills? If a testator intends to draft a new will and revoke her old will or a portion thereof but the attempted new will is found invalid after the testator's death, what can the probate court do? There are two doctrines that are helpful to courts in these circumstances. The first is a statutory doctrine called "revival" that applies when a testator creates a first will, properly revokes it and creates a second will and then properly revokes the second will. The second doctrine is a common law doctrine called "dependent relative revocation" or "conditional revocation." This doctrine applies when the testator creates a valid will, revokes it in whole or in part and then an attempt at a second will to replace it is later found to be invalid. We examine revival first.

UPC §2-509. Revival of Revoked Will.

> (a) If a subsequent will that wholly revoked a previous will is thereafter revoked by a revocatory act under Section §2-507(a)(2), the previous will remains revoked unless it is revived. The previous will is revived if it is evident from the circumstances of the revocation of the subsequent will or from the testator's contemporary or subsequent declarations that the testator intended the previous will to take effect as executed.
>
> (b) If a subsequent will that partly revoked a previous will is thereafter revoked by a revocatory act under Section §2-507(a)(2), a revoked part of the previous will is revived unless it is evident from the circumstances of the revocation of the subsequent will or from the testator's contemporary or subsequent declarations that the testator did not intend the revoked part to take effect as executed.
>
> (c) If a subsequent will that revoked a previous will in whole or in part is thereafter revoked by another, later, will, the previous will remains revoked in whole or in part, unless it or its revoked part is revived. The previous will or its revoked part is revived to the extent it appears from the terms of the later will that the testator intended the previous will to take effect.

The statutory doctrine of revival addresses the question of whether a previous will (Will #1) that was revoked by a later will (Will #2) should be revived when the later will is itself effectively revoked, either by another will (Will #3) or by a revocatory act. UPC §2-509(c) presumes that the previous will (Will #1) remains revoked regardless of the revocation of the later will (Will #2) by a third will (Will #3).

Example 1:   Angel wrote a will in 1995 leaving all his property to his children. In 1999, Angel wrote a new will leaving all his property to his new wife, explicitly stating in the will that he was revoking all prior wills. In 2008, Angel wrote a new will leaving all his property to his grandchildren, explicitly stating in the will that he was revoking all prior wills. UPC §2-507(c) presumes that the revocation of the 1999 will by the 2008 will was not intended to revive the 1995 will. The 2008 will is the operative document.

A similar result occurs if the later will (Will #2) was revoked by an act (instead of by a later will). The presumption is that the previous will (Will #1) remains revoked and is not revived, unless Will #2 only revoked a portion of previous Will #1, in which case it is presumed the portion previously revoked is revived.

Example 2:   Angel executed a will in 1995 leaving all his property to his children. In 1999, Angel wrote a new will leaving all his property to his new wife, explicitly stating in the will that he was revoking all prior wills. In 2008, Angel tore up the 1999 will. UPC §2-507(a) presumes that the destruction of the 1999 will was not intended to revive the 1995 will. Angel dies intestate.

Example 3:   Angel executed a will in 1995 leaving all his property to his children. In 1999, Angel drafted a codicil leaving his car to his newly driving nephew. By doing so, Angel revoked the 1995 will as to the car. In all other respects, the 1995 will remains in force. In 2008, Angel tore up the 1999 codicil. UPC §2-507(b) presumes that the destruction of the 1999 codicil was intended to revive the 1995 will with respect to the car; it will go to his children consistent with the provision in the 1995 document.

The presumptions supplied by UPC §2-507(a) and (b) can be rebutted with evidence that the testator intended otherwise. For example, in Example 1 the presumption can be rebutted with evidence that when Angel tore up his 1999 will he intended to revive the 1995 will. The burden of persuasion is on the proponent of the position contrary to the presumption. Testimony regarding the decedent's statements at the time of the revocation or at a later date can be admitted. Indeed, all relevant evidence of intention is to be considered by the court on this question. Extrinsic evidence is usually critical to decide the testator's intent since it is rare that the documents themselves explicitly speak to this. UPC §2-509 is a good example of the intent-furthering approach of the present UPC.

Some states do not permit revival under any circumstances, even if it can be shown that the testator intended to revive a prior will. In those states, the terms of the prior will can be given effect only if the testator executes a new will with those terms (or re-executes a copy of the old will).

2. Dependent Relative Revocation

Courts apply the statutory doctrine of revival when the testator has intentionally revoked a later will with the intent to revive all or part of an earlier will that had been previously revoked. If revival applies, the revocation is effective and the earlier will or a portion of it is revived and becomes the operative document.

However, while the UPC drafters note that courts should use revival more broadly than in the past because of the more modern intent-furthering aspects of the UPC, revival does not apply in all situations where there is revocation of one document with the intent that another document take effect. For example, revival may not accomplish what the testator has in mind if the testator revoked one will as part of a plan to leave property pursuant to a new will but the new will turns out to be invalid for one reason or another.

In this kind of situation, courts may employ the judicial doctrine of "dependent relative revocation" (DRR) to determine whether the intent of the testator would be better implemented if the revocation is given effect or if it is ignored. In other words, since the testator's first choice cannot be accomplished because the later will is actually invalid, what would the testator's second choice be — to die with the previous will revoked or not revoked? Put another way, should the revocation be upheld and the property pass pursuant to intestacy (since the testator will have died without a will that has not been revoked) or should the revocation be declared to be ineffective (and that document be held still in effect) since the revocation was dependent upon or conditional on the new will being declared valid and that condition has not been fulfilled?

Distinguishing Revival from DRR. Courts apply the statutory doctrine of revival when the testator has revoked the second will. The question for the court in revival is what the testator had in mind when she revoked the second will — did she mean to revive the provisions of the first will or did she mean to die intestate?

However, it would not make conceptual sense to use the revival doctrine if, as a factual matter, the testator did not intentionally revoke the second will but rather died thinking the second will was valid but turns out to have been wrong. In such a case, the question becomes what was in the testator's mind when she revoked the first will (as opposed to the second will as in the revival doctrine). Did she intend her revocation of the first will (or some part of it) to take effect only if the second will were later deemed to be valid? If the second will were later deemed invalid, would the testator have preferred the revocation of the first to not take effect?

That is the proper factual context in which to apply the common law doctrine of dependent relative revocation, sometimes also called conditional revocation. The court seeks to do the same thing in both revival and DRR cases — to decide whether it can actually probate the first will or whether it has to allow the testator to die intestate. But the two factual contexts require very different conceptual routes to achieve this same result.

For example, DRR is appropriate as a doctrinal solution for the probate court under the following scenario:

> **Example:**   Tina struck a provision out of her will that had left $100,000 to her brother, Javier. She then wrote in "$200,000 to my brother Javier." While the revocation does not need witnesses and a signature to be effective, the bequest of $200,000 does. If the $200,000 bequest fails due to the lack of witnesses or signature, Javier would receive nothing according to this provision of the will.

In the example above, a court could use the doctrine of DRR to ask what Tina would have preferred when one part (the intended bequest) of an interdependent two-part change in the estate plan is ineffective: Should the court also treat as ineffective the other half of the change (the revocation)? On the facts presented, it seems clear that Tina wanted Javier to receive more than $100,000. The court cannot give him $200,000, which appears to be Tina's first preference, because the new bequest does not comply with UPC §2-502. The court uses DRR to divine what the second-best choice is — is it to allow the revocation of the $100,000 gift to stand, in which case Javier will get nothing if there is a named residuary beneficiary, or is to treat the revocation as ineffective, thus allowing Javier to get $100,000? Thus, DRR is sometimes called "the law of second best."

The evidence that is used to determine the second-best choice is often the part of the transaction that failed in the first place. So, in the example above, though the court cannot give $200,000 to Javier, it is the best evidence that Tina would like to give Javier more than the amount in the original will, not less (or nothing). Therefore, the court might conclude that deeming the revocation ineffective and giving Javier $100,000 is more consistent with Tina's intent than allowing the revocation of the gift to stand; it is the best the court can do.

DRR is a common law doctrine. It involves a facts and circumstances analysis on a case-by-case basis. The kind of evidence that courts use to divine testator's intent as to conditional revocation include: (1) the nexus between the revocation of the old will (or a part of it) and the attempted execution of a new will or provision in terms of how close in time the two events were; and (2) how similar the terms of the two wills (or provisions) are. The closer in time revocation and execution are and the more similar the terms of the two documents, the more likely it is that a court will find that DRR is appropriate to apply.

As discussed in the following Comment to UPC §2-507, courts will find they less frequently need to employ DRR to resolve cases under the new provisions of the UPC since they are based more on an intent-furthering framework than an absolute concern about formalities.

Comment to UPC §2-507

Dependent Relative Revocation. Each court is free to apply its own doctrine of dependent relative revocation. . . . Note, however, that dependent relative revocation should less often be necessary under the revised provisions of the Code. Dependent relative revocation is the law of second best, i.e., its application does not produce the result the testator actually intended, but is designed to come as close as possible to that intent. A precondition to the application of dependent relative revocation is, or should be, good evidence of the testator's actual intention; without that, the court has no basis for determining which of several outcomes comes the closest to that actual intention.

When there is good evidence of the testator's actual intention, however, the revised provisions of the Code would usually facilitate the effectuation of the result the testator actually intended. If, for example, the testator by revocatory act revokes a second will for the purpose of reviving a former will, the evidence necessary to establish the testator's intent to revive the former will should be sufficient under Section §2-509 to effect a revival of the former will, making the application of dependent relative revocation as to the second will unnecessary. If, by revocatory act, the testator revokes a will in conjunction with an effort to execute a new will, the evidence necessary to establish the testator's intention that the new will be valid should, in most cases, be sufficient under Section §2-503 to give effect to the new will, making the application of dependent relative revocation as to the old will unnecessary. If the testator lines out parts of a will or dispositive provision in conjunction with an effort to alter the will's terms, the evidence necessary to establish the testator's intention that the altered terms be valid should be sufficient under Section §2-503 to give effect to the will as altered, making dependent relative revocation as to the lined-out parts unnecessary.

The doctrine of dependent relative revocation is in essence a legal fiction. The testator died having intentionally revoked the first will, albeit based on the erroneous belief that the second instrument was valid. The court must suspend its understanding of that reality of revocation when it concludes that the revocation of the first will, or a part of it as in the following case, was actually conditional. It must read in the condition — that the revocation of the first will or a portion of it was conditional on the validity of the second will — in order to find that the first will is still valid even though it is clear the testator intended to, and actually did, revoke it.

In the *Kirkeby* case, which we studied in Chapter 9, the court applied the doctrine of dependent relative revocation where the decedent's earlier will and codicil were both invalid. An earlier will was probated when the court found that DRR applied. The relevant part of the court's opinion states:

Kirkeby v. Covenant House
970 P.2d 241, 243-44 (Or. Ct. App. 1998)

. . . In June 1993, the court issued a memorandum opinion and sub-sequent order, determining that (1) the July 1992 will and the June 1992 codicil to the 1989 will were both invalid as improperly executed; but (2) Margaret did not die intestate because, applying the doctrine of "dependent relative revocation,"[3] the 1989 will remained valid.

The court's memorandum included the following pertinent findings and conclusions:

> The 1989 will is marked up and provisions are crossed out, but it is still legible . . . .
>
> The 1989 will is valid unless it was revoked. It is also clear to the Court that is was Decedent's intent to revoke the 1989 will and replace it with the 1992 will.
>
> Therefore, if the 1992 will is valid, there is no need to inquire further.
>
> The 1992 Will:
>
> Mrs. Horton's and Mr. Pullen's testimony and affidavits do not meet the requirements of the law to prove a will.
>
> Mrs. Ortega's testimony and affidavit does meet the requirement to prove a will . . . .
>
> Under the facts as found above by the Court, the 1992 will is simply not provable as a valid will under the law.
>
> Deceased certainly intended her estate to pass under a will and would not have revoked her 1989 will if she had realized that the 1992 will was not valid. The essential dispositions of these two wills are the same.
>
> The doctrine of dependent relative revocation applies . . . .
>
> The 1989 will is the valid Last Will of Decedent and shall be admitted to probate.

On June 25, 1993, the court entered its order admitting the 1989 will to probate.

In *Estate of Anderson* below, which involves the application of DRR in a situation where there is both ambiguity and mistake, note that the doctrine is applied in a context quite different than the paradigm presented above, reflecting its breadth. The court embraces an expansive use of DRR, allowing it in both cases that might result in intestacy and cases where the

---

3. [FN 5] Under the doctrine of dependent relative revocation, a court can probate a will that was revoked by a testator through the execution of a subsequent will where that subsequent will is later declared invalid. The applicable principle is that the court may declare the revoked will valid, if it determines that the testator did not intend to die intestate and would not have revoked the prior will if he or she had known that the subsequent will would prove to be invalid.

failure to use DRR would not result in intestacy but would defeat testator's intent.

Estate of Anderson
65 Cal. Rptr. 2d 307 (Ct. App. 1997)

The opinion of the court was delivered by Judge MASTERSON.

In 1982, Evelyn I. Anderson executed a will that exercised a testamentary power of appointment over a portion of a trust created by her deceased husband. In 1993, Anderson executed a second will that expressly revoked all prior wills and that inadvertently failed to exercise the power of appointment.

After Anderson died in 1995, the executor of her estate petitioned the trial court to admit to probate the 1993 will and that portion of the 1982 will exercising the power of appointment. One of Anderson's step-grandchildren initiated a will contest and objected to the admission of any portion of the 1982 will.

After conducting an evidentiary hearing, the trial court found that Anderson intended to exercise the power of appointment and that the 1993 will did not revoke the provision in the 1982 will exercising that power. Applying the doctrine of dependent relative revocation, the trial court admitted to probate the 1993 will and the portion of the 1982 will exercising the power of appointment.

The contestant challenges the trial court's order to the extent it admits to probate the provision in the 1982 will. We affirm.

BACKGROUND

[In 1982, while residing in Omaha, Nebraska, Evelyn executed a will that exercised the subject testamentary power of appointment, giving the trust property to Carole De Paul (referred to in the opinion as De Paul). In 1993, after moving to Pasadena, California, Evelyn met with a California lawyer to redo her will. She gave him a copy of the 1982 will to use as a model. She asked him "to carry forward its provisions into the new estate planning documents except as she directed otherwise." She requested that the lawyer convert her estate plan into a revocable trust with a pour-over will and to make a gift of $1,000 to each of Wilbur's grandchildren. The new will expressly revoked "all prior wills and codicils."

If the power of appointment is effectively exercised, Evelyn will give $500,000 to De Paul and $1,000 each to 20 grandchildren. (Step-relatives get $20,000.) If the power of appointment is not exercised, De Paul will receive one-sixth of the trust and five-sixths will go to Evelyn's step-relatives. In addition, the 20 grandchildren each will receive $1,000.]

DISCUSSION

Because the record in this case discloses no conflicts in the evidence and no issues of credibility, we independently determine whether the 1993 will revoked article eighth of the 1982 will.

The contestant argues that the trial court's order should be reversed because (1) the revocation clause in the 1993 will encompassed article eighth of the 1982 will, (2) the elements of the doctrine of dependent relative revocation were not satisfied in this case as a matter of law, and (3) sufficient evidence does not support the application of the doctrine of dependent relative revocation. We discuss each of these contentions in turn.

A. The Revocation Clause in the 1993 Will

[The court found that the revocation clause in the second will, which revoked all former wills, was sufficient to revoke article eighth of the first will, unless the doctrine of dependent relative revocation applies.]

B. The Doctrine of Dependent Relative Revocation

"Under the doctrine of dependent relative revocation, an earlier will, revoked only to give effect to a later one on the supposition that the later one will become effective, remains in effect to the extent that the latter proves ineffective. . . . The doctrine is designed to carry out the probable intention of the testator when there is no reason to suppose that he intended to revoke his earlier will if the later will became inoperative." Put another way, where a "question arises as to the effectiveness of the second instrument, . . . so that upon its failure to be operative for want of proper execution or other cause, the testator will be presumed to have intended the original instrument to stand to the extent that the later proves ineffective." "The doctrine thus requires that, in revoking a prior and executing a subsequent will, it be specifically intended that certain provisions in the former testament have a continuing effect, either through similar provisions in the new will or because it is intended to make only conditional changes which subsequently do not become effective for the reason that the conditions on which [they are] predicated fail to come into being."

As a leading authority has explained: "The testator doubtless has power to make an expressly conditional revocation. The cases, however, go further and hold that if he revokes *under some mistake*, the condition may be *implied or presumed*. With respect to certain situations, this has become crystallized into the doctrine of *dependent relative revocation*. Thus, if the testator destroys a first will in the mistaken belief that a second will is valid, the law presumes that he intended to revoke [the first] *only if the second were valid*; i.e., the revocation is not absolute, but is *relative*, and *dependent* upon the validity of the second will. Similarly, if the testator, in a new will or a codicil, revokes gifts to certain relatives, stating that they are dead, the doctrine may be applied to nullify the revocation if the belief turns out to be untrue." . . .

The contestant . . . argu[es] that, under California law, the doctrine of dependent relative revocation applies only where (1) the decedent's last will is wholly or partially invalid, resulting in intestacy and (2) the last will shows *on its face* that the revocation of the prior will was conditioned on the effectiveness of the last will. We reject this argument.

1.   Intestacy Under the Last Will

The doctrine of dependent relative revocation applies where a "question arises as to the *effectiveness* of the second instrument, . . . so that upon its failure to be operative for want of proper execution *or other cause*, the testator will be presumed to have intended the original instrument to stand to the extent that the later proves *ineffective*." Plainly, a will may prove "ineffective" if it results in total or partial intestacy, but that is not the only situation in which a will may "fail [] to be operative." A will may also be ineffective if, as a result of a mistake on the testator's part, it purports to revoke a prior will and fails in a material way to distribute the estate in accordance with the testator's intent.

"In the construction of wills the paramount rule, to which all others must yield, is that a will is to be construed according to the intention of the testator, as expressed therein, and this intention must be given effect as far as possible." The doctrine of dependent relative revocation is simply one means of implementing this paramount rule: "[T]he sole justification for the use of dependent relative revocation is to effectuate the decedent's intent as nearly as possible." No doubt, the purpose of the doctrine is often served by applying it where intestacy would otherwise result. By the same token, the doctrine should apply where the last will purports to revoke a prior exercise of a power of appointment, resulting in substantial gifts to the decedent's step-grandchildren contrary to her express intention to exercise that power solely for the benefit of her natural daughter.

As explained by one commentator: "The second instrument may be executed validly and apparently may be a good and sufficient disposition of the estate of the testator, yet operate neither as a disposition of the property nor as a revocation of a prior will. This result obtains if the testator executes the apparent will . . . under the mistaken notion that some fact or law does or does not exist. . . . In each case the problem is to discover the true intent when the second document is executed. Legal bars in the form of hard-and-fast rules not based on reason should never be permitted to interfere. Courts should be free to hold the revocation conditional on future events if the testator so intends it or to find [the intent to revoke] lacking if not present."

The facts of this case amply demonstrate why the doctrine of dependent relative revocation should not be limited to invalid final wills that would otherwise result in intestacy. Here, the trial court found that the second will was ineffective because it failed to carry out Anderson's intention to exercise the power of appointment in favor of De Paul. Under article eighth of the first will, De Paul was entitled to Anderson's entire 50 percent share of the Irwin trust, i.e., approximately $500,000. However, if the doctrine of dependent relative revocation does not save article eighth, then, under the default provisions of Irwin's will, De Paul will receive only one-sixth of Anderson's share — $83,333 instead of $500,000. The remaining five-sixths of Anderson's share ($416,667) will go to individuals who were to receive nothing under her first will (i.e., a stepson and several step-grandchildren).

Moreover, one of Anderson's primary reasons for executing the second will was to make gifts of $1,000 to each of Irwin's grandchildren (i.e., her step-grandchildren). The second will expressly stated that they were to receive that sum. Yet, if article eighth of the first will were deemed to be revoked, the *effect* of the second will would be to give 17 of Irwin's 22 grandchildren bequests ranging from approximately $14,900 to $28,800-gifts substantially greater than the $1,000 that Anderson wanted each of them to receive under the second will. The paramount goal in interpreting wills — to effectuate the testator's intent — would hardly be served if Anderson's desire to give each of Irwin's grandchildren a gift of $1,000 ultimately resulted in an average gift of more than $20,000 apiece, all at the expense of her only natural daughter. Indeed, we think it fair to assume that Anderson would have preferred that her share of the Irwin trust be distributed under the intestacy laws rather than in accordance with the default provisions of Irwin's will. If the intestacy laws were applicable, Anderson's entire 50 percent share of the trust would go to De Paul — the same disposition that Anderson made in her first will and the one she intended in the second.

Accordingly, we conclude that the doctrine of dependent relative revocation may be used to effectuate a testator's intent even if the last will would not otherwise result in total or partial intestacy.

2.   Consideration of Extrinsic Evidence

The contestant argues that the doctrine of dependent relative revocation does not apply unless the testator's last will shows on its face that the testator intended the revocation of the prior will to be conditioned on the effectiveness of the later will. We conclude that extrinsic evidence may be considered in determining whether Anderson intended to revoke article eighth of the 1982 will.

"[A] will is to be construed according to the intention of the testator, and not his imperfect attempt to express it." "Any conclusion as to the testator's intention must be considered in the light of his knowledge at the time he executed the will." "To constitute a valid revocation, acts of cancellation or interlineation must be done with sufficient present intent and purpose of revocation. . . . " (citations omitted.) In determining whether a will has been revoked, courts may consider extrinsic evidence of the testator's intent. . . .

As our Supreme Court has stated with regard to interpreting wills in general: "[E]xtrinsic evidence is admissible 'to explain any ambiguity arising on the face of a will, *or to resolve a latent ambiguity which does not so appear.*' . . . A latent ambiguity is one which is not apparent on the face of the will but is disclosed by some fact collateral to it. . . . 'The court must determine the true meaning of the instrument in the light of the evidence available. It can neither exclude extrinsic evidence relevant to that determination nor invoke such evidence to write a new or different instrument.' . . . [W]e think it is self-evident that in the interpretation of a will, a court cannot determine whether the terms of the will are clear and definite in the first place until it considers the circumstances under which the will was made so that the judge may be placed in the position of the testator whose language he is interpreting." (italics added, citations omitted.)

Applying these principles, we conclude that extrinsic evidence may be considered in determining whether Anderson conditioned the revocation of the first will on the exercise of the power of appointment in De Paul's favor. Even if we limit our focus to the written instruments — Irwin's will, Anderson's two wills, and the document creating Anderson's trust — we are left with an incomplete picture requiring the use of extrinsic evidence. The documentary evidence alone indicates that one of Anderson's primary reasons for executing the second will (and for purporting to revoke the prior will) was to leave a gift of $1,000 to each of Irwin's grandchildren. Yet the consequence of executing the second will, absent an exercise of the power of appointment, would be to give 17 of Irwin's 22 grandchildren an individual gift ranging from approximately $14,900 to $28,800. Thus, the effect of the second will appears to be inconsistent with the express provision leaving $1,000 to each of the grandchildren. Moreover, the circumstances surrounding the execution of the second will leave no doubt that Anderson conditioned the revocation of the first will on the exercise of the power of appointment in favor of De Paul. (See pt. C, *post.*) It follows that we may consider extrinsic evidence of Anderson's intention to revoke the first will.

C. *Sufficiency of the Evidence*

The contestant argues that there is insufficient evidence to support a determination that the revocation of the first will was conditioned on the exercise of the power of appointment. In particular, the contestant emphasizes that Anderson never specifically referred to the power of appointment in discussing the drafting or content of the second will. While that assertion is correct, it does not resolve the matter. . . .

As stated, the dispositive instruments alone raise a serious question about the interpretation of the second will. They indicate that Anderson executed the second will, in part, to provide each of Irwin's grandchildren with a gift of $1,000. However, the effect of the second will, absent an exercise of the power of appointment, would be to give most of the grand-children an average gift 20 times that amount. Further, the partner who supervised the drafting of the new estate planning documents testified that Anderson told him to make certain changes in the first will and otherwise to carry forward its existing provisions into the new documents. Anderson did not tell the partner to make any changes with respect to article eighth or the exercise of the power of appointment. The partner, in turn, conveyed those same instructions to the associate who drafted the new will and trust documents. As the partner indicated, the failure to explicitly reference the exercise of the power of appointment in the second will was the result of an error in drafting.

Given this evidence, we reject the contestant's assertion that Anderson never informed her attorneys that she wished to exercise the power of appointment in the second will. By telling her attorneys to carry forward the provisions of the first will except to the extent she directed otherwise, and by not requesting any changes in article eighth or the exercise of the power of appointment, Anderson effectively instructed her attorneys to exercise that power in the second will.

Nor do we doubt that Anderson made a *material* mistake in executing the second will. Instead of leaving a gift of $1,000 to each of Irwin's grand-children, Anderson signed a document that purported to give most of them a gift of at least $14,000. While article eighth of the first will left Anderson's entire share of the Irwin trust ($500,000) to her only natural daughter, the second will had the effect of giving five-sixths of that amount ($416,667) to steprelatives who, under the first will, were to receive nothing and, under the express terms of the second will, were to receive a collective gift of $20,000 (i.e., $1,000 for each of Irwin's grandchildren, not including De Paul's children). In other words, the second will, absent an exercise of the power of appointment, will mistakenly dispose of almost one-third of the assets over which Anderson had control.

On these facts, we conclude that a "question [has] arise[n] as to the effectiveness of the second instrument, . . . so that upon its failure to be operative for want of proper execution *or other cause*, the testator will be presumed to have intended the original instrument to stand *to the extent that the later proves ineffective*." Because the second will did not effectively exercise the power of appointment, article eighth of the first will remained in effect under the doctrine of dependent relative revocation.

DISPOSITION

The order is affirmed.

QUESTIONS

1. *Helping the lawyer.* In *Estate of Anderson*, the court used DRR to fix a lawyer's mistake. Do you think that the court was correct in admitting to probate the portion of the first will that exercised the power of appointment? Do you agree that this gave effect to Evelyn's intent? Why do you think courts are more willing to give effect to someone's intent when there is ineffective drafting or revocation than when there is no will at all?

2. *Even more help.* The Comment to UPC §2-507 suggests that DRR should not be needed as often as it was in the past due to the relaxed rules inherent in the Code. For a recent discussion about the appropriate use of DRR by courts, see Frank L. Schiavo, *Dependent Relative Revocation Has Gone Astray: It Should Return to Its Roots*, 13 WIDENER L. REV. 73 (2006).

PROBLEMS

As to each of the situations below, answer the following: Which will or testamentary scheme, if any, controls and why? Gertrude executed Will #1 eight years ago. Five years ago, she executed Will #2, which expressly revoked Will #1.

1. Last year, she executed Will #3, which expressly revoked all prior wills.

2. Recently, Gertrude revoked Will #3 by tearing it. There is no evidence suggesting that Gertrude wished Will #1 or #2 to control.
    a. What if Gertrude instead thought that by tearing Will #3, Will #2 would become her operative will?

3. Last year, she executed Will #3, which expressly revoked all prior wills. Will #3 lacked Gertrude's signature.
    a. What if Will #3 instead lacked one of the two required witnesses?

4. Will #3 was a codicil that redirected the gift of her house from Xavier (as provided in Will #2) to Yolanda. Recently, Gertrude revoked the codicil by writing "revoked" on it.
    a. What if it can be established that Gertrude revoked Will #2, believing that the property that was the subject of Will #2 would pass by intestacy.

E. WILL CONTESTS — IMPROPER EXECUTION, LACK OF CAPACITY OR INTENT AND UNDUE INFLUENCE

As noted in Chapter 9, there are legal requirements that must be met for a will to become valid: The testator must have testamentary intent, testamentary capacity and be at least age 18. Potential beneficiaries who are disappointed with their bequests may bring a will contest, in which they sue the personal representative of the estate in probate court. While the original burden is on those presenting the will for probate, "the proponents," to establish proper execution, the burden then shifts to those challenging the will, "the contestants," to establish that the will is invalid. Most contestants rely on one or more of the following theories to challenge the will: (1) lack of proper execution; (2) lack of testamentary capacity; (3) lack of testamentary intent; (4) undue influence; (5) fraud or duress. Lack of testamentary capacity and undue influence are often linked in the pleadings because the testator's level of capacity can influence both. If the testator has diminished capacity, a court may conclude that the individual's capacity was so low as to fail the sound mind requirement. Even if the testator's capacity is adequate to execute a will, the evidence may establish enough diminished capacity to sustain an argument that the conditions existed for the testator to be susceptible to undue influence.

Most will contests end in settlements. Many lawyers describe them as "nuisance suits" brought to extract some payment from a personal representative who is willing to pay off the contestants rather than run up the high costs of legal fees necessary to even do the initial groundwork to have the contest dismissed. *See* John H. Langbein, *Will Contests*, 103 Yale L.J. 2039, 2043 (1994) (reviewing David Margolick's book, *The Epic Battle for the Johnson and Johnson Fortune*, and noting that "the Johnson children's undue influence suit was a strike suit" and suggesting that "[m]aking contestants pay an estate's costs of defending an unsuccessful challenge would help to deter contestants from bringing such lawsuits.")

The following case implicates several of the theories noted above. As you read the case, identify the standard for each legal theory that is used to attack the validity of the will.

Estate of Graham
69 S.W.3d 598 (Tex. App. 2001)

The opinion of the court was delivered by Justice Dorsey.

This is a will contest. Frances Graham died in 1998 at the age of 83 years. His wife predeceased him, and he had no children. Two years before his death, Mr. Graham executed a will leaving his entire estate to the two daughters of his full sister. After Mr. Graham's will was admitted to probate, his seven remaining nieces and nephews brought suit to challenge the will. Those nieces and nephews are the children of Mr. Graham's half-sister. The two nieces who are beneficiaries under the will are the "will proponents," and the seven nieces and nephews who brought this are the "will contestants."

In their suit, the will contestants asserted that the will was invalid for the following reasons:

(1)   it was not executed with the formalities and solemnities required by the Texas Probate Code;
(2)   Mr. Graham lacked testamentary capacity when he executed it;
(3)   it was executed as a result of the undue influence and fraud;
(4)   Mr. Graham did not intend the document to be a will; and,
(5)   Mr. Graham was mistaken as to the contents of the instrument.

[I.]   Failure to Properly Execute the Will

We first address the will contestants' claim that Mr. Graham's will was not executed with the "formalities and solemnities required by the Texas Probate Code." Section 59 of the Texas Probate Code sets forth the requisites of a will. *See* Tex. Prob. Code Ann. §59(a) (Vernon Supp. 2001). It states that, except where otherwise provided by law, a will must be (1) in writing, (2) signed by the testator and (3) be attested by two or more credible witnesses above the age of fourteen years who shall subscribe their names thereto in their own handwriting in the presence of the testator. The will proponents provided summary judgment evidence establishing that Mr. Graham's will met those requirements.

The will itself shows that it was in writing and signed by the testator. The will proponents attached to their motion for summary judgment the affidavit of Cynthia L. Baumgardner, which stated, in relevant part:

> I am employed by Margaret Hoelscher, a bookkeeper and federal tax return preparer and consultant . . . . I was acquainted with Francis John Graham, who brought his income tax information to Ms. Hoelscher for her to prepare his income tax return.

> On March 8, 1996, Francis John Graham met with Margaret Hoelscher, and then he presented to me his handwritten notes on a will form dated March 6, 1996, and asked that I type up a will on a will form exactly as he had written and directed. I proceed [sic] to do so. After reviewing the Will, he asked that I, Alan Chait and Margaret Dreith, also employees of Margaret Hoelscher, act as witnesses. We three witnesses went to a nearby office where notary public Alta Garcia was asked to observe the signature and statements by Francis John Graham and each of the three witnesses, and then perform notarial services with respect to the signing of said Will. A true copy of the Will signed

by Francis John Graham, and witnessed by me and the other two witnesses, and notarized by Ms. Garcia, is attached hereto.

Also, the will proponents attached to their motion the affidavit of Altagracia Garcia, the notary who signed Mr. Graham's will. She confirmed that she notarized the will, that Mr. Graham stated to her that the document was his will, that he executed it in her presence and in the presence of the three witnesses, and that the witnesses signed the will in Mr. Graham's presence and in the presence of each other.

Section 59 also provides a method for self-proving a will. A will which is self-proved needs no further proof of its execution with the formalities and solemnities and under the circumstances required to make it a valid will. While a self-proved will can still be challenged, the self-proving affidavit constitutes prima facie evidence of the will's execution.

Thus, we turn to the specific question of whether Mr. Graham's will was self-proven. The will contained the following affidavit:

> We, FRANCIS JOHN GRAHAM, CYNTHIA L. BAUMGARDNER, MARGARET E. DREITH, and ALAN M. CHAIT, the testator and the witnesses, respectively, whose names are signed to the attached and foregoing instrument, were sworn and declared to the undersigned that the testator signed the instrument as his/her Last Will and that each of the witnesses, in the presence of the testator and each other, signed the will as a witness.
>
> [Signed by the testator and the witnesses]
>
> On 3-8-1996 before me, Altagracia Garcia appeared Francis John Graham, Cynthia L. Baumgardner, Margaret E. Dreith, Alan M. Chait, personally known to me (or proved to me on the basis of satisfactory evidence) to be the person(s) whose name(s) is/are subscribed to the within instrument and acknowledged to me that he/she/they executed the same in his/her/their authorized capacity(ies), and that by his/her/their signature(s) on the instrument the persons(s), or the entity upon behalf of which the person(s) acted, executed the instrument. WITNESS my hand and official seal.
> [Signed by the Notary Public].

An affidavit attached to a will that is in substantial compliance with the affidavit form set forth in Texas Probate Code §59(a) will make the will self-proved. *See* Tex. Prob. Code Ann. §59(b) (Vernon Supp. 2001). "For this purpose, an affidavit that is subscribed and acknowledged by the testator and subscribed and sworn to by the witnesses would suffice as being in substantial compliance." Thus, because Mr. Graham's will was subscribed and acknowledged by the testator and subscribed and sworn to by the witnesses, it is in substantial compliance with the affidavit form provided in probate code section 59(a). Accordingly, the will proponents' summary judgment evidence establishes that the will was self-proven. Thus, prima facie validity of its execution was established . . . .

[II.]   LACK OF TESTAMENTARY CAPACITY

Next, the will contestants alleged that Mr. Graham did not have testamentary capacity when he executed his will. In order to execute a valid will,

> [T]he testator must have been of sound mind at its execution; and by this is meant that he must have been capable of understanding the nature of the business he was engaged in, the nature and extent of his property, the persons to whom he meant to devise and bequeath it, the persons dependent upon his bounty, and the mode of distribution among them; that he must have had memory sufficient to collect in his mind the elements of the business to be transacted, and to hold them long enough to perceive, at least, their obvious relations to each other, and be able to form a reasonable judgment as to them; and that he was not under the influence of an insane delusion, either in regard to his property or the natural and proper objects of his bounty, which affected the disposition he was about to make.

This definition of testamentary capacity remains the benchmark in Texas.

While even the proponent of a self-proven will retains the burden of proving testamentary capacity when offering the will for probate, once the will has been admitted to probate, the burden shifts to any contestant to establish a *lack* of testamentary capacity.

The Texas Supreme Court has said that the proper inquiry in a will contest on grounds of testamentary incapacity is the condition of the testator's mind on the day the will was executed. If there is no direct testimony of acts, demeanor or condition indicating that the testator lacked testamentary capacity on the date of execution, the testator's mental condition on that date may be determined from lay opinion testimony based upon the witnesses' observations of testator's conduct either prior or subsequent to the execution. However, that evidence has probative force only if some evidence exists demonstrating that the condition persists and has some probability of being the same condition that existed at the time the will was made. Thus, to successfully challenge a testator's mental capacity with circumstantial evidence from time periods other than the day on which the will was executed, the will contestants must establish (1) that the evidence offered indicates a lack of testamentary capacity; (2) that the evidence is probative of the testator's capacity (or lack thereof) on the day the will was executed; and (3) that the evidence provided is of a satisfactory and convincing character, because probate will not be set aside on the basis of evidence that creates only a suspicion of mental incapacity.

[In the opinion of this court, the] will proponents established as a matter of law that Mr. Graham possessed testamentary capacity at the time he signed his will. Cynthia Baumgardner stated in her affidavit that Mr. Graham approached her at her job and asked her to type up his will for him. He then executed the will in front of her and two other witnesses. She stated that Mr. Graham had written out the terms of his will and asked her to type them up exactly as he had written. This indicates Mr. Graham knew what he was doing and desired to dispose of his estate in the manner outlined in the will. Baumgardner also stated that Mr. Graham told her that day that he wanted his property to go to his two nieces, Theresa A. Carollo and Bernadette P. Jaswith, the will proponents. She also stated that Graham "was acting solely on his own without influence or presence of any family member or any other person, and he stated that he just wanted to have things done in a legal and proper way so that his Estate would go to his two nieces as set out in the Will." This evidence indicates that Mr. Graham possessed the testamentary capacity required to make a valid will. . . .

Th[e] evidence negates the will contestants' allegation that Mr. Graham did not have the requisite testamentary capacity to execute a valid will in 1998. He was fully aware that he was making a will bequeathing his entire estate to his two nieces and not leaving anything to the contestants. By all accounts, Mr. Graham was lucid and comprehended what he was doing when he executed his will.

In contrast, the will contestants did not submit a scintilla of evidence raising a fact issue on the question of whether Mr. Graham possessed testamentary capacity at the time he executed his will. In fact, they made no argument whatever regarding testamentary capacity in their response and produced no evidence in that regard. Accordingly, we affirm the trial court's judgment in favor of the will proponents on the testamentary capacity cause of action . . . .

[III.]   LACK OF INTENT TO MAKE A WILL

Next, the will contestants alleged that Mr. Graham did not possess the required testamentary intent when he executed his March 1996 will. A document is not a will unless it is executed with testamentary intent. "To give the instrument the legal effect either of a will or other revocation of former wills it must be written and signed with the present intention to make it a will or revocation." "It is essential . . . that the maker shall have intended to express his testamentary wishes in the particular instrument." This concept has been explained to mean that in order for a document to possess the requisite testamentary intent, it must be evident that the testator intended that the very document at issue to be the instrument that actually makes the disposition of the testator's estate. A document that merely evidences an intention to dispose of the property is not a will.

We find abundant evidence that Mr. Graham intended the document signed on March 8, 1996, to be his will. Not only does the language on the document itself clearly indicate that it is Mr. Graham's Last Will and Testament, but it clearly bequeaths his estate to his two nieces. The will was properly executed, witnessed and self-proven. Also, the summary judgment evidence previously discussed shows that Mr. Graham intended the document he signed in March 1996 to be his will. The notary and a witness both stated that he knew he was signing his will and he asked them to witness and acknowledge it for him. Further, Cynthia Bumgardner stated in her affidavit that Mr. Graham approached her and asked her to re-type the handwritten will that he had made out. The fact that he wrote it out by hand before having it typed up indicates that Mr. Graham intended the document to be his will and understood the contents of the document. We hold that the will proponents have established their right to judgment on the issue of testamentary intent. Again, the will contestants offer no argument or evidence on the issue of testamentary intent in their response to the motion for summary judgment. Accordingly, they raised no evidence asserting a genuine issue of material fact that defeats the will proponents' right to judgment. We affirm the trial court's summary judgment on the claim of lack of testamentary intent. . . .

[IV.] MISTAKE AS TO CONTENTS OF INSTRUMENT

The will contestants also alleged that Mr. Graham was mistaken about the contents of his will. We can discern no indication that a mistake occurred in Mr. Graham's will. "A will is a unilateral instrument, and the court is concerned only with the intention of the testator as expressed in the document." We find the intention of Mr. Graham is quite clear from the language of the instrument. The will proponents offered further proof indicating that he intended exactly what the document said. Again, the will contestants did not offer argument or evidence regarding their allegation of mistake in their response. They thus failed to defeat the movants' right to judgment on this issue. Accordingly, we affirm the trial court's judgment in favor of the will proponents on this issue. . . .

[V.] UNDUE INFLUENCE

Courts have long recognized that the exertion of influence that was or became undue is usually a subtle thing and by its very nature usually involves an extended course of dealings and circumstances. Thus, it may be proved by circumstantial evidence. In the absence of direct evidence all of the circumstances shown or established by the evidence should be considered; and even though none of the circumstances standing alone would be sufficient to show the elements of undue influence, if when considered together they produce a reasonable belief that an influence was exerted that subverted or overpowered the mind of the testator and resulted in the execution of the testament in controversy, the evidence is sufficient to sustain such conclusion. *However, the circumstances relied on as establishing the elements of undue influence must be of a reasonably satisfactory and convincing character, and they must not be equally consistent with the absence of the exercise of such influence.* This is so because a solemn testament executed under the formalities required by law by one mentally capable of executing it should not be set aside upon a bare suspicion of wrongdoing.

Factors to be considered when determining whether undue influence exists in a particular case are:

(1)   the nature and type of relationship existing between the testator, the contestants and the party accused of exerting such influence;

(2)   the opportunities existing for the exertion of the type of influence or deception possessed or employed;

(3)   the circumstances surrounding the drafting and execution of the testament;

(4)   the existence of a fraudulent motive;

(5)   whether there has been an habitual subjection of the testator to the control of another;

(6)   the state of the testator's mind at the time of the execution of the testament;

(7)   the testator's mental or physical incapacity to resist or the susceptibility of the testator's mind to the type and extent of the influence exerted;

(8)   words and acts of the testator;

(9)   weakness of mind and body of the testator, whether produced by infirmities of age or by disease or otherwise;

(10)   whether the testament executed is unnatural in its terms of disposition of property.

. . . None of the will contestants had any knowledge regarding the specific circumstances surrounding the execution of Mr. Graham's will. None of them had ever been promised by Mr. Graham that he would leave anything to them in a will. They contend that the fact that he was warm to them and had a distant relationship with the nieces to whom he left his estate, in effect, raises an issue of material fact regarding undue influence. We disagree. Rather, we hold that evidence produced by the will contestants is not sufficient to raise a genuine issue of material fact on the issue of whether Mr. Graham's will was executed as a result of undue influence. . . .

[VI.]   FRAUD

Finally, the will contestants alleged that Mr. Graham's will was executed as a result of fraud. A claim that a will was procured through fraud requires proof of some kind of misrepresentation. The will proponents offered ample evidence to show that Mr. Graham's will was not the result of any type of fraud. The will contestants offered no controverting evidence showing any type of misrepresentation. Accordingly, we affirm summary judgment on the fraud claim.

The will proponents' motion for summary judgment is hereby AFFIRMED in all respects.

QUESTIONS

The requisite formalities. How did the proponents of the will in *Graham* establish compliance with all of the requisite formalities in connection with the will's execution? What kind of evidence did they present? How would you characterize the burden on the proponents of a will?

1.   Improper Execution

As noted above, the proponent of the will has the burden of presenting a properly executed document. If the will appears to be regular on its face, *i.e.*, if it is in writing and all the requisite signatures of the testator and the witnesses exist, then it will be deemed properly executed. If someone wants to challenge the validity of the will based on a failure to comply with the execution requirement, the contestant has the burden of establishing that the requisite legal requirements and formalities were not complied with.

2.   Testamentary Capacity — General Capacity and Insane Delusion

There are two theories of lack of testamentary capacity that may be used to attack a will: general capacity and insane delusion. First, the contestants may claim that the testator lacked a general understanding of who the natural objects of his bounty are, the fact that he is executing a will and the extent of his property. Based on this showing, the entire will would be invalid. Second, they may claim that the testator suffered from a specific delusion that involves a particular beneficiary and the delusion has no basis in reality. This challenge might invalidate only the bequest to that particular beneficiary.

a.   General Capacity

In order to have testamentary capacity, the testator must understand: (1) who the natural objects of his bounty are; (2) that he is making a will; and (3) the extent of his property. The testator's understanding of these three things must exist at the moment of execution. The testator may be a bit unsure of these things prior to or after execution, but as long as he is aware of them at the moment he signs his will, then he has met the standard of testamentary capacity.

Under the rules of professional responsibility, a lawyer who is involved in estate planning has a duty to assess the client's testamentary capacity. If there is any question about the client's capacity, a lawyer should consult with a physician or take similar action to confirm the testator's capacity. If the lawyer is not sure that the client has the requisite capacity, the Model Rules give guidance as to the steps the lawyer should take to assure herself that the client can validly execute the instruments.

MRPC 1.14. Client with Diminished Capacity

(b) When the lawyer reasonably believes that the client has diminished capacity, is at risk of substantial physical, financial or other harm unless action is taken and cannot adequately act in the client's own interest, the lawyer may take reasonably necessary protective action, including consulting with individuals or entities that have the ability to take action to protect the client and, in appropriate cases, seeking the appointment of a guardian ad litem, conservator or guardian.

Remember that the assessment of the client's capacity is based on capacity at the moment of execution. Elderly clients may have some forgetfulness, but as long as they understand the three important issues at the moment of execution — who their relatives are, what they own and that they are making a will — they have sufficient testamentary capacity. The following commentary gives more detailed guidance to the estate planning lawyer than the more general Model Rules.

ACTEC COMMENTARY ON MRPC 1.14

. . . *Determining Extent of Diminished Capacity.*   In determining whether a client's capacity is diminished, a lawyer may consider the client's overall circumstances and abilities, including the client's ability to express the reasons leading to a decision, the ability to understand the consequences of a decision, the substantive appropriateness of a decision, and the extent to which a decision is consistent with the client's values, long-term goals, and commitments. In appropriate circumstances, the lawyer may seek the assistance of a qualified professional. . . .

Testamentary Capacity.   If the testamentary capacity of a client is uncertain, the lawyer should exercise particular caution in assisting the client to modify his or her estate plan. The lawyer generally should not prepare a will, trust agreement, or other dispositive instrument for a client who the lawyer reasonably believes lacks the requisite capacity. On the other hand, because of the importance of testamentary freedom, the lawyer may properly assist clients whose testamentary capacity appears to be borderline. In any such case the lawyer should take steps to preserve evidence regarding the client's testamentary capacity.

In cases involving clients of doubtful testamentary capacity, the lawyer should consider, if available, procedures for obtaining court supervision of the proposed estate plan, including substituted judgment proceedings.

Lucid Interval. As noted above, elderly testators often have moments when they cannot remember certain people or places. However, as the *Restatement (Third) of Property: Wills & Other Donative Transfers* states in §8.1 m, "a person who is mentally incapacitated part of the time but who has lucid intervals during which he or she meets the standard for mental capacity can . . . make a valid will . . . provided such will is made during a lucid interval."

NOTE

Duty to assess competence. As noted above, it is incumbent on the lawyer who is drafting a will to assess the competence of the client prior to execution. Not only is it the lawyer's ethical duty, it also helps avoid future contests. However, some courts have found that lawyers owe no duty *to beneficiaries* of a will or estate to determine a testator's capacity. *See Moore v. Anderson Zeigler Disharoon Gallagher & Gray*, 135 Cal. Rptr. 2d 888 (Ct. App. 2003), in which the court dismissed a malpractice case against the law firm that represented testator and held that the law firm did not have any professional obligation to non-clients to assess testator's capacity. Upon determining, to the lawyer's satisfaction, the testator's capacity, the lawyer has met his or her "duty of loyalty to the testator."

b. The Insane Delusion

The contestant may base a challenge on a specific delusion allegedly held by the testator. The contestant must show that the delusion had no basis in reality and that there was a connection between the delusion and the testator's bequest in the will. The following case illustrates a challenge based on a theory of insane delusion.

Breeden v. Stone

992 P.2d 1167 (Colo. 2000)

I. Facts and Procedural History

This case involves a contested probate of a handwritten (holographic) will executed by Spicer Breeden, the decedent. Mr. Breeden died in his home on March 19, 1996, from a self-inflicted gunshot wound two days after he was involved in a highly publicized hit-and-run accident that killed the driver of the other vehicle.

Upon entering the decedent's home following his suicide, the Denver police discovered on his desk a handwritten document that read: "I want everything I have to go to Sydney Stone — 'houses,' 'jewelwry,' [sic] stocks[,] bonds, cloths [sic]. P.S. I was *Not* Driving the Vehical — [sic]." At the bottom of the handwritten document, the decedent printed, "SPICER H. BREEDEN" and signed beneath his printed name.

Sydney Stone (Respondent) offered the handwritten document for probate as the holographic will of the decedent. The decedent had previously executed a formal will in 1991 and a holographic codicil leaving his estate to persons other than Respondent. Several individuals filed objections to the holographic will, including Petitioners, who alleged lack of testamentary capacity. [The petitioners included Breeden's family members who alleged that the will was invalid based both on a lack of general testamentary capacity and the decedent's insane delusions about "threats against himself and his dog from government agents, friends, and others."] . . .

We granted certiorari to address whether the probate court correctly applied the insane delusion and *Cunningham* elements tests. . . .

II.   Testamentary Capacity

Underlying Colorado's law of wills is the fundamental concept of freedom of testation; namely that a testator "may dispose of his property as he pleases, and that [he] may indulge his prejudice against his relations and in favor of strangers, and that, if he does so, it is no objection to his will." This principle, however, is subject to the requirement that the maker of the will possess testamentary capacity at the time he executes the will. A person has testamentary capacity if he is an "individual eighteen or more years of age who is of sound mind."

Until 1973, the proponents of a will assumed the burden of proving that the testator had testamentary capacity at the time he executed a will. However, in 1973, the legislature shifted this burden to the contestants of a will. Under section 15-12-407, once a proponent of a will has offered prima facie proof that the will was duly executed, any contestant then assumes the burden of proving a lack of testamentary capacity, including a lack of sound mind, by a preponderance of the evidence. The issue of what constitutes sound mind has developed along two separate lines of inquiry, summarized below.

A. The Cunningham Test

We initially defined sound mind as having sufficient understanding regarding "the extent and value of [one's] property, the number and names of the persons who are the natural objects of [one's] bounty, their deserts with reference to their conduct and treatment toward [oneself], their capacity and necessity, and that [one] shall have sufficient active memory to retain all of these facts in [one's] mind long enough to have [one's] will prepared and executed."

After *Lehman,* this court further refined the test for sound mind in 1953 in the landmark case *Cunningham v. Stender,* when we held that mental capacity to make a will requires that: (1) the testator understands the nature of her act; (2) she knows the extent of her property; (3) she understands the proposed testamentary disposition; (4) she knows the natural objects of her bounty; and (5) the will represents her wishes.

B. The Insane Delusion Test

This court has also held that a person who was suffering from an insane delusion at the time he executed the will may lack testamentary capacity. We first defined an insane delusion in 1924 as "a persistent belief in that which has no existence in fact, and which is adhered to against all evidence." We held that a party asserting that a testator was suffering from an insane delusion must meet the burden of showing that the testator suffered from such delusion.

We also have addressed the issue of the causal relationship necessary between an individual's insane delusion and his capacity to contract. In *Hanks,* we noted that contractual capacity and testamentary capacity are the same . . . holding that

> [o]ne may have insane delusions regarding some matters and be insane on some subjects, yet [be] capable of transacting business concerning matters wherein such subjects are not concerned, and such insanity does not make one incompetent to contract unless the subject matter of the contract is so connected with an insane delusion as to render the afflicted party incapable of understanding the nature and effect of the agreement or of acting rationally in the transaction.

The *Hanks* case sets out a standard for the requisite causal connection between insane delusions and contractual capacity that is equally applicable to testamentary capacity. A number of other courts have applied a similar standard in the context of testamentary capacity by phrasing the inquiry as whether the delusion *materially* affects the contested disposition in the will. . . .

Based on Colorado precedent and the persuasive authority from other jurisdictions discussed above, we hold that before a will can be invalidated because of a lack of testamentary capacity due to an insane delusion, the insane delusion must materially affect the disposition in the will.

C.   *Cunningham and Insane Delusion Tests Are Not Mutually Exclusive*

As the preceding case law indicates, the *Cunningham* [as modified by *Lehman* as the test for general capacity] and the insane delusion tests [under *Hanks*] for sound mind have developed independently of each other.

The *Cunningham* test is most commonly applied in cases in which the objectors argue that the testator lacked general testamentary capacity due to a number of possible causes such as mental illness, physical infirmity, senile dementia, and general insanity. . . .

The insane delusion test ordinarily involves situations in which the testator, although in possession of his general faculties, suffers from delusions that often take the form of monomania or paranoia. . . .

As such, the *Cunningham* and insane delusion tests, although discrete, are not mutually exclusive. In order to have testamentary capacity, a testator must have a sound mind. In Colorado, a sound mind includes the presence of the *Cunningham* factors *and* the absence of insane delusions that materially affect the will. As noted above, insane delusions are often material to the making of the will, and thus will defeat testamentary capacity. However, just as in the *Hanks* case, not all insane delusions materially affect the making of a will. Nonetheless, a testator suffering from an immaterial insane delusion must still meet the *Cunningham* sound mind test.

Accordingly, we hold that an objector may challenge a testator's soundness of mind based on both or either of the *Cunningham* and insane delusion tests. . . .

E.   *Probate Court Decision*

. . . Then, the probate court applied the insane delusion test to hold that although the decedent was suffering from insane delusions at the time he executed his will, "[his] insane delusions did not affect or influence the disposition of property made in the will." . . . In so finding, the probate court considered the decedent's delusions regarding listening devices in his home and car and assassination plots against himself and his dog. In addition, the court weighed the testimony of numerous expert witnesses regarding the decedent's handwriting, his mental state near the time he executed the will, and the impact of his drug and alcohol use on his mental faculties. Further, the court considered testimony from several persons who stated that the decedent was not close to Petitioners, had infrequent contact with them, indicated to friends that he believed his father was irresponsible with money, disliked his sister's husband, and that his relationship with his brother was distant. . . . In fact, the decedent had not made provisions for either Breeden Sr. or Connell in his earlier 1991 will. (" . . . it is of special importance to note that [two years earlier, the testator] executed a will which was quite similar in the disposition"). As such, the probate court concluded that the insane delusions from which the decedent suffered did not materially affect or influence the disposition made in the holographic will.

. . . Our decision that the probate court correctly applied both tests for sound mind, by implication, holds that the court did not incorrectly merge the two tests. Although, at times, the probate court merged language from the *Cunningham* and insane delusion tests, the decision as a whole indicates that the court thoroughly analyzed all of the evidence presented and applied each of the tests to find that the decedent was of sound mind.

In sum, the probate court order reflects that the court thoroughly considered all of the evidence presented by the parties and concluded that (1) the testator met the *Cunningham* test for sound mind and (2) the insane delusions from which the decedent was suffering did not materially affect or influence his testamentary disposition.

NOTES AND QUESTIONS

1. *Ethical duties.* If a lawyer concludes that the client's mental soundness is questionable, should the lawyer allow the client to execute the will? If you conclude your client does not have testamentary capacity, what should you do? For an interesting case involving both a lawyer's failure to assess capacity and allegations of undue influence on his part, see Paula A. Monopoli, *Legal Ethics & Practical Politics: Musings on the Public Perception of Lawyer Discipline*, 10 Geo. J. Legal Ethics 423 (1997), in which the author describes the case of Boston lawyer, Michael Muse, and the disciplinary proceedings surrounding his drafting of a will for a homeless woman who turned out to have a significant estate.

2. *Professional judgment.* For a general discussion about the duties of an attorney when determining a client's incapacity, see *Persinger v. Holst*, 639 N.W.2d 594 (Mich. Ct. App. 2001), in which the court held that a lawyer was not liable when the testator was later found to be incapacitated because "at the time she executed the power of the attorney [the lawyer] exercised reasonable professional judgment with regard to its execution" and, at that time, she had no indication of testator's incapacity.

3.   *Creating a video record.* Video taping the execution of the will may help preserve evidence of the client's capacity for future contests. The benefits and drawbacks of such video taping are explored in Gerry Beyer, *Video-Recording the Will Execution Ceremony*, EST. PLAN. STUD. (Apr. 2010.)

3.   Lack of Testamentary Intent

As we noted in Chapter 9, one of the legal requirements for a valid will is that the testator have the proper testamentary intent. The *Graham* case above outlined the kind of factual evidence that courts consider when evaluating whether a testator had sufficient testamentary intent to create a valid will. Consider our discussion in Chapter 9 about "publication" — the requirement that a testator declare to the witnesses orally that, "This is my last will and testament." That section noted that states had moved away from this requirement and the UPC did not contain such a rule. Can you see the utility of such a rule in buttressing a finding of testamentary intent?

PROBLEMS

1.   Review the Marjorie M. Black will in the Appendix to Chapter 10. If you were representing the proponent of the will, what three phrases or sections in the will would help you establish that Marjorie had present, unconditional testamentary intent? When one says that testamentary intent is required, what precisely must the client intend?

2.   Sally drafted a document that begins, "I am going to Afghanistan and may never return. If I do not return, this is my will." Sally went to Afghanistan and returned, dying several years later without writing a new will. The document left all of Sally's property to her nephew, Jim. Sally's niece, Nancy, challenges the validity of the document as a will. If you represented Nancy, what arguments might you make regarding Sally's testamentary intent? If Nancy succeeds, how will Sally's property be distributed? What arguments would you make if you represented Jim?

4.   Undue Influence

A will can be challenged under the doctrine of undue influence. Undue influence is difficult to establish and requires the contestant to prove the following elements: (1) the existence and exertion of an influence; (2) the effective operation of that influence so as to subvert or overpower the testator's mind at the time of the execution of the will; and (3) the execution of a testament which the maker would not have executed but for such influence. The following case results in a finding of no undue influence. As the *Graham* court noted, "Although a contestant may prove undue influence by circumstantial evidence, the evidence must be probative of the issue and not merely create a surmise or suspicion that such influence existed at the time the will was executed."

Simmons v. Harms
695 S.E.2d 38 (Ga. 2010)

The opinion of the court was delivered by Justice BENHAM.

[Harriet Harms executed a will on September 13, 2005, and died 30 months later on March 18, 2008, at age 93. In her 2005 will, she named her son, appellee Edward Harms, as executor of her estate and devised to him the family "homeplace." She left the remainder of her estate, consisting of a brokerage account and an unimproved parcel of land in Savannah, to be divided among her four daughters, two of whom are appellants/caveators Marie Simmons and Frances Stockton. The 2005 will revoked a 1976 will, which distributed the decedent's estate equally among her five children and provided a life estate for her handicapped daughter in a small house on the property of the family homeplace].

. . . Appellants contend the probate court used the wrong legal standard in reaching its conclusion that appellants did not establish that the will was the product of appellee's undue influence on the testatrix.

A will is invalid "if anything destroys the testator's freedom of volition, such as . . . undue influence whereby the will of another is substituted for the wishes of the testator." OCGA §53-4-12. "A rebuttable presumption of undue influence arises when a beneficiary under a will occupies a confidential relationship with the testator, is not the natural object of [the testator's] bounty, and takes an active part in the planning, preparation, or execution of the will." "A confidential relationship is one where one party is so situated as to exercise a controlling influence over the will, conduct, and interest of another. . . . In order to give rise to the rebuttable presumption . . . , the evidence must show a confidential relationship wherein the primary beneficiary was capable of exerting the power of leadership over the submissive testator." One who is found to have held a confidential relationship with the testator may exercise influence to obtain a benefit, with that influence becoming what the law regards as undue when it gives dominion over the will to the extent that the testator's free agency is destroyed or the testator is constrained to do against his will what he is unable to refuse. Upon the introduction of evidence of circumstance which causes the presumption of undue influence to arise, the burden to produce evidence rebutting the presumption shifts to the propounder. It is for the trier of fact to determine whether a confidential relationship exists and whether someone has exerted undue influence over a testator, and the trier of fact's determination will be affirmed if there is any evidence to support it.

The probate court found that appellee lived with the testatrix when she executed her will but was not present when the will was executed; that appellee had discussed with the testatrix his receiving the homeplace; that there was no evidence the testatrix was isolated by appellee as she was in frequent contact with her family, friends, and neighbors before and after she executed the will and discussed its contents with several of them; and that the attorney who prepared the will testified the testatrix was competent and executed the will voluntarily. While the probate court's order does not contain the phrase "rebuttable presumption," the order noted that the influence exerted by one in a confidential relationship with the testator must be such that it "give[s] dominion over the will to such an extent as to destroy free agency or constrain[s] one to do against his will what he is unable to refuse" and the probate court found that appellee's conduct did not constitute the influence to render the will invalid because "[t]here was no evidence to support a finding that the testatrix was deprived of her free agency such that the will of the Propounder was substituted for her own will, that she was constrained or coerced into doing that which her own best judgment told her not to do, nor that such influence operated upon her at the moment of execution." In essence, the probate court's finding that there was no evidence of undue influence is also a finding that the propounder carried his burden of rebutting the presumption of undue influence. We conclude that the probate court used the appropriate legal standard to resolve the case. . . .

Judgment affirmed. All the Justices concur.

NOTES AND QUESTIONS

1.   As the court in *Simmons* notes, a confidential relationship with the testator may give rise to a presumption of undue influence. What kind of evidence should be required to establish that a confidential relationship exists between the testator and an alleged wrongdoer? See the *Restatement (Third) of Property: Wills & Other Donative Transfers* §8.3, cmt. g for a discussion of the three kinds of confidential relationships that may arise — fiduciary, reliant and dominant — and the kind of evidence that might give rise to each one. That section also states: "Traditionally, the single term 'confidential relationship' has been used to describe a relationship that gives rise to a presumption of undue influence if coupled with suspicious circumstances." Did the *Simmons* court discuss whether there were "suspicious circumstances" in finding that there was such a presumption? If not, why do you think they did not discuss this issue?

2. *Establishing undue influence.* Assume you represent a disgruntled beneficiary who believes she did not get her "fair share" due to the undue influence of her sister upon her mother. What kind of evidence would you seek to enter into the record, what is her burden of proof and what result would she be seeking if she is successful?

3. *Gay and lesbian testators.* Historically, the wills of gay and lesbian testators who left bequests to their partners were often challenged by families on the basis of undue influence. *See* Rhonda R. Rivera, *Lawyers, Clients and AIDS: Some Notes from the Trenches,* 49 Ohio St. L.J. 883 (1989), in which the author describes how undue influence was used historically to challenge the wills of homosexual testators. *See also* Jeffrey G. Sherman, *Undue Influence and the Homosexual Testator,* 42 U. Pitt. L. Rev. 225 (1981), in which the author analyzed whether a homosexual testator was more likely to have his will challenged under the doctrine of undue influence. But this traditional hostility to gay and lesbian couples has dissipated over the years, and contestants are much less likely to proceed on such grounds today.

5. Fraud and Duress

Fraud. Wills can be invalidated if the contestant can establish that they are the result of fraud. *See* Stephen Heffner, *Judge: Exeter Woman Who Left Handyman Her Estate Was Competent,* Providence J.-Bull., Feb. 26, 1992, and Tina Cassidy, *44 Cousins vs. a Caregiver Rhode Island Woman's Will Faces Challenge,* Bos. Globe, Sept. 22, 1991. The *Restatement (Third) of Property: Wills & Other Donative Transfers* states that, "a donative transfer is procured by fraud if the wrongdoer knowingly or recklessly made a false representation to the donor about a material fact that was intended to and did lead the donor to make a donative transfer that the donor would not otherwise have made."

> **Example:** Alonzo has been blind from birth. His, brother, Lorenzo, brought him a document to sign that he told Alonzo was a lease for 50 acres of Alonzo's land, which had valuable oil and gas reserves. In fact, the document was a will that bequeathed the 50 acres of land to Lorenzo. Lorenzo guides Alonzo's hand as he makes his mark on the will. The will would be invalidated by the underlying fraud.

In the *Pearl Rose* case detailed in the articles noted above, her heirs alleged that Mrs. Rose, the testator, was so badly disabled that she could not have signed the documents at issue and that Mr. Peck, the named personal representative and beneficiary, must have forged her signature. Consider the similarities between undue influence and fraud. What kind of evidence might be used to support each of these theories?

Duress.   The *Restatement (Third) of Property: Wills & Donative Transfers* provides that a donative transfer like a bequest has been procured by duress if someone threatens to or actually does something that coerces the testator into making the bequest. Such an act must be wrongful, *i.e.,* it must be something that the wrongdoer has no right to do. Again, note the connection with undue influence. While an act may not constitute coercion or duress because the person does have a right to do it, it may rise to the level of undue influence. For example, if Toby is afraid that Amanda will abandon him when he is ill and will not care for him, he may make a bequest to Amanda to try to ensure she will stay and take care of him. That is not duress, since it is not wrongful for Amanda if Amanda has no duty to care for him. However, depending on the other circumstances surrounding Amanda's relationship with Toby and her behavior with regard to the execution of the will, the *Restatement* notes such an act may constitute undue influence.

F.   PREVENTING CHALLENGES — *IN TERROREM* OR "NO-CONTEST" CLAUSES

If you are drafting a will for a client, how do you prevent a will contest from upsetting the estate plan? Many lawyers feel it is useful to include a penalty or no-contest clause in the will. This will cause a beneficiary to forfeit her bequest if she brings a challenge to the will. From a practical perspective, the beneficiary must receive something valuable under the will in order for such a clause to be effective. A beneficiary who has nothing to lose will go ahead and bring the contest despite the clause. The following language from the *Restatement (Third) of Property: Wills & Other Donative Transfers* §8.5, Illus. 1 is an example of such an *in terrorem* or "no-contest" clause:

> *If any beneficiary under my will should directly or indirectly contest, oppose or dispute this my last will and testament, I direct that such beneficiary shall received nothing under my will.*

Many state courts construe these clauses very narrowly since they have the effect of "closing the courthouse door" to potential beneficiaries. State statutes often provide a procedure whereby beneficiaries can ask for a preliminary hearing on the issue of whether the particular case they are contemplating will trigger the no-contest clause. If the court says it will not, then they may proceed without fear of forfeiting their inheritance. The UPC reflects this concern about access to the court in §2-517.

UPC §2-517. Penalty Clause for Contest.

A provision in a will purporting to penalize an interested person for contesting the will or instituting other proceedings relating to the estate is unenforceable if probable cause exists for instituting proceedings.

A number of courts have narrowed the applicability of no-contest clauses by finding that the challenge does not come within the ambit of a "contest." *See, e.g., Keener v. Keener*, 682 S.E.2d 545 (Va. 2009), in which the court held that a daughter's action "opening intestate administration of her father's estate," prior to the subsequent probate of the decedent's will, was not a contest within the meaning of the no-contest clause of the trust even if the action ultimately would have "thwarted the testator's purpose of funding the trust through the will" because "that purpose . . . was not a provision of the trust and the will contained no forfeiture provision." *See also Barr v. Dawson*, 158 P.3d 1073 (Okla. Civ. App. 2006), in which the court stated that moving for a spousal election was not a contest within the *in terrorem* clause because such statutory rights needed to be protected and, further, the plaintiff only moved for election under good-faith to provide for her incompetent mother prior to being given a copy of the trust, upon which she ultimately withdrew the contest when she agreed that the trust's terms would provide for her mother.

Note that lawyers have an ethical duty not to bring frivolous lawsuits. If they bring such a lawsuit, they may face disciplinary consequences and sanctions from the court. *See* Andrew Longstreth, *Paul Weiss and Lowenstein Ordered to Pay $1.6 Million for Filing Frivolous Suit against Ron Perelman's In-Laws*, Am. Law., Aug. 26, 2010. Lawyers in these circumstances should also be wary of having costs assessed against their clients. *See In re Estate of King*, 920 N.E.2d 820 (Mass. 2010), in which the court interpreted the Massachusetts statute to allow the award of costs and fees to a party in a will contest.

In recent years, alternative dispute resolution has become an attractive alternative to increasingly clogged court dockets. Mediation in particular has become a popular way to resolve disputes. Probate courts have explored the use of mediation in will contests with varying degrees of success. *See* Lela P. Love & Stewart E. Sterk, *Leaving More than Money: Mediation Clauses in Estate Planning Documents*, 65 Wash. & Lee L. Rev. 539 (2008), in which the authors argue that will mediation clauses can prevent contentious family litigation, and Yolanda Vorys, Note, *The Best of Both Worlds: The Use of Med-Arb for Resolving Will Disputes*, 22 Ohio St. J. on Disp. Resol. 871 (2007), in which the author argues that will disputes should be resolved with a hybrid of mediation and arbitration rather than litigation. Professors Mary Radford and Susan Gary have also explored the use of mediation in probate disputes in the following articles: Mary F. Radford, *Advantages and Disadvantages of Mediation in Probate, Trust, and Guardianship Matters*, 1 Pepp. Disp. Resol. L.J. 241 (2001) and *An Introduction to the Uses of Mediation and Other Forms of Dispute Resolution in Probate, Trust, and Guardianship Matters*, 34 Real Prop. Prob. & Tr. J. 601 (2000), and Susan N. Gary, *Mediating Probate Disputes*, Prob. & Prop., July-Aug. 1999, at 11.

NOTES

1. *Validate before you go.* Arkansas, Ohio, North Dakota and Alaska now allow for "pre-mortem" probate — a process whereby a will or trust can be validated before the testator dies, thus precluding a post-death attack on the instrument. *See Would the Actor's Heirs Have been Better off with an Alaskan Will?*, Trust Advisor (June 26, 2010), http://thetrustadvisor.com/news/premortem.

2. *Beyond will contests.* In addition to will contests, there are other kinds of claims that may be brought by disappointed heirs. For example, celebrity Anna Nicole Smith, whose legal name was Vickie Lynn Marshall, raised a claim for tortious interference with an inter vivos gift against her deceased husband's son, Pierce Marshall, in both a Texas probate court and in a federal bankruptcy court. Professor Irene Johnson explains the tort as follows: "An action for tortious interference with expectancy of inheritance or gift provides a plaintiff with the opportunity to recover for the loss of this expectancy if the defendant's tortious act deprives the plaintiff of an expected inheritance, benefit under a will, at-death benefit, or *inter vivos* gift." *See* Irene D. Johnson, *Tortious Interference with Expectancy of Inheritance or Gift — Suggestions for Resort to the Tort*, 39 U. Tol. L. Rev. 769, 770 (2008). This action sounds in tort rather than probate.

3. *The never-ending story.* The Ninth Circuit held that the federal bankruptcy court, which had ruled in Anna Nicole Smith's favor, did not have jurisdiction over her claim given the "probate exception" to federal jurisdiction, which reserves to state courts certain matters having to do with probate. The *Marshall* case was appealed to the United States Supreme Court, where the Court held that the "probate exception" to federal court jurisdiction did not extend to the kind of tort claim raised by Smith and it remanded the case. *See Marshall v. Marshall*, 547 U.S. 293 (2006). Anna Nicole Smith died on February 8, 2007. On remand, the Ninth Circuit vacated the prior decisions in favor of Anna Nicole Smith and effectively reinstated the Texas probate court decision adverse to Smith, the result of which was that her estate received nothing from her late husband's estate. Yet the story was not over. On September 28, 2010, the United States Supreme Court granted cert and heard the appeal from the Ninth Circuit's decision as this book went to press. *See Marshall v. Stern (In re Marshall)*, 600

F. 3d 1037 (9th Cir. 2009), cert. granted, 79 U.S.L.W 3092 (U.S. Sept. 28, 2010) (No. 10-179).

4. *Contracts to make wills.* In addition to the action in tort described above, disappointed heirs may bring an action in contract alleging that the decedent was contractually bound to either make a bequest or not change a bequest in her will. Contracts to make wills are governed by contract law, and UPC §2-514 requires that in order for a contract to make or not revoke a will to be enforceable, the material provisions of the contract must be in the will itself, or there must be an express reference in a will to such a contract and extrinsic evidence establishing its terms or there must be a writing signed by the decedent that establishes such a contract. It also provides that, "[t]he execution of a joint will or mutual wills does not create a presumption of a contract not to revoke the will or wills." *See Collins v. Estate of Collins*, 619 S.E.2d 531 (N.C. 2005), where the court found that mutual wills executed by a husband and wife did not create a contract not to revoke absent contractual language in the will or another document which evidenced their intent to enter into a binding contract.

5. *Beyond mere property distribution.* Part of the reason that will contests are brought is that wills have significant emotional significance for both the testator and the beneficiaries. For an interesting exploration of the expressive dimension of wills in addition to their legal function, see Daphna Hacker, *Soulless Wills*, 35 Law & Soc. Inquiry 957, 958 (2010), in which the author "argues that the unique, personal, and emotional voices of testators should be allowed to be heard in their wills . . .".

G. EXERCISE

Andrew Chang has been married to Linda Liu for 25 years, and they have two children: Betty and Michael. Andrew signed the will set out below in June of 2009.

Andrew has come to ask for your advice. He knows that you are a specialist in estate planning, and he has asked you to take a second look at the will. You should assume that the will was duly executed: It is in writing, and signed by the testator and three witnesses.

You are responsible for finding at least six issues where you can improve the drafting of the will as well as make alternative estate planning recommendations. Once you spot these issues, you should draft language to resolve them. You can either mark-up the existing language or draft entirely new language. You may work on this individually or in teams of up to three people.

Last Will and Testament

I, Andrew Chang, revoke any prior wills and codicils made by me and declare this to be my will.

Any references in this will to my spouse refer to Linda Liu. Any reference in my will to my children is to such children as well as any children subsequently born to or legally adopted by me. Any reference in my will to my issue is to my children and their issue.

(a) I give the sum of $10,000 to my son, Michael Chang.

(b) I give the engraved gold pocket watch and chain which I inherited from my grandfather to my daughter, Betty Chang.

(c) I give the sum of $25,000 to my sister, Heidi Chang, if she survives me, on the further condition that prior to receipt of this gift she shall establish to the satisfaction of my executor that she has refrained from smoking tobacco for a period of at least one full year.

Except as otherwise provided in a memorandum left at the time of my death, I give all my household goods, personal effects, and other articles of tangible personal property, except such property used in any business in which I may have any interest, together with any insurance policies covering such property and claims under such policies, to my children, to be divided between them as they may agree. I reserve the right to give such property in accordance with any memorandum directing their disposition signed by me or in my handwriting which I may leave at my death.

I nominate my spouse, Linda Liu, as my personal representative.

If both my children survive me and both have reached the age of forty-five years, I give my residuary estate outright in equal shares to each of them.

IN WITNESS WHEREOF, I have hereunto set my hand and seal this first day of June, 2009.

Andrew Chang

Jane Smith

Adam Good

12 PROTECTING THE FAMILY

A. INTRODUCTION

So far, you've seen how the law protects a testator's freedom of disposition, allowing the testator to include or exclude whomever he wishes or to place restrictions on the right to receive his property. However, when it comes to one's surviving spouse, the rules change, and may override the testator's planned disposition. Spouses *(and those treated as spouses pursuant to state law, such as those in a civil union)* are protected from disinheritance in several different ways. First, states typically provide a "homestead" exemption that permits a surviving spouse to continue to live in the marital home for a period of time and a family allowance to help with financial support in the period just after the decedent's death. Second, if a spouse has not been given a sufficient share of the marital property because the decedent made probate or nonprobate transfers to others, contemporary estate law typically remedies this by allowing the surviving spouse to "elect against the will" and take a greater share of the marital property than the decedent provided. Third, to protect against accidental disinheritance in situations where the decedent drafted a will before marrying the survivor, the omitted (sometimes called "pretermitted") spouse is provided a share of the probate estate equal to what would have been provided if the decedent died intestate. A final form of protection, outside of the trusts and estates context, is the spouse's entitlement to various survivor benefits through, for example, Social Security or private pensions.

As you learned in Chapter 2, only those family members with a recognized legal status are eligible for these protections. Children are generally not protected in the same way. Except in Louisiana, children are not entitled to a mandatory share of the estate if the testator has disinherited them. Under certain circumstances, however, if children are found to have been accidentally left out of a will, they may be entitled as pretermitted children to a limited share of the parent's estate.

This chapter explores the default and override rules for protecting the family, showing the tension between freedom to leave property as one chooses and protection of the "natural objects of one's bounty," or family members. In light of the assumptions of intestacy (discussed in Chapter 3) that the decedent would choose to leave property to family members, this chapter explores the opposite situation: What happens when the decedent chooses not to leave property to family members, or forgets to do so?

The chapter starts with a brief history of how surviving spouses have been protected through the concepts of dower and curtesy before turning to contemporary law on spousal protections and waiver of those protections. We also explore what happens to children and analyze why the protections for children are narrower than those for a spouse. The chapter concludes by comparing and contrasting the differing approaches that states have adopted towards omitted children. Along the way are problems and exercises that help you apply the law to different factual situations.

B.   HISTORY OF ADULT PARTNER PROTECTIONS

The decedent may have made lifetime gifts, drafted a will, forgotten to change a disposing document or entered into a spousal contract that denies passing wealth to her spouse. Each of these situations presents different issues when it comes to spousal protection. Before addressing them, consider Professor Gary's history of how the law has protected the surviving spouse from disinheritance. The article focuses on the elective share, and also provides a brief overview of other types of protections.

Susan N. Gary, The Oregon Elective Share Statute: Is Reform an Impossible Dream?
44 Willamette L. Rev. 337, 338, 339-40 (2007)

At a time when husbands held title to family property and wives did not, the law protected a widow who might otherwise be left without support when her husband died. The law provided a somewhat different sort of support for a surviving husband. Under English common law, dower gave the widow a life-estate in one-third of her husband's real property. Her husband could not extinguish her dower right, either during lifetime or at death. On her death, the widow did not control the ultimate disposition of the property; she held only a life estate. Protection for a surviving husband came in the form of curtesy. Curtesy provided a husband with a life estate in all of his deceased wife's property (not just her real property), but applied only if a child or children were born to the marriage.

Dower worked well when the bulk of assets consisted of real property, but as property interests diversified another system became necessary. Common law states in the United States began to shift from dower to elective share statutes. The early elective share statutes gave a surviving spouse the right to take a share of the deceased spouse's probate property. The statutes used one-third as the fraction, probably influenced by the one-third interest of dower. In contrast with dower, the statutes gave the surviving spouse a fee interest rather than a life estate in the elective share amount. . . .

Elective share statutes developed at a time when family structures created different needs for surviving spouses. Since then, changes in the way spouses hold title to property, the number of remarriages and short-term marriages, and federal programs that protect surviving spouses have all changed the stage on which the elective share currently plays. A few commentators have argued that the elective share has become unnecessary. Yet if each spouse receives a share of marital property when a marriage dissolves during the spouses' lifetimes, one can argue that each spouse should receive a share of marital property if the marriage ends when one spouse dies. All common law states except Georgia continue to apply elective share statutes.

QUESTIONS

1. *Real protection?* What accounts for the differing protections for husbands and wives?

2. *Rights to what? Why?* Given the historical reasons for protecting a spouse, are there any rationales that exist today for protecting a spouse from disinheritance? The article mentions that changes in the way spouses hold property has changed the impact of the elective share. You've learned about various lifetime transfers throughout the course. Consider whether any type of lifetime transfer should ever be subject to the elective share.

C. DIFFERING PROTECTIONS UNDER COMMUNITY PROPERTY AND COMMON LAW PROPERTY SYSTEMS

The forms of spousal protection depend on whether a state is a common-law or a community property state. If you are attending law school in Arizona, California, Idaho, Louisiana, Nevada, New Mexico, Texas, Washington or Wisconsin, you have probably already spent some time learning about the system of community property that controls ownership of marital property in those states. In Alaska, you can elect either community or common law. The other 40 states have a common law (or separate) system of property.

It is important to distinguish between the two systems of marital property ownership because, among other differences, each system provides a different form of protection for the surviving spouse. States typically have decided, based on general conflict of law principles, that the law of the marital domicile controls the classification of personal property acquired during marriage.

1. *Community Property*

In the nine community property states, property is held either as community property or separate property. *Community property* is property accumulated by either spouse from earnings or other work during the marriage. All property acquired during the marriage is jointly owned in a manner similar to tenancies in common (but which exists exclusively between spouses). With community property, title is irrelevant when it comes to actual ownership and control of the property. Each spouse owns an equal, undivided share in all of the property. Because each spouse has equal ownership, states have established various limits on each spouse's ability to give away or sell community property without the permission of the other spouse. By contrast, property that was acquired before the marriage, or that either spouse receives as a gift or an inheritance during the marriage, is considered *separate property* and remains under the ownership and control of that individual spouse. States vary as to whether, and under what circumstances, the earnings of separate property become community property. State community property concepts may not be applicable to assets governed by federal law, such as pensions subject to ERISA; federal law will preempt state law. *See Boggs v. Boggs*, 520 U.S. 833 (1997).

The community property system "is now generally viewed as 'explicitly recognizing marriage as a partnership'. . . . Each spouse's time and energy is thereby assumed to improve the marriage in some way, even if the market would not value such contributions. The classic example is the traditional division of labor between husband and wife, wherein the husband engages in work for wages while the wife stays at home to care for children and the household." Laura A. Rosenbury, *Two Ways to End a Marriage: Divorce or Death*, 2005 Utah L. Rev. 1227, 1234-35.

In community property states, community property is distributed at divorce either equally or by a system of equitable distribution based on a variety of factors, such as the need and contribution of each spouse. Upon death, the surviving spouse in a community property jurisdiction is entitled to retain her one-half of all community property. Title is irrelevant and does not affect the distribution of this property. The decedent's half of the community property is within his control to dispose through a will, by intestacy or by other methods. Because separate property retains its character, each spouse can dispose of it without the other spouse having any rights.

> **Example:** During their marriage, Waangari accumulated $200,000 in assets through her professional work (and not through inheritance) and Henry accumulated $1,000 of assets. The community property is thus $201,000. On Waangari's death, Henry is entitled to $100,500 of that property, and her estate controls the other half.

Notwithstanding the underlying principles of community property, the system does not always result in an equal division of the couple's marital assets. The surviving spouse may receive more or less than one-half of the community property if: (i) the couple migrated between community property and separate property states throughout the marriage (discussed later in subsection (3)); or (ii) the spouses have agreed otherwise in a marital agreement. (The use of marital agreements is discussed in Section E.)

2. Common Law Property

Common law states differ with respect to spousal rights in property acquired during the course of the marriage. In the common law system, title vests in the person who earns or otherwise acquires the property in his name. The spouse with title has sole ownership and control over the property during the marriage. Except to the extent the spouses acquire and title property jointly, the non-title holder has no rights in the property of the other.

At *divorce*, common law states distribute the property based on equitable distribution of all assets acquired during the marriage. In this way, property divisions at divorce in common law states and those in community property states tend to reach comparable outcomes.

The *death* of a spouse in a common law state, however, has a very different result than in community property states. In the absence of statutory spousal protections, the spouse who owns property can devise it without the surviving spouse obtaining any rights. As Professor Gary explained, to remedy the inadequate protection afforded by dower and to prevent disinherited widows and young children from becoming public charges, legislators in common law states enacted elective share statutes as a replacement or substitute for the surviving spouse's legal life estate (her dower interest). Consequently, if the testator's bequest to the widow is less than that required by the statute, she can take her statutory share instead. Unlike dower, what constitutes the estate for purposes of determining the elective share not only includes both realty and personalty but it may also include nonprobate property. While the traditional formula for the elective (sometimes also called a "forced") share allots a fixed portion of the estate (typically one-third) to the surviving spouse, regardless of the size of the estate, the surviving spouse's need or earning capacity or the duration of the marriage, the UPC takes these variables into account.

3.   *Division at Death for Migrating Couples*

It is not uncommon for couples to migrate between community property and common law states during their marriage. Courts have traditionally used the following rules to determine the classification of property as either community or common law that the couple has acquired in each state:

1) For real property, the law of the state in which the property is located controls its classification; and
2) For personal property, the law of the marital domicile at the time the property is acquired controls its classification.

If couples move between a common law and a community property state, the move does not affect the classification of the property interests. That is, property acquired while the couple is domiciled in California is community property, even if the spouses move to Missouri; property acquired in Missouri and titled in one spouse's name is separate property, even if the spouses move to California.

> **Example:** Sujatha and Sam lived in a common law state for 50 years. During the course of the marriage, Sujatha saved $100,000 from her earnings that she placed in a bank account in her own name. Sujatha and Sam retired and moved to a community property state. Sadly, Sujatha died shortly thereafter. Sam has no rights to the money in Sujatha's separately titled bank account as it is considered separate property. Because they are not needed with respect to community property, elective shares are not part of the law in community property states. As a result, without additional statutory assistance, Sam may be without anything on Sujatha's death.

In recognition of the unfairness to Sam of this result, four of the community property states have developed doctrines that recognize rights in the surviving spouse to property acquired in a common law state under the principle of "quasi-community property."[1] "Quasi-community property is generally defined as marital property acquired while domiciled in a common law state that would have been characterized as community property if the married couple had been domiciled in a community property state." Kenneth W. Kingma, *Property Division at Divorce or Death for Married Couples Migrating Between Common Law and Community Property States*, 35 ACTEC J. 74, 82 (2009). In effect, the property becomes community property to which the surviving spouse has equal rights.

The problem identified above for the surviving spouse does not exist when the opposite is true — the spouses acquired property in a community property state and then moved to a common law state. In this situation, the surviving spouse is typically entitled to one-half of the community property as well as an elective share in the common law property. The Uniform Disposition of Community Property Rights at Death Act (1971), which has been enacted in 14 common law states, provides explicit recognition of this principle, preserving the community property brought into the state as community property, unless the spouses have agreed otherwise. The community property is not, then, subject to the surviving spouse's elective share.

NOTES AND QUESTIONS

1.   *Divorce or death indeed.* Can the law be said to encourage divorce in a common law system for the lower-earning spouse?

2.   *Which distribution?* Pennsylvania law now provides that if death occurs after an action for divorce has been filed but before a decree in divorce has been entered, then the surviving spouse is entitled to equitable division of marital property under the divorce code rather than an elective share under the probate code. 20 Pa. Cons. Stat. §2203 (2008); 23 Pa. Cons. Stat. §3323 (D.1) (2008).

---

1. Surviving spouses may, alternatively, receive some protection based on conflict of law principles. *See* Mark Patton, Note, *Quasi-Community Property in Arizona: Why Just at Divorce and Not Death?*, 47 Ariz. L. Rev. 167, 177-80 (2005).

D. PROTECTION FOR THE SURVIVING SPOUSE — THE ELECTIVE SHARE

1. What Happens Without an Elective Share?

Before discussing the protections provided by the elective share and the mechanics of its operation, consider the rights of a surviving spouse who does not have the security afforded by the elective share rule. This will help put the protections against disinheritance, whether done innocently or by design, into perspective.

PROBLEMS

In each of the following problems, consider what property, if any, the surviving spouse (Sawyer) would be entitled to claim assuming there is no elective share statute. Tony and Sawyer have been married for 35 years, they live in a common law property state, have two children (Anya and Brad), all of Tony's property was acquired with funds earned during the marriage and Sawyer has no property in her name other than what is left to her by Tony. As you answer these questions, think about whose interests are favored, and whether anyone else's interests should be considered.

1. Tony dies with $1,000,000 in the probate estate and leaves everything to Sawyer in his will.

2. Tony dies with $1,000,000 in the probate estate and leaves nothing to Sawyer in his will. He devised a third each to Anya and Brad and his friend, Fred. Tony states in his will that he wishes to disinherit Sawyer because they have had so many disagreements over the years and he feels he wasted his life with her.

3. Tony dies with no property in his probate estate because he made gifts of $333,333 each to Anya and Brad and Fred a week before he died.

4. Tony dies with no property in his probate estate. He has a $1,000,000 life insurance policy on his life and named Anya and Brad and Fred as equal beneficiaries a year before he died.

5. Tony dies with no property in his probate estate. He has a $1,000,000 retirement plan and named his sole employee as the beneficiary a week before he died.

2. Current Approaches to the Elective Share

Now that you understand what happens in the absence of an elective share, we hope you can appreciate the need to provide some economic rights for a surviving spouse. In most common law states, this takes the form of the elective share. Elective share provisions are typically justified based on either an economic partnership or a dependency/support theory. The first theory views marriage as a partnership to which both spouses contribute, entitling both spouses to share in the assets. The second theory justifies the elective share as "a means of continuing the decedent's duty of support beyond the grave." Lawrence W. Waggoner, *The Uniform Probate Code's Elective Share: Time for a Reassessment (With an Addendum Reporting on Post-Publication Amendments)* (2010) (draft at 2).

This section first sets out the traditional approach to the elective share as codified in the Maryland elective share statute, and then turns to the UPC, which is a more expansive approach. As you read these statutes, consider whether they implement a support theory or a partnership theory.

a.   The Traditional Approach Exemplified in the Maryland Statute

Maryland Code Estates and Trusts Article §3-203 (2010). Right to Elective Share.

(a) "Net estate" defined. — In this section, "net estate" means the property of the decedent passing by testate succession, without a deduction for State or federal estate or inheritance taxes, and reduced by:

(1) Funeral and administration expenses;

(2) Family allowances; and

(3) Enforceable claims and debts against the estate.

(b) In general. — Instead of property left to the surviving spouse by will, the surviving spouse may elect to take a one-third share of the net estate if there is also a surviving issue, or a one-half share of the net estate if there is no surviving issue.

(c) Limitation. — The surviving spouse who makes this election may not take more than a one-half share of the net estate.

This provision was at issue in the following case, in which Maryland's highest court resolutely stuck to the statutory definition of "net estate."

Karsenty v. Schoukroun
959 A.2d 1147 (Md. 2008)

Opinion by HARRELL, J.

We are asked in this case to decide whether an *inter vivos* transfer, in which a deceased spouse retained control over the transferred property during his lifetime, constitutes a *per se* violation of the surviving spouse's statutory, elective right to a percentage of the deceased spouse's net estate under Maryland Code. The Circuit Court for Anne Arundel County held that it does not, concluding that the decedent did not intend to defraud his surviving spouse when he transferred assets to a revocable trust that he created for his daughter (by a prior marriage) and named that trust as the beneficiary of two IRA accounts. The Court of Special Appeals reversed the trial court in a reported opinion, where it held that, although the trial court was not clearly erroneous in finding that the decedent did not intend to defraud his surviving spouse, the decedent's retained control of the transferred assets rendered the transfer a fraud *per se* on the surviving spouse's marital rights.

We granted the trustee's Petition for a Writ of Certiorari. The successful petition posed the following question:

> Whether Maryland has a bright-line rule establishing that in every case in which a deceased spouse has transferred property with a retained interest, the transfer constitutes a fraud on the surviving spouse's elective share regardless of motive, the extent of control, and other equitable factors?

For the reasons to be explained, we shall reverse the judgment of the intermediate appellate court; however, because we remain concerned by the apparent legal test applied by the trial court in its ruling, we shall direct remand of this case to the trial court with further guidance. As we shall explain, the body of precedents forming the doctrine that, until now, has been referred to as "fraud on marital rights" has really little to do with common law fraud as typically understood. We reject that phraseology as inconsistent with the weight of Maryland precedent. We also shall take this opportunity to clarify somewhat the applicable primary factors to consider when determining whether to set aside an *inter vivos* transfer that frustrates a surviving spouse's right to an elective share of the deceased spouse's estate.

FACTS

This case arises from a decedent's *inter vivos* distribution of his assets through the use of both probate and non-probate estate planning arrangements. On 10 October 1987, Gilles H. Schoukroun ("Gilles" or "Decedent") married his first wife, Bernadette. The marriage produced one child, Lauren Schoukroun ("Lauren"), who was born on 20 April 1990. When Lauren was six years old, Gilles and Bernadette ended their marriage. . . .

Sometime in 1999, Gilles met Kathleen Sexton ("Kathleen") and, by October of that year, they became engaged to be married. Kathleen had been married previously and had a child from that marriage. In the Spring of 2000, before they married, Gilles and Kathleen took out life insurance policies from Zurich Kemper. Gilles purchased a policy on his life, naming

Kathleen as the beneficiary, in the amount of $200,000. Kathleen made her policy benefits payable to her estate in the amount of $200,000, with her son from her prior marriage as the beneficiary of her estate. Gilles and Kathleen were married in Worcester County on 3 July 2000. At the time, they were 40 and 45 years old, respectively. . . .

[Gilles developed lymphoma.] This case centers on the estate planning arrangements that Gilles made in the last three to four months of his life. On 23 June 2004, Gilles prepared and executed his Last Will and Testament and a document known as the Gilles H. Schoukroun Trust (the "Trust"). In his will, Gilles named his sister, Maryse Karsenty ("Maryse"), the Personal Representative of his estate. The will provided, "I give all my tangible personal property, together with any insurance providing coverage thereon, to my wife, KATHLEEN SEXTON . . . "Gilles bequeathed the "rest, residue and remainder" of the estate to the Trust.

With respect to the Trust, Gilles named Lauren the beneficiary. He named himself settlor and trustee during his lifetime, and he appointed Maryse trustee upon his death. In the event Maryse could not serve as trustee, Gilles named Kathleen as the alternative trustee. Clause Two of the Trust provided:

> The Settlor reserves the right to amend or terminate this trust from time to time by notice in writing delivered to the Trustee during the lifetime of the Settlor, and any amendment or termination shall be effective immediately upon delivery thereof to the Trustee, except that changes with respect to the Trustee's duties, liabilities or compensation shall not be effective without its consent.
>
> Upon the death of the Settlor, this trust shall be irrevocable and there shall be no right to alter, amend, revoke or terminate this trust or any of its provisions.

Clause Three of the Trust, in pertinent part, provided:

> The Trustee shall pay the net income from this trust to or for the benefit of the Settlor during the Settlor's lifetime, in such annual or more frequent installments as the Trustee and the Settlor may agree, and the Trustee shall pay so much or all of the principal of the trust to the Settlor as he shall from time to time request in a signed writing delivered to the Trustee.

On the same day that he created the Trust, Gilles transferred into the Trust assets from three financial accounts: (1) one at E*Trade Financial, worth approximately $29,037.15; (2) one at Fidelity Investments, worth approximately $75,257.25; and (3) a second at Fidelity Investments, worth approximately $49,034.67. On 12 July 2004, Gilles named the Trust as the beneficiary of two IRA transfer-on-death ("TOD") accounts at Fidelity Investments, one worth approximately $257,863.31, the other worth approximately $14,069.51. It was clear that Fidelity managed the investments in the larger TOD account (there was no similar evidence offered as to the smaller). It appears from the record that Gilles took no distributions from either of the TOD accounts during his lifetime.

When Gilles died, Lauren became the sole beneficiary of the Trust. Kathleen received the $200,000 proceeds from Gilles's Zurich Kemper life insurance policy. In accordance with Gilles's will, Kathleen also received his 2003 Toyota Highlander, the outstanding loan balance for which he had recently paid off. The vehicle was valued at approximately $22,000. . . .

ANALYSIS

Kathleen renounced her inheritance under Gilles's will and invoked her right to an elective share of his estate, which she contends should include the Trust and the TOD accounts. Accordingly, the starting point of our analysis of her claims is Maryland's elective share statute, Maryland Code Estates and Trusts Article, §3-203. . . .

Section 3-203 is clear and unambiguous with respect to the Trust and the TOD accounts in this case. The term "net estate," as it is used in Maryland's elective share statute, "means the property of the decedent passing by *testate succession*." Estates and Trusts Art. §3-203(a) (italics added). This includes only property in which the decedent "has some interest . . . which will survive his death." Here, the Trust and the TOD accounts fall outside the definition of "net estate" because Gilles did not have any interest in either that survived his death.[2] When Gilles created the Trust, Lauren received a vested, albeit revocable, interest therein; accordingly, Lauren became the sole beneficiary of the Trust by operation of law when Gilles died. Likewise, the TOD accounts transferred to the Trust upon Gilles's death "by reason of the contract" between him and Fidelity Investments with which the accounts were registered. *See* Maryland Code §16-109(a). Thus, by its plain language, Section 3-203 does not permit Kathleen to take a share of the Trust assets or the TOD accounts.

We must respect the "net estate" model chosen by the General Assembly. Many of our sister states, however, have taken a different approach with respect to their elective share statutes, adopting some form of the "augmented estate" concept. Although there are differences between the models adopted by the various augmented estate jurisdictions, the pith of the augmented estate concept is that a surviving spouse's elective share is calculated by including non-probate assets over which the decedent had dominion and control during her or his lifetime. . . .

Maryland precedent long has recognized that a court may invalidate a deceased spouse's *inter vivos* transfer where equity requires that the transferred property be considered part of her or his estate for the purpose of calculating the surviving spouse's statutory share. To determine whether

---

2. [FN 14] In other words, "net estate" does not include assets that are disposed of by "non-probate arrangements—such as living trusts, life insurance, joint ownership, and retirement."

equity requires that a transfer be set aside, a court must ask whether the decedent intended to part with ownership of the property in form only, while remaining the true owner of the property during her or his lifetime; if the decedent intended that the transfer divest her or him of ownership in form, but not in substance, the transaction unlawfully frustrates the statutory protection of the decedent's surviving spouse and, accordingly, is invalid.

. . . The pertinent case-law makes clear that all of the relevant facts and circumstances should be considered and a determination made on a case-by-case basis. Moreover, we long have recognized that an *inter vivos* transfer in which a decedent retained sole lifetime control over the transferred property is not, by itself, violative of the surviving spouse's statutory share. . . .

In the present case, Gilles retained the power to revoke the Trust at anytime "by notice in writing." He named himself as trustee and retained a life-estate in the net income of the Trust. Gilles also retained the power to invade the principal of the Trust. With respect to the TOD accounts, Gilles retained the power to change the beneficiary of those accounts. It is clear that Gilles retained absolute control over the Trust; however, this Court has not made that characteristic the sole touchstone of an *inter vivos* transfer that will be invalidated as to a surviving spouse. While retained control is a significant fact to consider, it is not, by itself, a sufficient justification for invalidating an *inter vivos* trust. Accordingly, we reverse the judgment of the intermediate appellate court and direct a remand of this case to the trial court for further proceedings not inconsistent with this opinion. . . .

To summarize, when a surviving spouse seeks to invalidate the nonprobate disposition of an asset, a scrutinizing court must focus on the nature of the underlying *inter vivos* transfer. If it was "complete and bona fide" or done in "good faith" (both phrases meaning the same thing in this context), the court must respect the estate planning arrangements of the decedent and may not invalidate the transaction; however if it was "a mere device or contrivance," "a mere fiction," "a sham," or "colorable" (each also sharing the same meaning in this context), the court shall invalidate the underlying transaction as to the surviving spouse. In order to answer this question, a court must consider whether the decedent truly intended that the *inter vivos* transfer divest her or him of ownership in form, but not in substance. Stated in more practical language, the question for a court to decide is whether the decedent intended that the transfer change nothing, except how the property is directed at the decedent's death. Notwithstanding our previous references to "fraud" on marital rights, because we ultimately are not concerned with whether a decedent intended to deprive her or his surviving spouse of property, we emphasize today that it is more helpful for a court to think of a sham transfer in this context as an unlawful frustration of the surviving spouse's statutory share. . . .

We admit that determining whether someone intended that an *inter vivos* transfer be a sham that changes nothing may be difficult, as it is an ethereal touchstone. There also is the complicating fact that the person whose intent matters most is deceased when the judicial inquiry typically engages itself. We believe, however, that three considerations lessen somewhat the difficulty of this analysis.

First, as a threshold matter, a surviving spouse must show that the decedent retained an interest in or otherwise continued to enjoy the transferred property. . . .

Second, as a guiding principle, courts should not employ their equity powers to second-guess reasonable and legitimate estate planning arrangements. For this reason, we think that a surviving spouse has a high hurdle to overcome.

Third, our case-law offers considerable guidance with respect to what factors are relevant to determining, in this context, whether a decedent intended that an *inter vivos* transfer be a sham. . . .

[W]e are not certain what the trial court meant when it found that Gilles did not intend to defraud Kathleen. If the trial court was looking solely for fraud, it applied the wrong standard; however, we may not substitute our judgment on the facts for that of the trial court. Accordingly, we must remand this case for further proceedings not inconsistent with this opinion and, if necessary, the taking of additional evidence.

NOTES AND QUESTIONS

1. *Sham on you.* The court listed various considerations to guide courts in determining the decedent's good faith, including the nature of the control retained by the decedent, the decedent's motives, the extent to which the surviving spouse was deprived of property and the reasonableness of the inter vivos transfer as part of the decedent's estate plan. At the end of its opinion, the court said its case law offered considerable guidance in the factors to consider when determining if the transfer was a sham. What factors do you think should be most relevant? One person's sham is another person's testamentary freedom. Does the court strike the appropriate balance between spousal protection and testamentary freedom?

2. *The right result?* In an omitted footnote, the court contrasted its conclusion with that of the Supreme Judicial Court of Massachusetts in *Sullivan v. Burkin*, 460 N.E.2d 572 (Mass. 1984). In *Sullivan*, the Court broke with precedent and announced that, in the future, the decedent's estate:

> shall include the value of assets held in an inter vivos trust created by the deceased spouse as to which the deceased spouse alone retained the power during his or her life to direct the disposition of those trust assets for his or her benefit, as, for example, by the exercise of a power of appointment or by revocation of the trust.

Id. at 574-75. The decedent's intent in setting up the trust would be irrelevant. From a policy perspective, what incentives with respect to estate planning does each state's approach create? In your view, which is "better" in terms of fairness? In terms of efficiency?

b. The UPC Approach

In developing the UPC approach to the elective share, the drafters considered both the dependency and the partnership theories of marriage. Professor Gary, whose article you read in part at the beginning of the chapter, provides additional history for the development of the elective share and the UPC approach in the following excerpt from the same article:

Susan N. Gary, The Oregon Elective Share Statute: Is Reform an Impossible Dream?
44 Willamette L. Rev. 337, 340-43 (2007)

As property ownership continued to change, elective share statutes based on the decedent's probate property became outmoded. Property owners held increasingly large amounts of property in ways that meant the property did not pass through probate when the property owners died. Property held in trust, under a contract with a beneficiary designation, or in joint tenancy or tenancy by the entirety passes outside probate. Life insurance, retirement plans, bank accounts, and stock accounts can all be held with the direction to pay the proceeds of the account to a beneficiary at death. Revocable trusts became a standard tool in estate planning, used to plan for incapacity as well as to avoid probate. With the proliferation of these alternatives to probate, less and less property remained subject to the elective share. A spouse who wanted to avoid the application of an elective share statute could do so simply by transferring the property to other beneficiaries through nonprobate means.

In some states courts stepped in to solve the problem, using theories such as illusory transfer or fraud on the widow's share to apply the elective share to property held in revocable trusts. A judicial solution, however, meant that each case required a fact-specific analysis, so legislatures in a few states began applying the elective share to an expanded "estate" that included property that passed outside of probate as well as within the probate process. New York was an early example of a state whose elective share statute extended its reach beyond the probate estate, and the New York statute influenced the Drafting Committee of the first Uniform Probate Code ("1969 UPC"). Promulgated in 1969, the Uniform Probate Code included an elective share statute that provided for an elective share of one-third of an "augmented estate," the term used in the 1969 UPC to indicate that the estate to which the elective share applied included both probate and nonprobate assets.

The 1969 UPC version of the elective share statute solved one problem with the early elective share statutes by expanding the reach of the elective share beyond the decedent's probate estate. The 1969 UPC worked well, or at least adequately, when most couples followed a paradigm common in the 1950s and 1960s. The husband worked outside the home and managed the household's assets, keeping title to the assets in his own name. The wife worked as an unpaid homemaker and had neither outside income nor assets titled in her name. The spouses stayed married throughout their joint lives, and if disinheritance came, it was on the death of the husband at the end of a long marriage.

By the late 1980s, two problems with the 1969 UPC became evident. The 1969 UPC ignored any property the surviving spouse might own in his or her own name, and many people married more than once. In addition, the development of a partnership theory of marriage suggested changes in the way property owned by spouses should be treated. The partnership theory posits that both spouses contribute equally to a marriage, whether economically or otherwise, and both spouses deserve to share equally in the economic fruits of the marriage. Under the partnership theory, an elective share statute reflects a surviving spouse's entitlement to a share of marital property, not just a need for support.

The Uniform Law Commission convened another Drafting Committee to revise the 1969 UPC. . . . The 1990 Uniform Probate Code ("1990 UPC") made several changes to the elective share statute, attempting to address several issues. The statute determines the elective share amount by considering assets held by both spouses, which reduces the elective share if the surviving spouse already has assets in his or her own name. While the Drafting Committee sought to incorporate the partnership theory of marriage into elective share law, it chose not to try to limit the elective share to marital property, and instead tried to approximate marital property through a mechanical phased-in percentage for the elective share. The longer the marriage, the larger the percentage: the share is three percent after one year of marriage and increases over fifteen years up to fifty percent. The 1990 UPC increased the maximum share from one-third under the 1969 UPC to fifty percent to reflect the partnership theory and each spouse's entitlement to one-half of the couple's marital property. The Drafting Committee thought that after fifteen years of marriage, property of the two spouses was likely to be property acquired during the marriage (other than by gift or inheritance) or to be commingled with marital property and so would all be considered marital property by the spouses. The Drafting Committee concluded that trying to determine marital property more precisely would be too difficult and that a mechanical solution was best.

Numerous problems remained with elective share statutes even after the improvements made by the 1990 UPC. A late-in-life marriage can create a situation in which, even after 15 years of marriage, a husband or wife may own a significant amount of separate (nonmarital) property and may prefer to leave property to children from a prior marriage rather than to a surviving spouse. Spouses may engage in estate planning using a variety of trusts to provide for each other and then for children from prior marriages. An elective share that undoes this estate planning may adversely affect a spouse who relied on plans agreed to when both spouses were alive. In the face of debilitating illnesses, some spouses find it necessary to engage in Medicaid planning. . . .

States that have adopted the 1990 UPC have not adopted the elective share provisions uniformly. Some states prefer to limit the property considered in determining the elective share to the deceased spouse's property, presumably because doing so makes a determination of the elective share amount easier. . . .

In light of the history and purpose of the elective share discussed in Professor Gary's article, important questions remain on how to structure it. The legislature of each state has had to decide the extent to which each of the following should affect the share to which the survivor was entitled:

- What property to include in the marital estate against which the election could be made. Should the marital estate include only probate assets titled in the name of the decedent, or should it also be augmented by property transferred by the decedent to others inter vivos, property transferred at death by nonprobate instruments and/or property owned separately by the surviving spouse?
- Must the parties have been living together when the testator died?
- Would the length of the marriage affect the amount to which the survivor would be entitled?
- Whose inheritance should be abated to make up a deficiency in the amount due the surviving spouse?
- Should the quality of the relationship between the decedent and the survivor affect the elective share? In other words, if the two were on bad terms or had begun divorce proceedings, should this decrease the share?

The UPC, set out below, has made one set of choices on these issues. Different states have made other choices, including states which have otherwise adopted the UPC. As you review the UPC structure, you may wish to look at your own state's statute and ask yourself what you think about the differing rationales and approaches.

You will notice that the UPC's elective share system considers both the length of the marriage and the financial situation of the surviving spouse. It also guarantees a minimum amount of $75,000 (in the 2008 version) to which the survivor is entitled, in recognition of the support theory behind the elective share concept. UPC §2-202(b). The UPC's elective share provisions lead to a distribution of property in common law states that may be comparable to the distribution in community property states, despite the very different methods used by each property system to calculate the amount to which the surviving spouse is entitled. However, unlike the community property system, the UPC does not distinguish between separate and community property and includes both in determining the marital property. As a result, the surviving spouse could end up with more via the elective share rules than under the community property approach.

While it is frequently said that the elective share rules permit the surviving spouse to "elect against the will," it is important to understand that the elective share rules apply whether the decedent died testate or intestate. That is, even if the decedent did not have a will, the surviving spouse is still entitled to an elective share portion of the augmented marital estate. Consequently, these rules provide the surviving spouse with the option to take the larger of: 1) the elective share (UPC §2-202); or 2) the share to which she is entitled from the probate estate, which, if the decedent died testate, would be pursuant to the will or, if the decedent died intestate, then would be pursuant to the intestacy provisions under UPC §2-102. As you review the elective share provisions, think about when a surviving spouse would choose the elective share.

Unless the time has been extended, the election is made "by filing in the Court and mailing or delivering to the personal representative, if any, a petition for the elective share within nine months after the date of the decedent's death, or within six months after the probate of the decedent's will, whichever limitation later expires;" if the election is not timely filed, then "the decedent's nonprobate transfers to others are not included within the augmented estate for the purpose of computing the elective-share." UPC §2-211(a).

The UPC allows the surviving spouse a one-half share of the "marital-property" portion of the estate. UPC §2-202 (set out below). Determining what constitutes the "marital-property" portion can be quite complex. The discussion of the UPC approach will be as follows:

- Identifying the property subject to the elective share; and
- Determining the sources for satisfying the elective share.

3.   The Marital-Property Portion

UPC §2-202. Elective Share.

> **(a) [Elective-Share Amount.]** The surviving spouse of a decedent who dies domiciled in this State has a right of election, under the limitations and conditions stated in this Part, to take an elective-share amount equal to 50 percent of the value of the marital-property portion of the augmented estate.

UPC §2-203. Composition of the Augmented Estate; Marital-Property Portion.

(a) [To be discussed in the next section]

(b) The value of the marital-property portion of the augmented estate consists of the sum of the values of the four components of the augmented estate as determined under subsection (a) multiplied by the following percentage:

If the decedent and the spouse were married to each other:	The percentage is:
Less than 1 year	3%
1 year but less than 2 years	6%
2 years but less than 3 years	12%
3 years but less than 4 years	18%
4 years but less than 5 years	24%
5 years but less than 6 years	30%
6 years but less than 7 years	36%
7 years but less than 8 years	42%
8 years but less than 9 years	48%
9 years but less than 10 years	54%
10 years but less than 11 years	60%
11 years but less than 12 years	68%
12 years but less than 13 years	76%
13 years but less than 14 years	84%
14 years but less than 15 years	92%
15 years or more	100%

Putting UPC §2-202 and UPC §2-203 together, we learn that the procedure for calculating the elective-share amount is as follows:

- Step One — Determine the augmented estate.
- Step Two — Identify the percentage of the augmented estate to which the spouse is vested pursuant to UPC §2-203.
- Step Three — Multiply the augmented estate in step one by the percentage in step two to calculate the "marital-property portion."
- Step Four — Multiply the marital-property portion by 50% to determine the amount to which the surviving spouse is entitled.

PROBLEM

The decedent's augmented estate is worth $1,000,000. What is the marital-property portion per UPC §2-203 and the elective-share amount per UPC §2-202 if the couple had been married three years as of decedent's death? Seven years? 12 years? 23 years?

NOTES AND QUESTIONS

1.   *Marching to a different schedule.* Other states have chosen different vesting schedules. For example, in Colorado, the survivor is entitled to 5% of the augmented estate for each year of marriage. After 10 years, the survivor has reached the maximum available, *i.e.*, 50%. COLO. REV. STAT. §15-11-201 (2009). Which approach seems more appropriate? Many states still allow the surviving spouse to receive approximately one-third of the property regardless of the length of the marriage. In Florida, for example, the surviving spouse can receive 30% of the augmented estate. FLA. STAT. §§732.201-732.2155 (2009). In New York, as in Maryland, the elective share percentage depends on the existence of children; it is one-half if there are no issue, while it is one-third if any children survive the decedent. N.Y. EST. POWERS & TRUSTS LAW §5.1.1(c) (2009). Should the length of the marriage make a difference with respect to the surviving spouse's share? What about the existence of children?

2.   *Beyond length.* The UPC uses a sliding scale based simply on years of marriage to determine the amount of the marital-property portion of the augmented estate. Should a court consider other factors in deciding on the appropriate amount of the marital-property portion? Should it matter whether both spouses worked throughout the marriage or whether one stayed home to raise children? Should it matter that the spouses married after both were retired? Should the elective share account for financial dependency between spouses? Note that upon divorce, the length of the marriage does not determine the outcome of property distribution, and the property acquired before marriage and kept separate may not be subject to division.

3.   *Fair elections of what?* As Professor Gary's article notes, some states allow election against the probate estate only while many allow election against an augmented estate that includes the probate estate along with other property that the decedent owned in substance (if not outright) around the time of death, including gifts *causa mortis* and property that passed outside of probate via will substitutes. This ensures that the decedent does not, in anticipation of death, quickly transfer assets out of the estate. Should the decedent's intent in making a gift make a difference as to whether the property is included in the augmented estate? What are the drawbacks to using an augmented estate as opposed to a probate estate?

4. *Composition of the Augmented Estate*

a. The General Rules

By far, the most difficult aspect of determining the surviving spouse's elective-share amount is figuring out what property to include in the augmented estate. We look first at the UPC provisions for guidance. Section 2-203 sets out the general rule for determining what is included, followed by more specific provisions establishing which transfers are included. Following this, we present a few policy questions about the UPC, a discussion of each of the sections with many examples and then problems that ask you to apply the UPC to various fact patterns.

UPC §2-203. Composition of the Augmented Estate . . .

> (a) Subject to Section 2-208, the value of the augmented estate . . . consists of the sum of the values of all property, whether real or personal, movable or immovable, tangible or intangible, wherever situated, that constitute:
>   (1) the decedent's net probate estate [per UPC §2-204];
>   (2) the decedent's nonprobate transfers to others [per UPC §2-205];
>   (3) the decedent's nonprobate transfers to the surviving spouse [per UPC §2-206]; and
>   (4) the surviving spouse's property and nonprobate transfers to others [per UPC §2-207].

UPC §2-204. Decedent's Net Probate Estate.

> The value of the augmented estate includes the value of the decedent's probate estate, reduced by funeral and administration expenses, homestead allowance, family allowances, exempt property, and enforceable claims.

UPC §2-205. Decedent's Nonprobate Transfers to Others.

> The value of the augmented estate includes the value of the decedent's nonprobate transfers to others, not included under Section 2-204, of any of the following types, in the amount provided respectively for each type of transfer:

(1) Property owned or owned in substance by the decedent immediately before death that passed outside probate at the decedent's death. Property included under this category consists of:

(A) Property over which the decedent alone, immediately before death, held a presently exercisable general power of appointment. The amount included is the value of the property subject to the power, to the extent the property passed at the decedent's death, by exercise, release, lapse, in default, or otherwise, to or for the benefit of any person other than the decedent's estate or surviving spouse.

(B) The decedent's fractional interest in property held by the decedent in joint tenancy with the right of survivorship. The amount included is the value of the decedent's fractional interest, to the extent the fractional interest passed by right of survivorship at the decedent's death to a surviving joint tenant other than the decedent's surviving spouse.

(C) The decedent's ownership interest in property or accounts held in POD, TOD, or co-ownership registration with the right of survivorship. The amount included is the value of the decedent's ownership interest, to the extent the decedent's ownership interest passed at the decedent's death to or for the benefit of any person other than the decedent's estate or surviving spouse. . . .

(2) Property transferred in any of the following forms by the decedent during marriage:

(A) Any irrevocable transfer in which the decedent retained the right to the possession or enjoyment of, or to the income from, the property if and to the extent the decedent's right terminated at or continued beyond the decedent's death. . . .

(B) Any transfer in which the decedent created a power over income or property, exercisable by the decedent alone or in conjunction with any other person, or exercisable by a nonadverse party, to or for the benefit of the decedent, creditors of the decedent, the decedent's estate, or creditors of the decedent's estate. . . .

(3) Property that passed during marriage and during the two-year period next preceding the decedent's death as a result of a transfer by the decedent if the transfer was of any of the following types:

(A) Any property that passed as a result of the termination of a right or interest in, or power over, property that would have been included in the augmented estate under paragraph (1)(A), (B), or (C), or under paragraph (2), if the right, interest, or power had not terminated until the decedent's death. The amount included is the value of the property that would have been included under those paragraphs if the property were valued at the time the right, interest, or power terminated, and is included only to the extent the property passed upon termination to or for the benefit of any person other than the decedent or the decedent's estate, spouse, or surviving spouse. . . .

(C) Any transfer of property, to the extent not otherwise included in the augmented estate, made to or for the benefit of a person other than the decedent's surviving spouse. The amount included is the value of the transferred property to the extent the aggregate transfers to any one donee in either of the two years exceeded [$13,000] [the amount excludable from taxable gifts under 26 U.S.C. Section 2503(b) [or its successor] on the date next preceding the date of the decedent's death].

UPC §2-206. Decedent's Nonprobate Transfers to the Surviving Spouse.

Excluding property passing to the surviving spouse under the federal Social Security system, the value of the augmented estate includes the value of the decedent's nonprobate transfers to the decedent's surviving spouse, which consist of all property that passed outside probate at the decedent's death from the decedent to the surviving spouse by reason of the decedent's death, including:

. . .(3) all other property that would have been included in the augmented estate under Section 2-205(1) or (2) had it passed to or for the benefit of a person other than the decedent's spouse, surviving spouse, the decedent, or the decedent's creditors, estate, or estate creditors.

UPC §2-207. Surviving Spouse's Property and Nonprobate Transfers to Others.

(a) **[Included Property.]** Except to the extent included in the augmented estate under Section 2-204 or 2-206, the value of the augmented estate includes the value of:

(1) property that was owned by the decedent's surviving spouse at the decedent's death, including,

(i) the surviving spouse's fractional interest in property held in joint tenancy with the right of survivorship,

(ii) the surviving spouse's ownership interest in property or accounts held in co-ownership registration with the right of survivorship, and

(iii) property that passed to the surviving spouse by reason of the decedent's death . . . and

(2) property that would have been included in the surviving spouse's nonprobate transfers to others . . . had the spouse been the decedent.

b.   The Spousal Equivalent Rule — UPC §2-207

The fourth item in UPC §2-203(a) is the most interesting and the one we start with because it affects our discussion of all of the other sections. UPC §2-207 most clearly reflects the partnership theory of marriage adopted by the UPC drafters. It is unique. The 1969 version of the UPC included only the surviving spouse's property that could be traced to the decedent. The current section provides that the augmented estate includes not only the decedent's probate estate and nonprobate transfers but it also includes the equivalent property owned or transferred by the surviving spouse (with a few minor exceptions). We call the inclusion of the surviving spouse's property the "spousal equivalent rule." In other words, in order to determine the entirety of the marital property at the time of the decedent's death, we must look not only at what was owned or controlled by the decedent but also at what was owned or controlled by the survivor, regardless of the source. Why does the UPC include the survivor's property?

c.   The Net Probate Estate — UPC §2-204

Decedent.   We continue our discussion of how to calculate the augmented estate with the net probate estate of the decedent. This is the most obvious item for inclusion. The probate estate is included in the augmented estate regardless of whom the beneficiaries are — the spouse or others.

Note that it is the "net" probate estate that gets included in the augmented estate. Thus, it is all the interests in property owned by the decedent at death less several items: expenses of and claims against the estate, homestead and family allowances and exempt property. The term "claims" is defined in section UPC §1-201(5) as including "liabilities of the decedent or protected person whether arising in contract, in tort, or otherwise, and liabilities of the estate which arise at or after the death of the decedent or after the appointment of a conservator, including funeral expenses and expenses of administration."

The Spousal Equivalent Rule of UPC §2-207.   Also included in the augmented estate is the property of the survivor equivalent to what would have been included in her probate estate had she been the decedent instead of her spouse.

> **Example:**   On Darrell's death, he owned 100% of the stock in the family business in his own name, worth $1,000,000. Among other debts, he personally owed State Bank $150,000. At Darrell's death, Darrell's surviving spouse (Cindy) owns a vacation home in the mountains in her own name worth $500,000 that has a mortgage of $200,000 on it. Under UPC §2-204 and the spousal equivalent rule of UPC §2-207, the augmented estate is increased by $1,150,000 for these items ($850,000 plus $300,000).

d. Nonprobate Transfers

Expanding the survivor's rights beyond just the probate estate, the value of the augmented estate also includes the value of the decedent's nonprobate transfers — the step that a few states, including Maryland, are still reluctant to take. UPC §2-205 augments the estate with the decedent's nonprobate transfers to persons other than the surviving spouse and UPC §2-206 increases it by the decedent's nonprobate transfers to the surviving spouse. While these property transfers are addressed separately in the statute, they are discussed together here. They are alike, except as we note in the discussion.

These sections basically provide that the surviving spouse should have rights to the property via the elective share rules if the decedent had the benefits of the property at the time of death. In essence, if the decedent had the equivalent of ownership during life and possessed it at death, the surviving spouse should have rights in the property at the decedent's death. Thus, the approach values "substance over form."

(1). Property owned in fact or in substance by the decedent immediately before death transferred to others (UPC §2-205(1)) and to the surviving spouse (UPC §2-206)

In this group is property in which the decedent had, at the moment before his death, the ability to make all or a portion of the property his own and available for the surviving spouse. Each subsection addresses a different type of asset of which the decedent could have become the full, technical owner by merely exercising his power of appointment, incident of ownership, or right of severance or withdrawal. Had the decedent exercised these powers or rights to become the owner, the property would have been included in the augmented estate as probate property; by not exercising these powers or rights, the decedent allowed the assets to pass outside probate, possibly to persons other than the surviving spouse.

Property included under this category need not have been property that the decedent owned at one time and transferred away; it may have been gifted to the decedent by another. It does not matter whether the interest was created before or after marriage, which is in contrast to the second and third categories that are discussed below.

Subsection A. Property over which the decedent had a presently exercisable general power of appointment.

This section only applies to property over which the decedent had *presently exercisable* general powers of appointment, *i.e.*, ones exercisable during life. If the decedent's power was exclusively a testamentary one, exercisable only by will, the property subject to the power is not included in the augmented estate because the decedent could not have made the property subject to the power into marital property while he was alive. In addition, the power must be a *general* one, *i.e.*, exercisable in favor of the decedent, the decedent's estate, his creditors or creditors of his estate. The subsection is demonstrated by the following example from the comments to UPC §§2-205 and 2-206.[3]

Example 3 — Revocable Inter-Vivos Trust.

G created a revocable inter-vivos trust, providing for the income to go to G for life, remainder in corpus to such persons, except G, G's creditors, G's estate, or the creditors of G's estate, as G by will appoints; in default of appointment, to X. G died, survived by [spouse] and X. G never exercised his power to revoke, and the corpus of the trust passed at G's death to X.

Regardless of whether G created the trust before or after marrying [his spouse], the value of the corpus of the trust at G's death is included in the augmented estate under paragraph [(1)(A)] because, immediately before G's death, the trust corpus was subject to a presently exercisable general power of appointment . . . held by G. [That is, he could have revoked it, bringing the corpus into the marriage, but did not.]

So long as G had a presently exercisable general power of appointment immediately before death, it is irrelevant *for purposes of this paragraph* whether the trust was created before or during the marriage or whether the property that went into the trust was marital property or not. In fact, the trust could have been created by a third person, such as G's parent. The key to inclusion is whether G had the ability to make the corpus marital property immediately before his death.

The spousal equivalent rule of UPC §2-207(a)(2) requires augmented estate inclusion for any presently exercisable powers, if any, owned by the surviving spouse at the time of the decedent's death.

Subsection B. Real property held by the decedent in joint tenancy with the right of survivorship.

This category is almost exclusively limited to joint tenancies in real property, as joint ownership in stocks, securities and bank accounts is covered by subsection C. If the other joint tenant is someone other than the surviving spouse, UPC §2-205 applies; if the other joint tenant is the surviving spouse, then UPC §2-206 controls.

The amount included by this subsection is the "fractional interest." UPC §2-201(2) defines fractional interest as a fraction with one as the numerator and the number of joint tenants as the denominator. For example, if there are two joint tenants, then half is included; if there are three, then a third is included, and so on. In addition, the spousal equivalent rule requires augmentation of the estate for the fractional interest of any real property joint tenancy interest owned by the surviving spouse at the death of the decedent. If the decedent was the other joint tenant, UPC §2-207(a)(1)(A) and (b) value the interest immediately before the decedent's death.

---

3. Numbered examples throughout this discussion are from the UPC comments.

The philosophy underlying this subsection's inclusion in the augmented estate is that during his life the decedent could have exercised his right of severance or partition, thus bringing his fractional share of the property into the marital estate.

Example 21 — Joint Tenancy.

> G, S [spouse], and X own property in joint tenancy. G died more than two years after the property was titled in that form, survived by S and X.
>
> In total, two-thirds of the value of the property at G's death is included in the augmented estate — one-sixth under Section 2-205, one-sixth under Section 2-206, and one-third under Section 2-207.

Subsection C. Personal property or accounts held in POD, TOD, or JTWROS.

UPC §2-205(1)(C) brings into the augmented estate the decedent's joint ownership in stocks, securities and bank accounts, as well as those with a POD or TOD registration. If the other joint tenant is the surviving spouse, UPC §2-206 applies; if another person, UPC §2-205 does. With respect to these will substitutes, the decedent controlled the property until death but arranged for the property to transfer outside probate.

This section is different from the previous one in that the amount included is the value of the decedent's "ownership interest," not the fractional interest, as that is the only amount the law would have allowed him to exercise control over during life. One's ownership interest equals the percentage toward the cost of the joint tenancy contributed by the decedent. *See also* UPC §6-211. The difference between the two sections is explained in the following example.

Example 6 — Joint Checking Account.

> G, X [son], and Y [daughter] were registered as co-owners of a joint checking account. G contributed 75 percent of the funds in the account. G died, survived by S [spouse], X, and Y.
>
> G's ownership interest in the account immediately before death, determined under Section 6-211, was 75 percent of the account. Because that percentage ownership interest passed by right of survivorship to X and Y at G's death, 75 percent of the value of the account at G's death is included in the augmented estate under paragraph (1)(iii). [Had this been real estate and the previous section applied, the fractional interest of one-third would have been included.]

Under the spousal equivalent rule of UPC §2-207(a)(1)(B), any ownership interest the survivor had (at the decedent's death) in stocks, securities and bank accounts, as well as other assets subject to POD and TOD registration, would likewise be included in the augmented estate.

(2). Certain transfers during marriage with interests retained by the decedent (UPC §2-205(2))

Property the decedent *irrevocably* transferred away during the marriage normally does not get included in the augmented estate. There are a few exceptions. One exception is a transfer in the two-year period prior to the decedent's death. It is discussed after this section. A second exception, discussed here, is a transfer where the decedent retained sufficient rights over the property so that the underlying property is treated as if it were still owned by the decedent for purposes of calculating the value of the augmented estate.

To fall into the second category, (i) the nonprobate transfer must have occurred during the marriage, and (ii) the decedent must have retained certain "strings of ownership." By doing the transfer in this manner during the marriage, the decedent retained the benefits from the marital property for himself during life but caused the principal to pass outside his probate estate at death.

For this section to apply, it is irrelevant whether the property was originally owned by the decedent before the marriage or earned during it. The critical precondition is that the property was transferred away during marriage. Most commonly, the section applies to a transfer of "marital property" into an irrevocable trust in which the decedent retained for himself the right to income for life with the remainder going somewhere other than to his estate. If the transferee of the future interest (for example, any remaining income interest or the corpus) is someone other than the surviving spouse, UPC §2-205 applies; if it is the surviving spouse, UPC §2-206 controls.

Assuming this section applies, what is included? UPC §2-205(2) requires inclusion of the value of the underlying corpus from which income is being drawn or over which the power may be exercised. For example, if the decedent was entitled to all the income from the property, 100% of the value of the corpus at the date of his death is added to the augmented estate. Similarly, if he was entitled to only 75% of the income, then only 75% of the corpus is included. The rationale for including the value of the corpus rather than the value of the life interest is that when he irrevocably transferred the property away during the marriage, the decedent deprived the other spouse of that property yet retained for himself the benefits associated with the corpus for the rest of his life. He may not "have his cake and eat it too."

> *Example 22 — Income Interest Passing to Surviving Spouse.*
>
> Before death, and during marriage, G created an irrevocable inter-vivos trust [and transferred to the trustee ownership of some stock he received as an inheritance many years before marrying and other stock he bought since being married. The terms of the trust provide] for the income to go to G for life, then for the income to go to [his spouse] S for life, then for the corpus of the trust to go to X. G died, survived by S and X.

The full value of the corpus of the trust at G's death is included in the augmented estate under a combination of Sections 2-205 and 2-206.

Spousal Equivalent Rule of UPC §2-207.   Also included in the augmented estate is equivalent property owned or owned in substance by the surviving spouse immediately before the death of the decedent that would have passed outside probate at the survivor's death had the survivor been the decedent instead of the spouse who did die.

(3). Transfers to persons other than surviving spouse during marriage and within two years of decedent's death (UPC §2-205(3))

As stated above, most property the decedent *irrevocably* transferred away during the marriage as to which he has not retained any strings of ownership does not get included in the augmented estate. However, an exception applies for transfers made during the marriage that took place during the two-year period just prior to the decedent's death. In a sense, they were in contemplation of death. This category of inclusion is unlike the other sections we've discussed because it only applies if the transfer was to someone other than the spouse. UPC §2-206 does not have a parallel provision since any property transferred to the survivor was within the family and either was spent as of the decedent's death or is included in the augmented estate under the spousal equivalent rule for probate property.

To appreciate the breadth of this section, it is critical to understand the meaning of the term "transfer." While transfer clearly encompasses the normal meaning ascribed to it, UPC §2-201(9) says that transfer also includes, "(A) an exercise or release of a presently exercisable general power of appointment held by the decedent, (B) a lapse at death of a presently exercisable general power of appointment held by the decedent, and (C) an exercise, release, or lapse of a general power of appointment that the decedent created in himself. . . ." Thus, an exercise, release or lapse of a general power of appointment during the proscribed two-year period requires inclusion in the augmented estate.

Example 16 — Retained Income Interest Terminating Within Two Years Before Death.

Before death, and during marriage, G created an irrevocable inter-vivos trust, providing for the income to go to G for ten years, then for the corpus of the trust to go to X. G died 11 years after the trust was created, survived by S [spouse] and X. G was married to S when the trust terminated.

The full value of the corpus of the trust at the date of its termination is included in the augmented estate under paragraph [(3)(A)]. The full value of the corpus at death would have been included in the augmented estate under paragraph [(2)(A)] had G's income interest not terminated until death; G's income interest terminated within the two-year period next preceding G's death; G was married to S when the trust was created and when the income interest terminated; and the trust corpus upon termination passed to a person other than S, G, or G's estate.

[A similar result would follow if G had created a revocable trust many years ago and released the power to revoke five months before he died.]

Example

Gertrude gave her good friend Xenon $100,000 16 months before she died in a car accident. Assuming the gift tax exclusion for the year of the transfer is $13,000, the amount included in the augmented estate is $87,000. If Gertrude had made the gift 27 months before her death, the transfer would be disregarded for augmented estate inclusion purposes.

Of course, the spousal equivalent rule of UPC §2-207 requires inclusion in the augmented estate of property transfers by the surviving spouse to someone other than the decedent in the two years before the death of the decedent.

QUESTIONS

1.   *Having your cake?* Professor Waggoner suggests that the UPC elective share implements both a dependency and a support approach. *See* Waggoner, *The Uniform Probate Code's Elective Share*, *supra*. Do you agree? And in which sections do you see these approaches codified?

2.   *Separation issues.* Note — again — that the elective share grants the surviving spouse rights, regardless of whether the surviving spouse is intentionally omitted from the estate plan, whether the parties are separated or whether a divorce is pending. Why? Consider that in New York, for example, a surviving spouse who has "abandoned" the decedent is not entitled to claim an elective share. N.Y. Est. Powers & Trusts Law 5-1.2 (McKinney 2009). In Oregon, regardless of the existence of a court order for legal separation, a court can deny entirely or reduce the elective share amount, if the spouses are living apart. Or. Rev. Stat. §114.135 (2009); *see* Pamela Paul, *The Un-Divorced*, N.Y. Times, July 30, 2010, http://www.nytimes.com/2010/08/01/fashion/01Undivorced .html?pagewanted=all.

PROBLEMS

The following problems provide you with extensive opportunities to work through the intricacies of the elective share provisions. The complexity of the problems show that, although there is a plethora of ways in which a survivor can be disinherited either accidentally or by design, the statute attempts to address as many as possible, sometimes through language that is very specific and sometimes in broad terms. As you work through the UPC elective share provisions, think about how a surviving spouse is protected against disinheritance from various types of the decedent's transfers, and how equity is done between spouses who may have unequal resources.

Tomasita is the decedent in the problem below. She is survived by her husband (Humberto), their daughter (Delia), son (Spencer), grandchild (Georgia) and Tomasita's sister (Sally). Tomasita and Humberto were married 25 years at her death. You are Humberto's attorney and he is trying to decide his rights to marital property. As to each of the following, advise him:

- **Is the asset probate property or nonprobate property of Tomasita?** This reviews material covered in Chapter 4 and contrasts the differences between one's probate estate and one's augmented estate. [If your class has already discussed estate and gift taxes, determine whether the asset is included in the gross estate or not. What you will find is that what is included in the gross estate for tax purposes and what is included in the augmented estate are similar and expansive, whereas what is included in the probate estate is much narrower.]
- **At Tomasita's death, is this item attributable to Tomasita and included in the augmented estate? If so, please identify the section: UPC §§2-204 to 2-206. How much is included?**
- **At Tomasita's death, is this item attributable to Humberto and included in the augmented estate per the spousal equivalent rule of UPC §2-207? How much is included?**

1. Houses and other property at Tomasita's death:
    a. Tomasita owned a $1,000,000 house and other real and personal property. Tomasita owned the house and all the other property in fee simple. Tomasita died with a valid will leaving all her property to Humberto.
    b. At Tomasita's death, Humberto owned a $450,000 house in the mountains and other property, including personal effects, in fee simple in his own name.
    c. The house and other property were owned by Tomasita as a tenant in common with Sally.
    d. Humberto's house and other property were owned by Humberto as a tenant in common with Sally.
    e. The house and other property were owned by Tomasita and Humberto as community property.
    f. The house was owned by Tomasita as joint tenants with right of survivorship with Spencer. Many years ago, Tomasita bought the property entirely with her own funds and titled it in joint tenancy with Spencer.
    g. Humberto's house was owned by Humberto as joint tenants with his brother, each contributing one-half.

2. Checking and investment accounts at Tomasita's death:
    a. Tomasita owned a checking account and an investment account in her name alone. Tomasita died without a will.
    b. Humberto has a checking account and stocks and securities that are in his name alone worth $450,000.
    c. Tomasita owned a checking account and an investment account that was registered in Tomasita's name and Spencer's names jointly. All the money in the account was contributed by Tomasita.
    d. Humberto owned a checking account and an investment account that was registered in his name and Spencer's names jointly. Humberto had contributed 75% and Spencer 25% to the balance.
    e. Tomasita owned a checking account and an investment account that was registered in her name alone but there is a "payable-on-death" (POD) or a "transfer-on-death" (TOD) designation in favor of Spencer.
3. Gifts to Spencer:
    a. Ten years before her death, Tomasita gifted stock to Spencer in fee simple that was worth $100,000 at the time. Tomasita died this year and the stock was worth $175,000.
    b. Ten years before Tomasita's death, Humberto gifted stock to Spencer in fee simple that was worth $100,000 at the time. When Tomasita died this year, the stock was worth $175,000.
    c. One year before her death, Tomasita gifted stock to Spencer in fee simple that was worth $100,000 at the time. Tomasita died this year and the stock was worth $175,000.

e. Whose Interest Is Going to Be Abated to Fund the Elective Share?

Once we determine the elective share, the surviving spouse has to decide whether to make the election or not. Assuming she elects against the will (or intestacy), the issue that surfaces is from what source will her share come? This is what UPC §2-209 seeks to answer. While the language of the statute appears complicated, it can be boiled down to a fairly easy statement: To the extent the surviving spouse already owns or receives property as the result of the decedent's death, whether it comes from probate or non-probate sources, these amounts are the first to fund the elective share. It is only if the survivor does not end up with ownership of property equal to the elective-share amount, *i.e.*, there is a deficiency, that others will have their inheritances abated to satisfy the amount to which the survivor is entitled.

UPC §2-209. Sources from Which Elective Share Payable.

(a) [Elective-Share Amount Only.] In a proceeding for an elective share, the following are applied first to satisfy the elective-share amount and to reduce or eliminate any contributions due from the decedent's probate estate and recipients of the decedent's nonprobate transfers to others:

   (1) amounts included in the augmented estate under Section 2-204 which pass or have passed to the surviving spouse by testate or intestate succession and amounts included in the augmented estate under Section 2-206; and

   (2) the marital-property portion of amounts included in the augmented estate under Section 2-207.

(b) [Marital Property Portion.] The marital-property portion under subsection (a)(2) is computed by multiplying the value of the amounts included in the augmented estate under Section 2-207 by the percentage of the augmented estate set forth in the schedule in Section 2-203(b) appropriate to the length of time the spouse and the decedent were married to each other.

(c) [Unsatisfied Balance of Elective-Share Amount. . . .] If, after the application of subsection (a), the elective-share amount is not fully satisfied . . . amounts included in the decedent's net probate estate, other than assets passing to the surviving spouse by testate or intestate succession, and in the decedent's nonprobate transfers to others . . . are applied [] to satisfy the unsatisfied balance of the elective-share amount. . . . The decedent's net probate estate and that portion of the decedent's nonprobate transfers to others are so applied that liability for the unsatisfied balance of the elective-share amount . . . is apportioned among the recipients of the decedent's net probate estate and of that portion of the decedent's nonprobate transfers to others in proportion to the value of their interests therein.

Example: After a 20-year marriage, Dieter died leaving $1,000,000, his entire probate estate, to Sarai, his spouse. Sarai already owned $500,000 in her own name. Dieter also left a $2,000,000 life insurance policy to his two children equally. The augmented estate is $3,500,000 and Sarai's elective share is one-half, or $1,750,000. Between the $1,000,000 she inherited and what she already owned, she is responsible for covering the first $1,500,000 of the elective share. If Sarai makes the election, the interest of the two children must be abated to satisfy her $250,000 deficiency. Each will be responsible to contribute in proportion to the value of the interests they received. Since they received equal nonprobate transfers, each must give Sarai $125,000.

PROBLEM

Harlan and Wendy were legally married at the time of Harlan's death. They had no premarital or post-marital agreement. Harlan's heirs are Amy, Bill and Carlos (Harlan's children from a prior marriage) and Wendy. Harlan's net probate estate is valued at $250,000. By his will, Harlan devised $100,000 of property to Wendy and the $150,000 residue to a charity. Harlan also arranged nonprobate transfers at his death of $30,000 to Wendy and $100,000 to Amy, $200,000 to Bill and $150,000 to Carlos. The value of Wendy's personal assets, not including any inheritance or allowances from Harlan's estate, is $20,000. During her marriage to Harlan, Wendy transferred money into a joint bank account with right of survivorship, which she maintains with her sister, Sally. The account's balance as of Harlan's death is $30,000, all of which is attributable to contributions made by Wendy.

Assume Harlan and Wendy were married for 20 years at the time of Harlan's death. Determine Wendy's elective-share amount under the UPC. From what sources is the elective-share amount, if any, payable? (*Compare* UPC §2-209(b) & (c) to §3-902.)

E.   PRENUPTIALS AND OTHER MARITAL AGREEMENTS

Potential spouses are increasingly likely to sign prenuptial agreements, particularly where they are entering into a second marriage. Spouses may also enter into agreements during a marriage. Estate planning attorneys provide critical perspectives on what to include concerning the surviving spouse's rights when it comes to drafting these agreements.

A spouse may waive the right to inherit from the other spouse. The elective share and the omitted spouse share (discussed later in the chapter) are default rules; parties can contract about the scope — or existence — of these protections and, indeed, even in community property states, spouses can enter into contracts about their rights to marital property. Usually, these waivers take the form of premarital agreements, although enforceable waivers can also be included in post-marital agreements entered into during the marriage or in separation agreements entered into as the marriage is dissolving. Waivers are more likely to be used in second (or subsequent) marriages, when a spouse wishes to leave property to children from an earlier relationship. Since such agreements are usually drafted to cover divorce, they tend to be used when one person has significant wealth and wants to protect it from a divorce property transfer in case the marriage does not last.

1.   When Is a Waiver Valid?

States have adopted varying approaches to determining the validity of a waiver. Because of the relationship between the contracting parties, courts or legislatures may adopt stricter standards for enforceability than would be applicable to parties not in an intimate relationship. Professor Gary observes that a statute addressing spousal waiver should include the following protections:

> The statute should require the waiver to be in writing and should require adequate disclosure of information by both spouses. The level of disclosure required for the waiver of an elective share right could be the same as that required for a prenuptial or postnuptial agreement, or a lower level of disclosure may be adequate. A surviving spouse seeking to prove that his or her waiver was unconscionable must show that the deceased spouse did not provide a fair and reasonable disclosure of his or her property and financial obligations, that the surviving spouse did not voluntarily waive that disclosure, and that the surviving spouse did not or reasonably could not have had adequate knowledge of that information. Although an elective share statute may not require separate representation, separate representation will strengthen the enforceability of the waiver.

Gary, *supra*, 44 WILLAMETTE L. REV. at 355. Consider whether these requirements were met in the following case, which considers the validity of a prenuptial agreement waiver.

In re Estate of Hollett
834 A.2d 348 (N.H. 2003)

DUGGAN, J.

The petitioner, Erin Hollett, appeals an order by the Merrimack County Probate Court (Patten, J.) declaring the prenuptial agreement made between Erin and the decedent, John Hollett, to be valid. Erin argues that the agreement should be set aside because of duress, undue influence, insufficient financial disclosure, and lack of effective independent counsel. The respondents, Kathryn Hollett, the decedent's first wife, and their five children, argue that the agreement is valid and the probate court's order should be affirmed. We reverse and remand.

The following facts were found by the trial court or are evident from the record. John and Erin married on August 18, 1990. Their courtship had begun in 1984, when John was fifty-two and Erin was twenty-two. John was a successful real estate investor and developer who regularly bought and sold property in New Hampshire and Florida. He had considerable experience with attorneys and accountants because of his business dealings. Erin had dropped out of high school in the eleventh grade, and had no work or business experience aside from several low level jobs. Throughout their relationship and marriage, Erin had almost no involvement in or understanding of John's business.

John had previously been married to Kathryn C. Hollett, with whom he had five children. Under the terms of their divorce, John owed Kathryn a substantial property settlement, and still owed her millions of dollars at the time of his death. Erin was unaware of this property settlement.

In 1988, the same year that John and Erin became engaged, Erin found a newspaper article about prenuptial agreements that John had left on the kitchen counter. When Erin confronted John with the article, he explained that his first wife had given it to him, and stated that he would not get married without a prenuptial agreement. This statement provoked a "heated and unpleasant" discussion during which Erin said she would not sign such an agreement, particularly because John's first wife had insisted upon it. John said nothing to Erin about a prenuptial agreement again until several days before the August 18, 1990 wedding.

In May 1990, apparently in anticipation of the impending marriage, John sent a statement of his net worth to his attorneys in the law firm of McLane, Graf, Raulerson, and Middleton. After meeting with John on July 18, 1990, his lawyers drafted a prenuptial agreement that was sent to him on July 26. Erin testified that she did not learn about the agreement until the evening of August 16, less than forty-eight hours before the wedding. Under the original draft, Erin was to renounce any claim to alimony or a property settlement in the event of a divorce, and would receive only $25,000 and an automobile.

Several days before the wedding, John's lawyers contacted Brian Shaughnessy, a recent law school graduate, and requested that he counsel Erin regarding the prenuptial agreement. The lawyers told Shaughnessy that John would pay his fee. Shaughnessy first called Erin on August 16 to obtain her consent to act as counsel and to set up a meeting at the McLane law firm office the next day. Shaughnessy had never before negotiated a prenuptial agreement, but prior to the meeting he studied the law of prenuptial agreements and reviewed the draft agreement.

Erin, accompanied by her mother, met with Shaughnessy in person for the first and only time at the McLane law firm on August 17, the day before the wedding. At that time, all of the plans and arrangements for the elaborate wedding, at which over 200 guests were expected, had already been made and paid for; Erin's mother and father had already flown in from Thailand. During the meeting and subsequent negotiations with John's attorneys, Shaughnessy noted that Erin was under considerable emotional distress, sobbing throughout the three or four hours he was with her and at times so distressed that he was unable to speak with her. Erin testified that she remembered almost nothing about the conference. Shaughnessy, however, testified that he carefully reviewed John's financial disclosure and draft of the agreement with Erin, explained their legal significance, and asked her what she sought to obtain from the agreement. He testified that he advised her that the settlement offer in the draft was inadequate, and reminded her that the wedding could be put off if necessary.

Shaughnessy also testified that he believed the financial disclosure provided by John, which had not been audited or reviewed by any other party, was inadequate. Shaughnessy, however, had no time to independently verify any of John's finances. . . .

At the end of the negotiations, the prenuptial agreement was considerably more favorable to Erin, allowing her to obtain as much as one-sixth of John's estate in the event of a divorce or John's death. John's lawyers prepared a final version of the agreement, which John and Erin signed on the morning of August 18, the day of their wedding.

The parties remained married until John's death on April 30, 2001. John was survived by Erin, his first wife, and his children from his first marriage. Erin subsequently petitioned the probate court to invalidate the prenuptial agreement, while John's first wife and children argued in favor of upholding it. After four days of hearings, the probate court concluded that the prenuptial agreement was valid and enforceable.

On appeal, Erin argues that the prenuptial agreement was invalid for three reasons: (1) the agreement was not voluntary because it was the product of duress and undue influence; (2) John's financial disclosures were inadequate; and (3) she did not have independent counsel. We need only address the issue of duress. . . .

RSA 460:2–a (1997) permits a man and a woman to enter into a written contract "in contemplation of marriage." A prenuptial agreement is presumed valid unless the party seeking the invalidation of the agreement proves that: (1) the agreement was obtained through fraud, duress or mistake, or through misrepresentation or nondisclosure of a material fact; (2) the agreement is unconscionable; or (3) the facts and circumstances have so changed since the agreement was executed as to make the agreement unenforceable. *See In the Matter of Yannalfo and Yannalfo*, 794 A.2d 795, 797 (N.H. 2002).

"As a practical matter, the claim of undue duress is essentially a claim that the agreement was not signed voluntarily." 3 C. Douglas, New Hampshire Practice, Family Law §1.05, at 12 (2002). To establish duress, a party must ordinarily "show that it involuntarily accepted the other party's terms, that the coercive circumstances were the result of the other party's acts, that the other party exerted pressure wrongfully, and that under the circumstances the party had no alternative but to accept the terms set out by the other party." *Yannalfo*, [794 A.2d at 797]. However, "the State has a special interest in the subject matter" of prenuptial agreements and "courts tend to scrutinize [them] more closely than ordinary commercial contracts." *MacFarlane v. Rich (MacFarlane)*, 567 A.2d 585, 589 (N.H. 1989). Moreover, because such agreements often involve persons in a confidential relationship, "the parties must exercise the highest degree of good faith, candor and sincerity in all matters bearing on the terms and execution of the proposed agreement, with fairness being the ultimate measure."

Under the heightened scrutiny afforded to prenuptial agreements, the timing of the agreement is of paramount importance in assessing whether it was voluntary. Fairness demands that the party presented with the agreement have "an opportunity to seek independent advice and a reasonable time to reflect on the proposed terms." . . .

The agreement in this case[], involves the post-marriage disbursement of an estate that totaled over six million dollars at the time of the agreement, and the relinquishment of marital rights such as alimony. Such a complicated and important agreement will require more time for negotiation and reflection. . . .

Second, [] Erin's bargaining position was vastly inferior to that of her husband. John was much older than Erin, and he had already been married. According to their financial disclosures, John had approximately six million dollars in assets, while Erin owned approximately five thousand dollars worth of personal property at the time of the agreement. Erin's work experience during the relationship was limited to stints as a bartender and a grocery store cashier. She had little understanding of and no real involvement in John's business ventures. According to Erin, in fact, John had encouraged Erin to stop working after they began their relationship. If Erin refused to sign the agreement, she thus not only stood to face the embarrassment of canceling a two hundred guest wedding, but also stood to lose her means of support. Prenuptial agreements that result from such a vast disparity in bargaining power must meet a high standard of procedural fairness.

Finally, John's conduct before the wedding raises serious questions regarding his good faith in dealing with Erin. John had contemplated a prenuptial agreement at least two years before the wedding, as evidenced by his argument with Erin in 1988. Despite Erin's opposition to the idea, however, he did not discuss the agreement with her again. Moreover, although John's lawyers had drafted a prenuptial agreement almost a month before the wedding, John did not obtain counsel for his wife or even inform her of the agreement until several days before the ceremony. . . .

. . . In upholding the agreement, the trial court cited as a factor in its reasoning Erin's failure to "repudiate or rescind" the agreement during her ten years of marriage to John. Public policy, however, limits the consideration of such evidence. As one court has stated:

> The law frowns upon litigation between husband and wife. Where their relations are friendly and affectionate, it takes account of the fact that she would be loath to institute legal proceedings against him. . . . [A]ny other policy would be apt to beget disagreements and contentions in the family fatal to domestic peace. . . .

. . . [In upholding the validity of the prenuptial contract,] the trial court focused upon the assistance Erin received from Brian Shaughnessy before the execution of the agreement. The respondents, in fact, suggest that the presence of counsel should be dispositive of the issue of voluntariness. We note that the trial court itself found that the time constraints limited the quality of Shaughnessy's representation: for example, he was unable to verify the accuracy of John's disclosures. Even assuming, however, that Shaughnessy provided Erin with effective independent counsel, and that the financial representations upon which he relied were accurate, we cannot agree that his counsel by itself was sufficient to validate this agreement. . . .

. . . [W]e conclude as a matter of law that her signing of the agreement was involuntary under the heightened standard applied to prenuptial agreements.

Reversed and remanded.

NOTES AND QUESTIONS

1. *A wing to stand on.* Do you agree that Erin did not sign the agreement voluntarily? Consider that she first knew of the potential existence of the prenuptial agreement two years before the wedding, and her husband found a lawyer who was able to procure some changes. Had you been advising John, what, if anything, would you have done differently?

2. *Whose prayers went unanswered?* Consider which family members are protected and which are not as a result of the court's decision. To what extent is the decedent's intent relevant here?

3. *Explaining the result.* Courts are far more likely today to uphold prenuptial waivers of the elective share than you might think or than this case suggests. In a Florida case, the wife claimed that she had not explicitly relinquished her elective share when she signed an agreement providing that she would "not claim or acquire any interest in any [of her husband's] property during the marriage or in the event of dissolution of the marriage." *Wiesfeld-Ladd v. Estate of Ladd*, 920 So. 2d 1148 (Fla. Dist. Ct. App. 2006). The court upheld the waiver, finding that the parties intended that the surviving spouse was not entitled to an elective share.

4. *Intimate fiduciary relationships.* Consider under what circumstances family members should be held to the heightened standards that *Hollett* articulates. John and Erin were not married when the agreement was signed. Should courts treat waiver agreements between engaged couples, married couples, separated couples and cohabiting couples differently?

2.   *The UPC Response*

Consider whether the UPC meets the standards set out by Professor Gary, and how it would have affected the outcome in *Hollett*.

UPC §2-213. Waiver of Right to Elect and of Other Rights.

> (a) The right of election of a surviving spouse and the rights of the surviving spouse to homestead allowance, exempt property, and family allowance, or any of them, may be waived, wholly or partially, before or after marriage, by a written contract, agreement, or waiver signed by the surviving spouse.
>
> (b) A surviving spouse's waiver is not enforceable if the surviving spouse proves that:
>
> (1) he [or she] did not execute the waiver voluntarily; or
>
> (2) the waiver was unconscionable when it was executed and, before execution of the waiver, he [or she]:
>
> (i) was not provided a fair and reasonable disclosure of the property or financial obligations of the decedent;
>
> (ii) did not voluntarily and expressly waive, in writing, any right to disclosure of the property or financial obligations of the decedent beyond the disclosure provided; and
>
> (iii) did not have, or reasonably could not have had, an adequate knowledge of the property or financial obligations of the decedent.
>
> (c) An issue of unconscionability of a waiver is for decision by the court as a matter of law.
>
> (d) Unless it provides to the contrary, a waiver of "all rights," or equivalent language, in the property or estate of a present or prospective spouse or a complete property settlement entered into after or in anticipation of separation or divorce is a waiver of all rights of elective share, homestead allowance, exempt property, and family allowance by each spouse in the property of the other and a renunciation by each of all benefits that would otherwise pass to him [or her] from the other by intestate succession or by virtue of any will executed before the waiver or property settlement.

In terms of best practices, it is important for the person seeking the agreement to make sure the other person has independent representation. It is safest if the parties pay for their own attorneys. Also, to avoid any perception of unconscionability associated with having to make a rushed decision, the agreement should be negotiated well before the wedding. Lastly, as the "poorer" person is giving up important rights, there should be adequate consideration given by the "richer" person.

QUESTIONS

1. *The same or different standard for waiver, round 1.* Should the spousal waiver context be subject to the same standards as other contracts? Should there be a requirement of separate representation? Who benefits when the law allows a spouse to waive these rights?

2. *The same or different, round 2.* Should the requirements for spousal waiver of inheritance rights be subject to a different standard than the standard applicable to other interspousal agreements? Consider the situation of Ted Will (yes, that was really his name) and Gertrude Fochs, who signed a prenuptial agreement by which each agreed to forgo any rights to inherit from the other. After Ted's death, Gertrude claimed a share of Ted's estate, arguing that her waiver was ineffective because the prenuptial agreement was invalid. The court decided that even though the premarital agreement itself did not entirely comply with California family law on premarital agreements, the waiver itself was valid under estate law: California's Probate Code has different standards for the validity of a waiver of inheritance rights, and the agreement at issue met those standards. *See Estate of Will*, 88 Cal. Rptr. 3d 502 (Ct. App. 2009).

PROBLEMS

Tyrone and Shana married late in life. They both had been married before and had children. Tyrone had accumulated a sizeable fortune before their marriage. Just prior to the marriage, Tyrone indicated he wanted Shana to complete a premarital agreement waiving "all rights" each had in the property of the other upon divorce or death. In exchange for executing this, Tyrone was willing to transfer to Shana, in trust, a fully paid $1,000,000 life insurance policy on his life. Tyrone is otherwise worth about $8,000,000.

1. Can you represent both Tyrone and Shana in drafting the agreement? Why or why not? Should you? Return to the ACTEC Commentaries to Model Rules 1.6-1.8 and your answers to a similar question in the first chapter.

2. Assume a prenuptial agreement was not executed. Upon Tyrone's death, to what, if anything, is Shana entitled per UPC §2-102 or UPC §2-202?

3. Without doing the actual drafting, identify four issues or concerns you would want to address in planning to draft or drafting a premarital agreement to avoid its subsequently being considered unenforceable by a court and detail in what manner you would address them. *See* Jeffrey A. Baskies, *A Practical Guide to Preparing and Using Premarital Agreements*, 27 Est. Plan. 347 (2000).

F.   THE SPECIAL CASE OF OMITTED SPOUSES AND CHILDREN

It is not uncommon for testators to forget to change their wills following a major life event, such as a marriage, divorce or the birth of a child. You have already learned that divorce serves to revoke a will in most states, but what happens when the individual marries or has children and forgets to revise a previously drafted will?

When family members are not included in someone's will, courts struggle to determine whether the disinheritance was intentional or accidental. While the elective share and homestead exemption are designed to protect a spouse regardless of the testator's intent, the statutory protections for an omitted spouse and child create a presumption meant to effectuate the testator's intent. Of course, the presumed intent can be overridden, in many states, by sufficient evidence of a contrary actual intent. Like the elective share, the omitted spouse and child protections rules allow the affected family member to override the testator's explicit provisions.

1.   *Omitted Spouses*

Russell Shannon, a divorced man who lived in California, drafted a will which gave his estate to his daughter and her son. The will included a clause that specifically prevented all other living persons from inheriting any part of his estate. Twelve years later, Russell married Lila, but did not change his will to include her. Russell died without ever updating his will. *In re Estate of Shannon*, 274 Cal. Rptr. 338 (Ct. App. 1990). Based on what you've learned already, does Lila have rights to any of Russell's property?

Presumably, you considered the elective share rules or the community property approach to ownership of property. Indeed, public policy, as is clearly expressed in the elective share and intestacy rules, favors providing for a surviving spouse on the death of the other spouse. Moreover, as we will discuss here, Russell's wife may have rights as an *omitted or pretermitted* spouse. A pretermitted spouse is a person who was left out of a spouse's will that was written prior to the marriage. States have developed different legal presumptions concerning the testator's intention with respect to a preter-mitted spouse, with many states providing explicit protection to an omitted spouse. These statutes generally give the spouse rights to property included in the **probate** estate, not the more expansive "augmented estate."

Omitted spouse statutes usually presume that the decedent would have wanted to change a premarital will to cover the new spouse, but just never got around to doing so. This presumption can typically be rebutted if one of three events occurs: (1) the parties entered into a premarital or marital agreement to waive inheritance rights; (2) after the marriage, the decedent uses other means, such as trusts or insurance policy benefits to provide substantially for the surviving spouse; or (3) the spouse was given something in the will even though the will was written prior to the marriage *and* the will expressly states that it excludes any persons the testator might marry in the future. Applying similar presumptions, the California Court of Appeal determined that there was insufficient evidence that Russell intentionally disinherited his wife, and that the clause preventing anyone else from inheriting was too general and not meant to include his wife. The court held Lila was able to collect her share under the pretermitted spouse statute in California.

a. The Testator's Intent?

Spouses may be intentionally or unintentionally omitted from the testator's will. In *Bay*, the court struggles to determine the testator's intent as it balances the interests (financial and otherwise) of affected family members. Think about what policies justify the court's decision.

Bay v. Estate of Bay

105 P.3d 434 (Wash. Ct. App. 2005)

BECKER, J.

Laura Bay, who was not named or provided for in her late husband's will, challenges a trial court's decision to deny her a share of his estate. Although she was presumptively entitled to an intestate share as an "omitted spouse," the statute permits this presumption to be rebutted by clear and convincing evidence "that a smaller share, including no share at all, is more in keeping with the decedent's intent." Wash. Rev. Code §11.12.095(3). Substantial evidence in this case supports the court's conclusion that it was more in keeping with the decedent's intent that his estate go entirely to his children. We affirm.

John Bay created a will in 1983, 16 years before his death. The will left everything to Cathy, his wife at the time, then in trust to their children. John's will emphasized his desire that his estate provide for his children's post-secondary education.

John and Cathy divorced in 1986 after having two children, Kelly and Eric. By statute, the divorce revoked any provisions in John's will in favor of Cathy. His estate would pass "as if the former spouse failed to survive the testator." Wash. Rev. Code §11.12.051. This left Kelly and Eric as the sole beneficiaries of the will.

John Bay married appellant Laura Bay in November 1999. He changed the beneficiary designation of his 401(k) retirement plan so that Laura was an 80 percent beneficiary. He designated his two children as equal beneficiaries of the remaining 20 percent. John did not make any changes to his will.

John Bay committed suicide in October 2000. At the time, Kelly was 18 and Eric was 15.

It was undisputed that John's 401(k) retirement plan, a non-probate asset, should be distributed according to the percentages he designated. Laura received approximately $290,000, and Kelly and Eric each received their 10 percent share.

John's probate estate was administered by his first wife's brother, who was the personal representative designated by the will. John's probate assets consisted almost entirely of separate property, amounting to a net of some $108,000. The personal representative proposed to distribute this sum equally between Kelly and Eric, with nothing for Laura.

Laura Bay protested the proposed distribution. She claimed that as an omitted spouse she was entitled to her intestate share of the probate estate. Her intestate share under the descent and distribution statute would have been "one-half of the net separate estate" because John was "survived by issue." Wash. Rev. Code §11.04.015(1)(b). Laura accordingly proposed that she receive $54,000 from the probate estate, with Kelly and Eric to receive $27,000 each.

The dispute came to the superior court where Judge Thorpe rejected Laura's claim and ordered the $108,000 to be distributed equally between Kelly and Eric Bay. Each child's total receipts, including their shares of the retirement account and some other non-probate accounts, amounted to approximately $100,000. Laura appeals the final order confirming the proposed distribution to the Bay children.

In confirming the distribution of John's set separate estate entirely to his children, the trial court applied Washington's 10-year-old omitted spouse statute, which provides as follows:

> (1) If a will fails to name or provide for a spouse of the decedent whom the decedent marries after the will's execution and who survives the decedent, referred to in this section as an "omitted spouse," the spouse must receive a portion of the decedent's estate as provided in subsection (3) of this section, unless it appears either from the will or from other clear and convincing evidence that the failure was intentional.
>
> (2) In determining whether an omitted spouse has been named or provided for, the following rules apply:
>
> > (a) A spouse identified in a will by name is considered named whether identified as a spouse or in any other manner.
> > (b) A reference in a will to the decedent's future spouse or spouses, or words of similar import, constitutes a naming of a spouse whom the decedent later marries. A reference to another class such as the decedent's heirs or family does not constitute a naming of a spouse who falls within the class.
> > (c) A nominal interest in an estate does not constitute a provision for a spouse receiving the interest.

(3) The omitted spouse must receive an amount equal in value to that which the spouse would have received [] if the decedent had died intestate, unless the court determines on the basis of clear and convincing evidence that a smaller share, including no share at all, is more in keeping with the decedent's intent. In making the determination the court may consider, among other things, the spouse's property interests under applicable community property or quasi-community property laws, the various elements of the decedent's dispositive scheme, and a marriage settlement or other provision and provisions for the omitted spouse outside the decedent's will.

. . . [The purpose of the omitted spouse statute is] "to prevent the unintentional disinheritance of the surviving spouse of a testator who marries after making a will and then dies without ever changing it" . . . [and] it establishes a presumption that the omitted spouse will receive the same amount as if the decedent had died intestate. . . .

Our analysis [] focuses on subsection (3). This part of the statute defines the presumption and states that it can be rebutted by evidence of the decedent's intent. The omitted spouse will receive her intestate share "unless the court determines on the basis of clear and convincing evidence that a smaller share, including no share at all, is more in keeping with the decedent's intent."

The statute provides a nonexclusive list of things the court may consider in relation to this question, including the decedent's dispositive scheme and provisions for the omitted spouse outside of the decedent's will. Here, the trial court considered John's desire to support a college education for his children, an interest he expressed not only in his will but also in the property settlement agreement he made with his first wife. The court made significant findings concerning John's sustained intent in seeing that Kelly and Eric could afford to go to college:

Even before the birth of his second child, Eric, the Decedent evidenced a keen interest in ensuring that his children had the financial ability to complete a college education, including post-graduate work.

Paragraph 3 of Article IV of his Last Will and Testament reads as follows:

At such time as my children have completed their formal education, the trust assets shall be spent sparingly, in the discretion of my Trustee, so that my children do not become dependent upon the trust for their support. It is my desire that each of my children who desire it shall complete a college education, including post-graduate work. Any educational expenditures after the normal four-year bachelor's degree shall be considered as an advancement to be charged against that child's share without interest at distribution.

The Decedent's interest in insuring that his children had funds to assist their post-secondary education continued to the time of his divorce from Cathy L. Smith in 1986, where this issue was addressed in their property settlement agreement . . . .

The court found that both children had excelled in school and in their extracurricular activities.

The court also took into consideration John's gift to Laura of 80 percent of the retirement account, his largest single asset. The court ultimately concluded that the facts set forth in the findings, which are uncontested on appeal, "provide clear and convincing evidence that it was the Decedent's intent for the omitted spouse to receive no share of the Decedent's remaining separate property."

When the burden of proof is "clear, cogent and convincing evidence," the factfinder's determination of an ultimate fact will be upheld on review "if supported by substantial evidence which the lower court could reasonably have found to be clear, cogent and convincing." *In re LaBelle*, 728 P.2d 138 (Wash. 1986).

Laura contends that the record falls short of meeting this test. She argues that the will "does not provide any evidence of intent on the part of John to disinherit his surviving spouse."

Laura takes as a premise the rule that the intent of a "testator" is generally determined as of the time of execution of the will. She argues that it is impossible to determine what John as a testator intended with respect to Laura, as he was not married to her when he executed the will. But the issue in this case does not involve the construction of a will. Under the omitted spouse statute, the trial court is concerned with the intent of the "decedent," not the "testator,". . . In a case such as this one, the court may consider manifestations of intent at times other than the execution of the will.

Laura's emphasis on the lack of evidence that John intended to "disinherit" her confuses the potential inquiry under subsection (1) with the inquiry into intent that the court was conducting under subsection (3). Evidence of intent to "disinherit" a new spouse would inform an inquiry under subsection (1), the purpose of which is to determine whether the failure to name or provide for the new spouse in the will was intentional. As discussed above, the trial court concluded under subsection (1) that John's failure to provide for Laura in his will was unintentional. Consequently, Laura was entitled to the presumption that she would receive a full intestate share. The purpose of an inquiry under subsection (3) is to determine whether the presumption — once established — is rebutted by clear and convincing evidence that a smaller share or no share at all is more in keeping with the decedent's intent.

We conclude that John's dispositive scheme, his property settlement agreement with his former wife, and the provision he made for Laura outside the will, provide substantial evidence that the trial court could reasonably have found to be clear, cogent and convincing evidence in support of rebutting the presumption.

NOTES AND QUESTIONS

1.   *Omitted spouse share vs. elective share.* Can a general statement be made about whether a spouse should claim the omitted spouse share or the elective share? Note that not all states protect spouses omitted from pre-marital wills. For example, Illinois protects only descendants, not spouses. Ronald Z. Domsky, *'Til Death Do Us Part . . . After That, My Dear, You're On Your Own: A Practitioner's Guide to Disinheriting a Spouse in Illinois,* 29 S. ILL. U. L.J. 207, 225 (2005).

2.   *Does the statute apply to someone named in the will who subsequently becomes a spouse?* It can. This depends on the statute and the facts. If the will is never changed, then the outcome can go either way. One argument is that because the person is specifically named in the will, the individual can-not be considered omitted. This argument is particularly strong when the parties were in a romantic relationship when the will was drafted, or married shortly thereafter, and the amount was not insubstantial.

Even if a person *is* named in the decedent's premarital will, however, the will may not have adequately "provided for" the surviving spouse. Depending on the statute, this argument can be particularly strong when the amount is not substantial. *See In Re Estate of Moi*, 151 P.3d 995 (Wash. Ct. App. 2006). And, as the *Shannon* case discussed at the beginning of this section illustrates, where the premarital will makes no reference at all to the later-married spouse, courts presume the spouse is entitled to a share.

3.   *Does the statute apply only to a spouse, or does it apply to a domestic partner as well?* Notwithstanding today's political climate, there is still very little discussion of pretermitted domestic partners. Several states have provided explicitly for omitted domestic partners, including New Jersey, Vermont and Washington. Stephen J. Hyland, *Domestic Partners and the New State Probate Code*, N.J. LAW., Apr. 2006, at 20, 22; Stephanie J. Willbanks, *Parting Is Such Sweet Sorrow, But Does It Have to Be So Complicated? Transmission of Property at Death in Vermont*, 29 VT. L. REV. 895 (2005); WASH. REV. CODE §11.12.095 (2009). In some states, the registered domestic partner statute simply adds registered domestic partners to every statute that applied to a spouse. In those states the omitted spouse statute will apply to a registered domestic partner. *See, e.g.,* OR. REV. STAT. §§106.340,112.305 (2009).

4.   The UPC and the *Restatement* focus on "surviving spouses" rather than partners. Paul J. Buser, *Domestic Partner and Non-Marital Claims Against Probate Estates:* Marvin *Theories Put to a Different Use*, 38 FAM. L.Q. 315, 319 (2004). What are your thoughts on whether estate protections should include surviving partners? *See* Christine A. Hammerle, Note, *Free Will to Will? A Case for the Recognition of Intestacy Rights for Survivors to a Same-Sex Marriage or Civil Union*, 104 MICH. L. REV. 1763 (2006).

5.   *What is the amount/share? From what property might that share be satisfied?* The amount to which the omitted spouse is entitled varies between states, but is typically somewhere between one-third of the estate and the entire estate. Virginia F. Coleman, *Planning Techniques for Large Estates:*

Selected Issues in Planning for the Second Marriage, American Law Institute-American Bar Association Continuing Legal Education, ALI-ABA Course of Study (Nov. 17-21, 2008).

Generally, the only portion of the estate available for distribution to omitted spouses is the property available for probate. The omitted spouse statutes typically only apply to property that could be passed by will, not will substitutes such as life insurance, individual retirement accounts, joint tenancies or other payable-on-death contractual arrangements. Alan Newman, *Revocable Trusts and the Law of Wills: An Imperfect Fit*, 43 Real Prop. Tr. & Est. L.J. 523 (2008).

b.   The UPC Approach

Under the UPC, a pretermitted spouse has the right to receive a share of the estate, with a few exceptions. Consider whom the UPC protects through these exceptions.

As you read the statute, notice several of its features:

- The share the survivor gets is the amount she would have gotten if the testator had died intestate. This makes sense because, with respect to the surviving spouse, the testator did die without a will. This requires returning to UPC §§2-102(1)-(4). Since the surviving spouse's portion is treated as an intestate share (even though there is a will), the surviving spouse may only draw this entitlement from the probate estate. Importantly, the survivor may alternatively seek her elective share of the augmented estate per UPC §2-202 if it is larger.
- The survivor is not necessarily entitled to a share of the entire probate estate. Subject to various exceptions, the survivor may not take an intestate share from the portion devised to children of the testator who were born prior to the marriage.

UPC §2-301. Entitlement of Spouse; Premarital Will.

> (a) If a testator's surviving spouse married the testator after the testator executed his [or her] will, the surviving spouse is entitled to receive, as an intestate share, no less than the value of the share of the estate he [or she] would have received if the testator had died intestate as to that portion of the testator's estate, if any, that is neither devised to a child of the testator who was born before the testator married the surviving spouse and who is not a child of the surviving spouse nor devised to a descendant of such a child or passes under sections 2-603 or 2-604 to such a child or to a descendant of such a child, unless:

(1) it appears from the will or other evidence that the will was made in contemplation of the testator's marriage to the surviving spouse;

(2) the will expresses the intention that it is to be effective notwithstanding any subsequent marriage; or

(3) the testator provided for the spouse by transfer outside the will and the intent that the transfer be in lieu of a testamentary provision is shown by the testator's statements or is reasonably inferred from the amount of the transfer or other evidence.

(b) In satisfying the share provided by this section, devises made by the will to the testator's surviving spouse, if any, are applied first, and other devises, other than a devise to a child of the testator who was born before the testator married the surviving spouse and who is not a child of the surviving spouse or a devise or substitute gift under Section 2-603 or 2-604 to a descendant of such a child, abate as provided in Section 3-902.

NOTES AND QUESTIONS

What policies justify the UPC approach? Note that the UPC protects devises made to the decedent's children who are not children of the surviving spouse as well. Why do you think it is so limited? Does UPC §2-301 provide adequate protection to the surviving spouse?

PROBLEMS

1.   When Sam wrote his will in 1994, he and Sally were good friends. In his will, he specifically named her in this bequest, "I leave Sally $10,000." Later, in 2002, Sam and Sally married. Sam never updated his will and died in 2011 with a probate estate worth $250,000. Can Sally be considered an omitted spouse even though she is specifically named in the will?

2.   In *Bay v. Bay*, what would the result be under the UPC? In what manner would the analysis differ?

3.   Joe wrote his will, leaving half of his property to his son, Joe Jr., and half to his sister. Six years later he met and married Cassie. Joe then took out a life insurance policy and named Cassie as beneficiary. Joe also set up a trust with Cassie as the beneficiary. Joe died without ever changing his will. To what is Cassie entitled?

4.   Ted and Sammy were getting married and planned an extensive honeymoon. A few days before the wedding, Ted met with his lawyer and signed a will leaving his entire estate to his two children from an earlier marriage. Sixteen years after the wedding, Ted died in a hang-gliding accident. Ted has a $2,000,000 probate estate. He acquired a life insurance

policy of $500,000 five years ago and named Sammy as the beneficiary. He also owned a $1,000,000 parcel of real estate in joint tenancy with one of his two children. This constitutes all of the property that passes as the result of Ted's death. What rights under UPC §2-301 does Sammy have? What elective share rights does Sammy have and from what sources will it come?

EXERCISE

You are advising your state legislature's Committee on Estate Planning and the Family. The Committee is considering adopting a new omitted spouse statute, and has asked you to develop a proposal. What would be the main features of your omitted spouse statute? In what ways would it be similar to or different from the UPC statute? How will you justify your proposal?

2. Omitted Children

Unlike omitted spouses, children intentionally omitted from a will are not entitled to demand a share of the estate. The one exception is in Louisiana, where children who are under the age of 24 or are incapable of caring for themselves, mentally or physically, are forced heirs. LA. CIV. CODE ANN. art. 1493 (2009). In the other 49 states, a testator can intentionally disinherit a child by giving the property to someone else in the will, and the testator's decision will be enforced — although, as discussed in the article below, it may be subject to a will contest.

Even though children have no right to inherit from their parents, most states do protect children who have been disinherited unintentionally through pretermitted or omitted child statutes. These statutes protect children born after the execution of their parent's will, and some even protect children alive at the time of the will's execution under some circumstances. Because it is not always clear whether the testator intentionally left out a child, states have adopted different approaches to determine the rights of an omitted child. Statutes vary on numerous issues, including the following:

- Which children have standing to contest their exclusion? Some statutes include grandchildren and other descendants as pretermitted heirs.
- Do the protections only include children who were born or adopted after the execution of the will, or all children omitted from the will, regardless of whether they were living when the will was executed?
- Does an omitted child take an intestate share or some other amount?

- Is the share limited to taking against probate property or does it include nonprobate property as well?
- What types of evidence, if any, are admissible to show the testator's intent?

a.   History of Protections

In the following article, Professor Tate provides an overview of the U.S. approach to the disinheritance of children and the justifications for the general rule.

Joshua C. Tate, Caregiving and the Case for Testamentary Freedom
42 U.C. Davis L. Rev. 129, 137-43, 148, 156, 163-65 (2008)

In the United States, the basic rule is that a parent can disinherit a child or grandchild for any reason or no reason. However, this general rule is subject to some limitations. For instance, when a child is born or adopted after the making of the will, and the testator fails to provide for that child, the child may have a claim as a "pretermitted" — overlooked — child. In some jurisdictions, a child born before the will's execution may also have a claim if the testator failed to mention the child in the will. In every American state except Louisiana, however, a child or other descendant alive at the time of the will's execution and expressly disinherited in the will has no claim to receive a share of the estate. This is true regardless of the age of the disinherited individual, although in the case of a child of divorced parents, some states provide that child support obligations survive the death of the parent obligated to furnish such support. With this limited qualification, a parent has no obligation to provide support even for a minor child after death.

The approach of the United States contrasts sharply with those of civil law and Commonwealth jurisdictions around the world. In most civil law jurisdictions, descendants are generally entitled to a reserved share of the estate unless interested parties show some specific grounds for disinheritance. In Austria, for example, a child is entitled to one-half of the amount she would have inherited under the intestacy rules unless the child was (1) convicted of a crime and sentenced to twenty years or more as punishment; (2) committed an offense against the testator that involved intent and was punishable by more than a year's imprisonment; or (3) grossly neglected duties of care and support to the testator when the testator was in a position of need. Similar provisions are found in most Continental legal systems, although the grounds for disinheritance vary. In these jurisdictions, therefore, the baseline rule is precisely the opposite of the U.S. rule — a presumption in favor of inheritance notwithstanding the testamentary disposition.

Because of its civil law tradition, Louisiana has a system of forced heirship similar to that in place in Continental Europe. However, the state legislature amended the system in 1995 to apply only to children who are under the age of twenty-four, permanently disabled, or likely to become permanently disabled in the future due to an "inherited, incurable disease or condition." Although the testator has the freedom to bequeath a substantial part of the estate to persons of the testator's choosing, the statute reserves a certain portion, called the legitime, for qualified children and other lineal descendants entitled to take by representation. . . .

Certain countries of the British Commonwealth, including England, Wales, New Zealand, Australia, and some parts of Canada follow another alternative to the U.S. rule that may be referred to as the "family maintenance" system. In these jurisdictions, courts have wide discretion to depart from a testator's estate plan to provide for a class of persons protected by legislation, typically including specified members of the testator's family. The statute of New South Wales, Australia is illustrative. It begins by defining a list of "eligible persons," including spouses, domestic partners, former spouses, children, and dependent grandchildren. It then provides that when the testator insufficiently provides for an eligible person, the court "may order that such provision be made out of the estate . . . as, in the opinion of the Court, ought, having regard to the circumstances at the time the order is made, to be made for the maintenance, education, or advancement in life of the eligible person." The statute allows the court to consider (1) contributions that eligible persons make to "the acquisition, conservation, or improvement of property of the deceased person" or "the welfare of the deceased person"; (2) the "character and conduct of the eligible person before and after the death of the deceased person"; (3) "circumstances existing before and after the death of the deceased person"; and (4) "any other matter which it considers relevant in the circumstances." . . .

Nevertheless, this power to disinherit is more limited in reality than the black-letter law suggests. Through substantive doctrines and procedural mechanisms, the U.S. legal system has checked absolute testamentary freedom. These legal institutions include the doctrine of undue influence; rules concerning mental capacity, fraud, and duress; and the right to trial by jury in probate proceedings.

In practice, when a testator disinherits his descendants, a postmortem will contest may follow. . . .

The doctrine of undue influence, therefore, may serve in reality as a check on testamentary freedom. A similar analysis could be applied to will contests involving the testator's mental capacity, fraud, or duress. All of these doctrines allow courts to undo testamentary dispositions that fail to provide for the testator's children or other close relatives. . . .

Ironically, the tale of inheritance in the common law begins not with complete freedom of testation, but with the exact opposite — primogeniture, a rule providing that all of a father's qualified land is inherited automatically by his eldest son. Testamentary freedom in England emerged in the shadow of primogeniture, and this fact is key to understanding why an absolute power of disinheritance had already developed in England by the time the American colonies were settled. Disinheritance in the common law came into being as a byproduct of reform, not as an independent policy. . . .

III. Contemporary Justifications for Testamentary Freedom

If the historical development of unlimited disinheritance in the common law does not necessarily justify its continued existence, many other explanations can be offered that may carry more weight. These include the positive incentives that freedom of testation may create; a noted American tendency toward individualism; a shift to human capital as the dominant form of inheritance; and obvious problems with the U.S. probate system. All of these arguments must be considered in evaluating whether unlimited disinheritance has some justification besides its historical pedigree. . . .

C. Inheritance and Human Capital

One possible contemporary justification for the U.S. rule that does not depend on American individualism is the change in the nature of wealth transmitted from parent to child. In a classic article published in 1988, John Langbein argued that the nature of wealth transmission changed dramatically over the course of the twentieth century. In the nineteenth century, Langbein argued, wealth transmitted from parent to child typically took the form of the family farm or firm. During the twentieth century, however, this form of wealth was gradually supplanted by human capital — the investment of the parents in the skills of the child. Consequently, "the business of educating children [became] the main occasion for intergenerational wealth transfer." At the same time, increasing life expectancy meant that parents needed to consume more of their assets during retirement, leaving children with less of an expectation that they would inherit property from their parents at death. Langbein predicted that wealth transfer at death would continue to decline in importance, at least with respect to the middle classes, while educational expenditures would become more prominent.

Although this transformation in the nature of family wealth transmission cannot explain why an absolute right to disinherit descendants became embedded in U.S. law, it helps to justify the continued existence of that rule. As increases in college tuition continue to outpace inflation, the amount of money parents invest in their children's education could also increase, and this lifetime investment may satisfy any moral obligation parents might have to provide for their adult children. According to this view, when the parents adequately provided for a child during their lifetime by an investment in the child's skills, that child has no reason to complain if the parents choose to devise what little remains at death to someone else.

The fact that human capital has become the dominant mode of family wealth transmission goes a long way toward justifying the U.S. rule allowing disinheritance of descendants. Taken to its logical extreme, however, it might call into question a central principle of the law of intestate succession in every American state, namely, the rule that parents of the intestate do not take when the intestate is survived by descendants. If children are adequately provided for through the human capital transferred to them by their parents, one would expect the law of intestacy to favor an elderly parent of the intestate over an adult child, but this is not the case. The apparent assumption is that the typical decedent would prefer for her children to inherit even if they are adults and the decedent is also survived by her own parent. If this assumption is incorrect, we should rethink not only the rules regarding disinheritance of children, but also the shares children take when the parent dies intestate.

The human capital justification for disinheritance is related to a broader argument, namely, that inheritance of any sort exacerbates the gap between rich and poor and increases concentration of wealth in the hands of a few. . . .

When courts consider the interests of omitted children, they must balance the potentially differing interests of parent and child. Whose interests does Professor Tate favor? Do you agree with his reasons for this balance? What other interests might be articulated by both parent and child? For example, think about the *Feinberg* case, discussed in Chapter 1, which involved dead hand control by grandparents.

As the article also points out, other countries have made different choices, and protect children, even from intentional disinheritance. Do any of these systems provide a good model? Consider the fact that there are fewer will contests in civil law countries as the result of forced heirship. Why do you think that is?

b.   Intentional Disinheritance

In this next case, do you think the court accurately describes the testator's intent? What could the drafting lawyer have done to make the testator's intentions more clear and less likely to be subject to a will contest? This is a good case to demonstrate how imprecise language can cause troubles.

In re Estate of Robbins
756 A.2d 602 (N.H. 2000)

NADEAU, J.

The petitioners, Pamela Robbins and Michael Robbins, file this interlocutory appeal, from the decision of the Cheshire County Probate Court (*Espiefs,* J.) granting a motion for partial summary judgment filed by the respondents, Bertha Johnson and Susan Wright. The petitioners argue that the probate court erred by ruling that the phrase "any other heir of mine" in the testator's will was sufficient reference to the testator's children to prevent application of the pretermitted heir statute. *See* N.H. Rev. Stat. Ann. §551:10 (1997). We reverse and remand.

The petitioners are the natural daughter and adopted son of the testator, Elizabeth C. Robbins. The respondents are the testator's sister and niece.

The testator's will did not devise any of her estate to the petitioners, but rather contained the following provision:

> *PRETERMITTED HEIR*: Except as otherwise expressly provided by this will and the Elizabeth C. Robbins Revocable Trust, I intentionally make no provisions for the benefit of any other heir of mine except as their [sic] rights are expressly set out in Elizabeth C. Robbins Revocable Trust.

The probate court found that the trust neither directly nor indirectly referred to the petitioners.

After the testator's death, the petitioners sought a distribution pursuant to RSA 551:10. . . .

RSA 551:10 provides:

> Every child born after the decease of the testator, and every child or issue of a child of the deceased not named or referred to in his will, and who is not a devisee or legatee, shall be entitled to the same portion of the estate, real and personal, as he would be if the deceased were intestate.

The purpose of the statute is to prevent a mistake or unintended failure by the testator or testatrix to remember the natural object of his or her bounty. Consequently, if a child is not named or referred to in the will, and is not a devisee or legatee under the will, then the statute creates a conclusive rule of law that pretermission of the child was accidental. "This rule is conclusive unless there is *evidence in the will itself* that the omission was intentional."

"[N]o testator should be understood to intend to disinherit one of his children or grandchildren upon any less clear evidence than his actually naming or distinctly referring to them personally so as to show that he had them in his mind."

The testator's reference to the child need not be direct. *See In re Estate of Laura*, 690 A.2d 1011, 1015-16 (N.H. 1997). In *Laura*, we held that by naming the father of the great-grandchildren, the testator sufficiently referred to the great-grandchildren to preclude them from invoking the statute.

The petitioners were neither named nor devisees or legatees under the testator's will. The respondents argue, however, that the testator's statement in the will that "I intentionally make no provisions for the benefit of any other heir of mine" sufficiently refers to the petitioners so as to deprive them of the statute's protection.

Two cases control the outcome of this case. In *MacKay*, the testator's will did not directly refer to the daughter-claimant, but provided that the residue of the estate would go to the testator's "heirs at law" and "next of kin." Similarly, in *Jackson*, the testator's will devised the residue of his estate to his brother and sister and "to their heirs and assigns forever," but did not directly name his three adopted children. We held in both cases that the testator's use of a generic term such as "heirs" was insufficient to preclude application of RSA 551:10.

In a similar context, when determining whether language in a will is sufficient to render a claimant a legatee for purposes of RSA 551:10, we have stated that although

> a devise or legacy to a class circumscribed by the terms "children" or "issue" may be a sufficient recognition of a child of the testator to exclude the child from the ambit of RSA 551:10, a devise or legacy to a class which *may include* children, such as "heirs-at-law" or "next-of-kin" is not sufficient recognition.

In the instant case, the reference to "any other heirs of mine" is insufficient to establish that the testator had her children in mind when she omitted them from the will. *See Jackson*, 379 A.2d at 835. We hold, therefore, that the probate court erred in concluding that the petitioners are not pretermitted heirs pursuant to RSA 551:10.

The respondents argue that *Smith v. Sheehan* (N.H. 1892), controls the outcome of this case. In Smith, the testator's son was not expressly mentioned in the testator's will, but the will contained a residual clause providing that the residue go "to my legal heirs." We held that the use of the term "heirs" was sufficient to deprive a child of the protection of the pretermitted heir statute.

Our holding in *Smith* rested not only on the fact that the term "heirs" was sufficient under the statute, but also on the fact that the testator's son was a legatee under the will. Thus, we did not have before us the question of whether the use of the term "heirs," alone, was sufficient under the predecessor [statute]. . . .

Accordingly, we hold today that a testator's use of the term "heirs" is insufficient to preclude application of the pretermitted heir statute. The words "children" or "issue" must be used. To the extent the holding in the *Smith* decision is inconsistent, it is overruled.

Reversed and remanded.

NOTES AND QUESTIONS

1. *Before or after?* Were Pamela and Michael born before or after the will was executed? Is that an important distinction under the New Hampshire statute? Should it be?

2. *Is $1 enough?* What if the will had provided, "I leave $1 to each of my children who survive me"? In that case, of course, no child is omitted from the will. Do you see any problems with such a bequest?

3. *Looking for clarity?* In *Estate of Mowry*, 131 Cal. Rptr. 2d 855 (Ct. App. 2003), the decedent's adopted daughter, Toni, argued she was unintentionally omitted from her father's holographic will, which was written after her adoption. Her position was that California public policy protected omitted heirs. The court, however, relied on the statute which legislatively overruled such a policy. The relevant section of the California Probate Code provided: "Except as provided in Section 21621, if a decedent fails to provide in a testamentary instrument for a child of decedent born or adopted after the execution of all of the decedent's testamentary instruments, the omitted child shall receive a share in the decedent's estate equal in value to that which the child would have received if the decedent had died without having executed any testamentary instrument." CAL. PROB. CODE §21620. On the other hand, Section 21621 stated: "A child shall not receive a share of the estate under Section 21620 if any of the following is established: (a) The decedent's failure to provide for the child in the decedent's testamentary instruments was intentional and that intention appears from the testamentary instruments." CAL. PROB. CODE §21621. The court read the sections together to mean that an omitted child was entitled to a share only where she was born or adopted *after* execution of the testamentary document unless she could prove the omission was the product of a mistake and was not intentional. What result in New Hampshire?

4. *Who's your Daddy? Your Mommy?* Omitted children who are non-marital also must prove that they are the decedent's child. Generally, maternity is relatively easy to prove, but paternity can be more difficult, as you know from Chapter 2, although it can be established by a DNA test, *see In re Estate of Johnson*, No. ADM 23-05, 2006 WL 3302857 (D.C. Super. Ct. June 21, 2006) (holding that since omitted nonmarital child could prove paternity and where the will did not explicitly indicate an intent to exclude

subsequent children, he could recover part of the decedent's estate), or through acknowledgement of the decedent prior to his death. *See* Ark. Code Ann. §28-9-209 (2009); *see also In re Estate of Keathley*, 242 S.W.3d 223 (Ark. 2006) (holding that child did not fulfill any of the requirements to be recognized by decedent or court as decedent's child, and so could not recover as omitted child). Before deploying overseas, or before undergoing cancer treatment, men are visiting sperm banks to preserve their sperm in case they die or become unable to conceive (chemical or biological warfare, or infertility). When their wives or girlfriends later use the sperm to have children, can those children recover from their deceased fathers' estates as omitted children? Possibly. *See* Charles P. Kindregan, Jr., *Dead Dads: Thawing an Heir from the Freezer*, 35 Wm. Mitchell L. Rev. 433 (2009); Kristine S. Knaplund, *Postmortem Conception and a Father's Last Will*, 46 Ariz. L. Rev. 91 (2004). For more information on posthumously conceived children, see the discussion in Chapter 2.

c.   The UPC Approach

As you read the UPC, think about the assumptions it makes concerning the testator's intentions in omitting a child. As with the pretermitted spouse rule, the testator's presumed intent (reflected in the statute) gives way to a contrary proven actual intent.

UPC §2-302. Omitted Children.

(a) Except as provided in subsection (b), if a testator fails to provide in his [or her] will for any of his [or her] children born or adopted after the execution of the will, the omitted after-born or after-adopted child receives a share in the estate as follows:

(1) If the testator had no child living when he [or she] executed the will, an omitted after-born or after-adopted child receives a share in the estate equal in value to that which the child would have received had the testator died intestate, unless the will devised all or substantially all of the estate to the other parent of the omitted child and that other parent survives the testator and is entitled to take under the will.

(2) If the testator had one or more children living when he [or she] executed the will, and the will devised property or an interest in property to one or more of the then-living children, an omitted after-born or after-adopted child is entitled to share in the testator's estate as follows:

(i) The portion of the testator's estate in which the omitted after-born or after-adopted child is entitled to share is limited to devises made to the testator's then-living children under the will.

(ii) The omitted after-born or after-adopted child is entitled to receive the share of the testator's estate, as limited in subparagraph (i), that the child would have received had the testator included all omitted after-born and after-adopted children with the children to whom devises were made under the will and had given an equal share of the estate to each child.

(iii) To the extent feasible, the interest granted an omitted after-born or after-adopted child under this section must be of the same character, whether equitable or legal, present or future, as that devised to the testator's then-living children under the will.

(iv) In satisfying a share provided by this paragraph, devises to the testator's children who were living when the will was executed abate ratably. In abating the devises of the then-living children, the court shall preserve to the maximum extent possible the character of the testamentary plan adopted by the testator.

(b) Neither subsection (a)(1) nor subsection (a)(2) applies if:

(1) it appears from the will that the omission was intentional; or

(2) the testator provided for the omitted after-born or after-adopted child by transfer outside the will and the intent that the transfer be in lieu of a testamentary provision is shown by the testator's statements or is reasonably inferred from the amount of the transfer or other evidence.

(c) If at the time of execution of the will the testator fails to provide in his [or her] will for a living child solely because he [or she] believes the child to be dead, the child is entitled to share in the estate as if the child were an omitted after-born or after-adopted child.

(d) In satisfying a share provided by subsection (a)(1), devises made by the will abate under Section 3-902.

Comment to UPC §2-302

. . . No Child Living When Will Executed.   If the testator had no child living when he or she executed the will, subsection (a)(1) provides that an omitted after-born or after-adopted child receives the share he or she would have received had the testator died intestate, unless the will devised, under trust or not, all or substantially all of the estate to the other parent of the omitted child. If the will did devise all or substantially all of the estate to the other parent of the omitted child, and if that other parent survives the testator and is entitled to take under the will, the omitted after-born or after-adopted child receives no share of the estate. In the case of an after-adopted child, the term "other parent" refers to the other adopting parent. (The other parent of the omitted child might survive the testator, but not be entitled to take under the will because, for example, that devise to the other parent was revoked under Section 2-803 or 2-804.)

One or More Children Living When Will Executed.   If the testator had one or more children living when the will was executed, subsection (a)(2), which implements the second basic objective stated above, provides that an omitted after-born or after-adopted child only receives a share of the testator's estate if the testator's will devised property or an equitable or legal interest in property to one or more of the children living at the time the will was executed; if not, the omitted after-born or after-adopted child receives nothing. . . .

Subsection (a)(2) is illustrated by the following example.

> *Example.* When G executed her will, she had two living children, A and B. Her will devised $7500 to each child. After G executed her will, she had another child, C.
>
> C is entitled to $5,000. $2,500 (1/3 of $7,500) of C's entitlement comes from A's $7,500 devise (reducing it to $5,000); and $2,500 (1/3 of $7,500) comes from B's $7,500 devise (reducing it to $5,000).
>
> *Variation.* If G's will had devised $10,000 to A and $5,000 to B, C would be entitled to $5,000. $3,333 (1/3 of $10,000) of C's entitlement comes from A's $10,000 devise (reducing it to $6,667); and $1,667 (1/3 of $5,000) comes from B's $5,000 devise (reducing it to $3,333).

Subsection (b) Exceptions.   To preclude operation of subsection (a)(1) or (a)(2), the testator's will need not make any provision, even nominal in amount, for a testator's present or future children; under subsection (b)(1), a simple recital in the will that the testator intends to make no provision for then living children or any the testator thereafter may have would be sufficient.

NOTES AND QUESTIONS

1. *Failure to mention under the UPC.* What requirements are there for an omitted child to inherit under the Uniform Probate Code? UPC §2-302 presumes that the failure to mention children born or adopted after execution of the will is unintentional and allows those children to inherit a share of the estate as if the decedent had died intestate. Why does this presumption make sense? Should it include pre-born or adopted children? However, if the decedent arranged for a transfer outside the will that was intended to be in lieu of the will, the child is not also entitled to a share of the estate. What might such a transfer look like?

2. *Live or dead?* Children omitted from the will because they are thought to be dead may also be able to inherit as pretermitted children in

some states, such as Connecticut, as well as in states that have adopted UPC §2-302(c). *See, e.g.,* Conn Gen. Stat §45a-257b(c) (2010).

3.   *Exception to a pretermitted child statute.* Under the UPC and in some states, an omitted child is not entitled to a share of the decedent's estate if all or "substantially all" of the estate is left to the other parent of that child. *See Gray v. Gray*, 947 So. 2d 1045 (Ala. 2006) (finding that the exception applied even when the children living at the time of execution of the will were not the children of the decedent's then spouse). Other states with this exception include Florida, California, Idaho and Indiana. What constitutes "substantially all"?

4.   *Trusting actions.* Under the UPC, trusts are not included in the property to which an omitted child can receive a share. This varies between jurisdictions. Some states include the decedent's revocable trust as property to which an omitted child can receive a share, in addition to the probate estate. *See, e.g.,* Iowa Code Ann. §633A.3106 (West Supp. 2009) (giving intestate share to a child born to or adopted by the settlor after creation of a revocable trust if the settlor unintentionally omitted that child from the trust). Other states, like the UPC, do not apply omitted child statutes to inter vivos trusts. *See, e.g., Kidwell v. Rhew*, 268 S.W.3d 309 (Ark. 2007) (holding that the pretermitted heir statute did not apply to revocable inter vivos trusts); *Welch v. Crow*, 206 P.3d 599 (Okla. 2009) (pretermitted heir statute does not apply to inter vivos trusts).

5.   *Defining descendants.* The UPC, and most states, specifically refer only to a "child." Consequently, pursuant to such a statute, a gift to grandchildren A and B would not include C (an after-born grandchild). In other jurisdictions, however, a grandchild can be a pretermitted "child." Some pretermitted child statutes apply to both omitted children of the testator and omitted issue of a deceased child of the testator. *See, e.g., Alexander v. Estate of Alexander*, 93 S.W.3d 688, 691 (Ark. 2002) (Arkansas's omitted child statute explicitly refers to the "issue of a deceased child of the testator," and the court refused to permit extrinsic evidence of the testator's intent); *In re Estate of Treloar*, 859 A.2d 1162 (N.H. 2004) (New Hampshire's omitted child statute, which refers to "issue of a child," gave grandchildren inheritance rights).

EXERCISES

1.   You've just finished meeting with a new client, Denaya. Her father recently died, and his will left none of his assets to her or to her younger sister. Her older brother and her mother each received one-half of her father's estate pursuant to the will. What advice will you give Denaya? What additional facts do you need to know? What would she need to demonstrate in a jurisdiction that had enacted the UPC?

2. Advise a client who wants to exclude his son from his will. What language should he use? What if he wants to exclude all children that may exist or may be born after he writes the will?

PROBLEMS

1. When Heath Ledger died, his daughter, Matilda, born outside of marriage with actor Michelle Williams, was not mentioned in his will because he had not updated it since her birth. If Heath Ledger's will were to be probated in a UPC state (instead of Australia), what would Matilda have to show in order to inherit a share of the estate?

2. Tim, an unmarried man with no children, wrote a will 12 years ago leaving all of his probate property, which is valued at $1,000,000, to his brother, Arnie. Tim married Winnie four years after his will was drafted. Two years later, Tim and Winnie had a child, Kala. In addition, Tim recently fathered a child, Tiger, out of wedlock and acknowledged the child as his. Tim has just died.

    a. Winnie predeceased Tim but Kala, Tiger and Arnie survived him. Who gets what? [See UPC §2-302(d) for source of payment.]

    b. Tim wrote a new will (after the marriage to Winnie but before the births of Kala and Tiger) leaving a total of $500,000 to his brother, Arnie. The rest he left to Winnie. The newer will was not amended or revoked in any way to reflect the birth of the children. As it turns out, Tim's probate and augmented estates are both $3,000,000. Since their marriage lasted 10 years, Winnie's elective share is 30% of the augmented estate. Winnie, Kala, Tiger and Arnie all survive Tim. To what would Kala and Tiger each be entitled?

        i. To what would Kala and Tiger be entitled if the probate and augmented estates were $700,000? The newer will was not amended or revoked in any way to reflect the fact that the economic bust changed his worth from $3,000,000 to $700,000 at his death. [Note: This seems to be an area where the strict reading of the statute and the policy underlying the section are in conflict.]

    c. Same as basic facts of (b), except Winnie did not survive Tim. Who gets what?

3. Tosca had an estate of $900,000. In his will, Tosca left $600,000 to his nephew, Nick, $200,000 to his child, Amy, $100,000 to his child, Biff, and $0 to his child, Cara. Tosca later married Willa and had a child, Kim.

    a. Willa predeceased Tosca, but Amy, Biff, Cara, Kim and Nick survived him. Who gets what? Pay special attention to UPC

§2-302(a)(2)(A), (B) and (D). [Note as you do this that a new child can only share from the portion left to existing children. Does Kim get one-fourth or one-third of the share left to other children?]

b.   What if Willa survived Tosca also? [Note as you do this that a new spouse can only share from the portion not left to existing children.]

13 | PLANNING FOR INCAPACITY

A. INTRODUCTION

Estate planning involves more than the transfer of wealth; it also involves the management of wealth and health throughout an individual's life. What happens to individuals and their property while they are alive but disabled, either physically or mentally, is of critical importance to them in their ongoing lives as well as to those around them. If, for example, a woman develops Alzheimer's or becomes involved in an accident and suffers severe brain damage, who will make financial decisions for her, like depositing income, paying bills and running a business? Likewise, who will make health care decisions, such as whether to operate or to request a physician's aid in removing life support? If she has dependents, who will care for them? This chapter is important to your understanding of the many facets of working with clients in matters affecting them, their property and their families.

The demographics make it easy to understand the need to plan for incapacity. The number of people over the age of 65 is continuously increasing; in 2009, the number of people over 65 was approximately 37.8 million; by 2020, that number is expected to be 55.0 million, with 6.6 million over the age of 85. U.S. ADMINISTRATION ON AGING, A PROFILE OF OLDER AMERICANS: 2009.[1] Moreover, Alzheimer's disease (which is associated with aging) and related dementias are becoming increasingly

---

1. *Available at* http://www.aoa.gov/AoAroot/Aging_Statistics/Profile/2008/docs/2008 profile.pdf.

prevalent with more than 5.3 million people having this disease in the United States in 2010. ALZHEIMER'S ASSOCIATION, 2010 ALZHEIMER'S DISEASE FACTS AND FIGURES (2010).[2]

It is not just the elderly, however, who need to plan for their incapacity; younger adults should do so as well. About 1.7 million people per year experience a traumatic brain injury, which may cause some forms of mental disability. Theresa Schiavo, in the case presented below, for example, was only 27 years old when she suffered a cardiac arrest as a result of a potassium imbalance.

Moreover, since children under the age of 18 are presumed to be legally incapacitated, parents should plan for the care of their children in the event they die or become incompetent. It is particularly important to plan for the ongoing care of children with disabilities.

As with all of trust and estate law, statutory default rules determine what will happen if the individual did not engage in advance planning and did not prepare written instructions. In addition to the fact that default rules do not necessarily reach the result the individual may have wished, they may not be efficient in an emergency, requiring a petition to, and an order from, the court.

This chapter analyzes the default and override rules relating to financial and health care issues in the event of incapacity, showing how planning can lead to results that are more consistent with the desires of the individual involved. Because Medicaid and Medicare have become an integral part of estate planning, the chapter includes a discussion of these programs. Additionally, the chapter examines planning for the care of children if their parents are unable to care for them. The chapter concludes with a presentation of ethical questions associated with representing people who may be suffering from cognitive disability. The issues addressed in this chapter are relevant to all clients, regardless of their financial wealth.

B. FINANCIAL DECISIONS DURING INCAPACITY

This section first discusses how the law approaches incapacitated individuals who have not engaged in any planning, and then turns to the steps individuals can take to be prepared. As you will see, even with planning, there still may be problems in effectuating the individual's interests.

---

2. *Available at* http://www.alz.org/documents_custom/report_alzfactsfigures2010.pdf.

1.   *What Happens When There Is No Planning?*

Adults presumptively have the mental capacity and the power to make financial and health care arrangements for themselves and their children. While they are healthy, they can make arrangements to delegate their authority to others should they become disabled and incapable of making their own decisions. This is normally accomplished by appointing someone as an agent pursuant to a power of attorney or naming someone to fulfill that role in a trust.

If the individual does not appoint someone, a court may have to select a guardian and/or a conservator to assume these responsibilities for the person and/or his minor children. A guardian is someone who is given legal responsibility for the health and welfare of another person (the ward) because the ward is unable to care for herself. A court may appoint a guardian: 1) to care for children whose parents have died, are incapacitated or whose rights have been terminated; or 2) to care for adults who have become incapacitated. The guardian's authority extends not only to physical and legal control over the ward, but also to medical and other personal decisions.

A conservator (sometimes called a guardian of the estate) is a fiduciary who is responsible for the financial aspects of the ward's property. *See* UPC §§5-102(1) and (3), 5-418. Once appointed by a court, a conservator can receive, invest, manage and distribute the ward's property. Conservators are most likely to be appointed when the ward has a substantial amount of property.

To start the appointment process, someone — often a relative — must file a petition with a court that sets out why the individual needs a guardian or conservator and who is qualified to serve. After a hearing and possible examination by a medical professional, the court will decide whether to approve the appointment of a guardian and/or a conservator. A court will choose individuals based on the order of preference among alternative decision makers specified in the applicable state statute, an order that is similar to the list of individuals who would receive the estate through intestacy.

Article V of the UPC incorporates the Uniform Guardianship and Protective Proceedings Act (UGPPA) (1997), which establishes procedures for guardians and conservators appointed for adults who are incapacitated as well as for minors. An incapacitated person is defined as someone who "is unable to receive and evaluate information or make or communicate decisions to such an extent that the individual lacks the ability to meet essential requirements for physical health, safety, or self-care, even with appropriate technological assistance." UPC §5-102(4). The Act does not specify how to determine incapacity; the method and factors used depends on the particular task. *See, e.g.,* ALI-ABA, Elder Law: Issues, Answers, and Opportunities (2007). For example, the level of capacity necessary to execute a will is much lower than the capacity to enter into a contract. *See* Lawrence A. Frolik & Mary F. Radford, *"Sufficient" Capacity: The Contrasting Capacity Requirements for Different Documents*, 2 NAELA J. 303 (2006).

The UGPPA emphasizes procedural protections for the potential ward, and provides limits on the powers of guardians and conservators. The UGPPA specifies that a "court, whenever feasible, shall grant to a guardian only those powers necessitated by the ward's limitations and demonstrated needs and make appointive and other orders that will encourage the development of the ward's maximum self-reliance and independence." UPC §5-311(b). Unlike powers of attorney (discussed next), where there is no ongoing court supervision of the agent's actions, a conservator or guardian is generally required to provide periodic reports or accountings to the court.

Not all states have adopted the UGPPA, and state practices vary substantially with respect to the scope of guardianships and conservatorships, the definition of "incapacity" that supports appointment of a guardian or conservator and the person's accountability. States also vary with respect to whether the ward (in either a guardianship or a conservatorship) retains any rights, such as the right to enter into a contract or to initiate a lawsuit. For example, the Connecticut statute specifies that the ward retains rights that are not specifically delegated to the guardian, CONN. GEN. STAT. §45a-650(k) (2010); Florida explicitly addresses the rights that may be delegated to a guardian of the person or property, as well as those that are retained by the ward, including an annual review of the guardianship plan, FLA. STAT. §744.3215 (2010).

2.   *What Is Possible with Advance Planning?*

Advance planning allows an individual to control who should make financial decisions in the event of the individual's incapacity, keeping the process private rather than court-supervised. The individual can choose representatives whom she believes will effectuate her plan and her wishes. While, as we discussed in Chapter 5, revocable living trusts (RLT) are a good way to plan for disability, the trust may not include all of a person's property — and many people will not have a trust at all. As a result, an individual who wants to ensure that someone else will step in when she becomes disabled is likely to use a power of attorney.

a.   **Powers of Attorney**

i.   *General*

A "power of attorney" authorizes one person (the "agent," who is sometimes also called the "attorney-in-fact") to act on behalf of someone else (the "principal") in a legal, health or business matter. Powers of attorney are routine instruments. They are frequently used for single transactions, such as by one spouse to the other spouse to act on his behalf in the sale of their home if he anticipates being out-of-town during the closing, or on a more comprehensive basis, allowing the agent to act for the principal in numerous matters when the principal is incapacitated. This chapter focuses on the latter use.

The capacity standard to appoint an agent is typically the same as that required to enter into a contract, a high standard which requires that the individual have a reasonable understanding of the act in which he is engaging. Frolik & Radford, *supra*, at 313, 315-16. A sample Durable Power of Attorney (and Appointment of Guardianship of Children) is included in Appendix A.

While powers of attorney typically expire once the principal is incapacitated, a *durable* power of attorney is designed to operate even after the principal is incapacitated. A *springing* power of attorney is dormant until the occurrence of some event specified in the power, such as the principal's incapacity.

Every state authorizes durable powers of attorney. When used properly, powers of attorney can enhance the principal's autonomy and ensure continuity in an individual's financial matters. Unfortunately, there is little independent oversight of them. This section explores issues involved in the implementation of powers of attorney, including the parameters for the agent's authority and the potential for abuse.

EXERCISES

1. As an example of what a power of attorney can do, please review the sample in Appendix A. What does the form provide with respect to a determination of the principal's incapacity? Do you see any ambiguities in the form? How might you address those ambiguities?

2. It is useful to look at the statutes in the jurisdiction where you plan to practice that set out the parameters of both financial and health care powers of attorney. What do the statutes provide with respect to a determination of the principal's incapacity? Do the statutes include authorized forms one may use?

ii. Agent's Responsibilities

The utility of a power of attorney depends on the trustworthiness of the agent. The agent has a fiduciary obligation to the principal, but the parameters of this obligation are not entirely clear. Moreover, the two model acts dealing with powers of attorney (parts of the UPC as well as the Uniform Power of Attorney Act) do not specify the scope of this fiduciary obligation. Accordingly, common law concepts of fiduciary obligations such as loyalty and due care, similar to those discussed in Chapter 6, are highly relevant. This section provides a brief review of those principles, but with a focus on powers of attorney. Note that these concepts are also relevant in the health care context discussed later in the chapter.

An agent's fiduciary duty is described generally by the *Restatement* as a "duty to act loyally for the principal's benefit in all matters connected with the agency relationship." RESTATEMENT (THIRD) OF AGENCY §8.01 (2006). Nonetheless, the *Restatement* also notes that "conduct by an agent that would otherwise constitute a breach of duty . . . does not constitute a breach of duty if the principal consents to the conduct. . . . " *Id.* at §8.06(10).

Many state statutes do not specifically state the agent's duties, and there is wide variation even among those states that do. "On one end of the spectrum, the agent is merely referred to as a fiduciary without further specification of duties; on the other, an extensive list of duties is provided. The statutory standards of care to be exercised by agents vary as well and range from a due care to a trustee-type standard." Linda S. Whitton, *Durable Powers as an Alternative to Guardianship: Lessons We Have Learned*, 37 STETSON L. REV. 7, 25 (2007).

But what happens when the agent is someone "who likely has inherent conflicts of interest, such as those arising from inheritance expectations or joint property ownership"? *Id.* at 24. Unfortunately, elder law attorneys and probate judges routinely deal with cases where a "trustworthy" agent has defrauded a trusting principal. Breaches can begin at the time the power of attorney is created, as when the principal is defrauded into signing a form; breaches may also occur when the agent engages in:

1)   "Transactions that exceed the intended scope of authority," such as making gifts of the principal's property when not granted gift-making authority;

2)   "Transactions conducted for self-dealing purposes," as when an agent spends the principal's money to buy himself a car rather than pay for the principal's nursing home care; or

3)   "Transactions conducted in contravention of the principal's expectations," such as when an agent has gift-making authority, but makes gifts that undermine the principal's estate plan.

LORI A. STIEGEL & ELLEN VANCLEAVE KLEM, ABA COMM. ON LAW AND AGING, POWER OF ATTORNEY ABUSE: WHAT STATES CAN DO ABOUT IT 4 (2008).[3]

Consider which of the breaches just mentioned are at issue in the case that follows.

In re Ferrara
852 N.E.2d 138 (N.Y. 2006)

READ, J.

Article 5, title 15 of the General Obligations Law prescribes what a statutory short form power of attorney must contain, specifies the powers

---

3. *Available at* http://assets.aarp.org/rgcenter/consume/2008_17_poa.pdf.

that the form may authorize and defines their scope. On this appeal, we hold that an agent acting under color of a statutory short form power of attorney that contains additional language augmenting the gift-giving authority must make gifts pursuant to these enhanced powers in the principal's best interest.

I.

On June 10, 1999, decedent George J. Ferrara, a retired stockbroker who was residing in Florida at the time, executed a will "mak[ing] no provision . . . for any family member . . . or for any individual person" because it was his "intention to leave [his] entire residuary estate to charity." Accordingly, in the same instrument he bequeathed his estate to a sole beneficiary, the Salvation Army, "to be held, in perpetuity, in a separate endowment fund to be named the 'GEORGE J. FERRARA MEMORIAL FUND' with the annual net income therefrom to be used by the Salvation Army to further its charitable purposes in the greater Daytona Beach, Florida area." On August 16, 1999, decedent executed a codicil naming the Florida attorney who had drafted his will and codicil as his executor, and otherwise "ratif[ied], confirm[ed] and republish[ed] [his] said Will of June 10, 1999." Decedent was single, and had no children. His closest relatives were his brother, John, and a sister, and their respective children.

According to John Ferrara's son, Dominick Ferrara, after decedent was hospitalized in Florida in December 1999, he and his father "were called to assist." . . .

On January 15, 2000, Dominick Ferrara accompanied decedent on a flight from Florida to New York. He brought along [a] blue bag and a box containing decedent's 1998 federal income tax returns and other personal papers or records and memorabilia; he testified that there was no will among these papers, which he apparently culled after decedent's death, and that decedent never mentioned any will to him. Immediately upon arriving in New York, decedent was admitted to an assisted living facility. He was thin, malnourished and weak, and was suffering from an array of serious chronic maladies.

On January 25, 2000, ten days later, decedent signed, and initialed where required, multiple originals of a "Durable General Power of Attorney: New York Statutory Short Form," thereby appointing John and Dominick Ferrara as his attorneys-in-fact, and allowing either of them to act separately

> "IN [HIS] NAME, PLACE AND STEAD in any way which [he] [him]self could do, if [he] were personally present, with respect to the following matters [listed in lettered subdivisions (A) through (O)] as each of them is defined in Title 15 of Article 5 of the New York General Obligations Law to the extent that [he was] permitted by law to act through an agent."

Subdivisions (A) through (O) of the pre-printed form listed various kinds of transactions; in particular, subdivision (M) specified "making gifts to my spouse, children and more remote descendants, and parents, not to exceed in the aggregate $10,000 to each of such persons in any year." Decedent authorized his attorneys-in-fact to carry out all of the matters listed in subdivisions (A) through (O). Critically, decedent also initialed a typewritten addition to the form, which stated that "[t]his Power of Attorney shall enable the Attorneys-in-Fact to make gifts without limitation in amount to John Ferrara and/or Dominick Ferrara."

Dominick Ferrara insists that this provision authorizing him to make unlimited gifts to himself was added "[i]n furtherance of [decedent's] wishes," because decedent repeatedly told him in December 1999 and January 2000 that he "wanted [Dominick Ferrara] to have all of [decedent's] assets to do with as [he] pleased." When asked if he and decedent had discussed making gifts to other family members—including his father, John, the other attorney-in-fact—Dominick Ferrara replied that they had not, again because "[m]y Uncle George gave me his money to do as I wished." Dominick Ferrara acknowledges that decedent made no memorandum or note to this effect, and only once expressed these donative intentions in the presence of anyone else—Dominick's wife, Elizabeth. Dominick Ferrara sought out an attorney in New York City "to discuss [his] Uncle's wishes," and this attorney provided him with the power of attorney that decedent ultimately executed.

The power of attorney was notarized by an attorney with whom Dominick and Elizabeth Ferrara were acquainted. This attorney testified that she attended the signing at the Ferraras' behest, and was acting as a notary only, not as an attorney for either the Ferraras or decedent. Specifically, she rendered no legal advice to decedent, who read the form in her presence before signing it. The attorney and Dominick Ferrara generally agree that it was Dominick who explained the form's provisions to decedent; she does not recall the word "gift" having been mentioned.

Decedent's condition deteriorated. He was admitted to the hospital on January 29, 2000, and never left. Decedent died on February 12, 2000, less than a month after moving to New York, and approximately three weeks after executing the power of attorney. During those three weeks, Dominick Ferrara transferred about $820,000 of decedent's assets to himself, including [] IBM stock and about $300,000 in cash from the certificates of deposit, multiple bank accounts and the sale of [decedent's] Florida property. After decedent's death, he filed a 1999 federal income tax return for decedent, and collected a refund in the amount of roughly $9,500. Dominick Ferrara testified that he does not recall what happened to any of the $300,000 in cash, but that he still owns the IBM stock.

The Salvation Army found out about decedent's will . . . [and] commenced a proceeding [in NY Surrogate Court]. . . .

II.

Section 5-1501 of the General Obligations Law sets out the forms creating a durable and nondurable statutory short form power of attorney. By these forms, the principal appoints an attorney-in-fact to act "IN [HIS] NAME, PLACE AND STEAD" with respect to any or all of 15 categories of matters listed in lettered subdivisions (A) through (O) "as each of them is defined in Title 15 of Article 5 of the New York General Obligations Law"; specifically, the 15 categories in subdivisions (A) through (O) are interpreted in corresponding sections 5-1502A through 5-1502O of the General Obligations Law (*id.*).[4]

As relevant to this case, in 1996 the Legislature amended section 5-1501 (1) to add lettered subdivision (M), authorizing the attorney-in-fact to "mak[e] gifts to [the principal's] spouse, children and more remote descendants, and parents, not to exceed in the aggregate $10,000 to each of such persons in any year." Section 5-1502M construes this gift-giving authority

"to mean that the principal authorizes the agent . . . [t]o make gifts . . . either outright or to a trust for the sole benefit of one or more of [the specified] persons . . . *only for purposes which the agent reasonably deems to be in the best interest of the principal,* specifically including minimization of income, estate, inheritance, generation-skipping transfer or gift taxes."

. . . Thus, section 5-1502M unambiguously imposes a duty on the attorney-in-fact to exercise gift-giving authority in the best interest of the principal. . . .

[T]he best interest requirement is consistent with the fiduciary duties that courts have historically imposed on attorneys-in-fact. "[A] power of attorney . . . is clearly given with the intent that the attorney-in-fact will utilize that power for the benefit of the principal" (*Mantella v. Mantella,* [3d Dept. 2000]). Because "[t]he relationship of an attorney-in-fact to his principal is that of agent and principal . . . , the attorney-in-fact must act in the utmost good faith and undivided loyalty toward the principal, and must act in accordance with the highest principles of morality, fidelity, loyalty and fair dealing."

---

4. [FN 2] . . . The 15 categories are real estate transactions; chattel and goods transactions; bond, share and commodity transactions; banking transactions; business operating transactions; insurance transactions; estate transactions; claims and litigation; personal relationships and affairs; benefits from military service; records, reports and statements; retirement benefit transactions; gifts to specified beneficiaries not to exceed $10,000 to each per year; tax matters; and all other matters. Subdivision (P) on the form authorizes the attorney-in-fact to delegate any or all of the matters selected to anyone whom he chooses. Subdivision (Q), which reads "each of the above matters identified by the following letters," allows the principal to list the letters of all the matters authorized and then to initial in one place on the document, as decedent did here, rather than separately initial each selected lettered subdivision.

In short, [regardless of the form of the gift-giving power], the best interest requirement remains. Thus, Dominick Ferrara was only authorized to make gifts to himself insofar as these gifts were in decedent's best interest, interpreted by section 5-1502M as gifts to carry out the principal's financial, estate or tax plans. Here, Dominick Ferarra clearly did not make gifts to himself for such purposes. Rather, he consistently testified that he made the self-gifts "[i]n furtherance of [decedent's] wishes" to give him "all of his assets to do with as [Dominick] pleased." The term "best interest" does not include such unqualified generosity to the holder of a power of attorney, especially where the gift virtually impoverishes a donor whose estate plan, shown by a recent will, contradicts any desire to benefit the recipient of the gift. Accordingly, the order of the Appellate Division should be reversed, without costs, and the matter remitted to Surrogate's Court for further proceedings in accordance with this opinion.

NOTES AND QUESTIONS

1. *Can the funds be recovered?* Consider what Dominick Ferrara did with the money he obtained, and the likelihood of any disgorgement. There are a range of potential civil claims against the agent, including fraud and conversion. Some states have adopted laws that criminalize abuse or exploitation of the authority granted by a power of attorney. For example, in Utah, an individual who "unjustly or improperly uses a vulnerable adult's power of attorney or guardianship for the profit or advantage of someone other than the vulnerable adult" is guilty of "exploitation." UTAH CODE ANN. §76-5-111 (4)(a)(2009). Of course, by the time a civil or criminal action begins, the agent may have already spent the money, so there may be nothing left to recover. Banks or other financial institutions that respect the power of attorney are generally protected if they can show that they relied on the agent in good faith, and states may even have laws that impose liability on an entity which does not honor the agent's request. *See* Lawrence Frolik, *Keep Powers of Attorney in Check*, 45 TRIAL 42, 44 (Apr. 2009).

2. *What steps might be taken to minimize abuses like the ones in* Ferrara? Should notaries who witness powers of attorney be required to administer competency tests? Should entities to which a power of attorney is presented have an obligation to perform further investigations? Would you add any more protections? For example, should an agent be required to give periodic accountings? Who should have the power to request those accountings? Should the principal be advised to inform relevant family members about the existence and scope of the power of attorney? *See* Frolik, *supra*.

3. *Signature complete*. New York now requires that principals and agents both sign the power of attorney. If the principal grants the agent the authority to make total annual gifts of more than $500 to one person or charity, then that power must be included in a separate Statutory Major Gifts Rider that must be signed in the presence of two witnesses or in a comparable form. N.Y. GEN. OBLIG. LAW §§51501-1514 (2010). Does this seem effective at guarding against abuse? If this precaution is taken, then what are its benefits and drawbacks to the principal and the agent?

iii. Uniform Power of Attorney Act

In an effort to curb abuses like those on display in *Ferrara*, NCCUSL (now ULC) drafted the Uniform Power of Attorney Act (UPAA) in 2006. The Act establishes relatively straightforward procedures so that individuals can arrange for a surrogate to handle their property if they are incapacitated. It also focuses on protecting the principal by promoting her autonomy and preventing fraud. In 2010, the UPAA became Article 5B of the UPC. The provisions of the UPAA excerpted below concern some of the more problematic issues that arise with powers of attorney, including the duration of the power, liability of third parties who rely on the power and the agent's obligations.

UPAA §110. Termination of Power of Attorney or Agent's Authority

> (a) A power of attorney terminates when:
>   (1) the principal dies;
>   (2) the principal becomes incapacitated, if the power of attorney is not durable;
>   (3) the principal revokes the power of attorney;
>   (4) the power of attorney provides that it terminates;
>   (5) the purpose of the power of attorney is accomplished; or
>   (6) the principal revokes the agent's authority or the agent dies. . . .
> (b) An agent's authority terminates when:
>   (1) the principal revokes the authority;
>   (2) the agent dies, becomes incapacitated, or resigns;
>   (3) an action is filed for the [dissolution] or annulment of the agent's marriage to the principal or their legal separation, unless the power of attorney otherwise provides; or
>   (4) the power of attorney terminates.
> (c) Unless the power of attorney otherwise provides, an agent's authority is exercisable until the authority terminates under subsection (b), notwithstanding a lapse of time since the execution of the power of attorney.

(d) Termination of an agent's authority or of a power of attorney is not effective as to the agent or another person that, without actual knowledge of the termination, acts in good faith under the power of attorney. An act so performed, unless otherwise invalid or unenforceable, binds the principal and the principal's successors in interest.

UPAA §114. Agent's Duties.

(a) Notwithstanding provisions in the power of attorney, an agent that has accepted appointment shall:

(1) act in accordance with the principal's reasonable expectations to the extent actually known by the agent and, otherwise, in the principal's best interest;

(2) act in good faith; and

(3) act only within the scope of authority granted in the power of attorney.

(b) Except as otherwise provided in the power of attorney, an agent that has accepted appointment shall:

(1) act loyally for the principal's benefit;

(2) act so as not to create a conflict of interest that impairs the agent's ability to act impartially in the principal's best interest;

(3) act with the care, competence, and diligence ordinarily exercised by agents in similar circumstances;

(4) keep a record of all receipts, disbursements, and transactions made on behalf of the principal;

(5) cooperate with a person that has authority to make healthcare decisions for the principal to carry out the principal's reasonable expectations to the extent actually known by the agent and, otherwise, act in the principal's best interest; and

(6) attempt to preserve the principal's estate plan, to the extent actually known by the agent, if preserving the plan is consistent with the principal's best interest based on all relevant factors. . . .

(d) An agent that acts with care, competence, and diligence for the best interest of the principal is not liable solely because the agent also benefits from the act or has an individual or conflicting interest in relation to the property or affairs of the principal. . . .

(f) Absent a breach of duty to the principal, an agent is not liable if the value of the principal's property declines. . . .

(h) Except as otherwise provided in the power of attorney, an agent is not required to disclose receipts, disbursements, or transactions conducted on behalf of the principal unless ordered by a court or requested by the principal, a guardian, a conservator, another fiduciary acting for the principal. . . .

Comment to UPAA §114

Although well settled that an agent under a power of attorney is a fiduciary, there is little clarity in state power of attorney statutes about what that means. . . .

Subsection (d) provides that an agent acting with care, competence, and diligence for the best interest of the principal is not liable solely because the agent also benefits from the act or has a conflict of interest. This position is a departure from the traditional common law duty of loyalty which required an agent to act solely for the benefit of the principal. . . . The public policy which favors best interest over sole interest as the benchmark for agent loyalty comports with the practical reality that most agents under powers of attorney are family members who have inherent conflicts of interest with the principal arising from joint property ownership or inheritance expectations. . . .

Subsection (h) codifies the agent's common law duty to account to a principal. . . . Rather than create an affirmative duty of periodic accounting, subsection (h) states that the agent is not required to disclose receipts [except in certain limited circumstances].

UPAA §119. Acceptance of and Reliance upon Acknowledged Power of Attorney.

. . . (c) A person that in good faith accepts an acknowledged power of attorney without actual knowledge that the power of attorney is void, invalid, or terminated, that the purported agent's authority is void, invalid, or terminated, or that the agent is exceeding or improperly exercising the agent's authority may rely upon the power of attorney as if the power of attorney were genuine, valid and still in effect, the agent's authority were genuine, valid and still in effect, and the agent had not exceeded and had properly exercised the authority. . . .

UPAA §201. Authority That Requires Specific Grant; Grant of General Authority.

(a) An agent under a power of attorney may do the following on behalf of the principal or with the principal's property only if the power of attorney expressly grants the agent the authority and exercise of the authority is not otherwise prohibited by another agreement or instrument to which the authority or property is subject:

> (1) create, amend, revoke, or terminate an inter vivos trust;
> (2) make a gift;
> (3) create or change rights of survivorship;
> (4) create or change a beneficiary designation;
> (5) delegate authority granted under the power of attorney;
> (6) waive the principal's right to be a beneficiary of a joint and survivor annuity, including a survivor benefit under a retirement plan; [or]
> (7) exercise fiduciary powers that the principal has authority to delegate. . . .

NOTES AND QUESTIONS

1.   *Helping* Ferrara. Would the provisions of the Uniform Act have prevented the *Ferrara* outcome?

2.   *Enacting the Act.* The Act is relatively new, and only a few states have adopted it. It attempts to ensure less interstate variation on a series of issues, including the agent's gift-giving authority and the applicable standards for the agent's conduct. Indeed, while the power to gift may seem inherently suspect, it is often (notwithstanding the facts of *Ferrara*) just a good way to continue a gift-giving plan to reduce the size of the estate for tax purposes.

3.   *Limited authority.* Some scholars and practitioners believe the Act provides too many constraints on the agent's authority by requiring specific grants of authority for actions such as amending a trust. The Comment to Section 201(a) notes that the Act "follows a growing trend among states to require express specific authority for such actions as making a gift, creating or revoking a trust, and using other non-probate estate planning devices such as survivorship interests and beneficiary designations" because these actions may threaten "the principal's property estate plan." Do you think the Act provides too many, or not enough, constraints in light of the problems that the Act seeks to address?

PROBLEMS

Rani and Sasha have each executed a durable power of attorney (DPOA) naming the other as agent. Please answer the questions below based on the Uniform Act.

1.   Rani and Sasha are married. Sasha withdraws all of the assets from Rani's account at Brattle Bank, and then leaves the country. Is this within Sasha's authority?

2.   Rani and Sasha are married. Rani obtains a civil protection order requiring Sasha to stay away based on past acts of domestic violence. Sasha then withdraws all of the assets from Rani's account at Brattle Bank. Is this within Sasha's authority? Does Rani have any recourse against the Bank?

3. Rani and Sasha are not married, and they have not seen each other in five years. Sasha withdraws all of the assets from Rani's account at Brattle Bank, and then leaves the country. Does Rani have any recourse against the Bank?

b. Differences Between Powers of Attorney and Conservators

Conservators appointed by the court and agents acting under a power of attorney have different roles and responsibilities. Their authority with respect to revocable trusts provides an example of the differing authority. Of course, as you know from Chapter 5, a revocable trust serves as an extremely useful option to help the settlor plan for future disabilities. Indeed, as you can see from UTC §602, the UTC tries to limit disruption of the settlor's estate plan by providing safeguards for revocation or modification by both an agent and a conservator. Its underlying assumption is that a revocable trust serves as the primary device chosen by the settlor to hold her property in case of incapacity, with the power of attorney as a supplement to handle any unexpected issues and a conservator as an involuntary court-appointed agent. Nonetheless, it serves as a reminder that whatever planning for incapacity the settlor undertakes, such as a revocable trust, can be unraveled.

UTC §602. Revocation or Amendment of Revocable Trust.

> (e) A settlor's powers with respect to revocation, amendment, or distribution of trust property may be exercised by an agent under a power of attorney only to the extent expressly authorized by the terms of the trust or the power.
>
> (f) A [conservator] of the settlor or, if no [conservator] has been appointed, a [guardian] of the settlor may exercise a settlor's powers with respect to revocation, amendment, or distribution of trust property only with the approval of the court supervising the [conservatorship] or [guardianship].

Consider the differences between the authority granted to the agent versus the conservator, and the reasons for these differences. Section 602 provides that an agent acting pursuant to a power of attorney can act only in a manner consistent with the authorizing document, and a conservator can act only in a manner consistent with an order of the court. Indeed, even if the revocable trust document specifies that a conservator shall not have the power to revoke, a court may nonetheless approve the revocation "if it concludes that the action is necessary in the interests of justice." Comment to UTC §602. Given the settlor's purposes in establishing a revocable trust, this grants enormous power to the conservator. Why should the agent pursuant to a power of attorney have fewer rights?

Cases in states that have not adopted a rule by statute have established different standards concerning revocation by agents acting under a power of attorney or by a conservator. In *In re Mosteller*, 719 A.2d 1067 (Pa. Super. Ct. 1998), for example, the court permitted an agent acting under a power of attorney to revoke the trust because the power of attorney provided a broad general grant of powers that included other actions with respect to the trust, even though it did not specifically authorize revocation. In the following case, the court permitted an agent acting under a power of attorney to revoke a trust. As you read the case, think about what other information you would like to help decide whether revocation should be permitted.

In re Franzen
955 P.2d 1018 (Colo. 1998)

On February 4, 1992, James Franzen, the settlor, executed an instrument creating a trust designed to provide for himself and his wife, Frances Franzen, in their old age. The corpus of the trust initially consisted of three bank accounts containing a total of $74,251.19, but it did not include certain other assets held by Mr. and Mrs. Franzen as joint tenants, such as the family home. Norwest Bank, then known as United Bank of Denver, was named as the sole trustee in the trust agreement.

James Franzen was terminally ill when he created the trust, and he died four months later. Upon Mr. Franzen's death, a trust officer at the bank sent a letter to Frances Franzen, who was living in a nursing home, notifying her that she had "certain rights regarding the trust." A copy of the trust agreement was enclosed, and the letter referred to Article 5.1, which states:

> At . . . [James's] death, if Frances survives . . . [him], she may direct . . . [the] trustee in writing to deliver the residuary trust estate to her within three months of [James's] death. If she does not so direct, this trust shall continue to be administered as provided in Article 3. If she so directs, the trust shall terminate on the date the trust estate is distributed to her.

The letter asked Mrs. Franzen for a decision in writing by August 1, 1992, "so that we have time to make arrangements for the transfer of assets if necessary." A handwritten note at the bottom of the letter, signed by Mrs. Franzen and dated July 14, 1992, says, "I wish to leave the trust intact for my lifetime."

The bank, concerned about the disposition of the vacant house and other assets not included in the trust, contacted Mrs. Franzen's nephews, who were named as remaindermen of the trust. The two nephews were reluctant to assume responsibility for Mrs. Franzen's affairs, though, and Mrs. Franzen's brother, James O'Brien, intervened. O'Brien moved Mrs. Franzen to a nursing home in Kentucky, where he lived, and asked the bank to turn over Mrs. Franzen's assets to him.

In the course of dealing with the bank, the nephews expressed concerns about O'Brien's motives. The bank declined to comply with O'Brien's request, and filed a Petition for Instruction and Advice in the Denver Probate Court (probate court). Before the hearing, O'Brien sent the bank a copy of a power of attorney purporting to authorize him to act in Mrs. Franzen's behalf and a letter attempting to revoke the trust and to remove the bank as trustee, citing Article 6.2 and Article 8 of the trust agreement.

Article 6.2 of the trust provides that after the death of James Franzen, Frances Franzen "may remove any trustee," and that "[a]ny removal under this . . . [paragraph] may be made without cause and without notice of any reason and shall become effective immediately upon delivery of . . . [written notice] to the trustee" unless Frances Franzen and the trustee agree otherwise.

Article 8 of the trust agreement gives James Franzen "the right to amend or revoke this trust in whole or in part . . . by a writing delivered to . . . [the] trustee. . . . After my death, Frances may exercise these powers with respect to the entire trust estate."

The hearing was continued, and the bank filed a Petition for Appointment of a Conservator, asking the probate court to appoint someone to manage and protect Mrs. Franzen's assets. When the hearing on both petitions was held, the probate court ruled that the power of attorney had created a valid agency but that the trust had not been revoked and continued in existence. The probate court found that Mrs. Franzen needed protection, but a conservator was not available, so the Court appointed the bank as "special fiduciary" with responsibility for both trust and non-trust assets pursuant to sections 15-14-408 and 15-14-409, 5 C.R.S. (1997). The probate court ordered the bank to use the assets to make payments for Mrs. Franzen's benefit.

Franzen appealed the probate court rulings. On appeal, the court of appeals reversed, holding that the power of attorney authorized O'Brien to remove the bank as trustee and to revoke the trust. The court of appeals also held, however, that the bank was not liable for expenditures made in good faith after receiving the removal and revocation letter, including the legal fees incurred in the course of opposing O'Brien's efforts. . . .

The basic rule recognized in these cases [involving other actions under powers of attorney] logically might extend by analogy to situations where a power of attorney gives an agent wide authority to make decisions on behalf of the principal but makes no mention of the power to alter the principal's rights under any trust. We are willing to assume, for the sake of argument, that the scope of the agent's authority under the common law in such circumstances would not extend to revocation of a trust established to benefit the principal.

Even so, we are not persuaded that under the common law, an agency instrument must expressly refer to a particular trust by name in order to confer authority on the agent to revoke it. Under the reasoning of the cases previously cited, the terms of the power of attorney need only evince an intention to authorize the agent to make decisions concerning the principal's interests in trusts generally, not necessarily a particular trust.

Section 1(c) of the power of attorney executed by Mrs. Franzen expressly authorizes O'Brien to "manage . . . and in any manner deal with any real or personal property, tangible or intangible, or any interest therein . . . in my name and for my benefit, upon such terms as . . . [O'Brien] shall deem proper, *including the funding, creation, and/or revocation of trusts* or other investments." (Emphasis added.)

We have little trouble concluding that the quoted language expressly authorizes O'Brien to revoke the Franzen trust, even though it does not mention the trust specifically by name.

NOTES AND QUESTIONS

1. *Yes grants.* Do you think the court correctly interpreted the authority granted to Mr. O'Brien? Are there are any other reasonable interpretations? *See* RESTATEMENT (THIRD) OF TRUSTS §63, cmt. L.

2. *No grants.* By contrast, courts have been reluctant to allow revocation when neither the trust document nor the power of attorney specifically permitted someone to act on behalf of the settlor to revoke the trust. In *Murphey v. Murphey*, 819 P.2d 1029 (Ariz. Ct. App. 1991), the trust document specifically declared that all rights reserved to the settlors were personal rights that could not be exercised by "any guardian or personal representative." The court held that a person acting under a power of attorney could not revoke the trust. Likewise, in *Muller v. Bank of America, N.A.*, 12 P.3d 899 (Kan. Ct. App. 2000), neither the trust document nor the power of attorney mentioned revocation by an agent, and the court refused to permit an agent to revoke the trust.

PROBLEMS

1. You are the attorney for your state's Elder Law Committee. Would you recommend that your state law permit revocation of a revocable trust by a conservator? By someone acting under a power of attorney? In your mind, is there a distinction between the two from a policy standpoint? What reasoning supports your recommendation? As you consider these issues in the context of a revocable trust, do they lead to any other recommendations about how incapacity should affect will substitutes or estate plans more generally? A finding of incapacity might, for example, automatically transform all revocable trusts into irrevocable trusts. Should the state establish more limits on the authority of conservators and agents?

2. Marian creates a revocable trust, leaving her estate to her daughter, Delilah. Marian dislikes her son, Sanford, and has excluded him from her estate plan. Marian is the trustee of the trust, and she names Big Bank as the successor trustee. When Marian begins to need more care, Sanford moves her to the state where he lives. He has her sign a power of attorney, naming him as her agent. Using the power of attorney, he revokes the trust. If the revocation is valid, Marian's estate will go by intestacy equally to her two children.

      a.   Advise Delilah. Is there anything she can do to protect the trust? Can she move her mother back home, to the state where Delilah lives?

      b.   Advise Big Bank. Is there anything Big Bank should do before sending the trust assets to Sanford?

      c.   Now assume that Sanford was able to get himself appointed conservator for Marian. As conservator, he revokes her trust. Advise Delilah with respect to the trust and with respect to moving Marian home.

EXERCISE

If you are drafting a revocable trust for a client, how would you advise the client about including a provision that allows possible revocation of the trust by someone acting on behalf of the client? What would such a provision say?

C.   HEALTH CARE DECISIONS DURING INCAPACITY

In the event of incapacity, an individual may be unable to make his own decisions about health care, treatment and end of life matters. This section first discusses the default rules of what happens without planning before turning to the primary means of delegating decisional authority. While the previous section discussed financial planning issues, this section addresses health care and treatment issues.

1.   What Happens Without Planning?

Most states have laws that establish a hierarchy of default health care decision makers, often called "surrogates," for any medical decision that must be made while the person is incapacitated. Under these statutes, spouses, sometimes along with recognized domestic partners, are generally listed first. For example, New Mexico's statute allows a spouse and then "an individual in a long-term relationship of indefinite duration with the patient in which the individual has demonstrated an actual commitment to the patient similar to the commitment of a spouse and in which the individual and patient consider themselves to be responsible for each other's well-being" to serve as surrogates. N.M. Stat. Ann. §24-7A-5 (2008). These individuals are generally followed in descending order of priority by the patient's adult children, parents, adult siblings and other blood relatives. Some states, such as Illinois and New York, recognize the possibility that "close friends" may serve as surrogate decision makers, but these individuals are generally placed at or near the bottom of the hierarchy. In states that do not recognize domestic partners, a long-term partner would be at the bottom of the list, entitled to act as a surrogate only if no one else on the list — parents, siblings or other relatives — wanted to act. Courts may appoint specific guardians in contested cases.

The parameters of the decisions authorized, specifically those involving whether an individual can choose to continue or end life-sustaining treatment and the standards on which a surrogate can make this choice, are framed by numerous high profile court cases over the past few decades. End of life (EOL) decision making and health care planning are particularly significant as medical technology increases the length of time during which individuals can live with terminal illness. Not only is there the question of who can act, but all this must be decided by a court where there is a conflict. That means time, expense and heart-wrenching differences of opinion. In an emergency, all this compounds the problems.

a.   History

In 1976, the New Jersey Supreme Court issued a landmark decision involving Karen Ann Quinlan. Just before her twenty-first birthday, Ms. Quinlan apparently ingested tranquilizers and alcohol at a party; she collapsed, went into a coma and then continued to live in a chronic vegetative state. She had not executed any advance health care directives. Her father petitioned to be appointed her guardian, with the intention of removing her from life support. The Supreme Court of New Jersey found that Ms. Quinlan should have the choice to be removed from life support, with that right exercised by her father, and that doctors could not face criminal punishment for ending medical treatment pursuant to a patient's right of privacy. The court based its decision on the right to privacy, presuming that it "is broad enough to encompass a patient's decision to decline medical treatment under certain circumstances." *In re Quinlan*, 355 A.2d 647, 663 (N.J.), *cert. denied, sub nom. Garger v. New Jersey*, 429 U.S. 922 (1976).

The next major case on EOL matters, *Cruzan v. Dir., Missouri Dep't of Health*, was decided by the U.S. Supreme Court in 1990. 497 U.S. 261

(1990). *Cruzan* involved parents who requested that their daughter, who was in a persistent vegetative state, no longer receive life-sustaining treatment. Unlike the *Quinlan* court's reliance on the right to privacy, the Supreme Court found: "It cannot be disputed that the Due Process Clause [of the Fourteenth Amendment] protects an interest in life as well as an interest in refusing life-sustaining medical treatment." *Id.* at 281. The Court, applying a seemingly heightened standard of review, found that the state had several interests, including preserving life, preventing suicide and guarding the integrity of the medical profession. The individual's interests included a right to autonomy and self-determination, encompassed in the right to a dignified death. Balancing those interests, the Court ruled that a state may apply a standard of clear and convincing evidence to ascertain the desire of the patient in discontinuing treatment when a guardian attempts to terminate these treatments. The Court held that Ms. Cruzan's parents had not met the proper evidentiary requirements. While the Court upheld Missouri's use of a "clear and convincing" standard before the termination of life-sustaining treatment, the Court did not reject an individual's right to EOL decision making. Indeed, in her concurring opinion, Justice O'Connor suggested that the Constitution may actually require that states comply with an individual's wishes set out through advance directives. *Id.* at 289, 290 (O'Connor, J., concurring).

As a result, "the basic decisional boundaries" involving a right to privacy with respect to medical treatment in *Quinlan* "and *Cruzan* (the right to die is within the individual's constitutionally protected interests and can be expressed by a proxy via clear and convincing evidence of the patient's intent) facilitated the creation of a basic rubric under which state courts could, within the confines of their state constitutions, decide EOL disputes." Judith D. Moran, *Schiavo and Its Implications for the Family Justice System*, 46 Fam. Ct. Rev. 297, 301 (2008). Moreover, in 1990, Congress enacted the Patient Self Determination Act, which requires that federally funded health care institutions and health maintenance organizations show that their patients have been informed that they have the right to make decisions concerning medical treatment, including through advance health directives. *See* Moran, *supra.*

b. *Schiavo*

In the early years of the twenty-first century, the Florida case of [Governor Jeb] *Bush v. Schiavo* once again dramatized the issues at stake when an individual does not plan for her disability and a loved one seeks to end life support. Terri Schiavo went into cardiac arrest at the age of 27, and the ensuing battles over who would make health care decisions for her ultimately resulted in appeals to Congress and the President to intervene.

In re Guardianship of Theresa Marie Schiavo
780 So. 2d 176 (Fla. Dist. Ct. App. 2001)

Altenbernd, Judge.

Robert and Mary Schindler, the parents of Theresa Marie Schiavo, appeal the trial court's order authorizing the discontinuance of artificial life support to their adult daughter. Michael Schiavo, Theresa's husband and guardian, petitioned the trial court in May 1998 for entry of this order. We have carefully reviewed the record. The trial court made a difficult decision after considering all of the evidence and the applicable law. We conclude that the trial court's decision is supported by competent, substantial evidence and that it correctly applies the law. Accordingly, we affirm the decision.

Theresa Marie Schindler was born on December 3, 1963, and lived with or near her parents in Pennsylvania until she married Michael Schiavo on November 10, 1984. Michael and Theresa moved to Florida in 1986. They were happily married and both were employed. They had no children.

On February 25, 1990, their lives changed. Theresa, age 27, suffered a cardiac arrest as a result of a potassium imbalance. Michael called 911, and Theresa was rushed to the hospital. She never regained consciousness.

Since 1990, Theresa has lived in nursing homes with constant care. She is fed and hydrated by tubes. The staff changes her diapers regularly. She has had numerous health problems, but none have been life threatening.

The evidence is overwhelming that Theresa is in a permanent or persistent vegetative state. It is important to understand that a persistent vegetative state is not simply a coma. She is not asleep. She has cycles of apparent wakefulness and apparent sleep without any cognition or awareness. As she breathes, she often makes moaning sounds. Theresa has severe contractures of her hands, elbows, knees, and feet.

Over the span of this last decade, Theresa's brain has deteriorated because of the lack of oxygen it suffered at the time of the heart attack. By mid-1996, the CAT scans of her brain showed a severely abnormal structure. At this point, much of her cerebral cortex is simply gone and has been replaced by cerebral spinal fluid. Medicine cannot cure this condition. Unless an act of God, a true miracle, were to recreate her brain, Theresa will always remain in an unconscious, reflexive state, totally dependent upon others to feed her and care for her most private needs. She could remain in this state for many years.

Theresa has been blessed with loving parents and a loving husband. Many patients in this condition would have been abandoned by friends and family within the first year. Michael has continued to care for her and to visit her all these years. He has never divorced her. He has become a professional respiratory therapist and works in a nearby hospital. As a guardian, he has always attempted to provide optimum treatment for his wife. He has been a diligent watch guard of Theresa's care, never hesitating to annoy the nursing staff in order to assure that she receives the proper treatment.

Theresa's parents have continued to love her and visit her often. No one questions the sincerity of their prayers for the divine miracle that now is Theresa's only hope to regain any level of normal existence. No one questions that they have filed this appeal out of love for their daughter.

This lawsuit is affected by an earlier lawsuit. In the early 1990's, Michael Schiavo, as Theresa's guardian, filed a medical malpractice lawsuit. That case resulted in a sizable award of money for Theresa. This fund remains sufficient to care for Theresa for many years. If she were to die today, her husband would inherit the money under the laws of intestacy. If Michael eventually divorced Theresa in order to have a more normal family life, the fund remaining at the end of Theresa's life would presumably go to her parents.

Since the resolution of the malpractice lawsuit, both Michael and the Schindlers have become suspicious that the other party is assessing Theresa's wishes based upon their own monetary self-interest. The trial court discounted this concern, and we see no evidence in this record that either Michael or the Schindlers seek monetary gain from their actions. Michael and the Schindlers simply cannot agree on what decision Theresa would make today if she were able to assess her own condition and make her own decision.

There has been discussion among the parties that the money remaining when Theresa dies should be given to a suitable charity as a lasting memorial. If anything is undeniable in this case, it is that Theresa would never wish for this money to drive a wedge between the people she loves. We have no jurisdiction over the disposition of this money, but hopefully these parties will consider Theresa's desires and her memory when a decision about the money is ultimately required.

This is a case to authorize the termination of life-prolonging procedures under chapter 765, Florida Statutes (1997), and under the constitutional guidelines enunciated in *In re Guardianship of Browning*, 568 So. 2d 4 (Fla. 1990). The Schindlers have raised three legal issues that warrant brief discussion.

First, the Schindlers maintain that the trial court was required to appoint a guardian ad litem for this proceeding because Michael stands to inherit under the laws of intestacy. When a living will or other advance directive does not exist, it stands to reason that the surrogate decision-maker will be a person who is close to the patient and thereby likely to inherit from the patient. Thus, the fact that a surrogate decision-maker may ultimately inherit from the patient should not automatically compel the appointment of a guardian. On the other hand, there may be occasions when an inheritance could be a reason to question a surrogate's ability to make an objective decision.

In this case, however, Michael Schiavo has not been allowed to make a decision to disconnect life-support. The Schindlers have not been allowed to make a decision to maintain life-support. Each party in this case, absent their disagreement, might have been a suitable surrogate decision-maker for Theresa. Because Michael Schiavo and the Schindlers could not agree on the proper decision and the inheritance issue created the appearance of conflict, Michael Schiavo, as the guardian of Theresa, invoked the trial court's jurisdiction to allow the trial court to serve as the surrogate decision-maker.

In this court's decision in *In re Guardianship of Browning*, 543 So. 2d 258, 273-74 (Fla. 2d DCA 1989), we described, in dicta, a method for judicial review of a surrogate's decision. The supreme court's decision affirming *In re Guardianship of Browning* did not squarely approve or reject the details of our proposed method. However, the supreme court recognized that the circuit court's jurisdiction could be invoked in two manners:

> We emphasize, as did the district court, that courts are always open to adjudicate legitimate questions pertaining to the written or oral instructions. First, the surrogate or proxy may choose to present the question to the court for resolution. Second, interested parties may challenge the decision of the proxy or surrogate.

In re Guardianship of Browning, 568 So. 2d at 16 (footnote omitted).

In this case, Michael Schiavo used the first approach. Under these circumstances, the two parties, as adversaries, present their evidence to the trial court. The trial court determines whether the evidence is sufficient to allow it to make the decision for the ward to discontinue life support. In this context, the trial court essentially serves as the ward's guardian. Although we do not rule out the occasional need for a guardian in this type of proceeding, a guardian ad litem would tend to duplicate the function of the judge, would add little of value to this process, and might cause the process to be influenced by hearsay or matters outside the record. Accordingly, we affirm the trial court's discretionary decision in this case to proceed without a guardian ad litem.

Second, the Schindlers argue that the trial court should not have heard evidence from Beverly Tyler, the executive director of Georgia Health Decisions. Although it is doubtful that this issue is preserved for appeal, we have reviewed the issue as if it were. Ms. Tyler has studied American values, opinions, and attitudes about the decision to discontinue life-support systems. As a result, she has some special expertise concerning the words and expressions that Americans often use in discussing these difficult issues. She also has knowledge about trends within American attitudes on this subject.

We have considerable doubt that Ms. Tyler's testimony provided much in the way of relevant evidence. She testified about some social science surveys. Apparently most people, even those who favor initial life-supporting medical treatment, indicate that they would not wish this treatment to continue indefinitely once their medical condition presented no reasonable basis for a cure. There is some risk that a trial judge could rely upon this type of survey evidence to make a "best interests" decision for the ward. In this case, however, we are convinced that the trial judge did not give undue weight to this evidence and that the court made a proper surrogate decision rather than a best interests decision.

Finally, the Schindlers argue that the testimony, which was conflicting, was insufficient to support the trial court's decision by clear and convincing evidence. We have reviewed that testimony and conclude that the trial court had sufficient evidence to make this decision. The clear and convincing standard of proof, while very high, permits a decision in the face of inconsistent or conflicting evidence.

In *Browning*, we stated:

> In making this difficult decision, a surrogate decision-maker should err on the side of life. . . . In cases of doubt, we must assume that a patient would choose to defend life in exercising his or her right of privacy.

In re Guardianship of Browning, 543 So. 2d at 273. We reconfirm today that a court's default position must favor life.

The testimony in this case establishes that Theresa was very young and very healthy when this tragedy struck. Like many young people without children, she had not prepared a will, much less a living will. She had been raised in the Catholic faith, but did not regularly attend mass or have a religious advisor who could assist the court in weighing her religious attitudes about life-support methods. Her statements to her friends and family about the dying process were few and they were oral. Nevertheless, those statements, along with other evidence about Theresa, gave the trial court a sufficient basis to make this decision for her.

In the final analysis, the difficult question that faced the trial court was whether Theresa Marie Schindler Schiavo, not after a few weeks in a coma, but after ten years in a persistent vegetative state that has robbed her of most of her cerebrum and all but the most instinctive of neurological functions, with no hope of a medical cure but with sufficient money and strength of body to live indefinitely, would choose to continue the constant nursing care and the supporting tubes in hopes that a miracle would somehow recreate her missing brain tissue, or whether she would wish to permit a natural death process to take its course and for her family members and loved ones to be free to continue their lives. After due consideration, we conclude that the trial judge had clear and convincing evidence to answer this question as he did.

Affirmed.

PARKER, A.C.J., and BLUE, J., Concur.

NOTES

1.   *What happened next?* Numerous appeals, as well as a special Florida statute intended to keep Ms. Schiavo alive that was declared unconstitutional by the Florida Supreme Court, did not change the outcome. On March 18, 2005, doctors at a Florida hospice removed Terri Schiavo's feeding tube. She died on March 31. For an overview of the reaction to Terri Schiavo's death and the court battle that preceded it, see Abby Goodnough, *Schiavo Dies, Ending Bitter Case Over Feeding Tube*, N.Y. Times, Apr. 1, 2005.[5]

2.   *And what about Florida law?* The Florida proxy statute is set out below. As you read it, note which potential decision makers are preferred.

Fla. Stat. §765.401 (2009).

The proxy.

(1) If an incapacitated or developmentally disabled patient has not executed an advance directive, or designated a surrogate to execute an advance directive, or the designated or alternate surrogate is no longer available to make health care decisions, health care decisions may be made for the patient by any of the following individuals, in the following order of priority, if no individual in a prior class is reasonably available, willing, or competent to act:

(a) The judicially appointed guardian of the patient. . . ;

(b) The patient's spouse;

(c) An adult child of the patient, or if the patient has more than one adult child, a majority of the adult children who are reasonably available for consultation;

(d) A parent of the patient;

(e) The adult sibling of the patient or, if the patient has more than one sibling, a majority of the adult siblings who are reasonably available for consultation;

(f) An adult relative of the patient who has exhibited special care and concern for the patient and who has maintained regular contact with the patient and who is familiar with the patient's activities, health, and religious or moral beliefs; or

(g) A close friend of the patient.

(h) A clinical social worker licensed pursuant to chapter 491, or who is a graduate of a court-approved guardianship program. Such a proxy must be selected by the provider's bioethics committee and must not be employed by the provider. . . .

---

5. *Available at* http://www.nytimes.com/2005/04/01/national/01schiavo.html?page wanted=1.

(2) Any health care decision made under this part must be based on the proxy's informed consent and on the decision the proxy reasonably believes the patient would have made under the circumstances. If there is no indication of what the patient would have chosen, the proxy may consider the patient's best interest in deciding that proposed treatments are to be withheld or that treatments currently in effect are to be withdrawn.

(3) Before exercising the incapacitated patient's rights to select or decline health care, the proxy must comply with the provisions of [other relevant provisions of the Florida statute], except that a proxy's decision to withhold or withdraw life-prolonging procedures must be supported by clear and convincing evidence that the decision would have been the one the patient would have chosen had the patient been competent or, if there is no indication of what the patient would have chosen, that the decision is in the patient's best interest.

3. *Sum, substance, and procedure.* Note the issues of both procedure and substance that are involved in surrogate decision making. First, someone must be selected to decide for the incompetent patient. Second, a state may establish substantive principles to guide the decision maker. Finally, the decision maker chooses the appropriate treatment. Which of these steps is at issue in *Schiavo*? What guidance does the Florida proxy statute provide?

c. State Standards

In the absence of an advance directive, all 50 states allow a surrogate to make decisions on behalf of an incapacitated individual to decline life-sustaining treatment. States differ on the burden of proof and the standard. New York requires clear and convincing evidence of the patient's wishes, rather than relying on a surrogate's substituted judgment. Some states, such as California, require that the surrogate decision maker consider only the best interests of the patient, focusing on whether it is in the patient's best interests to withhold life-sustaining treatment. By contrast, other states, such as Maryland, require the surrogate to exercise "substituted judgment," a standard based on what the patient would choose if she could speak on her own behalf. Some states have developed a hybrid that allows the surrogate to exercise substituted judgment when the patient's wishes are known, but to make a decision in the patient's best interests where these wishes are unknown. Alicia Ouellette, *Disability and the End of Life*, 85 Or. L. Rev. 123, 145-46 (2006). Look back at the Florida statute: Which standard(s) do you see?

Regardless of the evidentiary standard in a particular state, the type of evidence that will satisfy that standard is, however, often far from clear. For example, in *In re Biersack*, 2004 Ohio 6491 (Ohio Ct. App. 2004), Christine Biersack became a quadriplegic after an automobile crash. She remained unconscious and was fed through a tube. The court held that even though Biersack had never specifically referred to life support in the form of nutrition and hydration, there was sufficient evidence to show that she would have wanted the tube withdrawn. This evidence included testimony from her sons. One stated that Christine once said she "would never want to be 'kept alive by machine or any type of life support.'" A second son testified that when he and his mother watched a TV program about a woman in a vegetative state, his mother stated that she would not want to live in a similar situation. The court also noted that the son believed his mother would not want to be kept alive and would want to remove the feeding tube.

By contrast, in *In re Univ. Hosp. of the State Univ. of N.Y. Upstate Med. Univ.*, 754 N.Y.S.2d 153 (Sup. Ct. 2002), a hospital petitioned to terminate the life of a patient, Yvette Casimiro, who had signed a health proxy allowing for such an action. However, the agents whom Casimiro had named in the health proxy refused to consent to the withdrawal of life support because they believed that ending life support violated her intent and religious beliefs. They testified that soon after Casimiro signed the health proxy, she informed them that she probably would not have signed it if she had fully understood it included the possibility of terminating life support. Although the court acknowledged that the health proxy was executed in a legally sufficient manner, it held that "the patient's words and actions [before she became incompetent] indicate her desire to remain alive." The court also emphasized that Casimiro was a devout Catholic, and that she repeatedly told the agents she believed that "only God can take a life." Finally, the court took into account the fact that "other than the execution of the health care proxy and living will/power of attorney, there was absolutely no evidence offered by petitioner that the patient vocalized or represented a desire to be removed from life sustaining measures or to have medical treatment discontinued if she was presented with such a circumstance." Therefore, the court ruled that the hospital had not met its burden in demonstrating clear and convincing evidence that Casimiro would have wanted to terminate her life.

PROBLEMS

1. The following case is before Judge Johnson of the Columbia state court. You are Judge Johnson's law clerk, and the Judge has requested your advice on the appropriate ruling. What advice will you provide?

Amy Chen suffered severe brain damage when she almost drowned at a beach. Although doctors managed to save her life, she has been comatose for five months, is fed through a tube, and it is undisputed that she will never regain consciousness. Amy, who is 40 years old, has two young children, who are 5 and 7 years old. Her husband, Joe, has asked the hospital to withdraw life support because when the couple had discussed the possibility of being unable to make decisions for themselves, Amy said she "never wanted to be kept on life support if she were a vegetable and things looked hopeless." Amy's parents, however, argue that Amy should be allowed to continue living and that she would not want her treatment ended if she were competent today. Her father cited his Catholic faith and testified that he believed that Amy agreed with him when he had stated that "God, not doctors, can decide when one's life is over." Caroline, Amy's best friend, also testified that after she and Amy saw a movie involving a character in a vegetative state, Amy told Caroline that she "hopes [she is] never in a similar state and that her relatives would make the right decision for her."

2.   Consider what factors should most heavily influence a proxy in deciding whether to terminate a patient's life under either a substituted judgment or a best interest standard.

2.   *What Is Possible with Advance Planning?*

a.   **Advance Medical Directives**

Of course, a default provision is only necessary when an individual has not made plans in an instrument. Planning for health care incapacity involves two major types of advance directives: living wills and health care powers of attorney. A living will is a written document in which an individual specifies preferences regarding life-sustaining medical care in case of incapacity. A living will is limited to EOL decisions. State statutes generally allow an individual to indicate a preference for no further medical treatment in the case of terminal illness, imminent death or "an irreversible injury or illness that results in a persistent vegetative state or permanent unconsciousness." LAWRENCE A. FROLIK & MELISSA C. BROWN, ADVISING THE ELDERLY OR DISABLED CLIENT 23-52 (2d ed. 2009). In a living will, a person may, for example, state a preference not to receive life-sustaining artificial nutrition and hydration if there is no reasonable expectation of recovery. While the execution requirements for a living will vary, states typically require certain formalities; most require that the document be in writing and be signed, and many also require witnesses and a notary. States generally provide immunity to medical professionals who follow their patient's instructions in a living will, although most states do not impose liability if a medical professional fails to comply with a living will. *Id.* at 23-59. Attached as Appendix B is a copy of a living will.

Living wills generally provide guidance with respect to the desirability of life-sustaining measures, such as ventilators and tube feeding, but they also have limitations. "They typically contain broad pronouncements about the patient's wishes that are insufficiently flexible to deal with the ambiguities of real clinical decisions. In addition, living wills are based on people's predictions about how they will react to hypothetical situations that may occur far in the future. Research has shown that people often respond to real-world medical situations very differently than they might have anticipated from the standpoint of good health." Carl H. Coleman, *Research with Decisionally Incapacitated Human Subjects: An Argument for a Systemic Approach to Risk-Benefit Assessment,* 83 IND. L.J. 743, 774 (2008). Another limitation is that a living will does not become effective until certain requirements are met, such as the need to have two physicians certify that the individual is terminally ill and unable to make her own medical decisions.

While a living will is directed to medical professionals and concerns specific treatment decisions, a health care power of attorney appoints a surrogate decision maker. A health care power of attorney (sometimes also called a "health care proxy") is a written document that gives legal authority to another adult to make health care decisions on behalf of the principal. The health care power of attorney is far more comprehensive than a living will and typically addresses the principal's preferences concerning not only continuation or termination of artificial life support but also instructions about any medical treatments that the principal may wish to undergo or to avoid, such as surgery or chemotherapy. A sample Durable Power of Attorney for Health Care is included in Appendix C. *See also* http://caringinfo.org/i4a/pages/index.cfm?pageid=3289.

Even though living wills and health care proxies are fairly simple documents, a majority of Americans (more than 70%) have not executed them. Michelle Andrews, *Life-or-Death Decisions Call for Advance Planning,* WASH. POST, Jan. 18, 2011, at E4. Why? First, people may be reluctant to prepare such documents because the process requires facing up to one's own mortality. Second, people may not be aware of the option. It may take a dramatic case, such as Terri Schiavo's, to help people understand the availability — and the importance of executing — advance medical directives. In the week preceding her death, 27,000 people downloaded living wills and related forms from the Office of the Maryland Attorney General's Web site, compared to just over 600 during a one-week period in January 2005. Eric Rich, *Before Schiavo, 1991 Case Led to Landmark Md. Law,* WASH. POST, Mar. 30, 2005, at B1.

In April 2010, President Obama directed that all hospitals that participate in Medicare or Medicaid respect patients' advance directives and their designated visitors, regardless of the existence of a legal relationship between the patient and the visitor. The resulting regulations protect, among others, same-sex partners and widows and widowers with no children, as well as others who would not want various family members to make decisions for them. 42 C.F.R. §§482.13, 485.635(f)(2011).

NOTES

1.   *Keeping the documents.* The designated agent should presumably have a copy of the documents. What about the lawyer who may have helped draft them? Would a bank safe deposit box be appropriate? Consider the need for the availability of these directives during non-office hours. What about storing a scanned copy on a computer? Some states have now established state-wide electronic registries to ensure storage for, and access to, advance care directives. Thaddeus Mason Pope, *Legal Briefing: Advance Care Planning*, 20 J. CLINICAL ETHICS 362 (2009).

2.   *Moving clients.* It is all well and good for an individual to execute advance medical directives and to ensure that they are easily accessible. But what happens if the individual is traveling outside of her domicile state and becomes sick? Will medical officials and family members always respect the agent's authority?

Most states specify that they will grant reciprocity to out-of-state directives, even if the directive has not satisfied that state's specific conditions for such documents. *See, e.g.*, 755 ILL. COMP. STAT. 35/9(h) (2010).

3.   *But who really decides?* Family members or health care professionals may disagree about how to apply the advance medical directive under a given set of facts, or they may even challenge the authority of the agent. Some medical centers have begun to use alternative dispute resolution techniques to assist in decision making in such cases, and even include specialists in bioethics in the discussions. John Schwartz, *For the End of Life, Hospital Pairs Ethics and Medicine: A Team Effort to Resolve Family Bedside Conflicts*, N.Y. TIMES, July 4, 2005, at B1. How and in what manner might this affect the drafting of these documents?

D.   COVERING THE COSTS OF MEDICAL AND LONG-TERM CARE

Health care and long-term care in the United States are very costly. While the vast majority of people have health insurance, either through their workplace or through a privately purchased plan, very few have long-term care insurance. Of those who do have health or long-term care insurance, many are under-insured. This means paying for some or all of the expense from their own funds or those of family members, or seeking creative ways to cover the expense, such as reverse mortgages. Unless the person is wealthy, the extreme cost of these services will eventually drain their resources and cause them to have to seek some kind of government assistance. The principal government plans are Medicare and Medicaid. Almost 9.0 million people are dually enrolled in Medicare and Medicaid. *See* John Holahan, Dawn M. Miller & David Rousseau, *Dual Eligibles: Medicaid Enrollment and Spending for Medicare Beneficiaries in 2005*, Issue Paper, KAISER COMMISSION ON MEDICAID AND THE UNINSURED (Feb. 2009).

1. *Medicare*

Medicare, which was established in 1965, is the federal health care insurance program that provides coverage for people age 65 or older, people under age 65 with certain disabilities and people of all ages with end-stage renal disease. Coverage is automatic for those who qualify; for example, Medicare eligibility for those age 65 and older generally depends on whether the individual (or the individual's spouse) was employed for 10 years or longer in a Medicare-covered workplace and is a citizen or permanent resident of the United States.[6] The individual's present wealth and earnings are irrelevant. It is an entitlement program and is not based on need. The program helps with the cost of health care, but it does not cover all medical expenses or the cost of most long-term care.

There are four different Medicare programs — Parts A-D:

- Subject to certain deductibles and copays, Medicare Part A generally covers the first 90 days of most semi-private inpatient services provided by hospitals.[7] In addition, if the patient spent three days as an inpatient in a hospital first and the doctor ordered the services, Medicare Part A pays the costs while the patient is in a skilled nursing or hospice facility for 100 days.

  - Most people who have worked during their lives (or whose spouse worked) and paid Medicare taxes automatically get Medicare Part A when they turn 65 without having to pay premiums for coverage.
  - Those who do not automatically receive Medicare Part A upon reaching 65 may be able to purchase coverage.

- Part B, or Supplementary Medical Insurance, is optional.[8] If the individual or her spouse is working, the insurance at the workplace may cover these costs. Part B generally covers medical services and procedures not covered by Part A, such as services provided by physicians and other practitioners (including those while in the hospital), hospitals' outpatient departments, laboratories, and

---

6. For general information, *see* http://www.medicare.gov/default.aspx.

7. Medicare Part A (Hospital Insurance), *available at* http://www.medicare.gov/navigation/medicare-basics/medicare-benefits/part-a.aspx.

8. Medicare Part B (Medical Insurance), *available at* http://www.medicare.gov/navigation/medicare-basics/medicare-benefits/part-b.aspx.

suppliers of medical equipment. Part B also covers a limited number of drugs, most of which must be administered by injection in a physician's office. Depending on the circumstances, home health care may be covered by either Part A or Part B. Part B premiums range from $110 to $369 per month depending on one's income.

- Part C allows those eligible for Medicare to receive Medicare through private insurance plans in what are referred to as Medicare Advantage Plans. If an individual elects to join one of these plans, the plan pays for all the Medicare-covered Parts A and B health care. This plan can also include prescription drug coverage. Medicare Advantage Plans include:

  - Medical Health Maintenance Organizations (HMOs)
  - Preferred Provider Organizations (PPO)
  - Private Fee-for Service Plans
  - Medicare Special Needs Plans

- In most of these plans there are generally extra benefits and lower copayments than in the Original Medicare Plan. However, an individual may be restricted to certain doctors or hospitals belonging to the specific plan chosen.[9]
- Part D, which began in January 2006, provides prescription drug coverage.[10] Medicare prescription drug coverage is insurance that covers both brand-name and generic prescription drugs at participating pharmacies in an eligible recipient's area. Medicare prescription drug coverage provides protection for people who have very high drug costs or from unexpected prescription drug bills in the future. Everyone with Medicare is eligible for this coverage, regardless of income and resources, health status or current prescription expenses.[11]

2. *Medicaid*

While Medicare covers numerous aspects of health care, it does not cover long-term care for individuals who need help with the activities of daily living. Medicare also generally does not cover the costs of health care for people under the age of 65 who do not have adequate private insurance. Medicaid is a program that can provide financial assistance for qualified low-income individuals.

---

9. Medicare Advantage (Part C), *available at* http://www.medicare.gov/navigation/medicare-basics/medicare-benefits/part-c.aspx.

10. Medicare Prescription Drug Coverage (Part D), *available at* http://www.medicare.gov/navigation/medicare-basics/medicare-benefits/part-d.aspx.

11. Prescription Drug Coverage: Basic Information, *available at* http://www.medicare.gov/pdp-basic-information.asp.

Long-term care is very expensive: One year of care in a nursing home with a semi-private room can cost approximately $75,000,[12] and one year of care at home, with periodic help for personal care from a home health aide (the average is about three times a week), is approximately $18,000 a year.[13] Twenty-four hour a day in-home care can be as much as $80,000-$100,000 per year. Unless an individual has significant financial resources to pay for these costs, eventually he will need to turn to the government for help.

Medicaid is a governmental program that offers health and long-term care coverage for low-income individuals regardless of age. Medicaid receives funding from both state and federal governments, and, subject to the federally established minimum standards, each state has developed its own rules for determining eligibility and benefits offered. Medicaid is a needs-based program, so it has strict asset and income thresholds. In addition, a person must be able to establish that he requires medical assistance.

The discussion that follows will focus on the qualifications for the long-term care aspect of Medicaid. To obtain coverage, one must require medical assistance and not have too many assets or too much income.

a. Requires Medical Assistance

According to Medicaid standards, applicants must "need assistance" with some or all of the following to qualify for long-term care coverage:

- Activities of Daily Living (ADL): getting out of bed, bowel and bladder care, mobility, transferring, eating and bathing
- Basic Instrumental ADL: meal preparation, housework, laundry, shopping
- Supportive Services: managing medicine, appointments, money, arranging for services, using the phone.

b. Cannot Have Too Many Assets

In most states, to qualify for Medicaid an individual must have no more than $2,000 in liquid assets. The limit exempts the value of a home and a few other assets, such as household goods and an irrevocable burial contract. If a person owns more property than that, he must first "spend down" his existing assets to be eligible.

In order to ensure that individuals do not try to qualify for Medicaid by giving away their assets to family members or others, the law imposes a

---

12. Market Survey of Long-Term Care Costs (Oct. 2010), *available at* http://www .metlife.com/assets/cao/mmi/publications/studies/2010/mmi-2010-market-survey-long-term- care-costs.pdf.

13. U.S. Dep't of Health & Human Svcs. National Clearinghouse for Long-Term Care Information, Understanding LTC: Costs & Paying (Jan. 2010), *available at* http://www .longtermcare.gov/LTC/Main_Site/Understanding_Long_Term_Care/Costs_Paying/index.aspx.

60-month "look back" period. At the time of applying for Medicaid, the applicant must list all gratuitous transfers made within the previous 60 months. If there were any gifts made during that period, the person is denied Medicaid coverage for the number of months the transfers would have paid for care at the prevailing average monthly cost of care.[14] This is known as the "penalty period."

> **Example:** Janet had a medical emergency in January 2006, and had to move into an assisted care facility. By February 2011, after having paid the costs of assisted living for five years, her savings have dwindled to $50,000. Medicaid is clearly on the horizon in the next year or two. She would like to transfer $48,000 to her grandchildren now (to get her assets down to $2,000) so they have "a little something from Grandmom to remember her by," and apply for Medicaid immediately.
>
> Will this work? No. If the average monthly cost of care in her state is $6,000, she will be penalized for eight months ($48,000 ÷ $6,000).[15]
>
> Solution? Make whatever transfers are contemplated outside the 60-month look-back period. If Janet had transferred the $48,000 to her grandchildren when she entered the assisted care facility in January 2006, the transfer would be disregarded in determining her available assets if she did not apply for Medicaid until February 2011. This requires significant advance planning.

There are some exceptions to the transfer rules, such as an asset transferred to a spouse or a third party for the sole benefit of the spouse, or transfer of an asset with a purpose other than to qualify for Medicaid. Consequently, estate planning lawyers may, within the bounds of the rules of professional responsibility, discuss with their clients the legal parameters under which they can "spend down" or transfer their assets and still qualify for Medicaid. Practically speaking, however, clients generally are not interested in planning to make themselves impoverished five years in the future.

Special Needs Trusts Exception. Since Medicaid is a means-tested program, determining what property to include in the calculation of an applicant's available resources is of great significance. As discussed above, the limit is $2,000, though there are exemptions and exceptions. Generally, trusts for the benefit of the applicant are treated as an available resource and will jeopardize eligibility. There are exceptions that allow the individual to

---

14. The 60-month period was introduced by the Deficit Reduction Act of 2005.

15. To make matters worse, now that she no longer has the money given away, she may have difficulty paying for her care at the assisted living facility during the penalty period unless her family helps out.

receive Medicaid and also to benefit from a trust. Of greatest importance is the **Special Needs Trust** (SNT), also called *Supplemental Needs Trusts*. The beneficiary of a SNT is someone who has a severe and chronic or persistent disability and who, when the trust is established, is under 65 years of age. Because of the age factor, SNTs are most often used for the benefit of children.

The purpose of the trust is to "supplement," not replace, public benefits by enhancing the individual's life. To retain the beneficiary's eligibility for public benefits, SNTs may not be designed to provide for the basic needs of the individual that are covered by Medicaid — food, shelter or any asset which could be converted into food or shelter (including cash). Supplemental needs trusts might be used, for example, for physical therapy, medical treatment, education, entertainment, a television, travel, clothing, eyeglasses or a computer. Generally, cash may not be distributed.

There are two types of supplemental trusts for persons with disabilities: third-party trusts and self-settled trusts.

Third-party SNTs are often established and funded by parents (or other relatives) for the benefit of their developmentally disabled or mentally ill children. There are few rules with respect to excluding third-party SNTs as a resource since the beneficiary was never the owner of the money and is therefore not attempting to qualify by creating an artifice to hide assets. The most important rule that must be followed to exclude the assets of an SNT from being counted as a resource is that the trust terms do not entitle the beneficiary to either income or principal. Instead, whatever rights to income or principal the beneficiary is entitled to should be at the trustee's complete discretion. Contrary to a self-settled SNT, as discussed next, a third-party SNT rarely has a "pay-back" provision, nor is one required.

Self-Settled SNTs are established by a judge, a court-appointed guardian or the parents or grandparents of the beneficiary with the property of the disabled individual. Generally, the money comes from a personal injury settlement (perhaps, but not necessarily, arising out of the incident that caused the disability) or an inheritance. Because it is holding the property of the disabled person, self-settled SNTs must meet more requirements to ensure that the trust property will be excluded as a resource for Medicaid purposes. The most important requirement is that self-settled SNTs must include a provision repaying state Medicaid agencies for any benefits, payable at the death of the beneficiary. Such a provision is often called a "pay-back" provision.

A self-settled trust can be a private trust administered by a trustee or a "pooled income trust," which is run by a nonprofit association with a separate account maintained for each individual beneficiary. In the case of a pooled income trust, all accounts are pooled for investment and management purposes.

c.   Cannot Have Too Much Income

All states set a limit on the amount applicants for Medicaid can earn and still be eligible for nursing home care. States generally use one of two alternative standards for determining eligibility. In most states, an individual is qualified if the monthly income is less than the cost of the nursing home; in a minority of states, the "income cap" states, the monthly income must be less than a set amount. *See* LAWRENCE FROLIK & MELISSA BROWN, ADVISING THE ELDERLY OR DISABLED CLIENT, §14.03[1][c] (2d ed. 2009). Regardless of the state, individuals who earn below the designated amount through pensions, social security, rents, dividends, interest, etc., are qualified.

Miller Trust Exception.   In the "income cap" states, individuals who earn more than the average monthly cost of care must pay for the care themselves and cannot get assistance from Medicaid. If they fall in between the limit on earnings and the average monthly cost of care, it would appear they are in a classic "Catch-22"; earning too much to qualify for state assistance but not enough to pay for care on their own. This problem is often solved by use of a "Miller Trust,"[16] sometimes also called an "Income Trust" or a "Utah Gap Trust."

> All of the individual's current monthly income will need to go into an Income Trust each month. From the trust, the trustee can pay the individual's monthly income allowance (usually $50-$60) [and a few other items]. The balance of the individual's current monthly income will be paid from the Income Trust to the nursing home as the individual's monthly patient contribution amount. The balance of the individual's covered nursing home costs for the month will be paid by Medicaid.[17]

Example: Steve has earnings of $3,800 per month, which is above the $2,500 limit set by the state. The average monthly cost of care in his state is $6,000. If he sets up a Miller Trust to receive all of his income and pay his nursing care costs, the trust will essentially pay $3,750 ($3,800 less $50 monthly allowance), and Medicaid will pay the $2,250 balance.

d.   Estate Recovery Liens

Under federal law, states are required to pass laws to recover from the estates of recipients amounts paid for long-term care. Since Medicaid recipients are presumably asset poor, one might wonder to what property

---

16. *Miller v. Ibarra*, 746 F. Supp. 19 (D. Colo. 1990); *see* 42 USC §1396p(d)(4)(B)(2010).
17. *Available at* http://www.cobar.org/Docs/NewMedicaidColoradoDRA.doc.

the statute is referring. The answer is that some assets are exempted for purposes of determining eligibility but are not exempted from the lien, including one's home and the SNTs discussed in the previous section. This gives rise to a lien on the estate. According to the U.S. Dept. of Health and Human Services, at a minimum, the lien covers:

> all property and assets that pass from a deceased person to his or her heirs under state probate law, which governs both property conveyed by will and property of persons who die intestate. A state's ability to recover from probate estates depends in some measure on Medicaid's standing vis-à-vis other claimants. The order of payment of debt is established under state law. Mortgages, unpaid tax or public utility bills, child support arrears, burial costs, or other debts may be paid before the Medicaid lien and reduce the amount that is actually recovered. The State's standing is also influenced by locally determined state priorities. For example, some state laws protect the family home in an estate from some or all claims against it, including Medicaid claims.
>
> States may use the narrow Federal definition of "estate" and limit Medicaid estate recoveries to only those assets that pass through probate. Alternatively, they may choose to define "estate" in a broader context, which enables them to recover from some or all property that bypasses probate. Such property includes assets that pass directly to a survivor, heir or assignee through joint tenancy, rights of survivorship, life estates, living trusts, annuity remainder payments, or life insurance payouts. . . .
>
> The home is considered to be part of the recoverable estate unless it is protected for the spouse or certain other close relatives, or is conveyed outside of the State's definition of "estate" (e.g., through a life estate). . . .

HOW MUCH IS SUBJECT TO RECOVERY?

> At a minimum, states must recover amounts spent by Medicaid for long-term care and related drug and hospital benefits, including Medicaid payments for Medicare cost sharing related to these services. However, they have the option of recovering the costs of *all* Medicaid services paid on the recipient's behalf. The majority of states recover spending for more than the minimum of long-term care and related expenses.
>
> States can waive estate recovery when it is not cost-effective, as defined by the State and made public through their official State Medicaid plan. . . .
>
> Recoveries may not exceed the total amount spent by Medicaid on the individual's behalf at or after age 55. Nor may they exceed the amount remaining in the estate after the claims of other creditors against the estate have been satisfied in the order of payment of debt delineated by state law. [18]

---

18. U.S. Dept. of Health & Human Svcs. Medicaid Estate Recovery (Apr. 2005), *available at* http://aspe.hhs.gov/daltcp/reports/estaterec.htm.

PROBLEMS

You and a colleague are attorneys with some expertise in elder law and trusts and estates issues. Your clients, Chandra, and her mother, Sakina, have come to you for advice. Sakina is 77 years old and has always been able to live independently. She has assets of about $250,000 (her condominium worth $300,000 that has a mortgage of $150,000, a car worth $25,000 and stocks, securities, cash, rings and other personal property of $75,000) and income from a pension and social security combined of $2,500 per month. Her monthly expenses include $750 for mortgage on a condominium in an adult living community, $400 for insurance, taxes, electricity, telephone and fees on the condo, $250 for food, $200 per month for drugs and $200 per month for everything else, like clothing, hair styling, etc. She saves the rest and uses it for gifts to the grandchildren and vacations for herself.

Some things have happened recently that concern Chandra and Sakina, the most significant of these being that Sakina slipped in the bathtub and broke her hip. She went into the hospital for two nights and then into a nursing home for 30 days for round-the-clock care and rehabilitation therapy. While Medicare covered most of the costs of the hospital, it did not cover the nursing home costs of $200 per day because she did not need three days of hospitalization first — a Medicare requirement. The cost of this experience (over $6,000) and the fact that they can see that assisted living and maybe even a nursing home could be in Sakina's future have gotten them worried. Sakina's personal finances are not adequate to cover the exorbitant costs of these expenses if she lives a long life. (Her mother lived to be 104 years old!)

Chandra also believes that Sakina is confused about her finances. Sakina pays bills for items she did not buy and subscribes to many magazines despite the fact that her eyesight is limited. She recently agreed to buy some "miracle" cures for her ailments that cost $2,500.

While having her move into Chandra's house would be feasible, if necessary, it would be very disruptive to the family and, besides, Chandra and her partner work and cannot give Sakina the care she needs.

Chandra and Sakina are totally unfamiliar with the legal and health care systems. They would like you to explain how things operate, including what expenses they are likely to incur and how decisions are normally made. They would like you to advise them on what can be done now to make the transition go more smoothly. Please discuss the following issues.

1.   If they do no advance planning:

- How will Sakina pay for an assisted living facility if it costs about $3,500 per month, 24-hour in-home care at about $8,000 per month, or a nursing home that costs about $6,000-$7,000 per month?

- Who will be responsible for her medical decisions if she ends up in a hospital and cannot speak or is in a coma?
- Who will be responsible for paying her bills and taking care of other financial matters for her in the future if she continues to deteriorate?

2. It is clear to both of them that Sakina will not be able to afford medical and long-term care for as long as she is likely to live. What will happen when Sakina runs out of money? It is depressing to her that she might have to spend everything she's accumulated on medical and long-term care costs before she can get Medicaid to cover her long-term care. If she is going to have to become impoverished to get Medicaid, she would just as soon give what she owns to her daughter and grandchildren. Can she do so? What are the risks? Consider also your legal role as a counselor discussed in Chapter 1. What advice may you ethically provide? To whom?

3. Sakina would like Chandra to manage her finances and make any important medical decisions if she is not able to do so, rather than her other family members. Can you help make this possible?

4. As stated, Sakina's income is $2,500 per month. Assume this is above the limits to qualify for Medicaid by $500 per month. Assume also that it is less than the $6,000 she would need to pay for staying at a nursing home. Does this mean she cannot get Medicaid to cover her nursing home costs or is there some way to deal with this "gap"?

5. What costs does Medicaid cover and which ones does it not cover? What can you do so that mom has a little extra to pay for outings, hair styling, etc.? Sakina needs significant additional services due to the fact she has macular degeneration, is wheelchair-bound and is almost deaf. What advice can you give her about how to cover these costs?

E. PLANNING FOR THE CARE OF CHILDREN ON THE DEATH OR DISABILITY OF A PARENT

The law presumes that all individuals under the age of 18 are legally incapacitated, albeit with a few limited exceptions (such as a court finding otherwise). Consequently, parents face a series of legal issues concerning planning for their minor child or for a child with disabilities as they decide who should have custody of the children and in what manner to manage their own and their children's finances.

1.   Death of a Parent

When one parent dies, the surviving parent is generally assumed to be the custodian of the child, regardless of what the deceased parent's will provides. When both parents die, their wills may nominate a guardian, who will be given physical custody of the child, and/or a conservator, who becomes legally responsible for managing the child's financial assets. The guardian and conservator may be, and usually are, the same person, though the parents may make other choices, such as designating a relative to serve as a guardian, and a bank as a conservator. Look at the Appendix in Chapter 1 to see how Michael Jackson addressed these issues in his will.

While the parents' nominations are not legally binding, most courts will give great deference to the parents' preferences. Statutes in some states, however, such as Arkansas, merely direct that the court give "due regard" to the parents' testamentary request. A.C.A. §28-65-204 (2010). In some states, including Florida, the court must consider the preferences of a minor who is 14 or older as well as the person designated by the will. *See* Naomi Cahn, *Planning Options for the Daily Care of a Minor in the Event of an Adult's Incapacity or Death, in* Tax, Estate and Lifetime Planning for Minors 125 (Carmina d'Aversa ed., 2007).

A guardian must accept an appointment before it becomes effective; merely probating a will is insufficient. If the parents have not appointed a guardian or the appointed guardian declines, then courts will typically choose a relative who is the "next of kin." Gay and lesbian parents, and parents with partners who have not legally adopted the children, can try to protect the surviving partner's ability to serve as a guardian, but courts do not always respect such testamentary choices.

Once the appointment is effective, guardians typically do not have to file reports with the court concerning the health and welfare of their wards, although the will can provide otherwise. However, the Revised Uniform Guardianship and Protective Proceedings Act, as well as some states, authorize the court to require that the guardian submit reports to the court concerning the health and welfare of the minor. UPC §5-207(b)(5).

Guardians typically take physical custody of the minor, decide where the child will live, make educational and medical decisions and decide on religious training. Because they function as the parent, they may also consent to the minor's marriage or adoption in a majority of states. As guardians of the person, however, they do not have the same financial responsibility as parents. Guardians are not legally obligated to provide from their own funds for the minor and may receive money payable for the support of the minor to the minor's parent or guardian under the terms of any statutory benefit or insurance system or any private contract, devise or trust; a minority of states permit a guardian to petition the court for a reasonable compensation for their services as guardian. Additionally, guardians are not liable to third persons by reason of the parental relationship for acts of the minor.

The guardianship typically ends when the child is no longer a minor. In addition, the child or another person may petition the court for removal of the guardian. Generally, removal is justified only where the guardian has neglected her duties, rather than where removal would be in the best interest of the child. In some states, in recognition of the seriousness of the petition, the guardian is entitled to representation in removal proceedings.

On the other hand, there are several uncertainties associated with testamentary guardians. First, the parent cannot be certain that the court will accept her nomination because the appointment only takes effect once the will is probated. To overcome this uncertainty, Colorado, Hawaii and a few other states allow for court confirmation of the appointment prior to the parent's death in certain limited circumstances. In California, a parent with a terminal illness can request that the court appoint a joint guardian who will serve concurrently with the parent during her lifetime and who assumes sole responsibility when the parent dies. CAL. PROB. CODE §2105(f) (2010).

Second, if the other parent is still living and is not legally incapacitated, then that parent generally assumes legal custody upon the death of the first parent, and the testamentary appointment is irrelevant. Although divorced parents may believe that they can use a testamentary guardianship to preclude custody in the other parent, this is inaccurate. So long as her rights have not been legally terminated, the surviving parent is presumed to be the guardian regardless of the circumstances of the divorce and the provisions of the testamentary instrument. Third, testamentary guardians only assume power after the death of the testator, not upon her incapacity.

2.   Standby Guardianship

Unlike more conventional forms of guardianship, a standby guardian can be appointed before the death or incapacity of parents. Although states have typically been suspicious of inter vivos guardianship appointments, the increasing number of single parents and the AIDS epidemic led states to develop improved mechanisms for confirming the parents' choice of standby guardian while the parents are still alive. The more traditional inter vivos guardianship transfers custody and most other parental rights to a third party upon court approval of the guardianship and can be terminated, for example, if the delegating parent withdraws her consent. By contrast, rather than displacing parental authority completely and at the time of the guardianship petition, standby guardians exercise authority at the same time as the parent in most states, although a few states specify that a standby guardian becomes the sole parental authority once she is appointed.

The first standby guardianship law was enacted in New York, in 1992. Joyce McConnell, *Standby Guardianship: Sharing the Legal Responsibility for Children*, 7 MD. J. CONTEMP. L. ISSUES 249, 261 (1995-96). The 1997 federal Adoption and Safe Families Act also encouraged states to adopt procedures for standby guardianships, and approximately half of the states now have standby guardianship statutes. They are typically placed in a state's probate codes.

State approaches to standby guardianship statutes vary, but the statutes generally have the following attributes:[19]

First, they provide a process for a legal writing, generally witnessed by two people, that designates a person to act as a standby guardian. Aside from a few states, including Florida, Pennsylvania, Illinois and Massachusetts, parents can only use the standby guardianship process if they have a terminal or chronic illness. Depending on the statutory scheme, parents can petition for the appointment of a standby guardian before their incapacity, or they can designate a standby guardian, who then must petition the court for appointment before the guardianship can become effective;

Second, the non-custodial parent has an opportunity to be heard on the issue of standby guardianship through notice of a court hearing, if the parent can be located, and some states require that the preferences of a child who has reached a certain age be considered;

Third, a standby guardian does not assume authority until the happening of a triggering event, such as the parent's extended hospitalization or death. Typically, the standby guardian must provide the court with information concerning the occurrence of the triggering event, and some states require that a physician provide documentation of the parent's incapacity; and

Fourth, a court determines whether the standby guardianship is in the best interests of the child.

The UPC allows for court appointment of a standby guardian upon "a finding that the appointing parent will likely become unable to care for the child within [two] years." UPC §5-202(b). Depending on the state procedure, standby guardianships are often time-limited, lasting, typically, for two years. The UPC allows a parent to set out "the desired limitations on the powers to be given to the guardian." UPC §5-202(a). Consider what limits a parent might wish to impose. In addition to their use in cases of parental incapacity, standby guardianships can provide a useful bridging authority between the death of a parent and the probate of a will and appointment of a longer-term guardian. They can also provide security to the increasing number of single-parent families.

---

19. This description is drawn from: JUDITH LARSEN, STANDBY GUARDIAN LAWS: A GUIDE FOR LEGISLATORS, LAWYERS, AND CHILD WELFARE PROFESSIONALS 1-4 (2000), *available at* http://standbyguardianship.org/pdf/ABA-SBGlaws.pdf; Child Welfare Information Gateway, Standby Guardianship State Statutes (2008), *available at* http://www.childwelfare.gov/systemwide/laws_policies/statutes/guardianship.cfm.

3.   Partial Delegation — Educational and Medical Consents

Medical and educational consent laws authorize caregivers to make a specific set of limited decisions on behalf of a child when the parent or guardian consents to such a delegation. Like powers of attorney, but unlike formal guardianships, these can be done without court involvement, and statutes often include the forms for making such a delegation. The delegation generally must be in writing, although some states permit oral consent. These delegations are sometimes limited to relatives or to caregivers with whom the child resides, may be limited in duration and are generally quite restrictive in the scope of delegation.

These laws basically allow caregivers, who do not have legal custody of a child, to consent to a child's medical treatment and to enroll the child in school. They are useful in situations otherwise demanding parental consent so that third parties can proceed, for example, in the absence of authorization from a legal parent.

In California, a parent may authorize another person who is caring for the child to consent to medical and dental care. CAL. FAM. CODE §6910 (2009). In other jurisdictions, the caregiver can choose the child's school. In some states, parents can delegate authority to another person for purposes of consenting to the immunization of a minor.

4.   Child with Disabilities

Parents must plan for the long-term custodial and financial needs of children with disabilities. For custody decision making, parents can use the same options for minor children discussed above, appointing either a testamentary or standby guardian. Planning for financial needs depends on the parents' income. If the child qualifies for public benefits, then financial planning may involve techniques designed to ensure continued eligibility while providing for the child's special needs. Planning for the financial needs of children with disabilities takes the same form (discussed earlier in the chapter) of planning for any other individual with disabilities.

5.   Financial Planning for a Child

In addition to nominating a conservator, parents may establish trusts for their children or may transfer funds more directly. Typically, when an account is opened in the minor's name at a bank or brokerage company, it will be a custodial account under the state's enactment of the Uniform Transfer to Minors Act (UTMA), with the property registered as follows: "X as custodian for [minor's name] under the [state UTMA]." *See* UTMA §9(a)(1). Once the donor has made the transfer, it is irrevocable; the custodian holds title to the property on behalf of the minor. The custodian has broad powers regarding the use of the funds for the minor. UTMA accounts expire when the minor reaches the age of 21, and the beneficiary then owns the property outright.

A custodian may attempt to transfer the funds into a trust to delay the minor's outright ownership rights. This may raise problems, given that the UTMA account ends when the beneficiary reaches the age of 21:

> a custodian under the Act has the same rights and authority over the property "as unmarried adult owners have over their own property." The concern, however, is whether such a transfer is effectively a breach of fiduciary duty considering that by statute, the funds are to be turned over at age 21 "in an appropriate manner." Although the custodian may have numerous well-grounded reasons for desiring to delay the distribution including, for example, legitimate planning for creditor protection purposes (or protecting the child from his own lack of judgment), the fact remains the custodian would effectively be terminating what would otherwise be the child's right to obtain the funds at age 21, and the question arises whether such delay constitutes a delivery "in an appropriate manner." . . . [N]o custodian wishes to open the door for a potential fiduciary claim when the child reaches legal age or the custodianship would have otherwise terminated. In the end, the test should be whether the fiduciary acted in the beneficiary's best interest.

Bradley R. Coppedge, *Transfers to Trust and Use of UTMA Custodial Accounts*, 23 Prob. & Prop. 34, 37 (2009). To ensure maximum flexibility with respect to timing and method of distribution, parents may want to establish a trust rather than an UTMA account. On the other hand, establishing a trust can be expensive and difficult, particularly compared to the ease of opening an UTMA account, which is generally available for minimal or no cost.

EXERCISE

Your new clients, Mel and Devon, have 2 children: Georgia, age 13, and Dakota, age 8. Among other issues of estate planning, they would like to designate guardians for their children in case of their deaths or incapacity. How will you counsel them?

F.   ETHICAL ISSUES IN REPRESENTING A PERSON WITH DISABILITIES

A lawyer is sometimes asked to engage in estate planning for a client who has a mental disability. This presents a potential dilemma for an attorney who is responsible for zealous representation and pursuit of the client's objectives, and yet who may be concerned that the client may not have a full understanding of the legal process. The Model Rules of Professional Conduct provide for this contingency, setting out a lawyer's basic responsibilities to a client who may be impaired by a mental condition or through the legal disability of age. The American College of Trust and Estate Counsel (ACTEC) has developed guidelines for lawyers in the trusts and estates area.

MRPC 1.14. Client with Diminished Capacity

(a) When a client's capacity to make adequately considered decisions in connection with a representation is diminished, whether because of minority, mental impairment or for some other reason, the lawyer shall, as far as reasonably possible, maintain a normal client-lawyer relationship with the client.

(b) When the lawyer reasonably believes that the client has diminished capacity, is at risk of substantial physical, financial or other harm unless action is taken and cannot adequately act in the client's own interest, the lawyer may take reasonably necessary protective action, including consulting with individuals or entities that have the ability to take action to protect the client and, in appropriate cases, seeking the appointment of a guardian ad litem, conservator or guardian. . . .

* * *

ACTEC COMMENTARY ON MRPC 1.14

Preventive Measures for Competent Clients.   As a matter of routine, the lawyer who represents a competent adult in estate planning matters should provide the client with information regarding the devices the client could employ to protect his or her interests in the event of diminished capacity, including ways the client could avoid the necessity of a guardianship or similar proceeding. Thus, as a service to a client, the lawyer should inform the client regarding the costs, advantages and disadvantages of durable powers of attorney, directives to physicians or living wills, health care proxies, and revocable trusts. A lawyer may properly suggest that a competent client consider executing a letter or other document that would authorize the lawyer to communicate to designated parties (e.g., family members, health care providers, a court) concerns that the lawyer might have regarding the client's capacity. . . .

Implied Authority to Disclose and Act.   Based on [] MRPC 1.14, a lawyer has implied authority to make disclosures of otherwise confidential information and take protective actions when there is a risk of substantial harm to the client. Under those circumstances, the lawyer may consult with individuals or entities that may be able to assist the client, including family members, trusted friends, and other advisors. However, in deciding whether others should be consulted, the lawyer should also consider the client's wishes, the impact of the lawyer's actions on potential challenges to the client's estate plan, and the impact on the lawyer's ability to maintain the client's confidential information. In determining whether to act and in determining what action to take on behalf of a client, the lawyer should consider the impact a particular course of action could have on the client, including the client's right to privacy and the client's physical, mental and emotional well-being. In appropriate cases, the lawyer may seek the appointment of a guardian ad litem, conservator or guardian or take other protective action.

Testamentary Capacity. If the testamentary capacity of a client is uncertain, the lawyer should exercise particular caution in assisting the client to modify his or her estate plan. The lawyer generally should not prepare a will, trust agreement, or other dispositive instrument for a client who the lawyer reasonably believes lacks the requisite capacity. On the other hand, because of the importance of testamentary freedom, the lawyer may properly assist clients whose testamentary capacity appears to be border-line. In any such case the lawyer should take steps to preserve evidence regarding the client's testamentary capacity.

In cases involving clients of doubtful testamentary capacity, the lawyer should consider, if available, procedures for obtaining court supervision of the proposed estate plan, including substituted judgment proceedings.

Lawyer Retained by Fiduciary for Person with Diminished Capacity. The lawyer retained by a person seeking appointment as a fiduciary or retained by a fiduciary for a person with diminished capacity, including a guardian, conservator, or attorney-in-fact, stands in a lawyer-client relationship with respect to the prospective or appointed fiduciary. A lawyer who is retained by a fiduciary for a person with diminished capacity, but who did not previously represent the disabled person, represents only the fiduciary. Nevertheless, in such a case the lawyer for the fiduciary owes some duties to the disabled person. If the lawyer represents the fiduciary, as distinct from the person with diminished capacity, and is aware that the fiduciary is improperly acting adversely to the person's interests, the lawyer may have an obligation to disclose, to prevent, or to rectify the fiduciary's misconduct. *See* MRPC 1.2(d).

NOTES AND QUESTIONS

1.   *Capacity to determine capacity.* The ABA suggests that a lawyer who is concerned about the potential of diminished capacity should weigh different factors, such as the client's ability to understand the implications of any decision, whether the client's wishes signify an abrupt change in an existing estate plan and the client's mental state, with the reminder that an attorney can seek help in this determination. MRPC Rule 1.14, Comment 6.

2.   *Privileged communications.* The comments to Model Rule 1.14 recognize that when a client would like to include others in a meeting with the lawyer, this will typically not affect the attorney-client evidentiary privilege if the other individuals are needed to help the representation process. MRPC Rule 1.14, Comment 3, *available at* http://www.abanet.org/cpr/mrpc/rule_1_14_comm.html.

3.   *Professionally responsible planning.* Consider the existence of potential ethical issues in working with a client who wants to provide supplemental financial care for an individual with disabilities while ensuring that the person with disabilities retains Medicaid eligibility. Is there a public interest at stake? *See* Timothy L. Takacs & David L. McGuffey, *Medicaid Planning: Can it be Justified? Legal and Ethical Implications of Medicaid Planning,* 29 WM. MITCHELL L. REV. 111 (2002); Timothy L. Takacs & David L. McGuffey, *Revisiting the Ethics of Medicaid Planning,* 17 NAELA Q. 29 (2004).

PROBLEM

Carla called to ask you to represent her to redraft estate planning documents that she last revised three years ago. In your initial phone conversation, you learn that Carla is an 80-year old woman who lives independently. Her husband died several years ago, and she has two daughters, Donna and Maria, but they live out of town and only visit her occasionally. She arrives at your office with her daughter, Donna. As you begin to explain the types of steps that Carla might consider, she interrupts, asking, "Who are you?" When you explain that you are a lawyer who can help her plan for her future, she shouts out, "I don't need you." What should/would you do? How do you feel about drafting her will? What steps should you take with respect to her competence? What other things might you consider doing for her?

G.   THE END OF LIFE — PHYSICIAN-ASSISTED SUICIDE

If an individual can choose to end life-sustaining treatment, then can she also request physician assistance in ending her life? Physician-assisted suicide involves constitutional, moral, ethical and medical issues. The courts began examining the constitutional issues surrounding physician-assisted suicide in the 1970s through the right-to-die cases, with *In re Quinlan* and *Cruzan*, discussed above, as the first major opinions in this area. States have addressed physician-assisted suicide in a variety of ways, and the Supreme Court has issued several relevant opinions.

1.   State Approaches

There are very few states that explicitly permit physician-assisted suicide. In fact, more than 40 states have statutes that create civil or criminal penalties for those who assist suicide, with the majority of those criminalizing the conduct. Six states criminalize the practice under common law.

As of December 31, 2010, physician-assisted suicide was only permitted in three states: Washington, Oregon and Montana. In 1994, Oregon voters, through a ballot initiative, enacted the Oregon Death with Dignity Act, allowing physician-assisted suicide. In 2008, Washington state voters passed an initiative based on the Oregon law.

The statutory requirements in both states are similar. The patient must be at least 18 years of age and a resident of the state. Two independent doctors must verify that the patient is suffering from a terminal illness that will end the patient's life within six months, and that the patient is of sound mind to make medical decisions. The physician must also make sure the patient is making an informed decision, and is required to tell the patient: (1) his medical diagnosis; (2) his prognosis; (3) the potential risks associated with taking the medication to be prescribed; (4) the probable result of taking the medication to be prescribed; and (5) the feasible alternatives, including, but not limited to, comfort care, hospice care and pain control.

The Washington and Oregon statutes also both require a 15-day waiting period between a patient's initial oral request for life-ending medication and the patient's written request for the medication. Additionally, at least 48 hours must pass between the written request and the writing of the prescription by the physician. The written request must be witnessed by at least two independent witnesses. Each state also has reporting requirements for physicians who prescribe the lethal medication.

In Montana, the right to physician-assisted suicide was recognized by a court, and not the legislature or a ballot initiative. In *Baxter v. Montana*, the court observed that a physician's assistance in dying was not contrary to state public policy, although it did not address the constitutional issues that might be involved. *Baxter v. Montana*, 224 P.3d 1211 (Mont. 2009).

2.   Is Physician-Assisted Suicide Constitutional?

In 1997, the Supreme Court addressed the legality of a Washington state statute criminalizing physician-assisted suicide, examining the issue under the Fourteenth Amendment Due Process Clause in *Washington v. Glucksberg*, 521 U.S. 702 (1997). The Court first discussed the history of Anglo-American law with regard to suicide, acknowledging that suicide or assisting suicide has been subject to disapproval for centuries. The Court then found that because committing suicide is not recognized as a fundamental liberty interest protected by the Due Process Clause, a rational relationship standard of review was appropriate. The Court found several state interests at stake, including preserving human life; preventing the public-health problems of suicide; protecting the integrity of the medical profession; protecting poor, elderly, disabled and vulnerable people who are susceptible to pressure to end their lives; and preventing a slide down the slippery slope to euthanasia. The Court found that the law prohibiting physician-assisted suicide was at least rationally related to these legitimate and important interests, so the statute did not violate the Due Process Clause. In 2008, as discussed *supra*, Washington voters approved a Death with Dignity Act, so the statute upheld by the Supreme Court is no longer in existence.

The Supreme Court considered another set of issues relating to physician-assisted suicide in 2006 in *Gonzales v. Oregon*, 546 U.S. 243 (2006). The U.S. Attorney General had issued an interpretive rule in 2001 concerning the relationship of the Controlled Substances Act (CSA), which regulates the drugs typically involved in physician-assisted suicide, and the Oregon statute. The rule declared that it was not a "legitimate medical practice" to use controlled substances in physician-assisted suicide. Consequently, any such use would be illegal under federal law. Based on administrative law principles, the Court held that the Attorney General did not have the rulemaking power to issue such a regulation that would delegitimize a medical standard for treatment of patients authorized by state law.

NOTES

1.   *Pulling the plug.* Who chooses physician-assisted suicide? As of the end of 2010, about 12 years after Oregon's law became effective, 525 people (282 males and 243 females) had taken prescribed lethal medication. Not everyone who was given a prescription for the lethal medication in Oregon took it. In 2010, 96 prescriptions for lethal medication were written,

but 65 people died as a result of taking these medication; the vast majority of the others died as a result of their underlying disease. *See* OREGON PUBLIC HEALTH DIVISION, PRESCRIPTION HISTORY — OREGON DEATH WITH DIGNITY ACT (2010);[20] OREGON PUBLIC HEALTH DIVISION, 2008 SUMMARY OF OREGON'S DEATH WITH DIGNITY ACT (2011).[21]

The first reported person to die under Washington's Death with Dignity Act was Linda Fleming, who took a lethal medication prescribed by a doctor on May 21, 2009. She had been diagnosed with Stage 4 pancreatic cancer a month before her death. William Yardley, *First Death for Washington Assisted-Suicide Law*, N.Y. TIMES, May 22, 2009.[22]

Because Oregon's Death with Dignity Act requires reporting by doctors who write the prescriptions, Oregon has been able to follow the demographics of those who use its procedures. In 2008, there were 88 prescriptions written, and 54 of them were used. Among those who used the prescriptions, 78% were between 55 and 84 years old, with the median age being 72, and 98% of the patients were white. About half of the patients were married at the time of their deaths. At least 60% of the participants had at least a baccalaureate degree, which was up from 41% in previous years. Ninety-seven percent of the patients had some health insurance — 88% had private insurance, and only 8% had Medicare or Medicaid (down from 36% in previous years). Eighty percent of the participants had cancer.

Patients who died under Oregon's Death with Dignity Act cited three main EOL concerns: loss of autonomy (95%), decreasing ability to participate in activities that made life enjoyable (92%) and loss of dignity (92%). About one-third stated they were concerned about being a burden on family, friends or caregivers, and only 3% stated they were concerned about the financial implications of treatment. OREGON PUBLIC HEALTH DIVISION, OREGON'S DEATH WITH DIGNITY ACT 2008 ANNUAL REPORT, TABLE 1 (2009).[23]

2.   *Advance directives.* Health care proxies and living wills provide general direction as to the patient's wishes. In a state that allows for physician-assisted suicide, should an individual be able to specify her wishes concerning this outcome?

3.   *Suicide or euthanasia?* Some see no distinction between physician-assisted suicide and euthanasia, "a term that conjures up for many people images of the Nazis putting the elderly, the sick, and the retarded to death"; on the other hand, "leaving the final decision in the hands of the patient increases personal autonomy and may provide legal as well as psychological defenses for the physician." Melvin I. Urofsky, *Do Not Go Gentle into That Good Night: Thoughts on Death, Suicide, Morality and the Law*, 59 ARK. L. REV. 819, 828-30 (2007). Which perspective reflects your views?

---

20. *Available at* http://www.oregon.gov/DHS/ph/pas/docs/year13.pdf.

21. *Available at* http://www.oregon.gov/DHS/ph/pas/docs/year11.pdf.

22. *Available at* http://www.nytimes.com/2009/05/23/us/23suicide.html?scp=4&sq=physician%20assisted%20suicide&st=cse.

23. *Available at* http://oregon.gov/DHS/ph/pas/docs/yr11-tbl-1.pdf.

APPENDIX A[24]

GENERAL DURABLE POWER OF ATTORNEY (AND APPOINTMENT OF GUARDIANSHIP OF CHILDREN)

I, Steven Smith, the Principal, of the City and County of Denver, Colorado, by my execution hereof, designate Howard E. Shaw, as my attorney in fact and agent (subsequently called "agent") in my name and for my benefit for the 20__ calendar year or upon my disability, if at that time, my wife, Marjorie M. Black, is incapable of fulfilling the duties given by me to her in a General Durable Power of Attorney executed this same date:

ARTICLE I — GENERAL GRANT OF POWER

1.1   Except as expressly provided to the contrary in Articles VI and VII below, to exercise or perform any act, power, duty, right or obligation whatsoever that I now have or may hereafter acquire, relating to any person, including myself, any matter, and any transaction relating to property, real or personal, tangible or intangible, now owned or hereafter acquired by me, including without limitation, the following specifically enumerated powers. I grant to my agent full power and authority to do everything necessary in exercising any of the powers herein granted as fully as I might or could do if personally present, with full power of substitution or revocation, hereby ratifying and confirming all that my agent shall lawfully do or cause to be done by virtue of this power of attorney and the powers herein granted.

Powers of Collection and Payment. To forgive, request, demand, sue for, recover, collect, receive, and hold all such sums of money, debts, dues, commercial paper, checks, drafts, accounts, deposits, legacies, bequests, devises, notes, interests, stock certificates, bonds, dividends, certificates of deposit, annuities, pension, profit sharing, retirement, social security, insurance and other contractual benefits and proceeds, all documents of title, all property real or personal, intangible and tangible property and property rights, and demands whatsoever, liquidated or unliquidated, now or hereafter owned by, or due, owing, or payable or belonging to me, or in which I have or may hereafter acquire an interest, to have, use and take all lawful means and equitable and legal remedies and proceedings in my name for the collection and recovery thereof, and to adjust, sell, compromise, and agree for the same, and to execute and deliver for me, on my behalf, and in my name, all endorsements, releases, receipts, or other such sufficient discharges for the same;

---

24. The model forms have been adapted and substantially modified for pedagogical purposes.

Power to Acquire and Sell. To acquire, purchase, exchange, grant options to sell, and sell and convey real or personal property, tangible or intangible, or interest therein, on such terms and conditions as my agent shall deem proper;

Management Powers. To maintain, repair, improve, invest, manage, insure, rent, lease, encumber, and in any manner deal with any real or personal property, tangible or intangible, or any interest therein, that I now own or may hereafter acquire, in my name and for my benefit, upon such terms and conditions as my agent shall deem proper;

Banking Powers. To make, receive and endorse checks and drafts, deposit and withdraw funds, acquire and redeem certificates of deposit, in banks, savings and loan associations and other institutions, execute or release such deeds of trust or other security agreements as may be necessary or property in the exercise of the rights and powers herein granted;

Motor Vehicles. To apply for a Certificate of Title upon, and endorse and transfer a title thereto, for any automobile, truck, pickup, van, motorcycle or other motor vehicle, and to represent in such transfer assignment that the title to said motor vehicle is free and clear of all liens and encumbrances except those specifically set forth in such transfer assignment;

Business Interests. To conduct or participate in any lawful business of whatever nature for me and in my name; execute partnership agreements and amendments thereto; incorporate, reorganize, merge, consolidate, recapitalize, sell, liquidate or dissolve any business; elect or employ officers, directors and agents; carry out the provisions of any agreement for the sale of any business interest or stock therein; and exercise voting rights with respect to stock, either in person or by proxy, and exercise stock options; all as may be permitted by law and by the regulations of all professional organizations and associations of which I am a member;

Tax Powers. To prepare, sign and file joint or separate income tax returns or declarations of estimated tax for any year or years; to prepare, sign and file gift tax returns with respect to gifts made by me for any year or years; to consent to any gift and to utilize any gift-splitting provision or other tax election; and to prepare, sign and file any claims for refund of any tax;

Safe Deposit Boxes. To have access at any time or times to any safe deposit box rented by me, wheresoever located, and to remove all or any part of the contents thereof, and to surrender or relinquish said safe deposit box, and any institution in which any such safe deposit box may be located shall not incur any liability to me or to my estate as a result of permitting my agent to exercise this power;

Government Obligations. To acquire, purchase, sell, exchange and redeem any obligations or securities (of every nature including bills, notes and bonds, all regardless of series) of the United States or any of its agencies, of any state or any agencies thereof, of any other government or municipality, of any obligations or securities backed by the full faith and credit of the United States or any other government, and any obligations or securities for which the United States Treasury Department or any other governmental agency acts as transfer agency.

ARTICLE II — GUARDIANSHIP OF CHILDREN

2.1.   If this General Durable Power of attorney takes effect under Article X (B), I hereby appoint Howard Shaw as Guardian and Custodian of my children, Spencer Richard and Georgia Britton with the same duties, powers and order of succession as stated in my will, executed this same date.

ARTICLE III — INTERPRETATION

3.1.   This instrument is to be construed and interpreted as a General Power of Attorney under the laws of the State of Colorado. The enumeration of specific powers herein is not intended to, nor does it, limit or restrict the general powers herein granted to my agent.

ARTICLE IV — THIRD-PARTY RELIANCE

4.1.   Third parties may rely upon the representations of my agent as to all matters relating to any power granted to my agent, and no person who may act in reliance upon the representations of my agent or the authority granted to my agent shall incur any liability to me or to my estate as a result of permitting my agent to exercise any power.

ARTICLE V — SCHEDULE OF ASSETS

5.1.   This General Power of Attorney shall specifically apply to all assets listed in attached Schedules A and B and shall also apply to any and all other assets which I now have any interest in or which I may hereafter acquire any interest in.

ARTICLE VI — LIFE INSURANCE ON LIFE OF AGENT

6.1.   Notwithstanding any other provision of this General Power of Attorney, my agent shall have no rights or powers hereunder with respect to any policy of insurance, owned by me, insuring the life of my agent.

ARTICLE VII — FIDUCIARY POWERS

7.1.   Notwithstanding any other provision of this General Durable Power of Attorney, my agent shall have no rights or powers hereunder with respect to any act, power, duty, right or obligation, relating to any person, matter, transaction or property, owned by me or in my custody as a trustee, custodian, personal representative or other fiduciary capacity.

ARTICLE VIII — COLORADO FIDUCIARIES' POWERS ACT

8.1.   In addition to the powers described above, the agent, or successor agent, shall have all the powers conferred upon fiduciaries by the Colorado Fiduciaries' Act, as it is enacted as of the date of this document.

ARTICLE IX — ESTABLISHMENT OF OR ADDITIONS TO TRUST

9.1.   My agent may create a funded or unfunded revocable trust with dispositive provisions substantially identical to my then existing Will, if in my agent's sole discretion my agent determines that a trust would be in my best interest and the best interest of the devisees under my Will; and at any time and from time to time, may transfer any property, real or personal, tangible or intangible, now owned or hereafter acquired by me, to the persons or corporation then serving as the Trustee of the Trust thus created or of any revocable or irrevocable Trust created by me as Settlor, to be held, administered, and disposed of by the Trustee in accordance with the terms of the instrument.

ARTICLE X — TIME POWER OF ATTORNEY IS TO TAKE EFFECT

10.1. This General Durable Power of Attorney shall be effective:
During the calendar year 20__ while I am traveling in Europe, and,
Upon my disability if at that time, my wife, Marjorie M. Black, is incapable of fulfilling the duties given by me to her in a General Durable Power of Attorney executed this same date. For purposes of determining disability, the agent, successor agent, or any third party may rely upon the certification of my personal physician or the certification of two other practicing physicians who are medical doctors, that I am disabled and am unable to adequately exercise the powers described in this document.

ARTICLE XI — SUBSTITUTE OR SUCCESSOR AGENT

11.1.   If Howard Shaw fails to qualify or ceases to act as my agent due to his death, incapacity, resignation, or for any other reason, I appoint Steven R. Anderson, as my agent. If he fails to qualify or ceases to act as an agent due to his death, incapacity, resignation, or for any other reason, I appoint Kattrin Kinder as my agent.
If this General Durable Power of attorney takes effect pursuant to Article X(A) and if Howard Shaw fails to qualify or ceases to act as my agent due to his death, incapacity, resignation, or for any other reason, and if my children are placed with someone as their Guardian and Custodian,

notwithstanding the order of succession above, that person should succeed Howard Shaw.

ARTICLE XII — MISCELLANEOUS PROVISIONS

12.1. The following additional provisions shall apply to this document:

Execution of Documents. My agent shall be entitled to sign, execute and deliver and acknowledge any contract or other document that may be necessary, desirable, convenient, or proper in order to exercise any of the powers described in this document and to incur reasonable costs in the exercise of any such powers.

Delegation. From time to time, any agent may delegate to any other co-agent the exercise of any powers, discretionary or otherwise, and may revoke any such delegation. Such delegation and revocation shall be evidenced by a writing delivered to the other co-agent. While any delegation is in effect, any of the powers, discretionary or otherwise, so delegated may be exercised and action may taken with the same force and effect as if the delegating agent had personally joined in the exercise of such power and the taking of such action. Anyone dealing with the co-agent shall be absolutely protected in relying upon the written statements of the co-agent relative to the fact and extent of such delegation.

Reimbursement of Costs. My agent shall be entitled to reimbursement for all reasonable costs and expenses actually incurred and paid by my agent on my behalf under any provision of this document, and my agent shall be entitled to reasonable compensation for services rendered hereunder. My agent may also render bills for all reasonable costs and expenses incurred in the exercise of the powers granted in this document to the Trustee of any revocable living trust executed by me.

Revocation of Previous Powers of Attorney. I hereby revoke, annul, and cancel any and all General Powers of Attorney previously executed by me, if any, and the same shall be of no further force or effect. However, I do not intend in any way in this instrument to affect, modify, or terminate any special, restrictive, or limited Powers of Attorney I previously may have granted in connection with any banking, borrowing, or commercial transaction.

Dissolution of Marriage. If my spouse has been appointed my agent or successor agent hereunder and subsequent to the execution of this document an action is filed to dissolve our marriage, then the filing of such action shall automatically remove my spouse as agent or successor agent.

Incapacity of Agent. For purposes of determining the fact of an agent's incapacity, a successor agent or any third party may rely upon the certification of such agent's personal physician or the certification of two other practicing physicians who are medical doctors, that such agent is incapacitated and is unable to adequately exercise the powers described in this document.

Exculpation. My agent and my agent's estate, heirs, successors, and assigns are hereby released and forever discharged by me, my estate, my heirs, successors and assigns from all liability and from all claims or demands of all kinds arising out of the acts or admissions of my agent, except for willful misconduct or gross negligence.

Applicable Law. This instrument is executed and delivered in the State of Colorado and is to be construed pursuant to the laws of this state.

Photographic Copy. A photographic copy hereof shall for all purposes be deemed an original.

Severability. If any part of any provision of this document shall be invalid or unenforceable under applicable law, such part shall be ineffective to the extent of such invalidity only, without in any way affecting the remaining parts of such provision or the remaining provisions of this document.

Executed by me this ___ day of _____, 20___.

_____, Principal

SPECIMEN SIGNATURE OF AGENT:

_____
Agent

_____

[Notary execution here]

APPENDIX B

COLORADO "LIVING WILL"

DECLARATION AS TO MEDICAL OR SURGICAL TREATMENT

I, _____(name of declarant), being of sound mind and at least 18 years of age, direct that my life shall not be artificially prolonged under the circumstances set forth below and hereby declare that:

If at any time my attending physician and one other qualified physician certify in writing that:

I have an injury, disease, or illness which is not curable or reversible and which, in their judgment, is a terminal condition, and

For a period of seven consecutive days or more, I have been unconscious, comatose, or otherwise incompetent so as to be unable to make or communicate responsible decisions concerning my person,

then I direct that, in accordance with Colorado law, life-sustaining procedures shall be withdrawn and withheld pursuant to the terms of this declaration, it being understood that life-sustaining procedures shall not include any medical procedure or intervention for nourishment considered necessary by the attending physician to provide comfort or alleviate pain. However, I may specifically direct, in accordance with Colorado law, that artificial nourishment be withdrawn or withheld pursuant to the terms of this declaration.

In the event that the only procedure I am being provided is artificial nourishment, I direct that one of the following actions be taken:

_____(initials of declarant) a. Artificial nourishment shall not be continued when it is the only procedure being provided: or

_____(initials of declarant) b. Artificial nourishment shall be continued for _____ days when it is the only procedure being provided; or

_____(initials of declarant) c. Artificial nourishment shall be continued when it is the only procedure being provided.

I execute this declaration, as my free and voluntary act, this _____ [date].

By [Signature of declarant] _____

The foregoing instrument was signed and declared by _____ to be _____ [his or her] declaration, in the presence of us, who, in _____[his or her] presence, in the presence of each other, and at [his or her] request, have signed our names below as witnesses, and we declare that at the time of the execution of this instrument, the declarant, according to our best knowledge and belief, was of sound mind and under no constraint or undue influence.

Dated at _____, Colorado, this _____[date].

[Notary execution here]

APPENDIX C

DURABLE POWER OF ATTORNEY FOR HEALTH CARE

I, Marjorie M. Black, the Principal, of the City and County of Denver, Colorado, by my execution hereof, designate my husband, Steven Smith, to serve as my attorney in fact and agent (subsequently called "agent") in my name and for my benefit to exercise the powers set forth below.

By this document, I intend to create a Durable Power of Attorney for Health Care. If for any reason this document is held to be invalid or no agent designated in this document is available or able to serve, I request that my desires as expressed in this document be given full force and effect as a written expression of intent under applicable law.

I desire that my wishes as expressed herein be carried out through the authority given to my agent by this document despite any contrary feelings, beliefs or opinions of members of my family, relatives, friends, conservator, or guardian.

ARTICLE I — GENERAL POWERS REGARDING MY HEALTH CARE

1.1. My agent is authorized in my agent's sole and absolute discretion to exercise the powers granted herein relating to matters involving my health and medical care. In exercising such powers, my agent should first try to discuss with me the specifics of any proposed decision regarding medical care and treatment if I am able to communicate in any manner, however rudimentary. My agent is further instructed that if I am unable to give an informed consent to a proposed medical treatment, my agent shall give, withhold, withdraw, or modify such consent for me based upon any treatment choices that I have expressed while competent, whether under this document or otherwise. If my agent cannot determine the treatment choice I would want made under the circumstances, then my agent should make such choice for me based upon what my agent believes to be in my best interests. Accordingly, my agent is authorized as follows:

<u>Gain Access to Medical Records and Other Personal Information</u>. To request, receive and review any information, verbal or written, regarding my physical or mental health, including medical and hospital records, to execute any releases or other documents that may be required in order to obtain such information, and to disclose such information to such persons or entities as my agent shall deem appropriate.

I specifically authorize anyone to release to my agent any information governed by the Health Insurance Portability Act of 1996, (also known as HIPAA), and any amendments thereto.

Employ and Discharge Health Care Personnel. To employ and discharge medical personnel including physicians, psychiatrists, dentists, nurses, and therapists as my agent shall deem necessary for my physical, mental and emotional well-being, and to arrange for them to be paid reasonable compensation.

Give, Withhold, Withdraw or Modify Consent to Medical Treatment. To give, withhold or withdraw consent to any medical procedure, test or treatment, including surgery; to arrange for my hospitalization, convalescent care, hospice or home care; to summon paramedics or other emergency medical personnel and seek emergency treatment for me, as my agent shall deem appropriate. Under circumstances in which my agent determines that certain medical procedures, tests or treatments are no longer of any benefit to me or, where the benefits are outweighed by the burdens imposed, my agent may, in my agent's sole discretion, but after making every effort to communicate with me first, revoke, withdraw, modify or change consent to such procedures, tests and treatments, as well as hospitalization, convalescent care, hospice or home care which I or my agent may have previously allowed or consented to or which may have been implied due to emergency conditions. My agent's decisions should be guided by taking into account: (1) The provisions of this document; (2) any reliable evidence of preferences that I may have expressed on the subject, whether before or after the execution of this document; (3) what my agent believes I would want done in the circumstances if I were able to express myself; and (4) any information given to my agent by the physicians treating me as to my medical diagnosis and prognosis, and the intrusiveness, pain, risks and side effects associated with the treatment. My agent may act pursuant to these instructions, even though to do so might hasten the moment of my death or be against conventional medical advice or the advice of my attending physician.

Authorize Relief from Pain. To consent to and arrange for the administration of pain-relieving drugs of any kind or other surgical or medical procedures calculated to relieve my pain, including unconventional pain-relief therapies which my agent believes may be helpful, even though such drugs or procedures may have adverse side effects, may cause addiction, or may hasten the moment of my death.

Grant Releases. To grant, in conjunction with any instructions given under this Article, releases to hospital staff, physicians, nurses and other medical and hospital administrative personnel who act in reliance on instructions given by my agent or who render written opinions to my agent in connection with any matter described in this Article from all liability for damages suffered or to be suffered by me; to sign documents titled or purporting to be a "Refusal to Treatment" and "Leaving Hospital Against Medical Advice" as well as any necessary waivers of or releases from liability required by a hospital or physician to implement my wishes regarding medical treatment or non-treatment.

Exercise and Protect My Rights. To exercise my right of privacy and my right to make decisions regarding my medical treatment even though the exercise of my rights might hasten the moment of my death or be against conventional medical advice.

ARTICLE II — POWERS REGARDING LIFE SUSTAINING MEDICAL TREATMENT

2.1.   I wish to live and enjoy life as long as possible. However, I do not wish to receive medical treatment which will only postpone the moment of my death from an incurable and terminal condition or prolong an irreversible coma. Therefore, I have executed a Declaration as to Medical or Surgical Treatment (Living Will), pursuant to the Colorado Medical Treatment Decision Act (C.R.S., Title 15, Article 18). If there is a conflict between this document and any other document I may have signed concerning my health care, such as a Living Will, then the directions given by my agent under this document shall control.

2.2.   To further express my wishes regarding life-sustaining medical treatment, and without in any way attempting to create a conflict between this document and my Living Will (if there is any conflict this document shall control), my agent is authorized to:

Direct that treatment or procedures which will only postpone the moment of my death or prolong an irreversible coma be withheld or, if previously instituted, direct that they be withdrawn;

Direct that procedures other than manual feeding used to provide me with nourishment and hydration (including, for example, all forms of intravenous and parenteral feeding, all forms of tube feeding and misting) be withheld or, if previously instituted, direct that they be withdrawn;

Sign on my behalf any documents necessary to carry out the powers granted in this Article (including waivers or releases of liability required by any health care provider);

Direct and consent to the writing of a "No Code" or "Do Not Resuscitate" order by any health care provider;

Order whatever is appropriate to keep me as comfortable and as free of pain as is reasonably possible, including the administration of pain-relieving drugs, surgical or medical procedures calculated to relieve my pain, and unconventional pain-relief therapies which my agent believes may be helpful, even though such drugs or procedures may have adverse side effects, may cause addiction, or may hasten the moment of my death; and

Present to my attending physician an unrevoked declaration I have executed pursuant to the Colorado Medical Treatment Decision Act, and to transport me to a jurisdiction which will recognize any such unrevoked declaration.

For purposes of this Article: (1) "terminal condition" shall refer to a condition that is reasonably expected to result in my death within twelve months regardless of the treatment that I may receive; and (2) "irreversible coma" shall refer to a permanent loss of consciousness from which there is no reasonable possibility that I will return to a cognitive and sapient life, and shall include, but not be limited to, a persistent vegetative state.

ARTICLE III — POWERS REGARDING CARE AND CONTROL OF MY BODY

3.1.   My agent is authorized as follows with respect to my care and the control of my body:

<u>Provide for My Residence</u>. To make all necessary arrangements for me at any hospital, hospice, nursing home, convalescent home or similar establishment and to assure that all my essential needs are provided for at such a facility.

<u>Provide for Treatment, Care and Companionship</u>. To contract for medical treatment or any type of health care service in my name and on my behalf and to bind me to pay for all such services and facilities; to provide for such companionship for me as will meet my needs and preferences at a time when I am disabled or otherwise unable to arrange for such companionship myself.

<u>Make Advance Funeral Arrangements</u>. To make advance arrangements for my funeral and burial, (including the purchase of a burial plot and marker), cremation, or such other related arrangements as my agent shall deem appropriate, if I have not already done so myself.

<u>Make Anatomical Gifts</u>. To make anatomical gifts which will take effect at my death to such persons and organizations as my agent shall deem appropriate and to execute such papers and perform such acts as shall be necessary, appropriate, incidental or convenient in connection with such gifts.

<u>Subsequent Instructions</u>. Notwithstanding the powers given my agent under this Article, my agent shall follow any other subsequent instruction, oral or written, which I may give my agent while I still have the capacity to give informed consent.

ARTICLE IV — THIRD PARTY RELIANCE

4.1.   For the purpose of inducing any individual, organization, or entity (including, but not limited to any physician, hospital, nursing home, insurer, or other party), all of whom will be referred to in this Article as a "person" to act in accordance with the instructions of my agent as authorized in this document, I hereby represent, warrant and agree that:

<u>Reliance on Agent's Authority and Representation</u>. No person who relies in good faith upon the authority of my agent under this document

shall incur any liability to me, my estate, my heirs, successors or assigns. In addition, no person who relies in good faith upon any representation my agent may make as to (1) the fact that my agent's powers are then in effect, (2) the scope of my agent's authority granted under this document, (3) my competency at the time this document is executed, (4) the fact that this document has not been revoked, or (5) the fact that my agent continues to serve as my agent, shall incur any liability to me, my estate, my heirs, successors or assigns for permitting my agent to exercise any such authority.

No Liability for Unknown Revocation or Amendment. If this document is revoked or amended for any reason, I, my estate, my heirs, successors and assigns will hold any person harmless from any loss suffered or liability incurred as a result of such person acting in good faith upon the instructions of my agent prior to the receipt by such person of actual notice of such revocation or amendment.

Agent May Act Alone. The powers conferred on my agent by this document may be exercised by my agent alone and my agent's signature or act under the authority granted in this document may be accepted by persons as fully authorized by me and with the same force and effect as if I were personally present, competent, and acting on my own behalf. Consequently, all acts lawfully done by my agent hereunder are done with my consent and shall have the same validity and effect as if I were personally present and personally exercised the powers myself, and shall inure to the benefit of and bind me, my estate, my heirs, successors, assigns and personal representatives.

Release of Information. I hereby authorize all physicians and psychiatrists who have treated me, and all other providers of health care, including hospitals, to release to my agent all information or photocopies of any records which my agent may request. *I specifically authorize anyone to release to my agent any information governed by the Health Insurance Portability Act of 1996, (also known as HIPAA), and any amendments thereto.* If I am incompetent at the time, my agent shall request such information, all persons are authorized to treat any such request for information by my agent at the request of my legal representatives and to honor such requests on that basis. I hereby waive all privileges, to the extent that my agent deems appropriate, that may be applicable to such information and records and to any communication pertaining to me and made in the course of any confidential relationship recognized by law. My agent may also disclose such information to such persons as my agent shall deem appropriate.

Resort to Courts. I hereby authorize my agent to seek on my behalf and at my expense:

A declaratory judgment from any court of competent jurisdiction interpreting the validity of this document or any of the acts authorized by this document, but such declaratory judgment shall not be necessary in order for my agent to perform any act authorized by this document; and/or

A mandatory injunction requiring compliance with my agent's instructions by any person obligated to comply with instructions given by my agent; and/or

Actual and punitive damages against any person obligated to comply with instructions given by my agent who negligently or willfully fails or refuses to follow such instructions.

ARTICLE V — EFFECTIVE UPON DISABILITY OF PRINCIPAL

5.1.   THIS POWER OF ATTORNEY SHALL BECOME EFFECTIVE UPON MY DISABILITY. For purposes of determining my disability, the agent, successor agent, or any third party may rely upon the certification of my personal physician or the certification of two other practicing physicians who are medical doctors that I am disabled and am unable to adequately exercise the powers described in this document.

ARTICLE VI — SUBSTITUTE OR SUCCESSOR AGENT

6.1.   If my husband fails to qualify or ceases to act as my agent due to his death, incapacity, resignation, or for any other reason, I appoint Howard Shaw as my agent. If he fails to qualify or ceases to act as an agent due to his death, incapacity, resignation, or for any other reason, I appoint Kattrin Kinder, as my agent. If she fails to qualify or ceases to act as an agent due to her death, incapacity, resignation, or for any other reason, I appoint Steven R. Anderson, as my agent.

ARTICLE VII — MISCELLANEOUS PROVISIONS

7.1.   The following additional provisions shall apply to this document:

Execution of Documents. My agent shall be entitled to sign, execute, deliver and acknowledge any contract or other document that may be necessary, desirable, convenient or proper in order to exercise any of the powers described in this document and to incur reasonable costs in the exercise of any such powers. In addition, my agent shall render bills for all costs incurred in the exercise of the powers granted in this document to the agent then serving under any General Durable Power of Attorney I may have executed, or to the trustee of any revocable living trust, or to any other person then in charge of my financial affairs, or to my estate or personal representative.

Delegation. From time to time, any agent may delegate to any other co-agent the exercise of any powers, discretionary or otherwise, and may revoke any such delegation. Such delegation and revocation shall be evidenced by a writing delivered to the other co-agent. While any delegation is in effect, any of the powers, discretionary or otherwise, so delegated may be exercised and action may be taken with the same force and effect as if the delegating agent had personally joined in the exercise of such power and the taking of such action. Anyone dealing with the co-agent shall be absolutely protected in relying upon the written statements of the co-agent relative to the fact and extent of such delegation.

Reimbursement of Costs. My agent shall be entitled to reimbursement for all reasonable costs and expenses actually incurred and paid by my agent on my behalf under any provision of this document, and my agent shall be entitled to reasonable compensation for services rendered hereunder.

Nomination of Representative. To the extent that I am permitted by law to do so, I hereby nominate and appoint my agent to serve as my guardian, conservator or in any similar representative capacity, and if I am not permitted by law to so nominate, then I request in the strongest possible terms that any court of competent jurisdiction which may receive and be asked to act upon by any person to appoint a guardian, conservator or similar representative for me, give the greatest possible weight to this request.

If my agent is unwilling or unable to serve or to continue to serve in such capacity, then I nominate my successor agents to continue to serve in such capacity in the order that I have named them in this document, and if I am not permitted by law to so nominate, then I request in the strongest possible terms that any court of competent jurisdiction which may receive and be asked to act upon a petition by any person to appoint a guardian, conservator or similar representative for me, give the greatest possible weight to this request.

Revocation and Amendment. I revoke all prior Durable Powers of Attorney for Health Care that I may have executed, and I retain the right to revoke or amend this document. Revocation or amendments to this document shall be made in writing by me personally (and not by any agent named herein) and shall be attached to the original of this document.

Dissolution of Marriage. If my spouse has been appointed my agent or successor agent hereunder and subsequent to the execution of this document an action is filed to dissolve our marriage, then the filing of such action shall automatically remove my spouse as agent or successor agent.

Resignation of Agent. My agent and any successor agent may resign by the execution of a written resignation delivered to me or, if I am mentally incapacitated, by delivery to the agent then serving under any General Durable Power of Attorney I may have executed, or to the trustee of any revocable living trust, or to any other person then in charge of my financial affairs, or to my estate or personal representative, and absent such person, then to any person with whom I am residing or who has the care and custody of me, or, in the case of the resignation of a successor agent, by delivery to my agent.

In addition, the incapacity of my agent or any successor agent (as defined below) shall be deemed a resignation by such individual as agent or successor agent, as the case may be.

Incapacity of Agent. For purposes of determining the fact of an agent's incapacity, incapacity shall be deemed to exist when 1) the person's incapacity has been declared by a court of competent jurisdiction, or 2) when a conservator for such person has been appointed, or 3) upon execution of a certificate by two (2) physicians (neither of whom is related to such person and each of whom is licensed to practice medicine in the state of such person's residence) which states the physicians' opinions that the person is unable to make or communicate responsible decisions concerning the person's body, mental health or physical health and well-being. The effective date of such incapacity shall be the date of the decree adjudicating the incapacity, the date of the decree appointing the conservator, or the date of the physicians' certificate, as the case may be.

Relocation. My agent is authorized to transport me to another jurisdiction, or to establish a new residence or domicile for me, from time to time, and at any time, within or without the State of Colorado, and within or without the United States, for the purpose of exercising effectively the powers granted to my agent in this document.

Applicable Law. This document shall be governed by the laws of the State of Colorado in all respects, including its validity, construction, interpretation, and termination. I intend for this Durable Power of Attorney for Health Care to be honored in any jurisdiction and to refer to Colorado law to interpret and determine the validity of this document and any of the powers granted under this document.

Photographic Copy. A photographic copy hereof shall for all purposes be deemed an original.

Severability. If any part of any provision of this document shall be invalid or unenforceable under applicable law, such part shall be ineffective to the extent of such invalidity only, without in any way affecting the remaining parts of such provision or the remaining provisions of this document.

Conflict with Living Will. If there is a conflict between this document and any other document I may have signed concerning my health care, such as a Living Will, then the directions given by my agent under this document shall control.

Executed by me this _____ day of _____, 20__.

_____, Principal

SPECIMEN SIGNATURE OF AGENT:

_____, Agent

[Notary execution here]

APPENDIX D

COMPARISON OF COSTS AND COVERAGE OF MEDICARE AND MEDICAID[25]

Long-Term Care Service	Medicare	Private Medigap Insurance	Medicaid	You Pay on Your Own
Nursing Home Care	Pays in full for days 0-20 if you are in a Skilled Nursing Facility following a recent hospital stay. If your need for skilled care continues, may pay for the difference between your co-payment of $133.50/day for days 21-100. After day 100 does not pay.	May cover the $133.50/day co-payment if your nursing home stay meets all other Medicare requirements.	May pay for care in a Medicaid-certified nursing home if you meet functional and financial eligibility criteria.	If you need only personal or supervisory care in a nursing home and/or have not had a prior hospital stay, or if you choose a nursing home that does not participate in Medicaid or is not Medicare-certified.
Assisted Living Facility (and similar facility options)	Does not pay	Does not pay	In some states, may pay care-related costs, but not room and board	You pay on your own except as noted under Medicaid if eligible.
Continuing Care Retirement Community	Does not pay	Does not pay	Does not pay	You pay on your own
Adult Day Services	Not covered	Not Covered	Varies by state, financial and functional eligibility required	You pay on your own [except as noted under Medicaid if eligible.]

---

25. This chart is reprinted from: U.S. Dep't of Health and Human Services, National Clearinghouse for Long-Term Care Information, Paying for Long-Term Care: Overview (Mar. 8, 2011), *available at* http://www.longtermcare.gov/LTC/Main_Site/Paying_LTC/Costs_Of_Care/Costs_Of_Care.aspx.

Long-Term Care Service	Medicare	Private Medigap Insurance	Medicaid	You Pay on Your Own*
Home Health Care	Limited to reasonable, necessary part-time or intermittent skilled nursing care and home health aide services, and some therapies that are ordered by your doctor and provided by Medicare-certified home health agency. Does not pay for on-going personal care or custodial care needs only (help with activities of daily living).	Not covered	Pay for, but states have option to limit some services, such as therapy	You pay on your own for personal or custodial care, except as noted under Medicaid, if you are eligible.

14 ESTATE AND GIFT TAX PLANNING

A. INTRODUCTION

The possibility that taxes may be imposed on the transfer of property is central to any discussion of estate planning. Students are often surprised — and maybe a bit scared — at the need to discuss planning for gift and estate taxes in a basic trusts and estates course. We feel your pain. It is impossible, however, to understand the practical significance of much of the subject matter of this course without understanding the basics of transfer taxes. In this chapter, we discuss the topic in brief; we do not cover every nuance of transfer taxation.

We believe it is important for students to understand what property is included in the federal gross estate (and how that differs from the probate estate) and the availability of a host of exemptions, credits, exclusions and deductions. This knowledge will provide you with the basic tools for thinking about estate planning.

You have already learned that in a very high percentage of cases, elaborate planning for the transfer of property is not necessary. This follows from the fact that even if a person does not draft a will or trust, his property will pass to his designated beneficiaries or heirs either by the terms of a contract, like a life insurance contract, by operation of property law, such as a joint tenancy with right of survivorship, or by intestacy.

Likewise, sophisticated planning to avoid estate, gift and generation-skipping transfer (GST) taxes, sometimes referred to as the transfer tax regime, is not necessary. Because there are generous transfer tax exemptions and credits, **an individual who is not likely to acquire significant wealth,** *i.e.,* **not more than $5.0 million ($10.0 million for a married couple), does not need to plan to avoid transfer taxes.**[1]

But, for individuals or married couples with estates valued at more than $5.0 and $10.0 million, respectively, there is more to estate planning than deciding to whom to leave one's property. Unless these individuals engage in tax planning, large portions of their wealth may go to the government in the form of taxes rather than to their heirs or beneficiaries. For many people, this is a fate worse than death. Fortunately, for them, there are quite a few legal steps available to minimize or eliminate the transfer tax bite.[2]

This chapter first introduces you to the history of federal transfer taxes and some of the politics that surround the different views on these taxes. After that, we present the basics of transfer taxes beginning with the estate tax and followed by the gift tax and, modestly, the generation-skipping tax.

However, before we begin, it is important to understand the unsettled state that presently exists in the United States regarding transfer taxation. As we will see later, among a host of other far-reaching changes, the Economic Growth and Tax Relief Reconciliation Act of 2001 (EGTRRA)[3] repealed the federal estate and generation-skipping transfer taxes for persons dying in 2010. However, due to the sunset provisions in EGTRRA, decedents dying thereafter faced a return of the law that existed in 2001. On December 17, 2010, President Obama signed the Tax Relief, Unemployment Insurance Reauthorization, and Job Creation Act of 2010 (the "2010 Tax Relief Act").[4] This act is effective for only two years, 2011 and 2012, after which the law as it existed pre-EGTRRA is supposed to return. Since it is likely that the 2010 Tax Relief Act will be continued in some form when Congress considers legislation to deal with its expiration, the authors have decided to discuss the transfer tax laws in this chapter as if the 2010 Tax Relief Act continues beyond its expiration date. One other matter worth noting before we proceed is that while the casebook seeks to incorporate same-sex marriage and civil unions and the like into the discussion, it is not presently possible to do so in the federal transfer tax area. Although legally married same-sex partners are recognized as spouses in some states, for all federal purposes these couples are considered unmarried due to the

---

1. The exact number of decedents who must file and pay transfer taxes is unclear; ranging from 0.3% to about 2%. Regardless, the number is small. With the exemptions increased to $5.0 million for an individual and $10.0 million for couples beginning in 2011, the number of people subject to transfer tax will be even smaller.

2. Because of the many transfer tax reduction or elimination techniques available, tax professionals frequently refer to transfer taxes as a voluntary tax because much of it can be avoided with proper planning. While an overstatement, there is a lot of truth to this, as we will see.

3. Pub. L. No. 107-16, 115 Stat. 38 (2001).

4. Pub. L. No. 111-312, 124 Stat. 3296 (2010).

Defense of Marriage Act (DOMA).[5] In other words, the spousal rules discussed in this chapter do not include same-sex couples even if they are legally married under state law.

B.   A LITTLE HISTORY (AND AN UNCERTAIN FUTURE)

John R. Luckey, A History of Federal Estate, Gift, and Generation-Skipping Taxes

United States Congressional Research Service, Report Number 95-444
January 3, 2008

The concept of a death tax and the controversies surrounding such taxes have ancient roots. There is evidence of a 10 percent tax on transfers of property at death in ancient Egypt, as early as 700 B.C. Later, the Greeks and Romans adopted death taxes. Critics of such taxes may trace their grievances at least to Pliny the Younger, who charged that a death tax was "an unnatural tax augmenting the grief and sorrow of the bereaved."

The gift tax has developed as a necessary concomitant to the death tax because the easiest way to escape a tax on the gratuitous transfer of property at death is to divest oneself of the property during life. The impact of either tax alone would be diminished by the escape offered by the alternate transfer. . . .

Prior to 1916, the United States did not make regular use of death and gift taxes. The federal government turned to them only in time of extraordinary revenue demands, such as wartime, although individual states used them extensively. . . .

A history of the modern federal estate and gift taxes must begin in 1916. Though since extensively reexamined and revised numerous times, legislation enacted that year is the direct ancestor of current law. . . .

In 1916, Congress reacted to a mixture of changing attitudes and revenue shortages, the latter caused by a reduction in United States trade tariff receipts in the early years of World War I. It became apparent that greater reliance would have to be placed on internal taxes and that dependence on tariffs would have to be reduced. One internal tax was a federal estate tax.

The estate tax adopted in the Revenue Act of 1916 had many features of the current taxes. It was measured by the value of the property owned by a decedent at the date of death and the value of a decedent's estate was increased for tax purposes by certain lifetime transfers, including transfers for inadequate consideration, transfers not intended to take effect until

---

5. Pub. L. No. 104-199, 110 Stat. 2419 (1996).

death, and transfers in contemplation of death. The full value of property owned concurrently by a decedent and another person would be included in the decedent's gross estate, unless it could be established that the surviving joint owner had contributed part of the property's acquisition cost.

The 1916 estate tax allowed the executor to reduce a decedent's estate for tax purposes by a $50,000 exemption and the amount of any funeral expenses, administration expenses, debts, losses, and claims against the estate. The tax rates ranged from 1 percent on net estates of up to $50,000, to 10 percent on net estates over $5,000,000. . . .

Starting in 1976, Congress enacted major revisions to the federal transfer tax system. The estate and gift tax laws were significantly altered. A new tax on generation-skipping transfers was added. The greatest structural change was the unification of the estate and gift taxes.

The Tax Reform Act of 1976 created a unified estate and gift tax framework, consisting of a single graduated rate of tax imposed on both lifetime gifts and testamentary dispositions. The gift tax remained cumulative, so that the rate of tax on each successive taxable gift was higher throughout the donor's entire lifetime. Transfers made at death are treated as the last taxable gift of the deceased donor. Therefore, the amount of lifetime taxable gifts affects the rate of tax imposed on the donor's taxable estate, though it does not affect the actual size of the taxable estate. The estate and gift tax rates were graduated to a maximum tax rate of 70 percent on cumulative gifts or taxable estates of more than $5,000,000.

The Tax Reform Act of 1976 also merged the estate tax exclusion and the lifetime gift tax exclusion into a single, unified estate and gift tax credit, which may be used to offset gift tax liability during the donor's lifetime but which, if unused at death, is available to offset the deceased donor's estate tax liability. . . .

The 1976 Act also increased the limitation on the estate tax marital deductions for moderate-sized estates. . . .

One of the major changes in the 1976 Act was the adoption of a new tax on certain generation-skipping transfers. . . .

The Economic Recovery Tax Act of 1981 (ERTA) made substantial changes in the estate tax apparently designed to reduce the number of taxable estates and to prevent the imposition of an estate or gift tax on interspousal transfers [and reduce the top rate from 70% to 50%]. . . .

ERTA made substantial changes in the marital deduction. The quantitative limits on the estate and gift tax marital deductions were eliminated, thereby allowing unlimited interspousal tax-free transfers after December 31, 1981. The marital deduction was permitted for transfers of certain lifetime income interests in trust or otherwise, if the donor or executor elects to include the full value of the transferred property in the estate of the donee or surviving spouse. . . .

ERTA increased the annual gift tax per donee exclusion from $3,000 to $10,000, with respect to taxable gifts after December 31, 1981. The act also permitted an unlimited annual exclusion for the payment of a donee's tuition or medical expenses. . . .

A qualified disclaimer for estate and gift tax purposes was permitted even if the disclaimer was invalid under applicable State law, if the disclaimant actually transferred the property to the person who would have taken it if the disclaimer had been valid. . . .

The Economic Growth and Tax Relief Reconciliation Act of 2001 (EGTRRA) generally repealed the federal estate and generation-skipping transfer taxes at the end of the year 2009, provided for the phasing out of these taxes over the period 2002 to 2009, lowered and modified the gift tax, provided new income tax carry-over basis rules for property received from a decedent, and made other general amendments applicable in the phase-out period. . . .

The phaseout of the estate tax is being accomplished primarily by adjusting three features of the tax. The top rate is being gradually lowered. The applicable exclusion amount is being gradually raised. The credit for death taxes (estate or inheritance taxes) paid to a State was gradually lowered and replaced by a deduction for such taxes. Also, the 5% surtax used to recapture the benefits of the graduated tax rates on taxable estates of over $10,000,000 was repealed, and, after the applicable exclusion amount had surpassed the $1,300,000 level used to protect family owned businesses, the family owned business deduction was repealed. . . .

As stated in the above excerpt, EGTRRA repealed the estate tax for those dying in 2010 and imposed a carry-over in basis rule for property received as the result of a decedent's death. It also resurrected the estate tax to its pre-EGTRRA position for decedent's dying in 2011 and later. To almost everyone's surprise, Congress did not act to extend transfer taxes at the end of 2009 nor clarify the tax in future years. Its failure to act led to the estates of some very wealthy people avoiding estate taxes.[6] The article that follows presents one.

---

6. Section 301(c) of the 2010 Tax Relief Act gives estates of persons dying in 2010 the choice of whether to use the 2010 or 2011 tax rules. For some estates, it may be better to be subject to estate taxes because of the new higher exemptions and the ability to avoid the carry-over basis rules that apply to beneficiaries receiving property from a decedent dying in 2010. However, for most estates and especially where trusts for the benefit of later generations were established to avoid the generation-skipping tax, the "no taxation" alternative will be more beneficial.

Billionaire's Heirs First to Win 2010 Estate Tax Jackpot[7]

Houston gas pipeline mogul Dan Duncan was the 74th richest person in the world when he died on March 28. If he'd passed away three months earlier or ten months later, his $9 billion estate could have generated up to $4 billion for the IRS. But because there's no federal estate tax this year, the government gets nothing.

As the first billionaire to die in this year without an estate tax, Duncan presents a tempting opportunity for a revenue-strapped Congress to follow through on threats to reinstate the tax for 2010 and possibly even make it retroactive to the beginning of the year.

However, probate gurus say the sheer amount of money on the table makes a retroactive tax more unlikely. Big estates mean big lawyers ready to fight to see those billions of dollars go to the deceased's heirs, and the headaches could go on for years.

"I never imagined it would get this far," Joel Dobris, an estate planning professor at University of California-Davis, told me.

"The longer they wait, the stronger the 'no retroactivity' argument sounds," he added. "Maybe they waited too long."

The lack of clarity has already weighed on less monumental estates for months, says Don Ford, founder of Houston law firm Ford & Mathiason.

"We've had two clients fall into this already," he told me. "They've died this year and would have had taxable estates under either last year's rule or next year's rule. But now we've just got to hang on and see what happens."

---

7. The Trust Advisor Blog, http://thetrustadvisor.com/news/billionaire (Apr. 10, 2010). It is worth noting that a representative of the estate says that the timing of Duncan's death in 2010 had little effect on the estate taxes paid by Duncan's estate because his children have owned almost all of the economic interests for years and the majority of the remainder of his assets will pass to his charitable foundation and his wife, both estate tax-free transfers. *See* Clifford Pugh, *No Benefit to Dan Duncan's Heirs from Estate Tax Loophole* (Oct. 18, 2010), http://culturemap.com/newsdetail/10-12-10-no-benefit-to-duncan-heirs-from-estate-tax-loophole-spokesman-says/.

TICKING CLOCK, HIGH STAKES

Ford has heard that all the movers and shakers in Washington agree that the hole in the estate tax has got to be fixed, but nobody can agree on how to do it.

If nothing happens, the tax will reset in 2011 with an exemption of $1 million and a maximum rate of 50%. That would make a lot of upper-middle-class voters unhappy, Joel Dobris says, so the prospect of doing nothing isn't popular in Congress.

Late last year, the House approved an eleventh-hour plan to keep the tax alive in 2010 under the 2009 rules, which impose a maximum 45% tax rate on estates worth over $3.5 million. But the bill went nowhere in the Senate, feeding speculation that when and if Congress reinstates the tax for this year, it would be on a retroactive basis to cover those who died after January 1....

NOT A BIG REVENUE SOURCE

Nobody in Congress really expected a billionaire of Dan Duncan's caliber to die this year without significant estate protection already in place.

In fact, the Congressional Joint Committee on Taxation estimated last year that restoring the estate tax at 2009 levels would have only added about $468 million to the federal government's 2010 revenue.

That kind of cash really wouldn't have made much more than a symbolic difference in a $3.5 trillion operating budget. But symbolism matters a lot in Washington these days, UC-Davis professor Joel Dobris told me....

LOOKING AHEAD

For the rest of us, the clock is ticking and the spring and summer Congressional recesses are ahead. It's theoretically possible that gridlock and inertia will leave the door open for more billionaires to leave tax-free estates this year, in which case Houston lawyer Don Ford worries that the retroactivity issue could come back in 2011.

"Does this get pushed back to next year when it becomes a real issue, and then they try to make the new exemption and rates retroactive?" he wonders. "That's when it becomes a little unsettling."

No matter what happens to the estate tax, Ford told me that his clients take comfort in the trusts and other estate planning instruments he's put in place for them. "Uncertainty like this only demonstrates the value of what we do," he told me.

C. THE POLITICS OF TAXING TRANSFERS OF WEALTH

Due to the conflict between the desire of individuals to retain their property and the interest of the government to collect tax and redistribute wealth, there has been a sharp policy debate for many years over the fairness and wisdom of taxing the transfer of wealth from one generation of a family to the next.[8] The principal arguments advanced against the imposition of transfer taxes (or, as the opponents of the tax like to refer to it, the "death tax"), and the responses to them, summarized quite nicely in "The Estate Tax: Myths and Realities," Center for Budget and Policy Priorities, (rev. Jan. 13, 2009),[9] are as follows:

Argument Against Tax	Response
The estate tax constitutes "double taxation" because it applies to assets that already have been taxed once as income.	Large estates are comprised to a large degree of "unrealized" capital gains that have never been taxed; the estate tax is the only means of taxing this income.
The estate tax unfairly punishes success.	The estate tax affects only those most able to pay, and the funds it raises are used to support a range of programs that benefit the nation.
If the estate tax is reformed and retained, the logical top tax rate would be 15 percent, the same as the capital gains rate.	To match the effective tax rate on capital gains, the top estate tax rate needs to be about 45 percent.
Eliminating the estate tax would encourage people to save and thereby make more capital available for investment.	Eliminating the estate tax would not substantially affect private saving, and it would greatly increase government dissaving (*i.e.*, deficits); as a result, it would be more likely to *reduce* the capital available for investment than to increase it.
The estate tax is best characterized as the "death tax."	The estates of nearly all people who die are tax free.

---

8. *Compare* William W. Beach, *The Case for Repealing the Estate Tax*, Heritage Foundation Backgrounder No. 1091 (Aug. 21, 1996), *available at* http://www.heritage.org/Research/Taxes/BG1091.cfm *with The Estate Tax: Myths and Realities*, Center for Budget and Policy Priorities, (rev. Jan. 13, 2009), *available at* http://www.cbpp.org/cms/index.cfm? fa=view&id=2655&zoom_highlightsub=estate+tax.

9. *Available at* http://www.cbpp.org/cms/index.cfm?fa=view&id=2655&zoom_highlightsub=estate+tax.

Argument Against Tax	Response
The United States taxes estates highly compared to other countries.	U.S. estate tax revenues as a share of GDP are below the international average for taxes on wealth.
Many small, family-owned farms and businesses must be liquidated to pay estate taxes.	The number of small, family-owned farms and businesses that owe any estate tax at all is tiny, and virtually no such farms and businesses have to be liquidated to pay the tax.
The estate tax forces estates to turn over half of their assets to the government.	The few estates that pay any estate tax generally pay less than one-fifth of the value of the estate.
Weakening the estate tax wouldn't significantly worsen the deficit because the tax doesn't raise much revenue.	Repealing the estate tax, or weakening it well beyond its 2009 parameters, would add trillions of dollars to future deficits and be fiscally irresponsible.
The cost of complying with the estate tax is nearly equal to the total amount of revenue the tax raises.	The costs of estate tax compliance are relatively modest and are consistent with the costs of complying with other taxes.

Since 1976, the "anti-death tax" forces have been the clear victors in the debate. Tax legislation enacted during the terms of three recent Republican presidents significantly reduced the number of decedents subject to transfer taxes and, for those who are unable to escape it entirely, lessened the transfer tax bite. As the Luckey report excerpted above shows, it began with "The Tax Reform Act of 1976,"[10] which was enacted during the term of President Gerald Ford, continued with "The Economic Recovery Tax Act of 1981"[11] of President Ronald Reagan, and culminated in "The Economic Growth and Tax Relief Reconciliation Act of 2001,"[12] enacted under President George W. Bush. During these presidencies, the amount of property that could pass tax-free increased in stages from $60,000 to $3.5 million (for transfers made in 2009) and the top rate lowered from 70% to 45%. This trend continued in 2010 when President Obama signed the 2010 Tax Relief Act, which raised the tax-free exemption amount for transfers by gift or bequest in 2011 and 2012 for individuals and married couples to $5.0 and $10.0 million (subject to being adjusted for inflation after 2011), respectively, and lowered the top rate to 35%.

---

10. Pub. L. No. 94-455, 90 Stat. 1520 (1976).
11. Pub. L. No. 97-34, 95 Stat. 256 (1981).
12. Pub. L. No. 107-16, 115 Stat. 38 (2001).

EXERCISE

You are the aide to Senator Abrianna. The Senate is considering whether to extend the transfer tax provisions in the 2010 Tax Relief Act. As the law now stands, all the cuts that were enacted will disappear for decedents dying in 2013 and thereafter. In essence, beginning in 2013, the law will be as it was in 2000, with higher rates (as high as 50%) and lower exemptions ($1.0 million). The Senator would like your views on whether to let the law go into effect as it is, to permanently extend the tax cuts or to repeal the tax entirely. If you can offer any middle ground as a basis for a compromise, as one of a dying breed of centrists, he would be very interested in hearing that.

D.   INTRODUCTION TO TRANSFER TAXES

There are three transfer taxes at the federal level in the Internal Revenue Code (the IRC or Code):[13] estate tax, gift tax and generation-skipping tax (GST). In addition, most states have either estate taxes that tax the decedent's estate or inheritance taxes that tax the recipient of property. In this chapter, we focus exclusively on federal estate and gift taxes and, to a modest degree, GST; state taxes are beyond this chapter's scope.[14]

Transfer taxes are imposed on the *gratuitous* transfer of property or financial benefit to another during life or at death. In other words, transfer taxes are assessed when property ownership or the functional equivalent of ownership is gifted from one person to another. This general rule, however, is subject to a number of exceptions discussed below.

Estate taxes are at the core of federal transfer taxation. Gift taxes and GST complement the estate tax regime: If gifts and generation-skipping transfers were not taxed, individuals could give away unlimited amounts of property during their lifetimes, die with a small estate and thus avoid the estate tax.

---

13. The Internal Revenue Code of 1986 is Title 26 of the United States Code. This chapter will cite the Internal Revenue Code as IRC.

14. While coverage of state regimes to tax the transfer of wealth is beyond the scope of this chapter, it is worth noting that as of December 31, 2010, there are 21 states with different systems or exemption levels than the federal structure that is the subject of this chapter. It is anticipated that the loss of revenue resulting from the 2010 Tax Relief Act may serve as the catalyst for action by these and other states to depart even more from the federal estate tax approach. *See* Ashlea Ebeling (Dec. 21, 2010), *State Estate Taxes Loom As Big 2011 Issue*, http://www.forbes.com/2010/12/21/state-federal-estate-tax-planning-2011-personal-finance-state-estate-tax-map.html.

The amount of a transfer subject to tax is the difference between the fair market value (FMV)[15] of property gifted or devised and any consideration received by the donor. If the transfer occurs during the donor's life, FMV is determined on the date of the gift; if the transfer occurs at death, the property is valued at date of death.[16] IRC §§2512 and 2031. The definition of FMV derives from the Treasury Regulations: "the price at which the property would change hands between a willing buyer and a willing seller, neither being under any compulsion to buy or sell and both having knowledge of relevant facts."[17] Treas. Reg. §§20.2031-1(b) and 25.2512-1. FMV is normally determined by a property's "highest and best use," rather than its current, actual use.[18] *Symington v. Commissioner*, 87 T.C. 892 (1986).

The entire value of all transfers is not taxed. There are exclusions and credits in the Code that allow some property to pass transfer tax-free. An individual can transfer a total of $5.0 million ($10.0 million for a married couple) by gift and/or bequest before transfer taxes are imposed. In addition, each year a person can make gifts of $13,000 to an unlimited number of donees.

1. But First — Income Tax Consequences to Recipient of a Gift or Bequest

While you probably are not familiar with estate and gift taxes, you may have some familiarity with income taxes. Each year, you have to file a Form 1040 reporting your income and deductions to the IRS. Generally, income tax is levied on the receipt of money or property derived from any source. The most common sources of taxable income include wages, interest, dividends, rents and the gain or loss from the sale of stocks and other property. These are all taxable and must be reported on Form 1040.

The Internal Revenue Code does, however, exclude the receipt of certain kinds of income and property from an individual's taxable income. Notably, for purposes of this course, gifts and inheritances are not taxable

---

15. From the transferor's perspective, obviously the lower the FMV the better. As there is normally a wide range of values that could constitute FMV, and as there are many factors that influence FMV, quite a bit of tax planning involves efforts to reduce FMV. Undervaluing assets too aggressively, however, may result in accuracy-related penalties of 20% to 40% of a deficiency under IRC §6662(g)-(h). Not surprisingly, valuation is the issue most frequently raised by the Internal Revenue Service when examining estate tax returns.

16. There is, however, a special rule that allows real property used in certain family farms and closely held businesses to, under certain circumstances, be valued for estate tax purposes at less than its highest and best use. IRC §2032A.

17. Valuation for GST purposes is the same as valuation for the underlying gift tax or estate tax. IRC §§2624, 2642(b).

18. For this reason, undeveloped land and farms near a city are frequently valued based on what they would be worth if the land were subdivided and a residential neighborhood developed.

to the recipient. IRC §102 says, "[g]ross income does not include the value of property acquired by gift, bequest, devise, or inheritance." Thus, whether received as a gift or an inheritance, the transaction is income tax-free to the recipient, regardless of the amount received. If Bob's mother, for example, gave him $200,000 to buy a home, he would not have to include this as income on his individual income tax return. Similarly, if Margaret's dad left her $3,000,000 in his will, she would not have to report this as income.

Although there is no current income effect to the recipient of a gift or inheritance, there may be future tax consequences if the gift took the form of property instead of cash. This is because when the beneficiary later disposes of the property, any gain or loss may have to be reported on the donee's Form 1040. Gain occurs if the sales price exceeds the property's basis, and loss results if the sales price is less than the property's basis. IRC §1001.

A property's basis usually equals its cost. However, when a person receives property by gift or inheritance, the Code establishes special basis rules because no purchase is involved. A recipient of a gift is assigned the same basis in the gifted property as the donor had (generally referred to as "carry-over basis" because the donor's basis carries over to the recipient). IRC §1015. By contrast, the basis a devisee takes with respect to inherited property equals the property's fair market value at the time of the decedent's death. IRC §1014. This is often referred to as "stepped up" basis, because the basis of the property to the recipient steps up from the decedent's basis to its fair market value at the decedent's death.[19]

Since a gift of property carries the basis of the donor over to the donee, any "built-in gain" on appreciated property becomes the future income tax burden of the donee. By contrast, any built-in gain on appreciated property transferred by inheritance is never taxed due to the stepped up basis rule. This suggests an obvious estate planning strategy: If possible, hold onto property that has already appreciated and pass it at death rather than gift it inter vivos.

> **Example:**   Mom owned High Flying Corp. stock that she bought for $100,000. Mom gifted the stock to Child when it had a fair market value of $1.0 million. Child has no taxable income on the receipt of the transfer, and Child takes the stock with a carryover basis of $100,000. Shortly after receiving the stock, Child sells it for $1.0 million. Child has gain of $900,000 to report on her Form 1040.

> **Example:**   Mom owned High Flying Corp stock that she bought for $100,000. When Mom died, the stock was worth $1.0 million. She left the stock to Child in her will. Child has no taxable income on the

---

19. It is worth noting that if the value of the property decreased after its purchase by the decedent, the basis would step down to fair market value.

receipt of the stock, and Child takes the stock with a date of death basis of $1.0 million. Shortly after receiving the stock, Child sells it for $1.0 million. Child has no gain to report on her Form 1040.

While it is good planning to delay until death the transfer of property that is *already* appreciated, it may be wise to presently gift property that is projected to significantly increase in value in the *future* rather than hold onto it until death. Because of the difference in tax rates incurred by the donee for capital gains (generally 15%) and by the decedent for estate taxes (up to 35%), gifting property before it appreciates can save the family as much as 20% of the future appreciation.

For example, if Bill Gates had gifted his Microsoft stock when the company was just a startup and worth only a few cents per share, his transfer tax bill would have been minor or non-existent. By contrast, if he holds on to it until his death when it is likely to be worth billions of dollars, his transfer tax bill will be astronomical. Thus, even though donees of startup stock will have an enormous capital gain when they sell their stock many years later, because capital gains rates are well below transfer tax rates, the trade-off is worth it.[20]

E.   TAXATION OF ESTATES

In order to calculate the estate tax, we must determine the "taxable estate." IRC §2001(a)-(b). To reach the taxable estate, we start with the "gross estate," *i.e.*, the value of all property the decedent owned at death, and reduce it by a series of deductions. IRC §2051. The most significant deductions are for the value of money and other property transferred to the decedent's surviving spouse or to charities, as well as to pay estate administration expenses and debts of the decedent. The resulting tax liability, if any, is then reduced by several credits, the most significant of which is the unified tax credit.

To expand on the above, there are five steps to determine how much estate tax is due, if any:

1. Determine the federal *gross estate*, which is the sum of the following property interests:
    *   Property in which the decedent had an interest.
    *   Property in which the decedent held retained interests.

---

20. In fact, Bill Gates has avoided the tax problem with some of his stock by creating a charity, the Bill and Melinda Gates Foundation. Contributing to a private foundation has many tax and non-tax benefits. *See Private Foundation Tax Benefits*, https://www.fidelityprivatefoundations.com/resources_planning_taxbenefits.html.

- Life insurance proceeds.
- Certain transfers within three years of death.
- Annuities with a survivorship feature.
- Joint tenancies with a right of survivorship.
- Property over which the decedent had a general power of appointment.
- Property in a marital trust as to which a special election had earlier been made by the estate of the decedent's spouse (called QTIP trusts).

2. Determine allowable deductions:
   - Administrative expenses.
   - Decedent's debts and other claims against the estate.
   - The value of property contributed to charities.
   - The value of property transferred to the decedent's surviving spouse.
3. Calculate the *taxable estate* by subtracting #2 from #1.[21]
4. Calculate the *preliminary estate tax* by multiplying the taxable estate (the amount determined in #3) by the tax rates in the Internal Revenue Code.
5. Determine the *net estate tax* due, which is the preliminary estate tax (per #4) reduced by various credits, the most important of which is the unified tax credit equal to the tax on an estate of $5.0 million ($10.0 million for a married couple).[22]

In all cases where the gross estate (*i.e.*, before deductions) at the decedent's death plus the post-1976 gifts exceeds $5.0 million, the executor must file an estate tax return on Form 706. IRC §§6018(a)(1), (3), 6019(a)-(b). The return must be filed within nine months of the decedent's death, though a six-month extension to file is generally available. IRC §6075(a); Treas. Reg. §20.6081-1.

With this as background, we turn to a detailed discussion of what is included in the gross estate, what can be deducted to determine the taxable estate and what credits are available to offset the tax imposed, if any.

1.   Determining the "Gross Estate"

As compared to the more limited nature of property included in the *probate* estate, the property comprising the *gross* estate for tax purposes is made up

---

21. There is actually an intermediate step after this. To the taxable estate (the amount determined in #2), add gifts made subsequent to 1976. This results in the "grossed up taxable estate." This effectively taxes all transfers, both during life and at death, using the same graduated tax rates.

22. If there were any gift taxes paid on post-1976 gifts, they would be subtracted also. This avoids double taxation of lifetime gifts.

not only of property owned by the decedent at the time of death, *i.e.*, probate property, but also of property over which the decedent had control or incidents of ownership at the time of death. Therefore, while property that is subject to will substitutes is typically excluded from the probate estate, it is usually included in the gross estate. For example, though they are not included in the probate estate, checking accounts with a "payable-on-death" (POD) designation, investment accounts with a "transfer-on-death" (TOD) designation and property in a revocable trust are included in the gross estate pursuant to IRC §2031.[23]

Determining what to include in the gross estate is far from straightforward. To illustrate, although some of the decedent's interests in a trust or other investment are included in the gross estate, others are not. *A good standard to determine whether a decedent has interests or powers over trust property sufficient to treat the corpus as if it were owned by the decedent, and thus, includible in decedent's gross estate, is to ask (i) whether the decedent had the equivalent of ownership during life, and (ii) whether the decedent's death resulted in the transfer of the property to another.* Generally, if the decedent possessed this level of interest up to the moment of death, the subject property is included in the decedent's gross estate.

We next examine different kinds of property interests for inclusion in the gross estate.

a. Property in Which the Decedent Had an Interest[24]

All probate property owned at the moment of death[25] and any other property in which the decedent had an interest is included in the gross

---

23. **IRC §2031(a). Definition of Gross Estate.**

> The value of the gross estate of the decedent shall be determined by including to the extent provided for in this part, the value at the time of his death of all property, real or personal, tangible or intangible, wherever situated.

You will notice that in this chapter, the authors have decided to place the statutes in footnotes rather than in the text. This was done to avoid distracting the student from the difficult discussion of estate taxation by frequent Internal Revenue Code section citation and quotation. A student who wishes to review the statute has it available while the student who wishes to focus on only the textual presentation may do so.

24. **IRC §2033. Property in Which the Decedent Had an Interest.**

> The value of the gross estate shall include the value of all property to the extent of the interest therein of the decedent at the time of his death.

25. *See Goodman v. Granger*, 243 F.2d 264, 268 (3d Cir. 1957) ("Since death is the propelling force for the imposition of the [estate] tax, it is death which determines the interests to be includible in the gross estate").

estate. IRC §2033. Consequently, the gross estate includes property held in fee simple and the decedent's interest in a tenancy in common and community property. IRC §2033 also causes gross estate inclusion of a non-probate favorite — single-party accounts owned by the decedent that have a pay- or transfer-on-death provision (POD or TOD).

b.   Revocable Trusts[26]

Because the settlor of a revocable trust can revoke, alter, amend or terminate the trust and retake its corpus at any time, the settlor's powers are tantamount to owning the property in the trust. Thus, there is no gift when the settlor transfers property into the trust and, pursuant to IRC §2038, the FMV of trust corpus is included in the settlor's gross estate upon his death.[27]

> **Example:**   Jorell created a trust in 2000 and transferred $500,000 to it. The terms gave him the right to income during his life. On his death, the trust would terminate and be distributed to his daughter. He retained the right to revoke the trust during his life but never did so. The corpus was worth $3.0 million on his death.
>
> There are no gift tax consequences in 2000 when Jorell funded the trust since Jorell is not deemed to have parted with anything at that

---

26. **IRC §2038. Revocable Transfers.**

> (a)(1) The value of the gross estate shall include the value of all property . . . to the extent of any interest therein of which the decedent has at any time made a transfer (except in case of a bona fide sale for an adequate and full consideration in money or money's worth), by trust or otherwise, where the enjoyment thereof was subject at the date of his death to any change through the exercise of a power (in whatever capacity exercisable) by the decedent alone or by the decedent in conjunction with any other person (without regard to when or from what source the decedent acquired such power), to alter, amend, revoke, or terminate, or where any such power is relinquished during the 3 year period ending on the date of the decedent's death.

27. If the settlor retained the power to revoke less than all the trust, then only the corresponding portion of the trust corpus is includible. It should be clear that while revocable trusts are valuable as will substitutes to avoid probate, they do not result in transfer tax savings. Although no tax benefits derive from a settlor's use of a revocable trust, other benefits may exist. For example, if a settlor owns real property in multiple states, the use of a revocable living trust may avoid ancillary probate proceedings.

time. On his death, Jorell's gross estate includes the $3.0 million in the trust since he had the functional equivalent of ownership over the corpus at the time of his death and his death resulted in the transfer of the property to another — the keys to estate taxation mentioned above.

c. Transfers with a Retained Life Estate[28]

To the extent an individual transferred property into trust and retained the right until death to receive income from it or to use it, the FMV of the trust corpus is includible in the decedent's gross estate. IRC §2036. As far as the Code is concerned, it is treated as the practical equivalent of owning an income-generating asset. IRC §2036 is very broad, including in the estate a trust in which the settlor kept only the right to the income (even if he did not retain control over the principal) or the right to designate the persons who should possess or enjoy the property or the income therefrom. Does it make sense to you that a right to income alone would subject the entire interest to estate taxation?

Example: Donald created a trust in 2000 and transferred $500,000 to it. The terms of the trust give him the right to income during his life. On his death, the trust is to terminate and the corpus distributed to his daughter. He did *not* retain a right to revoke the trust. The corpus was worth $3.0 million on his death.

As we will discuss later, there is a gift to the extent of the actuarial value of the remainder interest multiplied by $500,000.[29] On Donald's death, all $3.0 million in the trust is included in his gross

---

28. **IRC §2036. Transfers with Retained Life Estate.**

> (a) The value of the gross estate shall include the value of all property to the extent of any interest therein of which the decedent has at any time made a transfer (except in case of a bona fide sale for an adequate and full consideration in money or money's worth), by trust or otherwise, under which he has retained for his life or for any period not ascertainable without reference to his death or for any period which does not in fact end before his death —
>
> > (1) the possession or enjoyment of, or the right to the income from, the property, or
> >
> > (2) the right, either alone or in conjunction with any person, to designate the persons who shall possess or enjoy the property or the income therefrom.

29. The gift of the remainder interest to Donald's daughter is taxed at the time of the transfer in 2000 based on the value assigned to it in the actuarial tables used by the IRS. The estate will get a credit for the gift tax paid in 2000.

estate because, at the moment of his death, he had the right to income from the $3.0 million and his death precipitated the transfer of the entire sum to his daughter — the keys to estate taxation. If Donald had only retained the right to half the income from the trust, only half of the corpus ($1.5 million) would be included in his gross estate.

Example: Assume in the above example that Donald's right to income was for the shorter of his life or 10 years. If Donald lived for 15 years, none of the trust corpus would be included in his estate because he did not have a prohibited power at the time of his death nor did his death cause the property to be transferred to his daughter. Of course, had he died in year seven, the result would be the same as in the example above.

IRC §2036 encompasses more than just trust assets. Any property transferred by the decedent in which the decedent retains the power to use, enjoy or possess the property or its income, or the right to appoint the present interest, is included in decedent's estate.

Example: Chinatsu transferred a vacation home worth $500,000 to her child, but retained the right for life to use the property without paying rent. As above, there is a gift to the extent of the actuarial value of the remainder interest multiplied by $500,000. When Chinatsu dies, the vacation home is included in her estate at its then-FMV because she had the right to use and enjoy the home at the time of her death, and ownership of the home transferred to her son at that time.

d.   Life Insurance Proceeds[30]

The proceeds of a life insurance policy are included in a decedent's estate if the decedent owned the policy at the time of death, if at any time in the three-year period prior to death the decedent had "incidents of ownership" in the policy or if the estate is named as the beneficiary of the policy.

---

30. **IRC §2042. Proceeds of Life Insurance.**

The value of the gross estate shall include the value of all property —

    (1) To the extent of the amount receivable by the executor as insurance under policies on the life of the decedent.

    (2) To the extent of the amount receivable by all other beneficiaries as insurance under policies on the life of the decedent with respect to which the decedent possessed at his death any of the incidents of ownership, exercisable either alone or in conjunction with any other person. . . .

[T]he term "incidents of ownership" is not limited in its meaning to ownership of the policy in the technical legal sense. Generally speaking, the term has reference to the right of the insured or his estate to the economic benefits of the policy. Thus, it includes the power to change the beneficiary, to surrender or cancel the policy, to assign the policy, to revoke an assignment, to pledge the policy for a loan, or to obtain from the insurer a loan against the surrender value of the policy, etc. Treas. Reg. §20.2042-1(c)(2).

Life insurance is a valuable estate planning tool. In addition to transferring wealth from the decedent to the beneficiaries of the policy, life insurance is frequently used to provide liquidity for an estate to pay taxes and other debts so that the decedent's interests in businesses, real estate, restricted securities or stock options or limited partnerships do not have to be sold at "fire sale" prices. Life insurance is also used to replace the income of the decedent.[31]

The amount of wealth transferred will be greater if estate taxes do not reduce the amount going to the beneficiaries. This requires that the purchase and ownership of the policies be structured correctly to avoid inclusion of the proceeds in the gross estate. The safest way to assure this result is for the decedent never to have owned the policy, never to have had any incidents of ownership and, of course, not to name his estate as the beneficiary of the policy. Therefore, estate planners frequently recommend that a family member purchase and own the policy from its inception and that the insured avoid having any rights associated with it. As among family members, it is best to have a child or grandchild be the owner instead of the other spouse so that the proceeds bypass the estates of both parents.[32]

An alternative strategy is to have an Irrevocable Life Insurance Trust (ILIT) acquire the policy. The ILIT owns the policy and, according to the terms of the trust, either distributes the proceeds after the insured's death or continues to exist after the insured's death for the benefit of family members. Typical terms for ILITs provide the surviving spouse with an income interest for life and, on her death, either (i) the trust terminates and the trust property gets distributed to the children or grandchildren or (ii) the trust continues and provides income to lower generation family members until it is finally terminated and the trust property distributed.[33]

---

31. Carolyn B.R. Decker, *Beyond High Net Worth: Insurance Needs of the Ultra Wealthy,* *available at* http://www.wealthstrategiesjournal.com/articles/2010/11/beyond-high-net-worth-insuranc.html.

32. It is likely a child or grandchild would need financial assistance to pay the premiums on the policy. It is perfectly acceptable for the insured to gift the amount of money needed to the owners, subject to the $13,000 annual exclusion rules, and let the owners pay the premiums. This does not make the insured the owner.

33. As with direct ownership by family members, the insured can make gifts to the trust of the amount needed to pay the premiums, though the gift will not automatically qualify for the annual exclusion because it is a gift of a future interest. There are ways to obtain the annual exclusion but their discussion is beyond the scope of this chapter. *Crummey v. Commissioner,* 397 F.2d 82 (9th Cir. 1968).

The strategy just discussed assumes a policy will be acquired in the future. If the insured already owns a policy, planning involves transferring ownership to a family member or an ILIT and hoping the insured survives the three-year inclusion window of IRC §2035, discussed in the next section.[34]

e.   Transfers of Certain Interests Within Three Years of Death[35]

In each of the three situations just discussed, *i.e.*, those covered by IRC §2038 (revocable transfers), IRC §2036 (transfers with a retained life interest) and IRC §2042 (life insurance), a taxpayer's attempt to avoid estate tax by transferring away the tainted property interest (either by direct transfer or by the exercise, release or lapse of the right) is ineffective if done within three years of death. IRC §2035. If this section applies, the FMV of the property subject to the forbidden powers or the face value of life insurance is included in the decedent's gross estate even though the decedent no longer owned the property at death.

> **Example:**   Tammy created a trust in 2000 and transferred $500,000 to it. The terms gave her the right to income during life. On her death, the trust would terminate and be distributed to her daughter. She retained the right to revoke the trust during life, but never did so. In March 2010, Tammy relinquished the life income interest and the right to revoke the trust.[36] If Tammy dies within the three years following the relinquishment of the income interest and the right to revoke, the trust corpus is includible in her estate. If she survives until March 2013, however, the trust corpus is excluded from her estate.

---

34. Even if the owner-insured is elderly, transferring ownership of the policy is a risk worth taking as there is no penalty if the person dies within the following three years.

35. **IRC §2035. Adjustments for Certain Gifts Made Within 3 Years of Decedent's Death.**

> (a) If —
> (1) the decedent made a transfer (by trust or otherwise) of an interest in any property, or relinquished a power with respect to any property, during the 3-year period ending on the date of the decedent's death, and
> (2) the value of such property (or an interest therein) would have been included in the decedent's gross estate under section 2036, . . . 2038, or 2042 if such transferred interest or relinquished power had been retained by the decedent on the date of his death,
> the value of the gross estate shall include the value of any property (or interest therein) which would have been so included [plus any gift tax paid on such transfer].

36. Tammy will be subject to gift taxation at the time she relinquishes her interests in the trust.

f. Annuities[37]

An annuity is a contract between the annuitant and an insurance company that promises to pay the annuitant a certain amount of money, on a periodic basis, for a specified period. Some annuities are purchased by the annuitant directly and others are acquired by the annuitant as a result of being a participant in the employer's retirement plan.

There are a variety of annuity types, but for our purposes we will distinguish between those that make payments only during the life of the annuitant and those that have a survivorship feature and make payments to others after the death of the annuitant. Since the essence of transfer taxation is the passing along of a valuable right to property to others at one's death, only annuities that have the survivorship feature are subject to estate taxation. The amount included in the gross estate is, correspondingly, the actuarial value of the amount receivable by the surviving beneficiaries.

While the transfer tax treatment of annuities and retirement plans is generally straightforward, the rules on when and in what manner the distributions from an inherited plan must be made are very complicated.[38] In addition, and contrary to most inheritances, the beneficiary has income to report on the receipt of the payments to the extent the payments represent income that was not taxed to the decedent (known as "income in respect of the decedent").[39]

---

37. **IRC §2039. Annuities**

> **(a) General**. — The gross estate shall include the value of an annuity or other payment receivable by any beneficiary by reason of surviving the decedent under any form of contract or agreement entered into after March 3, 1931 (other than as insurance under policies on the life of the decedent), if, under such contract or agreement, an annuity or other payment was payable to the decedent, or the decedent possessed the right to receive such annuity or payment, either alone or in conjunction with another for his life or for any period not ascertainable without reference to his death or for any period which does not in fact end before his death.
>
> **(b) Amount includible**. — Subsection (a) shall apply to only such part of the value of the annuity or other payment receivable under such contract or agreement as is proportionate to that part of the purchase price therefor contributed by the decedent. For purposes of this section, any contribution by the decedent's employer or former employer to the purchase price of such contract or agreement (whether or not to an employee's trust or fund forming part of a pension, annuity, retirement, bonus or profit sharing plan) shall be considered to be contributed by the decedent if made by reason of his employment.

38. *See, e.g.*, Deborah Jacobs, *Five Rules for Inherited IRAs* (June 9, 2010), *available at* http://www.forbes.com/forbes/2010/0628/investment-guide-stretch-ira-beneficiary-five-rules-inherited-iras.html.

39. The negative effects to the beneficiary of having to report the payments on her Form 1040 are partially offset by an income tax deduction for the portion of the estate taxes attributable to the inclusion of the annuity in the estate of the decedent.

g.   Joint Tenancy with Right of Survivorship[40]

The fact that a decedent's interest in a joint tenancy is included in her gross estate should come as no surprise since she would have had an ownership interest in the property until death and the interest passes to the other tenant upon death. What is surprising is the amount that is included. The Code requires the full value of the entire asset owned in joint tenancy with the right of survivorship to be included in the gross estate, except to the extent the decedent's estate can establish the percentage of the cost of the joint tenancy asset contributed by others. For example, if the decedent's estate can establish that the other tenant paid 75% toward the cost of the joint tenancy, only 25% of the value of the property is included in the decedent's gross estate. If the estate cannot meet its burden, then 100% is taxable.

If the joint tenancy is between spouses, different rules apply. Half the value of property held by spouses as joint tenants with the right of survivorship is included in the estate of the first spouse to die, regardless of which spouse contributed the funds needed to purchase the property.

Similarly, if the decedent was gifted an interest in property as a joint tenant, the FMV of the property in proportion to the interest the decedent was gifted is includible in decedent's estate. For example, assume mom gave her two sons a parcel of real estate in joint tenancy with right of survivorship. At that time, mom would be subject to gift tax on the FMV of the entire parcel of real estate. Upon the first son's death, his estate would include 50% of the real estate's FMV.

---

40. **IRC §2040. Joint Interests.**

> (a) The value of the gross estate shall include the value of all property to the extent of the interest therein held as joint tenants with right of survivorship by the decedent and any other person, or as tenants by the entirety by the decedent and spouse, or deposited, with any person carrying on the banking business, in their joint names and payable to either or the survivor, except such part thereof as may be shown to have originally belonged to such other person and never to have been received or acquired by the latter from the decedent for less than an adequate and full consideration in money or money's worth: Provided further, [t]hat where any property has been acquired by gift, bequest, devise, or inheritance, as a tenancy by the entirety by the decedent and spouse, then to the extent of one-half of the value thereof, or, where so acquired by the decedent and any other person as joint tenants with right of survivorship and their interests are not otherwise specified or fixed by law, then to the extent of the value of a fractional part to be determined by dividing the value of the property by the number of joint tenants with right of survivorship.

h. General Power of Appointments (GPOA)[41]

The tax treatment of the holder of a GPOA is complicated. A "pure" GPOA, *i.e.*, one in which the holder of the power has the current right to appoint property to herself, her creditors, her estate or the creditors of her estate, is treated as the substantive equivalent of ownership. The general rule is that the value of property subject to a presently exercisable GPOA is included in a decedent's gross estate.

This general rule is subject to a massive exception. If the power to appoint to oneself is limited by ascertainable standards, for example, health, education, maintenance, support (HEMS) or the like, the power is not considered a general one for tax purposes and the property subject to the power of appointment is *not* included in the donee's gross estate. Therefore, if the goal is to keep the property subject to the power of appointment out of the estate of the donee power holder, the GPOA should be limited by ascertainable standards. However, if the goal is to subject the property to taxation in the estate of the donee of the power, as might be the situation where the donee is the surviving spouse of the decedent, then the GPOA should not be limited by these standards. GPOA marital trusts are discussed in greater detail below in Section E.2.c., entitled "Transfers to Surviving Spouse."

Example: Bayette died and left the residue of her estate in trust for her husband, Blake. The terms of the trust gave Blake an income interest for life and the unlimited right to invade the principal of the trust for whatever reason he deemed necessary. Bayette's estate is entitled to a marital deduction for the value of the property transferred to the trust. IRC §2056(b)(5). On Blake's death, the value of corpus is included in his gross estate under IRC §2041, because he had the

---

41. **IRC §2041. Powers of Appointment.**

(a) The value of the gross estate shall include the value of all property . . .

(2) To the extent of any property with respect to which the decedent has at the time of his death a general power of appointment created after October 21, 1942, or with respect to which the decedent has at any time exercised or released such a power of appointment by a disposition which is of such nature that if it were a transfer of property owned by the decedent, such property would be includible in the decedent's gross estate under sections 2035 to 2038, inclusive. . . .

(b) For purposes of subsection (a) —

(1) The term "general power of appointment" means a power which is exercisable in favor of the decedent, his estate, his creditors, or the creditors of his estate; except that —

(A) A power to consume, invade, or appropriate property for the benefit of the decedent which is limited by an ascertainable standard relating to the health, education, support, or maintenance of the decedent shall not be deemed a general power of appointment.

functional equivalent of ownership over the property at the time of his death, and the corpus passes to another as the result of his death.

Example: Polly died and left the residue of her estate to a trust. Her son, Tyler, is trustee and income beneficiary. Polly's granddaughter is the remainder beneficiary. The trustee may appoint property to Tyler if needed for his health, education or support. While Tyler holds what appears to be a presently exercisable GPOA over trust corpus (the power to distribute trust property to himself), the fact that the power is limited by ascertainable standards transforms it into a non-general power of appointment for tax purposes. Thus, the trust corpus is *not* includible in Tyler's gross estate.

i. Qualified Terminable Interest Property (QTIP) Trusts[42]

The FMV of the principal in a Qualified Terminable Interest Property (QTIP) trust is included in the gross estate of the beneficiary of the trust. IRC §2044. A QTIP is a fairly standard marital trust, *i.e.*, income to surviving spouse, remainder to children, but with a tax twist. To qualify as a QTIP, the trust must satisfy two requirements: (1) the trust must provide the surviving spouse with an exclusive income interest for life, and (2) the estate of the decedent spouse must make a special QTIP election.

If a QTIP trust exists, the estate of the first spouse to die gets a marital deduction for the value of the property transferred into the trust. This makes the inter-spousal transfer estate-tax-free. The quid pro quo for this deduction is that the gross estate of the second spouse includes the FMV (as of the date of the second spouse's death) of any property remaining in the trust.

Example: Kasumi established a testamentary trust with $2.5 million. The terms provide his spouse, Keiko, with all the income for her life. On her death, the remainder goes to the children of his first marriage. His estate makes the appropriate QTIP election. Kasumi's estate gets a marital deduction for $2.5 million. Upon Keiko's death 18 years later, the QTIP trust corpus (valued, we will assume, at Keiko's death at $3.9 million) is included in her gross estate.

---

42. **IRC §2044. Certain Property for Which Marital Deduction Was Previously Allowed.**

> The value of the gross estate shall include the value of any property to which this section applies [any property if a deduction was allowed with respect to the transfer of such property to the decedent under §2056(b)(7) — the QTIP deduction section] in which the decedent had a qualifying income interest for life.

QTIP marital trusts are discussed in greater detail below in Section E.2.c., entitled "Transfers to Surviving Spouse."

2.   Deductions Allowable in Determining the "Taxable Estate"

Once the value of the gross estate is determined, deductions are allowed for, among other things, administrative expenses, debts of the decedent, transfers to the decedent's spouse, gifts to charities and payments to states and the District of Columbia for estate or inheritance taxes. The net result equals the "taxable estate." IRC §2051.

a.   Administrative Expenses, Etc.[43]

Administrative expenses include funeral expenses, executor expenses and other professional expenses. The estate may deduct these outlays to the extent they are paid.

b.   Debts of the Decedent

The determination of the *gross estate* has no deductions for the debts of the decedent. However, since it is only the decedent's net worth (assets less liabilities) that is transferred, there must be a place for a deduction for the decedent's debts. IRC §§2053(3) and (4) provide the authority for a deduction of claims against the estate to the extent paid, reasonably ascertainable or passed along to the beneficiaries. If, for example, a decedent owed $24,000 to credit card companies and the estate paid the balances due, the estate is entitled to a $24,000 deduction. Likewise, if the decedent's house is transferred to her children subject to the mortgage, the estate is reduced by the amount of the mortgage.

---

43. **IRC §2053(a). Expenses, Indebtedness, and Ttaxes.**

> . . . the value of the taxable estate shall be determined by deducting from the value of the gross estate such amounts —
>   (1) for funeral expenses,
>   (2) for administration expenses,
>   (3) for claims against the estate, and
>   (4) for unpaid mortgages on, or any indebtedness in respect of, property where the value of the decedent's interest therein, undiminished by such mortgage or indebtedness, is included in the value of the gross estate . . .

c. Transfers to Surviving Spouse[44]

The marital deduction permits unlimited tax-free transfers of property between spouses.[45] The surviving spouse receives the decedent's portion of marital property undiminished by taxes, thus providing the survivor with a greater likelihood of being able to support herself in the manner to which she was accustomed. Since the surviving spouse must include in her gross estate whatever property she receives from the decedent that she has not consumed, a marital deduction is really nothing more than a tax deferral

---

44. **IRC §2056. Bequests, Etc. to Surviving Spouse.**

> (a) . . . the value of the taxable estate shall, except as limited by subsection (b), be determined by deducting from the value of the gross estate an amount equal to the value of any interest in property which passes or has passed from the decedent to his surviving spouse, but only to the extent that such interest is included in determining the value of the gross estate.
>
> (b)(1) Where, on the lapse of time, on the occurrence of an event or contingency, or on the failure of an event or contingency to occur, an interest passing to the surviving spouse will terminate or fail [and pass to another person], no deduction shall be allowed under this section with respect to such interest . . . .
>
> (b)(5) In the case of an interest in property passing from the decedent, if his surviving spouse is entitled for life to all the income from the entire interest, or all the income from a specific portion thereof, payable annually or at more frequent intervals, with power in the surviving spouse to appoint the entire interest, or such specific portion (exercisable in favor of such surviving spouse, or of the estate of such surviving spouse, or in favor of either, whether or not in each case the power is exercisable in favor of others), and with no power in any other person to appoint any part of the interest, or such specific portion, to any person other than the surviving spouse [a marital deduction is allowed]. . . .
>
> (b)(7) In the case of qualified terminable interest property [QTIP] [a marital deduction is allowed].
>
> (B)(i) — The term "qualified terminable interest property" means property —
>
> (I) which passes from the decedent,
> (II) in which the surviving spouse has a qualifying income interest for life [the surviving spouse is entitled to all the income from the property, payable annually or at more frequent intervals, and no person has a power to appoint any part of the property to any person other than the surviving spouse] and
> (III) to which an [irrevocable] election [is made by the executor on the return.

45. Due to the Defense of Marriage Act (DOMA), the marital deduction is presently available only between spouses one of whom was a man and the other a woman. It is not available to same-sex or other long-term committed couples. Pub. L. No. 104-199, 110 Stat. 2419 (1996). Many lawsuits have been filed challenging DOMA's constitutionality and most have been successful, but the Supreme Court has not yet agreed to hear any of them. For a compendium of cases, see the DOMA Watch Web site, http://www.domawatch.org/case_names_index.html.

technique — from the decedent spouse's estate to the surviving spouse's estate.[46]

A marital deduction is allowed to the decedent's estate if the manner in which the transfer occurs assures that the surviving spouse will have to include the transferred property not otherwise consumed in her estate when she dies. The philosophy behind linking the allowance of the marital deduction for the estate of the first spouse with the inclusion in the gross estate of the second spouse is to assure that the marital property gets taxed at least once when passing between family generations.

Consistent with this analysis, a *transfer in fee simple* to one's surviving spouse gives rise to an unlimited marital deduction for the full value of the property transferred. IRC §2056(a).

> **Example:** Harvey dies leaving spouse, Tara, a fee simple interest in Blackacre, worth $350,000. Harvey's estate can take a marital deduction for $350,000. This is because Blackacre will be included in Tara's estate if she does not dispose of it before she dies. Transfers in fee simple to the surviving spouse are common in first marriages where there is no need to place the money into a trust for either asset protection or asset management purposes and the decedent wishes to leave to the survivor the decision of what happens to the property upon her death.

Transfers into trust (or a trust equivalent) may or may not qualify for the marital deduction. The answer depends on the type of interest the surviving spouse receives. No marital deduction is generally allowed if the recipient spouse merely acquires a life estate. This is because the interest of the recipient spouse is "terminable." As such, there would be nothing to tax upon the survivor's death. If the transferor spouse were allowed a marital deduction for the value of the terminable interest transferred to the recipient spouse and the recipient had nothing to include in her estate at her death, the property would never be taxed.

> **Example:** Jacob dies leaving spouse, Cynthia, a life interest in Blackacre. According to the terms of the transfer, on Cynthia's death, title to Blackacre passes to their children. Because Blackacre would not be included in Cynthia's gross estate at her death due to the fact that her interest terminates, the Code denies Jacob's estate a marital deduction for the transfer of Blackacre to Cynthia.

However, the "no deduction" terminable interest rule for transfers into a trust in which the spouse has an income interest for life is subject to two exceptions. A marital deduction is available if, in addition to an income

---

46. In addition to deferral, there may be some real tax savings associated with postponing taxation from the estate of the first spouse to die to the estate of the second spouse. As tax rates have gone down and the unified credit has gone up, the estates of surviving spouses

interest for life, the trust (1) gives the surviving spouse a General Power of Appointment (GPOA),[47] or (2) meets the QTIP trust requirements.[48] In both instances, the trust corpus will be taxed in the recipient spouse's estate, by IRC §2041 and IRC §2044, respectively.

> **Example:**   Afon dies leaving spouse, Sasha, a life interest in a testamentary trust. Sasha is also given a GPOA over the trust corpus that is exercisable during life or at death. Afon's estate is entitled to a marital deduction for the full value of the property transferred to the trust despite the fact that Sasha is getting a terminable life estate. This is because the value of the remaining corpus will be included in Sasha's gross estate on her death because she holds a GPOA over the trust property. IRC §2041. Normally, a marital GPOA trust is used in first marriages where the decedent would like to give the survivor discretion in deciding to whom to leave the property when she dies but wishes to have a trustee help with asset management.

> **Example:**   Rocco dies leaving spouse, Simka, a life interest in a testamentary trust. The trustee has the discretion to invade the corpus of the trust for Simka's support needs. On Simka's death, the trust terminates and the property is to be distributed to Rocco's descendants by representation. Without more, the terminable interest rule would disallow Rocco's estate a marital deduction for the property transferred into trust. If, however, a QTIP election is made, Rocco's estate is entitled to a marital deduction. This is because IRC §2044 will include the remaining corpus of the trust in Simka's gross estate. A QTIP is often employed in a second marriage because the rules allow the decedent to direct who the remaindermen are, normally his children from an earlier marriage. It also has the advantages of asset protection, if the spouse is not named the trustee, and professional asset management. The QTIP is an estate planner's dream in that its application is elective in whole or in part.

d.   Other Deductions

Deductions are allowed for the FMV of property transferred to charity, IRC §2055, and any estate, inheritance, legacy or succession taxes actually paid to a state or the District of Columbia in respect to property included in the gross estate. IRC §2058.

---

have experienced significantly reduced tax liabilities. If the estate tax is eliminated altogether, major tax savings would occur.

  47. *See* IRC §2056(b)(5).
  48. *See* IRC §2056(b)(7).

3.   Calculating the Estate Tax

After the gross estate is reduced by the allowable deductions to determine the taxable estate, the next step is to calculate the estate tax. The transfer tax regime requires that all taxable transfers made by the individual, whether made during life or at death, be accounted for when applying the applicable tax rate, which progress from 18% to 35%. IRC §2001(c).[49] In other words, the estate tax base is "grossed up," or combined with lifetime transfers. IRC §2001(b)(1). However, to avoid double taxation, gift tax previously paid is subtracted from the computed tax liability. IRC §2001(b)(2).

> **Example:**   Carole dies with a taxable estate of $5.5 million. She previously gave $2.0 million in taxable lifetime gifts (amounts in excess of the available exclusions), paying $500,000 in gift taxes. The estate tax is computed on the full $7.5 million. Along with the other credits discussed below, the $500,000 gift tax paid is also credited against the estate tax liability.

4.   Estate Tax Credits

Once the estate tax is computed, there are several credits that reduce the tax liability dollar-for-dollar. IRC §§2010-2016. By far, the most important is the unified tax credit in IRC §2010. As discussed earlier, the present credit is equal to the tax that would be due on an estate of $5.0 million. In addition, IRC §2010(c)(3) adjusts the credit in the future in $10,000 increments based on the cost of living index.

The 2010 Tax Relief Act includes a "portability" provision. IRC §2010(c) allows a surviving spouse to take advantage of the decedent's unused exclusion amount. As a condition to doing this, however, the personal representative of the deceased spouse must make an irrevocable election on a timely filed estate tax return. This could be a trap for the unwary as the election is lost if the executor of an estate under $5.0 million does not file an estate tax return because it is below the level required to file.

> **Example:**   Max dies leaving a gross estate of $4.5 million. He dies intestate and the entire estate goes to his wife, Carolina. As his taxable estate is zero due to the $4.5 million marital deduction, no unified credit is needed to reduce the tax liability. If Max's executor files a timely return and makes an election under IRC §2010(c)(5), Carolina may combine Max's unused $5.0 million exclusion with her own exclusion and pass $10.0 million tax-free to noncharitable donees. If

---

49. However, since all the rates below 35% pertain to estates worth less than $5.0 million and the unified credit eliminates tax liability on estates below $5.0 million, the actual tax rate imposed on the portion of estates *that are subject to tax* is 35%.

the executor fails to do so, Carolina is limited to her own $5.0 million exclusion.

Prior to the passage of the 2010 Tax Relief Act, significant estate planning was required for married couples. One planning device involved the execution of two testamentary trusts in the will of the first spouse to die (sometimes referred to as A and B trusts or as Marital and Family Trusts), one trust to take full advantage of the unified tax credit (a "credit shelter" trust or a "bypass" trust) and the other trust to qualify the decedent's remaining property for the marital deduction (a marital GPOA or QTIP trust). Planning also involved making inter vivos gifts from the richer spouse to the poorer spouse to raise the poorer spouse's wealth to the full unified credit equivalent. However, with the inclusion of the portability provision and an increase in the credit to $5.0 million in the 2010 Tax Relief Act, much of this planning is no longer important, assuming that both provisions continue after the 2010 Tax Relief Act expires. In states that have a lower credit that is not portable from the first spouse to the surviving spouse, credit shelter planning will continue to be important.

5.   *Liability for Estate Tax*

The personal representative is obligated to pay the estate tax. IRC §2002. If the personal representative does not pay the tax before paying other creditors or distributing the estate to the beneficiaries, the personal representative could be personally liable to the government. 31 USC §3713(b). A wise personal representative will not distribute property prematurely. Rather, a personal representative should withhold distributions until all tax liabilities are satisfied or until the personal representative is certain there are sufficient assets left in the estate to satisfy any tax liabilities that might arise when the return is filed or upon audit by the Internal Revenue Service.[50]

Clearly, when agreeing to serve, the personal representative does not intend to bear the burden of paying the estate's tax liability. The beneficiaries of probate and nonprobate transfers normally bear the tax

---

50. Executors should be cautious. If the executor or appraisers engaged in valuation that the IRS will potentially challenge, the executor should withhold sufficient assets to pay estate tax resulting from an unfavorable audit. There are two notable steps an executor can take to mitigate personal liability for estate tax. First, the executor may submit a written request to the IRS office where the return is filed for a determination of the amount of tax due and discharge from personal liability. IRC §2204(a); Treas. Reg. §20.2204-1; *but see* IRC §6324(a)(3). The IRS then has nine months from the date of request to respond. If the IRS does not respond within nine months, the executor is released from personal liability. Importantly, however, this does not release the estate from liability for a later determined tax deficiency. Furthermore, if the IRS determines a tax deficiency exists, the executor discharges personal liability after paying the deficiency determined by the IRS. Second, the executor may wait to receive a closing letter from the IRS stating that all tax liabilities have been satisfied.

burdens.[51] State law generally determines how estate tax liability is apportioned among beneficiaries when a decedent's will is silent.[52] But, federal law apportions estate tax among beneficiaries who receive three types of assets: life insurance proceeds on the decedent's life;[53] property over which decedent had a GPOA;[54] and property for which a marital deduction was previously allowed.[55]

F. TAXATION OF GIFTS

The taxation of gifts has always been perceived as a backstop for the estate tax regime to prevent individuals from gifting all of their property during their lifetimes to avoid the estate tax. Consequently, even though the gift tax is assessed first chronologically, we cover it after estate taxes.

Gift taxes are calculated on "taxable gifts." IRC §2503. Taxable gifts are the "total amount of gifts" made during the taxable year (at their FMV) minus exclusions for certain gifts and minus deductions for transfers to charities and to the donor's spouse. IRC §§2501, 2503(a).

The donor must file a Form 709 by April 15th for gifts made in the previous year to persons other than spouses and charities that exceed the exclusion amounts discussed below. The gift tax form is quite different from, and less complicated than, the estate tax return.

Determining the amount of the gift tax requires the following steps:

1. Determine *taxable gifts*, which equals the FMV of all gifts made during a taxable year *less* the following items:
    *   The annual exclusion.
    *   Gifts made for certain tuition and medical expenses.
    *   Gifts subject to the marital deduction.
    *   Gifts subject to the charitable deduction.
2. The *preliminary gift tax* is calculated by multiplying the taxable gifts (the amount determined in #1) by the tax rates found in the Internal Revenue Code.[56]

---

51. Will provisions, state statutes or state common law may apportion estate tax liability among beneficiaries. *See e.g.*, COLO. REV. STAT. §15-12-916 (2010).

52. *See, e.g., Riggs v. Del Drago*, 317 U.S. 95 (1942).

53. *See* IRC §2206.

54. *See* IRC §2207.

55. *See* IRC §2207A.

56. There is actually an intermediate step after this. To the taxable gifts (the amount determined in #1) is added gifts made subsequent to 1976. This results in the "grossed up taxable gifts." This effectively taxes all lifetime transfers using the same graduated tax rates. Then, after calculating the preliminary gift tax, the donor deducts the gift tax actually paid on post-1976 gifts to determine the net gift tax. This avoids double taxation of lifetime gifts.

3. The *net gift tax* equals the preliminary gift tax (under #2) reduced by various credits, the most important of which is the unified gift tax credit equal to the tax on a gift of $5.0 million.

1. Determining "Total Amount of Gifts"

Subject to the exceptions noted below, all transfers of property for less than FMV give rise to the imposition of gift taxes. The term "transfer" in the gift tax area is much broader than merely a gratuitous conveyance of a fee simple interest. It may include a transfer of property into trust, as well as the exercise, release or lapse of certain rights or powers over property.

Gifts only occur to the extent interests are transferred to others; the portion of any interest retained by the donor is not taxed. When a donor gifts property in fee simple to another person, the full FMV of the property is taxed since the donor has retained nothing. Likewise, an inter vivos fee simple transfer to an irrevocable trust in which the donor has not retained any interests or powers is a completed gift for its FMV.

If the settlor transfers property to a trust in which she has retained an interest, only the value of the interests irrevocably given to others is subject to gift tax.

> **Example:** Margaret, age 67, transfers $100,000 of stocks into a trust on January 25, 2011, the terms of which provide her with all the income for her life. On her death, the trust will terminate and be distributed to Margaret's descendants, per stirpes. The value of the transfer attributable to her life income interest is not considered a gift; rather, it is viewed as if she merely moved some of her money from one of her pockets to another. On the other hand, the remainder interest given to her descendants is a completed gift and taxed at its FMV. The IRS publishes actuarial tables[57] that allocate the value of a transfer between the retained income interest and the gifted remainder interest based on the interest rate and age of the person with the present interest at the time of transfer.[58] In Margaret's case, and using a 2.4% interest factor, her retained interest would be .30776 ($30,776) and the remainder would be .69224 ($69,224).[59] As discussed below, the annual exclusion does not apply here since the gift is of a future interest.

---

57. Treas. Reg. §§25.7520-1T; 1.642(c)-6T. *See also* http://www.federalregister.gov/articles/2009/05/07/E9-10111/use-of-actuarial-tables-in-valuing-annuities-interests-for-life-or-terms-of-years-and-remainder-or#g-6.

58. *See* Rev. Rul. 2011-2, 2011-2 IRB 1 (Table 5 for January 2011).

59. If Margaret has not relinquished her income interest before she dies, IRC §2036 will require the trust property be included in her gross estate at its date of death FMV. While it may appear the trust is being taxed twice, the fact is that it is only being taxed once but at two different times as the estate will get a reduction of its liability for taxes paid as a result of

Inter vivos transfers to a *revocable* trust are not considered gifts at all because nothing is deemed to have been given away. Gift taxes will be imposed, however, if the settlor later acts in a manner for the benefit of another. This may happen if the settlor invades the corpus and gives it to another, releases the power or lets it lapse.[60]

a. Gifting Within the Annual Exclusion Amount

Some portion of gratuitous inter vivos transfers may escape taxation. One of the most simple and often-used ways to remove a lot of property from an estate without incurring gift taxes is to take advantage of the annual gift exclusion.[61] "In the case of gifts (other than gifts of future interests in property)[62] made to any person by the donor during the calendar year, the first . . . [$13,000] of such gifts to such person shall not . . . be included in the total amount of gifts made during such year." IRC §2503(b)(1). Simply put, the donor can annually give up to $13,000 in present interest gifts to any number of people. Importantly, gifts within the annual exclusion do not count against the lifetime unified tax credit equivalent of $5.0 million. IRC §2503(b).

> **Example:**   Jared and Lesley have two children, two children-in-law, and 6 grandchildren, for a total of 10 potential donees. At $13,000 per year to each of the 10 donees, Jared and Lesley can each give away $130,000 per year gift tax-free without reducing the available unified credit. In other words, together they can give away more than a quarter million dollars per year. Over a long enough period, a significant amount of property can be removed from their estates free of tax.

Sometimes married couples have the bulk of their property in the name of only one spouse. This is especially true in common law property states. If the property-owning spouse is the only donor but the husband and wife wish to utilize both of their annual exclusions, they may do so by completing the consent line on the gift tax return (Form 709). IRC §2513. This is often referred to as gift-splitting.[63]

---

the January 11, 2011, gift. If Margaret does relinquish her income interest during life, she will be gift taxed again on the actuarial value of her remaining income interest.

60. If the exercise, release or lapse occurs within three years of the settlor's death, the corpus and any gift taxes paid are pulled back into the gross estate, as discussed above, due to IRC §2035(a)(2) and (b). Also, to the extent of any remaining corpus in the trust subject to the decedent's power to revoke at the time of death, it is included in the gross estate.

61. Not to be lost in the myopia of saving taxes are the many other reasons gifting is helpful to family members in need, such as to help buy a car, a home, start a business or get over difficult financial times.

62. Gifts must be of a present interest to qualify for the annual exclusion. Clearly, a gift of a fee simple interest meets this requirement. When the settlor establishes a trust that includes a future interest, the future interest does not qualify for the annual exclusion.

63. If the spouses gift-split, they are jointly and severally liable for gift tax due. IRC §2513(d).

b.   Gifting for Medical and Educational Needs

In addition to the $13,000 annual exclusion, a donor can make
unlimited gifts directly to educational institutions or medical providers for a
donee's tuition or medical expenses. IRC §2503(e). Importantly, only
tuition is excluded from taxable gifts; gifts for room, board and books are
taxable, even if paid directly to the school. *See* Treas. Reg. §25.2503-6(b)(2).
This is not only a great way to reduce the property subject to transfer taxes,
but it is also a wonderful vehicle for helping family members in school or in
serious medical situations when they need assistance the most. In the
example in the previous subsection, Jared and Lesley can pay tuition to private schools or colleges for their family members on top of the $26,000 they
give each of them annually.

c.   Section 529 College Savings Plans, or Qualified Tuition Programs[64]

Another way to provide for the education of children and grandchildren is through what are referred to as "Section 529 plans." (The name
comes from IRC §529.) Today, all 50 states and the District of Columbia
offer 529 college savings plans. They are tax-advantaged investment opportunities operated by the state's treasury office. Neither the contributing
parent (or grandparent or other donor) nor the child needs to live in the
sponsoring state to participate in a state's program. Section 529 plans can
be used to cover all "qualified higher education expenses," including
tuition, room and board, mandatory fees and books and computers (if
required).

An individual can use the $13,000 annual exclusion by contributing
to a 529 plan ($26,000 for married couples). If the limits are not exceeded,
the transfers are not subject to gift tax and the plan assets are excluded from
the transferor's estate.[65] Unlike education IRAs, there are no income limits.
Section 529 plans offer a special gifting feature. Specifically, a donor can
make a lump-sum contribution to a 529 plan of up to $65,000, elect to
spread the gift evenly over five years and completely avoid federal gift tax,
provided no other gifts are made to the same beneficiary during the five-
year period. As discussed above, a married couple can double the exclusion,
which here means they can gift up to $130,000.

For example, if Mother contributes $65,000 to Son's 529 account in
one year and makes the election, the contribution will be treated as if she

---

64. Portions of this discussion are excerpted from Money-Zine.com, Estate Planning
with 529 Plans, http://www.money-zine.com/Financial-Planning/College-Loan/Estate-
Planning-with-529-Plans/.

65. Note that 529 plans are subject to the annual exclusion limits. This is in contrast to
the exclusion available for payments for tuition per IRC §2503(e), discussed in the previous
section.

had made a $13,000 gift for each year of a five-year period. The entire $65,000 gift will be non-taxable, assuming Mother does not make any additional gifts to Son in any of those five years.

With 529 plans, the account owner always remains in control of the plan's assets. Even though the contributions are considered completed gifts, and therefore outside of the donor's estate, the donor, and not the beneficiary, remains in control of the money. In fact, the donor can reclaim the money at any time and for any reason or change the designated beneficiary.

2. Deductions Allowable in Determining "Taxable Gifts"

As was true with estate taxes, the value of gifts to the donor's spouse or to charities[66] is deductible to determine taxable gifts. IRC §2523. The rules for gift tax deductibility are almost identical to those for estate tax deductibility, as discussed above, and are not repeated here.

3. Gift Tax Rates and Credits

After the amount of taxable gifts is determined, gift tax is calculated in much the same manner and at the same rates as the estate tax. IRC §2502(a). Like the computation of estate taxes, calculating the gift tax liability requires combining (also known as "grossing up") the donor's current year taxable gifts with those made after 1976. IRC §2502(a)(1). Any gift taxes paid in previous years reduce the tax liability calculated for the current year. IRC §2502(a)(2).

Next, any remaining tax liability is reduced by the unified tax credit, which is equal to the tax that would be imposed on $5.0 million of taxable gifts, adjusted in $10,000 increments in the future based on the cost of living. Therefore, if the total of gifts made during a donor's lifetime does not exceed $5.0 million, no gift tax is due.[67] IRC §2505. The $5.0 million unified tax credit is increased by any unused exclusion amount attributable to the individual's spouse for which an election was made by the executor on a timely filed estate tax return. IRC §2010(c)(4)-(5). In addition, gift splitting is possible if husband and wife elect.

When the annual exclusion and the medical/tuition exclusion are combined with the unified tax credit, an individual can pass a large amount of wealth to her descendants without having to pay a penny of gift tax.

---

66. In addition, there may be an income tax deduction available equal to the value of the interest given and, to the extent the property appreciated, gains will not be taxed.

67. To the extent there were taxable gifts, whether taxed or not because of the unified credit, they reduce the amount of the transfers at death that are tax free. For example, if T gave $500,000 in excess of the $13,000 annual exclusion to donors other than her husband during her life, T could only give $4.5 million tax-free at death.

Example: Mike and Brittany have two children, two children-in-law, and 6 grandchildren, for a total of 10 potential donees. At $13,000 per year to each of the 10 donees, Mike and Brittany could each give away $130,000 per year ($260,000 combined) gift tax-free. Since gifts within the annual exclusion and for tuition and medical expenses do not count against the lifetime unified credit, each can give another $5.0 million (either alone or via gift-splitting per IRC §2513) during their lives without paying any gift tax. Thus, if they fully used the planning ideas suggested, after 10 years they can remove over $12,600,000 ($260,000 per year for 10 years — $2.6 million — plus $10.0 million) from their combined estates without paying any taxes!

G. THE GENERATION-SKIPPING TRANSFER (GST) TAX — AN ASIDE

As stated earlier, the mechanics of the GST tax are too complicated for a chapter designed to introduce students to the basics of transfer taxation.[68] Nonetheless, it is worth understanding the purpose and basic mechanics of the GST tax. The purpose of the tax is to ensure that persons do not avoid gift and estate taxes at each generation by passing property to family members in lower generations. GST concerns arise when a person makes a gratuitous transfer, either during life or at death, which skips a generation of the person's family. Credits similar to those available under the gift and estate tax regimes are available to offset GST tax liability, including the $5.0 million lifetime exemption.

H. POST-MORTEM PLANNING USING DISCLAIMERS

It is obvious that most estate planning is done while the client is alive. However, sometimes the decedent did not engage in estate planning or the law changed since the planning was done or the planning was done incorrectly, in which case some after-the-fact planning may be needed. The principal way to engage in post-mortem tax planning is through the use of disclaimers. IRC §§2518 and 2046. With disclaimers, the survivors may be able to rearrange who gets what without additional transfer taxes. This is because the disclaimant is treated as never becoming the owner of the

---

68. *See* Mark E. Powell, *The Generation Skipping Transfer Tax: A Quick Guide*, J. Accountancy, Oct. 2009, at 30.

property to which she is entitled by the will, intestacy or will substitute. After a disclaimer, when the property passes to a different person, it is as if it went from the decedent directly to that person and not from the decedent to the beneficiary to the third person.

> **Example:** Charlotte, a 90-year old widow, leaves her entire estate to her children, per stirpes. Her children and grandchildren are independently wealthy and do not need the inheritance. If her children were to accept the inheritance, Charlotte will have failed to take advantage of her GST lifetime exemption of $5.0 million and the children will be taxed when they transfer the property to their descendants, Charlotte's grandchildren and great-grandchildren. If, on the other hand, the children and the grandchildren disclaim $5.0 million, Charlotte's personal representative could elect to allocate her $5.0 million GST exemption and the property will pass to the great-grandchildren with no tax to anyone.

Disclaimers are an excellent tool to use to take advantage of tax exemptions, deductions and credits, although their importance has diminished with the portability of the decedent spouse's unused unified credit to the surviving spouse.

> **Example:** Rafael is married to Consuela. Rafael's will leaves all of his property, totaling $8.0 million, to a trust. The terms of the trust give the trustee discretion to sprinkle income among Consuela and their children. On Consuela's death, the trust terminates and the principal is to be distributed to the children by representation. Because Consuela's interest is terminable, it does not qualify for the marital deduction unless a QTIP election is made. However, because the QTIP rules require that a surviving spouse be the sole income beneficiary and sole permissible distributee, a QTIP election is not possible under the present terms of the trust. The estate wishes to qualify $3.0 million of the trust for the marital deduction, leaving the other $5.0 million to be eligible for the unified credit. If the children disclaim their right to income from three-eighths of the trust, the trust will leave Consuela as the sole income beneficiary of $3.0 million and thus qualify that portion of the trust for QTIP treatment.

The procedural requirements are complex for an effective disclaimer. They sometimes differ between state law (UPC §2-1101 *et seq.*) and IRC §2518. For tax purposes, the following requirements must be met to make a disclaimer qualify under the Internal Revenue Code:

- The disclaimer must be filed within nine months of the decedent's death;

- The disclaimed interest must pass without direction of the disclaim-ant;
- The disclaimant may not have received any benefits from property disclaimed nor received consideration in money or money's worth, directly or indirectly, from anyone in exchange for the disclaimer.

As a deemed predeceasing person who never took control of the interest, the disclaimant may not direct who will receive the disclaimed interest. Probate property passes by the terms of the will of the decedent or by operation of law. If there is no will, then the interest passes by intestate succession. If there is a will, it passes to the specified alternative taker, if one is named. If there is no alternative taker in it, then the interest passes either as a lapsed gift or into the residuary. Property held in will substitutes may be disclaimed, and the will substitute will direct the succession of interests.

NOTES

1.   Disclaimers are used for non-tax reasons also, such as for asset protection. For example, if a beneficiary has a lot of debt, he might disclaim his inheritance, with the property passing to his children rather than to him and then to his creditors. A disclaimer might also be used if the decedent's child is in the process of a nasty divorce and the child does not want to put the inheritance at risk of going to her spouse. A disclaimer is effective to defeat creditors' rights and is not treated as a fraudulent conveyance because the disclaimant is treated as being dead so that her interest is deemed never to have arisen. *Matter of Colacci's Estate*, 549 P.2d 1096, 37 Colo. App. 369 (App.1976).

2.   A contrary result occurs when federal tax obligations are involved. *Drye v. United States*, 528 U.S. 49 (1999) (cannot avoid tax lien by disclaimer).

3.   The effect of a disclaimer on government services is mixed. The majority view is exemplified by *Tannler v. Wisc. Dept. of Health & Soc. Serv.*, 564 N.W.2d 735 (Wis. 1997) (the disclaimed assets are counted toward the eligibility requirements for Medicaid benefits); the minority view by *Estate of Kirk*, 564 N.W.2d 735 (Iowa 1999) (disclaimer was allowed to defeat government from collecting Medicaid claims).

PROBLEMS

1. With a couple of exceptions, Tomasita is the decedent in the problems below. She is survived by her spouse (Humberto), daughter

(Delia), son (Spencer), grandchild (Georgia) and sister (Sally). As to each of the following, answer:

- Is the asset probate property or nonprobate property of the decedent? [This is for review of material covered in Chapter 4, and to contrast the differences between the probate estate and the taxable estate].
- Is there a transfer subject to gift tax and, if so, in what amount?
- At death, is there a transfer subject to estate tax and, if so, in what amount?

    a.   At her death, Tomasita had an ownership interest in a $1.0 million house and other real and personal property. Tomasita died with a valid will leaving all her property to Humberto. Answer the questions assuming:

       i.   Tomasita owned the house and all the other property in fee simple.

      ii.   Tomasita owned the house and other property as a tenant in common with Sally.

    iii.   Tomasita owned the house and other property as community property with Humberto.

    iv.   Tomasita and Spencer owned the house and other property as joint tenants with right of survivorship. Many years ago, Tomasita bought the property with her own funds and subsequently titled it in joint tenancy with Spencer.

    b.   At her death, Tomasita had an ownership interest in a checking account and an investment account in her name alone. Tomasita died without a will. Answer the questions assuming:

       i.   Tomasita owned accounts in fee simple.

      ii.   Tomasita owned the accounts in her name and Spencer's name jointly, with right of survivorship.

    iii.   Tomasita owned the accounts in her name alone, but there is a "pay-on-death" (POD) or a "transfer-on-death" (TOD) designation in favor of Spencer.

    c.   Ten years before her death, Tomasita gifted stock worth $100,000 to Spencer in fee simple. Tomasita died this year; the stock was worth $175,000 on her date of death.

    d.   Ten years before her death, Tomasita created an irrevocable trust to which she transferred $400,000 of stocks. She named Sally as the trustee and her cousin, Corinne, as the successor trustee on Sally's death. Tomasita is entitled to all the income from the trust for her life, paid monthly, and on her death the corpus is distributed to Spencer, if living. If Spencer does not survive Tomasita, the corpus is to be distributed to Georgia or her estate. Assume that at the time Tomasita funded the trust the actuarial value of Tomasita's interest is $250,000 and the remainder interest is $150,000. Answer the questions assuming:

i. Tomasita dies. At her death, the trust corpus is worth $1,000,000.

ii. Spencer was the first to die, survived by Tomasita, Sally, Delia, and Georgia. Would anything be included in his gross estate? What if Georgia had been the first to die?

iii. The income interest Tomasita reserved for herself was not for life but was for 15 years instead.

    (a) Advise Tomasita what the tax consequences will be if she dies in year 14.

    (b) Advise Tomasita what the tax consequences will be if she dies in year 20.

e. Ten years before her death, Tomasita created a revocable trust and transferred $400,000 of stocks and bonds to herself as trustee, with Sally specified as successor trustee upon her death or disability. Tomasita named herself the income beneficiary while she was alive. On her death, the trust terminates and the principal is to be distributed to Delia.

i. Tomasita dies. At her death, the trust corpus is worth $1,000,000.

ii. In each of the last five years, Tomasita invaded the trust and gave Georgia $20,000.

f. Tomasita owned a $1,000,000 whole life insurance policy on her own life. The primary beneficiary is Delia; the second beneficiary is Tomasita's estate. What happens on Tomasita's death?

i. What if Tomasita had transferred ownership of the policy to Spencer six years ago when its cash surrender value was $75,000.

2. For each of the following questions, determine the deduction or credit. Assume Tomasita's gross estate is $15.0 million. Is a deduction or credit available and, if so, in what amount?

a. Tomasita leaves everything to her surviving spouse, Humberto.

b. Tomasita leaves $5.0 million in trust, income to her children and, on the death of the last child, the remainder to her grandchildren, to be distributed per stirpes. The balance of the estate is left to Humberto, in fee simple.

c. Tomasita leaves the entire $15.0 million in trust, income payable quarterly to Humberto. On the death of Humberto, income is to be paid to her children and, on the death of the last child, the remainder is to be distributed to her grandchildren, by representation.The trust authorizes the trustee to invade corpus as needed for Humberto's comfort and support.

    i.   Does your answer change if the personal representative makes a QTIP election as to $10.0 million in the trust (QTIP Trust) but not as to the other $5.0 million?

    ii.   Assume the election is made as in the previous question. Humberto dies 12 years later. The value of the principal in the QTIP and Credit Shelter Trusts at Humberto's death is $12.0 million and $7.0 million, respectively. With respect to these trusts, what, if anything, is included in Humberto's estate?

EXERCISE

Harry and Winny Fortunata are in their late 40s and in good health. They have two children, one is in college and the other has recently graduated and entered the workforce, gotten married and started a family. Clients own a successful business, and its value has increased over the years. They own a home jointly; each has a retirement plan; an insurance policy on their life; stocks and bonds; and cash in a checking account. While their combined net wealth is presently about $3.0 million, they have great hopes of becoming quite wealthy when their business hits it big. They would like to do some estate planning at this time but not get too sophisticated. The Fortunatas cannot afford to give away (or tie up) a lot of their property at this time because they feel they still need it for their own support. They are not opposed to using trusts if you recommend them but do not want to go overboard with them.

    Write Clients a one- to two-page letter recommending four or five things for them to consider that you think fits their situation that might save taxes now or in the future. Make sure you explain what each planning idea is, how it works and why it might be right for them. You should not just copy the ideas mentioned above but should instead tailor the advice to their family situation and stated goals.

15 ADMINISTRATION OF THE PROBATE ESTATE

A. INTRODUCTION

1. General

Having explored the substantive law associated with estate planning during life, the book now turns to the procedural aspects of administering the estate of a decedent.

The probate process is a useful tool for transferring ownership of the decedent's probate property free of the claims of the decedent's creditors or other potential beneficiaries. However, the decedent's successors sometimes skip probate and simply divide the property among themselves when there is little or no property and where title to the property either is not the kind that involves a change in its registration, such as would be true for household items, or can be changed by methods other than through probate, such as registration of motor vehicles.

Probate procedures are state-specific; no two states are exactly the same.[1] The law of the states is built upon their own statutes, common law and court rules. Nevertheless, there are some common themes and, as we have throughout the book, we will use the Uniform Probate Code (UPC) as a basis for exploring those themes. We also present alternative approaches when states depart significantly from these rules.

---

1. In Appendix A, we have included an exhaustive checklist of matters that the attorney for the personal representative must consider doing when administering an estate. While specific to Pennsylvania, much of what is included pertains to all states.

While simplified in recent years, there are many procedural rules and they require strict adherence. Compliance with the law of the state where probate is being administered is critical to pass good title to the beneficiaries. Many lawyers assume that estate administration is a fairly straightforward process that they can learn as they go. However, lawyers who are not experienced with administering a probate estate can easily find themselves subject to disciplinary action by the state bar association, as the following case illustrates.

Lewis v. State Bar of California
621 P.2d 258 (CA. 1981)

This is a proceeding to review a recommendation of the Disciplinary Board of the State Bar (Disciplinary Board) that petitioner [Rider Reynolds Lewis] be suspended from the practice of law for a period of thirty days, but that such suspension be stayed and petitioner placed on probation for a period of one year.

Petitioner was admitted to the practice of law in California in June of 1972 and has no prior disciplinary record. He was a solo practitioner at all times relevant to this inquiry. He is charged with violating his oath and duties as an attorney in that he (1) negligently and improperly conducted the administration of an estate without any previous probate experience and without associating or consulting a sufficiently experienced attorney (Rules Prof. Conduct, rule 6-101);[2] (2) obtained a loan from a client without appropriate disclosure and without the client's written consent (rule 5-101);[3] and (3) failed to maintain complete and accurate records of funds belonging to a client (rule 8-101(B)(3)).[4]

---

2. [FN 1] Rule 6-101 became effective on January 1, 1975, and provides as follows:

A member of the State Bar shall not willfully or habitually

(1) Perform legal services for a client or clients if he knows or reasonably should know that he does not possess the learning and skill ordinarily possessed by lawyers in good standing who perform, but do not specialize in, similar services practicing in the same or similar locality and under similar circumstances unless he associates or, where appropriate, professionally consults another lawyer who he reasonably believes does possess the requisite learning and skill . . .

3. [FN 2] Rule 5-101 provides as follows:

A member of the State Bar shall not enter into a business transaction with a client or knowingly acquire an ownership, possessory, security or other pecuniary interest adverse to a client unless (1) the transaction and terms in which the member of the State Bar acquires the interest are fair and reasonable to the client and are fully disclosed and transmitted in writing to the client in manner and terms which should have reasonably been understood by the client, (2) the client is given a reasonable opportunity to seek the advice of independent counsel of the client's choice on the transaction, and (3) the client consents in writing thereto.

4. [FN 3] Rule 8-101(B) provides in relevant part: A member of the State Bar shall:

The facts of this matter are not in dispute. In November of 1973, petitioner was retained by Edward Vacha, an inmate at the state prison in Chino, to handle the administration of Vacha's deceased wife's estate. The estate was valued at approximately $100,000 and consisted primarily of some securities and a note secured by a deed of trust. Shortly thereafter, petitioner also agreed to make some contacts aimed at securing Vacha's release on parole.

In January of 1974, petitioner had himself appointed as administrator of the estate of Joan Cullinane Vacha. Having no previous experience in probate matters, he selected Thomas Middleton, an attorney familiar with probate practice, to serve as the attorney for the estate. Middleton prepared the petition to the probate court requesting petitioner's appointment as administrator. He also caused to be published the required notice to creditors of the estate. Thereafter, however, petitioner did not consult Middleton, who rendered no further services to the estate.

Over the following six months, petitioner made various contacts which resulted in a parole hearing for Vacha in July of 1974. At that hearing, it was determined that Vacha should be released on parole in October. Petitioner and Vacha then met at Chino to discuss petitioner's fee for securing Vacha's release. Petitioner requested and Vacha agreed to a fee of $20,000. Vacha informed petitioner that he did not have sufficient funds to pay the fee, but that petitioner could withdraw the $20,000 from the estate proceeds since Vacha was the sole heir.

In September, petitioner, as administrator of Joan Vacha's estate, obtained an order from the probate court authorizing the sale of certain securities belonging to the estate having an approximate value of $38,000. Although the petition to the probate court did not so state, one of petitioner's purposes in selling the securities was to obtain sufficient funds with which to pay himself the $20,000 fee which had been agreed upon. Following the sale, petitioner did not place the proceeds in an interest-bearing account or any account bearing the name of the estate or himself as the administrator of the estate. Instead, he deposited the entire amount in his clients' trust fund checking account. Over the next two months, he disbursed to himself a total of $20,000 from the account in satisfaction of the fee previously agreed to by Vacha. He also disbursed approximately $14,000 to Vacha over a seven-month period for a variety of living expenses and a new automobile. At no time did petitioner seek probate court approval for any of these disbursements.

In November of 1974, Vacha orally authorized petitioner to borrow up to $10,000 from the estate proceeds at 10 percent interest. That same month, petitioner actually borrowed $4,000 from the estate proceeds. Petitioner did not borrow the previously discussed amount of $10,000 because the estate

---

. . . (3) Maintain complete records of all funds, securities, and other properties of a client coming into the possession of the member of the State Bar and render appropriate accounts to his client regarding them. . . .

proceeds left in the client's trust account were insufficient. The loan was unsecured. Vacha never gave written consent for the loan, nor did petitioner encourage Vacha to seek independent counsel on the matter. A promissory note evidencing the debt was not executed by petitioner until approximately one month after the $4,000 was withdrawn. Petitioner kept the note in the estate files in his possession rather than delivering it to Vacha.

Petitioner also failed to keep an accurate record of the estate proceeds which he was holding in his client's trust fund account. As a result, in April of 1975, petitioner issued a $500 check to Vacha for living expenses which the bank refused to honor due to insufficient funds in the account.

In August of 1975, Vacha sought and received a probate court order removing petitioner as the administrator of Joan Vacha's estate. It was then discovered that during the 18-month period during which petitioner served as administrator of the estate, he had failed to prepare an inventory of the estate's assets and in addition failed to file any of the required state or federal income, estate, or inheritance tax returns. In fact, petitioner performed no services for the estate after he obtained the probate court approval for the sale of the estate's securities.

The Disciplinary Board hearing panel found that petitioner's performance in administering the estate of Joan Vacha constituted a violation of rule 6-101 in that, knowing that he did not possess sufficient skill in probate matters, he failed to associate or consult another lawyer who did possess the requisite learning and skill, and that he willfully failed and refused to perform all of the services for which he was retained. The panel further concluded that the manner in which petitioner obtained a personal loan from the estate violated rule 5-101 and that his failure to keep accurate account of the estate proceeds violated rule 8-101(B)(3).

The sole issue presented by this petition is the propriety of the discipline recommended by respondent State Bar. . . .

This court has long recognized the problems inherent in using disciplinary proceedings to punish attorneys for negligence, mistakes in judgment, or lack of experience or legal knowledge. . . .

There is no showing in the instant case that any of petitioner's actions were motivated by bad faith or a desire to benefit himself at the expense of his client.[5] Nearly all of his problems appear to be a direct or indirect result of his complete lack of familiarity with probate law.

Based on petitioner's demonstrated good faith as well as the fact that rule 6-101 only became effective some 13 months after he was retained to handle the probate of the estate, this court adopts the Disciplinary Board's recommendation that petitioner be suspended for thirty days, but that such suspension be stayed and petitioner placed on probation for one year under the terms and conditions as specified by the State Bar.

---

5. [FN 13] Each of the other rule violations with which petitioner is charged (rule 5-101; rule 8-101(B)(3)) appears to have been a technical violation of the disciplinary rules which resulted in no permanent loss to client Vacha or his wife's estate. . . .

BIRD, Chief Justice, concurring.

I fully concur with the court's opinion in this case. I only wish to note some additional concerns which I have regarding rule 6-101 of the Rules of Professional Conduct.

Rule 6-101 seems to provide for the discipline of careless, negligent, or incompetent attorneys. Its interpretation, however, has never been an issue before this court since the rule's enactment in 1975. As a result, the applicability of the rule to specific fact situations is far from clear.

The burden of this rule unfortunately appears to fall disproportionately on younger members of the legal profession who begin their careers as solo practitioners. It is they who are most likely to lack "the learning and skill ordinarily possessed by lawyers . . . who perform . . . similar services. . . ," yet be unable to easily "associate" or "professionally consult" another lawyer possessing the requisite learning and skill. It has been suggested that rule 6-101 may implicitly mandate an apprenticeship system for beginning lawyers.

Despite recent trends in legal education, graduates of law schools in this state or in other parts of the country are seldom prepared to begin the practice of law on their own. Law schools have traditionally emphasized training in legal reasoning as opposed to legal practice: "how to think" rather than "how to do." While this may be a necessary predicate to the practice of law, it places increasingly severe burdens on law school graduates who are unable to secure employment with large law firms or government agencies where they have access to advice from experienced colleagues. . . .

In the instant case, it seems clear that petitioner was aware that he lacked the requisite skill and training to handle the probate of the estate since he initially consulted an experienced probate attorney. It is therefore unnecessary for this court to address the issue as to whether or not rule 6-101 would apply if it had only been shown that petitioner "should have known" he was not competent to handle the case. It is my hope that before a case raising that issue comes before this court, the State Bar will consider an appropriate clarification of the rule.

PROBLEM

How do you think the *Lewis* case would be decided today using the Model Rules of Professional Conduct? Look specifically at Rules 1.1, 1.8 and 1.15 and the comments to them. What would you have done differently if you were Mr. Lewis? We return to issues of professional responsibility in estate administration in Section M below.

EXERCISE

All courts have standardized forms that need to be completed for some of the steps in the probate process. Locate the Web site of the court that has jurisdiction over probate in the state and county in which you plan to practice. Find the link that has the standardized probate forms. The exercises throughout the chapter will build on a set of facts for which you will be asked to complete the forms required by the court. If your jurisdiction does not have the forms posted online, use those of Denver, Colorado, http://www.denverprobatecourt.org/forms.htm or California, http://www.courtinfo.ca.gov/cgi-bin/forms.cgi.

In this chapter, we first provide a brief history and overview of the probate process, its purpose and how it functions via an excerpt from *American Probate: Protecting the Public, Improving the Process* by Professor Paula Monopoli. We continue by examining the probate process from a chronological perspective. We complete the chapter by reflecting on professional responsibility issues.

As we noted above, the particular procedures required in your state to probate a will and administer an estate may be very different from that in another state, and such procedures can even vary from county to county within a state. In addition, the treatment of same-sex partners varies widely from state to state. Same-sex partners are generally considered legal strangers unless they are spouses under state law or live in a state that extends spousal benefits. Thus, whether a same-sex partner is entitled to priority for appointment as a personal representative or guardian, who may make decisions about burials and donating organs or is entitled to maintenance and other benefits, is state-specific.[6]

There are some general principles that have evolved over the years that govern the process. These include a general duty on the part of the personal representative to gather the assets, account for and protect them, distribute them as provided in the will after paying expenses due to the government, attorneys for the estate and creditors and then account to the court. In order to accomplish all these steps, the personal representative must be given fairly broad power by the probate court. As you read the following excerpt, pay attention to the functions of the personal representative and how he obtains his authority through the "letters" or papers he is granted by the probate court.

---

6. For example, while same-sex marriages and civil unions are not allowed in Colorado, the state created "designated beneficiary agreements," which allow an individual to designate who they wish to serve in these roles and to inherit. CoLo. Rev. Stat. §15-22-101 *et seq.*

Paula Monopoli, American Probate: Protecting
The Public, Improving The Process
(2003)

The term *probate* is derived from the Latin *probare*, which means to show or demonstrate. Its canon law connection dates back to [the ecclesiastical and king's common law courts of] feudal England. . . .

The American colonies, later states, each developed their own methods of probating estates. . . . Twenty-one states and the District of Columbia have a formal probate court or division. Some of these states use the term "probate" to designate the court that handles these cases, while states like New Jersey and New York use the term "surrogate.". . .

A majority of states "have no formal probate court structure." For example, Arizona is one of thirty states where courts of general jurisdiction may have a probate department set up by local rule. Whether there is a separate court or not, there is wide variation in the jurisdiction of courts that handle matters loosely labeled "probate." The essential cases in a probate court's jurisdiction are wills, testamentary trusts, and decedents' estates. . . .

The probate process is intended to perform several useful functions. An executor is supposed to (1) collect or "marshal" all the decedent's assets and detail them on a list or "inventory"; (2) manage those assets during the several months or years it might take to administer the estate; (3) pay all those to whom the decedent owed debts, including hospital, doctor, and funeral bills and state and federal tax authorities; and (4) distribute what remains in the estate to the persons named in the will.

These important functions are performed by a "personal representative," either an "executor" [one appointed in the decedent's will] or "administrator" [one appointed by the court, normally with respect to the estate of an intestate decedent]. . . . Most probate courts oblige the decedent by making the person the decedent nominates the executor, but the court is not bound to do this. If someone objects, or if the court has misgivings about the nominee's ability to perform as a fiduciary, the court can name someone else. However, they rarely do.

. . . In the event of intestacy, the probate court names an "administrator" rather than an "executor," usually a spouse, child or relative of the decedent. If there are no such relatives, then a lawyer or other court appointee will serve in this role. All fiduciaries must answer to the probate court, and judicial oversight is one of the major benefits the probate process offers. . . .

The personal representative must inventory and transfer the decedent's assets to a "common pot." There are rules governing the transfer of a decedent's real property, securities, bank accounts, and other assets. Banks, brokerage houses, and county Registrars of deeds must be contacted to have the title to these assets transferred. The personal representative must present to the institution proof as to the rightful owner of the property. Someone must arrange for a new title to be prepared. This is a time-consuming process and, while it is not legally complicated, it is essential to creating clear title for the property's new owners.

Next, the estate is required to provide creditors with notice of the debtor's death unless the death was more than a year earlier. The personal representative must publish notices in the newspaper and send specific notices to known creditors of the decedent. Again, this requires time and effort. The court requires proof that notice to creditors has been given, which may require appearing in court.

Paying taxes is another important step in the probate process, and the rules of the estate tax, like all tax rules, are remarkably complex. Laypeople, and many lawyers, are unable to complete a federal estate tax return. They must hire an accountant. The federal estate tax form, Form 706, is complicated, and may require the preparer to secure a number of documents, including forms from insurance companies and, most time-consuming, a costly set of asset appraisals for real property, jewelry, artwork, and any stock in closely held corporations. Experts for each asset must be contacted, given the necessary information, and paid for their expertise.[7]

When the money remaining in an estate is to be distributed, the probate system has rules to determine who is entitled to it. The personal representative must be acquainted with the rules that determine who is an heir and what happens if a beneficiary is dead. The personal representative often must search for heirs. This too may require the assistance of an expert and costs money. When the heirs or beneficiaries are paid, the personal representative must get receipts and releases.

Finally, in some jurisdictions, the personal representative must file an accounting, detailing the assets she received at the beginning of the process, all the money spent for creditors, tax authorities, and, finally, heirs and beneficiaries. This accounting is a time-consuming process, but it is necessary for the fiduciary to be released from liability at the end of the probate process. Each of these activities is more difficult if the heirs or beneficiaries are minors and cannot consent to financial decisions. If minors or unborn beneficiaries may benefit from a trust or estate, a guardian ad litem court-appointed attorney to review the accounts and consent on behalf of the minor) may be required. The personal representative of an estate must be familiar with the rules governing the form of the account and the peculiarities of local court procedure. . . .

The underlying philosophy of the UPC [is] that the state should act in probate matters only when called upon by the parties. While it does provide an alternative for a supervised process, the UPC assumes that most estates

---

7. [In addition to the estate tax return, which lists the property included in the gross estate and gives rise to the estate tax, the personal representative is required to file income tax returns for the estate on income earned by assets in the estate and for any other income earned during administration of the estate. This is accomplished on Form 1041 — U.S. Income Tax Return for Estates and Trusts — EDS.]

will not require a supervised process. The drafters have moved away from court intervention to the realm of unsupervised probate. The theory of unsupervised probate is that "unless there is a compelling reason, once an executor or trustee is appointed, the court should step back and let the fiduciary administer the estate and close it without court intervention." Academics, some judges, and many lawyers have moved toward this position in large part because of public complaints that probate involves excessive delay and cost. The movement toward unsupervised probate also reflects the growing importance of nonprobate assets and the desire to pull the probate process closer to the model for the transfer of nonprobate assets like joint property, living trusts, and life insurance.

This academic and legislative response to the real and perceived problems of probate is laudable, as it attempts to bring real world solutions to real people. While unsupervised probate responds to public concerns about expense and delay, for some people, and in some special circumstances, there well may be a need for increased supervision of the probate process. For example, the court should be given the discretion to inquire more closely and to order supervised administration where a lawyer both drafted the instrument in question and is named in it as executor or trustee. And there is an argument for mandatory supervised probate when the court appoints a lawyer unknown to the decedent.

Under the UPC, a court may approve a petition for supervised administration in three different circumstances: (1) if the will directs it, unless circumstances have changed and it is no longer necessary; (2) if the will directs unsupervised administration, but the court concludes that there is a real need to protect the beneficiaries; or (3) if the will is silent and "the Court finds that supervised administration is necessary under the circumstances." . . .

Supervised administration under the UPC does not mean that the personal representative must check with the court prior to every action. It does mean that the personal representative's letters of appointment [also called "letters testamentary"] must be endorsed, to indicate to third parties, like banks or brokerage houses, that the personal representative needs permission from the court to take actions like buying or selling securities. . . .

While the current probate system, with its option to proceed informally, is a far cry from the complex rules of the past, it is still built upon an adversarial model. So, even though much of what needs to be filed is purely administrative paperwork, the parties have the right to force formal court proceedings when they wish. Personal representatives are at special risk of having their actions brought into court after-the-fact by disgruntled beneficiaries, whether taken in good faith or not.

We begin our discussion of the probate process by looking at UPC §3-101, which introduces its scope.

UPC §3-101. Devolution of Estate at Death; Restrictions.

> The power of a person to leave property by will, and the rights of creditors, devisees, and heirs to his property are subject to the restrictions and limitations contained in this Code to facilitate the prompt settlement of estates. Upon the death of a person, his real and personal property devolves to the persons to whom it is devised by his last will . . . , or in the absence of testamentary disposition, to his heirs . . . subject to homestead allowance, exempt property and family allowance, to rights of creditors, elective share of the surviving spouse, and to administration.

2.   Nonprobate Property Is Outside the Process

Before we launch into a discussion of the procedures associated with probating a will, remember that the only property subject to administration is probate property; nonprobate property, by definition, does not go through this process. Therefore, property in trust, insurance proceeds, retirement plan investments, property owned in joint tenancy with right of survivorship, payable- or transfer-on-death property and the like normally pass via will substitutes and bypass estate administration. Unless the decedent's estate is the named beneficiary, ownership of these types of property transfer automatically to the designated beneficiary or co-owner once proof of death is provided.

As noted above, the family may wish to avoid probate if the estate is small. The probate estate may be small because most of the decedent's property passes via will substitutes. Sometimes, avoiding probate was a conscious decision and sometimes it was not. (Chapter 4 on Will Substitutes introduced the concept of nonprobate transfers, and you might consider reviewing it after you read this material.)

Most nonprobate assets require that the beneficiary notify the company, trustee or the government of the decedent's death and provide them with a death certificate.[8] In addition to notification, the company, trustee or government entity may require the completion of certain of their forms.

---

8. In *Irwin v. Irwin*, 307 S.W.3d 383 (Tex. App. 2009), the appellate court determined that an executor of an estate lacked standing to litigate issues regarding whether the payment of life insurance proceeds to the decedent's former wife was proper because of the language of the divorce decree; only the designated secondary beneficiaries have standing.

a. Responsibility of Nonprobate Property to Pay Claims of Creditors and Taxes

While nonprobate property is not subject to administration, nonprobate property may still be liable for the claims of creditors and taxes if the probate estate is insufficient to pay them. UPC §6-102. The comments to UPC §6-102 explain the liability for debts this way:

> [T]his section clarifies that the recipients of nonprobate transfers can be required to contribute to pay allowed claims and statutory allowances to the extent the probate estate is inadequate. The maximum liability for a single nonprobate transferee is the value of the transfer. Values are determined . . . as of the time when the benefits are "received or controlled by the transferee." This would be the date of the decedent's death for nonprobate transfers made by means of a revocable trust, and date of receipt for other nonprobate transfers. [If a probate estate was not opened,] a creditor or other person seeking to use this Section 6-102 would first need to secure appointment of a personal representative to invoke Code procedures for establishing a creditor's claim as "allowed."

The General Comment to Part 9A of the Uniform Probate Code explains that the recipients of nonprobate property may be liable for taxes also:

> The Internal Revenue Code (IRC) places the primary responsibility for paying federal estate taxes on the decedent's executor and empowers, but does not direct, the executor to collect from recipients of certain nonprobate transfers included in the taxable estate a prorated portion of the estate tax attributable to those types of property. In the absence of specific contrary directions of the decedent, the IRC generally provides as to other transfers that taxes are to be borne by the persons who would bear that cost if the taxes were paid by the executor prior to distributing the estate. The determination of who should bear the ultimate burden of the estate taxes is left to the decedent's will or, if nothing is expressed therein, to the state [apportionment] law.
>
> If a state does not have a statutory apportionment law, the burden of the estate taxes generally will fall on residuary beneficiaries of the probate estate. This means that recipients of many types of nonprobate assets (such as beneficiaries of revocable trusts and surviving joint tenants) may be exonerated from paying a portion of the tax. Also, it generates a risk that residual gifts to the spouse or a charity may result in a smaller deduction and a larger tax. A number of states have adopted legislation apportioning the burden of estate taxes among the beneficiaries. . . .
>
> Under the statutory scheme, marital and charitable beneficiaries generally are insulated from bearing any of the estate tax, while all other beneficiaries bear the burden proportionate to the value of the property included in the gross estate.

It is important to note, however, that these rules do not supersede existing state legislation protecting certain nonprobate transfers from claims by creditors, such as a survivorship interest in joint tenancy real estate, death benefits in life insurance, retirement plans or IRAs. *See, e.g.,* Colo. Rev. Stat. §15-15-103.

B. MATTERS THAT NEED IMMEDIATE ATTENTION

1. The Decedent Has Just Died—Appointing Someone to Take Charge

Needless to say, when a loved one dies, one of the last things family members are thinking about is "taking care of business." The survivors are often in a state of emotional shock and not sure what to do. That said, there are some decisions that must be made very quickly, even before a probate estate is opened and a permanent personal representative is appointed. Someone has to take charge of funeral arrangements, protect the decedent's property, get a guardian appointed for a minor, and attend to a variety of other matters immediately. Often this is a family member, a friend, the family's lawyer or a newly engaged lawyer. Great compassion and understanding is called for at this time.

All states provide a summary procedure for appointing someone to act at this critical time. The executor named in the will generally may request appointment as the "special administrator" even before being appointed as the estate's personal representative.[9] If the executor is not available or qualified, any interested person may seek appointment. This can be accomplished informally by an *ex parte* application or by order of the court in a formal proceeding on petition of an interested person. UPC §§3-614 to 3-616. Once appointed and until the appointment of the permanent personal representative, the special administrator is authorized to act in the best interests of the estate and is cloaked with the powers of and assumes the duties associated with being a fiduciary. UPC §3-616.

2. What to Do with Decedent's Body

While most of trust and estate law focuses on disposition of the decedent's property, the family must also be concerned with disposing of the

---

9. Because appointment as the personal representative may be accomplished in a summary manner by filing an application with the Registrar, it is possible the personal representative will be appointed quickly so as to moot the need for the appointment of a special administrator.

decedent's body. There are often highly contentious fights between family members over what to do with the decedent's remains. *See, e.g.,* Frances H. Foster, *Individualized Justice in Disputes Over Dead Bodies,* 61 VAND. L. REV. 1351 (2008); Tanya K. Hernandez, *The Property of Death,* 60 U. PITT. L. REV. 971 (1999). Issues involve whether any part of the decedent's body will be donated, as well as how, where and sometimes whether the decedent will be buried or cremated.[10]

a. Anatomical Gifts

Assuming there is no autopsy or coroner's inquest, one of the first things that needs to be determined is whether the individual gifted all or some of his body parts to a research or education facility, such as a hospital or university, an eye or tissue bank or to an individual for transplantation. Most states have adopted, or are in the process of adopting, a version of the Uniform Anatomical Gift Act (UAGA). Other states have their own law on the subject.

Under §5 of the UAGA, a donor may make an anatomical gift by authorizing a statement or symbol to that effect to be imprinted on her driver's license or identification card, in her will or in some other manner that clearly indicates the donor's wishes, such as on a donor card. A gift of body parts may be revoked by the donor. UAGA §6. However, the cancellation of the donor's driver's license or invalidation of the will does not result in revocation. If the decedent left no instructions concerning the disposal of body organs, the UAGA gives the decedent's agent or specified family members the right to decide whether or not to donate some or all of the decedent's body. UAGA §9.

b. Funeral, Burial or Cremation

An individual has the right to direct her funeral, burial or cremation either by a signed instrument or by prearrangement with a funeral service. She may use her will or another document to specify the precise mode of dealing with the body. Relatives, however, may have different ideas. Indeed, "[f]amily disputes over bodily remains are common. Some of these disputes are highly publicized because of the deceased's identity. The families of Kirby Puckett, Ted Williams, Anna Nicole Smith, James Brown, Gram Parsons, and the Reverend Billy Graham have all had very bitter and very public disputes." Ann M. Murphy, *Please Don't Bury Me Down in That Cold Cold Ground: The Need for Uniform Laws on the Disposition of Human Remains,* 15 ELDER L.J. 381, 408 (2007). *See generally* Tanya Hernandez, *The*

---

10. *See* http://www.alcor.org/Library/html/pr2010-03-01.html for an interesting situation involving cryonics.

Property of Death, 60 U. Pitt. L. Rev. 971 (1999); Frances H. Foster, *Individualized Justice in Disputes Over Dead Bodies*, 61 Vand. L. Rev. 1351 (2008).

Approximately 15 states have statutes that specifically designate the individuals who are authorized to control the remains. In states that don't have such statutes, courts must decide who is entitled to determine what happens with the remains. "A survey of state cases reflects that in almost every jurisdiction, courts first look to the wishes, if any, of the deceased. If the deceased has left no clear instructions, the courts generally next look to the surviving spouse, and then to the next of kin." Murphy, *supra*, at 401.

3.   Protecting the Decedent's Property

Later in this chapter, we will discuss managing and distributing the decedent's property. However, immediately upon the decedent's death, some action may be needed to preserve the property, such as getting or maintaining insurance on it,[11] taking care of pets and livestock, disposing of perishable goods, cultivating and harvesting crops and managing an ongoing business or completing pending transactions.

For personal property in the decedent's home, the personal representative or the special administrator should gain access to the home as quickly as possible. Once that is done, the personal representative or special administrator should inventory the items and store the valuable property in a safe location, such as a storage unit,[12] and insure the contents. If valuable paintings need storage in a temperature controlled environment, this should be done. It is important to make sure family members and others do not enter the decedent's home and begin to take some of the property for their own benefit.

4.   Getting a Guardian and Conservator Appointed for Minors and Incapacitated Persons

On the death of the decedent, there may be individuals whose needs must be considered and for whom guardians and conservators need to be

---

11. The extent of the coverage of decedent's insurance may not be adequate to protect the property as the value of the property may have increased since the policy was purchased. In addition, some insurance companies either will refuse to continue coverage or decline to pay on claims made under a homeowner's policy if the house is no longer occupied by the owner. Likewise, automobile insurance may not cover drivers after the policy owner's death. Thus, it is critical to make sure there is coverage and in the needed amount.

12. Where the executor or special administrator deems it necessary, she may change the locks on the house or hire a guard.

appointed, such as for those who are minors, disabled or incapacitated. The decedent's will should be consulted as it is the usual place where decedents provide for the appointment of a guardian and conservator. If there is no such document, then judicial proceedings to determine guardianship and conservatorship will be needed. Except to the extent discussed in Chapter 13, such proceedings are beyond the scope of this book. *See* UPC §5-101 *et seq.*

5. *Providing for the Family Financially While the Estate Gets Administered*

The administration of a probate estate can take a long time, especially if there are formal proceedings and litigation over the validity of the will or disputes about the claims of creditors or beneficiaries. During this time, the decedent's family members may need money from the estate to pay their expenses of living, especially if the decedent was the principal income earner and the survivors were financially dependent on the decedent. They also may need to be assured that they can remain in the family home.

States generally allow the surviving spouse (or domestic partner) and dependent children a family allowance, designed to maintain the family during the period of probate administration. States may impose conditions on the availability of the family allowance. For example, Texas requires that a court examine the adequacy of a spouse's separate property (and property received through nonprobate transfers) for maintenance before allowing a family allowance and determining the appropriate amount. *Est. of Wolfe*, 268 S.W.3d 780 (Tex. App. 2008).

Dependent children are entitled to a family allowance in their own right; not through the surviving parent. Therefore, regardless whether the spouse survives or qualifies for the allowance, dependent children may do so. *Est. of Houston*, 270 P. 939, 942 (CA. 1928).

The UPC grant of a family allowance is stated as follows:

UPC §2-404. Family Allowance.

(a) In addition to the right to homestead allowance and exempt property, the decedent's surviving spouse and minor children whom the decedent was obligated to support and children who were in fact being supported by the decedent are entitled to a reasonable allowance in money out of the estate for their maintenance during the period of administration, which allowance may not continue for longer than one year if the estate is inadequate to discharge allowed claims. The allowance may be paid as a lump sum or in periodic installments. It is payable to the surviving spouse, if living, for the use of the surviving spouse and minor and dependent children; otherwise to the children, or persons having their care and custody.... The family allowance is exempt from and has priority over all claims except the homestead allowance.[13]

(b) The family allowance is not chargeable against any benefit or share passing to the surviving spouse or children by the will of the decedent, unless otherwise provided, by intestate succession or by way of elective share. The death of any person entitled to family allowance terminates the right to allowances not yet paid.

The Comment to UPC §2-404 explains how a reasonable allowance should be calculated:

In determining the amount of the family allowance, account should be taken of both the previous standard of living and the nature of other resources available to the family to meet current living expenses until the estate can be administered and assets distributed. While the death of the principal income producer may necessitate some change in the standard of living, there must also be a period of adjustment. If the surviving spouse has a substantial income, this may be taken into account. Whether life insurance proceeds payable in a lump sum or periodic installments were intended by the decedent to be used for the period of adjustment or to be conserved as capital may be considered. A living trust may provide the needed income without resorting to the probate estate.

How much is reasonable is determined on a case-by-case basis; however, the UPC says that the personal representative is only allowed to grant an allowance of up to $1,500 per month for 12 months ($18,000 for a year). In some states that have adopted the UPC, the amount of the allowance is different. Colorado, for example, permits an allowance of $2,000 per month or $24,000 for the year. COLO. REV. STAT. §15-11-404 and 405. If the surviving spouse and/or minor children want a larger allowance, they must petition the court and get a court order. Comment to UPC §2-404. Courts routinely grant allowances for larger amounts and for longer periods where the need is demonstrated.

In addition to the family allowance, some states allow the surviving spouse or the decedent's dependent children, or both, to occupy the decedent's principal residence for some period after the decedent's death. *See, e.g.,* OR. REV. STAT. §114.005 (one year).

---

13. In some states, the priority is different. For example, COLO. REV. STAT. §15-11-404(1) reads: "The family allowance is exempt from and has priority over all claims except claims for the costs and expenses of administration, and reasonable funeral and burial, interment, or cremation expenses . . . "

QUESTIONS

1. Why do you think the family allowance is initially limited to one year?

2. Surprisingly, when the UPC was amended in 2008 to include a cost of living adjustment for certain amounts elsewhere in the Code, UPC §2-404 was not among them. Why do you think the family allowance was treated differently?

3. The UPC provides that the family allowance is in addition to "any benefit or share passing to the surviving spouse or children by the will of the decedent, unless otherwise provided, by intestate succession or by way of elective share." This also means that the family allowance is available regardless of the decedent's testamentary intentions. Why do you think this is the case?

4. As you have learned, children receive very few protections from disinheritance. What protection does the UPC give them here? What rationale supports this different approach?

6. Obtaining the Will and Other Important Documents

Upon the decedent's death, it is critical for the personal representative to find any instructions that the decedent left with respect to disposing of his body and his property. Whoever has a copy of the decedent's will or other document that states the decedent's wishes should come forward as quickly as possible. This may be the drafting attorney, a family member or an agent. The UPC makes the responsibility mandatory; failure to do so may result in sanctions.

UPC §2-516. Duty of Custodian of Will; Liability.

> After the death of a testator and on request of an interested person, a person having custody of a will of the testator shall deliver it with reasonable promptness to a person able to secure its probate and if none is known, to an appropriate court. A person who willfully fails to deliver a will is liable to any person aggrieved for any damages that may be sustained by the failure. A person who willfully refuses or fails to deliver a will after being ordered by the court in a proceeding brought for the purpose of compelling delivery is subject to penalty for contempt of court.

Often, these types of documents are retained in a person's safe deposit box. If that is the case, co-signers on the box who have the key or specified family members and interested persons are allowed to gain access to the safe deposit box, so long as they are accompanied by an employee of the institution. Any documents removed must be duplicated and the copy placed back in the box. If a will is found, the original must be given to the personal representative named in the will or, if that is not possible, filed with the court having jurisdiction of the decedent's estate.

If the will is not in the safe deposit box or in the possession of the drafting attorney or family member, an exhaustive search is necessary. This may entail contacting agents, trustees, trust department of the decedent's bank and trusted friends, as well as looking in the decedent's desk at home and at work. It is also possible that the will was lodged with a court during the decedent's lifetime. UPC §2-515.

If the will is located, the original must be submitted with either the petition for formal probate (UPC §3-402) or the application for informal probate (UPC §3-301). Filing the will with the court (formal probate) or the Registrar (informal probate) is the first step in the probate proceedings.

If the original is not available, a copy (either authenticated or a photocopy) may suffice. In this situation, the personal representative should be able to open the estate and place the burden on a challenging party to show why the copy should not be admitted.

However, if neither the original nor a copy is available, there is a presumption that either the decedent never executed a written will or revoked it, in which case the decedent dies intestate. See Chapter 3. In such case, the applicant for "appointment of an administrator in intestacy shall state that after the exercise of reasonable diligence, the applicant is unaware of any unrevoked testamentary instrument. . . . " UPC §§3-301(a)(4), 3-304(b). To overcome the presumption, the proponents not only must prove that there was a will and that it was properly executed and witnessed but they must also prove that the testator did not intend to revoke the will. This is frequently accomplished with the oral evidence of someone who has seen and read the will or who had conversations with the decedent about these matters.

C. WHERE TO PROBATE THE ESTATE—JURISDICTION AND VENUE

Once the attorney has taken care of the matters needing immediate attention and has either located an unrevoked will or has concluded there is none, it is time to initiate probate proceedings. But where? In what state? In what court?

The estate of the decedent is administered pursuant to the laws of the state in which the decedent was domiciled at the time of death, regardless of whether the decedent died testate or intestate. If all of the decedent's property, real and personal, was located in the domiciliary state, the appropriate court in that state has jurisdiction to decide all matters associated with the estate, including the validity and interpretation of the will, if any, and all other matters of administration. For purposes of venue, probate must be filed in the county where the decedent was domiciled or resided at death.

Some states have special courts with exclusive jurisdiction to administer probate. These courts go by a variety of names, such as Probate Court, Chancery Court, Surrogate's Court or Orphans' Court. In other states, courts of general jurisdiction, such as superior or district courts, are granted probate jurisdiction. *See, e.g.,* Calif. Prob. Code §7050.

Ancillary Probate. If the decedent owned any real property outside of the state of last domicile that is subject to probate (*e.g.,* not held as joint tenancy with right of survivorship or in a trust), then a separate action must be filed in each situs state. UPC §3-201. Such proceedings are generally referred to as "ancillary probate." Other than the fact that such proceedings tend to be limited to specific parcels of property, ancillary probate is like "regular" probate. This means that in each such state, an estate needs to be opened by filing a will or getting intestacy adjudicated, creditors have to be notified, taxes have to be paid and after the property is distributed to the appropriate beneficiaries, the estate has to be closed. A personal representative has to be appointed who fulfills all the functions of the position and local counsel needs to be retained. This can add significant cost and time to the process.[14]

D. PROCEDURE TO PROBATE SMALL ESTATES BY AFFIDAVIT

The UPC and most states have a variety of methods available for administering probate estates. Alternative procedures exist to administer small estates by affidavit and larger estates by formal and informal means. We will present the procedures for small estates by affidavit in full here as they are unique and require limited continuing discussion. We will discuss the formal and informal procedures as each aspect of the probate process is addressed.

The UPC Article III, Part 12 (§3-1201 *et seq.*) provides a simplified alternative procedure for estates where the net value does not exceed $5,000. These estates can be administered either (1) under a special collection procedure by mere affidavit; or (2) in the normal formal or informal manner

---

14. It is to avoid ancillary probate that attorneys frequently advise clients who own real property in other jurisdictions to hold it in a manner that qualifies it as nonprobate property, such as in a joint tenancy or in a trust.

with the appointment of a personal representative (though with simplified procedures).

Rather than getting a personal representative appointed and letters of administration issued, interested parties frequently choose to have a small estate administered via the production of an affidavit from an individual who is a successor of the decedent, such as a spouse or child.[15] Employing the expedited collection-by-affidavit procedure, a successor of the decedent merely presents an affidavit (stating the facts specified in UPC §3-1201) to a person in possession of such property or debts due the decedent and makes a demand for its delivery and payment. If the person complies with the demand, he "is discharged and released to the same extent as if he dealt with a personal representative of the decedent." UPC §3-1202.

UPC §3-1201. Collection of Personal Property by Affidavit.[16]

(a) Thirty days after the death of a decedent, any person indebted to the decedent or having possession of tangible personal property or an instrument evidencing a debt, obligation, stock or chose in action belonging to the decedent shall make payment of the indebtedness or deliver the tangible personal property or an instrument evidencing a debt, obligation, stock or chose in action to a person claiming to be the successor of the decedent upon being presented an affidavit made by or on behalf of the successor stating that:

(1) the value of the entire [probate] estate, wherever located, less liens and encumbrances, does not exceed $5,000;

(2) 30 days have elapsed since the death of the decedent;

(3) no application or petition for the appointment of a personal representative is pending or has been granted in any jurisdiction; and

(4) the claiming successor is entitled to payment or delivery of the property.

Alternatively, a personal representative can be appointed. If so, that individual has relatively minimal duties. "Letters may be obtained quickly without notice or judicial involvement. Immediately, the personal representative is in a position to distribute to successors whose deeds or transfers will protect purchasers. This route accommodates the need for quick and inexpensive transfers of land of small value as well as other assets." General

---

15. According to UPC §1-201(39), a successor is defined as "persons, other than creditors, who are entitled to property of a decedent under his [or her] will or this Code."

16. The time frame and the amount of the estate will vary state by state. For example, in Colorado, this method may be employed after 10 days have elapsed since the death of the decedent and fair market value of the estate may not exceed $50,000. Colo. Rev. Stat. §15-12-1201.

Comment, UPC Article III, Part 12.

When a personal representative is appointed, certain small estates may be distributed to the beneficiaries immediately and closed by filing with the court a verified statement that affirms, among other things, that he has sent a closing statement to all distributees of the estate and to all creditors or other claimants of whom he is aware whose claims are neither paid nor barred and has furnished a full account in writing of his administration to the distributees whose interests are affected. UPC §3-1204. The same procedures apply if a personal representative is not appointed, except that nothing needs to be filed with the court to close the estate.

UPC §3-1203. Small Estates; Summary Administration Procedure.

If it appears from the inventory and appraisal that the value of the entire estate, less liens and encumbrances, does not exceed [the total of the] homestead allowance, exempt property, family allowance, costs and expenses of administration, reasonable funeral expenses, and reasonable and necessary medical and hospital expenses of the last illness of the decedent, the personal representative, without giving notice to creditors, may immediately disburse and distribute the estate to the persons entitled thereto and file a closing statement as provided in Section 3-1204.

E. FORMAL AND INFORMAL PROCEDURES TO PROBATE ESTATES — IN GENERAL

The General Comments to Article III of the UPC state: "The provisions of this Article describe the Flexible System of Administration of Decedents' Estates. Designed to be applicable to both intestate and testate estates and to provide persons interested in decedents' estates with as little or as much by way of procedural and adjudicative safeguards as may be suitable under varying circumstances, this system is the heart of the Uniform Probate Code."

Most estates are probated employing either the formal or informal procedures. Formal probate is the traditional model of probate and involves judicial oversight. In the past, this meant that every step of the probate process would require judicial approval and a hearing. For example, this would necessitate a hearing to name the personal representative and another hearing to determine the validity of the will, even if its validity was not contested. Then, judicial approval would be needed for each action of the personal representative and for closing the estate. At each step, attorney fees would be due and the process could become expensive and time-consuming.

Today, formal probate comes in two varieties — "supervised administration" and "formal proceedings." Supervised administration is similar to the traditional method presented above. As stated in UPC §3-501: "Supervised administration is a single in rem proceeding to secure complete administration and settlement of a decedent's estate under the continuing authority of the Court which extends until entry of an order approving distribution of the estate and discharging the personal representative or other order terminating the proceeding." We will not cover supervised administration in this chapter as interested parties rarely request it.

Formal proceedings (sometimes referred to as probate "in solemn form") involve court supervision also but on a much less continuous basis than supervised administration. Formal proceedings are those where an interested party seeks the court's involvement in selected aspects of the process.

Informal probate (sometimes referred to as probate "in common form") is a newer procedure that requires much less judicial involvement. It is the method used in the vast majority of probates today. The UPC creates a presumption of informal probate. Rather than having a hearing in court and getting a decision or order for each proposed action by the personal representative, the personal representative performs most functions without any involvement of the court or the Registrar, except upon opening and closing the estate. Interested parties may file a demand for notice of any order or filing pertaining to the decedent's estate with the court, which then imposes that duty on the personal representative. UPC §3-204. *See also* UPC §§3-306 and 3-310. It is left to anyone who wishes a judge to be involved on an issue that arises in the probate process to petition the court to request a formal proceeding. Informal probate enhances speed, reduces cost and increases efficiency because a personal representative does not have to wait for a hearing on an overcrowded docket, request permission to routinely pay attorneys' fees or continually take time off work for court appearances.

F. OPENING THE ESTATE — GETTING THE WILL ACCEPTED FOR PROBATE AND THE PERSONAL REPRESENTATIVE APPOINTED

1. General

The probate estate does not "open" or begin automatically upon the death of the decedent. A surviving spouse cannot find the will and just start distributing the decedent's property, even if doing so is consistent with the will's provisions.

An estate cannot be distributed until the will, if there is one, is declared to be the will of the decedent and a personal representative is appointed to assume legal responsibility for the estate and to perform a variety of required functions. This can be accomplished informally by filing the required paperwork directly with the Registrar *ex parte* or by instituting a formal testacy proceeding with the court. While getting the will probated (or intestacy adjudicated) and a personal representative appointed are technically two separate procedures, they are frequently handled together, especially in states with more modern probate procedures, such as in those states that have adopted the UPC. *See, e.g.,* UPC §§3-301, 3-402.

2. Probating the Will or Adjudicating Intestacy

Informal. If informal probate of a will is sought, the moving party must file the will with the Registrar along with the application no earlier than 120 hours after the decedent's death. Certain information must be verified by the applicant to be accurate and complete to the best of his knowledge and belief. UPC §3-301. The moving party must provide notice of his application to any person demanding it pursuant to UPC §3-204, and to any personal representative of the decedent whose appointment has not been terminated. The application or petition must state that after the exercise of reasonable diligence, the applicant is unaware of any unrevoked testamentary instrument relating to property in the domiciliary state, and identify the priority of the person whose appointment is sought and the names of any other persons having a prior or equal right to the appointment under UPC §3-203.

"The Registrar, upon making the findings required by Section 3-303 shall issue a written statement of informal probate if at least 120 hours have elapsed since the decedent's death. The Registrar's determination of informal probate is conclusive as to all persons until superseded by an order in a formal testacy proceeding." UPC §3-302. Among the findings the Registrar must make under UPC §3-303 is the validity of the will, if any. "A will which appears to have the required signatures and which contains an attestation clause showing that requirements of execution under Section 2-502, 2-503 or 2-506 have been met shall be probated without further proof. In other cases, the Registrar may assume execution if the will appears to have been properly executed, or he may accept a sworn statement or affidavit of any person having knowledge of the circumstances of execution, whether or not the person was a witness to the will." UPC §3-303(c).

An applicant who seeks to probate a will informally does not have to give *advance* notice of the application to anyone other than the appointed personal representative and anyone who has filed a request with the court that they be notified of all actions. If the will is accepted by the Registrar for probate, the applicant must provide written information of the probate to the heirs and devisees within 30 days *after* acceptance. Failure to do so does not affect the probate but is considered a breach of the duty owed to the beneficiaries. UPC §3-306. *Ex post facto* notice in this manner affords interested parties an opportunity to challenge the Registrar-approved will by filing a petition with the court for a formal proceeding. If no petition is filed, the Registrar's determination becomes final and conclusive.

Formal.   Petitions for formal probate of a will must be directed to the Court and contain statements similar to those required in an informal application. UPC §3-402. If the moving party seeks to have a will probated, the original of the will, including all codicils, should be filed with the application. The applicant must also state that he is unaware of any instrument revoking the will, and that the applicant believes that the instrument which is the subject of the application is the decedent's last will.

"A formal testacy proceeding is litigation to determine whether a decedent left a valid will." UPC §3-401. "The word 'testacy' is used to refer to the general status of a decedent in regard to wills. Thus, it embraces the possibility that he left no will, any question of which of several instruments is his valid will, and the possibility that he died intestate as to a part of his estate, and testate as to the balance." Comments to UPC §3-401. After all interested parties have been provided with notice and been afforded the right to a hearing, the court "shall determine the decedent's domicile at death, his heirs and his state of testacy [whether he died testate or intestate. The interested parties may contest the will on a variety of grounds, such as the capacity of the testator, whether the formalities were satisfied and whether there was undue influence, fraud or mistake.] Any will found to be valid and unrevoked shall be formally probated." UPC §3-409.

Petitions for adjudication of intestacy must be directed to the Court and request a judicial order. That is, a determination of intestacy and heirship can only be accomplished in a formal proceeding. UPC §§3-402 and 3-407 (burden of proof).

3. *Appointing the Personal Representative*

UPC §3-103 requires that a person be appointed "to acquire the powers and undertake the duties and liabilities of a personal representative . . . and be issued letters." UPC §3-203 governs who may be appointed the personal representative. It provides for a hierarchy of appointees.

UPC §3-203. Priority Among Persons Seeking Appointment as Personal Representative.

> (a) Whether the proceedings are formal or informal, persons who are not disqualified have priority for appointment in the following order:
>
> (1) the person with priority as determined by a probated will including a person nominated by a power conferred in a will;
>
> (2) the surviving spouse of the decedent who is a devisee of the decedent;
>
> (3) other devisees of the decedent;
>
> (4) the surviving spouse of the decedent;
>
> (5) other heirs of the decedent;
>
> (6) 45 days after the death of the decedent, any creditor.

Formal. Where formal proceedings are initially filed or where informal appointment is contested, the court will normally decide who to appoint as the personal representative based on the order provided in UPC §3-203. However, in such proceedings, the court may deviate from the statutory order and make an independent judgment of the person to appoint as the personal representative if it is established that the more superior person had a conflict of interest, lacked mental capacity or was too young. The fact that the person seeking appointment is not a resident of the state is considered but rarely precludes the appointment.

Informal. If informal probate is sought, the Registrar of the court is bound by the hierarchy of persons entitled to appointment in UPC §3-203; deviation is not permitted. The Registrar's determination is conclusive unless superseded by an order of the court in a formal testacy proceeding or agreement of or renunciation by those with superior rights. UPC §§3-203 and 3-302. The applicant must provide renouncements and nomination forms signed by anyone with an equal or superior right of appointment.

In contrast to the determination of heirship, which requires a formal proceeding, appointment as an administrator in intestacy may be sought by application with the Registrar. The application or petition must state that after the exercise of reasonable diligence, the applicant is unaware of any unrevoked testamentary instrument relating to property in the domiciliary state, and identify the priority of the person whose appointment is sought and the names of any other persons having a prior or equal right to the appointment under UPC §3-203.

Once the personal representative is determined, whether via formal or informal means, the personal representative assumes the powers and duties pertaining to the office. UPC §3-307.

4. *Obtaining Letters and Notifying Heirs and Devisees*

Assuming all the requirements are met and verified by the Registrar (informal) or adjudicated by the court (formal), "letters testamentary," "letters of [intestate] administration," or, more simply, "letters" are issued to the person appointed as the personal representative of the decedent. Once issued, letters demonstrate that the personal representative has the legal authority to administer the estate, including gathering the assets, notifying and paying creditors, disposing of assets and distributing property to the beneficiaries. Most persons and businesses dealing with the personal representative will ask for an original or copy of the letters before complying with a request for property or the like.

As with probate of the will, the moving party does not have to give *advance* notice that he is informally seeking appointment as the personal representative to anyone other than the named personal representative and anyone who has filed a request with the court that they be notified of all actions. UPC §3-310. However, within 30 days of appointment, the personal representative must send notice of the appointment to heirs and any devisees of the probated will. In addition, if the decedent is believed to have died intestate as the result of the revocation of a prior will, notice must be given to those named in the prior will. "The information shall include the name and address of the personal representative, indicate that it is being sent to persons who have or may have some interest in the estate being administered, indicate whether bond has been filed, and describe the Court where papers relating to the estate are on file. The information shall state that the estate is being administered by the personal representative under the Probate Code without supervision by the Court but that recipients are entitled to information regarding the administration from the personal representative and can petition the Court in any matter relating to the estate, including distribution of assets and expenses of administration." UPC §3-705. In many states, the information must also include a description of the essential terms of the will, *i.e.*, what property is left to whom.

EXERCISE

You have been retained by Jennifer Donnelly (of 1815 Brentwood Street, Your City, Your State), former wife of Daniel Moe and mother of his two children, Connor Ryan Moe (born August 13, six years ago) and Grace Eryn Moe (born June 7, four years ago). After a diligent search did not produce a will, it appears Daniel Moe died intestate. He resided at 2640 East Mississippi Avenue, Your City, Your State. He was not married at the time of his death 30 days ago on December 24, 20xx.

Ms. Donnelly would like (i) to be appointed the personal representative of her former husband's estate, (ii) have Daniel Moe declared to have died intestate and (iii) have the children determined to be his heirs. She would like you to prepare the form(s) necessary to accomplish these matters and to obtain "letters." Please do so using the forms prescribed by the court in the city or county in which you plan to practice. If your state does not have the forms posted online, use those of Denver, Colorado, http://www.denverprobatecourt.org/forms.htm or California, http://www.courtinfo.ca.gov/cgi-bin/forms.cgi.

NOTES

1. *Renunciation by personal representative.* The designated personal representative in a will may not wish to serve, in which case someone else will need to be appointed. There are many reasons why someone would decline the nomination, such as being unwilling to assume personal liability for the estate, suffering stress and grief resulting from the death of the decedent, declining health, having moved out of state or not having the time necessary for the job. If the personal representative does not accept the appointment, hopefully, the will provides for a successor executor. If the will is silent as to a successor, the court will need to select from the interested persons in much the same manner and in the same order as discussed above. Consistent with the present informal procedures avoiding court involvement, the person nominated in the will may file a form renouncing the appointment and nominating another qualified person. Unless contested, the renunciation and nomination will be accepted.

2. *Resignation by personal representative.* If the personal representative was already appointed and now wishes to resign, the UPC allows the personal representative to do so informally by filing a written statement of resignation with the Registrar, so long as the personal representative "has given at least 15 days written notice to the persons known to be interested in the estate." UPC §3-610. If, however, no one applies or petitions the court to be appointed, the filed statement of resignation is ineffective as a termination of appointment and the personal representative must file a formal objection to their own appointment with the court to be relieved of the duties of the position. UPC §§3-610 and 3-414.

3. *Removal of the personal representative.* To remove an appointed personal representative, an interested person may petition the court and establish cause for the removal. "Cause for removal exists when removal would be in the best interests of the estate, or if it is shown that a personal representative or the person seeking his appointment intentionally misrepresented material facts in the proceedings leading to his appointment, or that the personal representative has disregarded an order of the Court, has become incapable of discharging the duties of his office, or has mismanaged the estate or failed to perform any duty pertaining to the office." UPC §3-611. Other reasons, like those that would have precluded the appointment in the first place or permitted the personal representative to resign, may justify removal.

4.   *Bond.* Most states require the personal representative to give a bond to assure fulfillment of the person's duties and to give the estate's beneficiaries a source of payment in case of breach. Generally, a bond will not be required when the will waives the requirement.

The UPC has moved away from automatically requiring bond when informal proceedings are invoked. The Comments to UPC §3-603 explain the reason:

> This section must be read with the next three sections [bond amount, demand for bond and terms and conditions of bond]. The purpose of these provisions is to move away from the idea that bond always should be required of a probate fiduciary, or required unless a will excuses it. Also, it is designed to keep the Registrar acting pursuant to applications in informal proceedings, from passing judgment in each case on the need for bond. The point is that the Court and Registrar are not responsible for seeing that personal representatives perform as they are supposed to perform. Rather, performance is coerced by the remedies available to interested persons. Interested persons are protected by their ability to demand prior notice of informal proceedings (Section 3-204), to contest a requested appointment by use of a formal testacy proceeding or by use of a formal proceeding seeking the appointment of another person.

If bond is required and if the will does not state an amount, bond is normally in the amount of the estimated value of the estate plus the income expected to be earned by the estate during the first year of administration. UPC §3-604. The bond premium can and should be paid from the estate assets and not from the personal representative personally.

G.   GENERAL DUTIES, POWERS AND LIABILITY OF THE PERSONAL REPRESENTATIVE

Upon issuance of the letters, the personal representative acquires a host of duties and powers. This is so regardless of whether the administration is supervised or unsupervised, formal or informal.

1.   *Duties of the Personal Representative*

The duties imposed by the law on the personal representative fall into two broad categories: (1) general fiduciary duties, and (2) probate-specific procedural duties.

The personal representative owes general fiduciary duties to the estate and to all persons entitled to the estate, including creditors, surviving spouses, children and other devisees. The general fiduciary duties owed to an estate by a personal representative are similar to fiduciary duties owed to beneficiaries of a trust by a trustee, UPC §3-703, which are discussed in detail in Chapter 6. The UPC codifies common law obligations. The most common of the general fiduciary duties are: the duty of loyalty, the duty of care and prudence, the duty not to commingle assets of the estate with the personal assets of the representative, the duty to maintain accurate records, the duty of impartiality and the duty to avoid self-dealing.

In addition to general fiduciary obligations, the personal representative has other duties which are unique to probate administration. Broadly, the personal representative is responsible "to settle and distribute the estate of the decedent in accordance with the terms of any probated and effective will and this Code [*e.g.,* intestate succession], and as expeditiously and efficiently as is consistent with the best interests of the estate." UPC §3-703. The personal representative normally may satisfy the duty to settle and distribute the estate "without adjudication, order, or direction of the Court, [however, when necessary, the personal representative] may invoke the jurisdiction of the Court, in proceedings authorized by this Code, to resolve questions concerning the estate or its administration." UPC §3-704.

While the powers and duties of a trustee of a trust and of a personal representative to an estate are similar, the focus of a personal representative is different than that of a trustee. Whereas the trustee manages the property of the trust on an ongoing basis for long-term investment and must be impartial between beneficiaries with present and future interests, the personal representative of an estate manages the property with the goals of quickly paying the creditors, distributing the remaining property to the beneficiaries and winding up the administration.

The specific probate duties and responsibilities discussed in this chapter include:

- The duty to notify the heirs and devisees and certain other interested parties of his appointment. UPC §3-705. This duty was previously discussed in Section F above.
- The duty to gather the assets of the decedent and to "prepare and file or mail an inventory of property owned by the decedent at the time of his death, listing it with reasonable detail, and indicating as to each listed item, its fair market value as of the date of the decedent's death, and the type and amount of any encumbrance that may exist with reference to any item," UPC §3-706, supplement it as needed, UPC §3-708, and file a final report. Consistent with this duty is the right to employ appraisers, if needed. UPC §3-707. This duty is discussed in Section H below.
- The duty to take control of the estate property and to take all reasonably necessary steps for the management, protection and preservation of those assets. The personal representative must also pay any taxes due on the property. This duty is discussed in Section I below.

- The duty to notify creditors, determine the validity of their claims and pay amounts properly due. This duty is discussed in Section J below.
- The duty to prepare a financial accounting of the administration of the estate and to distribute the property to the devisees and heirs. This duty is discussed in Sections K and L below.

UPC §3-715 (21) allows the personal representative to "employ persons, including attorneys, auditors, investment advisors, or agents, even if they are associated with the personal representative, to advise or assist the personal representative in the performance of his administrative duties; act without independent investigation upon their recommendations; and instead of acting personally, employ one or more agents to perform any act of administration, whether or not discretionary." This provision effectively absolves the personal representative of all liability that may occur because of a poor decision by the trusted agent, unless there is gross negligence or fraud involved.

2.   Powers of the Personal Representative

The powers and authority of the personal representative to act emanate from two sources: the will and the probate law of the domiciliary state. Keeping in mind that the function of the personal representative is to collect, preserve, manage, settle and distribute the property of the estate, it is not surprising that the law grants the personal representative "the same power over the title to property of the estate that an absolute owner would have, in trust however, for the benefit of the creditors and others interested in the estate." UPC §3-711. Consistent with the function of the personal representative, UPC §3-711 authorizes 27 powers, including managing (retaining, selling, insuring, voting stock, abandoning, repairing, etc.) the decedent's assets and business, litigating, settling and paying debts and taxes, retaining other professionals to assist and advise the personal representative and the like. Many of these powers are discussed in greater detail below in the context of certain specific duties of the personal representative.

3.   Liability of the Personal Representative

Failing to adhere to the duties expected can make the personal representative individually liable for damages that occur as a result. In other words, the personal representative may have to reimburse injured parties from his own funds if the personal representative breached fiduciary duties to the estate or violated the state's probate law. Furthermore, in addition to being personally liable for the losses, there may be a penalty or surcharge of up to 100%

imposed on the personal representative by statute. However, a "personal representative may not be surcharged for acts of administration or distribution if the conduct in question was authorized at the time." UPC §3-703.

H. DUTY TO GATHER, INVENTORY AND VALUE THE ESTATE

All states require the personal representative to gather, inventory and value the estate's assets. This duty is fundamental to the estate administration process.

1. Gather the Decedent's Property

Immediately upon appointment, the personal representative should begin to identify and gather the decedent's property. UPC §3-709. The process of gathering the property is sometimes referred to as "marshalling." Besides having the legal obligation to do so, the personal representative has the fiduciary duty of prudent administration, which includes the duty to identify, control, protect and conserve estate property. UTC §809.

But where does one look to discover a decedent's property and debts? In other words, to what sources should the personal representative turn to identify the property owned and amounts owed by a dead person?

First, it is possible a decedent made an inventory of all assets and liabilities before death. The decedent's home should be thoroughly searched for financial records. This is more likely true for someone who was a fastidious record keeper or for someone who knew he was dying and wanted to put everything in order to minimize the problems for the executor and the family. Someone like this may have a record of property scheduled or maintained on the computer using a software program, like Quickbooks or Excel, in the safe deposit box or among personal papers.

Second, the personal representative may benefit from discussing the estate with partners, family members, attorneys and, especially, accountants, financial planners and insurance agents. Tax returns are another fruitful source as the income and expenses of some property is likely reported. IRS Form 4506T can be utilized to request copies of income transcripts (as well as copies of income tax returns and transcripts of returns) from the IRS, which will identify all income-producing assets owned by a decedent. This is extremely helpful in identifying previously unknown assets. Real property records in places where the decedent has lived also should be checked.

Third, the personal representative should obtain the bank records of the decedent. Bank deposits may indicate previously unknown sources of income. In addition to identifying possible sources of income, checks and charges on bank records and credit cards may disclose payees to whom the decedent was indebted.

Fourth, the personal representative should peruse the decedent's mail. Checks representing income and bills for debts and normal household charges like utilities and credit cards will be delivered on a regular basis. If the decedent was recently sick, hospitalized or in a nursing home, there should be associated bills. A change of address should be filed with the post office in order to get the decedent's mail coming to the personal representative rather than being delivered to the house where it could be lost or intercepted by family members.

EXERCISE

Draft a letter to Daniel Moe's accountant requesting property, tax and accounting records of the decedent and assistance locating any other sources of property ownership.

2.   *Inventory and Value the Decedent's Property*

Within a short time of being appointed (three months per UPC §3-706), the personal representative "shall prepare and file or mail an inventory of property owned by the decedent at the time of his death, listing it with reasonable detail, and indicating as to each listed item, its fair market value as of the date of the decedent's death, and the type and amount of any encumbrance that may exist with reference to any item."[17] UPC §3-706. This statutory duty is consistent with the fiduciary duties to identify trust assets, to keep adequate records and to inform and report.

Depending on the state, the inventory must either be sent (i) to all interested persons, (ii) to interested persons who have requested a copy of the inventory and/or (iii) to the court. Under UPC §3-706, while the personal representative's decision to file the inventory with the court is optional, doing so with interested parties is mandatory. "The Court's role in respect to [this] alternative is simply to receive and file the inventory with the file relating to the estate. *See* [UPC §]3-204, which permits any interested person to demand notice of any document relating to an estate which may be filed with the Court." Comments to UPC §3-706.

---

17. A supplemental inventory is required if "any property not included in the original inventory comes to the knowledge of a personal representative or if the personal representative learns that the value or description indicated in the original inventory for any item is erroneous or misleading, . . ." UPC §3-708.

While the statute only requires an inventory of probate property, it is critical to obtain this information for nonprobate property and gifted property as well. The personal representative will need this information to have a broader view of the property of the decedent, such as the effect on the elective share, and to prepare the estate tax return (Form 706), which must report all assets owned by the decedent or in which he held an interest as defined by the Internal Revenue Code. Knowing about the nonprobate property also may be vital as a source of funds where the probate assets are inadequate to pay off the creditors. In addition, transfers by the decedent to family members for inadequate consideration should be scrutinized because the personal representative might be obligated to recover property that was transferred in fraud of creditors. UPC §3-710.

Besides the purposes an inventory serves for the personal representative, it also provides interested persons with some of the information they need to determine how well the personal representative is performing her functions and whether to bring an action for dereliction. In addition, without an inventory of the property, those persons who have an interest in the estate are at a disadvantage in making decisions whether to contest a will, make an election against the will for a marital share and the like.

"If the personal representative breaches his duty concerning the inventory, he may be removed. Section 3-611. Or, an interested person seeking to surcharge a personal representative for losses incurred as a result of his administration might be able to take advantage of any breach of duty concerning inventory." Comments to UPC §3-706.

Most states require the inventory to be listed at fair market value as of the date of death. How does a personal representative estimate fair market value (FMV)? The answer depends on the item listed. Some assets are relatively easy to value, such as stocks traded on the recognized exchanges, like the New York Stock Exchange. The value of other assets can be reasonably estimated by reference to information on the Internet. For example, Kelly Blue Book (www.kbb.com) and Edmunds (www.edmunds.com) give information on the value of automobiles. Likewise, the value of real estate may be available either through property tax assessment statements or on the Web site of the county recorder.

The FMV of other assets may be more difficult to determine. In such cases, the probate law of all states permits either the court or the personal representative to retain the services of an appraiser. *See, e.g.,* UPC §3-707. Examples of areas where an appraiser may be necessary include real estate, oil and gas interests, art, coins, stamps, baseball cards, antiques, stock of closely held businesses and jewelry.

EXERCISE

You have diligently sought to identify all of Daniel Moe's assets and liabilities. The following represents the product of your work. On the forms prescribed by the court in the city or county in which you plan to practice, please file an inventory of the *probate* assets. If your state does not have the forms posted online, use those of Denver, Colorado, http://www.denverprobatecourt.org/forms.htm or California, http://www.courtinfo.ca.gov/cgi-bin/forms.cgi.

Residence at 2640 East Mississippi Ave., Your City, Your State	$375,000
Land in Another City, Another State	$40,000
Cash in bank from final paychecks of Xcel Energy, employer	$5,248
Cash in bank from automobile insurance refund	$46
Life insurance policy, children named as equal beneficiaries, face amount	$100,000
401(k) retirement, children named as equal beneficiaries	$25,000
First Mortgage owed to Bank of America on residence	$273,235
Second mortgage owed to JP Morgan on residence	$79,948

I. DUTY TO MANAGE THE PROPERTY OF THE ESTATE

Once the assets of the estate are identified and inventoried, the personal representative has the duty and the power to manage the property in a fiduciary capacity for the benefit of the estate, the creditors and others interested in the estate. UPC §§3-703(a) and 3-711.

In many states, real estate and personal property are handled differently, with title to the former passing directly to the heirs and legatees and title to the latter passing to the personal representative. The UPC makes no distinction. UPC §3-709 directs that the personal representative may allow the property to remain where it is or may take title to it if doing so is in the best interest of the estate. If the personal representative claims it is necessary to take possession of the assets, the claim is "conclusive evidence" that he needs the property. If a beneficiary believes otherwise, the only recourse is an action for surcharge for breach of fiduciary duty. *See* Comments to UPC §3-709.

Unless the will or a court order provides otherwise, the powers of the personal representative to manage the property of the estate are extensive. With a few exceptions, they are identical to the powers of a trustee with respect to trust property. See the general fiduciary duties discussed in Chapter 6. One exception under the UPC is that when disposing of or otherwise engaging in transactions with property, the personal representative must be mindful of the priorities in UPC §3-902. UPC §3-715. For example, since UPC §3-902 says the residuary bequest is abated first and specific bequests are abated last to pay the decedent's debts and the estate's expenses, the personal representative should not sell a specifically devised asset to obtain the cash to pay the creditors when there are plenty of assets in the residuary to do so. See the more extended discussion of UPC §3-902 in Section J.4 below.

J.   DUTIES ASSOCIATED WITH CREDITORS

1.   *General*

Among the most important functions served by the personal representative is that of notifying existing creditors of the decedent of the death, requesting that they submit their claims, determining the validity of the claims, litigating those that the personal representative believes are not valid and paying amounts properly due. If done properly and in a timely manner, the beneficiaries of the decedent emerge from probate with the property of the decedent free of the claims of general creditors. Title clearing and placing a time limit on the right of creditors to enforce debts are major reasons to put property through probate.

Creditors of the decedent of the estate are interested parties. UPC §1-201(23). As such, the personal representative owes fiduciary duties to the creditors comparable to those owed to potential distributees. To the extent other interested parties are entitled to notification of various events and to take certain action, creditors have the same rights. Creditors may even be appointed as the personal representative. To be sure, it is rare, but possible.

2.   *Notification and the Statute of Limitations*

All states have statutes that require creditors to submit their claims to the personal representative within a prescribed time period before they can institute legal proceedings against the estate to collect. If they do not follow this procedure in a timely manner, their claims are disallowed. **These are called "nonclaim statutes."** While different than a statute of limitations because they cannot be waived or tolled, such statutes place a time limit on the actions of the creditors after which their claims are untimely and barred. *See In the Matter of the Estate of Ongaro*, 998 P.2d 1097 (Colo. 2000) (creditor who failed to file notice of a claim against the estate with the personal representative within the one-year time limit set by the statute for doing so was barred from filing claim even though personal representative was aware of the debt and did not follow proper notification procedures, actions that might justify tolling if this were a statute of limitations). To assure that the creditors know of the decedent's death and of the duty to submit their claims timely, due process and state statutes require that the personal representative promptly provide notification to this effect by one of several methods intended to reach creditors.

The Supreme Court case which follows discusses the extent to which the statute must require more than mere publication in newspapers to satisfy due process standards for known or reasonably ascertainable creditors. How do you think this case would have been decided if Oklahoma had both kinds of nonclaim statutes mentioned in the first paragraph of section I of the opinion: proceeding-triggered and self-executing statutes of limitations?

Tulsa Professional Collection Services, Inc. v. Pope
485 U.S. 478 (1988)

This case involves a provision of Oklahoma's probate laws requiring claims "arising upon a contract" generally to be presented to the executor or executrix of the estate within two months of the publication of a notice advising creditors of the commencement of probate proceedings. Okla. Stat., Tit. 58, §333 (1981). The question presented is whether this provision of notice solely by publication satisfies the Due Process Clause.

I

Oklahoma's Probate Code requires creditors to file claims against an estate within a specified time period, and generally bars untimely claims. Such "nonclaim statutes" are almost universally included in state probate codes. See Uniform Probate Code §3-801.[18] Giving creditors a limited time in which to file claims against the estate serves the State's interest in facilitating the administration and expeditious closing of estates. Nonclaim statutes come in two basic forms. Some provide a relatively short time period, generally two to six months, that begins to run after the commencement of probate proceedings. [These nonclaim statutes might be referred to as "proceeding-triggered statutes of limitations."] Others call for a longer period, generally one to five years, which runs from the decedent's death. [These nonclaim statutes are referred to as "self-executing statutes of limitations."] Most States include both types of nonclaim statutes in their probate codes, typically providing that if probate proceedings are not commenced and the shorter period therefore never is triggered, then claims nonetheless may be barred by the longer period. Most States also provide that creditors are to be notified of the requirement to file claims imposed by the nonclaim statutes solely by publication. See Uniform Probate Code §3-801. Indeed, in most jurisdictions it is the publication of notice that

---

18. [The UPC cited here and elsewhere in the opinion is an older version — Eds.]

triggers the nonclaim statute. The Uniform Probate Code, for example, provides that creditors have four months from publication in which to file claims. Uniform Probate Code §3-801.

The specific nonclaim statute at issue in this case, Okla. Stat., Tit. 58, §333 (1981), provides for only a short time period and is best considered in the context of Oklahoma probate proceedings as a whole. Under Oklahoma's Probate Code, any party interested in the estate may initiate probate proceedings by petitioning the court to have the will proved. The court is then required to set a hearing date on the petition and to mail notice of the hearing "to all heirs, legatees and devisees, at their places of residence." If no person appears at the hearing to contest the will, the court may admit the will to probate on the testimony of one of the subscribing witnesses to the will. After the will is admitted to probate, the court must order appointment of an executor or executrix, issuing letters testamentary to the named executor or executrix if that person appears, is competent and qualified, and no objections are made.

Immediately after appointment, the executor or executrix is required to "give notice to the creditors of the deceased." Proof of compliance with this requirement must be filed with the court. This notice is to advise creditors that they must present their claims to the executor or executrix within two months of the date of the first publication. As for the method of notice, the statute requires only publication: "[S]uch notice must be published in some newspaper in [the] county once each week for two (2) consecutive weeks." A creditor's failure to file a claim within the 2-month period generally bars it forever. . . .

II

H. Everett Pope, Jr., was admitted to St. John Medical Center, a hospital in Tulsa, Oklahoma, in November 1978. On April 2, 1979, while still at the hospital, he died testate. His wife, appellee JoAnne Pope, initiated probate proceedings in the District Court of Tulsa County [and after letters were issued] the court ordered appellee to fulfill her statutory obligation by directing that she "immediately give notice to creditors." Appellee published notice in the Tulsa Daily Legal News for two consecutive weeks beginning July 17, 1979. The notice advised creditors that they must file any claim they had against the estate within two months of the first publication of the notice.

Appellant Tulsa Professional Collection Services, Inc., is a subsidiary of St. John Medical Center and the assignee of a claim for expenses connected with the decedent's long stay at that hospital. Neither appellant, nor its parent company, filed a claim with appellee within the 2-month time period following publication of notice. In October 1983, however, appellant filed an Application for Order Compelling Payment of Expenses of Last Illness. In making this application, appellant relied on Okla. Stat., Tit. 58, §594 (1981), which indicates that an executrix "must pay . . . the expenses of the last sickness." Appellant argued that this specific statutory command made compliance with the 2-month deadline for filing claims unnecessary [and that the nonclaim statute's notice provisions violated due process. The state courts, including the Supreme Court of Oklahoma rejected these positions]. . . .

III

Mullane v. Central Hanover Bank & Trust Co., 339 U.S. 306, 314 (1950) established that state action affecting property must generally be accompanied by notification of that action: "An elementary and fundamental requirement of due process in any proceeding which is to be accorded finality is notice reasonably calculated, under all the circumstances, to apprise interested parties of the pendency of the action and afford them an opportunity to present their objections." In the years since *Mullane* the Court has adhered to these principles, balancing the "interest of the State" and "the individual interest sought to be protected by the Fourteenth Amendment." The focus is on the reasonableness of the balance, and, as *Mullane* itself made clear, whether a particular method of notice is reasonable depends on the particular circumstances.

The Court's most recent decision in this area is *Mennonite Board of Missions v. Adams*, 462 U.S. 791 (1983), which involved the sale of real property for delinquent taxes. State law provided for tax sales in certain circumstances and for a 2-year period following any such sale during which the owner or any lienholder could redeem the property. After expiration of the redemption period, the tax sale purchaser could apply for a deed. The property owner received actual notice of the tax sale and the redemption period. All other interested parties were given notice by publication. 462 U.S., at 792-794, 103 S. Ct., at 2708-2709. In *Mennonite*, a mortgagee of property that had been sold and on which the redemption period had run complained that the State's failure to provide it with actual notice of these proceedings violated due process. The Court agreed, holding that "actual notice is a minimum constitutional precondition to a proceeding which will adversely affect the liberty or property interests of *any* party, whether unlettered or well versed in commercial practice, if its name and address are reasonably ascertainable." Because the tax sale had "immediately and drastically diminishe[d] the value of [the mortgagee's] interest," and because the mortgagee could have been identified through "reasonably diligent efforts," the Court concluded that due process required that the mortgagee be given actual notice.

Applying these principles to the case at hand leads to a similar result. Appellant's interest is an unsecured claim, a cause of action against the estate for an unpaid bill. Little doubt remains that such an intangible interest is property protected by the Fourteenth Amendment. . . .

The Fourteenth Amendment protects this interest, however, only from a deprivation by state action. Private use of state-sanctioned private remedies or procedures does not rise to the level of state action. Nor is the State's involvement in the mere running of a general statute of limitations generally sufficient to implicate due process. But when private parties make use of state procedures with the overt, significant assistance of state officials, state action may be found. The question here is whether the State's involvement with the nonclaim statute is substantial enough to implicate the Due Process Clause.

Appellee argues that it is not, contending that Oklahoma's nonclaim statute is a self-executing statute of limitations. . . .

It is true that nonclaim statutes generally possess some attributes of statutes of limitations. They provide a specific time period within which particular types of claims must be filed and they bar claims presented after expiration of that deadline. Many of the state court decisions upholding nonclaim statutes against due process challenges have relied upon these features and concluded that they are properly viewed as statutes of limitations.

As we noted in *Texaco, Inc. v. Short*, 454 U.S. 516, 533 (1982), however, it is the "self-executing feature" of a statute of limitations that makes *Mullane* and *Mennonite* inapposite. The State's interest in a self-executing statute of limitations is in providing repose for potential defendants and in avoiding stale claims. The State has no role to play beyond enactment of the limitations period. While this enactment obviously is state action, the State's limited involvement in the running of the time period generally falls short of constituting the type of state action required to implicate the protections of the Due Process Clause.

Here, in contrast, there is significant state action. The probate court is intimately involved throughout, and without that involvement the time bar is never activated. The nonclaim statute becomes operative only after probate proceedings have been commenced in state court. The court must appoint the executor or executrix before notice, which triggers the time bar, can be given. Only after this court appointment is made does the statute provide for any notice; §331 directs the executor or executrix to publish notice "immediately" after appointment. Indeed, in this case, the District Court reinforced the statutory command with an order expressly requiring appellee to "immediately give notice to creditors." The form of the order indicates that such orders are routine. Finally, copies of the notice and an affidavit of publication must be filed with the court. It is only after all of these actions take place that the time period begins to run, and in every one of these actions, the court is intimately involved. This involvement is so pervasive and substantial that it must be considered state action subject to the restrictions of the Fourteenth Amendment.

Where the legal proceedings themselves trigger the time bar, even if those proceedings do not necessarily resolve the claim on its merits, the time bar lacks the self-executing feature that *Short* indicated was necessary to remove any due process problem. Rather, in such circumstances, due process is directly implicated and actual notice generally is required. . . . In sum, the substantial involvement of the probate court throughout the process leaves little doubt that the running of Oklahoma's nonclaim statute is accompanied by sufficient government action to implicate the Due Process Clause.

Nor can there be any doubt that the nonclaim statute may "adversely affect" a protected property interest. In appellant's case, such an adverse effect is all too clear. The entire purpose and effect of the nonclaim statute is to regulate the timeliness of such claims and to forever bar untimely claims, and by virtue of the statute, the probate proceedings themselves have completely extinguished appellant's claim. Thus, it is irrelevant that the notice seeks only to advise creditors that they may become parties rather than that they are parties, for if they do not participate in the probate proceedings, the nonclaim statute terminates their property interests. It is not necessary for a proceeding to directly adjudicate the merits of a claim in order to "adversely affect" that interest. . . .

In assessing the propriety of actual notice in this context consideration should be given to the practicalities of the situation and the effect that requiring actual notice may have on important state interests. As the Court noted in *Mullane*, "[c]hance alone brings to the attention of even a local resident an advertisement in small type inserted in the back pages of a newspaper." Creditors, who have a strong interest in maintaining the integrity of their relationship with their debtors, are particularly unlikely to benefit from publication notice. As a class, creditors may not be aware of a debtor's death or of the institution of probate proceedings. Moreover, the executor or executrix will often be, as is the case here, a party with a beneficial interest in the estate. This could diminish an executor's or executrix's inclination to call attention to the potential expiration of a creditor's claim. There is thus a substantial practical need for actual notice in this setting.

At the same time, the State undeniably has a legitimate interest in the expeditious resolution of probate proceedings. Death transforms the decedent's legal relationships and a State could reasonably conclude that swift settlement of estates is so important that it calls for very short time deadlines for filing claims. As noted, the almost uniform practice is to establish such short deadlines, and to provide only publication notice. Providing actual notice to known or reasonably ascertainable creditors, however, is not inconsistent with the goals reflected in nonclaim statutes. Actual notice need not be inefficient or burdensome. We have repeatedly recognized that mail service is an inexpensive and efficient mechanism that is reasonably calculated to provide actual notice. . . . As the Court indicated in *Mennonite*, all that the executor or executrix need do is make "reasonably diligent efforts" to uncover the identities of creditors. For creditors who are not "reasonably ascertainable," publication notice can suffice. Nor is everyone who may conceivably have a claim properly considered a creditor entitled to actual notice. Here, as in *Mullane*, it is reasonable to dispense with actual notice to those with mere "conjectural" claims.

On balance then, a requirement of actual notice to known or reasonably ascertainable creditors is not so cumbersome as to unduly hinder the dispatch with which probate proceedings are conducted. Notice by mail is already routinely provided at several points in the probate process. In Oklahoma, for example, §26 requires that "heirs, legatees, and devisees" be mailed notice of the initial hearing on the will. Accord, Uniform Probate Code §3-403. Indeed, a few States already provide for actual notice in connection with short nonclaim statutes. *See, e.g.,* Calif. Prob. Code Ann. §§9050, 9100 (West Supp.1988); Nev. Rev. Stat. §§147.010, 155.010, 155.020 (1987); W. Va. Code §§44-2-2, 44-2-4 (1982). We do not believe that requiring adherence to such a standard will be so burdensome or impracticable as to warrant reliance on publication notice alone. . . .

IV

We hold that Oklahoma's nonclaim statute is not a self-executing statute of limitations. Rather, the statute operates in connection with Oklahoma's probate proceedings to "adversely affect" appellant's property interest. Thus, if appellant's identity as a creditor was known or "reasonably ascertainable," then the Due Process Clause requires that appellant be given "[n]otice by mail or other means as certain to ensure actual notice." Accordingly, the judgment of the Oklahoma Supreme Court is reversed and the case is remanded for further proceedings not inconsistent with this opinion.

It is so ordered.

In response to *Pope*, states around the country modified their statutes to conform the notice requirements to the decision. *See, e.g.,* Ohio Rev. Code Ann. §2117.07; Mass Ann. Laws ch. 197 §9; Cal. Prob. Code §9050. The UPC, for example, now provides for both actual notification procedures and notification by publication in proceeding-triggered statute of limitations nonclaim statutes. If the personal representative uses notice by publication, all interested creditors must be notified to present their claims within four months of the publication or they will be denied. However, if the creditor's claims are reasonably ascertainable or within the personal representative's personal knowledge, the personal representative may shorten the time period to 60 days by giving written notice directly to the creditor. Creditors who provide statements and invoices on a regular basis, such as utilities, credit cards, mortgages and the like, normally do not need to be notified since their bills serve as the equivalent of filing a claim.

UPC §3-801. Notice to Creditors.

(a) Unless notice has already been given under this section, a personal representative upon appointment [may] [shall] publish a notice to creditors once a week for three successive weeks in a newspaper of general circulation in the [county] announcing the appointment and the personal representative's address and notifying creditors of the estate to present their claims within four months after the date of the first publication of the notice or be forever barred.

(b) A personal representative may give written notice by mail or other delivery to a creditor, notifying the creditor to present his [or her] claim within four months after the published notice, if given as provided in subsection (a), or within 60 days after the mailing or other delivery of the notice, whichever is later, or be forever barred. Written notice must be the notice described in subsection (a) above or a similar notice.

UPC §3-803. Limitations on Presentation of Claims.

(a) All claims against a decedent's estate which arose before the death of the decedent . . . if not barred earlier by another statute, contract, tort, or other legal basis of limitations or non-claim statute, are barred against the estate, the personal representative, the heirs and devisees and non-probate transferees of the decedent, unless presented within the earlier of the following:

(1) one year after the decedent's death; or

(2) the time provided by Section 3-801(b) for creditors who are given actual notice, and within the time provided in Section 3-801(a) for all creditors barred by [notified by] publication. . . .

(c) All claims against a decedent's estate which arise at or after the death of the decedent . . . are barred against the estate, the personal representative, and the heirs and devisees of the decedent, unless presented as follows:

(1) a claim based on a contract with the personal representative, within four months after performance by the personal representative is due; or

(2) any other claim, within the later of four months after it arises, or the time specified in subsection (a)(1). (Emphasis added).

NOTES AND QUESTIONS

1. *Notice under UPC §3-803(a)(1).* Most states, regardless of whether there has been any notice given, deny claims if the creditors do not present their claims within a certain time after the decedent's death, generally ranging from one to three years. The UPC provides that even without notification, claims shall be barred one year from the decedent's death. The Comments to UPC §3-803 state that the shorter one-year period was

selected "to prevent concerns stemming from the possible applicability to this Code of *Tulsa Professional Collection Services v. Pope*, 108 S. Ct. 1340, 485 U.S. 478 (1988) from unduly prolonging estate settlements and closings." The one-year period is most likely going to apply when as estate has not been opened for administration and no personal representative was appointed.

2.   *Gaming the system.* It is interesting to note in the Comments that "[t]he Joint Editorial Board recognized that the new bar running one year after death [in UPC §3-803(a)(1)] may be used by some sets of successors to avoid payment of claims against their decedents of which they are aware. Successors who are willing to delay receipt and enjoyment of inheritances may consider waiting out the non-claim period running from death simply to avoid any public record of an administration that might alert known and unknown creditors to pursue their claims. The scenario was deemed to be unlikely, however" for a variety of reasons.

3.   *Enough information? Pope* seems to require notification in the manner most likely to inform the creditor before their claims can be denied as untimely. With that in mind, how can the UPC and other states have no-notice nonclaim statutes, like UPC §3-803(a)(1)?

4.   *Pope* and many statutes require actual notice to creditors who are reasonably ascertainable or within the personal representative's personal knowledge. Which creditors likely fall into this category, and what should you do to determine who they are when performing your due diligence? Creditors not known or reasonably ascertainable by the personal representative may be given notice by publication and may not demand actual notice. Contingent and conjectural creditors fall into the latter class. *U.S. Trust Co. of Florida Savings Bank v. Haig*, 694 So. 2d 769 (D.C. Fl. 1997).

EXERCISES

1.   Do a search of your local newspapers and find a notice to creditors informing them of a decedent's death and requesting that they submit their claims by a certain date. What information is provided, and what must creditors do and by when? (If you do not find something in a newspaper of general circulation, you may need to check legal newspapers.)

2.   You represent the estate of Daniel Moe. Write a letter to Mastercard (P.O. Box 645, Reno, NV 90218) notifying them of the death of Daniel Moe and requesting that they submit any claims they have against his estate by whatever date you believe is appropriate. You should calculate the due date based on UPC §3-801 and include it in the letter. Also identify what documentation you believe you should attach to the demand. It is possible the court in the city or county in which you plan to practice has a standard form letter. If your state does not have the forms posted online, use those of Denver, Colorado, http://www.denverprobatecourt.org/forms.htm or California, http://www.courtinfo.ca.gov/cgi-bin/forms.cgi.

3.   *Presenting Claims and Determining Validity*

The UPC allows creditors to present their claims in a number of ways, including filing with the court, filing with the personal representative or by bringing a suit against the personal representative within the allowed statutory period. UPC §3-804. The claimant should provide sufficient information about the basis for the claim, the name and address of the claimant and the amount claimed.

In some jurisdictions, debts may not be paid by the personal representative without a claim having been filed, even if the personal representative knows of an amount due, such as past-due utilities or credit card balances. Under UPC §3-807(b), the personal representative "may pay any just claim that has not been barred, with or without formal presentation, but [may find himself] personally liable to any other claimant whose claim is allowed and who is injured by its payment [*i.e.,* there is not enough money left in the estate to pay the claim]. . . ." With respect to property "encumbered by mortgage, pledge, lien, or other security interest, the personal representative may pay the encumbrance or any part thereof, renew or extend any obligation secured by the encumbrance or convey or transfer the assets to the creditor in satisfaction of his lien, in whole or in part, whether or not the holder of the encumbrance has presented a claim, if it appears to be for the best interest of the estate." UPC §3-814. This is true also for creditors who provide regular bills and statements, like utilities and credit cards, as their monthly statements are the equivalent of filing a claim.

Once claims are made, the personal representative must decide whether they are valid or not. The personal representative is not required to pay all claims. If the personal representative does not feel the claim is rightfully due, she may "disallow" the claim by mailing notice to the creditor that their claim has been denied.[19] The creditor then has 60 days to challenge the disallowance.

UPC §3-806. Allowance of Claims.

> (a) As to claims presented in the manner described in Section 3-804 within the time limit prescribed in 3-803, the personal representative may mail a notice to any claimant stating that the claim has been disallowed. . . . Every claim which is disallowed in whole or in part by the personal representative is barred so far as not allowed unless the claimant files a petition for allowance in the Court or

---

19. While the insolvency of the estate is not a basis for disallowing a claim, it has a similar effect; the creditor will not be paid.

commences a proceeding against the personal representative not later than 60 days after the mailing of the notice of disallowance or partial allowance if the notice warns the claimant of the impending bar. Failure of the personal representative to mail notice to a claimant of action on his claim for 60 days after the time for original presentation of the claim has expired has the effect of a notice of allowance. . . .

(c) Upon the petition of the personal representative or of a claimant in a proceeding for the purpose, the Court may allow in whole or in part any claim or claims presented to the personal representative or filed with the Clerk of Court in due time and not barred by subsection (a) of this section. Notice in this proceeding shall be given to the claimant, the personal representative and those other persons interested in the estate as the Court may direct by order entered at the time the proceeding is commenced.

If litigation is necessary, the personal representative is authorized to pursue the action. UPC §3-715(22). The personal representative also "may, if it appears for the best interest of the estate, compromise, i.e., settle, the claim, whether due or not due, absolute or contingent, liquidated or unliquidated." UPC §§3-715(17) and 3-813. To the extent the estate has a counterclaim against the creditor, the personal representative may offset the counterclaim against the claim. UPC §3-811.

EXERCISES

For the following exercises, if your state does not have the needed forms posted online, use those of Denver, Colorado, http://www .denverprobatecourt.org/forms.htm or California, http://www.courtinfo. ca.gov/cgi-bin/forms.cgi.

1.   You represent Mastercard. Daniel Moe had a credit card with Mastercard that had an outstanding balance of $23,887.09 as of the date of his death. Your client received notice from Mr. Moe's personal representative requiring that it submit a claim within 60 days of the date of the notice. Submit a claim on behalf of Mastercard on the form prescribed by the court in the city or county in which you plan to practice.

2.   You represent the executor of the estate of Daniel Moe. Mastercard submitted the claim above. There is a charge on the claim for $5,000 for first class tickets to Norway on United Airlines. Daniel Moe never charged such an item. You believe he was the subject of identity theft and the charge is clearly the result of fraud. File a Notice of Disallowance of the Claim.

4. *Payment of Claims and Priority of Payment*

Once the valid claims have been determined, if there is enough money in the estate to cover all the claims, the personal representative is authorized to pay them. UPC §§3-715(22) and 3-807(a). However, not all estates will be able to pay all the expenses of and claims against the estate. In these cases, the estate is deemed to be "insolvent." Where estates are insolvent, probate laws typically provide a specific order of payment. *See, e.g.,* VA. CODE ANN. §64.1-157; 755 ILL. COMP. STAT. 5/18-10. Thus, it may be necessary to wait until the expiration of the creditor claims period and all creditors are known before payment is made on any claims.

The UPC order is established in UPC §3-805. It is subject to part 4 of Article II, the exempt property and allowances rules, thus elevating these items to a higher priority. Expenses of the estate are paid by class. If a class cannot be paid in full, the class will split the available funds proportionate with how much each creditor is owed within that class.

UPC §3-805. Classification of Claims.

> (a) If the applicable assets of the estate are insufficient to pay all claims in full, the personal representative shall make payment in the following order:
>   (1) costs and expenses of administration;
>   (2) reasonable funeral expenses;
>   (3) debts and taxes with preference under federal law;
>   (4) reasonable and necessary medical and hospital expenses of the last illness of the decedent, including compensation of persons attending him;
>   (5) debts and taxes with preference under other laws of this state [*e.g.,* Medicaid];
>   (6) all other claims.
> (b) No preference shall be given in the payment of any claim over any other claim of the same class, and a claim due and payable shall not be entitled to a preference over claims not due.

The type of claim or expense that falls into each category listed in subsection (a) should not be difficult to determine. However, there are a few items that warrant additional explanation.

a. Secured Creditors

A general creditor is one who only has recourse to the debtor's general assets if the debtor defaults on an obligation to pay. A secured creditor, by contrast, has been given an interest in identifiable property and may, upon default by the debtor, foreclose upon the collateral that securitizes the loan and seize it. For example, the bank that holds a mortgage on the decedent's house is a "secured creditor" since they have recourse to the house itself if the decedent's estate is insufficient to pay all debts.[20]

The priority rules of UPC §3-805 apply only to unsecured debts; secured creditors are entitled to foreclose on their collateral directly. "If any assets of the estate are encumbered by mortgage, pledge, lien, or other security interest, the personal representative may pay the encumbrance or any part thereof, renew or extend any obligation secured by the encumbrance or convey or transfer the assets to the creditor in satisfaction of his lien, in whole or in part, whether or not the holder of the encumbrance has presented a claim, if it appears to be for the best interest of the estate." UPC §3-814.

In addition, unless the will indicates to the contrary, a specific devisee of mortgaged property takes subject to the lien without right to have other assets sold off to pay the secured obligation. UPC §2-609.

b.   Family Allowances

After the rights of secured creditors to their collateral, the family allowance has the highest priority. We discussed the family allowance to which the spouse and minor children who were dependent on the decedent are entitled during the administration of the estate in Section B.5 above. The family allowance is a claim against the estate and does not, absent a will provision to the contrary, affect the amount to which the recipients are otherwise entitled under the will or statute.

c.   Homestead Allowance and Exempt Property

The homestead exemption and family allowance are statutory protections that allow spouses, and sometimes other dependents, to retain property after the death of the homeowner. They take priority over other creditors' claims against the estate and result in the set-aside of certain property that cannot be used currently to pay the claims of unsecured creditors.

Homestead   Exemption/Allowance.   The   homestead   exemption/ allowance protects a specific piece of property — the homestead — for the use of a family. *See* Alison D. Morantz, *There's No Place Like Home: Homestead Exemption and Judicial Constructions of Family in Nineteenth-Century America,*

---

20. To the extent the collateral is insufficient to fully pay the outstanding debt, the creditor is unsecured for the difference and falls under the "all other claims" category of creditors in UPC §3-805.

24 LAW & HIST. REV. 245, 246 (2006). The rules with respect to the homestead exemption or allowance vary greatly among the states. In some states, the homestead is an exemption and in others it is an allowance. There are certain requirements that must be met both for the property to qualify for protection and for the family members to be entitled to protection. For example, in order for a plot of land to be protected, it must typically be occupied by a head of household and function as the family home; a vacation home is not protected.

Homestead laws were developed to provide a financial shelter for the family property, especially in bankruptcy. Homestead exemptions do not provide unlimited protection and they vary widely by state. The protection is typically a life estate that continues until the death or remarriage of the surviving spouse or until the marriage of the minor beneficiaries, or when the youngest attains majority. The homestead can then be sold to satisfy any debts.

A state may choose not to exempt the entire property from claims; depending on the statute, the full value of the home may be immune from sale, or only a specific value may be protected. *See* Lorna Fox, *Re-Possessing "Home": A Re-Analysis of Gender, Homeownership and Debtor Default for Feminist Legal Theory*, 14 WM. & MARY J. WOMEN & L. 423, 432 (2008). Where only a partial exemption is available because the house is valued higher than the statutory exemption, the creditor may force a sale and satisfy the debt with the funds exceeding the protected value. Forty-six out of 50 states offer some form of homestead exemption. The basic exemption amount ranges from $500 in Iowa to $200,000 in Minnesota, with five states and the District of Columbia offering a complete exemption. Stephanie M. Stern, *Residential Protectionism and the Legal Mythology of Home*, 107 MICH. L. REV. 1093, 1100 (2009).

Not only does the amount of protection differ by state, but the mechanism for allotting the benefit varies also. In an effort to recognize the reduced earning potential and the increased needs of the elderly, some states have created a system that increases the value of the basic protection based on the age of the beneficiary and/or the number of years the marriage lasted.[21] For example, California varies the amount of homestead exemptions between $50,000 and $150,000 based on age, and South Dakota's homestead exemption increases from $30,000 to $170,000 for owners 70 years of age or older.[22]

The UPC protects the decedent's family from the claims of creditors by granting a relatively small homestead allowance in the decedent's property.

---

21. *Id.*
22. *Id.*

UPC §2-402. Homestead Allowance.

> A decedent's surviving spouse is entitled to a homestead allowance of [$22,500]. If there is no surviving spouse, each minor child and each dependent child of the decedent is entitled to a homestead allowance amounting to [$22,500] divided by the number of minor and dependent children of the decedent. The homestead allowance is exempt from and has priority over all claims against the estate. Homestead allowance is in addition to any share passing to the surviving spouse or minor or dependent child by the will of the decedent, unless otherwise provided, by intestate succession, or by way of elective share. . . .

The homestead allowance provided for in the UPC is different from a homestead exemption, discussed above. Instead of protecting a particular piece of property, it offers a monetary payment to the surviving spouse or minor children, with the intent that the payment be used to cover the cost of housing, whether that is a mortgage or rent. Instead of the traditional homestead exemption, this method "protects all surviving spouses and minor children, including those of renters, owners of mobile homes not classified as real estate, and decedents who owned no interest in a residence of any sort." Jeffrey I. Roth, *Fraud on the Surviving Spouse in Jewish and American Law: A Model Chapter for a Jewish Law Casebook*, 28 CASE W. RES. J. INT'L L. 101, 125-26 (1996). The comments to the section also describe the rationale for using the set dollar amount, stating "the desirability of having a certain level below which administration may be dispensed with or be handled summarily, without regard to the size of allowances under Section 2-404." Comment to UPC §2-402. Additionally, the set amount is intended to minimize the fact that the homestead allowance can cause minor children of the decedent to be favored over the decedent's children who have reached the age of majority. *Id.*

Exempt Property. Unlike the homestead allowance, the exempt property statute does not provide a payment to the surviving spouse or children; rather, it allows the surviving spouse or children to designate certain personal property or money as exempt from creditors. The amount varies from state to state, with the UPC exempting $15,000. If there is no surviving spouse, the adult children of the decedent can still claim exempt property (whereas the homestead allowance is only available to minor or dependent children).

UPC §2-403. Exempt Property.

> In addition to the homestead allowance, the decedent's surviving spouse is entitled from the estate to a value, not exceeding $15,000 in excess of any security interests therein, in household furniture, automobiles, furnishings, appliances, and personal effects. If there is no surviving spouse, the decedent's children are entitled jointly to the same value. . . . These rights are in addition to any benefit or share passing to the surviving spouse or children by the decedent's will, unless otherwise provided, by intestate succession, or by way of elective share. . . .

PROBLEM

Sue and John were married 30 years ago. They have three children, Christine (age 26 and who lives in Turkey), Chase (age 15) and Casey (age 12). John died in a car accident recently. He did not have a will. The family lives in a state that adopted the UPC. The administration of the estate is going to take eight months.

   a.   John had $150,000 in cash, a house worth $400,000 on which there was a $225,000 mortgage and another $175,000 in assets, net of debts like credit cards, when he died. Assuming Sue and all the children survived John, how will his estate be divided, taking into account UPC §§2-402 to 2-404 and the intestate rules of your state? (For now, do not concern yourself with the elective share rules of UPC §2-201 *et seq.*)

       i.   Assume the monthly mortgage payments on the house are $1,400, food costs are $350, minimum payments on the credit cards and bank loan are $250 and insurance, gas and other expenses total $500. Sue did not have a job at John's death and is panicked about how to make these payments while the estate is tied up in administration. Do you have any suggestions?

   b.   Assume Sue and John got a divorce six years ago. How does this affect the estate division after John died?

   c.   Assume John had a will that left 75% of his estate to Sue and 25% to his five siblings to be divided equally among them. Everyone survived his death — Sue, the children and the siblings. How, if at all, does this affect the estate division? Does your answer change if he had left the $500,000 in an inter vivos, revocable trust which directed that its proceeds be distributed to his brother upon his death?

K.   IMPORTANT MATTERS TO BE ADDRESSED BEFORE FINALIZING THE ESTATE

1.   *Will Contests and Other Estate Controversies*

As the administration of the estate progresses from the issuance of letters to the final settlement, the personal representative and the attorney for the estate must resolve many issues, such as the validity of the will, if there is one, who the rightful recipients of the estate property are, and what amounts and which property are they entitled to. These and all other questions should be presented to the interested parties during administration to allow time for challenges by them or for a petition to the court for instructions of declaratory judgment so as not to delay the final settlement and closing of the estate.

In Chapter 11, we discussed will contests. We discovered the issues most often raised by contestants are whether the testator:

- Was of sound mind and had the required capacity to draft a will;
- Intended the document to be his last will and testament;
- Complied with the statutory formalities; or,
- Was unduly influenced by someone to leave them a disproportionately large bequest or was otherwise the object of fraud, duress or mistake.

In addition, a legal challenge may ensue to interpret provisions of the will, determine the rights of creditors, heirs and devisees, assert or defend legal claims to the estate's property, respond to deficiency determinations by the taxing authorities and a host of other issues. The following represents some, but not all, of the matters that need to be addressed and should be resolved before the plan of disposition is proposed. The substantive discussion of these is in previous chapters:

- Is the will clear or ambiguous in any regard about who the beneficiaries are and to what property they are entitled?
- Who are the family members? Are there any pretermitted spouses or children?
- Was a bequest revoked either because of divorce or murder or by any other means?
- If there is no will, what does the intestacy statute provide for each heir?
- What was the actual or deemed order of death as between the decedent and the devisees and heirs? Was there a valid disclaimer?

- If a named beneficiary predeceased the decedent or is deemed to have predeceased the decedent, does the devise lapse or is an alternate taker mentioned in the will or does the antilapse statute create a substitute gift in favor of the beneficiary's descendants?

- If there was a specific devise and if the specific asset is not owned by the decedent at death, does the gift adeem or is an alternate gift mentioned in the will or does the ademption statute create a replacement gift?

- Are there any debts of the decedent that are not exonerated and should pass to the devisee along with the property to which it is related, such as the mortgage on real estate?

- Did a devisee or heir receive an advancement or partial distribution that would reduce the amount to which they would otherwise be entitled in the final distribution?

- What property constitutes the augmented estate, and has the surviving spouse made an election against the will or against the intestate portion that would alter the amount to which he is entitled? Was there a premarital agreement affecting the rights of a surviving spouse? Was either the surviving spouse or any child omitted from a will drafted before the marriage or birth (*i.e.*, a pretermitted family member)?

- Should an election by the surviving spouse be made with respect to a QTIP trust (Qualified Terminable Interest Property)?

- If property of the estate needs to be disposed of to satisfy the claims of creditors, in what order should the property be sold?

- Was there a provision in the will purporting to penalize any interested person for contesting the will or instituting other proceedings relating to the estate? If so, did someone institute such proceedings without probable cause? UPC §3-905.

- Did the successors agree among themselves to alter the interests, shares or amounts to which they are entitled under the will of the decedent, or under the laws of intestacy, by written contract executed by all who are affected by its provisions? If so, the "personal representative shall abide by the terms of the agreement subject to his obligation to administer the estate for the benefit of creditors, to pay all taxes and costs of administration, and to carry out the responsibilities of his office for the benefit of any successors of the decedent who are not parties." UPC §3-912.

In all of these, the personal representative is authorized to act on behalf of the estate either to litigate the matter or to settle it. UPC §3-715. Where the issue is the rightful amount to which each family member is entitled, the family can enter into a "family settlement." So long as the settlement does not prejudice the creditors of the decedent or a non-participating beneficiary, courts are generally willing to accept them as a reasonable means of avoiding expensive and family-destroying litigation.

The UPC authorizes such settlements in §3-912.

UPC §3-912. Private Agreements Among Successors to Decedent Binding on Personal Representative.

> Subject to the rights of creditors and taxing authorities, competent successors may agree among themselves to alter the interests, shares, or amounts to which they are entitled under the will of the decedent, or under the laws of intestacy, in any way that they provide in a written contract executed by all who are affected by its provisions. The personal representative shall abide by the terms of the agreement subject to his obligation to administer the estate for the benefit of creditors, to pay all taxes and costs of administration, and to carry out the responsibilities of his office for the benefit of any successors of the decedent who are not parties. . . .

UPC §3-1101 also allows the settlement or compromise "of any controversy as to admission to probate of any instrument offered for formal probate as the will of a decedent, the construction, validity, or effect of any governing instrument, the rights or interests in the estate of the decedent, of any successor, or the administration of the estate, if approved in a formal proceeding in the Court for that purpose . . ."[23]

To the extent the personal representative incurs expenses and legal fees to defend or prosecute any proceeding in good faith, whether successful or not, the estate is the party liable to pay the costs. UPC §3-720. Of course, if a beneficiary or a purported beneficiary institutes proceedings against the estate or the will offered for probate, that party is responsible for their own costs.

2.   Tax Issues

In Chapter 14, we discussed estate and gift tax planning. That chapter covered the substantive aspects of tax while this one covers the procedural aspects. There are a host of tax matters that need to be addressed by the executor at this time. To establish the right to act on behalf of the estate of

---

23. The procedure for getting the settlement approved is to present to the probate court the entire written agreement that has been executed by all competent persons and parents acting for any minor child having beneficial interests or having claims which will or may be affected by the compromise. After notice to all interested persons or their representatives, the court shall approve the agreement if it finds that the contest or controversy is in good faith and that the effect of the agreement upon the interests of persons represented by fiduciaries or other representatives is just and reasonable. UPC §3-1102.

the decedent, the personal representative must file a Form 56 (Notice of Fiduciary Capacity) with the Internal Revenue Service.

The most obvious of the tax responsibilities of the personal representative is to file any federal and state tax returns that need to be filed. This may include the decedent's final income tax return (Form 1040), gift tax return (Form 709) and, of course, the estate tax return (Form 706). It also includes any returns for previous years that the decedent failed to file. As the estate will likely earn income during administration on property owned by it, such as gains on the sale of property, dividends, interest and rents, the personal representative must file income tax returns of the estate (Form 1041).

There are certain tax elections that may need to be made by the executor that will affect beneficiaries differently. As the personal representative has the duty to act impartially in the best interest of all beneficiaries equally and the duty to use reasonable care to achieve the greatest tax savings for the estate and as some elections help one beneficiary over another or the estate over either beneficiary, this creates an interesting balancing act for the personal representative. It is wisest for the personal representative to get written approval from those affected after fully explaining the situation. Among the important tax elections the personal representative must consider are:

- Whether to make the election to file a joint income tax return with the surviving spouse for any unfiled Forms 1040. IRC §6212(b).
- Whether to take the expenses of the last illness paid by the estate as a deduction on the final income tax return (IRC §213) or on the estate tax return (IRC §2053(a)). Similar decisions need to be made with respect to administrative expenses and losses incurred by the estate.
- Whether any gifts made by the decedent and the surviving spouse should be treated as made equally by both, *i.e.*, consenting to splitting gifts. IRC §2513.
- What should be the taxable year of the estate?
- Whether to make a QTIP (Qualified Terminable Interest Property) election for property passing to the surviving spouse via an income trust for the survivor's life. IRC §2056(b)(7).
- Whether the decedent's unused estate tax unified credit should be transferred to the surviving spouse. IRC §2010.
- Whether to extend (over a 10-year period) the time to pay any estate tax attributable to closely held business interests. IRC §6166.

Tax disclaimers also need to be considered by the beneficiaries. As discussed in Chapter 14, in order for a disclaimer to be effective for tax purposes, it must be made within nine months of the decedent's death in writing and delivered to the personal representative (and possibly a bank or investment company), the disclaimant cannot accept any benefits from the disclaimed property and the disclaimant cannot direct who receives the property. If done correctly, the disclaimant is deemed to have never owned the property and the interest passes to the alternate beneficiary as if the disclaimant predeceased the decedent.

The tax laws say that the executor is liable to file unfiled income and gift tax returns and the estate tax return and to pay tax due. Because the personal representative will be held personally liable for any taxes not paid by the estate if the personal representative distributed the property of the estate to others before making provision for taxes, the personal representative has a stake in making sure the taxes get paid first. IRS Form 4506T can be utilized by the personal representative to verify whether the decedent had filed all required income tax returns.

In order to fulfill the tax responsibilities, the personal representative will want to be sure of the exact amount of taxes due. The Internal Revenue Code provides a mechanism for the personal representative (1) to file a Form 4810 asking the Internal Revenue Service to make a prompt assessment (18 months instead of 36 months) of any income taxes due and (2) to request a discharge from personal liability for a decedent's income, gift and estate taxes (Form 5495).[24] IRC §§2204 and 6501(d). While these procedures provide the personal representative with liability relief, they may generate an examination by the IRS. Even if the IRS grants relief to the personal representative, the distributees of decedent's property remain liable as transferees and take the property subject to an estate tax lien. IRC §§6324 and 6901.

3.   Partial Distributions

Under the law of some states, distributions may not be made until the court orders them. However, under most state laws today and the UPC, distributions may be made without an order of the court once the nonclaim statute has run. This means distributions should not be made before four months have run where publication notice was employed and, more safely, one year for all debts. That being said, if the decedent was current on bills and very little is otherwise owed to creditors, partial distributions can safely be made earlier.

Making partial distributions is fraught with danger, however. While authorized to make distributions "as expeditiously and efficiently as is consistent with the best interests of the estate, [this] does not affect the duty of the personal representative to administer and distribute the estate in accordance with the rights of claimants whose claims have been allowed,

---

24. The request must be made after the returns for those taxes are filed. Within nine months after receipt of the request, the IRS will notify the executor of the amount of taxes due. If this amount is paid, the executor will be discharged from personal liability for any future deficiencies. If the IRS has not notified the executor, he or she will be discharged from personal liability at the end of the nine-month period.

the surviving spouse, any minor and dependent children and any preter-mitted child of the decedent as described elsewhere in this Code." UPC §3-703. Thus, personal liability can be levied on the personal representative for distributions that make the estate unable to pay creditors with a more senior status. *See also* UPC §3-807(b). In addition, "a distributee of property improperly distributed or paid, or a claimant who was improperly paid, is liable to return the property improperly received and its income since distribution if he has the property." UPC §3-909. Therefore, unless there are plenty of assets left in the estate subsequent to any distributions, it is wisest for the personal representative to uniformly deny calls for distributions from the beneficiaries. To the extent distributions are made, the personal representative should obtain a release from the distributee of personal liability.

L.   CLOSING THE ESTATE — THE FINAL ACCOUNTING AND THE FINAL DISTRIBUTION

1.   *The Procedure for Closing the Estate*

The final accounting and the distribution of the estate to devisees and heirs are the last stages of the personal representative's responsibilities leading to the closing of the estate. Closing an estate, like most aspects of estate administration, can be accomplished in formal proceedings by petition for an order of the court per UPC §3-1001 or UPC §3-1002 or informally by verified statement per UPC §3-1003.[25] Because formal proceedings better protect the personal representative from personal liability and more quickly relieve her of authority and responsibility, personal representatives occasionally choose the formal proceedings route, regardless whether prior aspects of administration were handled formally or informally. The reasons for the infrequency of employing this procedure despite its advantages to the personal representative are: (a) it is not preferred to get the court involved at the end of what has, so far, been an informal proceeding and to put in the public record what has been private information up to then; (b)

---

25. If the estate was never administered, UPC §3-901 says "the heirs and devisees are entitled to the estate in accordance with the terms of a probated will or the laws of intestate succession. Devisees may establish title by the probated will to devised property. Persons entitled to property by homestead allowance, exemption or intestacy may establish title thereto by proof of the decedent's ownership, his death, and their relationship to the decedent. Successors take subject to all charges incident to administration, including the claims of creditors and allowances of surviving spouse and dependent children, and subject to the rights of others resulting from abatement, retainer, advancement, and ademption." *See also* UPC §3-101.

a formal closing could delay what would otherwise be a straightforward matter; and (c) there are additional costs to the estate to do a formal closing.

Formal Closing.   If the nonclaim statute has run for presenting claims and after giving notice to all interested persons, the personal representative may petition the court for a complete settlement of the estate. Since the purpose of the petition is to finalize all open matters, "[t]he petition may request the Court to determine testacy, if not previously determined, to consider the final account or compel or approve an accounting and distribution, to construe any will or determine heirs and adjudicate the final settlement and distribution of the estate . . [and discharge] the personal representative from further claim or demand of any interested person." UPC §3-1001.

The judge reviews the accounting and the personal representative's request in the petition and allows all interested parties to challenge the disposition. After a hearing, if one is requested and the court finds that one is necessary, the judge will order whatever she deems is appropriate.

This process of obtaining a judicial order for disposition of the assets generally discharges the personal representative of any liability she may have in regard to the estate and the disposition thereof. It is the fact that all interested parties have a "last chance" to challenge the actions of the personal representative before the probate court that is the justification for the discharge under the formal procedures. However, if an interested party was not given notice of the formal proceedings terminating the estate, they may still have a claim against the personal representative. Therefore, a personal representative must be diligent in notifying all interested parties to be sure to discharge her liability.

Informal Closing.   The UPC also provides for an "informal" or court-free closing of the estate. UPC §3-1003 says "a personal representative may close an estate by filing with the court no earlier than six months after the date of original appointment of a general personal representative for the estate, a verified statement stating that the personal representative" has fulfilled all the responsibilities associated with administering the estate consistent with the law, including paying all expenses and claims, except those specified in the statement. The statement must also state that the personal representative "sent a copy of the statement to all distributees of the estate and to all creditors or other claimants of whom the personal representative is aware whose claims are neither paid nor barred and has furnished a full account in writing of the personal representative's administration to the distributees whose interests are affected thereby."

Contrary to the court supervised closing process, "a 'closing' statement under 3-1003 is only an affirmation by the personal representative that he believes the affairs of the estate to be completed. The statement is significant because it reflects that assets have been distributed. Any creditor whose claim has not been barred and who has not been paid is permitted

by Section 3-1004 to assert his claim against distributees [as transferees]."
Comment to UPC §3-1003.

Informal closing does not discharge the personal representative of
personal liability at the time of disposition or terminate her authority.
Instead, the liability of the personal representative using the informal
process terminates six months after the filing of the closing statement if no
claims are pending. UPC §3-1005. In addition, the personal representative
is still fully subject to suit under UPC §§3-602 and 3-608, for her authority
is not "terminated" under UPC §3-610(a) until one year after a closing
statement is filed. A receipt and release from all who have received a
distribution generally protects the personal representative from those who
might claim error.

2.   The Final Accounting

You will recall that one of the first things the personal representative must
do after being appointed is to prepare an inventory of the estate assets and
to supplement the inventory if the original was incorrect in some manner.
The inventory provides interested parties with a starting point in monitoring the personal representative's administration of the estate.

After the inventory is filed, the financial aspects of the personal
representative's duties during administration are substantiated by means of
a detailed accounting of all income, expenditures, receipts from property
disposed of or payments for property acquired and of allocations of these
between income and principal and among beneficiaries.[26] The accounting
will also reflect any distributions to beneficiaries and heirs and payments to
creditors and taxing authorities to satisfy valid claims. If the financial
display does not tell the whole story or is complicated and difficult to understand, the personal representative should include a narrative that explains
certain items.

> **Example.**   If the decedent's rental property was sold, the narrative
> might say: "The decedent's rental property at 2034 Albion Street was
> sold on December 2, 20XX, for $500,000. After the $200,000 mortgage
> to First Mortgage and other expenses of closing were paid, the balance
> of $275,000 was deposited in the Bank of the West, account number
> 1239756. A copy of the seller's closing statement is attached to this
> accounting."

Under the law of most states, the personal representative must provide
the beneficiaries with an interim accounting if the administration takes
longer than a year or when ordered to do so by the court.

---

26. Receipts, invoices, contracts or sale, vouchers and other documentation should be
retained as verification.

A final accounting is required when seeking to close the estate.[27] UPC §§3-1001 to 3-1003. The inventory of the assets (at date of distribution fair market value) and the final accounting provide the basis as to what is there for distribution. The UPC does not require that a final accounting be sent to the court or the Registrar; it only needs to be sent to all interested persons. The beneficiaries should review the accounting carefully to be sure the estate was properly administered and petition the court if there are problems. Once the accounting is approved, the personal representative is generally relieved of any liability associated with administering the estate.

Under the UPC and the law of all states, the personal representative may perform the accounting personally or hire a professional. In the event a professional is hired, the personal representative is relieved of liability or deficiency by the hired accountant and is not required to independently investigate the records to verify their accuracy.

3.   *The Final Distribution*

After everything else has been taken care of and accounted for, it is time for the estate to be distributed to the devisees and heirs. Who gets what property would seem like a relatively simple question to answer: just look at the will, a memorandum for the disposition of personal property or the intestacy statute. However, things are not so clear. For example, assume a decedent died with a potpourri of assets, including real estate, stocks, bonds and bank accounts. Most of the assets are not liquid. Debts and taxes have to be paid. There are mortgages on the real estate. There are expenses of managing the estate during administration. Some of the assets need to be sold to pay the debts and expenses. Some of the property that exists in the estate has increased in value and some decreased.

Which assets should be sold and which retained? Which beneficiaries' rights to the property should be abated to pay the debts and expenses? Are distributions affected by appreciation or depreciation in the value of the property? These and many more questions, including the reasonableness of the personal representative's fees, need to be resolved by the personal representative and/or the court before final distribution is made.

In order to pay debts and expenses, someone's bequest or inheritance has to be reduced to pay them. UPC §3-902 tells us that "shares of distributees abate, without any preference or priority as between real and personal

---

27. The UPC does not require that interim reports be filed with the court. The fiduciary duty to keep beneficiaries informed, however, requires that the personal representative provide interim accountings and reports to beneficiaries often enough to keep them fully advised about the administration of the estate. It is recommended that a copy of every check written is kept and maintained. The personal representative may be personally liable for any loss so a detailed accounting is necessary. These records are also very important for tax reasons. In addition, income produced by the assets such as dividends from stock must also be accounted for and included in the final report.

property [therefore bequests and devises are treated equally], in the following order," but that within each classification, abatement is pro-rata:

(1) residuary devises;
(2) general and pecuniary devises;
(3) specific devises.

The statutory order of abatement is overridden if "the will expresses an order of abatement, or if the testamentary plan or the express or implied purpose of the devise would be defeated by the order of abatement stated in subsection (a) [and would be inconsistent with the testator's intention]. . . ."

> **Example:** Decedent died with $500,000 in property and $320,000 in debts, exclusive of mortgages on real estate. Another $30,000 was spent in administering the estate. Decedent's will left a $25,000 ring to son and $35,000 of stock in the family business to daughter. Cash gifts were made to the television ministries of The New Life Church and the Old Life Church of $40,000 and $60,000, respectively. The residue, which would have amounted to $340,000 if there were no debts and expenses, was left to spouse. Unless the will provides for a different order or it is established that the order would be intent-defeating, spouse's residuary bequest will be eliminated to pay the $350,000 in debts and expenses of administration. The gifts to the charities will be reduced proportionate to the amount they were gifted to pay the remaining $10,000 in debts and expenses with New Life's bequest being abated by $4,000 and Old Life's bequest being abated by $6,000. The specific devises to the children are not disturbed.

Other matters also need to be considered before a final plan of distribution can be decided upon. These should have been resolved earlier when the proposed plan of disposition was presented. See Section K.1 above for a list of many of the issues that need to be considered.

These and other matters having been addressed by the personal representative, a statement of the proposed distribution must be filed with the court (assuming the informal procedure in UPC §3-1103 of a verified statement is not utilized) along with a Petition for Final Settlement and Distribution of the Estate. The personal representative must also give notice to the interested parties. After a hearing, if one is needed due to an objection raised by an interested party, the court will issue an Order of Final Settlement and Distribution. Only then may the personal representative begin to distribute assets of the estate.

"Unless a contrary intention is indicated by the will, the distributable assets of a decedent's estate shall be distributed in kind to the extent possible. . . ." UPC §3-906. "If distribution in kind is made, the personal representative shall execute an instrument or deed of distribution assigning, transferring or releasing the assets to the distributee as evidence of the distributee's title to the property." UPC §3-907. Where the beneficiaries are minors or are under some other disability, special rules apply. UPC §3-915. Receipts should be obtained by the personal representative for all distributions.

Once the distribution is complete, the personal representative will pay herself whatever amount she is still owed (keeping in mind that, as an administrative expense, the personal representative has likely been paid periodically as the case moved forward) and file for a Decree of Final Discharge.

EXERCISE

You represent the executor of the estate of Daniel Moe. Please file (1) the final accounting and (2) petition for final settlement and distribution. To the extent not provided here, use the Daniel Moe facts in previous exercises. If your state does not have the forms posted online, use those of Denver, Colorado, http://www.denverprobatecourt.org/forms.htm or California, http://www.courtinfo.ca.gov/cgi-bin/forms.cgi.

Receipts:

Refund of Insurance from State Farm	$47
Final paycheck from Xcel	$2,791
Incentive payment from Xcel	$2,458
Proceeds from sale of Residence at 2640 East Mississippi Ave	$179
Refund of escrow Residence at 2640 East Mississippi Ave	$266
Refund of overpayment to your law firm	$1,602

Expenditures:

Check to funeral home	$953
Various checks to Your law firm for legal services	$5,810
Expenses of sale of 2640 East Mississippi Ave	$580

4. Finality of Final Settlement and Reopening the Estate

Generally, once the Decree of Final Discharge is granted, the settlement is final and the estate cannot be reopened. However, there are exceptions. The personal representative may move to reopen the estate if other property of the decedent is later discovered and it was not administered, if he must perform a necessary act that requires his authority, like signing a tax return, or for any other proper purpose determined by the court; for example, the decedent was originally deemed to have died intestate and a will is later discovered.

UPC §3-1008. Subsequent Administration.

> If other property of the estate is discovered after an estate has been settled and the personal representative discharged or after one year after a closing statement has been filed, the Court upon petition of any interested person and upon notice as it directs may appoint the same or a successor personal representative to administer the subsequently discovered estate. If a new appointment is made, unless the Court orders otherwise, the provisions of this Code apply as appropriate; but no claim previously barred may be asserted in the subsequent administration.

The Decree of Final Discharge also provides protection to the personal representative for actions taken, except where there was misconduct or nondisclosure.

M.   ETHICAL ISSUES IN ESTATE ADMINISTRATION

Early in the chapter, we looked at one question of professional responsibility: Does the attorney have the competence and skill necessary to advise a personal representative? Now, we are going to circle back and look at two other professional responsibility issues that arise frequently in the context of estate administration. To help you understand the framework, we will use both the Model Rule and the Commentaries of the American College of Trusts and Estate Counsel (ACTEC), which help give more context in applying the Model Rules specifically to estate planning.

1.   Who Is the Client?

An attorney may be retained by any one of the many parties in the estate administration drama: the personal representative, a creditor, a named beneficiary, a family member or any other person not named as a beneficiary that thought they had a right to an inheritance, a charity or a variety of others. The focus of this discussion is on the situation where the attorney is retained by the personal representative. To what extent does the attorney owe a duty to the beneficiaries in addition to the personal representative, the breach of which may be actionable?

MRPC 1.2. Scope of Representation and Allocation of Authority Between Client and Lawyer

(a) Subject to paragraphs (c) and (d), a lawyer shall abide by a client's decisions concerning the objectives of representation and, as required by Rule 1.4, shall consult with the client as to the means by which they are to be pursued. A lawyer may take such action on behalf of the client as is impliedly authorized to carry out the representation. A lawyer shall abide by a client's decision whether to settle a matter. In a criminal case, the lawyer shall abide by the client's decision, after consultation with the lawyer, as to a plea to be entered, whether to waive jury trial and whether the client will testify.

(b) A lawyer's representation of a client, including representation by appointment, does not constitute an endorsement of the client's political, economic, social or moral views or activities.

(c) A lawyer may limit the scope of the representation if the limitation is reasonable under the circumstances and the client gives informed consent.

(d) A lawyer shall not counsel a client to engage, or assist a client, in conduct that the lawyer knows is criminal or fraudulent, but a lawyer may discuss the legal consequences of any proposed course of conduct with a client and may counsel or assist a client to make a good faith effort to determine the validity, scope, meaning or application of the law.

* * *

ACTEC COMMENTARY ON MRPC 1.2

General Principles.   The client and the lawyer, working together, are relatively free to define the scope and objectives of the representation, including the extent to which information will be shared among multiple clients and the nature and extent of the obligations that the lawyer will have to the client. If multiple clients are involved, the lawyer should discuss with them the scope of the representation and any actual or potential conflicts and determine the basis upon which the lawyer will undertake the representation. As stated in the Comment to MRPC 1.7 (Conflict of Interest: General Rule) with respect to estate administration, "the lawyer should make clear the lawyer's relationship to the parties involved." Also, as indicated in the ACTEC Commentary on MRPC 1.6 (Confidentiality of Information), 1.7 (Conflict of Interest: General Rule) and former Rule 2.2 (Intermediary), it is often permissible for a lawyer to represent more than one client in a single matter or in related matters. . . .

In the estate planning context, the lawyer should discuss with the client the functions that a personal representative, trustee, or other fiduciary will perform in the client's estate plan. In addition, the lawyer should describe to the client the role that the lawyer for the personal representative, trustee, or other fiduciary usually plays in the administration of the fiduciary estate, including the possibility that the lawyer for the fiduciary may owe duties to the beneficiaries of the fiduciary estate. By doing so the lawyer better equips the client to select and give directions to fiduciaries. The lawyer should be alert to the multiplicity of relationships and challenging ethical issues that may arise when the representation involves employee benefit plans, charitable trusts or foundations. . . .

Communication with Beneficiaries of Fiduciary Estate. The lawyer engaged by a fiduciary to represent the fiduciary generally in connection with a fiduciary estate may communicate directly with the beneficiaries regarding the nature of the relationship between the lawyer and the beneficiaries. However, the fiduciary is primarily responsible for communicating with the beneficiaries regarding the fiduciary estate. An early meeting between the fiduciary, the lawyer, and the beneficiaries may provide all parties with a better understanding of the proceeding and lead to a more efficient administration. . . .

As a general rule, the lawyer for the fiduciary should inform the beneficiaries that the lawyer has been retained by the fiduciary regarding the fiduciary estate and that the fiduciary is the lawyer's client; that while the fiduciary and the lawyer will, from time-to-time, provide information to the beneficiaries regarding the fiduciary estate, the lawyer does not represent them; and that the beneficiaries may wish to retain independent counsel to represent their interests. As indicated in MRPC 2.3 (Evaluation for Use by Third Persons), the lawyer may, at the request of a client, evaluate a matter affecting a client for the use of others.

Representation   of   Fiduciary   in   Representative   and   Individual Capacities.   The lawyer may represent the fiduciary in a representative capacity and as a beneficiary except as otherwise proscribed, as it may be in some cases by MRPC 1.7 (Conflict of Interest: General Rule).

Example 1.2-1:   Lawyer (L) drew a will for X in which X left her entire estate in equal shares to A and B and appointed A as executor. X died survived by A and B. A asked L to represent her both as executor and as beneficiary. L explained to A the duties A would have as personal representative, including the duty of impartiality toward the beneficiaries. L also described to A the implications of the common representation, to which A consented. L may properly represent A in both capacities. However, L should inform B of the dual representation and indicate that B may, at his or her own expense, retain independent counsel. In addition, L should maintain separate records with respect to the individual representation of A, who should be charged a separate fee (payable by A individually) for that representation. L may

properly counsel A with respect to her interests as beneficiary. However, L may not assert A's individual rights on A's behalf in a way that
conflicts with A's duties as personal representative. If a conflict develops that materially limits L's ability to function as A's lawyer in both
capacities, L should withdraw from representing A in one or both
capacities. . . .

Defining and Refining the Scope of Representation. As the lawyer obtains
information from a client, the lawyer and the client are typically working
together toward defining further the scope and objectives of the representation, which are often revised as the representation progresses. One of the
lawyer's goals should be to educate the client sufficiently about the process
and the options available to allow the client to make informed decisions
regarding the representation. See ACTEC Commentary on MRPC 1.4
(Communication). In furtherance of that goal many lawyers review with
an estate planning client the appropriate alternative methods by which the
client's general estate planning objectives could be implemented. In the
course of doing so the lawyer should express to the client the relative cost
advantages of the alternatives, including the present and future tax, legal
and other costs, such as trustee's fees. See ACTEC Commentary on MRPC
2.1 (Advisor).

Formal and Informal Agreements. Variations in the circumstances and
needs of trusts and estates clients and in the approach and practice of individual lawyers naturally result in lawyers and clients adopting different
methods of working together. The agreement between a lawyer and client
regarding the scope and objectives of the representation is often best
expressed in an engagement letter or other written communication. However, often their agreement is implicit—reflected in the manner in which
lawyer and client choose to work together. Their approach will reflect the
client's needs (as perceived by the client and the lawyer) and the lawyer's
judgment regarding the client's needs and objectives and the ways in which
they may reasonably be fulfilled. . . .

Disclosure of Acts or Omissions by Fiduciary Client. In some jurisdictions a
lawyer who represents a fiduciary generally with respect to the fiduciary
estate may disclose to a court or to the beneficiaries acts or omissions by the
fiduciary that might constitute a breach of fiduciary duty. In deciding
whether to make such a disclosure, the lawyer should consider MRPC 1.8
(b). See ACTEC Commentary on MRPC 1.6 (Confidentiality of Information). In jurisdictions that do not require or permit such disclosures, a
lawyer engaged by a fiduciary may condition the representation upon the
fiduciary's agreement that the creation of a lawyer-client relationship
between them will not preclude the lawyer from disclosing to the beneficiaries of the fiduciary estate or to an appropriate court any actions of the
fiduciary that might constitute a breach of fiduciary duty. The lawyer may
wish to propose that such an agreement be entered into in order better to

assure that the intentions of the creator of the fiduciary estate to benefit the beneficiaries will be fulfilled. Whether or not such an agreement is made, the lawyer for the fiduciary ordinarily owes some duties (largely restrictive in nature) to the beneficiaries of the fiduciary estate. The nature and extent of the duties of the lawyer for the fiduciary are shaped by the nature of the fiduciary estate and by the nature and extent of the lawyer's representation. . . .

General and Individual Representation Distinguished.   A lawyer represents the fiduciary generally (i.e., in a representative capacity) when the lawyer is retained to advise the fiduciary regarding the administration of the fiduciary estate or matters affecting the estate. On the other hand, a lawyer represents a fiduciary individually when the lawyer is retained for the limited purpose of advancing the interests of the fiduciary and not necessarily the interests of the fiduciary estate or the persons beneficially interested in the estate. For example, a lawyer represents a fiduciary individually when the lawyer, who may or may not have previously represented the fiduciary generally with respect to the fiduciary estate, is retained to negotiate with the beneficiaries regarding the compensation of the fiduciary or to defend the fiduciary against charges or threatened charges of mal-administration of the fiduciary estate. A lawyer who represents a fiduciary generally may normally also undertake to represent the fiduciary individually. If the lawyer has previously represented the fiduciary generally and is now representing the fiduciary individually, the lawyer should advise the beneficiaries of this fact.

Lawyer Should Not Attempt to Diminish Duties of Lawyer to Beneficiaries Without Notice to Them.   Without having first given written notice to the beneficiaries of the fiduciary estate, a lawyer who represents a fiduciary generally should not enter into an agreement with the fiduciary that attempts to diminish or eliminate the duties that the lawyer otherwise owes to the beneficiaries of the fiduciary estate. For example, without first giving notice to the beneficiaries of the fiduciary estate, a lawyer should not agree with a fiduciary not to disclose to the beneficiaries of the fiduciary estate any acts or omissions on the part of the fiduciary that the lawyer would otherwise be permitted or required to disclose to the beneficiaries. In jurisdictions that permit the lawyer for a fiduciary to make such disclosures, the lawyer generally should not give up the opportunity to make such disclosures when the lawyer determines the disclosures are needed to protect the interests of the beneficiaries.

Duties to Beneficiaries.   The nature and extent of the lawyer's duties to the beneficiaries of the fiduciary estate may vary according to the circumstances, including the nature and extent of the representation and the terms of any understanding or agreement among the parties (the lawyer, the fiduciary, and the beneficiaries). The lawyer for the fiduciary owes some duties to the beneficiaries of the fiduciary estate although he or she does not represent them. The duties, which are largely restrictive in nature, prohibit the lawyer from taking advantage of his or her position to the disadvantage of the fiduciary estate or the beneficiaries. In addition, in some circumstances the lawyer may be obligated to take affirmative action to protect the interests of the beneficiaries. Some courts have characterized the beneficiaries of a fiduciary estate as derivative or secondary clients of the lawyer for the fiduciary. The beneficiaries of a fiduciary estate are generally not characterized as direct clients of the lawyer for the fiduciary merely because the lawyer represents the fiduciary generally with respect to the fiduciary estate.

The scope of the representation of a fiduciary is an important factor in determining the nature and extent of the duties owed to the beneficiaries of the fiduciary estate. For example, a lawyer who is retained by a fiduciary individually may owe few, if any, duties to the beneficiaries of the fiduciary estate other than duties the lawyer owes to other third parties generally. Thus, a lawyer who is retained by a fiduciary to advise the fiduciary regarding the fiduciary's defense to an action brought against the fiduciary by a beneficiary may have no duties to the beneficiaries beyond those owed to other adverse parties or nonclients. In resolving conflicts regarding the nature and extent of the lawyer's duties some courts have considered the source from which the lawyer is compensated. . . .

Lawyer Serving as Fiduciary and Counsel to Fiduciary.   Some states permit a lawyer who serves as a fiduciary to serve also as lawyer for the fiduciary. Such dual service may be appropriate where the lawyer previously represented the decedent or is a primary beneficiary of the fiduciary estate. It may also be appropriate where there has been a long standing relationship between the lawyer and the client. Generally, a lawyer should serve in both capacities only if the client insists and is aware of the alternatives, and the lawyer is competent to do so. A lawyer who is asked to serve in both capacities should inform the client regarding the costs of such dual service and the alternatives to it. A lawyer undertaking to serve in both capacities should attempt to ameliorate any disadvantages that may come from dual service, including the potential loss of the benefits that are obtained by having a separate fiduciary and lawyer, such as the checks and balances that a separate fiduciary might provide upon the amount of fees sought by the lawyer and vice versa.

---

2.   Conflict of Interest — Dual Representation

Closely related to the question of who the client is and the duty the attorney owes to the other parties is whether the attorney has a conflict of interest.

MRPC 1.7. Conflict Of Interest: Current Clients

(a) Except as provided in paragraph (b), a lawyer shall not represent a client if the representation involves a concurrent conflict of interest. A concurrent conflict of interest exists if:

(1) the representation of one client will be directly adverse to another client; or

(2) there is a significant risk that the representation of one or more clients will be materially limited by the lawyer's responsibilities to another client, a former client or a third person or by a personal interest of the lawyer.

(b) Notwithstanding the existence of a concurrent conflict of interest under paragraph (a), a lawyer may represent a client if:

(1) the lawyer reasonably believes that the lawyer will be able to provide competent and diligent representation to each affected client;

(2) the representation is not prohibited by law;

(3) the representation does not involve the assertion of a claim by one client against another client represented by the lawyer in the same litigation or other proceeding before a tribunal; and

(4) each affected client gives informed consent, confirmed in writing.

* * *

ACTEC COMMENTARY ON MRPC 1.7

General Nonadversary Character of Estates and Trusts Practice; Representation of Multiple Clients. It is often appropriate for a lawyer to represent more than one member of the same family in connection with their estate plans, more than one beneficiary with common interests in an estate or trust administration matter, co-fiduciaries of an estate or trust, or more than one of the investors in a closely held business. See ACTEC Commentary on MRPC 1.6 (Confidentiality of Information). In some instances the clients may actually be better served by such a representation, which can result in more economical and better coordinated estate plans prepared by counsel who has a better overall understanding of all of the relevant family and property considerations. The fact that the estate planning goals of the clients are not entirely consistent does not necessarily preclude the lawyer from representing them: Advising related clients who have somewhat differing goals may be consistent with their interests and the lawyer's traditional role as the lawyer for the "family." Multiple representation is also generally appropriate because the interests of the clients in cooperation, including obtaining cost effective representation and achieving common objectives, often clearly predominate over their limited inconsistent interests. Recognition should be given to the fact that estate planning is fundamentally nonadversarial in nature and estate administration is usually nonadversarial.

Disclosures to Multiple Clients.   Before, or within a reasonable time after, commencing the representation, a lawyer who is consulted by multiple parties with related interests should discuss with them the implications of a joint representation (or a separate representation if the lawyer believes that mode of representation to be more appropriate and separate representation is permissible under the applicable local rules). See ACTEC Commentary on MRPC 1.6 (Confidentiality of Information). In particular, the prospective clients and the lawyer should discuss the extent to which material information imparted by either client would be shared with the other and the possibility that the lawyer would be required to withdraw if a conflict in their interests developed to the degree that the lawyer could not effectively represent each of them. The information may be best understood by the clients if it is discussed with them in person and also provided to them in written form, as in an engagement letter or brochure. As noted in the ACTEC Commentary on MRPC 1.2 (Scope of Representation and Allocation of Authority Between Client and Lawyer), a lawyer may represent co-fiduciaries whose interests do not conflict to an impermissible degree. A lawyer who represents co-fiduciaries may also represent one or both of them as beneficiaries so long as no disabling conflict arises.

Before accepting a representation involving multiple parties a lawyer may wish to consider meeting with the prospective clients separately, which may allow each of them to be more candid and, perhaps, reveal conflicts of interest.

Consider Possible Presence and Impact of Any Conflicts of Interest.   A lawyer who is asked to represent multiple clients regarding related matters must consider at the outset whether the representation involves or may involve impermissible conflicts, including ones that affect the interests of third parties or the lawyer's own interests. The lawyer must also bear this concern in mind as the representation progresses: What was a tolerable conflict at the outset may develop into one that precludes the lawyer from continuing to represent one or more of the clients.

Example 1.7-3:   Lawyer (L) represented Husband (H) and Wife (W) jointly with respect to estate planning matters. H died leaving a will that appointed Bank (B) as executor and as trustee of a trust for the benefit of W that meets the QTIP requirements under I.R.C. 2056(b)(7). L has agreed to represent B and knows that W looks to him as her lawyer. L may represent both B and W if the requirements of MRPC 1.7 are met. If a serious conflict arises between B and W, L may be required to withdraw as counsel for B or W or both. L may inform W of her elective share, support, homestead or other rights under the local law without violating MRPC 1.9 (Duties to Former Clients).

However, without the informed consent of all affected parties confirmed in writing, L should not represent W in connection with an attempt to set aside H's will or to assert an elective share.

Conflicts of Interest May Preclude Multiple Representation.   Some conflicts of interest are so serious that the informed consent of the parties is insufficient to allow the lawyer to undertake or continue the representation (a "non-waivable" conflict). Thus, a lawyer may not represent clients whose interests actually conflict to such a degree that the lawyer cannot adequately represent their individual interests. A lawyer may never represent opposing parties in the same litigation. A lawyer is almost always precluded from representing both parties to a pre-nuptial agreement or other matter with respect to which their interests directly conflict to a substantial degree. Thus, a lawyer who represents the personal representative of a decedent's estate (or the trustee of a trust) should not also represent a creditor in connection with a claim against the estate (or trust). This prohibition applies whether the creditor is the fiduciary individually or another party. On the other hand, if the actual or potential conflicts between competent, independent parties are not substantial, their common interests predominate, and it otherwise appears appropriate to do so, the lawyer and the parties may agree that the lawyer will represent them jointly subject to MRPC 1.7 (Conflict of Interest: General Rule) or act as an intermediary pursuant to former MRPC 2.2 (Intermediary).

Prospective Waivers.   A client who is adequately informed may waive some conflicts that might otherwise prevent the lawyer from representing another person in connection with the same or a related matter. These conflicts are said to be "waivable." Thus, a surviving spouse who serves as the personal representative of her husband's estate may give her informed consent confirmed in writing to permit the lawyer who represents her as personal representative also to represent a child who is a beneficiary of the estate. The lawyer also would need an informed consent from the child that is confirmed in writing before undertaking such a dual representation. However, a conflict might arise between the personal representative and the beneficiary that would preclude the lawyer from continuing to represent both, or either, of them.

PROBLEM

You have been retained by Jennifer Donnelly (of 1815 Brentwood Street, Your City, Your State), wife of Daniel Moe and mother of his two children, Connor Ryan Moe (born August 13, six years ago) and Grace Eryn Moe (born June 7, four years ago) to represent her as the personal representative of Daniel Moe's estate. Assume for purposes of this problem that Jennifer and Daniel were still married at the time of his death. As part of the administration of the intestate estate, it comes to light that Daniel had another child (Georgia Ming Britton) by another woman. To what extent may you also give advice to Jennifer about her intestate share and elective share? To the guardians of Connor and Grace about their intestate share? To the guardian of Georgia about her intestate share? To the extent you may give advice, what precautions would you take?

APPENDIX A

ESTATE ADMINISTRATION CHECKLIST[28]

Estate of:_____   Letters issued:_____

Date of Death:_____3 month:_____9 month:_____

EIN:_____   County:_____   File No.:_____

Initial Tasks:

_____   Obtain death certificates

_____   Determine citizenship of Decedent and spouse

_____   Obtain **AND READ** Will (and any codicils), revocable trust (and any amendments)

_____   If Decedent was divorced, obtain a copy of the settlement agreement and divorce decree

_____   Obtain names, addresses, telephone numbers, birth dates, social security numbers of heirs, beneficiaries and fiduciaries

_____   Enter estate administration deadlines so that they appear for both attorney and paralegal assigned

_____   Prepare probate petition (including renunciations, if any)

_____   Attend probate; arrange for witnesses to be present or affidavits prepared if Will not self-proved

_____   Consider filing change of address form with the post office

_____   Prepare engagement letter

_____   Obtain IRS Employer Identification Number (EIN) for estate

_____   Obtain IRS Employer Identification Number (EIN) for revocable trust, if applicable

_____   Open estate checking account and advise fiduciary about record keeping

_____   Contact Social Security Administration for death benefits, if applicable

_____   If Decedent was over age 55, contact Pennsylvania Department of Public Welfare to confirm Decedent was not receiving state benefits and that no lien for such benefits exists

_____   Contact Veterans Administration for death benefits, if applicable

_____   File IRS Form 56 (Notice Concerning Fiduciary Relationship)

---

28. *Note*: This list is not an exhaustive list of all items that must be considered in every estate. While it has been designed for decedents dying in Pennsylvania, it may be useful in other states also. © 2011 Heckscher, Teillon, Terrill & Sager, P.C., West Conshohocken, Pennsylvania. All rights reserved.

_____ Advertise the estate and/or revocable trust (once per week for three weeks in newspaper of general circulation and legal periodical in county of residence); this is critical in order to cut off possible claims

_____ Search Pennsylvania Unclaimed Property Database

_____ If Decedent was the settlor of a revocable trust, send Notices to Beneficiaries within 30 days of Decedent's death (for deaths after 11/6/2006)

_____ Send notice of death/probate to beneficiaries named in Decedent's will, and certain intestate heirs even if not named (Pennsylvania Orphans' Court Rule 5.6) within 90 days of fiduciary's Appointment

_____ File Certification of 5.6 Notices with Register of Wills within 3 months of probate

_____ Determine if Decedent owned a safe deposit box exists, how it is registered, and arrange to open and inventory, obtaining permission from Pennsylvania Department of Revenue, if required

_____ Obtain Ancillary Letters Testamentary/Administration for out-of-state real estate, if applicable; contact local counsel, if necessary

_____ Direct executor to retain and provide to cancelled checks, registers, and bank statements for 3 years prior to death

_____ Obtain funeral, medical and administrative expenses

_____ Determine if Decedent ever lived in or owned property in a community property state (CA, WA, NV, AZ, NM, TX, LA, UT, WI)

_____ Determine if Decedent had any eggs, sperm, or other reproductive material stored that may result in after-death children

_____ Determine if Decedent was the plaintiff or defendant in any ongoing or potential legal proceeding (including divorce)

_____ Secure decedent's computer(s) and obtain and secure decedent's passwords

_____ Determine if Decedent had any outstanding charitable pledges

_____ Consider liquidity needs of the estate

Life Insurance:

_____ Obtain name and policy numbers of all life insurance on Decedent's life

_____ Determine owner and beneficiary of each policy

_____ Apply for proceeds

_____ Obtain IRS Form 712 (Life Insurance Statement) for each policy

_____ Determine if the Decedent was the owner of any policy on another individual's life

Health Insurance:

_____ File medical claims

_____ Determine coverage for surviving family members; cancel policy and obtain refund, if applicable

Homeowner's Insurance:

_____ Notify agent/ insurance company of homeowner's death, and obtain new coverage for estate (or surviving spouse)

Employee Benefits:

_____ Collect any unpaid salary, bonus, commissions

_____ Contact employer

_____ Receive accrued vacation/holiday and sick compensation pay

_____ Apply for retirement and/or pension

_____ Apply for group life insurance

_____ Apply for death benefits

Retirement Benefits (401(k), 403(b), 457, IRA, Roth IRA, Roth 401(k), etc.) and Annuities:

_____ Contact plan administrator

_____ Obtain copy of plan documents

_____ Obtain copy of beneficiary designation forms

_____ If Decedent had reached his or her required beginning date (April 1st of the year after the year Decedent reached age 70½), determine if Decedent had taken the required minimum distribution for the year of death. If not, arrange for the beneficiary to take this distribution no later than December 31st of the year of death

_____ Consider rollover to spouse's IRA, if spouse is beneficiary

_____ Consider trustee to trustee transfer to an inherited IRA, if non-spouse is beneficiary

_____ If payable to a trust, determine oldest potential beneficiary (remember options to remove non-qualifying beneficiaries by September 30th of the year after Decedent's death)

_____ If payable to a trust, provide required documentation to plan administrator by October 31st of the year after death

_____ If multiple beneficiaries, consider dividing account by December 31st of the year after death so that each beneficiary may use his or her life expectancy

_____ If federal estate tax is paid, provide beneficiaries with information on Income in Respect of Decedent (IRD) deduction

_____ Suggest that beneficiaries obtain advice on distribution options from attorney or other advisors

Real Property:

_____ Obtain copy of deed or title search

_____ Determine if property was subject to a conservation easement

_____ Obtain date of death balance of mortgage

_____ Discuss with executor protection, upkeep and expenses (i.e. insurance, utilities — particularly if property is vacant — and real estate taxes)

_____ Obtain date of death appraisal

_____ If property was for sale or recently sold, obtain copies of listing agreements and/or settlement sheet, if applicable

_____ Prepare new deed, if applicable

_____ Consider applicability of <u>Gallenstein</u> Doctrine (if real estate was purchased by husband and wife before 1977)

Automobiles, Boats and Airplanes:

_____ Determine value

_____ Transfer ownership

_____ Obtain amounts of any loans and discuss with client payment of same

_____ Cancel insurance and/or obtain new insurance in name of estate or new owner, if applicable

Tangible Personal Property:

_____ Determine if Decedent left any notes or memoranda as to the distribution of tangible personal property

_____ Determine ownership (such as joint with spouse)

_____ Determine if appraisal is necessary

_____ Address storage and insurance

_____ Discuss method of distribution

_____ Cancel insurance and/or obtain new insurance in name of estate or new owner, if applicable

Cash Accounts:

_____ Obtain registration information (sole name, joint name, pay on death, etc.) and date of death balances

_____ Transfer balance to estate account or joint tenant or pay on death beneficiary, and close accounts

Securities (including mutual funds):

_____ Obtain registration information (sole name, joint name, transfer on death, etc.) and date of death balances

_____ Obtain accrued interest on bonds to date of death

_____ Consider applicability of <u>Gallenstein</u> Doctrine (if purchased by husband and wife before 1977)

_____ Transfer balance to estate account or joint tenant or pay on death beneficiary, and close accounts

Business Interests:

_____ Obtain tax returns, balance sheets, and financial records for last five years

_____ Determine type of entity (S-corp, C-corp, LLC, sole proprietorship, etc.)

_____ Obtain ownership information and valuation

_____ Consider IRS section 754 election for partnerships

_____ Consider ESBT, QSST elections, or prompt distributions. Consider S-corp issues in all funding decisions

_____ Determine whether Decedent/Estate subject to shareholders or partnership agreement and, if so, obtain those documents

_____ Determine if the governing instruments include a transfer restriction

Other Assets:

_____   Any claims? (accident insurance?)

_____   Pooled Income Funds where decedent received an annuity and balance is paid to charity

_____   Frequent Flier Accounts

Cash and Specific Bequests:

_____   Distribute cash and specific bequests

_____   Pay interest on cash bequests, if required by state law

_____   Prepare and obtain Receipt and Releases

Elections:

_____   Consider spousal election issues (elective share)

Disclaimers:

_____   File timely with the court (nine months after date of death for Pennsylvania; for other states, check the statute)

Gift and Lifetime Taxes:

_____   Obtain copies of all Gift Tax Returns filed; order from the IRS if applicable

_____   Obtain list of all gift(s) within year of death, including education and medical payments, charitable contributions, and contributions to 529 plans; determine ifany require a gift tax return

_____   Obtain name of accountant preparing life period final lifetime Income Tax Return; determine if additional estimated payment need be made; obtain copies of individual income tax returns for the last three years

Death Taxes:

_____   Obtain copies of Federal Estate Tax Return and Pennsylvania Inheritance Tax Return for pre-deceased spouse. Determine if any marital trusts need to be included on the Federal Estate Tax Return (QTIP and general power marital trusts) or the Pennsylvania Inheritance Tax Return (sole-use trust)

_____   Determine if a Pennsylvania remainder inheritance tax return needs to be filed (for trusts created before 1982 in which Decedent had an interest)

_____   Inquire if Decedent had inherited assets from another person in the 10 years before death. If so, obtain copies of the federal estate tax return filed in that estate, for possible use in claiming the TPT (tax on prior transfers) credit against federal estate tax

_____   Make Pennsylvania Inheritance Tax Prepayment (three months after date of death) in order to obtain 5% discount on tax due

_____   File Pennsylvania Inheritance Tax Return (due nine months after date of death, with a six month extension possible)

_____   Consider Pennsylvania election to tax for sole use property, including out-of-state real estate and life insurance

_____   Check six month alternate valuations for federal taxable estates

_____   File U.S. Estate Tax Return (due nine months after date of death, with a six month extension possible)

_____ Consider IRS section 6161, 6166, and 303 elections, and Graegin loans

_____ File Non-Resident Inheritance Tax Return or Non-Resident Estate Tax Return in PA or other state, if applicable. Confirm filing date; note that New Jersey inheritance tax return is due 8 months after death, not 9 months

_____ Consider tax apportionment issues

_____ Obtain and file signed IRS Power of Attorney (Form 2848)

Fiduciary Income Taxes:

_____ Prepare income projection and consider timing of income distributions; review one month before end of fiscal year and sixty-five days after end of fiscal year

_____ Select fiscal year and consider the impact on partnerships

_____ File Fiduciary Income Tax Returns (in accordance with selected fiscal year end)

_____ Consider IRS section 645 election if a revocable trust (File Form 8855)

_____ Forward K-1s and Pennsylvania RK-1 and NRK-1 to beneficiaries

_____ Prepare IRS form 1099s

_____ File Extensions, if necessary

_____ File Final Fiduciary Income Tax Return

Foreign Bank Account Reports

_____ Prepare and file Report of Foreign Bank and Financial Accounts (Form TD F 90-22) by June 30th

Commissions/Fees:

_____ Determine counsel fees for estate

_____ Compute and distribute commissions

_____ Determine if commission and fees should be claimed on federal estate tax return or federal estate income tax return

Trusts:

_____ Obtain Revocable Trust (and any amendments)

_____ Obtain all trusts created by Decedent

_____ Obtain all trusts of which Decedent was a beneficiary. If so, determine if Decedent had any five and five powers, and consider tax implications

_____ Obtain all trusts of which Decedent was a trustee

_____ Determine if Decedent was the donor or custodian of any UTMA account or 529 plan. If so, determine the state of situs

Accounting:

_____ Judicial

_____ Informal with Receipt and Release Agreement

_____ Waived in Family Settlement Agreement or Receipt and Release Agreement

Closing Estate:

_____   Determine timing for fund of trusts

_____   Distribute Assets (following court approval of Account or Receipt and Release Agreement)

_____   Cancel bond and obtain refund (if applicable)

_____   File Status Report (due 2 years after date of death and each year thereafter)

_____   Complete summary and fee card

00557906

16 *CHARITABLE TRUSTS*

A charitable trust is a trust with a charitable purpose. The trust law that applies to private express trusts — the trust law we studied earlier in the course — applies to charitable trusts as well. The first significant difference is that a charitable trust need not have an ascertainable beneficiary. Instead, a charitable trust must have a charitable purpose, and this chapter explores what qualifies as a charitable purpose.

A second significant difference is that the Rule Against Perpetuities, which we studied in Chapter 8, does not apply to charitable trusts. Because a charitable trust can, in theory, last forever, the law developed special modification rules called "*cy pres*" and "deviation." This chapter examines the development and application of these rules.

If a charitable trust does not have an ascertainable beneficiary, then who can enforce the trust? We will look at the roles of the state attorney general, donors, the Internal Revenue Service and even the public in supervising and enforcing the terms of a charitable trust.

Charitable organizations play a significant role in the United States, and the nonprofit sector continues to grow in size and importance. We will focus on charities organized as charitable trusts, but a charity can also be organized as a nonprofit corporation or as an unincorporated association. Many of the rules and problems we will examine apply to all types of charities, however organized. Some of the rules that apply to all charities derive from trust law, due in part to the idea that someone (a director or trustee) is managing property for the benefit of others and therefore should be subject to fiduciary principles. The American Law Institute is engaged in a project to provide guidance on the law of nonprofit organizations, and many observers expect that project to unify to an even greater extent the rules that apply to charitable trusts and nonprofit corporations. *See* PRINCIPLES OF THE LAW OF NONPROFIT ORGS, *available at* http://www.ali.org/index.cfm?fuseaction=projects.proj_ip&projectid=3.

A.   CHARITABLE PURPOSE

What constitutes a charitable purpose? The original articulation of charitable purpose appeared in the Statute of Elizabeth. *See* Statute of Charitable Uses, 43 Eliz. I, c.4 (1601). Something similar to this statement of what constitutes a charitable purpose continues to be used to this day, for example in the UTC definition and in other uniform acts that relate to charities. Even the definition used in the Internal Revenue Code derives from the concepts developed in early English law.

UTC §103. Definitions.

> (4) "Charitable trust" means a trust, or portion of a trust, created for a charitable purpose described in Section 405(a).

UTC §405. Charitable Purposes.

> (a) A charitable trust may be created for the relief of poverty, the advancement of education or religion, the promotion of health, governmental or municipal purposes, or other purposes the achievement of which is beneficial to the community.

B.   CHARITABLE NOT BENEVOLENT

Trust law distinguishes between charitable purposes and benevolent purposes. Gifts may be benevolent, but they are not charitable unless they alleviate poverty or contribute to education, religion or one of the other listed purposes. The following case describes the difference between a charitable purpose and a benevolent purpose.

Shenandoah Valley National Bank v. Taylor
63 S.E.2d 786 (1951)

MILLER, J.

Charles B. Henry, a resident of Winchester, Virginia, died testate on the 23rd day of April, 1949. His will dated April 21, 1949, was duly admitted to probate and the Shenandoah Valley National Bank of Winchester, the designated executor and trustee, qualified thereunder.

Subject to two inconsequential provisions not material to this litigation, the testator's entire estate valued at $86,000, was left as follows:

> SECOND: All the rest, residue and remainder of my estate, real, personal, intangible and mixed, of whatsoever kind and wherever situate, . . . , I give, bequeath and devise to the Shenandoah Valley National Bank of Winchester, Virginia, in trust, to be known as the "Charles B. Henry and Fannie Belle Henry Fund," for the following uses and purposes:

> (a) My Trustee shall invest and reinvest my trust estate, shall collect the income therefrom and shall pay the net income as follows:

> (1) On the last school day of each calendar year before Easter my Trustee shall divide the net income into as many equal parts as there are children in the first, second and third grades of the John Kerr School of the City of Winchester, and shall pay one of such equal parts to each child in such grades, to be used by such child in the furtherance of his or her obtainment of an education.

> (2) On the last school day of each calendar year before Christmas my trustee shall divide the net income into as many equal parts as there are children in the first, second and third grades of the John Kerr School of the City of Winchester, and shall pay one of such equal parts to each child in such grades, to be used by such child in the furtherance of his or her obtainment of an education.

By paragraphs (3) and (4) it is provided that the names of the children in the three grades shall be determined each year from the school records, and payment of the income to them "shall be as nearly equal in amounts as it is practicable" to arrange.

Paragraph (5) provides that if the John Kerr School is ever discontinued for any reason the payments shall be made to the children of the same grades of the school or schools that take its place, and the School Board of Winchester is to determine what school or schools are substituted for it.

Under clause "THIRD" the trustee is given authority, power, and discretion to retain or from time to time sell and invest and reinvest the estate, or any part thereof, as it shall deem to be to the best interest of the trust.

The John Kerr School is a public school used by the local school board for primary grades and had an enrollment of 458 boys and girls so there will be that number of pupils or thereabouts who would share in the distribution of the income.

The testator left no children or near relatives. Those who would be his heirs and distributees in case of intestacy were first cousins and others more remotely related. One of these next of kin filed a suit against the executor and trustee, and others challenging the validity of the provisions of the will which undertook to create a charitable trust.

Paragraph No. 10 of the bill alleges:

"That the aforesaid trust does not constitute a charitable trust and hence is invalid in that it violates the rule against the creation of perpetuities." . . . From decrees that adjudicated the principles of the cause and held that the trust was not charitable but a private trust and thus violative of the rule against perpetuities and void, this appeal was awarded.

The sole question presented is: does the will create a valid charitable trust?

Construction of the challenged provisions is required and in this undertaking the testator's intent as disclosed by the words used in the will must be ascertained. If his dominant intent as expressed was charitable, the trust should be accorded efficacy and sustained.

But on the other hand, if the testator's intent as expressed is merely benevolent, though the disposition of his property be meritorious and evince traits of generosity, the trust must nevertheless be declared invalid because it violates the rule against perpetuities. . . .

Authoritative definitions of charitable trusts may be found in 4 Pomeroy's Equity Jurisprudence, 5th Ed., sec. 1020, and Restatement of the Law of Trusts, sec. 368, p. 1140. The latter gives a comprehensive classification definition. It is:

Charitable purposes include:

    (a) the relief of poverty;
    (b) the advancement of education;
    (c) the advancement of religion;
    (d) the promotion of health;
    (e) governmental or municipal purposes; and
    (f) other purposes the accomplishment of which is beneficial to the community.

In the recent decision of *Allaun v. First, etc., Nat. Bank*, 190 Va. 104, 56 S.E.(2d) 83, the definition that appears in 3 M. J., Charitable Trust, sec. 2, p. 872, was approved and adopted. It reads:

"A charity," in a legal sense, may be described as a gift to be applied, consistently with existing laws, for the benefit of an indefinite number of persons, either by bringing their hearts under the influence of education or religion, by relieving their bodies from disease, suffering or constraint, by assisting them to establish themselves for life, or by erecting or maintaining public building or works, or otherwise lessening the burdens of government. It is immaterial whether the purpose is called charitable in the gift itself, if it is so described as to show that it is charitable. Generally speaking, any gift not inconsistent with existing laws which is promotive of science or tends to the education, enlightening, benefit or amelioration of the condition of mankind or the diffusion of useful knowledge, or is for the public convenience is a charity. It is essential that a charity be for the benefit of an indefinite number of persons; for if all the beneficiaries are personally designated, the trust lacks the essential element of indefiniteness, which is one characteristic of a legal charity.(190 Va. P. 108). . . .

In the law of trusts there is a real and fundamental distinction between a charitable trust and one that is devoted to mere benevolence. The former is public in nature and valid; the latter is private and if it offends the rule against perpetuities, it is void. . . .

Appellant contends that the gift qualifies as a charitable trust under the definition in *Allaun v. First, etc., Nat. Bank, supra*. It is also said that it not only meets the requirements of a charitable trust as defined in Restatement of the Law of Trusts, *supra*, but specifically fits two of those classifications, *viz.:*

(b) trusts for the advancement of education;

(f) other purposes the accomplishment of which is beneficial to the community.

We now turn to the language of the will for from its context the testator's intent is to be derived. . . .

In clause "SECOND" of the will the trust is set up, and by clause "THIRD" full power is bestowed upon the trustee to invest and reinvest the estate and collect the income for the purposes and uses of the trust. In paragraphs (1) and (2), respectively, of clause "SECOND" in clear and definite language the discretion, power and authority of the trustee in its disposition and application of the income are specified and limited. Yearly on the last school day before Easter and Christmas each youthful beneficiary of the testator's generosity is to be paid an equal share of the income. In mandatory language the duty and the duty alone to make cash payments to each individual child just before Easter and Christmas is enjoined upon the trustee by the certain and explicit words that it "shall divide the net income . . . and shall pay one of such equal shares to each child in such grades."

Without more, that language and the occasions specified for payment of the funds to the children being when their minds and interests would be far removed from studies or other school activities definitely indicate that no educational purpose was in the testator's mind. It is manifest that there was no intent or belief that the funds would be put to any use other than such as youthful impulse and desire might dictate. But in each instance immediately following the above-quoted language the sentence concludes with the words or phrase "to be used by such child in the furtherance of his or her obtainment of an education." It is significant that by this latter phrase the trustee is given no power, control or discretion over the funds so received by the child. Full and complete execution of the mandate and trust imposed upon the trustee accomplishes no educational purpose. Nothing toward the advancement of education is attained by the ultimate performance by the trustee of its full duty. It merely places the income irretrievably and forever beyond the range of the trust.

. . . In our opinion, the words of the will import an intent to have the trustee pay to each child his allotted share. If that be true, — and it is directed to be done in no uncertain language — we know that the admonition to the children would be wholly impotent and of no avail. . . .

If it be determined that the will fails to create a charitable trust for *educational purposes* (and our conclusion is that it is inoperative to create such a trust), it is earnestly insisted that the trust provided for is nevertheless charitable and valid. In this respect it is claimed that the two yearly payments to be made to the children just before Christmas and Easter produce "a desirable social effect" and are "promotive of public convenience and needs, and happiness and contentment" and thus the fund set up in the will constitutes a charitable trust. . . .

"The word 'charity', as used in law, has a broader meaning and includes substantially any scheme or effort to better the condition of society or any considerable portion thereof. It has been well said that any gift not inconsistent with existing laws, which is promotive of science or tends to the education, enlightenment, benefit, or amelioration of the condition of mankind or the diffusion of useful knowledge, or is for the public convenience, is a charity."

Numerous cases that deal with and construe specific provisions of wills or other instruments are cited by appellant to uphold the contention that the provisions of this will, without reference to and deleting the phrase "to be used by such child in the furtherance of his or her obtainment of an education" meet the requirements of a charitable trust. . . .

Upon examination of these decisions, it will be found that where a gift results in mere financial enrichment, a trust was sustained only when the court found and concluded from the entire context of the will that the ultimate intended recipients were poor or in necessitous circumstances.

A trust from which the income is to be paid at stated intervals to each member of a designated segment of the public, without regard to whether or not the recipients are poor or in need, is not for the relief of poverty, nor is it a social benefit to the community. It is a mere benevolence — a private trust — and may not be upheld as a charitable trust. . . .

Payment to the children of their cash bequests on the two occasions specified would bring to them pleasure and happiness and no doubt cause them to remember or think of their benefactor with gratitude and thanksgiving. That was, we think, Charles B. Henry's intent. Laudable, generous and praiseworthy though it may be, it is not for the relief of the poor or needy, nor does it otherwise so benefit or advance the social interest of the community as to justify its continuance in perpetuity as a charitable trust. . . .

No error is found in the decrees appealed from and they are affirmed.

The *Shenandoah Valley National Bank* case dates from 1951. At that time the Rule Against Perpetuities applied to invalidate a noncharitable trust that violated the Rule. Now that many states have abolished the Rule or adopted a 90-year wait-and-see rule, a trust that violates the common law Rule may still be valid.

When Mr. Henry attempted to create his trust, a noncharitable trust had to have an ascertainable beneficiary to be a valid trust. A charitable trust can operate without a beneficiary, but a trust without a charitable purpose can not — or could not at the time. The UTC now provides for trusts with a purpose in §409, so in a state that has enacted the UTC, a benevolent trust might be given effect. Many states have not yet adopted the UTC, however, and in those states a trust must have either an identifiable beneficiary or a charitable purpose.

QUESTIONS

1. *Who benefits?* A charitable trust benefits the public rather than specified persons. What does this mean?

2. *How many people?* What if a trust were to grant a scholarship each year to one student graduating from a particular high school? Is that a public purpose if only one person benefits each year? What if a trust provides scholarships for any niece or nephew of the settlor who graduates from high school with a 3.5 GPA?

3. *What is a public purpose?* Would providing an ice cream treat at the end of the school year serve a public purpose? What about giving each child a book before summer break? Would restricting a gift of money to needy students work? How would the trustee determine who should receive the gifts?

EXERCISE

Assume that Mr. Henry asked you to assist him. Because your state still follows the common law Rule Against Perpetuities, Mr. Henry wants to be certain that the trust he creates is a charitable trust. Draft distribution provisions for a trust that would both carry out Mr. Henry's wishes and qualify as charitable.

C. TAX PURPOSES

Tax law provides significant incentives for establishing a charitable trust. A donor creating an inter vivos trust can take an income tax deduction if the trust qualifies as a charitable trust. IRC §170. In addition, the trust will qualify for a deduction from the gift tax. IRC §2522. If the settlor creates a testamentary trust, there is no income tax deduction, but the estate will have a deduction from the estate tax. IRC §2055. The rules for qualification for a tax deduction require that the gift have a charitable purpose and, although the meaning of the term is not identical to the meaning of charitable purpose under trust law, in most cases a charitable purpose will be charitable under both trust law and tax law. We will not discuss the tax consequences further, but you should be aware that much legal work involving charitable trusts has a tax aspect.

D. MODIFICATION OF CHARITABLE TRUSTS

Charitable trusts can last in perpetuity, so the law developed doctrines to permit modification of provisions in charitable trusts. The doctrine of *cy pres* applies to restrictions on the purpose of a charitable trust, and the doctrine of deviation applies to restrictions on administrative provisions. As we will see, when courts apply these two doctrines, the distinction can get blurred. Both *cy pres* and deviation are, like most of trust law, default rules. A settlor can specify what should happen if a purpose becomes too difficult later on, and a settlor can authorize the trustee to make changes that become necessary. After looking at how courts apply *cy pres* and deviation, we will consider ways the settlor can plan for modification that may become necessary over time.

1. Cy Pres

If the terms of a trust do not provide for what should happen when changed circumstances affect a purpose restriction, *cy pres* permits a court to modify the restriction, under certain circumstances. Historically, under the common law, a court could modify a restriction that had become illegal, impossible or impracticable. *See* RESTATEMENT (SECOND) OF TRUSTS §399. In addition, a court could apply *cy pres* only if the court found that the settlor had a general charitable intent. If a court did not find a general charitable intent, the property reverted to the settlor or the settlor's estate. Courts typically found general charitable intent, and the doctrine then assumed that the settlor would want the restriction to be modified so that the trust could be used for another charitable purpose. Under *cy pres* the modification should be "as near as possible" to the original purpose. The term *"cy pres"* comes from Norman French, and the longer version is "cy pres comme possible" ("cy" has become "si" in modern French). The doctrine is changing, as we discuss following the *Buck* case.

A trustee cannot apply *cy pres* to modify a charitable trust without court approval. Courts approve *cy pres* petitions sparingly, and have construed "impracticable" as close to impossible and not just difficult or inefficient. The *Buck Trust* case is a famous *cy pres* case and is a good example of a court's reluctance to apply *cy pres*.

a. Buck Trust

In 1975, Beryl Buck died and under her will created a trust with instructions that the trust:

> shall always be held and used for exclusively non-profit charitable, religious or educational purposes in providing care for the needy in Marin County, California, and for other non-profit charitable, religious or education purposes in that county.

Mrs. Buck named the San Francisco Foundation, a community foundation serving five counties in the Bay Area, as the trustee. When Mrs. Buck died, the trust assets consisted primarily of stock in Beldridge Oil Company, valued at her death at $7.0 -10.0 million. When the value of the trust increased to $340.0 million just 10 years later, the trustee asked the court for permission to change the geographic restriction on the gift. The court refused to apply *cy pres* to do so.

The dramatic increase in value of the trust meant that huge annual distributions would be made in Marin County, one of the wealthiest counties in the country. (As a private foundation for tax purposes, the Buck Trust must distribute 5% of the value of its assets each year. IRC §4942.) The increase in value was something Mrs. Buck did not anticipate, so thoughts about her "intent" proved contentious. We will look first at a part of the court's opinion and then at an excerpt from an article by Professor John Simon. Professor Simon adapted the article from two documents he filed in support of the petition for *cy pres*.

In the Matter of the Estate of Beryl Buck
No. 23259 (Cal. Super. Ct., Marin County, Aug. 15, 1986) Reprinted in 21 U.S.F.L. Rev. 691, 749, 751, 752-53, 755 (1986-87)

By resolution dated January 26, 1984, the Distribution Committee of the San Francisco Foundation ("Foundation"), by a bare majority vote, resolved that it was "impracticable and inexpedient" to continue to spend all of the income from the Leonard and Beryl Buck Foundation ("Buck Trust") within Marin County, as required by Mrs. Buck's Will, and authorized the filing of a petition to modify the geographic restriction. . . .

"Impracticability" has been defined as "impossible" as early as 1850 in Dr. Johnson's famous dictionary *(A Dictionary of the English Language* (Henry G. Bohn: London, 1850), p. 616). . . .

California courts have never adopted a broad interpretation of the term "impracticable" in charitable trust cases. . . .

Like California courts, courts from other states often describe the standard for *cy pres* as one of "illegality, impossibility or impracticability." In many of those jurisdictions, however, "impracticability" is equated with "impossibility." *Dunbar v. Board of Trustees* (1969) 170 Colo. 327, 461 P.2d 28, 32 (dicta).

The Restatement (Second) of Trusts, (1959) section 399, comment q at 306, does not require a literal impossibility. Rather, it defines "impracticability" as follows:

> The doctrine of cy pres is applicable even though it is possible to carry out the particular purpose of the settler, if to carry it out would *fail to accomplish the general charitable intention* of the settler. In such case it is "impracticable" to carry out the particular purpose . . . . (Emphasis added).

Ineffective philanthropy, inefficiency and relative inefficiency, that is, inefficiency of trust expenditures in one location given greater relative needs or benefits elsewhere, do not constitute impracticability under either view. Such situation is not the equivalent of impossibility; nor is there any threat that the operation of the trust will fail to fulfill the general charitable intention of the settler. . . .

The *cy pres* doctrine should not be so distorted by the adoption of subjective, relative, and nebulous standards such as "inefficiency" or "ineffective philanthropy" to the extent that it becomes a facile vehicle for charitable trustees to vary the terms of a trust simply because they believe that they can spend the trust income better or more wisely elsewhere, or as in this case, prefer to do so. There is no basis in law for the application of standards such as "efficiency" or "effectiveness" to modify a trust, nor is there any authority that would elevate these standards to the level of impracticability . . . .

Where the income of a charitable trust can be used for the purpose specified by the testator, *cy pres* may not be invoked on the grounds that a different use of the income would be more useful or desirable. . . .

Thus, *cy pres* may not be invoked on the grounds that it would be more "fair," "equitable" or "efficient" to spend the Trust funds in a manner different from that specified by the testator.

Professor Simon takes a different view of the proper application of *cy pres*, although he concedes that if the California Supreme Court had reviewed the *cy pres* petition in the *Buck* case, the final result "would not have been an easy call."

John G. Simon, American Philanthropy and the Buck Trust
21 U.S.F. L. Rev. 641, 642-45, 660-61, 667 (1986-87)

For several months before filing the petition, the Distribution Committee and officers of the Foundation went through the process of trying to construe Beryl Buck's intentions in the light of drastically changed circumstances — the posthumous increase in the value of her gift from $7-10 million to $340 million, all to be spent in one small and very affluent county — and, in the light of these changed circumstances, figuring out how to discharge the Distribution Committee's trusteeship duties. . . .

Following much study and intense debate, and the changes in course that are an inevitable part of the business of making difficult decisions, the Foundation determined two things:

> 1. That, despite the indisputably "clear language" of Mrs. Buck's will, unprecedented later economic events, resulting in an enormous posthumous increase of her gift, had created, at a minimum, uncertainty concerning Mrs. Buck's intentions, and that this uncertainty could best be resolved by concluding that Mrs. Buck would have permitted *some part* of this massive gift to benefit neighboring counties served by the Foundation.

> 2. That a narrower resolution of the interpretive uncertainty not only would fail to honor the Foundation's obligations to Mrs. Buck but would force the Foundation to allocate these resources in an unacceptably inefficient manner, inconsistent with the Foundation's obligations as a charitable trustee.

In light of the foregoing, but mindful of conflicting community views, the Foundation decided to adopt what has to be viewed as a compromise position: grants would not be confined to Marin County, but Marin would enjoy a preferred position at all times, and this new policy would not commence until after three more years, or roughly $90 million more, of Marin-only grantmaking. This position would likely have provided Marin County with many times the amount of resources that Mrs. Buck thought she was allocating to Marin County.

The determinations made by the Foundation were congruent with two principles that are at the heart of the cy pres doctrine. *First,* cy pres, which is properly understood as an intent-enforcing doctrine, seeks to avoid a frustration of donor intention arising out of changed circumstances. In other words, cy pres deals with the fact of *surprise* — either because the gift is irrevocable or, as in Mrs. Buck's case, because the donor is dead.

Surprise was the subject of the first of the Foundation's determinations. *Second*, cy pres seeks to avoid charitable waste — to preserve what Professor Karst called "the efficiency of the charitable dollar." Where the donor's plan, if carried out in unreconstructed fashion would be "illegal," "impossible," "impractical," "inexpedient," "unsuitable," "unwise," or of diminished "usefulness" or "significance," to use the language of judicial, legislative, and scholarly authorities over the years, cy pres offers a way to restore the benefaction to full power. This theme of efficiency was the subject of the Foundation's second determination to which I have referred.

The two factors of surprise and efficiency interact. Where the charitable purpose is illegal, no specific finding of surprise resulting from changed circumstances is required. Even in this situation it could be said that cy pres plays an intent-enforcing or surprise-avoiding role for no donor would have wanted to see his or her gift wiped out on the grounds of illegality. But as one moves away from clear cases of "illegality" or "impossibility," the importance of surprise increases. Thus, a determination by charitable trustees that they cannot operate effectively under donor-imposed constraints (whether they assert "impracticability" or one of the other difficulties listed above) probably would not support a cy pres order in the absence of significant surprise. Where the conditions that produce charitable inefficiency are not very different from those the donor experienced, or might reasonably have anticipated, the donor may be assumed to have known what he or she was doing. In such a case there is no basis for others (including trustees) "to substitute their judgment for that of the trustor — however wrong-headed most people might consider that judgment to have been."

Where there has been major surprise, however, one cannot assume that the donor acted knowingly, that he or she intended or contemplated the inefficient outcome, and it is therefore appropriate for the trustees, with court approval, to reinterpret the donor's will to protect the donor gift from an unintended miscarriage caused by changed circumstances. . . .

The interaction between the factors of surprise and efficiency has a second consequence: the fact of surprise alone, without a finding of inefficiency, is not likely to support cy pres. Where the trustees find that they can continue to make productive use of the gift, even though the underlying conditions have significantly changed, adherence to the donor's express language will probably not, in Richard Posner's words, frustrate either "the donor's purposes [or] the efficient use of resources." . . .

In short, the trial court rejected the trustees' assessment of efficiency and substituted its own philanthropic preferences. Some readers of this Article may find the court's philanthropic views more appealing than the Foundation's. But it is a fact that Mrs. Buck did not name the superior court of California as her trustee; for better or for worse, she named the Foundation. Moreover, the court's rejection of the trustee's role in the cy pres process ignores the role charitable trustees play in the nonprofit sector. The result allows an agency of the state to become the grantmaking supervisor, thus undermining the decentralized, or "privatized," structure so carefully nurtured in our legal order.

The court's role, indeed, has been carried a step further. On July 25, 1986, the Attorney General of the State of California, the County of Marin, and the Marin Council of Agencies entered into an agreement, which was adopted by the court six days later, providing that 20 to 25% of income from the newly reconstituted Buck Trust would be set aside for one to three "major projects" of "national and international importance," that a hearing would be held by the court in July 1987, and that at the conclusion of the hearing, "the court may select one or more projects to be funded by the Buck Trust as determined by the court."

On August 7, 1987, the court directed that Buck Trust funds be allocated in certain prescribed amounts to three "major projects": The Buck Center on Aging, Institute on Alcohol and Other Drug Problems, and Marin Educational Institute. The court appointed a special master to monitor all three "major projects," approve their budgets, and attend all meetings of their governing bodies. The court ordered that it would "review the progress and operations of each major project annually" and reserved the right to impose additional conditions, to alter any project's Buck Trust funding, or to modify or terminate it as a Buck Trust beneficiary....

... Under the terms of Mrs. Buck's will, therefore, it is, to put it mildly, very difficult to justify a national-international "major projects" scheme.

One might, however, explain the "major projects" order not as a straightforward implementation of the Buck will but as the court's effort to interpret what Mrs. Buck *might have wanted to* do with some of her income if she knew its true magnitude. In that context, the notion that she would have wanted some Buck Trust funds to go to projects that do not primarily benefit Marin residents, but that assist larger national or international purposes, would be an arguable inference. It must be observed, however, that this explanation of the "major projects" order assumes that changed circumstances have forced the court to look beyond the express language of the testator and to search for the next-closest solution. There is a name for this approach. It is called cy pres! ...

Assuming that the court in reality stepped into a cy pres mode, the next question must be whether cy pres principles were correctly applied. From Mrs. Buck's point of view, would the next-closest solution take the form of grants to three national programs on aging, on alcohol and drug abuse, and on education?

Professor Simon suggests in his conclusion that the court may have applied *cy pres* after all, but that the court applied its own view of the changes that would be appropriate. Rather than expanding the geographic restriction to include the five counties served by the San Francisco Foundation, the court instead directed that a portion of the Buck Trust's income be used for three national-international projects, to be based in Marin County but to serve "all of humankind." *Cy pres* may be appropriate under the circumstances, but the question is whose interpretation should control a determination of what is "as near as possible" to the settlor's intent.

Many scholars have urged the liberalization of the *cy pres* doctrine. *See, e.g.,* Rob Atkinson, *Reforming Cy Pres Reform,* 44 HASTINGS L.J. 1111 (1993). The UTC did so, adding the term "wasteful" to the reasons a court can apply *cy pres.* UTC §413. The UTC also deletes the requirement that a court find general charitable intent, recognizing that donors who make charitable gifts and settlors who create charitable trusts usually have a general charitable intent. The UTC changed the language of modification, directing a court to apply the funds "in a manner consistent with the settlor's charitable purposes." The change from "as near as possible" gives the court a bit more flexibility but does not significantly change the requirement that the focus should be the intent of the settlor who created the trust. *See also* RESTATEMENT (THIRD) OF TRUSTS §67.

UTC §413. Cy pres.

(a) Except as otherwise provided in subsection (b), if a particular charitable purpose becomes unlawful, impracticable, impossible to achieve, or wasteful:

(1) the trust does not fail, in whole or in part;

(2) the trust property does not revert to the settlor or the settlor's successors in interest; and

(3) the court may apply cy pres to modify or terminate the trust by directing that the trust property be applied or distributed, in whole or in part, in a manner consistent with the settlor's charitable purposes.

(b) A provision in the terms of a charitable trust that would result in distribution of the trust property to a noncharitable beneficiary prevails over the power of the court under subsection (a) to apply cy pres to modify or terminate the trust only if, when the provision takes effect:

(1) the trust property is to revert to the settlor and the settlor is still living; or

(2) fewer than 21 years have elapsed since the date of the trust's creation.

QUESTIONS

1. Cy pres *or not* cy pres. What do you think Mrs. Buck would have wanted had she known about the increase in the value of the trust? Should that (what Mrs. Buck would have wanted) matter? Professor Simon suggests that the court actually applied *cy pres* in the *Buck Trust* case but did so without saying so. Do you think creating the three "major projects" constituted a change in the restriction on the gift?

2. *Was it wasteful?* If UTC §413 had applied to the Buck Trust, would the court have reached a different resolution?

3. *How long for dead hand control?* Should the level of deference to the donor/settlor's intent change after the passage of time? At some point (50 years, 100 years, 200 years), should the charity be able to modify restrictions more easily? If so, who should decide how to modify the restriction?

2. Deviation

Courts have been more willing to apply the doctrine of deviation—also known as administrative deviation or equitable deviation—to modify the terms of a trust. The common law doctrine of deviation permits a court to make changes to administrative terms of a trust. *See* RESTATEMENT (SECOND) OF TRUSTS §381. Deviation furthers the settlor's intent, because a court uses the doctrine to modify a restriction when continued compliance with the restriction will impair the accomplishment of the charitable purpose. Whether a restriction is a purpose restriction subject to *cy pres*, or an administrative restriction subject to deviation, sometimes seems to depend on whether the court wants to modify the trust.

The distinction between a purpose restriction and an administrative restriction is not always clear. In 1869, Ebenezer Woodward died and left property to the town of Quincy, to found a school for girls. His will provided that the school was "for the education of females . . . who are native born, born, I wish it to be understood, in the town of Quincy, and none other than these, to be allowed to attend this Institute. . . . " *Dartmouth Coll. v. City of Quincy*, 258 N.E.2d 745, 747(Mass. 1970). In the 1960s, the school had financial difficulties due to insufficient numbers of Quincy-born girls attending the school, and the school requested modification. The court applied the doctrine of deviation to allow non-Quincy-born girls to attend the school, filling spots not taken by Quincy-born girls. The court determined that Mr. Woodward's primary purpose was to create a school for girls and that the modification would make continued operation of the school possible.

In the Barnes Foundation case, a Pennsylvania trial court applied deviation to permit the Barnes Foundation to move its art collection to a new building in downtown Philadelphia. As you read about this case, compare the changes the court made to the original trust with the changes the California court was unwilling to make to the Buck Trust.

Dr. Albert Barnes made a great deal of money as a chemist who invented Argyrol, a compound used to treat gonorrhea, prevent blindness in infants and do other useful things. The drug earned Dr. Barnes a fortune, and he used it to buy art, first locally and then in Paris. In 1922, Dr. Barnes created the Barnes Foundation and built a building in Merion, Pennsylvania, to house his growing art collection. As the Web site of the Barnes Foundation states, "the Foundation is home to one of the world's largest collections of Impressionist, Post-Impressionist and early Modern paintings, with extensive holdings by Picasso, Matisse, Cézanne, Renoir and Modigliani, as well as important examples of African sculpture." *See* www.barnesfoundation.org/h_main.html. The following article provides more history about Dr. Barnes and the foundation.

Jonathan Scott Goldman, Just What the Doctor Ordered? The Doctrine of Deviation, the Case of Doctor Barnes's Trust and the Future Location of the Barnes Foundation
39 Real Prop. Prob. & Tr. J. 711, 720 (2005)

Dr. Barnes began to collect art around 1910. In 1912, he began to hone his focus on modern art when he sent his high school friend and Philadelphia painter William Glackens to Paris with a budget of $20,000 to buy the best modern art available at the best prices possible. Glackens returned with paintings by Manet, Gauguin, Cézanne, and Degas. Dr. Barnes was more than a collector who made purchases for investment; he studied his paintings diligently, seeking to learn from them and to understand their genius. After this initial shopping spree, Dr. Barnes developed his own knowledge of modern art and made all future purchases himself. He bought his art using aggressive tactics and at a feverish pitch, and he relished a good bargain. In 1922, when Dr. Barnes first saw the works of Chaim Soutine in Paris, he bought all the painter's work on the spot — between fifty and one hundred canvases — for approximately $3,000. By the next year, Dr. Barnes had purchased fifty paintings by one of his favorite artists, Cézanne. Ultimately, Dr. Barnes collected thousands of pieces of art, which are still at the Barnes Foundation in Lower Merion . . . .

In 1922, Dr. Barnes bought a large estate adjoining his home in Lower Merion and hired an architect to build the Barnes Foundation galleries, which would house his art collection. On December 4, 1922, Pennsylvania granted the Barnes Foundation a charter, designating it as an educational institution and not a museum. On December 6, Dr. Barnes executed the trust agreement and Bylaws, laying out his wishes with extreme specificity and endowing it with $6 million. The stated purpose of Dr. Barnes's eponymous foundation was "[t]o promote the advancement of education and the appreciation of the fine arts." In these documents, Dr. Barnes made specifications to control the Barnes Foundation after his death as he had controlled it during his lifetime. Among these were provisions mandating that his collection be permanently closed when he died, that the paintings remain exactly as he left them, and that the restrictive admissions policy of the Barnes Foundation remain in place.

Although Dr. Barnes left an endowment for the care of the art and buildings, he imposed restrictions on the types of investments the trustees could make and also restricted access to the art. By the 1990s, the Foundation had serious financial difficulties, due in part to these restrictions but also due to a series of lawsuits with the neighbors in Merion and other problems. The trustees brought a series of lawsuits that ultimately permitted some deviation from the restrictions Dr. Barnes had imposed. The court permitted greater discretion in investments, an increase in the admission fee and increased museum hours. The court also allowed a one-time traveling exhibition of some of the art. The changes raised money, but the foundation's financial problems continued to worsen.

By 2002, the trustees proposed a new plan with the backing of the Pew Charitable Trusts, the Lenfest Foundation and the Annenberg Foundation. The other foundations offered to help raise $150.0 million provided that the foundation could obtain changes to the trust indenture that would permit an increase in the size of the board of trustees of the Barnes Foundation (from 5 to 15) and permit the foundation to move the collection to downtown Philadelphia. The foundation would keep the building in Merion as an administrative building.

Lincoln University, which under the terms of Dr. Barnes's trust nominated four of the five trustees, opposed the move, and art students filed an amicus brief arguing against the move. The attorney general remained silent, thus tacitly supporting the move. After the first hearing, the trial court approved the increase in the number of trustees, and after a second hearing at which the court heard extensive evidence of the various options open to the museum, the court approved the move to Philadelphia.

The Barnes Foundation

*Court of Common Pleas, Montgomery County, PA Orphans'
Court Division, No. 58788, Dec. 13, 2004*

OTT, J.

[Page 1] In this opinion, we consider the evidence presented at the second round of hearings on The Barnes Foundation's second amended petition to amend its charter and bylaws. In its pleading, The Foundation sought permission, *inter alia*, to increase the number of trustees on its governing board and to relocate the art collection in its gallery in Merion,

Pennsylvania, to a new facility in Philadelphia. After the first hearings in December of 2003, we ruled that expanding the size of the Board of Trustees was appropriate in today's sophisticated world of charitable fund-raising. We also determined that The Foundation was on the brink of financial collapse, and that the provision in Dr. Barnes' indenture mandating that the gallery be maintained in Merion was not sacrosanct, and could yield under the "doctrine of deviation," provided we were convinced the move to Philadelphia represented the least drastic modification of the indenture that would accomplish the donor's desired end.

[Pages 39-40] In view of the foregoing [detailed testimony on the economic feasibility of the move], we find that The Foundation showed clearly and convincingly the need to deviate from the terms of Dr. Barnes' indenture;[1] and we find that the three-campus model represents the least drastic modification necessary to preserve the organization. By many interested observers, permitting the gallery to move to Philadelphia will be viewed as an outrageous violation of the donor's trust. However, some of the archival materials introduced at the hearings led us to think otherwise. Contained therein were signals that Dr. Barnes expected the collection to have much greater public exposure after his death. To the court's thinking, these clues make the decision — that there is no viable alternative — easily reconcilable with the law of charitable trusts. When we add this revelation to The Foundation's absolute guarantee that Dr. Barnes' primary mission — the formal education programs — will be preserved and, indeed, enhanced as a result of these changes, we can sanction this bold new venture with a clear conscience.

On October 7, 2009, the Barnes Foundation unveiled the design of the new building. The new structure will house classrooms and an auditorium, in keeping with the educational mission of the foundation, and will house the art collection "in 12,000 square feet of exhibition space that replicates the scale, proportion and configuration of the original galleries in Merion." *See* Press Release, http://www.barnesfoundation.org/v_pr_100709.html.

Although construction of the new building is underway, an organization called the Friends of the Barnes continues to challenge the move, and

---

1. [FN 13] As we have cited many times in the course of the litigation involving The Foundation, Section 381 of the Restatement (Second) of Trusts states: "[A] court will direct or permit the trustee of a charitable trust to deviate from a term of the trust if it appears to the court that compliance is impossible or illegal or that owing to circumstances not known to the settlor and not anticipated by him compliance would defeat or substantially impair the accomplishment of the purposes of the trust." It is only the administrative provisions of a trust that are subject to deviation, *i.e.*, "the details of administration which the settlor has prescribed in order to secure the more important result of obtaining for the beneficiaries the advantages which the settlor stated he wished them to have." Section 561 of Bogert, The Law of Trust and Trustees, at 27.

a documentary movie, "The Art of the Steal," released in 2010, presents a decidedly anti-move look at the Barnes saga. *See* www.barnesfriends.org.

The UTC further muddies the distinction between *cy pres* and deviation. UTC §412, which we discussed in Chapter 7, applies to both private trusts and charitable trusts. Recall that in UTC §412(a), the court can modify the administrative or *dispositive* terms of a trust if the modification is needed due to circumstances not anticipated by the settlor.

UTC §412. Modification or Termination Because of Unanticipated Circumstances or Inability to Administer Trust Effectively.

> (a) The court may modify the administrative or dispositive terms of a trust or terminate the trust if, because of circumstances not anticipated by the settlor, modification or termination will further the purposes of the trust. To the extent practicable, the modification must be made in accordance with the settlor's probable intention.
>
> (b) The court may modify the administrative terms of a trust if continuation of the trust on its existing terms would be impracticable or wasteful or impair the trust's administration.
>
> (c) Upon termination of a trust under this section, the trustee shall distribute the trust property in a manner consistent with the purposes of the trust.

QUESTION

1.   *Geography and politics.* Can you reconcile the different outcomes in the controversies involving the City of Quincy, the Buck Trust and the Barnes Foundation? Each involved geographic restrictions. To what extent do you think local politics played a role?

2.   *Deviation or* cy pres. UTC §412(a) talks about unanticipated circumstances. This provision is similar to the argument John Simon made for the application of *cy pres*. Could a court apply §412(a) to a situation like the one in the *Buck Trust*?

PROBLEMS

1.   Morisha created a charitable trust under her will. The trust directed that distributions be made to preserve polar bear habitat. Fifty years after Morisha's death, the Arctic ice has vanished and polar bears live only in zoos. What should the trustee do with the assets remaining in the trust?

2.   When Zeke died, he left his entire estate to a trustee to be held in trust for the purpose of building a cancer treatment center in his hometown. His hometown has a hospital, but cancer patients have to go to a cancer facility two hours away for treatment. Although Zeke had a substantial fortune when he wrote his will, by the time of his death medical expenses had depleted his assets. The trustee received $50,000 for the trust. What should the trustee do with the money?

3.   Maggie's trust directs the trustee to invest only in U.S. Treasury notes and bonds. After 10 years, the trustee is worried that the value of the trust is shrinking due to inflation. What are the trustee's options? Does she have a fiduciary duty to petition the court?

4.   Joyce created a trust to provide college scholarships for needy students graduating from the high school she attended. The high school has a graduating class of only 50 students each year and in last year's class none of the students could be considered "needy." Joyce funded the trust with $5.0 million. Advise the trustees.

3.   UPMIFA

Courts have applied the doctrine of *cy pres* to modify restrictions on gifts to charities organized as nonprofit corporations, but the application of modification rules to nonprofit corporations has been unclear. In 2006, the Uniform Law Commission approved the Uniform Prudent Management of Institutional Funds Act (UPMIFA), an act that applies versions of UTC §§412, 413 to investment assets held by nonprofit corporations. Forty-seven states plus the District of Columbia and the Virgin Islands have adopted the act. UPMIFA applies primarily to nonprofit corporations, but the act also applies to charitable trusts if a charity serves as the trustee.

UPMIFA adds a new way to modify a restriction. If a restriction on a charitable fund covered by UPMIFA meets the requirements for *cy pres* — the restriction has become unlawful, impracticable, impossible to achieve or wasteful — and the fund is small (less than $25,000) and old (more than 20 years old), the charity can modify the restriction itself, without court approval. The charity must give notice to the attorney general, who can block the modification if it seems inappropriate, but if the modification is in keeping with the settlor's intent, the charity will be able to proceed without the expense of a court proceeding. This "self-help" modification is not available to charitable trusts, unless a charity is the trustee.

E.   ENFORCEMENT OF CHARITABLE TRUSTS

A private trust must have a beneficiary, because someone must be able to enforce the trust. If the trustee commits a breach of trust by engaging in self-dealing or violating the terms of the trust, the beneficiary has standing to bring a lawsuit against the trustee. A charitable trust has a charitable purpose but usually does not have an identifiable beneficiary. Who has standing to enforce the trust?

The attorney general, as the representative of the public's interest in a charity, has standing to sue a charity regardless of whether the charity is organized as a trust or a corporation. While the powers of the attorney general are substantial, the extent of the supervision the attorney general provides is limited due to limited resources. Due to a lack of clarity about the scope of the authority of the attorney general, the Uniform Law Commission has appointed a committee to draft an act called the Protection of Charitable Assets Act. See www.nccusl.org for the most recent draft of this act.

States vary in the number of staff allocated to supervising nonprofits. In some states, several assistant attorneys general form a charitable division of the attorney general's office. In other states, however, one assistant attorney general supervises the nonprofit sector as only one part of her job responsibilities, and some states may not have *any* attorneys specifically assigned to charitable matters.

In the discussion that follows, a reference to the "attorney general" includes any state regulator assigned to supervise charities. Typically, charity officials hold the position of assistant attorney general, but in some states the regulator will have a different title and may not be in the office of the attorney general.

The attorney general always has standing to take an action involving a charitable trust, but the attorney general may choose not to act, either because the attorney general determines that no action is warranted or because the office does not have sufficient resources to pursue the problem. Politics can play a role in these decisions.

If someone other than the attorney general were to have standing, who would that be? The possible options are the donors to the charity, the people served by the charity (who have "special interests" in the charity) or an interested person willing to take on the role of a "relator" and fund the litigation. We will examine donor standing first and then take a quick look at the special interests doctrine and the use of relators.

1. *Donor Standing*

Once a donor makes a gift to a charity, the donor relinquishes all control over the gift. The donor must trust the charity to carry out the donor's wishes. But what if the charity accepts a gift subject to a restriction and then fails to honor the restriction? If the donor does not have standing to enforce the restriction, and the attorney general lacks the resources to enforce the restriction, then what can the donor do? And what if the donor has died?

In most cases, a charity will want to carry out the donor's intent, both because the charity agreed to the terms and because donor relations are important in future fundraising. Sometimes, however, a charity will ignore or intentionally violate a donor agreement. Other times, the donor's surviving spouse, children or grandchildren may disagree with the charity about what the deceased donor intended.

Before we look at two donor standing cases, consider the change the UTC has made to the common law. The UTC gives the settlor of a charitable trust standing to enforce the trust. Although the UTC limits standing to a "settlor," so descendants would not have rights under this provision, the change is significant. A charitable trust is defined as a trust or portion of a trust, so it appears that a donor has standing with respect to the donor's gift, even if the donor made the gift to a large charity organized as a trust (and the donor did not create the trust). No cases have yet applied the provision.

UTC §405. Charitable Purposes; Enforcement.

> (c) The settlor of a charitable trust, among others, may maintain a proceeding to enforce the trust.

UTC §105. Definitions.

> (4) "Charitable trust" means a trust, or portion of a trust, created for a charitable purpose described in Section 405(a).

Now we will look at two cases involving donor intent and donor standing. The first case, *Smithers*, permits donor standing under limited circumstances. This case has not been followed elsewhere. The second case, *Hardt v. Vitae Foundation*, involves a charity organized as a nonprofit corporation, but the court's analysis of the standing rule is the traditional one and may continue to apply to charitable trusts in states that have not adopted UTC §405.

Smithers v. St. Luke's Roosevelt Hosp. Center
281 A.D. 2d 127, 723 N.Y.S.2d 426 (N.Y.A.D. 1 Dept. 2001)

ELLERIN, J.

The issue before us is whether the estate of the donor of a charitable gift has standing to sue the donee to enforce the terms of the gift. We conclude that in the circumstances here present plaintiff estate does have the necessary standing.

. . . Plaintiff Adele Smithers is the widow of R. Brinkley Smithers, a recovered alcoholic who devoted the last 40 years of his life to the treatment and understanding of the disease of alcoholism. In 1971 Smithers announced his intention to make a gift to defendant St. Luke's-Roosevelt Hospital Center (the "Hospital") of $10 million over time for the establishment of an alcoholism treatment center (the "Gift"). In his June 16, 1971 letter to the Hospital creating the Gift, Smithers stated, "Money from the $10 million grant will be supplied as needed. It is understood, however, that the detailed project plans and staff appointments must have my approval."

. . . With $1 million from the first installment of the Gift, the Hospital purchased a building at 56 East 93rd Street in Manhattan to house the rehabilitation program, and in 1973 the Smithers Alcoholism Treatment and Training Center opened there. . . .

[After several years and some disagreements between Smithers and the hospital, a hospital administrator engaged in discussions with Smithers and repaired the relationship. In 1983, Smithers agreed to complete the gift and signed a letter restricting the gift for use for the Smithers Center, which he described as follows: "In this letter I will refer to all aspects of the existing alcoholism program, including in-patient, out-patient and rehabilitation services, and any future extension thereof, collectively as the 'Smithers Center.'" A representative of the hospital signed the letter, agreeing to the restrictions. Smithers died in January 1994, and just over a year later the Hospital announced its plan to sell the building and move the Smithers Center into a hospital ward.]

Mrs. Smithers notified the Hospital of her objections to the proposed relocation of the program and demanded an accounting of the Smithers Center's finances.

The Hospital at first resisted disclosing its financial records, but Mrs. Smithers persisted, and in May 1995 the Hospital disclosed that it had been misappropriating monies from the Endowment Fund since before Smithers's death, transferring such monies to its general fund where they were used for purposes unrelated to the Smithers Center. Mrs. Smithers notified the Attorney General, who investigated the Hospital's plan to sell the building and discovered that the Hospital had transferred restricted assets from the Smithers Endowment Fund to its general fund in what it called "loans." The Attorney General demanded the return of these assets and in August 1995 the Hospital returned nearly $5 million to the Smithers

Endowment Fund, although it did not restore the income lost on those funds during the intervening years.

In the next three years, Mrs. Smithers tried to negotiate a resolution with the Hospital. The Attorney General participated in the negotiations, seeking, according to an affidavit in support of his motion to dismiss the complaint, "to effectuate a settlement that would resolve the plaintiff's concerns and benefit the Smithers Alcoholism Program." When the negotiations proved unsuccessful, the Attorney General, according to the affidavit, "proceeded to conclude his investigation . . . and to resolve those issues identified during the course of the investigation.". . .

In July 1998, the Attorney General entered into an Assurance of Discontinuance . . . with the Hospital. Under the terms of this assurance the Hospital agreed to make no more transfers or loans from Gift funds for any purpose other than the benefit of the Smithers Center and to return to the Gift fund $1 million from the proceeds of any sale of the building. The Attorney General did not require the Hospital to return the entire proceeds of such a sale, because he found that, contrary to Mrs. Smithers's contention, the terms of the Gift did not preclude the Hospital from selling the building.

[Mrs. Smithers had herself appointed as Special Administratrix for Mr. Smither's Estate for purposes of bringing suit against the Hospital for specific performance of the terms of the gift. Motions by the Hospital and the Attorney General to dismiss for lack of standing were granted.]

On appeal, the Attorney General's office, having reevaluated the matter "under the direction of the newly elected Attorney General," reversed its position and urged this Court to remand for a hearing on the merits to determine whether or not the building was subject to gift restrictions. If it were, then all proceeds of the sale would be subject to the same restrictions and could not be used for the Hospital's general purposes. . . . [T]he Attorney General urged that the issue of Mrs. Smithers's standing to bring the suit need not, and should not, be reached in this action, since he certainly had standing and had joined with her in seeking reversal and remand. . . .

While this appeal was pending, the Attorney General and the Hospital reached another agreement. This agreement raised some issues for the first time, but it brought the position of the Attorney General and the Hospital on other issues into accord with Mrs. Smithers's position. For example, the Hospital agreed to allocate the entire net proceeds of the sale of the building to the restricted purposes of the Gift and to restore the income lost as a result of the transfer of Gift funds to its general fund. Reversing his position again, the Attorney General returned to his predecessor's contention that Mrs. Smithers has no standing to bring this suit, and asked this Court to modify the decision dismissing the complaint for lack of standing so as to hold only that plaintiff does not have standing as special administratrix of the donor's estate and affirm, as modified, on that narrow ground.

He sought a remand of the matter, not for further proceedings on the merits, but for the court's approval and implementation of his settlement stipulation with the Hospital.

The sole issue before us is whether Mrs. Smithers, on behalf of Smithers's estate, has standing to bring this action. The Attorney General maintains that, with a few exceptions inapplicable here, standing to enforce the terms of a charitable gift is limited to the Attorney General. Most recently, the Attorney General has urged that, pursuant to the above-mentioned proposed settlement stipulation between himself and the Hospital, he has achieved all the relief that is appropriate in this case. . . .

The Supreme Court incorrectly characterized Mrs. Smithers as one who "positions herself as the champion and representative of the possible beneficiaries of the Gift," with no tangible stake because she has no position or property to lose if the Hospital alters its administration of the Gift. Mrs. Smithers did not bring this action on her own behalf or on behalf of beneficiaries of the Smithers Center. She brought it as the court-appointed special administratrix of the estate of her late husband to enforce his rights under his agreement with the Hospital through specific performance of that agreement. Therefore, the general rule barring beneficiaries from suing charitable corporations has no application to Mrs. Smithers. Moreover, the desire to prevent vexatious litigation by "irresponsible parties who do not have a tangible stake in the matter and have not conducted appropriate investigations" has no application to Mrs. Smithers either. Without possibility of pecuniary gain for himself or herself, only a plaintiff with a genuine interest in enforcing the terms of a gift will trouble to investigate and bring this type of action. Indeed, it was Mrs. Smithers's accountants who discovered and informed the Attorney General of the Hospital's misdirection of Gift funds, and it was only after Mrs. Smithers brought her suit that the Attorney General acted to prevent the Hospital from diverting the entire proceeds the sale of the building away from the Gift fund and into its general fund. The Attorney General, following his initial investigation of the Hospital's administration of the Gift, acquiesced in the Hospital's sale of the building, its diversion of the appreciation realized on the sale, and its relocation of the rehabilitation unit, even as he ostensibly was demanding that the Hospital continue to act "in accordance with the donor's gift" (*see* April 21, 1998 letter, *supra*). Absent Mrs. Smithers's vigilance, the Attorney General would have resolved the matter between himself and the Hospital in that manner and without seeking permission of any court.

The donor of a charitable gift is in a better position than the Attorney General to be vigilant and, if he or she is so inclined, to enforce his or her own intent. . . .

Moreover, the circumstances of this case demonstrate the need for co-existent standing for the Attorney General and the donor. The Attorney General's office was notified of the Hospital's misappropriation of funds by Mrs. Smithers, whose accountants performed the preliminary review of the Hospital's financial records, and it learned of the Hospital's closing of the detox unit — a breach, according to the Attorney General, of a specific representation — from Mrs. Smithers's papers in this action. Indeed, there is no substitute for a donor, who has a "special, personal interest in the enforcement of the gift restriction. . . . "In any event, the Attorney General's interest in enforcing gift terms is not necessarily congruent with that of the donor. The donor seeks to have his or her intent faithfully executed, which by definition will benefit the beneficiaries, and perhaps also to erect a tangible memorial to himself or herself. . . . We conclude that the distinct but related interests of the donor and the Attorney General are best served by continuing to accord standing to donors to enforce the terms of their own gifts concurrent with the Attorney General's standing to enforce such gifts on behalf of the beneficiaries thereof.

Mrs. Smithers, appointed the Special Administratrix of Smithers's estate for the purpose of pursuing claims by the estate against the Hospital in connection with its administration of the Smithers Center, therefore has standing to sue the Hospital for enforcement of the Gift terms

FRIEDMAN, J. (dissenting)

. . . Distilled to their essentials, what emerges from the foregoing authorities is that there are three rules governing standing in this genre of litigation. First, a donor does not have standing to seek enforcement of a gift merely because he is the donor. Second, a donor who has retained certain rights to control the gift, i.e., a right to make staff appointments or exercise other decision-making authority concerning the use of the gift, may very well have standing. Third, the donor or his heirs may also have standing if the gift reverts to the donor or his heirs upon the failure to use the gift for its intended purpose. The corollary to these rules is that the estate will lack standing if it has no interest in the gift after the donor's death, i.e., there is no provision for the gift, upon misuse, to revert to the estate. Bearing these rules in mind, the fundamental flaw in the majority's grant of standing in this case becomes evident.

The principal focus of the majority's analysis centers upon the question of whether Mr. Smithers had standing to commence an action. As to this question, I agree with the majority that *Associate Alumni*, [57 N.E. 626 (1900),] supports the view that he did since he seems to have retained the right to make appointments to key staff positions. This observation, however, is irrelevant to the question presented on this appeal. Here, we are not required to determine whether Mr. Smithers would have had standing, but whether his estate has standing.

With regard to this issue, and applying the rules of standing noted above, it is uncontroverted that the estate was not the donor of the gift. Thus, even if pure donor standing were recognized (as the majority concludes), this could not be a basis for granting standing to Mr. Smithers's estate. Next, to the extent that Mr. Smithers may have had standing based upon his right to exercise discretionary control over the gift, i.e., via the right to appoint key staffing positions, that right was personal to him, abated upon his death, and did not devolve to his estate. Hence, as plaintiff concedes that the estate has no right to exercise control over the gift, this may not be a basis of standing. Finally, since it is uncontroverted that the estate does not have a right of reverter in the gift or, in fact, any right to control the gift by way of appointment to staff positions or otherwise, it follows that there is no retained interest that could support a claim of standing. In view of this, I fail to perceive the legal basis for the majority's grant of standing to plaintiff.

NOTES AND QUESTIONS

1. *Can a niece bring the suit?* A few years after *Smithers*, another plaintiff asked a New York court to grant standing to enforce restrictions on a gift. In *Rettek v. Ellis Hospital*, No. 1:08-CV-844 (GLS/DRH), 2009 U.S. Dist. LEXIS 1607, (N.D.N.Y. Jan. 12, 2009), a niece of the deceased donors brought suit against the hospital that had received the gifts to enforce restrictions on the use of the gifts. Norma Rettek raised her concerns about misappropriation of funds with the Charities Bureau of the Attorney General's office and discussions occurred between Rettek's counsel and the Charities Bureau and between the Charities Bureau and the hospital. After two years with no resolution, Ms. Rettek filed the suit. The court refused to grant her standing, noting that she did not represent the estate of the deceased donors.

2. *Switching sides.* What role did the Attorney General play in *Smithers*? Why did the Attorney General ask the court to find that Mrs. Smithers lacked standing? Why did the Attorney General switch sides?

3. *Whose interest?* Whose interest does the Attorney General protect?

Hardt v. Vitae Foundation

302 S.W.3d 133 (Mo. App. W.D. 2009)

[The will of Selma J. Hartke gave the executors of her estate, Edwin and Karl Hardt, the authority to distribute the residue of her estate to charitable organizations they chose. The Hardts met with Sandra Faucher and Carl Landwehr of the Vitae Foundation, "a non-profit charitable corporation describing itself as an 'advertising campaign for life . . . [that] research[es], produce[s] and purchase[s] airtime in an effort to encourage a greater respect for human life, restore traditional values in our American culture, and reduce the number of abortions by using mass media education.'" The Hardts agreed to support a proposal prepared by the foundation to air media campaigns in 10 markets. The Hardts made a gift of over $4.0 million from the estate in 2001 and then in 2002 made a second gift of $4.0 million (only

$3.0 million of which was involved in the dispute), in each case on the terms and conditions proposed by the foundation and agreed to by the foundation when it accepted the gift.]

In August of 2003, Ms. Faucher contacted the Hardts' counsel and informed him that some portions of the Hardts' grant to Vitae were not being used in accordance with the conditions placed on the gifts but, instead, were being expended for administrative expenses, including the hiring of significant new staff members, and were being spent without the receipt of matching funds [a term of the grant]. She also told the Hardts' counsel that Vitae promised expansion of media campaigns in new markets was not occurring. [Ms. Faucher was no longer employed by Vitae at this time.]

On September 8, 2003, the Hardts requested an accounting from Vitae with respect to both gifts. On September 26, 2003, Landwehr sent a letter to the Hardts indicating that subsequent to their gifts, Vitae had adopted a new development strategy. The Hardts later learned that little money was being used for media campaigns at all. . . .

On August 6, 2008, the Hardts filed a petition in the Cole County Circuit Court seeking: (a) a detailed accounting of both the 2001 and 2002 gifts, (b) the restoration of any part of either gift spent in contravention of conditions placed on the gifts, (c) an injunction preventing any future expenditure of funds from either gift in any manner inconsistent with the applicable conditions, or (d) in the alternative, the transfer of the 2001 gift to another charitable organization of the Hardts' choosing.

. . . On December 5, 2008, the trial court granted the [foundation's] motion to dismiss and held that the Hardts lacked standing to bring their claims. . . .

LEGAL ANALYSIS

At common law, only the Attorney General had standing to enforce the terms of a charitable gift. This rule applied to gifts both to charitable trusts and charitable corporations and was made primarily to prevent potential beneficiaries without a "special interest" in the gift from "vex[ing]" public charities with "frequent suits, possibly based on an inadequate investigation." Since the Attorney General represents the public at large, he can enforce the terms of the charitable donation on behalf of all of the beneficiaries, which for public charities means the general public.

Donors were also prevented from enforcing their gifts in court, because non-trustee donors retained no interest in the gift, "except the sentimental one that every person who contributed" to the charity would be presumed to have. Accordingly, the donor was left with no ability to make sure the charitable organization used the gift according to the gift's terms and conditions.

An exception to this rule existed, however, when the donor specifically made the charitable gift subject to a condition subsequent to the donation. In these cases, if the charitable trust or charitable corporation failed to perform the specified act, the gift would revert back to the donor or to a designated third party. The donor of such a gift had standing to enforce the conditions placed on the gift because it retained an interest in the property. The parties agree that this exception does not apply in this case.

Recently, there has been a trend in the law to give donors more control over the enforcement of the terms of their charitable gifts. In 2005, Missouri adopted the Uniform Trust Code ("MUTC"). This law specifically granted settlors of charitable trusts the ability to "maintain a proceeding to enforce the trust." §456.4-405.3 RSMo. The law was also made retroactive to apply to trusts created before its enactment. The law, on its face, clearly applies only to trusts. . . .

The Hardts argue that because common law charitable trust principles have often applied to charitable corporations, newly enacted statutes addressing only charitable trusts must also apply to charitable corporations. The extension of common law charitable trust principles to gifts to charitable corporations is not enough to authorize this court's extension of the MUTC, a statutory provision that on its face applies only to charitable trusts, to gifts made outright to charitable corporations. . . .

Where the language of a statute is clear and unambiguous, there is no room for construction. If a term is defined within a statute, a court must give effect to the legislature's definition. . . . [T]he MUTC is limited by its unambiguous terms to charitable trusts, and this court lacks the authority to apply common law precedent to construe the legislation in a manner that is inconsistent with the express language of the MUTC.

Moreover, just this year, Missouri adopted the Uniform Prudent Management of Institutional Funds Act ("UPMIFA"), which expressly applies to both charitable trusts and nonprofit corporations. This law grants charitable organizations more discretion than they may have had under the common law to make prudent investment decisions regarding charitable funds and endowments. While the UPMIFA stresses that charitable fund managers give primary consideration to the donor's intent as expressed in the gift instrument, it does not expressly grant the donor standing to enforce this intent as the MUTC does in the case of charitable trusts. . . .

The Hardts' second argument is that even if there is no statutory authority giving them standing to sue, Missouri should follow New York, which recently expanded the common law to allow donors to sue to enforce the terms of charitable gifts. . . . [The court then discusses, and distinguishes, the *Smithers* case.]

Arguing that "public policy" favors granting donors standing to enforce restrictions on charitable gifts, the Hardts urge this court to follow New York's example. They claim that the donor's interest is distinct from that of the Attorney General and hint that the Attorney General might not be vigilant or might even have a conflict of interest in enforcing the restrictions of the gift. This argument is not persuasive. In this case, unlike in *Smithers*, there is no indication in the record that the Attorney General was even notified of Vitae's failure to comply with the conditions. The Hardts apparently did not attempt to involve the Attorney General in the matter, taking it directly to court based upon their own interests. While it is conceivable that there may be times when the Attorney General does not sufficiently represent a donor's interest, it has not been shown to be the case here, and we find no reason to expand the common law to give standing to the Hardts. Indeed, in light of the legislature's passage of the UPMIFA, it would not be appropriate for us to do so.

[The Hardts also argued that the court should apply *cy pres* to transfer the gift to another charity. The court said that *cy pres* did not apply on the facts.]

Assuming the Hardts' gift to Vitae is subject to legitimate, enforceable restrictions and that Vitae is not using the gift appropriately pursuant to those restrictions, the Hardts' course of action should be to notify the Attorney General and to ask him to enforce the restrictions. Therefore, and for all of the above reasons, we affirm the judgment of the trial court.

NOTES AND QUESTIONS

1. *Politics.* Why do you think the Hardts did not contact the Missouri Attorney General about their problems with the Vitae Foundation?

2. *Impossible?* Why does *cy pres* not apply on these facts?

3. *Reversion.* The dissent explains that a donor will have standing if the gift agreement provides that if the charity fails to carry out the terms of the gift the gift will revert to the donor (a reversionary interest in the donor). Why do few donors keep a reversion?

4. *What can the donor do?* The Connecticut court denied standing to a donor of a restricted gift in *Carl J. Herzog Foundation, Inc. v. University of Bridgeport*, 699 A.2d 995 (Conn. 1997). The Herzog Foundation had given Bridgeport University a gift to use for nursing scholarships. The university closed its nursing school due to financial troubles and redirected the money to the general endowment. The foundation sued to enforce the restriction, and the court denied standing. In this case the donor was the plaintiff, but the court followed the traditional rule — only the attorney general has standing. In *Herzog* the court noted that UMIFA (the Uniform Management of Institutional Funds Act), the predecessor to UPMIFA, did not provide for standing.

2. Special Interests Doctrine

Although beneficiaries of a charitable trust generally do not have standing as beneficiaries, courts have occasionally permitted identifiable beneficiaries to sue a charity by finding that the persons have a "special interest" in the charity. The plaintiffs must have a specific interest that will be directly affected by the charity's failure to carry out its purpose or by a breach of fiduciary duties. The persons with a special interest must be members of an identifiable class of beneficiaries of the charity and not merely members of the general public who are concerned that the charity be run properly. Courts have been willing to let such beneficiaries sue the charity to protect the "special interest" in a manner analogous to a suit by a beneficiary of a private trust, but the remedy sought must be a benefit to the charity itself and not money damages for the plaintiffs.

A study published in 1993 identified factors most likely to induce a court to grant standing to private persons: (a) the extraordinary nature of the acts complained of and the remedy sought by the plaintiff; (b) the presence of fraud or misconduct on the part of the charity or its directors; (c) the state attorney general's availability or effectiveness; and (d) the nature of the benefitted class and its relationship to the charity. *See* Mary G. Blasko et al., *Standing to Sue in the Charitable Sector*, 28 U.S.F. L. Rev. 37 (1993).

If the attorney general has already reviewed the case and decided not to act, a court is unlikely to grant standing, at least if the attorney general in that state has a record of charitable enforcement. If, however, the court perceives lax enforcement efforts or lack of resources or interest on the part of the attorney general, the court may be willing to grant standing to a private person with special interests. *See id.*

3. Relators

A relator is a private person who sues a charity on behalf of the attorney general. A statute enacted in 1980 provides for relators in California. Cal. Corp. Code §5142(a) (2010). The statute permits persons granted relator status by the attorney general to sue a charity on behalf of the attorney general. Pursuant to the statute, a private person can notify the attorney general of abuse by the charity or its fiduciaries. If the attorney general agrees, the relator can proceed with the suit on behalf of the attorney general. The private relator pays the court costs, but the attorney general remains in control of the action. The suit must be one which the attorney general within his or her discretion could have brought, and the attorney general must authorize the suit before the relator can proceed. Because the attorney general will supervise the suit, a relator may be more troublesome to the attorney general than helpful.

4.   Internal Revenue Service

In addition to the enforcement of the fiduciary duties of trustees and directors provided by the state attorney general and others, the IRS enforces tax rules that regulate charities. In order to be exempt for tax purposes under IRC §501(c)(3), a charity must operate "exclusively" for exempt purposes, essentially charitable purposes. Exclusively has been interpreted to mean primarily, but if trustees operate a charity for their own benefit and not for charitable purposes, the charity may lose its tax-exempt status. In addition, the tax code prohibits private inurement. If a trustee or other person takes advantage of the charitable trust by taking excessive salary or by engaging in a self-dealing transaction that benefits the individual and harms the organization, the charity and the trustee may face penalties. If the behavior is egregious, the charity may lose its exempt status. In recent years, concern about whether adequate monitoring of charities exists at the state level has led to increasing monitoring through the IRS. The annual return filed by charities with the IRS, Form 990, was expanded in 2009 to include questions about management of the charity, including conflicts of interests between trustees and the charity.

5.   Role of the General Public — The Bishop Estate

In the 1990s, the trustees of the Bishop Estate, a charitable trust with an estimated value of $10.0 billion in 1995, engaged in self-dealing, paid themselves huge salaries and took other personal benefits from the trust. The trustees also failed to carry out the purposes of the trust. The trust and its trustees had political connections that made any challenge to the trust difficult, but the work of students, parents, teachers, alumni and private citizens eventually prompted investigations by the attorney general and the IRS that forced the resignation of all five trustees. A bestselling book written about the creation of the trust and the events of the late 1990s makes compelling reading. *See* Samuel P. King & Randall W. Roth, Broken Trust — Greed, Mismanagement & Political Manipulation at America's Largest Charitable Trust. The information that follows comes from the book.

When Princess Bernice Pauahi Bishop died in 1884, she was the last surviving member of the Hawaiian dynasty founded by her great-grandfather, Kamehameha, the ruler who united the Hawaiian islands as the Kingdom of Hawaii. She owned 378,569 acres of land, and she had no children. Her will made some specific bequests, gave her husband, Charles Bishop, a life estate in some of the property, and then gave the remainder interest and the rest of the land to five trustees "to erect and maintain in the Hawaiian Islands two schools, each for boarding and day scholars, one for boys and one for girls, to be known as, and called the Kamehameha Schools." The custom at the time of Pauahi's death was to call a trust an "estate" so the trust became know as the Bishop Estate. Charles Bishop later gave his life estate and much of his own property to the trust. According to Pauahi's will, justices of the Kingdom's Supreme Court were to select new trustees as vacancies occurred.

In the 1980s and 1990s, the Bishop Estate was forced to sell much of its land under a law enacted to reduce large landholdings. Prior to that, the trust had been land-rich but cash-poor, paying relatively low compensation to employees and trustees. Finding themselves with billions in cash, the trustees had the look of "shell-shocked lottery winners," according to the *Wall Street Journal*. They began investing in risky deals based on "relationships," without first developing an overall investment plan.

The trustees developed a "lead trustee" system, ceding much authority to one trustee for each of five areas: asset management; education and communication; government relations; legal affairs; and alumni relations. A lead trustee could make major decisions without the agreement or even knowledge of other trustees, in violation of basic fiduciary principles (the duty not to delegate discretionary duties). The trustees referred to themselves as CEOs and took the position that $1.0 million dollars per trustee per year was reasonable compensation because each functioned as a CEO. Never mind that being a trustee was only a part-time job and that most of the trustees had never held a job that paid even one-tenth of what they were now paying themselves.

Prior to 1997, the five justices of Hawaii's Supreme Court selected Bishop Estate trustees even though jurisdiction for trust matters had long before shifted to the probate court. Acting officially, the justices ruled that they were the proper parties to select Bishop Estate trustees so long as they did it unofficially. That presumably meant that they were not protected by judicial immunity when selecting trustees (creating possible personal exposure if they acted negligently in selecting trustees who harmed the trust), yet the justices continued to decide cases involving the trustees.

Bishop Estate trusteeships reportedly became prized political chits under this selection process, which became intertwined with the state's judicial appointment system: Seven of the nine members of the Hawaii Judicial Selection Commission were appointed by the chief justice, House speaker, Senate president and governor, and during the cash-rich times the justices filled trustee vacancies with a chief justice, a House speaker, a Senate president and a governor's closest adviser — who also chaired the Judicial Selection Commission at the time — as well as various other political leaders.

The probate court appointed a master each year to review the annual accounts filed by the trustees, but the masters made only a cursory review and evidently accepted as accurate any information provided by the trustees. Criticism was rare and muted, and seemed not to matter in any event. For example, the trustees simply ignored recommendations made by the master in the 1992, 1993 and 1995 reports.

The state attorney general also had the power and responsibility to hold the trustees of charitable trusts accountable, but during these years the attorney general seemed not to notice any problems with the trust.

Things started to change during the mid-1990s when Lokelani Lindsey, the lead trustee for education, began to micromanage the Kamehameha schools, including making decisions about curriculum, line-item budgeting and hiring. As she became more and more involved in the daily management of the schools, the morale of teachers, students and administrators sank. Rumors circulated that the well-liked president of the schools would be fired and that several teachers who had dared to challenge Lindsey would also be fired.

The authors of *Broken Trust* put it this way:

> The Kamehameha *ohana* [Hawaiian word meaning extended family] — students, teachers, parents, and alumni — gradually came to realize that Lokelani Lindsey had transformed their campus into a place of suspicion and fear, a place where no one could act on his or her conscience without fear of reprisal. They saw that the other trustees had done nothing to stop her. Nor had the justices, attorney general, master, or probate judge. This prompted the *ohana* to consider drastic action. Although many of them had a lot to lose, there was too much at stake — their children, their school, Pauahi's legacy — simply to look away. At first one by one, and then together, they acted.

BROKEN TRUST, p. 125.

On May 15, 1997, nearly 1,000 members of the Kamehameha *ohana* staged a protest march. At about the same time, several individual students and their parents sought standing to bring an action against the trustees. In July, trustee Oswald Stender went public with his criticisms of the other four trustees. Then, on August 17, 1997, the *Honolulu Star-Bulletin* published "Broken Trust," a lengthy essay that detailed the abuses of the trust. The five authors were prominent people, active in civic affairs and well known in the community. Four were Hawaiian elders and the fifth was Randall W. Roth, a trusts and estates professor who had been on the faculty at the University of Hawaii for 17 years and who had spent years gathering information about the notoriously secretive Bishop Estate.

The public response was loud and clear, and the political winds shifted dramatically. Within days the governor instructed the attorney general to investigate the trustees and the circumstances of their selection. Within weeks, four other investigations commenced. The justices almost immediately announced that they would no longer have anything to do with trustee selection, but steadfastly refused to cooperate in any of the investigations. They said it would violate separation-of-power principles. The probate judge, who had been appointed by the chief justice, seemed disinclined to make a definitive decision about the trustees. Commentators called it a legal logjam.

Then something remarkable happened. The IRS threatened to revoke the trust's tax-exempt status if the five trustees were not replaced *immediately*. The probate court's failure to act would cost the charity nearly $1.0 billion upfront, and more in future years. Reminiscent of the first *Godfather* movie, it was an offer that the probate court "couldn't refuse." Although wildly popular with the public in Hawaii, the former trustees called the IRS's action "extortion" and at least one professor expressed concern about the precedent it set. *See* Evelyn Brody, *A Taxing Time for the Bishop Estate: What Is the I.R.S. Role in Charity Governance?*, 21 U. Haw. L. Rev. 537 (1999). *See also* Samuel King & Randall Roth, *Erosion of Trust* 93 A.B.A. J. 48 (Aug. 2007).

NOTES

Misbehaving trustees. The trustees of the Bishop Estate engaged in self-dealing and conflict of interest transactions. Unfortunately, other trustees have given in to similar temptations. In 2003, a series of articles published in the *Boston Globe* revealed gross abuse of a number of charitable foundations. One situation involved the Paul and Virginia Cabot Charitable Trust, a grant-making foundation. The trustee, a son of the settlors of the trust, began to pay himself a substantial salary at about the time the energy company of which he was the chairman began having financial difficulties. He paid himself over $5.0 million in salary over five years, and in one of those years he increased his salary to help pay for his daughter's $200,000 wedding. During that time period the trust made total grants of only $400,000 a year to charities, usually to the same charities each year. The article describes financial abuses at a number of charities. *See* http://www.boston.com/news/nation/articles/2003/10/09/some_officers_of_charities_steer_assets_to_selves/.

F. DRAFTING FOR DONOR INTENT

Nearly all of the cases we have looked at in this chapter involve the donor's intent and alleged failure by the charity to carry out that intent. Charities generally want to give effect to a donor's intent. Honoring the intent of a contributor is important for a charity's reputation and may influence future donors. Problems arise, however, when different views of what a donor intended develop over time. Sometimes the circumstances change, as we saw in the *Buck Trust* and the *Barnes Foundation*. In other cases the parties may disagree about what the donor meant. In *Smithers*, for example, Mrs. Smithers argued that Mr. Smithers had intended the hospital to use the building purchased with his gift while the attorney general thought that Mr. Smithers' restrictions did not include keeping the building.

1. Robertson v. Princeton

In *Robertson v. Princeton Univ.*, No. C99-02 (N.J. Super. Ct. Ch. Div. filed July 17, 2002), the largest donor intent case yet, each side argued that it was trying to protect the donor's intent against the other side. In 1961, Marie Robertson, with the advice of her husband, Charles Robertson, gave Princeton University $35.0 million in A&P stock (a grocery chain—the Atlantic & Pacific Tea Company) for use by the Woodrow Wilson School. The detailed gift agreement directed that the funds be used to expand the graduate school "where men and women dedicated to public service may prepare themselves for careers in government service, with particular emphasis on the education of such persons for careers in those areas of the Federal Government that are concerned with international relations and affairs." The gift agreement contained a number of other provisions and was drafted with enough flexibility to allow Princeton to adapt to changes over time, within the framework of the gift. The gift was held in a separate organization, the Robertson Foundation, which was controlled by Princeton (Princeton appointed four of the seven members) but also had family members as trustees.

The Woodrow Wilson School grew over the years, and the family stayed involved as trustees, even after the deaths of Marie and Charles. In 2002, when the Robertson Foundation had grown in value to $600.0 million, four children and a cousin of the Robertsons filed suit against Princeton, alleging misuse of the funds and asking that the foundation be transferred to their control. Both sides argued about the restrictions spelled out in the Certificate of Incorporation of the Robertson Foundation. The litigation lasted six years and ended with a settlement agreement. Princeton paid $50.0 million to the Robertson Foundation for Government, a new organization managed by the Robertson family, to be held as a separate fund and managed according to the family's view of the Roberstons' intent. Princeton also paid $40.0 million to the Banbury Foundation, which had paid the legal fees incurred by the family. The rest of the Robertson Foundation will be held by Princeton as a separate fund within its endowment and will be managed according to Princeton's view of the Robertsons' intent.

The *Robertson* case is complicated, but part of the problem may have been different interpretations of "government service." The family interpreted the term narrowly, meaning employed directly by the federal government. Princeton viewed the term as what it meant over time—the meaning of the type of work the Robertsons' envisioned and how that work had evolved by the turn of the twenty-first century. For example, the Woodrow Wilson School prepares students to work with the government through non-governmental organizations (NGOs) and in other ways that support U.S. interests in international work.

The Certificate of Incorporation of the Robertson Foundation (which lays out the terms of the gift), various background documents and legal documents and the Settlement Agreement, can be found at www .princeton.edu/robertson.

The document that created the Robertson Foundation evidences a negotiated agreement and careful drafting. The Certificate of Incorporation reflects the intent of the donors, with a reasonable amount of detail, and at the same time provides the flexibility a university would need to adapt to changes over time. We turn next to a discussion about how to advise donors in making gifts to charity or setting up charitable trusts. As you think about drafting for donor intent, keep the *Robertson* case in mind. If family members disagree about the interpretation of a document after the death of the original donor, relying on the written document may not avoid a lengthy court battle.

2.   *Leona M. and Harry B. Helmsley Trust*

When Leona Helmsley died in 2007, her will gave the residue of her estate to the Leona M. and Harry B. Helmsley Charitable Trust, a trust established by Ms. Helmsley on April 23, 1999. The trust instrument states that the trustees "may establish and administer programs for the charitable purposes authorized by [a prior paragraph in the trust instrument] or they may, in their sole discretion, distribute the net income and principal of the Trust Fund to and among such one or more Charitable Organizations and in such amounts or proportions as the Trustees, in their sole discretion, shall determine." In 2003, Ms. Helmsley wrote a "mission statement" for the trust. This mission statement expressed two priorities: indigent people and dogs. A year later she crossed out the provision for indigents, so the mission statement directed the trustees to make grants for "(1) purposes related to the provision of care for dogs; and (2) such other charitable activities as the Trustees shall determine." Based on the mission statement, Ms. Helmsley seems to have intended that the primary focus of the trust be on dog welfare, but the legal language of the trust does not limit the distributions to organizations that benefit dogs.

After Ms. Helmsley's death, the trustees asked the Surrogate Court for instructions about the legal effect the mission statement. The court ruled that the mission statement did not bind the trustees, based on the language in the trust instrument giving them discretion over distributions. Shortly after the court's decision, the trustees announced initial distributions from the trust. The trustees distributed $135.0 million to medical centers, health care organizations, and to educational, conservation and anti-poverty programs. They distributed $1.0 million to 10 animal-related organizations, and many of those organizations focused on human, rather than animal, welfare; for example, by training guide dogs. The trustees acted in a legally correct manner, but Ms. Helmsley might not have been pleased that only a small percentage of her trust was being used for the care of dogs.

In the case of the Helmsley trust, the written mission statement provided information about the settlor's intent, but the trustees could ignore that statement given the flexible provision in the trust instrument. For other trusts, the trust instrument may be the only written evidence of intent. Years later, the flexibility of broadly drafted purpose provisions may prove useful and may, in fact, be what the settlor intended all along. A broadly drafted purpose provision will give the trustees the ability to adjust to changes over time, but a flexible provision will also give the trustees authority to make distributions that may not reflect the intent of the settlor.

NOTES

The Surrogate Court opinion can be found at *In the Matter of the Trustees of the Leona M. and Harry B. Helmsley Charitable Trust*, for Advice and Direction, No. 2968/2007 (N.Y. Surrogate's Court filed February 19, 2009), *available at* http://graphics8.nytimes.com/packages/pdf/nyregion/20090 226decision.pdf. For more information about the trust and the interpretation of Ms. Helmsley's intent, you may want to read Sam Roberts, *Trustees Begin to Parcel Leona Helmsley's Estate*, N.Y. Times, Apr. 22, 2009; Stephanie Strom, *Not All of Helmsley's Trust Has to Go to Dogs*, N.Y. Times, Feb. 26, 2009.

G. DRAFTING CONSIDERATIONS

1. Non-Perpetual Trusts

Some donors intentionally create a charitable trust (or a nonprofit corporation) that will terminate in a fixed number of years, either during the donor's lifetime or perhaps extending through the lifetimes of the donors' children. By creating a trust that will not last in perpetuity, the donor and the donor's immediate family can maintain control over the trust. For example, Aaron and Irene Diamond created a foundation with $200.0 million and a plan to spend the entire amount in 10 years. The foundation terminated on schedule, while Irene was still alive. The Bill and Melinda Gates Foundation will terminate in 100 years. *See* Susan N. Gary, *The Problems with Donor Intent: Interpretation, Enforcement, and Doing the Right Thing*, 74 Chi-Kent L. Rev. 101 (2010).

2. *Clear Statement of Intent*

Careful thought should go into the drafting of a trust agreement or a gift agreement. The lawyer can help the donor identify the donor's specific interests and also think about possible changes that could affect the donor's plans. Just as a lawyer asks "what if" questions when drafting a will, she should also ask questions like what should happen if a program ends or is no longer feasible, if the charity changes direction or if the need for a particular service changes.

3. *Flexibility*

Although the donor may want a gift used for a particular purpose, giving the charity some flexibility in carrying out the planned purpose will benefit both the charity and donor. For example, a donor might want to create a scholarship for a student with a specific interest in the Civil War. The donor might consider broadening the restriction to a scholarship for a student interested in American history, with a preference for a student focusing on the Civil War. The broader category would make it more likely that the university could make the award each year, furthering the donor's intent, and would make a need for modification later on less likely.

4. *Provisions for Modification*

The donor should think about what should happen should a change to the original purpose become necessary. One option is to permit the charity to modify the restriction, without going to court, in keeping with the donor's general purposes for the gift. By giving the charity the authority to modify the gift if that becomes necessary, the donor will save the charity from spending money on a *cy pres* court proceeding. The drafted language could permit modification only if the restriction becomes "impossible," or could provide for modification if the restriction is "necessary" or something in between.

   The donor may not want to give the charity complete authority to modify the purpose of the trust. In that case, the donor could require the charity to consult with family members (identified specifically or by relationship to the donor) or to get the approval of specified persons. If the donor wants to require approval, the donor should keep in mind the time-frame. Approval of a child might make sense, but approval of "descendants" far into the future may not.

5.   *Standing*

What if a gift agreement provides that the donor will have standing to enforce a restriction on a gift? Will the provision in the gift agreement be effective to grant standing? The answer is not clear, because the right to determine standing lies with the court, but a provision in a gift agreement might sway a court to permit standing. If a donor includes a standing provision in a gift agreement, the next question will be standing for whom? Standing for the donor is one thing, but a charity may be reluctant to sign an agreement that purports to give standing to descendants of the donor in perpetuity. If the donor is a foundation, the foundation may have perpetual life so the right to standing may in fact continue for a very long time, even as the trustees of the foundation change.

6.   *Mediation or Arbitration*

Another way to handle disputes that arise about the meaning of a restriction or the use of funds is to use mediation or arbitration. The gift agreement could include a requirement that the donor and charity engage in good faith in mediation if a disagreement arises. The difficulty with using mediation in this context is that because the donor may not have standing to go to court if the mediation fails, the charity has less incentive to work toward a settlement than in other situations. A clause requiring arbitration may be a better choice for that reason.

NOTES

Advising clients. A lawyer cannot assure a client that a particular purpose restriction will be enforceable in perpetuity. Even a carefully drafted restriction may require modification over time. For more discussion of the problems with drafting charitable gifts with restrictions intended to last in perpetuity, see RAY MADOFF, IMMORTALITY AND THE LAW — THE RISING POWER OF THE AMERICAN DEAD (2010).

EXERCISES

1.   Alexi wants to make a gift to the college she attended. She wants the gift to be used to create summer programs in chemistry for junior high school students. Her goal is to encourage students to go into science in college. The university would run the summer programs and has agreed to do so. Alexi is willing to give the college $5.0 million to endow this project. Advise Alexi. What should her gift agreement require? Advise the university. What should it be willing to accept and what should it require?

2.   Grady gave the art museum in his small town several paintings by local artists. None of the paintings are terribly valuable, although one is worth $30,000. When he made the gift, he and the museum signed an agreement in which the museum agreed to keep the paintings as part of its permanent collection and display the paintings at least three months each year.

    a.   Grady visits the museum frequently and is distressed to find that the paintings are not on display. Indeed, they have not been on display for the past two years. What can Grady do?

    b.   Grady learned that the museum sold the one relatively valuable painting to pay for maintenance costs. The museum is struggling to stay afloat. What can Grady do?

TABLE OF CASES

Principal cases in italics.

TABLE OF LAWS AND OTHER MATERIAL

INDEX